# Collins

BESTSELLING BILINGUAL DICTIONARIES

# Russian
# Dictionary

Collins

**HarperCollins Publishers**
Westerhill Road
Bishopbriggs
Glasgow
G64 2QT
Great Britain

First Edition 2008

Reprint  10 9 8 7 6 5 4

© HarperCollins Publishers 2008

ISBN 978-0-00-726375-2

Collins® is a registered trademark of
HarperCollins Publishers Limited

www.collinslanguage.com

A catalogue record for this book is
available from the British Library

Supplement typeset by
Wordcraft, Glasgow

Printed in Italy by
LEGO Spa, Lavis (Trento)

**Acknowledgements**
We would like to thank those authors
and publishers who kindly gave
permission for copyright material to be
used in the Collins Word Web. We would
also like to thank Times Newspapers Ltd
for providing valuable data.

| СОДЕРЖАНИЕ | | CONTENTS | |
|---|---|---|---|

Авторский коллектив/Contributors
Albina Ozieva • Olga Stott

Заведующий редакцией/Editorial Management
Catherine Love

Ведущий редактор/Managing Editor
Gaëlle Amiot-Cadey

Редакторы/Editorial Staff
Pat Cook • Genevieve Gerrard • Isobel Gordon • Andrew Knox

Компьютерное обслуживание/Computing
Thomas Callan • André Gautier • Robert McMillan • Thomas Widmann

Редактор серии/Series Editor
Rob Scriven

## ВВЕДЕНИЕ

Мы рады, что вы выбрали словарь, подготовленный издательством Коллинз. Мы надеемся, что он окажется вам полезен, где бы вы им ни пользовались – дома, на отдыхе или на работе.

В настоящем введении излагаются некоторые советы по эффективному использованию данного издания: его обширного словника и сведений, содержащихся в каждой словарной статье. Данная информация поможет вам не только читать и понимать современный английский, но также овладеть устной речью.

## INTRODUCTION

We are delighted that you have decided to use the Collins Russian Dictionary and hope that you will enjoy and benefit from using it at home, on holiday or at work.

This introduction gives you a few tips on how to get the most out of your dictionary – not simply from its comprehensive wordlist but also from the information provided in each entry. This will help you to read and understand modern Russian, as well as communicate and express yourself in the language.

# О ПОЛЬЗОВАНИИ СЛОВАРЁМ

**Заглавные слова**
**Заглавными** называются слова, начинающие словарную статью. Они напечатаны жирным шрифтом и расположены в алфавитном порядке. При многих из них приводятся словосочетания и сращения. Они напечатаны жирным шрифтом меньшего размера.

**Перевод**
Перевод заглавных слов напечатан обычным шрифтом. Варианты перевода, разделённые запятой синонимичны. Различные значения многозначного слова разделены точкой с запятой.

Переводы для значений производных слов часто разделены только точкой с запятой и перед ними даётся одна помета типа (*см прил*). Это означает, что последовательное разделение значений рассматриваемого слова и его переводов даётся при слове, от которого это слово образовано. Например, **careful/carefully**.

В случаях, когда точный перевод невозможен, даётся приблизительный эквивалент. Он обозначается знаком ≈. Если же таковой отсутствует, то приводится толкование.

**Пометы**
*Пометы* служат для разделения значений многозначного слова. Их цель – помочь читателю выбрать перевод, наиболее подходящий в том или ином контексте. Пометы напечатаны курсивом и заключены в круглые скобки.

При заглавных словах даны необходимые стилистические пометы. Нецензурные слова помечены восклицательным знаком (!).

**Произношение**
В англо-русской части словаря все заглавные слова снабжены транскрипцией. Транскрипция не даётся для производных слов, о произношении которых можно судить, исходя из произношения исходного слова, например, **enjoy/enjoyment**. Список фонетических знаков приводится на страницах xv–xvi.

В русско-английской части словаря все русские слова снабжены знаком ударения. Омографы (слова, имеющие одинаковое написание, но различное ударение и значение) приводятся как отдельные заглавные слова в том порядке, в котором в них проставлено ударение, например, первым даётся слово за́мок, затем – замо́к. Более подробную информацию о принципах русского произношения читатель может найти в разделе на страницах xiv–xv.

## Служебные слова

В словаре уделяется особое внимание русским и английским словам, которые обладают сложной грамматической структурой. Таковыми являются в первую очередь служебные слова, вспомогательные глаголы, местоимения, частицы итп. Они обозначены пометой **KEYWORD**.

## Английские фразовые глаголы

Фразовыми глаголами называются устойчивые сочетания глагола с элементами **in**, **up** итп, типа **blow up**, **cut down** итп. Они приводятся при базовых глаголах, таких как **blow**, **cut**, и расположены в алфавитном порядке.

## Культурные реалии

Описание культурных реалии даётся соответствующих словарных статьей и оттеняется серым светом.

## Употребление *or*/*или*, косой черты и скобок

Между взаимозаменяемыми вариантами перевода фраз в англо-русской части употребляется союз "*or*", в русско-английской – "*или*". Косая черта (/) означает, что приведённые варианты перевода не являются взаимозаменяемыми. В круглые скобки заключаются возможные, но необязательные в данном выражении слова.

## Употребление тильды (~)

Тильда в англо-русской части заменяет заглавное слово в словосочетаниях. Например, если заглавным является слово "**order**", то фраза "**out of order**" будет представлена следующим образом: **out of** ~. В русско-английской части тильда заменяет: 1) целое заглавное слово: например, в статье "**до́бр|ый**" фраза "**до́брый день**" показана следующим образом: ~ **день**. 2) тильда заменяет часть заглавного слова, предшествующую вертикальной черте: например, в статье "**до́бр|ый**" фраза "**до́брое у́тро**" показана следующим образом: **~ое у́тро**.

# USING THE DICTIONARY

## Headwords
The **headword** is the word you look up in a dictionary. They are listed in alphabetical order, and printed in bold type. Each headword may contain phrases, which are in smaller bold type. The two headwords appearing at the top of each page indicate the first and last word dealt with on that page.

Where appropriate, words related to headwords are grouped in the same entry (eg. **enjoy**, **enjoyment**) in smaller bold type than the headword.

## Translations
The translations of the headword are printed in ordinary roman type. Translations separated by a comma are interchangeable, those separated by a semi-colon are not interchangeable. Where the indicator refers to a different part of speech eg. (*see adj*), the translations mirror the splits shown at the other part of speech eg. **careful/carefully**.

Where it is not possible to give an exact translation equivalent, an approximate (cultural) equivalent is given preceded by ≈. If this also isn't possible, then a gloss is given to explain the source item.

## Indicators
*Indicators* are pieces of information given in italic type and in brackets. They offer contexts in which the headword might appear or provide synonyms, guiding you to the most appropriate translation.

Colloquial and informal language in the dictionary is marked at the headword. Rude or offensive translations are also marked with (!).

## Pronunciation
On the English-Russian side of the dictionary you will find the phonetic spelling of the word in square brackets after the headword, unless the word is grouped under another headword and the pronunciation can be easily derived eg. **enjoy/enjoyment**. A list of the symbols used is given on pages xv–xvi.

For Russian-English, stress is given on all Russian words as a guide to pronunciation. Words which are spelt in the same way, but have different stress positions are treated as separate entries, the order following the order of the stress eg. **за́мок** comes before **замо́к**. The section on pages xiv–xv explains Russian phonetics in more detail.

## Keywords
In the dictionary special status is given to "key" Russian and English words. These words can be grammatically complex, often having many different usages, and are labelled **KEYWORD**.

**Cultural boxes**
On both sides of the dictionary cultural information is shown in a shaded grey box.

**"You" in phrases**
The Russian formal form is used to translate "you/your" and imperative phrases, unless the phrase is very colloquial and the informal form would be more natural.

**Use of or/или, oblique and brackets**
"*or*" on the English-Russian side, and "*или*" on the Russian-English side are used between interchangeable parts of a translation or phrase, whereas the oblique (/) is used between non-interchangeable alternatives. Round brackets are used to show optional parts of the translation or phrase.

**Use of the swung dash (~)**
The swung dash (~) is used on the English-Russian side to stand for the headword in phrases eg. at "**order**" the phrase "**out of order**" is shown as "**out of ~**". On the Russian-English side the swung dash can either stand for the full headword eg. at "**до́бр|ый**" the phrase "**до́брый день**" is shown as "**~ день**", or it can stand for the part of the word before the hairline eg. at "**до́бр|ый**" the phrase "**до́брое у́тро**" appears as "**~ое у́тро**".

**American variants**
American spelling variants are generally shown at the British headword eg. **colour/color** and may also be shown as a separate entry. Variant forms are generally shown as separate headwords eg. **trousers/pants**, unless the British and American forms are alphabetically adjacent, when the American form is only shown separately if phonetics are required eg. **cut-price/cut-rate**.

**Russian reflexive verbs**
Russian reflexive verbs eg. **мы́ться, кра́ситься** are listed under the basic verb eg. **мыть, кра́сить**.

# STYLE AND LAYOUT OF THE DICTIONARY
## RUSSIAN-ENGLISH

### Inflectional and grammatical information

Inflectional information is shown in the dictionary in brackets straight after the headword and before the part of speech eg. **стол (-á)** *м*.

Grammatical information is shown after the part of speech and refers to the whole entry eg. **завид|овать (-ую**; *pf* **позавидовать)** *несов*: – +*dat*. Note that transitive verbs are labelled *перех*, and intransitive verbs have no label other than aspect. Where grammatical information eg. *no pf* is given in the middle of the entry, it then governs all the following senses.

### Use of the hairline (|)

The hairline is used in headwords to show where the inflection adds on eg. **книг|а (-и)**.

### Stress

Stress changes are shown where they occur, the last form given being indicative of the rest of the pattern eg. **игр|á (-ы́**; *nom pl* **-ы)**. In this example the stress is on the last syllable in the singular moving to the first syllable in the plural.

### Nouns, numerals and pronouns

In order to help you determine the declension and stress pattern of nouns, numerals and pronouns, we have shown the genitive in each case.

This is given as the first piece of information after the headword and is not labelled eg. **стол (-á)**.

Where the headword has further irregularities in declension these are shown at the headword and labelled eg. **я́блок|о (-а**; *nom pl* **-и)**.

### Verbs

The majority of verbs are dealt with in aspectual pairs, and the translation is shown at the base form of the pair. The other aspect is generally shown separately and cross-referred to the base form. To help you see how a verb conjugates, inflections are shown immediately after the headword.

In phrases both aspects are shown if both work in the context.

The past tense is shown at the headword if it is irregularly formed.

### Inflections given as separate entries

Some irregular inflected forms are also shown at their alphabetical position and cross-referred to the base headword.

### Spelling rules

The following spelling rules apply to Russian:

– after **ж, ч, ш, щ, г, к** and **х, ы** is replaced by **и, я** by **а** and **ю** by **у**.
– after **ж, ч, ш, щ** and **ц, е** replaces an unstressed **о**.

# ENGLISH-RUSSIAN

## Gender

The gender of Russian noun translations is only shown for:
– nouns ending in **-ь**
– neuter nouns ending in **-я**
– masculine nouns ending in **-а**
– nouns with a common gender
– indeclinable nouns
– substantivized adjectives
– plural noun translations if a singular form exists.

## Feminine forms

The feminine forms of masculine nouns are shown as follows:
– the feminine ending adds on to the masculine form, eg. учи́тель(ница)
– the feminine ending substitutes part of the masculine form, the last common letter of both forms being shown before the feminine ending (unless it is a substantivized adjective), eg. актёр(три́са).
– the feminine form is given in full, eg. чех (че́шка).

## Adjectives

Russian translations of adjectives are always given in the masculine, unless the adjective relates only to a feminine noun eg. бере́менная.

## Verbs

Imperfective and perfective aspects are shown in translation where they both apply eg. **to do** де́лать (сде́лать *pf*). If only one aspect is shown, it means that only one aspect works for this sense. The same applies to translations of infinitive phrases eg. **to buy sth** покупа́ть (купи́ть *pf*) что-н.

Where the English phrase contains the construction "to do" standing for any verb, it has been translated by *+infin/+impf infin/+pf infin*, depending on which aspects of the Russian verb work in the context.

Where the English phrase contains the past tense of a verb in the 1st person singular, the Russian translation gives only the masculine form eg. **I was glad** я был рад

## Prepositions

Unless bracketed, prepositions and cases which follow verbs, adjectives etc are obligatory as part of the translation eg. **to inundate with** зава́ливать (завали́ть *pf*) *+instr*

Where they are separated by *or* they are interchangeable.

An oblique (/) is used to separate prepositions when the preposition depends on the following noun not the preceding verb eg. идти́ в/на.

# RUSSIAN ABBREVIATIONS

| aviation | **АВИА** | авиация |
|---|---|---|
| automobiles | **АВТ** | автомобильное дело |
| administration | **АДМИН** | администрация |
| anatomy | **АНАТ** | анатомия |
| architecture | **АРХИТ** | архитектура |
| impersonal | **безл** | безличный |
| biology | **БИО** | биология |
| botany | **БОТ** | ботаника |
| parenthesis | **вводн сл** | вводное слово |
| military | **ВОЕН** | военный термин |
| reflexive | **возв** | возвратный глагол |
| geography | **ГЕО** | география |
| geometry | **ГЕОМ** | геометрия |
| verb | **глаг** | глагол |
| offensive | **груб!** | грубо |
| singular | **ед** | единственное число |
| feminine | **ж** | женский род |
| zoology | **ЗООЛ** | зоология |
| history | **ИСТ** | история |
| et cetera | **итп** | и тому подобное |
| predicate | **как сказ** | как сказуемое |
| commercial | **КОММ** | коммерция |
| computing | **КОМП** | компьютер |
| somebody | **кто-н** | кто-нибудь |
| culinary | **КУЛИН** | кулинария |
| linguistics | **ЛИНГ** | лингвистика |
| masculine | **м** | мужской род |
| mathematics | **МАТ** | математика |
| medicine | **МЕД** | медицина |
| exclamation | **межд** | междометие |
| pronoun | **мест** | местоимение |
| plural | **мн** | множественное число |
| nautical | **МОР** | морской термин |
| music | **МУЗ** | музыка |
| adverb | **нареч** | наречие |
| invariable | **неизм** | неизменяемое |
| intransitive | **неперех** | непереходный глагол |
| indeclinable | **нескл** | несклоняемое |
| imperfective | **несов** | несовершенный вид |
| figurative | **перен** | в переносном значении |
| transitive | **перех** | переходный |
| subject | **подлеж** | подлежащее |
| politics | **ПОЛИТ** | политика |
| superlative | **превос** | превосходная степень |

| preposition | **предл** | предлог |
| pejorative | **пренебр** | пренебрежительное |
| adjective | **прил** | прилагательное |
| possessive | **притяж** | притяжательный |
| school | **ПРОСВЕЩ** | просвещение |
| psychology | **ПСИХОЛ** | психология |
| informal | **разг** | разговорное |
| religion | **РЕЛ** | религия |
| agriculture | **С.-Х.** | сельское хозяйство |
| see | **см** | смотри |
| collective | **собир** | собирательное |
| perfective | **сов** | совершенный вид |
| abbreviation | **сокр** | сокращение |
| neuter | **ср** | средний род |
| comparative | **сравн** | сравнительная степень |
| construction | **СТРОИТ** | строительство |
| noun | **сущ** | имя существительное |
| television | **ТЕЛ** | телевидение |
| technology | **ТЕХ** | техника |
| printing | **ТИПОГ** | типографский термин |
| diminutive | **уменьш** | уменьшительное |
| physics | **ФИЗ** | физика |
| photography | **ФОТО** | фотография |
| chemistry | **ХИМ** | химия |
| particle | **част** | частица |
| somebody's | **чей-н** | чей-нибудь |
| numeral | **чис** | числительное |
| something | **что-н** | что-нибудь |
| economics | **ЭКОН** | экономика |
| electricity | **ЭЛЕК** | электроника |
| law | **ЮР** | юридический термин |
| registered trademark | ® | зарегистрированный товарный знак |
| introduces a cultural equivalent | ≈ | вводит культурный эквивалент |

## АНГЛИЙСКИЕ СОКРАЩЕНИЯ

| сокращение | **abbr** | abbreviation |
| винительный падеж | **acc** | accusative |
| прилагательное | **adj** | adjective |
| администрация | **ADMIN** | administration |
| наречие | **adv** | adverb |
| сельское хозяйство | **AGR** | agriculture |
| анатомия | **ANAT** | anatomy |
| архитектура | **ARCHIT** | architecture |

| | | |
|---|---|---|
| автомобильное дело | *AUT* | automobiles |
| вспомогательный глагол | *aux vb* | auxiliary verb |
| авиация | *AVIAT* | aviation |
| биология | *BIO* | biology |
| ботаника | *BOT* | botany |
| британский английский | *BRIT* | British English |
| химия | *CHEM* | chemistry |
| коммерция | *COMM* | commerce |
| компьютер | *COMPUT* | computing |
| союз | *conj* | conjunction |
| строительство | *CONSTR* | construction |
| сращение | *cpd* | compound |
| кулинария | *CULIN* | culinary |
| дательный падеж | *dat* | dative |
| склоняется | *decl* | declines |
| определённый артикль | *def art* | definite article |
| уменьшительное | *dimin* | diminutive |
| экономика | *ECON* | economics |
| электроника | *ELEC* | electricity |
| особенно | *esp* | especially |
| и тому подобное | *etc* | et cetera |
| междометие | *excl* | exclamation |
| женский род | *f* | feminine |
| в переносном значении | *fig* | figurative |
| родительный падеж | *gen* | genitive |
| география | *GEO* | geography |
| геометрия | *GEOM* | geometry |
| безличный | *impers* | impersonal |
| несовершенный вид | *impf* | imperfective verb |
| несклоняемое | *ind* | indeclinable |
| неопределённый артикль | *indef art* | indefinite article |
| разговорное | *inf* | informal |
| грубо | *inf!* | offensive |
| инфинитив | *infin* | infinitive |
| творительный падеж | *instr* | instrumental |
| неизменяемое | *inv* | invariable |
| неправильный | *irreg* | irregular |
| лингвистика | *LING* | linguistics |
| местный падеж | *loc* | locative |
| мужской род | *m* | masculine |
| субстантивированное прилагательное | *m/f/nt adj* | adjectival noun |
| математика | *MATH* | mathematics |
| медицина | *MED* | medicine |
| военный термин | *MIL* | military |
| музыка | *MUS* | music |

| | | |
|---|---|---|
| существительное | **n** | noun |
| морской термин | **NAUT** | nautical |
| именительный падеж | **nom** | nominative |
| существительное во множественном числе | **npl** | plural noun |
| средний род | **nt** | neuter |
| числительное | **num** | numeral |
| себя | **o.s.** | oneself |
| разделительный | **part** | partitive |
| пренебрежительное | **pej** | pejorative |
| совершенный вид | **pf** | perfective verb |
| фотография | **PHOT** | photography |
| физика | **PHYS** | physics |
| физиология | **PHYSIOL** | physiology |
| множественное число | **pl** | plural |
| политика | **POL** | politics |
| страдательное причастие | **pp** | past participle |
| предлог | **prep** | preposition |
| местоимение | **pron** | pronoun |
| предложный падеж | **prp** | prepositional |
| психология | **PSYCH** | psychiatry |
| прошедшее время | **pt** | past tense |
| религия | **REL** | religion |
| кто-нибудь | **sb** | somebody |
| просвещение | **SCOL** | school |
| единственное число | **sg** | singular |
| что-нибудь | **sth** | something |
| подлежащее | **subj** | subject |
| превосходная степень | **superl** | superlative |
| техника | **TECH** | technology |
| телесвязь | **TEL** | telecommunications |
| театр | **THEAT** | theatre |
| телевидение | **TV** | television |
| типографский термин | **TYP** | printing |
| американский английский | **US** | American English |
| обычно | **usu** | usually |
| глагол | **vb** | verb |
| непереходный глагол | **vi** | intransitive verb |
| звательный падеж | **voc** | vocative case |
| фразовый глагол | **vt fus** | inseparable verb |
| переходный глагол | **vt** | transitive verb |
| зоология | **ZOOL** | zoology |
| зарегистрированный торговый знак | **®** | registered trademark |
| вводит культурный эквивалент | **≈** | introduces a cultural equivalent |

# RUSSIAN PRONUNCIATION

## Vowels and diphthongs

| Letter | Symbol | Russian Example | English Example/Explanation |
|--------|--------|-----------------|------------------------------|
| А,а | [a] | д*а*ть | *a*fter |
| Е,е | [ɛ] | с*е*л | g*e*t |
| Ё,ё | [jo] | *ё*лка, мо*ё* | *ya*wn |
| И,и | [i] | *и*х, н*и*ва | sh*ee*t |
| Й,й | [j] | *й*од, мо*й* | *yi*eld |
| Ó,ó | [o] | к*о*т | d*o*t |
| О,о | [ʌ] | н*о*гá | c*u*p |
| У,у | [u] | *у*м | sh*oo*t |
| Ы,ы | [ɨ] | с*ы*н | *pronounced like "ee", but with the tongue arched further back in the mouth* |
| Э,э | [æ] | *э*то | c*a*t |
| Ю,ю | [ju] | *ю*г | *yo*u, *you*th |
| Я,я | [ja] | *я*сно | *ya*k |

## Consonants

| Letter | Symbol | Russian Example | English Example/Explanation |
|--------|--------|-----------------|------------------------------|
| Б,б | [b] | *б*анк | *b*ut |
| В,в | [v] | *в*от | *v*at |
| Г,г | [g] | *г*од | *g*ot |
| Д,д | [d] | *д*ом | *d*og |
| Ж,ж | [ʒ] | *ж*енá | mea*s*ure |
| З,з | [z] | *з*áвтра | do*z*e |
| К,к | [k] | *к*от | *c*at |
| Л,л | [l] | *л*óдка | *l*ot |
| М,м | [m] | *м*ать | *m*at |
| Н,н | [n] | *н*ас | *n*o |
| П,п | [p] | *п*асть | *p*ut |
| Р,р | [r] | *р*от | *pronounced like rolled Scots "r"* |
| С,с | [s] | *с*ад | *s*at |
| Т,т | [t] | *т*ок | *t*op |
| Ф,ф | [f] | *ф*óрма | *f*at |
| Х,х | [x] | *х*од | *pronounced like Scots "ch" in "loch"* |
| Ц,ц | [ts] | *ц*ель | bi*ts* |
| Ч,ч | [tʃ] | *ч*áсто | *ch*ip |
| Ш,ш | [ʃ] | *ш*ýтка | *sh*oot |
| Щ,щ | [ʃʃ] | *щ*ит | fre*sh sh*eets |

xvi

Russian vowels are inherently short. Russian stressed vowels tend to be slightly longer than unstressed vowels. In unstressed positions all vowels are "reduced". Unstressed "**o**" sounds like "**a**" eg. **города́** [gərʌ'da], except in some loanwords and acronyms eg. **ра́дио** ['raḍio], **госба́нк** [gos'bank]. Unstressed "**e**" is pronounced like "**bit**" eg. **село́** [şi'lo]. The same is true of "**я**" before stressed syllables eg. **пяти́** [pi'ṭi], and of "**a**" when it follows "**ч**" or "**щ**" eg. **щади́ть**[ʃʃi'ḍiṭ].

The letter "**ё**" is used only in grammar books, dictionaries etc. to avoid ambiguity eg. **нéбо** and **нёбо**.

# АНГЛИЙСКОЕ ПРОИЗНОШЕНИЕ

## Гласные и Дифтонги

| Знак | Английский Пример | Русское Соответствие/Описание |
|---|---|---|
| [ɑ:] | f**a**ther | .м**а́**ма |
| [ʌ] | b**u**t, c**o**me | **а**лья́нс |
| [æ] | m**a**n, c**a**t | **э́**тот |
| [ə] | f**a**ther, **a**go | ра́н**а** |
| [ə:] | b**i**rd, h**ea**rd | ф**ё**дор |
| [ɛ] | g**e**t, b**e**d | г**е**н |
| [ɪ] | **i**t, b**i**g | к**и**т |
| [i:] | t**ea**, s**ea** | **и́**ва |
| [ɔ] | h**o**t, w**a**sh | х**о**д |
| [ɔ:] | s**aw**, **a**ll | **о́**чень |
| [u] | p**u**t, b**oo**k | б**у**к |
| [u:] | t**oo**, y**ou** | **у́**лица |
| [aɪ] | fl**y**, h**i**gh | л**а́й** |
| [au] | h**ow**, h**ou**se | **а́у**т |
| [ɛə] | th**ere**, b**ear** | *произно́сится как сочета́ние "э" и кра́ткого "а"* |
| [eɪ] | d**ay**, ob**ey** | **эй** |
| [ɪə] | h**ere**, h**ear** | *произно́сится как сочета́ние "и" и кра́ткого "а"* |
| [əu] | g**o**, n**o**te | **о́у** |
| [ɔɪ] | b**oy**, **oi**l | б**о́й** |

| [uə] | p**oor**, s**ure** | *произносится как сочетание "у" и кра́ткого "а"* |
| [juə] | p**ure** | *произносится как сочетание "ю" и кра́ткого "а"* |

## Согласные

| [b] | **b**ut | **б**ом |
| [d] | **d**ot | **д**ом |
| [g] | **g**o, **g**et, bi**g** | **г**ол, ми**г** |
| [dʒ] | **g**in, **judg**e | **дж**и́нсы, и́ми**дж** |
| [ŋ] | si**ng** | *произносится как ру́сское "н", но не ко́нчиком языка́, а за́дней ча́стью его́ спи́нки* |
| [h] | **h**ouse, **h**e | **х**а́ос, **х**и́мия |
| [j] | **y**oung, **y**es | **й**од, **й**е́мен |
| [k] | **c**ome, mo**ck** | **к**а́мень, ро**к** |
| [r] | **r**ed, t**r**ead | **р**от, т**р**ава́ |
| [s] | **s**and, ye**s** | **с**ад, ри**с** |
| [z] | ro**s**e, **z**ebra | ро́**з**а, **з**е́бра |
| [ʃ] | **sh**e, ma**ch**ine | **ш**и́на, ма**ш**и́на |
| [tʃ] | **ch**in, ri**ch** | **ч**ин, кули́**ч** |
| [v] | **v**alley | **в**альс |
| [w] | **w**ater, **wh**ich | **у**о́тергейт, **у**и́к-э́нд |
| [ʒ] | vi**s**ion | ва́**ж**ный |
| [θ] | **th**ink, my**th** | *произносится как ру́сское "с", но ко́нчик языка́ нахо́дится ме́жду зуба́ми* |
| [ð] | **th**is, **th**e | *произносится как ру́сское "з", но ко́нчик языка́ нахо́дится ме́жду зуба́ми* |
| [f] | **f**ace | **ф**акт |
| [l] | **l**ake, **l**ick | **л**ай, **л**ом |
| [m] | **m**ust | **м**ат |
| [n] | **n**ut | **н**ет |
| [p] | **p**at, **p**ond | **п**ар, **п**от |
| [t] | **t**ake, ha**t** | э́**т**от, не**т** |
| [x] | lo**ch** | **х**од |

# А, а

---

KEYWORD

**a** *союз* 1 but; **он согласи́лся, а я отказа́лась** he agreed, but I refused

2 (*выражает присоединение*) and

3 (*во фразах*): **а (не) то** or (else); **а вот** but

♦ *част* (*обозначает отклик*): **иди́ сюда́! - а, что тако́е!** come here! - yes, what is it?; **а как же** (*разг*) of course, certainly

♦ *межд* ah; (*выражает ужас, боль*) oh; **а ну** (*разг*) go on; **а ну́ его́!** (*разг*) stuff him!

---

**абажу́р** (**-а**) *м* lampshade
**абза́ц** (**-а**) *м* paragraph
**абитурие́нт** (**-а**) *м entrant to university, college etc*
**абонеме́нт** (**-а**) *м* season ticket
**абоне́нт** (**-а**) *м* subscriber
**або́рт** (**-а**) *м* abortion
**абрико́с** (**-а**) *м* (*плод*) apricot
**абсолю́тный** *прил* absolute
**абстра́ктный** *прил* abstract
**абсу́рдный** *прил* absurd
**аванга́рд** (**-а**) *м* vanguard; (*ИСКУССТВО*) avant-garde
**ава́нс** (**-а**) *м* (*КОММ*) advance
**авантю́р|а** (**-ы**) *ж* adventure
**авари́йный** *прил* emergency; (*дом*) unsafe; **~ сигна́л** alarm signal
**ава́ри|я** (**-и**) *ж* accident; (*повреждение*) breakdown
**а́вгуст** (**-а**) *м* August
**а́виа** *нескл* (*авиапочта*) air mail
**авиакомпа́ни|я** (**-и**) *ж* airline

**авиано́с|ец** (**-ца**) *м* aircraft carrier
**авиа́ци|я** (**-и**) *ж* aviation
**Австра́ли|я** (**-и**) *ж* Australia
**А́встри|я** (**-и**) *ж* Austria
**автоба́з|а** (**-ы**) *ж* depot
**автобиогра́фи|я** (**-и**) *ж* autobiography
**авто́бус** (**-а**) *м* bus
**автовокза́л** (**-а**) *м* bus station
**авто́граф** (**-а**) *м* autograph
**автозаво́д** (**-а**) *м* car (*BRIT*) *или* automobile (*US*) plant
**автозапра́вочн|ая** (**-ой**) *ж* (*также*: **~ ста́нция**) filling station
**автомагистра́л|ь** (**-и**) *ж* motorway (*BRIT*), expressway (*US*)
**автома́т** (**-а**) *м* automatic machine; (*ВОЕН*) sub-machine-gun
**автомаши́н|а** (**-ы**) *ж* (motor)car, automobile (*US*)
**автомеха́ник** (**-а**) *м* car mechanic
**автомоби́л|ь** (**-я**) *м* (motor)car, automobile (*US*); **легково́й ~** (passenger) car
**автоно́мный** *прил* autonomous
**автоотве́тчик** (**-а**) *м* answering machine
**а́втор** (**-а**) *м* author
**авторите́т** (**-а**) *м* authority
**авторите́тный** *прил* authoritative
**а́вторск|ий** *прил* author's; **~ое пра́во** copyright; **~ое свиде́тельство** patent
**авторуч|ка** (**-ки**; *gen pl* **-ек**) *ж* fountain pen
**автостра́д|а** (**-ы**) *ж* motorway (*BRIT*), expressway (*US*)
**аге́нт** (**-а**) *м* agent
**аге́нтств|о** (**-а**) *ср* agency
**агити́р|овать** (**-ую**) *несов*: **~ (за** +*acc*) to campaign (for)
**аго́ни|я** (**-и**) *ж* death throes *мн*
**агра́рный** *прил* agrarian
**агрега́т** (**-а**) *м* machine
**агре́сси|я** (**-и**) *ж* aggression

**агроно́м** (-а) м agronomist

**ад** (-а) м hell

**адапти́р|оваться** (-у́юсь) *(не)сов возв* to adapt

**адвока́т** (-а) м counsel; *(в суде)* ≈ barrister *(BRIT)*, ≈ attorney *(US)*

**адеква́тный** *прил* adequate

**администра́тор** (-а) м administrator; *(в гости́нице)* manager

**администра́ци|я** (-и) ж administration; *(гости́ницы)* management

**а́дрес** (-а; *nom pl* -á) м address

**а́дресный** *прил*: ~ **стол** residents' registration office

**адрес|ова́ть** (-у́ю) *(не)сов перех*: ~ **что-н кому́-н** to address sth to sb

**ажу́рный** *прил* lace

**аза́рт** (-а) м ardour *(BRIT)*, ardor *(US)*

**аза́ртн|ый** *прил* ardent; **~ая игра́** gambling

**а́збук|а** (-и) м alphabet; *(буква́рь)* first reading book

**Азербайджа́н** (-а) м Azerbaijan

**А́зи|я** (-и) ж Asia

**азо́т** (-а) м nitrogen

**а́ист** (-а) м stork

**ай** *межд (выража́ет боль)* ow, ouch

**а́йсберг** (-а) м iceberg

**акаде́мик** (-а) м academician

**акаде́ми|я** (-и) ж academy

**акваре́л|ь** (-и) ж watercolours мн *(BRIT)*, watercolors мн *(US)*; *(карти́на)* watercolo(u)r

**аква́риум** (-а) м aquarium, fish tank

**аккомпани́р|овать** (-ую) *несов*: ~ +dat to accompany

**акко́рд** (-а) м chord

**аккредити́в** (-а) м letter of credit

**аккумуля́тор** (-а) м accumulator

**аккура́тный** *прил (посеще́ние)* regular; *(рабо́тник)* meticulous; *(рабо́та)* accurate; *(костю́м)* neat

**акселера́тор** (-а) м accelerator

**акт** (-а) м act; *(докуме́нт)* formal document

**актёр** (-а) м actor

**акти́в** (-а) м assets мн

**акти́вный** *прил* active

**актри́с|а** (-ы) ж actress

**актуа́льный** *прил* topical; *(зада́ча)* urgent

**аку́л|а** (-ы) ж shark

**акуше́р** (-а) м obstetrician

**акуше́р|ка** (-ки; *gen pl* -ок) ж midwife

**акце́нт** (-а) м accent

**акци́з** (-а) м excise (tax)

**акционе́р** (-а) м shareholder

**акционе́рный** *прил* joint-stock

**а́кци|я** (-и) ж *(КОММ)* share; *(де́йствие)* action

**а́лгебр|а** (-ы) ж algebra

**а́либи** *ср нескл* alibi

**алиме́нт|ы** (-ов) мн alimony ед, maintenance ед

**алкого́лик** (-а) м alcoholic

**алкого́л|ь** (-я) м alcohol

**аллерге́н** (-а) м allergen

**аллерги́|я** (-и) ж allergy

**алле́|я** (-и) ж alley

**алло́** *межд* hello

**алма́з** (-а) м diamond

**алта́р|ь** (-я́) м chancel

**алфави́т** (-а) м alphabet

**а́лый** *прил* scarlet

**альбо́м** (-а) м album

**альмана́х** (-а) м anthology

**альпини́зм** (-а) м mountaineering

**альт** (-á) м *(инструме́нт)* viola

**альтернати́в|а** (-ы) ж alternative

**алья́нс** (-а) м alliance

**алюми́ни|й** (-я) м aluminium *(BRIT)*, aluminum *(US)*

**амбулато́ри|я** (-и) ж doctor's

surgery (*BRIT*) или office (*US*)

**Аме́рик|а (-и)** ж America

**америка́нск|ий**

**амети́ст (-а)** м amethyst

**ами́нь** *част* (*РЕЛ*) amen

**амнисти́р|овать (-ую)** *(не)сов*
*перех* to grant (an) amnesty to

**амни́сти|я (-и)** ж amnesty

**амора́льный** *прил* immoral

**амортиза́тор (-а)** м (*ТЕХ*) shock
absorber

**амортиза́ци|я (-и)** ж (*ТЕХ*) shock
absorption; (*ЭКОН*) depreciation

**а́мпул|а (-ы)** ж ampoule (*BRIT*),
ampule (*US*)

**ампути́р|овать (-ую)** *(не)сов*
*перех* to amputate

**АН** ж *сокр* (= Акаде́мия нау́к)
Academy of Sciences

**ана́лиз (-а)** м analysis

**анализи́р|овать (-ую;** *pf* про~)
*несов перех* to analyse (*BRIT*),
analyze (*US*)

**анали́тик (-а)** м analyst

**аналоги́чный** *прил* analogous

**анало́ги|я (-и)** ж analogy; **по ~и**
**(с** +*instr*) in a similar way (to)

**анана́с (-а)** м pineapple

**ана́рхи|я (-и)** ж anarchy

**анато́ми|я (-и)** ж anatomy

**анаш|а́ (-и́)** ж hashish

**анга́р (-а)** м hangar

**а́нгел (-а)** м (*также разг*) angel

**анги́н|а (-ы)** ж tonsillitis

**англи́йский** *прил* English; **~ язы́к**
English

**англича́н|ин (-ина;** *nom pl* **-е,** *gen*
*pl* **-)** м Englishman

**А́нгли|я (-и)** ж England

**анекдо́т (-а)** м joke

**анеми́|я (-и)** ж anaemia (*BRIT*),
anemia (*US*)

**анестезио́лог (-а)** м anaesthetist
(*BRIT*), anesthiologist (*US*)

**анестези́|я (-и)** ж anaesthesia

(*BRIT*), anesthesia (*US*)

**анке́т|а (-ы)** ж (*опросный лист*)
questionnaire; (*бланк для*
*сведений*) form; (*сбор сведений*)
survey

**аннота́ци|я (-и)** ж précis

**аннули́р|овать (-ую)** *(не)сов*
*перех* (*брак, договор*) to annul

**анони́мный** *прил* anonymous

**анса́мбл|ь (-я)** м ensemble;
(*танцевальный*) company;
(*эстрадный*) group

**Антаркти́д|а (-ы)** ж Antarctica

**Анта́рктик|а (-и)** ж the Antarctic

**анте́нн|а (-ы)** ж aerial (*BRIT*),
antenna (*US*); **~ косми́ческой**
**свя́зи** satellite dish

**антибио́тик (-а)** м antibiotic

**антивое́нный** *прил* antiwar

**антиква́рный** *прил* antique

**антисанита́рный** *прил*
unhygienic, insanitary

**антисемити́зм (-а)** м anti-
Semitism

**антифаши́стский** *прил* antifascist

**анти́чный** *прил* classical; **~ мир**
the Ancient World

**антра́кт (-а)** м interval

**аню́тины** *прил*: **~ гла́зки** pansy
*ед*

**А/О** *ср сокр* (= акционе́рное
о́бщество) joint-stock company

**апа́ти|я (-и)** ж apathy

**апелли́р|овать (-ую)** *(не)сов*
(*ЮР*) to appeal

**апелля́ци|я (-и)** ж (*также ЮР*)
appeal

**апельси́н (-а)** м orange

**аплоди́р|овать (-ую)** *несов*: **~**
+*dat* to applaud

**аплодисме́нт|ы (-ов)** *мн*
applause *ед*

**апо́стол (-а)** м apostle

**аппара́т (-а)** м apparatus;
(*ФИЗИОЛОГИЯ*) system; (*штат*) staff

**аппарату́р|а (-ы)** ж собир equipment

**аппендици́т (-а)** м appendicitis

**аппети́т (-а)** м appetite; **прия́тного ~!** bon appétit!

**апре́л|ь (-я)** м April

**апте́к|а (-и)** ж pharmacy

**апте́кар|ь (-я)** м pharmacist

**ара́б (-а)** м Arab

**ара́бский** прил (страны) Arab; **~ язы́к** Arabic

**ара́хис (-а)** м peanut

**арби́тр (-а)** м (в спорах) arbitrator; (в футболе) referee

**арбитра́ж (-а)** м arbitration

**арбу́з (-а)** м watermelon

**аргуме́нт (-а)** м argument

**аргументи́р|овать (-ую)** (не)сов перех to argue

**аре́н|а (-ы)** ж arena; (цирка) ring

**аре́нд|а (-ы)** ж (наём) lease

**аре́ндн|ый** прил lease; **~ая пла́та** rent

**аренд|ова́ть (-у́ю)** (не)сов перех to lease

**аре́ст (-а)** м (преступника) arrest

**аресто́ванн|ый (-ого)** м person held in custody

**арест|ова́ть (-у́ю);** impf **аресто́вывать** сов перех (преступника) to arrest

**аристокра́ти|я (-и)** ж aristocracy

**арифме́тик|а (-и)** ж arithmetic

**а́ри|я (-и)** ж aria

**а́р|ка (-ки;** gen pl **-ок)** ж arch

**Арктик|а (-и)** ж the Arctic

**армату́р|а (-ы)** ж steel framework

**арме́йский** прил army

**Арме́ни|я (-и)** ж Armenia

**а́рми|я (-и)** ж army

**армяни́н (-а;** nom pl **армя́не,** gen pl **армя́н)** м Armenian

**армя́н|ка (-ки;** gen pl **-ок)** ж Armenian

**арома́т (-а)** м (цветов) fragrance; (кофе итп) aroma

**арсена́л (-а)** м (склад) arsenal

**арте́ри|я (-и)** ж (также перен) artery

**арти́кл|ь (-я)** м (линг) article

**артилле́ри|я (-и)** ж artillery

**арти́ст (-а)** м actor

**арти́ст|ка (-ки;** gen pl **-ок)** ж actress

**артри́т (-а)** м arthritis

**а́рф|а (-ы)** ж harp

**арха́нгел (-а)** м archangel

**архео́лог (-а)** м archaeologist (BRIT), archeologist (US)

**архи́в (-а)** м archive

**архиепи́скоп (-а)** м archbishop

**архипела́г (-а)** м archipelago

**архите́ктор (-а)** м architect

**архитекту́р|а (-ы)** ж architecture

**асбе́ст (-а)** м asbestos

**аспе́кт (-а)** м aspect

**аспира́нт (-а)** м postgraduate (doing PhD)

**аспиранту́р|а (-ы)** ж postgraduate studies мн (leading to PhD)

**аспири́н (-а)** м aspirin

**ассамбле́|я (-и)** ж assembly

**ассигн|ова́ть (-у́ю)** (не)сов перех to allocate

**ассимили́р|оваться (-уюсь)** (не)сов возв to become assimilated

**ассисте́нт (-а)** м assistant; (в вузе) assistant lecturer

**ассортиме́нт (-а)** м range

**ассоциа́ци|я (-и)** ж association

**ассоции́р|овать (-ую)** (не)сов перех to associate

**а́стм|а (-ы)** ж asthma

**а́стр|а (-ы)** ж aster

**астроло́ги|я (-и)** ж astrology

**астроно́м (-а)** м astronomer

**астрономи́ческий** прил (также перен) astronomic(al)

**асфа́льт** (-а) м asphalt
**асфальти́р|овать** (-ую; *pf* **за~**)
*(не)сов перех* to asphalt
**ата́к|а** (-и) ж attack
**атак|ова́ть** (-у́ю) *(не)сов перех*
to attack
**атама́н** (-а) м ataman (*Cossack
leader*)
**атеи́ст** (-а) м atheist
**ателье́** *ср нескл* studio; *(мод)*
tailor's shop; **телевизио́нное ~**
television repair shop; **~ прока́та**
rental shop
**атланти́ческий** *прил*:
**Атланти́ческий океа́н** the Atlantic
(Ocean)
**а́тлас** (-а) м atlas
**атле́тик|а** (-и) ж: **лёгкая ~** track
and field events: **тяжёлая ~** weight
lifting
**атмосфе́р|а** (-ы) ж atmosphere
**а́том** (-а) м atom
**атрофи́р|оваться** (*3sg* -**уется**)
*(не)сов возв* to atrophy
**АТС** ж *сокр* (= **автомати́ческая
телефо́нная ста́нция**) automatic
telephone exchange
**атташе́** м *нескл* attaché
**аттеста́т** (-а) м certificate; **~
зре́лости** ≈ GCSE

> **аттеста́т зре́лости** - Certificate
> of Secondary Education. This is
> obtained by school-leavers after
> sitting their final exams. This
> document records all the marks
> the pupils have attained during
> their exams and enables them to
> apply to a higher education
> institution. See also note at
> **проходно́й балл**.

**аттест|ова́ть** (-у́ю) *(не)сов
перех* to assess
**аттракцио́н** (-а) м (*в ци́рке*)

attraction; (*в па́рке*) amusement
**ауди́т** (-а) м audit
**аудито́ри|я** (-и) ж lecture hall
♦ *собир (слу́шатели)* audience
**аукцио́н** (-а) м auction
**а́ут** (-а) м (*в те́ннисе*) out; (*в
футбо́ле*): **мяч в а́уте** the ball is
out of play
**афери́ст** (-а) м swindler
**афи́ш|а** (-и) ж poster
**Африк|а** (-и) ж Africa
**ах** *межд*: **~!** oh!, ah!; **~ да!** (*разг*)
ah yes!
**ацето́н** (-а) м acetone
**аэро́бик|а** (-и) ж aerobics
**аэро́бус** (-а) м airbus
**аэровокза́л** (-а) м air terminal (*esp
BRIT*)
**аэродро́м** (-а) м aerodrome
**аэрозо́л|ь** (-я) м aerosol, spray
**аэропо́рт** (-а; *loc sg* -**у́**) м airport
**АЭС** ж *сокр* (= **а́томная
электроста́нция**) atomic power
station

# Б, б

**б** *част см*. **бы**
**ба́б|а** (-ы) ж (*разг*) woman
**ба́б|а-яг|а́** (-ы, -и́) ж Baba Yaga
(*old witch in Russian folk-tales*)
**ба́б|ий** *прил* womanish; **~ье ле́то**
Indian summer
**ба́б|ка** (-ки; *gen pl* -**ок**) ж
grandmother
**ба́боч|ка** (-ки; *gen pl* -**ек**) ж
butterfly; (*га́лстук*) bow tie
**бабуш|ка** (-ки; *gen pl* -**ек**) ж
grandmother, grandma
**бага́ж** (-а́) м luggage (*BRIT*),
baggage (*US*)
**бага́жник** (-а) м (*в автомоби́ле*)
boot (*BRIT*), trunk (*US*); (*на*

*велосипеде)* carrier

**багро́вый** *прил* crimson

**бадминто́н (-а)** *м* badminton

**ба́з|а (-ы)** *ж* basis; (*ВОЕН, АРХИТ*) base; (*для туристов*) centre (*BRIT*), center (*US*); (*товаров*) warehouse

**база́р (-а)** *м* market; (*книжный*) fair; (*перен: разг*) racket

**бази́р|овать (-ую)** *несов перех*: ~ что-н на +*prp* to base sth on; **~ся** *несов возв*: **~ся (на** +*prp*) to be based (on)

**байда́р|ка (-ки;** *gen pl* **-ок)** *ж* canoe

**Байка́л (-а)** *м* Lake Baikal

**бак (-а)** *м* tank

**бакале́|я (-и)** *ж* grocery section; (*товары*) groceries *мн*

**ба́кен (-а)** *м* buoy

**бакенба́рд|ы (-)** *мн* sideburns *мн*

**баклажа́н (-а;** *gen pl* **- или -ов)** *м* aubergine (*BRIT*), eggplant (*US*)

**бакс (-а)** *м* (*разг*) dollar

**бакте́ри|я (-и)** *ж* bacterium

**бал (-а;** *loc sg* **-у́,** *nom pl* **-ы́)** *м* ball

**балала́|йка (-йки;** *gen pl* **-ек)** *ж* balalaika

**бала́нс (-а)** *м* balance

**баланси́р|овать (-ую)** *несов*: ~ **(на** +*prp*) to balance (on)

**балери́н|а (-ы)** *ж* ballerina

**бале́т (-а)** *м* ballet

**ба́л|ка (-ки;** *gen pl* **-ок)** *ж* beam

**балка́нский** *прил* Balkan

**Балка́н|ы (-)** *мн* the Balkans

**балко́н (-а)** *м* (*АРХИТ*) balcony; (*ТЕАТР*) circle (*BRIT*), balcony (*US*)

**балл (-а)** *м* mark; (*СПОРТ*) point

**балла́д|а (-ы)** *ж* ballad

**баллисти́ческий** *прил* ballistic

**балло́н (-а)** *м* (*газовый*) cylinder; (*для жидкости*) jar

**баллоти́р|овать (-ую)** *несов перех* to vote for; **~ся** *несов*

*возв*: **~ся в** +*acc* или **на пост** +*gen* to stand (*BRIT*) или run (*US*) for

**бал|ова́ть (-у́ю;** *pf* **из~)** *несов перех* to spoil; **~ся** *несов возв* (*ребёнок*) to be naughty

**балти́йск|ий** *прил*: **Балти́йское мо́ре** the Baltic (Sea)

**бальза́м (-а)** *м* balsam

**ба́льн|ый** *прил*: **~ое пла́тье** ball gown

**ба́мпер (-а)** *м* bumper

**бана́льный** *прил* banal, trite

**бана́н (-а)** *м* banana

**ба́нд|а (-ы)** *ж* gang

**бандеро́л|ь (-и)** *ж* package

**банди́т (-а)** *м* bandit

**банк (-а)** *м* bank

**ба́н|ка (-ки;** *gen pl* **-ок)** *ж* jar; (*жестяная*) tin (*BRIT*), can (*US*)

**банке́т (-а)** *м* banquet

**банки́р (-а)** *м* banker

**банкно́т (-а;** *gen pl* **-)** *м* banknote

**ба́нковский** *прил* bank

**банкома́т (-а)** *м* cash machine

**банкро́т (-а)** *м* bankrupt

**банкро́тств|о (-а)** *ср* bankruptcy

**бант (-а)** *м* bow

**ба́н|я (-и;** *gen pl* **-ь)** *ж* bathhouse

**бапти́ст (-а)** *м* Baptist

**бар (-а)** *м* bar

**бараба́н (-а)** *м* drum

**бараба́н|ить (-ю, -ишь)** *несов* to drum

**бараба́нн|ый** *прил*: **~ая перепо́нка** eardrum

**бара́к (-а)** *м* barracks *мн*

**бара́н (-а)** *м* sheep

**бара́ний** *прил* (*котлета*) lamb; (*тулуп*) sheepskin

**бара́нин|а (-ы)** *ж* mutton; (*молодая*) lamb

**барахл|о́ (-а́)** *ср собир* junk

**барахо́л|ка (-ки;** *gen pl* **-ок)** *ж* flea market

**барда́к (-á)** м (*груб!*: *беспоря́док*) hell broke loose (!)

**барелье́ф (-а)** м bas-relief

**ба́рж|а (-и)** ж barge

**барито́н (-а)** м baritone

**ба́рмен (-а)** м barman bartender (*US*)

**баро́метр (-а)** м barometer

**баррика́д|а (-ы)** ж barricade

**барсу́к (-á)** м badger

**ба́ртер (-а)** м barter

**ба́рхат (-а)** м velvet

**барье́р (-а)** м (*в беге*) hurdle; (*на ска́чках*) fence; (*перен*) barrier

**бас (-а; *nom pl* -ы́)** м bass

**баскетбо́л (-а)** м basketball

**ба́с|ня (-ни; *gen pl* -ен)** ж fable

**бассе́йн (-а)** м (swimming) pool; (*реки, озера итп*) basin

**баст|ова́ть (-у́ю)** *несов* to be on strike

**баталь́он (-а)** м batallion

**батаре́|йка (-йки; *gen pl* -ек)** ж (*ЭЛЕК*) battery

**батаре́|я (-и)** ж (*отопи́тельная*) radiator; (*ВОЕН, ЭЛЕК*) battery

**бати́ст (-а)** м cambric, lawn

**бато́н (-а)** м (white) loaf (*long or oval*)

**ба́тюш|ка (-ки; *gen pl* -ек)** м father

**бахром|а́ (-ы́)** ж fringe (*BRIT*), bangs мн (*US*)

**ба́ш|ня (-ни; *gen pl* -ен)** ж tower

**баю́ка|ть (-ю)** *несов перех* to lull to sleep

**бая́н (-а)** м bayan (*kind of concertina*)

**бди́тельный** *прил* vigilant

**бег (-а)** м run, running; **на ~у́** hurriedly; *см. также* **бега́**

**бег|á (-о́в)** мн the races мн

**бе́га|ть (-ю)** *несов* to run

**бегемо́т (-а)** м hippopotamus, hippo (*inf*)

**беги́(те)** *несов см.* **бежа́ть**

**бегле́ц (-á)** м fugitive

**бе́глый** *прил* escaped; (*речь, чте́ние*) fluent; (*обзор*) brief

**бегов|о́й** *прил* (*ло́шадь*) race; **~а́я доро́жка** running track

**бего́м** *нареч* quickly; (*перен: разг*) in a rush

**бе́гств|о (-а)** *ср* flight; (*из пле́на*) escape

**бегу́** *итп несов см.* **бежа́ть**

**бегу́н (-á)** м runner

**бегу́н|ья (-ьи; *gen pl* -ий)** ж runner

**бед|á (-ы́; *nom pl* -ы)** ж tragedy; (*несча́стье*) misfortune, trouble; **про́сто ~!** it's just awful!; **не ~!** (*разг*) (it's) nothing!, not to worry!

**бедне́|ть (-ю; *pf* о~)** *несов* to become poor

**бе́дност|ь (-и)** ж poverty

**бе́дный** *прил* poor

**бедня́г|а (-и)** м/ж (*разг*) poor thing

**бедня́к (-á)** м poor man

**бедр|о́ (-á; *nom pl* бёдра, *gen pl* бёдер)** *ср* thigh; (*таз*) hip

**бе́дственный** *прил* disastrous

**бе́дстви|е (-я)** *ср* disaster

**бе́дств|овать (-ую)** *несов* to live in poverty

**бе|жа́ть (*см. Table 20*)** *несов* to run; (*вре́мя*) to fly

**бе́жевый** *прил* beige

**бе́жен|ец (-ца)** м refugee

**без** *предл*: **~ +gen** without; **~ пяти́/десяти́ мину́т шесть** five to/ten to six

**безала́берный** *прил* (*разг*) sloppy

**безалкого́льный** *прил* nonalcoholic, alcohol-free; **~ напи́ток** soft drink

**безапелляцио́нный** *прил* peremptory

**безбиле́тник** (**-а**) *м* fare dodger
**безбо́жный** *прил* (*разг*)
  shameless
**безболе́зненный** *прил* painless
**безбре́жный** *прил* boundless
**безве́тренный** *прил* calm
**безвку́сный** *прил* tasteless
**безвла́сти|е** (**-я**) *ср* anarchy
**безвозвра́тн|ый** *прил*
  irretrievable; **~ая ссу́да**
  nonrepayable loan
**безво́льный** *прил* weak-willed
**безвы́ходный** *прил* hopeless
**безгра́мотный** *прил* illiterate;
  (*работник*) incompetent
**безграни́чный** *прил* boundless
**безда́рный** *прил* (*человек*)
  talentless; (*произведение*)
  mediocre
**безде́йств|овать** (**-ую**) *несов* to
  stand idle; (*человек*) to take no
  action
**безде́льник** (**-а**) *м* (*разг*) loafer
**безде́льнича|ть** (**-ю**) *несов*
  (*разг*) to loaf *или* lounge about
**безде́тный** *прил* childless
**бе́здн|а** (**-ы**) *ж* abyss; **у меня́ ~**
  **дел** (*разг*) I've got heaps of things
  to do
**бездо́мный** *прил* (*человек*)
  homeless; (*собака*) stray
**бездо́нный** *прил* bottomless
**безду́мный** *прил* thoughtless
**безду́шный** *прил* heartless
**безе́** *ср нескл* meringue
**безжа́лостный** *прил* ruthless
**безжи́зненный** *прил* lifeless
**беззабо́тный** *прил* carefree
**беззако́ни|е** (**-я**) *ср* lawlessness
**беззасте́нчивый** *прил* shameless
**беззащи́тный** *прил* defenceless
  (*BRIT*), defenseless (*US*)
**беззву́чный** *прил* inaudible
**беззу́бый** *прил* toothless
**безли́чный** *прил* impersonal

**безлю́дный** *прил* deserted
**безме́рный** *прил* boundless
**безмо́лвный** *прил* silent
**безмяте́жный** *прил* tranquil
**безнадёжный** *прил* hopeless
**безнака́занный** *прил*
  unpunished
**безнали́чный** *прил* noncash; **~**
  **расчёт** clearing settlement
**безнра́вственный** *прил* immoral
**безо** *предл см.* **без**
**безоби́дный** *прил* harmless
**безо́блачный** *прил* cloudless;
  (*перен: жизнь*) carefree
**безобра́зи|е** (**-я**) *ср* ugliness;
  (*поступок*) outrage; **~!** it's an
  outrageous!, it's a disgrace!
**безобра́зный** *прил* ugly;
  (*поступок*) outrageous, disgraceful
**безогово́рочный** *прил*
  unconditional
**безопа́сность** (**-и**) *ж* safety;
  (*международная*) security
**безопа́сный** *прил* safe
**безору́жный** *прил* unarmed
**безотве́тный** *прил* (*любовь*)
  unrequited; (*существо*) meek
**безотве́тственный** *прил*
  irresponsible
**безотка́зный** *прил* reliable
**безотлага́тельный** *прил* urgent
**безотноси́тельно** *нареч*: **~ к**
  +*dat* irrespective of
**безоши́бочный** *прил* correct
**безрабо́тиц|а** (**-ы**) *ж*
  unemployment
**безрабо́тн|ый** *прил* unemployed
  ♦ (**-ого**) *м* unemployed person
**безра́достный** *прил* joyless
**безразли́чно** *нареч* indifferently
  ♦ *как сказ*: **мне ~** it doesn't matter
  *или* makes no difference to me; **~**
  **кто/что** no matter who/what
**безразли́чный** *прил* indifferent
**безразме́рн|ый** *прил*: **~ые**

носки́ one-size socks
**безрезульта́тный** *прил* fruitless
**безрука́в|ка (-ки;** *gen pl* **-ок)** *ж*
(*кофта*) sleeveless top; (*куртка*)
sleeveless jacket
**безукори́зненный** *прил*
irreproachable; (*работа*) flawless
**безу́ми|е (-я)** *ср* madness; **до ~я**
madly
**безу́мно** *нареч* (*любить*) madly;
(*устать*) terribly
**безу́мный** *прил* mad; (*о чувстве*)
wild
**безупре́чный** *прил*
irreproachable; (*работа*) flawless
**безусло́вно** *нареч* (*доверять*)
unconditionally ♦ *част*
(*несомненно*) without a doubt;
(*конечно*) naturally
**безуспе́шный** *прил* unsuccessful
**безуча́стный** *прил* indifferent
**безъя́дерный** *прил* nuclear-free
**безымя́нный** *прил* (*герой*,
*автор*) anonymous; **~ па́лец** ring
finger
**бей(ся)** *несов см.* **би́ть(ся)**
**Белару́с|ь (-и)** *ж* Belarus
**белору́с (-а)** *м* Belorussian
**беле́|ть (-ю;** *pf* **по~)** *несов* (*лицо*)
to go *или* turn white; (*no pf;*
*цветы*) to show white
**бели́л|а (-)** *мн* emulsion *ед*
**бел|и́ть (-ю́, -ишь;** *pf* **по~)** *несов*
*перех* to whitewash
**бе́личий** *прил* squirrel's; (*шуба*)
squirrel (fur)
**бе́л|ка (-ки;** *gen pl* **-ок)** *ж* squirrel
**белко́вый** *прил* proteinous
**бел|о́к (-ка́)** *м* protein; (*яйца*)
(egg) white; (*АНАТ*) white (of the
eye)
**белокро́ви|е (-я)** *ср* (*МЕД*)
leukaemia (*BRIT*), leukemia (*US*)
**белоку́рый** *прил* (*человек*)
fair(-haired); (*волосы*) fair

**белосне́жный** *прил* snow-white
**бе́лый** *прил* white; **~ медве́дь**
polar bear
**Бе́льги|я (-и)** *ж* Belgium
**бель|ё (-я́)** *ср собир* linen;
**ни́жнее ~** underwear
**бельэта́ж (-а)** *м* (*ТЕАТР*) dress
circle
**бемо́л|ь (-я)** *м* (*МУЗ*) flat
**бензи́н (-а)** *м* petrol (*BRIT*), gas
(*US*)
**бензоба́к (-а)** *м* petrol (*BRIT*) *или*
gas (*US*) tank
**бензоколо́н|ка (-ки;** *gen pl* **-ок)**
*ж* petrol (*BRIT*) *или* gas (*US*) pump
**Бенилю́кс (-а)** *м* Benelux
**бенуа́р (-а)** *м* (*ТЕАТР*) boxes *мн*
**бе́рег (-а;** *loc sg* **-ý,** *nom pl* **-á)** *м*
(*моря, озера*) shore; (*реки*) bank
**бережли́вый** *прил* thrifty
**бе́режный** *прил* caring
**берёз|а (-ы)** *ж* birch (tree)
**берём** *несов см.* **брать**
**бере́мене|ть (-ю;** *pf* **за~)** *несов*
to get pregnant
**бере́менн|ая** *прил* pregnant
♦ **(-ой)** *ж* pregnant woman
**бере́менность (-и)** *ж* pregnancy
**бере́т (-а)** *м* beret
**берёт** *etc несов см.* **брать**
**бер|е́чь (-егу́, -ежёшь** *etc*,
**-егу́т;** *pt* **-ёг, -егла́)** *несов перех*
(*здоровье, детей*) to look after,
take care of; (*деньги*) to be careful
with; (*время*) to make good use of;
**~ся** (*pf* **по~ся**) *несов возв:* **~ся**
*+gen* to watch out for; **~еги́тесь!**
watch out!
**Берли́н (-а)** *м* Berlin
**беру́(сь)** *etc несов см.* **брать(ся)**
**бесе́д|а (-ы)** *ж* conversation;
(*популярный доклад*) talk
**бесе́д|ка (-ки;** *gen pl* **-ок)** *ж*
pavilion
**бесе́д|овать (-ую)** *несов:* **~ (с**

+*instr*) to talk (to)

**бе|си́ть** (**-шу́**, **-сишь**) *несов перех* to infuriate; **~ся** *несов возв* (*разг*) to run wild; (*pf* **вз~ся**; *раздражаться*) to become furious

**бескомпроми́ссный** *прил* uncompromising

**бесконе́чност|ь** (**-и**) *ж* infinity; **до ~и** (*очень долго*) endlessly; (*очень сильно*) infinitely

**бесконе́чный** *прил* endless; (*любовь, ненависть*) undying

**бесконтро́льный** *прил* uncontrolled

**бескоры́стный** *прил* unselfish

**бескро́вный** *прил* bloodless

**бесперспекти́вный** *прил* (*работа*) without prospects

**беспе́чный** *прил* carefree

**беспла́тный** *прил* free

**беспло́дный** *прил* (*женщина*) infertile; (*почва*) barren, infertile; (*попытки, дискуссии*) fruitless

**бесповоро́тный** *прил* irrevocable

**бесподо́бный** *прил* (*разг*) fantastic

**беспоко́|ить** (**-ю**, **-ишь**; *pf* **по~**) *несов перех* (*мешать*) to disturb, trouble; (*pf* **о~**; *тревожить*) to worry; **~ся** *несов возв* (*утруждать себя*) to trouble o.s. (*тревожиться*); **~ся о** +*prp или* **за** +*acc* to worry about

**беспоко́йный** *прил* anxious; (*ребёнок*) restless; (*время*) troubled

**беспоко́йств|о** (**-а**) *ср* anxiety; (*хлопоты*) trouble; **прости́те за ~!** sorry to trouble you!

**беспо́лезный** *прил* useless

**беспо́мощный** *прил* helpless

**беспоря́дк|и** (**-ов**) *мн* disturbances *мн*

**беспоря́д|ок** (**-ка**) *м* disorder; **в ~ке** (*комната, дела*) in a mess;

см. *также* **беспоря́дки**

**беспоря́дочный** *прил* disorderly; (*рассказ*) confused

**беспоса́дочный** *прил* nonstop

**беспо́чвенный** *прил* groundless

**беспо́шлинный** *прил* duty-free

**беспоща́дный** *прил* merciless

**беспра́вный** *прил* without (civil) rights

**беспреде́л** (**-а**) *м* lawlessness

**беспреде́льный** *прил* boundless; (*о чувстве*) immeasurable

**беспрекосло́вный** *прил* unquestioning

**беспрепя́тственный** *прил* unimpeded

**беспрецеде́нтный** *прил* unprecedented

**беспри́быльный** *прил* unprofitable

**беспризо́рный** *прил* homeless

**беспринци́пный** *прил* unscrupulous

**беспристра́стный** *прил* unbias(s)ed

**беспричи́нный** *прил* unfounded

**беспроце́нтный** *прил* interest-free

**бессвя́зный** *прил* incoherent

**бессерде́чный** *прил* heartless

**бесси́льный** *прил* feeble, weak; (*гнев*) impotent; (*президент*) powerless

**бессме́ртный** *прил* immortal

**бессмы́сленный** *прил* meaningless, senseless; (*бесполезный*) pointless; (*взгляд*) inane

**бессо́вестный** *прил* (*нечестный*) unscrupulous; (*наглый*) shameless

**бессодержа́тельный** *прил* (*речь*) empty

**бессозна́тельн|ый** *прил* (*действия*) instinctive; **быть** (*impf*) **в ~ом состоя́нии** to be

unconscious
**бессо́нниц|а (-ы)** ж insomnia
**бессо́нный** прил (ночь) sleepless
**бесспо́рный** прил indisputable
**бесстра́шный** прил fearless
**бессты́дный** прил shameless
**беста́ктный** прил tactless
**бестолко́вый** прил (глупый) stupid
**бестсе́ллер (-а)** м best seller
**бесхозя́йственный** прил (руководитель) inefficient
**бесцве́тный** прил colourless (BRIT), colorless (US)
**бесце́льный** прил futile
**бесце́нный** прил priceless
**бесце́нок** м: **за ~** dirt cheap, for next to nothing
**бесчелове́чный** прил inhuman
**бесче́|стить (-щу, -стишь;** pf **о~)** несов перех (девушку) to violate
**бесчи́сленный** прил countless
**бесчу́вственный** прил (жестокий) unfeeling; (без сознания) senseless
**бето́н (-а)** м concrete
**бетони́р|овать (-ую;** pf **за~)** несов перех to concrete
**бефстро́ганов** м нескл boeuf или beef stroganoff
**бе́шенств|о (-а)** ср (МЕД) rabies; (раздражение) rage
**бе́шеный** прил (взгляд) furious; (характер, ураган) violent; (разг: цены) crazy
**биатло́н (-а)** м biathlon
**Би-би-си** ж сокр (= Брита́нская радиовеща́тельная корпора́ция) BBC
**библе́йский** прил biblical
**библиогра́фи|я (-и)** ж bibliography
**библиоте́к|а (-и)** ж library
**библиоте́кар|ь (-я)** м librarian
**библиоте́чный** прил library

**Би́бли|я (-и)** ж the Bible
**бигуди́** ср/мн нескл curlers мн
**бидо́н (-а)** м (для молока) churn
**бижуте́ри|я (-и)** ж costume jewellery
**биле́т (-а)** м ticket; (членский) (membership) card; **обра́тный ~** return (BRIT) или roundtrip (US) ticket; **входно́й ~** entrance ticket (for standing room)
**биллио́н (-а)** м billion (one thousand million)
**билья́рд (-а)** м (игра) billiards
**бино́кл|ь (-я)** м binoculars мн
**бинт (-а́)** м bandage
**бинт|ова́ть (-у́ю;** pf **за~)** несов перех to bandage
**биогра́фи|я (-и)** ж biography
**био́лог (-а)** м biologist
**биоло́ги|я (-и)** ж biology
**биосфе́р|а (-ы)** ж biosphere
**би́рж|а (-и)** ж (КОММ) exchange; **фо́ндовая ~** stock exchange или market
**биржеви́к (-а́)** м stockbroker
**биржево́й** прил (сделка) stock-exchange; **~ бро́кер** stockbroker
**би́р|ка (-ки;** gen pl **-ок)** ж tag
**бирюз|а́ (-ы́)** ж turquoise
**бис** межд: **Бис!** encore!
**би́сер (-а)** м собир glass beads мн
**бискви́т (-а)** м sponge (cake)
**бит (-а)** м (КОМП) byte
**би́тв|а (-ы)** ж battle
**битко́м** нареч: **~ (наби́т)** (разг) jam-packed
**бить (бью, бьёшь;** imper **бей(те);** pf **поби́ть)** несов перех to beat; (стёкла) to break ♦ (pf **проби́ть)** неперех (часы) to strike; **~** (impf) **в** +acc (в дверь) to

bang at; (*дождь, ветер*) to beat against; (*орудие*) to hit; **его́ бьёт озно́б** he's got a fit of the shivers; **би́ться** *несов возв* (*сердце*) to beat; (*стекло*) to be breakable; (*сражаться*) to fight; **би́ться** (*impf*) **о** +*acc* to bang against; **би́ться** (*impf*) **над** +*instr* (*над зада́чей*) to struggle with

**бифште́кс** (-а) *м* steak

**бла́г|а** (-) *мн* rewards *мн*; **всех благ!** all the best!

**бла́г|о** (-а) *ср* benefit; *см. также* **бла́га**

**благови́дный** *прил* plausible

**благодар|и́ть** (-ю́, -и́шь; *pf* по~) *несов перех* to thank

**благода́рност|ь** (-и) *ж* gratitude, thanks *мн*

**благода́р|ный** *прил* grateful; (*тема*) rewarding; **я Вам о́чень ~ен** I am very grateful to you

**благодаря́** *предл*: ~ +*dat* thanks to ♦ *союз*: ~ **тому́, что** owing to the fact that

**благ|о́й** *прил*: ~**и́е наме́рения** good intentions *мн*

**благополу́чи|е** (-я) *ср* (*в семье*) welfare; (*материа́льное*) prosperity

**благополу́чн|ый** *прил* successful; ~**ая семья́** good family

**благоприя́тный** *прил* favourable (*BRIT*), favorable (*US*)

**благоразу́мный** *прил* prudent

**благоро́дный** *прил* noble

**благослов|и́ть** (-лю́, -и́шь; *impf* **благослов|ля́ть**) *сов перех* to bless

**благосостоя́ни|е** (-я) *ср* well-being, prosperity

**благотвори́тел|ь** (-я) *м* benefactor

**благотвори́тельност|ь** (-и) *ж* charity

**благотвори́тельн|ый** *прил*

charitable; ~**ая организа́ция** charity (organization); ~ **конце́рт** charity concert

**благоустро́енный** *прил* (*дом*) with all modern conveniences

**блаже́нный** *прил* blissful; (*РЕЛ*) Blessed

**блаже́нств|о** (-а) *ср* bliss

**бланк** (-а) *м* form; (*организа́ции*) headed notepaper

**блат** (-а) *м* (*разг*) connections *мн*; **по бла́ту** (*разг*) through (one's) connections

**бледне́|ть** (-ю; *pf* по~) *несов* to (grow) pale

**бле́дный** *прил* pale; (*перен*) dull

**блеск** (-а) *м* (*огне́й*) brilliance, brightness; (*мета́лла*) shine; **с бле́ском** (*сде́лать*) brilliantly

**блесн|у́ть** (-у́, -ёшь) *сов* to flash; (*на экза́мене*) to do brilliantly

**бле|сте́ть** (-щу́, -сти́шь или, **блеще́шь**) *несов* (*звёзды, мета́лл*) to shine; (*глаза́*) to sparkle

**блестя́щий** *прил* (*звезда́*) bright; (*мета́лл*) shining; (*глаза́*) sparkling; (*студе́нт*) brilliant

**бле́|ять** (-ю) *несов* to bleat

**ближа́йший** *прил* (*го́род, дом*) the nearest; (*год*) the next; (*пла́ны*) immediate; (*друг, уча́стие*) closest; ~ **ро́дственник** next of kin

**бли́же** *сравн прил от* **бли́зкий** ♦ *сравн нареч от* **бли́зко**

**ближневосто́чный** *прил* Middle-Eastern

**бли́жний** *прил* (*го́род*) neighbouring; **бли́жнее зарубе́жье** former Soviet republics; **Бли́жний Восто́к** Middle East

**близк|ие** (-их) *мн* relatives *мн*

**бли́зкий** *прил* close; (*коне́ц*) imminent; ~ **кому́-н** (*интере́сы,* *тема*) close to sb's heart; ~ **по** +dat (*по содержанию, по цели*) similar *или* close in

**бли́зко** *нареч* near *или* close by ♦ *как сказ* not far off; ~ **от** +gen near, close to

**близне́ц** (-**а́**) *м* (*обычно мн*) twin; **бра́тья/сёстры-близнецы́** twin brothers/sisters; *см. также* **Близнецы́**

**Близнецы́** (-**ов**) *мн* Gemini *ед*

**близору́кий** *прил* short-sighted (*BRIT*), nearsighted (*US*)

**бли́зость** (-**и**) *ж* proximity; (*интересов, мнений*) closeness

**блин** (-**а́**) *м* pancake

**блок** (-**а**) *м* bloc; (*ТЕХ*) unit

**блока́д**|**а** (-**ы**) *ж* (*ВОЕН*) siege; (*экономическая*) blockade

**блоки́р**|**овать** (-**ую**) (*не*)*сов перех* to block; (*город*) to blockade

**блокно́т** (-**а**) *м* notebook, jotter

**блонди́н** (-**а**) *м*: **он - ~** he is blond

**блонди́н**|**ка** (-**ки**; *gen pl* -**ок**) *ж* blonde

**блох**|**а́** (-**и́**; *nom pl* -**и**) *ж* flea

**блужда́**|**ть** (-**ю**) *несов* to wander *или* roam (around)

**блу́з**|**ка** (-**ки**; *gen pl* -**ок**) *ж* blouse

**блю́д**|**о** (-**а**) *ср* dish

**блю**|**сти́** (-**ду́**, -**дёшь**; *pt* -**л**, -**ла́**, -**ло́**; *pf* **со~**) *несов перех* (*интересы*) to guard; (*чистоту*) to maintain

**боб** (-**а́**) *м* (*обычно мн*) bean

**бобр** (-**а́**) *м* beaver

**Бог** (-**а**; *voc* **Бо́же**) *м* God; **не дай ~!** God forbid!; **ра́ди Бо́га!** for God's sake!; **сла́ва Бо́гу** (*к счастью*) thank God

**богате́**|**ть** (-**ю**; *pf* **раз~**) *несов* to become rich

**бога́тств**|**а** (-) *мн* (*природные*) resources *мн*

**бога́тств**|**о** (-**а**) *ср* wealth, riches *мн*; *см. также* **бога́тства**

**бога́тый** *прил* rich; ~ **урожа́й** bumper harvest

**богаты́р**|**ь** (-**я́**) *м* warrior hero of Russian folk epics; (*перен*) Hercules

**бога́ч** (-**а́**) *м* rich man

**боги́н**|**я** (-**и**) *ж* goddess

**Богоро́диц**|**а** (-**ы**) *ж* the Virgin Mary

**богослови**|**е** (-**я**) *ср* theology

**богослуже́ни**|**е** (-**я**) *ср* service

**боготвор**|**и́ть** (-**ю́**, -**и́шь**) *несов перех* to worship

**бо́дрый** *прил* energetic; (*настроение, музыка*) cheerful

**боеви́к** (-**а́**) *м* militant; (*фильм*) action movie

**боево́й** *прил* military; (*настроение, дух*) fighting

**боеголо́в**|**ка** (-**ки**; *gen pl* -**ок**) *ж* warhead

**боеприпа́с**|**ы** (-**ов**) *мн* ammunition *ед*

**бо**|**е́ц** (-**йца́**) *м* (*солдат*) soldier

**Бо́же** *сущ см.* **Бог** ♦ *межд*: ~ (**ты мой**)! good Lord *или* God!; ~! **кака́я красота́!** God, it's beautiful!; ~ **упаси́** (*разг*) God forbid

**бо́жеский** *прил* (*РЕЛ*) divine; (*разг: цены, условия*) half-decent

**боже́ственный** *прил* divine

**Бо́ж**|**ий** *прил* God's; **ка́ждый бо́жий день** (*разг*) every single day; **бо́жья коро́вка** ladybird

**бо**|**й** (-**я**; *loc sg* -**ю́**, *nom pl* -**и́**, *gen pl* -**ёв**) *м* battle; (*боксёров*) fight; (*барабанов*) beating; (*часов*) striking

**бо́йкий** *прил* (*речь, ответ*) quick; (*продавец*) smart; (*место*) busy

**бойко́т** (-**а**) *м* boycott

**бойкоти́р**|**овать** (-**ую**) (*не*)*сов перех* to boycott

**бо́|йня** (**-йни**; gen pl **-ен**) ж slaughterhouse, abattoir; (на войне) carnage

**бок** (**-а**; loc sg **-ý**, nom pl **-á**) м side

**бока́л** (**-а**) м (wine)glass, goblet

**бо́ком** нареч sideways

**бокс** (**-а**) м (СПОРТ) boxing; (МЕД) isolation ward

**боксёр** (**-а**) м boxer

**болва́н** (**-а**) м (разг) blockhead

**Болга́ри|я** (**-и**) ж Bulgaria

**бо́лее** нареч more; ~ **или ме́нее** more or less; ~ **того́** what's more; **тем** ~ all the more so

**боле́зненный** прил sickly; (укол) painful; (перен: подозри́тельность) unhealthy; (самолюбие) unnatural

**боле́зн|ь** (**-и**) ж illness; (заразная) disease

**боле́льщик** (**-а**) м fan

**бол|е́ть** (**-е́ю**) несов: ~ (+instr) to be ill (with); (СПОРТ): ~ **за** +acc to be a fan of; (3sg **-и́т**; руки итп) to ache

**болеутоля́ющ|ий** прил: ~**ее сре́дство** painkiller

**боло́н|ка** (**-ки**; gen pl **-ок**) ж lapdog

**боло́нь|я** (**-и**) ж (ткань) lightweight waterproof material

**боло́т|о** (**-а**) ср marsh, bog

**болт** (**-á**) м bolt

**болта́|ть** (**-ю**) несов перех (разг: вздор) to talk ♦ неперех (разговаривать) to chat; (: много) to chatter; ~ (impf) **нога́ми** to dangle one's legs

**болтовн|я́** (**-и́**) ж (разг) waffle

**болту́н** (**-á**) м chatterbox

**болту́ш|ка** (**-ки**; gen pl **-ек**) ж см. **болту́н**

**бол|ь** (**-и**) ж pain; **зубна́я** ~ toothache; **головна́я** ~ headache

**больни́ц|а** (**-ы**) ж hospital

**больни́чный** прил hospital; ~ **лист** medical certificate

**бо́льно** нареч (удариться, упасть) badly, painfully; (обидеть) deeply; ~! that hurts!; **мне** ~ I am in pain

**больн|о́й** прил (рука итп) sore; (воображение) morbid; (нездоров) ill, sick ♦ (**-о́го**) м (болеющий) sick person; (пациент) patient; ~ **вопро́с** a sore point

**бо́льше** сравн прил от **большо́й** ♦ сравн нареч от **мно́го** ♦ нареч: ~ +gen (часа, килограмма итп) more than; (не хотеть, не жить) anymore; ~ **не бу́ду** (разг) I won't do it again; ~ **так не де́лай** don't do that again

**большинств|о́** (**-á**) ср majority

**больш|о́й** прил big, large; (радость) great; (дети) grown-up; **бо́льшей ча́стью, по бо́льшей ча́сти** for the most part; ~**áя бу́ква** capital letter

**боля́ч|ка** (**-ки**; gen pl **-ек**) ж sore

**бо́мб|а** (**-ы**) ж bomb

**бомбардиро́в|ка** (**-ки**; gen pl **-ок**) ж bombing

**бомбардиро́вщик** (**-а**) м bomber

**бомб|и́ть** (**-лю́**, **-и́шь**) несов перех to bomb

**бомбоубе́жищ|е** (**-а**) ср bomb shelter

**бомж** (**-á**) м homeless person

**бордо́вый** прил dark red, wine

**бордю́р** (**-а**) м (тротуара) kerb (BRIT), curb (US); (салфетки) border

**бор|е́ц** (**-ца́**) м (за свободу итп) fighter; (СПОРТ) wrestler

**борм|ота́ть** (**-очу́**, **-о́чешь**) несов перех to mutter

**бор|ода́** (acc sg **-оду**, gen sg **-оды́**, nom pl **-о́ды**, gen pl **-о́д**, dat pl

**-ода́м)** ж beard

**борода́в|ка (-ки;** gen pl **-ок)** ж wart

**бор|о́ться (-ю́сь, -ешься)** несов возв (СПОРТ) to wrestle; **~** (impf) **(c** +instr) to fight (with или against)

**борт (-а;** acc sg **за́ ~** или **за бо́рт,** instr sg **за бо́ртом** или **за ~о́м,** loc sg **-у́,** nom pl **-á)** м side; **на ~у́** или **~** on board, aboard; **челове́к за ~о́м!** man overboard!

**бортпроводни́к (-á)** м steward (on plane)

**бортпроводни́ц|а (-ы)** ж air hostess, stewardess (on plane)

**борщ (-á)** м borsch (beetroot-based soup)

**борьб|á (-ы́)** ж (за мир) fight, struggle; (СПОРТ) wrestling

**босико́м** нареч barefoot

**босо́й** прил barefoot

**босоно́ж|ка (-ки;** gen pl **-ек)** ж (обычно мн) sandal; (: с закрытым носом) slingback

**бота́ник|а (-и)** ж botany

**боти́н|ок (-ка)** м (обычно мн) ankle boot

**бо́цман (-а)** м boatswain, bosun

**бо́ч|ка (-ки;** gen pl **-ек)** ж barrel

**бо|я́ться (-ю́сь, -и́шься)** несов возв: **~** (+gen) to be afraid (of); **~** (impf) +infin to be afraid of doing или to do

**бра́во** межд bravo

**бразды́** мн: **~ правле́ния** the reins мн of power

**брак (-а)** м (супружество) marriage; (продукция) rejects мн; (деффект) flaw

**брако́ванный** прил reject

**брак|ова́ть (-у́ю;** pf **за~)** несов перех to reject

**браконье́р (-а)** м poacher

**браконье́рств|о (-а)** ср poaching

**бракосочета́ни|е (-я)** ср marriage ceremony

**бран|и́ть (-ю́, -и́шь)** несов to scold

**брасле́т (-а)** м (на часах) bracelet; (украшение) bangle

**брасс (-а)** м breaststroke

**брат (-а;** nom pl **-ья,** gen pl **-ьев)** м brother; **двою́родный ~** cousin

**бра́тск|ий** прил brotherly, fraternal; **~ая моги́ла** communal grave

**бра́тств|о (-а)** ср brotherhood

**бра|ть (беру́, берёшь;** pt **-л,** **-лá, -ло;** pf **взять)** несов перех to take; (билет) to get; (работника) to take on; (барьер) to clear; (разг: арестовать) to nick; **бра́ться** (pf **взя́ться)** несов возв: **бра́ться за** +acc (хватать рукой) to take hold of; (за работу) to get down to; (за книгу) to begin (за решение проблемы) to begin; **бра́ться (взя́ться** pf**) за ум** to see sense

**бра́тья** etc сущ см. **брат**

**бра́чный** прил (контракт) marriage; (союз) conjugal

**бревн|о́ (-á;** nom pl **брёвна,** gen pl **брёвен)** ср log; (СПОРТ) the beam

**бред (-а;** loc sg **-ý)** м delirium; (вздор) nonsense

**бре́|дить (-жу, -дишь)** несов to be delirious; **~** (impf) **кем-н/чем-н** to be mad about sb/sth

**брезгли́вый** прил (человек) fastidious; (взгляд) disgusted

**бре́зг|овать (-ую;** pf **по~)** несов: **~** +instr to be fastidious about

**брезе́нт (-а)** м tarpaulin

**бре́м|я (-ени;** как **вре́мя;** см. Table 4) ср burden

**бр|ести́ (-еду́, -едёшь;** pt **-ёл,** **-елá, -ело́)** несов to trudge

**брига́д|а (-ы)** ж (ВОЕН) brigade,

(work) team

**бригади́р** (**-а**) м team leader

**бриллиа́нт** (**-а**) м (cut) diamond

**брита́н|ец** (**-ца**) м Briton; **~цы** the British

**Брита́ни|я** (**-и**) ж Britain

**брита́нский** прил British

**бри́тв|а** (**-ы**) ж razor; **безопа́сная ~** safety razor

**бритоголо́в|ый** (**-ого**) м skinhead

**бр|ить** (**-е́ю, -е́ешь**; pf **по~и́ть**) несов перех (человека) to shave; (бо́роду) to shave off; **~и́ться** (pf **по~и́ться**) несов возв to shave

**бри́финг** (**-а**) м briefing

**бров|ь** (**-и**; gen pl **-е́й**) ж eyebrow

**бро|ди́ть** (**-жу́, -дишь**) несов to wander

**бродя́г|а** (**-и**) м/ж tramp

**брожѐни|е** (**-я**) ср fermentation; (перен: в обществе) ferment

**бро́кер** (**-а**) м broker

**бронежиле́т** (**-а**) м bullet-proof jacket

**бронетранспортёр** (**-а**) м armoured (BRIT) или armored (US) personnel carrier

**бро́нз|а** (**-ы**) ж bronze

**брони́р|овать** (**-ую**; pf **за~**) (не)сов перех to reserve

**бронх** (**-а**) м bronchial tube

**бронхи́т** (**-а**) м bronchitis

**бро́н|я** (**-и**) ж reservation

**брон|я́** (**-и́**) ж armour (BRIT) или armor (US) plating

**броса́|ть** (**-ю**) несов от **бро́сить; ~ся** несов от **бро́ситься** ♦ возв: **~ся снежка́ми/камня́ми** to throw snowballs/stones at each other

**бро́|сить** (**-шу, -сишь**; impf **броса́ть**) сов перех (ка́мень, мяч итп) to throw; (я́корь, се́ти) to cast; (семью́, дру́га) to abandon; (войска́) to dispatch;

(спорт) to give up; **меня́ ~си́ло в жар** I broke out in a sweat; **броса́ть** (**~** pf) +infin to give up doing; **~ся** (impf **броса́ться**) сов возв: **~ на** +acc (на врага́) to throw o.s. at; **броса́ться** (**~ся** pf) в **ата́ку** to rush to the attack

**бро́сов|ый** прил (разг: вещь) trashy; **~ая цена́** giveaway price

**бро́ш|ка** (**-ки**; gen pl **-ек**) ж brooch

**брош|ь** (**-и**) ж см. **бро́шка**

**брошю́р|а** (**-ы**) ж (книжка) booklet

**брус** (**-а**; nom pl **-ья**, gen pl **-ьев**) м beam; см. также **бру́сья**

**брусни́к|а** (**-и**) ж cowberry

**брус|о́к** (**-ка́**) м (для точки) whetstone; (мыла) bar

**бру́сь|я** (**-ев**) мн parallel bars мн

**бру́тто** прил неизм gross

**бры́з|гать** (**-жу, -жешь**) несов to splash; (**-гаю**; опры́скивать): **~ на** +acc to spray

**бры́зг|и** (**-**) мн splashes мн; (мелкие) spray ед

**бры́нз|а** (**-ы**) ж feta cheese

**брю́кв|а** (**-ы**) ж swede

**брю́к|и** (**-**) мн trousers мн, pants мн (US)

**брюне́т** (**-а**) м: **он ~** he has dark hair

**брюне́т|ка** (**-ки**; gen pl **-ок**) ж brunette

**Брюссе́л|ь** (**-я**) м Brussels

**брюшно́й** прил abdominal; **~ тиф** typhoid (fever)

**БТР** сокр = **бронетранспортёр**

**бу́блик** (**-а**) м ≈ bagel

**бу́б|ны** (**-ён**; dat pl **-нам**) мн (КАРТЫ) diamonds мн

**буг|о́р** (**-ра́**) м mound; (на коже) lump

**Будапе́шт** (**-а**) м Budapest

**будди́ст** (**-а**) м Buddhist

**бу́дем** *несов см.* **быть**

**бу́дет** *несов см.* **быть** ♦ *част* that's enough; ~ **тебе́!** that's enough from you!

**бу́дешь** *etc несов см.* **быть**

**буди́льник** (-**а**) *м* alarm clock

**бу|ди́ть** (-**жу́, -дишь**; *pf* **раз~**) *несов перех* to wake (up), awaken

**бу́д|ка** (-**ки**; *gen pl* -**ок**) *ж* (*сторожа*) hut; (*для собаки*) kennel; **телефо́нная** ~ phone box

**бу́дн|и** (-**ей**) *мн* working *или* week days *мн*; (*перен: повседневность*) routine *ед*

**бу́дто** *союз* (*якобы*) supposedly; (*словно*): (**как**) ~ (**бы**) as if; **он уверя́ет, ~ сам её ви́дел** he claims to have seen her himself

**бу́ду** *etc несов см.* **быть**

**бу́дущ|ее** (-**его**) *ср* the future; **в ~ем** in the future

**бу́дущ|ий** *прил* (*следующий*) next; (*предстоящий*) future; **~ее вре́мя** future tense

**бу́дь(те)** *несов см.* **быть** ♦ *союз*: **будь то** be it

**бужени́н|а** (-**ы**) *ж* cold cooked and seasoned pork

**бу|й** (-**я**; *nom pl* -**и**) *м* buoy

**бу́йвол** (-**а**) *м* buffalo

**бу́йный** *прил* wild; (*растительность*) luxuriant, lush

**бук** (-**а**) *м* beech

**бу́кв|а** (-**ы**) *ж* letter

**буква́льный** *прил* literal

**буква́р|ь** (-**я**) *м* first reading book

**буке́т** (-**а**) *м* bouquet

**букинисти́ческий** *прил*: ~ **магази́н** second-hand bookshop

**букле́т** (-**а**) *м* booklet

**букси́р** (-**а**) *м* tug; (*трос*) towrope

**була́в|ка** (-**ки**; *gen pl* -**ок**) *ж* pin

**бу́л|ка** (-**ки**; *gen pl* -**ок**) *ж* roll; (*белый хлеб*) loaf

**бу́лоч|ка** (-**ки**; *gen pl* -**ек**) *ж* small roll

**бу́лочн|ая** (-**ой**) *ж* baker, baker's

**булы́жник** (-**а**) *м* cobblestone

**булы́жн|ый** *прил*: ~**ая мостова́я** cobbled street

**бульва́р** (-**а**) *м* boulevard

**бульва́рн|ый** *прил* boulevard; ~**ая пре́сса** gutter press

**бульдо́г** (-**а**) *м* bulldog

**бульдо́зер** (-**а**) *м* bulldozer

**бульо́н** (-**а**; *part gen* -**у**) *м* stock

**бум** (-**а**) *м* boom

**бума́г|а** (-**и**) *ж* paper; **це́нные ~и** securities

**бума́ж|ка** (-**ки**; *gen pl* -**ек**) *ж* piece of paper

**бума́жник** (-**а**) *м* wallet, pocketbook (*US*)

**бума́жный** *прил* paper

**бу́нкер** (-**а**) *м* bunker

**бунт** (-**а**) *м* (*мятеж*) riot; (: *на корабле*) mutiny

**бунт|ова́ть** (-**у́ю**) *несов* (*см сущ*) to riot; to mutiny

**бура́в|ить** (-**лю, -ишь**; *pf* **пробура́вить**) *несов перех* to drill

**бура́н** (-**а**) *м* blizzard, snowstorm

**буре́ни|е** (-**я**) *ср* boring, drilling

**буржуази́|я** (-**и**) *ж* bourgeoisie; **ме́лкая** ~ petty bourgeoisie

**буржуа́зный** *прил* bourgeois

**бур|и́ть** (-**ю́, -и́шь**; *pf* **про~**) *несов перех* to bore, drill

**бурл|и́ть** (-**ю́, -и́шь**) *несов* (*ручей*) to bubble; (*толпа*) to seethe

**бу́рный** *прил* (*погода, океан*) stormy; (*чувство*) wild; (*рост*) rapid

**буров|о́й** *прил* boring, drilling; ~**ая вы́шка** derrick; ~**ая сква́жина** bore(hole)

**бу́рый** *прил* brown

**бу́р|я** (-**и**) *ж* storm

**бу́с|ы** (-) *мн* beads *мн*

**бутафо́ри|я** (-и) *ж* (*ТЕАТР*) props *мн*; (*перен*) sham

**бутербро́д** (-а) *м* sandwich

**буто́н** (-а) *м* bud

**бу́тс|а** (-ы) *ж* football boot

**буты́л|ка** (-ки; *gen pl* -ок) *ж* bottle

**буты́лочный** *прил* bottle; (*цвет*) bottle-green

**бу́фер** (-а; *nom pl* -á) *м* buffer

**буфе́т** (-а) *м* snack bar; (*шкаф*) sideboard

**буфе́тчик** (-а) *м* barman

**буха́н|ка** (-ки; *gen pl* -ок) *ж* loaf

**Бухаре́ст** (-а) *м* Bucharest

**бухга́лтер** (-а) *м* accountant, book-keeper

**бухгалте́ри|я** (-и) *ж* accountancy, book-keeping; (*отдел*) accounts office

**бухга́лтерск|ий** *прил* book-keeping, accountancy; **~ие кни́ги** books; **~ учёт** book-keeping, accountancy

**бу́хт|а** (-ы) *ж* bay

**буш|ева́ть** (-у́ю) *несов* (*пожар, ураган*) to rage

---

KEYWORD

---

**бы** *част* 1 (*выражает возможность*): **купи́л бы, е́сли бы бы́ли де́ньги** I would buy it if I had the money; **я бы давно́ уже́ купи́л э́ту кни́гу, е́сли бы у меня́ бы́ли де́ньги** I would have bought this book long ago if I had had the money

2 (*выражает пожелание*): **я бы хоте́л поговори́ть с тобо́й** I would love to speak to you

3 (*выражает совет*): **ты бы написа́л ей** you should write to her

4 (*выражает опасение*): **не захвати́л бы нас дождь** I hope

we don't get caught in the rain; **отдохну́ть/погуля́ть бы** it would be nice to have a rest/go for a walk

---

**быва́ло** *част* expresses repeated action in the past; **~ сиди́м и разгова́риваем** we used to *или* would sit and talk

**быва́|ть** (-ю) *несов* (*посещать*) to be; (*случаться*) to happen, take place; **он ~ет у нас ча́сто** he often comes to see us; **как ни в чём не ~ло** (*разг*) as if nothing had happened

**бы́вший** *прил* former

**бык** (-а́) *м* bull; (*рабочий*) ox

**был** *etc несов см.* **быть**

**были́н|а** (-ы) *ж* heroic poem

**бы́л|ь** (-и) *ж* true story

**бы́стро** *нареч* quickly

**быстрот|а́** (-ы́) *ж* speed; (*ума, рук*) quickness

**бы́стрый** *прил* (*машина итп*) fast; (*руки, взгляд, речь*) quick

**быт** (-а; *loc sg* -у́) *м* life; (*повседневность*) everyday life; **слу́жба бы́та** consumer services

**бытов|о́й** *прил* everyday; **~о́е обслу́живание населе́ния** consumer services; **~а́я те́хника** household electrical appliances

---

KEYWORD

---

**быть** (*см. Table 21*) *несов* 1 (*omitted in present tense*) to be; **кни́га на столе́** the book is on the table; **за́втра я бу́ду в шко́ле** I will be at school tomorrow; **дом был на краю́ го́рода** the house was *или* stood on the edge of the town; **на ней краси́вое пла́тье** she is wearing a beautiful dress; **вчера́ был дождь** it rained yesterday

2 (*часть составного сказ*) to be; **я хочу́ быть учи́телем** I want to

be a teacher; **я был рад ви́деть тебя́** I was happy to see you; **так и быть!** so be it!; **как быть?** what is to be done?; **э́того не мо́жет быть** that's impossible; **кто/како́й бы то ни́ был** whoever/whatever it might be; **бу́дьте добры́!** excuse me!; **бу́дьте добры, позвони́те его́!** would you be so good *или* kind as to call him?; **бу́дьте здоро́вы!** take care!
3 (*образует будущее время*; *+impf vb*): **ве́чером я бу́ду писа́ть пи́сьма** I'll be writing letters this evening; **я бу́ду люби́ть тебя́ всегда́** I'll love you forever

---

**бью(сь)** *etc несов см.* **бить(ся)**
**бюдже́т (-а)** *м* budget; **дохо́дный ~** revenue; **расхо́дный ~** expenditure
**бюдже́тник (-а)** *м person working in a state-funded institution*
**бюдже́тный** *прил* budgetary; (*организация*) state-funded
**бюллете́н|ь (-я)** *м* bulletin; (*на выборах*) ballot paper; (*справка*) medical certificate
**бюро́** *ср нескл* office; **~ нахо́док** lost property office
**бюрокра́т (-а)** *м* bureaucrat
**бюрокра́ти|я (-и)** *ж* bureaucracy
**бюст (-а)** *м* bust
**бюстга́льтер (-а)** *м* bra

# В, в

**В** *сокр* (= **вольт**) v.

**в** *предл*; *+acc* 1 (*о месте направления*) in(to); **я положи́л кни́гу в портфе́ль** I put the book

in(to) my briefcase; **я сел в маши́ну** I got in(to) the car
2 (*уехать, пойти*) to; **он уе́хал в Москву́** he went to Moscow
3 (*об изменении состояния*): **погружа́ться в рабо́ту** to be absorbed in one's work
4 (*об объекте физического действия*): **он постуча́л в дверь** he knocked on the door; **он посмотре́л мне в глаза́** he looked me in the eyes; **мать поцелова́ла меня́ в щёку** mother kissed me on the cheek
5 (*о времени совершения чего-н*): **он пришёл в понеде́льник** he came on Monday; **я ви́дел его́ в про́шлом году́** I saw him last year; **я встре́тил его́ в два часа́** I met him at two o'clock; **э́то случи́лось в ма́рте/в двадца́том ве́ке** it happened in March/in the twentieth century
6 (*о размере, количестве*): **ве́сом в 3 то́нны** 3 tons *или* tonnes in weight; (*+prp*): **дра́ма в трёх частя́х** a drama in three acts; **в пяти́ ме́трах от доро́ги** five metres (*BRIT*) *или* meters (*US*) from the road
7 (*о соотношении величин*): **в два ра́за бо́льше/длинне́е** twice as big/long; **во мно́го раз лу́чше/умне́е** much better/cleverer
8 (*обозначает форму, вид*): **брю́ки в кле́тку** checked trousers; **лека́рство в табле́тках** medicine in tablet form
9 (*+prp*; *о месте*) in; **ко́шка сиди́т в корзи́не** the cat is sitting in the basket; **я живу́ в дере́вне** I live in the country; **сын у́чится в шко́ле** my son is at school
10 (*о чём-н облегающем, покрыва́ющем*): **ру́ки в кра́ске/**

**са́же** hands covered in paint/soot;
**това́р в упако́вке** packaged
goods
**11** (*об одежде*) in; **мужчи́на в
очка́х/в ша́пке** a man in *или*
wearing glasses/a hat
**12** (*о состоянии*): **быть в у́жасе/
негодова́нии** to be terrified/
indignant

**в.** *сокр* (= **век**) с; (= **восто́к**) E
**ваго́н** (-а) *м* (*пассажирский*)
carriage (*BRIT*), coach (*BRIT*), car
(*US*); (*товарный*) wagon (*BRIT*),
truck; **спа́льный ~** couchette car;
**мя́гкий ~** ≈ sleeping car;
**~-рестора́н** dining (*BRIT*) *или* club
(*US*) car
**ва́жный** *прил* important
**ва́з**|**а** (-ы) *ж* vase
**вазели́н** (-а) *м* Vaseline ®
**вака́нси**|**я** (-и) *ж* vacancy
**вака́нтн**|**ый** *прил* vacant; **~ая
до́лжность** vacancy
**ва́куум** (-а) *м* vacuum
**вакци́н**|**а** (-ы) *ж* vaccine
**вакцини́р**|**овать** (-ую) (*не*)*сов
перех* to vaccinate
**вал** (-а; *loc sg* -у́, *nom pl* -ы́) *м*
(*насыпь*) bank; (*ТЕХ, стержень*)
shaft; (*волна*) breaker
**ва́лен**|**ок** (-ка) *м* felt boot
**валериа́нк**|**а** (-и) *ж* valerian drops
**вале́т** (-а) *м* (*КАРТЫ*) jack
**ва́лик** (-а) *м* (*в механизме*)
cylinder; (*для краски*) roller;
(*подушка*) bolster
**вал**|**и́ть** (-ю́, -ишь; *pf* **с~** *или*
**по~**) *несов перех* (*заставить
падать*) to knock over; (*рубить*) to
fell; (*pf* **с~**; *разг: бросать*) to
dump ♦ *неперех* (*дым, пар*) to
pour out; **~** (**с~** *pf*) **вину́ на** +*acc*
(*разг*) to point the finger at; **~ся**
(*pf* **с~ся** *или* **по~ся**) *несов возв*

(*падать*) to fall; **~ся** (*impf*) **с ног**
(*разг*) to be dead on one's feet
**валово́й** *прил* (*доход*) gross
**валу́н** (-а́) *м* boulder
**вальс** (-а) *м* waltz
**валю́т**|**а** (-ы) *ж* currency ♦ *собир*
foreign currency
**валю́тн**|**ый** *прил* currency; **~ курс**
rate of exchange
**валя́**|**ть** (-ю) *несов перех*
(*катать*) to roll; (*pf* **с~**; *скатывать*)
to shape; **~ся** *несов возв*
(*кататься*) to roll about; (*разг:
человек, бумаги итп*) to lie about
**вам** *etc мест см.* **вы**
**вампи́р** (-а) *м* vampire
**вани́л**|**ь** (-и) *ж* vanilla
**ва́нн**|**а** (-ы) *ж* bath
**ва́нн**|**ая** (-ой) *ж* bathroom
**ва́рвар** (-а) *м* barbarian
**ва́рварств**|**о** (-а) *ср* barbarism;
(*жестокость*) barbarity
**ва́реж**|**ка** (-ки; *gen pl* -ек) *ж*
mitten
**варёный** *прил* boiled
**варе́нь**|**е** (-я) *ср* jam
**вариа́нт** (-а) *м* variant
**вар**|**и́ть** (-ю́, -ишь; *pf* **с~**) *несов
перех* (*обед*) to cook; (*суп, кофе*)
to make; (*картофель*) to boil;
(*ТЕХ*) to weld; **~ся** (*pf* **с~ся**) *несов
возв* (*обед*) to be cooking
**Варша́в**|**а** (-ы) *ж* Warsaw
**варьете́** *ср нескл* variety show
**варьи́р**|**овать** (-ую) *несов
(не)перех* to vary
**вас** *мест см.* **вы**
**ва́т**|**а** (-ы) *ж* cotton wool (*BRIT*),
(absorbent) cotton (*US*)
**ва́тман** (-а) *м heavy paper for
drawing etc*
**ва́тный** *прил* cotton-wool (*BRIT*),
absorbent cotton (*US*)
**ватру́ш**|**ка** (-ки; *gen pl* -ек) *ж* curd
tart

**ватт** (-a) м watt

**ва́учер** (-a) м voucher

**ва́ф|ля** (-ли; gen pl -ель) ж wafer

**ва́хт|а** (-ы) ж watch; **стоя́ть** (impf) **на ~e** to keep watch

**вахтёр** (-a) м caretaker, janitor (esp US, SCOTTISH)

**ваш** (-его; f -a, nt -e, pl -и; как **наш**; см. Table 9) притяж мест your; **э́то ва́ше** this is yours

**Вашингто́н** (-a) м (ГЕО) Washington

**вбе|жа́ть** (как **бежа́ть**; см. Table 20; impf **вбега́ть**) сов: ~ (в +acc) to run in(to)

**вбить** (вобью́, вобьёшь; impf **вбива́ть**) сов перех: ~ (в +acc) to drive или hammer in(to)

**вблизи́** нареч nearby ♦ предл: ~ +gen или **от** +gen near (to)

**вбок** нареч sideways

**вбро́|сить** (-шу, -сишь; impf **вбра́сывать**) сов перех to throw in

**ввал|и́ться** (-ю́сь, -ишься; impf **вва́ливаться**) сов возв (щеки, глаза) to become sunken

**введе́ни|е** (-я) ср introduction

**ввез|ти́** (-у́, -ёшь; pt ввёз, -ла́, -ло́; impf **ввози́ть**) сов перех (в дом итп) to take in; (в страну) to import

**вверх** нареч up ♦ предл: ~ **по** +dat up; ~ **по тече́нию** upstream; **в до́ме всё ~ дном** (разг) everything in the house is topsy-turvy; ~ **нога́ми** (разг) upside down

**вверху́** нареч up ♦ предл: ~ +gen at the top of

**вв|ести́** (-еду́, -едёшь; pt -ёл, -ела́, impf **вводи́ть**) сов перех to take in; (лекарство) to inject; (в компьютер) to enter; (закон) to introduce; (сделать действующим): ~ **что-н в** +acc to put sth into

**ввиду́** предл: ~ +gen in view of ♦ союз: ~ **того́, что** in view of the fact that

**ввод** (-a) м bringing in; (данных) input, feeding in

**вво|ди́ть** (-жу́, -дишь) несов от **ввести́**

**вво́дн|ый** прил introductory; ~**ое сло́во** parenthesis

**ввоз** (-a) м (процесс) importation; (импорт) imports мн

**вво|зи́ть** (-жу́, -зишь) несов от **ввезти́**

**ввозн|о́й** прил imported; ~**ые по́шлины** import duty

**ВВП** м сокр (= валово́й вну́тренний проду́кт) GDP

**вглубь** нареч (down) into the depths ♦ предл: ~ +gen (вниз) into the depths of; (внутрь) into the heart of

**вда|ва́ться** (-ю́сь) несов от **вда́ться**

**вдав|и́ть** (-лю́, -ишь; impf **вда́вливать**) сов перех: ~ (в +acc) to press in(to)

**вдалеке́** нареч in the distance; ~ **от** +gen a long way from

**вдали́** нареч = **вдалеке́**

**вдаль** нареч into the distance

**вда́ться** (как **дать**; см. Table 16; impf **вдава́ться**) сов возв: ~ **в** +acc to jut out into (перен): **в рассужде́ния**) to get caught up in; **вдава́ться** (~ pf) **в подро́бности** to go into details

**вдво́е** нареч (сложить) in two; ~ **сильне́е** twice as strong

**вдвоём** нареч: **они́ живу́т** ~ the two of them live together

**вдвойне́** нареч double (the amount)

**вде|ть** (-ну, -нешь; impf

**вдева́ть**) *сов перех* to put in

**вдоба́вок** *нареч* (*разг*) in addition ♦ *предл*: ~ к +*dat* in addition to

**вдов|а́** (-ы́; *nom pl* -ы) *ж* widow

**вдов|е́ц** (-ца́) *м* widower

**вдо́воль** *нареч* to one's heart's content

**вдоль** *нареч* (*сломаться*) lengthways ♦ *предл*: ~ +*gen* along

**вдох** (-а) *м* inhalation; **де́лать** (**сде́лать** *pf*) ~ to breathe in

**вдохнове́ни|е** (-я) *ср* inspiration

**вдохнов|и́ть** (-лю́, -и́шь; *impf* **вдохновля́ть**) *сов перех* to inspire

**вдохн|у́ть** (-у́; *impf* **вдыха́ть**) *сов перех* (*воздух*) to breathe in; (*дым, лекарство*) to inhale

**вдре́безги** *нареч* to smithereens

**вдруг** *нареч* suddenly; (*а если*) what if

**вду́ма|ться** (-юсь; *impf* **вду́мываться**) *сов возв*: ~ в +*acc* to think over

**вдыха́|ть** (-ю) *несов от* **вдохну́ть**

**вегетариа́н|ец** (-ца) *м* vegetarian

**вегетариа́нский** *прил* vegetarian

**ве́да|ть** (-ю) *несов*: ~ +*instr* (*управля́ть*) to be in charge of

**ве́дени|е** (-я) *ср* authority

**веде́ни|е** (-я) *ср* conducting; (*войны*) waging; ~ **хозя́йства** housekeeping

**ведёт(ся)** *etc несов см.* **вести́(сь)**

**ве́дом|о** *ср*: с/без ~а кого́-н (*согла́сие*) with/without sb's consent; (*уведомле́ние*) with/without sb's knowledge

**ве́домост|ь** (-и; *gen pl* -е́й) *ж* register; **расчётная** *или* **платёжная** ~ payroll

**ве́домств|о** (-а) *ср* department

**ведр|о́** (-а́; *nom pl* **вёдра**, *gen pl* **вёдер**) *ср* bucket, pail

**веду́щ|ий** *прил* leading ♦ (-его) *м* presenter

**ведь** *нареч* (*в вопросе*): ~ **ты хо́чешь пое́хать?** you do want to go, don't you?; (*в утвержде́нии*): ~ **она́ не спра́вится одна́!** she can't surely manage alone! ♦ *союз* (*о причи́не*) seeing as; **пое́шь, ~ ты го́лоден** you should eat, seeing as you're hungry

**ве́дьм|а** (-ы) *ж* witch

**ве́ер** (-а; *nom pl* -а́) *м* fan

**ве́жливый** *прил* polite

**везде́** *нареч* everywhere; ~ **и всю́ду** everywhere you go

**вездехо́д** (-а) *м* ≈ Landrover ®

**везе́ни|е** (-я) *ср* luck

**вез|ти́** (-у́, -ёшь) *несов перех* to transport, take; (*сани*) to pull; (*тачку*) to push ♦ (*pf* **по~**) *безл*: ~ +*dat* (*разг*) to be lucky

**век** (-а; *nom pl* -а́) *м* century; (*период*) age; **на ~а́, во ве́ки ~о́в** forever

**ве́к|о** (-а) *ср* eyelid

**вексово́й** *прил* ancient

**ве́ксел|ь** (-я; *nom pl* -я́) *м* promissory note

**вел|е́ть** (-ю́, -и́шь) (*не*)*сов*: ~ +*dat* to order

**велика́н** (-а) *м* giant

**вели́к|ий** *прил* great ♦ *как сказ*: **сапоги́ мне велики́** the boots are too big for me; ~**ие держа́вы** the Great Powers

**Великобрита́ни|я** (-и) *ж* Great Britain

**великоду́шный** *прил* magnanimous, big-hearted

**великору́сский** *прил* Great Russian

**великоле́пный** *прил* magnificent

**вели́чественный** *прил* majestic

**величин|а́** (-ы́) *ж* size; (*МАТ*) quantity

**велого́н|ка** (-ки; gen pl -ок) ж
cycle race

**велосипе́д** (-а) м bicycle

**вельве́т** (-а) м corduroy

**Ве́н|а** (-ы) ж Vienna

**ве́н|а** (-ы) ж vein

**Ве́нгри|я** (-и) ж Hungary

**венери́ческий** прил venereal

**ве́ник** (-а) м broom

**вен|о́к** (-ка́) м wreath

**вентиля́тор** (-а) м (ventilator) fan

**венча́|ть** (-ю; pf об~ или по~)
несов перех to marry (in church); ~
(impf) на ца́рство кого́-н to crown
sb; ~ся (pf об~ся) несов возв to
be married (in church)

**ве́р|а** (-ы) ж faith; (в Бога) belief

**вера́нд|а** (-ы) ж verandah

**ве́рб|а** (-ы) ж pussy willow

**верблю́д** (-а) м camel

**ве́рбн|ый** прил: Ве́рбное
воскресе́нье ≈ Palm Sunday

**верб|ова́ть** (-у́ю; pf за~) несов
перех to recruit

**верёв|ка** (-ки; gen pl -ок) ж
(толстая) rope; (тонкая) string

**ве́р|ить** (-ю, -ишь; pf по~)
несов: ~ +dat to believe;
(доверять) to trust; ~ (по~ pf) в
кого́-н/что-н to believe in sb/sth; ~
(по~ pf) на́ слово кому́-н to take
sb at his итп word; ~ся несов
безл: не ~ится, что э́то пра́вда
it's hard to believe it's true

**вермише́л|ь** (-и) ж vermicelli

**ве́рмут** (-а) м vermouth

**верне́е** вводн сл or rather; ~
всего́ most likely

**ве́рно** нареч (преданно) faithfully;
(правильно) correctly ♦ как сказ
that's right

**верн|у́ть** (-у́, -ёшь) сов перех to
return, give back; (долг) to pay
back; (здоровье, надежду) to
restore; ~ся сов возв: ~ся (к +dat)

to return (to)

**ве́рный** прил (друг) faithful;
(надёжный) sure; (правильный)
correct; ~ сло́ву true to one's word

**ве́ровани|е** (-я) ср (обычно мн)
faith

**вероиспове́дани|е** (-я) ср faith

**вероло́мный** прил (друг)
treacherous; (нападение) deceitful

**вероя́тно** как сказ it is probable
♦ вводн сл probably

**вероя́тн|ый** прил probable; ~ее
всего́ most likely или probably

**ве́рси|я** (-и) ж version

**верста́к** (-а́) м (ТЕХ) (work)bench

**вер|те́ть** (-чу́, -тишь) несов
перех (руль) to turn; ~ (impf) в
рука́х что-н to fiddle with sth; ~ся
несов возв (колесо) to spin;
(человек) to fidget

**вертика́льный** прил vertical

**вертолёт** (-а) м helicopter

**ве́рующ|ий** (-его) м believer

**верф|ь** (-и) ж shipyard

**верх** (-а; loc sg -у́, nom pl -и́) м
(дома, стола) top; (обуви) upper;
~ соверше́нства/глу́пости the
height of perfection/stupidity; см.
также верхи́

**верх|и́** (-о́в) мн: в ~а́х at the top;
встре́ча/перегово́ры в ~а́х
summit meeting/talks

**ве́рхн|ий** прил top; ~яя оде́жда
outer clothing или garments;
Ве́рхняя пала́та Upper Chamber

**верхо́вный** прил supreme;
Верхо́вный Суд High Court
(BRIT), Supreme Court (US)

**верхо́в|ой** прил: ~а́я езда́ horse
(BRIT) или horseback (US) riding

**верхо́м** нареч astride

**верху́ш|ка** (-ки; gen pl -ек) ж
(дерева, насыпи) top; (перен:
правящая) elite

**верши́н|а** (-ы) ж top; (горы)

summit

**вес** (-а; *nom pl* -**а́**) *м* weight; (*перен: влияние*) authority

**веселе́ть** (-ю; *pf* по~) *несов* to cheer up

**весел|и́ть** (-ю́, -и́шь; *pf* раз~) *несов перех* to amuse; **~ся** *несов возв* to have fun

**ве́село** *нареч* (*сказать*) cheerfully ♦ *как сказ*: **здесь ~** it's fun here; **мне ~** I'm having fun

**весёлый** *прил* cheerful

**весе́ль|е** (-я) *ср* merriment

**весе́нний** *прил* spring

**ве́|сить** (-шу, -сишь) *несов* to weigh

**ве́ский** *прил* (*аргумент*) potent

**весл|о́** (-а́; *nom pl* **вёсла**, *gen pl* **вёсел**) *ср* oar

**весн|а́** (-ы́; *nom pl* **вёсны**, *gen pl* **вёсен**) *ж* spring

**весно́й** *нареч* in (the) spring

**весну́ш|ка** (-ки; *gen pl* -ек) *ж* freckle

**весо́мый** *прил* (*вклад*) substantial

**ве|сти́** (-ду́, -дёшь; *pt* вёл, -ла́, -ло́) *несов перех* to take; (*машину*) to drive; (*корабль*) to navigate; (*отряд*) to lead; (*заседание*) to chair; (*работу*) to conduct; (*хозяйство*) to run; (*записи*) to keep ♦ (*pf* **привести́**) *неперех*: **вести́ к** +*dat* to lead to; **вести́** (*impf*) **себя́** to behave; **вести́сь** *несов возв* (*расследование*) to be carried out; (*переговоры*) to go on

**вестибю́л|ь** (-я) *м* lobby

**вест|ь** (-и) *ж* news; **пропада́ть** (**пропа́сть** *pf*) **бе́з ~и** (*ВОЕН*) to go missing; **бе́з ~и пропа́вший** (*ВОЕН*) missing feared dead; **Бог ~ кто/что** (*разг*) God knows who/ what

**вес|ы́** (-о́в) *мн* scales *мн*;

(*созвездие*): **Весы́** Libra

**весь** (*всего́*; *f* вся, *nt* всё, *pl* все; *см. Table 13*) *мест* all; **всего́ хоро́шего** *или* **до́брого!** all the best!

**ветв|ь** (-и; *gen pl* -е́й) *ж* branch

**ве́т|ер** (-ра) *м* wind

**ветера́н** (-а) *м* veteran

**ветерина́р** (-а) *м* vet (*BRIT*), veterinarian (*US*)

**ве́т|ка** (-ки; *gen pl* -ок) *ж* branch

**ве́то** *ср нескл* veto

**ве́треный** *прил* windy

**ветров|о́й** *прил*: ~**о́е стекло́** windscreen (*BRIT*), windshield (*US*)

**ветря́н|ка** (-ки) *ж* (*МЕД*) chickenpox

**ветрян|о́й** *прил* wind-powered; ~**а́я о́спа** chickenpox

**ве́тхий** *прил* (*дом*) dilapidated; (*одежда*) shabby; **Ве́тхий Заве́т** the Old Testament

**ветчин|а́** (-ины́; *nom pl* -и́ны) *ж* ham

**ве́х|а** (-и) *ж* landmark

**ве́чер** (-а; *nom pl* -а́) *м* evening; (*праздник*) party

**вече́рний** *прил* evening

**вече́рнее отделе́ние** - People who do not want to give up their job may opt to do a degree by taking courses in the evening. This course runs over 4 days a week with over 20 contact hours a week and is very much like the day-time course. Because of the reduced hours the entire degree takes 6 years to complete. See also notes at **зао́чный** and **о́чный**.

**ве́чером** *нареч* in the evening

**ве́чно** *нареч* eternally; (*разг*: *жаловаться*) perpetually

**ве́чност|ь** (-и) ж eternity

**ве́чный** прил eternal, everlasting

**ве́шал|ка** (-ки; gen pl -ок) ж (планка) rack; (стойка) hatstand; (плечики) coat hanger; (гардероб) cloakroom; (петля) loop

**ве́ша|ть** (-ю; pf **пове́сить**) несов перех to hang; (pf **с~**; товар) to weigh; **~ся** (pf **пове́ситься**) несов возв to hang o.s.

**веща́|ть** (3sg -ет) несов to broadcast

**веще́ственный** прил material

**веществ|о́** (-а́) ср substance

**вещ|ь** (-и; gen pl -е́й) ж thing; (книга, фильм) piece

**ве́|ять** (-ю, -ешь) несов (ветер) to blow lightly

**взаи́мный** прил mutual

**взаимоде́йстви|е** (-я) ср (связь) interaction

**взаимоотноше́ни|е** (-я) ср (inter)relationship

**взаимопо́мощ|ь** (-и) ж mutual assistance или aid

**взаимопонима́ни|е** (-я) ср mutual understanding

**взаимосвя́з|ь** (-и) ж interconnection

**взаймы́** нареч: дава́ть/брать де́ньги ~ to lend/borrow money

**взаме́н** нареч in exchange
♦ предл: ~ +gen (вместо) instead of; (в обмен) in exchange for

**взаперти́** нареч under lock and key

**взбить** (**взобью́, взобьёшь**; imper **взбей(те)**, impf **взбива́ть**) сов перех (яйца) to beat; (сливки) to whip; (волосы) to fluff up; (подушки) to plump up

**взва́л|ить** (-ю, -ишь; impf **взва́ливать**) сов перех: ~ что-н на +acc to haul sth up onto

**взве́|сить** (-шу, -сишь; impf **взве́шивать**) сов перех (товар) to weigh; (факты) to weigh up*

**взве|сти́** (-ду́, -дёшь; pt **взвёл**, -ла́; impf **взводи́ть**) сов перех: ~ куро́к to cock a gun

**взве́шенный** прил considered

**взве́шива|ть** (-ю) несов от **взве́сить**

**взвин|ти́ть** (-чу́, -ти́шь; impf **взви́нчивать**; сов перех (разг: цены) to jack up

**взвод** (-а) м platoon; **на взво́де** (курок) cocked

**взво|ди́ть** (-жу́, -дишь) несов от **взвести́**

**взволно́ванный** прил agitated; (радостный) excited

**взволн|ова́ть(ся)** (-у́ю(сь)) сов от **волнова́ть(ся)**

**взв|ыть** (-о́ю, -о́ешь) сов to howl; (сирена) to wail

**взгляд** (-а) м glance; (выражение) look; (перен: мнение) view; **на мой/твой ~** in my/your view

**взгля́н|уть** (-у́, -ешь) сов: ~ на +acc to look at

**вздор** (-а) м (разг) rubbish

**вздо́рный** прил (нелепый) absurd

**вздох** (-а) м sigh; (ужаса) gasp

**вздохн|у́ть** (-у́, -ёшь) сов to sigh

**вздро́гн|уть** (-у; impf **вздра́гивать**) сов to shudder

**взду́ма|ть** (-ю) сов (разг): не ~йте лгать! don't even think of lying!

**вздыха́|ть** (-ю) несов to sigh

**взима́|ть** (-ю) несов перех (налоги) to collect

**взлёт** (-а) м (самолёта) takeoff

**взле|те́ть** (-чу́, -ти́шь; impf **взлета́ть**) сов (птица) to soar; (самолёт) to take off; **взлета́ть** (~

*pf)* **на во́здух** to explode

**взлётн|ый** *прил*: ~**ая полоса́** runway, airstrip

**взлома́|ть (-ю;** *impf* **взла́мывать)** *сов перех* to break open, force; (*КОМП*) to hack into

**взло́мщик (-а)** *м* burglar

**взмахн|у́ть (-у́, -ёшь)** *impf* **взма́хивать)** *сов*: ~ +*instr* (*рукой*) to wave; (*крылом*) to flap

**взмо́рь|е (-я)** *ср* seashore

**взнос (-а)** *м* payment; (*в фонд*) contribution; (*членский*) fee

**взойти́** (*как* **идти́**; *см. Table 18;* *impf* **всходи́ть** *или* **восходи́ть)** *сов* to rise; (*семена*) to come up; (*на трон*) to ascend

**взорв|а́ть (-у́, -ёшь;** *impf* **взрыва́ть)** *сов перех* (*бомбу*) to detonate; (*дом, мост*) to blow up; ~**ся** (*impf* **взрыва́ться)** *сов возв* (*бомба*) to explode; (*мост, дом*) to be blown up

**взрев|е́ть (-у́, -ёшь)** *сов* to roar

**взросле́|ть (-ю;** *pf* **по~)** *несов* to grow up; (*духовно*) to mature

**взро́сл|ый** *прил* (*человек*) grown-up; (*фильм*) adult ♦ **(-ого)** *м* adult

**взрыв (-а)** *м* explosion; (*дома*) blowing up; ~ +*gen* (*возмущения*) outburst of

**взрыва́|ть(ся) (-ю(сь))** *несов от* **взорва́ть(ся)**

**взрывоопа́сный** *прил* explosive

**взрывча́т|ка (-ки;** *gen pl* **-ок)** *ж* explosive (substance)

**взы|ска́ть (-щу́, -щешь;** *impf* **взы́скивать)** *сов перех* (*долг*) to recover; (*штраф*) to exact ♦ *неперех*: ~ **с кого́-н** to call sb to account

**взя́т|ка (-ки;** *gen pl* **-ок)** *ж* bribe

**взя́точник (-а)** *м* bribe-taker

**взя|ть (возьму́, возьмёшь)** *сов*

*от* **брать** ♦ *перех*: **возьму́ (да) и откажу́сь** (*разг*) I could refuse just like that; **с чего́** *или* **отку́да ты** ~**л?** (*разг*) whatever gave you that idea?; **взя́ться** *сов от* **бра́ться**

**вид (-а;** *part gen* **-у,** *loc sg* **-у́)** *м* (*внешность*) appearance; (*предмета, искусства*) form; (*панорама*) view; (*растений, животных*) species; (*спорта*) type; (*линг*) aspect; **в ви́де** +*gen* in the form of; **на ~у́ у** +*gen* in full view of; **под ви́дом** +*gen* in the guise of; ~ **на о́зеро/го́ры** a view of the lake/hills; **име́ть** (*impf*) **в ~у́** to mean; (*учитывать*) to bear in mind; **де́лать (сде́лать** *pf*) ~ to pretend; **упуска́ть (упусти́ть** *pf*) **из ви́ду что-н** (*факт*) to lose sight of sth; **теря́ть (потеря́ть** *pf*) **кого́-н из ви́ду** to lose sight of sb; ~ **на жи́тельство** residence permit

**вида́|ть (***pt* **-л, -ла, -ло;** *pf* **по~)** *несов перех* (*разг*) to see; (*испытать*) to know; ~**ся** (*pf* **по~ся)** *несов возв* (*разг*) to see each other

**ви́део** *ср нескл* video

**видеоза́пис|ь (-и)** *ж* video recording

**видеоигр|а́ (-ы́;** *nom pl* **-ы)** *ж* video game

**видеока́мер|а (-ы)** *ж* camcorder, videocamera

**видеокассе́т|а (-ы)** *ж* video cassette

**видеомагнитофо́н (-а)** *м* video (recorder)

**ви́|деть (-жу, -дишь)** *несов* to see ♦ (*pf* **у~)** *перех* to see; (*испытать*) to know; ~**дите ли** you see; ~**ся** (*pf* **у~ся)** *несов возв* to see each other

**ви́димо** *вводн сл* apparently

**ви́димо-неви́димо** *нареч* (*разг*): **наро́ду в го́роде** ~ there are masses of people in the city

**ви́димост|ь (-и)** ж visibility; (*подобие*) appearance; **по все́й ~и** apparently

**видне́|ться** (*3sg* **-ется**) *несов возв* to be visible

**ви́дно** *как сказ* one can see; (*понятно*) clearly ♦ *вводн сл* probably; **тебе́ видне́е** you know best; **там ~ бу́дет** we'll see

**ви́дный** *прил* (*заметный*) visible; (*известный*) prominent

**ви́жу(сь)** *несов см.* **ви́деть(ся)**

**ви́з|а (-ы)** ж visa

**визажи́ст (-а)** м make-up artist

**визг (-а)** м (*собаки*) yelp; (*ребёнка*) squeal; (*металла*) screech

**визж|а́ть (-у́, -и́шь)** *несов* (*см сущ*) to yelp; to squeal

**визи́т (-а)** м visit

**визи́т|ка (-ки;** *gen pl* **-ок)** ж business card

**визи́тн|ый** *прил*: ~**ая ка́рточка** (business) card

**виктори́н|а (-ы)** ж quiz game

**ви́л|ка (-ки;** *gen pl* **-ок)** ж fork; (**штéпсельная**) ~ plug

**ви́лл|а (-ы)** ж villa

**ви́л|ы (-)** мн pitchfork *ед*

**виля́|ть (-ю)** *несов*: ~ +*instr* (*хвостом*) to wag; (*бёдрами*) to wiggle

**вин|а́ (-ы́)** м blame; (*чувство*) guilt

**винегре́т (-а)** м beetroot salad

**вини́тельный** *прил*: ~ **паде́ж** accusative (case)

**вин|и́ть (-ю́, -и́шь)** *несов перех*: ~ **кого́-н в** +*prp* to blame sb for; (*упрекать: за лень*): ~ **кого́-н за** +*acc* to accuse sb of

**вин|о́ (-а́;** *nom pl* **-а)** *ср* wine

**винова́тый** *прил* (*взгляд итп*) guilty; ~ (**в** +*prp*) (*в неудаче*) responsible *или* to blame (for); **винова́т!** sorry!, excuse me!

**вино́вност|ь (-и)** ж guilt

**вино́вн|ый** *прил* guilty ♦ **(-ого)** м guilty party

**виногра́д (-а)** м (*растение*) (grape)vine; (*ягоды*) grapes *мн*

**виногра́дник (-а)** м vineyard

**винт (-а́)** м screw

**винто́в|ка (-ки;** *gen pl* **-ок)** ж rifle

**виолонче́л|ь (-и)** ж cello

**вира́ж (-а́)** м (*поворот*) turn

**виртуа́льный** *прил* virtual

**виртуо́з (-а)** м virtuoso

**виртуо́зн|ый** *прил* masterly; ~**ое исполне́ние** a virtuoso performance

**ви́рус (-а)** м virus

**ви́селиц|а (-ы)** ж gallows

**ви|се́ть (-шу́, -си́шь)** *несов* to hang; (*КОМП*) to freeze

**ви́ски** *ср нескл* whisky (*BRIT*), whiskey (*US, IRELAND*)

**вис|о́к (-ка́)** м (*АНАТ*) temple

**високо́сный** *прил*: ~ **год** leap year

**витами́н (-а)** м vitamin

**вита́|ть (-ю)** *несов* to hang in the air

**вито́й** *прил* twisted

**вит|о́к (-ка́)** м (*спирали*) twist

**витра́ж (-а́)** м stained-glass window

**витри́н|а (-ы)** ж (*в магазине*) shop window; (*в музее*) display case

**ви|ть (вью, вьёшь;** *imper* **вей(те)**; *pf* **с~**) *несов перех* (*венок*) to weave; (*гнездо*) to build; **ви́ться** *несов возв* (*растения*) to trail; (*волосы*) to curl

**вихр|ь (-я)** м whirlwind

ви́це-президе́нт (-а) м vice president

ВИЧ м сокр (= ви́рус иммунодефици́та челове́ка) HIV; ~-инфици́рованный HIV-positive

ви́ш|ня (-ни; gen pl -ен) ж cherry

вка́лыва|ть (-ю) несов от вколо́ть

вка|ти́ть (-чу́, -тишь; impf вка́тывать) сов перех (что-н на колёсах) to wheel in; (что-н кру́глое) to roll in

вклад (-а) м (в нау́ку) contribution; (в ба́нке) deposit

вкла́дчик (-а) м investor

вкла́дыва|ть (-ю) несов от вложи́ть

включа́|ть (-ю) несов от включи́ть ♦ перех: ~ (в себя́) to include; ~ся несов от включи́ться

включа́я предл: ~ +acc including

включи́тельно нареч inclusive

включ|и́ть (-у́, -и́шь; impf включа́ть) сов перех to turn или switch on; включа́ть (~ pf) кого́-н/ что-н во что-н to include sb/sth in sth; ~ся (impf включа́ться) сов возв to come on; (в спор): ~ся в +acc to join in

вкол|о́ть (-ю́, -ешь; impf вка́лывать) сов перех to stick in

вкра́тце нареч briefly

вкривь нареч: ~ и вкось (разг) all over the place

вкру|ти́ть (-чу́, -тишь; impf вкру́чивать) сов перех to screw in

вкруту́ю нареч: яйцо́ ~ hard-boiled egg

вкус (-а) м taste; она́ оде́та со вку́сом she is tastefully dressed

вку́сно нареч tastily ♦ как сказ: о́чень ~ it's delicious; она́ ~ гото́вит she is a good cook

вку́сный прил tasty; (обед) delicious

вла́г|а (-и) ж moisture

владе́л|ец (-ьца) м owner

владе́ни|е (-я) ср ownership; (поме́щика) estate

владе́|ть (-ю) несов: ~ +instr (облада́ть) to own, possess; (языко́м) to be proficient in; (ору́жием) to handle proficiently; ~ (impf) собо́й to control o.s.; ~ (impf) рука́ми/нога́ми to have the use of one's arms/legs

вла́жность (-и) ж humidity

вла́жный прил damp; (глаза́, ко́жа) moist

власт|вовать (-ую) несов: ~ над +instr to rule; (перен) to hold sway over

вла́ст|и (-е́й) мн authorities мн

вла́ст|ный прил (челове́к) imperious; (структу́ра) holding power; он не ~ен +infin ... it's not within his power to ...

власт|ь (-и; gen pl -е́й) ж power; (роди́тельская) authority; см. та́кже вла́сти

вле́во нареч (to the) left

влез|ть (-у, -ешь; pt -, -ла; impf влеза́ть) сов: ~ на +acc to climb (up); (на кры́шу) to climb onto; (в дом) to break in

вле|те́ть (-чу́, -ти́шь; impf влета́ть) сов: ~ в +acc to fly into

влече́ни|е (-я) ср: ~ (к +dat) attraction (to)

вле|чь (-ку́, -чёшь etc, -ку́т; pt влёк, -кла́, pf повле́чь) несов перех: ~ за собо́й to lead to; его́ ~чёт нау́ка he is drawn to science

влива́ни|е (-я) ср (де́нег) injection

вли|ть (волью́, вольёшь; pt -л, -ла́, -ло, imper влей(те); impf влива́ть) сов перех to pour in;

(де́ньги) to inject

**влия́ни|е** (-я) *ср* influence

**влия́тельный** *прил* influential

**влия́|ть** (-ю) *несов*: ~ **на** +*acc* to influence; (*на органи́зм*) to affect

**влож|и́ть** (-у́, -ишь; *impf* **вкла́дывать**) *сов перех* to insert; (*сре́дства*) to invest

**влюб|и́ться** (-лю́сь, -ишься; *impf* **влюбля́ться**) *сов возв*: ~ **в** +*acc* to fall in love with

**влюблённ|ый** *прил* in love; (*взгляд*) loving ♦ (**-ого**) *м*: ~**ые** lovers

**вме́сте** *нареч* together; ~ **с тем** at the same time

**вмести́тельный** *прил* spacious

**вме|сти́ть** (-щу́, -сти́шь; *impf* **вмеща́ть**) *сов перех* (*о за́ле*) to hold; (*о гости́нице*) to accommodate; ~**ся** (*impf* **вмеща́ться**) *несов возв* to fit in

**вме́сто** *предл*: ~ +*gen* (*взаме́н*) instead of ♦ *союз*: ~ **того́ что́бы** instead of, rather than

**вмеша́тельств|о** (-а) *ср* interference; (*ЭКОН*) intervention

**вмеша́|ть** (-ю; *impf* **вме́шивать**) *сов перех* (*доба́вить*) to mix in; (*перен*): ~ **кого́-н в** +*acc* to get sb mixed up in; ~**ся** (*impf* **вме́шиваться**) *сов возв* to interfere; (*в перегово́ры итп*) to intervene

**вмеща́|ть(ся)** (-ю(сь)) *несов от* **вмести́ть(ся)**

**вмиг** *нареч* instantly

**вмя́тин|а** (-ы) *ж* dent

**внаём** *нареч*: **отдава́ть** ~ to let, rent out

**внача́ле** *нареч* at first

**вне** *предл*: ~ +*gen* outside; ~ **о́череди** out of turn; **он был** ~ **себя́** he was beside himself

**внебра́чный** *прил* extramarital;

(*ребёнок*) illegitimate

**внедоро́жник** (-а) *м* 4-wheel drive

**внедре́ни|е** (-я) *ср* introduction

**внеза́пный** *прил* sudden

**внеочередно́й** *прил* unscheduled

**вне|сти́** (-у́, -ёшь; *pt* **внёс, -ла́**; *impf* **вноси́ть**) *сов перех* (*ве́щи*) to carry *или* bring in; (*су́мму*) to pay; (*законопрое́кт*) to bring in; (*попра́вку*) to insert

**внешко́льный** *прил* extracurricular

**вне́шн|ий** *прил* (*стена́*) exterior; (*споко́йствие*) outward; (*свя́зи*) external; ~ **мир** outside world; ~ **вид** appearance; ~**яя поли́тика/ торго́вля** foreign policy/trade

**вне́шност|ь** (-и) *ж* appearance

**внешта́тный** *прил* freelance

**вниз** *нареч*: ~ (**по** +*dat*) down; ~ **по тече́нию** downstream

**внизу́** *нареч* below; (*в зда́нии*) downstairs ♦ *предл*: ~ **страни́цы** at the foot *или* bottom of the page

**вни́к|нуть** (-ну; *pt* -, -ла; *impf* **вника́ть**) *сов*: ~ **во что-н** to understand sth well; (*изуча́ть*) to scrutinize sth

**внима́ни|е** (-я) *ср* attention

**внима́тельный** *прил* attentive; (*рабо́та*) careful; (*сын*) caring

**вничью́** *нареч* (*СПОРТ*): **сыгра́ть** ~ to draw

**вновь** *нареч* again

**вно|си́ть** (-шу́, -сишь) *несов от* **внести́**

**внук** (-а; *nom pl* -**ки** *или* -**ча́та**) *м* grandson; *см. также* **вну́ки**

**вну́к|и** (-ов) *мн* grandchildren *мн*

**вну́тренн|ий** *прил* interior; (*побужде́ние, го́лос*) inner; (*поли́тика, ры́нок*) domestic; (*ра́на*) internal; **Министе́рство** ~**их дел** ≈ the Home Office

(BRIT), ≈ the Department of the Interior (US)

**внутри́** нареч inside ♦ предл: ~ +gen (дома) inside; (организации) within

**внутрь** нареч inside ♦ предл: ~ +gen inside

**вну́ч|ка (-ки**; gen pl **-ек) ж** granddaughter

**внуша́|ть (-ю)** несов от **внуши́ть**

**внуши́тельный** прил imposing; (сумма, успех) impressive

**внуш|и́ть (-у́, -и́шь**; impf **внуша́ть)** сов перех: ~ **что-н кому́-н** (чувство) to inspire sb with sth; (идею) to instil (BRIT) или instill (US) sth in sb

**вня́тный** прил articulate, audible

**во** предл см. **в**

**вовл|е́чь (-еку́, -ечёшь** etc **-еку́т**; pt **-ёк, -екла́**; impf **вовлека́ть)** сов перех: ~ **кого́-н в** +acc to draw sb into

**во́время** нареч on time

**во́все** нареч (разг) completely; ~**нет** not at all

**во-вторы́х** вводн сл secondly, in the second place

**вод|а́ (**acc sg **-у**, gen sg **-ы́**, nom pl **-ы) ж** water; см. также **во́ды**

**води́тел|ь (-я) м** driver

**води́тельск|ий** прил: ~**ие права́** driving licence (BRIT), driver's license (US)

**во|ди́ть (-жу́, -дишь)** несов перех (ребёнка) to take; (машину, поезд) to drive; (самолёт) to fly; (корабль) to sail; ~**ся** несов возв (рыба итп) to be (found)

**во́дк|а (-и) ж** vodka

**во́дный** прил water

**водоём (-а) м** reservoir

**водола́з (-а) м** diver

**Водоле́|й (-я) м** Aquarius

**водонепроница́емый** прил waterproof

**водоочистно́й** прил water-purifying

**водопа́д (-а) м** waterfall

**водопрово́д (-а) м** water supply system; **у них в до́ме есть** ~ their house has running water

**водопрово́дный** прил (труба, кран) water; (система) plumbing

**водопрово́дчик (-а) м** plumber

**водоро́д (-а) м** hydrogen

**во́доросл|ь (-и) ж** algae; (разг: в реке) waterweed; (в море) seaweed

**водосто́чн|ый** прил: ~**ая труба́** drainpipe; ~**ая кана́ва** gutter

**водохрани́лищ|е (-а) ср** reservoir

**во́д|ы (-)** мн (государственные) waters мн; (минеральные) spa ед

**водяни́стый** прил watery

**водяно́й** прил water; ~ **знак** watermark

**во|ева́ть (-ю́ю)** несов (страна) to be at war; (человек) to fight

**военача́льник (-а) м** (military) commander

**военкома́т (-а) м** сокр (= **вое́нный комиссариа́т**) office for military registration and enlistment

**вое́нно-возду́шн|ый** прил: ~**ые си́лы** (the) air force

**вое́нно-морско́й** прил: ~ **флот** (the) navy

**военнообя́занн|ый (-ого) м** person eligible for compulsory military service

**военноплённ|ый (-ого) м** prisoner of war

**вое́нно-промы́шленный** прил: ~ **ко́мплекс** military-industrial complex

**военнослу́жащ|ий (-его) м** serviceman

**вое́нн|ый** *прил* military; (*врач*) army ♦ (**-ого**) *м* serviceman **~ое положе́ние** martial law

**вожде́ни|е (-я)** *ср* (*машины*) driving; (*судна*) steering

**вожд|ь (-я́)** *м* (*племени*) chief, chieftain; (*партии*) leader

**вожж|а́ (-и́;** *nom pl* **-и,** *gen pl* **-е́й)** *ж* rein

**возб|уди́ть (-ужу́, -у́дишь;** *impf* **возбужда́ть)** *сов перех* (*вызвать*) to arouse; (*взволновать*) to excite; **возбужда́ть (~** *pf*) **де́ло** *или* **проце́сс про́тив** +*gen* to bring a case *или* institute proceedings against; **~ся** *сов возв* (*человек*) to become excited

**возбужде́ни|е (-я)** *ср* (*волнение*) agitation; (: *радостное*) excitement

**возбуждённый** *прил* (*см сущ*) agitated; excited

**возве|сти́ (-ду́, -дёшь;** *pt* **возвёл, -ла́;** *impf* **возводи́ть**) *сов перех* to erect

**возвра́т (-а)** *м* return; (*долга*) repayment; **без ~а** irrevocably

**возвра|ти́ть (-щу́, -ти́шь;** *impf* **возвраща́ть**) *сов перех* to return; (*долг*) to repay; (*здоровье, счастье*) to restore; **~ся** (*impf* **возвраща́ться**) *сов возв*: **~ся (к** +*dat*) to return *или* come back (to)

**возвраще́ни|е (-я)** *ср* return

**возвы́шенный** *прил* (*идея, цель*) lofty; (*натура, музыка*) sublime

**возгла́в|ить (-лю, -ишь;** *impf* **возглавля́ть**) *сов перех* to head

**во́зглас (-а)** *м* exclamation

**возда́ть** (*как* **дать;** *см. Table 16*; *impf* **воздава́ть**) *сов перех*: **~ кому́-н по заслу́гам (в награду)** to reward sb for their services; (*в*

*наказание*) to give sb what they deserve; **воздава́ть (~** *pf*) **до́лжное кому́-н** to give sb their due

**воздви́г|нуть (-ну;** *pt* **-,** **-ла;** *impf* **воздвига́ть**) *сов перех* to erect

**возде́йстви|е (-я)** *ср* effect; (*идеологическое*) influence

**возде́йств|овать (-ую)** (*не)сов*: **~ на** +*acc* to have an effect on

**возде́ла|ть (-ю;** *impf* **возде́лывать**) *сов перех* (*поле*) to cultivate

**воздержа́вш|ийся (-егося)** *м* (*полит*) abstainer

**возд|ержа́ться (-ержу́сь, -е́ржишься;** *impf* **возде́рживаться**) *сов возв*: **~ от** +*gen* to refrain from; (*от голосования*) to abstain from

**во́здух (-а)** *м* air; **на (откры́том) ~е** outside, outdoors

**возду́шный** *прил* air; (*десант*) airborne; **возду́шный флот** civil aviation; (*ВОЕН*) air force

**воззва́ни|е (-я)** *ср* appeal

**во|зи́ть (-жу́, -зишь)** *несов перех* to take; **~ся** *несов возв* to potter about; **~ся** (*impf*) **с** +*instr* (*разг*: *с работой итп*) to dawdle over; (*с детьми итп*) to spend a lot of time with

**во́зле** *нареч* nearby ♦ *предл*: **~** +*gen* near

**возлож|и́ть (-у́, -ишь;** *impf* **возлага́ть**) *сов перех* (*венок*) to lay; (*задачу*) to entrust

**возлю́бленн|ый (-ого)** *м* beloved

**возме́зди|е (-я)** *ср* retribution

**возме|сти́ть (-щу́, -сти́шь;** *impf* **возмеща́ть**) *сов перех* (*убытки*) to compensate for; (*затраты*) to refund, reimburse

**возмо́жно** *как сказ* it is possible

♦ *вводн сл* (*может быть*) possibly
**возмо́жност|и (-ей)** *мн*
(*творческие*) potential *ед*;
**фина́нсовые ~** financial resources
**возмо́жност|ь (-и)** *ж* opportunity;
(*вероятность*) possibility; **по
(ме́ре) ~и** as far as possible; *см.
также* **возмо́жности**
**возмо́жный** *прил* possible
**возмужа́|ть (-ю)** *сов от* **мужа́ть**
**возмути́тельный** *прил* appalling
**возму|ти́ть (-щу́, -ти́шь;** *impf*
**возмуща́ть)** *сов перех* to appal
(*BRIT*), appall (*US*); **~ся** (*impf*
**возмуща́ться)** *сов возв* to be
appalled
**возмуще́ни|е (-я)** *ср* indignation
**вознагра|ди́ть (-жу́, -ди́шь;** *impf*
**вознагражда́ть)** *сов перех* to
reward
**возникнове́ни|е (-я)** *ср*
emergence
**возни́к|нуть (-ну;** *pt* **-, -ла;** *impf*
**возника́ть)** *сов* to arise
**возн|я́ (-и́)** *ж* (*при игре*) frolicking;
**~ с** +*instr* (*хлопоты*) bother with
**возобнов|и́ть (-лю́, -и́шь;** *impf*
**возобновля́ть)** *сов перех*
(*работу*) to resume; (*контракт*) to
renew; **~ся** (*impf*
**возобновля́ться)** *сов возв* to
resume
**возраже́ни|е (-я)** *ср* objection
**возра|зи́ть (-жу́, -зи́шь;** *impf*
**возража́ть)** *сов*: **~** (+*dat*) to
object (to)
**во́зраст (-а)** *м* age; **он был уже́ в
~е** he was getting on in years
**возр|асти́ (3sg** **-асте́т,** *pt* **-о́с,
-осла́;** *impf* **возраста́ть)** *сов* to
grow
**возро|ди́ть (-жу́, -ди́шь;** *impf*
**возрожда́ть)** *сов перех* to revive;
**~ся** (*impf* **возрожда́ться)** *сов
возв* to revive

**возрожде́ни|е (-я)** *ср* revival;
(*нации, веры*) rebirth;
**Возрожде́ние** Renaissance
**возьму́(сь)** *etc сов см.* **взя́ть(ся)**
**во́ин (-а)** *м* warrior
**во́инск|ий** *прил* military; **~ая
обя́занность** conscription
**во́инственный** *прил* belligerent;
(*депутат*) militant
**во|й (-я)** *м* howl
**во́йлок (-а)** *м* felt
**войн|а́ (-ы́;** *nom pl* **-ы)** *ж* war
**во́йск|о (-а;** *nom pl* **-а́)** *ср* (the)
forces *мн*
**войти́** (*как* **идти́;** *см. Table 18; impf*
**входи́ть)** *сов*: **~ (в** +*acc*) to enter,
go in(to); (*в комитет*) to become a
member (of); (*уместиться*) to fit
in(to)
**вока́льный** *прил* vocal; (*конкурс*)
singing
**вокза́л (-а)** *м* station
**вокру́г** *нареч* around, round
♦ *предл*: **~** +*gen* (*кругом*) around,
round; (*по поводу*) about, over;
**ходи́ть** (*impf*) **~ да о́коло** (*разг*) to
beat about the bush
**вол (-а́)** *м* ox bullock
**вола́н (-а)** *м* (*на одежде*) flounce;
(*СПОРТ*) shuttlecock
**волды́р|ь (-я́)** *м* blister
**волево́й** *прил* strong-willed
**волейбо́л (-а)** *м* volleyball
**волк (-а;** *gen pl* **-о́в)** *м* wolf
**волн|а́ (-ы́;** *nom pl* **во́лны)** *ж* wave
**волне́ни|е (-я)** *ср* (*радостное*)
excitement; (*нервное*) agitation;
(*обычно мн: в массах*) unrest *ед*
**волни́стый** *прил* (*волосы*) wavy
**волн|ова́ть (-у́ю;** *pf* **вз~)** *несов
перех* to be concerned about;
(*подлеж:музыка*) to excite; **~ся**
(*pf* **вз~ся)** *несов возв* (*море*) to
be rough; (*человек*) to worry
**вол|окно́ (-окна́;** *nom pl* **-о́кна,**

gen pl **-о́кон**) ср fibre (BRIT), fiber (US)

**во́лос** (-а; gen pl **воло́с**, dat pl **-а́м**) м hair только ед

**волос**|**о́к** (-ка́) м hair; **быть** (impf) или **находи́ться** (impf) **на ~** или **на ~ке́ от** +gen to be within a hair's-breadth of

**волоч**|**и́ть** (-у́, -и́шь) несов перех to drag

**во́лчий** прил wolf

**волше́бник** (-а) м wizard

**волше́бниц**|**а** (-ы) ж (good или white) witch

**волше́бный** прил magic; (музыка) magical

**во́льно** нареч freely; **~!** (ВОЕН) at ease!

**во́л**|**ьный** прил (свободный) free
♦ как сказ: **~ен** +infin he is free to do

**вольт** (-а; gen pl **-**) м volt

**во́л**|**я** (-и) ж will; (стремление): **~ к побе́де** the will to win

**вон** нареч (разг: прочь) out; (: там) (over) there; **~ отсю́да!** get out of here!; **~ (оно́) что** so that's it!

**вон**|**ь** (-и) ж (разг) pong

**воня́**|**ть** (-ю) несов (разг) to pong

**вообра**|**зи́ть** (-жу́, -зи́шь; impf **вообража́ть**) сов перех to imagine

**вообще́** нареч (в общем) on the whole; (совсем) absolutely; (+noun: без частностей) in general; **~ говоря́** generally speaking

**воодушев**|**и́ть** (-лю́, -и́шь; impf **воодушевля́ть**) сов перех to inspire; **~ся** сов возв: **~ся** +instr to be inspired by

**воодушевле́ни**|**е** (-я) ср inspiration

**вооружа́**|**ть(ся)** (-ю(сь)) несов см. **вооружи́ть(ся)**

**вооруже́ни**|**е** (-я) ср (процесс) arming; (оружие) arms мн

**вооружённ**|**ый** прил armed; **~ые си́лы** (the) armed forces

**вооруж**|**и́ть** (-у́, -и́шь; impf **вооружа́ть**) сов перех to arm; (перен) to equip; **~ся** (impf **вооружа́ться**) сов возв to arm o.s.

**во-пе́рвых** нареч firstly, first of all

**вопло**|**ти́ть** (-щу́, -ти́шь; impf **воплоща́ть**) сов перех to embody; **воплоща́ть** (**~** pf) **в жизнь** to realize; **~ся** (impf **воплоща́ться**) сов возв: **~ся в** +prp to be embodied in; **воплоща́ться** (**~ся** pf) **в жизнь** to be realized

**воплоще́ни**|**е** (-я) ср embodiment

**вопл**|**ь** (-я) м scream

**вопреки́** предл: **~** +dat contrary to

**вопро́с** (-а) м question; (проблема) issue; **задава́ть (зада́ть** pf) **~** to ask a question

**вопроси́тельный** прил (взгляд) questioning; (ЛИНГ) interrogative; **~ знак** question mark

**вор** (-а; gen pl **-о́в**) м thief

**ворв**|**а́ться** (-у́сь, -ёшься; impf **врыва́ться**) сов возв to burst in

**воробе́й** (-ья́) м sparrow

**вор**|**ова́ть** (-у́ю) несов перех to steal

**воровств**|**о́** (-а́) ср theft

**во́рон** (-а) м raven

**воро́н**|**а** (-ы) ж crow

**воро́н**|**ка** (-ки; gen pl **-ок**) ж (для переливания) funnel; (после взрыва) crater

**во́рот** (-а) м neck (of clothes)

**воро́т**|**а** (-) мн gates мн; (СПОРТ) goal ед

**воротни́к** (-а́) м collar

**воро́ча**|**ть** (-ю) несов перех to shift ♦ неперех: **~** +instr (разг:

деньга́ми) to have control of; **~ся**
*несов возв* to toss and turn

**ворс** (-а) *м* (*на тка́ни*) nap

**ворч|а́ть** (-у́, -и́шь) *несов*
(*зверь*) to growl; (*челове́к*) to
grumble

**ворчли́вый** *прил* querulous

**восемна́дцатый** *чис* eighteenth

**восемна́дцат|ь** (-и; *как пять;
см. Table 26*) *чис* eighteen

**во́с|емь** (-ьми́; *как пять; см.
Table 26*) *чис* eight

**во́с|емьдесят** (-ьми́десяти; *как
пятьдеся́т; см. Table 26*) *чис*
eighty

**вос|емьсо́т** (-ьмисо́т; *как
пятьсо́т; см. Table 28*) *чис* eight
hundred

**воск** (-а) *м* wax

**воскли́кн|уть** (-у; *impf
восклица́ть*) *сов* to exclaim

**восклица́ни|е** (-я) *ср* exclamation

**восклица́тельный** *прил*
exclamatory; **~ знак** exclamation
mark (*BRIT*) и́ли point (*US*)

**восково́й** *прил* wax

**воскреса́|ть** (-ю) *несов от
воскре́снуть*

**воскресе́ни|е** (-я) *ср* resurrection

**воскресе́нь|е** (-я) *ср* Sunday

**воскре|си́ть** (-шу́, -си́шь; *impf
воскреша́ть*) *сов перех* to
resurrect; (*перен*) to revive

**воскре́с|нуть** (-ну; *pt* -, -ла; *impf
воскреса́ть*) *сов* to be
resurrected; (*перен*) to be revived

**воскре́сный** *прил* Sunday

**воспале́ни|е** (-я) *ср* inflammation;
**~ лёгких** pneumonia

**воспал|и́ться** (3sg -и́тся; *impf
воспаля́ться*) *сов возв* to
become inflamed

**воспита́ни|е** (-я) *ср* upbringing;
(*гра́ждан*) education; (*че́стности*)
fostering

**воспи́танный** *прил* well-brought-
up

**воспита́тел|ь** (-я) *м* teacher; (*в
ла́гере*) instructor

**воспита́|ть** (-ю; *impf
воспи́тывать*) *сов перех*
(*ребёнка*) to bring up;
(*трудолю́бие*) to foster

**воспо́льз|оваться** (-уюсь) *сов
от по́льзоваться*

**воспомина́ни|е** (-я) *ср*
recollection; *см. также*
**воспомина́ния**

**воспомина́ни|я** (-й) *мн* memoirs
*мн*, reminiscences *мн*

**воспрепя́тств|овать** (-ую) *сов
от препя́тствовать*

**воспреща́|ться** (3sg -ется) *несов
возв* to be forbidden

**восприи́мчивый** *прил* receptive

**воспр|иня́ть** (-иму́, -и́мешь;
*impf воспринима́ть*) *сов перех*
(*смысл*) to comprehend

**воспроизв|ести́** (-еду́, -едёшь;
*pt* -ёл, -ела́, -ело́; *impf
воспроизводи́ть*) *сов перех* to
reproduce

**воспроти́в|иться** (-люсь,
-ишься) *сов от проти́виться*

**восста|ва́ть** (-ю́, -ёшь) *несов от
восста́ть*

**восста́ни|е** (-я) *ср* uprising

**восстан|ови́ть** (-овлю́, -о́вишь;
*impf восстана́вливать*) *сов
перех* to restore

**восста́|ть** (-ну, -нешь; *impf
восстава́ть*) *сов*: **~(про́тив** +gen)
to rise up (against)

**восто́к** (-а) *м* east; **Восто́к** the
East, the Orient

**восто́рг** (-а) *м* rapture

**восто́рженный** *прил*
(*покло́нник*) ecstatic; (*похвала́*)
rapturous

**восторжеств|ова́ть** (-ую) *сов*

от **торжествова́ть**

**восто́чный** *прил* eastern; ~ **ве́тер** east wind

**востре́бовани|е (-я)** *ср (багажа)* claim; **письмо́ до ~я** a letter sent poste restante (*BRIT*) *или* general delivery (*US*)

**восхити́тельный** *прил* delightful

**восхи|ти́ть (-щу́, -ти́шь;** *impf* **восхища́ть)** *сов перех:* **меня́** ~**ща́ет он/его́ хра́брость** I admire him/his courage; ~**ся** (*impf* **восхища́ться)** *сов возв:* ~**ся** +*instr* to admire

**восхище́ни|е (-я)** *ср* admiration

**восхо́д (-а)** *м:* ~ **со́лнца** sunrise; ~ **луны́** moonrise

**восх|оди́ть (-ожу́, -о́дишь)** *несов от* **взойти́**

**восьмёр|ка (-ки;** *gen pl* **-ок)** *ж* (*разг: цифра*) eight

**восьмидеся́тый** *чис* eightieth

**восьмиуго́льник (-а)** *м* octagon

**восьмичасово́й** *прил* eight-hour; (*поезд*) eight-o'clock

**восьмо́й** *чис* eighth

---

KEYWORD

---

**вот** *част* **1** (*о близком предмете*): **вот моя́ ма́ма** here is my mother; **вот мои́ де́ти** here are my children

**2** (*выража́ет указа́ние*) this; **вот в чём де́ло** this is what it's about; **вот где ну́жно иска́ть** this is where we need to look

**3** (*при эмфатике*): **вот ты и сде́лай э́то** YOU do this; **вот негодя́й!** what a rascal!

**4** (*во фра́зах*): **вот-во́т** (*разг: вот и́менно*) that's it; **он вот-во́т ля́жет спать** he is just about to go to bed; **вот ещё!** (*разг*) not likely!; **вот (оно́) как** *или* **что!** is that so *или* right?; **вот тебе́ и на** *или* **те**

---

**раз!** (*разг*) well I never!

**воткн|у́ть (-у́, -ёшь;** *impf* **втыка́ть)** *сов перех* to stick in

**во́тум (-а)** *м:* ~ **дове́рия/ недове́рия** vote of confidence/no confidence

**вошёл** *etc сов см.* **войти́**

**вошь (вши;** *instr sg* **во́шью,** *nom pl* **вши)** *ж* louse

**впада́|ть (-ю)** *несов от* **впасть**

♦ *неперех:* ~ **в** +*acc* to flow into

**впа́дин|а (-ы)** *ж* (*в земле́*) gully

**впа|сть (-ду́, -дёшь;** *impf* **впада́ть)** *сов* (*щёки, глаза́*) to become sunken; **впада́ть (~** *pf*) **в** +*prp* (*в истерику*) to go into

**впервы́е** *нареч* for the first time

**вперёд** *нареч* (*идти́*) ahead, forward; (*заплати́ть*) in advance

**впереди́** *нареч* in front; (*в будущем*) ahead ♦ *предл:* ~ +*gen* in front of

**впечатле́ни|е (-я)** *ср* impression

**впечатли́тельный** *прил* impressionable

**впечатля́|ть (-ю)** *несов* to be impressive

**впи|са́ть (-шу́, -шешь;** *impf* **впи́сывать)** *сов перех* to insert

**впита́|ть (-ю;** *impf* **впи́тывать)** *сов перех* to absorb; ~**ся** *сов возв* to be absorbed

**вплавь** *нареч* by swimming

**вплотну́ю** *нареч* close (by)

♦ *предл:* ~ **к** +*dat* (*к го́роду*) right up close to; (*к стене́*) right up against

**вплоть** *предл:* ~ **до** +*gen* (*зимы́*) right up till; (*включая*) right up to

**вполго́лоса** *нареч* softly

**впо́ру** *как сказ:* **пла́тье/шля́па мне** ~ the dress/hat fits me nicely

**впосле́дствии** *нареч* subsequently

**впра́ве** *как сказ:* ~ +*infin* (*знать,*

требовать) to have a right to do

**впра́во** *нареч* to the right

**впредь** *нареч* in future ♦ *предл*: ~ **до** +*gen* pending

**впро́голодь** *нареч*: **жить** ~ to live from hand to mouth

**впро́чем** *союз* however, though ♦ *вводн сл* but then again

**впу|сти́ть** (-**щу́**, -**стишь**; *impf* **впуска́ть**) *сов перех* to let in

**враг** (-**а́**) *м* enemy

**вражд|а́** (-**ы́**) *ж* enmity, hostility

**вражде́бный** *прил* hostile

**вражд|ова́ть** (-**у́ю**) *несов*: ~ (**с** +*instr*) to be on hostile terms (with)

**вразре́з** *нареч*: ~ **с** +*instr* in contravention of

**вразуми́тельный** *прил* comprehensible

**врань|ё** (-**я́**) *ср* (*разг*) lies *мн*

**врасплóх** *нареч* unawares

**врата́р|ь** (-**я́**) *м* goalkeeper

**вр|ать** (-**у́**, -**ёшь**; *pf* **совра́ть**) *несов* (*разг*: *человек*) to fib

**врач** (-**а́**) *м* doctor

**враче́бный** *прил* medical

**враща́|ть** (-**ю**) *несов перех* (*колесо*) to turn; ~**ся** *несов возв* to revolve, rotate

**враще́ни|е** (-**я**) *ср* rotation

**вред** (-**а́**) *м* damage; (*человеку*) harm ♦ *предл*: **во** ~ +*dat* to the detriment of

**вреди́тел|ь** (-**я**) *м* (*насекомое*) pest

**вре|ди́ть** (-**жу́**, -**ди́шь**; *pf* **на~**) *несов*: ~ +*dat* to harm; (*здоровью*) to damage; (*врагу*) to inflict damage on

**вре́дно** *нареч*: ~ **влия́ть на** +*acc* to have a harmful effect on ♦ *как сказ*: **кури́ть** ~ smoking is bad for you

**вре́дный** *прил* harmful; (*разг*: *человек*) nasty

**вре́|заться** (-**жусь**, -**жешься**; *impf* **вреза́ться**) *сов возв*: ~ **в** +*acc* (*верёвка*) to cut into; (*машина*) to plough (*BRIT*) *или* plow (*US*) into; (*в па́мять*) to engrave itself on

**времена́ми** *нареч* at times

**вре́менный** *прил* temporary

**вре́м|я** (-**ени**; *см. Table 4*) *ср* time; (*линг*) tense ♦ *предл*: **во** ~ +*gen* during ♦ *союз*: **в то** ~ **как** *или* **когда́** while; (**а**) **в то же** ~ (but) at the same time; ~ **от ~ени** from time to time; **в после́днее** ~ recently; **в своё** ~ (*когда́ необходи́мо*) in due course; **в своё** ~ **она́ была́ краса́вицей** she was a real beauty in her day; **на** ~ for a while; **со ~енем** *или* in time; **тем ~енем** meanwhile; **ско́лько ~ени?** what time is it?; **хорошо́ проводи́ть** (**провести́** *pf*) ~ to have a good time; ~ **го́да** season

**вро́вень** *нареч*: ~**с** +*instr* level with

**вро́де** *предл*: ~ +*gen* like ♦ *част* sort of

**врождённый** *прил* innate; (*боле́знь*) congenital

**врозь** *нареч* (*жить*) apart

**вруч|и́ть** (-**у́**, -**и́шь**; *impf* **вруча́ть**) *сов перех*: ~ **что-н кому́-н** to hand sth (over) to sb

**вручну́ю** *нареч* (*разг*) by hand

**врыва́|ться** (-**юсь**) *несов от* **ворва́ться**

**вряд** *част*: ~**ли** hardly; ~**ли она́ придёт** she's unlikely to come

**вса́дник** (-**а**) *м* rider, horseman

**все** *мест см.* **весь**

┌─────────────┐
│ KEYWORD │
└─────────────┘

**всё** (**всего́**) *мест см.* **весь** ♦ *ср* (*как сущ*: *без исключе́ния*) everything; **вот и всё**, **э́то всё** that's all; **ча́ще всего́** most often;

лу́чше всего́ написа́ть ей письмо́ it would be best to write to her; **меня́ э́то волну́ет ме́ньше всего́** that is the least of my worries; **мне всё равно́** it's all the same to me; **Вы хоти́те чай и́ли ко́фе? - всё равно́** do you want tea or coffee? - I don't mind; **я всё равно́ пойду́ туда́** I'll go there all the same

♦ *нареч* 1 (*разг*: *всё время*) all the time

2 (*только*) all; **э́то всё он винова́т** it's all his fault

3 (*о нарастании признака*): **шум всё уси́ливается** the noise is getting louder and louder

4 (*о постоянстве признака*): **всё так же** still the same; **всё там же** still there; **всё же** all the same; **всё ещё** still

**всевозмо́жный** *прил* all sorts of
**всегда́** *нареч* always
**всего́** *мест см.* **весь**; **всё** ♦ *нареч* in all ♦ *част* only; **~ лишь** (*разг*) only; **~-на́всего** (*разг*) only, mere
**вселе́нн|ая (-ой)** *ж* the whole world; **Вселе́нная** universe
**всел|и́ть (-ю́, -и́шь;** *impf* **вселя́ть)** *сов перех* (*жильцов*) to install; **~ся** (*impf* **вселя́ться)** *сов возв* (*жильцы*) to move in
**всем** *мест см.* **весь**; **всё**; **все**
**всеме́рный** *прил* all possible
**всеми́рн|ый** *прил* worldwide; (*конгресс*) world; **~ая паути́на** (*комп*) World-Wide Web
**всемогу́щий** *прил* omnipotent
**всенаро́дный** *прил* national
**всено́щн|ая (-ой)** *ж* vespers
**всео́бщ|ий** *прил* universal; **~ая забасто́вка** general strike
**всеобъе́млющий** *прил* comprehensive

**всеросси́йский** *прил* all-Russia
**всерьёз** *нареч* in earnest; **ты э́то говори́шь**~? are you serious?
**всесторо́нний** *прил* comprehensive
**всё-таки** *част* still, all the same
♦ *союз:* **а** ~ all the same, nevertheless
**всеуслы́шание** *ср:* **во** ~ publicly
**всех** *мест см.* **все**
**вска́кива|ть (-ю)** *несов от* **вскочи́ть**
**вскачь** *нареч* at a gallop
**вски́н|уть (-у;** *impf* **вски́дывать)** *сов перех* (*мешок, ружьё*) to shoulder; (*голову*) to jerk up
**вскип|е́ть (-лю́, -и́шь;** *impf* **кипе́ть)** *сов* to boil; (*перен*) to flare up
**вскользь** *нареч* in passing
**вско́ре** *нареч* soon ♦ *предл:* ~ **по́сле** +*gen* soon *или* shortly after
**вскоч|и́ть (-у́, -ишь;** *impf* **вска́кивать)** *сов:* ~ **в/на** +*acc* to leap up onto
**вскри́кн|уть (-у;** *impf* **вскри́кивать)** *сов* to cry out
**вскр|ы́ть (-о́ю, -о́ешь;** *impf* **вскрыва́ть)** *сов перех* (*сейф*) to open; (*недостатки*) to reveal; (*нарыв*) to lance; (*труп*) to carry out a postmortem on; **вскры́ться** *сов возв* (*недостатки*) to come to light, be revealed
**вслед** *нареч* (*бежать*) behind
♦ *предл:* ~ (**за** +*instr*) after; ~ +*dat* (*другу, поезду*) after
**вследствие** *предл:* ~ +*gen* as a result of, because of ♦ *союз:* ~ **того́ что** because; ~ **чего́** as a result of which
**вслух** *нареч* aloud
**всмя́тку** *нареч:* **яйцо́** ~ soft-boiled egg
**всплеск (-а)** *м* (*волны*) splash

**всплесн|у́ть** (**-у́**, **ёшь**; *impf* **вспле́скивать**) *сов* (*рыба*) to splash; ~ (*pf*) **рука́ми** to throw up one's hands

**всплы|ть** (**-ву́**, **-вёшь**; *impf* **всплыва́ть**) *сов* to surface

**вспо́мн|ить** (**-ю**, **-ишь**; *impf* **вспомина́ть**) *сов перех* to remember ♦ *неперех*: ~ **о** +*prp* to remember about

**вспомога́тельный** *прил* supplementary; (*судно, отряд*) auxiliary; ~ **глаго́л** auxiliary verb

**вспорхн|у́ть** (**-у́**, **-ёшь**) *сов* to fly off

**вспоте́|ть** (**-ю**) *сов от* **потеть**

**вспугн|у́ть** (**-у́**, **ёшь**; *impf* **вспу́гивать**) *сов перех* to scare away *или* off

**вспу́хн|уть** (**-у**) *сов от* **пу́хнуть**

**вспы́льчивый** *прил* short-tempered

**вспы́хн|уть** (**-у**; *impf* **вспы́хивать**) *сов* (*зажечься*) to burst into flames; (*конфликт*) to flare up; (*покраснеть*) to blush

**вспы́ш|ка** (**-ки**; *gen pl* **-ек**) *ж* flash; (*гнева*) outburst; (*болезни*) outbreak

**вста|ва́ть** (**-ю́**; *imper* **-ва́й(те)**) *несов от* **встать**

**вста́в|ить** (**-лю**, **-ишь**; *impf* **вставля́ть**) *сов перех* to insert, put in

**вста́в|ка** (**-ки**; *gen pl* **-ок**) *ж* insertion

**вставн|о́й** *прил* (*рамы*) removable; **~ы́е зу́бы** dentures, false teeth

**вста|ть** (**-ну**, **-нешь**; *impf* **встава́ть**) *сов* (*на ноги*) to stand up; (*с постели*) to get up; (*солнце*) to rise; (*вопрос*) to arise

**встрево́ж|ить(ся)** (**-у(сь)**, **-ишь(ся)**) *несов от* **трево́жить(ся)**

**встре́|тить** (**-чу**, **-тишь**; *impf* **встреча́ть**) *сов перех* to meet; (*факт*) to come across; (*оппозицию*) to encounter; (*праздник итп*) to celebrate; **~ся** (*impf* **встреча́ться**) *сов возв*: **~ся с** +*instr* to meet; **мне ~тились интере́сные фа́кты** I came across some interesting facts

**встре́ч|а** (**-и**) *ж* meeting

**встреча́|ть(ся)** (**-ю(сь)**) *несов от* **встре́тить(ся)**

**встре́чный** *прил* (*машина*) oncoming; (*мера*) counter; **~ ве́тер** head wind

**встряхн|у́ть** (**-у́**, **-ёшь**; *impf* **встря́хивать**) *сов перех* to shake (out)

**вступи́тельный** *прил* (*речь, статья*) introductory; **~ экза́мен** entrance exam

**вступи́тельные экза́мены** - entrance exams. All higher education institutions in Russia require the applicants to sit entrance exams, both written and oral. Normally the candidates sit four exams, the subjects depend on what the applicants want to specialize in. An essay on Russian literature is a requirement for all departments.

**вступ|и́ть** (**-лю́**, **-ишь**; *impf* **вступа́ть**) *сов*: **~ в** +*acc* to enter; (*в партию*) to join; (*в переговоры*) to enter into; **~ся** (*impf* **вступа́ться**) *сов возв*: **~ся за** +*acc* to stand up for

**вступле́ни|е** (**-я**) *ср* entry; (*в партию*) joining; (*в книге*) introduction

**всхли́пыва|ть** (**-ю**) *несов* to sob

**всхо|ди́ть** (-жу́, -дишь) *несов от* **взойти́**

**всхо́д|ы** (-ов) *мн* shoots *мн*

**всю́ду** *нареч* everywhere

**вс|я** (-ей) *мест см.* **весь**

**вся́к|ий** *мест* (*каждый*) every; (*разнообразный*) all kinds of; (*любой*) any ♦ (-ого) *м* (*любой*) anyone; (*каждый*) everyone

**вся́ческий** *мест* all possible; (*товары*) all kinds of

**вся́чин|а** (-ы) *ж* (*разг*): **вся́кая ~** all sorts of things

**Вт** *сокр* (= *ватт*) W

**втащ|и́ть** (-у́, -ишь); *impf* **вта́скивать**) *сов перех*: **~ (в** +*acc*) to drag in(to)

**втере́ть** (вотру́, вотрёшь; *pt* втёр, втёрла; *impf* **втира́ть**) *сов перех*: **~ (в** +*acc*) to rub in(to)

**вти́сн|уть** (-у; *impf* **вти́скивать**) *сов перех*: **~ (в** +*acc*) to cram in(to)

**вто́ргн|уться** (-усь; *impf* **вторга́ться**) *сов возв*: **~ в** +*acc* to invade

**втори́чный** *прил* (*повторный*) second; (*фактор*) secondary

**вто́рник** (-а) *м* Tuesday

**втор|о́е** (-о́го) *ср* main course

**втор|о́й** *прил* second; **сейча́с ~ час** it's after one; **сейча́с полови́на ~о́го** it's half past one

**второпя́х** *нареч* in a hurry

**второстепе́нный** *прил* secondary

**в-тре́тьих** *вводн сл* thirdly, in the third place

**втро́е** *нареч* (*больше*) three times; (*увеличить*) threefold

**втроём** *нареч* in a group of three

**втройне́** *нареч* three times as much

**втыка́|ть** (-ю) *несов от* **воткну́ть**

**втян|у́ть** (-у́; *impf* **втя́гивать**) *сов*

*перех* (*втащить*) to pull in; **втя́гивать** (**~** *pf*) **кого́-н в** +*acc* (*в дело*) to involve sb in

**вуа́л|ь** (-и) *ж* veil

**вуз** (-а) *м сокр* (= *вы́сшее уче́бное заведе́ние*) higher education establishment

**вулка́н** (-а) *м* volcano

**вульга́рный** *прил* vulgar

**вход** (-а) *м* (*движение*) entry; (*место*) entrance; (*ТЕХ*) inlet; (*КОМП*) input

**вхо|ди́ть** (-жу́, -дишь) *несов от* **войти́**

**входно́й** *прил* (*дверь*) entrance; (*КОМП*) input

**вцеп|и́ться** (-лю́сь, -ишься) *сов возв*: **~ в** +*acc* to seize

**вчера́** *нареч, м нескл* yesterday

**вчера́шний** *прил* yesterday's

**вче́тверо** *нареч* four times

**вчетверо́м** *нареч* in a group of four

**вши** *etc сущ см.* **вошь**

**вширь** *нареч* in breadth

**въезд** (-а) *м* (*движение*) entry; (*место*) entrance

**въездно́й** *прил* entry

**въе́|хать** (*как* **е́хать**; *см. Table 19*; *impf* **въезжа́ть**) *сов* to enter; (*в новый дом*) to move in; (*наверх: на машине*) to drive up; (*: на коне, велосипеде*) to ride up

**Вы** (**Вас**; *см. Table 6b*) *мест* you (*formal*)

**вы** (**вас**; *см. Table 6b*) *мест* you (*plural*)

**вы́бе|жать** (*как* **бежа́ть**; *см. Table 20*; *impf* **выбега́ть**) *сов* to run out

**выбива́|ть(ся)** (-ю(сь)) *несов от* **вы́бить(ся)**

**выбира́|ть** (-ю) *несов от* **вы́брать**

**вы́б|ить** (-ью, -ьешь; *impf*

**выбива́ть**) *сов перех* to knock out; (*противника*) to oust; (*ковёр*) to beat; (*надпись*) to carve;

**выбива́ть** (~ *pf*) **чек** (*кассир*) to ring up the total; **~ся** (*impf* **выбива́ться**) *сов возв*: **~ся из** +*gen* (*освободиться*) to get out of

**вы́бор** (-а) *м* choice

**вы́борный** *прил* (*кампания*) election; (*пост, орган*) elective

**вы́борочный** *прил* selective; **~ая прове́рка** spot check

**вы́боры** (-ов) *мн* election *ед*

**выбра́сыва|ть(ся)** (-ю(сь)) *несов от* **вы́бросить(ся)**

**вы́б|рать** (-еру, -ерешь; *impf* **выбира́ть**) *сов перех* to choose; (*голосованием*) to elect

**вы́брос** (-а) *м* (*газа*) emission; (*отходов*) discharge; (*нефти*) spillage

**выбро|сить** (-шу, -сишь; *impf* **выбра́сывать**) *сов перех* to throw out; (*отходы*) to discharge; (*газы*) to emit; **~ся** (*impf* **выбра́сываться**) *сов возв* to throw oneself out; **выбра́сываться** (**~ся** *pf*) **с парашю́том** to bale out

**вы́б|ыть** (*как* **быть**; *см. Table 21*; *impf* **выбыва́ть**) *сов*: **~ из** +*gen* to leave

**выведе́ни|е** (-я) *ср* (*формулы*) deduction; (*породы*) breeding; (*вредителей*) extermination

**вы́вез|ти** (-у, -ешь; *impf* **вывози́ть**) *сов перех* to take; (*товар: из страны*) to take out

**вы́верн|уть** (-у; *impf* **вывора́чивать**) *сов перех* (*винт*) to unscrew; (*карманы, рукава*) to turn inside out; **~ся** (*impf* **вывора́чиваться**) *сов возв* (*винт*) to come unscrewed

**вы́ве|сить** (-шу, -сишь; *impf* **вывешивать**) *сов перех* (*флаг*)

to put up; (*бельё*) to hang out

**вы́вес|ка** (-ки; *gen pl* -ок) *ж* sign

**вы́ве|сти** (-ду, -дешь; *impf* **выводи́ть**) *сов перех* to take out; (*войска: из города*) to pull out, withdraw; (*формулу*) to deduce; (*птенцов*) to hatch; (*породу*) to breed; (*уничтожить*) to exterminate; (*исключить*) to expel: **~ кого́-н из** +*gen* (*из партии*) to expel sb from; **выводи́ть** (~ *pf*) **кого́-н из терпе́ния** to exasperate sb; **выводи́ть** (~ *pf*) **кого́-н из себя́** to drive sb mad; **~сь** (*impf* **выводи́ться**) *сов возв* (*цыпля́та*) to hatch (out); (*исчезнуть*) to be eradicated

**вывешива|ть** (-ю) *несов от* **вы́весить**

**вы́вих** (-а) *м* dislocation

**вы́вихн|уть** (-у) *сов перех* to dislocate

**вы́вод** (-а) *м* (*войск*) withdrawal; (*умозаключение*) conclusion

**вы|води́ть(ся)** (-вожу́(сь), -во́дишь(ся)) *несов от* **вы́вести(сь)**

**вы́воз** (-а) *м* removal; (*товаров*) export

**вы|вози́ть** (-вожу́, -во́зишь) *несов от* **вы́везти**

**вывора́чива|ть(ся)** (-ю(сь)) *несов от* **вы́вернуть(ся)**

**выгиба́|ть** (-ю) *несов от* **вы́гнуть**

**вы́гля|деть** (-жу, -дишь) *несов* to look

**вы́глян|уть** (-у; *impf* **выгля́дывать**) *сов* to look out

**вы́г|нать** (-оню, -онишь; *impf* **выгоня́ть**) *сов перех* to throw out; (*стадо*) to drive out

**вы́гн|уть** (-у; *impf* **выгиба́ть**) *сов перех* to bend; (*спину*) to arch

**вы́говор** (-а) *м* (*произношение*)

accent; (*наказание*) reprimand

**вы́говор|ить** (-ю, -ишь; *impf*
**выгова́ривать**) *сов перех*
(*произнести*) to pronounce

**вы́год|а** (-ы) *ж* advantage, benefit;
(*прибыль*) profit

**вы́годно** *нареч* (*продать*) at a
profit ♦ *как сказ* it is profitable;
**мне э́то ~** this is to my advantage;
(*прибыльно*) this is profitable for
me

**вы́годный** *прил* (*сделка*)
profitable; (*условия*) advantageous

**выгоня́|ть** (-ю) *несов от*
**вы́гнать**

**вы́гор|еть** (*3sg* -ит; *impf*
**выгора́ть**) *сов* (*сгореть*) to burn
down; (*выцвести*) to fade

**вы́гре|сти** (-бу, -бешь; *pt* -б,
-бла, -бло; *impf* **выгреба́ть**) *сов
перех* to rake out

**вы́гру|зить** (-жу, -зишь; *impf*
**выгружа́ть**) *сов перех* to
unload; **~ся** (*impf* **выгружа́ться**)
*сов возв* to unload

**выда|ва́ть(ся)** (-ю́(сь)) *несов от*
**вы́дать(ся)**

**вы́дав|ить** (-лю, -ишь; *impf*
**выда́вливать**) *сов перех*
(*лимон*) to squeeze

**вы́да|ть** (*как* **дать**; *см. Table 16*;
*impf* **выдава́ть**) *сов перех* to give
out; (*патент*) to issue;
(*продукцию*) to produce; (*тайну*)
to give away; **выдава́ть** (~ *pf*)
**кого́-н/что́-н за** +*acc* to pass sb/sth
off as; **выдава́ть** (~ *pf*) **де́вушку
за́муж** to marry a girl off; **~ся** (*impf*
**выдава́ться**) *сов возв* (*берег*) to
jut out

**вы́дач|а** (-и) *ж* (*справки*) issue;
(*продукции*) output;
(*заложников*) release

**выдаю́щийся** *прил* outstanding

**выдвига́|ть(ся)** (-ю(сь)) *несов*

*от* **вы́двинуть(ся)**

**выдвиже́ни|е** (-я) *ср*
(*кандидата*) nomination

**вы́двин|уть** (-у; *impf* **выдвига́ть**)
*сов перех* to put forward; (*ящик*)
to pull out; (*обвинение*) to level;
**~ся** (*impf* **выдвига́ться**) *сов возв*
to slide out; (*работник*) to advance

**выделе́ни|е** (-я) *ср* (*средств*)
allocation; (*физиология*) secretion

**вы́дел|ить** (-ю, -ишь; *impf*
**выделя́ть**) *сов перех* to assign,
allocate; (*отличить*) to pick out;
(*газы*) to emit; **~ся** (*impf*
**выделя́ться**) *сов возв* (*пот*) to
be secreted; (*газ*) to be emitted;
**выделя́ться** (**~ся** *pf*) **чем-н** to
stand out by virtue of sth

**выдёргива|ть** (-ю) *несов от*
**вы́дернуть**

**вы́держанный** *прил* (*человек*)
self-possessed; (*вино, сыр*) mature

**вы́держ|ать** (-у, -ишь; *impf*
**выде́рживать**) *сов перех*
(*давление*) to withstand; (*боль*)
to bear; (*экзамен*) to get through
♦ *неперех* (*человек*) to hold out;
(*мост*) to hold; **не ~** (*pf*) (*человек*)
to give in

**вы́держ|ка** (-ки; *gen pl* -ек) *ж*
(*самообладание*) self-control;
(*отрывок*) excerpt; (*фото*)
exposure

**вы́дерн|уть** (-у; *impf*
**выдёргивать**) *сов перех* to pull
out

**вы́дох** (-а) *м* exhalation; **де́лать**
(**сде́лать** *pf*) **~** to breathe out

**вы́дохн|уть** (-у; *impf* **выдыха́ть**)
*сов перех* to exhale, breathe out

**вы́дума|ть** (-ю; *impf*
**выду́мывать**) *сов перех*
(*историю*) to make up, invent;
(*игру*) to invent

**вы́дум|ка** (-ки; *gen pl* -ок) *ж*

invention

**выдыхáни|е (-я)** *ср* exhalation

**выдыхá|ть (-ю)** *несов от* **вы́дохнуть**

**вы́езд (-а)** *м* (*отъезд*) departure; (*место*) way out; **игрá на ~е** (*СПОРТ*) away game

**выездной** *прил* (*документ*) exit; **~ спектáкль** guest performance; **~ матч** away match

**вы́е|хать** (*как éхать; см. Table 19*; *impf* **выезжáть**) *сов* (*уехать*) to leave; (*машина*) to drive out

**выж|ать (-му, -мешь;** *impf* **выжимáть**) *сов перех* (*лимон*) to squeeze; (*бельё*) to wring (out)

**выж|ечь (-гу, -жешь** *итп* **-гут;** *pt* **-ег, -гла;** *impf* **выжигáть**) *сов перех* to burn; (*подлеж: солнце*) to scorch

**выживáни|е (-я)** *ср* survival

**выживá|ть (-ю)** *несов от* **вы́жить**

**выжигá|ть (-ю)** *несов от* **вы́жечь**

**выжимá|ть (-ю)** *несов от* **вы́жать**

**вы́жи|ть (-ву, -вешь;** *impf* **выживáть**) *сов* to survive ♦ *перех* (*разг*) to drive out

**вы́з|вать (-ову, -овешь;** *impf* **вызывáть**) *сов перех* to call; (*гнев, критику*) to provoke; (*восторг*) to arouse; (*пожар*) to cause; **вызывáть (~ pf) когó-н на что-н** to challenge sb to sth; **~ся** (*impf* **вызывáться**) *сов возв*: **~ся +infin** to volunteer to do

**вы́здорове|ть (-ю, -ешь;** *impf* **выздорáвливать**) *сов* to recover

**вы́зов (-а)** *м* call; (*в суд*) summons; **~ +dat** (*обществу, родителям итп*) challenge to; **бросáть (брóсить pf) ~ комý-н/чемý-н** to challenge sb/sth

**вы́зубр|ить (-ю, -ишь)** *сов от* **зубри́ть**

**вызывá|ть(ся) (-ю(сь))** *несов от* **вы́звать(ся)**

**вызывáющий** *прил* challenging

**вы́игра|ть (-ю;** *impf* **выи́грывать**) *сов перех* to win

**вы́игрыш (-а)** *м* (*матча*) winning; (*денежный*) winnings *мн*; (*выгода*) advantage

**вы́игрышный** *прил* (*выгодный*) advantageous; **~ вклад** ≈ premium bonds

**вы́|йти** (*как идти́; см. Table 18*; *impf* **выходи́ть**) *сов* to leave; (*из игры*) to drop out; (*из автобуса*) to get off; (*книга*) to come out; (*случиться*) to ensue; (*оказаться*): **~ +instr** to come out; **выходи́ть (~ pf) зáмуж (за) +acc** to marry (*of woman*); **выходи́ть (~ pf) из больни́цы** to leave hospital

**выкáлыва|ть (-ю)** *несов от* **вы́колоть**

**выкáпыва|ть (-ю)** *несов от* **вы́копать**

**выкáрмлива|ть (-ю)** *несов от* **вы́кормить**

**вы́кача|ть (-ю;** *impf* **выкáчивать**) *сов перех* to pump out

**вы́кидыш (-а)** *м* miscarriage

**вы́кин|уть (-у;** *impf* **выки́дывать**) *сов перех* to throw out; (*слово*) to omit

**вы́кип|еть (3sg -ит;** *impf* **выкипáть**) *сов* to boil away

**выклáдыва|ть (-ю)** *несов от* **вы́ложить**

**выключáтел|ь (-я)** *м* switch

**вы́ключ|ить (-у, -ишь;** *impf* **выключáть**) *сов перех* to turn off; **~ся** (*impf* **выключáться**) *сов возв* (*мотор*) to go off; (*свет*) to go out

**вы́к|овать (-ую;** *impf*

**вико́вывать**) *сов перех*
(*металл*) to forge

**ви́кол**|**оть** (**-ю, -ешь**; *impf*
**вика́лывать**) *сов перех* to poke
out

**ви́копа**|**ть** (**-ю**) *сов от* **копа́ть**
♦ (*impf* **вика́пывать**) *перех* (*яму*)
to dig; (*овощи*) to dig up

**ви́корм**|**ить** (**-лю, -ишь**; *impf*
**выка́рмливать**) *сов перех* to
rear

**ви́крик** (**-а**) *м* shout

**ви́крикн**|**уть** (**-у**; *impf*
**выкри́кивать**) *сов перех* to
shout *или* cry out

**ви́кро**|**йка** (**-йки**; *gen pl* **-ек**) *ж*
pattern

**ви́кру**|**тить** (**-чу, -тишь**; *impf*
**выкру́чивать**) *сов перех* to
unscrew; **~ся** *сов возв* to come
unscrewed

**ви́куп** (**-а**) *м* (*заложника*)
ransoming; (*вещей*) redemption;
(*плата*) ransom

**ви́купа**|**ть(ся)** (**-ю(сь)**) *сов от*
**купа́ть(ся)**

**ви́куп**|**ить** (**-лю, -ишь**; *impf*
**выкупа́ть**) *сов перех*
(*заложника*) to ransom; (*вещи*) to
redeem

**выла́влива**|**ть** (**-ю**) *несов от*
**ви́ловить**

**выла́мыва**|**ть** (**-ю**) *несов от*
**ви́ломать**

**ви́лез**|**ти** (**-у, -ешь**; *pt* **-, -ла**; *impf*
**вылеза́ть**) *сов* (*волосы*) to fall
out; **вылеза́ть** (**~** *pf*) **из** +*gen* to
climb out of

**ви́леп**|**ить** (**-лю, -ишь**) *сов от*
**лепи́ть**

**ви́лет** (**-а**) *м* departure

**ви́ле**|**теть** (**-чу, -тишь**; *impf*
**вылета́ть**) *сов* to fly out; **его́ и́мя**
**~тело у меня́ из головы́** his
name has slipped my mind

**ви́леч**|**ить** (**-у, -ишь**; *impf*
**выле́чивать**) *сов перех* to cure;
**~ся** *несов возв* to be cured

**ви́л**|**ить** (**-ью, -ьешь**; *impf*
**вылива́ть**) *сов перех* to pour
out; (*impf* **лить**; *деталь, ста́тую*)
to cast; **~ся** (*impf* **вылива́ться**)
*сов возв* to pour out; **вылива́ться**
(**~ся** *pf*) **в** +*acc* to turn into

**ви́лов**|**ить** (**-лю, -ишь**; *impf*
**выла́вливать**) *сов перех* to
catch

**ви́лож**|**ить** (**-у, -ишь**; *impf*
**выкла́дывать**) *сов перех* to lay
out; **выкла́дывать** (**~** *pf*) **что-н**
**чем-н** (*пли́ткой*) to face sth with
sth

**ви́лома**|**ть** (**-ю**; *impf*
**выла́мывать**) *сов перех* to break
open

**ви́луп**|**иться** (*3sg* **-ится**; *impf*
**вылу́пливаться**) *сов возв*
(*птенцы*) to hatch (out)

**выма́чива**|**ть** (**-ю**) *несов от*
**ви́мочить**

**ви́м**|**ереть** (*3sg* **-рет**; *impf*
**вымира́ть**) *сов* (*диноза́вры*) to
become extinct; (*город*) to be
dead

**ви́ме**|**сти** (**-ту, -тешь**; *pt* **-л, -ла**;
*impf* **вымета́ть**) *сов перех* to
sweep out

**ви́ме**|**стить** (**-щу, -стишь**; *impf*
**вымеща́ть**) *сов перех*: **~ что-н**
**на ком-н** to take sth out on sb

**вымета́**|**ть** (**-ю**) *несов от*
**ви́мести**

**вымира́**|**ть** (*3sg* **-ет**) *несов от*
**ви́мереть**

**вымога́тельств**|**о** (**-а**) *ср*
extortion

**вымога́**|**ть** (**-ю**) *несов перех* to
extort

**ви́мок**|**нуть** (**-ну, -нешь**; *pt* **-,**
**-ла**) *сов* to get soaked through

**вы́моч|ить** (-у, -ишь; *impf* **выма́чивать**) *сов перех* to soak

**вы́мпел** (-а) *м* (*на корабле*) pennant; (*награда*) trophy (*in the form of a pennant*)

**вы́мыс|ел** (-ла) *м* fantasy; (*ложь*) fabrication

**вы́м|ыть** (-ою, -оешь) *сов от* **мыть**

**вы́мышленный** *прил* fictitious

**вы́м|я** (-ени; *как* **вре́мя**; *см.* Table 4) *ср* udder

**вына́шива|ть** (-ю) *несов перех* to nurture

**вы́нес|ти** (-у, -ешь; *pt* -, -ла; *impf* **выноси́ть**) *сов перех* to carry *или* take out; (*приговор*) to pass, pronounce; (*впечатления, знания*) to gain; (*боль, оскорбление*) to bear

**вынима́|ть** (-ю) *несов от* **вы́нуть**

**вын|оси́ть** (-ошу́, -о́сишь) *несов от* **вы́нести** ♦ *перех*: я его́ не ~ошу́ I can't bear *или* stand him

**выно́сливый** *прил* resilient

**вы́ну|дить** (-жу, -дишь; *impf* **вынужда́ть**) *сов перех*: ~ кого́-н/что-н к чему́-н to force sb/sth into sth

**вы́нужденн|ый** *прил* forced; ~ая поса́дка emergency landing

**вы́н|уть** (-у; *impf* **вынима́ть**) *сов перех* to take out

**вы́нырн|уть** (-у) *сов* (*из воды*) to surface; (*разг: из-за угла*) to pop up

**выпада́|ть** (-ю) *несов от* **вы́пасть**

**выпаде́ни|е** (-я) *ср* (*осадков*) fall; (*зубов, волос*) falling out

**вы́па|сть** (-ду, -дешь; *impf* **выпада́ть**) *сов* to fall out; (*осадки*) to fall; (*задача итп*): ~

+*dat* to fall to; **мне ~л слу́чай/~ло сча́стье встре́тить его́** I chanced to/had the luck to meet him

**вы́пивк|а** (-и) *ж* booze

**вы́пи|сать** (-шу, -шешь; *impf* **выпи́сывать**) *сов перех* to copy *или* write out; (*пропуск, счёт, рецепт*) to make out; (*газету*) to subscribe to; (*пациента*) to discharge; ~ся (*impf* **выпи́сываться**) *несов возв* (*из больницы*) to be discharged; (*с адреса*) to change one's residence permit

**вы́пис|ка** (-ки; *gen pl* -ок) *ж* (*цитата*) extract

**вы́п|ить** (-ью, -ьешь; *imper* -ей(те)) *сов от* **пить**

**вы́плав|ить** (-лю, -ишь; *impf* **выплавля́ть**) *сов перех* to smelt

**вы́плат|а** (-ы) *ж* payment

**вы́пла|тить** (-чу, -тишь; *impf* **выпла́чивать**) *сов перех* to pay; (*долг*) to pay off

**вы́плесн|уть** (-у; *impf* **выплёскивать**) *сов перех* to pour out

**вы́плы|ть** (-ву, -вешь; *impf* **выплыва́ть**) *сов* to swim out

**вы́полз|ти** (-у; *pt* -, -ла, -ло; *impf* **выполза́ть**) *сов* to crawl out

**выполни́мый** *прил* feasible

**вы́полн|ить** (-ю, -ишь; *impf* **выполня́ть**) *сов перех* (*задание, заказ*) to carry out; (*план, условие*) to fulfil (*BRIT*), fulfill (*US*)

**вы́потрош|ить** (-у, -ишь) *сов от* **потроши́ть**

**выпра́шива|ть** (-ю) *несов перех* to beg for

**вы́про|сить** (-шу, -сишь) *сов перех*: **он ~сил у отца́ маши́ну** he persuaded his father to give him the car

**вы́прыгн|уть** (-у; *impf*
**выпры́гивать**) *сов* to jump out

**вы́прям|ить** (-лю, -ишь; *impf*
**выпрямля́ть**) *сов перех* to
straighten (out); ~**ся** (*impf*
**выпрямля́ться**) *несов возв* to
straighten (up)

**вы́пуклый** *прил* (*лоб итп*)
bulging; (*линза*) convex

**вы́пуск** (-а) *м* (*продукции*)
output; (*газа*) emission, release;
(*книги*) publication; (*денег,
акций*) issue; (*учащиеся*) school-
leavers *мн* (*BRIT*), graduates *мн* (*US*)

**выпуска́|ть** (-ю) *несов от*
**вы́пустить**

**выпускни́к** (-а́) *м* (*вуза*)
graduate; ~ **шко́лы** school-leaver
(*BRIT*), graduate (*US*)

**выпускно́й** *прил* (*класс*) final-
year; (*ТЕХ*): ~ **кла́пан** exhaust
valve; ~ **ве́чер** graduation; ~
**экза́мен** final exam, finals *мн*

---

**выпускны́е экза́мены** - final
exams. These exams are sat by
pupils at the end of their
secondary education. Pupils have
no choice as to the subjects they
study and the exams they
subsequently take. They have to
study all the subjects in the
curriculum. All exams, except an
essay on Russian literature and an
exam in maths, are oral.

---

**вы́пу|стить** (-щу, -стишь; *impf*
**выпуска́ть**) *сов перех* to let out;
(*дым*) to exhale; (*заключённого*)
to release; (*специалистов*) to turn
out; (*продукцию*) to produce;
(*книгу*) to publish; (*заём, марки*)
to issue; (*акции*) to put into
circulation; (*исключить:
параграф*) to omit

**вы́пью** *etc сов см.* **вы́пить**

**вы́работа|ть** (-ю; *impf*
**выраба́тывать**) *сов перех* to
produce; (*план*) to work out;
(*привычку*) to develop

**выра́внива|ть** (-ю) *несов от*
**вы́ровнять**

**выража́|ть(ся)** (-ю(сь)) *несов от*
**вы́разить(ся)**

**выраже́ни|е** (-я) *ср* expression

**вырази́тельный** *прил* expressive

**вы́ра|зить** (-жу, -зишь; *impf*
**выража́ть**) *сов перех* to express;
~**ся** (*impf* **выража́ться**) *сов возв*
(*чувство*) to manifest *или* express
itself; (*человек*) to express o.s.

**вы́р|асти** (-асту, -астешь; *pt*
-ос, -осла, -осли) *сов от* **расти́**
♦ (*impf* **выраста́ть**) *неперех*
(*появиться*) to rise up; **выраста́ть**
(~ *pf*) **в** +*acc* to (grow to)
become

**вы́ра|стить** (-щу, -стишь) *сов*
*от* **расти́ть**

**выра́щива|ни|е** (-я) *ср*
(*растений*) cultivation;
(*животных*) rearing

**выра́щива|ть** (-ю; *pf* **вы́растить**)
*несов перех* = **расти́ть**

**вы́рв|ать** (-у, -ешь; *impf*
**вырыва́ть**) *сов перех* to pull out;
(*отнять*): ~ **что-н у кого́-н** to
snatch sth from sb ♦ (*impf* **рвать**)
*безл* (*разг*): **её ~ало** she threw
up; **ему́ ~али зуб** he had his tooth
taken out; ~**ся** (*impf* **вырыва́ться**)
*сов возв* (*из тюрьмы́*) to escape;
(*перен: в театр*) to manage to get
away; (*пламя*) to shoot out

**вы́рез** (-а) *м*: **пла́тье с больши́м
~ом** a low-cut dress

**вы́ре|зать** (-жу, -жешь; *impf*
**выреза́ть**) *сов перех* to cut out;
(*опухоль, гнойник*) to remove;
(*из де́рева, из ко́сти итп*) to

carve; (на камне, на металле итп) to engrave; (убить) to slaughter

**вы́рез|ка** (**-ки**; gen pl **-ок**) ж (газетная) cutting, clipping; (мясная) fillet

**вы́ровня|ть** (**-ю**) сов от **ровня́ть** ♦ (impf **выра́внивать**) перех to level

**вы́род|иться** (3sg **-ится**; impf **вырожда́ться**) сов возв to degenerate

**вырожде́ни|е** (**-я**) ср degeneration

**вы́рон|ить** (**-ю, -ишь**) сов перех to drop

**вы́рос** etc сов см. **вы́расти**

**вы́руб|ить** (**-лю, -ишь**; impf **выруба́ть**) сов перех (деревья) to cut down; (свет) to cut off

**вы́руга|ть(ся)** (**-ю(сь)**) сов от **руга́ть(ся)**

**вы́руч|ить** (**-у, -ишь**; impf **выруча́ть**) сов перех to help out; (деньги) to make

**вы́ручк|а** (**-и**) ж rescue; (деньги) takings мн

**вырыва́|ть(ся)** (**-ю(сь)**) несов от **вы́рвать(ся)**

**вы́р|ыть** (**-ою, -оешь**) сов от **рыть** ♦ (impf **вырыва́ть**) перех to dig up; (яму) to dig

**вы́са|дить** (**-жу, -дишь**; impf **выса́живать**) сов перех (растение) to plant out; (пассажира: дать выйти) to drop off; (: силой) to throw out; (войска) to land; **~ся** (impf **выса́живаться**) сов возв: **~ся** (**из** +gen) to get off; (войска) to land

**выса́сыва|ть** (**-ю**) несов от **вы́сосать**

**вы́свобо|дить** (**-жу, -дишь**; impf **высвобожда́ть**) сов перех

(ногу, руку) to free; (время) to set aside

**вы́сел|ить** (**-ю, -ишь**; impf **выселя́ть**) сов перех to evict

**вы́си|деть** (**-жу, -дишь**; impf **выси́живать**) сов перех to hatch; (перен: лекцию) to sit out

**вы́с|иться** (3sg **-ится**) несов возв to tower

**выска|за́ть** (**-жу, -жешь**; impf **выска́зывать**) сов перех to express; **~ся** (impf **выска́зываться**) сов возв to speak one's mind; **выска́зываться** (**~ся** pf) **про́тив** +gen/**за** +acc to speak out against/in favour of

**выска́зывани|е** (**-я**) ср statement

**выска́кива|ть** (**-ю**) несов от **вы́скочить**

**вы́скользн|уть** (**-у**; impf **выска́льзывать**) сов to slip out

**вы́скоч|ить** (**-у, -ишь**; impf **выска́кивать**) сов to jump out; **его́ и́мя ~ило у меня́ из головы́** (разг) his name has slipped my mind

**вы́|слать** (**-шлю, -шлешь**; impf **высыла́ть**) сов перех to send off; (изгнать) to deport

**вы́сле|дить** (**-жу, -дишь**; impf **выслё́живать**) сов перех to track down

**вы́слуг|а** (**-и**) ж: **за ~у лет** for long service

**вы́слуша|ть** (**-ю**; impf **выслу́шивать**) сов перех to hear out

**вы́сме|ять** (**-ю**; impf **высме́ивать**) сов перех to ridicule

**вы́сморка|ть(ся)** (**-ю(сь)**) сов от **сморка́ть(ся)**

**высо́выва|ть(ся)** (**-ю(сь)**) несов от **вы́сунуть(ся)**

**высо́кий** прил high; (человек)

tall; (*честь*) great; (*гость*) distinguished

**высоко́** *нареч* high (up) ♦ *как сказ* it's high (up)

**высокого́рный** *прил* alpine

**высокоме́рный** *прил* haughty

**высокопа́рный** *прил* (*речь*) high-flown, pompous

**высокопоста́вленный** *прил* high-ranking

**высос|а́ть** (-у, -ешь; *impf* **выса́сывать**) *сов перех* to suck out; (*насосом*) to pump out

**высот|а́** (-ы́; *nom pl* -**ы**) *ж* height; (*гео*) altitude; (*звука*) pitch

**высо́тный** *прил* (*здание*) high-rise

**высох|нуть** (-ну; *pt* -, -ла, -ло) *сов от* **со́хнуть**

**высо́честв|о** (-а) *ср*: Ва́ше *итп* Высо́чество Your *etc* Highness

**вы́сп|аться** (-люсь, -ишься; *impf* **высыпа́ться**) *сов возв* to sleep well

**вы́став|ить** (-лю, -ишь; *impf* **выставля́ть**) *сов перех* (*поставить наружу*) to put out; (*грудь*) to stick out; (*кандидатуру*) to put forward; (*товар*) to display; (*охрану*) to post; (*разг: выгнать*) to chuck out

**вы́став|ка** (-ки; *gen pl* -ок) *ж* exhibition

**выставля́|ть** (-ю) *несов от* **вы́ставить**

**выстира́|ть** (-ю) *сов от* **стира́ть**

**вы́стрел** (-а) *м* shot

**вы́стрел|ить** (-ю, -ишь) *сов* to fire

**вы́стро|ить(ся)** (-ю(сь), -ишь(ся)) *сов от* **стро́ить(ся)**

**вы́ступ** (-а) *м* ledge

**выступа́|ть** (-ю) *несов от* **вы́ступить** ♦ *неперех* (*берег*) to jut out; (*скулы*) to protrude

**вы́ступ|ить** (-лю, -ишь; *impf* **выступа́ть**) *сов* (*против, в защиту*) to come out; (*из толпы*) to step out; (*актёр*) to perform; (*пот, сыпь*) to break out; (*в поход, на поиски*) to set off *или* out

**выступле́ни|е** (-я) *ср* (*актёра*) performance; (*в печати*) article; (*речь*) speech

**вы́сун|уть** (-у; *impf* **высо́вывать**) *сов перех* to stick out; ~**ся** (*impf* **высо́вываться**) *сов возв* (*из окна*) to lean out; (*рука, нога*) to stick out

**вы́суш|ить(ся)** (-у(сь), -ишь(ся)) *сов от* **суши́ть(ся)**

**вы́счита|ть** (-ю; *impf* **высчи́тывать**) *сов перех* to calculate

**вы́сш|ий** *прил* (*орган власти*) highest, supreme; **в ~ей сте́пени** extremely; ~**ая ме́ра наказа́ния** capital punishment; ~**ее образова́ние** higher education; ~**ее уче́бное заведе́ние** = **вуз**

**высыла́|ть** (-ю) *несов от* **вы́слать**

**высып|а́ть** (-лю, -лешь; *impf* **высыпа́ть**) *сов перех* to pour out; ~**ся** (*impf* **высыпа́ться**) *сов возв* to pour out

**выта́лкива|ть** (-ю) *несов от* **вы́толкнуть**

**вы́тащ|ить** (-у, -ишь) *сов от* **тащи́ть** ♦ (*impf* **выта́скивать**) *перех* (*мебель*) to drag out

**вытека́|ть** (*3sg* -ет) *несов от* **вы́течь** ♦ *неперех* (*вывод*) to follow; (*река*) to flow out

**вы́т|ереть** (-ру, -решь; *impf* **вытира́ть**) *сов перех* to wipe up; (*посуду*) to dry (up); (*руки, глаза*) to wipe; ~**ся** (*impf* **вытира́ться**) *сов возв* (*человек*) to dry o.s.

**вы́тесн|ить** (-ю, -ишь; *impf* **вытесня́ть**) *сов перех* (*удалить*) to oust; (*заменить собой*) to supplant

**вы́те|чь** (*3sg* -чет, *3pl* -кут, *pt* -к, -кла; *impf* **вытека́ть**) *сов* to flow out

**вытира́|ть(ся)** (-ю(сь)) *несов от* **вы́тереть(ся)**

**вы́толкн|уть** (-у; *impf* **выта́лкивать**) *сов перех* to push out

**вы́трав|ить** (-лю, -ишь; *impf* **вытра́вливать**) *сов перех* (*пятно*) to remove; (*крыс*) to exterminate; (*рисунок*) to etch

**вытрезви́тел|ь** (-я) *м overnight police cell for drunks*

**вы́тряхн|уть** (-у; *impf* **вытря́хивать**) *сов перех* to shake out

**выть** (**во́ю**, **во́ешь**) *несов* (*зверь, ветер*) to howl; (*сирена*) to wail

**вы́тян|уть** (-у; *impf* **вытя́гивать**) *сов перех* to pull out; (*дым*) to extract; (*руки*) to stretch; ~**ся** (*impf* **вытя́гиваться**) *сов возв* (*на диване, вдоль берега*) to stretch out; (*встать смирно*) to stand at attention

**вы́у|дить** (-жу, -дишь; *impf* **выу́живать**) *сов перех* (*рыбу*) to catch; (*разг: сведения*) to wheedle out

**вы́уч|ить(ся)** (-у(сь), -ишь(ся)) *сов от* **учи́ть(ся)**

**выха́жива|ть** (-ю) *несов от* **выходи́ть**

**вы́хва|тить** (-чу, -тишь; *impf* **выхва́тывать**) *сов перех* to snatch

**выхлопн|о́й** *прил* exhaust; ~**ые га́зы** exhaust fumes

**вы́ход** (-а) *м* (*войск*) withdrawal; (*из кризиса*) way out; (*на сцену*) appearance; (*в море*) sailing; (*книги*) publication; (*на экран*) showing; (*место*) exit

**выхо|ди́ть** (-жу, -дишь; *impf* **выха́живать**) *сов перех* (*больного*) to nurse (back to health)

**вых|оди́ть** (-ожу́, -о́дишь) *несов от* **вы́йти** ♦ *неперех*: ~ **на** +*acc* (*юг, север*) to face; **окно́** ~**о́дит в парк** the window looks out onto the park

**вы́хо|дка** (-ки) *ж* prank

**выходн|о́й** *прил* exit; (*платье*) best ♦ (-о́го) *м* (*также*: ~ **день**) day off (work); **сего́дня** ~ (*разг*) today is a holiday; ~**ые** weekend *ед*

**вы́цве|сти** (*3sg* -тет; *impf* **выцвета́ть**) *сов* to fade

**вы́черкн|уть** (-у; *impf* **вычёркивать**) *сов перех* to cross *или* score out

**вы́ч|есть** (-ту, -тешь; *impf* **вычита́ть**) *сов перех* (*МАТ*) to subtract; (*долг, налог*) to deduct

**вы́чет** (-а) *м* deduction ♦ *предл*: **за** ~**ом** +*gen* minus

**вычисле́ни|е** (-я) *ср* calculation

**вычисли́тельн|ый** *прил* (*операция*) computing; ~**ая маши́на** computer; ~**ая те́хника** computers *мн*; ~ **центр** computer centre (*BRIT*) *или* center (*US*)

**вы́числ|ить** (-ю, -ишь; *impf* **вычисля́ть**) *сов перех* to calculate

**вычита́ни|е** (-я) *ср* subtraction

**вычита́|ть** (-ю) *несов от* **вы́честь**

**вы́ше** *сравн прил от* **высо́кий** ♦ *сравн нареч от* **высоко́** ♦ *нареч* higher; (*в тексте*) above ♦ *предл*: ~ +*gen* above

**вы́шел** *сов см.* **вы́йти**
**вышестоя́щий** *прил* higher
**вышива́|ть (-ю)** *несов от* **вы́шить**
**вы́шив|ка (-ки;** *gen pl* **-ок)** *ж* embroidery
**вы́ш|ить (-ью, -ешь;** *impf* **вышива́ть)** *сов перех* to embroider
**вы́ш|ка (-ки;** *gen pl* **-ек)** *ж* (*строение*) tower; (*СПОРТ*) diving board; **бурова́я** *или* **нефтяна́я ~** derrick
**вы́шла** *etc сов см.* **вы́йти**
**вы́яв|ить (-лю, -ишь;** *impf* **выявля́ть)** *сов перех* (*талант*) to discover; (*недостатки*) to expose; **~ся** (*impf* **выявля́ться**) *сов возв* to come to light, be revealed
**вы́ясн|ить (-ю, -ишь;** *impf* **выясня́ть)** *сов перех* to find out; **~ся** (*impf* **выясня́ться**) *сов возв* to become clear
**Вьетна́м (-а)** *м* Vietnam
**вью́г|а (-и)** *ж* snowstorm, blizzard
**вя́жущий** *прил* (*вкус*) acerbic; (*материал*) binding
**вяз (-а)** *м* elm
**вяза́ни|е (-я)** *ср* knitting
**вя́заный** *прил* knitted
**вя|за́ть (-жу́, -жешь;** *pf* **с~)** *несов перех* to tie up; (*свитер*) to knit
**вя́зкий** *прил* (*тягучий*) viscous; (*топкий*) boggy
**вя́з|нуть (-ну;** *pt* **-, -ла, -ло;** *pf* **за~** *или* **у~)** *несов:* **~ (в** +*prp*) to get stuck (in)
**вя́лый** *прил* (*листья, цветы*) wilted, withered; (*человек, речь*) sluggish
**вя́н|уть (-у;** *pf* **за~** *или* **у~)** *несов* (*цветы*) to wilt, wither; (*красота*) to fade

# Г, г

**г** *сокр* (= **грамм**) g, gm
**г.** *сокр* = **год, го́род**
**Гаа́г|а (-и)** *ж* The Hague
**габари́т (-а)** *м* (*ТЕХ*) dimension
**Гава́йи** *м нескл* Hawaii
**га́ван|ь (-и)** *ж* harbour (*BRIT*), harbor (*US*)
**гада́|ть (-ю)** *несов* (*предполагать*) to guess; **~ (по~** *pf*) **кому́-н** to tell sb's fortune
**га́дост|ь (-и)** *ж* filth
**гадю́к|а (-и)** *ж* viper, adder
**га́ечный** *прил:* **~ ключ** spanner
**газ (-а)** *м* gas; *см. также* **га́зы**
**газе́т|а (-ы)** *ж* newspaper
**газиро́ванн|ый** *прил:* **~ая вода́** carbonated water
**га́зов|ый** *прил* gas; **~ая плита́** gas cooker
**газо́н (-а)** *м* lawn
**газопрово́д (-а)** *м* gas pipeline
**га́з|ы (-ов)** *мн* (*МЕД*) wind *ед*
**ГАИ** *ж сокр* (= **Госуда́рственная автомоби́льная инспе́кция**) *state motor vehicle inspectorate*
**га́|йка (-йки;** *gen pl* **-ек)** *ж* nut
**галантере́|я (-и)** *ж* haberdashery (*BRIT*), notions store (*US*)
**галере́|я (-и)** *ж* gallery
**га́л|ка (-ки;** *gen pl* **-ок)** *ж* jackdaw
**галло́н (-а)** *м* gallon
**галлюцина́ци|я (-и)** *ж* hallucination
**га́лоч|ка (-ки;** *gen pl* **-ек)** *ж* (*в тексте*) tick, check (*US*)
**га́лстук (-а)** *м* tie, necktie (*US*)
**га́льк|а (-и)** *ж собир* pebbles *мн*
**га́мбургер (-а)** *м* hamburger
**га́мм|а (-ы)** *ж* (*МУЗ*) scale
**гангре́н|а (-ы)** *ж* gangrene

**га́нгстер** (-а) м gangster
**гандбо́л** (-а) м handball
**ганте́ль** (-и) ж dumbbell
**гара́ж** (-а́) м garage
**гара́нт** (-а) м guarantor
**гаранти́йный** прил guarantee
**гаранти́р|овать** (-ую) (не)сов перех to guarantee
**гара́нти|я** (-и) ж guarantee
**гардеро́б** (-а) м wardrobe; (в общественном здании) cloakroom
**гармони́р|овать** (-ую) несов: ~ с +instr (со средой) to be in harmony with; (одежда) to go with
**гармони́ст** (-а) м concertina player
**гармо́ни|я** (-и) ж harmony
**гармо́ш|ка** (-ки; gen pl -ек) ж (разг) ≈ squeeze-box
**гарнизо́н** (-а) м garrison
**гарни́р** (-а) м side dish
**гарниту́р** (-а) м (мебель) suite
**гар|ь** (-и) ж (угля) cinders мн
**га|си́ть** (-шу́, -сишь; pf по~) несов перех (свет) to put out; (пожар) to extinguish, put out
**га́с|нуть** (-ну; pt - или -нул, -ла; pf по~ или у~) несов (огни) to go out
**гастри́т** (-а) м gastritis
**гастро́л|и** (-ей) мн performances of touring company; **е́здить/е́хать** (пое́хать pf) на ~ to go on tour
**гастроли́р|овать** (-ую) несов to be on tour
**гастроно́м** (-а) м food store
**гастроно́ми|я** (-и) ж delicatessen
**гаши́ш** (-а) м cannabis
**гва́рди|я** (-и) ж (ВОЕН) Guards мн
**гвозди́к|а** (-и) ж (цветок) carnation; (пряность) cloves мн
**гвозд|ь** (-я́) м nail
**гг** сокр = **го́ды, господа́**
**где** нареч where; (разг: где-нибудь) somewhere, anywhere ♦ союз where; ~ **Вы живёте?** where do you live?
**где́-либо** нареч = **где́-нибудь**
**где́-нибудь** нареч somewhere; (в вопросе) anywhere
**где́-то** нареч somewhere
**гекта́р** (-а) м hectare
**гемmorро́|й** (-я) м piles мн
**ген** (-а) м gene
**генера́л** (-а) м (ВОЕН) general
**генера́льн|ый** прил general; (главный) main; ~ая убо́рка spring-clean; ~ая репети́ция dress rehearsal
**генера́тор** (-а) м generator
**гене́тик|а** (-и) ж genetics
**генети́ческ|ий** прил genetic; ~и модифици́рованный genetically modified
**гениа́льный** прил great
**ге́ни|й** (-я) м genius
**ге́нный** прил (терапия) gene
**геноци́д** (-а) м genocide
**геогра́фи|я** (-и) ж geography
**гео́лог** (-а) м geologist
**геоме́три|я** (-и) ж geometry
**гера́н|ь** (-и) ж geranium
**герб** (-а́) м coat of arms; **госуда́рственный** ~ national emblem
**ге́рбов|ый** прил: ~ая бума́га stamped paper
**геркуле́с** (-а) м (КУЛИН) porridge oats мн
**Герма́ни|я** (-и) ж Germany
**герма́нский** прил German
**гермети́чный** прил hermetic
**геро́изм** (-а) м heroism
**геро́ин|я** (-и) ж heroine
**герои́ческий** прил heroic
**геро́|й** (-я) м hero
**г-жа** м сокр = **госпожа́**
**ги́бел|ь** (-и) ж (человека) death; (армии) destruction; (самолёта,

*надежды*) loss; (*карьеры*) ruin

**ги́бкий** *прил* flexible

**ги́б|нуть** (**-ну**; *pt* **-**, **-ла**; *pf* **по~**) *несов* to perish; (*перен*) to come to nothing

**гибри́д** (**-а**) *м* hybrid

**гига́нт** (**-а**) *м* giant

**гига́нтский** *прил* gigantic

**гигие́н|а** (**-ы**) *ж* hygiene

**гигиени́чный** *прил* hygienic

**гид** (**-а**) *м* guide

**гидравли́ческий** *прил* hydraulic

**гидрометеоце́нтр** (**-а**) *м сокр* (= *Гидрометеорологи́ческий центр*) meteorological office

**гидроэлектроста́нци|я** (**-и**) *ж* hydroelectric power station

**гимн** (**-а**) *м*: **госуда́рственный ~** national anthem

**гимна́зи|я** (**-и**) *ж* ≈ grammar school

gimnázija ~ grammar school. This institution of secondary education strives for higher academic standards than comprehensive schools. Pupils can study subjects which are not offered by mainstream education, e.g. classics and two modern languages.

**гимна́ст** (**-а**) *м* gymnast

**гимна́стик|а** (**-и**) *ж* exercises *мн*; (**спорти́вная**) ~ gymnastics; **худо́жественная** ~ modern rhythmic gymnastics

**гинеко́лог** (**-а**) *м* gynaecologist (*BRIT*), gynecologist (*US*)

**гипертони́|я** (**-и**) *ж* high blood pressure

**гипно́з** (**-а**) *м* hypnosis

**гипнотизи́р|овать** (**-ую**; *pf* **за~**) *несов перех* to hypnotize

**гипо́тез|а** (**-ы**) *ж* hypothesis

**гипотони́|я** (**-и**) *ж* low blood pressure

**гиппопота́м** (**-а**) *м* hippopotamus, hippo (*inf*)

**гипс** (**-а**) *м* (*ИСКУССТВО*) plaster of Paris; (*МЕД*) plaster

**гирля́нд|а** (**-ы**) *ж* garland

**ги́р|я** (**-и**) *ж* (*весов*) weight; (*СПОРТ*) dumbbell

**гита́р|а** (**-ы**) *ж* guitar

**глав|а́** (**-ы́**; *nom pl* **-ы**) *ж* (*книги*) chapter; (*здания*) dome ♦ *м* (*делегации*) head; **во -é с** +*instr* headed by; **во -é** +*gen* at the head of

**глава́р|ь** (**-я́**) *м* (*банды*) leader

**главнокома́ндующ|ий** (**-его**) *м* commander in chief

**гла́вн|ый** *прил* main; (*старший по положению*) senior, head; **~ым о́бразом** chiefly, mainly

**глаго́л** (**-а**) *м* verb

**гла́ди́льн|ый** *прил*: **~ая доска́** ironing board

**гла́|дить** (**-жу**, **-дишь**; *pf* **по~**) *несов перех* to iron; (*волосы*) to stroke

**гла́дкий** *прил* (*ровный*) smooth

**глаз** (**-а**; *loc sg* **-ý**, *nom pl* **-á**, *gen pl* **-**) *м* eye; **с гла́зу на́ ~** tête à tête; **на ~** roughly

**глазно́й** *прил* eye

**глазу́нь|я** (**-и**) *ж* fried egg

**гла́нд|а** (**-ы**) *ж* (*обычно мн*) tonsil

**гла́сность** (**-и**) *ж* openness

**гла́сн|ый** (**-ого**) *м* vowel; (*открытый*) open, public

**гли́н|а** (**-ы**) *ж* clay

**гли́няный** *прил* clay

**глоба́льный** *прил* universal

**гло́бус** (**-а**) *м* globe

**глота́|ть** (**-ю**; *pf* **проглоти́ть**) *несов перех* to swallow

**глот|о́к** (**-ка́**) *м* gulp, swallow; (*воды, чая*) drop

**гло́х|нуть** (**-ну**; *pt* **-**, **-ла**; *pf* **о~**)

*несов* to grow deaf; (*мотор*) to stall

**глу́бже** *сравн прил от* **глубо́кий**
♦ *сравн нареч от* **глубоко́**

**глуб|ина́ (-ины́;** *nom pl* **-и́ны)** *ж* depth; (*леса*) heart; (*перен*): **в ~ине́ души́** in one's heart of hearts

**глубо́кий** *прил* deep; (*провинция*) remote; (*мысль*) profound

**глубоко́** *нареч* deeply ♦ *как сказ*: **здесь ~** it's deep here

**глубокоуважа́емый** *прил* dear

**глупе́|ть (-ю;** *pf* **по~)** *несов* to grow stupid

**глу́по** *как сказ* it's stupid *или* silly

**глу́пост|ь (-и)** *ж* stupidity, silliness; (*поступок*) stupid *или* silly thing; (*слова*) nonsense

**глу́пый** *прил* stupid, silly

**глухо́й** *прил* deaf; (*звук*) muffled

**глухонем|о́й** *прил* deaf-and-dumb ♦ **(-о́го)** *м* deaf-mute

**глуши́тел|ь (-я)** *м* (*ТЕХ*) silencer; (*АВТ*) silencer (*BRIT*), muffler (*US*)

**глуш|и́ть (-у́, -и́шь;** *pf* **за~)** *несов перех* (*звуки*) to muffle; (*мотор*) to turn off

**глуш|ь (-и́;** *instr sg* **-ью,** *loc sg* **-и́)** *ж* wilderness

**глы́б|а (-ы)** *ж* (*ледяна́я*) block

**глюко́з|а (-ы)** *ж* glucose

**гля|де́ть (-жу́, -ди́шь;** *pf* **по~)** *несов* to look

**гля́нцевый** *прил* glossy

**гна|ть (гоню́, го́нишь;** *pt* **-л, -ла́)** *несов перех* (*стадо*) to drive; (*человека*) to throw out; (*машину*) to drive fast; **гна́ться** *несов возв*: **гна́ться за** +*instr* to pursue

**гнев (-а)** *м* wrath

**гнезд|о́ (-а́;** *nom pl* **гнёзда,** *gen pl* **гнёзд)** *ср* (*птиц*) nest

**гне|сти́ (-ту́, -тёшь)** *несов перех*

to gnaw

**гнёт (-а)** *м* (*бедности итп*) yoke

**гнету́щий** *прил* depressing

**гнило́й** *прил* rotten

**гнил|ь (-и)** *ж* rotten stuff

**гни|ть (-ю́, -ёшь;** *pf* **с~)** *несов* to rot

**гно|и́ть (-ю́, -и́шь;** *pf* **с~)** *несов перех* to let rot; **~ся** *несов возв* (*рана*) to fester

**гно|й (-я)** *м* pus

**ГНС** *сокр* (= *Госуда́рственная нало́говая слу́жба*) ≈ Inland Revenue

**гн|уть (-у, -ёшь;** *pf* **согну́ть)** *несов перех* to bend; **гну́ться** *несов возв* (*ветка*) to bend

**говор|и́ть (-ю́, -и́шь;** *pf* **сказа́ть)** *несов перех* to say; (*правду*) to tell ♦ *неперех; no pf* to speak, talk; (*обсуждать*): **~ о** +*prp* to talk about; (*общаться*): **~ с** +*instr* to talk to *или* with

**говя́дин|а (-ы)** *ж* beef

**год (-а;** *loc sg* **-у́,** *nom pl* **-ы,** *gen pl* **-о́в/лет)** *м* year; **прошло́ 3 го́да/5 лет** 3/5 years passed; **из го́да в ~** year in year out; **кру́глый ~** all year round

**го|ди́ться (-жу́сь, -ди́шься)** *несов возв*: **~** +*dat* to suit; **~** (*impf*) **для** +*gen* to be suitable for

**го́д|ный** *прил*: **~ к** +*dat или* **для** +*gen* fit *или* suitable for; **биле́т ~ен до ...** the ticket is valid until ...

**годовщи́н|а (-ы)** *ж* anniversary

**гол (-а;** *nom pl* **-ы)** *м* goal

**Голла́нди|я (-и)** *ж* Holland

**голла́ндский** *прил* Dutch; **~ язы́к** Dutch

**гол|ова́ (-овы́;** *acc sg* **-ову,** *dat sg* **-ове́,** *nom pl* **-овы,** *gen pl* **-о́в,** *dat pl* **-ова́м)** *ж* head

**головно́й** *прил* (*офис*) main; (*боль*) head

**головокруже́ни|е (-я)** *ср*
giddiness
**го́лод (-а)** *м* hunger;
(*недоедание*) starvation;
(*бедствие*) famine
**голода́ни|е (-я)** *ср*
(*воздержание*) fasting;
кислоро́дное ~ oxygen
deficiency
**голода́|ть (-ю)** *несов* to starve;
(*воздерживаться от пищи*) to
fast
**голо́дный** *прил* hungry; (*год,
время*) hunger-stricken
**голодо́в|ка (-ки; *gen pl* -ок)** *ж*
hunger strike
**гололёд (-а)** *м* black ice
**го́лос (-а; *part gen* -у, *nom pl* -á)** *м*
voice; (*полит*) vote; **во весь ~** at
the top of one's voice
**голосова́ни|е (-я)** *ср* ballot
**голос|ова́ть (-у́ю; *pf* про~)**
*несов* to vote; (*разг: на дороге*)
to hitch (a lift)
**голуб|о́й** *прил* light blue ♦ **(-ого)**
*м* (*разг*) gay
**го́луб|ь (-я; *gen pl* -е́й)** *м* pigeon;
dove
**го́лый** *прил* (*человек*) naked
**гольф (-а)** *м* golf; (*обычно мн:
чулки*) knee sock
**гомеопа́т (-а)** *м* homoeopath
(*BRIT*), homeopath (*US*)
**го́мик (-а)** *м* (*разг*) homo(sexual)
**гомосексуали́ст (-а)** *м*
homosexual
**гоне́ни|е (-я)** *ср* persecution
**го́н|ка (-ки; *gen pl* -ок)** *ж* (*разг:
спешка*) rush; (*соревнования*)
race; **~ вооруже́ний** arms race
**гонора́р (-а)** *м* fee; **а́вторский ~**
royalty
**го́ночный** *прил* racing
**го́нщик (-а)** *м* racing (*BRIT*) *или*
race car (*US*) driver;
(*велосипедист*) racing cyclist

**гоня́|ть (-ю, -ешь)** *несов перех*
(*ученика*) to grill ♦ *неперех* to
race; **~ся** *несов возв*: **~ся за** +*instr*
(*преследовать*) to chase (after);
(*перен*) to pursue
**гор.** *сокр* = **го́род**
**гор|а́ (*acc sg* -у, *gen sg* -ы́, *nom pl*
-ы, *dat pl* -а́м)** *ж* mountain;
(*небольшая*) hill
**гора́здо** *нареч* much
**горб (-а́; *loc sg* -у́)** *м* hump
**горба́тый** *прил* hunchbacked
**горб|ить (-лю, -ишь; *pf* с~)**
*несов перех*: **~ спи́ну** to stoop;
**~ся** (*pf* с~ся) *несов возв* to stoop
**горбу́ш|ка (-ки; *gen pl* -ек)** *ж*
crust
**гор|ди́ться (-жу́сь, -ди́шься)**
*несов возв*: **~** +*instr* to be proud of
**го́рдост|ь (-и)** *ж* pride
**го́рдый** *прил* proud
**го́р|е (-я)** *ср* (*скорбь*) grief;
(*несчастье*) misfortune
**гор|ева́ть (-ю́ю)** *несов* to grieve
**горе́лый** *прил* burnt
**гор|е́ть (-ю́, -и́шь; *pf* с~)** *несов*
to burn; (*no pf; дом*) to be on fire;
(*больной*) to be burning hot;
(*глаза*) to shine
**го́реч|ь (-и)** *ж* bitter taste;
(*потери*) bitterness
**горизо́нт (-а)** *м* horizon
**горизонта́л|ь (-и)** *ж* horizontal;
(*на карте*) contour
**горизонта́льный** *прил* horizontal
**гори́лл|а (-ы)** *ж* gorilla
**гори́стый** *прил* mountainous
**го́р|ка (-ки; *gen pl* -ок)** *ж* hill;
(*кучка*) small pile
**го́рл|о (-а)** *ср* throat
**го́рлыш|ко (-ка; *nom pl* -ки, *gen pl*
-ек)** *ср* (*бутылки*) neck
**гормо́н (-а)** *м* hormone
**гормона́льный** *прил* hormonal
**го́рный** *прил* mountain; (*лыжи*)

downhill; (*промышленность*)
mining

**го́род** (**-а**; *nom pl* **-а́**) *м* (*большой*)
city; (*небольшой*) town

**горожа́н|ин** (**-ина**; *nom pl* **-е**, *gen
pl* **-**) *м* city dweller

**гороско́п** (**-а**) *м* horoscope

**горо́х** (**-а**) *м собир* peas *мн*

**горо́ш|ек** (**-ка**) *м собир* peas *мн*;
(*на платье итп*) polka dots *мн*;
**ткань в ~** spotted material

**горо́шин|а** (**-ы**) *ж* pea

**горст|ь** (**-и**; *gen pl* **-е́й**) *ж* handful

**горч|и́ть** (*3sg* **-и́т**) *несов* to taste
bitter

**горчи́ц|а** (**-ы**) *ж* mustard

**горчи́чник** (**-а**) *м* mustard plaster

**горш|о́к** (**-ка́**) *м* pot

**го́рький** *прил* bitter

**го́рько** *нареч* (*плакать*) bitterly
♦ *как сказ*: **во рту ~** I have a bitter
taste in my mouth

**горю́ч|ее** (**-его**) *ср* fuel

**горю́чий** *прил* flammable

**горя́ч|ий** *прил* hot; (*перен:
любовь*) passionate; (: *спор*)
heated; (: *желание*) burning;
(: *человек*) hot-tempered; **~ая
ли́ния** hot line

**горячо́** *нареч* (*спорить, любить*)
passionately ♦ *как сказ* it's hot

**гос.** *сокр* = **госуда́рственный**

**Госба́нк** (**-а**) *м сокр* (=
*госуда́рственный банк*) state
bank

**госбезопа́сност|ь** (**-и**) *ж сокр* (=
*госуда́рственная безопа́сность*)
national security

**госбюдже́т** (**-а**) *м сокр* (=
*госуда́рственный бюдже́т*) state
budget

**госпитализи́р|овать** (**-ую**)
(*не*)*сов перех* to hospitalize

**го́спитал|ь** (**-я**) *м* army hospital

**господа́** *итп сущ см.* **господи́н**

♦ *мн* (*при фамилии, при звании*)
Messrs

**го́споди** *межд*: **Го́споди!** good
Lord!

**госп|оди́н** (**-оди́на**; *nom pl* **-ода́**,
*gen pl* **-о́д**) *м* gentleman; (*хозяин*)
master; (*при обращении*) sir; (*при
фамилии*) Mr

**госпо́дств|о** (**-а**) *ср* supremacy

**госпо́дств|овать** (**-ую**) *несов* to
rule; (*мнение*) to prevail

**Госпо́дь** (**Го́спода**; *voc* **Го́споди**)
*м* (*также*: **~ Бог**) the Lord; **не дай
Го́споди!** God forbid!; **сла́ва тебе́
Го́споди!** Glory be to God!; (*разг*)
thank God!

**госпож|а́** (**-и́**) *ж* lady; (*хозяйка*)
mistress; (*при обращении, при
звании*) Madam; (*при фамилии:
замужняя*) Mrs; (: *незамужняя*)
Miss; (: *замужняя или
незамужняя*) Ms

**госстра́х** (**-а**) *м сокр* (=
*госуда́рственное страхова́ние*)
≈ national insurance

**гостеприи́мный** *прил* hospitable

**гости́н|ая** (**-ой**) *ж* living *или*
sitting room, lounge (*BRIT*)

**гости́ниц|а** (**-ы**) *ж* hotel

**го|сти́ть** (**-щу́, -сти́шь**) *несов* to
stay

**гост|ь** (**-я**; *gen pl* **-е́й**) *м* guest;
**идти́ (пойти́** *pf*) **в го́сти к кому́-н**
to go to see sb; **быть** (*impf*) **в ~я́х
у кого́-н** to be at sb's house

**госуда́рственный** *прил* state

**госуда́рств|о** (**-а**) *ср* state

**гото́в|ить** (**-лю, -ишь**; *pf* **при~**)
*несов перех* to get ready; (*уроки*)
to prepare; (*обед*) to prepare,
make; (*pf* **под~**; *специалиста*) to
train ♦ *неперех* to cook; **~ся** (*pf*
**при~ся**) *несов возв*: **~ся к** +*dat*
(*к отъезду*) to get ready for; **~ся**
(**под~ся** *pf*) **к** +*dat* (*к экзамену*) to

prepare for

**гото́вност|ь** (**-и**) *ж*: ~ +*infin* readiness *или* willingness to do

**гото́во** *как сказ* that's it

**гото́вый** *прил* (*изделие*) ready-made; **я/обе́д гото́в** I am/dinner is ready; ~ **к** +*dat*/ +*infin* prepared for/to do

**гр.** *сокр* (= **граждани́н**) Mr (= **гражда́нка**) Mrs

**граб|ёж** (**-ежа́**) *м* robbery; (*дома*) burglary

**граби́тел|ь** (**-я**) *м* robber

**граби́тельск|ий** *прил* (*война*) predatory; ~**ое нападе́ние** (*на дом*) burglary; (*на банк*) robbery

**гра́б|ить** (**-лю, -ишь**; *pf* **о~**) *несов перех* (*человека*) to rob; (*дом*) to burgle; (*город*) to pillage

**гра́б|ли** (**-ель** *или* **-лей**) *мн* rake *ед*

**гра́ви|й** (**-я**) *м* gravel

**гравир|ова́ть** (**-у́ю**; *pf* **вы́~**) *несов перех* to engrave

**гравю́р|а** (**-ы**) *ж* (*оттиск*) engraving; (*офорт*) etching

**град** (**-а**) *м* (*также перен*) hail

**гра́дус** (**-а**) *м* degree

**гра́дусник** (**-а**) *м* thermometer

**граждани́н** (**-а**; *nom pl* **гра́ждане**, *gen pl* **гра́ждан**) *м* citizen

**гражда́н|ка** (**-ки**; *gen pl* **-ок**) *ж* citizen

**гражда́нский** *прил* civil; (*долг*) civic; (*платье*) civilian

**гражда́нств|о** (**-а**) *ср* citizenship

**грамм** (**-а**) *м* gram(me)

**грамма́тик|а** (**-и**) *ж* grammar

**граммати́ческий** *прил* grammatical; (*упражнение*) grammar

**гра́мот|а** (**-ы**) *ж* (*документ*) certificate

**гра́мотный** *прил* (*человек*) literate; (*текст*) correctly written; (*специалист, план*) competent

**грампласти́нк|а** (**-и**) *ж* record

**грана́т|а** (**-ы**) *ж* grenade

**грандио́зный** *прил* grand

**гранёный** *прил* (*стакан*) cut-glass

**грани́ц|а** (**-ы**) *ж* (*государства*) border; (*участка*) boundary; (*обычно мн: перен*) limit; **éхать (поéхать** *pf*) **за ~у** to go abroad; **жить** (*impf*) **за ~ей** to live abroad; **из-за ~ы** from abroad

**грани́ч|ить** (**-у, -ишь**) *несов*: ~ **с** +*instr* to border on (*перен*) to verge on

**грант** (**-а**) *м* grant

**гран|ь** (**-и**) *ж* (*ГЕОМ*) face; (*алмаза*) facet; **на гра́ни** +*gen* on the brink *или* verge of

**граф|а́** (**-ы́**) *ж* column

**гра́фик** (**-а**) *м* (*МАТ*) graph; (*план*) schedule, timetable

**графи́н** (**-а**) *м* (*для вина*) decanter; (*: открытый*) carafe

**графи́ческий** *прил* graphic

**гра́ци|я** (**-и**) *ж* grace

**гребён|ка** (**-ки**; *gen pl* **-ок**) *ж* comb

**гребеш|о́к** (**-ка́**) *м* comb

**гребл|я** (**-и**) *ж* rowing

**гре́йпфрут** (**-а**) *м* grapefruit

**грек** (**-а**) *м* Greek (man)

**гре́л|ка** (**-ки**; *gen pl* **-ок**) *ж* hot-water bottle

**грем|е́ть** (**-лю́, -и́шь**; *pf* **про~**) *несов* (*поезд*) to thunder by; (*гром*) to rumble; ~ (**про~** *pf*) +*instr* (*ведром*) to clatter

**грен|ка** (**-ки**; *gen pl* **-ок**) *ж* toast

**гре|сти́** (**-бу́, -бёшь**; *pt* **грёб, -бла́**) *несов* to row; (*веслом, руками*) to paddle ♦ *перех* (*листья*) to rake

**гре|ть** (**-ю**) *несов перех* (*подлеж: солнце*) to heat, warm; (*: шуба*) to keep warm; (*воду*) to heat (up); (*руки*) to warm; **грéться** *несов возв* (*человек*) to warm o.s. (*вода*) to warm *или* heat up

**грех** (**-á**) *м* sin

**Грéци|я** (**-и**) *ж* Greece

**грéцкий** *прил*: ~ **орéх** walnut

**грéческий** *прил* Greek; ~ **язы́к** Greek

**грéчк|а** (**-и**) *ж* buckwheat

**грéчневый** *прил* buckwheat

**греш|и́ть** (**-ý, -и́шь**; *pf* **со~**) *несов* to sin

**гриб** (**-á**) *м* (*съедобный*) (edible) mushroom; **несъедóбный** ~ toadstool

**грибнóй** *прил* (*суп*) mushroom

**гриб|óк** (**-кá**) *м* (*на коже*) fungal infection; (*на дереве*) fungus

**грим** (**-а**) *м* stage make-up, greasepaint

**гримáс|а** (**-ы**) *ж* grimace

**гримир|овáть** (**-ýю**; *pf* **за~**) *несов перех*: ~ **кого́-н** to make sb up

**грипп** (**-а**) *м* flu

**гриф** (**-а**) *м* (*муз*) fingerboard

**гри́фел|ь** (**-я**) *м* (pencil)lead

**гроб** (**-а**; *loc sg* **-ý**, *nom pl* **-ы́**) *м* coffin

**гр|озá** (**-озы́**; *nom pl* **-óзы**) *ж* thunderstorm

**грозд|ь** (**-и**; *gen pl* **-éй**) *ж* (*винограда*) bunch; (*сирени*) cluster

**гро|зи́ть** (**-жý, -зи́шь**) *несов* (*опасность*) to loom; ~ (*impf*) +*instr* (*катастрофой*) to threaten to become; ~ (**при~** *pf*) **кому́-н чем-н** to threaten sb with sth

**грóзный** *прил* threatening; (*противник, оружие*) formidable

**грозов|óй** *прил*: ~**áя тýча** storm cloud

**гром** (**-а**; *gen pl* **-óв**) *м* thunder

**громáдный** *прил* enormous, huge

**гром|и́ть** (**-лю́, -и́шь**) *несов перех* to destroy

**грóмкий** *прил* (*голос*) loud; (*скандал*) big

**грóмко** *нареч* loudly

**громóздкий** *прил* cumbersome

**грóмче** *сравн прил от* **грóмкий ♦** *сравн нареч от* **грóмко**

**грóхот** (**-а**) *м* racket

**грох|отáть** (**-очý, -óчешь**; *pf* **про~**) *несов* to rumble

**грубé|ть** (**-ю**; *pf* **о~**) *несов* (*человек*) to become rude; (*pf* **за~**; *кожа*) to become rough

**груб|и́ть** (**-лю́, -и́шь**; *pf* **на~**) *несов*: ~ +*dat* to be rude to

**грубия́н** (**-а**) *м* rude person

**грýбо** *нареч* (*отвечать*) rudely; (*подсчитать*) roughly; ~ **говоря́** roughly speaking

**грýбост|ь** (**-и**) *ж* rudeness

**грýбый** *прил* (*человек*) rude; (*ткань, пища*) coarse; (*кожа, подсчёт*) rough; (*ошибка, шутка*) crude; (*нарушение правил*) gross

**грýд|а** (**-ы**) *ж* pile, heap

**груди́нк|а** (**-и**) *ж* (*говядина*) brisket; (*копчёная свинина*) bacon

**груднóй** *прил* (*молоко*) breast; (*кашель*) chest; ~ **ребёнок** baby

**гр|удь** (**-уди́**; *instr sg* **-ýдью**, *nom pl* **-ýди**) *ж* (*анат*) chest; (*: женщины*) breasts *мн*; **корми́ть** (*impf*) ~**ýдью** to breast-feed

**гружёный** *прил* loaded

**груз** (**-а**) *м* (*тяжесть*) weight; (*товар*) cargo

**грузи́н** (**-а**) *м* Georgian

**гр|узи́ть** (**-ужý, -ýзишь**; *pf* **за~** *или* **на~**) *несов перех* (*корабль итп*) to load (up); ~ (**по~** *pf*) (в/на +*acc*) (*товар*) to load (onto)

**Грýзи|я** (**-и**) *ж* Georgia

**грузови́к** (-á) м lorry (BRIT), truck (US)

**грузов|о́й** прил (судно, самолёт) cargo; ~**áя маши́на** goods vehicle; ~**о́е такси́** removal (BRIT) или moving (US) van

**грузоподъёмност|ь** (и) ж freight или cargo capacity

**гру́зчик** (-а) м porter; (в магазине) stockroom worker

**грунт** (-а) м soil; (краска) primer

**гру́пп|а** (-ы) ж group; ~ **кро́ви** blood group

**группир|ова́ть** (-у́ю; pf с~) несов перех (отдел) to set up; (данные, цифры) to group, classify

**гру|сти́ть** (-щу́, -сти́шь) несов to feel melancholy или very sad; ~ (impf) **по** +dat или **о** +prp to pine for, miss

**гру́стно** нареч sadly ♦ как сказ: **мне** ~ I feel sad

**гру́стный** прил sad

**груст|ь** (-и) ж sadness

**гру́ш|а** (-и) ж pear

**грыз|ть** (-у́, -ёшь; pt -, -ла) несов перех (яблоки) to nibble (at); (pf **разгры́зть**; кость) to gnaw (on)

**гря́д|ка** (-ки; gen pl -ок) ж row

**гря́зно** как сказ безл: **до́ма/на у́лице** ~ the street/house is filthy

**гря́зный** прил dirty

**гряз|ь** (-и; loc sg -и́) ж dirt; (на доро́ге) mud; (перен) filth

**губ|а́** (-ы́; nom pl -ы, dat pl -а́м) ж lip

**губе́рни|я** (-и) ж gubernia (administrative region)

**губерна́тор** (-а) м governor

**губ|и́ть** (-лю́, -ишь; pf **по~**) несов перех to kill; (здоровье) to ruin

**гу́б|ка** (-ки; gen pl -ок) ж sponge

**губн|о́й** прил: ~**áя пома́да** lipstick; ~**áя гармо́шка** harmonica

**гу|де́ть** (-жу́, -ди́шь) несов (шмель, провода) to hum; (ветер) to moan

**гуд|о́к** (-ка́) м (автомобиля) horn; (парохода, завода) siren; (звук) hoot

**гул** (-а) м (голосов) drone

**гу́лкий** прил (шаги) resounding; (свод) echoing

**гуля́|ть** (-ю; pf **по~**) несов to stroll; (быть на улице) to be out; (на свадьбе) to have a good time, enjoy o.s.; **идти́ (пойти́** pf) ~ to go for a walk

**гуманита́рный** прил (помощь) humanitarian; (образование) arts

**гума́нный** прил humane

**гу́сениц|а** (-ы) ж caterpillar; (трактора) caterpillar track

**гуси́н|ый** прил (яйцо) goose; ~**áя ко́жа** goose flesh, goose pimples (BRIT) или bumps (US)

**густе́|ть** (3sg -ет; pf **по~**) несов (туман) to become denser; (pf **за~**; каша) to thicken

**густо́й** прил (лес) dense; (брови) bushy; (облака, суп, волосы) thick; (цвет, бас) rich

**густонаселённый** прил densely populated

**гус|ь** (-я; gen pl -е́й) м goose, gander

**гуся́тниц|а** (-ы) ж casserole (dish)

**гу́щ|а** (-и) ж (кофе́йная) grounds мн; (заросли) thicket; **в ~е собы́тий** at the centre of events

**ГЭС** ж сокр = **гидроэлектроста́нция**

# Д, д

---
KEYWORD
---

**да** *част* 1 (*выражает согласие*)
yes
2 (*не так ли*): **ты придёшь, да?**
you're coming, aren't you?; **ты**
**меня́ лю́бишь, да?** you love me,
don't you?
3 (*пусть: в лозунгах, в*
*призы́вах*); **да здра́вствует**
**демокра́тия!** long live democracy!
4 (*во фра́зах*): **вот э́то да!** (*разг*)
cool!; **ну да!** (*разг*) sure!;
(*выражает недоверие*) I'll bet!;
**да ну́!** (*разг*) no way!
♦ *союз* (*и*) and; **у неё то́лько**
**одно́ пла́тье, да и то ста́рое** she
only has one dress and even that's
old

---

**дава́й(те)** *несов см.* **дава́ть**
♦ *част* let's; **~ пить чай** let's have
some tea; **дава́й-дава́й!** (*разг*)
come on!, get on with it!
**дава́|ть (-ю;** *imper* **~а́й(те))**
*несов от* **дать**
**дав|и́ть (-лю́, -ишь)** *несов перех*
(*подлеж: обувь*) to pinch; (*pf* **за~**;
*кале́чить*) to crush, trample;
(*подлеж: машина*) to run over; (*pf*
**раз~**; *насекомых*) to squash; **~**
(*impf*) **на** +*acc* (*налега́ть*) to press
*или* weigh down on; **~ся** *несов*
*возв*: **~ся (по~ся** *pf*) +*instr*
(*ко́стью*) to choke on
**да́в|ка (-ки;** *gen pl* **-ок)** *ж* crush
**давле́ни|е (-я)** *ср* pressure
**да́вн|ий** *прил*: **с ~их пор** for a
long time
**давно́** *нареч* (*случи́ться*) a long

time ago; (*до́лго*) for a long time;
**~ бы так!** about time too!
**давны́м-давно́** *нареч* (*разг*) ages
ago
**дади́м** *etc сов см.* **дать**
**да́же** *част* even
**да́й(те)** *сов см.* **дать**
**дал** *etc сов см.* **дать**
**да́лее** *нареч* further; **и так ~** and
so on
**далёкий** *прил* distant, far-off
**далеко́** *нареч* (*о расстоянии*) far
away ♦ *как сказ* it's a long way
away; **~ за** +*acc* long after; **~ не** by
no means
**дало́** *etc сов см.* **дать**
**дальне́йш|ий** *прил* further; **в ~ем**
in the future
**да́льний** *прил* distant; (*поезд*)
long-distance; **Да́льний Восто́к**
the Far East
**дальнови́дный** *прил* far-sighted
**дальнозо́ркий** *прил* long-sighted
(*BRIT*), far-sighted (*US*)
**да́льше** *сравн прил от* **далёкий**
♦ *сравн нареч от* **далеко́**
**дам** *сов см.* **дать**
**да́м|а (-ы)** *ж* lady; (*КАРТЫ*) queen
**да́мский** *прил* (*одежда*) ladies'
**Да́ни|я (-и)** *ж* Denmark
**да́нн|ые (-ых)** *мн* (*сведения*)
data *ед*; (*способности*) talent *ед*
**да́нный** *прил* this, the given
**дан|ь (-и)** *ж* tribute
**дар (-а;** *nom pl* **-ы́)** *м* gift
**дар|и́ть (-ю́, -ишь;** *pf* **по~)** *несов*
*перех* to give
**да́ром** *нареч* (*беспла́тно*) free, for
nothing; (*бесполе́зно*) in vain
**даст** *сов см.* **дать**
**да́т|а (-ы)** *ж* date
**да́тельный** *прил*: **~ паде́ж** the
dative (case)
**дати́р|овать (-ую)** (*не*)*сов перех*
to date

**дать** (см. Table 16; impf **дава́ть**) сов to give; (позволить): ~ **кому́-н** +infin to allow sb to do, let sb do; **я тебе́ дам!** (угроза) I'll show you!

**да́ч|а** (-и) ж (дом) dacha (holiday cottage in the country); (показаний) provision

**дашь** сов см. **дать**

**дв|а** (-ух; см. Table 23; f ~**е**, nt ~) м чис two ♦ м нескл (ПРОСВЕЩ) ≈ poor (school mark)

**двадцатиле́тний** прил (период) twenty-year; (человек) twenty-year-old

**двадца́тый** чис twentieth

**два́дцат|ь** (-и; как **пять**; см. Table 26) чис twenty

**два́жды** нареч twice; ~ **три** — **шесть** two times three is six

**две** ж чис см. **два**

**двена́дцатый** чис twelfth

**двена́дцат|ь** (-и; как **пять**; см. Table 26) чис twelve

**двер|ь** (-и; loc sg -**и́**, gen pl -**е́й**) ж door

**дв|е́сти** (-ухсо́т; см. Table 28) чис two hundred

**дви́гател|ь** (-я) м engine, motor

**дви́га|ть** (-ю; pf **дви́нуть**) несов перех to move; (no pf; механизм) to drive; ~**ся** (pf **дви́нуться**) несов возв to move; (отправляться): ~**ся в/на** +acc to set off или start out for

**движе́ни|е** (-я) ср movement; (дорожное) traffic; (души) impulse; **пра́вила доро́жного** или **у́личного** ~ ≈ the Highway Code

**дви́н|уть(ся)** (-у(сь)) сов от **дви́гать(ся)**

**дво́|е** (-и́х; см. Table 30a) м чис two

**двоебо́рь|е** (-я) ср biathlon

**двоето́чи|е** (-я) ср (ЛИНГ) colon

**дво́|йка** (-йки; gen pl -ек) ж (цифра, карта) two; (ПРОСВЕЩ) ≈ fail, ≈ E (school mark)

**двойно́й** прил double

**дво́|йня** (-йни; gen pl -ен) ж twins мн

**дво́йственный** прил (позиция) ambiguous

**двор** (-а́) м yard; (короле́вский) court

**двор|е́ц** (-ца́) м palace

**дво́рник** (-а) м (работник) road sweeper; (АВТ) windscreen (BRIT) или windshield (US) wiper

**дворня́ж|ка** (-ки; gen pl -ек) ж mongrel

**дворя́нств|о** (-а) ср nobility

**двою́родн|ый** прил: ~ **брат** (first) cousin (male); ~**ая сестра́** (first) cousin (female)

**двузна́чный** прил (число) two-digit; (слово) with two senses

**двукра́тн|ый** прил: ~ **чемпио́н** two-times champion; **в ~ом разме́ре** twofold

**двум** etc чис см. **два**

**двумста́м** etc чис см. **две́сти**

**двусмы́сленный** прил ambiguous

**двуспа́льн|ый** прил: ~**ая крова́ть** double bed

**двусторо́нний** прил (движение) two-way; (соглашение) bilateral

**двух** чис см. **два**

**двухле́тний** прил (период) two-year; (ребёнок) two-year-old

**двухме́стный** прил (номер) double; (купе, каюта) two-berth

**двухсо́т** etc чис см. **две́сти**

**двухсо́тый** чис two hundredth

**двухста́х** чис см. **две́сти**

**двуязы́чный** прил bilingual

**дебати́р|овать** (-ую) несов перех to debate

**деба́т|ы** (-ов) мн debate ед

**дебет** (-а) м debit

**дебил** (-а) м mentally handicapped person; (*разг: глупый*) idiot

**дебильный** *прил* mentally handicapped

**дебют** (-а) м debut; (*в шахматах*) opening

**дева** (-ы) ж: **старая ~** spinster; (*созвездие*): **Дева** Virgo

**девальвация** (-и) ж devaluation

**девать(ся)** (-ю(сь)) *несов от* **деть(ся)**

**девиз** (-а) м motto

**девичий** *прил*: **~ья фамилия** maiden name

**девочка** (-ки; *gen pl* -ек) ж (*ребёнок*) little girl

**девушка** (-ки; *gen pl* -ек) ж girl

**девяносто** (-а; *как сто; см. Table 27*) *чис* ninety

**девяностый** *чис* ninetieth

**девятисотый** *чис* nine-hundredth

**девятка** (-ки; *gen pl* -ок) ж nine

**девятнадцатый** *чис* nineteenth

**девятнадцать** (-и; *как пять; см. Table 26*) *чис* nineteen

**девятый** *чис* ninth

**девять** (-и; *как пять; см. Table 26*) *чис* nine

**девятьсот** (-исот; *как пятьсот; см. Table 28*) *чис* nine hundred

**дёготь** (-тя) м tar

**деградировать** (-ую) (*не*)*сов* to degenerate

**дед** (-а) м grandfather; **Дед Мороз** ≈ Father Christmas, ≈ Santa (Claus)

**дедовщина** (-ы) ж *mental and physical harassment in the army by older conscripts*

**дедушка** (-ки; *gen pl* -ек) м grandpa

**деепричастие** (-я) *ср* gerund

**дежурить** (-ю, -ишь) *несов* to be on duty

**дежурный** *прил*: **~ врач** doctor on duty ♦ (**-ого**) м person on duty

**дезинфицировать** (-ую) (*не*)*сов перех* to disinfect

**дезинформировать** (-ую) (*не*)*сов перех* to misinform

**дезодорант** (-а) м antiperspirant, deodorant

**действенный** *прил* effective

**действие** (-я) *ср* (*механизма*) functioning; (*романа итп*) action; (*часть пьесы*) act; (*лекарства*) effect; *см. также* **действия**

**действительно** *нареч, вводн сл* really

**действительность** (-и) ж reality

**действительный** *прил* real, actual; (*документ*) valid

**действия** (-й) *мн* (*поступки*) actions *мн*

**действовать** (-ую) *несов* (*человек*) to act; (*механизмы, закон*) to operate; (*pf* по~; *влиять*): **~ на** +acc to have an effect on

**действующий** *прил*: **~ие лица** (*персонажи*) characters *мн*; **~ая армия** standing army; **~ вулкан** active volcano

**декабрь** (-я) м December

**декан** (-а) м dean

**деканат** (-а) м faculty office

**декларация** (-и) ж declaration; **таможенная ~** customs declaration

**декольте** *ср нескл, прил неизм* décolleté

**декоративный** *прил* ornamental; (*искусство*) decorative

**декорация** (-и) ж (*ТЕАТР*) set

**декрет** (-а) м (*приказ*) decree; (*разг: отпуск*) maternity leave

**декретный** *прил*: **~ отпуск** maternity leave

**делать** (-ю; *pf* с~) *сов перех* to make; (*упражнения, опыты итп*) to do; ~ **не́чего** there is nothing to be done; **~ся** (pf **с~ся**) несов возв: **~ся** +instr to become

**делега́т** (-а) м delegate

**делега́ци**|я (-и) ж delegation

**деле́ни**|е (-я) ср division; (на линейке, в термометре) point

**дел**|**е́ц** (-ьца́) м dealer

**деликате́с** (-а) м delicacy

**дел**|**и́ть** (-ю́, -ишь; pf **по~** или **раз~**) несов перех (также МАТ) to divide; ~ (**раз~** pf) **что-н на** +acc to divide sth by; ~ (**раз~** pf) **что-н с** +instr to share sth with; **~ся** (pf **раз~ся**) несов возв: **~ся** (**на** +acc) (отряд) to divide или split up (into); **~ся** (**по~ся** pf) **чем-н с кем-н** to share sth with sb

**де́л**|о (-а; nom pl -а́) ср matter; (надобность, также КОММ) business; (положение) situation; (поступок) act; (ЮР) case; (АДМИН) file; **э́то моё ~** that's my business; **э́то не твоё ~** it's none of your business; **как дела́?** how are things?; **в чём ~?** what's wrong?; **в том, что ...** the thing is that ...; **на (са́мом) ~е** in (actual) fact; **на ~е** in practice; **то и ~** every now and then

**делово́й** прил business; (дельный) efficient; (вид, тон) businesslike

**де́льный** прил (человек) efficient; (предложение) sensible

**дельфи́н** (-а) м dolphin

**демаго́ги**|я (-и) ж demagogy

**демисезо́нн**|**ый** прил: **~ое пальто́** coat for spring and autumn wear

**демобилиз**|**ова́ться** (-у́юсь) (не)сов возв to be demobilized

**демокра́т** (-а) м democrat

**демократи́ческий** прил democratic

**демокра́ти**|я (-и) ж democracy

**де́мон** (-а) м demon

**демонстра́нт** (-а) м demonstrator

**демонстра́ци**|я (-и) ж demonstration; (фильма) showing

**демонстри́р**|**овать** (-ую) (не)сов (ПОЛИТ) to demonstrate ♦ несов перех to show

**демонти́р**|**овать** (-ую) (не)сов to dismantle

**де́нежный** прил monetary; (рынок) money; **~ знак** banknote

**день** (дня) м day; **на днях** (скоро) in the next few days; (недавно) the other day; **~ рожде́ния** birthday

**де́нь**|**ги** (-ег; dat pl -ьга́м) мн money ед

**депо́** ср нескл depot

**депорти́р**|**овать** (-ую) (не)сов перех to deport

**депре́сси**|я (-и) ж depression

**депута́т** (-а) м deputy (POL)

**дёрга**|**ть** (-ю) несов перех to tug или pull (at) ♦ неперех: ~ +instr (плечом, головой) to jerk; **~ся** несов возв (машина, лошадь) to jerk; (лицо, губы) to twitch

**дереве́нский** прил country, village; (пейзаж) rural

**дере́в**|**ня** (-ни; gen pl -е́нь, dat -ня́м) ж (селение) village; (местность) the country

**дёр**|**ево** (-ева; nom pl -е́вья, gen pl -е́вьев) ср tree; (древесина) wood

**деревя́нный** прил wooden

**держа́в**|а (-ы) ж power

**держа́тел**|ь (-я) м holder

**держ**|**а́ть** (-у́, -ишь) сов перех to keep; (в руках, во рту, в зубах) to hold; ~ (impf) **себя́ в рука́х** to keep one's head; **~ся** несов возв to stay; (на колоннах, на сваях) to be supported; (иметь *оса́нку*) to stand; (*вести́ себя́*) to behave; **~ся** (*impf*) +*gen* (*берега́, сте́ны итп*) to keep to

**де́рзкий** *прил* (*гру́бый*) impertinent; (*сме́лый*) audacious

**дёрн** (**-а**) *м* turf

**дёрн|уть** (**-у**) *несов перех* to tug (at) ♦ *непepex*: **~** +*instr* (*плечо́м, голово́й*) to jerk; **~ся** *несов возв* (*маши́на*) to start with a jerk; (*гу́бы*) to twitch

**деса́нт** (**-а**) *м* landing troops *мн*

**деса́нтник** (**-а**) *м* paratrooper

**десе́рт** (**-а**) *м* dessert

**десн|а́** (**-ы́**; *nom pl* **дёсны**, *gen pl* **дёсен**) *ж* (*АНАТ*) gum

**десятибо́рь|е** (**-я**) *ср* decathlon

**десятиле́ти|е** (**-я**) *ср* (*срок*) decade

**десяти́чный** *прил* decimal

**деся́тк|и** (**-ов**) *мн*: **~ люде́й/книг** scores *мн* of people/books

**деся́т|ок** (**-ка**) *м* ten

**деся́тый** *прил* tenth

**де́сят|ь** (**-и́**; *как* **пять**; *см. Table 26*) *чис* ten

**дета́л|ь** (**-и**) *ж* detail; (*механи́зма*) component, part

**дета́льный** *прил* detailed

**детдо́м** (**-а**; *nom pl* **-а́**) *м сокр* = **де́тский дом**

**детекти́в** (**-а**) *м* (*фильм*) detective film; (*кни́га*) detective novel

**детёныш** (**-а**) *м* cub

**де́т|и** (**-е́й**; *dat pl* **-я́м**, *instr pl* **-ьми́**, *prp pl* **-я́х**, *nom sg* **ребёнок**) *мн* children *мн*

**де́тск|ий** *прил* (*го́ды, боле́знь*) childhood; (*кни́га, игра́*) children's; (*рассужде́ние*) childish; **~ая площа́дка** playground; **~ дом** children's home; **~ сад** kindergarten

**де́тский сад** - kindergarten or nursery. Children go to kindergarten from around the age of three and stay there until they are six or seven. The kindergartens provide full-time childcare and pre-primary education five days a week.

**де́тств|о** (**-а**) *ср* childhood

**де́|ть** (**-ну, -нешь**; *impf* **~ва́ть**) *сов перех* (*разг*) to put; (*вре́мя, де́ньги*) to do with; **де́ться** (*impf* **дева́ться**) *сов возв* (*разг*) to get to

**дефе́кт** (**-а**) *м* defect

**дефи́с** (**-а**) *м* hyphen

**дефици́т** (**-а**) *м* deficit; (*нехва́тка*): **~** +*gen* и́ли **в** +*prp* shortage of

**дефици́тный** *прил* in short supply

**деформи́р|овать** (**-ую**) (*не*)*сов перех* to deform

**дециме́тр** (**-а**) *м* decimetre (*BRIT*), decimeter (*US*)

**дешеве́|ть** (*3sg* **-ет**; *pf* **по~**) *несов* to go down in price

**дешёвый** *прил* cheap

**де́ятел|ь** (**-я**) *м*: **госуда́рственный ~** statesman; **полити́ческий ~** politician

**де́ятельност|ь** (**-и**) *ж* work; (*се́рдца, мо́зга*) activity

**де́ятельный** *прил* active

**джаз** (**-а**) *м* jazz

**джем** (**-а**) *м* jam

**джи́нс|ы** (**-ов**) *мн* jeans *мн*

**джу́нгл|и** (**-ей**) *мн* jungle *ед*

**дзюдо́** *ср нескл* judo

**диа́гноз** (**-а**) *м* diagnosis

**диагности́р|овать** (**-ую**) (*не*)*сов перех* to diagnose

**диагона́л|ь** (**-и**) *ж* diagonal

**диагра́мм|а** (**-ы**) *ж* diagram

**диале́кт** (**-а**) *м* dialect

**диало́г** (**-а**) *м* dialogue

**диа́метр** (-а) м diameter

**диапазо́н** (-а) м range; (*частот*) waveband

**диапозити́в** (-а) м (*ФОТО*) slide

**диафра́гм|а** (-ы) ж diaphragm

**дива́н** (-а) м sofa

**дива́н-крова́т|ь** (-и) ж sofa bed

**диверса́нт** (-а) м saboteur

**диве́рси|я** (-и) ж sabotage

**дивиде́нд** (-а) м dividend

**дивизи|я** (-и) ж division

**ди́в|о** (-а) *ср* wonder; **на ~** wonderfully

**дие́з** (-а) м (*МУЗ*) sharp

**дие́т|а** (-ы) ж diet

**диза́йн** (-а) м design

**диза́йнер** (-а) м designer

**дизентери́|я** (-и) ж dysentery

**дика́р|ь** (-я́) м savage

**ди́кий** *прил* wild; (*поступок*) absurd; (*нравы*) barbaric

**ди́кост|ь** (-и) ж (*см прил*) wildness; absurdity; barbarity

**дикта́нт** (-а) м dictation

**дикта́тор** (-а) м dictator

**диктату́р|а** (-ы) ж dictatorship

**дикт|ова́ть** (-у́ю; *pf* **про~**) *несов перех* to dictate

**ди́ктор** (-а) м newsreader, newscaster; (*на вокзале*) announcer

**ди́лер** (-а) м: **~** (**по** +*prp*) dealer (in)

**дина́мик** (-а) м (loud)speaker

**дина́мик|а** (-и) ж dynamics *мн*

**динами́чный** *прил* dynamic

**дина́сти|я** (-и) ж dynasty

**диноза́вр** (-а) м dinosaur

**дипло́м** (-а) м (*университета*) degree certificate; (*училища*) diploma; (*работа*) dissertation (*for undergraduate degree*)

**диплома́т** (-а) м diplomat; (*разг: портфель*) briefcase

**дир.** *сокр* (= **дире́ктор**) dir.

**директи́в|а** (-ы) ж directive

**дире́ктор** (-а; *nom pl* **-á**) м director; **~ шко́лы** headmaster

**дире́кци|я** (-и) ж (*завода*) management; (*школы*) senior management

**дирижёр** (-а) м (*МУЗ*) conductor

**дирижи́р|овать** (-ую) *несов*: **~** +*instr* to conduct

**диск** (-а) м (*также КОМП*) disc, disk (*esp US*); (*СПОРТ*) discus; (*МУЗ*) record; **ги́бкий/жёсткий ~** floppy/ hard disk

**дисквалифици́р|овать** (-ую) (*не)сов перех* (*врача, юриста*) to strike off; (*спортсмена*) to disqualify

**диске́т** (-а) м diskette

**дисково́д** (-а) м (*КОМП*) disk drive

**дискоте́к|а** (-и) ж discotheque; (*пластинки*) record collection

**дискримина́ци|я** (-и) ж discrimination

**диску́сси|я** (-и) ж discussion

**диспансе́р** (-а) м *specialized health centre*

**диспе́тчер** (-а) м controller

**диссерта́ци|я** (-и) ж ≈ PhD thesis

**диссиде́нт** (-а) м dissident

**дистанцио́нн|ый** *прил*: **~ое управле́ние** remote control

**диста́нци|я** (-и) ж distance

**дистрибью́тор** (-а) м distributor

**дисципли́н|а** (-ы) ж discipline

**дисциплини́рованный** *прил* disciplined

**дифтери́т** (-а) м diphtheria

**дич|ь** (-и) ж *собир* game

**длин|а́** (-ы́) ж length; **в ~у́** lengthways

**дли́нный** *прил* long; (*разг: человек*) tall

**дли́тельный** *прил* lengthy

**дл|и́ться** (*3sg* **-и́тся**; *pf* **про~**) *несов возв* (*урок, беседа*) to last

**для** *предл*; +*gen* for; (*в отношении*): ~ **меня́ э́то о́чень ва́жно** this is very important to me; ~ **того́ что́бы** in order to; **крем ~ лица́** face cream; **альбо́м ~ рисова́ния** sketch pad

**дневни́к** (-а́) *м* diary; (*ПРОСВЕЩ*) register

**дневн|о́й** *прил* daily; ~**ое вре́мя** daytime

**днём** *сущ см.* **день** ♦ *нареч*: ~ in the daytime; (*после обеда*) in the afternoon

**дни** *etc сущ см.* **день**

**дн|о́** (-а) *ср* (*ямы*) bottom; (*моря, реки*) bottom, bed

---
KEYWORD
---

**до** *предл*; +*gen* **1** (*о пределе движения*) as far as, to; **мы дое́хали до реки́** we went as far as *или* to the river; **я проводи́л его́ до ста́нции** I saw him off at the station

**2** (*о расстоянии*) to; **до го́рода 3 киломе́тра** it is 3 kilometres (*BRIT*) *или* kilometers (*US*) to the town

**3** (*о временно́м пределе*) till, until; **я отложи́л заседа́ние до утра́** I postponed the meeting till *или* until morning; **до свида́ния!** goodbye!

**4** (*перед*) before; **мы зако́нчили до переры́ва** we finished before the break

**5** (*о пределе состояния*): **мне бы́ло оби́дно до слёз** I was so hurt I cried

**6** (*полностью*): **я отда́л ей всё до копе́йки** I gave her everything down to my last kopeck; **он вы́пил буты́лку до дна́** he drank the bottle dry

**7** (*направление действия*): **ребёнок дотро́нулся до**

**игру́шки** the child touched the toy

---

**доба́в|ить** (-лю, -ишь; *impf* **добавля́ть**) *сов перех* to add

**добавле́ни|е** (-я) *ср* addition

**добежа́ть** (*как* **бежа́ть**; *см. Table 20*; *impf* **добега́ть**) *сов*: ~ **до** +*gen* to run *или* as far as

**доб|и́ться** (-ью́сь, -ьёшься; *impf* **добива́ться**) *сов возв*: ~ +*gen* to achieve

**доб|ра́ться** (-еру́сь, -ерёшься; *impf* **добира́ться**) *сов возв*: ~ **до** +*gen* to get to, reach

**добре́|ть** (-ю; *pf* **по**~) *несов* to become kinder

**добр|о́** (-а́) *ср* good; (*разг: имущество*) belongings *мн*, property; ~ **пожа́ловать (в Москву́)!** welcome (to Moscow)!; **э́то не к** ~**у́** this is a bad omen

**доброво́л|ец** (-ьца) *м* volunteer

**доброво́льный** *прил* voluntary

**доброду́шный** *прил* good-natured

**доброжела́тельный** *прил* benevolent

**доброка́чественный** *прил* quality; (*опухоль*) benign

**добросо́вестный** *прил* conscientious

**доброт|а́** (-ы́) *ж* kindness

**до́бр|ый** *прил* kind; (*совет, имя*) good; **бу́дьте добры́!** excuse me!; **бу́дьте добры́, позвони́те нам за́втра!** would you be so good as to phone us tomorrow?; **всего́** ~**ого!** all the best!; ~**ого здоро́вья!** take care!; ~ **день/ве́чер!** good afternoon/evening!; ~**ое у́тро!** good morning!

**добы́ть** (*как* **быть**; *см. Table 21*; *impf* **добыва́ть**) *сов перех* to get; (*нефть*) to extract; (*руду*) to mine

**добы́ч|а** (-и) *ж* (*нефти*)

extraction; (*руды*) mining, extraction; (*то, что добыто*) output; (*на охоте*) catch

**дове|зти́** (-у́; *pt* довёз, -ла́; *impf* **довози́ть**) *сов перех*: ~ кого́-н до +*gen* to take sb to *или* as far as

**дове́ренност|ь** (-и) *ж* power of attorney

**дове́ренн|ый** (-ого) *м* (*также*: ~ое лицо́) proxy

**дове́ри|е** (-я) *ср* confidence, trust; **телефо́н** *or* **Слу́жба** ~я help line

**дове́р|ить** (-ю, -ишь; *impf* **доверя́ть**) *сов перех*: ~ что-н кому́-н to entrust sb with sth

**дове́рчивый** *прил* trusting

**дове|сти́** (-ду́, -дёшь; *pt* довёл, -ла́; *impf* **доводи́ть**) *сов перех*: ~ кого́-н/что-н до +*gen* to take sb/ sth to *или* as far as; **доводи́ть** (~ *pf*) что-н до конца́ to see sth through to the end; **доводи́ть** (~ *pf*) что-н до све́дения кого́-н to inform sb of sth

**дов|оди́ться** (-ожу́сь, -о́дишься) *несов*: ~ +*dat* to be related to

**довое́нный** *прил* prewar

**дов|ози́ть** (-ожу́, -о́зишь) *несов* от **довезти́**

**дово́льно** *нареч* (*сильный*) quite
♦ *как сказ* (*that is* ) enough

**дово́льный** *прил* satisfied, contented

**догада́|ться** (-юсь; *impf* **дога́дываться**) *сов возв* to guess

**дога́д|ка** (-ки; *gen pl* -ок) *ж* guess

**до́гм|а** (-ы) *ж* dogma

**дог|на́ть** (-оню́, -о́нишь; *impf* **догоня́ть**) *сов перех* to catch up with

**догово́р** (-а) *м* (*полит*) treaty; (*комм*) agreement

**договорённост|ь** (-и) *ж*

agreement

**догово́р|ить** (-ю, -ишь; *impf* **догова́ривать**) *сов (не)перех* to finish

**догово́р|иться** (-ю́сь, -и́шься; *impf* **догова́риваться**) *сов возв*: ~ с кем-н о чём-н (*о встрече*) to arrange sth with sb; (*о цене*) to agree sth with sb

**догово́рный** *прил* (*цена*) agreed; (*обязательство*) contractual

**догола́** *нареч*: разде́ться ~ to strip bare *или* naked

**догоня́|ть** (-ю) *несов от* **догна́ть**

**догор|е́ть** (-ю, -и́шь; *impf* **догора́ть**) *сов* to burn out

**доде́ла|ть** (-ю; *impf* **доде́лывать**) *сов перех* to finish

**доду́ма|ться** (-юсь; *impf* **доду́мываться**) *сов возв*: ~ до +*gen* to hit on; **как ты мог до тако́го** ~? what on earth gave you that idea?

**доеда́|ть** (-ю) *несов от* **дое́сть**

**дое́ду** *etc сов см.* **дое́хать**

**доезжа́|ть** (-ю) *несов от* **дое́хать**

**дое́м** *сов см.* **дое́сть**

**дое́сть** (*как* **есть**; *см. Table 15*; *impf* **доеда́ть**) *сов перех* to eat up

**дое́хать** (*как* **е́хать**; *см. Table 19*; *impf* **доезжа́ть**) *сов*: ~ до +*gen* to reach

**дожд|а́ться** (-у́сь, -ёшься; *imper* -и́(те)сь) *сов возв*: ~ кого́-н/ чего́-н to wait until sb/sth comes

**дождли́вый** *прил* rainy

**дожд|ь** (-я́) *м* rain; ~ **идёт** it's raining; ~ **пошёл** it has started to rain

**дожида́|ться** (-юсь) *несов возв*: ~ +*gen* to wait for

**дожи|ть** (-ву́, -вёшь; *impf* **дожива́ть**) *сов неперех*: ~ до

+*gen* to live to

**до́з|а (-ы)** *ж* dose

**дозвон|и́ться (-ю́сь, -и́шься;** *impf* **дозва́нива́ться)** *сов возв* to get through

**доигра́|ть (-ю;** *impf* **дои́грывать)** *сов перех* to finish playing

**доистори́ческий** *прил* prehistoric

**до|и́ть (-ю́, -ишь;** *pf* **по~)** *несов перех* to milk

**дойти́ (как идти́; см. Table 18;** *impf* **доходи́ть)** *сов:* ~ до +*gen* to reach

**док (-а)** *м* dock

**доказа́тельств|о (-а)** *ср* proof, evidence

**док|аза́ть (-ажу́, -а́жешь;** *impf* **дока́зывать)** *сов перех* (*правду, виновность*) to prove

**докла́д (-а)** *м* (*на съезде итп*) paper; (*начальнику*) report

**докла́дчик (-а)** *м* speaker

**докла́дыва|ть (-ю)** *несов от* **доложи́ть**

**до́ктор (-а;** *nom pl* **-а́)** *м* doctor; ~ **нау́к** Doctor of Sciences (*postdoctoral research degree in Russia*)

**до́кторский** *прил* (*МЕД*) doctor's; (*ПРОСВЕЩ*) postdoctoral

**доктри́н|а (-ы)** *ж* doctrine

**докуме́нт (-а)** *м* document

**документа́льный** *прил* documentary; ~ **фильм** documentary

**документа́ци|я (-и)** *ж собир* documentation

**долг (-а;** *loc sg* **-у́,** *nom pl* **-и́)** *м* debt; **дава́ть (дать** *pf*)/**брать (взять** *pf*) **что-н в** ~ to lend/ borrow sth; **быть (***impf***) в** ~**у́ пе́ред кем-н** *или* **у кого́-н** to be indebted to sb

**до́лгий** *прил* long

**до́лго** *нареч* for a long time; **как** ~ **...?** how long ...?

**долгов|о́й** *прил:* ~**а́я распи́ска** IOU

**долгожда́нный** *прил* long-awaited

**долгоигра́ющ|ий** *прил:* ~**ая пласти́нка** LP

**долгосро́чный** *прил* long-term

**долгот|а́ (-ы́)** *ж* length; (*ГЕО*) longitude

---

KEYWORD

---

**до́лж|ен (-на́, -но́, -ны́)** *часть сказуемого;* +*infin* **1** (*обязан*): **я до́лжен уйти́** I must go; **я до́лжен бу́ду уйти́** I will have to go; **она́ должна́ была́ уйти́** she had to go

**2** (*выражает предположение*): **он до́лжен ско́ро прийти́** he should arrive soon

**3** (*о долге*): **ты до́лжен мне 5 рубле́й** you owe me 5 roubles

**4**: **должно́ быть** (*вероятно*) probably; **должно́ быть, она́ о́чень уста́ла** she must have been very tired

---

**должни́к (-а́)** *м* debtor

**должностн|о́й** *прил* official; ~**о́е лицо́** official

**до́лжност|ь (-и;** *gen pl* **-е́й)** *ж* post

**до́лжный** *прил* required

**доли́н|а (-ы)** *ж* valley

**до́ллар (-а)** *м* dollar

**дол|ожи́ть (-ожу́, -о́жишь;** *impf* **докла́дывать)** *сов перех* to report

**дол|ото́ (-ота́;** *nom pl* **-о́та)** *ср* chisel

**до́льше** *сравн прил от* **до́лгий**
 ♦ *сравн нареч от* **до́лго**

**до́л|ька (-ьки;** *gen pl* **-ек)** *ж* segment

**до́л|я (-и;** *gen pl* **-е́й)** *ж* share; (*пирога*) portion; (*судьба*) fate; ~

**секу́нды** a fraction of a second

**дом (-а;** *nom pl* **-á)** *м* house; (*своё жильё*) home; (*семья*) household; **дом моде́лей** fashion house; **дом о́тдыха** ≈ holiday centre (*BRIT*) *или* center (*US*)

**до́ма** *нареч* at home

**дома́шн|ий** *прил* (*адрес*) home; (*еда*) home-made; (*животное*) domestic; **~яя хозя́йка** housewife; **~ее зада́ние** homework

**домини́р|овать (-ую)** *несов* to dominate

**домино́** *ср нескл* (*игра*) dominoes; (*фишка, костюм*) domino

**домкра́т (-а)** *м* (*ТЕХ*) jack

**домовладе́л|ец (-ьца)** *м* home owner

**домовладе́ни|е (-я)** *ср* (*дом*) *house with grounds attached*

**домово́дств|о (-а)** *ср* home economics

**домо́й** *нареч* home

**домоуправле́ни|е (-я)** *ср* ≈ housing department

**домохозя́|йка (-йки;** *gen pl* **-ек)** *ж* = **дома́шняя хозя́йка**

**домрабо́тниц|а (-ы)** *ж* (= *дома́шняя рабо́тница*) domestic help (*BRIT*), maid (*US*)

**до́мысел (-ла)** *м* conjecture

**донесе́ни|е (-я)** *ср* report

**донес|ти́ (-у́, -ёшь;** *pt* **донёс, -ла́;** *impf* **доноси́ть)** *сов перех* to carry ♦ *неперех*: **~ на** +*acc* to inform on; **~** (*pf*) **о** +*prp* to report on; **~сь** (*impf* **доноси́ться**) *сов возв*: **~сь до** +*gen* to reach

**до́низу** *нареч* to the bottom; **све́рху ~** from top to bottom

**до́нор (-а)** *м* (*МЕД*) donor

**доно́с (-а)** *м*: **~ (на** +*acc*) denunciation (of)

**дон|оси́ть (-ошу́, -о́сишь)**

**несов от донести́**

**доно́счик (-а)** *м* informer

**допива́|ть (-ю)** *несов от допи́ть*

**до́пинг (-а)** *м* drugs *мн*

**допи|са́ть (-шу́, -шешь;** *impf* **допи́сывать)** *сов перех* to finish (writing)

**допи́|ть (допью́, допьёшь;** *imper* **допе́й(те);** *impf* **допива́ть)** *сов перех* to drink up

**допла́т|а (-ы)** *ж* surcharge; **~ за бага́ж** excess baggage (charge)

**доплы́|ть (-ву́, -вёшь;** *impf* **доплыва́ть)** *сов*: **~ до** +*gen* (*на корабле*) to sail to; (*вплавь*) to swim to

**дополне́ни|е (-я)** *ср* supplement; (*ЛИНГ*) object; **в ~ (к** +*dat*) in addition (to)

**дополни́тельный** *прил* additional

**допо́лн|ить (-ю, -ишь;** *impf* **дополня́ть)** *сов перех* to supplement

**допра́шива|ть (-ю)** *несов от допроси́ть*

**допро́с (-а)** *м* interrogation

**допро|си́ть (-шу́, -сишь;** *impf* **допра́шивать)** *сов перех* to interrogate, question

**до́пуск (-а)** *м* (*в здание*) admittance; (*к документам*) access

**допуска́|ть (-ю;** *pf* **допусти́ть)** *несов перех* to admit, allow in; (*предположить*) to assume

**допу́стим** *вводн сл* let us assume

**допуще́ни|е (-я)** *ср* assumption

**дораст|и́ (-у́, -ёшь;** *pt* **доро́с, доросла́, доросло́;** *impf* **дораста́ть)** *сов*: **~ до** +*gen* to grow to

**доро́г|а (-и)** *ж* road, way; **по ~е** on the way

**до́рого** *нареч* (*купить, продать*) at a high price ♦ *как сказ* it's expensive

**дорог|óй** *прил* expensive; (*цена*) high; (*друг, мать*) dear; (*воспоминания, подарок*) cherished ♦ (**-óго**) *м* dear, darling

**дорожá|ть** (*3sg* -ет; *pf* по~) *несов* to go up *или* rise in price

**дорóже** *сравн прил от* **дорогóй** ♦ *сравн нареч от* **дóрого**

**дорож|и́ть** (-ý, -и́шь) *несов*: ~ +*instr* to value

**дорóж|ка** (-ки; *gen pl* -ек) *ж* pathway; (*для плавания*) lane; (*для бега, на магнитофоне*) track; (*ковёр*) runner

**дорóжный** *прил* road; (*костюм, расходы*) travelling (*BRIT*), traveling (*US*); (*сумка*) travel

**досáд|а** (-ы) *ж* annoyance; **какáя ~** what a pity!

**досáдный** *прил* annoying; (*печальный*) upsetting

**доск|á** (-ки́; *nom pl* -ки, *gen pl* -óк) *ж* board; (*деревянная*) plank; (*мраморная*) slab; (*чугунная*) plate; **~ объявлéний** notice (*BRIT*) *или* bulletin (*US*) board

**досконáльный** *прил* thorough

**дослóвно** *нареч* word for word

**дослóвный** *прил* literal, word-for-word

**дослýша|ть** (-ю; *impf* **дослýшивать**) *сов перех* to listen to

**досмóтр** (-а) *м*: **тамóженный ~** customs examination

**досм|отрéть** (-отрю́, -óтришь; *impf* **досмáтривать**) *сов перех* to watch the end of; (*багаж*) to check

**досрóчно** *нареч* ahead of time

**досрóчный** *прил* early

**доста|вáть(ся)** (-ю́(сь)) *несов от* **достáть(ся)**

**достáв|ить** (-лю, -ишь; *impf* **доставлять**) *сов перех* (*груз*) to deliver; (*пассажиров*) to carry, transport; (*удовольствие, возможность*) to give

**достáв|ка** (-ки; *gen pl* -ок) *ж* delivery

**достáт|ок** (-ка) *м* prosperity

**достáточно** *нареч*: ~ **хорошó/ подрóбно** good/detailed enough ♦ *как сказ* that's enough

**достá|ть** (-ну, -нешь; *imper* ~**нь(те)**; *impf* **доставáть**) *сов перех* to take; (*раздобыть*) to get ♦ *неперех*: ~ **до** +*gen* to reach; ~**ся** (*impf* **доставáться**) *сов возв* (*при разделе*): **мне ~лся дом** I got the house

**достигá|ть** (-ю) *несов от* **дости́чь**

**достижéни|е** (-я) *ср* achievement; (*предела, возраста*) reaching

**дости́|чь** (-гну, -гнешь; *pt* -г, -гла; *impf* **достигáть**) *сов*: ~ +*gen* to reach; (*результата, цели*) to achieve; (*положения*) to attain

**достовéрный** *прил* reliable

**достóинств|о** (-а) *ср* (*книги, плана*) merit; (*уважение к себе*) dignity; (*КОММ*) value

**достóйный** *прил* (*награда, кара*) fitting; (*человек*) worthy

**достопримечáтельност|ь** (-и) *ж* sight; (*музея*) showpiece; **осмáтривать** (**осмотрéть** *pf*) **~и** to go sightseeing

**достоя́ни|е** (-я) *ср* property; **станови́ться** (**стать** *pf*) **~м общéственности** to become public knowledge

**дóступ** (-а) *м* access

**достýпный** *прил* (*место*) accessible; (*цены*) affordable; (*объяснение*) comprehensible

**досýг** (-а) *м* leisure (time); **на ~е** in one's spare *или* free time

**досьé** *ср нескл* dossier, file

**дота́ци|я** (**-и**) ж subsidy

**дотла́** нареч: **сгоре́ть ~** to burn down (to the ground)

**дотро́н|уться** (**-усь**; impf **дотра́гиваться**) сов возв: **~ до** +gen to touch

**дот|яну́ть** (**-яну́, -я́нешь**; impf **дотя́гивать**) сов перех: **~ что-н до** +gen to extend sth as far as; **~ся** (impf **дотя́гиваться**) сов возв: **~ся до** +gen to reach

**до́хлый** прил dead

**до́х|нуть** (**-ну**; pt **-**, **-ла**; pf **по~**) несов (животное) to die

**дохо́д** (**-а**) м income, revenue; (человека) income

**доходи́ть** несов от **дойти́**

**дохо́дный** прил profitable; (выгодный) revenue-generating; **дохо́дная статья́** credit side (of accounts)

**дохо́дчивый** прил clear, easy to understand

**доце́нт** (**-а**) м ≈ reader (BRIT), ≈ associate professor (US)

**до́ч|ка** (**-ки**; gen pl **-ек**) ж daughter

**доч|ь** (**-ери**; см. Table 2) ж daughter

**дошёл** сов см. **дойти́**

**дошко́льник** (**-а**) м preschool child

**дошла́** итп сов см. **дойти́**

**дою́р|ка** (**-ки**; gen pl **-ок**) ж milkmaid

**ДПР** ж сокр = **Демократи́ческая Па́ртия Росси́и** см. **ЛДПР**

**драгоце́нность** (**-и**) ж jewel

**драгоце́нный** прил precious

**дразн|и́ть** (**-ю́, -ишь**) несов перех to tease

**дра́к|а** (**-и**) ж fight

**драко́н** (**-а**) м dragon

**дра́м|а** (**-ы**) ж drama

**драматизи́р|овать** (**-ую**) (не)сов перех to dramatize

**драмати́ческий** прил dramatic; (актёр) stage

**драмату́рг** (**-а**) м playwright

**драматурги́|я** (**-и**) ж drama
♦ собир plays мн

**драпир|ова́ть** (**-у́ю**; pf **за~**) несов перех: **~ что-н (чем-н)** to drape sth (with sth)

**драть** (**деру́, дерёшь**; pf **разодра́ть**) несов перех (бумагу, одежду) to tear или rip up; (pf **задра́ть**; подлеж: волк) to tear to pieces; (pf **содра́ть**; кору, обои) to strip; **дра́ться** (pf **подра́ться**) несов возв: **подра́ться (с** +instr) to fight (with)

**дре́безг** м: **в ~и** to smithereens

**дребезж|а́ть** (3sg **-и́т**) несов to jingle; (стёкла) to rattle

**древеси́н|а** (**-ы**) ж собир timber

**древе́сный** прил wood; **~ у́голь** charcoal

**дре́вний** прил ancient

**дрейф|ова́ть** (**-у́ю**) несов to drift

**дрел|ь** (**-и**) ж drill

**дрем|а́ть** (**-лю́, -лешь**) несов to doze

**дрессир|ова́ть** (**-у́ю**; pf **вы́~**) несов перех to train

**дроб|и́ть** (**-лю́, -и́шь**; pf **раз~**) несов перех to crush; (силы) to split

**дроб|ь** (**-и**; gen pl **-е́й**) ж fraction; (барабана) beat

**дров|а́** (**-**; dat pl **-а́м**) мн firewood ед

**дро́гн|уть** (**-у**) сов (стёкла, руки) to shake; (голос, лицо) to quiver

**дрож|а́ть** (**-у́, -и́шь**) несов to shake, tremble; (лицо) to quiver; **~** (impf) **за** +acc или **над** +instr (разг) to fuss over

**дро́жж|и** (**-е́й**) мн yeast ед

**дрозд** (**-а́**) м thrush; **чёрный ~**

blackbird

**друг** (-га; *nom pl* **-зья́**, *gen pl* **-зе́й**) *м* friend; ~ **~а́** each other, one another; ~ **дру́гу** (*говори́ть*) to each other *или* one another; ~ **за дру́гом** one after another; ~ **о дру́ге** (*говори́ть*) about each other *или* one another

**друг|о́й** *прил* (*ино́й*) another; (*второ́й*) the other; (*не тако́й, как э́тот*) different ♦ (**-о́го**) *м* (*кто́-то ино́й*) another (person); (*второ́й*) the other (one); **в ~ раз** another time; **и тот и ~** both

**дру́жб|а** (-ы) *ж* friendship

**дружелю́бный** *прил* friendly, amicable

**дру́жеский** *прил* friendly

**дру́жественный** *прил* friendly

**друж|и́ть** (-у́, -ишь) *несов*: ~ **с** +*instr* to be friends with

**дру́жный** *прил* close-knit; (*смех*) general; (*уси́лия*) concerted

**друж|о́к** (-ка́) *м* (*друг*) friend, pal (*inf*)

**друзья́** *etc сущ см.* **друг**

**дря́блый** *прил* sagging; (*те́ло*) flabby

**дрянь** (-и) *ж* (*разг*) rubbish (BRIT), trash (US)

**дуб** (-а; *nom pl* **-ы́**) *м* (БОТ) oak (tree); (*древеси́на*) oak

**дуби́н|ка** (-ки; *gen pl* **-ок**) *ж* cudgel; **рези́новая ~** truncheon

**дублён|ка** (-ки; *gen pl* **-ок**) *ж* sheepskin coat

**дублёр** (-а) *м* backup; (КИНО) double

**дублика́т** (-а) *м* duplicate

**дубли́р|овать** (-ую) *несов перех* to duplicate; (КИНО) to dub; (КОМП) to back up

**дуг|а́** (-и́; *nom pl* **-и**) *ж* (ГЕОМ) arc

**ду́л|о** (-а) *ср* muzzle; (*ствол*) barrel

**ду́м|а** (-ы) *ж* (*размышле́ние*) thought; **Ду́ма** (ПОЛИТ) the Duma (*lower house of Russian parliament*)

**ду́ма|ть** (-ю) *несов*: ~ (**о чём-н**) to think (about sth); ~ (*impf*) **над чем-н** to think sth over; **я ~ю, что да/нет** I think/don't think so

**дум|е́ц** (-ца́) *м* (*разг*) member of the Duma

**ду́мск|ой** *прил*: ~**о́е заседа́ние** meeting of the Duma

**ду́н|уть** (-у) *сов* to blow

**дуп|ло́** (-ла́; *nom pl* **-ла**, *gen pl* **-ел**) *ср* (*де́рева*) hollow

**ду́р|а** (-ы) *ж* (*разг*) fool

**дура́к** (-а́) *м* (*разг*) fool

**дура́цкий** *прил* (*разг*) foolish; (*шля́па*) silly

**дура́ч|ить** (-у, -ишь; *pf* **о~**) *несов перех* (*разг*) to con; ~**ся** *несов возв* (*разг*) to play the fool

**дур|и́ть** (-ю́, -ишь; *pf* **об~**) *несов перех* to fool

**ду́рно** *нареч* badly

**ду́роч|ка** (-ки; *gen pl* **-ек**) *ж* (*разг*) silly girl

**дуршла́г** (-а) *м* colander

**ду|ть** (-ю, -ешь) *несов* to blow ♦ (*pf* **вы́~**) *перех* (ТЕХ) to blow; **здесь ду́ет** it's draughty (BRIT) *или* drafty (US) in here

**дух** (-а; *part gen* **-у**) *м* spirit; **быть** (*impf*) **в ду́хе/не в ду́хе** to be in high/low spirits

**дух|и́** (-о́в) *мн* perfume *ед*, scent *ед*

**духове́нств|о** (-а) *ср собир* clergy; (*правосла́вное*) priesthood

**духо́вк|а** (-и) *ж* oven

**духо́вный** *прил* spiritual; (*религио́зный*) sacred, church

**духов|о́й** *прил* (МУЗ) wind; ~**ые инструме́нты** brass section (*in orchestra*); ~ **орке́стр** brass band

**духот|а́** (-ы́) *ж* stuffiness; (*жара́*)

closeness

**душ** (**-а**) *м* shower

**душ**|**á** (*acc sg* **-y**, *gen sg* **-й**, *nom pl* **-и**) *ж* soul; **на ду́шу (населе́ния)** per head (of the population); **он в ней ~й не ча́ет** she's the apple of his eye; **говори́ть** (*impf*)/**бесе́довать** (*impf*) **по ~м** to have a heart-to-heart talk/chat; **в глубине́ ~й** in one's heart of hearts

**душевнобольн**|**о́й** (**-о́го**) *м* mentally-ill person

**душе́вн**|**ый** *прил* (*силы, подъём*) inner; (*разговор*) sincere; (*человек*) kindly; **~ое потрясе́ние** shock

**душераздира́ющий** *прил* (*крик*) bloodcurdling; (*плач*) heart-rending

**души́стый** *прил* (*цветок*) fragrant; (*мыло*) perfumed, scented

**душ**|**и́ть** (**-у́**, **-ишь**; *pf* **за~** *или* **у~**) *несов перех* to strangle; (*свободу, прогресс*) to stifle; (*pf* **на~**; *платок*) to perfume, scent

**ду́шно** *как сказ* it's stuffy *или* close

**дуэ́т** (**-а**) *м* (*произведение*) duet; (*исполнители*) duo

**ды́бом** *нареч*: **встава́ть ~** (*волосы, шерсть*) to stand on end

**дыбы́** *мн*: **станови́ться на ~** (*лошадь*) to rear up

**дым** (**-а**; *loc sg* **-у́**) *м* smoke

**дым**|**и́ть** (**-лю́**, **-и́шь**; *pf* **на~**) *несов* (*печь, дрова*) to smoulder (*BRIT*), smolder (*US*); **~ся** *несов возв* (*труба*) to be smoking

**ды́мк**|**а** (**-и**) *ж* haze

**дымохо́д** (**-а**) *м* flue

**ды́мчатый** *прил* (*стёкла*) tinted

**ды́н**|**я** (**-и**) *ж* melon

**дыр**|**а́** (**-ы́**; *nom pl* **-ы**) *ж* hole

**ды́рк**|**а** (**-ки**; *gen pl* **-ок**) *ж* hole

**дыроко́л** (**-а**) *м* punch

**дыха́ни**|**е** (**-я**) *ср* breathing, respiration

**дыш**|**а́ть** (**-у́**, **-ишь**) *несов* to breathe; **~** (*impf*) +*instr* (*ненавистью*) to exude; (*любовью*) to radiate

**дья́вол** (**-а**) *м* devil

**дья́кон** (**-а**) *м* deacon

**дю́жин**|**а** (**-ы**) *ж* dozen

**дю́н**|**а** (**-ы**) *ж* (*обычно мн*) dune

**дя́д**|**я** (**-и**) *м* uncle; (*разг*) bloke

**дя́т**|**ел** (**-ла**) *м* woodpecker

# Е, е

**Ева́нгели**|**е** (**-я**) *ср* the Gospels *мн*; (*одна из книг*) gospel

**евре́**|**й** (**-я**) *м* Jew

**евре́йский** *прил* (*народ, обычаи*) Jewish; **~ язы́к** Hebrew

**е́вро** *м нескл* euro

**Евро́п**|**а** (**-ы**) *ж* Europe

**европе́**|**ец** (**-йца**) *м* European

**европе́йск**|**ий** *прил* European; **Европе́йский Сове́т** Council of Europe; **Европе́йское Соо́бщество** European Community

**его́** *мест см.* **он**; **оно́** ♦ *притяж мест* (*о мужчине*) his; (*о предмете*) its

**ед**|**а́** (**-ы́**) *ж* (*пища*) food; (*процесс*): **за ~о́й, во вре́мя ~ы́** at mealtimes

**едва́** *нареч* (*с трудом: нашёл, достал, доехал итп*) only just; (*только, немного*) barely, hardly; (*только что*) just ♦ *союз* (*как только*) as soon as; **~ ли** hardly

**е́дем** *etc сов см.* **е́хать**

**еди́м** *несов см.* **есть**

**едини́ц**|**а** (**-ы**) *ж* (*цифра*) one; (*измерения, часть целого*) unit;

**де́нежная** ~ monetary unit
**единобо́рств|о** (-a) *ср* single combat
**единовре́менн|ый** *прил*: ~ая су́мма lump sum
**единогла́сный** *прил* unanimous
**единоду́шный** *прил* unanimous
**еди́нственн|ый** *прил* (the) only; ~ое число́ (*линг*) singular
**еди́н|ый** *прил* (цельный) united; (*общий*) common; все до ~ого to a man; ~ (**проездно́й) биле́т** travel card (*for use on all forms of transport*)

**еди́ный проездно́й биле́т -** travel card. This is a cheap and convenient way of city travel. It covers all types of transport including the underground.

**еди́те** *несов см.* **есть**
**е́ду** *etc несов см.* **е́хать**
**едя́т** *несов см.* **есть**
**её** *мест см.* **она́** ♦ *притяж мест* (*о женщине итп*) her; (*о предмете итп*) its
**ёж** (-á) *м* hedgehog
**ежего́дный** *прил* annual
**ежедне́вник** (-a) *м* diary
**ежедне́вный** *прил* daily
**ежеме́сячный** *прил* monthly
**еженеде́льный** *прил* weekly
**езд|á** (-ы́) *ж* journey
**éз|дить** (-жу, -дишь) *несов* to go; ~ (*impf*) **на** +*prp* (*на лошади, на велосипеде*) to ride; (*на поезде, на автобусе итп*) to travel *или* go by
**ей** *мест см.* **она́**
**ел** *etc несов см.* **есть**
**éле** *нареч* (*с трудом*) only just; (*едва*) barely, hardly; ~-~ with great difficulty
**ёл|ка** (-ки; *gen pl* -ок) *ж* fir (tree);

(*праздник*) New Year party for children; (**рожде́ственская** *или* **нового́дняя**) ~ ≈ Christmas tree
**ело́вый** *прил* fir
**ёлочн|ый** *прил*: ~ые игру́шки Christmas-tree decorations *мн*
**ел|ь** (-и) *ж* fir (tree)
**ем** *несов см.* **есть**
**ёмкост|ь** (-и) *ж* (*объём*) capacity; (*вместилище сосуд*) container
**ему́** *мест см.* **он**; **оно́**
**ерунд|á** (-ы́) *ж* rubbish, nonsense
**ЕС** *сокр* (= **Европе́йский Сою́з**) EU

---
KEYWORD
---

**éсли** *союз* **1** (*в том случае когда*) if; **éсли она́ придёт, дай ей э́то письмо́** if she comes, give her this letter; **éсли ..., то ...** (*если*) if ..., then ...; **éсли он опозда́ет, то иди́ оди́н** if he is late, (then) go alone
**2** (*об условном действии*): **éсли бы(, то** *или* **тогда́)** if; **éсли бы я мог, (то) помо́г бы тебе́** if I could, I would help you
**3** (*выражает сильное желание*): (**ах** *или* **о**) **éсли бы** if only; **ах éсли бы он пришёл!** oh, if only he would come!; **éсли уж на то пошло́** if it comes to it; **что éсли...?** (*а вдруг*) what if...?

**ест** *несов см.* **есть**
**есте́ственно** *нареч* naturally ♦ *вводн сл* (*конечно*) of course
**есте́ственный** *прил* natural
**есть** *несов* (*один предмет*) there is; (*много предметов*) there are; **у меня́** ~ **друг** I have a friend
**есть** (*см. Table 15; pf* **пое́сть** *или* **съ~**) *несов перех* (*питаться*) to eat; (*pf* **съ~**; *металл*) to corrode; **мне хо́чется** ~ I'm hungry

**éхать** (см. Table 19) несов to go; (поезд, автомобиль: приближаться) to come; (: двигаться) to go; (разг: скользить) to slide; ~ (impf) **на** +prp (на лошади, на велосипеде) to ride; ~ (impf) +instr или **на** +prp (на поезде, на автобусе) to travel или go by

**ехи́дный** прил spiteful

**ешь** несов см. **есть**

**ещё** нареч (дополнительно) more; **хочу́ ~ ко́фе** I want more coffee

**ЕЭС** ср сокр (= Европе́йское экономи́ческое соо́бщество) EEC

**éю** мест см. **она́**

# Ж, ж

**ж** союз, част см. **же**

**жа́б|а** (-ы) ж (ЗООЛ) toad

**жа́бр|а** (-ы) ж (ЗООЛ) gill

**жа́воронок** (-ка) м (ЗООЛ) lark

**жа́днича|ть** (-ю; pf по~) несов (разг) to be mingy

**жа́дност|ь** (-и) ж: ~ (к +dat) (к вещам, к деньгам) greed (for)

**жа́дный** прил greedy

**жа́жд|а** (-ы) ж thirst

**жаке́т** (-а) м (woman's) jacket

**жале́|ть** (-ю; pf по~) несов перех to feel sorry for; (скупиться) to grudge ♦ неперех: ~ о +prp to regret; не ~я сил sparing no effort

**жа́л|ить** (-ю, -ишь; pf у~) несов перех (подлеж: оса) to sting; (: змея) to bite

**жа́лкий** прил (вид) pitiful, pathetic

**жа́лко** как сказ = **жаль**

**жа́л|о** (-а) ср (пчелы) sting; (змеи) bite

**жа́лоб|а** (-ы) ж complaint

**жа́лобн|ый** прил plaintive

**жа́лованье** (-я) ср salary

**жа́л|оваться** (-уюсь; pf по~) несов возв: ~ на +acc to complain about; (ябедничать) to tell on

**жа́лост|ь** (-и) ж: ~ к +dat sympathy for; **кака́я ~!** what a shame!

---
KEYWORD
---

**жаль** как сказ 1; (+acc; о сострадании): **(мне) жаль дру́га** I am sorry for my friend
2 (+acc или +gen; о сожалении, о досаде): **(мне) жаль вре́мени/ де́нег** I grudge the time/money
3 (+infin): **жаль уезжа́ть** it's a pity или shame to leave

---

**жанр** (-а) м genre

**жар** (-а) м heat; (МЕД) fever

**жар|а́** (-ы́) ж heat

**жарго́н** (-а) м slang; (профессиональный) jargon

**жа́реный** прил (на сковороде) fried; (в духовке) roast

**жа́р|ить** (-ю, -ишь; pf за~) несов перех (на сковороде) to fry; (в духовке) to roast; ~ся (pf за~ся) несов возв to fry

**жа́ркий** прил hot; (спор) heated

**жа́рко** нареч heatedly ♦ как сказ it's hot; **мне ~** I'm hot

**жасми́н** (-а) м jasmine

**жа́тв|а** (-ы) ж harvest

**жать** (**жму, жмёшь**) несов перех (руку) to shake; (лимон, сок) to squeeze; **сапоги́ мне жмут** my boots are pinching (my feet)

**жать** (**жну, жнёшь**; pf с~) несов перех to harvest

**жва́ч|ка** (-ки; gen pl -ек) ж (разг: резинка) chewing gum

**ж.д.** сокр (= желе́зная доро́га)

R., r., RR (US)

**жд|ать** (-у, -ёшь; pt -ал, -ала,
-а́ло) несов (не)перех: ~ +acc
или +gen (письмо, гостей) to
expect; (поезда) to wait for

---

KEYWORD

---

**же** союз 1 (при
противопоставлении) but; **я не
люблю матема́тику, литерату́ру
же обожа́ю** I don't like
mathematics, but I love literature
2 (вводит дополнительные
сведения) and; **успе́х зави́сит от
нали́чия ресу́рсов, ресу́рсов же
ма́ло** success depends on the
presence of resources, and the
resources are insufficient

♦ част 1 (ведь): **вы́пей ещё ча́ю,
хо́чешь же!** have more tea, you
want some, don't you?
2 (именно): **приду́ сейча́с же** I'll
come right now
3 (выражает сходство): **тако́й
же** the same; **в э́том же году́** this
very year

---

**ж|ева́ть** (-у́ю) несов перех to
chew
**жела́ни|е** (-я) ср (просьба)
request; ~ +gen/ +infin desire for/to
do
**жела́тельный** прил desirable
**жела́|ть** (-ю; pf по~) несов: ~
+gen to desire; ~ (по~ pf) +infin to
wish или want to do; ~ (по~ pf)
кому́-н сча́стья/всего́ хоро́шего
to wish sb happiness/all the best
**жела́ющ|ий** (-его) м: ~ие
пое́хать/порабо́тать those
interested in going/working
**желе́** ср нескл jelly (BRIT), jello (US)
**жел|еза́** (-езы́; nom pl -езы, gen pl
-ёз, dat pl -еза́м) ж gland
**железнодоро́жный** прил

(вокза́л) railway (BRIT), railroad
(US); (транспорт) rail
**желе́зн|ый** прил iron; ~ая
доро́га railway (BRIT), railroad (US)
**желе́з|о** (-а) ср iron
**железобето́н** (-а) м reinforced
concrete
**жёлоб** (-а; nom pl -а́) м gutter
**желте́|ть** (-ю; pf по~) несов to
turn yellow
**желт|о́к** (-ка́) м yolk
**желту́х|а** (-и) ж jaundice
**жёлтый** прил yellow
**желу́д|ок** (-ка) м (АНАТ) stomach
**желу́дочный** прил (боль)
stomach; (сок) gastric
**жёлуд|ь** (-я) м acorn
**жёлчный** прил: ~ пузы́рь gall
bladder
**жёлч|ь** (-и) ж (также перен) bile
**жемчуг** (-а; nom pl -а́) м pearls мн
**жемчу́жин|а** (-ы) ж pearl
**жен|а́** (-ы́; nom pl **жёны**, gen pl
**жён**) ж wife
**жена́т|ый** прил married (of man);
**он ~ на** +prp he is married to; **они́
~ы** they are married
**жене́в|а** (-ы) ж Geneva
**жен|и́ть** (-ю́, -ишь) (не)сов
перех (сына, внука): ~ кого́-н
(на +prp) to marry sb (off) (to); ~ся
(не)сов возв: ~ся на +prp to marry
(of man); (pf по~ся; разг) to get
hitched
**жени́х** (-а́) м (до свадьбы) fiancé;
(на свадьбе) (bride)groom
**жёнский** прил women's; (логика,
органы) female; ~ пол the female
sex; ~ род feminine gender
**жёнственный** прил feminine
**жёнщин|а** (-ы) ж woman
**жерд|ь** (-и; gen pl -е́й) ж pole
**жереб|ёнок** (-ёнка; nom pl -я́та,
gen pl -я́т) м foal
**жеребьёв|ка** (-ки; gen pl -ок) ж

casting *или* drawing of lots
**же́ртв|а (-ы)** ж victim; (*РЕЛ*)
sacrifice; **челове́ческие ~ы**
casualties
**же́ртв|овать (-ую;** *pf* **по~)** *несов*:
~ +*instr* (*жи́знью*) to sacrifice
♦ *перех* (*де́ньги*) to donate
**жест (-а)** м gesture
**жестикули́р|овать (-ую)** *несов*
to gesticulate
**жёсткий** *прил* (*крова́ть,*
*челове́к*) hard; (*мя́со*) tough;
(*во́лосы*) coarse; (*усло́вия*) strict;
~ **ваго́н** railway carriage with hard
seats; ~ **диск** hard disk
**жесто́кий** *прил* cruel; (*моро́з*)
severe
**жесто́кост|ь (-и)** ж cruelty
**жест|ь (-и)** ж tin-plated sheet metal
**жето́н (-а)** м tag; (*в метро́*) token
**жечь (жгу, жжёшь** *etc,* **жгут;** *pt*
**жёг, жгла;** *pf* **с~)** *несов перех* to
burn
**жже́ни|е (-я)** *ср* burning sensation
**живо́й** *прил* alive; (*органи́зм*)
living; (*живо́тное*) live; (*челове́к:*
*энерги́чный*) lively
**живопи́сный** *прил* picturesque
**жи́вопис|ь (-и)** ж painting
**живо́т (-а́)** м stomach; (*разг*)
tummy
**животново́дств|о (-а)** *ср* animal
husbandry
**живо́тн|ое (-ого)** *ср* animal
**живо́тный** *прил* animal
**живу́** *etc несов см.* **жить**
**жи́дкий** *прил* liquid
**жи́дкост|ь (-и)** ж liquid
**жи́ж|а (-и)** ж slurry
**жи́зненный** *прил* (*вопро́с,*
*интере́сы*) vital; (*необходи́мость*)
basic; ~ **у́ровень** standard of living;
~ **о́пыт** experience
**жизнера́достный** *прил* cheerful
**жизнеспосо́бный** *прил* viable

**жизн|ь (-и)** ж life
**жил** *etc несов см.* **жить**
**жиле́т (-а)** м waistcoat (*BRIT*), vest
(*US*)
**жил|е́ц (-ьца́)** м (*до́ма*) tenant
**жили́щный** *прил* housing
**жил|о́й** *прил* (*дом, зда́ние*)
residential; **~а́я пло́щадь**
accommodation
**жиль|ё (-я́)** *ср* accommodation
**жир (-а;** *nom pl* **-ы́)** м fat;
(*расти́тельный*) oil
**жира́ф (-а)** м giraffe
**жи́рный** *прил* (*пи́ща*) fatty;
(*челове́к*) fat; (*во́лосы*) greasy
**жи́тел|ь (-я)** м resident
**жи́тельств|о (-а)** *ср* residence
**жи|ть (-ву́, -вёшь;** *pt* **-л, -ла́,**
**-ло)** *несов* to live; **~л-был** there
once was, once upon a time there
was
**жму́р|ить (-ю, -ишь;** *pf* **за~)**
*несов*: ~ **глаза́** to screw up one's
eyes; **~ся (***pf* **за~ся)** *несов возв* to
squint
**жоке́|й (-я)** м jockey
**жонглёр (-а)** м juggler
**жонгли́р|овать (-ую)** *несов*: ~
+*instr* to juggle (with)
**жре́би|й (-я)** м: **броса́ть ~** to cast
lots
**ЖСК** м *сокр* (= **жи́лищно-**
**строи́тельный кооперати́в**) ≈
housing cooperative
**жужж|а́ть (-у́, -и́шь)** *несов* to
buzz
**жук (-а́)** м beetle
**жу́лик (-а)** м swindler; (*в игре́*)
cheat
**жу́льничеств|о (-а)** *ср*
underhandedness; (*в игре́*)
cheating
**журна́л (-а)** м magazine;
(*кла́ссный*) register
**журнали́ст (-а)** м journalist

**журнали́стик|а (-и)** ж journalism
**журч|а́ть (-у́, -и́шь)** несов
 (ручей, вода) to babble, murmur
**жу́ткий** прил terrible
**жЭК (-а)** м сокр (= жи́лищно-
 эксплуатаци́онная конто́ра) ≈
 housing office
**жюри́** ср нескл panel of judges

## З, з

**з** сокр (= за́пад) W; (=
 за́падный) W

---
KEYWORD
---

**за** предл; +асс **1** out (of);
 **выходи́ть (вы́йти** pf) **за дверь** to
 go out of the door
 **2** (позади) behind; **пря́таться
 (спря́таться** pf) **за де́рево** to hide
 behind a tree
 **3** (около: сесть, встать) at;
 **сади́ться (сесть** pf) **за стол** to sit
 down at the table
 **4** (свыше какого-н предела)
 over; **ему́ за со́рок** he is over forty
 **5** (при указании на расстояние,
 на время): **за пять киломе́тров
 отсю́да** five kilometres (BRIT) или
 kilometers (US) from here; **за три
 часа́ до нача́ла спекта́кля** three
 hours before the beginning of the
 show
 **6** (при указании объекта
 действия): **держа́ться за** +асс to
 hold onto; **ухвати́ться** (pf) **за** +асс
 to take hold of; **брать (взять** pf)
 **кого́-н за́ руку** to take sb by the
 hand; **бра́ться (взя́ться** pf) **за
 рабо́ту** to start work
 **7** (об объекте чувств) for;
 **ра́доваться** (impf) **за сы́на** to be
 happy for one's son;

**беспоко́иться** (impf) **за му́жа** to
worry about one's husband
 **8** (о цели) for; **сража́ться** (impf)
 **за побе́ду** to fight for victory
 **9** (в пользу) for, in favour (BRIT)
 или favor (US) of; **голосова́ть
 (проголосова́ть** pf) **за
 предложе́ние** to vote for или in
 favour of a proposal
 **10** (по причине, в обмен) for;
 **благодарю́ Вас за по́мощь** thank
 you for your help; **плати́ть** (impf)
 **за что-н** to pay for sth
 **11** (вместо кого-н) for; **рабо́тать**
 (impf) **за дру́га** to fill in for a friend
 ♦ предл; +instr **1** (по другую
 сторону) on the other side of;
 **жить** (impf) **за реко́й** to live on
 the other side of the river
 **2** (вне) outside; **жить** (impf) **за́
 го́родом** to live outside the town;
 **за грани́цей** abroad
 **3** (позади) behind; **стоя́ть** (impf)
 **за две́рью** to stand behind the
 door
 **4** (около: стоять, сидеть) at;
 **сиде́ть** (impf) **за столо́м** to sit at
 the table
 **5** (о смене событий) after; **год за
 го́дом** year after year
 **6** (во время чего-н) over; **за
 за́втраком** over breakfast
 **7** (о объекте внимания):
 **смотре́ть** или **уха́живать за**
 +instr to look after
 **8** (с целью получить, достать
 что-н) for; **я посла́л его́ за
 газе́той** I sent him out for a paper
 **9** (по причине) owing to
 ♦ как сказ (согласен) in favour;
 **кто за?** who is in favour?
 ♦ ср нескл pro; **взве́сить** (pf) **все
 за и про́тив** to weigh up all the
 pros and cons

**заба́вный** _прил_ amusing

**забасто́в|ка** (**-ки**; _gen pl_ **-ок**) _ж_ strike

**забасто́вщик** (**-а**) _м_ striker

**забе́г** (**-а**) _м_ (_СПОРТ_) race (_in running_); (: _отборочный_) heat

**забежа́ть** (_как_ **бежа́ть**; _см. Table 20; impf_ **забега́ть**) _сов_: ~ (**в** +_acc_) (_в дом, в деревню_) to run in(to); (_разг: на недолго_) to drop in(to); **забега́ть** (~ _pf_) **вперёд** to run ahead

**забира́|ть(ся)** (**-ю(сь)**) _несов от_ **забра́ть(ся)**

**заб|и́ть** (**-ью́, -ьёшь**) _сов_ (_часы_) to begin to strike; (_вода_) to begin to flow ♦ (_impf_ **забива́ть**) _перех_ (_гвоздь, сваю_) to drive in; (_СПОРТ, гол_) to score; (_наполнить_) to overfill; (_засорить_) to clog (up); (_скот, зверя_) to slaughter; ~**ся** _сов возв_ (_сердце_) to start beating; (_impf_ **забива́ться**; _спрятаться_) to hide (away)

**забле|сте́ть** (**-щу́, -сти́шь**) _сов_ (_слёзы_) to glisten; (_глаза_) to light up; (_металл_) to gleam

**забл|уди́ться** (**-ужу́сь, -у́дишься**) _сов возв_ to get lost

**заблужда́|ться** (**-юсь**) _несов возв_ to be mistaken

**заблужде́ни|е** (**-я**) _ср_ misconception

**заболева́ни|е** (**-я**) _ср_ illness

**заболе́|ть** (**-ю**; _impf_ **заболева́ть**) _сов_ (_нога, горло_) to begin to hurt; **заболева́ть** (~ _pf_) +_instr_ (_гриппом_) to fall ill with

**забо́р** (**-а**) _м_ fence

**забо́т|а** (**-ы**) _ж_ (_беспокойство_) worry; (_уход_) care; (_обычно мн: хлопоты_) trouble _ед_

**забо́|титься** (**-чусь, -тишься**; _pf_ **по~**) _несов возв_: ~ **о** +_prp_ to take care of

**забо́тливый** _прил_ caring

**забра́сыва|ть** (**-ю**) _несов от_ **заброса́ть, забро́сить**

**заб|ра́ть** (**-еру́, -ерёшь**; _impf_ **забира́ть**) _сов перех_ to take; ~**ся** (_impf_ **забира́ться**) _сов возв_ (_влезть_): ~**ся на** +_acc_ to climb up; (_проникнуть_): ~**ся в** +_acc_ to get into

**заброса́|ть** (**-ю**; _impf_ **забра́сывать**) _сов перех_: ~ +_instr_ (_канаву, яму_) to fill with; (_цветами_) to shower with

**забро́|сить** (**-шу, -сишь**; _impf_ **забра́сывать**) _сов перех_ (_мяч, камень_) to fling; (_десант_) to drop; (_учёбу_) to neglect

**забро́шенный** _прил_ (_дом_) derelict; (_сад, ребёнок_) neglected

**забры́зга|ть** (**-ю**; _impf_ **забры́згивать**) _сов перех_ to splash

**забы́ть** (_как_ **быть**; _см. Table 21; impf_ **забыва́ть**) _сов перех_ to forget

**зав.** _сокр_ = **заве́дующий**

**зава́л** (**-а**) _м_ obstruction

**зав|али́ть** (**-алю́, -а́лишь**; _impf_ **зава́ливать**) _сов перех_ (_вход_) to block off; (_разг: экзамен_) to mess up; **зава́ливать** (~ _pf_) +_instr_ (_дорогу: снегом_) to cover with; (_яму: землёй_) to fill with; ~**ся** (_impf_ **зава́ливаться**) _сов возв_ (_забор_) to collapse; (_разг: на экзамене_) to come a cropper

**зав|ари́ть** (**-арю́, -а́ришь**; _impf_ **зава́ривать**) _сов перех_ (_чай, кофе_) to brew; (_TEX_) to weld

**зава́рк|а** (**-и**) _ж_ (_действие: чая_) brewing; (_заваренный чай_) brew

**заварно́й** _прил_: ~ **крем** custard

**заведе́ни|е** (**-я**) _ср_ establishment

**заве́д|овать** (**-ую**) _несов_: ~ +_instr_ to be in charge of

**заве́дующ|ий (-его)** *м* manager; (*лаборато́рией, ка́федрой*) head; **~ хозя́йством** (*в шко́ле*) bursar; (*на заво́де*) *person in charge of supplies*

**заве́р|ить (-ю, -ишь;** *impf* **заверя́ть)** *сов перех* (*ко́пию, по́дпись*) to witness; **заверя́ть (~** *pf*) **кого́-н в чём-н** to assure sb of sth

**заверн|у́ть (-у́, -ёшь;** *impf* **завора́чивать)** *сов перех* (*рука́в*) to roll up; (*га́йку*) to tighten up; (*нале́во, напра́во, за у́гол*) to turn; **завора́чивать (~** *pf*) **(в** +*acc*) (*посы́лку, кни́гу, ребёнка*) to wrap (in); **~ся** (*impf* **завора́чиваться**) *сов возв:* **~ся в** +*acc* (*в полоте́нце, в плед*) to wrap o.s. up in

**заверша́|ть (-ю)** *несов от* **заверши́ть**

**заверша́ющий** *прил* final

**заверше́ни|е (-я)** *ср* completion; (*разгово́ра, ле́кции*) conclusion

**заверш|и́ть (-у́, - и́шь;** *impf* **заверша́ть)** *сов перех* to complete; (*разгово́р*) to end

**заверя́|ть (-ю)** *несов от* **заве́рить**

**зав|ести́ (-еду́, -едёшь;** *pt* **-ёл, -ела́, -ело́;** *impf* **заводи́ть)** *сов перех* to take; (*приобрести́*) to get; (*установи́ть*) to introduce; (*перепи́ску, разгово́р*) to initiate; (*часы́*) to wind up; (*маши́ну*) to start; **~сь** (*impf* **заводи́ться**) *сов возв* (*появи́ться*) to appear; (*мото́р, часы́*) to start working

**заве́т (-а)** *м* (*наставле́ние*) precept; (*РЕЛ*): **Ве́тхий/Но́вый Заве́т** the Old/New Testament

**завеща́ни|е (-я)** *ср* (*докуме́нт*) will, testament

**завеща́|ть (-ю)** (*не*)*сов перех:* ~ **что-н кому́-н** (*насле́дство*) to bequeath sth to sb

**завива́|ть(ся) (-ю(сь))** *несов от* **зави́ть(ся)**

**зави́вк|а (-и)** *ж* (*воло́с*) curling; (*причёска*) curly hair

**зави́дно** *как сказ:* **ему́ ~** he feels envious

**зави́д|овать (-ую;** *pf* **по~**) *несов:* **~** +*dat* to envy, be jealous of

**завин|ти́ть (-чу́, -ти́шь;** *impf* **зави́нчивать)** *сов перех* to tighten (up)

**зави́|сеть (-шу, -сишь)** *несов:* **~ от** +*gen* to depend on

**зави́симост|ь (-и)** *ж* (*отноше́ние*) correlation; **~ (от** +*gen*) dependence (on); **в ~и от** +*gen* depending on

**зави́стливый** *прил* envious, jealous

**за́вист|ь (-и)** *ж* envy, jealousy

**завит|о́к (-ка́)** *м* (*ло́кон*) curl

**зав|и́ть (-ью, -ьёшь;** *impf* **завива́ть)** *сов перех* (*во́лосы*) to curl; **~ся** (*impf* **завива́ться**) *сов возв* (*во́лосы*) to curl; (*сде́лать зави́вку*) to curl one's hair

**заво́д (-а)** *м* (*в часа́х, у игру́шки*) factory; clockwork

**зав|оди́ть(ся) (-ожу́(сь), -о́дишь(ся))** *несов от* **завести́(сь)**

**заводно́й** *прил* (*механи́зм*) clockwork; (*ру́чка*) winding

**завоева́ни|е (-я)** *ср* (*страны́*) conquest; (*успе́х*) achievement

**завоева́тел|ь (-я)** *м* conqueror

**завоева́тельный** *прил* aggressive

**заво|ева́ть (-ю́ю;** *impf* **завоёвывать**) *сов перех* to conquer

**завора́чива|ть(ся) (-ю(сь))** *несов от* **заверну́ть(ся)**

**за́втра** *нареч, ср нескл* tomorrow;

до ~! see you tomorrow!

**за́втрак** (-а) *м* breakfast

**за́втрака|ть** (-ю; *impf* **по~**) *несов* to have breakfast

**за́втрашний** *прил* tomorrow's; ~ **день** tomorrow

**за́вуч** (-а) *м сокр* ≈ deputy head

**завхо́з** (-а) *м сокр* = **заве́дующий хозя́йством**

**зав|яза́ть** (-яжу́, -я́жешь; *impf* **завя́зывать**) *сов перех* (*верёвку*) to tie; (*руку, посылки*) to bind; (*разговор*) to start (up); (*дружбу*) to form; **~ся** (*impf* **завя́зываться**) *сов возв* (*шнурки*) to be tied; (*разговор*) to start (up); (*дружба*) to form

**зага́да|ть** (-ю; *impf* **зага́дывать**) *сов перех* (*загадку*) to set; (*желание*) to make

**зага́д|ка** (-ки; *gen pl* -ок) *ж* riddle; (*перен*) puzzle

**зага́дочный** *прил* puzzling

**зага́р** (-а) *м* (sun)tan

**загиба́|ть(ся)** (-ю(сь)) *несов от* **загну́ть(ся)**

**загла́ви|е** (-я) *ср* title

**загла́вн|ый** *прил*: **~ая бу́ква** capital letter; **~ая роль** title role

**загла́|дить** (-жу, -дишь; *impf* **загла́живать**) *сов перех* (*складки*) to iron

**заглóхн|уть** (-у) *сов от* **глóхнуть**

**заглуш|и́ть** (-у́, -и́шь) *сов от* **глуши́ть**

**загл|яну́ть** (-яну́, -я́нешь; *impf* **загля́дывать**) *сов* (*в окно, в комнату*) to peep; (*в книгу, в словарь*) to glance; (*разг: посетить*) to pop in

**заг|на́ть** (-оню́, -о́нишь; *pt* -на́л, -нала́, -на́ло; *impf* **загоня́ть**) *сов перех* (*коров, детей*) to drive

**загн|и́ть** (-ию́, -иёшь; *impf*

**загнива́ть**) *сов* to rot

**загно|и́ться** (-ю́сь, -и́шься) *сов возв* (*рана*) to fester; (*глаз*) to become inflamed

**загн|у́ть** (-у́, -ёшь; *impf* **загиба́ть**) *сов перех* to bend; (*край*) to fold; **~ся** (*impf* **загиба́ться**) *сов возв* (*гвоздь*) to bend; (*край*) to fold

**за́говор** (-а) *м* conspiracy

**заговор|и́ть** (-ю́, -и́шь) *сов* (*начать говори́ть*) to begin to speak

**заголо́в|ок** (-ка) *м* headline

**заго́н** (-а) *м* (*для коров*) enclosure; (*для овец*) pen

**загоня́|ть** (-ю) *несов от* **загна́ть**

**загора́жива|ть** (-ю) *несов от* **загороди́ть**

**загора́|ть(ся)** (-ю(сь)) *несов от* **загоре́ть(ся)**

**загоре́лый** *прил* tanned

**загор|е́ть** (-ю́, -и́шь; *impf* **загора́ть**) *сов* to go brown, get a tan; **~ся** (*impf* **загора́ться**) *сов возв* (*дрова, костёр*) to light; (*здание итп*) to catch fire; (*лампочка, глаза*) to light up

**за́город** (-а) *м* (*разг*) the country

**загор|оди́ть** (-ожу́, -о́дишь; *impf* **загора́живать**) *сов перех* to block off; (*свет*) to block out

**за́городный** *прил* (*экскурсия*) out-of-town; (*дом*) country

**загото́в|ить** (-лю, -ишь; *impf* **загота́вливать**) *сов перех* to lay in; (*документы итп*) to prepare

**загражде́ни|е** (-я) *ср* barrier

**заграни́ц|а** (-ы) *ж* (*разг*) foreign countries *мн*

**заграни́чный** *прил* foreign, overseas; ~ **па́спорт** passport (*for travel abroad*)

**загрем|е́ть** (-лю́, -и́шь) *сов* (*гром*) to crash

**загро́бн|ый** прил: ~ый мир the next world; ~ая жизнь the afterlife

**загр|узи́ть** (-ужу́, -у́зишь) сов от **грузи́ть** ♦ (impf **загружа́ть**) перех (машину) to load up; (КОМП) to boot up

**загрязне́ни|е** (-я) ср pollution; ~ окружа́ющей среды́ (environmental) pollution

**загрязн|и́ть** (-ю́, -и́шь; impf **загрязня́ть**) сов перех to pollute; ~ся (impf **загрязня́ться**) сов возв to become polluted

**ЗАГС** (-а) м сокр (= за́пись а́ктов гражда́нского состоя́ния) ≈ registry office

**зад** (-а; nom pl -ы́, gen pl -о́в) м (человека) behind; (животного) rump; (маши́ны) rear

**зада|ва́ть(ся)** (-ю́(сь), -ёшь(ся)) несов от **зада́ть(ся)**

**зад|ави́ть** (-авлю́, -а́вишь) сов от **дави́ть** ♦ перех to crush; его́ ~ави́ла маши́на he was run over by a car

**зада́ни|е** (-я) ср task; (уче́бное) exercise; (ВОЕН) mission; дома́шнее ~ homework

**зада́т|ок** (-ка) м deposit

**зада́ть** (как **дать**; см. Table 16; impf **задава́ть**) сов перех to set; **задава́ть** (~ pf) кому́-н вопро́с to ask sb a question; ~ся (impf **задава́ться**) сов возв: ~ся це́лью +infin to set o.s. the task of doing

**зада́ч|а** (-и) ж task; (МАТ) problem

**задви́га|ть** (-ю) сов: ~ +instr to begin to move; ~ся сов возв to begin to move

**задви́жк|а** (-и) ж bolt

**задви́н|уть** (-у) сов перех to push; (я́щик, занаве́ски) to close

**задева́|ть** (-ю) несов от **заде́ть**

**заде́ла|ть** (-ю; impf **заде́лывать**) сов перех to seal up

**задёргива|ть** (-ю) несов от **задёрнуть**

**зад|ержа́ть** (-ержу́, -е́ржишь; impf **заде́рживать**) сов перех to delay, hold up; (престу́пника) to detain; **я не хочу́ Вас заде́рживать** I don't want to hold you back; ~ся (impf **заде́рживаться**) сов возв to be delayed или held up; (ждать) to pause

**заде́рж|ка** (-ки; gen pl -ек) ж delay, hold-up

**задёрн|уть** (-у; impf **задёргивать**) сов перех (што́ры) to pull shut

**заде́|ть** (-ну, -нешь; impf **задева́ть**) сов перех (перен: самолю́бие) to wound; **задева́ть** (~ pf) за +acc (за стол) to brush against; (кость) to graze against

**задира́|ть(ся)** (-ю) несов от **задра́ть(ся)**

**за́дн|ий** прил back; помеча́ть (поме́тить pf) ~им число́м to backdate; опла́чивать (оплати́ть pf) ~им число́м to make a back payment; ~ие но́ги hind legs

**задо́лго** нареч: ~ до +gen long before

**задо́лженност|ь** (-и) ж debts мн

**за́дом** нареч backwards (BRIT), backward (US); ~ наперёд back to front

**задохн|у́ться** (-у́сь, -ёшься; impf **задыха́ться**) сов возв (в дыму́) to suffocate; (от бе́га) to be out of breath; (от зло́сти) to choke

**зад|ра́ть** (-еру́, -ерёшь; impf **задира́ть**) сов перех (пла́тье) to hitch или hike up; ~ся (impf **задира́ться**) сов возв (пла́тье итп) to ruck up

**задр|ема́ть** (**-емлю́, -е́млешь**) *сов* to doze off

**задрож|а́ть** (**-у́, -и́шь**) *сов* (*человек, голос*) to begin to tremble; (*здание*) to begin to shake

**заду́ма|ть** (**-ю**; *impf* **заду́мывать**) *сов перех* (*план*) to think up; (*карту, число*) to think of; **заду́мывать** (**~** *pf*) +*infin* (*уехать итп*) to think of doing; **~ся** (*impf* **заду́мываться**) *сов возв* to be deep in thought

**заду́мчивый** *прил* pensive, thoughtful

**заду́мыва|ть(ся)** (**-ю(сь)**) *несов от* **заду́мать(ся)**

**зад|уши́ть** (**-ушу́, -у́шишь**) *сов от* **души́ть**

**задыха́|ться** (**-юсь**) *несов от* **задохну́ться**

**заеда́|ть** (**-ю**) *несов от* **зае́сть**

**зае́зд** (**-а**) *м* (*СПОРТ*) race (*in horse-racing, motor-racing*)

**заезжа́|ть** (**-ю**) *несов от* **зае́хать**

**заём** (**за́йма**) *м* loan

**заёмщик** (**-а**) *м* borrower

**зае́|сть** (*как* **есть**; *см. Table 15*; *impf* **заеда́ть**) *сов перех* (*подлеж: комары*) to eat ♦ *безл* (*разг: ружьё*) to jam; **пласти́нку ~ло** (*разг*) the record is stuck

**зае́|хать** (*как* **е́хать**; *см. Table 19*; *impf* **заезжа́ть**) *сов*: **~ за кем-н** to go to fetch sb; **заезжа́ть** (**~** *pf*) **в** +*асс* (*в канаву, во двор*) to drive into; (*в Москву, в магазин итп*) to stop off at

**заж|а́ть** (**-му́, -мёшь**; *impf* **зажима́ть**) *сов перех* to squeeze; (*рот, уши*) to cover

**заж|е́чь** (**-гу́, -жёшь** *итп*, **-гу́т**; *pt* **-ёг, -гла́**; *impf* **зажига́ть**) *сов перех* (*спичку*) to light; (*свет*) to turn on; **~ся** (*impf* **зажига́ться**) *сов возв* (*спичка*) to light; (*свет*) to go on

**зажива́|ть** (**-ю**) *несов от* **зажи́ть**

**зажига́л|ка** (**-ки**; *gen pl* **-ок**) *ж* (cigarette) lighter

**зажига́ни|е** (**-я**) *ср* (*АВТ*) ignition

**зажига́|ть(ся)** (**-ю(сь)**) *несов от* **заже́чь(ся)**

**зажима́|ть** (**-ю**) *несов от* **зажа́ть**

**заж|и́ть** (**-иву́, -ивёшь**; *impf* **зажива́ть**) *сов* (*рана*) to heal (up)

**заземле́ни|е** (**-я**) *ср* (*ЭЛЕК, устройство*) earth (*BRIT*), ground (*US*)

**заземл|и́ть** (**-ю́, -и́шь**; *impf* **заземля́ть**) *сов перех* to earth (*BRIT*), ground (*US*)

**зазу́брин|а** (**-ы**) *ж* serration

**заигра́|ть** (**-ю**) *сов (не)перех* to begin to play ♦ *неперех* (*музыка*) to begin

**заи́грыва|ть** (**-ю**) *несов*: **~ с** +*instr* (*разг: любезничать*) to flirt with; (*заискивать*) to woo

**заика́|ться** (**-юсь**) *несов возв* to have a stutter; **~** (**заикну́ться** *pf*) **о** +*prp* (*упомянуть*) to mention

**займств|овать** (**-ую**; *impf* **по~**) *(не)сов перех* to borrow; (*опыт*) to take on board

**заинтересо́ванный** *прил* interested; **я заинтересо́ван в э́том де́ле** I have an interest in the matter

**заинтерес|ова́ть** (**-у́ю**) *сов перех* to interest; **~ся** *сов возв*: **~ся** +*instr* to become interested in

**заи́скива|ть** (**-ю**) *несов*: **~ пе́ред** +*instr* to ingratiate o.s. with

**зайти́** (*как* **идти́**; *см. Table 18*; *impf* **заходи́ть**) *сов* (*солнце, луна*) to go down; (*спор, разговор*) to start up; (*посетить*): **~ (в/на** +*асс*/**к** +*dat*) to call in (at); (*попасть*): **~ в/**

**на** +acc to stray into; **заходи́ть (~** pf**) за кем-н** to go to fetch sb; **заходи́ть (~** pf**) спра́ва/сле́ва** to come in from the right/left

**закавка́зский** прил Transcaucasian

**зака́з (-а)** м (см глаг) ordering; booking; commissioning; (заказанный предмет) order; **по ~у** to order

**зак|аза́ть (-ажу́, -а́жешь;** impf **зака́зывать)** сов перех to order; to book; (портрет) to commission

**заказн|о́й** прил: **~о́е уби́йство** contract killing; **~о́е письмо́** registered letter

**зака́зчик (-а)** м customer

**закалённый** прил resistant

**закал|и́ть (-ю́, -и́шь;** impf **закаля́ть)** сов перех (сталь) to temper; (ребёнка, организм) to toughen up; **~ся** (impf **закаля́ться)** сов возв to toughen

**зака́лк|а (-и)** ж (см глаг) tempering; toughening up

**зака́лыва|ть (-ю)** несов от **заколо́ть**

**зака́нчива|ть(ся) (-ю)** несов от **зако́нчить(ся)**

**зака́па|ть (-ю;** impf **зака́пывать)** сов перех (запачкать) to splatter; (лекарство) to apply

**зака́пыва|ть (-ю)** несов от **зака́пать, закопа́ть**

**зака́т (-а)** м (перен: жизни) twilight; **~ (со́лнца)** sunset

**заката́|ть (-ю;** impf **зака́тывать)** сов перех to roll up

**зак|ати́ть (-ачу́, -а́тишь;** impf **зака́тывать)** сов перех (что-н кру́глое) to roll; (что-н на колёсах) to wheel; **~ся** (impf **зака́тываться)** сов возв to roll

**закида́|ть (-ю;** impf **заки́дывать)** сов = **заброса́ть**

**заки́н|уть (-у;** impf **заки́дывать)** сов перех to throw

**закип|е́ть (3sg -и́т;** impf **закипа́ть)** сов to start to boil; (перен: работа) to intensify

**заки́с|нуть (-ну;** pt -, -ла; impf **закиса́ть)** сов to turn sour

**за́кис|ь (-и)** ж oxide

**закла́дк|а (-и)** ж (в книге) bookmark

**закладн|а́я (-о́й)** ж mortgage deed

**закла́дыва|ть (-ю)** несов от **заложи́ть**

**закле́|ить (-ю, -ишь;** impf **закле́ивать)** сов перех to seal (up)

**заклина́ни|е (-я)** ср plea; (магические слова) incantation

**заклина́|ть (-ю)** несов перех (духов, змея) to charm; (перен: умолять) to plead with

**заклин|и́ть (-ю, -ишь;** impf **закли́нивать)** сов перех to jam

**заключа́|ть (-ю)** несов от **заключи́ть; ~ся** несов возв: **~ся в** +prp (состоять в) to lie in; (содержаться в) to be contained in; **пробле́ма ~ется в том, что ...** the problem is that ...

**заключе́ни|е (-я)** ср conclusion; (в тюрьме) imprisonment, confinement

**заключённ|ый (-ого)** м prisoner

**заключи́тельный** прил concluding, final

**заключ|и́ть (-у́, -и́шь;** impf **~а́ть)** сов перех (договор, сделку) to conclude

**заколдо́ванный** прил enchanted; **~ круг** vicious circle

**зако́лк|а (-и)** ж (для волос) hairpin

**зак|оло́ть (-олю́, -о́лешь)** сов от **коло́ть ♦** (impf **зака́лывать)**

*перех* (*волосы*) to pin up

**зако́н** (**-а**) *м* law; **объявля́ть** (**объяви́ть** *pf*) кого́-н вне ~а to outlaw sb

**зако́нность** (**-и**) *ж* (*документа*) legality; (*в стране*) law and order

**зако́нный** *прил* legitimate, lawful; (*право*) legal

**законода́тельный** *прил* legislative

**законода́тельство** (**-а**) *ср* legislation

**закономе́рный** *прил* predictable; (*понятный*) legitimate

**законопрое́кт** (**-а**) *м* (*полит*) bill

**зако́нченный** *прил* complete

**зако́нч**|**ить** (**-у, -ишь**; *impf* **зака́нчивать**) *сов перех* to finish; ~**ся** (*impf* **зака́нчиваться**) *сов возв* to finish, end

**закопа́**|**ть** (**-ю**; *impf* **зака́пывать**) *сов перех* to bury; (*яму*) to fill in

**закоп**|**ти́ть** (**-чу́, -ти́шь**) *сов от* **копти́ть**; ~**ся** *сов возв* to be covered in smoke

**закреп**|**и́ть** (**-лю́, -и́шь**; *impf* **закрепля́ть**) *сов перех* to fasten; (*победу, пози́цию*) to consolidate; (*ФОТО*) to fix

**закрич**|**а́ть** (**-у́, -и́шь**) *сов* to start shouting

**закругл**|**и́ть** (**-ю́, -и́шь**; *impf* **закругля́ть**) *сов перех* (*край, бесе́ду*) to round off

**закр**|**ути́ть** (**-учу́, -у́тишь**; *impf* **закру́чивать**) *сов перех* (*волосы*) to twist; (*га́йку*) to screw in

**закрыва́**|**ть(ся)** (**-ю(сь)**) *несов от* **закры́ть(ся)**

**закры́тие** (**-я**) *ср* closing (time)

**закры́т**|**ый** *прил* closed, shut; (*терра́са, маши́на*) enclosed; (*стадио́н*) indoor; (*собра́ние*) closed, private; (*ра́на*) internal; в

~ом помеще́нии indoors

**закр**|**ы́ть** (**-о́ю, -о́ешь**; *impf* **закрыва́ть**) *сов перех* to close, shut; (*заслони́ть, накры́ть*) to cover (up); (*прохо́д, грани́цу*) to close (off); (*во́ду, газ итп*) to shut off; ~**ся** (*impf* **закрыва́ться**) *сов возв* to close, shut; (*магази́н*) to close *или* shut down; (*запере́ться: в до́ме итп*) to close o.s. up

**зак**|**ури́ть** (**-урю́, -у́ришь**; *impf* **заку́ривать**) *сов перех* to light (up)

**зак**|**уси́ть** (**-ушу́, -у́сишь**; *impf* **заку́сывать**) *сов* (*пое́сть*) to have a bite to eat

**заку́ск**|**а** (**-и**) *ж* snack; (*обычно мн: для во́дки*) zakuska nibbles *мн*; (*в нача́ле обе́да*) hors d'oeuvre

**заку́сочн**|**ая** (**-ой**) *ж* snack bar

**закута́**|**ть(ся)** (**-ю(сь)**) *сов от* **кута́ть(ся)**

**зал** (**-а**) *м* hall; (*в библиоте́ке*) room; ~ **ожида́ния** waiting room

**заледене́лый** *прил* covered in ice; (*ру́ки*) icy

**заледене́**|**ть** (**-ю**) *сов* (*доро́га*) to ice over; (*перен: ру́ки*) to freeze

**зале́з**|**ть** (**-у, -ешь**; *impf* **залеза́ть**) *сов*: ~ **на** +*acc* (*на кры́шу*) to climb onto; (*на де́рево*) to climb (up); (*разг*): ~ **в** +*acc* (*в кварти́ру*) to break into; (*в до́лги*) to fall into

**зале**|**те́ть** (**-чу́, -ти́шь**; *impf* **залета́ть**) *сов*: ~ (**в** +*acc*) to fly in(to)

**зал**|**ечи́ть** (**-ечу́, -е́чишь**; *impf* **зале́чивать**) *сов перех* to heal

**зали́в** (**-а**) *м* bay; (*дли́нный*) gulf

**зал**|**и́ть** (**-ью́, -ьёшь**; *impf* **залива́ть**) *сов перех* to flood; (*костёр*) to extinguish; **залива́ть** (~ *pf*) **бензи́н в маши́ну** to fill a

car with petrol; **~ся** (*impf*
**залива́ться**) *сов возв* (*вода*) to
seep; **залива́ться** (**~ся** *pf*)
**слеза́ми/сме́хом** to burst into
tears/out laughing

**зало́г** (**-а**) *м* (*действие: вещей*)
pawning; (*: квартиры*)
mortgaging; (*заложенная вещь*)
security; (*линг*) voice

**зал|ожи́ть** (**-ожу́, -о́жишь**; *impf*
**закла́дывать**) *сов перех*
(*покрыть*) to clutter up;
(*отметить*) to mark; (*кольцо,
шубу*) to pawn; (*дом*) to
mortgage; (*заполнить*) to block
up; **у меня́ ~ожи́ло нос/го́рло**
(*разг*) my nose/throat is all bunged
up

**зало́жник** (**-а**) *м* hostage

**залп** (**-а**) *м* salvo volley

**за́лпом** *нареч* all in one go

**зам.** *м сокр* (= **замести́тель**)
dep.

**зама́|зать** (**-жу, -жешь**; *impf*
**зама́зывать**) *сов перех* (*щели*)
to fill with putty; (*запачкать*) to
smear

**зама́зк|а** (**-и**) *ж* putty

**зам|ани́ть** (**-аню́, -а́нишь**; *impf*
**зама́нивать**) *сов перех* to lure,
entice

**зама́нчивый** *прил* tempting

**замахн|у́ться** (**-у́сь, -ёшься**;
*impf* **зама́хиваться**) *сов возв*: **~
на** +*acc* (*на ребёнка*) to raise one's
hand to; (*перен*) to set one's sights
on

**зама́чива|ть** (**-ю**) *несов от*
**замочи́ть**

**заме́дл|ить** (**-ю, -ишь**; *impf*
**замедля́ть**) *сов перех* to slow
down; **~ся** (*impf* **замедля́ться**)
*сов возв* to slow down

**заме́н|а** (**-ы**) *ж* replacement;
(*СПОРТ*) substitution

**зам|ени́ть** (**-еню́, -е́нишь**; *impf*
**заменя́ть**) *сов перех* to replace

**зам|ере́ть** (**-ру́, -рёшь**; *pt* **-ер,
-ерла́**; *impf* **замира́ть**) *сов*
(*человек*) to stop dead; (*перен*:
*сердце*) to stand still; (*: работа,
страна*) to come to a standstill;
(*звук*) to die away

**замёрз|нуть** (**-ну**; *pt* **-, -ла**; *impf*
**замерза́ть**) *сов* to freeze; (*окно*)
to ice up; **я ~** I'm freezing

**зам|еси́ть** (**-ешу́, -е́сишь**; *impf*
**заме́шивать**) *сов перех* to
knead

**замести́тел|ь** (**-я**) *м* (*директора*)
deputy

**заме|сти́ть** (**-щу́, -сти́шь**) *сов от*
**замеща́ть**

**заме́|тить** (**-чу, -тишь**; *impf*
**замеча́ть**) *сов перех* to notice;
(*сказать*) to remark

**заме́т|ка** (**-ки**; *gen pl* **-ок**) *ж* note;
(*в газете*) short piece *или* article

**заме́тно** *нареч* noticeably ♦ *как
сказ* (*видно*) it's obvious

**заме́тный** *прил* noticeable;
(*личность*) prominent

**замеча́ни|е** (**-я**) *ср* comment,
remark; (*выговор*) reprimand

**замеча́тельно** *нареч* (*красив,
умён*) extremely; (*делать что-н*)
wonderfully, brilliantly ♦ *как сказ*:
**~!** that's wonderful *или* brilliant!

**замеча́тельный** *прил* wonderful,
brilliant

**замеча́|ть** (**-ю**) *несов от*
**заме́тить**

**замеша́тельств|о** (**-а**) *ср*
confusion

**заме́шива|ть** (**-ю**) *несов от*
**замеси́ть**

**замеща́|ть** (**-ю**) *несов перех*
(*временно*) to stand in for; (*pf*
**замести́ть**: *заменять*:
*работника итп*) to replace;

(: *игрока*) to substitute; (*вакансию*) to fill

**замеще́ни|е** (**-я**) *ср* (*работника*) replacement; (*игрока*) substitution

**зами́н|ка** (**-ки**; *gen pl* **-ок**) *ж* hitch

**замира́|ть** (**-ю**) *несов от* **замере́ть**

**за́мкнутый** *прил* (*жизнь*) cloistered; (*человек*) reclusive

**замкн|у́ть** (**-у́**, **-ёшь**; *impf* **замыка́ть**) *сов перех* to close; **~ся** (*impf* **замыка́ться**) *сов возв* to close; (*перен: обособиться*) to shut o.s. off

**за́м|ок** (**-ка**) *м* castle

**зам|о́к** (**-ка́**) *м* lock; (*также*: **вися́чий ~**) padlock

**замо́лк|нуть** (**-ну**; *pt* **-**, **-ла**; *impf* **замолка́ть**) *сов* to fall silent

**замолч|а́ть** (**-у́**, **-и́шь**) *сов* (*человек*) to go quiet; **~и́!** be quiet!, shut up!

**заморажива́ни|е** (**-я**) *ср* (*продуктов*) refrigeration; **~ цен/ зарпла́ты** price/wage freeze

**заморо́|зить** (**-жу**, **-зишь**; *impf* **замора́живать**) *сов перех* to freeze

**за́морозк|и** (**-ов**) *мн* frosts *мн*

**зам|очи́ть** (**-очу́**, **-о́чишь**; *impf* **зама́чивать**) *сов перех* to soak

**за́муж** *нареч*: **выходи́ть ~** (**за** +*acc*) to get married (to), marry

**за́мужем** *нареч* married

**заму́жеств|о** (**-а**) *ср* marriage

**заму́жняя** *прил* married

**замуч|ить** (**-у**, **-ишь**) *сов от* **му́чить** ♦ *перех*: **~** (*pf*) **кого́-н до сме́рти** to torture sb to death; **~ся** *сов от* **му́читься**

**за́мш|а** (**-и**) *ж* suede

**замыка́ни|е** (**-я**) *ср* (*также*: **коро́ткое ~**) short circuit

**замыка́|ть(ся)** (**-ю(сь)**) *несов от* **замкну́ть(ся)**

**за́мыс|ел** (**-ла**) *м* scheme

**замы́сл|ить** (**-ю**, **-ишь**; *impf* **замышля́ть**) *сов перех* to think up

**за́навес** (**-а**) *м* (*ТЕАТР*) curtain

**занаве́|сить** (**-шу**, **-сишь**; *impf* **занаве́шивать**) *сов перех* to hang a curtain over

**занаве́с|ка** (**-ки**; *gen pl* **-ок**) *ж* curtain

**зан|ести́** (**-есу́**, **-есёшь**; *pt* **-ёс**, **-есла́**; *impf* **заноси́ть**) *сов перех* (*принести*) to bring; (*записать*) to take down; (*доставить*): **доро́гу ~есло́ сне́гом** the road is covered (over) with snow

**занима́тельный** *прил* engaging

**занима́|ть** (**-ю**) *несов от* **заня́ть**; **~ся** *несов возв* (*на рояле итп*) to practise (*BRIT*), practice (*US*); **~ся** (*impf*) +*instr* (*учиться*) to study; (*уборкой*) to do; **~ся** (*impf*) **спо́ртом/му́зыкой** to play sports/ music; **чем ты сейча́с ~ешься?** what are you doing at the moment?

**за́ново** *нареч* again

**зано́з|а** (**-ы**) *ж* splinter

**зано́с** (**-а**) *м* (*обычно мн*) drift

**зан|оси́ть** (**-ошу́**, **-о́сишь**) *несов от* **занести́**

**зано́счивый** *прил* arrogant

**за́нят** *прил* busy; **он был о́чень ~** he was very busy; **телефо́н ~** the phone *или* line is engaged

**заня́ти|е** (**-я**) *ср* occupation; (*в школе*) lesson, class; (*времяпрепровождение*) pastime

**за́нятост|ь** (**-и**) *ж* employment

**заня́ть** (**займу́**, **займёшь**; *impf* **занима́ть**) *сов перех* to occupy; (*позицию*) to take up; (*деньги*) to borrow; (*время*) to take; **~** (*pf*) **пе́рвое/второе ме́сто** to take first/second place; **~ся** *сов возв*:

~**ся** +*instr* (*языком, спортом*) to take up; (*бизнесом*) to go into; ~**ся** (*pf*) **собо́й/детьми́** to devote time to o.s./one's children

**заодно́** *нареч* (*вместе*) as one

**зао́чный** *прил* part-time

**зао́чное отделе́ние** - Part-time study is one of the ways of obtaining a degree, and is for people who do not want to give up their job. Most students work independently with regular postal communication with their tutors. Two exam sessions a year are preceded by a month of intensive lectures and tutorials which prepare students for the exams. See also notes at **о́чный** and **вече́рний**.

**за́пад** (**-а**) *м* west; **За́пад** (*полит*) the West

**западноевропе́йский** *прил* West European

**за́падный** *прил* western; (*ветер*) westerly

**западн|я́** (**-и́**) *ж* trap

**запа́с** (**-а**) *м* store; (*руды*) deposit; (*ВОЕН*) the reserves *мн*

**запаса́|ть(ся)** (**-ю(сь)**) *несов от* **запасти́(сь)**

**запасн|о́й** *прил* spare ♦ (**-о́го**) *м* (*СПОРТ: также*: ~ **игро́к**) substitute; **~áя часть** spare part

**зап|асти́** (**-асу́, -асёшь**; *impf* **запаса́ть**) *сов перех* to lay in; **~сь** (*impf* **запаса́ться**) *сов возв*: **~сь** +*instr* to stock up (on)

**за́пах** (**-а**) *м* smell

**запая́|ть** (**-ю**) *сов перех* to solder

**зап|ере́ть** (**-ру́, -рёшь**; *impf* **запира́ть**) *сов перех* (*дверь*) to lock; (*дом, человека*) to lock up; ~**ся** (*impf* **запира́ться**) *сов возв* (*дверь*) to lock; (*человек*) to lock

o.s. up

**зап|е́ть** (**-ою́, -оёшь**) *сов* (*не*)*перех* to start singing

**запеча́та|ть** (**-ю**; *impf* **запеча́тывать**) *сов перех* to seal up

**запира́|ть(ся)** (**-ю(сь)**) *несов от* **запере́ть(ся)**

**зап|иса́ть** (**-ишу́, -и́шешь**; *impf* **запи́сывать**) *сов перех* to write down; (*концерт, пластинку*) to record; (*на курсы*) to enrol; ~**ся** (*impf* **запи́сываться**) *сов возв* (*на курсы*) to enrol (o.s.); (*на плёнку*) to make a recording; ~**ся** (*pf*) (**на приём**) **к врачу́** to make a doctor's appointment

**запи́ск|а** (**-и**) *ж* note; (*служебная*) memo

**записн|о́й** *прил*: **~áя кни́жка** notebook

**запи́сыва|ть(ся)** (**-ю(сь)**) *несов от* **записа́ть(ся)**

**за́пис|ь** (**-и**) *ж* record; (*в дневнике*) entry; (*МУЗ*) recording; (*на курсы*) enrolment (*BRIT*), enrollment (*US*); (*на приём к врачу*) appointment

**запла́ка|ть** (**-чу, -чешь**) *сов* to start crying *или* to cry

**запла́т|а** (**-ы**) *ж* patch

**запл|ати́ть** (**-ачу́, -а́тишь**) *сов от* **плати́ть**

**запл|ести́** (**-ету́, -етёшь**; *pt* **-ёл, -ела́, -ело́**; *impf* **заплета́ть**) *сов перех* (*волосы*) to plait

**заплы́в** (**-а**) *м* (*СПОРТ*) race (*in swimming*); (: *отборочный*) heat

**запл|ы́ть** (**-ыву́, -ывёшь**; *impf* **заплыва́ть**) *сов* (*человек*) to swim off; (*глаза*) to become swollen

**запове́дник** (**-а**) *м* (*природный*) nature reserve

**за́повед|ь** (**-и**) *ж* commandment

**заподо́зр|ить** (**-ю, -ишь**) *сов перех* to suspect

**запо́лн|ить** (**-ю, -ишь**; *impf* **заполня́ть**) *сов перех* to fill; (*анкету, бланк*) to fill in *или* out; **~ся** (*impf* **заполня́ться**) *сов возв* to fill up

**заполя́рный** *прил* polar

**запо́мн|ить** (**-ю, -ишь**; *impf* **запомина́ть**) *сов перех* to remember

**за́понк|а** (**-и**) *ж* cuff link

**запо́р** (**-а**) *м* (*МЕД*) constipation; (*замок*) lock

**запоте́|ть** (**-ю**) *сов* to steam up

**запра́в|ить** (**-лю, -ишь**; *impf* **заправля́ть**) *сов перех* (*рубашку*) to tuck in; (*салат*) to dress; **заправля́ть** (**~** *pf*) **маши́ну** to fill up the car; **~ся** (*impf* **заправля́ться**) *сов возв* (*разг: горючим*) to tank up

**запра́в|ка** (**-ки**; *gen pl* **-ок**) *ж* (*машины, самолёта итп*) refuelling; (*кулин*) dressing; (*разг: станция*) filling station

**запра́вочн|ый** *прил*: **~ая ста́нция** filling station

**запре́т** (**-а**) *м*: **~** (**на что-н**/ +*infin*) ban (on sth/on doing)

**запре|ти́ть** (**-щу́, -ти́шь**; *impf* **запреща́ть**) *сов перех* to ban; **запреща́ть** (**~** *pf*) **кому́-н** +*infin* to forbid sb to do

**запре́тный** *прил* forbidden

**запреще́ни|е** (**-я**) *ср* banning; **суде́бное ~** injunction

**запрещённый** *прил* banned

**запро́с** (**-а**) *м* inquiry; (*обычно мн: требования*) expectation

**запр|я́чь** (**-ягу́, -яжёшь** итп, **-ягу́т**; *pt* **-я́г, -ягла́**; *impf* **запряга́ть**) *сов перех* (*лошадь*) to harness

**запуга́|ть** (**-ю**; *impf* **запу́гивать**) *сов перех* to intimidate

**за́пуск** (**-а**) *м* (*станка*) starting; (*ракеты*) launch

**зап|усти́ть** (**-ущу́, -у́стишь**; *impf* **запуска́ть**) *сов перех* (*бросить*) to hurl; (*станок*) to start (up); (*ракету*) to launch; (*хозяйство, болезнь*) to neglect ♦ *неперех*: **~ чем-н в кого́-н** to hurl sth at sb; **запуска́ть** (**~** *pf*) **что-н в произво́дство** to launch (production of) sth

**запу́танный** *прил* (*нитки, волосы*) tangled; (*дело, вопрос*) confused

**запу́та|ть** (**-ю**) *сов от* **пу́тать**; **~ся** *сов от* **пу́таться** ♦ (*impf* **запу́тываться**) *возв* (*человек*) to get caught up; (*дело, вопрос*) to become confused

**запу́щенный** *прил* neglected

**запча́ст|ь** (**-и**) *ж сокр* = **запасна́я часть**

**запя́ст|ье** (**-ья**; *gen pl* **-ий**) *ср* wrist

**запят|а́я** (**-о́й**) *ж* comma

**зарабо́та|ть** (**-ю**; *impf* **зараба́тывать**) *сов перех* to earn ♦ *неперех*; (*no impf*; *начать рабо́тать*) to start up

**за́работн|ый** *прил*: **~ая пла́та** pay, wages *мн*

**за́работ|ок** (**-ка**) *м* earnings *мн*

**заража́|ть(ся)** (**-ю(сь)**) *несов от* **зарази́ть(ся)**

**зараже́ни|е** (**-я**) *ср* infection; (*местности*) contamination

**зара́з|а** (**-ы**) *ж* infection

**зара|зи́ть** (**-жу́, -зи́шь**; *impf* **заража́ть**) *сов перех* to infect; (*местность*) to contaminate; **~ся** (*impf* **заража́ться**) *сов возв*: **~ся** +*instr* (*гриппом итп*) to catch

**зара́зный** *прил* infectious

**зара́нее** *нареч* in advance

**зар|асти́** (**-асту́, -астёшь**; *pt* **-о́с,**

**-осла́;** *impf* **зараста́ть)** *сов*
(*зажить: рана*) to close up;
**зараста́ть** (~ *pf*) +*instr* (*травой*) to
be overgrown with

**заре́|зать (-жу, -жешь)** *сов от*
**ре́зать ♦** *перех* (*человека*) to
stab to death

**зарекомендова́ть (-у́ю)** *сов:* ~
**себя́** +*instr* to prove oneself to be

**зарод|и́ться** (*3sg* **-и́тся;** *impf*
**зарожда́ться)** *сов возв*
(*явление*) to emerge; (*перен:
чувство*) to arise

**заро́дыш (-а)** *м* (*БИО*) embryo;
(*растения, также перен*) germ

**зарожде́ни|е (-я)** *ср* emergence;
(*идеи, чувства*) conception

**за́росл|ь (-и)** *ж* (*обычно мн*)
thicket

**зарпла́т|а (-ы)** *ж сокр* (=
*за́работная пла́та*) pay

**зарубе́жный** *прил* foreign

**зарубе́жь|е (-я)** *ср* overseas;
**бли́жнее** ~ former Soviet republics

**зар|ы́ть (-о́ю, -о́ешь)** *impf*
**зарыва́ть)** *сов перех* to bury;
**~ся** (*impf* **зарыва́ться)** *сов возв:*
**~ся в** +*acc* to bury o.s. in

**зар|я́ (-и́;** *nom pl* **зо́ри,** *gen pl*
**зорь,** *dat pl* **зо́рям)** *ж* dawn;
(*вечерняя*) sundown; **ни свет ни**
~ at the crack of dawn

**заря́д (-а)** *м* (*ВОЕН, ЭЛЕК*) charge;
(*перен: бодрости*) boost

**заря|ди́ть (-жу́, -ди́шь)** *impf*
**заряжа́ть)** *сов перех* to load;
(*батарейку*) to charge; **~ся** (*impf*
**заряжа́ться)** *сов возв* to
recharge

**заря́дк|а (-и)** *ж* (*СПОРТ*) exercises
*мн*; (*батареи*) charging

**заса́д|а (-ы)** *ж* ambush; (*отряд*)
ambush party

**заса́сыва|ть** (*3sg* **-ет)** *несов от*
**засоса́ть**

**засверка́|ть (-ю)** *сов* to flash

**засв|ети́ть (-ечу́, -е́тишь;** *impf*
**засве́чивать)** *сов перех* (*ФОТО*)
to expose

**заседа́ни|е (-я)** *ср* meeting;
(*парламента, суда*) session

**заседа́тел|ь (-я)** *м:* **прися́жный** ~
member of the jury

**заседа́|ть (-ю)** *несов* (*на
совещании*) to meet; (*в
парламенте, в суде*) to sit;
(*парламент, суд*) to be in session

**засека́|ть (-ю)** *несов от* **засе́чь**

**засел|и́ть (-ю́, -и́шь;** *impf*
**заселя́ть)** *сов перех* (*земли*) to
settle; (*дом*) to move into

**засе́|чь (-ку́, -чёшь** *etc,* **-ку́т;**
*pt* **-ёк, -екла́, -екло́)** *impf*
**засека́ть)** *сов перех* (*место*) to
locate; **засека́ть** (~ *pf*) **вре́мя** to
record the time

**засе́|ять (-ю;** *impf* **засева́ть)** *сов
перех* to sow

**засло́н (-а)** *м* shield

**заслон|и́ть (-ю́, -и́шь;** *impf*
**заслоня́ть)** *сов перех* to shield

**заслу́г|а (-и)** *ж* (*обычно мн*)
service; **наградить** (*pf*) **кого́-н по**
~**м** to fully reward sb; **его́
наказа́ли по** ~**м** he got what he
deserved

**заслу́женный** *прил* well-
deserved; (*врач, учёный итп*)
renowned

**засл|ужи́ть (-ужу́, -у́жишь;** *impf*
**заслу́живать)** *сов перех* to earn

**заслу́ша|ть (-ю;** *impf*
**заслу́шивать)** *сов перех* to
listen to

**засме|я́ться (-ю́сь, -ёшься)** *сов
возв* to start laughing

**засн|у́ть (-у́, -ёшь;** *impf*
**засыпа́ть)** *сов* to go to sleep, fall
asleep

**засо́в** (-а) м bolt
**засо́выва|ть** (-ю) несов от **засу́нуть**
**засоре́ни|е** (-я) ср (рек) pollution; (туалета) blockage
**засор|и́ть** (-ю́, -и́шь; impf **засоря́ть**) сов перех (туалет) to clog up, block; **~ся** (impf **засоря́ться**) сов возв (туалет) to become clogged up или blocked
**засос|а́ть** (-у́, -ёшь; impf **заса́сывать**) сов перех to suck in
**засо́хн|уть** (-у; impf **засыха́ть**) сов (грязь) to dry up; (растение) to wither
**заста́в|а** (-ы) ж (также: **пограни́чная ~**) frontier post
**заста|ва́ть** (-ю́, -ёшь) несов от **заста́ть**
**заста́в|ить** (-лю, -ишь; impf **заставля́ть**) сов перех (занять) to clutter up; **заставля́ть (~ pf) кого́-н** +infin to force sb to do, make sb do
**заста́|ть** (-ну, -нешь; impf **застава́ть**) сов перех to catch, find
**застегн|у́ть** (-у́, -ёшь; impf **застёгивать**) сов перех to do up; **~ся** (impf **застёгиваться**) сов возв (на пуговицы) to button o.s. up; (на молнию) to zip o.s. up
**застёж|ка** (-ки; gen pl -ек) ж fastener
**застекл|и́ть** (-ю́, -и́шь; impf **застекля́ть**) сов перех to glaze
**застел|и́ть** (-ю́, -ишь; impf **застила́ть**) сов перех (кровать) to make up
**засте́нчивый** прил shy
**застига́|ть** (-ю) несов от **засти́чь**
**застила́|ть** (-ю) несов от **застели́ть**
**засти́|чь** (-гну, -гнешь; pt -г,

-гла, -гло; impf **застига́ть**) сов перех to catch
**засто́|й** (-я) м (в делах) standstill; (в жизни) stagnation
**засто́йный** прил stagnant
**застра́ива|ть** (-ю) несов от **застро́ить**
**застрах|ова́ть(ся)** (-у́ю(сь)) сов от **страхова́ть(ся)**
**застрева́|ть** (-ю) несов от **застря́ть**
**застр|ели́ть** (-елю́, -е́лишь) сов перех to gun down; **~ся** сов возв to shoot o.s.
**застро́|ить** (-ю, -ишь; impf **застра́ивать**) сов перех to develop
**застря́|ть** (-ну, -нешь; impf **застрева́ть**) сов to get stuck
**заст|упи́ться** (-уплю́сь, -у́пишься; impf **заступа́ться**) сов возв: **~ за** +acc to stand up for
**засты́|ть** (-ну, -нешь; impf **застыва́ть**) сов to freeze; (цемент) to set
**засу́н|уть** (-у; impf **засо́вывать**) сов перех: **~ что-н в** +acc to thrust sth into
**за́сух|а** (-и) ж drought
**зас|уши́ть** (-ушу́, -у́шишь; impf **засу́шивать**) сов перех to dry up
**засу́шливый** прил dry
**засчита́|ть** (-ю; impf **засчи́тывать**) сов перех (гол) to allow (to stand)
**засы́п|ать** (-лю, -лешь; impf **засыпа́ть**) сов перех (яму) to fill (up); (покрыть) to cover; **засыпа́ть (~ pf) кого́-н вопро́сами** to bombard sb with questions; **засыпа́ть (~ pf) кого́-н пода́рками** to shower sb with gifts
**засыпа́|ть** (-ю) несов от **засну́ть**
**засыха́|ть** (-ю) несов от

**засо́хнуть**

**зата́|и́ть** (**-ю́**, **-и́шь**; *impf*
**зата́ивать**) *сов перех*
(*неприязнь*) to harbour (*BRIT*),
harbor (*US*); ~ (*pf*) **дыха́ние** to hold
one's breath; **~ся** *сов возв* to hide

**зата́плива|ть** (**-ю**) *несов от*
**затопи́ть**

**зат|ащи́ть** (**-ащу́**, **-а́щишь**; *impf*
**зата́скивать**) *сов перех* to drag

**затверде́|ть** (*3sg* **-ет**; *impf*
**затвердева́ть**) *сов* to harden;
(*раствор*) to solidify

**затво́р** (**-а**) *м* shutter

**затева́|ть** (**-ю**) *несов от* **зате́ять**

**затека́|ть** (**-ю**) *несов от* **зате́чь**

**зате́м** *нареч* (*потом*) then; (*для
того*) for that reason; ~ **что́бы** in
order to

**затемн|и́ть** (**-ю́**, **-и́шь**; *impf*
**затемня́ть**) *сов перех* to darken

**зат|е́чь** (*3sg* **-ече́т**, *pt* **-ёк**, **-екла́**,
**-екло́**; *impf* **затека́ть**) *сов*
(*опухнуть*) to swell up; (*онеметь*)
to go numb; **затека́ть** (~ *pf*) **за**
+*acc*/**в** +*acc* (*вода*) to seep behind/
into

**зате́|я** (**-и**) *ж* (*замысел*) idea,
scheme

**зате́|ять** (**-ю**; *impf* **затева́ть**) *сов
перех* (*разговор, игру*) to start
(up)

**затих|нуть** (**-ну**; *pt* **-**, **-ла**; *impf*
**затиха́ть**) *сов* to quieten (*BRIT*)
*или* quiet (*US*) down; (*буря*) to die
down

**зати́шь|е** (**-я**) *ср* lull

**заткн|у́ть** (**-у́**, **-ёшь**; *impf*
**затыка́ть**) *сов перех* to plug; ~
(*pf*) **что-н за** +*acc*/**в** +*acc* to stuff sth
behind/into; **затыка́ть** (~ *pf*)
**кого́-н** *или* **рот кому́-н** (*разг*) to
shut sb up; **~ся** (*impf* **затыка́ться**)
*сов возв* (*разг*: *замолчать*) to
shut up; **~йсь!** (*разг*: *пренебр*)

shut it!

**затме́ни|е** (**-я**) *ср* eclipse

**зато́** *союз* (*также*: **но ~**) but then
(again)

**зат|ону́ть** (**-ону́**, **-о́нешь**) *сов* to
sink

**зат|опи́ть** (**-оплю́**, **-о́пишь**; *impf*
**зата́пливать**) *сов перех* (*печь*)
to light; (*impf* **затопля́ть**;
*деревню*) to flood; (*судно*) to sink

**зато́р** (**-а**) *м* congestion; (*на
улице*) traffic jam

**затра́гива|ть** (**-ю**) *несов от*
**затро́нуть**

**затра́т|а** (**-ы**) *ж* expenditure

**затра́|тить** (**-чу**, **-тишь**; *impf*
**затра́чивать**) *сов перех* to
expend

**затро́н|уть** (**-у**; *impf*
**затра́гивать**) *сов перех* (*перен*:
*тему*) to touch on; (: *человека*) to
affect

**затрудне́ни|е** (**-я**) *ср* difficulty

**затрудни́тельный** *прил* difficult,
awkward

**затрудн|и́ть** (**-ю́**, **-и́шь**; *impf*
**затрудня́ть**) *сов перех*: ~ **что-н**
to make sth difficult; **е́сли Вас не
~и́т** if it isn't too much trouble; **~ся**
(*impf* **затрудня́ться**) *сов возв*:
**~ся** +*infin*/**с чем-н** to have difficulty
doing/with sth

**зат|упи́ть(ся)** (**-уплю́**, **-у́пишь**)
*сов от* **тупи́ть(ся)**

**зат|уши́ть** (**-ушу́**, **-у́шишь**) *сов
от* **туши́ть**

**затыка́|ть(ся)** (**-ю(сь)**) *несов от*
**заткну́ть(ся)**

**заты́л|ок** (**-ка**) *м* the back of the
head

**зат|яну́ть** (**-яну́**, **-я́нешь**; *impf*
**затя́гивать**) *сов перех* (*шнурки,
гайку*) to tighten; (*дело*) to drag
out; (*вовлечь*): ~ **кого́-н в** +*acc* to
drag sb into; **~ся** (*impf*

**зати́гиваться**) *сов возв* (*петля, узел*) to tighten; (*рана*) to close up; (*дело*) to overrun; (*при курении*) to inhale

**заура́дный** *прил* mediocre

**зау́трен|я** (-и) *ж* (*РЕЛ*) dawn mass

**за|учи́ть** (-учу́, -у́чишь; *impf* ~у́чивать) *сов перех* to learn, memorize

**захва́т** (-а) *м* seizure, capture; (*СПОРТ*) hold; (*ТЕХ*) clamp

**захв|ати́ть** (-ачу́, -а́тишь; *impf* **захва́тывать**) *сов перех* to seize, capture; (*взять с собой*) to take; (*подлеж: музыка*) to captivate; (*болезнь, пожар*) to catch (in time); **дух ~а́тывает** it takes your breath away; **у меня́ дух ~ати́ло от волне́ния** I was breathless with excitement

**захва́тнический** *прил* aggressive

**захва́тчик** (-а) *м* invader

**захва́тывающий** *прил* gripping; (*вид*) breathtaking

**захлебн|у́ться** (-у́сь, -ёшься; *impf* **захлёбываться**) *сов возв* to choke

**захло́па|ть** (-ю) *сов*: ~ (**в ладо́ши**) (*зрители*) to start clapping

**захло́пн|уть** (-у; *impf* **захло́пывать**) *сов перех* to slam (shut); ~**ся** (*impf* **захло́пываться**) *сов возв* to slam (shut)

**захо́д** (-а) *м* (*также*: ~ **со́лнца**) sundown; (*в порт*) call; (*попытка*) go; **с пе́рвого/второ́го ~а** at the first/second go

**зах|оди́ть** (-ожу́, -о́дишь) *несов от* **зайти́**

**захор|они́ть** (-оню́, -о́нишь) *сов перех* to bury

**зах|оте́ть** (*как* **хоте́ть**; *см. Table 14*) *сов перех* to want; ~**ся** *сов безл*: **мне ~оте́лось есть/пить** I

started to feel hungry/thirsty

**зац|епи́ть** (-еплю́, -е́пишь; *impf* **зацепля́ть**) *сов перех* (*поддеть*) to hook up; (*разг: задеть*) to catch against; ~**ся** *сов возв*: ~**ся за** +*acc* (*задеть за*) to catch *или* get caught on; (*ухватиться за*) to grab hold of

**зача́ти|е** (-я) *ср* conception

**зача́т|ок** (-ка; *nom pl* -ки) *м* (*идеи итп*) beginning, germ *ед*

**заче́м** *нареч* why

**заче́м-то** *нареч* for some reason

**зачеркн|у́ть** (-у́, -ёшь; *impf* **зачёркивать**) *сов перех* to cross out

**зачерпн|у́ть** (-у́, -ёшь; *impf* **заче́рпывать**) *сов перех* to scoop up

**зач|еса́ть** (-ешу́, -е́шешь; *impf* **зачёсывать**) *сов перех* to comb

**зачёт** (-а) *м* (*ПРОСВЕЩ*) test; **сдава́ть** (*impf*)/**сдать** (*pf*) ~ **по фи́зике** (*BRIT*) to sit *или* take/pass a physics test

**зачётн|ый** *прил*: ~**ая рабо́та** assessed essay (*BRIT*), term paper (*US*); ~**ая кни́жка** student's record book

**зачётная кни́жка** - student's record book. This is a special booklet into which all exam marks attained by the students are entered. It is the students' responsibility to look after their own record books.

**зачи́нщик** (-а) *м* instigator

**зачи́сл|ить** (-ю, -ишь; *impf* **зачисля́ть**) *сов перех* (*в институ́т*) to enrol; (*на рабо́ту*) to take on; (*на счёт*) to enter

**зачита́|ть** (-ю; *impf* **зачи́тывать**) *сов перех* to read out

**зашёл** *сов см.* **зайти́**

**заш|и́ть** (**-ью́, -ьёшь**; *impf* **зашива́ть**) *сов перех* (*дырку*) to mend; (*шов, рану*) to stitch

**зашла́** *etc сов см.* **зайти́**

**заштопа|ть** (**-ю**) *сов от* **што́пать**

**защёлк|а** (**-и**) *ж* (*на двери*) latch

**защёлкн|уть** (**-у**; *impf* **защёлкивать**) *сов перех* to shut

**защи́т|а** (**-ы**) *ж* (*также ЮР, СПОРТ*) defence (*BRIT*), defense (*US*); (*от комаров, от пыли*) protection; (*диплома*) (public) viva

**защи|ти́ть** (**-щу́, -ти́шь**; *impf* **защища́ть**) *сов перех* to defend; (*от солнца, от комаров итп*) to protect; **~ся** (*impf* **защища́ться**) *сов возв* to defend o.s.; (*студент*) to defend one's thesis

**защи́тник** (**-а**) *м* (*также СПОРТ*) defender; (*ЮР*) defence counsel (*BRIT*), defense attorney (*US*); **ле́вый/пра́вый ~** (*футбол*) left/right back

**защи́тный** *прил* protective; **~ цвет** khaki

**защища́|ть** (**-ю**) *несов от* **защити́ть** ♦ *перех* (*ЮР*) to defend; **~ся** *несов от* **защити́ться**

**за|яви́ть** (**-явлю́, -я́вишь**; *impf* **заявля́ть**) *сов перех* (*протест*) to make ♦ *неперех*: **~ о** *+prp* to announce; **заявля́ть** (**~** *pf*) **на кого́-н в мили́цию** to report sb to the police

**зая́в|ка** (**-ки**; *gen pl* **-ок**) *ж*: **~ (на** *+acc*) application (for)

**заявле́ни|е** (**-я**) *ср* (*правительства*) statement; (*просьба*): **~ (о** *+prp*) application (for)

**заявля́|ть** (**-ю**) *несов от* **заяви́ть**

**за́|яц** (**-йца**) *м* (*ЗООЛ*) hare

**зва́ни|е** (**-я**) *ср* (*воинское*) rank; (*учёное, почётное*) title

**звать** (**зову́, зовёшь**; *pf* **позва́ть**) *несов перех* to call; (*приглашать*) to ask; (*no pf*; *называть*): **~ кого́-н кем-н** to call sb sth; **как Вас зову́т?** what is your name?; **меня́/его́ зову́т Алекса́ндр** my/his name is Alexander; **~ (позва́ть** *pf*) **кого́-н в го́сти/в кино́** to ask sb over/to the cinema

**звезд|а́** (**-ы́**; *nom pl* **звёзды**) *ж* star

**звен|е́ть** (**-ю́, -и́шь**) *несов* (*звонок*) to ring; (*голос*) to ring out; (*стаканы*) to clink

**звен|о́** (**-а́**; *nom pl* **-ья**, *gen pl* **-ьев**) *ср* link; (*конструкции*) section

**звери́ный** *прил* (wild) animal

**зве́рский** *прил* (*поступок*) brutal

**зве́рств|о** (**-а**) *ср* (*жестокость*) brutality; (*поступок*) atrocity

**зве́рств|овать** (**-ую**) *несов* to commit atrocities

**звер|ь** (**-я**; *gen pl* **-е́й**) *м* (wild) animal, beast

**звон** (**-а**) *м* clinking; (*колокола*) chime

**звон|и́ть** (**-ю́, -и́шь**; *pf* **по~**) *несов* to ring; (*ТЕЛ*): **~ кому́** to ring *или* phone *или* call (*US*) sb

**зво́нкий** *прил* sonorous

**звон|о́к** (**-ка́**; *nom pl* **-ки́**) *м* bell; (*звук*) ring; (*по телефону*) (telephone) call

**звук** (**-а**) *м* sound

**звуков|о́й** *прил* sound, audio; **~а́я доро́жка** track (*on audio tape*); **~а́я аппарату́ра** hi-fi equipment

**звукоза́пис|ь** (**-и**) *ж* sound recording

**звуч|а́ть** (*3sg* **-и́т**) *несов* (*гитара*) to sound; (*гнев*) to be heard

**зда́ни|е** (**-я**) *ср* building

**здесь** *нареч* here

**здоро́ва|ться** (**-юсь**; *pf* **по~**)

*несов возв:* ~ **с** +*instr* to say hello to

**здо́рово** *нареч (разг: отлично)* really well ♦ *как сказ (разг)* it's great

**здоро́в|ый** *прил* healthy; *(перен: идея)* sound; *(разг: большой)* hefty; **бу́дьте ~ы!** *(при прощании)* take care!; *(при чихании)* bless you!

**здоро́вь|е (-я)** *ср* health; **как Ва́ше ~?** how are you keeping?; **за Ва́ше ~!** (to) your good health!; **на ~!** enjoy it!

**здравомы́слящий** *прил* sensible

**здравоохране́ни|е (-я)** *ср* health care; **министе́рство ~я** ≈ Department of Health

**здра́вств|овать (-ую)** *несов* to thrive; **~уйте** hello; **да ~ует...!** long live ...!

**здра́вый** *прил* sound

**зе́бр|а (-ы)** *ж* zebra; *(переход)* zebra crossing *(BRIT)*, crosswalk *(US)*

**зева́|ть (-ю)** *несов* to yawn *(pf* **про~)** ♦ *перех (разг)* to miss out

**зевну́|ть (-у́, -ёшь)** *сов* to yawn

**зелене́|ть (-ю); *pf* по~)** *несов* to go *или* turn green

**зелён|ый** *прил* green

**зе́лен|ь (-и)** *ж (цвет)* green ♦ *собир (растительность)* greenery; *(овощи и травы)* greens *мн*

**земе́льный** *прил* land; **~ наде́л** *или* **уча́сток** plot of land

**землевладе́л|ец (-ьца)** *м* landowner

**землевладе́ни|е (-й)** *ср* landownership

**земледе́ли|е (-я)** *ср* arable farming

**земледе́льческий** *прил (район)* agricultural; *(машины)* farming

**землетрясе́ни|е (-я)** *ср* earthquake

**зем|ля́ (-ли́;** *acc sg* **-лю,** *nom pl* **-ли,** *gen pl* **-е́ль)** *ж* land; *(поверхность)* ground; *(почва)* earth, soil; *(планета)*: **Земля́** Earth

**земля́к (-а́)** *м* compatriot

**земляни́к|а (-и)** *ж (растение)* wild strawberry (plant) ♦ *собир (ягоды)* wild stawberries *мн*

**земно́й** *прил (поверхность, кора)* earth's; *(перен: желания)* earthly; **~шар** the globe

**зени́т (-а)** *м* zenith

**зени́тный** *прил (ВОЕН)* anti-aircraft

**зе́рк|ало (-ала;** *nom pl* **-ала́,** *gen pl* **-а́л,** *dat pl* **-ала́м)** *ср* mirror

**зерка́льный** *прил* glassy

**зерн|о́ (-а́;** *nom pl* **зёрна,** *gen pl* **зёрен)** *ср (пшеницы)* grain; *(кофе)* bean; *(мака)* seed ♦ *собир (семенное, на хлеб)* grain

**зернохрани́лищ|е (-а)** *ср* granary

**зигза́г (-а)** *м* zigzag

**зим|а́ (-ы́;** *acc sg* **-у,** *dat sg* **-е́,** *nom pl* **-ы)** *ж* winter

**зи́мний** *прил (день)* winter's; *(погода)* wintry; *(лес, одежда)* winter

**зим|ова́ть (-у́ю); *pf* про~)** *несов (человек)* to spend the winter; *(птицы)* to winter

**зимо́в|ка (-ки;** *gen pl* **-ок)** *ж* wintering place; *(для птиц)* wintering ground

**зимо́й** *нареч* in the winter

**зл|ить (-ю, -ишь); *pf* разозли́ть)** *несов перех* to annoy; **зли́ться** *(pf* **разозли́ться)** *несов возв* to get angry

**зл|о (-а;** *gen pl* **зол)** *ср* evil; *(неприятность)* harm ♦ *нареч (посмотре́ть, сказа́ть)* spitefully; **со ~а** out of spite; **меня́ ~ берёт**

(*разг*) it makes me angry; **у меня́ на неё ~а не хвата́ет** (*разг*) she annoys me no end

**зло́б|а (-ы)** ж malice; **на ~у дня** on a topical issue

**зло́бный** *прил* mean; (*улыбка*) evil; (*голос*) nasty

**злободне́вный** *прил* topical

**злове́щий** *прил* sinister

**злоде́|й (-я)** *м* villain

**злоде́йский** *прил* wicked

**злой** *прил* evil; (*собака*) vicious; (*глаза, лицо*) mean; (*карикатура*) scathing; **я зол на тебя́** I'm angry with you

**злока́чественный** *прил* malignant

**злора́дный** *прил* gloating

**зло́стный** *прил* malicious

**зло́ст|ь (-и)** ж malice

**злоупотреб|и́ть (-лю́, -и́шь;** *impf* **злоупотребля́ть**) *сов*: ~ +*instr* to abuse; (*дове́рием*) to breach

**злоупотребле́ни|е (-я)** *ср* (*обычно мн: преступле́ние*) malpractice *ед*; ~ **нарко́тиками** drug abuse; ~ **дове́рием** breach of confidence

**зме́йный** *прил* (*кожа*) snake; ~ **яд** venom

**зме́|й (-я;** *gen pl* **-ев)** *м* serpent; (*также*: **возду́шный ~**) kite

**зм|ея́ (-еи́;** *nom pl* **-е́и,** *gen pl* **-е́й**) ж snake

**знак (-а)** *м* sign, symbol; (*КОМП*) character; **в ~** +*gen* as a token of; **под зна́ком** +*gen* in an atmosphere of; ~ **ра́венства** equals sign; **зна́ки зодиа́ка** signs of the Zodiac

**знако́м|ить (-лю, -ишь;** *pf* **по~)** *несов перех*: ~ **кого́-н с** +*instr* to introduce sb to; **~ся** (*pf* **по~ся**) *несов возв*: **~ся с** +*instr* (с

челове́ком) to meet; (*pf* **о~ся**) to study

**знако́мств|о (-а)** *ср* acquaintance

**знако́м|ый** *прил*: ~ (**с** +*instr*) familiar (with) ♦ **(-ого)** *м* acquaintance

**знамена́тел|ь (-я)** *м* denominator

**знамена́тельный** *прил* momentous

**знамени́тый** *прил* famous

**зна́м|я (-ени;** *как* **вре́мя;** *см.* Table 4) *ср* banner

**зна́ни|е (-я)** *ср* knowledge *ед*; **со ~м де́ла** expertly

**зна́тный** *прил* (*род, челове́к*) noble

**знато́к (-а́)** *м* (*литерату́ры*) expert; (*вин*) connoisseur

**зна|ть (-ю)** *несов перех* to know; **как зна́ешь** as you wish; **ну, зна́ешь!** well I never!

**значе́ни|е (-я)** *ср* (*слова, взгля́да*) meaning; (*побе́ды*) importance

**зна́чит** *вводн сл* (*разг*) so ♦ *союз* (*сле́довательно*) that means

**значи́тельный** *прил* significant; (*вид, взгляд*) meaningful

**зна́ч|ить (-у, -ишь)** *несов* (*не*)*перех* to mean; **~ся** *несов возв* (*состоя́ть*) to appear

**знач|о́к (-ка́)** *м* badge; (*поме́тка*) mark

**зна́ющий** *прил* knowledgeable

**зноб|и́ть (3sg -и́т)** *несов безл*: **его́ ~и́т** he's shivery

**зно|й (-я)** *м* intense heat

**зно́йный** *прил* scorching

**зов (-а)** *м* call

**зову́** *итп несов см.* **звать**

**зодиа́к (-а)** *м* zodiac

**зол|а́ (-ы́)** ж cinders *мн*

**золо́в|ка (-ки;** *gen pl* **-ок**) ж sister-in-law, husband's sister

**золоти́стый** *прил* golden

**золо|ти́ть (-чу́, -ти́шь;** pf **по~)** несов перех to gild

**зо́лот|о (-а)** ср gold

**золото́й** прил golden; (перен: человек, время) wonderful

**Зо́лушк|а (-и)** ж Cinderella

**зо́н|а (-ы)** ж zone; (лесная) area; (для заключённых) prison camp

**зона́льный** прил (граница, деление) zone; (местный) regional

**зонд (-а)** м probe

**зонт (-а́)** м (от дождя) umbrella; (от солнца) parasol

**зо́нтик (-а)** м = зонт

**зооло́ги|я (-и)** ж zoology

**зоомагази́н (-а)** м pet shop

**зоопа́рк (-а)** м zoo

**зрач|о́к (-ка́)** м (АНАТ) pupil

**зре́лищ|е (-а)** ср sight; (представление) show

**зре́лый** прил mature; (плод) ripe

**зре́ни|е (-я)** ср (eye)sight

**зре|ть (-ю;** pf **созре́ть)** несов to mature; (плод) to ripen

**зри́мый** прил visible

**зри́тел|ь (-я)** м (в театре, в кино) member of the audience; (на стадионе) spectator; (наблюдатель) onlooker

**зри́тельный** прил (память) visual; **~ зал** auditorium

**зря** нареч (разг: без пользы) for nothing, in vain; **~ тра́тить (потра́тить** pf**) де́ньги/вре́мя** to waste money/time; **~ ты ему́ э́то сказа́л** you shouldn't have told him about it

**зуб (-а;** nom pl **-ы,** gen pl **-о́в)** м tooth; (nom pl **-ья,** gen pl **-ьев;** пилы) tooth; (грабель, вилки) prong

**зубн|о́й** прил dental; **~а́я щётка** toothbrush; **~ врач** dentist

**зубр|и́ть (-ю́, -и́шь;** impf

**вы́зубрить)** несов перех (разг) to swot

**зуд (-а)** м itch

**зы́бкий** прил shaky

**зыб|ь (-и)** ж ripple

**зят|ь (-я)** м (муж дочери) son-in-law; (муж сестры) brother-in-law

# И, и

KEYWORD

**и** союз 1 and; **я и мой друг** my friend and I; **и вот показа́лся лес** and then a forest came into sight

2 (тоже): **и он пошёл в теа́тр** he went to the theatre too; **и он не пришёл** he didn't come either

3 (даже) even; **и сам не рад** even he himself is not pleased

4 (именно): **о том и речь!** that's just it!

5 (во фразах): **ну и нагле́ц же ты!** what a cheek you have!; **туда́ и сюда́** here and there; **и ... и ...** both ... and ...

**и́в|а (-ы)** ж willow

**игл|а́ (-ы́;** nom pl **-ы)** ж needle; (ежа) spine; (проигрывателя) needle, stylus

**иглоука́лывани|е (-я)** ср acupuncture

**иго́л|ка (-ки;** gen pl **-ок)** ж = игла́

**иго́рный** прил: **~ дом** gaming club

**игр|а́ (-ы́;** nom pl **-ы)** ж game; (на скрипке итп) playing; (актёра) performance; **~ слов** play on words

**игра́льн|ый** прил: **~ые ка́рты** playing cards мн

**игра́|ть (-ю)** несов to play ♦ (pf **сыгра́ть)** перех to play; (пьесу)

to perform; ~ (**сыгра́ть** *pf*) **в** +*асс*
(*СПОРТ*) to play
**игри́стый** *прил* sparkling
**игро́в|о́й** *прил*: ~**ая ко́мната**
playroom; ~ **автома́т** fruit
machine
**игро́к** (-**а́**) *м* player
**игру́шечный** *прил* toy
**игру́ш|ка** (-    *gen pl* -**ек**) *ж* toy;
**ёлочные** ~**ки** Christmas tree
decorations
**идеализи́р|овать** (-**ую**) *(не)сов*
*перех* to idealize
**идеа́льный** *прил* ideal
**иде́йный** *прил* ideological
**идём** *несов см.* **идти́**
**идеологи́ческий** *прил*
ideological
**идеоло́ги|я** (-**и**) *ж* ideology
**идёшь** *etc несов см.* **идти́**
**иде́|я** (-**и**) *ж* idea; **по** ~**е** (*разг*)
supposedly
**идио́м|а** (-**ы**) *ж* idiom
**идио́т** (-**а**) *м* idiot
**идти́** (*см. Table 18*) *несов* to go;
(*пешко́м*) to walk; (*го́ды*) to go
by; (*фильм*) to be on; (*часы́*) to
work; (*подходи́ть: оде́жда*): ~ **к**
+*dat* to go with; **иди́ сюда́!** come
here!; **иду́!** (I'm) coming!; **идёт**
**по́езд/авто́бус** the train/bus is
coming; **идёт дождь/снег** it's
raining/snowing; **дела́ иду́т**
**хорошо́/пло́хо** things are going
well/badly; **Вам идёт э́та шля́па**
the hat suits you; ~ (**пойти́** *pf*)
**пешко́м** to walk, go on foot
**ие́н|а** (-**ы**) *ж* yen

---

**из** *предл*; +*gen* **1** (*о направлении*)
out of; **он вы́шел из ко́мнаты** he
went out of the room
**2** (*об исто́чнике*) from; **све́дения**
**из кни́ги** information from a book;

**я из Москвы́** I am from Moscow
**3** (*при выделе́нии ча́сти из*
*це́лого*) of; **вот оди́н из**
**приме́ров** here is one of the
examples
**4** (*о материа́ле*) made of; **э́тот**
**стол сде́лан из сосны́** this table is
made of pine; **ва́за из стекла́** a
glass vase; **варе́нье из я́блок**
apple jam
**5** (*о причи́не*) out of; **из**
**осторо́жности/за́висти** out of
wariness/envy; **из эконо́мии** in
order to save money
**6** (*во фра́зах*): **из го́да в год** year
in, year out; **я бежа́л изо всех**
**сил** I ran at top speed

---

**изб|а́** (-**ы́**; *nom pl* -**ы**) *ж* hut
**изба́в|ить** (-**лю**, -**ишь**; *impf*
**избавля́ть**) *сов перех*: ~ **кого́-н**
**от** +*gen* (*от пробле́м*) to free sb
from; (*от враго́в*) to deliver sb
from; ~**ся** (*impf* **избавля́ться**) *сов*
*возв*: ~**ся от** +*gen* to get rid of;
(*от стра́ха*) to get over
**избало́ванный** *прил* spoilt
**избега́|ть** (-**ю**) *несов от*
**избежа́ть** ♦ *неперех*: ~ **чего́-н**/
+*infin* to avoid sth/doing
**избежа́ть** (*как* **бежа́ть**; *см. Table*
*20*; *impf* **избега́ть**) *сов*: ~ +*gen* to
avoid
**избива́|ть** (-**ю**) *несов от* **изби́ть**
**избира́тел|ь** (-**я**) *м* voter
**избира́тельн|ый** *прил* (*систе́ма*)
electoral; ~**ая кампа́ния** election
campaign; ~ **уча́сток** polling
station; ~ **бюллете́нь** ballot paper
**избира́|ть** (-**ю**) *несов от*
**избра́ть**
**изби́ть** (-**обью́**, -**обьёшь**; *impf*
**избива́ть**) *сов перех* to beat up
**и́збранный** *прил* (*расска́зы*)
selected; (*лю́ди, круг*) select

**изб|ра́ть** (-еру́, -ерёшь; *pt* -ра́л, -рала́, -ра́ло; *impf* **избира́ть**) *сов перех* (*профессию*) to choose; (*президента*) to elect

**избы́т|ок** (-ка) *м* (*излишек*) surplus; (*обилие*) excess

**избы́точный** *прил* (*вес*) excess

**изверже́ни|е** (-я) *ср* eruption

**изве́сти|е** (-я) *ср* news; *см. также* **изве́стия**

**изве|сти́ть** (-щу́, -сти́шь; *impf* **извеща́ть**) *сов перех*: ~ кого́-н о +*prp* to inform sb of

**изве́сти|я** (-й) *мн* (*издание*) bulletin *ед*

**изве́стк|а** (-и) *ж* slaked lime

**изве́стно** *как сказ*: ~, что ... it is well known that ...; мне э́то ~ I know about it; наско́лько мне ~ as far as I know; как ~ as is well known

**изве́стност|ь** (-и) *ж* fame; ста́вить (поста́вить *pf*) кого́-н в ~ to inform sb

**изве́стный** *прил* famous, well-known; (*разг: лентяй*) notorious; (*условия*) certain

**и́звест|ь** (-и) *ж* lime

**извеща́|ть** (-ю) *несов от* **извести́ть**

**извеще́ни|е** (-я) *ср* notification

**извива́|ться** (-юсь) *несов возв* (*змея*) to slither; (*человек*) to writhe

**изви́листый** *прил* winding

**извине́ни|е** (-я) *ср* apology; (*оправдание*) excuse

**извини́тельный** *прил* (*тон, улыбка*) apologetic

**извин|и́ть** (-ю́, -и́шь; *impf* **извиня́ть**) *сов перех* (*простить*): ~ что-н (кому́-н) to excuse (sb for) sth; ~и́те! excuse me!; ~и́те, Вы не ска́жете, где вокза́л? excuse me, could you tell me where the station is?; ~ся (*impf* **извиня́ться**) *сов возв*: ~ся (за +*acc*) to apologize (for)

**извл|е́чь** (-еку́, -ечёшь *итп*, -еку́т; *pt* -ёк, -екла́, -екло́; *impf* **извлека́ть**) *сов перех* (*осколок*) to remove; (*перен*) to derive

**извраще́ни|е** (-я) *ср* distortion; полово́е ~ sexual perversion

**изги́б** (-а) *м* bend

**изгиба́|ть(ся)** (-ю(сь)) *несов от* **изогну́ть(ся)**

**изгна́ни|е** (-я) *ср* (*ссылка*) exile

**изг|на́ть** (-оню́, -о́нишь; *pt* -на́л, -нала́, -на́ло; *impf* **изгоня́ть**) *сов перех* to drive out; (*сослать*) to exile

**и́згород|ь** (-и) *ж* fence; жива́я ~ hedge

**изгото́в|ить** (-лю, -ишь; *impf* **изготовля́ть**) *сов перех* to manufacture

**изда|ва́ть** (-ю́, -ёшь) *несов от* **изда́ть**

**издалека́** *нареч* from a long way off

**и́здали** *нареч* = **издалека́**

**изда́ни|е** (-я) *ср* publication; (*изданная вещь*) edition

**изда́тел|ь** (-я) *м* publisher

**изда́тельств|о** (-а) *ср* publisher, publishing house

**изда́ть** (*как* **дать**; *см. Table 16*; *impf* **издава́ть**) *сов перех* (*книгу*) to publish; (*закон*) to issue; (*стон*) to let out

**издева́тельств|о** (-а) *ср* mockery; (*жестокое*) abuse

**издева́|ться** (-юсь) *несов возв*: ~ над +*instr* (*над подчинёнными*) to make a mockery of; (*над чьей-н одеждой*) to mock, ridicule

**изде́ли|е** (-я) *ср* (*товар*) product, article

**изде́рж|ки** (-ек) *мн* expenses *мн*;

суде́бные ~ legal costs

**изжо́г|а (-и)** ж heartburn

**из-за** предл: ~ +gen (занавески) from behind; (угла) from around; (по вине) because of; ~ того́ что because

**излага́|ть (-ю)** несов от **изложи́ть**

**излече́ни|е (-я)** ср (выздоровление) recovery

**изл|ечи́ться (-ечу́сь, -е́чишься;** impf **излечиваться)** сов возв: ~ от +gen to be cured of

**изли́ш|ек (-ка)** м (остаток) remainder; ~ +gen (веса) excess of

**изли́шний** прил unnecessary

**изложе́ни|е (-я)** ср presentation

**изл|ожи́ть (-ожу́, -о́жишь;** impf **излага́ть)** сов перех (события) to recount; (просьбу) to state

**излуча́|ть (-ю)** несов перех to radiate

**излуче́ни|е (-я)** ср radiation

**изме́н|а (-ы)** ж (родине) treason; (другу) betrayal; супру́жеская ~ adultery

**измене́ни|е (-я)** ср change; (поправка) alteration

**изм|ени́ть (-еню́, -е́нишь;** impf **изменя́ть)** сов перех to change ♦ непperex: ~ +dat (родине, другу) to betray; (супругу) to be unfaithful to; (память) to fail; **~ся** (impf **изменя́ться)** сов возв to change

**изме́нник (-а)** м traitor

**измере́ни|е (-я)** ср measurement; (величина) dimension

**измери́тельный** прил measuring

**измер|ить (-ю, -ишь)** сов от **ме́рить** ♦ (impf **измеря́ть)** перех to measure

**изму́ченный** прил (человек) worn-out; (лицо) haggard

**изму́ч|ить (-у, -ишь)** сов от **му́чить**

**измышле́ни|е (-я)** ср fabrication

**из|мя́ть (-омну́, -омнёшь)** сов от **мять**

**изна́нк|а (-и)** ж (одежды) inside; (ткани) wrong side

**изнаси́ловани|е (-я)** ср rape

**изнаси́л|овать (-ую)** сов от **наси́ловать**

**изна́шива|ть(ся) (-ю(сь))** несов от **износи́ть(ся)**

**изнемога́|ть (-ю)** несов от **изнемо́чь**

**изнеможе́ни|е (-я)** ср exhaustion

**изнем|о́чь (-огу́, -о́жешь** итп, **-о́гут;** pt **-о́г, -огла́, -огло́;** impf **изнемога́ть)** сов to be exhausted

**изно́с (-а)** м (механизмов) wear

**изн|оси́ть (-ошу́, -о́сишь;** impf **изна́шивать)** сов перех to wear out; **~ся** (impf **изна́шиваться)** сов возв to wear out

**изнури́тельный** прил exhausting

**изнур|и́ть (-ю́, -и́шь;** impf **изнуря́ть)** сов перех to exhaust

**изнутри́** нареч from inside

**изо** предл = **из**

**изоби́ли|е (-я)** ср abundance

**изобража́|ть (-ю)** несов от **изобрази́ть**

**изображе́ни|е (-я)** ср image; (действие: событий) depiction, portrayal

**изобрази́тельн|ый** прил descriptive; **~ое иску́сство** fine art

**изобра|зи́ть (-жу́, -зи́шь;** impf **изобража́ть)** сов перех to depict, portray

**изобр|ести́ (-ету́, -етёшь;** pt **-ёл, -ела́;** impf **изобрета́ть)** сов перех to invent

**изобрета́тель (-я)** м inventor

**изобрета́тельный** прил

inventive

**изобрете́ни|е (-я)** *ср* invention

**изогн|у́ть (-у́, -ёшь;** *impf* **изгиба́ть)** *сов перех* to bend; **~ся** (*impf* **изгиба́ться)** *сов возв* to bend

**изоли́рованный** *прил* (*провод*) insulated; (*комната*) separate

**изоли́р|овать (-ую)** (*не*)*сов перех* to isolate; (*вход*) to cut off; (*ТЕХ, ЭЛЕК*) to insulate

**изоля́тор (-а)** *м* (*ТЕХ, ЭЛЕК*) insulator; (*в больнице*) isolation unit

**изоля́ци|я (-и)** *ж* (*см глаг*) isolation; cutting off; insulation

**изощрённый** *прил* sophisticated

**из-под** *предл*: **~** +*gen* from under(neath); (*около*) from outside; **ба́нка ~ варе́нья** jam jar

**Изра́и|ль (-я)** *м* Israel

**израильтя́н|ин (-ина;** *nom pl* **-е)** *м* Israeli

**изра́ильский** *прил* Israeli

**и́зредка** *нареч* now and then

**изрече́ни|е (-я)** *ср* saying

**изуве́ч|ить (-у, -ишь;** *impf* **изуве́чивать)** *сов перех* to maim

**изуми́тельный** *прил* marvellous (*BRIT*), marvelous (*US*), wonderful

**изум|и́ть (-лю́, -и́шь;** *impf* **изумля́ть)** *сов перех* to amaze, astound; **~ся** (*impf* **изумля́ться)** *сов возв* to be amazed *или* astounded

**изумле́ни|е (-я)** *ср* amazement

**изумру́д (-а)** *м* emerald

**изуча́|ть (-ю)** *несов от* **изучи́ть**
♦ *перех* (*о процессе*) to study

**изуче́ни|е (-я)** *ср* study

**из|учи́ть (-учу́, -у́чишь;** *impf* **изуча́ть)** *сов перех* (*язык, предмет*) to learn; (*понять*) to get to know; (*исследовать*) to study

**изъ|яви́ть (-явлю́, -я́вишь;** *impf* **изъявля́ть)** *сов перех* to indicate

**изъя́н (-а)** *м* defect

**изъя́ть (изыму́, изы́мешь;** *impf* **изыма́ть)** *сов перех* to withdraw

**изы́сканный** *прил* refined, sophisticated

**изю́м (-а)** *м собир* raisins *мн*

**изя́щный** *прил* elegant

**ика́|ть (-ю)** *несов* to hiccup

**ико́н|а (-ы)** *ж* (*РЕЛ*) icon

**икр|а́ (-ы́)** *ж* (*чёрная, красная*) caviar(e); (*nom pl* **-ы;** *АНАТ*) calf

**ИЛ (-а)** *м сокр* = **самолёт констру́кции С.В. Илью́шина**

**ил (-а)** *м* silt

**и́ли** *союз* or; **~ ... ~ ...** either ... or ...

**иллюмина́тор (-а)** *м* (*корабля*) porthole; (*самолёта*) window

**иллюстра́ци|я (-и)** *ж* illustration

**иллюстри́р|овать (-ую;** *pf* **~** *или* **про~)** *несов перех* to illustrate

**им** *мест см.* **он; оно́; они́**

**им.** *сокр* = **и́мени**

**и́мени** *etc сущ см.* **и́мя**

**име́ни|е (-я)** *ср* estate

**имени́нник (-а)** *м person celebrating his name day or birthday*

**имени́тельный** *прил* (*ЛИНГ*): **~ паде́ж** the nominative (case)

**и́менно** *част* exactly, precisely
♦ *союз* (*перед перечислением*): **а ~** namely; **вот ~!** exactly!, precisely!

**име́|ть (-ю)** *несов перех* to have; **~** (*impf*) **ме́сто** (*событие*) to take place; **~** (*impf*) **де́ло с** +*instr* to deal with; **~** (*impf*) **в виду́** to bear in mind; (*подразумевать*) to mean; **~ся** *несов возв* (*сведения*) to be available

**и́ми** *мест см.* **они́**

**иммигра́нт (-а)** *м* immigrant

**иммиграцио́нный** *прил* immigration

**иммигра́ци|я (-и)** *ж* immigration

**иммигри́р|овать (-ую)** *(не)сов*
to immigrate

**иммуните́т (-а)** *м (МЕД, перен):* ~
**(к** +*dat*) immunity (to)

**импера́тор (-а)** *м* emperor

**импе́ри|я (-и)** *ж* empire

**и́мпорт (-а)** *м (ввоз)* importation

**импорти́р|овать (-ую)** *(не)сов*
*перех* to import

**и́мпортный** *прил* imported

**импровизи́р|овать (-ую)** *pf* ~
*или* **сымпровизи́ровать)**
*(не)сов перех* to improvise

**и́мпульс (-а)** *м* impulse

**иму́ществ|о (-а)** *ср* property;
*(принадле́жности)* belongings *мн*

**и́м|я (-ени;** *как* **вре́мя;** *см. Table*
*4) ср (также перен)* name;
*(также:* **ли́чное ~)** first *или*
Christian name; **во** +*gen (ра́ди)*
in the name of; **на** ~ +*gen*
*(письмо́)* addressed to; **от ~ени**
+*gen* on behalf of

**ина́че** *нареч (по-друго́му)*
differently ♦ *союз* otherwise, or else

**инвали́д (-а)** *м* disabled person

**инвали́дн|ый** *прил:* ~**ая коля́ска**
wheelchair; ~ **дом** home for the
disabled

**инвали́дност|ь (-и)** *ж* disability;
**получа́ть (получи́ть,** *pf)* ~**ь** to be
registered as disabled

**инвалю́т|а (-ы)** *ж сокр (=*
*иностра́нная валю́та)* foreign
currency

**инвести́р|овать (-ую)** *(не)сов*
*(не)перех (ЭКОН)* to invest

**инвести́ци|я (-и)** *ж* investment

**инде́|ец (-йца)** *м* Native American,
North American Indian

**инде́|йка (-йки;** *gen pl* **-ек)** *ж*
turkey

**и́ндекс (-а)** *м (цен, книг)* index;
*(также:* **почто́вый ~)** post *(BRIT)*
*или* zip *(US)* code

**индивидуа́льный** *прил*
individual

**инди́|ец (-йца)** *м* Indian

**инди́йский** *прил* Indian;
**Инди́йский океа́н** the Indian
Ocean

**Инди|я (-и)** *ж* India

**индустриа́льный** *прил* industrial

**индустри́|я (-и)** *ж* industry

**и́не|й (-я)** *м* hoarfrost

**ине́рци|я (-и)** *ж* inertia

**инжене́р (-а)** *м* engineer

**инициа́л|ы (-ов)** *мн* initials *мн*

**инициати́в|а (-ы)** *ж* initiative

**инициати́вн|ый** *прил*
enterprising; ~**ая гру́ппа** ≈
pressure group

**инициа́тор (-а)** *м* initiator

**инкасса́тор (-а)** *м* security guard
*(employed to collect and deliver money)*

**инкуба́тор (-а)** *м* incubator

**иногда́** *нареч* sometimes

**иногоро́дн|ий** *прил* from another
town ♦ **(-его)** *м person from another*
*town*

**ин|о́й** *прил* different ♦ *мест*
*(некоторый)* some (people); ~**ыми**
**слова́ми** in other words; **не что**
~**о́е, как ...,** **не кто ~, как ...** none
other than ...

**иномар|ка (-ки;** *gen pl* **-ок)** *ж*
foreign car

**инопланетя́н|ин (-ина;** *nom pl*
**-е)** *м* alien

**иноро́дн|ый** *прил* alien; ~**ое**
**те́ло** *(МЕД)* foreign body

**иностра́н|ец (-ца)** *м* foreigner

**иностра́нн|ый** *прил* foreign;
**Министе́рство** ~**ых дел** Ministry
of Foreign Affairs, ≈ Foreign Office
*(BRIT),* ≈ State Department *(US)*

**инспекти́р|овать (-ую;** *pf* **про~)**
*несов перех* to inspect

**инспе́ктор (-а)** *м* inspector

**инспе́кци|я (-и)** *ж* inspection

**инста́нци|я** (-и) ж authority

**инсти́нкт** (-а) м instinct

**институ́т** (-а) м institute

**инструкти́р|овать** (-ую; pf **про~**) (не)сов перех to instruct

**инстру́кци|я** (-и) ж instructions мн; (также: ~ **по эксплуата́ции**) instructions (for use)

**инструме́нт** (-а) м instrument

**инсули́н** (-а) м insulin

**инсу́льт** (-а) м (МЕД) stroke

**инсцени́р|овать** (-ую) (не)сов перех (роман) to adapt

**интегра́ци|я** (-и) ж integration

**интелле́кт** (-а) м intellect

**интеллектуа́л** (-а) м intellectual

**интеллектуа́льный** прил intellectual

**интеллиге́нт** (-а) м member of the intelligentsia

**интеллиге́нтный** прил cultured and educated

**интеллиге́нци|я** (-и) ж собир the intelligentsia

**интенси́вный** прил intensive; (окраска) intense

**интерва́л** (-а) м interval

**интервью́** ср нескл interview

**интервьюи́р|овать** (-ую; pf **про~**) (не)сов перех to interview

**интере́с** (-а) м: ~ (**к** +dat) interest (in)

**интере́сно** нареч: **он о́чень ~ расска́зывает** he is very interesting to listen to ♦ как сказ: ~(, **что ...**) it's interesting (that ...); **мне э́то о́чень ~** I find it very interesting; ~, **где он э́то нашёл** I wonder where he found that

**интере́сный** прил interesting; (внешность, женщина) attractive

**интерес|ова́ть** (-у́ю) несов перех to interest; ~**ся** несов возв: ~**ся** +instr to be interested in; (осведомляться) to inquire after;

**он ~ова́лся, когда́ ты приезжа́ешь** he was asking when you would be arriving

**интерна́т** (-а) м boarding school

**интернациона́льный** прил international

**Интерне́т** (-а) м Internet

**интерпрета́ци|я** (-и) ж interpretation

**интерье́р** (-а) м (здания) interior

**инти́мный** прил intimate

**интона́ци|я** (-и) ж intonation; (недовольная итп) note

**интри́г|а** (-и) ж (политическая) intrigue; (любовная) affair

**интриг|ова́ть** (-у́ю; pf **за~**) несов перех to intrigue

**интуити́вный** прил intuitive

**интуи́ци|я** (-и) ж intuition

**Интури́ст** (-а) м сокр (= Гла́вное управле́ние по иностра́нному тури́зму) Russian tourist agency dealing with foreign tourism

**интури́ст** (-а) м сокр = **иностра́нный тури́ст**

**инфа́ркт** (-а) м (также: ~ **миока́рда**) heart attack

**инфекцио́нный** прил infectious

**инфе́кци|я** (-и) ж infection

**инфинити́в** (-а) м infinitive

**инфля́ци|я** (-и) ж (ЭКОН) inflation

**информацио́нн|ый** прил information; ~**ая програ́мма** news programme (BRIT) или program (US)

**информа́ци|я** (-и) ж information

**информи́р|овать** (-ую; pf ~ или **про~**) несов перех to inform

**инфраструкту́р|а** (-ы) ж infrastructure

**инциде́нт** (-а) м incident

**инъе́кци|я** (-и) ж injection

**иня́з** (-а) м сокр (= факульте́т иностра́нных языко́в) modern languages department

**и.о.** *сокр* (= исполня́ющий обя́занности) acting

**Иорда́ни|я (-и)** ж Jordan

**ипоте́к|а (-и)** ж (*КОММ*) mortgage

**ипоте́чн|ый** *прил* mortgage; **~ая ссу́да** mortgage; **~ банк** ≈ building society

**ипподро́м (-а)** м racecourse (*BRIT*), racetrack (*US*)

**Ира́к (-а)** м Iraq

**Ира́н (-а)** м Iran

**и́рис (-а)** м (*БОТ*) iris

**ирла́нд|ец (-ца)** м Irishman

**Ирла́нди|я (-и)** ж Ireland

**ирла́нд|ка (-ки;** *gen pl* **-ок)** ж Irishwoman

**ионизи́р|овать (-ую)** *несов*: ~ (**над** +*instr*) to be ironic (about)

**иро́ни|я (-и)** ж irony

**иск (-а)** м lawsuit; **предъявля́ть (предъяви́ть** *pf*) **кому́-н ~** to take legal action against sb

**искажа́|ть(ся) (-ю(сь))** *несов от* **искази́ть(ся)**

**искаже́ни|е (-я)** *ср* distortion

**иска|зи́ть (-жу́, -зи́шь;** *impf* **искажа́ть)** *сов перех* (*факты*) to distort; (*лицо́*) to contort; **~ся** (*impf* **искажа́ться)** *сов возв* to be distorted; (*го́лос*) to contort

**иска́ть (ищу́, и́щешь)** *несов перех* to look *или* search for

**исключе́ни|е (-я)** *ср* (*из спи́ска*) exclusion; (*из институ́та*) expulsion; (*отклоне́ние*) exception; **за ~** +*gen* with the exception of; **де́лать (сде́лать** *pf*) **что-н в ви́де ~я** to make an exception of sth

**исключи́тельно** *нареч* (*осо́бенно*) exceptionally; (*то́лько*) exclusively

**исключи́тельный** *прил* exceptional

**исключ|и́ть (-у́, -и́шь;** *impf* **исключа́ть)** *сов перех* to exclude;

(*из институ́та*) to expel; (*оши́бку*) to exclude the possibility of; **э́то ~ено́** that is out of the question

**иско́нный** *прил* (*населе́ние, язы́к*) native, original; (*пра́во*) intrinsic

**ископа́ем|ое (-ого)** *ср* fossil; (*та́кже*: **поле́зное ~**) mineral

**искорен|и́ть (-ю́, -и́шь;** *impf* **искореня́ть)** *сов перех* to eradicate

**и́скр|а (-ы)** ж spark

**и́скренне** *нареч* sincerely; **~ Ваш** Yours sincerely

**и́скренний** *прил* sincere

**и́скренност|ь (-и)** ж sincerity

**искрив|и́ть (-лю́, -и́шь;** *impf* **искривля́ть)** *сов перех* to bend

**искупа́|ть(ся) (-ю(сь))** *сов от* **купа́ть(ся)**

**иск|упи́ть (-уплю́, -у́пишь;** *impf* **искупа́ть)** *сов перех* to atone for

**иску́сный** *прил* (*рабо́тник*) skilful (*BRIT*), skillful (*US*); (*рабо́та*) fine

**иску́сственный** *прил* artificial; (*ткань*) synthetic; (*мех*) fake

**иску́сств|о (-а)** *ср* art

**искуша́|ть (-ю)** *несов перех* to tempt

**искуше́ни|е (-я)** *ср* temptation

**исла́м (-а)** м Islam

**исла́мский** *прил* Islamic

**Исла́нди|я (-и)** ж Iceland

**испа́н|ец (-ца)** м Spaniard

**Испа́ни|я (-и)** ж Spain

**испаре́ни|е (-я)** *ср* (*де́йствие: воды́*) evaporation; (*обы́чно мн: проду́кт*) vapour *ед* (*BRIT*), vapor *ед* (*US*)

**испар|и́ться (3sg -и́тся,** *сов возв* (*impf* **испаря́ться)** to evaporate

**испа́чка|ть(ся) (-ю(сь))** *сов от* **па́чкать(ся)**

**испове́дани|е (-я)** *ср* denomination

**исповедник** (-a) *м* (*РЕЛ*) confessor

**исповед|овать** (-ую) *несов перех* (*религию, идею*) to profess
♦ (*не*)*сов перех* (*РЕЛ*): ~ **кого-н** to hear sb's confession; ~**ся** (*не*)*сов возв*: ~**ся кому-н** *или* у **кого-н** to confess to sb

**исповед|ь** (-и) *ж* confession

**исполком** (-a) *м сокр* (= **исполнительный комитет**) executive committee

**исполнени|е** (-я) *ср* (*приказа*) execution; (*обещания*) fulfilment (*BRIT*), fulfillment (*US*); (*роли*) performance

**исполнитель** (-я) *м* (*роли*) performer; **судебный** ~ bailiff

**исполнительный** *прил* (*власть*) executive; (*работник*) efficient

**исполн|ить** (-ю, -ишь; *impf* **исполнять**) *сов перех* (*приказ*) to carry out; (*обещание*) to fulfil (*BRIT*), fulfill (*US*); (*роль*) to perform; ~**ся** (*impf* **исполняться**) *сов возв* (*желание*) to be fulfilled; **ему** ~**илось 10 лет** he is 10

**использовани|е** (-я) *ср* use

**использ|овать** (-ую) (*не*)*сов перех* to use

**исправ|ить** (-лю, -ишь; *impf* **исправлять**) *сов перех* (*повреждение*) to repair; (*ошибку*) to correct; (*характер*) to improve; ~**ся** (*impf* **исправляться**) *сов возв* (*человек*) to change (for the better)

**исправлени|е** (-я) *ср* (*повреждения*) repairing; (*преступника*) reforming; (*текста*) correction

**исправный** *прил* (*механизм*) in good working order

**испуг** (-a) *м* fright; **в** ~**e**, **с** ~**у** in *или* with fright

**испуганный** *прил* frightened

**испуга|ть(ся)** (-ю(сь)) *сов от* **пугать(ся)**

**испытани|е** (-я) *ср* (*машины*) testing

**испытательный** *прил*: ~ **срок** trial period, probation

**испыта|ть** (-ю; *impf* **испытывать**) *сов перех* (*механизм*) to test; (*нужду, радость*) to experience

**исследовани|е** (-я) *ср* (*см глаг*) research; examination; (*научный труд*) study

**исследователь** (-я) *м* researcher

**исследовательск|ий** *прил*: ~**ая работа** research; ~ **институт** research institute

**исслед|овать** (-ую) (*не*)*сов перех* to research; (*больного*) to examine

**исся́к|нуть** (*3sg* -**нет**, *pt* -, -**ла**; *impf* **иссякать**) *сов* (*запасы*) to run dry; (*перен: терпение*) to run out

**истека́|ть** (-ю) *несов от* **истечь**

**истерик|а** (-и) *ж* hysterics *мн*

**истеричный** *прил* hysterical

**ист|ец** (-ца) *м* plaintiff

**ист|ечь** (*3sg* -**ечёт**, *pt* -**ёк**, -**екла**, -**екло́**; *impf* **истекать**) *сов* (*срок*) to expire; (*время*) to run out

**истинный** *прил* true

**исток** (-a) *м* (*реки*) source

**историк** (-a) *м* historian

**исторический** *прил* historical; (*важный*) historic; ~ **факультет** history department

**истори|я** (-и) *ж* (*наука*) history; (*рассказ*) story

**источник** (-a) *м* (*водный*) spring; (*сил*) source

**истощени|е** (-я) *ср* exhaustion

**истощённый** *прил* (*человек*) malnourished; (*вид*) drained истра́|тить (-чу, -тишь) *сов от* тра́тить

истреби́тел|ь (-я) *м* (*самолёт*) fighter (plane); (*лётчик*) fighter pilot

истреб|и́ть (-лю́, -и́шь; *impf* истребля́ть) *сов перех* to destroy; (*крыс*) to exterminate

исхо́д (-а) *м* outcome

исх|оди́ть (-ожу́, -о́дишь) *несов*: ~ из +*gen* (*сведения*) to originate from; (*основываться*) to be based on; ~одя́ из +*gen или от* +*gen* on the basis of

исхо́дный *прил* primary

исходя́щий *прил* outgoing; ~ но́мер (*АДМИН*) reference number

исчéз|нуть (-ну, -нешь; *pt* -, -ла; *impf* исчеза́ть) *сов* to disappear

исчéрпа|ть (-ю; *impf* исчéрпывать) *сов перех* to exhaust

исчéрпывающий *прил* exhaustive

исчисля́|ться (*3pl* -ются) *несов возв*: ~ +*instr* to amount to

ита́к *союз* thus, hence

Ита́ли|я (-и) *ж* Italy

италья́н|ец (-ца) *м* Italian

италья́нский *прил* Italian; ~ язы́к Italian

и т.д. *сокр* (= и так да́лее) etc.

ито́г (-а) *м* (*работы итп*) result; (*общая сумма*) total; в ~е (*при подсчёте*) in total; в (коне́чном) ~е in the end; подводи́ть (подвести́ *pf*) ~и to sum up

итого́ *нареч* in total, altogether

ито́говый *прил* (*сумма*) total

и т.п. *сокр* (= и тому́ подо́бное) etc.

иудаи́зм (-а) *м* Judaism

их *мест см.* они́ ♦ *притяж мест* their

и́хн|ий *притяж мест* (*разг*) their;

по ~ему (in) their way

ищу́ *итп несов см.* иска́ть

июл|ь (-я) *м* July

июн|ь (-я) *м* June

# Й, й

йо́г|а (-и) *ж* yoga

йо́гурт (-а) *м* yoghurt

йод (-а) *м* iodine

# К, к

KEYWORD

к *предл*; +*dat* 1 (*о направлении*) towards; я пошёл к до́му I went towards the house; звать (позва́ть *pf*) кого́-н к телефо́ну to call sb to the phone; мы пое́хали к друзья́м we went to see friends; поста́вь ле́стницу к стене́ put the ladder against the wall

2 (*о добавлении, включении*) to; э́та ба́бочка отно́сится к о́чень ре́дкому ви́ду this butterfly belongs to a very rare species

3 (*об отношении*) of; любо́вь к му́зыке love of music; он привы́к к хоро́шей еде́ he is used to good food; к моему́ удивле́нию to my surprise

4 (*назначение*) with; припра́вы к мя́су seasonings for meat

каба́н (-а́) *м* (*дикий*) wild boar

кабач|о́к (-ка́) *м* marrow (*BRIT*), squash (*US*)

ка́бел|ь (-я) *м* cable

каби́н|а (-ы) *ж* (*телефонная*) booth; (*грузовика*) cab;

(*самолёта*) cockpit; (*лифта*) cage
**кабинет** (**-а**) *м* (*в доме*) study;
(*на работе*) office; (*школьный*)
classroom; (*врача*) surgery (*BRIT*),
office (*US*); (*ПОЛИТ: также*: ~
**министров**) cabinet
**каблук** (**-а**) *м* heel
**кавалери|я** (**-и**) *ж* cavalry
**Кавказ** (**-а**) *м* Caucasus
**кавказ|ец** (**-ца**) *м* Caucasian
**кавыч|ки** (**-ек**; *dat pl* **-кам**) *мн*
inverted commas *мн*, quotation
marks *мн*
**кадр** (**-а**) *м* (*ФОТО, КИНО*) shot
**кадр|ы** (**-ов**) *мн* (*работники*)
personnel *ед*, staff *ед*
**каждый** *прил* each, every
**каз|ак** (**-ака**; *nom pl* **-аки**) *м*
Cossack
**казарм|а** (**-ы**) *ж* barracks *мн*
**ка|заться** (**-жусь, -жешься**; *pf*
**по~**) *несов возв*: ~ +*instr* to look,
seem; (**мне**) **кажется, что ...** it
seems (to me) that ...
**казачий** *прил* Cossack
**казино** *ср нескл* casino
**казн|а** (**-ы**) *ж* treasury
**казн|ить** (**-ю, -ишь**) (*не*)*сов*
*перех* to execute
**казн|ь** (**-и**) *ж* execution
**ка|йма** (**-ймы**; *nom pl* **-ймы**, *gen pl*
**-ём**) *ж* hem

---
KEYWORD
---

**как** *местоимённое нареч* **1**
(*вопросительное*) how; **как Вы
себя чувствуете**? how do you
feel?; **как дела**? how are things?;
**как тебя зовут**? what's your
name?
**2** (*относительное*): **я сделал, как
ты просил** I did as you asked; **я не
знаю, как это могло случиться** I
don't know how that could have
happened

**3** (*насколько*): **как быстро/давно**
how quickly/long ago
**4** (*до какой степени*): **как
красиво**! how beautiful!; **как
жаль**! what a pity *или* shame!
**5** (*выражает возмущение*) what
♦ *союз* **1** (*подобно*) as; **мягкий,
как вата** as soft as cotton wool;
**как можно скорее/громче** as
soon/loud as possible; **он одет,
как бродяга** he is dressed like a
tramp
**2** (*в качестве*) as
**3** (*о временных отношениях: о
будущем, об одновременности*)
when; (: *о прошлом*) since; **как
закончишь, позвони мне** phone
(*BRIT*) *или* call (*US*) me when you
finish; **прошло два года, как она
исчезла** two years have passed
since she disappeared
**4**: **как будто, как бы** as if; **он
согласился как бы нехотя** he
agreed as if unwillingly; **как же** of
course; **как говорят** *или*
**говорится** as it were; **как ни**
however; **как никак** after all; **как
раз вовремя/то, что надо** just in
time/what we need; **это платье/
пальто мне как раз** this dress/
coat is just my size; **как ..., так и ...**
both ... and ...; **как только** as soon
as

**какао** *ср нескл* cocoa
**как-либо** *нареч* = **как-нибудь**
**как-нибудь** *нареч* (*так или
иначе*) somehow; (*когда-нибудь*)
sometime
**как-никак** *нареч* after all

---
KEYWORD
---

**как|ой** (**-ая, -ое, -ие**) *мест* **1**
(*вопросительное*) what; **какой
тебе нравится цвет**? what colour

do you like?

2 (*относительное*) which; **скажи́, кака́я кни́га интере́снее** tell me which book is more interesting

3 (*выража́ет оце́нку*) what; **како́й подле́ц!** what a rascal!

4 (*разг: неопределённое*) any; **нет ли каки́х вопро́сов?** are there any questions?

5 (*во фра́зах*): **ни в каку́ю** not for anything; **каки́м о́бразом** in what way

**како́й-либо** *мест* = **како́й-нибудь**

**как|о́й-нибудь** *мест* (*тот или ино́й*) any; (*приблизи́тельно*) some; **он и́щет ~ рабо́ты** he's looking for any kind of work

**как|о́й-то** *мест*: **Вам ~о́е-то письмо́** there's a letter for you; (*напомина́ющий*): **она́ ~а́я-то стра́нная сего́дня** she is acting kind of oddly today

**ка́к-то** *мест* (*каки́м-то о́бразом*) somehow; (*в не́которой сте́пени*) somewhat; (*разг*): **~ (раз)** once

**ка́ктус** (-а) *м* cactus

**кале́к|а** (-и) *м/ж* cripple

**календа́р|ь** (-я́) *м* calendar

**кале́ч|ить** (-у, -ишь; *pf* **по~** *или* **ис~**) *несов перех* to cripple; (*ми́на*) to maim

**кали́бр** (-а) *м* calibre (*BRIT*), caliber (*US*)

**ка́ли|й** (-я) *м* potassium

**кали́т|ка** (-ки; *gen pl* -ок) *ж* gate

**кало́ри|я** (-и) *ж* calorie

**калькуля́тор** (-а) *м* calculator

**ка́льци|й** (-я) *м* calcium

**ка́мбал|а** (-ы) *ж* flatfish

**камене́|ть** (-ю) *несов от* **окамене́ть**

**ка́менный** *прил* stone

**ка́менщик** (-а) *м* bricklayer

**ка́м|ень** (-ня; *gen pl* -не́й) *м* stone

**ка́мер|а** (-ы) *ж* (*тюре́мная*) cell; (*та́кже*: **теле~, кино~**) camera; **~ хране́ния** (*на вокза́ле*) left-luggage office (*BRIT*), checkroom (*US*); (*в музе́е*) cloakroom

**ка́мерный** *прил*: **~ая му́зыка** chamber music

**ками́н** (-а) *м* fireplace

**кампа́ни|я** (-и) *ж* campaign

**камы́ш** (-а́) *м* rushes *мн*

**кана́в|а** (-ы) *ж* ditch

**Кана́д|а** (-ы) *ж* Canada

**кана́л** (-а) *м* canal; (*СВЯЗБ ТЕЛ, перен*) channel

**канализацио́нн|ый** *прил*: **~ая труба́** sewer pipe

**канализа́ци|я** (-и) *ж* sewerage

**кана́т** (-а) *м* cable

**кана́тн|ый** *прил*: **~ая доро́га** cable car

**кандида́т** (-а) *м* candidate; (*ПРОСВЕЩ*): **~ нау́к** ≈ Doctor

**кандидату́р|а** (-ы) *ж* candidacy; **выставля́ть (вы́ставить** *pf*) **чью-н ~у** to nominate sb

**кани́кул|ы** (-) *мн* holidays *мн* (*BRIT*), vacation *ед* (*US*)

**кани́стр|а** (-ы) *ж* jerry can

**кано́э** *ср нескл* canoe

**кану́н** (-а) *м* eve; **в ~** +*gen* on the eve of

**канцеля́ри|я** (-и) *ж* office

**канцеля́рский** *прил* office

**ка́па|ть** (-ю) *несов* (*вода́*) to drip ♦ (*pf* **на~**) *перех*: **~ что-н** (*миксту́ру*) to pour sth out drop by drop

**капе́лл|а** (-ы) *ж* (*МУЗ*) choir

**ка́пельниц|а** (-ы) *ж* (*МЕД*) drip

**капита́л** (-а) *м* (*КОММ*) capital

**капитали́зм** (-а) *м* capitalism

**капиталисти́ческий** *прил* capitalist

**капиталовложе́ни|я** (-й) *мн*

capital investment *ед*

**капитáльный** *прил* (*ЭКОН, КОММ*) capital; (*сооружение, труд*) main; (*ремонт, покупка*) major

**капитáн** (**-а**) *м* captain

**капитули́р|овать** (**-ую**) (*не*)*сов* to capitulate

**капкáн** (**-а**) *м* trap

**кáп|ля** (**-ли**; *gen pl* **-ель**) *ж* (*также перен*) drop

**капóт** (**-а**) *м* (*АВТ*) bonnet (*BRIT*), hood (*US*)

**каприз** (**-а**) *ж* caprice, whim

**капри́знича|ть** (**-ю**) *несов* to behave capriciously

**капри́зный** *прил* (*человек*) capricious

**капрóн** (**-а**) *м* synthetic thread

**кáпсул|а** (**-ы**) *ж* capsule

**капýст|а** (**-ы**) *ж* cabbage; **цветнáя ~** cauliflower

**капюшóн** (**-а**) *м* hood

**карáбка|ться** (**-юсь**; *pf* **вс~**) *несов возв*: **~ на** +*асс* (*человек*) to clamber up

**карáкулевый** *прил* astrakhan

**карамéл|ь** (**-и**) *ж собир* (*леденцы*) caramels *мн*

**карандáш** (**-á**; *gen pl* **-éй**) *м* pencil

**карантин** (**-а**) *м* quarantine

**карá|ть** (**-ю**; *pf* **по~**) *несов перех* to punish

**караýл** (**-а**) *м* guard

**караýл|ить** (**-ю, -ишь**) *несов перех* to guard

**карбюрáтор** (**-а**) *м* carburettor (*BRIT*), carburetor (*US*)

**кардинáльный** *прил* cardinal, of cardinal importance

**кардиóлог** (**-а**) *м* cardiologist, heart specialist

**кардиолóги|я** (**-и**) *ж* cardiology

**кáрий** *прил* (*глаза*) hazel

**карикатýр|а** (**-ы**) *ж* caricature

**каркáс** (**-а**) *м* framework (*of building*)

**кáрка|ть** (**-ю**) *несов* to caw

**кáрлик** (**-а**) *м* dwarf

**кармáн** (**-а**) *м* pocket

**кармáнн|ый** *прил* (*деньги, часы*) pocket; **~ нож** pocketknife; **~ые расхóды** petty expenses

**карнавáл** (**-а**) *м* carnival

**карни́з** (**-а**) *м* (*для штор*) curtain rail

**карп** (**-а**) *м* carp

**кáрт|а** (**-ы**) *ж* (*ГЕО*) map; (*также*: **игрáльная ~**) (playing) card; **магни́тная ~** (swipe)card

**карти́н|а** (**-ы**) *ж* picture

**карти́н|ка** (**-ки**; *gen pl* **-ок**) *ж* (*иллюстрация*) picture (*in book etc*)

**картóн** (**-а**) *м* (*бумага*) cardboard

**картотéк|а** (**-и**) *ж* card index

**картóфелин|а** (**-ы**) *ж* potato

**картóфел|ь** (**-я**) *м* (*плод*) potatoes *мн*

**картóфельный** *прил* potato

**кáрточ|ка** (**-ки**; *gen pl* **-ек**) *ж* card; (*также*: **фóто~**) photo

**картóш|ка** (**-ки**; *gen pl* **-ек**) *ж* (*разг*) = **картóфелина**, **картóфель**

**кáртридж** (**-а**) *м* (*КОМП*) cartridge

**карусéл|ь** (**-и**) *ж* merry-go-round (*BRIT*), carousel (*US*)

**карьéр|а** (**-ы**) *ж* career

**касá|ться** (**-юсь**; *pf* **коснýться**) *несов возв*: **~** +*gen* (*дотрагиваться*) to touch; (*затрагивать*) to touch on; (*иметь отношение*) to concern; **э́то тебя не ~ется** it doesn't concern you; **что ~ется Вас, то ...** as far as you are concerned ...

**кáс|ка** (**-ки**; *gen pl* **-ок**) *ж* helmet

**каспи́йск|ий** *прил*: **Каспи́йское мóре** Caspian Sea

**кáсс|а** (**-ы**) *ж* (*ТЕАТР, КИНО*) box office; (*железнодорожная*) ticket office; (*в магазине*) cash desk

**кассе́т|а** (-ы) *ж* (*магнитофонная*) cassette; (*ФОТО*) cartridge

**касси́р** (-а) *м* cashier

**кастрю́л|я** (-и) *ж* saucepan

**катало́г** (-а) *м* catalogue (*BRIT*), catalog (*US*)

**ката́р** (-а) *м* catarrh

**катастро́ф|а** (-ы) *ж* disaster

**катастрофи́ческий** *прил* catastrophic, disastrous

**ката́|ть** (-ю) *несов перех* (*что-н круглое*) to roll; (*что-н на колёсах*) to wheel; ~ (*impf*) **кого́-н на маши́не** to take sb for a drive; **~ся** *несов возв*: **ката́ться на маши́не/велосипе́де** to go for a drive/cycle; **~ся** (*impf*) **на конька́х/ло́шади** to go skating/horse (*BRIT*) *или* horseback (*US*) riding

**категори́чный** *прил* categorical

**катего́ри|я** (-и) *ж* category

**ка́тер** (-а) *м* boat

**ка|ти́ть** (-чу́, -тишь) *несов перех* (*что-н круглое*) to roll; (*что-н на колёсах*) to wheel; **~ся** *несов возв* to roll; (*капли*) to run

**кат|о́к** (-ка́) *м* ice *или* skating rink; (*ТЕХ: также*: **асфа́льтовый ~**) steamroller

**като́лик** (-а) *м* Catholic

**католи́ческий** *прил* Catholic

**кату́ш|ка** (-ки; *gen pl* -ек) *ж* spool

**кафе́** *ср нескл* café

**ка́федр|а** (-ы) *ж* (*ПРОСВЕЩ*) department; (*РЕЛ*) pulpit; **заве́дующий ~ой** chair

**ка́фел|ь** (-я) *м собир* tiles *мн*

**ка́фельн|ый** *прил* (*пол*) tiled; **~ая пли́тка** (ceramic) tile

**кафете́ри|й** (-я) *м* cafeteria

**кача́|ть** (-ю) *несов перех* (*колыбель*) to rock; (*нефть*) to pump; **~** (*impf*) **голово́й** to shake one's head; **~ся** *несов возв* to

swing; (*на волнах*) to rock, roll

**каче́л|и** (-ей) *мн* swing *ед*

**ка́чественный** *прил* qualitative; (*товар, изделие*) high-quality

**ка́честв|о** (-а) *ср* quality ♦ *предл*: **в ~е** +*gen* as; **в ~е приме́ра** by way of example

**ка́ш|а** (-и) *ж* ≈ porridge

**ка́ш|ель** (-ля) *м* cough

**ка́шля|ть** (-ю) *несов* to cough

**кашта́н** (-а) *м* chestnut

**каю́т|а** (-ы) *ж* (*МОР*) cabin

**ка́|яться** (-юсь, -ешься; *pf* **по~**) *несов возв*: **~** (**в чём-н пе́ред кем-н**) to confess (sth to sb); (*pf* **рас~**; *грешник*) to repent

**кв.** *сокр* (= **квадра́тный**) sq.; (= **кварти́ра**) Apt.

**квадра́т** (-а) *м* square

**квадра́тный** *прил* square

**ква́ка|ть** (*3sg* -ет) *несов* to croak

**квалифика́ци|я** (-и) *ж* qualification; (*специальность*) profession

**квалифици́рованный** *прил* (*работник*) qualified; (*труд*) skilled

**кварта́л** (-а) *м* quarter

**кварте́т** (-а) *м* quartet

**кварти́р|а** (-ы) *ж* flat (*BRIT*), apartment (*US*); (*снимаемое жильё*) lodgings *мн*

**квартира́нт** (-а) *м* lodger

**квартпла́т|а** (-ы) *ж сокр* (= **кварти́рная пла́та**) rent (*for a flat*)

**квас** (-а) *м* kvass (*malted drink*)

**ква́шен|ый** *прил*: **~ая капу́ста** sauerkraut, pickled cabbage

**квита́нци|я** (-и) *ж* receipt

**кг** *сокр* (= **килогра́мм**) kg

**КГБ** *м сокр* (*ИСТ*) (= **Комите́т госуда́рственной безопа́сности**) KGB

**ке́д|ы** (-) *мн* pumps *мн*

**кекс** (-а) *м* (fruit)cake

**кем** *мест см.* **кто**

**ке́мпинг** (-а) *м* camping site, campsite

**ке́п|ка** (-ки; *gen pl* -ок) *ж* cap

**кера́мик|а** (-и) *ж собир* ceramics *мн*

**керами́ческий** *прил* ceramic

**кефи́р** (-а) *м* kefir (*yoghurt drink*)

**кива́|ть** (-ю) *несов*: ~ +*dat* to nod to

**кивн|у́ть** (-у́, -ёшь) *сов*: ~ (+*dat*) to nod (to)

**кида́|ть** (-ю) *несов от* **ки́нуть**; ~**ся** *несов от* **ки́нуться ♦** *возв*: ~**ся камня́ми** to throw stones at each other

**ки́ллер** (-а) *м* hitman

**килогра́мм** (-а) *м* kilogram(me)

**киломе́тр** (-а) *м* kilometre (*BRIT*), kilometer (*US*)

**кинематогра́фи|я** (-и) *ж* cinematography

**кино́** *ср нескл* cinema; (*разг*: *фильм*) film, movie (*US*); **идти́ (пойти́** *pf*) **в** ~ (*разг*) to go to the pictures (*BRIT*) *или* movies (*US*)

**киноактёр** (-а) *м* (film) actor

**киноактри́с|а** (-ы) *ж* (film) actress

**кинокарти́н|а** (-ы) *ж* film

**кинотеа́тр** (-а) *м* cinema

**кинофи́льм** (-а) *м* film

**ки́н|уть** (-у; *impf* **кида́ть**) *сов перех* (*камень*) to throw; (*взгляд*) to cast; (*друзей*) to desert; (*разг*: *обману́ть*) to cheat; ~**ся** (*impf* **кида́ться**) *сов возв*: ~**ся на** +*acc* (*на врага́*) to attack; (*на еду́*) to fall upon

**кио́ск** (-а) *м* kiosk

**ки́п|а** (-ы) *ж* bundle

**кипе́ни|е** (-я) *ср* boiling

**кип|е́ть** (-лю́, -и́шь; *pf* **вс~**) *несов* (*вода́*) to boil; (*стра́сти*) to run high

**кипя|ти́ть** (-чу́, -ти́шь; *pf* **вс~**) *несов перех* to boil; ~**ся** *несов*

возв (*овощи*) to boil

**кипят|о́к** (-ка́) *м* boiling water

**кипячёный** *прил* boiled

**кирпи́ч** (-а́) *м* brick

**кислоро́д** (-а) *м* oxygen

**кисл|ота́** (-оты́; *nom pl* -о́ты) *ж* acid

**ки́сл|ый** *прил* sour; ~**ая капу́ста** sauerkraut

**ки́с|нуть** (-ну; *pt* -, -ла; *pf* **про~** *или* **с~**) *несов* to go off

**кист|ь** (-и) *ж* (*АНАТ*) hand; (*гроздь: ряби́ны*) cluster; (*: виногра́да*) bunch; (*на ска́терти итп*) tassel; (*худо́жника, маля́ра*) (paint)brush

**кит** (-а́) *м* whale

**кита́|ец** (-йца) *м* Chinese

**Кита́|й** (-я) *м* China

**кита́йский** *прил* Chinese; ~ **язы́к** Chinese

**кише́чник** (-а) *м* intestines *мн*

**киш|ка́** (-ки́; *gen pl* -о́к, *dat pl* -ка́м) *ж* gut, intestine

**клавиату́р|а** (-ы) *ж* keyboard

**кла́виш|а** (-и) *ж* key

**клад** (-а) *м* treasure

**кла́дбищ|е** (-а) *ср* cemetery

**кладо́в|ка** (-ки; *gen pl* -ок) *ж* (*разг*) cubby-hole

**клад|у́** *etc несов см.* **класть**

**клад|ь** (-и) *ж*: **ручна́я** ~ hand luggage

**клал** *etc несов см.* **класть**

**кла́ня|ться** (-юсь; *pf* **поклони́ться**) *несов возв*: ~ +*dat* to bow to

**кла́пан** (-а) *м* valve

**класс** (-а) *м* class; (*комната*) classroom

**кла́ссик|а** (-и) *ж* classics *мн*

**классифици́р|овать** (-ую) (*не*)*сов перех* to classify

**класси́ческий** *прил* (*пример, работа*) classic; (*музыка,* литература) classical

**кла́ссный** *прил* (ПРОСВЕЩ) class;
(*разг: хороший*) cool

**кла|сть** (-ду́, -дёшь; *pt* -л, -ла; *pf*
**положи́ть**) *несов перех* to put;
(*pf* **сложи́ть**; *фундамент*) to lay

**кл|ева́ть** (-юю́) *несов перех*
(*подлеж: птица*) to peck ♦
*непереx* (*рыба*) to bite

**клевет|а́** (-ы́) *ж* (*устная*) slander;
(*письменная*) libel

**клев|ета́ть** (-ещу́, -е́щешь; *pf*
**на~**) *несов:* ~ **на** +*acc* (*см сущ*) to
slander; to libel

**клеён|ка** (-ки; *gen pl* -ок) *ж*
oilcloth

**кле́|ить** (-ю, -ишь; *pf* **с~**) *несов*
*перех* to glue; **~ся** *несов возв* to
stick

**кле|й** (-я) *м* glue

**кле́йк|ий** *прил* sticky; **~ая ле́нта**
sticky tape

**клейм|о́** (-а́; *nom pl* -а) *ср* stamp;
(*на скоте, на осуждённом*)
brand; **~ позо́ра** stigma

**клён** (-а) *м* maple (tree)

**кле́т|ка** (-ки; *gen pl* -ок) *ж* (*для*
*птиц, животных*) cage; (*на*
*ткани*) check; (*на бумаге*) square;
(*БИО*) cell; **ткань в ~ку** checked
material

**кле́тчатый** *прил* (*ткань итп*)
chequered (*BRIT*), checked

**клёш** *прил неизм:* **брю́ки ~** flares;
**ю́бка ~** flared skirt

**клешн|я́** (-и́; *gen pl* -е́й) *ж* claw,
pincer

**кле́щ|и** (-е́й) *мн* tongs *мн*

**клие́нт** (-а) *м* client

**клиенту́р|а** (-ы) *ж собир* clientèle

**кли́зм|а** (-ы) *ж* enema

**кли́макс** (-а) *м* (*БИО*) menopause

**кли́мат** (-а) *м* (*также перен*)
climate

**клин** (-а; *nom pl* -ья, *gen pl* -ьев) *м*
wedge

**кли́ник|а** (-и) *ж* clinic

**кли́пс|ы** (-ов) *мн* clip-on earrings
*мн*

**кли́ринговый** *прил* (*КОММ*)
clearing

**кли́ч|ка** (-ки; *gen pl* -ек) *ж* (*кошки*
*итп*) name; (*человека*) nickname

**клише́** *ср нескл* (*перен*) cliché

**кло|к** (-ка́; *nom pl* -чья, *gen pl*
-чьев) *м* (*волос*) tuft; (*ваты*) wad

**клони́р|овать** (-ую) (*не*)*сов*
*перех* to clone

**клон|и́ть** (-ю́, -ишь) *несов:* **его́**
**~и́ло ко сну** he was drifting off (to
sleep); **к чему́ ты кло́нишь?** what
are you getting *или* driving at?

**кло́ун** (-а) *м* clown

**клоч|о́к** (-ка́) *м уменьш от* **клок**;
(*земли*) plot; (*бумаги*) scrap

**клуб** (-а) *м* club; (*nom pl* -ы́;
*обычно мн: дыма, пыли*) cloud

**клуб|и́ться** (*3sg* -и́тся) *несов*
*возв* to swirl

**клубни́к|а** (-и) *ж собир* (*ягоды*)
strawberries *мн*

**клуб|о́к** (-ка́) *м* (*шерсти*) ball

**клу́мб|а** (-ы) *ж* flowerbed

**клык** (-а́) *м* (*животного*) fang

**клюв** (-а) *м* beak

**клю́кв|а** (-ы) *ж собир* (*ягоды*)
cranberries *мн*

**клю́н|уть** (-у) *сов перех* to peck

**ключ** (-а́) *м* (*также перен*) key;
(*родник*) spring; (*МУЗ*): **басо́вый/**
**скрипи́чный ~** bass/treble clef;
**га́ечный ~** spanner

**ключево́й** *прил* (*главный*) key

**клю́ш|ка** (-ки; *gen pl* -ек) *ж*
(*ХОККЕЙ*) hockey stick; (*ГОЛБФ*)
club

**кля́|сться** (-ну́сь, -нёшься; *pt*
-лся, -ла́сь; *pf* **по~**) *несов возв*
to swear; ~ (**по~** *pf*) **в чём-н** to
swear sth

**кля́тв|а (-ы)** ж oath

**км.** *сокр* (= **киломе́тр**) km

**кни́г|а (-и)** ж book

**кни́ж|ка (-ки;** *gen pl* **-ек)** ж уменьш от **кни́га;** (*разг*) book; **трудова́я ~** employment record book; **че́ковая ~** chequebook (*BRIT*), checkbook (*US*)

**кни́жный** *прил*: **~ магази́н** bookshop

**кни́зу** *нареч* downwards

**кно́п|ка (-ки;** *gen pl* **-ок)** ж (*звонка*) button; (*канцелярская*) drawing pin (*BRIT*), thumbtack (*US*); (*застёжка*) press stud, popper (*BRIT*)

**КНР** ж *сокр* (= **Кита́йская Наро́дная Респу́блика**) PRC

**княз|ь (-я;** *nom pl* **-ья́,** *gen pl* **-е́й)** м prince (*in Russia*)

**ко** *предл см.* **к**

**кобы́л|а (-ы)** ж mare

**кова́рный** *прил* devious

**ков|ёр (-ра́)** м carpet

**ко́врик (-а)** м rug; (*дверной*) mat; (*КОМП*) mouse mat

**ковш| (-а́)** м ladle

**ковыря́|ть (-ю)** *несов перех* to dig up; **~** (*impf*) **в зуба́х/носу́** to pick one's teeth/nose

**когда́** *нареч* when; **~ как** it depends

**когда́-либо** *нареч* = **когда́-нибудь**

**когда́-нибудь** *нареч* (*в вопросе*) ever; (*в утверждении*) some *или* one day; **Вы ~ там бы́ли?** have you ever been there?; **я ~ туда́ пое́ду** I'll go there some *или* one day

**когда́-то** *нареч* once

**кого́** *мест от* **кто**

**ко́г|оть (-тя;** *gen pl* **-те́й)** м claw

**код (-а)** м code

**ко́декс (-а)** м code

**коди́р|овать (-ую;** *pf* **за~)** *несов перех* to encode, code

**ко́е-где** *нареч* here and there

**ко́е-как** *нареч* (*небрежно*) any old how; (*с трудом*) somehow

**ко́е-како́й (ко́е-како́го)** *мест* some

**ко́е-кто́ (ко́е-кого́)** *мест* (*некоторые*) some (people)

**ко́е-что́ (ко́е-чего́)** *мест* (*нечто*) something; (*немногое*) a little

**ко́ж|а (-и)** ж skin; (*материал*) leather

**ко́жаный** *прил* leather

**ко́жн|ый** *прил*: **~ые боле́зни** skin diseases

**кожур|а́ (-ы́)** ж (*апельсина итп*) peel

**коз|а́ (-ы́;** *nom pl* **-ы)** ж (nanny) goat

**коз|ёл (-ла́)** м (billy) goat

**Козеро́г (-а)** м (*созвездие*) Capricorn

**ко́|йка (-йки;** *gen pl* **-ек)** ж (*в казарме*) bunk; (*в больнице*) bed

**кока́ин (-а)** м cocaine

**коке́тливый** *прил* flirtatious

**коке́тнича|ть (-ю)** *несов* to flirt

**коклю́ш (-а)** м whooping cough

**кокте́йл|ь (-я)** м cocktail

**кол (-а́;** *nom pl* **-ья)** м stake

**колбас|а́ (-ы́)** ж sausage

**колго́т|ки (-ок)** *мн* tights *мн* (*BRIT*), pantihose *мн* (*US*)

**колд|ова́ть (-у́ю)** *несов* to practise (*BRIT*) *или* practice (*US*) witchcraft

**колду́н (-а́)** м sorcerer, wizard

**колеба́ни|е (-я)** *ср* (*маятника*) swing; (*почвы, здания*) vibration; (*перен: цен*) fluctuation

**кол|еба́ть (-е́блю, -е́блешь)** *несов перех* to rock, swing; (*pf* **по~;** *авторитет*) to shake; **~ся** *несов возв* (*ФИЗ*) to oscillate;

(*пламя итп*) to flicker; (*цены*) to fluctuate; (*сомневаться*) to waver

**коле́н|о** (**-а**; *nom pl* **-и**, *gen pl* **-ей**) *cp* knee

**кол|есо́** (**-еса́**; *nom pl* **-ёса**) *cp* wheel

**колея́** (**-и́**) *ж* (*на доро́ге*) rut; (*железнодоро́жная*) track

**коли́честв|о** (**-а**) *cp* quantity

**ко́лкост|ь** (**-и**) *ж* (*насме́шка*) biting remark

**колле́г|а** (**-и**) *м/ж* colleague

**колле́ги|я** (**-и**) *ж*: **адвока́тская ~** ≈ the Bar; **редакцио́нная ~** editorial board

**колле́дж** (**-а**) *м* college

**коллекти́в** (**-а**) *м* collective

**коллекти́вный** *прил* collective

**коллекциони́р|овать** (**-ую**) *несов перех* to collect

**колле́кци|я** (**-и**) *ж* collection

**коло́д|а** (**-ы**) *ж* (*бревно́*) block; (*карт*) pack, deck

**коло́д|ец** (**-ца**) *м* well; (*в ша́хте*) shaft

**ко́локол** (**-а**; *nom pl* **-á**) *м* bell

**колоко́льчик** (**-а**) *м* bell; (*БОТ*) bluebell

**колониа́льный** *прил* colonial

**коло́ни|я** (**-и**) *ж* colony; **исправи́тельно-трудова́я ~** penal colony

**коло́н|ка** (**-ки**; *gen pl* **-ок**) *ж* column; (*га́зовая*) water heater; (*для воды́, для бензи́на*) pump

**коло́нн|а** (**-ы**) *ж* (*АРХИТ*) column

**колори́т** (**-а**) *м* (*перен: эпо́хи*) colour (*BRIT*), color (*US*)

**колори́тный** *прил* colourful (*BRIT*), colorful (*US*)

**ко́л|ос** (**-оса**; *nom pl* **-о́сья**, *gen pl* **-о́сьев**) *м* ear (*of corn, wheat*)

**колосса́льный** *прил* colossal

**кол|оти́ть** (**-очу́**, **-о́тишь**) *несов*: **~ по столу́/в дверь** to thump the table/on the door; **~ся** *несов возв* (*се́рдце*) to thump

**кол|о́ть** (**-ю́**, **-ешь**; *pf* **рас~**) *несов перех* (*дрова́*) to chop (up); (*оре́хи*) to crack; (*pf* **за~**; *штыко́м итп*) to spear; (*pf* **у~**; *иго́лкой*) to prick; (*разг: де́лать уко́л*): **~ кого́-н** to give sb an injection; **~** (*impf*) **кому́-н что́-н** (*разг*) to inject sb with sth; **у меня́ ко́лет в боку́** I've got a stitch; **~ся** *несов возв* (*ёж, шипо́вник*) to be prickly; (*наркома́н*) to be on drugs

**колыбе́льн|ая** (**-ой**) *ж* (*также*: **~ пе́сня**) lullaby

**кольцев|о́й** *прил* round, circular; **~а́я доро́га** ring road; **~а́я ли́ния** (*в метро́*) circle line

**коль|цо́** (**-ьца́**; *nom pl* **-ьца**, *gen pl* **-е́ц**) *cp* ring; (*в маршру́те*) circle

**колю́ч|ий** *прил* (*куст*) prickly; **~ая про́волока** barbed wire

**колю́ч|ка** (**-ки**; *gen pl* **-ек**) *ж* thorn

**коля́с|ка** (**-ки**; *gen pl* **-ок**) *ж*: (**де́тская**) **~** pram (*BRIT*), baby carriage (*US*); **инвали́дная ~** wheelchair

**ком** *мест см.* **кто ♦** (**-а**; *nom pl* **-ья**, *gen pl* **-ьев**) *м* lump

**кома́нд|а** (**-ы**) *ж* command; (*су́дна*) crew; (*СПОРТ*) team

**команди́р** (**-а**) *м* commander, commanding officer

**командиро́в|ка** (**-ки**; *gen pl* **-ок**) *ж* (*коро́ткая*) business trip; (*дли́тельная*) secondment (*BRIT*), posting

**кома́ндовани|е** (**-я**) *cp*: **~** (*+instr*) (*су́дном, во́йском*) command (of) **♦** *собир* command

**кома́нд|овать** (**-ую**; *pf* **с~**) *несов* to give orders; **~** (*impf*) *+instr* (*а́рмией*) to command; (*му́жем*) to order around

**кома́ндующ|ий** (**-его**) *м*

commanding officer, commander

**кома́р (-а́)** м mosquito

**комба́йн (-а)** м (С.-Х.) combine (harvester); **ку́хонный ~** food processor

**комбина́т (-а)** м plant

**комбина́ци|я (-и)** ж combination; (женское бельё) slip

**комбинезо́н (-а)** м overalls мн; (детский) dungarees мн

**комбини́р|овать (-ую;** pf **с~)** несов перех to combine

**коме́ди́йный** прил comic; (актёр) comedy

**коме́ди|я (-и)** ж comedy

**коме́т|а (-ы)** ж comet

**ко́мик (-а)** м comedian, comic

**комиссио́нный** прил: **~ магази́н** second-hand shop which sells goods on a commission basis

**коми́сси|я (-и)** ж commission

**комите́т (-а)** м committee

**ко́мка|ть (-ю;** pf **с~)** несов перех to crumple

**коммента́ри|й (-я)** м commentary

**коммента́тор (-а)** м commentator

**коммент́и́р|овать (-ую)** (не)сов перех (текст) to comment on; (матч) to commentate on

**коммерса́нт (-а)** м businessman

**комме́рческий** прил commercial; **~ магази́н** privately-run shop

**коммуна́льн|ый** прил communal; **~ые платежи́** bills; **~ые услу́ги** utilities

**коммуна́льные услу́ги** - The communal services include water supply, hot water and heating, public radio, rubbish collection and street sweeping, and building maintenance. All these are paid for on a standing charge basis.

Electricity and telephone are metered and hence paid for separately.

**коммуни́зм (-а)** м communism

**коммуника́ци|я (-и)** ж communication

**коммуни́ст (-а)** м communist

**ко́мнат|а (-ы)** ж room

**ко́мнатн|ый** прил indoor; **~ая температу́ра** room temperature; **~ое расте́ние** house plant

**компа́кт-ди́ск (-а)** м compact disc

**компа́ктный** прил compact

**компа́ни|я (-и)** ж (КОММ) company; (друзья) group of friends

**компаньо́н (-а)** м (КОММ) partner

**компа́рти|я (-и)** ж сокр (= коммунисти́ческая па́ртия) Communist Party

**ко́мпас (-а)** м compass

**компенса́ци|я (-и)** ж compensation

**компенси́р|овать (-ую)** (не)сов перех: **~ (кому́-н)** to compensate (sb) for

**компете́нтный** прил (человек) competent; (органы) appropriate

**ко́мплекс (-а)** м complex; (мер) range

**ко́мплексный** прил integrated

**компле́кт (-а)** м set

**компле́кт|овать (-у́ю;** pf **у~)** несов перех to build up

**комплиме́нт (-а)** м compliment

**компози́тор (-а)** м composer

**компоне́нт (-а)** м component

**компости́р|овать (-ую;** pf **за~)** сов перех to punch или clip (ticket)

**компо́т (-а)** м compote

**компре́сс (-а)** м.(МЕД) compress

**компромети́р|овать (-ую;** pf **с~)**

*несов перех* to compromise
**компроми́сс** (-а) *м* compromise
**компью́тер** (-а) *м* computer
**компью́терщик** (-а) *м* (*разг*)
computer specialist
**кому́** *мест см.* **кто**
**комфо́рт** (-а) *м* comfort
**комфорта́бельный** *прил*
comfortable
**конве́йер** (-а) *м* conveyor (belt)
**конве́рси**|**я** (-и) *ж* conversion
**конве́рт** (-а) *м* envelope
**конверти́р**|**овать** (-ую) *(не)сов*
*перех* (*деньги*) to convert
**конверти́руемый** *прил*
convertible
**конво́**|**й** (-я) *м* escort
**конгре́сс** (-а) *м* (*съезд*) congress
**конди́терск**|**ая** (-ой) *ж*
confectioner's
**конди́терский** *прил*
confectionery; **~ магази́н**
confectioner's
**кондиционе́р** (-а) *м* air
conditioner
**кон**|**ёк** (-ька́) *м* (*обычно мн,*
*СПОРТ*) skate; **ката́ться** *(impf)* **на**
**~ька́х** to skate; *см. также* **коньки́**
**кон**|**е́ц** (-ца́) *м* end; **без ~ца́**
endlessly; **в ~це́ ~цо́в** in the end;
**биле́т в оди́н ~** single (*BRIT*) *или*
one-way ticket; **под ~** towards the
end
**коне́чно** *вводн сл* of course,
certainly
**коне́чност**|**ь** (-и) *ж* (*АНАТ*) limb
**коне́чный** *прил* (*цель, итог*)
final; (*станция*) last
**конкре́тно** *нареч* (*говорить*)
specifically; (*именно*) actually
**конкре́тный** *прил* (*реальный*)
concrete; (*факт*) actual
**конкуре́нт** (-а) *м* competitor
**конкурентоспосо́бный** *прил*
competitive

**конкуре́нци**|**я** (-и) *ж* competition
**конкури́р**|**овать** (-ую) *несов:* **~**
**с** +*instr* to compete with
**ко́нкурс** (-а) *м* competition
**консе́нсус** (-а) *м* consensus
**консервати́вный** *прил*
conservative
**консерва́тор** (-а) *м* conservative
**консервато́ри**|**я** (-и) *ж* (*МУЗ*)
conservatoire (*BRIT*), conservatory
(*US*)
**консерви́р**|**овать** (-ую) *(не)сов*
*перех* to preserve; (*в жестяных*
*банках*) to can
**консе́рвн**|**ый** *прил:* **~ая ба́нка**
can
**консе́рв**|**ы** (-ов) *мн* canned food
*ед*
**конспе́кт** (-а) *м* notes *мн*
**конспекти́р**|**овать** (-ую; *pf* **за~**)
*несов перех* to take notes on
**конспира́ци**|**я** (-и) *ж* conspiracy
**конститу́ци**|**я** (-и) *ж* constitution
**констру́ир**|**овать** (-ую; *pf* **с~**)
*несов перех* to construct
**констру́ктор** (-а) *м* designer;
(*детская игра*) construction set
**констру́кторск**|**ий** *прил:* **~ое**
**бюро́** design studio
**констру́кци**|**я** (-и) *ж* construction
**ко́нсул** (-а) *м* consul
**ко́нсульств**|**о** (-а) *ср* consulate
**консульта́нт** (-а) *м* consultant
**консульта́ци**|**я** (-и) *ж* (*у врача, у*
*юриста*) consultation;
(*учреждение*) consultancy;
**же́нская ~** ≈ gynaecological and
antenatal (*BRIT*) *или* gynecological
and prenatal (*US*) clinic
**консульти́р**|**овать** (-ую; *pf*
**про~**) *несов перех* to give
professional advice to; **~ся** (*impf*
**про~ся**) *несов возв:* **~ся с**
**кем-н** to consult sb
**конта́кт** (-а) *м* contact

**контáктный** *прил* (*ли́нзы*)
contact; ~ **телефóн** contact
number

**контéйнер** (-а) *м* container

**контéкст** (-а) *м* context

**контингéнт** (-а) *м* contingent

**континéнт** (-а) *м* continent

**контóр|а** (-ы) *ж* office

**контóрский** *прил* office

**контрабáнд|а** (-ы) *ж* smuggling;
(*товáры*) contraband

**контрабанди́ст** (-а) *м* smuggler

**контрабáс** (-а) *м* double bass

**контрáкт** (-а) *м* contract

**контрáктный** *прил* contractual

**контрáст** (-а) *м* contrast

**контрацепти́в** (-а) *м*
contraceptive

**контролёр** (-а) *м* (*в пóезде*)
(ticket) inspector; (*театрáльный*)
≈ usher; (*сберкáссы*) cashier

**контроли́р|овать** (-ую) *несов
перех* to control

**контрóл|ь** (-я) *м* (*наблюдéние*)
monitoring; (*провéрка*) testing,
checking; (*в трáнспорте*) ticket
inspection; (*в магази́не*) checkout

**контрóльн|ая** (-ой) *ж* (*тáкже*: ~
**рабóта**) class test

**контрóльн|ый** *прил*: ~**ая
коми́ссия** inspection team; ~**ые
ци́фры** control figures

**контрразвéдк|а** (-и) *ж*
counterespionage

**кóнтур** (-а) *м* contour

**конур|á** (-ы́) *ж* (*собáчья*) kennel

**кóнус** (-а) *м* cone

**конферансьé** *ср нескл* compère

**конферéнц-зáл** (-а) *м* conference
room

**конферéнци|я** (-и) *ж* conference

**конфéт|а** (-ы) *ж* sweet

**конфиденциáльный** *прил*
confidential

**конфиск|овáть** (-у́ю) (*не*)*сов*

*перех* to confiscate

**конфли́кт** (-а) *м* (*вое́нный*)
conflict; (*в семьé, на рабóте*)
tension

**конфликт|овáть** (-у́ю) *несов*: ~
**с** +*instr* (*разг*) to be at loggerheads
with

**конфóр|ка** (-ки; *gen pl* -**ок**) *ж* ring
(*on cooker*)

**конфронтáци|я** (-и) *ж*
confrontation

**концентрáци|я** (-и) *ж*
concentration

**концентри́р|овать** (-ую; *pf* **с**~)
*несов перех* to concentrate; ~**ся**
(*pf* **с**~**ся**) *несов возв* (*капитáл*) to
be concentrated; (*ученик*) to
concentrate

**концéпци|я** (-и) *ж* concept

**концéрн** (-а) *м* (*ЭКОН*) concern

**концéрт** (-а) *м* concert

**концлáгер|ь** (-я; *nom pl* -**я́**) (=
*концентрацио́нный лáгерь*)
concentration camp

**конча́|ть(ся)** (-ю(сь)) *несов от*
**кóнчить(ся)**

**кóнчик** (-а) *м* tip (*of finger etc*)

**кóнч|ить** (-у, -ишь; *impf*
**конча́ть**) *сов перех* to end;
(*университéт, кни́гу, рабóту*) to
finish; ~**ся** (*impf* **конча́ться**) *сов
возв* (*разговóр, кни́га*) to end,
finish; (*запáсы*) to run out; (*лес
итп*) to end

**кон|ь** (-я́; *nom pl* -**и**, *gen pl* -**éй**) *м*
(*лóшадь*) horse; (*ШÁХМАТЫ*)
knight

**коньк|и́** (-óв) *мн* skates *мн*

**конья́к** (-á) *м* brandy, cognac

**конъюнкту́р|а** (-ы) *ж* (*КОММ*)
situation; ~ **ры́нка** market
conditions

**кооперати́в** (-а) *м* cooperative;
(*разг*: *кварти́ра*) flat in housing
cooperative; **жили́щный** ~

cooperative (*form of house or flat ownership*)

**кооперати́вный** *прил* cooperative; ~ **магази́н** *или* **ларёк** co-op

**коопера́тор (-а)** *м member of private enterprise*

**коопера́ци|я (-и)** *ж* cooperative enterprise

**координа́т|а (-ы)** *ж* (*ГЕОМ, обычно мн*) coordinate; (*разг: адрес*) number (and address)

**координи́р|овать (-ую)** (*не*)*сов перех* to coordinate

**копа́|ть (-ю)** *несов перех* (*землю*) to dig; (*pf* **вы́копать**; *колодец*) to sink; (*овощи*) to dig up; **~ся** *несов возв* (*в чужих вещах*) to snoop about; (*разг: возиться*) to dawdle

**копе́йка (-йки;** *gen pl* **-ек)** *ж* kopeck

**копира́йт (-а)** *м* copyright

**копирова́льн|ый** *прил*: **~ая маши́на** photocopying machine, photocopier; **~ая бума́га** carbon paper

**копи́р|овать (-ую;** *pf* **с~)** *несов перех* to copy

**коп|и́ть (-лю́, -ишь;** *pf* **на~** *или* **с~)** *несов перех* to save; **~ся** (*pf* **на~ся** *или* **с~ся)** *несов возв* to accumulate

**ко́пи|я (-и)** *ж* copy; (*перен: о человеке*) spitting image

**ко́пот|ь (-и)** *ж* layer of soot

**коп|ти́ть (-чу́, -ти́шь)** *несов* (*лампа*) to give off soot ♦ (*pf* **за~)** *перех* (*мясо, рыбу*) to smoke

**копчёный** *прил* smoked

**копы́т|о (-а)** *ср* hoof

**копь|ё (-я́;** *nom pl* **-я,** *gen pl* **-ий)** *ср* spear; (*СПОРТ*) javelin

**кор|а́ (-ы́)** *ж* (*дерева*) bark; **земна́я ~** the earth's crust

**кораблекруше́ни|е (-я)** *ср* shipwreck

**кораблестрое́ни|е (-я)** *ср* shipbuilding

**кора́бл|ь (-я́)** *м* ship

**кора́лл (-а)** *м* coral

**кордебале́т (-а)** *м* corps de ballet

**коренн|о́й** *прил* (*население*) indigenous; (*вопрос, реформы*) fundamental; **~ым о́бразом** fundamentally; **~ зуб** molar

**ко́р|ень (-ня;** *nom pl* **-ни,** *gen pl* **-не́й)** *м* root; **в ~не** fundamentally

**кореш|о́к (-ка́)** *м* (*переплёта*) spine

**Коре́|я (-и)** *ж* Korea

**корзи́н|а (-ы)** *ж* basket

**коридо́р (-а)** *м* corridor

**кори́ц|а (-ы)** *ж* cinnamon

**кори́чневый** *прил* brown

**ко́р|ка (-ки;** *gen pl* **-ок)** *ж* (*апельсинная*) peel

**корм (-а;** *nom pl* **-а́)** *м* (*для скота*) fodder, feed; (*диких животных*) food

**корм|а́ (-ы́)** *ж* stern

**корми́л|ец (-ьца)** *м* breadwinner

**корм|и́ть (-лю́, -ишь;** *pf* **на~)** *несов перех*: **~ кого́-н чем-н** to feed sb sth; (*pf* **про~;** *содержать*) to feed, keep; **~** (*impf*) **гру́дью** to breast-feed; **~ся** (*pf* **про~ся)** *несов возв* (*животное*) to feed; (*человек*): **~ся** +*instr* to survive

**коро́б|ка (-ки;** *gen pl* **-ок)** *ж* box; **~ скоросте́й** gearbox

**коро́в|а (-ы)** *ж* cow

**короле́в|а (-ы)** *ж* queen

**короле́вский** *прил* royal

**короле́вств|о (-а)** *ср* kingdom

**коро́л|ь (-я́)** *м* king

**коро́н|а (-ы)** *ж* crown

**коро́н|ка (-ки;** *gen pl* **-ок)** *ж* (*на зубе*) crown

**корон|ова́ть (-у́ю)** (*не*)*сов перех*

to crown

**коро́тк|ий** *прил* short; **~ие во́лны** short wave; **~ое замыка́ние** short circuit

**ко́ротко** *нареч* briefly; (*стричься*) short ♦ *как сказ*: **э́то пла́тье мне ~** this dress is too short for me

**коро́че** *сравн нареч*: **~ говоря́** to put it briefly, in short

**корпора́ци|я (-и)** *ж* corporation

**ко́рпус (-а;** *nom pl* **-ы)** *м* body; (*самолёта*) fuselage; (*nom pl* **-а́;** *судна, здания*) frame; (*здание*) block; (*дипломатический*) corps

**корректи́в (-а)** *м* amendment

**корректи́р|овать (-ую;** *pf* **от~)** *несов перех* (*ошибку*) to correct

**корреспонде́нт (-а)** *м* correspondent

**корреспонде́нци|я (-и)** *ж* correspondence

**корро́зи|я (-и)** *ж* corrosion

**коррумпи́рованный** *прил* corrupt

**корру́пци|я (-и)** *ж* corruption

**корт (-а)** *м* (tennis) court

**ко́рточ|ки (-ек)** *мн*: **присе́сть на ~** to squat down; **сиде́ть** (*impf*) **на ~ках** to squat

**корч|ева́ть (-у́ю)** *несов перех* to uproot; (*перен*) to root out

**ко́рч|иться (-усь, -ишься;** *pf* **с~)** *несов возв* (*от боли*) to double up

**кор|ь (-и)** *ж* measles *мн*

**коря́вый** *прил* (*дерево*) gnarled

**кос|а́ (-ы́;** *acc sg* **-у,** *dat sg* **-е́,** *nom pl* **-ы)** *ж* (*волосы*) plait; (*орудие*) scythe

**ко́свенный** *прил* indirect; (*дополнение, падеж*) oblique

**коси́л|ка (-ки;** *gen pl* **-ок)** *ж* mower (*machine*)

**ко|си́ть (-шу́, -сишь;** *pf* **с~)** *несов перех* (*газон, сено*) to mow; (*глаза*) to slant

**косме́тик|а (-и)** *ж* make-up ♦ *собир* cosmetics *мн*

**космети́ческий** *прил* cosmetic; **~ кабине́т** beauty salon

**космети́ч|ка (-ки;** *gen pl* **-ек)** *ж* (*специалистка*) beautician; (*сумочка*) make-up bag

**косми́ческ|ий** *прил* space; **~ое простра́нство** (outer) space

**космона́вт (-а)** *м* cosmonaut; (*в США итп*) astronaut

**ко́смос (-а)** *м* the cosmos

**косн|у́ться (-у́сь, -ёшься)** *сов от* **каса́ться**

**косогла́зый** *прил* cross-eyed

**косо́й** *прил* (*глаза*) squinty; (*дождь, лучи*) slanting

**кост|ёр (-ра́)** *м* campfire

**костля́вый** *прил* bony

**ко́стный** *прил* (*АНАТ*): **~ мозг** (bone) marrow

**ко́сточ|ка (-ки;** *gen pl* **-ек)** *ж* (*абрикосовая, вишнёвая*) stone; (*винограда*) seed; (*лимона*) pip

**костыл|ь (-я́)** *м* (*инвалида*) crutch

**кост|ь (-и;** *gen pl* **-е́й)** *ж* bone

**костю́м (-а)** *м* outfit; (*на сцене*) costume; (*пиджак и брюки/юбка*) suit

**костя́ш|ка (-ки;** *gen pl* **-ек)** *ж* (*пальцев*) knuckle

**косы́н|ка (-ки;** *gen pl* **-ок)** *ж* (triangular) scarf

**кося́к (-а́)** *м* (*двери*) jamb; (*рыб*) school, shoal

**кот (-а́)** *м* tomcat

**кот|ёл (-ла́)** *м* (*паровой*) boiler

**котел|о́к (-ка́)** *м* (*кастрюля*) billy(can); (*шляпа*) bowler (hat) (*BRIT*), derby (*US*)

**коте́льн|ая (-ой)** *ж* boilerhouse

**кот|ёнок (-ёнка;** *nom pl* **-я́та,** *gen pl* **-я́т)** *м* kitten

**ко́тик** (**-а**) м (*тюлень*) fur seal
**коти́р|оваться** (**-уюсь**) несов
возв (*КОММ*): **~** (**в** +*acc*) to be
quoted (at); (*также перен*) to be
highly valued
**котле́т|а** (**-ы**) ж rissole; (*также*:
**отбивна́я ~**) chop

---
KEYWORD
---

**кото́р|ый** (**-ая, -ое, -ые**) мест 1
(*вопросительное*) which;
**кото́рый час?** what time is it?
2 (*относительное*: *о предмете*)
which; (: *о человеке*) who;
**же́нщина, кото́рую я люблю́** the
woman I love
3 (*не первый*): **кото́рый день/
год мы не ви́делись** we haven't
seen each other for many days/
years

---

**ко́фе** м нескл coffee; **~ в зёрнах**
coffee beans
**кофева́р|ка** (**-ки**; *gen pl* **-ок**) ж
percolator
**кофе́йник** (**-а**) м coffeepot
**кофе́йный** прил coffee
**кофемо́л|ка** (**-ки**; *gen pl* **-ок**) ж
coffee grinder
**ко́фт|а** (**-ы**) ж blouse;
(*шерстяная*) cardigan
**коча́н** (**-а́**) м: **~ капу́сты** cabbage
**кочене́|ть** (**-ю**; *pf* **о~**) несов
(*руки*) to go stiff; (*человек*) to get
stiff
**коша́чий** прил (*мех, лапа*) cat's
**кошел|ёк** (**-ька́**) м purse
**ко́ш|ка** (**-ки**; *gen pl* **-ек**) ж cat
**кошма́р** (**-а**) м nightmare
**кошма́рный** прил nightmarish
**коэффицие́нт** (**-а**) м coefficient
**краб** (**-а**) м crab
**краево́й** прил regional
**кра́ж|а** (**-и**) ж theft; **~ со взло́мом**
burglary

**кра|й** (**-я**; *loc sg* **-ю́**, *nom pl* **-я́**, *gen pl*
**-ёв**) м edge; (*чашки, коробки*)
rim; (*местность*) land; (*ПОЛИТ*)
krai (*regional administrative unit*)
**кра́йне** нареч extremely
**кра́йн|ий** прил extreme; (*дом*)
end; (*пункт маршрута*) last, final;
**в ~ем слу́чае** as a last resort; **по
~ей ме́ре** at least; **Кра́йний
Се́вер** the Arctic; **~ срок** (final)
deadline
**кран** (**-а**) м tap, faucet (*US*);
(*СТРОИТ*) crane
**крапи́в|а** (**-ы**) ж nettle
**краси́вый** прил beautiful;
(*мужчина*) handsome; (*решение,
фраза*) fine
**краси́тел|ь** (**-я**) м dye
**кра́|сить** (**-шу, -сишь**; *pf* **по~**)
несов перех to paint; (*волосы*) to
dye; (*pf* **на~**; *губы итп*) to make
up; **~ся** (*pf* **на~ся**) несов возв to
wear make-up
**кра́с|ка** (**-ки**; *gen pl* **-ок**) ж paint;
(*обычно мн: нежные, весенние
итп*) colour (*BRIT*), color (*US*)
**красне́|ть** (**-ю**; *pf* **по~**) несов to
turn red; (*от стыда*) to blush,
flush; (*от гнева*) to go red
**красноречи́вый** прил (*оратор,
письмо*) eloquent; (*взгляд, жест*)
expressive; (*факты*) revealing
**кра́сн|ый** прил red; **~ая ры́ба**
salmon; **~ая строка́** new
paragraph
**крас|ота́** (**-оты́**; *nom pl* **-о́ты**) ж
beauty
**кра́сочный** прил colourful (*BRIT*),
colorful (*US*)
**кра|сть** (**-ду́, -дёшь**; *pf* **укра́сть**)
несов перех to steal; **кра́сться**
несов возв (*человек*) to creep,
steal
**кра́тер** (**-а**) м crater
**кра́тк|ий** прил short; (*беседа*)

brief, short; **~ое прилага́тельное** short-form adjective

**краткоvре́менный** *прил* short; **~ дождь** shower

**краткосро́чный** *прил* short; (*заём, ссуда*) short-term

**кра́тный** *прил* divisible

**крах** (-а) *м* collapse

**крахма́л** (-а) *м* starch

**крахма́л|ить** (-ю, -ишь; *pf* на~) *несов перех* to starch

**кра́шеный** *прил* (*мех, ткань*) dyed; (*стол, дверь*) painted

**креве́т|ка** (-ки; *gen pl* -ок) *ж* shrimp

**креди́т** (-а) *м* credit

**креди́тн|ый** *прил* credit; **~ая ка́рточка** credit card; **~ счёт** credit account

**кредито́р** (-а) *м* creditor

**кредитоспосо́бный** *прил* solvent

**кре́до** *ср нескл* credo

**кре́йсер** (-а) *м* (*ВОЕН*) battleship

**крем** (-а) *м* cream; **сапо́жный ~** shoe polish

**кремато́ри|й** (-я) *м* crematorium

**кремир|ова́ть** (-ую) (*не*)сов *перех* to cremate

**кремл|ь** (-я́) *м* citadel; **Кремль** the Kremlin

**кре́мовый** *прил* cream

**креп|и́ть** (-лю́, -и́шь) *несов перех* to fix

**кре́пкий** *прил* strong

**кре́пко** *нареч* strongly; (*спать, люби́ть*) deeply; (*завяза́ть*) tightly

**крепле́ни|е** (-я) *ср* reinforcement; (*обычно мн: лыжные*) binding

**креп|нуть** (-ну; *pt* -, -ла; *pf* о~) *несов* to get stronger; (*уве́ренность*) to grow

**кре́пост|ь** (-и) *ж* (*ВОЕН*) fortress

**кре́с|ло** (-ла; *gen pl* -ел) *ср* armchair; (*в теа́тре*) seat

**крест** (-а́) *м* cross

**кре|сти́ть** (-щу́, -стишь; *pf* о~) *несов перех* to christen, baptize; (*пере~ pf*) **кого́-н** to make the sign of the cross over sb; **~ся** (*не*)сов *возв* to be christened *или* baptized; (*pf* пере~ся; крести́ть себя́*) to cross o.s.

**крёстн|ый** *прил*: **~ая мать** godmother; **~ оте́ц** godfather

**крестья́н|ин** (-ина; *nom pl* -е, *gen pl* -) *м* peasant

**крестья́нский** *прил* peasant

**креще́ни|е** (-я) *ср* christening, baptism; (*праздник*): **Креще́ние** ≈ the Epiphany

**крив|и́ть** (-лю́, -и́шь; *pf* с~ *или* по~) *несов перех* to curve; (*лицо́, гу́бы*) to twist

**кривля́|ться** (-юсь) *несов возв* (*грима́сничать*) to squirm

**криво́й** *прил* (*линия, палка, улыбка*) crooked; (*ноги*) bandy

**кри́зис** (-а) *м* crisis

**крик** (-а; *part gen* -у) *м* cry

**крикли́вый** *прил* loud; (*голос*) yapping

**кри́кн|уть** (-у) *сов* to shout

**кримина́л** (-а) *м* crime

**криминали́ст** (-а) *м* specialist in crime detection

**кримина́льный** *прил* (*случай*) criminal; (*исто́рия, хро́ника*) crime

**криминоге́нный** *прил* (*райо́н*) crime-ridden; (*ситуа́ция*) conducive to crime

**криста́лл** (-а) *м* crystal

**крите́ри|й** (-я) *м* criterion

**кри́тик** (-а) *м* critic

**кри́тик|а** (-и) *ж* criticism

**критик|ова́ть** (-у́ю) *несов перех* to criticize

**крити́ческий** *прил* critical

**крич|а́ть** (-у́, -и́шь) *несов*

(*человек: от боли, от гнева*) to cry (out); (: *говорить громко*) to shout; ~ (*impf*) **на** +*acc* (*бранить*) to shout at

**крова́вый** *прил* bloodied; (*рана, битва*) bloody

**крова́т|ь** (-**и**) *ж* bed

**кро́в|ля** (-**ли**; *gen pl* -**ель**) *ж* roof

**кро́вн|ый** *прил* (*родство*) blood; ~**ые интере́сы** vested interest *ед*; ~ **враг** deadly enemy

**кровожа́дный** *прил* bloodthirsty

**кровообраще́ни|е** (-**я**) *ср* (*МЕД*) circulation

**кровопроли́тный** *прил* bloody

**кровотече́ни|е** (-**я**) *ср* bleeding

**кровоточ|и́ть** (*3sg* -**и́т**) *несов* to bleed

**кров|ь** (-**и**; *loc sg* -**и́**) *ж* blood

**кро|и́ть** (-**ю́**, -**и́шь**) *несов перех* to cut out

**крокоди́л** (-**а**) *м* crocodile

**кро́лик** (-**а**) *м* rabbit; (*мех*) rabbit fur

**кро́личий** *прил* rabbit

**кро́ме** *предл*: ~ +*gen* (*за исключе́нием*) except; (*сверх чего-н*) besides; ~ **того́** besides

**кро́н|а** (-**ы**) *ж* (*дерева*) crown

**кронште́йн** (-**а**) *м* (*балкона*) support; (*полки*) bracket

**кропотли́вый** *прил* painstaking

**кросс** (-**а**) *м* (*бег*) cross-country; (*гонки*) cross-country race

**кроссво́рд** (-**а**) *м* crossword

**кроссо́в|ка** (-**ки**; *gen pl* -**ок**) *ж* (*обычно мн*) trainer

**кро́хотный** *прил* tiny

**кро́шечный** *прил* (*разг*) teeny-weeny, tiny

**крош|и́ть** (-**у́**, -**ишь**) *несов перех* (*хлеб*) to crumble; ~**ся** *несов возв* (*хлеб, мел*) to crumble

**кро́ш|ка** (-**ки**; *gen pl* -**ек**) *ж*

(*кусочек*) crumb; (*ребёнок*) little one

**круг** (-**а**; *nom pl* -**и́**) *м* circle; (*СПОРТ*) lap; (*loc sg* -**у́**; *перен: знакомых*) circle; (: *обязанностей, интересов*) range

**круг|и́** (-**о́в**) *мн* (*литературные, политические*) circles *мн*

**круглосу́точный** *прил* (*работа*) round-the-clock; (*магазин*) twenty-four-hour

**кру́гл|ый** *прил* round; (*дурак*) total; ~ **год** all year (round); ~**ые су́тки** twenty-four hours

**круговоро́т** (-**а**) *м* cycle

**кругозо́р** (-**а**) *м*: **он челове́к широ́кого** ~**а** he is knowledgeable

**круго́м** *нареч* around

**кругосве́тный** *прил* round-the-world

**кружевно́й** *прил* lace

**кру́жев|о** (-**а**; *nom pl* -**а́**) *ср* lace

**круж|и́ть** (-**у́**, -**ишь**) *несов перех* to spin ♦ *неперех* (*птица*) to circle; ~**ся** *несов возв* (*в та́нце*) to spin (around); **у меня́ голова́ кру́жится** my head's spinning

**кру́ж|ка** (-**ки**; *gen pl* -**ек**) *ж* mug

**круж|о́к** (-**ка́**) *м* circle; (*организация*) club

**круи́з** (-**а**) *м* cruise

**круп|а́** (-**ы́**; *nom pl* -**ы**) *ж* grain

**кру́пно** *нареч* (*нарезать*) coarsely; **писа́ть** (**написа́ть** *pf*) ~ to write in big letters

**кру́пный** *прил* (*размеры, фирма*) large; (*песок, соль*) coarse; (*учёный, дело*) prominent; (*событие, успех*) major; ~ **план** close-up

**кру|ти́ть** (-**чу́**, -**тишь**) *несов перех* (*руль*) to turn; (*pf* **с**~; *руки*) to twist; ~**ся** *несов возв* (*вертеться*) to turn around; (: *колесо*) to spin; (: *дети*) to fidget

**кру́то** *нареч* (*подниматься*) steeply; (*повернуть*) sharply ♦ *как сказ* (*разг: хорошо*) it's cool

**круто́й** *прил* steep; (*перемены*) sharp; (*разг: хороший*) cool

**круше́ни**|**е** (**-я**) *ср* (*поезда*) crash; (*перен: надежд, планов*) shattering

**крыжо́вник** (**-а**) *м собир* (*ягоды*) gooseberries *мн*

**крыл**|**о́** (**-а́**; *nom pl* **-ья**, *gen pl* **-ьев**) *ср* wing

**крыльц**|**о́** (**-а́**) *ср* porch

**Крым** (**-а**; *loc sg* **-у́**) *м* Crimea

**кры́с**|**а** (**-ы**) *ж* rat

**кры́тый** *прил* covered

**кр**|**ыть** (**-о́ю**, **-о́ешь**; *pf* **покры́ть**) *несов перех* to cover

**кры́ш**|**а** (**-и**) *ж* roof; (*разг: перен*) protection

**кры́ш**|**ка** (**-ки**; *gen pl* **-ек**) *ж* (*ящика, чайника*) lid

**крю́**|**к** (**-ка́**; *nom pl* **-чья**, *gen pl* **-чьев**) *м* hook

**крюч**|**о́к** (**-ка́**) *м* hook; **~ для вяза́ния** crochet hook

**кря́ка**|**ть** (**-ю**) *несов* (*утка*) to quack

**крях**|**те́ть** (**-чу́**, **-ти́шь**) *несов* to groan

**ксероко́пи**|**я** (**-и**) *ж* photocopy, Xerox ®

**ксе́рокс** (**-а**) *м* photocopier; (*копия*) photocopy, Xerox ®

**кста́ти** *вводн сл* (*между прочим*) incidentally, by the way; (*случайно*) by any chance ♦ *нареч* (*сказать, прийти*) at the right time

KEYWORD

**кто** (**кого́**; *см. Table 7*) *мест* 1 (*вопросительное, относительное*) who; **кто там?** who is there?

2 (*разг: кто-нибудь*) anyone; **е́сли кто позвони́т, позови́ меня́** if anyone phones, please call me

3: **ма́ло ли кто** many (people); **ма́ло кто** few (people); **ма́ло кто пошёл в кино́** only a few of us went to the cinema; **кто из вас ...** which of you ...; **кто (его́) зна́ет!** who knows!

**кто́-либо** (**кого́-либо**; *как* **кто**; *см. Table 7*) *мест* = **кто́-нибудь**

**кто́-нибудь** (**кого́-нибудь**; *как* **кто**; *см. Table 7*) *мест* (*в вопросе*) anybody, anyone; (*в утвержде́нии*) somebody, someone

**кто́-то** (**кого́-то**; *как* **кто**; *см. Table 7*) *мест* somebody, someone

**куб** (**-а**) *м* (*ГЕОМ, МАТ*) cube

**ку́бик** (**-а**) *м* (*игру́шка*) building brick *или* block

**ку́б**|**ок** (**-ка**) *м* (*СПОРТ*) cup

**кубоме́тр** (**-а**) *м* cubic metre (*BRIT*) *или* meter (*US*)

**кувши́н** (**-а**) *м* jug (*BRIT*), pitcher (*US*)

**кувырка́**|**ться** (**-юсь**) *несов возв* to somersault

**куда́** *нареч* (*вопросительное, относительное*) where; **~ ты положи́л мою́ ру́чку?** where did you put my pen?; **скажи́, ~ ты идёшь** tell me where you are going

**куда́-либо** *нареч* = **куда́-нибудь**

**куда́-нибудь** *нареч* (*в вопросе*) anywhere; (*в утвержде́нии*) somewhere

**куда́-то** *нареч* somewhere

**ку́др**|**и** (**-е́й**) *мн* curls *мн*

**кудря́вый** *прил* (*волосы*) curly; (*человек*) curly-haired

**кузне́чик** (**-а**) *м* grasshopper

**ку́зов** (**-а**; *nom pl* **-а́**) *м* (*АВТ*) back (*of van, lorry etc*)

**кукаре́ка|ть (-ю)** *несов* to crow

**кукареку́** *межд* cock-a-doodle-doo

**ку́к|ла (-лы;** *gen pl* **-ол)** *ж* (*также перен*) doll; (*в театре*) puppet

**ку́кольный** *прил*: ~ **теа́тр** puppet theatre (*BRIT*) *или* theater (*US*)

**кукуру́з|а (-ы)** *ж* (*БОТ*) maize; (*КУЛИН*) (sweet)corn

**куку́ш|ка (-ки;** *gen pl* **-ек)** *ж* cuckoo

**кула́к (-а́)** *м* fist

**кул|ёк (-ька́)** *м* paper bag

**кулина́р (-а)** *м* master chef

**кулинари́|я (-и)** *ж* cookery; (*магазин*) ≈ delicatessen

**кули́с|а (-ы)** *ж* (*ТЕАТР*) wing

**куло́н (-а)** *м* (*украшение*) pendant

**кулуа́р|ы (-ов)** *мн* (*полит*) lobby *ед*

**кульмина́ци|я (-и)** *ж* (*перен*) high point, climax

**культ (-а)** *м* cult

**культу́р|а (-ы)** *ж* culture

**культу́рный** *прил* cultural; (*растение*) cultivated

**куми́р (-а)** *м* (*также перен*) idol

**купа́льник (-а)** *м* swimming *или* bathing costume (*BRIT*), bathing suit (*US*)

**купа́льный** *прил*: ~ **костю́м** swimming *или* bathing costume (*BRIT*), bathing suit (*US*)

**купа́|ть (-ю;** *pf* **вы́купать** *или* **ис~)** *несов перех* to bath; ~**ся** (*pf* **вы́купаться** *или* **ис~ся**) *несов возв* to bathe; (*плавать*) to swim; (*в ванне*) to have a bath

**купе́** *ср нескл* compartment (*in railway carriage*)

**купе́йный** *прил*: ~ **ваго́н** Pullman (car)

**купи́рованный** *прил* = **купе́йный**

**куп|и́ть (-лю́, -ишь;** *impf* **покупа́ть)** *сов перех* to buy

**купле́т (-а)** *м* couplet

**куплю́** *сов см.* **купи́ть**

**ку́пол (-а;** *nom pl* **-а́)** *м* cupola

**купо́н (-а)** *м* (*ценных бумаг*) ticket; **пода́рочный** ~ gift voucher

**купю́р|а (-ы)** *ж* (*ЭКОН*) denomination; (*сокращение*) cut

**куре́ни|е (-я)** *ср* smoking

**кури́льщик (-а)** *м* smoker

**кури́ный** *прил* (*бульон*) chicken

**кур|и́ть (-ю́, -ишь)** *несов (не)перех* to smoke

**ку́р|ица (-ицы;** *nom pl* ~**ы)** *ж* hen, chicken; (*мясо*) chicken

**кур|о́к (-ка́)** *м* hammer (*on gun*)

**куро́рт (-а)** *м* (*holiday*) resort

**курс (-а)** *м* course; (*полит*) policy; (*комм*) exchange rate; (*просвещ*) year (*of university studies*); **быть** (*impf*) **в ку́рсе (де́ла)** to be well-informed; **входи́ть (войти́** *pf*) **в** ~ **чего́-н** to bring o.s. up to date on sth; **вводи́ть (ввести́** *pf*) **кого́-н в** ~ (**чего́-н**) to put sb in the picture (about sth)

**курса́нт (-а)** *м* (*ВОЕН*) cadet

**курси́в (-а)** *м* italics *мн*

**курси́р|овать (-ую)** *несов*: ~ **ме́жду** +*instr* ... **и** +*instr* ... (*самолёт, автобус*) to shuttle between ... and ...; (*судно*) to sail between ... and ...

**курсов|о́й** *прил*: ~**а́я рабо́та** project; ~**а́я ра́зница** (*комм*) difference in exchange rates

**курсо́р (-а)** *м* cursor

**ку́рт|ка (-ки;** *gen pl* **-ок)** *ж* jacket

**курча́вый** *прил* (*волосы*) curly; (*человек*) curly-haired

**ку́р|ы (-)** *мн от* **ку́рица**

**курье́р (-а)** *м* messenger

**куря́тин|а (-ы)** *ж* chicken

**куса́|ть (-ю)** *несов перех* to bite; ~**ся** *несов возв* (*животное*) to bite

**кус|óк (-кá)** *м* piece; **~ сáхара** sugar lump; **~ мы́ла** bar of soap

**куст (-á)** *м* (*БОТ*) bush

**кустáрник (-а)** *м* shrubbery

**ку́та|ть (-ю)**; *pf* **за~** *несов перех* (*плечи*) to cover up; (*ребёнка*) to bundle up; **~ся** (*pf* **за~ся**) *несов возв*: **~ся в** +*acc* to wrap o.s. up in

**ку́х|ня (-ни)**; *gen pl* **-онь**) *ж* (*помещение*) kitchen; **ру́сская ~** Russian cuisine

**ку́хонный** *прил* kitchen

**ку́ч|а (-и)** *ж* (*песка, листьев*) pile, heap; (*разг*): **~** +*gen* (*денег, проблем*) heaps *или* loads of

**ку́ша|ть (-ю)**; *pf* **по~** *или* **с~**) *несов перех* to eat

**кушéт|ка (-ки)**; *gen pl* **-ок**) *ж* couch

**кювéт (-а)** *м* ditch

# Л, л

**лабири́нт (-а)** *м* maze; (*перен*) labyrinth

**лаборáнт (-а)** *м* lab(oratory) technician

**лаборатóри|я (-и)** *ж* laboratory

**лáв|ка (-ки)**; *gen pl* **-ок**) *ж* (*скамья*) bench; (*магазин*) shop

**лаврóвый** *прил*: **~ лист** bay leaf

**лáгер|ь (-я)** *м* camp

**лáдно** *част* (*разг*) O.K., all right

**ладóн|ь (-и)** *ж* palm

**лáзер (-а)** *м* laser

**лá|зить (-жу, -зишь)** *несов* to climb; (*под стол*) to crawl

**лай (-я)** *м* barking

**лáйнер (-а)** *м* liner

**лак (-а)** *м* (*для ногтей, для пола*) varnish; **~ для вóлос** hairspray

**лакир|овáть (-ýю)**; *pf* **от~**) *несов*

*перех* (*изделие*) to lacquer

**лакони́чный** *прил* (*речь*) laconic

**лáмп|а (-ы)** *ж* lamp; (*ТЕХ*) tube; **~ дневнóго свéта** fluorescent light

**лáмпоч|ка (-ки)**; *gen pl* **-ек**) *ж* lamp; (*для освещения*) light bulb

**лáндыш (-а)** *м* lily of the valley

**лáп|а (-ы)** *ж* (*зверя*) paw; (*птицы*) foot

**лаптóп (-а)** *м* laptop

**лар|ёк (-ькá)** *м* stall

**ласкá|ть (-ю)** *несов перех* (*ребёнка, девушку*) to caress; (*собаку*) to pet

**лáсковый** *прил* affectionate

**лáстик (-а)** *м* (*разг*) rubber (*BRIT*), eraser

**лáсточ|ка (-ки)**; *gen pl* **-ек**) *ж* swallow

**Лáтви|я (-и)** *ж* Latvia

**латýн|ь (-и)** *ж* brass

**латы́н|ь (-и)** *ж* Latin

**лауреáт (-а)** *м* winner (*of award*)

**лáцкан (-а)** *м* lapel

**лá|ять (-ю)**; *pf* **про~**) *несов* to bark

**лгать (лгу, лжёшь** *итп*, **лгут**; *pf* **солгáть)** *несов* to lie

**лгун (-á)** *м* liar

**ЛДПР** *ж сокр* = Либерáльно-демократи́ческая Пáртия Росси́и

**лéбед|ь (-я**; *gen pl* **-éй)** *м* swan

**лев (льва)** *м* lion; (*созвездие*): **Лев** Leo

**левосторóнний** *прил* on the left

**левш|á (-и́**; *gen pl* **-éй)** *м/ж* left-handed person

**лéвый** *прил* left; (*ПОЛИТ*) left-wing

**лёг** *итп сов см.* **лечь**

**легéнд|а (-ы)** *ж* legend

**лёгк|ий** *прил* (*груз*) light; (*задача*) easy; (*боль, насморк*) slight; (*характер, человек*) easy-going; **~ая атлéтика** athletics (*BRIT*), track (*US*)

**легкó** *нареч* easily ♦ *как сказ*: **э́то**

**легко** it's easy

**легкоатлéт** (**-а**) м athlete (*in track and field events*)

**легков|óй** *прил*: ~**áя маши́на**, ~**óй автомоби́ль** car, automobile (*US*)

**лёгк|ое** (**-ого**) *ср* (*обычно мн*) lung

**легкомы́сленный** *прил* frivolous, flippant; (*поступок*) thoughtless

**легкомы́сли|е** (**-я**) *ср* frivolity

**лёгкость|ь** (**-и**) ж (*задания*) simplicity, easiness

**лéгче** *сравн прил от* **лёгкий** ♦ *сравн нареч от* **легкó** ♦ *как сказ*: **больнóму сегóдня лéгче** the patient is feeling better today

**лёд** (**льда**; *loc sg* **льду**) м ice

**леден|éц** (**-цá**) м fruit drop

**ледянóй** *прил* (*покров*) ice; (*вода, взгляд*) icy

**леж|áть** (**-ý, -и́шь**) *несов* (*человек, животное*) to lie; (*предмет, вещи*) to be; ~ (*impf*) **в больни́це** to be in hospital

**лез** *etc несов см.* **лезть**

**лéзви|е** (**-я**) *ср* blade

**лез|ть** (**-у, -ешь**; *pt* **-, -ла**) *несов* (*выпадать: волосы*) to fall out; (*проникать*): ~ **в** +*acc* to climb in; ~ (*impf*) **на** +*acc* to climb (up)

**лéй|ка** (**-йки**; *gen pl* **-ек**) ж watering can

**лейкопла́стыр|ь** (**-я**) м sticking plaster (*BRIT*), adhesive tape (*US*)

**лейтена́нт** (**-а**) м lieutenant

**лека́рств|о** (**-а**) *ср* medicine; ~ **от** +*gen* medicine for; ~ **от ка́шля** cough medicine

**лéктор** (**-а**) м lecturer

**лéкци|я** (**-и**) ж lecture

**лён** (**льна**) м (*БОТ*) flax; (*ткань*) linen

**лени́вый** *прил* lazy

**лени́|ться** (**-юсь, -ишься**; *pf*

**по~**) *несов возв* to be lazy

**лéнт|а** (**-ы**) ж ribbon; (*ТЕХ*) tape

**лентя́|й** (**-я**) м lazybones

**лен|ь** (**-и**) ж laziness ♦ *как сказ*: **емý ~ учи́ться/рабóтать** he can't be bothered studying/working

**лепест|óк** (**-кá**) м petal

**леп|и́ть** (**-лю́, -ишь**; *pf* **вы́лепить**) *несов перех* to model; (*pf* **с~**; *соты, гнёзда*) to build

**лес** (**-а**; *loc sg* **-ý**, *nom pl* **-á**) м (*большой*) forest; (*небольшой*) wood ♦ *собир* (*материал*) timber (*BRIT*), lumber (*US*)

**лесбия́н|ка** (**-ки**; *gen pl* **-ок**) ж lesbian

**лéск|а** (**-и**) ж fishing line

**леснóй** *прил* forest

**лéстниц|а** (**-ы**) ж staircase; (*ступени*) stairs мн; (*переносная*) ladder; (*стремянка*) stepladder

**лéстничн|ый** *прил*: ~**ая клéтка** stairwell

**лéстный** *прил* flattering

**лест|ь** (**-и**) ж flattery

**летá** (**лет**) мн см. **год**; (*возраст*): **скóлько Вам лет?** how old are you?; **емý 16 лет** he is 16 (years old)

**летá|ть** (**-ю**) *несов* to fly

**ле|тéть** (**-чý, -ти́шь**) *несов* to fly

**лéтний** *прил* summer

**лётн|ый** *прил*: ~**ое пóле** airfield

**лéт|о** (**-а**) *ср* summer

**лéтом** *нареч* in summer

**летýч|ий** *прил*: ~**ая мышь** bat

**лётчик** (**-а**) м pilot

**лéчащий** *прил*: ~ **врач** ≈ consultant-in-charge (*BRIT*), ≈ attending physician (*US*)

**лечéбниц|а** (**-ы**) ж clinic

**лечéбный** *прил* (*учреждение*) medical; (*трава*) medicinal

**лечéни|е** (**-я**) *ср* (*больных*) treatment; (*от простуды*) cure

**лечи́|ть** (-у́, -ишь) *несов перех*
to treat; (*больного*): ~ **кого́-н от**
+*gen* to treat sb for; ~**ся** *несов*
*возв* to undergo treatment

**лечу́** *несов см.* **лете́ть**

**ле́|чь** (**ля́гу, ля́жешь** *итп,*
**ля́гут;** *pt* **лёг, -гла́,** *imper* **ля́г(те);**
*impf* **ложи́ться**) *сов* to lie down;
(*перен*): ~ **на** +*acc* (*задача*) to fall
on; **ложи́ться** (~ *pf*) **в больни́цу**
to go into hospital

**лжец** (-а́) *м* liar

**лжи** *сущ см.* **ложь**

**лжи́вый** *прил* (*человек*) deceitful

**ли** *част* (*в вопросе*): **зна́ешь ~
ты, что ...** do you know that ... (*в
косвенном вопросе*): **спроси́,
смо́жет ~ он нам помо́чь** ask if
he can help us; (*в
разделительном вопросе*): **она́
краси́вая, не так ~?** she's
beautiful, isn't she?

**либера́льный** *прил* liberal

**ли́бо** *союз* (*или*) or

**ли́в|ень** (-ня) *м* downpour

**ли́г|а** (-и) *ж* (*ПОЛИТ, СПОРТ*) league

**ли́дер** (-а) *м* leader

**лиди́р|овать** (-ую) *несов* to lead,
be in the lead

**ли|за́ть** (-жу́, -жешь) *несов
перех* (*тарелку, мороженое*) to
lick

**лизн|у́ть** (-у́, -ёшь) *сов перех* to
lick

**ликвиди́р|овать** (-ую) (*не)сов
перех* (*фирму*) to liquidate;
(*оружие*) to destroy

**ликви́дный** *прил* (*КОММ*) liquid;
(*фирма*) solvent

**ликёр** (-а) *м* liqueur

**ли́ли|я** (-и) *ж* lily

**лило́вый** *прил* purple

**лими́т** (-а) *м* (*на бензин*) quota;
(*цен*) limit

**лимити́р|овать** (-ую) (*не)сов*

*перех* to limit; (*цены*) to cap

**лимо́н** (-а) *м* lemon

**лимона́д** (-а) *м* lemonade

**лимо́нн|ый** *прил* lemon; ~**ая
кислота́** citric acid

**лине́йк|а** (-йки; *gen pl* -ек) *ж*
(*линия*) line; (*инструмент*) ruler;
**тетра́дь в ~йку** lined notebook

**ли́нз|а** (-ы) *ж* lens

**ли́ни|я** (-и) *ж* line; **по ~и** +*gen* in
the line of; **железнодоро́жная ~**
railway (*BRIT*) *или* railroad (*US*)
track

**лино́леум** (-а) *м* linoleum

**линя́|ть** (*3sg* -ет; *pf* **по~**) *несов* to
run (*colour*); (*pf* **об~**; *животные*) to
moult (*BRIT*), molt (*US*)

**ли́пкий** *прил* sticky

**ли́п|нуть** (-ну; *pt* -, -ла; *pf* **при~**)
*несов* (*грязь, тесто*) to stick

**липу́ч|ка** (-ки; *gen pl* -ек) *ж* (*разг:
застёжка*) Velcro ® fastening

**ли́рик|а** (-и) *ж* lyric poetry

**лири́ческий** *прил* lyrical

**лис|а́** (-ы́; *nom pl* -ы) *ж* fox

**лист** (-а́; *nom pl* -ья) *м* (*растения*)
leaf; (*nom pl* -ы; *бумаги, железа*)
sheet

**листа́|ть** (-ю) *несов перех*
(*страницы*) to turn

**листв|а́** (-ы́) *ж собир* foliage,
leaves *мн*

**листо́в|ка** (-ки; *gen pl* -ок) *ж*
leaflet

**лист|о́к** (-ка́) *м* (*бумаги*) sheet

**ли́стья** *итп сущ см.* **лист**

**Литв|а́** (-ы́) *ж* Lithuania

**литерату́р|а** (-ы) *ж* literature;
(*также*: **худо́жественная ~**)
fiction

**литерату́рный** *прил* literary

**литр** (-а) *м* litre (*BRIT*), liter (*US*)

**литро́вый** *прил* (*бутылка итп*)
(one-)litre (*BRIT*), (one-)liter (*US*)

**литурги́|я** (-и) *ж* liturgy

**ли|ть** (**лью, льёшь;** *pt* **-л, -ла́**) *несов перех* (*воду*) to pour; (*слёзы*) to shed; (*ТЕХ, детали, изделия*) to cast, mould (*BRIT*), mold (*US*) ♦ *неперех* (*вода, дождь*) to pour; **ли́ться** *несов возв* (*вода*) to pour out

**лифт** (**-а**) *м* lift

**ли́фчик** (**-а**) *м* bra

**лихора́дк|а** (**-и**) *ж* fever; (*на губах*) cold sore

**лицев|о́й** *прил*: **~а́я сторона́ мате́рии** the right side of the material

**лице́|й** (**-я**) *м* lycée, ≈ grammar school

**лицеме́р** (**-а**) *м* hypocrite

**лицеме́рный** *прил* hypocritical

**лице́нзи|я** (**-и**) *ж* licence (*BRIT*), license (*US*)

**ли|цо́** (**-ца́;** *nom pl* **-ца**) *ср* face; (*перен: индивидуальность*) image; (*ткани итп*) right side; (*ЛИНГ*) person; **от ~ца́** +*gen* in the name of, on behalf of

**ли́чно** *нареч* (*знать*) personally; (*встретить*) in person

**ли́чность|ь** (**-и**) *ж* individual

**ли́чный** *прил* personal; (*частный*) private

**лиша́|ть** (**-ю**) *несов от* **лиши́ть**

**лише́ни|е** (**-я**) *ср* (*прав*) deprivation; **~ свобо́ды** imprisonment

**лиш|и́ть** (**-у́, -и́шь;** *impf* **лиша́ть**) *сов перех*: **~ кого́-н/что-н** +*gen* (*отнять: прав, привилегий*) to deprive sb/sth of; (*покоя, счастья*) to rob sb/sth of

**ли́шний** *прил* (*вес*) extra; (*деньги, билет*) spare; **~ раз** once again *или* more

**лишь** *част* (*только*) only ♦ *союз* (*как только*) as soon as; **~ бы она́ согласи́лась!** if only she would agree!

**лоб** (**лба;** *loc sg* **лбу**) *м* forehead

**ло́бби** *ср нескл* lobby

**лобов|о́й** *прил* frontal; **~о́е стекло́** windscreen (*BRIT*), windshield (*US*)

**лов|и́ть** (**-лю́, -ишь;** *pf* **пойма́ть**) *несов перех* to catch; (*момент*) to seize; **~** (*impf*) **ры́бу** to fish

**ло́вкий** *прил* (*человек*) agile; (*движение*) nimble; (*удар*) swift

**ло́вл|я** (**-и**) *ж* (*действие*) catching; **ры́бная ~** fishing

**лову́шк|а** (**-и;** *gen pl* **-ек**) *ж* trap

**ло́гик|а** (**-и**) *ж* logic

**логи́чный** *прил* logical

**логоти́п** (**-а**) *м* logo

**ло́д|ка** (**-ки;** *gen pl* **-ок**) *ж* boat

**лоды́ж|ка** (**-ки;** *gen pl* **-ек**) *ж* ankle

**ло́дыр|ь** (**-я**) *м* (*разг*) idler

**ло́ж|а** (**-и**) *ж* (*в театре, в зале*) box

**лож|и́ться** (**-у́сь, -и́шься**) *несов от* **лечь**

**ло́ж|ка** (**-ки;** *gen pl* **-ек**) *ж* spoon

**ло́жный** *прил* false; (*вывод*) wrong

**ложь** (**лжи;** *instr sg* **ло́жью**) *ж* lie

**лоз|а́** (**-ы́;** *nom pl* **-ы**) *ж* vine

**ло́зунг** (**-а**) *м* (*призыв*) slogan; (*плакат*) banner

**ло́кон** (**-а**) *м* ringlet

**ло́к|оть** (**-тя;** *gen pl* **-те́й,** *dat pl* **-тя́м**) *м* elbow

**лом** (**-а**) *м* crowbar ♦ *собир* (*для переработки*) scraps *мн*

**лома́|ть** (**-ю;** *pf* **с~**) *несов перех* to break; (*традиции*) to challenge; (*планы*) to frustrate; (*pf* **с~** *или* **по~;** *механизм*) to break; **~** (*impf*) **го́лову над чем-то** to rack one's brains over sth; **~ся** (*pf* **с~ся**) *несов возв* to break

**ло́мтик** (**-а**) *м* slice

**Ло́ндон** (**-а**) *м* London

**ло́паст|ь** (-и; *gen pl* -**е́й**) ж blade

**лопа́т|а** (-ы) ж spade

**лопа́тк|а** (-ки; *gen pl* -**ок**) ж уменьш от **лопа́та**; (*АНАТ*) shoulder blade

**ло́пн|уть** (-у; *pf* **ло́паться**) *сов* (*шар*) to burst; (*стекло*) to shatter; (*разг: банк*) to go bust

**лоску́т** (-**а́**) *м* (*материи*) scrap

**лосо́с|ь** (-я) *м* salmon

**лос|ь** (-я; *gen pl* -**е́й**) *м* elk, moose

**лосьо́н** (-а) *м* lotion

**лотере́|я** (-и) ж lottery

**лото́** *ср нескл* lotto

**лот|о́к** (-**ка́**) *м* (*прилавок*) stall

**лохма́тый** *прил* (*животное*) shaggy; (*человек*) dishevelled

**лохмо́ть|я** (-ев) *мн* rags *мн*

**ло́шад|ь** (-и; *gen pl* -**е́й**) ж horse

**луг** (-а; *loc sg* -**у́**, *nom pl* -**а́**) *м* meadow

**лу́ж|а** (-и) ж (*на дороге*) puddle; (*на полу, на столе*) pool

**лук** (-а) *м собир* (*плоды*) onions *мн* ♦ *м* (*оружие*) bow; **зелёный ~** spring onion (*BRIT*), scallion

**лу́ковиц|а** (-ы) ж bulb

**лун|а́** (-ы) ж moon

**лу́н|ка** (-ки; *gen pl* -**ок**) ж hole

**лу́нный** *прил*: **~ свет** moonlight

**лу́п|а** (-ы) ж magnifying glass

**луч** (-**а́**) *м* ray; (*фонаря*) beam

**лучев|о́й** *прил*: **~а́я боле́знь** radiation sickness

**лу́чше** *сравн прил от* **хоро́ший** ♦ *сравн нареч от* **хорошо́** ♦ *как сказ*: **так ~** that's better ♦ *част*: **~ не опра́вдывайся** don't try and justify yourself ♦ *вводн сл*: **~ (всего́), позвони́ ве́чером** it would be better if you phone in the evening; **больно́му ~** the patient is feeling better; **нам ~, чем им** we're better off than them; **как нельзя́ ~** couldn't be better

**лу́чш|ий** *прил* (*самый хоро́ший*) best; **в ~ем слу́чае мы зако́нчим за́втра** the best-case scenario is that we'll finish tomorrow; **э́то (всё) к ~ему** it's (all) for the best

**лы́ж|а** (-и) ж (*обычно мн*) ski; *см. также* **лы́жи**

**лы́ж|и** (-) *мн* (*спорт*) skiing *ед*; **во́дные ~** water-skis; (*спорт*) water-skiing; **го́рные ~** downhill skis; (*спорт*) downhill skiing

**лы́жник** (-а) *м* skier

**лы́жный** *прил* (*крепления, мазь итп*) ski; (*соревнования*) skiing

**лыжн|я́** (-**и́**) ж ski track

**лысе́|ть** (-ю; *pf* **об~** *или* **по~**) *несов* to go bald

**лы́син|а** (-ы) ж bald patch

**лы́сый** *прил* bald

**ль** *част* = **ли**

**льго́т|а** (-ы) ж benefit; (*предприятиям итп*) special term; **нало́говые ~** tax relief

**льго́тный** *прил* (*тариф*) concessionary; (*условия*) privileged; (*заём*) special-rate; **~ биле́т** concessionary ticket

**льди́н|а** (-ы) ж ice floe

**льняно́й** *прил* (*полотенце*) linen

**ль|стить** (-**щу**, -**стишь**; *pf* **по~стить**) *несов*: **~ +***dat* (*хвалить*) to flatter; (*самолюбию*) to gratify

**любе́зност|ь** (-и) ж (*одолжение*) favour (*BRIT*), favor (*US*)

**любе́зн|ый** *прил* polite; **бу́дьте ~ы!** excuse me, please!; **бу́дьте ~ы, принеси́те нам ко́фе!** would you be so kind as to bring us some coffee?

**люби́м|ец** (-**ца**) *м* favourite (*BRIT*), favorite (*US*)

**люби́мый** *прил* (*женщина, брат*) beloved; (*писатель, занятие итп*) favourite (*BRIT*), favorite (*US*)

**люби́тель** (**-я**) *м* (*непрофессионал*) amateur; **~му́зыки/спо́рта** music-/sports-lover

**люби́тельский** *прил* amateur

**люб|и́ть** (**-лю́**, **-ишь**) *несов перех* to love; (*музыку, спорт итп*) to like

**люб|ова́ться** (**-у́юсь**; *pf* **по~**) *несов возв*: ~ +*instr* to admire

**любо́вник** (**-а**) *м* lover

**любо́вный** *прил* (*дела*) lover's; (*песня, письмо*) love; (*отношение, подход*) loving

**люб|о́вь** (**-ви́**; *instr sg* **-о́вью**) *ж* love; (*привязанность*): ~ **к** +*dat* (*к родине, к матери итп*) love for; (*к чтению, к искусству итп*) love of

**любозна́тельный** *прил* inquisitive

**люб|о́й** *мест* (*всякий*) any
♦ (**-о́го**) *м* (*любой человек*) anyone

**любопы́тный** *прил* (*случай*) interesting; (*человек*) curious

**любопы́тств|о** (**-а**) *ср* curiosity

**лю́бящий** *прил* loving

**лю́д|и** (**-е́й**; *dat pl* **-ям**, *instr pl* **-ьми́**, *prp pl* **-ях**) *мн* people *мн*; (*кадры*) staff *ед*; **молоды́е ~** young men; (*молодёжь*) young people; *см. также* **челове́к**

**лю́дный** *прил* (*улица итп*) busy

**людое́д** (**-а**) *м* (*человек*) cannibal

**людско́й** *прил* human

**люк** (**-а**) *м* (*танка*) hatch; (*на дороге*) manhole

**люкс** (**-а**) *м* (*о вагоне*) first-class carriage; (*о каюте*) first-class cabin
♦ *прил неизм* first-class

**лю́стр|а** (**-ы**) *ж* chandelier

**ляга́|ть** (**-ю**) *несов перех* (*подлеж: лошадь, корова*) to kick; **~ся** *несов возв* (*лошадь, корова*) to kick

**ля́гу** *итп сов см.* **лечь**

**лягу́ш|ка** (**-ки**; *gen pl* **-ек**) *ж* frog

**ля́жешь** *итп сов см.* **лечь**

**ля́ж|ка** (**-ки**; *gen pl* **-ек**) *ж* thigh

**ля́м|ка** (**-ки**; *gen pl* **-ок**) *ж* strap

# М, м

**М** *сокр* = **метро́**

**м** *сокр* (= **метр**) m

**мавзоле́|й** (**-я**) *м* mausoleum

**магази́н** (**-а**) *м* shop

**маги́стр** (**-а**) *м* master's degree

**магистра́л|ь** (**-и**) *ж* main line

**маги́ческий** *прил* magic

**магни́т** (**-а**) *м* magnet

**магнитофо́н** (**-а**) *м* tape recorder

**ма́|зать** (**-жу**, **-жешь**; *pf* **на~** *или* **по~**) *несов перех* to spread; (*pf* **из~**; *разг: пачкать*) to get dirty; **~ся** (*pf* **из~ся**) *несов возв* (*разг: пачкаться*) to get dirty; **~ (на~ся** *pf*) **кре́мом** to apply cream

**маз|о́к** (**-ка́**) *м* (*МЕД*) smear

**маз|ь** (**-и**) *ж* (*МЕД*) ointment; (*ТЕХ*) grease

**ма́|й** (**-я**) *м* May

**1 Ма́я** - International Day of Workers' solidarity. Although, as the name suggests, this holiday is highly political, for most people it is an opportunity to celebrate the spring and to enjoy a short holiday.

**ма́|йка** (**-йки**; *gen pl* **-ек**) *ж* vest (*BRIT*), sleeveless undershirt (*US*)

**майоне́з** (**-а**) *м* mayonnaise

**майо́р** (**-а**) *м* (*ВОЕН*) major

**мак** (**-а**) *м* poppy

**макаро́н|ы** (**-**) *мн* pasta *ед*

**мака́|ть** (**-ю**) *несов перех* to dip

**макéт** (**-а**) *м* model
**мáклер** (**-а**) *м* (*КОММ*) broker
**макн|ýть** (**-ý, -ёшь**) *сов перех* to dip
**максимáльный** *прил* maximum
**мáксимум** (**-а**) *м* maximum
**макулатýр|а** (**-ы**) *ж собир* wastepaper (*for recycling*)
**малахи́т** (**-а**) *м* malachite
**малéйший** *прил* (*ошибка*) the slightest
**мáленький** *прил* small, little
**мали́н|а** (**-ы**) *ж* (*кустарник*) raspberry cane *или* bush; (*ягоды*) raspberries *мн*

---
KEYWORD
---

**мáло** *чис*: **мáло** +*gen* (*друзей, книг*) only a few; (*работы, денег*) not much, little; **нам дáли мáло книг** they only gave us a few books; **у меня́ мáло дéнег** I don't have much money; **мáло рáдости** little joy
♦ *нареч* not much; **онá мáло измени́лась** she hasn't changed much
♦ *как сказ*: **мне э́того мáло** this is not enough for me; **мáло ли что** so what?; **мáло ли кто/где/когдá** it doesn't matter who/where/when; **мáло тогó** (and) what's more; **мáло тогó что** not only

---

**маловероя́тный** *прил* improbable
**малодýшный** *прил* cowardly
**малокрóви|е** (**-я**) *ср* (sickle-cell) anaemia (*BRIT*) *или* anemia (*US*)
**малолéтний** *прил* young
**малообеспéченный** *прил* disadvantaged
**малоразви́тый** *прил* underdeveloped
**малочи́сленный** *прил* small

**мáл|ый** *прил* small, little; (*доход, скорость*) low ♦ *как сказ*: **плáтье/пальтó мне мáло** the dress/coat is too small for me; **сáмое ~ое** at the very least
**малы́ш** (**-á**) *м* little boy
**малы́ш|ка** (**-ки**; *gen pl* **-ек**) *ж* little girl
**мáльчик** (**-а**) *м* boy
**малю́т|ка** (**-ки**; *gen pl* **-ок**) *м/ж* baby
**маля́р** (**-á**) *м* painter (and decorator)
**маляри́|я** (**-и**) *ж* malaria
**мáм|а** (**-ы**) *ж* mummy (*BRIT*), mommy (*US*)
**мамáш|а** (**-и**) *ж* mummy (*BRIT*), mommy (*US*)
**мандари́н** (**-а**) *м* tangerine
**мандáт** (**-а**) *м* mandate
**манёвр** (**-а**) *м* manoeuvre (*BRIT*), maneuver (*US*)
**манéж** (**-а**) *м* (*для верховой езды*) manège; (*цирка*) ring; (*для младенцев*) playpen; (*также*: **легкоатлети́ческий ~**) indoor stadium
**манекéн** (**-а**) *м* (*портного*) dummy; (*в витрине*) dummy, mannequin
**манекéнщиц|а** (**-ы**) *ж* model
**манéр|а** (**-ы**) *ж* manner; (*художника*) style
**манжéт|а** (**-ы**) *ж* cuff
**маникю́р** (**-а**) *м* manicure
**манипули́р|овать** (**-ую**) *несов*: **~** +*instr* to manipulate
**ман|и́ть** (**-ю́, -ишь**; *pf* **по~**) *несов перех* to beckon; (*no pf*; *привлекать*) to draw
**манифéст** (**-а**) *м* manifesto
**манифестáци|я** (**-и**) *ж* rally
**мáни|я** (**-и**) *ж* mania
**мáнн|ый** *прил*: **~ая кáша, ~ая крупá** semolina

**маньяк** (-а) м maniac

**марáзм** (-а) м (МЕД) dementia; (перен: разг) idiocy; **стáрческий** ~ senile dementia

**марафóн** (-а) м marathon

**марафóн|ец** (-ца) м marathon runner

**мáрган|ец** (-ца) м manganese

**маргарúн** (-а) м margarine

**маргарúт|ка** (-ки; gen pl -ок) ж daisy

**марин|овáть** (-ýю; pf за~) несов перех (овощи) to pickle; (мясо, рыбу) to marinate, marinade

**марионéт|ка** (-ки; gen pl -ок) ж puppet

**мáр|ка** (-ки; gen pl -ок) ж (почтовая) stamp; (сорт) brand; (качество) grade; (модель) make; (деньги) mark; **торгóвая** ~ trademark

**мáркетинг** (-а) м marketing

**марксúзм** (-а) м Marxism

**мáрл|я** (-и) ж gauze

**мармелáд** (-а) м fruit jellies мн

**мародёр** (-а) м looter

**мáрочный** прил (изделие) branded; (вино) vintage

**Марс** (-а) м Mars

**март** (-а) м March

**марш** (-а) м march

**мáршал** (-а) м marshal

**марш|ировáть** (-ýю; pf про~) несов to march

**маршрýт** (-а) м route

**маршрýтн|ый** прил: ~**ое таксú** fixed-route taxi

**мáс|ка** (-ки; gen pl -ок) ж mask; (косметическая) face pack

**маскарáд** (-а) м masked ball

**маскир|овáть** (-ýю; pf за~) несов перех to camouflage; ~**ся** (pf за~ся) несов возв to camouflage o.s.

**мáсленица** (-ы) ж ≈ Shrovetide

**маслён|ка** (-ки; gen pl -ок) ж butter dish; (ТЕХ) oilcan

**мáсленый** прил (в масле) buttery

**маслúн|а** (-ы) ж (дерево) olive (tree); (плод) olive

**мáс|ло** (-ла; nom pl -лá, gen pl -ел) ср oil; (сливочное) butter

**мáсляный** прил oil; (пятно) oily

**масóн** (-а) м (Free)mason

**мáсс|а** (-ы) ж (также ФИЗ) mass; (древесная) pulp; (много) loads мн

**массáж** (-а) м massage

**массажúст** (-а) м masseur

**массúв** (-а) м (водный) expanse; (земельный) tract; **гóрный** ~ massif; **жилóй** или **жилúщный** ~ housing estate (BRIT) или project (US)

**массúвный** прил massive

**мáссов|ый** прил mass; **товáры** ~**ого спрóса** consumer goods

**мáстер** (-а; nom pl -á) м master; (в цеху) foreman

**мастерск|áя** (-óй) ж workshop; (художника) studio

**мастерств|ó** (-á) ср skill

**мастúк|а** (-и) ж floor polish

**мастúт** (-а) м mastitis

**мáст|ь** (-и; gen pl -éй) ж (лошади) colour (BRIT), color (US); (КАРТЫ) suit

**масштáб** (-а) м scale

**масштáбный** прил scale;

(*большой*) large-scale

**мат** (**-а**) *м* (*ШАХМАТЫ*) checkmate; (*половик, также СПОРТ*) mat; (*ругательства*) bad language

**матема́тик** (**-а**) *м* mathematician

**матема́тик|а** (**-и**) *ж* mathematics

**ма́тери** *etc сущ см.* **мать**

**материа́л** (**-а**) *м* material; (*обычно мн: следствия*) document

**материа́льный** *прил* material; (*финансовый*) financial

**матери́к** (**-а́**) *м* continent; (*суша*) mainland

**матери́нский** *прил* maternal

**матери́нств|о** (**-а**) *ср* motherhood

**матери́|я** (**-и**) *ж* matter; (*разг: ткань*) cloth

**матёрый** *прил* (*зверь*) full-grown, mature; (*преступник*) hardened

**ма́тер|ь** (**-и**) *ж*: **Ма́терь Бо́жья** Mother of God

**ма́терью** *etc сущ см.* **мать**

**ма́т|ка** (**-ки**; *gen pl* **-ок**) *ж* uterus, womb; (*ЗООЛ: также*: **пчели́ная ~**) queen bee

**ма́товый** *прил* (*без блеска*) mat(t); **~ое стекло́** frosted glass

**матра́с** (**-а**) *м* mattress

**матрёш|ка** (**-ки**; *gen pl* **-ек**) *ж* Russian doll (*containing range of smaller dolls*)

**ма́тричный** *прил*: **~ при́нтер** (*КОМП*) dot-matrix printer

**матро́с** (**-а**) *м* sailor

**ма́туш|ка** (**-ки**; *gen pl* **-ек**) *ж* (*мать*) mother

**матч** (**-а**) *м* match

**мат|ь** (**-ери**; *см. Table 1*) *ж* mother; **~-одино́чка** single mother

**мафио́зный** *прил* mafia

**ма́фи|я** (**-и**) *ж* the Mafia

**мах** (**-а**) *м* (*крыла*) flap; (*рукой*) swing; **одни́м ~ом** in a stroke; **с ма́ху** straight away

**ма|ха́ть** (**-шу́, -шешь**) *несов*: ~ +*instr* to wave; (*крыльями*) to flap; ~ (*impf*) **кому́-н руко́й** to wave to sb

**махина́тор** (**-а**) *м* machinator

**махина́ци|я** (**-и**) *ж* machination

**махн|у́ть** (**-у́, -ёшь**) *сов* to wave

**махо́рк|а** (**-и**) *ж* coarse tobacco

**махро́в|ый** *прил* (*халат*) towelling; (*перен: отъявленный*) out-and-out; **~ая ткань** terry towelling

**ма́чех|а** (**-и**) *ж* stepmother

**ма́чт|а** (**-ы**) *ж* mast

**маши́н|а** (**-ы**) *ж* machine; (*автомобиль*) car

**маши́на́льный** *прил* mechanical

**машини́ст** (**-а**) *м* driver, operator

**машини́ст|ка** (**-ки**; *gen pl* **-ок**) *ж* typist

**маши́н|ка** (**-ки**; *gen pl* **-ок**) *ж* machine; **пи́шущая ~** typewriter

**маши́нн|ый** *прил* machine; **~ое отделе́ние** engine room

**машинопи́сн|ый** *прил* (*текст*) typewritten; **~ое бюро́** typing pool

**машинострое́ни|е** (**-я**) *ср* mechanical engineering

**ма́як** (**-а́**) *м* lighthouse

**ма́ятник** (**-а**) *м* (*часов*) pendulum

**МВД** *ср сокр* (= **Министе́рство вну́тренних дел**) ≈ the Home Office (*BRIT*), ≈ the Department of the Interior (*US*)

**МВФ** *м сокр* (= **Междунаро́дный валю́тный фонд**) IMF

**мгл|а** (**-ы**) *ж* haze; (*вечерняя*) gloom

**мгнове́ни|е** (**-я**) *ср* moment

**мгнове́нный** *прил* instant; (*злость*) momentary

**МГУ** *м сокр* (= **Моско́вский госуда́рственный университе́т**) Moscow State University

**ме́бел|ь** (-и) ж собир furniture

**мёд** (-а) м honey

**меда́л|ь** (-и) ж medal

**медальо́н** (-а) м medallion

**медве́диц|а** (-ы) ж she-bear;
**Больша́я Медве́дица** the Great
Bear

**медве́д|ь** (-я) м bear

**медвеж|о́нок** (-о́нка; nom pl
-а́та, gen pl -а́т) м bear cub

**ме́дик** (-а) м medic

**медикаме́нт** (-а) м medicine

**медици́н|а** (-ы) ж medicine

**ме́дленный** прил slow

**медли́тельный** прил slow

**ме́дл|ить** (-ю, -ишь) несов to
delay; ~ (impf) **с реше́нием** to be
slow in deciding

**ме́дный** прил copper; (МУЗ) brass

**медо́вый** прил honey; ~ **ме́сяц**
honeymoon

**медпу́нкт** (-а) м сокр (=
медици́нский пункт) ≈ first-aid
centre (BRIT) или center (US)

**медсестр|а́** (-ы́) ж сокр (=
медици́нская сестра́) nurse

**меду́з|а** (-ы) ж jellyfish

**мед|ь** (-и) ж copper

**междоме́ти|е** (-я) ср interjection

**ме́жду** предл: ~ +instr between; ~
+gen (в окружении) amongst; ~
**про́чим** (попутно) in passing;
(кстати) by the way; ~ **тем**
meanwhile; ~ **тем как** while; **они́
договори́лись** ~ **собо́й** they
agreed between them

**междугоро́дный** прил intercity

**междунаро́дный** прил
international

**мел** (-а) м chalk

**меле́|ть** (3sg -ет; pf об~) несов to
become shallower

**ме́лкий** прил small; (песок,
дождь) fine; (интересы) petty

**мело́ди|я** (-и) ж tune, melody

**ме́лочный** прил petty

**ме́лоч|ь** (-и; gen pl -е́й) ж
(пустяк) triviality; (подробность)
detail ♦ ж собир little things мн;
(деньги) small change

**мел|ь** (-и; loc sg -и́) ж shallows мн;
**сади́ться (сесть** pf**) на** ~ (МОР) to
run aground

**мелька́|ть** (-ю) несов to flash past

**мелькн|у́ть** (-у́, -ёшь) сов to
flash

**ме́льком** нареч in passing

**ме́льниц|а** (-ы) ж mill

**мельхио́р** (-а) м nickel silver

**ме́льче** сравн прил от **ме́лкий**

**мельч|и́ть** (-у́, -и́шь; pf из~ или
раз~) несов перех (ножом) to
cut up into small pieces; (в ступке)
to crush

**мемора́ндум** (-а) м
memorandum

**мемориа́л** (-а) м memorial

**мемуа́р|ы** (-ов) мн memoirs мн

**ме́неджер** (-а) м manager

**менеджме́нт** (-а) м management

**ме́нее** сравн нареч от **ма́ло**
♦ нареч (опасный) less; (года)
less than; **тем не** ~ nevertheless

**менинги́т** (-а) м meningitis

**менструа́ци|я** (-и) ж
menstruation

**ме́ньше** сравн прил от **ма́лый,
ма́ленький** ♦ сравн нареч от
**ма́ло** ♦ нареч less than; ~ **всего́**
least of all

**ме́ньш|ий** сравн прил от
**ма́лый, ма́ленький** ♦ прил: **по
~ей ме́ре** at least; **са́мое ~ее** no
less than

**меньшинств|о́** (-а́) ср собир
minority

**меню́** ср нескл menu

**меня́** мест см. **я**

**меня́|ть** (-ю; pf по~) несов перех
to change; ~ (**по~** pf) **что-н на** +acc

to exchange sth for; **~ся** (*pf* **по~ся**) *несов возв* to change

**ме́р|а (-ы)** *ж* measure; (*предел*) limit; **в по́лной ~е** fully; **по ~е** +*gen* with; **по ~е того́ как** as

**мерза́в|ец (-ца)** *м* scoundrel

**ме́рзкий** *прил* disgusting; (*погода, настроение*) foul

**мерзлот|а́ (-ы́)** *ж*: **ве́чная ~** permafrost

**мёрзлый** *прил* (*земля*) frozen

**мёрз|нуть (-ну;** *pt* **-, -ла;** *pf* **за~)** *несов* to freeze

**ме́р|ить (-ю, -ишь;** *pf* **с~** *или* **из~)** *несов перех* to measure; (*pf* **по~;** *примерять*) to try on

**ме́р|ка (-ки;** *gen pl* **-ок)** *ж* measurements *мн*; (*перен: критерий*) standard

**ме́рк|нуть (3sg** **-нет;** *pf* **по~)** *несов* (*также перен*) to fade

**ме́рный** *прил* measured

**мероприя́ти|е (-я)** *ср* measure; (*событие*) event

**мертве́|ть (-ю;** *pf* **о~)** *несов* (*от холода*) to go numb; (*pf* **по~;** *от страха, от горя*) to be numb

**мертве́ц (-а́)** *м* dead person

**мёртвый** *прил* dead

**мерца́|ть (3sg** **-ет)** *несов* to glimmer, flicker; (*звёзды*) to twinkle

**ме|си́ть (-шу́, -сишь;** *pf* **с~)** *несов перех* (*тесто*) to knead

**ме́сс|а (-ы)** *ж* (*РЕЛ*) Mass

**ме|сти́ (-ту́, -тёшь;** *pt* **мёл, -ла́;** *pf* **под~)** *несов перех* (*пол*) to sweep; (*мусор*) to sweep up

**ме́стность|ь (-и)** *ж* area

**ме́стный** *прил* local

**ме́ст|о (-а;** *nom pl* **-а́)** *ср* place; (*действия*) scene; (*в театре, в поезде итп*) seat; (*багажа*) item

**местожи́тельств|о (-а)** *ср* place of residence

**местоиме́ни|е (-я)** *ср* pronoun

**местонахожде́ни|е (-я)** *ср* location

**месторожде́ни|е (-я)** *ср* (*угля, нефти*) field

**месть|ь (-и)** *ж* revenge, vengeance

**ме́сяц (-а;** *nom pl* **-ы)** *м* month; (*часть луны*) crescent moon; (*диск луны*) moon

**ме́сячный** *прил* monthly

**мета́лл (-а)** *м* metal

**металлоло́м (-а)** *м* scrap metal

**металлу́рги|я (-и)** *ж* metallurgy

**ме|та́ть (-чу́, -чешь)** *несов перех* (*гранату, диск итп*) to throw; (*pf* **на~;** *шов*) to tack (*BRIT*), baste; **~ся** *несов возв* (*в постели*) to toss and turn; (*по комнате*) to rush about

**мете́ль|ь (-и)** *ж* snowstorm, blizzard

**метеоро́лог (-а)** *м* meteorologist

**метеосво́д|ка (-ки;** (*gen pl* **-ок)** *ж* сокр (= **метеорологи́ческая сво́дка**) weather forecast *или* report

**метеоста́нци|я (-и)** *ж* сокр (= **метеорологи́ческая ста́нция**) weather station

**ме́|тить (-чу, -тишь;** *pf* **по~)** *несов перех* to mark ♦ *неперех*: **~ в** +*acc* (*в цель*) to aim at; **~ся** (*pf* **на~ся**) *несов возв*: **~ся в** +*acc* to aim at

**ме́т|ка (-ки;** *gen pl* **-ок)** *ж* mark

**ме́ткий** *прил* (*точный*) accurate; (*замечание*) apt

**метл|а́ (-ы́)** *ж* broom

**метн|у́ть (-у́, -ёшь)** *сов перех* to throw; **~ся** *сов возв* to rush

**ме́тод (-а)** *м* method

**метр (-а)** *м* metre (*BRIT*), meter (*US*); (*линейка*) measure

**метрдоте́ль (-я)** *м* head waiter

**ме́трик|а (-и)** *ж* birth certificate

**метри́ческий** *прил* metric

**метро́** *ср нескл* metro, tube (*BRIT*), subway (*US*)

**мех** (**-а**; *nom pl* **-а́**) *м* fur

**мех**|**а́** (**-о́в**) *мн* (*кузнечный*) bellows *мн*

**механи́зм** (**-а**) *м* mechanism

**меха́ник** (**-а**) *м* mechanic

**механи́ческий** *прил* mechanical; (*цех*) machine

**мехово́й** *прил* fur

**мецена́т** (**-а**) *м* patron

**меч** (**-а́**) *м* sword

**мече́т**|**ь** (**-и**) *ж* mosque

**мечт**|**а́** (**-ы́**; *gen pl* **-а́ний**) *ж* dream

**мечта́ни**|**е** (**-я**) *ср* daydream

**мечта́**|**ть** (**-ю**) *несов*: ~ (**о** +*prp*) to dream (of)

**меша́**|**ть** (**-ю**; *pf* **по~**) *несов перех* (*суп, чай*) to stir; (*pf* **с~**; *напитки, краски*) to mix ♦ (*pf* **по~**) *неперех*: ~ +*dat* (*быть помехой*) to disturb, bother; (*реформам*) to hinder; ~ (**по~** *pf*) **кому́-н** +*infin* (*препятствовать*) to make it difficult for sb to do; **~ся** (*pf* **с~ся**) *несов возв* (*путаться*) to get mixed up

**меш**|**о́к** (**-ка́**) *м* sack

**мещ**|**ани́н** (**-ани́на**; *nom pl* **-а́не**, *gen pl* **-а́н**) *м* petty bourgeois

**меща́нский** *прил* (*взгляды*) petty-bourgeois; (*вкусы*) philistine

**миг** (**-а**) *м* moment

**мига́**|**ть** (**-ю**) *несов* to wink; (*огни*) to twinkle

**мигн**|**у́ть** (**-у́, -ёшь**) *сов* to wink

**ми́гом** *нареч* (*разг*) in a jiffy

**мигра́ци**|**я** (**-и**) *ж* migration

**МИД** (**-а**) *м сокр* (= *Министе́рство иностра́нных дел*) ≈ the Foreign Office (*BRIT*), ≈ the State Department (*US*)

**ми́довский** *прил* (*разг*) Foreign Office

**ми́зерный** *прил* meagre (*BRIT*), meager (*US*)

**мизи́н**|**ец** (**-ца**) *м* (*на руке*) little finger; (*на ноге*) little toe

**микроавто́бус** (**-а**) *м* minibus

**микро́б** (**-а**) *м* microbe

**микрорайо́н** (**-а**) *м* ≈ catchment area

---

**микрорайо́н** - These are modern housing estates with densely built blocks of flats and are a feature of all big Russian cities. They have their own infrastructure of schools, health centres, cinemas, and shops.

---

**микроско́п** (**-а**) *м* microscope

**микрофи́льм** (**-а**) *м* microfilm

**микрофо́н** (**-а**) *м* microphone

**ми́ксер** (**-а**) *м* mixer

**микстур**|**а** (**-ы**) *ж* mixture

**милитари́ст** (**-а**) *м* militarist

**милиционе́р** (**-а**) *м* policeman (*in Russia*)

**мили́ци**|**я** (**-и**) *ж, собир* police (*in Russia*)

**миллиа́рд** (**-а**) *м* billion

**миллигра́мм** (**-а**) *м* milligram(me)

**миллиме́тр** (**-а**) *м* millimetre (*BRIT*), millimeter (*US*)

**миллио́н** (**-а**) *м* million

**миллионе́р** (**-а**) *м* millionaire

**ми́л**|**овать** (**-ую**; *pf* **по~**) *несов перех* to have mercy on; (*преступника*) to pardon

**милови́дный** *прил* pleasing

**милосе́рди**|**е** (**-я**) *ср* compassion

**милосе́рдный** *прил* compassionate

**ми́лостын**|**я** (**-и**) *ж* alms *мн*

**ми́лост**|**ь** (**-и**) *ж* (*доброта*) kind-heartedness; **~и про́сим!** welcome!

**ми́лый** *прил* (*симпатичный*) pleasant, nice; (*дорогой*) dear

**ми́л**|**я** (**-и**) *ж* mile

**ми́мик|а (-и)** ж expression
**ми́мо** нареч past ♦ предл: ~ +gen
past
**мимолётный** прил fleeting
**мимохо́дом** нареч on the way;
(упомянуть) in passing
**ми́н|а (-ы)** ж (ВОЕН) mine
**минда́лин|а (-ы)** ж (МЕД) tonsil
**минда́л|ь (-я́)** м almond
**минера́л (-а)** м mineral
**минздра́в (-а)** м сокр (=
министе́рство
здравоохране́ния) Ministry of
Health
**миниатю́р|а (-ы)** ж miniature;
(ТЕАТР) short play
**миниатю́рный** прил miniature
**минима́льный** прил minimum
**ми́нимум (-а)** м minimum
♦ нареч at least, minimum;
**прожи́точный ~** minimum living
wage
**мини́р|овать (-ую;** pf **за~)**
(не)сов перех (ВОЕН) to mine
**министе́рств|о (-а)** ср ministry
**мини́стр (-а)** м (ПОЛИТ) minister
**ми́нн|ый** прил mine; **~ое по́ле**
minefield
**мин|ова́ть (-у́ю)** (не)сов перех
to pass
**мину́вший** прил past
**ми́нус (-а)** м minus
**мину́т|а (-ы)** ж minute
**мину́тный** прил (стрелка)
minute; (дело) brief
**ми́н|уть (3sg -ет)** сов
(исполниться): **ей/ему́ ~уло 16
лет** she/he has turned 16˚
**минфи́н (-а)** м сокр (разг. =
Министе́рство фина́нсов)
Ministry of Finance
**мир (-а;** nom pl **-ы́)** м world;
(Вселенная) universe; (loc sg **-у́**;
РЕЛ) (secular) world; (состояние
без войны) peace

**мир|и́ть (-ю́, -и́шь;** pf **по~** или
**при~) несов перех** to reconcile;
**~ся** (pf **по~ся) несов возв: ~ся с**
+instr to make up или be reconciled
with; (pf **при~ся; с**
недоста́тками) to reconcile o.s to,
come to terms with
**ми́рн|ый** прил peaceful; **~ое
вре́мя** peacetime; **~ое
населе́ние** civilian population;
**~ые перегово́ры** peace talks или
negotiations
**мировоззре́ни|е (-я)** ср
philosophy of life
**мирово́й** прил world
**миролюби́вый** прил peaceable
**миротво́р|ец (-ца)** м peacemaker,
peacekeeper
**миротво́рческ|ий** прил
peacemaking; **~ие войска́**
peacekeeping force
**мирско́й** прил secular, lay
**ми́сси|я (-и)** ж mission
**ми́стер (-а)** м Mr
**ми́стик|а (-и)** ж mysticism
**ми́тинг (-а)** м rally
**митрополи́т (-а)** м metropolitan
**миф (-а)** м myth
**мише́н|ь (-и)** ж target
**младе́н|ец (-ца)** м infant, baby
**мла́дше** сравн прил от
**молодо́й**
**мла́дший** прил younger;
(сотрудник, класс) junior
**млекопита́ющ|ее (-его)** ср
mammal
**мле́чный** прил: **Мле́чный Путь**
the Milky Way
**мм** сокр (= миллиме́тр) mm
**мне** мест см. **я**
**мне́ни|е (-я)** ср opinion
**мни́мый** прил imaginary;
(ложный) fake
**мни́тельный** прил suspicious
**мно́г|ие** прил many ♦ (-их) мн

(*мно́го люде́й*) many (people)
**мно́го** *чис*: ~ +*gen* (*книг, друзе́й*) many, a lot of; (*рабо́ты*) much, a lot of ♦ *нареч* (*разгова́ривать, пить итп*) a lot; (+*comparative*; *гора́здо*) much; ~ **книг тебе́ да́ли?** did they give you many *или* a lot of books?; ~ **рабо́ты тебе́ да́ли?** did they give you much *или* a lot of work?
**многоде́тный** *прил* with a lot of children
**мно́г|ое (-ого)** *ср* a great deal
**многозначи́тельный** *прил* significant
**многозна́чный** *прил* (*число́*) multi-digit; (*сло́во*) polysemous
**многокра́тный** *прил* repeated
**многоле́тний** *прил* (*пла́ны*) long-term; (*труд*) of many years; (*расте́ния*) perennial
**многолю́дный** *прил* crowded
**многонациона́льный** *прил* multinational
**многообеща́ющий** *прил* promising
**многообра́зи|е (-я)** *ср* variety
**многообра́зный** *прил* varied
**многосло́вный** *прил* verbose
**многосторо́нний** *прил* (*перегово́ры*) multilateral; (*ли́чность*) many-sided; (*интере́сы*) diverse
**многото́чи|е (-я)** *ср* (*ЛИНГ*) ellipsis
**многоуважа́емый** *прил* (*в обраще́нии*) Dear
**многочи́сленный** *прил* numerous
**многоэта́жный** *прил* multistorey (*BRIT*), multistory (*US*)
**мно́|жественн|ый** *прил*: ~**ое число́** (*ЛИНГ*) the plural (number)
**мно́жеств|о (-а)** *ср*: ~ +*gen* a great number of
**мно́жительн|ый** *прил*: ~**ая**

**те́хника** photocopying equipment
**мно́ж|ить (-у, -ишь;** *pf* **y~)** *несов перех* to multiply
**мной** *мест см.* **я**
**мобилиз|ова́ть (-у́ю) (не)сов перех** to mobilize
**моби́льник (-а)** *м* (*разг*) mobile
**моби́льный** *прил* mobile; ~ **телефо́н** mobile phone
**мог** *итп несов см.* **мочь**
**моги́л|а (-ы)** *ж* grave
**могу́** *etc несов см.* **мочь**
**могу́чий** *прил* mighty
**могу́ществ|о (-а)** *ср* power, might
**мо́д|а (-ы)** *ж* fashion; *см. та́кже* **мо́ды**
**модели́р|овать (-ую) (не)сов перех** (*оде́жду*) to design; (*pf* **с~**; *проце́сс, поведе́ние*) to simulate
**моде́л|ь (-и)** *ж* model
**модельер (-а)** *м* fashion designer
**моде́м (-а)** *м* (*КОМП*) modem
**модернизи́р|овать (-ую) (не)сов перех** to modernize
**мо́дный** *прил* fashionable
**мо́д|ы (-)** *мн* fashions *мн*; **журна́л мод** fashion magazine
**мо́жет** *несов см.* **мочь** ♦ *вводн сл* (*та́кже*: ~ **быть**) maybe
**мо́жно** *как сказ* (*возмо́жно*): ~ +*infin* it is possible to do; ~ (**войти́**)? may I (come in)?; **как** **лу́чше** as well as possible
**моза́ик|а (-и)** *ж* (*узо́р*) mosaic
**мозг (-а;** *loc sg* **-у́,** *nom sg* **-и́)** *м* brain; **спинно́й** ~ spinal cord
**мозгово́й** *прил* cerebral; ~ **центр** (*перен*) nerve centre (*BRIT*) *или* center (*US*)
**мозо́л|ь (-и)** *ж* callus
**мой (моего́;** *см. Table 8*; *f* **моя́,** *притяж мест* **моё,** *pl* **мой**) my; **по-мо́ему** my way; (*по моему́ мне́нию*) in my opinion

**МОК** (**-а**) *м сокр* (=
Междунаро́дный олимпи́йский
комите́т) IOC

**мо́к|нуть** (**-ну**; *pt* **-**, **-ла**) *несов* to
get wet; (*лежа́ть в воде́*) to be
soaking

**мо́крый** *прил* wet

**мол** (**-а**; *loc sg* **-у́**) *м* breakwater,
mole ♦ *част* (*разг*): **он**, **~**, **ничего́
не зна́ет** he says he knows nothing

**молв|а́** (**-ы́**) *ж* rumour (*BRIT*),
rumor (*US*)

**моле́б|ен** (**-на**) *м* (*РЕЛ*) service

**моле́кул|а** (**-ы**) *ж* molecule

**моли́тв|а** (**-ы**) *ж* prayer

**моли́твенник** (**-а**) *м* prayer book

**мол|и́ться** (**-ю́сь**, **-и́шься**; *pf*
**по~**) *несов возв*: **~** +*dat* to pray to

**мо́лни|я** (**-и**) *ж* lightning;
(*засте́жка*) zip (fastener) (*BRIT*),
zipper (*US*)

**молодёжный** *прил* youth; (*мо́да,
газе́та*) for young people

**молодёж|ь** (**-и**) *ж собир* young
people *мн*

**молоде́|ть** (**-ю**; *pf* **по~**) *несов* to
become younger

**молод|е́ц** (**-ца́**) *м* strong fellow; **~!**
(*разг*) well done!; **она́/он ~!** (*разг*)
she/he has done well!

**молодожён** (**-а**) *м* (*обы́чно мн*)
newlywed

**молодо́й** *прил* young;
(*карто́фель, листва́*) new

**мо́лодост|ь** (**-и**) *ж* youth

**моложа́вый** *прил* (*челове́к*)
young-looking; (*вид, лицо́*)
youthful

**моло́же** *сравн прил от* **молодо́й**

**молок|о́** (**-а́**) *ср* milk

**мо́лот** (**-а**) *м* hammer

**молот|о́к** (**-ка́**) *м* hammer

**мо́лотый** *прил* (*ко́фе, пе́рец*)
ground

**моло́ть** (**мелю́, ме́лешь**; *pf* **с~**
или **по~**) *несов перех* to grind

**моло́чник** (**-а**) *м* (*посу́да*) milk
jug

**моло́чный** *прил* (*проду́кты,
скот*) dairy; (*кокте́йль*) milk

**мо́лча** *нареч* silently;
(*согласи́ться*) tacitly

**молчали́вый** *прил* silent;
(*согла́сие*) tacit

**молча́ни|е** (**-я**) *ср* silence

**молч|а́ть** (**-у́**, **-и́шь**) *несов* to be
silent; **~** (*impf*) **о** +*prp* to keep silent
или quiet about

**мол|ь** (**-и**) *ж* moth

**мольбе́рт** (**-а**) *м* easel

**моме́нт** (**-а**) *м* moment; (*докла́да*)
point; **теку́щий ~** the current
situation

**момента́льный** *прил* instant

**монасты́р|ь** (**-я́**) *м* (*мужско́й*)
monastery; (*же́нский*) convent

**мона́х** (**-а**) *м* monk

**мона́хин|я** (**-и**; *gen pl* **-ь**) *ж* nun

**моне́т|а** (**-ы**) *ж* coin

**моне́тный** *прил*: **~ двор** mint

**монито́р** (**-а**) *м* monitor

**моногра́фи|я** (**-и**) *ж* monograph

**монопо́ли|я** (**-и**) *ж* monopoly

**моното́нный** *прил* monotonous

**монта́ж** (**-а́**) *ж* (*сооруже́ния*)
erection; (*механи́зма*) assembly;
(*ка́дров*) editing

**монтёр** (**-а**) *м* fitter; (*ЭЛЕК*)
electrician

**монти́р|овать** (**-ую**; *pf* **с~**) *несов
перех* (*обору́дование*) to
assemble; (*фильм*) to edit

**монуме́нт** (**-а**) *м* monument

**мора́л|ь** (**-и**) *ж* morals *мн*, ethics
*мн*; (*ба́сни, ска́зки*) moral

**мора́льный** *прил* moral

**морато́ри|й** (**-я**) *м* moratorium

**морг** (**-а**) *м* morgue

**морга́|ть** (**-ю**) *несов* to blink; (*под-
ми́гивать*): **~** (+*dat*) to wink (at)

**моргн|у́ть** (**-у́, -ёшь**) *сов* to blink; (*подмигнуть*): ~ (+*dat*) to wink (at)

**мо́рд|а** (**-ы**) *ж* (*животного*) muzzle; (*разг: человека*) mug

**мо́р|е** (**-я**; *nom pl* **-я́**, *gen pl* **-éй**) *ср* sea

**морехо́дный** *прил* naval

**морж** (**-а́**) *м* walrus

**мор|и́ть** (**-ю́, -и́шь**; *pf* **по~**) *несов перех* (*насекомых*) to exterminate

**морко́в|ь** (**-и**) *ж* carrots *мн*

**моро́жен|ое** (**-ого**) *ср* ice cream

**моро́женый** *прил* frozen

**моро́з** (**-а**) *м* frost

**морози́льник** (**-а**) *м* freezer

**морози́льн|ый** *прил*: **~ая ка́мера** deepfreeze

**моро́|зить** (**-жу, -зишь**) *несов перех* to freeze

**моро́зный** *прил* frosty

**морос|и́ть** (*3sg* **-и́т**) *несов* to drizzle

**моро́ч|ить** (**-у, -ишь**; *pf* **за~**) *несов перех*: ~ **го́лову кому́-н** (*разг*) to pull sb's leg

**морск|о́й** *прил* sea; (*БИО*) marine; (*курорт*) seaside; **~óе пра́во** maritime law; **~áя боле́знь** seasickness; **~áя сви́нка** guinea pig

**морщи́н|а** (**-ы**) *ж* (*на лице*) wrinkle

**морщи́нистый** *прил* wrinkled

**мо́рщ|ить** (**-у, -ишь**; *pf* **на~**) *несов перех* (*брови*) to knit; (*pf* **с~**; *нос, лоб*) to wrinkle; (*лицо*) to screw up; **~ся** (*pf* **с~ся**) *несов возв*: **~ся от** +*gen* (*от старости*) to become wrinkled from; (*от боли*) to wince in

**моря́к** (**-а́**) *м* sailor

**Москв|а́** (**-ы́**) *ж* Moscow

**москви́ч** (**-а́**) *м* Muscovite

**мост** (**-а́**; *loc sg* **-ý**) *м* bridge

**мо́стик** (**-а**) *м* bridge; **капита́нский ~** bridge (*NAUT*)

**мо|сти́ть** (**-щу́, -сти́шь**; *pf* **вы́мостить**) *несов перех* to pave

**мостов|а́я** (**-о́й**) *ж* road

**мота́|ть** (**-ю**; *pf* **на~**) *несов перех* (*нитки*) to wind ♦ (*pf* **по~**) *неперех*: ~ +*instr* (*головой*) to shake; **~ся** *несов возв* to swing

**моте́л|ь** (**-я**) *м* motel

**моти́в** (**-а**) *м* (*преступления*) motive; (*мелодия*) motif

**мотиви́р|овать** (**-ую**) (*не*)*сов перех* to justify

**мот|о́к** (**-ка́**) *м* skein

**мото́р** (**-а**) *м* motor; (*автомобиля, лодки*) engine

**моторо́ллер** (**-а**) *м* (motor) scooter

**мотоци́кл** (**-а**) *м* motorcycle

**мотыл|ёк** (**-ька́**) *м* moth

**мох** (**мха**; *loc sg* **мху**, *nom pl* **мхи**) *м* moss

**мохе́р** (**-а**) *м* mohair

**мохна́тый** *прил* (*животное*) shaggy

**моч|а́** (**-и́**) *ж* urine

**моча́л|ка** (**-ки**; *gen pl* **-ок**) *ж* sponge

**мочево́й** *прил*: ~ **пузы́рь** bladder

**моч|и́ть** (**-у́, -ишь**; *pf* **на~**) *несов перех* to wet; (*pf* **за~**; *бельё*) to soak

**мо|чь** (**-гу́, -жешь** *etc*, **-гут**; *pt* **-г, -гла́, -гло́**; *pf* **с~**) *несов*: ~ +*infin* can do, to be able to do; **я ~гу́ игра́ть на гита́ре/говори́ть по-англи́йски** I can play the guitar/speak English; **он мо́жет прийти́** he can come, he is able to come; **я сде́лаю всё, что ~гу́** I will do all I can; **за́втра мо́жешь не приходи́ть** you don't have to come tomorrow; **он мо́жет**

**оби́деться** he may well be offended; **не ~гу́ поня́ть э́того** I can't understand this; **мо́жет быть** maybe; **не мо́жет быть!** it's impossible!

**моше́нник** (-а) м swindler

**моше́нича|ть** (-ю; pf c~) несов to swindle

**мо́ш|ка** (-ки; gen pl -ек) ж midge

**мо́щность|ь** (-и) ж power

**мо́щный** прил powerful

**мощь** (-и) ж might, power

**мо|я́** (-е́й) притяж мест см. **мой**

**мрак** (-а) м darkness

**мра́мор** (-а) м marble

**мрачне́|ть** (-ю; pf по~) несов to grow dark; (лицо) to darken

**мра́чный** прил gloomy

**мсти́тел|ь** (-я) м avenger

**мсти́тельный** прил vindictive

**мстить** (мщу, мстишь; pf **отомсти́ть**) несов: ~ **кому́-н** to take revenge on sb

**МТС** ж сокр (= междугоро́дная телефо́нная ста́нция) ≈ intercity telephone exchange

**му́дрост|ь** (-и) ж wisdom

**му́дрый** прил wise

**муж** (-а; nom pl -**ья́**, gen pl -**е́й**) м husband

**мужа́|ть** (-ю; pf воз~) несов to mature; ~**ся** несов возв to take heart, have courage

**му́жественный** прил (поступок) courageous

**му́жеств|о** (-а) ср courage

**мужи́к** (-а́) м (разг: мужчина) geezer, guy

**мужско́й** прил men's; (характер) masculine; (органы, клетка) male; ~ **род** masculine gender

**мужчи́н|а** (-ы) м man

**музе́|й** (-я) м museum

**му́зык|а** (-и) ж music

**музыка́льн|ый** прил musical; ~**ая**

**шко́ла** music school

**музыка́нт** (-а) м musician

**му́к|а** (-и) ж torment

**мук|а́** (-и́) ж flour

**му́льтик** (-а) м (разг) cartoon

**мультимеди́йный** прил (КОМП) multimedia

**мультиплика́тор** (-а) м animator

**мультипликацио́нный** прил: ~ **фильм** cartoon, animation film

**мунди́р** (-а) м uniform; **карто́фель в ~е** jacket potatoes

**муниципалите́т** (-а) м municipality, city council

**мура́в|е́й** (-**ья́**) м ant

**мура́ш|ки** (-ек) мн: **у меня́ ~ по спине́ бе́гают** shivers are running down my spine

**мурлы́|кать** (-чу, -чешь) несов to purr

**муска́т** (-а) м (орех) nutmeg

**му́скул** (-а) м muscle

**мускули́стый** прил muscular

**му́сор** (-а) м rubbish (BRIT), garbage (US)

**му́сорн|ый** прил rubbish (BRIT), garbage (US); ~**ое ведро́** dustbin (BRIT), trash can (US)

**мусоропрово́д** (-а) м refuse или garbage (US) chute

**мусульма́нин** (-а) м Muslim

**мута́нт** (-а) м mutant

**мута́ци|я** (-и) ж mutation

**му|ти́ть** (-чу́, -ти́шь; pf вз~ или за~) несов перех (жидкость) to cloud; ~**ся** (pf за~**ся**) несов возв (вода́, раство́р) to become cloudy

**мутне́|ть** (3sg -ет; pf по~) несов (жидкость) to become cloudy; (взор) to grow dull

**му́тный** прил (жидкость) cloudy; (стекло) dull

**му́х|а** (-и) ж fly

**мухомо́р** (-а) м (БОТ) fly agaric

**муче́ни|е** (-я) ср torment, torture

**му́ченик** (**-а**) *м* martyr

**мучи́тел|ь** (**-я**) *м* tormentor

**мучи́тельный** *прил* agonizing

**му́ч|ить** (**-у, -ишь**) *pf* **за~** *или* **из~**) *несов перех* to torment; **~ся** (*pf* **за~ся**) *несов возв:* **~ся** +*instr* (*сомнениями*) to be tormented by; **~ся** (*impf*) **над** +*instr* to agonize over

**мч|ать** (**-у, -ишь**) *несов* (*машину*) to speed along; (*лошадь*) to race along; **мча́ться** *несов возв* (*поезд*) to speed along; (*лошадь*) to race along

**мще́ни|е** (**-я**) *ср* vengeance, revenge

**мы** (**нас;** *см. Table 6b*) *мест* we; **~ с тобо́й/жено́й** you/my wife and I

**мы́л|ить** (**-ю, -ишь;** *pf* **на~**) *несов перех* to soap; **~ся** (*pf* **на~ся**) *несов возв* to soap o.s.

**мы́л|о** (**-а**) *ср* soap

**мы́льниц|а** (**-ы**) *ж* soap dish

**мы́льн|ый** *прил* (*пена*) soap; **~ая о́пера** soap (opera)

**мыс** (**-а;** *loc sg* **-ý**, *nom pl* **-ы́**) *м* point

**мы́сленный** *прил* mental

**мысли́тел|ь** (**-я**) *м* thinker

**мы́сл|ить** (**-ю, -ишь**) *несов* to think ♦ *перех* to imagine

**мысл|ь** (**-и**) *ж* thought; (*идея*) idea; **за́дняя ~** ulterior motive; **о́браз мы́слей** way of thinking

**мыть** (**мо́ю, мо́ешь;** *pf* **вы~** *или* **помы́ть**) *несов перех* to wash; **мы́ться** (*pf* **вы́~ся** *или* **помы́ться**) *несов возв* to wash o.s.

**мыч|а́ть** (**-ý, -и́шь;** *pf* **про~**) *несов* (*корова*) to moo

**мышело́в|ка** (**-ки;** *gen pl* **-ок**) *ж* mousetrap

**мы́шечный** *прил* muscular

**мы́ш|ка** (**-ки;** *gen pl* **-ек**) *ж* mouse; **под ~кой** under one's arm

**мышле́ни|е** (**-я**) *ср* (*способность*) reason; (*процесс*) thinking

**мы́шц|а** (**-ы**) *ж* muscle

**мыш|ь** (**-и**) *ж* (*ЗООЛ, КОМП*) mouse

**мэр** (**-а**) *м* mayor

**мэ́ри|я** (**-и**) *ж* city hall

**мя́гкий** *прил* soft; (*движения*) smooth; (*характер, климат*) mild; (*наказание*) lenient; **~ ваго́н** *railway carriage with soft seats;* **~ знак** soft sign (*Russian letter*)

**мя́гко** *нареч* gently; (*отругать*) mildly; **~ говоря́** to put it mildly

**мя́кот|ь** (**-и**) *ж* flesh; (*мясо*) fillet

**мя́мл|ить** (**-ю, - ишь;** *pf* **про~**) *несов перех* to mumble

**мясни́к** (**-á**) *м* butcher

**мясно́й** *прил* (*котлета*) meat; **~ магази́н** the butcher's

**мя́с|о** (**-а**) *ср* meat

**мясору́б|ка** (**-ки;** *gen pl* **-ок**) *ж* mincer (*BRIT*), grinder (*US*); (*перен*) carnage

**мя́т|а** (**-ы**) *ж* mint

**мяте́ж** (**-á**) *м* revolt

**мя́тный** *прил* mint

**мя́тый** *прил* (*одежда*) creased

**мять** (**мну, мнёшь;** *pf* **измя́ть** *или* **с~**) *несов перех* (*одежду*) to crease; (*бумагу*) to crumple; **мя́ться** *несов возв* (*разг: человек*) to shilly-shally; (*pf* **помя́ться** *или* **смя́ться;** *одежда*) to get creased

**мяу́ка|ть** (**-ю;** *pf* **про~**) *несов* to miaow, mew

**мяч** (**-á**) *м* ball; **футбо́льный ~** football

# Н, н

**на** предл; +acc 1 (направление на поверхность) on; **положи тарéлку на стол** put the plate on the table

2 (направление в какое-нибудь место) to; **сесть** (pf) **на пóезд** to get on(to) the train

3 (об объекте воздействия): **обрати внимáние на этого человéка** pay attention to this man; **нажми на педáль/кнóпку** press the pedal/button; **я люблю смотрéть на детéй/на звёзды** I love watching the children/the stars

4 (о времени, сроке) for; **он уéхал на мéсяц** he has gone away for a month

5 (о цели, о назначении) for; **дéньги на книги** money for books

6 (о мере) into; **делить** (impf) **что-н на чáсти** to divide sth into parts

7 (при сравнении): **я получáю на сто рублéй мéньше** I get one hundred roubles less

8 (об изменении состояния) into; **нáдо перевести текст на английский** the text must be translated into English

♦ предл; +prp 1 (нахождение на поверхности) on; **книга на пóлке** the book is on the shelf; **на дéвочке шáпка/шýба** the girl has a hat/fur coat on

2 (о пребывании где-нибудь) in; **на Украйне/Кавкáзе** in the Ukraine/Caucasus; **на ýлице** in the street; **быть** (impf) **на рабóте/**заседáнии to be at work/at a meeting

3 (о времени осуществления чего-н): **встрéтимся на слéдующей недéле** let's meet next week

4 (об объекте воздействия) on; **сосредотóчиться** (pf)/**остановиться** (pf) **на чём-н** to concentrate/dwell on sth

5 (о средстве осуществления чего-н): **éздить на пóезде/велосипéде** to travel by train/bicycle; **игрáть** (impf) **на роя́ле/скрипке** to play the piano/violin; **катáться** (impf) **на лы́жах/конькáх** to go skiing/skating; **говорить** (impf) **на рýсском/английском языкé** to speak (in) English/Russian

6 (о составной части предмета): **кáша на водé** porridge made with water

---

**на** (**нáте**) част (разг) here (you are)

**набежáть** (как **бежáть**; см. Table 20; impf **набегáть**) сов (разг: тучи) to gather; (наскочить): ~ **на** +acc to run into; (волны: на берег) to lap against

**нáбело** нареч: переписáть что-н ~ to write sth out neatly

**нáбережн|ая** (**-ой**) ж embankment

**набивá|ть(ся)** (**-ю(сь)**) несов от **набить(ся)**

**набивк|а** (**-и**) ж stuffing

**набирá|ть** (**-ю**) несов от **набрáть**

**наб|ить** (**-ью, -ьёшь**; impf **набивáть**) сов перех: ~ (+instr) to stuff (with); **набивáть** (~ pf) **цéну** (разг) to talk up the price; **~ся** (impf **набивáться**) сов возв (разг): ~**ся в** +acc to be crammed into

**наблюда́тел|ь** (**-я**) м observer

**наблюда́тельный** прил
(*человек*) observant; ~ **пункт**
observation point

**наблюда́|ть** (**-ю**) несов перех to
observe ♦ неперех: ~ **за** +instr to
monitor

**на́бок** нареч to one side

**набо́р** (**-а**) м (*совокупность*) set;
(*типог*) typesetting

**набо́рщик** (**-а**) м typesetter

**набра́сыва|ть** (**-ю**) несов от
**наброса́ть**, **набро́сить**; **~ся**
несов от **набро́ситься**

**наб|ра́ть** (**-еру́, -ерёшь**; pt **-ра́л,
-рала́, -ра́ло**; impf **набира́ть**)
сов перех: ~ +gen (*цветы*) to pick;
(*воду*) to fetch; (*студентов*) to
take on; (*скорость, высоту,
баллы*) to gain; (*код*) to dial;
(*текст*) to typeset

**наброса́|ть** (**-ю**; impf
**набра́сывать**) сов перех (*план,
текст*) to sketch out ♦ (не)перех: ~
+acc или +gen (*вещей, окурков*)
to throw about

**набро́|сить** (**-шу, -сишь**; impf
**набра́сывать**) сов перех
(*пальто, платок*) to throw on; **~ся**
(impf **набра́сываться**) сов возв:
**~ся на** +acc (*на жертву*) to fall
upon

**набро́с|ок** (**-ка**) м (*рисунок*)
sketch; (*статьи*) draft

**набу́х|нуть** (3sg **-нет**, pt **-, -ла**;
impf **набуха́ть**) сов to swell up

**нав|али́ть** (**-алю́, -а́лишь**; impf
**нава́ливать**) сов (не)перех: ~
+acc или +gen (*мусору*) to pile up;
**~ся** (impf **нава́ливаться**) сов
возв: **~ся на** +acc (*на дверь итп*)
to lean into

**нава́лом** как сказ: ~ +gen (*разг*)
loads of; **у него́ де́нег** ~ he has

loads of money

**наведе́ни|е** (**-я**) ср (*порядка*)
establishment; (*справок*) making

**наве́к(и)** нареч (*навсегда*) forever

**наве́рно(е)** вводн сл probably

**наверняка́** вводн сл (*конечно*)
certainly ♦ нареч (*несомненно*)
definitely, for sure

**наверста́|ть** (**-ю**; impf
**навёрстывать**) сов перех
(*типог*) to typeset; **навёрстывать**
(**~** pf) **упу́щенное** или
**поте́рянное вре́мя** to make up for
lost time

**наве́рх** нареч up; (*на верхний
этаж*) upstairs; (*на поверхность*)
to the top

**наверху́** нареч at the top; (*на
верхнем этаже*) upstairs

**наве́с** (**-а**) м canopy

**нав|ести́** (**-еду́, -едёшь**; pt **-ёл,
-ела́, -ело́**; impf **наводи́ть**) сов
перех (*ужас, грусть итп*) to
cause; (*бинокль*) to focus;
(*орудие*) to aim; (*порядок*) to
establish; **наводи́ть** (**~** pf) **кого́-н
на** +acc (*на место, на след*) to
lead sb to; **наводи́ть** (**~** pf)
**спра́вки** to make inquiries

**наве|сти́ть** (**-щу́, -сти́шь**; impf
**навеща́ть**) сов перех to visit

**на́взничь** нареч on one's back

**навига́ци|я** (**-и**) ж navigation

**нави́с|нуть** (**-ну**; pt **-, -ла**; impf
**нависа́ть**) сов: ~ **на** +acc
(*волосы: на лоб*) to hang down
over

**нав|оди́ть** (**-ожу́, -о́дишь**)
несов от **навести́**

**наводне́ни|е** (**-я**) ср flood

**наво́з** (**-а**) м manure

**на́волоч|ка** (**-ки**; gen pl **-ек**) ж
pillowcase

**навре|ди́ть** (**-жу́, -ди́шь**) сов от
**вреди́ть**

**навсегда́** *нареч* forever; **раз и ~**
once and for all

**навстре́чу** *предл*: ~ *+dat* towards
♦ *нареч*: **идти́ ~ кому́-н** (*перен*)
to give sb a hand

**на́вык (-а)** *м* skill

**навы́нос** *нареч* to take away
(*BRIT*), to go (*US*)

**навы́пуск** *нареч* outside, over

**нав|яза́ть (-яжу́, -я́жешь;** *impf*
**навя́зывать)** *сов перех*: ~ **что-н**
**кому́-н** to impose sth on sb; **~ся**
(*impf* **навя́зываться**) *сов возв* to
impose o.s.

**навя́зчивый** *прил* persistent

**нагиба́|ть(ся) (-ю(сь))** *несов от*
**нагну́ть(ся)**

**нагле́|ть (-ю;** *pf* **об~)** *несов* to get
cheeky

**нагле́ц (-а́)** *м* impudent upstart

**на́глухо** *нареч* tight, securely

**на́глый** *прил* cheeky, impertinent

**нагля́дный** *прил* (*пример,*
*случай*) clear; (*метод обучения*)
visual

**наг|на́ть (-оню́, -о́нишь;** *impf*
**нагоня́ть)** *сов перех* (*беглеца*)
to catch up with; (*упущенное*) to
make up for; **нагоня́ть (~** *pf*)
**страх на кого́-н** to strike fear into
sb

**нагнета́|ть (-ю)** *несов перех*
(*воздух*) to pump; (*перен:*
*напряжение*) to heighten

**нагн|у́ть (-у́, -ёшь;** *impf*
**нагиба́ть)** *сов перех* (*ветку*) to
pull down; (*голову*) to bend; **~ся**
(*impf* **нагиба́ться**) *сов возв* to
bend down

**наговор|и́ть (-ю́, -и́шь)** *сов*
(*разг: наклеветать*): ~ **на** *+acc* to
slander; ~ (*pf*) **чепухи́** to talk a lot
of nonsense; **~ся** *сов возв* to talk
one's fill

**наго́й** *прил* (*человек*) naked, nude

**на́голо** *нареч*: **остри́чься ~** to
shave one's head

**нагоня́|ть (-ю)** *несов от* **нагна́ть**

**нагото́ве** *нареч* at the ready

**награ́д|а (-ы)** *ж* reward, prize;
(*ВОЕН*) decoration

**награ|ди́ть (-жу́, -ди́шь;** *impf*
**награжда́ть)** *сов перех*: ~ **кого́-н**
**чем-н** (*орденом*) to award sb sth,
award sth to sb; (*перен:*
*талантом*) to endow sb with sth

**нагрева́тельный** *прил*: ~
**прибо́р** heating appliance

**нагре́|ть (-ю;** *impf* **нагрева́ть)**
*сов перех* to heat, warm; **~ся**
(*impf* **нагрева́ться**) *сов возв* to
warm up

**нагроможде́ни|е (-я)** *ср* pile

**нагруб|и́ть (-лю́, -и́шь)** *сов от*
**груби́ть**

**нагру́дник (-а)** *м* bib

**нагру́дный** *прил*: ~ **карма́н**
breast pocket

**нагр|узи́ть (-ужу́, -у́зишь)** *сов*
*от* **грузи́ть** ♦ (*impf* **нагружа́ть**)
*перех* to load up

**нагру́зк|а (-и)** *ж* load

**над** *предл*: ~ *+instr* above;
**рабо́тать** (*impf*) ~ *+instr* to work on;
**ду́мать** (*impf*) ~ *+instr* to think
about; **сме́яться** (*impf*) ~ *+instr* to
laugh at; **сиде́ть** (*impf*) ~ **кни́гой** to
sit over a book

**над|ави́ть (-авлю́, -а́вишь;** *impf*
**нада́вливать)** *сов*: ~ **на** *+acc* (*на*
*дверь итп*) to lean against; (*на*
*кнопку*) to press

**надба́вк|а (-и)** *ж* (*к зарплате*)
rise; (*к цене*) mark-up

**надви́н|уть (-у;** *impf* **надвига́ть)**
*сов перех*: ~ **что-н** (**на** *+acc*) to
pull sth down (over); **~ся** (*impf*
**надвига́ться**) *сов возв*
(*опасность, старость*) to
approach

**на́двое** *нареч* in half

**надгро́би|е (-я)** *ср* gravestone

**надева́|ть (-ю)** *несов от* **наде́ть**

**наде́жд|а (-ы)** *ж* hope

**надёжный** *прил* reliable; (*механизм*) secure

**наде́ла|ть (-ю)** *сов (не)перех*: ~ +*acc или* +*gen (ошибок)* to make lots of; **что ты ~л?** what have you done?

**наде́л|и́ть (-ю́, -и́шь;** *impf* **наделя́ть)** *сов перех*: ~ **кого́-н чем-н (землёй)** to grant sb sth

**наде́|ть (-ну, -нешь;** *impf* **надева́ть)** *сов перех* to put on

**наде́|яться (-юсь)** *несов возв*: ~ +*infin* to hope to do; ~ **(по~** *pf)* **на** +*acc (на друга)* to rely on; (*на улучшение*) to hope for

**надзе́мный** *прил* overground

**надзира́тел|ь (-я)** *м* guard

**надзо́р (-а)** *м* control; (*орган*) monitoring body

**надл|оми́ть (-омлю́, -о́мишь;** *impf* **надла́мывать)** *сов перех* to break; (*здоровье, психику*) to damage

**надме́нный** *прил* haughty

---
KEYWORD
---

**на́до** *как сказ* **1** (*следует*): **на́до ему́ помо́чь** it is necessary to help him; **на́до, что́бы он пришёл во́время** he must come on time; **на́до всегда́ говори́ть пра́вду** one must always speak the truth; **мне/ему́ на́до зако́нчить рабо́ту** I/he must finish the job; **помо́чь тебе́? - не на́до!** can I help you? - there's no need!; **не на́до!** (*не делай этого*) don't!

**2** (*о потребности*): **на́до мно́го лет** it takes many years; **им на́до 5 рубле́й** they need 5 roubles; **что тебе́ на́до?** what do you want?;

**так ему́/ей и на́до** (*разг*) it serves him/her right; **на́до же!** (*разг*) of all things!

---

**на́до** *предл см.* **над**

**надое́дливый** *прил* tiresome

**надое́|сть (как есть;** *см. Table 15*; *impf* **надоеда́ть)** *сов*: ~ **кому́-н** (+*instr*) (*разговорами, упрёками*) to bore sb (with); **мне ~ло ждать** I'm tired of waiting; **он мне ~л** I've had enough of him

**надо́лго** *нареч* for a long time

**надорв|а́ть (-у́, -ёшь;** *impf* **надрыва́ть)** *сов перех* (*перен: силы*) to tax; (: *здоровье*) to put a strain on; ~**ся** (*impf* **надрыва́ться)** *сов возв* to do o.s. an injury; (*перен*) to overexhaust o.s.

**надп|иса́ть (-ишу́, -и́шешь;** *impf* **надпи́сывать)** *сов перех* to inscribe; (*конверт*) to address

**надруга́|ться (-юсь)** (*не)сов возв*: ~ **над** +*instr (над могилой, над женщиной)* to violate; (*над чувствами*) to abuse

**надсмо́трщик (-а)** *м* (*тюремный*) warden

**наду́|ть (-ю, -ешь;** *impf* **надува́ть)** *сов перех (мяч, колесо)* to inflate, blow up; (*разг: обмануть*) to con; ~**ся** (*impf* **надува́ться)** *сов возв (матрас, мяч)* to inflate; (*парус*) to billow; (*вены*) to swell; (*перен: от важности*) to swell up; (: *разг: обидеться*) to sulk

**наеда́|ться (-юсь)** *несов от* **нае́сться**

**наедине́** *нареч*: ~ **(с** +*instr*) alone (with); **они́ оста́лись** ~ they were left on their own

**нае́здник (-а)** *м* rider

**наезжа́|ть (-ю)** *несов от*

**нае́хать**

**на|ём (-йма́)** *м* hiring; (*квартиры*) renting

**наёмник (-а)** *м* mercenary; (*работник*) casual worker

**наёмный** *прил* (*труд, работник*) hired; **~ уби́йца** hitman

**нае́|сться** (*как* **есть**; *см. Table 15*; *impf* **наеда́ться**) *сов возв*: **~ +gen** (*сладкого*) to eat a lot of; **я ~лся** I'm full

**нае́хать** (*как* **е́хать**; *см. Table 19*; *impf* **наезжа́ть**) *сов* (*разг: гости*) to arrive in droves; **наезжа́ть (~** *pf*) **на +acc** (*на кнопку*) to drive into

**наж|а́ть (-му́, -мёшь;** *impf* **нажима́ть)** *сов* (*перен*): **~ на +acc** (*на кнопку*) to press

**нажда́чн|ый** *прил*: **~ая бума́га** emery paper

**нажи́м (-а)** *м* pressure

**нажима́|ть (-ю)** *несов от* **нажа́ть**

**нажи́|ть (-ву́, -вёшь;** *impf* **нажива́ть)** *сов перех* (*состояние*) to acquire; **~ся** (*impf* **нажива́ться)** *сов возв*: **~ся (на +prp)** to profiteer (from)

**наза́д** *нареч* back; (*нагнуться, катиться итп*) backwards; (*тому́*) **~** ago; **де́сять лет/неде́лю (тому́) ~** ten years/one week ago

**назва́ни|е (-я)** *ср* name; **торго́вое ~** trade name

**наз|ва́ть (-ову́, -овёшь;** *impf* **называ́ть)** *сов перех* (*дать имя*) to call; (*назначить*) to name

**назе́мн|ый** *прил* surface; **~ые войска́** ground troops

**на́земь** *нареч* to the ground

**назло́** *нареч* out of spite; **~ кому́-н** to spite sb; **как ~** to make things worse

**назначе́ни|е (-я)** *ср* (*цены итп*) setting; (*на работу*) appointment;

(*функция*) function; **пункт** *или* **ме́сто ~я** destination

**назна́ч|ить (-у, -ишь;** *impf* **назнача́ть)** *сов перех* (*на работу*) to appoint; (*цену*) to set; (*встречу*) to arrange; (*лекарство*) to prescribe

**назо́йливый** *прил* persistent

**назре́|ть (3sg -ет;** *impf* **назрева́ть)** *сов* (*вопрос*) to become unavoidable

**называ́емый** *прил*: **так называ́емый** so-called

**называ́|ть (-ю)** *несов от* **назва́ть**; **~ся** *несов возв* (*носить название*) to be called

**наибо́лее** *нареч*: **~ интере́сный/ краси́вый** the most interesting/ beautiful

**наибо́льший** *прил* the greatest

**наи́вный** *прил* naive

**наизна́нку** *нареч* inside out

**наизу́сть** *нареч*: **знать/вы́учить ~** to know/learn by heart

**наиме́нее** *нареч*: **~ уда́чный/ спосо́бный** the least successful/ capable

**наименова́ни|е (-я)** *ср* name; (*книги*) title, name

**наиме́ньший** *прил* (*длина, вес*) the smallest; (*усилие*) the least

**на|йти́ (-йду́, -йдёшь;** *pt* **-шёл, -шла́, -шло́;** *impf* **находи́ть)** *сов перех* to find; **на меня́ ~шёл смех** I couldn't help laughing; **~сь** (*impf* **находи́ться)** *сов возв* (*потерянное*) to turn up; (*добровольцы*) to come forward; (*не растеряться*) to regain control

**наказа́ни|е (-я)** *ср* punishment

**нак|аза́ть (-ажу́, -а́жешь;** *impf* **нака́зывать)** *сов перех* to punish

**нака́л (-а)** *м* (*борьбы*) heat

**накал|и́ть (-ю́, -и́шь;** *impf* **накаля́ть)** *сов перех* to heat up;

(*перен: обстано́вку*) to hot up;
~**ся** (*impf* **накаля́ться**) *сов возв*
to heat; (*перен: обстано́вка*) to
hot up

**накану́не** *нареч* the day before,
the previous day ♦ *предл*: ~ +*gen*
on the eve of

**нака́плива|ть(ся)** (-ю(сь)) *несов*
*от* **накопи́ть(ся)**

**нак|ати́ть** (-ачу́, -а́тишь; *impf*
**нака́тывать**) *сов*: ~ (**на** +*acc*)
(*волна́*) to roll up (onto)

**накача́|ть** (-ю; *impf* **нака́чивать**)
*сов перех* (*ка́меру*) to pump up

**наки́д|ка** (-ки; *gen pl* -**ок**) *ж*
(*оде́жда*) wrap; (*покрыва́ло*)
bedspread, throw

**наки́н|уть** (-у; *impf* **наки́дывать**)
*сов перех* (*плато́к*) to throw on;
~**ся** (*impf* **наки́дываться**) *сов*
*возв*: ~**ся на** +*acc* (*на челове́ка*)
to hurl o.s. at; (*разг: на еду́, на*
*кни́гу*) to get stuck into

**на́кип|ь** (-и) *ж* (*на бульо́не*)
scum; (*в ча́йнике*) fur (*BRIT*), scale
(*US*)

**накладн|а́я** (-о́й) *ж* (*КОММ*) bill of
lading (*BRIT*), waybill (*US*);
**грузова́я** ~ consignment note

**накладн|о́й** *прил*: ~**ые расхо́ды**
overheads *мн* (*BRIT*), overhead (*US*)

**накла́дыва|ть** (-ю) *несов от*
**наложи́ть**

**накле́|ить** (-ю, -ишь; *impf*
**накле́ивать**) *сов перех* to stick on

**накле́|йка** (-йка; *gen pl* -**ек**) *ж*
label

**накло́н** (-а) *м* incline, slope

**накл|они́ть** (-оню́, -о́нишь; *impf*
**наклоня́ть**) *сов перех* to tilt; ~**ся**
(*impf* **наклоня́ться**) *сов возв* to
bend down

**накло́нность|ь** (-и) *ж*: ~ **к** +*dat* (*к*
*му́зыке итп*) aptitude for;
**дурны́е/хоро́шие** ~**и** bad/good

habits

**накова́л|ьня** (-ьни; *gen pl* -**ен**) *ж*
anvil

**нак|оло́ть** (-олю́, -о́лешь; *impf*
**нака́лывать**) *сов перех* (*ру́ку*)
to prick; (*прикрепи́ть*): ~ (**на** +*acc*)
(*на шля́пу, на дверь*) to pin
on(to)

**наконе́ц** *нареч* at last, finally
♦ *вводн сл* after all; ~**-то!** at long
last!

**наконе́чник** (-а) *м* tip, end

**накоп|и́ть** (-лю́, -ишь) *сов от*
**копи́ть** ♦ (*impf* **нака́пливать**)
*перех* (*си́лы, информа́цию*) to
store up; (*сре́дства*) to
accumulate; ~**ся** *сов от* **копи́ться**
♦ (*impf* **нака́пливаться**) *возв*
(*си́лы*) to build up; (*сре́дства*) to
accumulate

**нак|орми́ть** (-ормлю́,
-о́рмишь) *сов от* **корми́ть**

**на́крест** *нареч* (*также*: **крест-**~)
crosswise

**накрич|а́ть** (-у́, -и́шь) *сов*: ~ **на**
+*acc* to shout at

**накр|ути́ть** (-учу́, -у́тишь; *impf*
**накру́чивать**) *сов перех*: ~ (**на**
+*acc*) (*га́йку*) to screw on(to);
(*кана́т*) to wind (round)

**накр|ы́ть** (-о́ю, -о́ешь; *impf*
**накрыва́ть**) *сов перех* to cover;
**накрыва́ть** (~ *pf*) (**на**) **стол** to lay
the table; ~**ся** (*impf* **накрыва́ться**)
*сов возв*: ~**ся** (+*instr*) (*одея́лом*)
to cover o.s. up (with)

**налага́|ть** (-ю) *несов от*
**наложи́ть**

**нала́|дить** (-жу, -дишь; *impf*
**нала́живать**) *сов перех*
(*механи́зм*) to repair, fix;
(*сотру́дничество*) to initiate;
(*хозя́йство*) to sort out; ~**ся** (*impf*
**нала́живаться**) *сов возв*
(*рабо́та*) to go well; (*отноше́ния*)

здоровье) to improve

**налéво** *нареч* (to the) left; (*разг: продать*) on the side

**налегкé** *нареч* (*ехать*) without luggage

**налёт** (-а) *м* raid; (*пыли, плесени*) thin coating *или* layer

**нале|тéть** (-чý, -тúшь; *impf* **налетáть**) *сов* (*буря*) to spring up; **налетáть** (~ *pf*) **на** +*acc* (*натолкнуться*) to fly against; (*напасть*) to swoop down on

**нал|úть** (-ью, -ьёшь; *impf* **наливáть**) *сов перех* to pour (out)

**налицó** *как сказ:* **фáкты** ~ the facts are obvious; **доказáтельство** ~ there is proof

**налúчи|е** (-я) *ср* presence

**налúчност|ь** (-и) *ж* cash

**налúчн|ые** (-ых) *мн* cash *ед*

**налúчн|ый** *прил:* ~**ые дéньги** cash; ~ **расчёт** cash payment; ~ **счёт** cash account

**налóг** (-а) *м* tax; ~ **на ввоз** +*gen* import duty on

**налóгов|ый** *прил* tax; ~**ая декларáция** tax return

**налóговик** (-а) *м* taxman

**налогоплатéльщик** (-а) *м* taxpayer

**налóженн|ый** *прил:* ~**ым платежóм** cash on delivery

**нал|ожúть** (-ожý, -óжишь; *impf* **наклáдывать**) *сов перех* to put *или* place on; (*компресс, бинт, лак*) to apply; (*impf* **налагáть**) *штраф*) to impose

**нам** *мест см.* **мы**

**нама́|зать** (-жу, -жешь) *сов от* **мáзать**

**намáтыва|ть** (-ю) *несов от* **намотáть**

**намёк** (-а) *м* hint

**намека́|ть** (-ю; *pf* **намекнýть**) *несов:* ~ **на** +*acc* to hint at

**намеревá|ться** (-юсь) *несов возв:* ~ +*infin* to intend to do

**намéрен** *как сказ:* **он** ~ **уéхать** he intends to leave

**намéрени|е** (-я) *ср* intention

**намéренный** *прил* deliberate

**намета́|ть** (-ю) *сов от* **метáть**

**намé|тить** (-чу, -тишь; *impf* **намечáть**) *сов перех* to plan; (*план*) to project; ~**ся** *сов от* **мéтиться** ♦ (*impf* **намечáться**) *возв* to begin to show; (*событие*) to be coming up

**нáми** *мест см.* **мы**

**намнóго** *нареч* much, far; ~ **хýже/интерéснее** much worse/ more interesting

**намóкн|уть** (-у; *impf* **намокáть**) *сов* to get wet

**намóрдник** (-а) *м* muzzle

**намóрщ|ить** (-у, -ишь) *сов от* **мóрщить**

**намота́|ть** (-ю) *сов от* **мотáть**

**нам|очúть** (-очý, -óчишь) *сов от* **мочúть**

**нан|ести́** (-есý, -есёшь; *pt* -ёс, -еслá, -еслó; *impf* **наносúть**) *сов перех* (*мазь, краску*) to apply; (*рисунок*) to draw; (*на карту*) to plot; (*удар*) to deliver; (*урон*) to inflict; ~ (*pf*) **комý-н визúт** to pay sb a visit

**нанúзыва|ть** (-ю) *несов перех* to string

**на|нять** (-йму́, -ймёшь; *impf* **нанимáть**) *сов перех* (*работника*) to hire; (*лодку, машину*) to hire, rent; ~**ся** (*impf* **нанимáться**) *сов возв* to get a job

**наоборóт** *нареч* (*делать*) the wrong way (round) ♦ *вводн сл, част* on the contrary

**наобýм** *нареч* without thinking

**наотрéз** *нареч* flatly, point-blank

**нападá|ть** (-ю) *несов от*

**напáсть**

**нападáющ|ий** (**-его**) *м* (*СПОРТ*) forward

**нападéни|е** (**-я**) *ср* attack; (*СПОРТ*) forwards *мн*

**напáд|ки** (**-ок**) *мн* attacks *мн*

**нап|áсть** (**-адý, -адёшь**; *impf* **нападáть**) *сов*: ~ **на** +*acc* to attack; (*обнаружить*) to strike; (*тоска, страх*) to grip, seize

**напéв** (**-а**) *м* tune, melody

**напевá|ть** (**-ю**) *несов от* **напéть** ♦ *перех* (*песенку*) to hum

**наперебóй** *нареч* vying with each other

**наперегонки** *нареч* (*разг*) racing each other

**наперёд** *нареч* (*знать, угадáть*) beforehand; **зáдом** ~ back to front

**наперекóр** *предл*: ~ +*dat* in defiance of

**наперст|óк** (**-кá**) *м* thimble

**нап|éть** (**-óю, -оёшь**; *impf* **напевáть**) *сов перех* (*мотив, песню*) to sing

**напивá|ться** (**-юсь**) *несов от* **напиться**

**напильник** (**-а**) *м* file

**напирá|ть** (**-ю**) *несов*: ~ **на** +*acc* (*теснить*) to push against

**написáни|е** (**-я**) *ср* writing; (*слова*) spelling

**нап|исáть** (**-ишý, -ишешь**) *сов от* **писáть**

**напит|óк** (**-кá**) *м* drink

**нап|иться** (**-ьюсь, -ьёшься**; *impf* **напивáться**) *сов возв*: ~ (+*gen*) to have a good drink (of); (*разг: опьянеть*) to get drunk

**напл|евáть** (**-юю**) *сов от* **плевáть**

**наплы́в** (**-а**) *м* (*туристов*) influx; (: *заявления, чувств*) flood

**наплы́|ть** (**-вý, -вёшь**; *impf* **наплывáть**) *сов* (*перен*:

*воспоминания*) to come flooding back; **наплывáть** (~ *pf*) **на** +*acc* (*на мель, на кáмень*) to run against

**наповáл** *нареч* (*убить*) outright

**наподóбие** *предл*: ~ +*gen* resembling

**нап|оить** (**-ою, -óишь**) *сов от* **поить**

**напокáз** *нареч* for show

**наполн|ить** (**-ю, -ишь**; *impf* **наполнять**) *сов перех*: ~ +*instr* to fill with; ~**ся** (*impf* **наполняться**) *сов возв*: ~**ся** +*instr* to fill with

**наполовину** *нареч* by half; (*наполнить*) half

**напоминá|ть** (**-ю**) *несов от* **напóмнить** ♦ *перех* (*иметь сходство*) to resemble

**напóмн|ить** (**-ю, -ишь**; *impf* **напоминáть**) *сов* (*не*)*перех*: ~ **комý-н** +*acc* или **о** +*prp* to remind sb

**напóр** (**-а**) *м* pressure

**напослéдок** *нареч* finally

**напрáв|ить** (**-лю, -ишь**; *impf* **направлять**) *сов перех* to direct; (*к врачý*) to refer; (*послáние*) to send; ~**ся** (*impf* **направляться**) *сов возв*: ~**ся в** +*acc*/**к** +*dat итп* to make for

**направлéни|е** (**-я**) *ср* direction; (*деятельности, также ВОЕН*) line; (*политики*) orientation; (*докумéнт: в больницу*) referral; (: **на рабóту, на учёбу**) directive; **по** ~**ю к** +*dat* towards

**напрáво** *нареч* (*идти*) (to the) right

**напрáсно** *нареч* in vain

**напрáсный** *прил* (*труд*) vain; (*тревóга*) unfounded

**напрáшива|ться** (**-юсь**) *несов от* **напроситься**

**напримéр** *вводн сл* for example или instance

**напрока́т** *нареч*: взять ~ to hire; **отдава́ть (отда́ть** *pf*) ~ to hire out

**напролёт** *нареч* without a break

**напроло́м** *нареч* stopping at nothing

**напр|оси́ться (-ошу́сь, -о́сишься**; *impf* **напра́шиваться**; *сов возв* (*разг: в гости*) to force o.s.; **напра́шиваться (~** *pf*) **на** +*acc* (*на комплимент*) to invite

**напро́тив** *нареч* opposite ♦ *вводн сл* on the contrary ♦ *предл*: ~ +*gen* opposite

**напряга́|ть(ся) (-ю(сь))** *несов от* **напра́чь(ся)**

**напряже́ни|е (-я)** *ср* tension; (*ФИЗ, механическое*) strain, stress; (: *электрическое*) voltage

**напряжённый** *прил* tense; (*отношения, встреча*) strained

**напрями́к** *нареч* (*идти*) straight

**напр|я́чь (-ягу́, -яжёшь** *итп*, **-ягу́т**; *pt* **-я́г, -ягла́**; *impf* **напряга́ть**) *сов перех* to strain; **~ся** (*impf* **напряга́ться**) *сов возв* (*мускулы*) to become tense; (*человек*) to strain o.s.

**напыл|и́ть (-ю́, -и́шь)** *сов от* **пыли́ть**

**напы́щенный** *прил* pompous

**наравне́** *нареч*: ~ с +*instr* (*по одной линии*) on a level with; (*на равных правах*) on an equal footing with

**нарас|ти́ (3sg -тёт**; *impf* **-та́ть)** *сов* (*проценты*) to accumulate; (*волнение, сопротивление*) to grow

**нарасхва́т** *нареч* like hot cakes

**нара́щива|ть (-ю)** *несов перех* (*темпы, объём итп*) to increase

**нарв|а́ть (-у́, -ёшь)** *сов* (*не)перех*: ~ +*acc или* +*gen* (*цветов, ягод*) to pick; **~ся** (*impf* **нарыва́ться**) *сов возв* (*разг*):

~**ся на** +*acc* (*на хулигана*) to run up against; (*на неприятность*) to run into

**наре́|зать (-жу, -жешь**; *impf* **нареза́ть)** *сов перех* to cut

**наре́чи|е (-я)** *ср* (*ЛИНГ, часть речи*) adverb; (: *говоры*) dialect

**нарис|ова́ть (-у́ю)** *сов от* **рисова́ть**

**наркоби́знес (-а)** *м* drug trafficking

**наркоде́л|ец (-ьца́)** *м* drug dealer

**нарко́з (-а)** *м* (*МЕД*) narcosis, anaesthesia (*BRIT*), anesthesia (*US*)

**наркологи́ческий** *прил*: ~ **диспансе́р** drug-abuse clinic

**наркома́н (-а)** *м* drug addict *или* abuser

**наркома́ни|я (-и)** *ж* (*МЕД*) drug addiction *или* abuse

**нарко́тик (-а)** *м* drug

**наркоти́ческий** *прил* (*средства*) drug

**наро́д (-а**; *part gen* **-у)** *м* people *мн*

**наро́дност|ь (-и)** *ж* nation

**наро́дный** *прил* national; (*фронт*) popular; (*искусство*) folk

**нарочи́тый** *прил* deliberate

**наро́чно** *нареч* purposely, on purpose; **как ~** (*разг*) to make things worse

**нар|уби́ть (-ублю́, -у́бишь**; *impf* **наруба́ть)** *сов* (*не)перех*: ~ +*acc или* +*gen* to chop

**нару́жност|ь (-и)** *ж* appearance

**нару́жный** *прил* (*дверь, стена*) exterior; (*спокойствие*) outward

**нару́жу** *нареч* out

**нару́чник (-а)** *м* (*обычно мн*) handcuff

**нару́чн|ый** *прил*: ~**ые часы́** (wrist)watch *ед*

**наруша́|ть(ся) (-ю(сь))** *несов от* **нару́шить(ся)**

**наруши́тел|ь (-я)** *м* (*закона*)

infringer, transgressor; (*ЮР, порядка*) offender; ~ **грани́цы** *person who illegally crosses a border*; ~ **дисципли́ны** troublemaker

**нару́ш**|**ить** (**-у, -ишь**) *impf* **наруша́ть**) *сов перех* (*покой*) to disturb; (*связь*) to break; (*правила, договор*) to violate; (*дисциплину*) to breach; **наруша́ть** (~ *pf*) **грани́цу** to illegally cross a border; ~**ся** (*impf* **наруша́ться**) *сов возв* to be broken *или* disturbed

**нарци́сс** (**-а**) *м* daffodil, narcissus

**нары́в** (**-а**) *м* (*МЕД*) abscess, boil

**нарыва́**|**ть** (*3sg* **-ет**) *несов* (*рана*) to fester

**наря́д** (**-а**) *м* (*одежда*) attire; (*красивый*) outfit; (*КОММ*) order; (*распоряжение*) directive

**нар**|**яди́ть** (**-яжу́, -я́дишь**) *impf* **наряжа́ть**) *сов перех* (*одеть*) to dress; **наряжа́ть** (~ *pf*) **ёлку** ≈ to decorate (*BRIT*) *или* trim (*US*) the Christmas tree; ~**ся** (*impf* **наряжа́ться**) *сов возв*: ~**ся** (**в** +*acc*) to dress o.s. (in)

**наря́дный** *прил* (*человек*) well-dressed; (*комната, улица*) nicely decorated; (*шляпа, платье*) fancy

**наряду́** *нареч*: ~ **с** +*instr* along with; (*наравне*) on an equal footing with

**наряжа́**|**ть(ся)** (**-ю(сь)**) *несов от* **наряди́ть(ся)**

**нас** *мест см.* **мы**

**насеко́м**|**ое** (**-ого**) *ср* insect

**населе́ни**|**е** (**-я**) *ср* population

**населённый** *прил* (*район*) populated; ~ **пункт** locality

**насел**|**и́ть** (**-ю́, -и́шь**) *impf* **населя́ть**) *сов перех* (*регион*) to settle

**населя́**|**ть** (**-ю**) *несов от* **насели́ть** ♦ *перех* (*проживать*) to inhabit

**насе́ч**|**ка** (**-ки**; *gen pl* **-ек**) *ж* notch

**наси́ли**|**е** (**-я**) *ср* violence

**наси́л**|**овать** (**-ую**; *pf* **из~**) *несов перех* (*женщину*) to rape

**наси́льно** *нареч* forcibly

**наси́льственный** *прил* violent

**наска́кива**|**ть** (**-ю**) *несов от* **наскочи́ть**

**наскво́зь** *нареч* through

**наско́лько** *нареч* so much

**наск**|**очи́ть** (**-очу́, -о́чишь**) *impf* **наска́кивать**) *сов*: ~ **на** +*acc* to run into

**наску́ч**|**ить** (**-у, -ишь**) *сов*: ~ **кому́-н** to bore sb

**насла**|**ди́ться** (**-жу́сь, -ди́шься**; *impf* **наслажда́ться**) *сов возв*: ~ +*instr* to relish

**наслажде́ни**|**е** (**-я**) *ср* enjoyment, relish

**насле́ди**|**е** (**-я**) *ср* (*культурное*) heritage; (*идеологическое*) legacy

**насле́дник** (**-а**) *м* heir; (*перен: преемник*) inheritor

**насле́д**|**овать** (**-ую**) (*не*)*сов перех* to inherit; (*престол*) to succeed to

**насле́дственный** *прил* inherited; (*черты, болезнь*) hereditary

**насле́дств**|**о** (**-а**) *ср* (*имущество*) inheritance; (*культурное*) heritage; (*идеологическое*) legacy

**наслы́шан** *как сказ*: **я** ~ **об э́том** I have heard a lot about it

**насма́рку** *нареч* (*разг*): **идти́** ~ to be wasted

**на́смерть** *нареч* (*сражаться*) to the death; (*ранить*) fatally

**насмеха́**|**ться** (**-юсь**) *несов возв*: ~ **над** +*instr* to taunt

**насмеш**|**и́ть** (**-у́, -и́шь**) *сов от* **смеши́ть**

**насме́ш**|**ка** (**-ки**; *gen pl* **-ек**) *ж* jibe

**насме́шливый** *прил* mocking

**насмея́|ться** (**-юсь**) *сов возв*: ~ **над** +*instr* to offend

**на́сморк** (**-а**) *м* runny nose

**насовсе́м** *нареч* (*разг*) for good

**насор|и́ть** (**-ю́, -и́шь**) *сов от* **сори́ть**

**насо́с** (**-а**) *м* pump

**на́спех** *нареч* hurriedly

**наста|ва́ть** (*3sg* **-ёт**) *несов от* **наста́ть**

**наста́вник** (**-а**) *м* mentor

**наста́ива|ть** (**-ю**) *несов от* **настоя́ть**

**наста́|ть** (*3sg* **-нет**; *impf* **наставать́**) *сов* to come; (*ночь*) to fall

**на́стежь** *нареч* (*открыть*) wide

**насти́|чь** (**-гну, -гнешь**; *pt* **-г, -гла**; *impf* **настига́ть**) *сов перех* to catch up with

**насто́|йка** (**-йки**; *gen pl* **-ек**) *ж* (*экстракт*) tincture; (*алкоголь*) liqueur

**насто́йчивый** *прил* persistent; (*просьба*) insistent

**насто́лько** *нареч* so

**насто́льный** *прил* (*лампа, часы*) table; (*календарь*) desk

**насторожé** *как сказ*: **он всегда́ ~** he is always on the alert

**насторож|и́ть** (**-у́, -и́шь**; *impf* **настора́живать**) *сов перех* to alert; **~ся** (*impf* **настора́живаться**) *сов возв* to become more alert

**настоя́ни|е** (**-я**) *ср*: **по ~ю кого́-н** on sb's insistence

**настоя́тельный** *прил* (*просьба*) persistent; (*задача*) urgent

**насто|я́ть** (**-ю́, -и́шь**; *impf* **наста́ивать**) *сов*: ~ **на** +*prp* to insist on ♦ *перех* (*травы*) to infuse

**настоя́щ|ий** *прил* real; (*момент*) present; **по-~ему** (*как надо*) properly; (*преданный*) really; **~ее**

**вре́мя** (*ЛИНГ*) the present tense

**настра́ива|ть(ся)** (**-ю(сь)**) *несов от* **настро́ить(ся)**

**настрое́ни|е** (**-я**) *ср* mood; (*антивоенное*) feeling; **не в ~и** in a bad mood

**настро́|ить** (**-ю, -ишь**; *impf* **настра́ивать**) *сов перех* (*пианино итп*) to tune; (*механизм*) to adjust; **настра́ивать** (~ *pf*) **кого́-н на** +*acc* to put sb in the right frame of mind for; **настра́ивать** (~ *pf*) **кого́-н про́тив** +*gen* to incite sb against; **~ся** (*impf* **настра́иваться**) *сов возв*: **~ся** (*pf*) +*infin* to be disposed to do

**настро́|й** (**-я**) *м* mood

**настро́йщик** (**-а**) *м*: **~ роя́ля** piano tuner

**наступа́|ть** (**-ю**) *несов от* **наступи́ть** ♦ *неперех* (*ВОЕН*) to go on the offensive

**наст|упи́ть** (**-уплю́, -у́пишь**; *impf* **наступа́ть**) *сов* to come; (*ночь*) to fall; **наступа́ть** (~ *pf*) **на** +*acc* (*на камень итп*) to step on

**наступле́ни|е** (**-я**) *ср* (*ВОЕН*) offensive; (*весны, старости*) beginning; (*темноты*) fall

**на́сухо** *нареч*: **вы́тереть что-н ~** to dry sth thoroughly

**насу́щный** *прил* vital

**насчёт** *предл*: **~** +*gen* regarding

**насчита́|ть** (**-ю**; *impf* **насчи́тывать**) *сов перех* to count

**насчи́тыва|ть** (**-ю**) *несов от* **насчита́ть** ♦ *неперех* to have

**насы́п|ать** (**-лю, -лешь**; *impf* **насыпа́ть**) *сов перех* to pour

**на́сып|ь** (**-и**) *ж* embankment

**насы́|тить** (**-щу, -тишь**; *impf* **насыща́ть**) *сов перех* (*накормить*) to satiate; (*водой,* *ра́достью*) to fill; (*рынок*) to saturate; **~ся** (*impf* **насыща́ться**) *сов возв* (*нае́сться*) to eat one's fill; (*рынок*) to be saturated

**ната́лкива|ть(ся)** (-ю(сь)) *несов от* **натолкну́ть(ся)**

**натвор|и́ть** (-ю́, -и́шь) *сов* (*не*)*перех*: **~** +*acc или* +*gen* (*разг*) to get up to

**нат|ере́ть** (-ру́, -рёшь; *pt* -ёр, -ёрла; *impf* **натира́ть**) *сов перех* (*боти́нки, полы́*) to polish; (*но́гу*) to chafe; (*морко́вь, сыр итп*) to grate

**на́тиск** (-а) *м* pressure

**наткн|у́ться** (-у́сь, -ёшься; *impf* **натыка́ться**) *сов возв*: **~ на** +*acc* to bump into

**НА́ТО** *ср сокр* NATO

**натолкн|у́ть** (-у́, -ёшь; *impf* **ната́лкивать**) *сов перех*: **~ кого́-н на** +*acc* (*на иде́ю*) to lead sb to; **~ся** (*impf* **ната́лкиваться**) *сов возв*: **~ся на** +*acc* to bump into

**натоща́к** *нареч* on an empty stomach

**на́три|й** (-я) *м* sodium

**нату́р|а** (-ы) *ж* (*хара́ктер*) nature; (*нату́рщик*) model (*ART*); **~ой, в ~е** (*ЭКОН*) in kind

**нату́ра́льный** *прил* natural; (*мех, ко́жа*) real

**нату́рщик** (-а) *м* model (*ART*)

**натыка́|ться** (-юсь) *несов от* **наткну́ться**

**натюрмо́рт** (-а) *м* still life

**натя́гива|ть(ся)** (-ю) *несов от* **натяну́ть(ся)**

**натя́нутый** *прил* strained

**нат|яну́ть** (-яну́, -я́нешь; *impf* **натя́гивать**) *сов перех* to pull tight; (*перча́тки*) to pull on; **~ся** (*impf* **натя́гиваться**) *сов возв* to tighten

**науга́д** *нареч* at random

**нау́к|а** (-и) *ж* science; **есте́ственные ~и** science; **гуманита́рные ~и** arts

**нау́тро** *нареч* next morning

**на|учи́ть(ся)** (-учу́(сь), -у́чишь(ся)) *сов от* **учи́ть(ся)**

**нау́чно-популя́рный** *прил* science

**нау́чно-техни́ческий** *прил* scientific

**нау́чный** *прил* scientific

**нау́шник** (-а) *м* (*обы́чно мн: та́кже*: **магнитофо́нные ~и**) headphones *мн*

**наха́л** (-а) *м* (*разг*) cheeky beggar

**наха́льный** *прил* cheeky

**нахлы́н|уть** (*3sg* -ет) *сов* to surge

**нахму́р|ить(ся)** (-ю(сь), -ишь(ся)) *несов от* **хму́рить(ся)**

**нах|оди́ть** (-ожу́, -о́дишь) *несов от* **найти́**; **~ся** *несов от* **найти́сь** ♦ *возв* (*дом, го́род*) to be situated; (*челове́к*) to be

**нахо́д|ка** (-ки; *gen pl* -ок) *ж* (*поте́рянного*) discovery; **он - ~ для нас** he is a real find for us; **Бюро́ ~ок** lost property office (*BRIT*), lost and found (*US*)

**нахо́дчивый** *прил* resourceful

**наце́л|ить** (-ю, -ишь; *impf* **наце́ливать**) *сов перех*: **~ кого́-н на** +*acc* to push sb towards; **~ся** *сов от* **це́литься**

**наце́н|ка** (-ки; *gen pl* -ок) *ж* (*на това́р*) surcharge

**наци́зм** (-а) *м* Nazism

**национализи́р|овать** (-ую) (*не*)*сов перех* to nationalize

**национали́зм** (-а) *м* nationalism

**национали́ст** (-а) *м* nationalist

**национа́льност|ь** (-и) *ж* nationality; (*на́ция*) nation

**национа́льный** *прил* national

**наци́ст** (-а) *м* Nazi

**на́ци|я (-и)** ж nation;
**Организа́ция Объединённых Наций** United Nations Organization

**знача|ди́ть (-жу́, -ди́шь)** сов от **чади́ть**

**нача́л|о (-а)** ср beginning, start; **быть** (impf) **под ~м кого́-н** или **у кого́-н** to be under sb

**нача́льник (-а)** м (руководитель) boss; (цеха) floor manager; (управления) head

**нача́льн|ый** прил (период) initial; (глава книги) first; **~ая шко́ла** (ПРОСВЕЩ) primary (BRIT) или elementary (US) school; **~ые кла́ссы** (ПРОСВЕЩ) the first three classes of school

**нача́льные кла́ссы** - Children start school at the age of six or seven. There are no separate primary schools in Russia. The first three classes of the 10-year education system are referred to as **нача́льные кла́ссы**. The main emphasis is on reading, writing and arithmetic. Other subjects taught include drawing, PE and singing.

**нача́льств|о (-а)** ср (власть) authority ♦ собир (руководители) management

**нач|а́ть (-ну́, -нёшь;** impf **начина́ть)** сов перех to begin, start

**начеку́** нареч: **быть ~** to be on one's guard

**на́черно** нареч roughly

**нач|ерти́ть (-ерчу́, -е́ртишь)** сов от **черти́ть**

**начёс (-а)** м (на ткани) nap; (вид причёски) bouffant

**начина́ни|е (-я)** ср initiative

**начина́|ть (-ю)** несов от **нача́ть**

**начина́ющ|ий** прил (писатель) novice ♦ **(-его)** м beginner

**начина́я** предл: **~ +instr** (включая) including; **~ с +gen** from; (при отсчёте) starting from; **~ от +gen** (включая) including

**начин|и́ть (-ю́, -и́шь;** impf **начиня́ть)** сов перех (пирог) to fill

**начи́н|ка (-ки;** gen pl **-ок)** ж filling

**начи́танный** прил well-read

**начну́** итп см. **нача́ть**

**наш (-его;** см. Table 9; f **-а,** притяж мест nt **-е,** pl **-и)** our; **чей э́то дом? - ~** whose is this house? - ours; **чьи э́то кни́ги? - на́ши** whose are these books? - ours; **по-на́шему** our way; (по нашему мнению) in our opinion

**нашаты́рный** прил: **~ спирт** (МЕД) liquid ammonia

**наше́стви|е (-я)** ср invasion

**нащу́па|ть (-ю;** impf **нащу́пывать)** сов перех to find

**наяву́** нареч in reality; **как ~** distinctly

**НДС** м сокр (= нало́г на доба́вленную сто́имость) VAT

**не** част not; **~ я написа́л э́то письмо́** I didn't write this letter; **я ~ рабо́таю** I don't work; **~ пла́чьте/опозда́йте** don't cry/be late; **~ могу́ ~ согласи́ться/~ возрази́ть** I can't help agreeing/ objecting; **~ мне на́до помо́чь, а ему́** I am not the one who needs help, he is; **~ до +gen** no time for; **мне ~ до тебя́** I have no time for you; **~ без того́** (разг) that's about it; **~ то** (разг: в противном случае) or else

**небе́сный** прил (тела) celestial; (перен) heavenly; **~ цвет** sky blue

**неблагода́рный** прил ungrateful; (работа) thankless

**не́б|о** (-а; *nom pl* **небеса́**, *gen pl* **небе́с**) *ср* (*РЕЛ*) Heaven

**нёб|о** (-а) *ср* (*АНАТ*) palate

**небольшо́й** *прил* small

**небоскло́н** (-а) *м* sky above the horizon

**небоскрёб** (-а) *м* skyscraper

**небре́жный** *прил* careless

**небыва́лый** *прил* unprecedented

**нева́жно** *нареч* (*де́лать что-н*) not very well ♦ *как сказ* it's not important

**нева́жный** *прил* unimportant; (*не о́чень хоро́ший*) poor

**неве́дени|е** (-я) *ср* ignorance; **он пребыва́ет в по́лном ~и** he doesn't know anything (about it)

**неве́ж|а** (-и) *м/ж* boor

**неве́жд|а** (-ы) *м/ж* ignoramus

**неве́жественный** *прил* ignorant

**неве́жеств|о** (-а) *ср* ignorance

**невезе́ни|е** (-я) *ср* bad luck

**неве́рный** *прил* (*оши́бочный*) incorrect; (*муж*) unfaithful

**невероя́тный** *прил* improbable; (*чрезвыча́йный*) incredible

**неве́рующ|ий** *прил* (*РЕЛ*) faithless ♦ (-его) *м* unbeliever

**неве́ст|а** (-ы) *ж* (*по́сле помо́лвки*) fiancée; (*на сва́дьбе*) bride

**неве́стк|а** (-ки; *gen pl* -ок) *ж* (*жена́ сы́на*) daughter-in-law; (*жена́ бра́та*) sister-in-law

**невзго́д|а** (-ы) *ж* adversity *ед*

**невзира́я** *предл*: ~ **на** +*acc* in spite of

**невзлюби́ть** (-юблю́, -ю́бишь) *сов перех* to take a dislike to

**невзнача́й** *нареч* (*разг*) by accident

**невзра́чный** *прил* dowdy

**неви́данный** *прил* unprecedented

**невиди́м|ка** (-ки; *gen pl* -ок) *ж* (*шпи́лька*) hairpin

**неви́димый** *прил* invisible

**неви́нный** *прил* innocent

**невино́вный** *прил* innocent

**невменя́емый** *прил* deranged

**невмеша́тельств|о** (-а) *ср* nonintervention; (*ЭКОН*) laissez faire

**невнима́тельный** *прил* (*ученик*) inattentive; (*муж*) inconsiderate

**невня́тный** *прил* muffled

**не́вод** (-а) *м* fishing net

**невозмо́жно** *нареч* (*большо́й, тру́дный*) impossibly ♦ *как сказ*: ~ +*infin* (*сде́лать, найти́ итп*) it is impossible to do; (*э́то*) ~ that's impossible

**невозмо́жный** *прил* impossible

**невозмути́мый** *прил* (*челове́к*) unflappable; (*тон*) unruffled

**нево́льный** *прил* (*улы́бка, свиде́тель*) involuntary; (*ложь*) unintentional

**нево́л|я** (-и) *ж* captivity

**невооружённ|ый** *прил* unarmed; **~ым гла́зом** (*без прибо́ров*) with the naked eye; **э́то ви́дно ~ым гла́зом** (*перен*) it's plain for all to see

**невоспи́танный** *прил* ill-bred

**невпопа́д** *нареч* (*разг*) out of turn

**неврасте́ник** (-а) *м* neurotic

**неврастени́|я** (-и) *ж* (*МЕД*) nervous tension

**невреди́мый** *прил* (*челове́к*) unharmed

**невро́з** (-а) *м* neurosis

**невропато́лог** (-а) *м* neurologist

**невыноси́мый** *прил* unbearable, intolerable

**негати́в** (-а) *м* (*ФОТО*) negative

**негати́вный** *прил* negative

**не́где** *как сказ*: ~ **отдохну́ть** итп there is nowhere to rest итп; **мне** ~ **жить** I have nowhere to live

**негла́сный** *прил* secret

**него́** *мест от* **он, оно́**

**него́дност|ь (-и)** *ж*: **приходи́ть
(прийти́** *pf*) **в ~** (*оборудование*)
to become defunct

**него́дный** *прил* unusable;
(*скверный*) good-for-nothing

**негодова́ни|е (-я)** *ср* indignation

**негод|ова́ть (-у́ю)** *несов* to be
indignant

**негодя́|й (-я)** *м* scoundrel

**негра́мотный** *прил* illiterate;
(*работа*) incompetent

**негрита́нский** *прил* black

**неда́вн|ий** *прил* recent; **до ~его
вре́мени** until recently

**неда́вно** *нареч* recently

**недалёк|ий** *прил* (*перен*:
*человек, ум*) limited; **в ~ом
бу́дущем** in the near future

**недалеко́** *нареч* (*жить, быть*)
nearby; (*идти, ехать*) not far ♦ *как
сказ*: **~ (до** +*gen*) it isn't far (to); **~
от** +*gen* not far from

**неда́ром** *нареч* (*не напрасно*)
not in vain; (*не без цели*) for a
reason

**недви́жимост|ь (-и)** *ж* property

**недви́жим|ый** *прил*: **~ое
иму́щество = недви́жимость**

**неде́льный** *прил* (*срок*) one-
week; (*запас, заработок*) *а или*
one week's

**неде́л|я (-и)** *ж* week; **че́рез ~ю** in
a week('s time); **на про́шлой/
э́той/сле́дующей ~e** last/this/next
week

**недове́ри|е (-я)** *ср* mistrust,
distrust

**недове́рчивый** *прил* mistrustful,
distrustful

**недово́льный** *прил* discontented,
dissatisfied

**недово́льств|о (-а)** *ср*: **~** (+*instr*)
dissatisfaction (with)

**недоговор|и́ть (-ю́, -и́шь;** *impf*

**недогова́ривать)** *сов перех* to
leave unsaid; **он что́-то
недогова́ривает** there is
something that he's not saying

**недоеда́|ть (-ю)** *несов* to eat
badly

**недолю́блива|ть (-ю)** *несов
перех* to dislike

**недомога́ни|е (-я)** *ср*:
**чу́вствовать** (*impf*) **~** to feel unwell

**недомога́|ть (-ю)** *несов* to feel
unwell

**недоно́шенный** *прил*: **~
ребёнок** premature baby

**недооц|ени́ть (-еню́, -е́нишь;**
*impf* **недооце́нивать**) *сов перех*
to underestimate

**недопусти́мый** *прил*
unacceptable

**недора́звитый** *прил*
underdeveloped

**недоразуме́ни|е (-я)** *ср*
misunderstanding

**недосмо́тр (-а)** *м* oversight

**недоста|ва́ть (3sg -ёт)** *несов
безл*: **мне ~ёт сме́лости** I lack
courage; **мне ~ёт де́нег** I need
money

**недоста́т|ок (-ка;** *nom pl* **-ки)** *м*:
**~** +*gen* shortage *или* lack of; (*в
работе*) shortcoming in

**недоста́точно** *нареч* insufficiently
♦ *как сказ*: **у нас ~ еды́/де́нег** we
don't have enough food/money; **я
~ зна́ю об э́том** I don't know
enough about it

**недоста́точный** *прил* insufficient

**недоста́ч|а (-и)** *ж* (*мало*) lack;
(*при проверке*) shortfall

**недоста́ющий** *прил* missing

**недосто́йный** *прил*: **~** (+*gen*)
unworthy (of)

**недоумева́|ть (-ю)** *несов* to be
perplexed *или* bewildered

**недоуме́ни|е (-я)** *ср* perplexity,

bewilderment

**недоу́ч|ка** (**-ки**; *gen pl* **-ек**) *м/ж*
(*разг*) drop-out

**недочёт** (**-а**) *м* (*в подсчётах*)
shortfall; (*в рабо́те*) deficiency

**не́др|а** (**-**) *мн* depths *мн*; **в ~х
земли́** in the bowels of the earth

**неё** *мест см.* **она́**

**нежда́нный** *прил* unexpected

**не́ж|иться** (**-усь, -ишься**) *несов
возв* to laze about

**не́жность|ь** (**-и**) *ж* tenderness

**не́жный** *прил* tender, gentle;
(*ко́жа, пух*) soft; (*за́пах*) subtle

**незабу́д|ка** (**-ки**; *gen pl* **-ок**) *ж*
forget-me-not

**незабыва́емый** *прил*
unforgettable

**незави́симо** *нареч* independently;
**~ от** +*gen* regardless of

**незави́симост|ь** (**-и**) *ж*
independence

**незави́симый** *прил* independent

**незадо́лго** *нареч*: **~ до** +*gen* или
**пе́ред** +*instr* shortly before

**незаме́тно** *нареч* (*изменя́ться*)
imperceptibly ♦ *как сказ* it isn't
noticeable; **он ~ подошёл** he
approached unnoticed

**незаме́тный** *прил* barely
noticeable; (*перен: челове́к*)
unremarkable

**неза́нят|ый** *прил* free; (*дом*)
unoccupied; **~ая часть населе́ния**
the non-working population

**незауря́дный** *прил* exceptional

**не́зачем** *как сказ* (*разг*): **~
ходи́ть/э́то де́лать** there's no
reason to go/do it

**нездоро́в|иться** (*3sg* **-ится**)
*несов безл*: **мне нездоро́вится** I
feel unwell, I don't feel well

**незнако́м|ец** (**-ца**) *м* stranger

**незначи́тельный** *прил* (*су́мма*)
insignificant; (*факт*) trivial

**неизбе́жный** *прил* inevitable

**неизве́стн|ый** *прил* unknown
♦ (**-ого**) *м* stranger

**неизгла́дмый** *прил* indelible

**неизлечи́мый** *прил* (*боле́знь*)
incurable; (*больно́й*) terminally ill

**неизме́нный** *прил* unchanging

**неиме́ни|е** (**-я**) *ср*: **за ~м** +*gen* for
want of

**неимове́рный** *прил* extreme

**неиму́щий** *прил* deprived

**неиссяка́емый** *прил*
inexhaustible

**нейстовый** *прил* intense

**неистощи́мый** *прил* inexhaustible

**ней** *мест см.* **она́**

**нейло́н** (**-а**) *м* nylon

**нейрохиру́рг** (**-а**) *м* neurosurgeon

**нейтралите́т** (**-а**) *м* neutrality

**нейтра́льный** *прил* neutral

**не́кем** *мест см.* **не́кого**

**не́к|ий** (**-ого**; *f* **-ая**, *nt* **-ое**, *pl* **-ие**)
*мест* a certain

**не́когда** *как сказ* (*чита́ть*) there is
no time; **ей ~** she is busy; **ей ~**
+*infin* ... she has no time to ...

**не́к|ого** (*как* **кто**; *см. Table 7*)
*мест*: **~ спроси́ть/позва́ть** there is
nobody to ask/call

**не́кому** *мест см.* **не́кого**

**не́котор|ый** (**-ого**; *f* **-ая** *nt* **-ое**, *pl*
**-ые**) *мест* some

**некроло́г** (**-а**) *м* obituary

**некста́ти** *нареч* at the wrong time
♦ *как сказ*: **э́то ~** this is untimely

**не́кто** *мест* a certain person

**не́куда** *как сказ* (*идти́*) there is
nowhere; **да́льше** или **ху́же/
лу́чше ~** (*разг*) it can't get any
worse/better

**нелегити́мный** *прил* illegitimate

**неле́пый** *прил* stupid

**нелётн|ый** *прил*: **~ая пого́да**
poor weather for flying

**нельзя́** *как сказ* (*невозмо́жно*) it

is impossible; (*не разрешается*) it is forbidden; **~ ли?** would it be possible?; **как ~ лу́чше** as well as could be expected

**нём** *мест см.* **он; оно́**

**неме́дленно** *нареч* immediately

**неме́дленный** *прил* immediate

**неме́|ть** (**-ю**; *pf* **о~**) *несов* (*от ужаса, от восторга*) to be struck dumb; (*нога, рука*) to go numb

**нём|ец** (**-ца**) *м* German

**неме́цкий** *прил* German; **~ язы́к** German

**неминýемый** *прил* unavoidable

**нём|ка** (**-ки**; *gen pl* **-ок**) *ж см.* **не́мец**

**немно́г|ие** (**-их**) *мн* few

**немно́го** *нареч* (*отдохну́ть, ста́рше*) a little, a bit; **~** +*gen* a few; (*де́нег*) a bit

**немно́жко** *нареч* (*разг*) = **немно́го**

**нем|о́й** *прил* (*челове́к*) dumb; (*перен: вопрос*) implied ♦ (**-о́го**) *м* mute; **~ фильм** silent film

**не́мощный** *прил* sick, ailing

**нему́** *мест от* **он; оно́**

**немы́слимый** *прил* unthinkable

**ненави́|деть** (**-жу, -дишь**) *несов перех* to hate

**ненави́стный** *прил* hated

**не́навист|ь** (**-и**) *ж* hatred

**ненаси́ли|е** (**-я**) *ср* non-violence

**нена́стный** *прил* wet and dismal

**нена́сть|е** (**-я**) *ср* awful weather

**ненасы́тный** *прил* insatiable

**ненорма́льн|ый** *прил* abnormal; (*разг: сумасше́дший*) mad ♦ (**-ого**) *м* (*разг*) crackpot

**необита́емый** *прил* (*ме́сто*) uninhabited; **~ о́стров** desert island

**необозри́мый** *прил* vast

**необосно́ванный** *прил* unfounded

**необходи́мо** *как сказ* it is

necessary; **мне ~ с Ва́ми поговори́ть** I really need to talk to you

**необходи́мост|ь** (**-и**) *ж* necessity

**необходи́мый** *прил* necessary

**необъя́тный** *прил* vast

**необыкнове́нный** *прил* exceptional

**необыча́йный** *прил* = **необыкнове́нный**

**необы́чный** *прил* unusual

**неожи́данност|ь** (**-и**) *ж* surprise

**неожи́данный** *прил* unexpected

**неопределённый** *прил* indefinite; (*отве́т, жест*) vague

**неоспори́мый** *прил* (*преиму́щество*) unquestionable; (*аргуме́нт*) incontrovertible

**неотврати́мый** *прил* inevitable

**неотдели́мый** *прил*: **~** (**от** +*gen*) inseparable (from)

**не́откуда** *как сказ*: **мне ~ де́нег взять** I can't get money from anywhere

**неотло́жн|ый** *прил* urgent; **~ая медици́нская по́мощь** emergency medical service

**неотрази́мый** *прил* irresistible; (*впечатле́ние*) powerful

**неотъе́млемый** *прил* (*пра́во*) inalienable; (*часть*) integral

**неофаши́зм** (**-а**) *м* Neo-fascism

**неофаши́ст** (**-а**) *м* Neo-fascist

**неохо́т|а** (**-ы**) *ж* (*разг: нежела́ние*) reluctance ♦ *как сказ*: **мне ~ спо́рить** I don't feel like arguing

**неоцени́мый** *прил* invaluable

**непереходный** *прил*: **~ глаго́л** (*линг*) intransitive verb

**неповтори́мый** *прил* unique

**непого́д|а** (**-ы**) *ж* bad weather

**неподви́жный** *прил* motionless; (*взгляд*) fixed

**неподде́льный** *прил* genuine

**неподкýпный** *прил* (*человек*)
incorruptible

**непоколебúмый** *прил*
unshakable

**непола́д|ки** (**-ок**) *мн* fault *ед*

**неполноцéнност|ь** (**-и**) *ж*
inadequacy; **кóмплекс ~и**
inferiority complex

**неполноцéнный** *прил*
inadequate, insufficient

**непоня́тно** *нареч*
incomprehensibly ♦ *как сказ* it is
incomprehensible; **мне э́то ~** I
cannot understand this

**непоня́тный** *прил*
incomprehensible

**непоправúмый** *прил* (*ошибка*)
irreparable

**непосрéдственный** *прил*
(*начальник*) immediate;
(*результат, участник*) direct

**непостижúмый** *прил* (*загадка,
сила*) incomprehensible

**непоча́тый** *прил*: **~ край** no end,
a great deal

**непра́вд|а** (**-ы**) *ж* lie, untruth
♦ *как сказ* it's not true; **э́то ~!** this
is a lie!

**непра́вильно** *нареч* (*решить*)
incorrectly, wrongly ♦ *как сказ*:
**э́то ~** it's wrong

**непра́вильный** *прил* wrong;
(*форма, глагол*) irregular

**непредвúденный** *прил*
unforeseen

**непредсказу́емый** *прил*
unpredictable

**непреклóнный** *прил* firm

**непремéнный** *прил* necessary

**непрерывный** *прил* continuous

**непривычно** *как сказ*: **мне ~**
+*infin* I'm not used to doing

**неприéмлемый** *прил*
unacceptable

**неприкосновéнност|ь** (**-и**) *ж*
inviolability; **дипломатúческая ~**
diplomatic immunity

**неприлúчный** *прил* indecent

**непримéтный** *прил* (*человек,
жизнь*) unremarkable

**непримирúмый** *прил*
irreconcilable

**непринуждённый** *прил* informal

**непристóйный** *прил* obscene

**непристу́пный** *прил* (*крепость*)
impregnable

**неприя́зн|ь** (**-и**) *ж* hostility

**неприя́тно** *как сказ*: **~** +*infin* it's
unpleasant to do; **мне ~ говорúть
об э́том** I don't enjoy talking about
it

**неприя́тност|ь** (**-и**) *ж* (*обычно
мн: на работе, в семьé*) trouble
*ед*

**неприя́тный** *прил* unpleasant

**непроизвóльный** *прил*
involuntary

**непромока́емый** *прил*
waterproof

**нера́венств|о** (**-а**) *ср* inequality

**неравнопра́ви|е** (**-я**) *ср*
inequality (of rights)

**нера́вный** *прил* unequal

**неразбери́х|а** (**-и**) *ж* (*разг*)
muddle

**неразрешúмый** *прил* insoluble

**неразрывный** *прил* indissoluble

**неразу́мный** *прил* unreasonable

**нерв** (**-а**) *м* (*АНАТ*) nerve; **нéрвы**
(*вся система*) nervous system

**нéрвнича|ть** (**-ю**) *несов* to fret

**нéрвный** *прил* nervous

**нервóзный** *прил* (*человек*)
nervous, highly (*BRIT*) *или* high (*US*)
strung

**нерешúтельный** *прил* indecisive

**нержавéющ|ий** *прил* rustproof;
**~ая ста́ль** stainless steel

**нерóвный** *прил* (*поверхность*)
uneven; (*характер*) unbalanced

**неря́шливый** прил (человек, одежда) scruffy; (работа) careless

**нёс** несов см. **нести́**

**несбы́точный** прил unrealizable

**несваре́ни|е (-я)** ср ~ **желу́дка** indigestion

**несгиба́емый** прил staunch

**несгора́емый** прил fireproof

**несклоня́емый** прил (линг) indeclinable

**не́скольк|о (-их)** чис ~ +gen a few ♦ нареч (обидеться) somewhat

**нескро́мный** прил (человек) immodest; (вопрос) indelicate; (жест, предложение) indecent

**неслы́ханный** прил unheard of

**неслы́шно** нареч (сделать) quietly ♦ как сказ: **мне ~** I can't hear

**неслы́шный** прил inaudible

**несмотря́** предл: ~ **на** +acc in spite of, despite; ~ **на то что ...** in spite of или despite the fact that ...; ~ **ни на что** no matter what

**несовершенноле́тн|ий (-его)** м minor ♦ прил: ~ **ребёнок** minor

**несоверше́нный** прил flawed; ~ **вид** (линг) imperfective (aspect)

**несовмести́мый** прил incompatible

**несогласо́ванный** прил (действия) uncoordinated

**несомне́нно** нареч (правильный, хороший итп) indisputably ♦ вводн сл without a doubt ♦ как сказ: **э́то ~** this is indisputable; ~, **что он придёт** there is no doubt that he will come

**несомне́нный** прил indisputable

**несостоя́тельный** прил (КОММ) insolvent; (начальник) incompetent

**несправедли́вост|ь (-и)** ж injustice

**несправедли́вый** прил (человек, суд, упрёк) unfair, unjust

**неспроста́** нареч (разг) for a reason

**нес|ти́ (-у́, -ёшь;** pt **нёс, -ла́)** несов от **носи́ть** ♦ перех to carry; (влечь: неприятности) to bring; (pf **по~;** службу) to carry out; (pf **с~;** яйцо) to lay; ~**сь** несов возв (человек, машина) to race; (pf **с~сь;** курица) to lay eggs

**несча́стный** прил unhappy; (разг: жалкий) wretched; ~ **слу́чай** accident

**несча́сть|е (-я)** ср misfortune; **к ~ю** unfortunately

**несъедо́бный** прил inedible

---
KEYWORD
---

**нет** част 1 (при отрицании, несогласии) no; **ты согла́сен? - нет** do you agree? - no; **тебе́ не нра́вится мой суп? - нет, нра́вится** don't you like my soup? - yes, I do

2 (для привлечения внимания): **нет, ты то́лько посмотри́ на него́!** would you just look at him!

3 (выражает недоверие): **нет, ты действи́тельно не се́рдишься?** so you are really not angry?

♦ как сказ: **нет** +gen (не имеется: об одном предмете) there is no; (: о нескольких предметах) there are no; **нет вре́мени** there is no time; **нет биле́тов** или **биле́тов нет** there are no tickets; **у меня́ нет де́нег** I have no money; **его́ нет в го́роде** he is not in town

♦ союз (во фразах): **нет - так нет** it can't be helped; **чего́ то́лько нет!** what don't they have!; **нет чтобы извини́ться** (*разг*) instead of saying sorry

---

**нетерпе́ни|е (-я)** *ср* impatience; **с ~м ждать** (*impf*)/**слу́шать** (*impf*) to wait/listen impatiently; **с ~м жду Ва́шего отве́та** I look forward to hearing from you

**нетерпи́мый** *прил* intolerable; (*непримиримый*): **~ к** +*dat* (**ко лжи**) intolerant of

**нетре́зв|ый** *прил* drunk; **в ~ом состоя́нии** drunk

**нетрудово́й** *прил*: **~ дохо́д** unearned income

**нетрудоспосо́бност|ь (-и)** *ж* disability; **посо́бие по ~и** disability living allowance

**нетрудоспосо́бный** *прил* unable to work through disability

**не́тто** *прил неизм* (*о весе*) net

**неуда́ч|а (-и)** *ж* bad luck; (*в дела́х*) failure

**неуда́чный** *прил* (*попытка*) unsuccessful; (*фильм, стихи*) bad

**неудо́бно** *нареч* (*расположенный, сиде́ть*) uncomfortably ♦ *как сказ* it's uncomfortable; (*неприли́чно*) it's awkward; **мне ~** I am uncomfortable; **~ задава́ть лю́дям таки́е вопро́сы** it's awkward to ask people such questions; (**мне**) **~ сказа́ть ему́ об э́том** I feel uncomfortable telling him that

**неудо́бный** *прил* uncomfortable

**неудовлетвори́тельный** *прил* unsatisfactory

**неудово́льстви|е (-я)** *ср* dissatisfaction

**неуже́ли** *част* really

**неузнава́емост|ь (-и)** *ж*: **до ~и** beyond (all) recognition

**неузнава́емый** *прил* unrecognizable

**неукло́нный** *прил* steady

**неуклю́жий** *прил* clumsy

**неулови́мый** *прил* imperceptible; (*челове́к*) elusive

**неуме́стный** *прил* inappropriate

**неумоли́мый** *прил* relentless; (*зако́н*) stringent

**неурожа́йный** *прил*: **~ год** year with a poor harvest

**неуро́чный** *прил* (*вре́мя*) unearthly

**неуря́диц|а (-ы)** *ж* (*разг: обы́чно мн: ссо́ры*) squabble

**неуста́нный** *прил* indefatigable

**неутоли́мый** *прил* insatiable; (*жа́жда*) unquenchable

**неутоми́мый** *прил* untiring

**неформа́льный** *прил* (*организа́ция*) non-formal

**нефри́т (-а)** *м* (*МЕД*) nephritis; (*ГЕО*) jade

**нефтедобыва́ющий** *прил* (*промы́шленность*) oil

**нефтедобы́ч|а (-и)** *ж* drilling for oil

**нефтеперерабо́тк|а (-и)** *ж* oil processing

**нефтепрово́д (-а)** *м* oil pipeline

**нефт|ь (-и)** *ж* oil, petroleum

**нефтя́ник (-а)** *м* worker in the oil industry

**нефтяно́й** *прил* oil

**нехва́тк|а (-и)** *ж*: **~** +*gen* shortage of

**нехорошо́** *нареч* badly ♦ *как сказ* it's bad; **мне ~** I'm not well

**не́хотя** *нареч* unwillingly

**неча́янный** *прил* unintentional; (*неожи́данный*) chance

**не́чего** *как сказ*: **~ рассказа́ть** there is nothing to tell; (*разг: не сле́дует*) there's no need to do; **не́ за что!** (*в отве́т на благода́рность*) not at all!, you're welcome! (*US*); **де́лать ~** there's

nothing else to be done
**нечётный** _прил_ (_число_) odd
**нечто** _мест_ something
**неясно** _нареч_: **он ~ объяснил положение** he didn't explain the situation clearly ♦ _как сказ_ it's not clear; **мне ~, почему он отказался** I'm not clear _или_ it's not clear to me why he refused
**неясный** _прил_ (_очертания, звук_) indistinct; (_мысль, вопрос_) vague

_KEYWORD_

**ни** _част_ 1 (_усиливает отрицание_) not a; **ни один** not one, not a single; **она не произнесла ни слова** she didn't say a word; **она ни разу не пришла** she didn't come once; **у меня не осталось ни рубля** I don't have a single rouble left
2: **кто/что/как ни** who-/what-/however; **сколько ни** however much; **что ни говори** whatever you say; **как ни старайся** however hard you try
♦ _союз_ (_при перечислении_): **ни ..., ни ...** neither ... nor ...; **ни за что** no way

**нигде** _нареч_ nowhere; **его ~ не было** he was nowhere to be found; **~ нет моей книги** I can't find my book anywhere, my book is nowhere to be found; **я ~ не мог поесть** I couldn't find anywhere to get something to eat
**ниже** _сравн прил от_ **низкий** ♦ _сравн нареч от_ **низко** ♦ _нареч_ (_далее_) later on ♦ _предл_: ~ +_gen_ below
**нижний** _прил_ (_ступенька, ящик_) bottom; ~ **этаж** ground (_BRIT_) _или_ first (_US_) floor; **~ее бельё** underwear; **~яя юбка** underskirt

**низ** (**-а**) _м_ (_стола, юбки_) bottom
**низкий** _прил_ low
**низко** _нареч_ low
**низкопробный** _прил_ (_золото_) low-grade; (_книга_) trashy
**низовой** _прил_ grass-roots
**низший** _сравн прил от_ **низкий**; (_звание_) junior
**НИИ** _м сокр_ (= **научно-исследовательский институт**) scientific research institute
**никак** _нареч_ (_никаким образом_) no way; **~ не могу запомнить это слово** I can't remember this word at all; **дверь ~ не открывалась** the door just wouldn't open
**никак|ой** _мест_: **нет ~ого сомнения** there is no doubt at all; **~ие деньги не помогли** no amount of money would have helped
**никел|ь** (**-я**) _м_ (_ХИМ_) nickel
**никогда** _нареч_ never; **как ~** as never before
**никого** _мест см._ **никто**
**ник|ой** _нареч_: **~им образом** not at all; **ни в коем случае** under no circumstances
**ни|кто** (**-кого**; _как_ **кто**; _см. Table 7_) _мест_ nobody
**никуда** _нареч_: **я ~ не поеду** I'm not going anywhere; **~ я не поеду** I'm not going anywhere; **это ~ не годится** that just won't do
**ниоткуда** _нареч_ from nowhere; **~ нет помощи** I get no help from anywhere
**нисколько** _нареч_ not at all; (_не лучше_) no; (_не рад_) at all
**нит|ка** (**-ки**; _gen pl_ **-ок**) _ж_ (_обычно мн: для шитья_) thread _ед_; (: _для вязания_) yarn _ед_
**нит|ь** (**-и**) _ж_ = **нитка**
**них** _мест см._ **они**

**ничего́** *мест см.* **ничто́** ♦ *нареч* fairly well; (э́то) ~, что ... it's all right that ...; извини́те, я Вас побеспоко́ю - ~! sorry to disturb you - it's all right!; как живёшь? - ~ how are you? - all right; ~ себе́ (*сносно*) fairly well; ~ себе́! (*удивление*) well, I never!

**нич|ей** (**-ьего́**; *f* **-ья́**, *nt* **-ьё**, *pl* **-ьи́**) (*как* **чей**; *см. Table 5*) *мест* nobody's

**ниче́йн|ый** *прил*: ~ результа́т/ ~ая па́ртия draw

**ничко́м** *нареч* face down

**нич|то́** (**-его́**; *как* **что**; *см. Table 7*) *мест*, *ср* nothing; **ничего́ подо́бного не ви́дел** I've never seen anything like it; **ничего́ подо́бного!** (*разг: совсем не так*) nothing like it!; **ни за что́!** (*ни в коем случае*) no way!; **ни за что́ не соглаша́йся** whatever you do, don't agree; **я здесь ни при чём** it has nothing to do with me; **ничего́ не поде́лаешь** there's nothing to be done

**ничто́жный** *прил* paltry

**ничу́ть** *нареч* (*нисколько*) not at all; (*не лучше, не больше*) no; (*не испуга́лся, не огорчи́лся*) at all

**ничь|я́** (**-е́й**) *ж* (*СПОРТ*) draw; **сыгра́ть** (*pf*) **в ~ю** to draw (*BRIT*), tie (*US*)

**ни́щенск|ий** *прил* (*зарплата*) meagre (*BRIT*), meager (*US*); ~ая жизнь life of begging

**нищет|а́** (**-ы́**) *ж* poverty

**ни́щ|ий** *прил* poverty-stricken ♦ (**-его**) *м* beggar

**но** *союз* but ♦ *межд*: ~! gee up!

**нова́тор** (**-а**) *м* innovator

**нове́лл|а** (**-ы**) *ж* novella

**но́венький** *прил* (*разг*) new

**новизн|а́** (**-ы́**) *ж* novelty

**нови́н|ка** (**-ки**; *gen pl* **-ок**) *ж* new product

**нович|о́к** (**-ка́**) *м* newcomer; (*в классе*) new pupil

**новобра́н|ец** (**-ца**) *м* new recruit

**новобра́чн|ый** (**-ого**) *м* newlywed

**нового́дн|ий** *прил* New Year; ~яя ёлка ≈ Christmas tree

**новорождённ|ый** *прил* newborn ♦ (**-ого**) *м* newborn boy

**новосёл** (**-а**) *м* (*дома*) new owner

**новосе́л|ье** (**-ья**; *gen pl* **-ий**) *ср* house-warming (party)

**но́вост|ь** (**-и**; *gen pl* **-е́й**) *ж* news

**но́вшеств|о** (**-а**) *ср* (*явление*) novelty; (*метод*) innovation

**но́в|ый** *прил* new; ~ая исто́рия modern history; **Но́вый Заве́т** the New Testament; **Но́вая Зела́ндия** New Zealand

**ног|а́** (**-и́**; *acc sg* **-у**, *nom pl* **-и**, *gen pl* **-**, *dat pl* **-а́м**) *ж* (*ступня*) foot; (*выше ступни*) leg; **вверх ~ми** upside down

**но́г|оть** (**-тя**; *gen pl* **-те́й**) *м* nail

**нож** (**-а́**) *м* knife

**но́ж|ка** (**-ки**; *gen pl* **-ек**) *ж уменьш от* **нога́**; (*стула, стола итп*) leg; (*циркуля*) arm

**но́жниц|ы** (**-**) *мн* scissors *мн*

**ножно́й** *прил* foot

**ножо́в|ка** (**-ки**; *gen pl* **-ок**) *ж* hacksaw

**ноздр|я́** (**-и́**; *nom pl* **-и**, *gen pl* **-е́й**) *ж* (*обычно мн*) nostril

**нол|ь** (**-я́**) *м* (*МАТ*) zero, nought; (*о температуре*) zero; (*перен: человек*) nothing; ~ це́лых пять деся́тых, 0.5 zero *или* nought point five, 0.5; **в де́сять ~~** at exactly ten o'clock

**номенклату́р|а** (**-ы**) *ж* (*товаров*) list ♦ *собир* (*работники*) nomenklatura

**но́мер** (-а; *nom pl* -**а́**) *м* number; (*журнала*) issue; (*в гостинице*) room; ~ **маши́ны** registration (number)

**номерно́й** *прил* ~ **знак (автомоби́ля)** (car) number (*BRIT*) *или* license (*US*) plate

**номер|о́к** (-ка́) *ж* (*для пальто*) ≈ ticket

**нор|а́** (-ы́; *nom pl* -ы) *ж* (*зайца*) burrow; (*лисы*) den; (*барсука*) set; (*перен*) hole

**Норве́ги|я** (-и) *ж* Norway

**но́р|ка** (-ки; *gen pl* -ок) *ж* mink

**но́рм|а** (-ы) *ж* standard; (*выработки*) rate

**нормализ|ова́ть** (-у́ю) (*не*)*сов перех* to normalize; ~**ся** (*не*)*сов возв* to stabilize

**норма́льно** *нареч* normally ♦ *как сказ*: **э́то вполне́** ~ this is quite normal; **как дела́?** - ~ how are things? - not bad; **у нас всё** ~ everything's fine with us

**норма́льный** *прил* normal

**нос** (-а; *loc sg* -**у́**, *nom pl* -**ы́**) *м* nose; (*корабля*) bow; (*птицы*) beak, bill; (*ботинка*) toe

**носи́л|ки** (-ок) *мн* stretcher *ед*

**носи́льщик** (-а) *м* porter

**носи́тел|ь** (-я) *м* (*инфекции*) carrier; ~ **языка́** native speaker

**но|си́ть** (-шу́, -сишь) *несов перех* to carry; (*платье, очки*) to wear; (*усы, причёску*) to sport; (*фамилию мужа*) to use; ~**ся** *несов возв* (*человек*) to rush; (*слухи*) to spread; (*одежда*) to wear; (*разг: увлекаться*): ~**ся с** +*instr* (*с идеей*) to be preoccupied with; (*с человеком*) to make a fuss over

**носов|о́й** *прил* (*звук*) nasal; ~**а́я часть** bow; ~ **плато́к** handkerchief

**нос|о́к** (-ка́; *gen pl* -**о́к**) *м* (*обычно мн: чулок*) sock; (*gen pl* -**ко́в**; *ботинка, чулка, ноги*) toe

**носоро́г** (-а) *м* rhinoceros, rhino

**ностальги́|я** (-и) *ж* nostalgia

**но́т|а** (-ы) *ж* note; *см. также* **но́ты**

**нотариа́льн|ый** *прил* (*услуги*) notarial; ~**ая конто́ра** notarial office

**нота́риус** (-а) *м* notary (public)

**но́т|ы** (-) *мн* (*МУЗ*) sheet music

**ноутбу́к** (-а) *м* (*КОМП*) notebook

**ноч|ева́ть** (-у́ю; *pf* **пере~**) *несов* to spend the night

**ночёв|ка** (-ки; *gen pl* -ок) *ж*: **останови́ться на ~ку** to spend the night

**ночле́г** (-а) *м* (*место*) somewhere to spend the night; **остана́вливаться (останови́ться** *pf*) **на** ~ to spend the night

**ночн|о́й** *прил* (*час, холод*) night; ~**а́я руба́шка** nightshirt

**ноч|ь** (-и; *loc sg* -**и́**, *nom pl* -**и**, *gen pl* -**е́й**) *ж* night; **на** ~ before bed; **споко́йной но́чи!** good night!

**но́чью** *нареч* at night

**но́шеный** *прил* second-hand

**ношу́(сь)** *несов см.* **носи́ть(ся)**

**ноя́бр|ь** (-я́) *м* November

**нрав** (-а) *м* (*человека*) temperament; *см. также* **нра́вы**

**нра́в|иться** (-люсь, -ишься; *pf* **по~**) *несов возв*: **мне/им ~ится э́тот фильм** I/they like this film; **мне ~ится чита́ть/гуля́ть** I like to read *или* reading/to go for a walk

**нра́вственный** *прил* moral

**нра́в|ы** (-ов) *мн* morals

**н.с.** *сокр* (= **но́вого сти́ля**) NS, New Style

**НТР** *ж сокр* = **нау́чно-техни́ческая револю́ция**

KEYWORD

**ну** межд 1 (выражает
побужде́ние) come on; **ну,
начина́й!** come on, get started!
2 (выражает восхище́ние) what;
**ну и си́ла!** what strength!
3 (выражает иро́нию) well (well)
♦ част 1 (неуже́ли): **(да) ну?!** not
really?!
2 (усиливает вырази́тельность):
**ну коне́чно!** why of course!; **ну, я
тебе́ покажу́!** why, I'll show you!
3 (допу́стим): **ты говори́шь по-
англи́йски? - ну, говорю́** do you
speak English? - what if I do?
4 (во фра́зах): **ну и ну!** (разг)
well well!; **ну-ка!** (разг) come on!;
**ну тебя́/его́!** (разг) forget it!

**ну́дный** прил tedious
**нужд|а́** (-ы́; nom pl -ы) ж (no pl;
бедность) poverty;
(потре́бность): **~ (в** +prp) need
(for)
**нужда́|ться** (-юсь) несов возв
(бе́дствовать) to be needy; **~**
(impf) **в** +prp to need, be in need of
**ну́жно** как сказ (необходи́мо): **~,
что́бы им помогли́, ~ им помо́чь**
it is necessary to help them; **мне ~
идти́** I have to go, I must go; **мне
~ 10 рубле́й** I need 10 roubles;
**о́чень ~!** (разг) my foot!
**ну́жный** прил necessary
**нулев|о́й** прил: **~а́я температу́ра**
temperature of zero; **~а́я отме́тка**
(mark of) zero
**нул|ь** (-я́) м (МАТ) zero, nought; (о
температу́ре) zero; (перен:
челове́к) nothing; **начина́ть
(нача́ть** pf) **с ~я́** to start from
scratch
**нумер|ова́ть** (-у́ю; pf про~)
несов перех to number

**ну́три|я** (-и) ж (ЗООЛ) coypu
**ны́не** нареч today
**ны́нешний** прил the present
**нырн|у́ть** (-у́, -ёшь) сов to dive
**ныря́|ть** (-ю) несов to dive
**ны|ть** (но́ю, но́ешь) несов
(ра́на) to ache; (жа́ловаться) to
moan
**Нью-Йо́рк** (-а) м New York
**н.э.** сокр (= на́шей э́ры) AD
**нюх** (-а) м (соба́ки) nose
**нюха|ть** (-ю; pf по~) несов перех
(цветы́, во́здух) to smell
**ня́неч|ка** (-ки; gen pl -ек) ж (разг)
= **ня́ня**
**ня́нч|ить** (-у, -ишь) несов перех
to mind; **~ся** несов возв: **~ся с**
+instr (с младе́нцем) to mind
**ня́н|ька** (-ьки; gen pl -ек) ж (разг:
ребёнка) nanny
**ня́н|я** (-и; gen pl -ь) ж nanny;
(рабо́тающая на дому́) child
minder; (в больни́це) auxiliary
nurse; (в де́тском саду́) cleaner;
**приходя́щая ~** babysitter

# О, о

**о** межд oh ♦ предл: **~** +prp about;
**~** +acc (опере́ться, уда́риться)
against; (споткну́ться) over
**об** предл = **о**
**о́б|а** (-о́их; см. Table 25; f **~е**, nt **~**)
м чис both
**обанкро́|титься** (-чусь,
-тишься) сов возв to go
bankrupt
**обая́ни|е** (-я) ср charm
**обая́тельный** прил charming
**обва́л** (-а) м (сне́жный)
avalanche; (зда́ния, эконо́мики)
collapse
**обвал|и́ться** (3sg -ится; impf

обва́ливаться) *сов возв* to collapse

**обв|ести́** (**-еду́, -едёшь**; *pt* **-ёл, -ела́**; *impf* **обводи́ть**) *сов перех* (*букву, чертёж*) to go over; **обводи́ть** (**~** *pf*) **вокру́г** +*gen* to lead *или* take round

**обвине́ни|е** (**-я**) *ср*: **~** (**в** +*prp*) accusation (of); (*ЮР*) charge (of) ♦ *собир* (*обвиняющая сторона*) the prosecution

**обвини́тел|ь** (**-я**) *м* accuser; (*ЮР*) prosecutor

**обвини́тельный** *прил* (*речь*) accusatory; **~ пригово́р** (*ЮР*) verdict of guilty; **~ акт** (*ЮР*) indictment

**обвин|и́ть** (**-ю́, -и́шь**; *impf* **обвиня́ть**) *сов перех*: **~ кого́-н** (**в** +*prp*) to accuse sb (of); (*ЮР*) to charge sb (with)

**обвиня́ем|ый** (**-ого**) *м* the accused, the defendant

**обвиня́|ть** (**-ю**) *несов от* **обвини́ть** ♦ *перех* (*ЮР*) to prosecute

**об|ви́ть** (**-овью́, -овьёшь**; *impf* **обвива́ть**) *сов перех* (*подлеж: плющ*) to twine around; **обвива́ть** (**~** *pf*) **кого́-н/что-н чем-н** to wind sth round sb/sth

**обв|оди́ть** (**-ожу́, -о́дишь**) *несов от* **обвести́**

**обв|яза́ть** (**-яжу́, -я́жешь**; *impf* **обвя́зывать**) *сов перех*: **~ кого́-н/что-н чем-н** to tie sth round sb/sth; **~ся** (*impf* **обвя́зываться**) *сов возв*: **~ся чем-н** to tie sth round o.s.

**обгоня́|ть** (**-ю**) *несов от* **обогна́ть**

**обгор|е́ть** (**-ю́, -и́шь**; *impf* **~а́ть**) *сов* (*дом*) to be burnt; (*на солнце*) to get sunburnt

**обгры́з|ть** (**-у́, -ёшь**; *impf*

**обгрыза́ть**) *сов перех* to gnaw

**обдира́|ть** (**-ю**) *несов от* **ободра́ть**

**обду́манный** *прил* considered

**обду́ма|ть** (**-ю**; *impf* **обду́мывать**) *сов перех* to consider, think over

**об|е** (**-е́их**) *ж чис см.* **о́ба**

**обега́|ть** (**-ю**) *несов от* **обежа́ть**

**обе́д** (**-а**) *м* lunch, dinner; (*время*) lunch *или* dinner time; **по́сле ~а** after lunch *или* dinner; (*после 12 часов дня*) in the afternoon

**обе́да|ть** (**-ю**; *pf* **по~**) *несов* to have lunch *или* dinner

**обе́денный** *прил* (*стол, сервиз*) dinner; (*время*) lunch, dinner

**обедне́|ть** (**-ю**) *сов от* **бедне́ть**

**обе́д|ня** (**-ни**; *gen pl* **-ен**) *ж* Mass

**обежа́ть** (*как* **бежа́ть**; *см. Table 20*; *impf* **обега́ть**) *сов*: **~ вокру́г** +*gen* to run round

**обезбо́ливающ|ее** (**-его**) *ср* painkiller

**обезбо́л|ить** (**-ю, -ишь**; *impf* **обезбо́ливать**) *сов перех* to anaesthetize (*BRIT*), anesthetize (*US*)

**обезвре́|дить** (**-жу, -дишь**; *impf* **обезвре́живать**) *сов перех ещ вуагыуж* (*преступника*) to disarm

**обездо́ленный** *прил* deprived

**обезору́ж|ить** (**-у, -ишь**; *impf* **обезору́живать**) *сов перех* to disarm

**обезу́ме|ть** (**-ю**) *сов*: **~ от** +*gen* to go out of one's mind with

**обезья́н|а** (**-ы**) *ж* (*с хвостом*) monkey; (*без хвоста*) ape; (*перен: разг*) copycat

**обе́их** *чис см.* **о́бе**

**оберега́|ть** (**-ю**) *несов перех* (*человека*) to protect

**оберн|у́ть** (**-у́, -ёшь**; *impf* **обёртывать** *или* **обора́чивать**) *сов перех* to wrap (up); **~ся** (*impf*

обора́чиваться) *сов возв*
(*повернуться назад*) to turn
(round); обора́чиваться (~ся *pf*)
+*instr* (*неприятностями*) to turn
out to be

обёрт|ка (-ки; *gen pl* -ок) *ж*
(*конфетная*) wrapper

обёрточн|ый *прил*: ~ая бума́га
wrapping paper

обёртыва|ть (-ю) *несов от*
оберну́ть

обеспе́чени|е (-я) *ср* (*мира,
догово́ра*) guarantee; ~ +*instr*
(*сырьём*) provision of;
материа́льное ~ financial security

обеспе́ченност|ь (-и) *ж*
(*material*) comfort; фина́нсовая ~
financial security

обеспе́ченный *прил* well-off,
well-to-do

обеспе́ч|ить (-у, -ишь; *impf*
обеспе́чивать) *сов перех*
(*семью*) to provide for; (*мир,
успех*) to guarantee;
обеспе́чивать (~ *pf*) кого́-н/что-н
чем-н to provide *или* supply sb/sth
with sth

обесси́ле|ть (-ю; *impf*
обесси́левать) *сов* to become
*или* grow weak

обесцве́|тить (-чу, -тишь; *impf*
обесцве́чивать) *несов перех* to
bleach

обесце́н|ить (-ю, -ишь; *impf*
обесце́нивать) *сов перех* to
devalue; ~ся (*impf*
обесце́ниваться) *сов возв* to be
devalued; (*вещь*) to depreciate

обеща́ни|е (-я) *ср* promise

обеща́|ть (-ю; *pf* ~ *или* по~)
*несов* (*не*)*перех* to promise

обжа́ловани|е (-я) *ср* appeal

обжа́л|овать (-ую) *сов перех* to
appeal against

об|же́чь (-ожгу́, -ожжёшь *etc*,

-ожгу́т; *pt* -жёг, -ожгла́,
-ожгло́; *impf* обжига́ть) *сов
перех* to burn; (*кирпич итп*) to
fire; (*подлеж: крапива*) to sting;
~ся (*impf* обжига́ться) *сов возв*
to burn o.s.

обзо́р (-а) *м* view; (*новостей*)
review

обзо́рный *прил* general

обива́|ть (-ю) *несов от* оби́ть

оби́вк|а (-и) *ж* upholstery

оби́д|а (-ы) *ж* insult; (*го́речь*)
grievance; кака́я ~! what a pity!;
быть (*impf*) в ~е на кого́-н to be
in a huff with sb

оби́|деть (-жу, -дишь; *impf*
обижа́ть) *сов перех* to hurt,
offend; ~ся (*impf* обижа́ться) *сов
возв*: ~ся (на +*acc*) to be hurt
*или* offended (by)

оби́дно *как сказ* (*см прил*) it's
offensive; it's upsetting; мне ~
слы́шать э́то it hurts me to hear
this

оби́дный *прил* offensive; (*разг:
доса́дный*) upsetting

оби́дчивый *прил* touchy

обижа́|ть(ся) (-ю(сь)) *несов от*
оби́деть(ся)

оби́женный *прил* aggrieved

оби́ли|е (-я) *ср* abundance

оби́льный *прил* abundant

обита́|ть (-ю) *несов* to live

об|и́ть (-обью, -обьёшь; *imper*
обе́й(те); *impf* обива́ть) *сов
перех*: ~ (+*instr*) to cover (with)

обихо́д (-а) *м*: быть в ~е to be in use

обкле́|ить (-ю, -ишь; *impf*
обкле́ивать) *сов перех*
(*плака́тами*) to cover; (*обоями*) to
(wall)paper

обкра́дыва|ть (-ю) *несов от*
обокра́сть

обл. *сокр* = о́бласть

обла́в|а (-ы) *ж* (*на

*преступников*) roundup

**облага́**|**ть** (**-ю**) *несов от* **обложи́ть**

**облада́**|**ть** (**-ю**) *несов*: ~ +*instr* to possess

**о́блак**|**о** (**-а**; *nom pl* **-а́**, *gen pl* **-о́в**) *ср* cloud

**областно́й** *прил* ≈ regional

**о́бласт**|**ь** (**-и**; *gen pl* **-е́й**) *ж* region; (*АДМИН*) ≈ region, oblast; (*науки, искусства*) field

**о́блачный** *прил* cloudy

**облега́**|**ть** (**-ю**) *несов от* **обле́чь**
♦ *перех* to fit

**облега́ющий** *прил* close-fitting

**облегче́ни**|**е** (**-я**) *ср* (*жизни*) improvement; (*успокоение*) relief

**облегч**|**и́ть** (**-у́, -и́шь**; *impf* **облегча́ть**) *сов перех* (*вес*) to lighten; (*жизнь*) to make easier; (*боль*) to ease

**обле́з**|**ть** (**-у, -ешь**; *impf* **облеза́ть**) *сов* (*разг*) to grow mangy; (*краска, обои*) to peel (off)

**облека́**|**ть** (**-ю**) *несов от* **обле́чь**

**обле**|**те́ть** (**-чу́, -ти́шь**; *impf* **облета́ть**) *сов перех* to fly round
♦ *непepex* (*листья*) to fall off

**обл**|**е́чь** (**-еку́, -ечёшь** *итп*, **-еку́т**; *pt* **-ёк, -екла́**; *impf* **облека́ть**; *сов перех*: ~ **кого́-н/ что-н чем-н** (*властью, доверием*) to vest sb/sth with sth; (*impf* **облега́ть**, *3sg* **-я́жет**, *pt* **-ёг, -егла́, -егло́**) *платье*) to envelop

**облива́**|**ть** (**-ю**) *несов от* **обли́ть**; ~**ся** *несов от* **обли́ться** ♦ *возв*: ~**ся слеза́ми** to be in floods of tears

**облига́ци**|**я** (**-и**) *ж* (*КОММ*) bond

**обл**|**иза́ть** (**-ижу́, -и́жешь**; *impf* **обли́зывать**) *сов перех* to lick

**о́блик** (**-а**) *м* appearance

**обл**|**и́ть** (**-олью́, -ольёшь**;

**облива́ть**; *сов перех*: ~ **кого́-н/ что-н чем-н** (*намеренно*) to pour sth over sb/sth; (*случайно*) to spill sth over sb/sth; ~**ся** (*impf* **облива́ться**) *сов возв*: ~**ся** **чем-н** (*водой*) to sluice o.s. with sth

**обл**|**ожи́ть** (**-ожу́, -о́жишь**; *impf* **облага́ть**) *сов перех*: ~ **нало́гом** to tax

**обло́ж**|**ка** (**-ки**; *gen pl* **-ек**) *ж* (*книги, тетради*) cover

**облок**|**оти́ться** (**-очу́сь, -о́тишься**) *сов возв*: ~ **на** +*acc* to lean one's elbows on

**обло́м**|**ок** (**-ка**) *м* fragment

**облуче́ни**|**е** (**-я**) *ср* irradiation

**облуч**|**и́ть** (**-у́, -и́шь**; *impf* **облуча́ть**) *сов перех* to irradiate; ~**ся** (*impf* **облуча́ться**) *сов возв* to be irradiated

**облысе́**|**ть** (**-ю**) *сов от* **лысе́ть**

**обмакн**|**у́ть** (**-у́, -ёшь**; *impf* **обма́кивать**) *сов перех*: ~ **что-н в** +*acc* to dip sth into

**обма́н** (**-а**) *м* deception

**обма́нн**|**ый** *прил*: ~**ым путём** fraudulently

**обм**|**ану́ть** (**-ану́, -а́нешь**; *impf* **обма́нывать**) *сов перех* to deceive; (*поступить нечестно*) to cheat

**обма́нчивый** *прил* deceptive

**обма́ныва**|**ть** (**-ю**) *несов от* **обману́ть**

**обма́тыва**|**ть** (**-ю**) *несов от* **обмота́ть**

**обме́н** (**-а**) *м* exchange; (*документов*) renewal; (*также*: ~ **веще́ств**: *БИО*) metabolism; (*также*: ~ **жилпло́щадью**) exchange (*of flats etc*)

**обме́нный** *прил* exchange

**обменя́**|**ть** (**-ю**; *impf* **обме́нивать**) *сов перех* (*вещи, билеты*) to change; ~**ся** (*impf*

обме́ниваться) *сов возв* ~**ся**
+*instr* to exchange

обморо́|зить (**-жу, -зишь**; *impf*
обмора́живать) *сов перех*: ~
но́гу to get frostbite in one's foot

о́бморок (**-а**) *м* faint; па́дать
(упа́сть *pf*) в ~ to faint

обмота́|ть (**-ю**; *impf*
обма́тывать) *сов перех*: ~
кого́-н/что-н чем-н to wrap sth
round sb/sth

обм|ы́ть (**-о́ю, -о́ешь**; *impf*
обмыва́ть) *сов перех* (*рану*) to
bathe; (*разг: событие*) to
celebrate (*by drinking*)

обнагле́|ть (**-ю**) *сов от* нагле́ть

обнадёж|ить (**-у, -ишь**; *impf*
обнадёживать) *сов перех* to
reassure

обнажённый *прил* bare

обнаж|и́ть (**-у́, -и́шь**; *impf*
обнажа́ть) *сов перех* to expose;
(*руки, ноги*) to bare; (*ветки*) to
strip bare; ~**ся** (*impf* обнажа́ться)
*сов возв* to be exposed; (*человек*)
to strip

обнаро́д|овать (**-ую**) *сов перех*
(*факты, статью*) to make public;
(*закон, указ*) to promulgate

обнару́ж|ить (**-у, -ишь**; *impf*
обнару́живать) *сов перех*
(*найти*) to find; (*проявить*) to
show; ~**ся** (*impf*
обнару́живаться) *сов возв*
(*найтись*) to be found; (*стать
явным*) to become evident

обн|ести́ (**-есу́, -есёшь**; *pt* **-ёс,
-есла́, -есло́**; *impf* обноси́ть) *сов
перех*: ~ что-н/кого́-н вокру́г
+*gen* to carry sth/sb round;
(*огородить*): ~ что-н чем-н to
surround sth with sth

обнима́|ть(ся) (**-ю(сь)**) *несов от*
обня́ть(ся)

обни́мк|а *ж*: в ~у (*разг*) with their

arms around each other

обнов|и́ть (**-лю́, -и́шь**; *impf*
обновля́ть) *сов перех*
(*оборудование, гардероб*) to
replenish; (*репертуар*) to refresh;
~**ся** (*impf* обновля́ться) *сов возв*
(*репертуар*) to be refreshed;
(*организм*) to be regenerated

обн|я́ть (**-иму́, -и́мешь**; *pt* **-ял,
-яла́, -яло**; *impf* обнима́ть) *сов
перех* to embrace; ~**ся** (*impf*
обнима́ться) *сов возв* to
embrace (each other)

обо *предл см.* о

обобщ|и́ть (**-у́, -и́шь**; *impf* ~а́ть)
*сов перех* (*факты*) to generalize
from; (*статью*) to summarize

обога|ти́ть (**-щу́, -ти́шь**; *impf*
обогаща́ть) *сов перех* to enrich;
~**ся** (*impf* обогаща́ться) *сов возв*
(*человек, страна*) to be enriched

об|огна́ть (**-гоню́, -го́нишь**; *impf*
обгоня́ть) *сов перех* to overtake;
(*перен*) to outstrip

обогре́|ть (**-ю**; *impf* обогрева́ть)
*сов перех* (*помещение*) to heat;
(*человека*) to warm

о́б|од (**-ода**; *nom pl* **-о́дья**, *gen pl*
**-о́дьев**) *м* rim; (*ракетки*) frame

обо́дранный *прил* (*одежда*)
shabby; (*руки*) scratched

об|одра́ть (**-деру́, -дерёшь**; *impf*
обдира́ть) *сов перех* (*кору,
шкуру*) to strip; (*руки*) to scratch

ободр|и́ть (**-ю́, -и́шь**; *impf*
ободря́ть) *сов перех* to
encourage

обо́з (**-а**) *м* convoy

обознача́|ть (**-ю**) *несов от*
обозна́чить ♦ *перех* to signify

обозна́ч|ить (**-у, -ишь**; *impf*
обознача́ть) *сов перех*
(*границу*) to mark; (*слово*) to
mean

обозрева́тел|ь (**-я**) *м* (*событий*)

observer; (*на радио итп*) editor

**обозре́ни|е (-я)** *ср* review

**обо́|и (-ев)** *мн* wallpaper *ед*

**обо́их** *чис см.* **о́ба**

**обойти́** (*как* **идти́**; *см.* Table 18; *impf* **обходи́ть**) *сов перех* to go round; (*закон*) to get round; (*обогнать*) to pass; **~сь** (*impf* **обходи́ться**) *сов возв* (*улади́ться*) to turn out well; (*сто́ить*): **~сь в** +*acc* to cost; **обходи́ться** (**~сь** *pf*) **с кем-н/ чем-н** to treat sb/sth; **обходи́ться** (**~сь** *pf*) **без** +*gen* (*разг*) to get by without

**об|окра́сть (-краду́, -крадёшь;** *impf* **обкра́дывать**) *сов перех* to rob

**оболо́ч|ка (-ки;** *gen pl* **-ек)** *ж* (*плода*) pericarp; (*Земли*) crust

**обоня́ни|е (-я)** *ср* sense of smell

**обора́чива|ть(ся) (-ю(сь))** *несов от* **оберну́ть(ся)**

**оборв|а́ть (-у́, -ёшь;** *pt* **-а́л, -ала́, -а́ло;** *impf* **обрыва́ть**) *сов перех* (*верёвку*) to break; (*ягоды, цветы*) to pick; (*перен: разговор, дружбу*) to break off; (: *разг: говоря́щего*) to cut short; **~ся** (*impf* **обрыва́ться**) *сов возв* (*верёвка*) to break; (*перен: жизнь, разговор*) to be cut short

**обо́р|ка (-ки;** *gen pl* **-ок)** *ж* frill

**оборо́н|а (-ы)** *ж* defence (*BRIT*), defense (*US*)

**оборо́нный** *прил* defence (*BRIT*), defense (*US*)

**обороня́|ть (-ю)** *несов перех* to defend; **~ся** *несов возв* (*защища́ться*) to defend o.s.

**оборо́т (-а)** *м* (*полный круг*) revolution; (*КОММ*) turnover; (*обратная сторона*) back; (*перен: поворот событий*) turn; (*линг*) turn of phrase; (*употребление*)

circulation

**обору́довани|е (-я)** *ср* equipment

**обору́д|овать (-ую)** *(не)сов перех* to equip

**обосн|ова́ть (-у́ю;** *impf* **обосно́вывать**) *сов перех* (*теорию, вывод*) to substantiate; **~ся** (*impf* **обосно́вываться**) *сов возв* (*расположи́ться*) to settle

**обосо́бленный** *прил* (*дом*) detached; (*жизнь*) solitary

**обостр|и́ть (-ю́, -и́шь;** *impf* **обостря́ть**) *сов перех* to sharpen; (*желания, конфликт*) to intensify; **~ся** (*impf* **обостря́ться**) *сов возв* (*см перех*) to sharpen; to intensify

**обошёл(ся)** *etc сов см.* **обойти́(сь)**

**обою́дный** *прил* mutual

**обрабо́та|ть (-ю;** *impf* **обраба́тывать**) *сов перех* (*камень*) to cut; (*кожу*) to cure; (*деталь*) to turn; (*текст*) to polish up; (*землю*) to till; (*перен: разг: человека*) to work on

**обра́д|овать(ся) (-ую(сь))** *сов от* **ра́довать(ся)**

**о́браз (-а)** *м* image; (*ЛИТЕРАТУРА*) figure; (*жизни*) way; (*икона*) icon; **каки́м ~ом?** in what way?; **таки́м ~ом** in this way; (*следовательно*) consequently; **гла́вным ~ом** mainly; **не́которым ~ом** to some extent

**образ|е́ц (-ца́)** *м* sample; (*скромности, мужества*) model

**образова́ни|е (-я)** *ср* formation; (*получение знаний*) education

**образо́ванный** *прил* educated

**образ|ова́ть (-у́ю;** *impf* **~**) *(не)сов перех* to form; **~ся** (*impf* **~ся**) *(не)сов возв* to form; (*группа, комиссия*) to be formed

**образцо́вый** *прил* exemplary

**обрати́мый** *прил* reversible; *(валюта)* convertible

**обра|ти́ть (-щу́, -ти́шь;** *impf* **обраща́ть)** *сов перех (взгляд, мысли)* to turn; **обраща́ть (~** *pf)* **кого́-н/что́-н в** +*acc* to turn sb/sth into; **обраща́ть (~** *pf)* **внима́ние на** +*acc* to pay attention to; **~ся** *(impf* **обраща́ться)** *сов возв (взгляд)* to turn; *(преврати́ться)*: **~ся в** +*acc* to turn into; **обраща́ться (~ся** *pf)* **к** +*dat (к врачу́ итп)* to consult; *(к пробле́ме)* to address; **обраща́ться (~ся** *pf)* **в суд** to go to court

**обра́тно** *нареч* back; **туда́ и ~** there and back; **биле́т туда́ и ~** return *(BRIT)* *или* round-trip *(US)* ticket

**обра́тн|ый** *прил* reverse; *(дорога, путь)* return; **на ~ом пути́** on the way back; **в ~ую сто́рону** in the opposite direction; **~ая сторона́** reverse (side); **~ а́дрес** return address

**обраща́|ть (-ю)** *несов от* **обрати́ть; ~ся** *несов от* **обрати́ться ♦** *возв (де́ньги, това́р)* to circulate; **~ся** *(impf)* **с** +*instr (с маши́ной)* to handle; *(с челове́ком)* to treat

**обраще́ни|е (-я)** *ср* address; *(ЭКОН)* circulation; **~ к** +*dat (к наро́ду итп)* address to; **~ с** +*instr (с прибо́ром)* handling of

**обремен|и́ть (-ю́, -и́шь;** *impf* **обременя́ть)** *сов перех*: **~кого́-н чем-н** to load sb down with sth

**о́бруч (-а)** *м* hoop

**обруча́льн|ый** *прил*: **~ое кольцо́** wedding ring

**обру́ш|ить (-у, -ишь;** *impf* **обру́шивать)** *сов перех (сте́ну, кры́шу)* to bring down; **~ся** *(impf* **обру́шиваться)** *сов возв (кры́ша, зда́ние)* to collapse; **обру́шиваться (~ся** *pf)* **на** +*acc (на го́лову)* to crash down onto; *(на врага́)* to fall upon

**обры́в (-а)** *м (ГЕО)* precipice

**обрыва́|ть(ся) (-ю(сь))** *несов от* **оборва́ть(ся)**

**обры́в|ок (-ка)** *м (бума́ги)* scrap; *(воспомина́ний)* fragment

**обры́вочный** *прил* fragmentary

**обры́зга|ть (-ю;** *impf* **обры́згивать)** *сов перех*: **~ кого́-н/что́-н** +*instr (водо́й)* to splash sb/sth with; *(гря́зью)* to splatter sb/sth with; **~ся** *(impf* **обры́згиваться)** *сов возв*: **~ся** +*instr (см перех)* to get splashed with; to get splattered with

**обря́д (-а)** *м* ritual

**обсле́д|овать (-ую)** *(не)сов перех* to inspect; *(больно́го)* to examine

**обслу́живани|е (-я)** *ср* service

**обсл|ужи́ть (-ужу́, -у́жишь;** *impf* **обслу́живать)** *сов перех (клие́нтов)* to serve; *(подлеж: поликли́ника)* to see to

**обста́в|ить (-лю, -ишь;** *impf* **обставля́ть)** *сов перех (кварти́ру)* to furnish

**обстано́в|ка (-ки;** *gen pl* **-ок)** *ж* situation; *(кварти́ры)* furnishings *мн*

**обстоя́тельств|о (-а)** *ср* circumstance; **смотря́ по ~ам** depending on the circumstances; *(как отве́т на вопро́с)* it depends

**обс|уди́ть (-ужу́, -у́дишь;** *impf* **обсужда́ть)** *сов перех* to discuss

**обсужде́ни|е (-я)** *ср* discussion

**обува́|ть(ся) (-ю(сь))** *несов от* **обу́ть(ся)**

**обувно́й** *прил* shoe

**о́був|ь (-и)** *ж* footwear

**обусло́в|ить (-лю, -ишь;** *impf* **обусла́вливать)** *сов перех* (*явиться причиной*) to lead to

**обу́|ть (-ю;** *impf* **обува́ть)** *сов перех* (*ребёнка*) to put shoes on; **~ся** (*impf* **обува́ться**) *сов возв* to put on one's shoes or boots

**обуче́ни|е (-я)** *ср*: **~** +*dat* (*преподавание*) teaching of

**обхв|ати́ть (-ачу́, -а́тишь;** *impf* **обхва́тывать)** *сов перех*: **~ что-н (рука́ми)** to put one's arms round sth

**обхо́д (-а)** *м* (*путь*) way round; (*в больнице*) round; **в ~** +*gen* (*озера, закона*) bypassing

**обх|оди́ть(ся) (-ожу́(сь), -о́дишь(ся))** *несов от* **обойти́(сь)**

**обходно́й** *прил* (*путь*) detour

**обши́рный** *прил* extensive

**обща́|ться (-юсь)** *несов возв*: **~ с** +*instr* to mix with; (*с одним человеком*) to see; (*вести разговор*) to communicate with

**общегосуда́рственный** *прил* state

**общедосту́пный** *прил* (*способ*) available to everyone; (*цены*) affordable; (*лекция*) accessible

**о́бщ|ее (-его)** *ср* similarity; **в ~ем** (*разг*) on the whole; **у них мно́го ~его** they have a lot in common

**общежи́ти|е (-я)** *ср* (*рабочее*) hostel; (*студенческое*) hall of residence (*BRIT*), dormitory *или* hall (*US*)

**общеизве́стный** *прил* well-known

**обще́ни|е (-я)** *ср* communication

**общеобразова́тельный** *прил* comprehensive

**общепри́знанный** *прил* universally recognized

**общепри́нятый** *прил* generally accepted

**обще́ственност|ь (-и)** *ж собир* community

**обще́ственн|ый** *прил* social; (*не частный*) public; (*организация*) civic; **~ое мне́ние** public opinion

**о́бществ|о (-а)** *ср* society

**о́бщ|ий** *прил* general; (*труд*) communal; (*дом*) shared; (*друзья*) mutual; (*интересы*) common; (*количество*) total; (*картина, описание*) general; **в ~ей сло́жности** altogether

**общи́тельный** *прил* sociable

**о́бщност|ь (-и)** *ж* (*идей*) similarity; (*социальная*) community

**объедине́ни|е (-я)** *ср* (*сил*) uniting; (*производственное*) association

**объединённый** *прил* joint

**объедин|и́ть (-ю, -и́шь;** *impf* **объединя́ть)** *сов перех* to join, unite; (*ресурсы*) to pool; (*компании*) to amalgamate; **~ся** (*impf* **объединя́ться**) *сов возв* to unite

**объе́зд (-а)** *м* detour; (*с целью осмотра*) tour

**объезжа́|ть (-ю)** *несов от* **объе́хать**

**объе́кт (-а)** *м* subject; (*СТРОИТ, ВОЕН*) site

**объекти́в (-а)** *м* lens

**объекти́вный** *прил* objective

**объём (-а)** *м* volume

**объёмный** *прил* voluminous

**объе́хать** (*как* **е́хать**; *см. Table 19*; *impf* **объезжа́ть)** *сов перех* (*яму*) to go *или* drive round; (*друзей, страны*) to visit

**объ|яви́ть (-явлю́, -я́вишь;** *impf* **объявля́ть)** *сов перех* to announce; (*войну*) to declare ♦

*непереход:* ~ **о** +*prp* to announce

**объявле́ни|е (-я)** *ср*
announcement; (*войны*)
declaration; (*реклама*)
advertisement; (*извещение*) notice

**объясне́ни|е (-я)** *ср* explanation

**объясн|и́ть (-ю́, -и́шь;** *impf*
**объясня́ть)** *сов перех* to explain;
~**ся** (*impf* **объясня́ться)** *сов*
*возв:* ~**ся (с** +*instr*) to clear things
up (with)

**объясня́|ться (-юсь)** *несов от*
**объясни́ться ♦** *возв* (*на*
*английском языке*) to
communicate; ~ (*impf*) +*instr*
(*трудностями*) to be explained by

**обы́денный** *прил* mundane

**обыкнове́нный** *прил* ordinary

**о́быск (-а)** *м* search

**об|ыска́ть (-ыщу́, -ы́щешь;** *impf*
**обы́скивать)** *сов перех* to
search

**обы́ча|й (-я)** *м* custom

**обы́чно** *нареч* usually

**обы́чный** *прил* usual;
(*заурядный*) ordinary

**обя́занност|и (-ей)** *мн* duties *мн*,
responsibilities *мн*; **исполня́ть**
(*impf*) ~ +*gen* to act as

**обя́занност|ь (-и)** *ж* duty; *см.*
*также* **обя́занности**

**обя́занный** *прил:* ~ +*infin*
(*сделать итп*) obliged to do

**обяза́тельно** *нареч* definitely; **не**
~ not necessarily

**обяза́тельный** *прил* (*правило*)
binding; (*исполнение, обучение*)
compulsory, obligatory; (*работник*)
reliable

**обяза́тельств|о (-а)** *ср*
commitment; (*обычно мн, комм*)
liability

**ова́л (-а)** *м* oval

**овдове́|ть (-ю)** *сов* (*женщина*) to
become a widow, be widowed;

(*мужчина*) to become a widower,
be widowed

**Ов|е́н (-на́)** *м* (*созвездие*) Aries

**ов|ёс (-са́)** *м собир* oats *мн*

**ове́чий** *прил* (*шерсть, сыр*)
sheep's

**ОВИ́Р (-а)** *м сокр* = **отде́л виз и**
**регистра́ций**

**овладе́|ть (-ю, -ешь;** *impf*
**овладева́ть)** *сов:* ~ +*instr*
(*городом, вниманием*) to
capture; (*языком, профессией*) to
master

**о́вощ (-а)** *м* vegetable

**овощно́й** *прил* (*суп, блюдо*)
vegetable; ~ **магази́н**
greengrocer's (*BRIT*), fruit and
vegetable shop

**овра́г (-а)** *м* ditch

**овся́нк|а (-и)** *ж собир* (*каша*)
porridge (*BRIT*), oatmeal (*US*)

**овся́ный** *прил* oat

**ов|ца́ (-цы́;** *nom pl* **-цы,** *gen pl* **-е́ц)**
*ж* sheep; (*самка*) ewe

**овча́р|ка (-ки;** *gen pl* **-ок)** *ж*
sheepdog

**овчи́н|а (-ы)** *ж* sheepskin

**оглавле́ни|е (-я)** *ср* (table of)
contents

**огло́хн|уть (-у)** *сов от* **гло́хнуть**

**огл|уши́ть (-ушу́, -у́ши́шь;** *impf*
**оглуша́ть)** *сов перех:* ~ **кого́-н**
**чем-н** to deafen sb with sth

**огля|де́ть (-жу́, -ди́шь;** *impf*
**огля́дывать)** *сов перех* to look
round; ~**ся** (*impf* **огля́дываться)**
*сов возв* to look around

**огл|яну́ться (-яну́сь, -я́нешься;**
*impf* **огля́дываться)** *сов возв* to
look back; (*я*) **не успе́л** ~, **как ...**
before I knew it ...

**о́гненный** *прил* fiery

**огнеопа́сный** *прил* (in)flammable

**огнестре́л|ьный** *прил:* ~**ое**
**ору́жие** firearms *мн*; ~**ая ра́на**

bullet wound

**огнетуши́тел|ь (-я)** м fire-extinguisher

**ог|о́нь (-ня́)** м fire; (*фонарей, в окне*) light

**огоро́д (-а)** м vegetable *или* kitchen garden

**огорче́ни|е (-я)** ср distress; **к моему ~ю** to my dismay

**огорч|и́ть (-у́, -и́шь**; *impf* **огорча́ть**) *сов перех* to distress; **~ся** (*impf* **огорча́ться**) *сов возв* to be distressed *или* upset

**огра́б|ить (-лю, -ишь)** *сов от* **гра́бить**

**ограбле́ни|е (-я)** ср robbery

**огра́д|а (-ы)** ж (*забор*) fence; (*решётка*) railings мн

**огра|ди́ть (-жу́, -ди́шь**; *impf* **огражда́ть**) *сов перех* (*сберечь*) to shelter, protect

**огражде́ни|е (-я)** ср = **огра́да**

**ограниче́ни|е (-я)** ср limitation; (*правило*) restriction

**ограни́ченный** *прил* limited; (*человек*) narrow-minded

**ограни́ч|ить (-у, -ишь**; *impf* **ограни́чивать**) *сов перех* to limit, restrict; **~ся** (*impf* **ограни́чиваться**) *сов возв*: **~ся** +*instr* (*удовлетвориться*) to content o.s. with; (*свестись*) to become limited to

**огро́мный** *прил* enormous

**огры́з|ок (-ка)** м (*яблока*) half-eaten bit; (*карандаша*) stub

**огур|е́ц (-ца́)** м cucumber

**ода́лжива|ть (-ю)** *несов от* **одолжи́ть**

**одарённый** *прил* gifted

**одева́|ть(ся) (-ю(сь))** *несов от* **оде́ть(ся)**

**оде́жд|а (-ы)** ж clothes мн

**одеколо́н (-а)** м eau de Cologne

**оде́ну(сь)** *etc сов см.* **оде́ть(ся)**

**од|ержа́ть (-ержу́, -е́ржишь**; *impf* **оде́рживать**) *сов перех*: **~ побе́ду** to be victorious

**оде́тый** *прил* dressed

**оде́|ть (-ну, -нешь**; *impf* **одева́ть**) *сов перех* to dress; **~ся** (*impf* **одева́ться**) *сов возв* to get dressed; (*тепло, красиво*) to dress

**одея́л|о (-а)** ср (*шерстяное*) blanket; (*стёганое*) quilt

---

KEYWORD

---

**од|и́н (-ного́**; *см. Table 22;* f **одна́**, nt **одно́**, pl **одни́**) м чис one; **одна́ кни́га** one book; **одни́ брю́ки** one pair of trousers

♦ *прил* alone; (*единственный, единый*) one; (*одинаковый, тот же самый*) the same; **он идёт в кино́ оди́н** he goes to the cinema alone; **есть то́лько оди́н вы́ход** there is only one way out; **у них одни́ взгля́ды** they hold similar views

♦ *мест* 1 (*какой-то*): **оди́н мой знако́мый** a friend of mine; **одни́ неприя́тности** nothing but problems

2 (*во фразах*): **оди́н из** +*gen pl* one of; **оди́н и то́т же** the same; **одно́ и то́ же** the same thing; **оди́н раз** once; **оди́н на оди́н** one to one; **все до одного́** all to a man; **ни оди́н** not one; **оди́н за други́м** one after the other; **по одному́** one by one; **оди́н-еди́нственный** only one

---

**одина́ковый** *прил* similar

**оди́ннадцатый** *чис* eleventh

**оди́ннадцат|ь (-и**; *как* **пять**; *см. Table 26*) *чис* eleven

**одино́кий** *прил* (*жизнь, человек*) lonely; (*не семейный*) single

**одино́честв|о (-а)** ср loneliness

**одино́чный** *прил* single

**одн|а́** (-о́й) *ж чис см.* **оди́н**

**одна́жды** *нареч* once

**одна́ко** *союз, вводн сл* however;
~! well, I never!

**одни́** (-х) *мн чис см.* **оди́н**

**одн|о́** (-о́го) *ср чис см.* **оди́н**

**одновреме́нно** *нареч:* ~ (с +*instr*)
at the same time (as)

**одного́** *etc чис см.* **оди́н; одно́**

**однозна́чн|ый** *прил*
(тождественный) synonymous; (с
одним значением: слово)
monosemous; (: выражение,
ответ) unambiguous; (МАТ)
single-figure; ~**ое число́** single-
digit number

**одноме́стный** *прил* (купе,
номер) single; (каюта) single-berth

**однообра́зный** *прил*
monotonous

**однора́зовый** *прил* disposable

**однородный** *прил* (явления)
similar; (масса) homogeneous

**односторо́нний** *прил* unilateral;
(движение) one-way

**одноцве́тный** *прил* plain

**одноэта́жный** *прил* single-storey
(*BRIT*), single-story (*US*), one-storey
(*BRIT*), one-story (*US*)

**одобре́ни|е** (-я) *ср* approval

**одобри́тельный** *прил* (отзыв)
favourable (*BRIT*), favorable (*US*);
(восклицание) approving

**одо́бр|ить** (-ю, -ишь; *impf*
**одобря́ть**) *сов перех* to approve

**одолже́ни|е** (-я) *ср* favour (*BRIT*),
favor (*US*)

**одолж|и́ть** (-у́, -и́шь; *impf*
**ода́лживать**) *сов перех:* ~ что-н
кому́-н to lend sth to sb;
**ода́лживать** (~ *pf*) что-н у кого́-н
(разг) to borrow sth from sb

**одува́нчик** (-а) *м* dandelion

**ожере́л|ье** (-ья; *gen pl* -ий) *ср*
necklace

**ожесточе́ни|е** (-я) *ср* resentment

**ожесточённый** *прил* (человек)
resentful, embittered; (спор) fierce

**ожива́|ть** (-ю) *несов от* **ожи́ть**

**ожив|и́ть** (-лю́, -и́шь; *impf*
**оживля́ть**) *сов перех* to revive;
(глаза, лицо) to light up; ~**ся**
(*impf* **оживля́ться**) *сов возв* to
liven up; (лицо) to brighten

**оживлённый** *прил* lively;
(беседа, спор) animated

**ожида́ни|е** (-я) *ср* anticipation;
(обычно мн: надежды)
expectation

**ожида́|ть** (-ю) *несов перех*
(ждать) to expect; (надеяться): ~
+*gen* to expect; **э́того мо́жно
бы́ло** ~ that was to be expected;
~**ся** *несов возв* to be expected

**ож|и́ть** (-иву́, -ивёшь; *impf*
**ожива́ть**) *сов* to come to life

**ожо́г** (-а) *м* burn

**озабо́ченный** *прил* worried

**озагла́в|ить** (-лю, -ишь) *сов
перех* to entitle

**озада́ч|ить** (-у, -ишь; *impf*
**озада́чивать**) *сов перех* to
puzzle, perplex

**оздорови́тельн|ый** *прил* health-
improving

**о́з|еро** (-ера; *nom pl* -ёра) *ср* lake

**озира́|ться** (-юсь) *несов возв:* ~
(по сторона́м) to glance about
или around

**означа́|ть** (-ю) *несов перех* to
mean, signify

**озно́б** (-а) *м* shivering

**озо́н** (-а) *м* ozone

**озо́нов|ый** *прил:* ~ **слой** ozone
layer; ~**ая дыра́** hole in the ozone
layer

**ой** *межд:* ~! (выражает испуг)
argh!; (выражает боль) ouch!,
ow!

**ок|аза́ть** (-ажу́, -а́жешь; *impf* **ока́зывать**) *сов перех*: ~ **по́мощь кому́-н** to provide help for sb; **ока́зывать** (~ *pf*) **влия́ние/давле́ние на** +*acc* to exert influence/pressure on; **ока́зывать** (~ *pf*) **внима́ние кому́-н** to pay attention to sb; **ока́зывать** (~ *pf*) **сопротивле́ние** (**кому́-н**) to offer resistance (to sb); **ока́зывать** (~ *pf*) **услу́гу кому́-н** to do sb a service; **~ся** (*impf* **ока́зываться**) *сов возв* (*найти́сь: на столе́ итп*) to appear; (*очути́ться: на остро́ве итп*) to end up; **ока́зываться** (**~ся** *pf*) +*instr* (*во́ром, шпио́ном*) to turn out to be; **ока́зывается, она́ была́ права́** it turns out that she was right

**окамене́|ть** (*impf* **камене́ть**) *сов* (*перен: лицо́*) to freeze; (*: се́рдце*) to turn to stone

**ока́нчива|ть** (-ю) *несов от* **око́нчить**; **~ся** *несов от* **око́нчиться** ♦ *возв*: **~ся на гла́сную/согла́сную** to end in a vowel/consonant

**океа́н** (-а) *м* ocean

**оки́н|уть** (-у; *impf* **оки́дывать**) *сов перех*: ~ **кого́-н/что-н взгля́дом** to glance over at sb/sth

**о́кис|ь** (-и) *ж* oxide

**оккупи́р|овать** (-ую) (*не*)*сов перех* to occupy

**окла́д** (-а) *м* (*зарпла́та*) salary

**оклев|ета́ть** (-ещу́, -е́щешь) *сов перех* to slander

**окле́|ить** (-ю, -ишь; *impf* **окле́ивать**) *сов перех*: ~ **что-н чем-н** to cover sth with sth

**ок|но́** (-на́; *nom pl* **-на**, *gen pl* **-он**) *ср* window

**о́коло** *нареч* nearby ♦ *предл*: ~ +*gen* (*ря́дом с*) near; (*приблизи́тельно*) about, around

**околозе́мный** *прил* around the earth

**око́нн|ый** *прил*: **~ая ра́ма** window frame; **~ое стекло́** windowpane

**оконча́ни|е** (-я) *ср* end; (*линг*) ending

**оконча́тельно** *нареч* (*отве́тить*) definitely; (*победи́ть*) completely; (*отредакти́ровать*) finally

**оконча́тельный** *прил* final; (*побе́да, сверже́ние*) complete

**око́нч|ить** (-у, -ишь; *impf* **ока́нчивать**) *сов перех* to finish; (*вуз*) to graduate from; **~ся** (*impf* **ока́нчиваться**) *сов возв* to finish; **~ся** (*pf*) +*instr* (*сканда́лом*) to result in

**око́п** (-а) *м* trench

**о́корок** (-а; *nom pl* **-а́**) *м* gammon

**окочене́|ть** (-ю) *сов от* **кочене́ть**

**окра́ин|а** (-ы) *ж* (*го́рода*) outskirts *мн*; (*страны́*) remote parts *мн*

**окра́с|ка** (-ки; *gen pl* **-ок**) *ж* (*стены́*) painting; (*живо́тного*) colouring (*BRIT*), coloring (*US*)

**окре́пн|уть** (-у) *сов от* **кре́пнуть**

**окре́стност|ь** (-и) *ж* (*обы́чно мн*) environs *мн*

**окре́стный** *прил* (*дере́вни*) neighbouring (*BRIT*), neighboring (*US*)

**о́крик** (-а) *м* shout

**окри́кн|уть** (-у; *impf* **окри́кивать**) *сов перех*: ~ **кого́-н** to shout to sb

**о́круг** (-а) *м* (*администрати́вный*) district; (*избира́тельный*) ward; (*национа́льный*) territory; (*го́рода*) borough

**округл|и́ть** (-ю́, -и́шь; *impf* **округля́ть**) *сов перех* (*фо́рму*) to round off; (*ци́фру*) to round up/down

**окружа́|ть** (-ю) *несов от*

**окружи́ть** ♦ *перех* to surround
**окружа́ющ|ее** (**-его**) *ср* environment
**окружа́ющ|ие** (**-их**) *мн* (*также*: **~ лю́ди**) the people around one
**окружа́ющий** *прил* surrounding
**окруже́ни|е** (**-я**) *ср* (*среда́*) environment; (*компа́ния*) circles *мн*; (*ВОЕН*) encirclement; **в ~и** +*gen* (*среди́*) surrounded by
**окруж|и́ть** (**-у́, -и́шь**; *impf* **окружа́ть**) *сов перех* to surround
**окружн|о́й** *прил* regional; **~а́я доро́га** bypass
**окру́жност|ь** (**-и**) *ж* circle
**октя́бр|ь** (**-я́**) *м* October
**окули́ст** (**-а**) *м* ophthalmologist
**окун|у́ть** (**-у́, -ёшь**; *impf* **~а́ть**) *сов перех* to dip
**окупа́емост|ь** (**-и**) *ж* viability
**ок|упи́ть** (**-уплю́, -у́пишь**; *impf* **окупа́ть**) *сов перех* (*расхо́ды*) to cover; (*пое́здку, прое́кт*) to cover the cost of
**оку́р|ок** (**-ка**; *nom pl* **-ки**) *м* stub, butt
**ола́д|ья** (**-ьи**; *gen pl* **-ий**) *ж* ≈ drop scone, ≈ (Scotch) pancake
**оле́н|ий** *прил* deer's; **~ьи рога́** antlers
**оле́н|ь** (**-я**) *м* deer
**оли́вк|а** (**-и**) *ж* olive
**олимпиа́д|а** (**-ы**) *ж* (*СПОРТ*) the Olympics *мн*; (*по фи́зике итп*) Olympiad
**олимпи́йск|ий** *прил* Olympic; **~ие и́гры** the Olympic Games
**о́лов|о** (**-а**) *ср* (*ХИМ*) tin
**омерзи́тельный** *прил* disgusting
**омле́т** (**-а**) *м* omelette
**ОМО́Н** *м сокр* (= **отря́д мили́ции осо́бого назначе́ния**) special police force
**омо́ним** (**-а**) *м* homonym
**омо́нов|ец** (**-ца**) *м member of the special police force*

**омрач|и́ть** (**-у́, -и́шь**; *impf* **омрача́ть**) *сов перех* (*лицо́*) to cloud; **~ся** (*impf* **омрача́ться**) *сов возв* to darken
**он** (**его́**; *см. Table 6а*) *мест* (*челове́к*) he; (*живо́тное, предме́т*) it
**она́** (**её**; *см. Table 6а*) *мест* (*челове́к*) she; (*живо́тное, предме́т*) it
**они́** (**их**; *см. Table 6b*) *мест* they
**онкологи́ческ|ий** *прил* oncological; **~ая кли́ника** cancer clinic
**онла́йновый** *прил* (*КОМП*) on-line
**оно́** (**его́**; *см. Table 6а*) *мест* it; **~ и ви́дно!** (*разг*) sure! (*used ironically*); **вот ~ что и как!** (*разг*) so that's what it is!
**ООН** *ж сокр* (= **Организа́ция Объединённых На́ций**) UN(O)
**опа́здыва|ть** (**-ю**) *несов от* **опозда́ть**
**опаса́|ться** (**-юсь**) *несов возв*: **~** +*gen* to be afraid of; **~** (*impf*) **за** +*acc* to be worried about
**опасе́ни|е** (**-я**) *ср* apprehension
**опа́сност|ь** (**-и**) *ж* danger
**опа́сный** *прил* dangerous
**опе́к|а** (**-и**) *ж* (*госуда́рства*) guardianship; (*ма́тери, отца́*) custody; (*забо́та*) care
**опека́|ть** (**-ю**) *несов перех* to take care of; (*сироту́*) to be guardian to
**о́пер|а** (**-ы**) *ж* opera
**операти́вн|ый** *прил* (*ме́ры*) efficient; (*хирурги́ческий*) surgical; **~ая гру́ппа** ≈ task force; **~ое запомина́ющее устро́йство** RAM
**опера́тор** (**-а**) *м* operator
**операцио́нный** *прил* surgical; **~ стол** operating table
**опера́ци|я** (**-и**) *ж* operation

**опере|ди́ть** (-жу́, -ди́шь; impf **опережа́ть**) сов перех to outstrip

**опере́тт|а** (-ы) ж operetta

**опер|е́ться** (обопру́сь, обопрёшься; pt опёрся, -ла́сь; impf **опира́ться**) сов: ~ на +acc to lean on

**опери́р|овать** (-ую; pf ~ или про~) несов перех (больного) to operate on ♦ неперех (no pf; ВОЕН) to operate; ~ (impf) +instr (акциями) to deal in; (перен: цифрами, фактами) to use

**о́перный** прил operatic; (певец) opera

**опеча́та|ть** (-ю; impf **опеча́тывать**) сов перех to seal

**опеча́т|ка** (-ки; gen pl -ок) ж misprint

**опи́л|ки** (-ок) мн (древесные) sawdust ед; (металлические) filings мн

**опира́|ться** (-юсь) несов от **опере́ться**

**описа́ни|е** (-я) ср description

**оп|иса́ть** (-ишу́, -и́шешь; impf **опи́сывать**) сов перех to describe

**опла́т|а** (-ы) ж payment

**опл|ати́ть** (-ачу́, -а́тишь; impf **опла́чивать**) сов перех (работу, труд) to pay for; (счёт) to pay

**оплодотвор|и́ть** (-ю́, -и́шь; impf **оплодотворя́ть**) сов перех to fertilize

**опло́т** (-а) м stronghold, bastion

**опове|сти́ть** (-щу́, -сти́шь; impf **оповеща́ть**) сов перех to notify

**опозда́ни|е** (-я) ср lateness; (поезда, самолёта) late arrival

**опозда́|ть** (-ю; impf **опа́здывать**) сов: ~ (в/на +acc) (в школу, на работу итп) to be late (for)

**опознава́тельный** прил (знак) identifying

**опозна́|ть** (-ю; impf **опознава́ть**) сов перех to identify

**опозо́р|ить(ся)** (-ю(сь)) сов от **позо́рить(ся)**

**опо́мн|иться** (-юсь, -ишься) сов возв (прийти в сознание) to come round; (одуматься) to come to one's senses

**опо́р|а** (-ы) ж support

**опо́рный** прил supporting; ~ прыжо́к vault; ~ пункт base

**оппозицио́нный** прил opposition

**оппози́ци|я** (-и) ж opposition

**оппоне́нт** (-а) м (в споре) opponent; (диссертации) external examiner

**опра́в|а** (-ы) ж frame

**оправда́ни|е** (-я) ср justification; (ЮР) acquittal; (извинение) excuse

**опра́вданный** прил justified

**оправда́|ть** (-ю; impf **опра́вдывать**) сов перех to justify; (надежды) to live up to; (ЮР) to acquit; ~ся (impf **опра́вдываться**) сов возв to justify o.s.; (расходы) to be justified

**опра́в|ить** (-лю, -ишь; impf **оправля́ть**) сов перех (платье, постель) to straighten; (линзы) to frame; ~ся (impf **оправля́ться**) сов возв: ~ся от +gen to recover from

**опра́шива|ть** (-ю) несов от **опроси́ть**

**определе́ни|е** (-я) ср determination; (ЛИНГ) attribute

**определённый** прил (установленный) definite; (некоторый) certain

**определ|и́ть** (-ю́, -и́шь; impf **определя́ть**) сов перех to determine; (понятие) to define

**оприхо́д|овать** (-ую) сов от **прихо́довать**

**опроверг|нуть** (**-у**; *impf*
**опровергать**) *сов перех* to
refute

**опрокин|уть** (**-у**; *impf*
**опрокидывать**) *сов перех*
(*стакан*) to knock over; **~ся** (*impf*
**опрокидываться**) *сов возв*
(*стакан, стул, человек*) to fall
over; (*лодка*) to capsize

**опрометчивый** *прил* precipitate

**опрос** (**-а**) *м* (*свидетелей*)
questioning; (*населения*) survey; **~**
**общественного мнения**
opinion poll

**опр|осить** (**-ошу́, -о́сишь**; *impf*
**опрашивать**) *сов перех*
(*свидетелей*) to question;
(*население*) to survey

**опросный** *прил*: **~ лист**
questionnaire

**опротест|овать** (**-у́ю**) *сов перех*
(*ЮР*) to appeal against

**опрятный** *прил* neat, tidy

**опт** (**-а**) *м* (*КОММ, крупная*
*партия*) wholesale

**оптимальный** *прил* optimum

**оптимизм** (**-а**) *м* optimism

**оптимистичный** *прил* optimistic

**оптический** *прил* optical

**опто́в|ый** *прил* wholesale; **~ые**
**закупки** (*КОММ*) bulk buying

**о́птом** *нареч*: **купить/продать ~**
to buy/sell wholesale

**опуска|ть(ся)** (**-ю(сь)**) *несов от*
**опустить(ся)**

**опусте́|ть** (*3sg* **-ет**) *сов от*
**пусте́ть**

**оп|устить** (**-ущу́, -у́стишь**; *impf*
**опускать**) *сов перех* to lower;
(*пропустить*) to miss out;
**опускать** (**~** *pf*) **в** +*acc* (*в ящик*) to
drop *или* put in(to); **~ся** (*impf*
**опускаться**) *сов возв* (*человек:*
*на диван, на землю*) to sit
(down); (*солнце*) to sink; (*мост,*

*шлагбаум*) to be lowered; (*перен:*
*человек*) to let o.s. go

**опустош|и́ть** (**-у́, -и́шь**; *impf*
**опустоша́ть**) *сов перех*
(*страну*) to devastate

**опу́хн|уть** (**-у**) *сов от* **пу́хнуть**
♦ (*impf* **опуха́ть**) *неперех* to swell
(up)

**о́пухол|ь** (**-и**) *ж* (*рана*) swelling;
(*внутренняя*) tumour (*BRIT*),
tumor (*US*)

**опу́хший** *прил* swollen

**о́пыт** (**-а**) *м* experience;
(*эксперимент*) experiment

**о́пытный** *прил* (*рабочий*)
experienced; (*лаборатория*)
experimental

**опьяне́|ть** (**-ю**) *сов от* **пьяне́ть**

**опя́ть** *нареч* again; **~ же** (*разг*) at
that

**ора́нжевый** *прил* orange

**ора́тор** (**-а**) *м* orator;
(*выступающий*) speaker

**ор|а́ть** (**-у́, -ёшь**) *несов* (*разг*) to
yell; (*ребёнок*) to bawl, howl

**орби́т|а** (**-ы**) *ж* orbit

**о́рган** (**-а**) *м* (*также АНАТ*) organ;
(*власти*) body; (*орудие*): **о́рган**
+*gen* (*пропаганды*) vehicle for;
**ме́стные ~ы вла́сти** local
authorities (*BRIT*) *или* government
(*US*); **половы́е ~ы** genitals

**орга́н** (**-а**) *м* (*МУЗ*) organ

**организа́тор** (**-а**) *м* organizer

**организа́ци|я** (**-и**) *ж* organization;
(*устройство*) system

**органи́зм** (**-а**) *м* organism

**организо́ванный** *прил* organized

**организ|ова́ть** (**-у́ю**) (*не*)*сов*
*перех* (*создать*) to organize

**органи́ческий** *прил* organic

**оргкомите́т** (**-а**) *м сокр* (=
*организацио́нный комите́т*)
organizational committee

**оргте́хник|а** (**-и**) *ж* office

automation equipment

**о́рден** (-а; *nom pl* -**а́**) *м* order

**о́рдер** (-а) *м* (*ЮР*) warrant; (*на кварти́ру*) authorization

**орёл** (орла́; *nom pl* орлы́) *м* eagle

**оре́х** (-а) *м* nut

**оригина́л** (-а) *м* original

**оригина́льный** *прил* original

**ориенти́р** (-а) *м* landmark

**орке́стр** (-а) *м* orchestra

**орна́мент** (-а) *м* (decorative) pattern

**оробе́|ть** (-ю) *сов от* **робе́ть**

**ороси́тельный** *прил* irrigation

**ороше́ни|е** (-я) *ср* irrigation

**ортодокса́льный** *прил* orthodox

**ортопе́д** (-а) *м* orthopaedic (*BRIT*) *или* orthopedic (*US*) surgeon

**ортопеди́ческий** *прил* orthopaedic (*BRIT*), orthopedic (*US*)

**ору́ди|е** (-я) *ср* tool; (*ВОЕН*) gun (*used of artillery*)

**ору́жи|е** (-я) *ж* weapon

**орфогра́фи|я** (-и) *ж* spelling

**ОС** *ж нескл сокр* (*КОМП*: = операцио́нная систе́ма) operating system

**ос|а́** (-ы́; *nom pl* о́сы) *ж* wasp

**оса́д|а** (-ы) *ж* siege

**оса́д|ок** (-ка) *м* sediment; *см. также* **оса́дки**

**оса́дки** (-ов) *мн* precipitation *ед*

**осва́ива|ть(ся)** (-ю(сь)) *несов от* **осво́ить(ся)**

**осве́дом|ить** (-лю, -ишь) *impf* **осведомля́ть** *сов перех* to inform; ~**ся** (*impf* **осведомля́ться**) *сов возв*: ~**ся о** +*prp* to inquire about

**освеж|и́ть** (-у́, -и́шь; *impf* **освежа́ть**) *сов перех* (*знания*) to refresh; ~**ся** (*impf* **освежа́ться**) *сов возв* (*воздух*) to freshen; (*челове́к*) to freshen up

**освети́тельный** *прил*: ~ **прибо́р** light

**осве|ти́ть** (-щу́, -ти́шь; *impf* **освеща́ть**) *сов перех* to light up; (*пробле́му*) to cover; ~**ся** (*impf* **освеща́ться**) *сов возв* to be lit up

**освеще́ни|е** (-я) *ср* lighting; (*пробле́мы, де́ла*) coverage

**освобо|ди́ть** (-жу́, -ди́шь) *impf* **освобожда́ть** *сов перех* (*из тюрьмы́*) to release; (*го́род*) to liberate; (*дом*) to vacate; (*вре́мя*) to free up; ~ (*pf*) кого́-н от до́лжности to dismiss sb; ~**ся** (*impf* **освобожда́ться**) *сов возв* (*из тюрьмы́*) to be released; (*дом*) to be vacated

**освобожде́ни|е** (-я) *ср* release; (*го́рода*) liberation; ~ **от** до́лжности dismissal

**осво́|ить** (-ю, -ишь; *impf* **осва́ивать**) *сов перех* (*те́хнику, язык*) to master; (*зе́мли*) to cultivate; ~**ся** (*impf* **осва́иваться**) *сов возв* (*на но́вой рабо́те*) to find one's feet

**освя|ти́ть** (-щу́, -ти́шь; *impf* **освяща́ть**) *сов перех* (*РЕЛ*) to bless

**оседа́|ть** (-ю) *несов от* **осе́сть**

**ос|ёл** (-ла́) *м* donkey

**осе́нний** *прил* autumn, fall (*US*)

**о́сен|ь** (-и) *ж* autumn, fall (*US*)

**о́сенью** *нареч* in autumn *или* the fall (*US*)

**ос|е́сть** (-я́ду, -я́дешь; *impf* **оседа́ть**) *сов* (*пыль, оса́док*) to settle

**осётр** (-етра́) *м* sturgeon (*ZOOL*)

**осетри́н|а** (-ы) *ж* sturgeon (*CULIN*)

**оси́н|а** (-ы) *ж* aspen

**оси́н|ый** *прил*: ~**ое гнездо́** (*перен*) hornet's nest

**оскверн|и́ть** (-ю́, -и́шь; *impf* **оскверня́ть**) *сов перех* to defile

**оско́л|ок** (**-ка**) *м* (*стекла*) piece; (*снаряда*) shrapnel *ед*

**оскорби́тельный** *прил* offensive

**оскорб|и́ть** (**-лю́, -и́шь**; *impf* **оскорбля́ть**) *сов перех* to insult; **~ся** (*impf* **оскорбля́ться**) *сов возв* to be offended, take offence *или* offense (*US*)

**оскорбле́ни|е** (**-я**) *ср* insult

**осла́б|ить** (**-лю, -ишь**; *impf* **ослабля́ть**) *сов перех* to weaken; (*дисциплину*) to relax

**ослепи́тельный** *прил* dazzling

**ослеп|и́ть** (**-лю́, -и́шь**; *impf* **ослепля́ть**) *сов перех* to blind; (*подлеж: красота*) to dazzle

**осле́п|нуть** (**-ну**; *pt* **-, -ла**) *сов от* **сле́пнуть**

**осложне́ни|е** (**-я**) *ср* complication

**осложн|и́ть** (**-ю́, -и́шь**; *impf* **осложня́ть**) *сов перех* to complicate; **~ся** (*impf* **осложня́ться**) *сов возв* to become complicated

**осма́трива|ть(ся)** (**-ю(сь)**) *несов от* **осмотре́ть(ся)**

**осмеле́|ть** (**-ю**) *несов от* **смеле́ть**

**осме́л|иться** (**-юсь, -ишься**; *impf* **осме́ливаться**) *сов возв* to dare

**осмо́тр** (**-а**) *м* inspection; (*больного*) examination; (*музея*) visit

**осм|отре́ть** (**-отрю́, -о́тришь**; *impf* **осма́тривать**) *сов перех* (*см сущ*) to inspect; to examine; to visit; **~ся** (*impf* **осма́триваться**) *сов возв* (*по сторонам*) to look around; (*перен: на новом месте*) to settle in

**осмотри́тельный** *прил* cautious

**осна|сти́ть** (**-щу́, -сти́шь**; *impf* **оснаща́ть**) *сов перех* to equip

**оснаще́ни|е** (**-я**) *ср* equipment

**осно́в|а** (**-ы**) *ж* basis;

(*сооружения*) foundations *мн*; **на ~е** +*gen* on the basis of; *см. также* **осно́вы**

**основа́ни|е** (**-я**) *ср* base; (*теории*) basis; (*поступка*) grounds *мн*; **без вся́ких ~й** without any reason; **до ~я** completely; **на ~и** +*gen* on the grounds of; **на како́м ~и?** on what grounds?

**основа́тел|ь** (**-я**) *м* founder

**основа́тельный** *прил* (*анализ*) thorough

**основа́|ть** (*pt* **-л, -ла, -ло**; *impf* **осно́вывать**) *сов перех* to found; **осно́вывать** (**~** *pf*) **что-н на** +*prp* to base sth on *или* upon; **~ся** (*impf* **осно́вываться**) *сов возв* (*компания*) to be founded

**основн|о́й** *прил* main; (*закон*) fundamental; **в ~о́м** on the whole

**осно́выва|ть(ся)** (**-ю(сь)**) *несов от* **основа́ть(ся)**

**осно́в|ы** (**-**) *мн* (*физики*) basics *мн*

**осо́бенно** *нареч* particularly; (*хорошо*) especially, particularly

**осо́бенный** *прил* special, particular

**особня́к** (**-а**) *м* mansion

**осо́бый** *прил* (*вид, случай*) special, particular; (*помещение*) separate

**осозна́|ть** (**-ю**; *impf* **осознава́ть**) *сов перех* to realize

**о́сп|а** (**-ы**) *ж* smallpox

**оспа́рива|ть** (**-ю**) *несов от* **оспо́рить ♦** *перех* (*первенство*) to contend *или* compete for

**оспо́р|ить** (**-ю, -ишь**; *impf* **оспа́ривать**) *сов перех* to question

**оста|ва́ться** (**-ю́сь, -ёшься**) *несов от* **оста́ться**

**оста́в|ить** (**-лю, -ишь**; *impf* **оставля́ть**) *сов перех* to leave; (*сохранить*) to keep;

(*прекратить*) to stop; (*перен: надежды*) to give up; ~ь! stop it!
**остальн|о́е** (-**о́го**) *ср* the rest *мн*; **в ~о́м** in other respects
**остально́й** *прил* (*часть*) the remaining
**остальн|ы́е** (-**ы́х**) *мн* the others *мн*
**остан|ови́ть** (-**овлю́**, -**о́вишь**; *impf* **остана́вливать**) *сов перех* to stop; ~**ся** (*impf* **остана́вливаться**) *сов возв* to stop; (*в гостинице, у друзей*) to stay; ~**ся** (*pf*) **на** +*prp* (*на вопросе*) to dwell on; (*на решении*) to come to; (*взгляд*) to rest on
**остано́вк|а** (-**и**) *ж* stop; (*мотора*) stopping; (*в работе*) pause
**оста́т|ок** (-**ка**) *м* (*пищи, дня*) the remainder, the rest; ~**ки** (*дома*) remains; (*еды*) leftovers
**оста́|ться** (-**нусь**; *impf* **остава́ться**) *сов возв* (*не уйти*) to stay; (*сохраниться*) to remain; (*оказаться*) to be left
**остекл|и́ть** (-**ю́**, -**и́шь**) *сов от* **стекли́ть**
**осторо́жно** *нареч* (*взять*) carefully; (*ходить, говорить*) cautiously; ~! look out!
**осторо́жност|ь** (-**и**) *ж* care; (*поступка, поведения*) caution
**осторо́жный** *прил* careful
**остри|ё** (-**я́**) *ср* point; (*ножа*) edge
**остр|и́ть** (-**ю́**, -**и́шь**; *pf* **с~**) *несов* to make witty remarks
**о́стров** (-**а**; *nom pl* -**а́**) *м* island
**остросюже́тный** *прил* (*пьеса*) gripping; ~ **фильм**, ~ **рома́н** thriller
**остро́т|а** (-**ы**) *ж* witticism
**острот|а́** (-**ы́**) *ж* (*зрения*) sharpness; (*ситуации*) acuteness
**остроу́мный** *прил* witty
**о́стрый** *прил* (*нож, память, вкус*) sharp; (*борода, нос*) pointed; (*зрение, слух*) keen; (*шутка, слово*) witty; (*еда*) spicy; (*желание*) burning; (*боль, болезнь*) acute; (*ситуация*) critical
**ост|уди́ть** (-**ужу́**, -**у́дишь**; *impf* **остужа́ть**) *сов перех* to cool
**осты́|ть** (-**ну**, -**нешь**) *сов от* **стыть** ♦ (*impf* **остыва́ть**) *неперех* to cool down
**ос|уди́ть** (-**ужу́**, -**у́дишь**; *impf* **осужда́ть**) *сов перех* to condemn; (*приговорить*) to convict
**осужде́ни|е** (-**я**) *ср* (*см глаг*) condemnation; conviction
**осуждённ|ый** (-**ого**) *м* convict
**ос|уши́ть** (-**ушу́**, -**у́шишь**; *impf* **осуша́ть**) *сов перех* to drain
**осуществ|и́ть** (-**лю́**, -**и́шь**; *impf* **осуществля́ть**) *сов перех* (*мечту, идею*) to realize; (*план*) to implement; ~**ся** (*impf* **осуществля́ться**) *сов возв* (*мечты, идея*) to be realized
**осчастли́в|ить** (-**лю**, -**ишь**) *сов перех* to make happy
**осы́п|ать** (-**лю**, -**лешь**; *impf* **осыпа́ть**) *сов перех*: **осыпа́ть** (~ *pf*) **кого́-н/что-н чем-н** to scatter sth over sb/sth; (*перен: подарками*) to shower sb/sth with sth; ~**ся** (*impf* **осыпа́ться**) *сов возв* (*насыпь*) to subside; (*штукатурка*) to crumble; (*листья*) to fall
**ос|ь** (-**и**; *loc sg* -**и́**) *ж* (*механизма*) axle; (*ГЕОМ*) axis
**осьмино́г** (-**а**) *м* octopus

┌─────────────┐
│ KEYWORD │
└─────────────┘

**от** *предл*; +*gen* **1** from; **он отошёл от стола́** he moved away from the table; **он узна́л об э́том от дру́га** he found out about it from a friend

2 (*указывает на причину*):
**бумáга размóкла от дождя** the
paper got wet with rain; **от злóсти**
with anger; **от рáдости** for joy; **от
удивлéния** in surprise; **от
разочарóвания/стрáха** out of
disappointment/fear
3 (*указывает на что-н, против
чего направлено действие*): for;
**лекáрство от кáшля** medicine for
a cough, cough medicine
4 (*о части целого*): **рýчка/ключ
от двéри** door handle/key; **я
потерял пýговицу от пальтó** I
lost the button off my coat
5 (*в датах*): **письмó от пéрвого
февраля** a letter of *или* dated the
first of February
6 (*о временной
последовательности*): **год от
гóда** from year to year; **врéмя от
врéмени** from time to time

---

**отáплива|ть (-ю)** *несов перех* to
heat; **~ся** *несов возв* to be heated
**отбежáть** (*как* **бежáть**; *см. Table
20*; *impf* **отбегáть**) *сов* to run off
**отб|елúть (-елю́, -éлишь;** *impf*
**отбéливать**) *сов перех* to bleach
**отбивн|áя (-óй)** *ж* tenderized
steak; (*также*: **~ котлéта**) chop
**отбирá|ть (-ю)** *несов от*
**отобрáть**
**от|бúть (-обью́, -обьёшь;** *impf*
**отбивáть**) *сов перех* (*отколоть*)
to break off; (*мяч, удар*) to fend
off; (*атаку*) to repulse; (*мясо*) to
tenderize; **~ся** (*impf* **отбивáться**)
*сов возв*: **~ся** (*pf*) (**от** +*gen*) (*от
нападающих*) to defend o.s.
(against); (*отстать*) to fall behind
**отблагодар|úть (-ю́, -úшь)** *сов
перех* to show one's gratitude to
**отбóр (-а)** *м* selection
**отбóрный** *прил* selected

**отбóрочный** *прил* (*СПОРТ*)
qualifying
**отбрó|сить (-шу, -сишь;** *impf*
**отбрáсывать**) *сов перех* to
throw aside; (*сомнения*) to cast
aside; (*тень*) to cast
**отбрóс|ы (-ов)** *мн*
(*производства*) waste *ед*;
(*пищевые*) scraps *мн*
**от|бы́ть** (*как* **бы́ть**; *см. Table 21*;
*impf* **отбывáть**) *сов*: **~ (из** +*gen*/**в**
+*acc*) to depart (from/for) ♦ (*pt
-ы́л, -ылá, -ы́ло*) *перех*: **~
наказáние** to serve a sentence
**отвáжный** *прил* brave
**отвáр (-а)** *м* (*мясной*) broth
**отв|арúть (-арю́, -áришь;** *impf*
**отвáривать**) *сов перех* to boil
**отв|езтú (-езу́, -езёшь;** *pt* **-ёз,
-езлá;** *impf* **отвозúть**) *сов перех*
(*увезти*) to take away; **отвозúть**
(**~** *pf*) **когó-н/чтó-н в гóрод/на
дáчу** to take sb/sth off to town/the
dacha
**отвéргн|уть (-у;** *impf* **отвергáть**)
*сов перех* to reject
**отверн|ýть (-ý, -ёшь;** *impf*
**отвёртывать**) *сов перех* (*гайку*)
to unscrew; (*impf* **отворáчивать;**
*лицо, голову*) to turn away; **~ся**
(*impf* **отворáчиваться**) *сов возв*
(*человек*) to turn away
**отвéрсти|е (-я)** *ср* opening
**отвёрт|ка (-ки;** *gen pl* **-ок)** *ж*
screwdriver
**отв|естú (-едý, -едёшь;** *pt* **-ёл,
-елá;** *impf* **отводúть**) *сов перех*
(*человека: домой, к врачу*) to
take (off); (: *от окна*) to lead away;
(*глаза*) to avert; (*кандидатуру*) to
reject; (*участок*) to allot;
(*средства*) to allocate
**отвéт (-а)** *м* (*на вопрос*) answer;
(*реакция*) response; (*на письмо,
на приглашение*) reply; **в ~ (на**

+*acc*) in response (to); **быть** (*impf*) **в**
**~е за** +*acc* to be answerable for
**ответвле́ни|е** (-**я**) *ср* branch
**отве́|тить** (-**чу**, -**тишь**; *impf*
**отвеча́ть**) *сов*: ~ (**на** +*acc*) to
answer, reply (to); ~ (*pf*) **за** +*acc* (*за*
*преступле́ние*) to answer for
**отве́тственност|ь** (-**и**) *ж* (*за*
*посту́пки*) responsibility;
(*зада́ния*) importance; **нести́**
(**понести́** *pf*) ~ **за** +*acc* to be
responsible for; **привлека́ть**
(**привле́чь** *pf*) **кого́-н к ~и** to call
sb to account
**отве́тственный** *прил*: ~ (**за** +*acc*)
responsible (for); (*ва́жный*)
important; ~ **рабо́тник** executive
**отвеча́|ть** (-**ю**) *несов от*
**отве́тить** ♦ *неперех*: ~ +*dat*
(*тре́бованиям*) to meet;
(*описа́нию*) to answer; ~ (*impf*) **за**
**кого́-н/что-н** to be responsible for
sb/sth
**отвл|е́чь** (-**еку́**, -**ече́шь** *итп*,
-**еку́т**; *pt* -**ёк**, -**екла́**; *impf*
**отвлека́ть**) *сов перех*: ~ (**от**
+*gen*) (*от дел*) to distract (from);
(*проти́вника*) to divert (from); ~**ся**
(*impf* **отвлека́ться**) *сов возв*: ~**ся**
(**от** +*gen*) to be distracted (from);
(*от те́мы*) to digress (from)
**отв|оди́ть** (-**ожу́**, -**о́дишь**)
*несов от* **отвести́**
**отво|ева́ть** (-**ю́ю**; *impf*
**отвоёвывать**) *сов перех* to win
back
**отв|ози́ть** (-**ожу́**, -**о́зишь**) *несов*
*от* **отвезти́**
**отвора́чива|ть(ся)** (-**ю(сь)**)
*несов от* **отверну́ть(ся)**
**отврати́тельный** *прил* disgusting
**отвраще́ни|е** (-**я**) *ср* disgust
**отвы́к|нуть** (-**ну**; *pt* -, -**ла**; *impf*
**отвыка́ть**) *сов*: ~ **от** +*gen* (*от*
*люде́й, от рабо́ты*) to become

unaccustomed to; (*от нарко́тиков*)
to give up
**отв|яза́ть** (-**яжу́**, -**я́жешь**; *impf*
**отвя́зывать**) *сов перех*
(*верёвку*) to untie; ~**ся** (*impf*
**отвя́зываться**) *сов возв* (*разг*):
~**ся от** +*gen* (*отде́латься*) to get
rid of
**отгада́|ть** (-**ю**; *impf* **отга́дывать**)
*сов перех* to guess
**отговор|и́ть** (-**ю́**, -**и́шь**; *impf*
**отгова́ривать**) *сов перех*: ~
**кого́-н от чего́-н**/ +*infin* to
dissuade sb from sth/from doing
**отгово́р|ка** (-**ки**; *gen pl* -**ок**) *ж*
excuse
**отгоня́|ть** (-**ю**) *несов от*
**отогна́ть**
**отгу́л** (-**а**) *м* day off
**отда|ва́ть** (-**ю́**, -**ёшь**) *несов от*
**отда́ть**
**отдалённый** *прил* distant;
(*ме́сто, схо́дство*) remote
**отда́ть** (*как* **дать**; *см. Table 16*;
*impf* **отдава́ть**) *сов перех*
(*возврати́ть*) to return; (*дать*) to
give; (*ребёнка: в шко́лу*) to send;
**отдава́ть** (~ *pf*) **кого́-н под суд** to
prosecute sb; **отдава́ть** (~ *pf*)
**кому́-н честь** to salute sb;
**отдава́ть** (~ *pf*) **себе́ отчёт в**
+*prep* to realize
**отде́л** (-**а**) *м* (*учрежде́ния*)
department; (*газе́ты*) section;
(*исто́рии, нау́ки*) branch; ~
**ка́дров** personnel department
**отде́ла|ть** (-**ю**; *impf* **отде́лывать**)
*сов перех* (*кварти́ру*) to do up;
**отде́лывать** (~ *pf*) **что-н чем-н**
(*пальто́: ме́хом*) to trim sth with
sth; ~**ся** (*impf* **отде́лываться**) *сов*
*возв*: ~**ся от** +*gen* (*разг*) to get
rid of; ~**ся** (*pf*) +*instr* (*разг*:
*испу́гом*) to get away with
**отделе́ни|е** (-**я**) *ср* section;

(*учрежде́ния*) department;
(*филиа́л*) branch; (*конце́рта*) part;
~ **свя́зи** post office; ~ **мили́ции**
police station

**отд|ели́ть** (**-елю́, -е́лишь**; *impf*
**отделя́ть**) *сов перех* to separate;
~**ся** (*impf* **отделя́ться**) *сов возв*:
~**ся** (**от** +*gen*) to separate (from)

**отде́л|ка** (**-ки**; *gen pl* **-ок**) *ж*
decoration; (*на пла́тье*) trimmings
*мн*

**отде́лыва|ть(ся)** (**-ю(сь)**) *несов*
*от* **отде́лать(ся)**

**отде́льный** *прил* separate

**отдохн|у́ть** (**-у́, -ёшь**; *impf*
**отдыха́ть**) *сов* to (have a) rest;
(*на мо́ре*) to have a holiday, take a
vacation (*US*)

**о́тдых** (**-а**) *м* rest; (*отпуск*)
holiday, vacation (*US*); **на ~е** (*в
отпуске*) on holiday; **дом ~а**
holiday centre (*BRIT*) *или* center
(*US*)

**отдыха́|ть** (**-ю**) *несов от*
**отдохну́ть**

**отдыха́ющ|ий** (**-его**) *м*
holidaymaker (*BRIT*), vacationer (*US*)

**отёк** (**-а**) *м* swelling

**отека́|ть** (**-ю**) *несов от* **оте́чь**

**оте́л|ь** (**-я**) *м* hotel

**от|е́ц** (**-ца́**) *м* father

**оте́чественн|ый** *прил*
(*промы́шленность*) domestic;
**Оте́чественная Война́** patriotic
war (*fought in defence of one's country*)

**оте́честв|о** (**-а**) *ср* fatherland

**от|е́чь** (**-еку́, -ечёшь** *итп*, **-еку́т**;
*pt* **~ёк, -екла́, -екло́**; *impf*
**отека́ть**) *сов* to swell up

**о́тзвук** (**-а**) *м* echo

**о́тзыв** (**-а**) *м* (*реце́нзия*) review

**отзыва́|ть(ся)** (**-ю(сь)**) *несов от*
**отозва́ть(ся)**

**отзы́вчивый** *прил* ready to help

**отка́з** (**-а**) *м* refusal; (*от реше́ния*)

rejection; (*механи́зма*) failure;
**закру́чивать** (**закрути́ть** *pf*) **что-н**
**до ~а** to turn sth full on; **набива́ть**
(**наби́ть** *pf*) **до ~а** to cram

**отк|аза́ть** (**-ажу́, -а́жешь**; *impf*
**отка́зывать**) *сов* (*мото́р,
не́рвы*) to fail; **отка́зывать** (~ *pf*)
**кому́-н в чём-н** to refuse sb sth; (*в
по́мощи*) to deny sb sth; ~**ся** (*impf*
**отка́зываться**) *сов возв*: ~**ся**
(**от** +*gen*) to refuse; (*от о́тдыха,
от мы́сли*) to give up;
**отка́зываться** (~**ся** *pf*) **от свои́х
слов** to retract one's words

**отка́лыва|ть(ся)** (**-ю(сь)**) *несов
от* **отколо́ть(ся)**

**отка́ча|ть** (**-ю**; *impf* **отка́чивать**)
*сов перех* to pump (out)

**отки́н|уть** (**-у**; *impf* **отки́дывать**)
*сов перех* to throw; (*верх,
сиде́ние*) to open; (*во́лосы,
го́лову*) to toss back; ~**ся** (*impf*
**отки́дываться**) *сов возв*: ~**ся на**
+*acc* to lean back against

**откла́дыва|ть** (**-ю**) *несов от*
**отложи́ть**

**откл|они́ть** (**-оню́, -о́нишь**; *impf*
**отклоня́ть**) *сов перех* (*перен:
про́сьбу, предложе́ние*) to reject;
~**ся** (*impf* **отклоня́ться**) *сов возв*
(*стре́лка*) to deflect; (*перен: в
сто́рону, от уда́ра*) to dodge; (*от
ку́рса, на се́вер*) to be deflected;
**отклоня́ться** (~**ся** *pf*) **от те́мы** to
digress

**отключ|и́ть** (**-у́, -и́шь**; *impf*
**отключа́ть**) *сов перех* to switch
off; (*телефо́н*) to cut off; ~**ся** (*impf*
**отключа́ться**) *сов возв* to switch
off

**отк|оло́ть** (**-олю́, -о́лешь**; *impf*
**отка́лывать**) *сов перех* (*кусо́к*)
to break off; (*бант, була́вку*) to
unpin; ~**ся** (*impf* **отка́лываться**)
*сов возв* to break off

**откорректи́р|овать (-ую)** *сов от* **корректи́ровать**

**открове́нно** *нареч* frankly

**открове́нный** *прил* frank; (*обман*) blatant

**откро́ю(сь)** *etc сов см.* **откры́ть(ся)**

**откр|ути́ть (-учу́, -у́тишь;** *impf* **откру́чивать) сов перех** to unscrew

**открыва́л|ка (-ки;** *gen pl* **-ок) ж** (*разг: для консервов*) tin-opener; (*для бутылок*) bottle-opener

**открыва́|ть(ся) (-ю(сь))** *несов от* **откры́ть(ся)**

**открыти|е (-я)** *ср* discovery; (*сезона, выставки*) opening

**откры́т|ка (-ки;** *gen pl* **-ок) ж** postcard

**откры́тый** *прил* open; (*голова*) bare; (*взгляд, человек*) frank

**откр|ы́ть (-о́ю, -о́ешь;** *impf* **открыва́ть) сов перех** to open; (*намерения, правду итп*) to reveal; (*воду, кран*) to turn on; (*возможность, путь*) to open up; (*закон*) to discover; **~ся** (*impf* **открыва́ться) сов возв** to open; (*возможность, путь*) to open up

**отку́да** *нареч* where from ♦ *союз* from where, whence; **Вы ~** ? where are you from?; **~ Вы прие́хали?** where have you come from?; **~ ты э́то зна́ешь?** how do you know about that?

**отку́да-нибудь** *нареч* from somewhere (or other)

**отку́да-то** *нареч* from somewhere

**отк|уси́ть (-ушу́, -у́сишь;** *impf* **отку́сывать) сов перех** to bite off

**отлага́тельств|о (-а)** *ср* delay

**отла́мыва|ть(ся) (-ю)** *несов от* **отломи́ть(ся)**

**отле|те́ть (-чу́, -ти́шь;** *impf*

**отлета́ть) сов** to fly off; (*мяч*) to fly back

**отли́в (-а) м** (*в море*) ebb; (*оттенок*) sheen

**отлича́|ть (-ю)** *несов от* **отличи́ть;** **~ся** *возв* (*быть другим*): **~ся (от** +*gen*) to be different (from)

**отличи|е (-я)** *ср* distinction; **в ~ от** +*gen* unlike

**отличи́тельный** *прил* (*черта*) distinguishing

**отлич|и́ть (-у́, -и́шь;** *impf* **отлича́ть) сов перех** (*наградить*) to honour (*BRIT*), honor (*US*); **отлича́ть (~** *pf*) **кого́-н/ что-н от** +*gen* to tell sb/sth from

**отли́чник (-а) м** 'A'grade pupil

**отли́чно** *нареч* extremely well ♦ *как сказ* it's excellent *или* great ♦ *ср нескл* (*ПРОСВЕЩ*) excellent *или* outstanding (*school mark*); **он ~ зна́ет, что он винова́т** he knows perfectly well that he's wrong; **учи́ться** (*impf*) **на ~** to get top marks

**отли́чный** *прил* excellent; (*иной*): **~ от** +*gen* distinct from

**отл|ожи́ть (-ожу́, -о́жишь;** *impf* **откла́дывать) сов перех** (*деньги*) to put aside; (*собрание*) to postpone

**отл|оми́ть (-омлю́, -о́мишь;** *impf* **отла́мывать) сов перех** to break off; **~ся** (*impf* **отла́мываться) сов возв** to break off

**отмахн|у́ться (-у́сь, -ёшься;** *impf* **отма́хиваться) сов возв:** **~ от** +*gen* (*от мухи*) to brush away; (*от предложения*) to brush *или* wave aside

**отме́н|а (-ы) ж** (*см глаг*) repeal; reversal; abolition; cancellation

**отм|ени́ть** (**-еню́, -е́нишь;** *impf* **отменя́ть**) *сов перех* (*закон*) to repeal; (*решение, приговор*) to reverse; (*налог*) to abolish; (*лекцию*) to cancel

**отме́|тить** (**-чу, -тишь;** *impf* **отмеча́ть**) *сов перех* (*на карте, в книге*) to mark; (*указать*) to note; (*юбилей*) to celebrate; **~ся** (*impf* **отмеча́ться**) *сов возв* to register

**отме́т|ка** (**-ки;** *gen pl* **-ок**) *ж* mark; (*в документе*) note

> **отме́тка** - mark. The Russian scale of marking is from 1 to 5, with 5 being the highest mark. + can be added to marks 3, 4 and 5.

**отмеча́|ть(ся)** (**-ю(сь)**) *несов от* **отме́тить(ся)**

**отморо́|зить** (**-жу, -зишь;** *impf* **отмора́живать**) *сов перех*: **~ ру́ки/но́ги** to get frostbite in one's hands/feet

**отм|ы́ть** (**-о́ю, -о́ешь;** *impf* **отмыва́ть**) *сов перех*: **~ что-н** to get sth clean; (*грязь*) to wash sth out; (*деньги*) to launder sth

**отн|ести́** (**-есу́, -есёшь;** *pt* **-ёс, -есла́;** *impf* **относи́ть**) *сов перех* to take (off); (*подлеж: течение*) to carry off; (*причислить к*): **~ что-н к** +*dat* (*к периоду, к году*) to date sth back to; (*к число группе*) to categorize sth as; (*к категории*) to put sth into; **относи́ть** (**~** *pf*) **что-н за или на счёт** +*gen* to put sth down to; **~сь** (*impf* **относи́ться**) *сов возв*: **~сь к** +*dat* (*к человеку*) to treat; (*к предложению, к событию*) to take

**отнима́|ть** (**-ю**) *несов от* **отня́ть**

**относи́тельно** *нареч* relatively ♦ *предл*: **~** +*gen* (*в отношении*) regarding, with regard to

**относи́тельный** *прил* relative

**отн|оси́ть** (**-ошу́, -о́сишь**) *несов от* **отнести́; ~ся** *несов от* **отнести́сь** ♦ *возв*: **~ся к** +*dat* to relate to; (*к классу*) to belong to; (*к году*) to date from; **он к ней хорошо́ ~о́сится** he likes her; **как ты ~о́сишься к нему́?** what do you think about him?; **э́то к нам не ~о́сится** it has nothing to do with us

**отноше́ни|е** (**-я**) *ср* (*МАТ*) ratio; **~ (к** +*dat*) attitude (to); (*связь*) relation (to); **в ~и** +*gen* with regard to; **по ~ю к** +*dat* towards; **в э́том ~и** in this respect *или* regard; **в не́котором ~и** in certain respects; **име́ть** (*impf*) **~ к** +*dat* to be connected with; **не име́ть** (*impf*) **~я к** +*dat* to have nothing to do with

**отню́дь** *нареч*: **~ не** by no means, far from; **~ нет** absolutely not

**отн|я́ть** (**-иму́, -и́мешь;** *impf* **отнима́ть**) *сов перех* to take away; (*силы, время*) to take up

**ото** *предл см.* **от**

**от|обра́ть** (**-беру́, -берёшь;** *pt* **-обра́л, -обрала́;** *impf* **отбира́ть**) *сов перех* (*отнять*) to take away; (*выбрать*) to select

**отовсю́ду** *нареч* from all around

**от|огна́ть** (**-гоню́, -го́нишь;** *impf* **отгоня́ть**) *сов перех* to chase away

**отодви́н|уть** (**-у;** *impf* **отодвига́ть**) *сов перех* (*шкаф*) to move; (*засов*) to slide back; (*срок, экзамен*) to put back; **~ся** (*impf* **отодвига́ться**) *сов возв* (*человек*) to move

**от|озва́ть** (**-зову́, -зовёшь;** *impf* **отзыва́ть**) *сов перех* to call back; (*посла, документы*) to recall; **отзыва́ть** (**~** *pf*) **кого́-н в сто́рону**

to take sb aside; **~ся** (*impf* **отзыва́ться**) *сов возв*: **~ся (на** +*acc*) to respond (to); **хорошо́/ пло́хо ~ся** (*pf*) **о** +*prp* to speak well/badly of

**отойти́** (*как* **идти́**; *см.* Table 18; *impf* **отходи́ть**) *сов* (*поезд, автобус*) to leave; (*пятно*) to come out; (*отлучиться*) to go off; **отходи́ть** (**~** *pf*) **от** +*gen* to move away from; (*перен: от друзей, от взглядов*) to distance o.s. from; (*от темы*) to depart from

**отом|сти́ть** (-щу́, -сти́шь) *сов от* **мстить**

**отопи́тельный** *прил* (*прибор*) heating; **~ сезо́н** the cold season

**отопи́тельный сезо́н** . The heating comes on around the middle of October and goes off around the middle of May. The central heating is controlled centrally and individual home owners do not have any say over it.

**отопле́ни|е** (-я) *ср* heating
**оторв|а́ть** (-у́, -ёшь; *impf* **отрыва́ть**) *сов перех* to tear off; **отрыва́ть** (**~** *pf*) (**от** +*gen*) to tear away (from); **~ся** (*impf* **отрыва́ться**) *сов возв* (*пуговица*) to come off; **отрыва́ться** (**~ся** *pf*) **от** +*gen* (*от работы*) to tear o.s. away (from); (*убежать*) to break away (from); (*от семьи́*) to lose touch (with); **отрыва́ться** (**~ся** *pf*) **от земли́** (*самолёт*) to take off

**отпева́ни|е** (-я) *ср* funeral service
**отпева́|ть** (-ю) *несов от* **отпе́ть**
**от|пере́ть** (-опру́, -опрёшь; *pt* -пер, -перла́, -перло; *impf* **отпира́ть**) *сов перех* to unlock

**отп|е́ть** (-ою́, -оёшь; *impf* **отпева́ть**) *сов перех* (РЕЛ) to conduct a funeral service for

**отпеча́та|ть** (-ю; *impf* **отпеча́тывать**) *сов перех* to print; **~ся** (*impf* **отпеча́тываться**) *сов возв* (*на земле́*) to leave a print; (*перен: в памяти*) to imprint itself

**отпеча́т|ок** (-ка) *м* imprint; **~ки па́льцев** fingerprints

**отпира́|ть** (-ю) *несов от* **отпере́ть**

**отпл|ати́ть** (-ачу́, -а́тишь; *impf* **отпла́чивать**) *сов*: **~** +*dat* (*наградить*) to repay; (*отомстить*) to pay back

**отплы́|ть** (-ву́, -вёшь; *impf* **отплыва́ть**) *сов* (*человек*) to swim off; (*корабль*) to set sail

**отполз|ти́** (-у́, -ёшь; *impf* **отполза́ть**) *сов* to crawl away

**отпо́р** (-а) *м*: **дать ~** +*dat* (*врагу*) to repel, repulse

**отправи́тел|ь** (-я) *м* sender
**отпра́в|ить** (-лю, -ишь; *impf* **отправля́ть**) *сов перех* to send; **~ся** (*impf* **отправля́ться**) *сов возв* (*человек*) to set off

**отпра́в|ка** (-ки; *gen pl* -ок) *ж* (*письма*) posting; (*груза*) dispatch
**отправле́ни|е** (-я) *ср* (*письма*) dispatch; (*почтовое*) item
**отправн|о́й** *прил*: **~ пункт** point of departure; **~а́я то́чка** (*перен*) starting point

**отпр|оси́ться** (-ошу́сь, -о́сишься; *impf* **отпра́шиваться**) *сов перех* to ask permission to leave

**о́тпуск** (-а) *м* holiday (BRIT), vacation (US); **быть** (*impf*) **в ~е** to be on holiday

**отп|усти́ть** (-ущу́, -у́стишь; *impf* **отпуска́ть**) *сов перех* to let out;

(*из рук*) to let go of; (*товар*) to sell; (*де́ньги*) to release; (*бо́роду*) to grow

**отрабо́та|ть (-ю;** *impf* **отраба́тывать)** *сов перех* (*како́е-то вре́мя*) to work; (*осво́ить*) to perfect, polish
♦ *неперех* (*ко́нчить рабо́тать*) to finish work

**отр|ави́ть (-авлю́, -а́вишь;** *impf* **отравля́ть)** *сов перех* to poison; (*перен: пра́здник*) to spoil; **~ся** *сов*, (*impf* **отравля́ться**) *возв* to poison o.s.; (*едо́й*) to get food-poisoning

**отравле́ни|е (-я)** *ср* poisoning

**отраже́ни|е (-я)** *ср* (*см глаг*) reflection; deflection

**отра|зи́ть (-жу́, -зи́шь;** *impf* **отража́ть)** *сов перех* to reflect; (*уда́р*) to deflect; **~ся** (*impf* **отража́ться**) *сов возв*: **~ся в** +*prp* to be reflected in; **отража́ться** (**~ся** *pf*) (*в зе́ркале*) to be reflected in; **отража́ться** (**~ся** *pf*) **на** +*prp* (*на здоро́вье*) to have an effect on

**о́трасл|ь (-и)** *ж* branch (*of industry*)

**отр|асти́ (**3sg **-астёт,** pt **-о́с, -осла́;** *impf* **отраста́ть)** *сов* to grow

**отра|сти́ть (-щу́, -сти́шь;** *impf* **отра́щивать)** *сов перех* to grow

**отре́з (-а)** *м* piece of fabric

**отре́|зать (-жу, -жешь;** *impf* **отреза́ть)** *сов перех* to cut off

**отре́з|ок (-ка)** *м* (*тка́ни*) piece; (*пути́*) section; (*вре́мени*) period

**отр|е́чься (-еку́сь, -ечёшься** etc, **-еку́тся;** pt **-ёкся, -екла́сь;** *impf* **отрека́ться)** *сов возв*: **~ от** +*gen* to renounce; **отрека́ться** (**~** *pf*) **от престо́ла** to abdicate

**отрица́ни|е (-я)** *ср* denial; (*линг*) negation

**отрица́тельный** *прил* negative

**отрица́|ть (-ю)** *несов перех* to deny; (*мо́ду итп*) to reject

**отро́ст|ок (-ка)** *м* (*побе́г*) shoot

**отр|уби́ть (-ублю́, -у́бишь;** *impf* **отруба́ть)** *сов перех* to chop off

**отруга́|ть (-ю)** *сов от* **руга́ть**

**отры́в (-а)** *м*: **~ от** +*gen* (*от семьи́*) separation from; **ли́ния ~а** perforated line; **быть** (*impf*) **в ~е от** +*gen* to be cut off from

**отрыва́|ть(ся) (-ю(сь))** *несов от* **оторва́ть(ся)**

**отры́в|ок (-ка)** *м* excerpt

**отры́вочный** *прил* fragmented

**отря́д (-а)** *м* party, group; (*воен*) detachment

**отряхн|у́ть (-у́, -ёшь;** *impf* **отря́хивать)** *сов перех* (*снег, пыль*) to shake off; (*пальто́*) to shake down

**отсе́к (-а)** *м* compartment

**отс|е́чь (-еку́, -ечёшь** etc, **-еку́т;** pt **-ёк, -екла́;** *impf* **отсека́ть)** *сов перех* to cut off

**отск|очи́ть (-очу́, -о́чишь;** *impf* **отска́кивать)** *сов* (*в сто́рону, наза́д*) to jump; (*разг: пу́говица, кно́пка*) to come off; **отска́кивать** (**~** *pf*) **от** +*gen* (*мяч*) to bounce off; (*челове́к*) to jump off

**отсоедин|и́ть (-ю́, -и́шь;** *impf* **отсоединя́ть)** *сов перех* to disconnect

**отсро́ч|ить (-у, -ишь;** *impf* **отсро́чивать)** *сов перех* to defer

**отста|ва́ть (-ю́, -ёшь)** *несов от* **отста́ть**

**отста́в|ка (-ки;** gen pl **-ок)** *ж* retirement; (*кабине́та*) resignation; **подава́ть** (**пода́ть** *pf*) **в ~ку** to offer one's resignation

**отста́ива|ть(ся) (-ю)** *несов от* **отстоя́ть(ся)**

**отста́лый** *прил* backward

**отста́|ть (-ну, -нешь;** *impf*

**отстава́ть)** *сов (перен: в учёбе, в работе)* to fall behind; *(часы)* to be slow; **отстава́ть (~ pf) (от** *+gen)* *(от группы)* to fall behind; *(от поезда, от автобуса)* to be left behind; **~нь от меня́!** stop pestering me!

**отстегн|у́ть (-у́, -ёшь;** *impf* **отстёгивать)** *сов перех* to unfasten

**отсто|я́ть (-ю́, -и́шь;** *impf* **отста́ивать)** *сов перех (город, своё мнение)* to defend; *(раствор)* to allow to stand; *(два часа итп)* to wait; **~ся (**impf **отста́иваться)** *сов возв* to settle

**отстран|и́ть (-ю́, -и́шь;** *impf* **отстраня́ть)** *сов перех (отодвинуть)* to push away; *(уволить):* **~ от** *+gen* to remove, dismiss; **~ся (**impf **отстраня́ться)** *сов возв:* **~ся от** *+gen (от должности)* to relinquish; *(отодвинуться)* to draw back

**отст|упи́ть (-уплю́, -у́пишь;** *impf* **отступа́ть)** *сов* to step back; *(ВОЕН)* to retreat; *(перен: перед трудностями)* to give up

**отступле́ни|е (-я)** *ср* retreat; *(от темы)* digression

**отсу́тстви|е (-я)** *ср (человека)* absence; *(денег, вкуса)* lack

**отсу́тств|овать (-ую)** *несов (в классе итп)* to be absent; *(желание)* to be lacking

**отсу́тствующ|ий** *прил (взгляд, вид)* absent ♦ **(-его)** *м* absentee

**отсчёт (-а)** *м (минут)* calculation; **то́чка ~а** point of reference

**отсчита́|ть (-ю;** *impf* **отсчи́тывать)** *сов перех (деньги)* to count out

**отсю́да** *нареч* from here

**отта́ива|ть (-ю)** *несов от* **отта́ять**

**отта́лкива|ть(ся) (-ю(сь))** *несов от* **оттолкну́ть(ся)**

**отт|ащи́ть (-ащу́, -а́щишь;** *impf* **отта́скивать)** *сов перех* to drag

**отта́|ять (-ю;** *impf* **отта́ивать)** *сов (земля)* to thaw; *(мясо)* to thaw out

**отте́н|ок (-ка)** *м* shade

**о́ттепел|ь (-и)** *ж* thaw

**о́ттиск (-а)** *м (ступни)* impression; *(рисунка)* print

**оттого́** *нареч* for this reason; **~ что** because

**оттолкн|у́ть (-у́, -ёшь;** *impf* **отта́лкивать)** *сов перех* to push away; **~ся (**impf **отта́лкиваться)** *сов возв:* **~ся от чего́-н** *(от берега)* to push o.s. away *или* back from sth; *(перен: от данных)* to take sth as one's starting point

**отту́да** *нареч* from there

**отт|яну́ть (-яну́, -я́нешь;** *impf* **оття́гивать)** *сов перех* to pull back; *(карман)* to stretch; *(разг: выполнение)* to delay; **оття́гивать (~ pf) вре́мя** to play for time

**от|учи́ть (-учу́, -у́чишь;** *impf* **отуча́ть)** *сов перех:* **~ кого́-н** *+gen (от курения)* to wean sb off; **отуча́ть (~ pf) кого́-н** *+infin (врать)* to teach sb not to do; **~ся (**impf **отуча́ться)** *сов возв:* **~ся** *+infin* to get out of the habit of doing

**отхлы́н|уть (**3sg **-ет)** *сов (волны)* to roll back

**отхо́д (-а)** *м* departure; *(ВОЕН)* withdrawal; *см. также* **отхо́ды**

**отх|оди́ть (-ожу́, -о́дишь)** *несов от* **отойти́**

**отхо́д|ы (-ов)** *мн* waste *ед*

**отца́** *etc сущ см.* **оте́ц**

**отцо́вский** *прил* father's; *(чувства, права́)* paternal

**óтчáива|ться** (**-юсь**) *несов от* **отчáяться**

**отчáл|ить** (**-ю**, **-ишь**; *impf* **отчáливать**) *сов* to set sail

**отчáсти** *нареч* partially

**отчáяни|е** (**-я**) *ср* despair

**отчáянно** *нареч* (*пытаться*) desperately; (*спорить*) fiercely

**отчáянный** *прил* desperate; (*смелый*) daring

**отчá|яться** (**-юсь**; *impf* **отчáиваться**) *сов возв*: ~ (+*infin*) to despair (of doing)

**отчегó** *нареч* (*почему*) why
♦ *союз* (*вследствие чего*) which is why

**отчегó-нибудь** *нареч* for any reason

**отчегó-то** *нареч* for some reason

**óтчеств|о** (**-а**) *ср* patronymic

**óтчество** - patronymic. The full name of a Russian person must include his or her patronymic. Besides being the formal way of addressing people, the use of the patronymic also shows your respect for that person. Patronymics are not as officious as they sound to some foreign ears. In fact, quite often the patronymic replaces the first name and is used as an affectionate way of addressing people you know well.

**отчёт** (**-а**) *м* account; **финáнсовый ~** financial report; (*выписка*) statement; **отдавáть** (**отдáть** *pf*) **себé ~ в чём-н** to realize sth

**отчётливый** *прил* distinct; (*объяснение*) clear

**отчётност|ь** (**-и**) *ж* accountability
♦ *собир* (*документы*) records

**отчётный** *прил* (*собрание*) review; (*период, год*) accounting; **~ доклáд** report

**отчúзн|а** (**-ы**) *ж* mother country

**óтчим** (**-а**) *м* stepfather

**отчислéни|е** (**-я**) *ср* (*работника*) dismissal; (*студента*) expulsion; (*обычно мн: на строительство*) allocation *ед*; (: *денежные: удержание*) deduction; (: *выделение*) assignment

**отчúсл|ить** (**-ю**, **-ишь**; *impf* **отчислять**) *сов перех* (*работника*) to dismiss; (*студента*) to expel; (*деньги: удержать*) to deduct; (: *выделить*) to assign

**отчитá|ть** (**-ю**; *impf* **отчúтывать**) *сов перех* (*ребёнка*) to tell off; **~ся** (*impf* **отчúтываться**) *сов возв* to report

**отчуждéни|е** (**-я**) *ср* estrangement

**отшéльник** (**-а**) *м* hermit

**отъéзд** (**-а**) *м* departure; **быть** (*impf*) **в ~е** to be away

**отъéхать** (*как* **éхать**; *см. Table 19*; *impf* **отъезжáть**) *сов* to travel; **отъезжáть** (**~** *pf*) **от** +*gen* to move away from

**отъявленный** *прил* utter

**отыгрá|ть** (**-ю**; *impf* **отыгрывать**) *сов перех* to win back; **~ся** (*impf* **отыгрываться**) *сов возв* (*в карты, в шахматы*) to win again; (*перен*) to get one's own back

**от|ыскáть** (**-ыщу́**, **-ыщешь**; *impf* **отыскивать**) *сов перех* to hunt out; (*КОМП*) to retrieve

**óфис** (**-а**) *м* office

**офицéр** (**-а**) *м* (*ВОЕН*) officer; (*разг: ШАХМАТЫ*) bishop

**официáльн|ый** *прил* official; **~ое лицó** official

**официáнт** (**-а**) *м* waiter

**оформúтел|ь** (**-я**) *м*: **~**

**спекта́кля** set designer: ~ **витри́н** window dresser

**оформ|ить (-лю, -ишь;** *impf* **оформля́ть)** *сов перех* (*документы, договор*) to draw up; (*книгу*) to design the layout of; (*витрину*) to dress; (*спектакль*) to design the sets for; **оформля́ть (~** *pf*) **кого́-н на рабо́ту** +*instr* to take sb on (as); **~ся** (*impf* **оформля́ться**) *сов возв* (*взгляды*) to form; **оформля́ться** (**~ся** *pf*) **на рабо́ту** (+*instr*) to be taken on (as)

**оформле́ни|е (-я)** *ср* design; (*документов, договора*) drawing up; **музыка́льное ~** music

**оформля́|ть(ся) (-ю(сь))** *несов от* **офо́рмить**

**оффшо́рный** *прил* (*КОММ*) off-shore

**охва|ти́ть (-чу́, -а́тишь;** *impf* **охва́тывать)** *сов перех* (*подлеж: пламя, чувства*) to engulf; (*население*) to cover; **охва́тывать** (**~** *pf*) **что-н чем-н** (*руками, лентой*) to put sth round sth

**охладе́|ть (-ю;** *impf* **охладева́ть)** *сов* (*отношения*) to cool; **охладева́ть** (**~** *pf*) **к** +*dat* (*к мужу*) to grow cool towards

**охла|ди́ть (-жу́, -ди́шь;** *impf* **охлажда́ть)** *сов перех* (*воду, чувства*) to cool; **~ся** (*impf* **охлажда́ться**) *сов возв* (*печка, вода*) to cool down

**охо́т|а (-ы)** *ж* hunt; (*разг: желание*) desire

**охо́|титься (-чусь, -тишься)** *несов возв:* ~ **на** +*acc* to hunt (*to kill*); ~ (*impf*) **за** +*instr* to hunt (*to catch*); (*перен: разг*) to hunt for

**охо́тник (-а)** *м* hunter

**охо́тничий** *прил* hunting

**охо́тно** *нареч* willingly

**охра́н|а (-ы)** *ж* (*защита*) security; (*группа людей*) bodyguard; (*растений, животных*) protection; (*здоровья*) care; ~ **труда́** health and safety regulations

**охра́нник (-а)** *м* guard

**охраня́|ть (-ю)** *несов перех* to guard; (*природу*) to protect

**оц|ени́ть (-еню́, -е́нишь;** *impf* **оце́нивать)** *сов перех* (*вещь*) to value; (*знания*) to assess; (*признать достоинства*) to appreciate

**оце́н|ка (-ки;** *gen pl* **-ок)** *ж* (*вещи*) valuation; (*работника, поступка*) assessment; (*отметка*) mark

**оц|епи́ть (-еплю́, -е́пишь;** *impf* **оцепля́ть)** *сов перех* to cordon off

**оча́г (-а́)** *м* hearth; (*перен: заболевания*) source

**очарова́ни|е (-я)** *ср* charm

**очарова́тельный** *прил* charming

**очар|ова́ть (-у́ю;** *impf* **очаро́вывать)** *сов перех* to charm

**очеви́д|ец (-ца)** *м* eyewitness

**очеви́дно** *нареч, част obviously* ♦ *как сказ:* ~, **что он винова́т** it's obvious that he is guilty ♦ *вводн сл:* ~, **он не придёт** apparently he's not coming

**очеви́дный** *прил* (*факт*) plain; (*желание*) obvious

**о́чень** *нареч* (+*adv*, +*adj*) very; (+*vb*) very much

**очередно́й** *прил* next; (*ближайший: задача*) immediate; (*: номер газеты*) latest; (*повторяющийся*) another

**о́черед|ь (-и)** *ж* (*порядок*) order; (*место в порядке*) turn; (*группа людей*) queue (*BRIT*), line (*US*); (*в строительстве*) section; **в пе́рвую** ~ in the first instance; **в поря́дке**

~и when one's turn comes; **в свою**
~ in turn; **по ~и** in turn
**óчерк (-а)** *м (литературный)*
essay; *(газетный)* sketch
**очертáни|е (-я)** *ср* outline *ед*
**очéчник (-а)** *м* spectacle case
**очисти́тельный** *прил* purification
**очи́|стить (-щу, -стишь;** *impf*
**очищáть)** *сов перех* to clean;
*(газ, воду)* to purify; *(город,*
*квартиру)* to clear; **~ся** *(impf*
**очищáться)** *сов возв (газ, вода)*
to be purified
**очи́стк|а (-и)** *ж* purification
**очистн|óй** *прил:* **~ые**
**сооружéния** purification plant
*ед*
**очищá|ть(ся) (-ю)** *несов от*
**очи́стить(ся)**
**очи́щенный** *прил (хим)* purified;
*(яблоко, картошка)* peeled
**очк|и́ (-ов)** *мн (для чтения)*
glasses *мн*, spectacles *мн; (для*
*плавания)* goggles *мн;* **защи́тные**
**~и́** safety specs
**очк|ó (-á)** *ср (СПОРТ)* point;
*(КАРТЫ)* pip
**очн|у́ться (-у́сь, -ёшься)** *сов*
*возв (после сна)* to wake up;
*(после обморока)* to come round
**óчн|ый** *прил (обучение,*
*институт итп)* with direct contact
between students and teachers; **~ая**
**стáвка** *(ЮР)* confrontation

**óчное отделéние** - This is one of
the ways of obtaining a degree. It
is a full time course with over 30
contact hours a week and two
exam sessions. See also notes at
**заóчный** and **вечéрнни**.

**оч|ути́ться (2sg -ýтишься)** *сов*
*возв* to end up
**ошéйник (-а)** *м* collar

**ош|иби́ться (-ибýсь, -ибёшься;**
*pt* **-и́бся, -и́блась;** *impf*
**ошибáться)** *сов возв* to make a
mistake; **ошибáться (~ *pf*) в ком-н**
to misjudge sb
**оши́б|ка (-ки;** *gen pl* **-ок)** *ж*
mistake, error; **по ~ке** by mistake
**оши́бочный** *прил (мнение)*
mistaken, erroneous; *(суждение,*
*вывод)* wrong
**ощýпа|ть (-ю;** *impf* **ощýпывать)**
*сов перех* to feel
**óщуп|ь (-и)** *ж:* **на ~** by touch;
**пробирáться** *(impf)* **на ~** to grope
one's way through
**ощу|ти́ть (-щý, -ти́шь;** *impf*
**ощущáть)** *сов перех (желание,*
*боль)* to feel
**ощущéни|е (-я)** *ср* sense;
*(радости, боли)* feeling

# П, п

**павильóн (-а)** *м* pavilion
**павли́н (-а)** *м* peacock
**пáгубный** *прил (последствия)*
ruinous; *(влияние)* pernicious
**пáда|ть (-ю;** *pf* **упáсть** *или*
**пасть)** *несов* to fall;
*(настроение)* to sink;
*(дисциплина, нравы)* to decline
**падéж (-á)** *м (ЛИНГ)* case
**падéни|е (-я)** *ср* fall; *(нравов,*
*дисциплины)* decline
**па|й (-я;** *nom pl* **-и́)** *м (ЭКОН)* share;
**на ~áх** jointly
**пáйщик (-а)** *м* shareholder
**пакéт (-а)** *м* package; *(мешок)*
(paper *или* plastic) bag
**пак|овáть (-ýю;** *pf* **за~** *или* **у~)**
*несов перех* to pack
**палáт|а (-ы)** *ж (в больнице)*
ward; *(ПОЛИТ)* chamber, house

палáт|ка (-ки; gen pl -ок) ж tent
пá|лец (-ьца) м (руки) finger;
(ноги) toe; большóй ~ (руки)
thumb; (ноги) big toe
палúтр|а (-ы) ж palette
пá|лка (-ки; gen pl -ок) ж stick
палóмничеств|о (-а) ср
pilgrimage
пáлоч|ка (-ки; gen pl -ек) ж
(муз): дирижёрская ~
(conductor's) baton; волшéбная ~
magic wand
пáлуб|а (-ы) ж (мор) deck
пáльм|а (-ы) ж palm (tree)
пальтó ср нескл overcoat
пáмятник (-а) м monument; (на
могиле) tombstone
пáмятный прил (день)
memorable; (подарок)
commemorative
пáмят|ь (-и) ж memory;
(воспоминание) memories мн
панáм|а (-ы) ж Panama (hat)
панéл|ь (-и) ж (строит) panel
пáник|а (-и) ж panic
паник|овáть (-ýю) несов (разг)
to panic
панихúд|а (-ы) ж (рел) funeral
service; граждáнская ~ civil funeral
панúческий прил panic-stricken
панорáм|а (-ы) ж panorama
пансионáт (-а) м boarding house
пáп|а (-ы) м dad; (также:
Рúмский ~) the Pope
папирóс|а (-ы) ж type of cigarette
папирóсн|ый прил: ~ая бумáга
(тонкая бумага) tissue paper
пáп|ка (-ки; gen pl -ок) ж folder
(BRIT), file (US)
пар (-а; nom pl -ы́) м steam; см.
также пары́
пáр|а (-ы) ж (туфель итп) pair;
(супружеская) couple
парáграф (-а) м paragraph
парáд (-а) м parade

парáдн|ое (-ого) ср entrance
парáдный прил (вход,
лестница) front, main
парадóкс (-а) м paradox
парадоксáльный прил
paradoxical
паразúт (-а) м parasite
парализ|овáть (-ýю) (не)сов
перех to paralyze
паралúч (-á) м paralysis
параллéл|ь (-и) ж parallel
парáметр (-а) м parameter
парашю́т (-а) м parachute
пáрен|ь (-я) м (разг) guy
парú ср нескл bet
Парú|ж (-а) м Paris
парúк (-á) м wig
парикмáхер (-а) м hairdresser
парикмáхерск|ая (-ой) ж
hairdresser's (BRIT), beauty salon
(US)
пáр|иться (-юсь, -ишься) несов
возв (в бане) to have a sauna
пар|úть (-ю́, -úшь) несов to glide
парк (-а) м park
паркéт (-а) м parquet
парк|овáть (-ýю) несов перех to
park
парлáмент (-а) м parliament
парлáментский прил
parliamentary
парнúк (-á) м greenhouse
парникóвый прил: ~ эффéкт
greenhouse effect
паровóз (-а) м steam engine
паров|óй прил steam; ~óе
отоплéние central heating
парóди|я (-и) ж: ~ (на +acc)
parody (of)
парóл|ь (-я) м password
парóм (-а) м ferry
парохóд (-а) м steamer, steamship
пáрт|а (-ы) ж desk (in schools)
партéр (-а) м the stalls мн
партизáн (-а; gen pl -) м partisan,

guerrilla

**парти́йный** *прил* party

**па́рти|я (-и)** *ж (ПОЛИТ)* party; *(МУЗ)* part; *(груза)* consignment; *(изделий: в производстве)* batch; *(СПОРТ)*: ~ **в ша́хматы/волейбо́л** a game of chess/volleyball

**партнёр (-а)** *м* partner

**партнёрств|о (-а)** *ср* partnership

**па́рус (-а;** *nom pl* **-а́)** *м* sail

**парфюме́ри|я (-и)** *ж собир perfume and cosmetic goods*

**пар|ы́ (-о́в)** *мн* vapour *ед (BRIT)*, vapor *ед (US)*

**пас (-а)** *м (СПОРТ)* pass

**па́смурный** *прил* overcast, dull

**па́спорт (-а;** *nom pl* **-а́)** *м* passport; *(автомобиля, станка)* registration document

**па́спорт** - passport. Russian citizens are required by law to have a passport at the age of 16. The passport serves as an essential identification document and has to be produced on various occasions ranging from applying for a job to collecting a parcel from the post office. Those who travel abroad have to get a separate passport for foreign travel.

**пассажи́р (-а)** *м* passenger

**пасси́вный** *прил* passive

**па́ст|а (-ы)** *ж* paste; *(томатная)* purée; **зубна́я ~** toothpaste

**пас|ти́ (-у́, -ёшь;** *pt* **-, -ла́)** *несов перех (скот)* to graze; **~сь** *несов возв* to graze

**паст|ила́ (-илы́;** *nom pl* **-и́лы)** *ж* ≈ marshmallow

**пасту́х (-а́)** *м (коров)* herdsman; *(овец)* shepherd

**па|сть (-ду́, -дёшь;** *pt* **-л, -ла, -ло)** *сов от* **па́дать** ♦ **(-сти)** *ж (зверя)* mouth

**Па́сх|а (-и)** *ж (в иудаизме)* Passover; *(в христианстве)* ≈ Easter

**пате́нт (-а)** *м* patent

**патент|ова́ть (-у́ю;** *pf* **за~)** *несов перех* to patent

**патоло́ги|я (-и)** *ж* pathology

**патриа́рх (-а)** *м* patriarch

**патрио́т (-а)** *м* patriot

**патриоти́зм (-а)** *м* patriotism

**патро́н (-а)** *м (ВОЕН)* cartridge; *(лампы)* socket

**патрули́р|овать (-ую)** *несов (не)перех* to patrol

**патру́л|ь (-я́)** *м* patrol

**па́уз|а (-ы)** *ж (также МУЗ)* pause

**пау́к (-а́)** *м* spider

**паути́н|а (-ы)** *ж* spider's web, spiderweb *(US)*; *(в помещении)* cobweb; *(перен)* web

**пах (-а;** *loc sg* **-у́)** *м* groin

**па|ха́ть (-шу́, -шешь;** *pf* **вс~)** *несов перех* to plough *(BRIT)*, plow *(US)*

**па́х|нуть (-ну;** *pt* **-, -ла)** *несов*: ~ *(+instr)* to smell (of)

**пацие́нт (-а)** *м* patient

**па́ч|ка (-ки;** *gen pl* **-ек)** *ж (бумаг)* bundle; *(чая, сигарет итп)* packet

**па́чка|ть (-ю;** *pf* **за~** *или* **ис~)** *несов перех*: ~ **что-н** to get sth dirty; **~ся** *(pf* **за~ся** *или* **ис~ся)** *несов возв* to get dirty

**паште́т (-а)** *м* pâté

**пая́|ть (-ю)** *несов перех* to solder

**пев|е́ц (-ца́)** *м* singer

**певи́ц|а (-ы)** *ж см.* **певе́ц**

**педаго́г (-а)** *м* teacher

**педагоги́ческий** *прил (коллектив)* teaching; ~ **институ́т** teacher-training *(BRIT)* или teachers' *(US)* college; ~ **сове́т** staff meeting

**педа́л|ь (-и)** ж pedal

**педиа́тр (-а)** м paediatrician (*BRIT*), pediatrician (*US*)

**пей** несов см. **пить**

**пе́йджер (-а)** м pager

**пейза́ж (-а)** м landscape

**пе́йте** несов см. **пить**

**пека́р|ня (-ни;** gen pl **-ен)** ж bakery

**пелена́|ть (-ю;** pf **за~)** несов перех to swaddle

**пелён|ка (-ки;** gen pl **-ок)** ж swaddling clothes мн

**пельме́н|ь (-я;** nom pl **-и)** м (*обычно* мн) ≈ ravioli ед

**пе́н|а (-ы)** ж (*мыльная*) suds мн; (*морская*) foam; (*бульонная*) froth

**пена́л (-а)** м pencil case

**пе́ни|е (-я)** ср singing

**пе́н|иться (**3sg **-ится;** pf **вс~)** несов возв to foam, froth

**пеницилли́н (-а)** м penicillin

**пе́нк|а (-и)** ж (*на молоке*) skin

**пенсионе́р (-а)** м pensioner

**пенсио́нный** прил (*фонд*) pension

**пе́нси|я (-и)** ж pension; **выходи́ть** (**вы́йти** pf) **на ~ю** to retire

**пень (пня)** м (tree) stump

**пе́п|ел (-ла)** м ash

**пе́пельниц|а (-ы)** ж ashtray

**пе́рвенств|о (-а)** ср championship; (*место*) first place

**перви́чный** прил (*самый ранний*) initial; (*низовой*) grass-root

**первобы́тный** прил primeval

**пе́рв|ое (-ого)** ср first course

**первокла́ссник (-а)** м pupil in first year at school

**первонача́льный** прил (*исходный*) original, initial

**первосо́ртный** прил top-quality,

top-grade

**первостепе́нный** прил (*задача, значение*) paramount

**пе́рв|ый** чис first; (*по времени*) first, earliest; **~ эта́ж** ground (*BRIT*) или first (*US*) floor; **~ое вре́мя** at first; **в ~ую о́чередь** in the first place или instance; **~ час дня/но́чи** after midday/midnight; **това́р ~ого со́рта** top grade product (*on a scale of 1-3*); **~ая по́мощь** first aid

**перебежа́ть** (*как* **бежа́ть;** *см.* Table 20; impf **перебега́ть)** сов: **~ (че́рез** +acc) to run across

**перебива́|ть (-ю)** несов от **переби́ть**

**перебира́|ть(ся) (-ю(сь))** несов от **перебра́ть(ся)**

**переб|и́ть (-ью́, -ьёшь;** impf **перебива́ть)** сов перех to interrupt; (*разбить*) to break

**перебо́|й (-я)** м (*двигателя*) misfire; (*задержка*) interruption

**переболе́|ть (-ю)** сов: **~** +instr to recover from

**переб|оро́ть (-орю́, -о́решь)** сов перех to overcome

**перебра́сыва|ть (-ю)** несов от **перебро́сить**

**переб|ра́ть (-еру́, -ерёшь;** impf **перебира́ть)** сов перех (*бумаги*) to sort out; (*крупу, ягоды*) to sort; (*события*) to go over или through (in one's mind); **~ся** (impf **перебира́ться**) сов возв (*через реку*) to manage to get across

**перебро́|сить (-шу, -сишь;** impf **перебра́сывать)** сов перех (*мяч*) to throw; (*войска*) to transfer

**перева́л (-а)** м (*в горах*) pass

**перева́лочный** прил: **~ пункт/ ла́герь** transit area/camp

**перев|арить** (-арю́, -а́ришь; *impf* **перева́ривать**) *сов перех* to overcook (*by boiling*); (*пищу, информацию*) to digest; ~**ся** (*impf* **перева́риваться**) *сов возв* to be overcooked *или* overdone; (*пища*) to be digested

**перев|езти́** (-езу́, -езёшь; *pt* -ёз, -езла́; *impf* **перевози́ть**) *сов перех* to take *или* transport across

**переверн|у́ть** (-у́, -ёшь; *impf* **перевора́чивать**) *сов перех* to turn over; (*изменить*) to change (completely); (*no impf*; *комнату*) to turn upside down; ~**ся** (*impf* **перевора́чиваться**) *сов возв* (*человек*) to turn over; (*лодка, машина*) to overturn

**перевес** (-а) *м* (*преимущество*) advantage

**перев|ести́** (-еду́, -едёшь; *pt* -ёл, -ела́; *impf* **переводи́ть**) *сов перех* (*помочь перейти́*) to take across; (*часы*) to reset; (*учреждение, сотрудника*) to transfer, move; (*текст*) to translate; (: *устно*) to interpret; (*переслать: деньги*) to transfer; (*доллары, метры итп*) to convert; ~**сь** (*impf* **переводи́ться**) *сов возв* to move

**перево́д** (-а) *м* transfer; (*стрелки часов*) resetting; (*текст*) translation; (*деньги*) remittance

**перев|оди́ть(ся)** (-ожу́(сь), -о́дишь(ся)) *несов от* **перевести́(сь)**

**перево́дчик** (-а) *м* translator; (*устный*) interpreter

**перев|ози́ть** (-ожу́, -о́зишь) *несов от* **перевезти́**

**перево́з|ка** (-ки; *gen pl* -ок) *ж* conveyance, transportation (*US*)

**перевора́чива|ть(ся)** (-ю(сь)) *несов от* **переверну́ться(ся)**

**переворо́т** (-а) *м* (*полит*) coup (d'état); (*в судьбе*) turning point

**перевоспита́|ть** (-ю; *impf* **перевоспи́тывать**) *сов перех* to re-educate

**перев|яза́ть** (-яжу́, -я́жешь; *impf* **перевя́зывать**) *сов перех* (*руку, раненого*) to bandage; (*рану*) to dress, bandage; (*коробку*) to tie up

**перевя́з|ка** (-ки; *gen pl* -ок) *ж* bandaging

**перег|на́ть** (-оню́, -о́нишь; *pt* -на́л, -нала́, -на́ло, *impf* **перегоня́ть**) *сов перех* (*обогнать*) to overtake; (*нефть*) to refine; (*спирт*) to distil (*BRIT*), distill (*US*)

**перегова́рива|ться** (-юсь) *несов возв*: ~ (**с** +*instr*) to exchange remarks with

**перегово́рный** *прил*: ~ **пункт** telephone office (*for long-distance calls*)

**перегово́р|ы** (-ов) *мн* negotiations *мн*, talks *мн*; (*по телефону*) call *ед*

**перегоня́|ть** (-ю) *несов от* **перегна́ть**

**перегор|е́ть** (*3sg* -и́т; *impf* ~а́ть) *сов* (*лампочка*) to fuse; (*двигатель*) to burn out

**перегоро|ди́ть** (-жу́, -ди́шь; *impf* **перегора́живать**) *сов перех* (*комнату*) to partition (off); (*дорогу*) to block

**перегр|узи́ть** (-ужу́, -у́зишь; *impf* **перегружа́ть**) *сов перех* to overload

**перегру́з|ка** (-ки; *gen pl* -ок) *ж* overload; (*обычно мн: нервные*) strain *ед*

KEYWORD

**пе́ред** *предл*; +*instr* **1** (*о*

положении, в присутствии) in front of
2 (раньше чего-н) before
3 (об объекте воздействия):
пе́ред тру́дностями in the face of difficulties; извиня́ться
(извини́ться pf) пе́ред кем-н to apologize to sb; отчи́тываться
(отчита́ться pf) пе́ред +instr to report to
4 (по сравнению) compared to
5 (как союз): пе́ред тем как before; пе́ред тем как зако́нчить before finishing

**переда|ва́ть** (-ю́; imper ~ва́й(те)) несов от **переда́ть**
**переда́м** etc сов см. **переда́ть**
**переда́тчик** (-а) м transmitter
**переда́|ть** (как дать; см. Table 16; impf **передава́ть**; сов перех: ~ что-н (кому́-н) (письмо, подарок) to pass или hand sth (over) (to sb); (известие, интерес) to pass sth on (to sb); ~йте ему́ (мой) приве́т give him my regards; ~йте ей, что я не приду́ tell her I am not coming; передава́ть (~ pf) что-н по телеви́дению/ра́дио to televise/broadcast sth
**переда́ч|а** (-и) ж (денег, письма) handing over; (матча) transmission; (ТЕЛ, РАДИО) programme (BRIT), program (US); програ́мма ~ television and radio guide
**переда́шь** сов см. **переда́ть**
**передвига́|ть(ся)** (-ю(сь)) несов от **передви́нуть(ся)**
**передвиже́ни|е** (-я) ср movement; сре́дства ~я means of transport
**передви́н|уть** (-у; impf **передвига́ть**) сов перех to move; ~ся (impf **передвига́ться**)

сов возв to move
**переде́ла|ть** (-ю; impf **переде́лывать**) сов перех (работу) to redo; (характер) to change
**пере́дний** прил front
**пере́дн|яя** (-ей) ж (entrance) hall
**пе́редо** предл = **пе́ред**
**передов|а́я** (-о́й) ж (также: ~ статья́) editorial; (также: ~ пози́ция: ВОЕН) vanguard
**передово́й** прил (технология) advanced; (писатель, взгляды) progressive
**передразни́ть** (-азню́, -а́знишь; impf **передра́знивать**) сов перех to mimic
**передыш|ка** (-ки; gen pl -ек) ж respite
**перее́зд** (-а) м (в новый дом) move
**перее́хать** (как е́хать; см. Table 19; impf **переезжа́ть**) сов (переселиться) to move; **переезжа́ть** (~ pf) (че́рез +acc) to cross
**пережива́ни|е** (-я) ср feeling
**пережива́|ть** (-ю) несов от **пережи́ть** ♦ неперех: ~ (за +acc) (разг) to worry (about)
**пережи́|ть** (-ву́, -вёшь; impf **пережива́ть**) сов перех (вытерпеть) to suffer
**перезвон|и́ть** (-ю́, -и́шь; impf **перезва́нивать**) сов to phone (BRIT) или call (US) back
**переизб|ра́ть** (-еру́, -ерёшь; pt -ра́л, -рала́; impf **переизбира́ть**) сов перех to re-elect
**переизда́|ть** (как дать; см. Table 16; impf **переиздава́ть**) сов перех to republish
**пере|йти́** (как идти́; см. Table 18; impf **переходи́ть**) сов (не)перех: ~ (че́рез +acc) to cross ♦ неперех:

~ в/на +*acc* (*поменять место*) to go (over) to; (*на другую работу*) to move to; **переходи́ть** (~ *pf*) **к** +*dat* (*к сыну итп*) to pass to; (*к делу, к обсуждению*) to turn to; **переходи́ть** (~ *pf*) **на** +*acc* to switch to

**переки́н|уть** (-у; *impf* **переки́дывать**) *сов перех* to throw

**перекла́дин|а** (-ы) *ж* crossbeam; (*СПОРТ*) (horizontal *или* high) bar

**перекла́дыва|ть** (-ю) *несов от* **переложи́ть**

**переключа́тел|ь** (-я) *м* switch

**переключ|и́ть** (-у́, -и́шь; *impf* **переключа́ть**) *сов перех* to switch; **~ся** (*impf* **переключа́ться**) *сов возв*: **~ся** (**на** +*acc*) (*внимание*) to shift (to)

**перекопа́|ть** (-ю) *сов перех* (*огород*) to dig up; (*разг: шкаф*) to rummage through

**перекр|ести́ть** (-ещу́, -е́стишь) *сов от* **крести́ть**; **~ся** *сов от* **крести́ться** ♦ (*impf* **перекре́щиваться**) *возв* (*дороги, интересы*) to cross

**перекрёст|ок** (-ка) *м* crossroads

**перекр|ы́ть** (-о́ю, -о́ешь; *impf* **перекрыва́ть**) *сов перех* (*реку*) to dam; (*воду, газ*) to cut off

**перек|упи́ть** (-уплю́, -у́пишь; *impf* **перекупа́ть**) *сов перех* to buy

**переку́пщик** (-а) *м* dealer

**перек|уси́ть** (-ушу́, -у́сишь) *сов* (*разг*) to have a snack

**переле́з|ть** (-у, -ешь; *pt* -, -ла; *impf* **перелеза́ть**) *сов (не)перех*: ~ (**че́рез** +*acc*) (*забор, канаву*) to climb (over)

**перелёт** (-а) *м* flight; (*птиц*) migration

**переле|те́ть** (-чу́, -ти́шь; *impf*

**перелета́ть**) *сов (не)перех*: ~ (**че́рез** +*acc*) to fly over

**перелётный** *прил* (*птицы*) migratory

**перелива́ни|е** (-я) *ср*: ~ **кро́ви** blood transfusion

**перелива́|ть** (-ю) *несов от* **перели́ть**

**перелиста́|ть** (-ю; *impf* **перели́стывать**) *сов перех* (*просмотреть*) to leaf through

**перел|и́ть** (-ью́, -ьёшь; *impf* **перелива́ть**) *сов перех* to pour (*from one container to another*); **перелива́ть** (~ *pf*) **кровь** кому́-н to give sb a blood transfusion

**перел|ожи́ть** (-ожу́, -о́жишь; *impf* **перекла́дывать**) *сов перех* to move; **перекла́дывать** (~ *pf*) **что-н на кого́-н** (*задачу*) to pass sth onto sb

**перело́м** (-а) *м* (*МЕД*) fracture; (*перен*) turning point

**перело́мный** *прил* critical

**перема́тыва|ть** (-ю) *несов от* **перемота́ть**

**переме́н|а** (-ы) *ж* change; (*в школе*) break (*BRIT*), recess (*US*)

**переме́нный** *прил* (*успех, ветер*) variable; ~ **ток** alternating current

**переме|сти́ть** (-щу́, -сти́шь; *impf* **перемеща́ть**) *сов перех* (*предмет*) to move; (*людей*) to transfer; **~ся** (*impf* **перемеща́ться**) *сов возв* to move

**перемеша́|ть** (-ю; *impf* **переме́шивать**) *сов перех* (*кашу*) to stir; (*угли, дрова*) to poke; (*вещи, бумаги*) to mix up

**перемеща́|ть(ся)** (-ю(сь)) *несов от* **перемести́ть(ся)**

**перемеще́ни|е** (-я) *ср* transfer

**переми́ри|е** (-я) *ср* truce

**перемота́|ть** (**-ю**; *impf* **перема́тывать**) *сов перех* (*нитку*) to wind; (*плёнку*) to rewind

**перенапряга́|ть** (**-ю**) *несов от* **перенапря́чь**

**перенапряже́ни|е** (**-я**) *ср* overexertion

**перенапря́|чь** (**-гу́**, **-жёшь** *итп*, **-гу́т**; *pt* **-г**, **-гла́**; *impf* **перенапряга́ть**) *сов перех* to overstrain

**перенаселённый** *прил* overpopulated

**перен|ести́** (**-есу́**, **-есёшь**; *pt* **-ёс**, **-есла́**, **-есло́**; *impf* **переноси́ть**) *сов перех*: ~ **что-н че́рез** +*acc* to carry sth over *или* across; (*поменять место*) to move; (*встречу, заседание*) to reschedule; (*болезнь*) to suffer from; (*голод, холод итп*) to endure

**перенима́|ть** (**-ю**) *несов от* **переня́ть**

**перено́с** (**-а**) *м* (*предмета*) transfer; (*встречи*) rescheduling; (*линг*) hyphen

**перен|оси́ть** (**-ошу́**, **-о́сишь**) *несов от* **перенести́** ♦ *перех*: **не** ~ **антибио́тиков/самолёта** to react badly to antibiotics/flying

**перено́сиц|а** (**-ы**) *ж* bridge of the nose

**переносно́й** *прил* portable

**перено́сный** *прил* (*значение*) figurative

**перено́счик** (**-а**) *м* (*МЕД*) carrier

**переноч|ева́ть** (**-у́ю**) *сов от* **ночева́ть**

**пере|ня́ть** (**-йму́**, **-ймёшь**; *pt* **-ня́л**, **-няла́**; *impf* **перенима́ть**) *сов перех* (*опыт, идеи*) to assimilate; (*обычаи, привычки*) to adopt

**переоде́|ть** (**-ну**, **-нешь**; *impf* **переодева́ть**) *сов перех* (*одежду*) to change (out of); **переодева́|ть** (~ *pf*) **кого́-н** to change sb *или* sb's clothes; ~**ся** (*impf* **переодева́ться**) *сов возв* to change, get changed

**переоц|ени́ть** (**-еню́**, **-е́нишь**; *impf* **переоце́нивать**) *сов перех* to overestimate

**перепа́д** (**-а**) *м*: ~ +*gen* fluctuation in

**перепеча́та|ть** (**-ю**) *сов перех* (*напечатанное*) to reprint; (*рукопись*) to type

**переп|иса́ть** (**-ишу́**, **-и́шешь**; *impf* **перепи́сывать**) *сов перех* (*написать заново*) to rewrite; (*скопировать*) to copy

**перепи́с|ка** (**-ки**; *gen pl* **-ок**) *ж* (*см глаг*) rewriting; copying; (*деловая, личная*) correspondence

**перепи́сыва|ть** (**-ю**) *несов от* **переписа́ть**; ~**ся** *несов возв*: ~**ся** (**с** +*instr*) to correspond (with)

**пе́репис|ь** (**-и**) *ж* (*населения*) census; (*имущества*) inventory

**перепл|ати́ть** (**-ачу́**, **-а́тишь**; *impf* **перепла́чивать**) *сов* to overpay

**перепл|ести́** (**-ету́**, **-етёшь**; *pt* **-ёл**, **-ела́**; *impf* **переплета́ть**) *сов перех* (*книгу*) to bind

**переплёт** (**-а**) *м* (*обложка*) binding; **око́нный** ~ window sash

**переплы́|ть** (**-ву́**, **-вёшь**; *pt* **-л**, **-ла́**; *impf* **переплыва́ть**) *сов* (*не*)*перех*: ~ (**че́рез** +*acc*) (*вплавь*) to swim (across); (*на лодке, на корабле*) to sail (across)

**перепол|зти́** (**-у́**, **-ёшь**; *pt* **-**, **-ла́**, **-ло́**; *impf* **переполза́ть**) *сов* (*не*)*перех*: ~ (**че́рез** +*acc*) to crawl across

**перепо́лн|ить** (**-ю**, **-ишь**; *impf*

**переполня́ть)** *сов перех* (*сосуд, контейнер*) to overfill; (*вагон, автобус итп*) to overcrowd; **~ся** (*impf* **переполня́ться**) *сов возв* (*сосуд*) to be overfilled

**переполо́х** (-a) *м* hullabaloo

**перепо́н|ка** (-ки; *gen pl* -ок) *ж* membrane

**переправа** (-ы) *ж* crossing

**переправ|ить** (-лю, -ишь; *impf* **переправля́ть)** *сов перех*: **~ кого́-н/что-н че́рез** +*acc* to take across; **~ся** (*impf* **переправля́ться**) *сов возв*: **~ся че́рез** +*acc* to cross

**перепрода́ть** (*как* **дать**; *см. Table 16*; *impf* **перепродава́ть)** *сов перех* to resell

**перепры́гн|уть** (-у; *impf* **перепры́гивать)** *сов* (*не)перех*: **~ (че́рез** +*acc*) to jump (over)

**перепуга́|ть** (-ю) *сов перех*: **~ кого́-н** to scare the life out of sb

**перепу́та|ть** (-ю) *сов* от **пу́тать**

**перерабо́та|ть** (-ю; *impf* **перераба́тывать)** *сов перех* (*сырьё, нефть*) to process; (*идеи, статью, теорию*) to rework

**перер|асти́** (-асту́, -астёшь; *pt* -о́с, -осла́; *impf* **перераста́ть)** *сов перех* to outgrow ♦ *неперех*: **~ в** +*acc* (*превратиться*) to turn into

**перере́|зать** (-жу, -жешь; *impf* **перереза́ть)** *сов перех* (*провод*) to cut in two; (*путь*) to cut off

**переры́в** (-a) *м* break; **де́лать (сде́лать** *pf*) **~** to take a break

**перес|ади́ть** (-ажу́, -а́дишь; *impf* **переса́живать)** *сов перех* to move; (*дерево, цветок, сердце*) to transplant; (*кость, кожу*) to graft

**переса́д|ка** (-ки; *gen pl* -ок) *ж* (*на

*поезд итп*) change; (*МЕД, сердца*) transplant; (*: кожи*) graft

**переса́жива|ть** (-ю) *несов от* **пересади́ть**; **~ся** *несов от* **пересе́сть**

**пересека́|ть(ся)** (-ю(сь)) *несов от* **пересе́чь(ся)**

**пересел|и́ть** (-ю́, -и́шь; *impf* **переселя́ть)** *сов перех* (*на новые земли*) to settle; (*в новую квартиру*) to move; **~ся** (*impf* **переселя́ться**) *сов возв* (*в новый дом*) to move

**перес|е́сть** (-я́ду, -я́дешь; *impf* **переса́живаться)** *сов* (*на другое место*) to move; **переса́живаться** (**~** *pf*) **на друго́й по́езд/самолёт** to change trains/planes

**пересече́ни|е** (-я) *ср* (*действие*) crossing; (*место*) intersection

**перес|е́чь** (-еку́, -ечёшь *etc*, -еку́т; *pt* -ёк, -екла́; *impf* **пересека́ть)** *сов перех* to cross; **~ся** (*impf* **пересека́ться**) *сов возв* to intersect; (*интересы*) to cross

**переска́з** (-a) *м* retelling

**переск|аза́ть** (-ажу́, -а́жешь; *impf* **переска́зывать)** *сов перех* to tell

**пере|сла́ть** (-шлю́, -шлёшь; *impf* **пересыла́ть)** *сов перех* (*отослать*) to send; (*по другому адресу*) to forward

**пересм|отре́ть** (-отрю́, -о́тришь; *impf* **пересма́тривать)** *сов перех* (*решение, вопрос*) to reconsider

**пересн|я́ть** (-иму́, -и́мешь; *pt* -я́л, -яла́, *impf* **переснима́ть)** *сов перех* (*документ*) to make a copy of

**перес|оли́ть** (-олю́, -о́лишь; *impf* **переса́ливать)** *сов перех*: **что-н** to put too much salt in sth

**пересо́х|нуть** (*3sg* **-нет**, *pt* **-**, **-ла**; *impf* **пересыха́ть**) *сов* (*почва, бельё*) to dry out; (*река*) to dry up

**переспр|оси́ть** (**-ошу́**, **-о́сишь**; *impf* **переспра́шивать**) *сов перех* to ask again

**переста|ва́ть** (**-ю́**) *несов от* **переста́ть**

**переста́в|ить** (**-лю**, **-ишь**; *impf* **переставля́ть**) *сов перех* to move; (*изменить порядок*) to rearrange

**перестара́|ться** (**-юсь**) *сов возв* to overdo it

**переста́|ть** (**-ну**, **-нешь**; *impf* **перестава́ть**) *сов* to stop; **перестава́ть** (**~** *pf*) +*infin* to stop doing

**перестра́ива|ть** (**-ю**) *несов от* **перестро́ить**

**перестре́л|ка** (**-ки**; *gen pl* **-ок**) *ж* exchange of fire

**перестро́|ить** (**-ю**, **-ишь**; *impf* **перестра́ивать**) *сов перех* (*дом*) to rebuild; (*экономику*) to reorganize

**перестро́|йка** (**-йки**; *gen pl* **-ек**) *ж* (*дома*) rebuilding; (*экономики*) reorganization; (*ИСТ*) perestroika

**перест|упи́ть** (**-уплю́**, **-у́пишь**; *impf* **переступа́ть**) *сов перех* (*закон*) to overstep ♦ (*не*)*перех*: **~** (**че́рез** +*acc*) (*порог, предмет*) to step over

**пересчёт** (**-а**) *м* count; (*повторный*) re-count

**пересчита́|ть** (**-ю**; *impf* **пересчи́тывать**) *сов перех* to count; (*повторно*) to re-count, count again; (*в других единицах*) to convert

**пересыла́|ть** (**-ю**) *несов от* **пересла́ть**

**пересы́п|ать** (**-лю**, **-лешь**; *impf* **пересыпа́ть**) *сов перех* (*насыпать*) to pour

**пересыха́|ть** (*3sg* **-ет**) *несов от* **пересо́хнуть**

**перет|ащи́ть** (**-ащу́**, **-а́щишь**; *impf* **перета́скивать**) *сов перех* (*предмет*) to drag over

**перетр|уди́ться** (**-ужу́сь**, **-у́дишься**; *impf* **перетружда́ться**) *сов возв* (*разг*) to be overworked

**перет|яну́ть** (**-яну́**, **-я́нешь**; *impf* **перетя́гивать**) *сов перех* (*передвинуть*) to pull, tow; (*быть тяжелее*) to outweigh

**переубе|ди́ть** (**-жу́**, **-ди́шь**; *impf* **переубежда́ть**) *сов перех*: **~ кого́-н** to make sb change his *итп* mind

**переу́л|ок** (**-ка**) *м* lane, alley

**переутом|и́ться** (**-лю́сь**, **-и́шься**; *impf* **переутомля́ться**) *сов возв* to tire o.s. out

**переутомле́ни|е** (**-я**) *ср* exhaustion

**переучёт** (**-а**) *м* stocktaking

**пере|учи́ть** (**-учу́**, **-у́чишь**; *impf* **переу́чивать**) *сов перех* to retrain; **~ся** (*impf* **переу́чиваться**) *сов возв* to undergo retraining

**перехитр|и́ть** (**-ю́**, **-и́шь**) *сов перех* to outwit

**перехо́д** (**-а**) *м* crossing; (*к другой системе*) transition; (*подземный, в здании*) passage

**перех|оди́ть** (**-ожу́**, **-о́дишь**) *несов от* **перейти́**

**перехо́дный** *прил* (*промежуточный*) transitional; **~ глаго́л** transitive verb

**пе́р|ец** (**-ца**) *м* pepper

**пе́реч|ень** (**-ня**) *м* list

**перечеркн|у́ть** (**-у́**, **-ёшь**; *impf* **перечёркивать**) *сов перех* to cross out

**перечи́сл|ить** (**-ю**, **-ишь**; *impf*

**перечисля́ть**) *сов перех*
(*упомянуть*) to list; (*КОММ*) to transfer

**перечита́|ть** (**-ю**; *impf* **перечи́тывать**) *сов перех* (*книгу*) to reread, read again

**перешагн|у́ть** (**-у́, -ёшь**; *impf* **переша́гивать**) *сов (не)перех*: ~ (**че́рез** +*acc*) to step over

**перешёл** *итп сов см.* **перейти́**

**переш|и́ть** (**-ью́, -ьёшь**; *impf* **перешива́ть**) *сов перех* (*платье*) to alter; (*пуговицу*) to move (*by sewing on somewhere else*)

**переэкзамено́в|ка** (**-ки**; *gen pl* **-ок**) *ж* resit

**пери́л|а** (**-**) *мн* railing *ед*; (*лестницы*) ban(n)isters *мн*

**пери́метр** (**-а**) *м* perimeter

**пери́од** (**-а**) *м* period; **пе́рвый/ второ́й ~ игры́** (*СПОРТ*) first/ second half (of the game)

**периоди́ческий** *прил* periodical

**перифери́|я** (**-и**) *ж* the provinces *мн*

**перламу́тр** (**-а**) *м* mother-of-pearl

**перло́вый** *прил* barley

**пер|о́** (**-а́**; *nom pl* **-ья**, *gen pl* **-ьев**) *ср* (*птицы*) feather; (*для письма*) nib

**перочи́нный** *прил*: ~ **нож** penknife

**перпендикуля́рный** *прил* perpendicular

**перро́н** (**-а**) *м* platform (*RAIL*)

**пе́рсик** (**-а**) *м* peach

**персона́ж** (**-а**) *м* character

**персона́л** (**-а**) *м* (*АДМИН*) personnel, staff

**персона́льный** *прил* personal; ~ **компью́тер** PC

**перспекти́в|а** (**-ы**) *ж* (*ГЕОМ*) perspective; (*вид*) view; (*обычно мн: планы*) prospects; **в ~е** (*в будущем*) in store

**перспекти́вный** *прил* (*изображе́ние*) in perspective; (*планирование*) long-term; (*ученик*) promising

**пе́рст|ень** (**-ня**) *м* ring

**перча́т|ка** (**-ки**; *gen pl* **-ок**) *ж* glove

**пе́рч|ить** (**-у, -ишь**; *pf* **на~**) *сов перех* to pepper

**перши́ть** (*3sg* **-и́т**) *несов безл* (*разг*): **у меня́ ~и́т в го́рле** I've got a frog in my throat

**пе́рья** *etc сущ см.* **перо́**

**пёс** (**пса**) *м* dog

**пес|е́ц** (**-ца́**) *м* arctic fox

**пе́с|ня** (**-ни**; *gen pl* **-ен**) *ж* song

**пес|о́к** (**-ка́**; *part gen* **-ку́**) *м* sand

**песо́чный** *прил* (*печенье*) short

**пессимисти́чный** *прил* pessimistic

**пёстрый** *прил* (*ткань*) multi-coloured (*BRIT*), multi-colored (*US*)

**песча́ный** *прил* sandy

**пе́т|ля** (**-ли**; *gen pl* **-ель**) *ж* loop; (*в вязании*) stitch; (*двери, крышки*) hinge; (*для пуговицы*) buttonhole

**петру́шк|а** (**-и**) *ж* parsley

**пету́х** (**-а́**) *м* cock, rooster (*US*)

**петь** (**пою́, поёшь**; *imper* **пой(те)**; *pf* **с~**) *несов перех* to sing

**пехо́т|а** (**-ы**) *ж* infantry

**печа́л|ь** (**-и**) *ж* (*грусть*) sadness, sorrow

**печа́льный** *прил* sad; (*ошибка, судьба*) unhappy

**печа́та|ть** (**-ю**; *pf* **на~**) *несов перех* (*также ФОТО*) to print; (*публиковать*) to publish; (*на компьютере*) to type

**печа́тн|ый** *прил* (*станок*) printing; ~**ые бу́квы** block letters

**печа́т|ь** (**-и**) *ж* stamp; (*на дверях, на сейфе*) seal; (*издательское дело*) printing; (*след: страданий*)

mark ♦ *собир* (*пресса*) press
**печён|ка** (**-ки**; *gen pl* **-ок**) ж liver
**печёный** *прил* baked
**пе́чен|ь** (**-и**) ж (*АНАТ*) liver
**печёнь|е** (**-я**) *ср* biscuit (*BRIT*), cookie (*US*)
**пе́ч|ка** (**-ки**; *gen pl* **-ек**) ж stove
**пе́ч|ь** (**-чи**; *loc sg* **-чи́**, *gen pl* **-е́й**) ж stove; (*ТЕХ*) furnace ♦ (**-ку́**, **-чёшь** *etc*, **-ку́т**; *pt* **пёк**, **-кла́**, *pf* **испе́чь**) *несов перех* to bake;
микроволно́ва́я ~ microwave oven; **пе́чься** (*pf* **испе́чься**) *несов возв* to bake
**пешехо́д** (**-а**) м pedestrian
**пешехо́дный** *прил* pedestrian
**пе́ш|ка** (**-ки**; *gen pl* **-ек**) ж pawn
**пешко́м** *нареч* on foot
**пеще́р|а** (**-ы**) ж cave
**пиани́но** *ср нескл* (upright) piano
**пиани́ст** (**-а**) м pianist
**пивн|а́я** (**-о́й**) ж ≈ bar, ≈ pub (*BRIT*)
**пивно́й** *прил* (*бар, бочка*) beer
**пи́в|о** (**-а**) *ср* beer
**пиджа́к** (**-а́**) м jacket
**пижа́м|а** (**-ы**) ж pyjamas *мн*
**пик** (**-а**) м peak ♦ *прил неизм* (*часы, период, время*) peak; **часы́** ~ rush hour
**пи́к|и** (**-**) *мн* (*в картах*) spades *мн*
**пи́ковый** *прил* (*в картах*) of spades
**пил|а́** (**-ы́**; *nom pl* **-ы**) ж saw
**пил|и́ть** (**-ю́**, **-ишь**) *несов перех* to saw; (*перен: разг*) to nag
**пи́л|ка** (**-ки**; *gen pl* **-ок**) ж nail file
**пило́т** (**-а**) м pilot
**пило́тный** *прил* (*пробный*) pilot, trial
**пина́|ть** (**-ю**) *несов перех* to kick
**пингви́н** (**-а**) м penguin
**пин|о́к** (**-ка́**) м kick
**пинце́т** (**-а**) м (*МЕД*) tweezers *мн*
**пионе́р** (**-а**) м pioneer; (*в СССР*)

member of Communist Youth organization
**пипе́т|ка** (**-ки**; *gen pl* **-ок**) ж pipette
**пир** (**-а**; *nom pl* **-ы́**) м feast
**пирами́д|а** (**-ы**) ж pyramid
**пира́т** (**-а**) м pirate
**пиро́г** (**-а́**) м pie
**пиро́жн|ое** (**-ого**) *ср* cake
**пирож|о́к** (**-ка́**) м (*с мясом*) pie; (*с вареньем*) tart
**писа́ни|е** (**-я**) *ср*: Свяще́нное Писа́ние Holy Scripture
**писа́тел|ь** (**-я**) м writer
**пи|са́ть** (**-шу́**, **-шешь**; *pf* **на~**) *несов перех* to write; (*картину*) to paint ♦ *неперех*; (*no pf*; *ребёнок*) to be able to write; (*ручка*) to write; **~ся** *несов возв* (*слово*) to be spelt *или* spelled
**писк** (**-а**) м squeak; (*птицы*) cheep
**пискля́вый** *прил* (*голос*) squeaky
**пистоле́т** (**-а**) м pistol
**пи́сьменно** *нареч* in writing
**пи́сьменн|ый** *прил* (*просьба, экзамен*) written; (*стол, прибор*) writing; **в ~ой фо́рме** in writing
**пись|мо́** (**-ьма́**; *nom pl* **-ьма**, *gen pl* **-ем**) *ср* letter; (*no pl*; *алфавитное*) script
**пита́ни|е** (**-я**) *ср* (*ребёнка*) feeding; (*ТЕХ*) supply; (*вегетарианское*) diet; **обще́ственное** ~ public catering
**пита́тельный** *прил* (*вещества*) nutritious; (*крем*) nourishing
**пита́|ть** (**-ю**) *несов перех* (*перен: любовь*) to feel; **~ся** *несов возв*: **~ся** +*instr* (*человек, растение*) to live on; (*животное*) to feed on
**пито́мник** (**-а**) м (*БОТ*) nursery
**пи|ть** (**пью**, **пьёшь**; *pt* **-л**, **-ла́**, *imper* **пе́й(те)**, *pf* **вы́~**) *несов перех* to drink ♦ *неперех*: ~ **за кого́-н/что-н** to drink to sb/sth

**питьев|ой** *прил*: ~**ая вода** drinking water

**пи́цц|а (-ы)** *ж* pizza

**пиццери́|я (-и)** *ж* pizzeria

**пи́чка|ть (-ю;** *pf* **на~)** *несов перех* to stuff

**пишу́** *etc несов см.* **писа́ть(ся)**

**пи́щ|а (-и)** *ж* food

**пищ|а́ть (-у́, -и́шь)** *несов* (*птицы*) to cheep; (*животные*) to squeak

**пищеваре́ни|е (-я)** *ср* digestion

**пищев|о́й** *прил* food; (*соль*) edible; ~**ая со́да** baking soda

**ПК** *м сокр* = **персона́льный компью́тер**

**пл.** *сокр* (= **пло́щадь**) Sq.

**пла́вани|е (-я)** *ср* swimming; (*на судне*) sailing; (*рейс*) voyage

**пла́вательный** *прил*: ~ **бассе́йн** swimming pool

**пла́ва|ть (-ю)** *несов* to swim; (*кора́бль*) to sail; (*в воздухе*) to float

**пла́в|ить (-лю, -ишь;** *pf* **рас~)** *несов перех* to smelt; ~**ся** (*pf* **рас~ся**) *несов возв* to melt

**пла́в|ки (-ок)** *мн* swimming trunks *мн*

**пла́вленый** *прил*: ~ **сыр** processed cheese

**плавни́к (-а́)** *м* (*у рыб*) fin

**пла́вный** *прил* smooth

**плаву́чий** *прил* floating

**плака́т (-а)** *м* poster

**пла́|кать (-чу, -чешь)** *несов* to cry, weep; ~ (*impf*) **от** +*gen* (*от боли итп*) to cry from; (*от радости*) to cry with; (*от горя*) to cry in

**пла́м|я (-ени;** *как* **вре́мя;** *см. Table 4*) *ср* flame

**план (-а)** *м* plan; (*чертёж*) plan, map; **пере́дний** ~ foreground; **за́дний** ~ background

**планёр (-а)** *м* glider

**плане́т|а (-ы)** *ж* planet

**планета́ри|й (-я)** *м* planetarium

**плани́р|овать (-ую)** *несов перех* to plan; (*pf* **за~;** *намерева́ться*) to plan

**планиро́вк|а (-и)** *ж* layout

**пла́н|ка (-ки;** *gen pl* -**ок)** *ж* slat

**пла́новый** *прил* planned; (*отдел, коми́ссия*) planning

**планоме́рный** *прил* systematic

**пласт (-а́)** *м* (*также перен*) stratum; **лежа́ть** (*impf*) ~**ом** to lie flat

**пла́стик (-а)** *м* = **пластма́сса**

**пластили́н (-а)** *м* plasticine

**пласти́н|а (-ы)** *ж* plate

**пласти́н|ка (-ки;** *gen pl* -**ок)** *ж* уменьш от **пласти́на;** (*муз*) record

**пласти́ческий** *прил* plastic

**пласти́чный** *прил* (*жесты, движения*) graceful; (*материалы, вещества*) plastic

**пластма́сс|а (-ы)** *ж сокр* (= **пласти́ческая ма́сса**) plastic

**пла́стыр|ь (-я)** *м* (*мед*) plaster

**пла́т|а (-ы)** *ж* (*за труд, за услуги*) pay; (*за кварти́ру*) payment; (*за прое́зд*) fee; (*перен: награ́да*) reward

**плат|ёж (-ежа́)** *м* payment

**платёжеспосо́бный** *прил* (*комм*) solvent

**платёжн|ый** *прил* (*комм*): ~ **бланк** payslip; ~**ая ве́домость** payroll

**пла́тин|а (-ы)** *ж* platinum

**пла|ти́ть (-чу́, -тишь;** *pf* **за~** *или* **у~)** *несов перех* to pay

**пла́тный** *прил* (*вход, стоя́нка*) chargeable; (*шко́ла*) fee-paying; (*больни́ца*) private

**плат|о́к (-ка́)** *м* (*головно́й*) headscarf; (*наплечный*) shawl;

(также: **носово́й ~**) handkerchief

**платфо́рм|а (-ы)** ж platform; (*станция*) halt; (*основание*) foundation

**пла́ть|е (-я**; *gen pl* **-ев)** *ср* dress ♦ *собир* (*одежда*) clothing, clothes *мн*

**плафо́н (-а)** *м* (*абажур*) shade (*for ceiling light*)

**плацда́рм (-а)** *м* (*ВОЕН*) bridgehead

**плаце́нт|а (-ы)** ж (*МЕД*) placenta

**плацка́ртный** *прил*: **~ ваго́н** railway car with open berths instead of compartments

**плач (-а)** *м* crying

**пла́чу** etc несов см. **пла́кать**

**плачу́** несов см. **плати́ть**

**плащ (-а́)** *м* raincoat

**пл|ева́ть (-юю́)** *несов* to spit; (*pf* **на~**; *перен*): **~ на** +*acc* (*разг* (*на правила, на мнение других*) to not give a damn about: **~ся** *несов возв* to spit

**плед (-а)** *м* (tartan) rug

**пле́йер (-а)** *м* Walkman ®

**пле́м|я (-ени**; *как* **вре́мя**; *см. Table 4*) *ср* (*также перен*) tribe

**племя́нник (-а)** *м* nephew

**племя́нниц|а (-ы)** ж niece

**плен (-а**; *loc sg* **-у́)** *м* captivity; **бра́ть (взять** *pf*) **кого́-н в ~** to take sb prisoner; **попада́ть (попа́сть** *pf*) **в ~** to be taken prisoner

**плён|ка (-ки**; *gen pl* **-ок)** ж film; (*кожица*) membrane; (*магнитофонная*) tape

**пле́нн|ый (-ого)** *м* prisoner

**пле́нум (-а)** *м* plenum

**пле́сен|ь (-и)** ж mould (*BRIT*), mold (*US*)

**плеск (-а)** *м* splash

**пл|еска́ться (-ещу́сь, -е́щешься)** *несов возв* to splash

**пле́сневе|ть (**3sg **-ет;** *pf* **за~)** несов to go mouldy (*BRIT*) или moldy (*US*)

**пл|ести́ (-ету́, -ете́шь;** *pt* **-ёл, -ела́;** *pf* **с~)** несов перех (*сети*) to weave; (*венок, волосы*) to plait

**плетёный** *прил* wicker

**плёт|ка (-ки**; *gen pl* **-ок)** ж whip

**пле́чик|и (-ов)** *мн* (*вешалка*) coat hangers *мн*; (*подкладки*) shoulder pads *мн*

**плеч|о́ (-а́**; *nom pl* **-и)** *ср* shoulder

**пли́нтус (-а)** *м* skirting board (*BRIT*), baseboard (*US*)

**плиссе́** *прил неизм*: **ю́бка/пла́тье ~** pleated skirt/dress

**плит|а́ (-ы́**; *nom pl* **-ы)** ж (*каменная*) slab; (*металлическая*) plate; (*печь*) cooker, stove

**пли́т|ка (-ки**; *gen pl* **-ок)** ж (*керамическая*) tile; (*шоколада*) bar; (*электрическая*) hot plate; (*газовая*) camping stove

**плов|е́ц (-ца́)** *м* swimmer

**плод (-а́)** *м* (*БОТ*) fruit; (*БИО*) foetus (*BRIT*), fetus (*US*); **~** +*gen* (*перен: усилий*) fruits of

**плод|и́ться (**3sg **-и́тся;** *pf* **рас~)** несов возв to multiply

**плодоро́дный** *прил* fertile

**плодотво́рный** *прил* fruitful

**пло́мб|а (-ы)** ж (*в зубе*) filling; (*на дверях, на сейфе*) seal

**пломби́р (-а)** *м* rich creamy ice-cream

**пломбир|ова́ть (-у́ю;** *pf* **за~)** несов перех (*зуб*) to fill; (*pf* **о~**; *дверь, сейф*) to seal

**пло́ский** *прил* flat

**плоскогу́бц|ы (-ев)** *мн* pliers *мн*

**пло́скост|ь (-и**; *gen pl* **-е́й)** ж plane

**плот (-а́**; *loc sg* **-у́)** *м* raft

**плоти́н|а (-ы)** ж dam

**пло́тник (-а)** *м* carpenter

**пло́тный** прил (туман) dense, thick; (толпа) dense; (бума́га, ко́жа) thick; (обед) substantial

**пло́хо** нареч (учи́ться, рабо́тать) badly ♦ как сказ it's bad; **мне ~** I feel bad; **у меня́ ~ с деньга́ми** I am short of money

**плохо́й** прил bad

**площа́д|ка** (-ки; gen pl -ок) ж (де́тская) playground; (спорти́вная) ground; (строи́тельная) site; (часть ваго́на) corridor; **ле́стничная ~** landing; **поса́дочная ~** landing pad

**пло́щад|ь** (-и; gen pl -е́й) ж (ме́сто) square; (простра́нство, та́кже MAT) area; (та́кже: жила́я ~) living space

**плуг** (-а; nom pl -и́) м plough (BRIT), plow (US)

**плы|ть** (-ву́, -вёшь; pt -л, -ла́) несов to swim; (су́дно) to sail; (о́блако) to float

**плю́н|уть** (-у) сов to spit; **плюнь!** (разг) forget it!

**плюс** м нескл, союз plus

**пляж** (-а) м beach

**пневмони́|я** (-и) ж pneumonia

**ПО** ср нескл сокр (= програ́ммное обеспе́чение) software; (КОММ: = произво́дственное объедине́ние) ≈ large industrial company

---
KEYWORD
---

**по** предл; +dat **1** (о ме́сте де́йствия, вдоль) along; **ло́дка плывёт по реке́** the boat is sailing on the river; **спуска́ться (спусти́ться** pf) **по ле́стнице** to go down the stairs
**2** (при глаго́лах движе́ния) round; **ходи́ть** (impf) **по ко́мнате/ са́ду** to walk round the room/ garden; **плыть** (impf) **по тече́нию** to go downstream
**3** (об объе́кте возде́йствия) on; **уда́рить** (impf) **по врагу́** to deal a blow to the enemy
**4** (в соотве́тствии с): **де́йствовать по зако́ну/ пра́вилам** to act in accordance with the law/the rules; **по расписа́нию/пла́ну** according to schedule/plan
**5** (об основа́нии): **суди́ть по вне́шности** to judge by appearances; **жени́ться** (impf/pf) **по любви́** to marry for love
**6** (всле́дствие) due to; **по необходи́мости** out of necessity
**7** (посре́дством): **говори́ть по телефо́ну** to speak on the phone; **отправля́ть (отпра́вить** pf) **что-н по по́чте** to send sth by post; **передава́ть (переда́ть** pf) **что-н по ра́дио/по телеви́дению** to broadcast/televise sth
**8** (с це́лью, для): **о́рганы по борьбе́ с престу́пностью** organizations in the fight against crime; **я позва́л тебя́ по де́лу** I called on you on business
**9** (о како́й-н характери́стике объе́кта) in; **по профе́ссии** by profession; **дед по ма́тери** maternal grandfather; **това́рищ по шко́ле** school friend
**10** (о сфе́ре де́ятельности) in
**11** (о ме́ре вре́мени): **по вечера́м/утра́м** in the evenings/ mornings; **по воскресе́ньям/ пя́тницам** on Sundays/Fridays; **я рабо́таю по це́лым дням** I work all day long; **рабо́та рассчи́тана по мину́там** the work is planned by the minute
**12** (о едини́чности предме́тов):

**мáма далá всем по я́блоку** Mum gave them each an apple; **мы купи́ли по одно́й кни́ге** we bought a book each

♦ *предл*; *+асс* **1** (*вплоть до*) up to; **с пéрвой по пя́тую главу́** from the first to (*BRIT*) или through (*US*) the fifth chapter; **я за́нят по го́рло** (*разг: перен*) I am up to my eyes in work; **он пó уши в неё влюблён** he is head over heels in love with her

**2** (*при обозначении цены*): **по два/три рубля́ за шту́ку** two/three roubles each

**3** (*при обозначении количества*): **по два/три человéка** in twos/threes

♦ *предл*; (*+prp; после*) on; **по приéзде** on arrival

**п/о** *сокр* (= *почто́вое отделéние*) post office
**по-англи́йски** *нареч* in English
**побéг** (**-а**) *м* (*из тюрьмы́*) escape; (*БОТ*) shoot, sprout
**побегу́** *etc сов см.* **побежáть**
**побéд|а** (**-ы**) *ж* victory
**победи́тел|ь** (**-я**) *м* (*в войне*) victor; (*в состязании*) winner
**победи́ть** (*2sg* **-и́шь**, *3sg* **-и́т**; *impf* **побеждáть**) *сов перех* to defeat ♦ *неперех* to win
**победоно́сный** *прил* victorious
**побежáть** (*как* **бежáть**; *см. Table 20*) *сов* (*человек, животное*) to start running; (*дни, годы*) to start to fly by; (*ручьи, слёзы*) to begin to flow
**побеждá|ть** (**-ю**) *несов от* **победи́ть**
**побелé|ть** (**-ю**) *сов от* **белéть**
**побел|и́ть** (**-ю́**, **-ишь**) *сов от* **бели́ть**
**побéлк|а** (**-и**) *ж* whitewash;

(*действие*) whitewashing
**побереж|ье** (**-ья**; *gen pl* **-ий**) *ср* coast
**побеспоко́|ить** (**-ю**, **-ишь**) *сов от* **беспоко́ить**
**поб|и́ть** (**-ью́**, **-ьёшь**) *сов от* **бить** ♦ *перех* (*повредить*) to destroy; (*разбить*) to break
**побли́зости** *нареч* nearby
♦ *предл*: ~ **от** *+gen* near (to), close to
**побо́рник** (**-а**) *м* champion (*of cause*)
**побор|о́ть** (**-ю́**, **-о́решь**) *сов перех* (*также перен*) to overcome
**побо́чный** *прил* (*продукт, реакция*) secondary; ~ **эффéкт** side effect
**побу|ди́ть** (**-жу́**, **-ди́шь**) *сов перех*: ~ **кого́-н к чему́-н**/ *+infin* to prompt sb into sth/to do
**побуждéни|е** (**-я**) *ср* (*к действию*) motive
**побывá|ть** (**-ю**) *сов*: ~ **в Áфрике/у роди́телей** to visit Africa/one's parents
**поб|ы́ть** (*как* **быть**; *см. Table 21*) *сов* to stay
**пов|али́ть(ся)** (**-алю́(сь)**, **-а́лишь(ся)**) *сов от* **вали́ть(ся)**
**по́вар** (**-а**; *nom pl* **-á**) *м* cook
**повáренн|ый** *прил*: ~**ая кни́га** cookery (*BRIT*) или cook (*US*) book; ~**ая соль** table salt
**поведéни|е** (**-я**) *ср* behaviour (*BRIT*), behavior (*US*)
**повез|ти́** (**-у́**, **-ёшь**; *pt* **-ёз**, **-езлá**) *сов от* **везти́** ♦ *перех* to take
**повéренн|ый** (**-ого**) *м*: ~ **в делáх** chargé d'affaires
**повéр|ить** (**-ю**, **-ишь**) *сов от* **вéрить**
**поверн|у́ть** (**-у́**, **-ёшь**; *impf* **повора́чивать**) *сов* (*не*)*перех* to turn; ~**ся** (*impf* **повора́чиваться**)

*сов возв* to turn

**пове́рх** *предл:* ~ +*gen* over

**пове́рхностный** *прил* surface; (*перен*) superficial

**пове́рхность** (-и) *ж* surface

**пове́р|ье** (-ья; *gen pl* -**ий**) *ср* (popular) belief

**пове́|сить(ся)** (-шу(сь), -сишь(ся)) *сов от* **ве́шать(ся)**

**повествова́ни|е** (-я) *ср* narrative

**пов|ести́** (-еду́, -едёшь; *pt* -ёл, -ла́) *сов перех* (*начать вести: ребёнка*) to take; (: *войска*) to lead; (*машину, поезд*) to drive; (*войну, следствие итп*) to begin ♦ (*impf* **поводи́ть**) *неперех:* ~ +*instr* (*бровью*) to raise; (*плечом*) to shrug; ~ (*pf*) **себя́** to start behaving

**повест|ка** (-ки; *gen pl* -**ок**) *ж* summons; (*также:* ~ **дня**) agenda

**по́вест|ь** (-и) *ж* story

**по-ви́димому** *вводн сл* apparently

**пови́дл|о** (-а) *ср* jam (*BRIT*), jelly (*US*)

**пови́нност|ь** (-и) *ж:* **во́инская** ~ conscription

**повин|ова́ться** (-у́юсь) *сов возв:* ~ +*dat* to obey

**повинове́ни|е** (-я) *ср* obedience

**пови́с|нуть** (-ну; *pt* -, -ла; *impf* **повиса́ть**) *сов* to hang; (*тучи*) to hang motionless

**повл|е́чь** (-еку́, -ечёшь итп, -еку́т; *pt* -ёк, -екла́, -екло́) *сов от* **влечь**

**по́в|од** (-ода; *loc sg* -**оду́**, *nom pl* -**о́дья**, *gen pl* -**ьев**) *м* (*лошади*) rein; (*nom pl* -**оды**, *причина*) reason ♦ *предл:* **по** ~**у** +*gen* regarding, concerning

**пово|ди́ть** (-ожу́, -о́дишь) *несов от* **повести́**

**повод|о́к** (-ка́) *м* lead, leash

**пово́з|ка** (-ки; *gen pl* -**ок**) *ж* cart

**повора́чива|ть(ся)** (-ю(сь)) *несов от* **поверну́ть(ся)**

**поворо́т** (-а) *м* (*действие*) turning; (*место*) bend; (*перен*) turning point

**поворо́тный** *прил* (*ТЕХ*) revolving; ~ **пункт** *или* **моме́нт** (*перен*) turning point

**повре|ди́ть** (-жу́, -ди́шь; *impf* **поврежда́ть**) *сов перех* (*поранить*) to injure; (*поломать*) to damage

**поврежде́ни|е** (-я) *ср* (*см глаг*) injury; damage

**повседне́вный** *прил* everyday, routine; (*занятия, встречи*) daily

**повсеме́стный** *прил* widespread

**повсю́ду** *нареч* everywhere

**по-вся́кому** *нареч* in different ways

**повторе́ни|е** (-я) *ср* repetition; (*урока*) revision

**повтор|и́ть** (-ю́, -и́шь; *impf* **повторя́ть**) *сов перех* to repeat; ~**ся** (*impf* **повторя́ться**) *сов возв* (*ситуация*) to repeat itself; (*болезнь*) to recur

**повто́рный** *прил* repeated

**повы́|сить** (-шу, -сишь; *impf* **повыша́ть**) *сов перех* to increase; (*интерес*) to heighten; (*качество, культуру*) to improve; (*работника*) to promote; **повыша́ть** (~ *pf*) **го́лос** to raise one's voice; ~**ся** (*impf* **повыша́ться**) *сов возв* to increase; (*интерес*) to heighten; (*качество, культура*) to improve

**повы́шенн|ый** *прил* (*спрос*) increased; (*интерес*) heightened; ~**ое давле́ние** high blood pressure

**пов|яза́ть** (-яжу́, -я́жешь; *impf* **повя́зывать**) *сов перех* to tie

**повя́з|ка** (-ки; *gen pl* -**ок**) *ж*

bandage

**пога́н|ка (-ки;** *gen pl* **-ок)** *ж* toadstool

**пог|аси́ть (-ашу́, -а́сишь)** *сов от* **гаси́ть ♦** (*impf* **погаша́ть**) *перех* (*заплати́ть*) to pay (off)

**пога́с|нуть (-ну;** *pt* **-, -ла)** *сов от* **га́снуть**

**погаша́|ть (-ю)** *несов от* **погаси́ть**

**поги́б|нуть (-ну;** *pt* **-, -ла)** *сов от* **ги́бнуть**

**поги́бш|ий (-его)** *м* casualty (*dead*)

**погл|оти́ть (-ощу́, -о́тишь;** *impf* **поглоща́ть)** *сов перех* to absorb; (*время*) to take up; (*фирму*) to take over

**поглоще́ни|е (-я)** *ср* absorption; (*КОММ*) takeover

**пог|на́ться (-оню́сь, -о́нишься)** *сов возв:* **~за кем-н/чем-н** to set off in pursuit of sb/sth

**поговор|ка (-ки;** *gen pl* **-ок)** *ж* saying

**пого́д|а (-ы)** *ж* weather

**пого́дный** *прил* weather

**поголо́вь|е (-я)** *ср* (*скота́*) total number

**пого́н (-а)** *м* (*обычно мн*) (shoulder) stripe

**пого́н|я (-и)** *ж:* **~ за** +*instr* pursuit of

**пограни́чник (-а)** *м* frontier *или* border guard

**пограни́чный** *прил* border

**по́греб (-а;** *nom pl* **-á)** *м* cellar

**погреба́льный** *прил* funeral

**погрему́ш|ка (-ки;** *gen pl* **-ек)** *ж* rattle

**погре́|ть (-ю)** *сов перех* to warm up; **~ся** *сов возв* to warm up

**погро́м (-а)** *м* pogrom; (*разг: беспоря́док*) chaos

**погр|узи́ть (-ужу́, -у́зишь)** *сов*

*перех от* **грузи́ть ♦** (**-ужу́, -у́зишь;** *impf***погружа́ть)** *перех:* **~ что-н в** +*acc* to immerse sth in; **~ся** (*impf* **погружа́ться**) *сов возв:* **~ся в** +*acc* (*челове́к*) to immerse o.s. in; (*предме́т*) to sink into

**погру́з|ка (-ки;** *gen pl* **-ок)** *ж* loading

**погру́зочный** *прил* loading

**погря́зн|уть (-у;** *impf* **погряза́ть)** *сов:* **~ в** +*prp* (*в долга́х, во лжи*) to sink into

---
| KEYWORD |
---

**под** *предл;* +*acc* **1** (*ниже*) under; **идти́** (*impf*) **под гору** to go downhill

**2** (*подде́рживая сни́зу*) by

**3** (*ука́зывает на положе́ние, состоя́ние*) under; **отдава́ть** (**отда́ть** *pf*) **кого́-н под суд** to prosecute sb; **попада́ть** (**попа́сть** *pf*) **под дождь** to be caught in the rain

**4** (*бли́зко к*): **под у́тро/ве́чер** towards morning/evening; **под ста́рость** approaching old age

**5** (*ука́зывает на функцию*) as; **мы приспосо́били помеще́ние под магази́н** we fitted out the premises as a shop

**6** (*в ви́де чего́-н*): **сте́ны под мра́мор** marble-effect walls

**7** (*в обме́н на*) on; **брать** (**взять** *pf*) **что-н под зало́г/че́стное сло́во** to take sth on security/trust

**8** (*в сопровожде́нии*): **под роя́ль/скри́пку** to the piano/violin; **мне э́то не под си́лу** that is beyond my powers

**♦** *предл* (+*instr*) **1** (*ниже чего́-н*) under

**2** (*о́коло*) near; **под но́сом у кого́-н** under sb's nose; **под руко́й** to hand, at hand

3 (*об усло́виях существова́ния объе́кта*) under; **быть** (*impf*) **под наблюде́нием/аре́стом** to be under observation/arrest; **под назва́нием, под и́менем** under the name of

4 (*всле́дствие*) under; **под влия́нием/тя́жестью чего́-н** under the influence/weight of sth; **понима́ть** (*impf*)/**подразумева́ть** (*impf*) **под чем-н** to understand/ imply by sth

пода|ва́ть (-ю́) *несов от* пода́ть
под|ави́ть (-авлю́, -а́вишь; *impf* подавля́ть) *сов перех* to suppress; ~ся *сов от* дави́ться
подавле́ни|е (-я) *ср* suppression
пода́вленный *прил* (*настрое́ние, челове́к*) depressed
подавля́|ть (-ю) *несов от* подави́ть
подавля́ющий *прил* (*большинство́*) overwhelming
под|ари́ть (-арю́, -а́ришь) *сов от* дари́ть
пода́р|ок (-ка) *м* present, gift
пода́рочный *прил* gift
пода́ть (*как* дать; *см. Table 16*; *impf* подава́ть) *сов перех* to give; (*еду́*) to serve up; (*по́езд, такси́ итп*) to bring; (*заявле́ние, жа́лобу итп*) to submit; (*СПОРТ, в те́ннисе*) to serve; (: *в футбо́ле*) to pass; подава́ть (~ *pf*) го́лос за +*acc* to cast a vote for; подава́ть (~ *pf*) в отста́вку to hand in *или* submit one's resignation; подава́ть (~ *pf*) на кого́-н в суд to take sb to court; подава́ть (~ *pf*) кому́-н ру́ку (*при встре́че*) to give sb one's hand
пода́ч|а (-и) *ж* (*де́йствие: заявле́ния*) submission; (*СПОРТ, в те́ннисе*) serve; (: *в футбо́ле*) pass

подбежа́ть (*как* бежа́ть; *см. Table 20*; *impf* подбега́ть) *сов* to run up
подбива́|ть (-ю) *несов от* подби́ть
подбира́|ть (-ю) *несов от* подобра́ть
под|би́ть (-обью́, -обьёшь; *impf* подбива́ть) *сов перех* (*пти́цу, самолёт*) to shoot down; (*глаз, крыло́*) to injure
подбо́р (-а) *м* selection
подборо́д|ок (-ка) *м* chin
подбро́|сить (-шу, -сишь; *impf* подбра́сывать) *сов перех* (*мяч, ка́мень*) to toss; (*нарко́тик*) to plant; (*разг: подвезти́*) to give a lift
подва́л (-а) *м* cellar; (*для жилья́*) basement
подва́льный *прил* (*помеще́ние*) basement
подведе́ни|е (-я) *ср*: ~ ито́гов summing-up
подв|езти́ (-езу́, -езёшь; *pt* -ёз, -езла́; *impf* подвози́ть) *сов перех* (*маши́ну, това́р*) to take up; (*челове́ка*) to give a lift
подве́рг|нуть (-ну; *pt* -, -ла; *impf* подверга́ть) *сов перех*: ~ кого́-н/ что-н чему́-н to subject sb/sth to sth; подверга́ть (~ *pf*) кого́-н ри́ску/опа́сности to put sb at risk/in danger; ~ся (*impf* подверга́ться) *сов возв*: ~ся +*dat* to be subjected to
подве́рженный *прил*: ~ +*dat* (*дурно́му влия́нию*) subject to (*просту́де*) susceptible to
подверн|у́ть (-у́, -ёшь; *impf* подвора́чивать) *сов перех* (*сде́лать коро́че*) to turn up; подвора́чивать (~ *pf*) но́гу to turn *или* twist one's ankle; ~ся (*impf* подвора́чиваться) *сов возв*

(*разг: попасться*) to turn up
**подве́|сить** (-шу, -сишь; *impf*
**подве́шивать**) *сов перех* to
hang up
**подв|ести́** (-еду́, -еде́шь; *pt* -ёл,
-ела́; *impf* **подводи́ть**) *сов перех*
(*разочаровать*) to let down;
**подводи́ть** (~ *pf*) +*dat*
(*человека*) to bring up to;
(*машину*) to drive up to; (*поезд*)
to bring into; (*корабль*) to sail up
to; (*электричество*) to bring to;
**подводи́ть** (~ *pf*) глаза́/гу́бы to
put eyeliner/lipstick on; **подводи́ть**
(~ *pf*) ито́ги to sum up
**подве́шива|ть** (-ю) *несов от*
**подве́сить**
**по́двиг** (-а) *м* exploit
**подвига́|ть(ся)** (-ю(сь)) *несов от*
**подви́нуть(ся)**
**подви́жный** *прил* agile
**подви́н|уть** (-у; *impf* **подвига́ть**)
*сов перех* (*передвинуть*) to
move; ~**ся** (*impf* **подвига́ться**)
*сов возв* (*человек*) to move
**подвла́стный** *прил*: ~ +*dat*
(*закону*) subject to; (*президенту*)
under the control of
**подв|оди́ть** (-ожу́, -о́дишь)
*несов от* **подвести́**
**подво́дн|ый** *прил* (*растение*,
*работы*) underwater; ~**ая ло́дка**
submarine
**подв|ози́ть** (-ожу́, -о́зишь)
*несов от* **подвезти́**
**подвора́чива|ть** (-ю) *несов от*
**подверну́ть**
**подгиба́|ть(ся)** (-ю(сь)) *несов от*
**подогну́ть(ся)**
**подгля|де́ть** (-жу́, -ди́шь; *impf*
**подгля́дывать**) *сов перех* to
peep through
**подгор|е́ть** (*3sg* -и́т; *impf*
**подгора́ть**) *сов* to burn slightly
**подготови́тельный** *прил*

(*работа*) preparatory
**подгото́в|ить** (-лю, -ишь; *impf*
**подгота́вливать**) *сов перех* to
prepare; ~**ся** (*impf*
**подгота́вливаться**) *сов возв* to
prepare (o.s.)
**подгото́вк|а** (-и) *ж* preparation;
(*запас знаний*) training
**подгу́зник** (-а) *м* nappy (*BRIT*),
diaper (*US*)
**подда|ва́ться** (-ю́сь) *несов от*
**подда́ться** ♦ *возв*: не ~
**сравне́нию/описа́нию** to be
beyond comparison/words
**по́дданн|ый** (-ого) *м* subject
**по́дданств|о** (-а) *ср* nationality
**подда́ться** (*как дать*; *см. Table
16*; *impf* **поддава́ться**) *сов возв*
(*дверь итп*) to give way;
**поддава́ться** (~ *pf*) +*dat*
(*влиянию, соблазну*) to give in to
**подде́ла|ть** (-ю; *impf* **под-
де́лывать**) *сов перех* to forge
**подде́л|ка** (-ки; *gen pl* -ок) *ж*
forgery
**подде́льный** *прил* forged
**подд|ержа́ть** (-ержу́, -е́ржишь;
*impf* **подде́рживать**) *сов перех*
to support; (*падающего*) to hold
on to; (*предложение итп*) to
second; (*беседу*) to keep up
**подде́ржива|ть** (-ю) *несов от*
**поддержа́ть** ♦ *перех*
(*переписку*) to keep up;
(*порядок, отношения*) to
maintain
**подде́ржк|а** (-и) *ж* support
**подде́ла|ть** (-ю) *сов перех* (*разг*)
to do; **что ~ешь** (*разг*) it can't be
helped
**под|ели́ть(ся)** (-елю́(сь),
-е́лишь(ся)) *сов от* **дели́ть(ся)**
**поде́ржанный** *прил* (*одежда,
мебель итп*) second-hand
**под|же́чь** (-ожгу́, -ожжёшь *etc*,

**-ожгу́т**; *impf* **поджига́ть**) *сов перех* to set fire to

**подзаты́льник** (**-а**) *м* (*разг*) clip round the ear

**подзе́мный** *прил* underground

**подзо́рн|ый** *прил*: **~ая труба́** telescope

**подк|ати́ть** (**-ачу́, -а́тишь**; *impf* **подка́тывать**) *сов перех* (*что-н круглое*) to roll; (*что-н на колёсах*) to wheel

**подка́шива|ть(ся)** (**-ю(сь)**) *несов от* **подкоси́ть(ся)**

**подки́н|уть** (**-у**; *impf* **подки́дывать**) *сов* = **подбро́сить**

**подкла́д|ка** (**-ки**; *gen pl* **-ок**) *ж* lining

**подкла́дыва|ть** (**-ю**) *несов от* **подложи́ть**

**подключ|и́ть** (**-у́, -и́шь**; *impf* **подключа́ть**) *сов перех* (*телефон*) to connect; (*лампу*) to plug in; (*специалистов*) to involve

**подко́в|а** (**-ы**) *ж* (*лошади итп*) shoe

**подк|ова́ть** (**-ую́**; *impf* **подко́вывать**) *сов перех* to shoe

**подк|оси́ть** (**-ошу́, -о́сишь**; *impf* **подка́шивать**) *сов перех* (*подлеж: несчастье*) to devastate; **~ся** (*impf* **подка́шиваться**) *сов возв*: **у него́ но́ги/коле́ни подкоси́лись** his legs/knees gave way

**подкр|а́сться** (**-аду́сь, -адёшься**; *impf* **подкра́дываться**) *сов возв* to sneak *или* steal up

**подкреп|и́ть** (**-лю́, -и́шь**; *impf* **подкрепля́ть**) *сов перех* to support, back up

**подкрепле́ни|е** (**-я**) *ср* (*ВОЕН*) reinforcement

**по́дкуп** (**-а**) *м* bribery

**подк|упи́ть** (**-уплю́, -у́пишь**; *impf* **подкупа́ть**) *сов перех* to bribe

**подлеж|а́ть** (*3sg* **-и́т**) *несов*: **~ +dat** (*проверке, обложению налогом*) to be subject to; **э́то не ~и́т сомне́нию** there can be no doubt about that

**подлежа́щ|ее** (**-его**) *ср* (*ЛИНГ*) subject

**подле́ц** (**-а́**) *м* scoundrel

**подли́в|ка** (**-ки**; *gen pl* **-ок**) *ж* (*КУЛИН*) sauce

**по́длинник** (**-а**) *м* original

**по́длинный** *прил* original; (*документ*) authentic; (*чувство*) genuine; (*друг*) true

**по́дло** *нареч* (*поступить*) meanly

**подло́г** (**-а**) *м* forgery

**подл|ожи́ть** (**-ожу́, -о́жишь**; *impf* **подкла́дывать**) *сов перех* (*бомбу*) to plant; (*добавить*) to put; (*дров, сахара*) to add

**подлоко́тник** (**-а**) *м* arm(rest)

**по́длост|ь** (**-и**) *ж* (*поступка*) baseness; (*сам поступок*) base thing

**по́длый** *прил* base

**подмен|и́ть** (**-ю́, -и́шь**; *impf* **подме́нивать**) *сов перех* to substitute; (*коллегу*) to stand in for

**подм|ести́** (**-ету́, -етёшь**; *pt* **-ёл, -ела́**) *сов от* **мести́** ♦ (*impf* **подмета́ть**) *перех* (*пол*) to sweep; (*мусор*) to sweep up

**подмётк|а** (**-и**) *ж* (*подошва*) sole

**подмигн|у́ть** (**-у́, -ёшь**; *impf* **подми́гивать**) *сов*: **~ кому́-н** to wink at sb

**подмы́ш|ка** (**-ки**; *gen pl* **-ек**) *ж* armpit

**поднес|ти́** (**-у́, -ёшь**; *impf* **подноси́ть**) *сов перех*: **~ что-н к чему́-н** to bring sth up to sth

**поднима́|ть(ся)** (**-ю(сь)**) *несов*

**от подня́ть(ся)**

**подно́жи|е (-я)** *ср* (*горы*) foot

**подно́жка (-ки;** *gen pl* **-ек)** *ж* (*автобуса итп*) step; **поста́вить** (*pf*) **~ку кому́-н** to trip sb up

**подно́с (-а)** *м* tray

**подн|оси́ть (-ошу́, -о́сишь)** *несов от* **поднести́**

**подн|я́ть (-иму́, -и́мешь;** *impf* **поднима́ть)** *сов перех* to raise; (*что-н лёгкое*) to pick up; (*что-н тяжёлое*) to lift (up); (*флаг*) to hoist; (*спящего*) to rouse; (*панику, восста́ние*) to start; (*экономику, дисциплину*) to improve; (*архивы, документацию итп*) to unearth; **поднима́ть (~** *pf*) **крик** *или* **шум** to make a fuss; **~ся** (*impf* **поднима́ться**) *сов возв* to rise; (*на этаж, на сцену*) to go up; (*с постели, со стула*) to get up; (*паника, метель, драка*) to break out; **поднима́ться (~ся** *pf*) **на́ го́ру** to climb a hill; **~я́лся крик** there was an uproar

**подо** *предл см.* **под**

**подоба́ющий** *прил* appropriate

**подо́бно** *предл*: **~** *+dat* like, similar to

**подо́бн|ый** *прил*: **~** *+dat* (*сходный с*) like, similar to; **и тому́ ~ое** et cetera, and so on; **ничего́ ~ого** (*разг*) nothing of the sort

**под|обра́ть (-беру́, -берёшь;** *impf* **подбира́ть)** *сов перех* to pick up; (*приподнять*) to gather (up); (*выбрать*) to pick, select

**подобре́|ть (-ю)** *сов от* **добре́ть**

**подогн|у́ть (-у́, -ёшь;** *impf* **подгиба́ть)** *сов перех* (*рукава*) to turn up; **~ся** (*impf* **подгиба́ться**) *сов возв* to curl under

**подогре́|ть (-ю;** *impf*

**подогрева́ть)** *сов перех* to warm up

**пододви́н|уть (-у;** *impf* **пододвига́ть)** *сов перех* to move closer

**пододея́льник (-а)** *м* ≈ duvet cover

**подожд|а́ть (-у́, -ёшь;** *pt* **-а́л, -ала́)** *сов перех* to wait for; **~** (*pf*) **с чем-н** to put sth off

**подозрева́|ть (-ю)** *несов перех* to suspect; **~** (*impf*) **кого́-н в чём-н** to suspect sb of sth; **~** (*impf*) (**о чём-н**) to have an idea (about sth)

**подозре́ни|е (-я)** *ср* suspicion

**подозри́тельный** *прил* suspicious

**подо|и́ть (-ю́, -ишь)** *сов от* **дои́ть**

**подойти́** (*как* **идти́**; *см. Table 18; impf* **подходи́ть**) *сов*: **~ к** *+dat* to approach; (*соответствовать*): **~ к** *+dat* (*юбка*) to go (well) with; **э́то мне подхо́дит** this suits me

**подоко́нник (-а)** *м* windowsill

**подо́л (-а)** *м* hem

**подо́лгу** *нареч* for a long time

**подо́пытный** *прил*: **~ кро́лик** (*перен*) guinea pig

**подорв|а́ть (-у́, -ёшь;** *pt* **-а́л, -ала́;** *impf* **подрыва́ть)** *сов перех* to blow up; (*перен: авторите́т*) to undermine; (*: здоро́вье*) to destroy

**подотчётн|ый** *прил* accountable; **~ые де́ньги** expenses

**подохо́дный** *прил*: **~ нало́г** income tax

**подо́шв|а (-ы)** *ж* (*обуви*) sole

**подошёл** *etc сов см.* **подойти́**

**под|пере́ть (-опру́, -опрёшь;** *pt* **-пёр, -пёрла;** *impf* **подпира́ть)** *сов перех*: **~ что-н чем-н** to prop sth up with sth

**подписа́ни|е (-я)** *ср* signing

**подп|иса́ть (-ишу́, -и́шешь;** *impf*

**подписывать**) *сов перех* to sign; **~ся** (*impf* **подписываться**) *сов возв*: **~ся под** +*instr* to sign; **подписываться** (**~ся** *pf*) **на** +*acc* (*на газету*) to subscribe to

**подпис|ка** (**-ки**; *gen pl* **-ок**) *ж* subscription; (*о невыезде*) signed statement

**подписчик** (**-а**) *м* subscriber

**подпис|ь** (**-и**) *ж* signature

**подплы|ть** (**-ву́, -вёшь**; *pt* **-л, -ла́**; *impf* **подплыва́ть**) *сов* (*лодка*) to sail (up); (*пловец, рыба*) to swim (up)

**подполко́вник** (**-а**) *м* lieutenant colonel

**подпо́льный** *прил* underground

**подпо́р|ка** (**-ки**; *gen pl* **-ок**) *ж* prop, support

**подпры́гн|уть** (**-у**; *impf* **подпры́гивать**) *сов* to jump

**подп|усти́ть** (**-ущу́, -у́стишь**; *impf* **подпуска́ть**) *сов перех* to allow to approach

**подрабо́та|ть** (**-ю**) *сов* (*не*)*перех*: **~** +*acc или* +*gen* to earn extra

**подра́внива|ть** (**-ю**) *несов от* **подровня́ть**

**подража́ни|е** (**-я**) *ср* imitation

**подража́|ть** (**-ю**) *несов*: **~** +*dat* to imitate

**подразделе́ни|е** (**-я**) *ср* subdivision; (*воинское*) subunit

**подразделя́|ться** (*3sg* **-ется**) *несов возв* to be subdivided

**подразумева́|ть** (**-ю**) *несов перех* to imply; **~ся** *несов возв* to be implied

**подр|асти́** (**-асту́, -астёшь**; *pt* **-о́с, -осла́**; *impf* **подраста́ть**) *сов* to grow

**под|ра́ться** (**-еру́сь, -ерёшься**) *сов от* **дра́ться**

**подре́|зать** (**-жу, -жешь**; *impf* **подреза́ть**) *сов перех* (*волосы*) to cut

**подро́бност|ь** (**-и**) *ж* detail

**подро́бный** *прил* detailed

**подровня́|ть** (**-ю**; *impf* **подра́внивать**) *сов перех* to trim

**подростко́вый** *прил* teenage; **~ во́зраст** adolescence

**подро́ст|ок** (**-ка**) *м* teenager, adolescent

**подру́г|а** (**-и**) *ж* (girl)friend

**по-друго́му** *нареч* (*иначе*) differently

**подр|ужи́ться** (**-ужу́сь, -у́жишься**) *сов возв*: **~ с** +*instr* to make friends with

**подру́чный** *прил*: **~ материа́л** the material to hand

**подрыва́|ть** (**-ю**) *несов от* **подорва́ть**

**подрывно́й** *прил* subversive

**подря́д** *нареч* in succession ♦ (**-а**) *м* (*рабочий догово́р*) contract; **все/всё ~** everyone/everything without exception

**подря́дный** *прил* contract

**подря́дчик** (**-а**) *м* contractor

**подса́жива|ться** (**-юсь**) *несов от* **подсе́сть**

**подсве́чник** (**-а**) *м* candlestick

**подс|е́сть** (**-я́ду, -я́дешь**; *impf* **подса́живаться**) *сов*: **~ к** +*dat* to sit down beside

**подск|аза́ть** (**-ажу́, -а́жешь**; *impf* **подска́зывать**) *сов перех* (*перен: идею*) to suggest; (*разг: адрес*) to give out; **подска́зывать** (**~** *pf*) **что-н кому́-н** to prompt sb with sth

**подска́з|ка** (**-ки**; *gen pl* **-ок**) *ж* prompt

**подслу́ша|ть** (**-ю**; *impf* **подслу́шивать**) *сов перех* to eavesdrop on

подсм|отре́ть (-отрю́, -о́тришь; *impf* подсма́тривать) *сов перех* (*увидеть*) to spy on

подсне́жник (-а) *м* snowdrop

подсо́бный *прил* subsidiary

подсо́выва|ть (-ю) *несов от* подсу́нуть

подсозна́ни|е (-я) *ср* the subconscious

подсозна́тельный *прил* subconscious

подсо́лнечн|ый *прил*: ~ое ма́сло sunflower oil

подсо́лнух (-а) *м* (*разг*) sunflower

подста́в|ить (-лю, -ишь; *impf* подставля́ть) *сов перех*: ~ под +*acc* to put under

подста́в|ка (-ки; *gen pl* -ок) *ж* stand

подставля́|ть (-ю) *несов от* подста́вить

подста́нци|я (-и) *ж* substation

подстере́|чь (-гу́, -жёшь *итп*, -гу́т; *impf* подстерега́ть) *сов перех* to lie in wait for

подстра́ива|ть (-ю) *несов от* подстро́ить

подстр|ели́ть (-елю́, -е́лишь; *impf* подстре́ливать) *сов перех* to wound

подстри́|чь (-гу́, -жёшь *итп*, -гу́т; *pt* -г, -ла; *impf* подстрига́ть) *сов перех* to trim; (*для укора́чивания*) to cut; ~ся (*impf* подстрига́ться) *сов возв* to have one's hair cut

подстро́|ить (-ю, -ишь; *impf* подстра́ивать) *сов перех* to fix

по́дступ (-а) *м* (*обычно мн*) approach

подст|упи́ть (-уплю́, -у́пишь; *impf* подступа́ть) *сов* (*слёзы*) to well up; (*рыда́ния*) to rise; подступа́ть (~ *pf*) к +*dat* (*к го́роду, к те́ме*) to approach

подсуди́м|ый (-ого) *м* (*ЮР*) the accused, the defendant

подсу́дный *прил* (*ЮР*) sub judice

подсу́н|уть (-у; *impf* подсо́вывать) *сов перех* to shove

подсчёт (-а) *м* counting; (*итог*) calculation

подсчита́|ть (-ю; *impf* подсчи́тывать) *сов перех* to count (up)

подта́лкива|ть (-ю) *несов от* подтолкну́ть

подтвер|ди́ть (-жу́, -ди́шь; *impf* подтвержда́ть) *сов перех* to confirm; (*фа́ктами*) to back up; ~ся (*impf* подтвержда́ться) *сов* to be confirmed

подтвержде́ни|е (-я) *ср* confirmation

подтолкн|у́ть (-у́, -ёшь; *impf* подта́лкивать) *сов перех* to nudge; (*побуди́ть*) to urge on

подтя́гива|ть(ся) (-ю(сь)) *несов от* подтяну́ть(ся)

подтя́ж|ки (-ек) *мн* (*для брюк*) braces *мн* (*BRIT*), suspenders *мн* (*US*)

подтя́нутый *прил* smart

подт|яну́ть (-яну́, -я́нешь; *impf* подтя́гивать) *сов перех* (*тяжёлый предме́т*) to haul up; (*га́йку*) to tighten; (*войска́*) to bring up; ~ся (*impf* подтя́гиваться *сов возв* (*на бру́сьях*) to pull o.s. up; (*войска́*) to move up

поду́ма|ть (-ю) *сов*: ~ (о +*prp*) to think (about); ~ (*pf*) над +*instr или* о +*prp* to think about; ~ (*pf*), что... to think that ...; кто бы мог ~! who would have thought it!

поду́|ть (-ю) *сов* to blow; (*ве́тер*) to begin to blow

под|уши́ть (-ушу́, -у́шишь) *сов*

*перех* to spray lightly with perfume

**поду́ш|ка** (**-ки**; *gen pl* **-ек**) *ж* (*для сидения*) cushion; (*под голову*) pillow

**подхв|ати́ть** (**-ачу́, -а́тишь**; *impf* **подхва́тывать**) *сов перех* (*падающее*) to catch; (*подлеж: течение, толпа*) to carry away; (*идею, болезнь*) to pick up

**подхо́д** (**-а**) *м* approach

**подх|оди́ть** (**-ожу́, -о́дишь**) *несов от* **подойти́**

**подходя́щий** *прил* (*дом*) suitable; (*момент, слова*) appropriate

**подчеркн|у́ть** (**-у́, -ёшь**; *impf* **подчёркивать**) *сов перех* (*в тексте*) to underline; (*в речи*) to emphasize

**подчине́ни|е** (**-я**) *ср* obedience

**подчинён|ный** *прил* subordinate ♦ (**-ого**) *м* subordinate

**подчин|и́ть** (**-ю́, -и́шь**; *impf* **подчиня́ть**) *сов перех* (*страну*) to subjugate; **подчиня́ть** (~ *pf*) **что-н кому́-н** to place sth under the control of sb; **~ся** (*impf* **подчиня́ться**) *сов возв*: **~ся** +*dat* to obey

**подше́фный** *прил*: **~ де́тский дом** children's home under patronage

**подшива́|ть** (**-ю**) *несов от* **подши́ть**

**подши́в|ка** (**-ки**; *gen pl* **-ок**) *ж* (*газет, документов*) file

**подши́пник** (**-а**) *м* (*ТЕХ*) bearing

**подш|и́ть** (**-ошью, -ошьёшь**; *imper* **-ше́й(те)**; *impf* **подшива́ть**) *сов перех* (*рукав*) to hem; (*подол*) to take up

**подш|ути́ть** (**-учу́, -у́тишь**; *impf* **подшу́чивать**) *сов*: **~ над** +*instr* to make fun of

**подъе́ду** *etc сов см.* **подъе́хать**

**подъе́зд** (**-а**) *м* (*к городу, к дому*) approach; (*в здании*) entrance

**подъезжа́|ть** (**-ю**) *несов от* **подъе́хать**

**подъём** (**-а**) *м* (*груза*) lifting; (*флага*) raising; (*на гору*) ascent; (*промышленный*) revival

**подъёмник** (**-а**) *м* lift (*BRIT*), elevator (*US*)

**подъёмный** *прил* lifting; **~ кран** crane

**подъе́хать** (*как* **е́хать**; *см. Table 19*; *impf* **подъезжа́ть**) *сов* (*на автомобиле*) to drive up; (*на коне*) to ride up

**под|ыша́ть** (**-ышу́, -ы́шешь**) *сов* to breathe

**пое́дешь** *etc сов см.* **пое́хать**

**поеди́м** *итп сов см.* **пое́сть**

**поеди́те** *сов см.* **пое́сть**

**пое́ду** *etc сов см.* **пое́хать**

**поедя́т** *сов см.* **пое́сть**

**по́езд** (**-а**; *nom pl* **-а́**) *м* train

**по́езд|ка** (**-ки**; *gen pl* **-ок**) *ж* trip

**поезжа́й(те)** *сов см.* **пое́хать**

**пое́сть** (*как* **есть**; *см. Table 15*) *сов от* **есть** ♦ *перех*: **~ чего́-н** to eat a little bit of sth

**пое́хать** (*как* **е́хать**; *см. Table 19*) *сов* to set off

**пое́шь** *сов см.* **пое́сть**

**пожале́|ть** (**-ю**) *сов от* **жале́ть**

**пожа́л|овать** (**-ую**) *сов*: **добро́ ~** welcome; **~ся** *сов от* **жа́ловаться**

**пожа́луйста** *част* please; (*в ответ на благодарность*) don't mention it (*BRIT*), you're welcome (*US*); **~, помоги́те мне** please help me; **скажи́те, ~, где вокза́л!** could you please tell me where the station is; **мо́жно здесь сесть? - ~!** may I sit here? - please do!

**пожа́р** (**-а**) *м* fire

**пожа́рник** (**-а**) *м* (*разг*) fireman

**пожа́рн|ый (-ого)** м fireman
♦ *прил*: **~ая кома́нда** fire brigade
(*BRIT*) *или* department (*US*); **~ая
маши́на** fire engine

**пож|а́ть (-му́, -мёшь;** *impf*
**пожима́ть) сов перех** to
squeeze; **он ~а́л мне ру́ку** he
shook my hand; **пожима́ть (~** *pf*)
**плеча́ми** to shrug one's shoulders

**пожела́ни|е (-я)** *ср* wish;
**прими́те мои́ наилу́чшие ~я**
please accept my best wishes

**пожела́|ть (-ю)** *сов от* **жела́ть**

**пож|ени́ться (-еню́сь,
-е́нишься)** *сов возв* to marry,
get married

**поже́ртвовани|е (-я)** *ср* donation

**пожива́|ть (-ю)** *несов* (*разг*): **как
ты ~ешь?** how are you?

**пожи́зненн|ый** *прил* lifelong;
**~ое заключе́ние** life
imprisonment

**пожило́й** *прил* elderly

**пожима́|ть (-ю)** *несов от*
**пожа́ть**

**пож|и́ть (-иву́, -ивёшь;** *pt* **-и́л,
-ила́)** *сов* (*пробы́ть*) to live for a
while

**по́з|а (-ы)** *ж* posture; (*перен*:
*поведе́ние*) pose

**позавчера́** *нареч* the day before
yesterday

**позади́** *нареч* (*сзади*) behind; (*в
прошлом*) in the past ♦ *предл*: **~
**+gen** behind

**позаи́мств|овать (-ую)** *сов от*
**займствовать**

**позапро́шлый** *прил* before last

**поз|ва́ть (-ову́, -овёшь)** *сов от*
**звать**

**позво́л|ить (-ю, -ишь;** *impf*
**позволя́ть) сов** to permit ♦
*перех*: **~ что-н кому́-н** to allow sb
sth; **позволя́ть (~** *pf*) **себе́ что-н**
(*поку́пку*) to be able to afford sth

**позвон|и́ть (-ю́, -и́шь)** *сов от*
**звони́ть**

**позвоно́чник (-а)** м spine, spinal
column

**поздне́е** *сравн нареч от* **по́здно**
♦ *нареч* later ♦ *предл*: **~** +gen
after; **(не)** +gen (no) later than

**по́здн|ий** *прил* late; **са́мое ~ее**
(*разг*) at the latest

**по́здно** *нареч* late ♦ *как сказ* it's
late

**поздоро́ва|ться (-юсь)** *сов от*
**здоро́ваться**

**поздрави́тельный** *прил*
greetings

**поздра́в|ить (-лю, -ишь;** *impf*
**поздравля́ть) сов перех*: **~
кого́-н с** +instr to congratulate sb
on; **поздравля́ть (~** *pf*) **кого́-н с
днём рожде́ния** to wish sb a
happy birthday

**поздравле́ни|е (-я)** *ср*
congratulation; (*с днём
рождения*) greetings *мн*

**по́зже** *нареч* = **поздне́е**

**позити́вный** *прил* positive

**пози́ци|я (-и)** *ж* position

**познако́м|ить(ся) (-лю(сь),
-ишь(ся))** *сов от* **знако́мить(ся)**

**позна́ни|я (-й)** *мн* knowledge *ед*

**позову́** *итп сов см.* **позва́ть**

**позо́р (-а)** м disgrace

**позо́р|ить (-ю, -ишь;** *pf* **о~)**
*несов перех* to disgrace; **~ся** (*pf*
**о~ся**) *несов возв* to disgrace o.s.

**позо́рный** *прил* disgraceful

**пои́м|ка (-ки;** *gen pl* **-ок)** *ж*
capture

**поинтерес|ова́ться (-у́юсь)** *сов
возв*: **~** +instr to take an interest in

**по́иск (-а)** м search; (*нау́чный*)
quest; *см. также* **по́иски**

**по|иска́ть (-ищу́, -и́щешь)** *сов
перех* to have a look for

**по́иск|и (-ов)** *мн*: **~** (+gen) search

*ед* (for); **в ~ах** +*gen* in search of
**по|и́ть** (-ю́, -ишь; *imper* **-й(те)**; *pf*
**на~**) *несов перех*: **~ кого́-н
чем-н** to give sb sth to drink
**пойду́** *etc сов см.* **пойти́**
**пойма́|ть** (-ю) *сов от* **лови́ть**
♦ *перех* to catch
**пойму́** *etc сов см.* **поня́ть**
**пойти́** (*как* **идти́**; *см. Table 18*) *сов*
to set off; (*по пути реформ*) to
start off; (*о механизмах, к цели*)
to start working; (*дождь, снег*)
to begin to fall; (*дым, пар*) to
begin to rise; (*кровь*) to start flowing;
(*фильм итп*) to start showing;
(*подойти*): **~** +*dat или* **к** +*dat*
(*шляпа, поведение*) to suit

KEYWORD

**пока́** *нареч* 1 (*некоторое время*)
for a while
**2** (*тем временем*) in the
meantime
♦ *союз* 1 (*в то время как*) while
**2** (*до того времени как*): **пока́ не**
until; **пока́!** so long!; **пока́ что** for
the moment

**покажу́(сь)** *etc сов см.*
**показа́ть(ся)**
**пока́з** (-а) *м* (*фильма*) showing;
(*опыта*) demonstration
**показа́ни|е** (-я) *ср* (ЮР, *обычно
мн*) evidence *ед*; (*на счётчике
итп*) reading
**показа́тел|ь** (-я) *м* indicator;
(МАТ, ЭКОН) index
**показа́тельный** *прил* (*пример*)
revealing
**пока|за́ть** (-жу́, -жешь; *impf*
**пока́зывать**) *сов перех* to show
♦ *неперех* (*на суде*) to testify;
**пока́зывать** (**~** *pf*) **приме́р** to set
an example; **~ся** *сов от* **каза́ться**
♦ (*impf* **пока́зываться**) *возв* to

appear; **пока́зываться** (**~ся** *pf*)
**врачу́** to see a doctor
**поката́|ть** (-ю) *сов перех*: **~
кого́-н на маши́не** to take sb for a
drive; **~ся** *сов возв* to go for a
ride
**пок|ати́ть** (-ачу́, -а́тишь) *сов
перех* (*что-н круглое*) to roll;
(*что-н на колёсах*) to wheel; **~ся**
*сов возв* to start rolling *или* to roll
**покача́|ть** (-ю) *сов перех* to rock
♦ *неперех*: **~ голово́й** to shake
one's head; **~ся** *сов возв* (*на
качелях*) to swing
**пока́чива|ться** (-юсь) *несов
возв* to rock
**покая́ни|е** (-я) *ср* repentance
**поки́н|уть** (-у; *impf* **покида́ть**)
*сов перех* to abandon
**поклада́я**: **не ~ рук** tirelessly
**покло́н** (-а) *м* (*жест*) bow;
(*приветствие*) greeting
**покл|они́ться** (-оню́сь,
-о́нишься) *сов от* **кла́няться**
**покло́нник** (-а) *м* admirer
**поклоня́|ться** (-юсь) *несов
возв*: **~** +*dat* to worship
**поко́|иться** (*3sg* **-ится**) *несов
возв*: **~ на** +*prp* to rest on
**поко́|й** (-я) *м* peace; **оставля́ть
(оста́вить** *pf*) **кого́-н в ~е** to leave
sb in peace
**поко́йный** *прил* the late ♦ (**-ого**)
*м* the deceased
**поколе́ни|е** (-я) *ср* generation
**поко́нч|ить** (-у, -ишь) *сов*: **~ с**
+*instr* (*с делами*) to be finished
with; (*с бедностью, с
проблемой*) to put an end to; **~**
(*pf*) **с собо́й** to kill o.s., commit
suicide
**покор|и́ть** (-ю́, -и́шь; *impf*
**покоря́ть**) *сов перех* (*страну,
народ*) to conquer; **покоря́ть** (**~**
*pf*) **кого́-н** (*заставить любить*) to

win sb's heart; **~ся** (impf
**покоря́ться**) сов возв: **~ся** +dat
to submit (to)
**покóрный** прил submissive
**покрови́тельств**|**о** (**-а**) ср
protection
**покрó**|**й** (**-я**) ср cut (of clothing)
**покрыва́л**|**о** (**-а**) ср bedspread
**покры́ти**|**е** (**-я**) ср covering
**покр**|**ы́ть** (**-óю, -óешь**) сов от
**крыть** ♦ (impf **покрыва́ть**) перех
(звуки) to cover up; (расходы,
расстояние) to cover; **~ся** (impf
**покрыва́ться**) сов возв: **~ся**
+instr (одеялом) to cover o.s. with;
(снегом итп) to be covered in
**покры́ш**|**ка** (**-ки**; gen pl **-ек**) ж
(АВТ) tyre (BRIT), tire (US)
**покупа́тель**|**ь** (**-я**) м buyer; (в
магазине) customer
**покупа́тельский** прил (спрос,
интересы) consumer
**покупа́**|**ть** (**-ю**) несов от **купи́ть**
**покýп**|**ка** (**-ки**; gen pl **-ок**) ж
purchase; **де́лать** (**сде́лать** pf) **~ки**
to go shopping
**покуша́**|**ться** (**-юсь**) несов возв:
**~ на** +acc to attempt to take
**покуше́ни**|**е** (**-я**) ср: **~** (**на** +acc)
(на свободу, на права)
infringement (of); (на жизнь)
attempt (on)
**пол** (**-а**; loc sg **-ý**, nom pl **-ы́**) м
floor; (nom pl **-ы**, gen pl **-óв**, dat pl
**-áм**) sex
**полага́**|**ть** (**-ю**) несов (думать) to
suppose; **на́до ~** supposedly
**пол**|**го́да** (**-уго́да**) ср/мн half a
year
**пóлдень** (**полу́дня** или
**пóлдня**) м midday, noon; **2 часа́
по́сле полу́дня** 2 p.m
**пóл**|**е** (**-я**; nom pl **-я́**, gen pl **-е́й**) ср
field; **~ де́ятельности** sphere of
activity; **~ зре́ния** field of vision

**полев**|**óй** прил (цветок) meadow;
**~ команди́р** warlord; **~ые рабо́ты**
work in the fields
**поле́зн**|**ый** прил useful; (пища)
healthy; **~ые ископа́емые**
minerals
**поле́з**|**ть** (**-у, -ешь**) сов: **~ на**
+acc (на гору) to start climbing
или to climb; (pf) **в** +acc (в
драку, в спор) to get involved in;
**~** (pf) **в карма́н** to put one's hand
in(to) one's pocket
**поле́мик**|**а** (**-и**) ж polemic
**поле́н**|**о** (**-а**; nom pl **-ья**, gen pl
**-ьев**) ср log
**полёт** (**-а**) м flight
**поле**|**те́ть** (**-чу́, -ти́шь**) сов
(птица, самолёт) to fly off;
(время) to start to fly by
**пóлза**|**ть** (**-ю**) несов to crawl
**полз**|**ти́** (**-ý, -ёшь**; pt **-, -ла́**)
несов to crawl
**ползунк**|**и́** (**-óв**) мн rompers мн
**полива́**|**ть** (**-ю**) несов от **поли́ть**
**поливитами́н**|**ы** (**-ов**) мн
multivitamins мн
**полиго́н** (**-а**) м (для учений)
shooting range; (для испытания
оружия) test(ing) site
**поликли́ник**|**а** (**-и**) ж health
centre (BRIT) или center (US)

**поликли́ника** - health centre.
These centres are staffed by a
range of specialist doctors:
surgeons, eye doctors,
dermatologists etc. Patients can
make an appointment with a
number of doctors at any time.

**поли́р**|**ова́ть** (**-у́ю**; pf **от~**) несов
перех to polish
**пóлис** (**-а**) м: **страхово́й ~**
insurance policy
**политехни́ческий** прил: **~**

**институ́т** polytechnic
**поли́тик** (-а) *м* politician
**поли́тик**|**а** (-и) *ж* (*курс*) policy; (*события, наука*) politics
**полити́ческий** *прил* political
**пол**|**и́ть** (-ью́, -ьёшь; *pt* -и́л, -ила́, *impf* **полива́ть**) *сов* (*дождь*) to start pouring *или* to pour down ♦ *перех*: ~ **что-н** **чем-н** (*соусом*) to pour sth over sth; **полива́ть** (~ *pf*) **цветы́** to water the flowers
**полице́йск**|**ий** *прил* police ♦ (-**ого**) *м* policeman ~ **уча́сток** police station
**поли́ци**|**я** (-и) *ж* the police
**поли́чн**|**ое** (-**ого**) *ср*: **пойма́ть кого́-н с ~ым** to catch sb at the scene of a crime; (*перен*) to catch sb red-handed *или* in the act
**полиэтиле́н** (-а) *м* polythene
**полк** (-а́; *loc sg* -**ý**) *м* regiment
**по́л**|**ка** (-ки; *gen pl* -**ок**) *ж* shelf; (*в поезде: для багажа*) luggage rack; (*: для лежания*) berth; **кни́жная** ~ bookshelf
**полко́вник** (-а) *м* colonel
**полне́**|**ть** (-ю; *pf* **по~**) *несов* to put on weight
**полномо́чи**|**е** (-я) *ср* authority; (*обычно мн: право*) power
**полномо́чный** *прил* fully authorized
**полноправный** *прил* (*гражданин*) fully-fledged; (*наследник*) rightful
**по́лностью** *нареч* fully, completely
**полноце́нный** *прил* proper
**пол**|**ночь** (-**ýночи**) *ж* midnight
**по́лный** *прил* full; (*победа, счастье итп*) complete, total; (*толстый*) stout; ~ +*gen или* +*instr* full of; (*тревоги, любви итп*) filled with

**полови́к** (-а́) *м* mat
**полови́н**|**а** (-ы) *ж* half; **на ~е доро́ги** halfway; **сейча́с ~ пе́рвого/второ́го** it's (now) half past twelve/one
**поло́вник** (-а) *м* ladle
**полово́дь**|**е** (-я) *ср* high water
**полово́й** *прил* (*тряпка, мастика*) floor; (*БИО*) sexual
**положе́ни**|**е** (-я) *ср* situation; (*географическое*) location, position; (*тела, головы итп*) position; (*социальное, семейное итп*) status; (*правила*) regulations *мн*; (*обычно мн: тезис*) point; **она́ в ~и** (*разг*) she's expecting; ~ **дел** the state of affairs
**поло́женный** *прил* due
**положи́тельный** *прил* positive
**пол**|**ожи́ть** (-ожу́, -о́жишь) *сов* **от класть**
**поло́м**|**ка** (-ки; *gen pl* -**ок**) *ж* breakdown
**полос**|**а́** (-ы́; *nom pl* **по́лосы**, *gen pl* **поло́с**, *dat pl* **по́ласам**) *ж* (*ткани, металла*) strip; (*на ткани, на рисунке итп*) stripe
**полоса́тый** *прил* striped, stripy
**поло́с**|**ка** (-ки; *gen pl* -**ок**) *ж* (*ткани, бумаги*) (thin) strip; (*на ткани*) (thin) stripe; **в ~ку** striped
**пол**|**оска́ть** (-ощу́, -о́щешь; *pf* **про~**) *несов перех* (*бельё, посуду*) to rinse; (*рот*) to rinse out
**по́лост**|**ь** (-и; *gen pl* -**е́й**) *ж* (*АНАТ*) cavity
**полоте́н**|**це** (-ца; *gen pl* -**ец**) *ср* towel
**пол**|**отно́** (-отна́; *nom pl* -**о́тна**, *gen pl* -**о́тен**) *ср* (*ткань*) sheet; (*картина*) canvas
**пол**|**о́ть** (-ю, -ешь; *pf* **про~**) *несов перех* to weed
**полпути́** *м нескл* half (*of journey*); **на ~** halfway

**пол|тора́** (-у́тора; (f ~торы́) м/ср чис one and a half

**полуботи́н|ок** (-ка) м ankle boot

**полуго́ди|е** (-я) ср (ПРОСВЕЩ) semester; (ЭКОН) half (of the year)

**полузащи́т|а** (-ы) ж midfield

**полузащи́тник** (-а) м midfielder

**полукру́г** (-а) м semicircle

**полумра́к** (-а) м semidarkness

**полуо́стров** (-а) м peninsular

**полупальто́** ср нескл jacket, short coat

**полупроводни́к** (-а́) м (ЭЛЕК) semiconductor

**полуфабрика́т** (-а) м (КУЛИН) partially prepared food

**полуфина́л** (-а) м semifinal

**получа́тель** (-я) м recipient

**получа́|ть(ся)** (-ю(сь)) несов от **получи́ть(ся)**

**получе́ни|е** (-я) ср receipt; (урожая, результата) obtaining

**пол|учи́ть** (-учу́, -у́чишь; impf **получа́ть**) сов перех to receive, get; (урожай, насморк, удовольствие) to get; (известность) to gain ♦ неперех (разг: быть наказанным) to get it in the neck; **~ся** (impf **получа́ться**) сов возв to turn out; (удасться) to work; (фотография) to come out; **из него́ ~у́чится хоро́ший учи́тель** he'll make a good teacher; **у меня́ э́то не ~уча́ется** I can't do it

**получ|ка** (-ки; gen pl -ек) ж (разг) pay

**полуша́ри|е** (-я) ср hemisphere

**пол|часа́** (-уча́са) м half an hour

**по́лый** прил hollow

**по́льз|а** (-ы) ж benefit; **в ~у** +gen in favour (BRIT) или favor (US) of

**по́льзовани|е** (-я) ср: **~** (+instr) use (of)

**по́льз|оваться** (-уюсь; pf вос~)

*несов возв*: **~** +instr to use; (no pf; авторитетом, успехом итп) to enjoy

**по́льский** прил Polish; **~ язы́к** Polish

**По́льш|а** (-и) ж Poland

**пол|юби́ть** (-юблю́, -ю́бишь) сов перех (человека) to come to love; **~** (pf) **что-н**/ +infin to develop a love for sth/doing

**по́люс** (-а; nom pl -а́) м pole

**пол|я́** (-е́й) мн (шляпы) brim ед; (на страни́це) margin ед

**поля́н|а** (-ы) ж glade

**поля́рный** прил (ГЕО) polar; (разные) diametrically opposed

**пома́д|а** (-ы) ж (также: губна́я **~**) lipstick

**пом|аха́ть** (-ашу́, -а́шешь) сов: **~** +instr to wave

**поме́дл|ить** (-ю, -ишь) сов: **~ с** +instr/ +infin to linger over sth/doing

**поменя́|ть(ся)** (-ю(сь)) сов от **меня́ть(ся)**

**поме́р|ить** (-ю, -ишь) сов от **ме́рить**

**поме|сти́ть** (-щу́, -сти́шь; impf **помеща́ть**) сов перех to put; **~ся** (impf **помеща́ться**) сов возв (уместиться) to fit

**помёт** (-а) м dung; (птиц) droppings мн; (детёныши) litter

**помёт|а** (-ы) ж note

**помё|тить** (-чу, -тишь) сов от **ме́тить** ♦ (impf **помеча́ть**) перех to note

**помё́т|ка** (-ки; gen pl -ок) ж note

**поме́х|а** (-и) ж hindrance; (СВЯЗЬ, обычно мн) interference ед

**помеча́|ть** (-ю) несов от **помётить**

**помеша́|ть** (-ю) сов от **меша́ть**

**помеща́|ть(ся)** (-ю(сь)) несов от **помести́ть(ся)**

**помеще́ни|е** (-я) ср room; (под

офис) premises мн; **жило́е ~** living space

**помидо́р (-а)** м tomato

**поми́л|овать (-ую)** сов от **ми́ловать**

**поми́мо** предл: **~** +gen besides; (без участия) bypassing; **~ того́/ всего́ про́чего** apart from that/ anything else

**поми́н|ки (-ок)** мн wake ед

**помину́тный** прил at one-minute intervals; (очень частый) constant

**помир|и́ть(ся) (-ю́(сь), -и́шь(ся))** сов от **мири́ть(ся)**

**по́мн|ить (-ю, -ишь)** несов (не)перех: **~ (о** +prp или **про** +асс) to remember

**помо́г** итп сов см. **помо́чь**

**помога́|ть (-ю)** несов от **помо́чь**

**по-мо́ему** нареч my way ♦ вводн сл in my opinion

**помо́|и (-ев)** мн dishwater ед; (отходы) slops мн

**помо́йка (-йки;** gen pl **-ек)** ж (яма) cesspit; (для мусора) rubbish (BRIT) или garbage (US) heap

**помолч|а́ть (-у́, -и́шь)** сов to pause

**помо́рщ|иться (-усь, -ишься)** сов возв to screw up one's face

**помо́ст (-а)** м (для обозрения) platform; (для выступлений) rostrum

**пом|о́чь (-огу́, -о́жешь** итп, **-о́гут;** pt **-о́г, -огла́;** impf **помога́ть)** сов: **~** +dat to help; (другой стране) to aid

**помо́щник (-а)** м helper; (должность) assistant

**по́мощ|ь (-и)** ж help, assistance

**пом|ы́ть(ся) (-о́ю(сь), -о́ешь(ся))** сов от **мы́ть(ся)**

**помя́тый** прил rumpled; (бок машины) dented

**пона́доб|иться (-люсь, -ишься)** сов возв to be needed

**по-настоя́щему** нареч properly

**по-на́шему** нареч our way

**понеде́льник (-а)** м Monday

**понемно́гу** нареч a little; (постепенно) little by little

**пон|ести́ (-есу́, -есёшь;** pt **-ёс, -есла́)** сов от **нести́; ~сь** сов возв (человек) to tear off; (лошадь) to charge off; (машина) to speed off

**по́ни** м нескл pony

**понижа́|ть(ся) (-ю(сь))** несов от **пони́зить(ся)**

**пониже́ни|е (-я)** ср reduction; (в должности) demotion

**пони́|зить (-жу, -зишь;** impf **понижа́ть)** сов перех to reduce; (в должности) to demote; (голос) to lower; **~ся** (impf **понижа́ться)** сов возв to be reduced

**понима́|ть (-ю)** несов от **поня́ть** ♦ перех to understand ♦ неперех: **~ в** +prp to know about; **~ете** you see

**поно́с (-а)** м diarrhoea (BRIT), diarrhea (US)

**пон|оси́ть (-ошу́, -о́сишь)** сов перех to carry for a while; (одежду) to wear

**поно́шенный** прил (одежда) worn

**понра́в|иться (-люсь, -ишься)** сов от **нра́виться**

**по́нчик (-а)** м doughnut (BRIT), donut (US)

**поня́ти|е (-я)** ср notion; (знание) idea; **~я не име́ю** (разг) I've no idea

**поня́тно** нареч intelligibly ♦ как сказ: **мне ~** I understand; **~!** I see!; **~?** got it?

**поня́тный** прил intelligible; (ясный) clear; (оправданный) understandable

**по|ня́ть (-йму́, -ймёшь;** *pt* **-нял, -няла́;** *impf* **понима́ть)** *сов перех* to understand

**поощре́ни|е (-я)** *ср* encouragement

**поощр|и́ть (-ю́, -и́шь;** *impf* **поощря́ть)** *сов перех* to encourage

**поп (-а́)** *м* (*разг*) priest

**попада́ни|е (-я)** *ср* hit

**попада́|ть(ся) (-ю(сь))** *несов от* **попа́сть(ся)**

**попа́рно** *нареч* in pairs

**попа́|сть (-ду́, -дёшь;** *impf* **попада́ть)** *сов:* ~ **в** +*acc* (*в цель*) to hit; (*в ворота*) to end up in; (*в чужой город*) to find o.s. in; (*в беду*) to land in; **мы́ло ~ло мне в глаза́** the soap got in my eyes; **попада́ть (~** *pf*) **в ава́рию** to have an accident; **попада́ть (~** *pf*) **в плен** to be taken prisoner; **попада́ть (~** *pf*) **под дождь** to be caught in the rain; **ему́ ~ло** (*разг*) he got a hiding; (**Вы**) **не туда́ ~ли** you've got the wrong number; ~**ся** (*impf* **попада́ться**) *сов возв* (*преступник*) to be caught; **мне ~лась интере́сная кни́га** I came across an interesting book; **попада́ться (~ся** *pf*) **кому́-н на глаза́** to catch sb's eye

**попе́й(те)** *сов см.* **попи́ть**

**поперёк** *нареч* crossways
♦ *предл:* ~ +*gen* across

**попере́чный** *прил* horizontal

**поперхн|у́ться (-у́сь, -ёшься)** *сов возв* to choke

**попе́рч|ить (-у, -ишь)** *сов от* **пе́рчить**

**попече́ни|е (-я)** *ср* (*о детях*) care; (*о делах, о доме*) charge

**попечи́тел|ь (-я)** *м* guardian; (*КОММ*) trustee

**поп|и́ть (-ью́, -ьёшь;** *pt* **-и́л, -ила́,** *imper* **-е́й(те))** *сов перех* to have a drink of

**попл|ы́ть (-ву́, -вёшь;** *pt* **-л, -ла́)** *сов* to start swimming; (*судно*) to set sail

**попола́м** *нареч* in half; ~ **с** +*instr* mixed with

**пополне́ни|е (-я)** *ср* (*запасов*) replenishment; (*коллекции*) expansion; (*воинское*) reinforcement

**попо́лн|ить (-ю, -ишь;** *impf* **пополня́ть)** *сов перех:* ~ **что-н** +*instr* (*запасы*) to replenish sth with; (*коллекцию*) to expand sth with; (*коллектив*) to reinforce sth with; ~**ся** (*impf* **пополня́ться**) *сов возв* (*запасы*) to be replenished; (*коллекция*) to be expanded

**попра́в|ить (-лю, -ишь;** *impf* **поправля́ть)** *сов перех* to correct; (*галстук, платье*) to straighten; (*причёску*) to tidy; (*здоровье, дела*) to improve; ~**ся** (*impf* **поправля́ться**) *сов возв* to improve; (*пополнеть*) to put on weight

**попра́в|ка (-ки;** *gen pl* **-ок)** *ж* (*ошибки*) correction; (*в решение, в закон*) amendment

**по-пре́жнему** *нареч* as before; (*всё ещё*) still

**попро́б|овать (-ую)** *сов от* **про́бовать**

**попр|оси́ть(ся) (-ошу́(сь), -о́сишь(ся))** *сов от* **проси́ть(ся)**

**попроща́|ться (-юсь)** *сов возв:* ~ **с** +*instr* to say goodbye to

**попуга́|й (-я)** *м* parrot

**популя́рност|ь (-и)** *ж* popularity

**популя́рный** *прил* popular; (*понятный*) accessible

**попу́тный** *прил* (*замечание*)

accompanying; (*машина*) passing; (*ветер*) favourable (*BRIT*), favorable (*US*)

**попу́тчик** (**-а**) *м* travelling (*BRIT*) *или* traveling (*US*) companion

**попы́т|ка** (**-ки**; *gen pl* **-ок**) *ж* attempt

**попью́** *итп сов см.* **попи́ть**

**попя́|титься** (**-чусь, -тишься**) *сов возв* to take a few steps backwards (*BRIT*) *или* backward (*US*)

**по́р|а** (**-ы**) *ж* pore

**пор|а́** (**-ы́**; *acc sg* **-у́**, *dat sg* **-е́**, *nom pl* **-ы**) *ж* time ♦ *как сказ* it's time; **до каки́х ~?** until when?; **до сих ~** (*раньше*) up till now; (*всё ещё*) still; **до тех ~** until then; **до тех ~, пока́** until; **с каки́х ~?** since when?

**поравня́|ться** (**-юсь**) *сов возв*: **~ с** +*instr* (*человек*) to draw level with; (*машина*) to come alongside

**пораже́ни|е** (**-я**) *ср* (*цели*) hitting; (*МЕД*) damage; (*проигрыш*) defeat; **наноси́ть** (**нанести́** *pf*) **кому́-н ~** to defeat sb; **терпе́ть** (**потерпе́ть** *pf*) **~** to be defeated

**порази́тельный** *прил* striking; (*о неприятном*) astonishing

**пора́н|ить** (**-ю, -ишь**) *сов перех* to hurt

**порв|а́ть(ся)** (**-у́, -ёшь**) *сов от* **рва́ть(ся)**

**поре́з** (**-а**) *м* cut

**поре́|зать** (**-жу, -жешь**) *сов перех* to cut; **~ся** *сов возв* to cut o.s.

**порногра́фи|я** (**-и**) *ж* pornography

**по́ровну** *нареч* equally

**поро́г** (**-а**) *м* (*также перен*) threshold

**поро́д|а** (**-ы**) *ж* (*животных*) breed

**поро́дистый** *прил* pedigree

**поро́й** *нареч* from time to time

**поро́к** (**-а**) *м* vice; (*МЕД*) abnormality

**пороло́н** (**-а**) *м* foam rubber

**порос|ёнок** (**-ёнка**; *nom pl* **-я́та**, *gen pl* **-я́т**) *м* piglet

**по́рох** (**-а**; *part gen* **-у**) *м* gunpowder

**порош|о́к** (**-ка́**) *м* powder

**порт** (**-а**; *loc sg* **-у́**, *nom pl* **-ы**, *gen pl* **-о́в**) *м* port

**портати́вный** *прил* portable

**портве́йн** (**-а**) *м* port (*wine*)

**по́р|тить** (**-чу, -тишь**; *pf* **ис~**) *несов перех* to damage; (*настроение, праздник, ребёнка*) to spoil; **~ся** (*pf* **ис~ся**) *сов возв* (*механизм*) to be damaged; (*здоровье, погода*) to deteriorate; (*настроение*) to be spoiled; (*молоко*) to go off; (*мясо, овощи*) to go bad

**портни́х|а** (**-и**) *ж* (*женская*) dressmaker; (*мужская*) tailor

**портн|о́й** (**-о́го**) *м* (*мужской*) tailor; (*женский*) dressmaker

**портре́т** (**-а**) *м* portrait

**Португа́ли|я** (**-и**) *ж* Portugal

**португа́льский** *прил* Portuguese; **~ язы́к** Portuguese

**портфе́л|ь** (**-я**) *м* briefcase; (*ПОЛИТ, КОММ*) portfolio

**портье́р|а** (**-ы**) *ж* curtain

**поруга́|ться** (**-юсь**) *сов от* **руга́ться** ♦ *возв* (*разг*): **~ся (с** +*instr*) to fall out (with)

**пору́к|а** (**-и**) *ж*: **брать кого́-н на ~и** to take sb on probation; (*ЮР*) to stand bail for sb

**по-ру́сски** *нареч* (*говорить, писать*) in Russian; **говори́ть** (*impf*)/**понима́ть** (*impf*) **~** to speak/ understand Russian

**поруча́|ть** (**-ю**) *несов от* **поручи́ть**

**поручéни|е** (-я) *ср* (*задание*)
errand; (: *важное*) mission
**пóруч|ень** (-ня) *м* handrail
**поручи́тельств|о** (-а) *ср*
guarantee
**пор|учи́ть** (-учý, -ýчишь; *impf*
**поруча́ть**) *сов*: ~ **комý-н что-н**
to entrust sb with sth; **поручи́ть** (~
*pf*) **комý-н** +*infin* to instruct sb to
do; **поруча́ть** (~ *pf*) **комý-н
когó-н/что-н** (*отдать на
попечение*) to leave sb/sth in sb's
care; **~ся** *сов от* **руча́ться**
**пóрци|я** (-и) *ж* portion
**пóрш|ень** (-ня) *м* (*в двигателе*)
piston; (*в насосе*) plunger
**поры́в** (-а) *м* (*ветра*) gust
**поры́вистый** *прил* (*ветер*) gusty
**поря́дков|ый** *прил* (*номер*)
ordinal; **~ое числи́тельное**
ordinal (number)
**поря́д|ок** (-ка) *м* order;
(*правила*) procedure; **в ~ке** +*gen*
(*в качестве*) as; **в ~ке** in order;
**всё в ~ке** everything's OK; **~ дня**
agenda
**поря́дочный** *прил* (*честный*)
decent; (*значительный*) fair
**пос|ади́ть** (-ажý, -áдишь) *сов
от* **сажа́ть**
**посáд|ка** (-ки; *gen pl* -ок) *ж*
(*овощей*) planting; (*пассажиров*)
boarding; (*самолёта итп*) landing
**посáдочный** *прил* (*талон*)
boarding; (*площадка*) landing
**по-свóему** *нареч* his *итп* way; **он
~ прав** in his own way, he is right
**посвя|ти́ть** (-щý, -ти́шь; *impf*
**посвяща́ть**) *сов перех*: **~ что-н**
+*dat* to devote sth to; (*книгу*) to
dedicate sth to
**посéв** (-а) *м* sowing
**посéв|ы** (-ов) *мн* crops *мн*
**поселéни|е** (-я) *ср* settlement
**пос|ели́ть(ся)** (-елю́(сь),

**-éлишь(ся)**) *сов от* **сели́ть(ся)**
**посёл|ок** (-ка) *м* village; **дáчный
~** village made up of dachas
**посереди́не** *нареч* in the middle
♦ *предл*: ~ +*gen* in the middle of
**посети́тел|ь** (-я) *м* visitor
**посе|ти́ть** (-щý, -ти́шь; *impf*
**посеща́ть**) *сов перех* to visit
**посещéни|е** (-я) *ср* visit
**посé|ять** (-ю, -ишь) *сов от*
**сéять**
**поси|дéть** (-жý, -ди́шь) *сов* to
sit for a while
**поскользн|ýться** (-ýсь, -ёшься)
*сов возв* to slip
**поскóльку** *союз* as
**послáни|е** (-я) *ср* message
**послáнник** (-а) *м* envoy
**по|слáть** (-шлю́, -шлёшь; *impf*
**посыла́ть**) *сов перех* to send
**пóсле** *нареч* (*потом*) afterwards
(*BRIT*), afterward (*US*) ♦ *предл*: ~
+*gen* after ♦ *союз*: ~ **тогó как** after
**послевоéнный** *прил* postwar
**послéдн|ий** *прил* last; (*новости,
мода*) latest; **за** или **в ~ее врéмя**
recently
**послéдовател|ь** (-я) *м* follower
**послéдовательност|ь** (-и) *ж*
sequence; (*политики*) consistency
**послéдовательный** *прил* (*один
за другим*) consecutive;
(*логический*) consistent
**послéд|овать** (-ую) *сов от*
**слéдовать**
**послéдстви|е** (-я) *ср*
consequence
**послезáвтра** *нареч* the day after
tomorrow
**послóвиц|а** (-ы) *ж* proverb,
saying
**послýша|ть** (-ю) *сов от*
**слýшать** ♦ *перех*: **~ что-н** to
listen to sth for a while; **~ся** *сов от*
**слýшаться**

**послу́шный** *прил* obedient

**посме́|ть** (-ю) *сов от* **сметь**

**посм|отре́ть** (-отрю́, -о́тришь) *сов от* **смотре́ть** ♦ *непepex*: ~о́трим (*разг*) we'll see; ~ся *сов от* **смотре́ться**

**посо́би|е** (-я) *ср* (*помощь*) benefit; (*ПРОСВЕЩ, учебник*) textbook; (: нагля́дное) visual aids *мн*; ~ по безрабо́тице unemployment benefit; ~ по инвали́дности disability living allowance

**пос|о́л** (-ла́) *м* ambassador

**посол|и́ть** (-олю́, -о́лишь) *сов от* **соли́ть**

**посо́льств|о** (-а) *ср* embassy

**посп|е́ть** (3sg -е́ет) *сов от* **спеть**

**поспеш|и́ть** (-у́, -и́шь) *сов от* **спеши́ть**

**поспо́р|ить** (-ю, -ишь) *сов от* **спо́рить**

**посреди́** *нареч* in the middle ♦ *предл*: ~ +gen in the middle of

**посреди́не** *нареч* in the middle ♦ *предл*: ~ +gen in the middle of

**посре́дник** (-а) *м* intermediary; (*при конфли́кте*) mediator; **торго́вый** ~ middleman

**посре́днический** *прил* (*КОММ*) intermediary; (*услуги*) agent's

**посре́дничеств|о** (-а) *ср* mediation

**посре́дственно** *нареч* (*учиться, писать*) averagely ♦ *ср нескл* (*ПРОСВЕЩ*) ≈ satisfactory (*school mark*)

**посре́дственный** *прил* mediocre

**посре́дством** *предл*: ~ +gen by means of; (*человека*) through

**поссо́р|ить(ся)** (-ю(сь), -ишь(ся)) *сов от* **ссо́рить(ся)**

**пост** (-а́; *loc sg* -у́) *м* (*лю́ди*) guard; (*место*) lookout post; (*до́лжность*) post; (*РЕЛ*) fast

**поста́в|ить** (-лю, -ишь) *сов от* **ста́вить** ♦ (*impf* **поставля́ть**) *перех* (*това́р*) to supply

**поста́в|ка** (-ки; *gen pl* -ок) *ж* (*снабже́ние*) supply

**поставщи́к** (-а́) *м* supplier

**постаме́нт** (-а) *м* pedestal

**постан|ови́ть** (-овлю́, -о́вишь; *impf* **постановля́ть**) *сов*: ~ +infin to resolve to do

**постано́в|ка** (-ки; *gen pl* -ок) *ж* (*ТЕАТР*) production; ~ вопро́са/ пробле́мы the formulation of the question/problem

**постановле́ни|е** (-я) *ср* (*реше́ние*) resolution; (*распоряже́ние*) decree

**постано́вщик** (-а) *м* producer

**постара́|ться** (-юсь) *сов от* **стара́ться**

**пост|ели́ть** (-елю́, -е́лишь) *сов от* **стели́ть**

**посте́л|ь** (-и) *ж* bed

**посте́льн|ый** *прил*: ~ое бельё bedclothes *мн*

**постепе́нно** *нареч* gradually

**постепе́нный** *прил* gradual

**постира́|ть** (-ю) *сов от* **стира́ть**

**по|сти́ться** (-щу́сь, -сти́шься) *несов возв* (*РЕЛ*) to fast

**по́стн|ый** *прил* (*суп*) vegetarian; ~ое ма́сло vegetable oil

**посто́льку** *союз*: ~ ... поско́льку insofar as ...

**посторо́нн|ий** *прил* (*чужо́й*) strange; (*по́мощь, влия́ние*) outside; (*вопро́с*) irrelevant ♦ (-его) *м* stranger, outsider; ~им вход воспрещён authorized entry only

**постоя́нн|ый** *прил* (*рабо́та, а́дрес*) permanent; (*шум*) constant; ~ое запомина́ющее устро́йство ROM

**посто|я́ть** (-ю́, -и́шь) *сов от*

**стоя́ть ♦** *неперех* (*стоять недолго*) to stand for a while
**постри|чь(ся)** (**-гу́(сь), -жёшь(ся)** *итп,* **-гу́т(ся);** *pt* **-г(ся), -гла́(сь)**) *сов от* **стри́чь(ся)**
**постро́|ить** (**-ю, -ишь**) *сов от* **стро́ить**
**постро́|йка** (**-йки;** *gen pl* **-ек**) *ж* construction; (*здание*) building
**пост|упи́ть** (**-уплю́, -у́пишь;** *impf* **поступа́ть**) *сов* (*человек*) to act; (*товар, известия*) to come in; (*жалоба*) to be received; **поступа́ть** (*~ pf*) **в/на** *+acc* (*в университет, на работу*) to start
**поступле́ни|е** (**-я**) *ср* (*действие: в университет, на работу*) starting; (*обычно мн: бюджетное*) revenue *ед*; (*в библиотеке*) acquisition
**посту́п|ок** (**-ка**) *м* deed
**посту́ч|а́ть(ся)** (**-у́(сь), -и́шь(ся)**) *сов от* **стуча́ть(ся)**
**посу́д|а** (**-ы**) *ж собир* crockery; **ку́хонная ~** kitchenware; **стекля́нная ~** glassware; **мыть** (**помы́ть** *pf*) **~у** to wash the dishes, wash up
**посчита́|ть** (**-ю**) *сов от* **счита́ть**
**посыла́|ть** (**-ю**) *несов от* **посла́ть**
**посы́л|ка** (**-ки;** *gen pl* **-ок**) *ж* (*действие: книг, денег*) sending; (*посланное*) parcel
**посы́п|ать** (**-лю, -лешь**) *сов перех* to sprinkle; **~ся** *сов от* **сы́паться**
**пот** (**-а;** *loc sg* **-у́**) *м* sweat
**по-тво́ему** *нареч* your way
**потенциа́л** (**-а**) *м* potential
**потенциа́льный** *прил* potential
**потепле́ни|е** (**-я**) *ср* warmer spell
**пот|ере́ть** (**-ру́, -рёшь;** *pt* **-ёр, -ёрла**) *сов перех* (*ушиб*) to rub;

(*морковь*) to grate
**потерпе́вш|ий** (**-его**) *м* (*ЮР*) victim
**пот|ерпе́ть** (**-ерплю́, -ерпишь**) *сов от* **терпе́ть**
**поте́р|я** (**-и**) *ж* loss
**потеря́|ть(ся)** (**-ю(сь)**) *сов от* **теря́ть(ся)**
**поте́|ть** (**-ю;** *impf* **вс~**) *несов* to sweat
**по́тный** *прил* sweaty
**пото́к** (**-а**) *м* stream
**потол|о́к** (**-ка́**) *м* ceiling
**пото́м** *нареч* (*через некоторое время*) later; (*после*) then ♦ *союз:* **а/и ~** and then, anyhow; **на ~** for later
**пото́мк|и** (**-ов**) *мн* descendants *мн*
**пото́мственный** *прил* hereditary; (*право*) inherited
**пото́мств|о** (**-а**) *ср собир* descendants *мн*; (*дети*) offspring *мн*
**потому́** *нареч:* **~ (и)** that's why; **~ что** because
**пото́п** (**-а**) *м* flood
**потороп|и́ть(ся)** (**-лю́(сь), -ишь(ся)**) *сов от* **торопи́ть(ся)**
**пото́чн|ый** *прил* (*производство*) mass; **~ая ли́ния** production line
**потра́|тить** (**-чу, -тишь**) *сов от* **тра́тить**
**потреби́тел|ь** (**-я**) *м* consumer
**потреби́тельский** *прил* (*спрос*) consumer
**потреб|и́ть** (**-лю́, -и́шь**) *сов от* **потребля́ть**
**потребле́ни|е** (**-я**) *ср* (*действие*) consumption; **това́ры широ́кого ~я** consumer goods
**потребля́|ть** (**-ю;** *pf* **потреби́ть**) *несов перех* to consume
**потре́бность|** (**-и**) *ж* need
**потре́б|овать(ся)** (**-ую(сь)**) *сов*

*от* **требовать(ся)**

**потрёпанный** *прил* (*книга, одежда*) tattered; (*вид, лицо*) worn

**потрох|а́** (*-о́в*) *мн* (*птицы*) giblets *мн*

**потрош|и́ть** (*-у́, -и́шь*; *pf* **вы́потрошить**) *несов перех* (*курицу, рыбу*) to gut

**потру|ди́ться** (*-жу́сь, -дишься*) *сов возв* to work; ~ (*pf*) +*infin* to take the trouble to do

**потряса́ющий** *прил* (*музыка, стихи*) fantastic; (*красота*) stunning

**потрясе́ни|е** (*-я*) *ср* (*нервное*) breakdown; (*социальное*) upheaval; (*впечатление*) shock

**потряс|ти́** (*-у́, -ёшь*; *pt* -, *-ла́*) *сов перех* to shake; (*взволновать*) to stun

**поту́хн|уть** (*3sg* -*ет*; *impf* **потуха́ть**) *сов* (*лампа, свет*) to go out

**пот|уши́ть** (*-ушу́, -у́шишь*) *сов от* **туши́ть**

**пот|яну́ться** (*-яну́сь, -я́нешься*; *impf* **потя́гиваться**) *сов возв* (*в постели, в кресле*) to stretch out

**поу́жина|ть** (*-ю*) *сов от* **у́жинать**

**поумне́|ть** (*-ю*) *сов от* **умне́ть**

**поучи́тельный** *прил* (*пример*) instructive; (*тон*) didactic

**похвал|а́** (*-ы́*) *ж* praise

**похва́ста|ться** (*-юсь*) *сов от* **хва́статься**

**похити́тел|ь** (*-я*) *м* (*см глаг*) thief; abductor; kidnapper

**похи́|тить** (*-щу, -тишь*; *impf* **похища́ть**) *сов перех* (*предмет*) to steal; (*человека*) to abduct; (: *для выкупа*) to kidnap

**похище́ни|е** (*-я*) *ср* (*см глаг*) theft; abduction; kidnap(ping)

**похло́па|ть** (*-ю*) *сов перех* to pat

**похме́ль|е** (*-я*) *ср* hangover

**похо́д** (*-а*) *м* (*военный*) campaign; (*туристический*) hike (*walking and camping expedition*)

**пох|оди́ть** (*-ожу́, -о́дишь*) *несов*: ~ **на кого́-н/что-н** to resemble sb/sth ♦ *сов* to walk

**похо́дк|а** (*-и*) *ж* gait

**похо́ж|ий** *прил*: ~ (**на** +*acc* или **с** +*instr*) similar (to); **он** ~ **на бра́та, они́ с бра́том** ~ he looks like his brother; **они́** ~**и** they look alike; ~**е на то, что ...** it looks as if ...; **э́то на него́ (не)** ~**e** it's (not) like him

**похолода́ни|е** (*-я*) *ср* cold spell

**похолода́|ть** (*3sg* -*ет*) *сов от* **холода́ть**

**похор|они́ть** (*-оню́, -о́нишь*) *сов от* **хорони́ть**

**похоро́нн|ый** *прил* funeral; ~**ое бюро́** undertaker's

**по́хор|оны** (*-о́н*; *dat pl* -**она́м**) *мн* funeral *ед*

**поцел|ова́ть(ся)** (*-у́ю(сь)*) *сов от* **целова́ть(ся)**

**поцелу́|й** (*-я*) *м* kiss

**почасово́й** *прил* (*оплата*) hourly

**поча́т|ок** (*-ка*) *м* (*кукурузы*) cob

**по́чв|а** (*-ы*) *ж* soil; (*перен*) basis; **на** ~**e** +*gen* arising from

**почём** *нареч* (*разг*) how much?

**почему́** *нареч* why; **вот** ~ that is why

**почему́-либо** *нареч* for some reason or other

**почему́-нибудь** *нареч* = **почему́-либо**

**почему́-то** *нареч* for some reason

**по́черк** (*-а*) *м* handwriting

**почерне́|ть** (*-ю*) *сов от* **черне́ть**

**поче|са́ть(ся)** (*-шу́(сь), -шешь(ся)*) *сов от* **чеса́ть(ся)**

**почёт** (*-а*) *м* honour (*BRIT*), honor (*US*)

**почётный** прил (гость) honoured (BRIT), honored (US); (член) honorary; (обязанность) honourable (BRIT), honorable (US); ~ **карау́л** guard of honour (BRIT) или honor (US)

**поч|ини́ть** (-иню́, -и́нишь) сов от **чини́ть**

**почи́н|ка** (-ки; gen pl -ок) ж repair

**почи́|стить** (-щу, -стишь) сов от **чи́стить**

**почита́тел|ь** (-я) м admirer

**почита́|ть** (-ю) сов перех (книгу) to read ♦ несов перех to admire

**по́ч|ка** (-ки; gen pl -ек) ж (БОТ) bud; (АНАТ) kidney

**по́чт|а** (-ы) ж (учрежде́ние) post office; (пи́сьма) post, mail

**почтальо́н** (-а) м postman (BRIT) mailman (US)

**почта́мт** (-а) м main post office

**почте́ни|е** (-я) ср respect, veneration

**почти́** нареч almost, nearly; ~ что (разг) almost

**почти́тельный** прил respectful

**почти́|ть** (как чтить; см. Table 17) сов перех (память) to pay homage to

**почто́в|ый** прил postal; (ма́рка) postage; ~ая откры́тка postcard; ~ и́ндекс postcode (BRIT), zip code (US); ~ перево́д (де́ньги) postal order; ~ я́щик postbox

**почу́вств|овать** (-ую) сов от **чу́вствовать**

**пошатн|у́ть** (-у́, -ёшь) сов перех (ве́ру) to shake; (здоро́вье) to damage; ~ся сов возв to sway; (авторите́т) to be undermined

**пошёл** сов см. **пойти́**

**поши́в** (-а) м (де́йствие) sewing; **индивидуа́льный** ~ tailoring

**пошла́** etc сов см. **пойти́**

**по́шлин|а** (-ы) ж duty

**пошло́** сов см. **пойти́**

**по́шлый** прил vulgar; (анекдо́т) corny

**пошлю́** итп сов см. **посла́ть**

**пош|ути́ть** (-учу́, -у́тишь) сов от **шути́ть**

**поща́д|а** (-ы) ж mercy

**поща|ди́ть** (-жу́, -ди́шь) сов от **щади́ть**

**пощёчин|а** (-ы) ж slap across the face

**поэ́зи|я** (-и) ж poetry

**поэ́м|а** (-ы) ж poem

**поэ́т** (-а) м poet

**поэте́сс|а** (-ы) ж см. **поэ́т**

**поэти́ческий** прил poetic

**поэ́тому** нареч therefore

**пою́** итп сов см. **петь**

**по|яви́ться** (-явлю́сь, -я́вишься; impf **появля́ться**) сов возв to appear; **у него́ ~яви́лись иде́и/сомне́ния** he has had an idea/begun to have doubts

**появле́ни|е** (-я) ср appearance

**появля́|ться** (-юсь) несов от **появи́ться**

**по́яс** (-а; nom pl -а́) м (реме́нь) belt; (та́лия) waist; (ГЕО) zone

**поясне́ни|е** (-я) ср explanation; (к схе́ме) explanatory note

**поясн|и́ть** (-ю́, -и́шь; impf **поясня́ть**) сов перех to explain

**поясни́ц|а** (-ы) ж small of the back

**пр.** сокр = **прое́зд, проспе́кт**

**прабабу́ш|ка** (-ки; gen pl -ек) ж great-grandmother

**прав|а́** (-) мн (также: **води́тельские** ~) driving licence ед (BRIT), driver's license ед (US); ~ **челове́ка** human rights

**пра́вд|а** (-ы) ж truth ♦ нареч really ♦ вводн сл true ♦ как сказ it's true; ~у или по ~е говоря́ или сказа́ть to tell the truth

**правди́вый** *прил* truthful

**правдоподо́бный** *прил* plausible

**пра́вил|о** (**-а**) *ср* rule; **э́то не в мои́х ~ах** that's not my way; **как ~** as a rule; **по всем ~ам** by the rules; **~а доро́жного движе́ния** rules of the road, ≈ Highway Code

**пра́вильно** *нареч* correctly ♦ *как сказ* that's correct *или* right

**пра́вильный** *прил* correct; (*вывод, ответ*) right

**прави́тел|ь** (**-я**) *м* ruler

**прави́тельственный** *прил* government

**прави́тельств|о** (**-а**) *ср* government

**пра́в|ить** (**-лю, -ишь**) *несов перех* (*исправлять*) to correct ♦ *неперех*: **~** *+instr* (*страной*) to rule, govern; (*машиной*) to drive

**правле́ни|е** (**-я**) *ср* government; (*орган*) board

**пра́внук** (**-а**) *м* great-grandson

**пра́в|о** (**-а**; *nom pl* **-á**) *ср* (*свобода*) right; (*нормы, наука*) law; **име́ть** (*impf*) **~ на что-н**/ *+infin* to be entitled *или* have the right to sth/to do; **на ра́вных права́х с** *+instr* on equal terms with; *см. также* **права́**

**правомо́чный** *прил* (*орган*) competent; (*лицо*) authorized

**правонаруше́ни|е** (**-я**) *ср* offence

**правонаруши́тел|ь** (**-я**) *м* offender

**правописа́ни|е** (**-я**) *ср* spelling

**правопоря́д|ок** (**-ка**) *м* law and order

**правосла́ви|е** (**-я**) *ср* orthodoxy

**правосла́вн|ый** *прил* (*церковь, обряд*) orthodox ♦ (**-ого**) *м* member of the Orthodox Church

**правосу́ди|е** (**-я**) *ср* justice

**правот|а́** (**-ы́**) *ж* correctness

**пра́вый** *прил* right; (*полит*) right-wing; **он прав** he is right

**пра́вящий** *прил* ruling

**Пра́г|а** (**-и**) *ж* Prague

**праде́душ|ка** (**-ки**; *gen pl* **-ек**) *м* great-grandfather

**пра́зднеств|о** (**-а**) *ср* festival

**пра́здник** (**-а**) *м* public holiday; (*религиозный*) festival; (*нерабочий день*) holiday; (*радость, торжество*) celebration; **с ~ом!** best wishes!

**пра́здничный** *прил* (*салют, обед*) celebratory; (*одежда, настроение*) festive; **~ день** holiday

**пра́здн|овать** (**-ую**) *несов перех* to celebrate

**пра́ктик|а** (**-и**) *ж* practice; (*часть учёбы*) practical experience *или* work; **на ~е** in practice

**практика́нт** (**-а**) *м* trainee (*on placement*)

**практик|ова́ть** (**-у́ю**) *несов перех* to practise (*BRIT*), practice (*US*); **~ся** *несов возв* (*обучаться*): **~ся в чём-н** to practise sth

**практи́чески** *нареч* (*на деле*) in practice; (*по сути дела*) practically

**практи́чный** *прил* practical

**прах** (**-а**) *м* (*умершего*) ashes *мн*

**пра́чечн|ая** (**-ой**) *ж* laundry

**пребыва́ни|е** (**-я**) *ср* stay

**пребыва́|ть** (**-ю**) *несов* to be

**превзойти́** (*как* **идти́**; *см. Table 18; impf* **превосходи́ть**) *сов перех* (*врага, соперника*) to beat; (*результаты, ожидания*) to surpass; (*доходы, скорость*) to exceed

**превосхо́|дить** (**-жу́, -дишь**) *несов от* **превзойти́**

**превосхо́дно** *нареч* superbly ♦ *как сказ* it's superb ♦ *част*: **~!** (*хорошо*) excellent!

**превосхо́дн|ый** *прил* superb;
~**ая сте́пень** superlative degree

**превосхо́дств|о** (-**а**) *ср*
superiority

**превра|ти́ть** (-**щу́**, -**ти́шь**; *impf*
**превраща́ть**) *сов перех*: ~
**что-н/кого́-н в** +*acc* to turn *или*
transform sth/sb into; ~**ся** (*impf*
**превраща́ться**) *сов возв*: ~**ся** (**в**
+*acc*) to turn (into)

**превраще́ни|е** (-**я**) *ср*
transformation

**превы́|сить** (-**шу́**, -**сишь**; *impf*
**превыша́ть**) *сов перех* to
exceed

**прегра́д|а** (-**ы**) *ж* barrier

**прегра|ди́ть** (-**жу́**, -**ди́шь**; *impf*
**прегражда́ть**) *сов перех*: ~
**кому́-н доро́гу/вход** to block *или*
bar sb's way/entrance

**преда|ва́ть** (-**ю́**) *несов от*
**преда́ть**

**пре́данный** *прил* devoted

**преда́тел|ь** (-**я**) *м* traitor

**преда́тельств|о** (-**а**) *ср* treachery

**преда́ть** (*как* **дать**; *см. Table 16*;
*impf* **предава́ть**) *сов перех* to
betray; (~ *pf*) **что-н**
**гла́сности** to make sth public

**предвари́тельный** *прил*
preliminary; (*прода́жа*) advance

**предвзя́тый** *прил* prejudiced

**предви́|деть** (-**жу**, -**дишь**) *сов*
*перех* to predict

**предводи́тел|ь** (-**я**) *м* leader

**предвы́борн|ый** *прил*
(*собра́ние*) pre-election; ~**ая**
**кампа́ния** election campaign

**преде́л** (-**а**) *м* (*обычно мн*:
*города́, страны́*) boundary;
(*перен*: *прили́чия*) bound;
(: *терпе́ния*) limit; (*по́длости*,
*соверше́нства*) height;
(*мечта́ний*) pinnacle; **на ~е** at
breaking point; **в ~ах** +*gen*

(*зако́на*, *го́да*) within; (*прили́чия*)
within the bounds of; **за ~ами** +*gen*
(*страны́*, *го́рода*) outside

**преде́льный** *прил* maximum;
(*восто́рг*, *ва́жность*) utmost; ~
**срок** deadline

**предисло́ви|е** (-**я**) *ср* foreword,
preface

**предлага́ть** (-**ю**) *несов от*
**предложи́ть**

**предло́г** (-**а**) *м* pretext; (*линг*)
preposition; **под ~ом** +*gen* on the
pretext of

**предложе́ни|е** (-**я**) *ср* suggestion,
proposal; (*заму́жества*) proposal;
(*КОММ*) offer; (*ЛИНГ*) sentence;
**де́лать** (**сде́лать** *pf*) ~ **кому́-н**
(*де́вушке*) to propose to sb;
(*КОММ*) to make sb an offer;
**вноси́ть** (**внести́** *pf*) ~ (**на**
*собра́нии*) to propose a motion

**предл|ожи́ть** (-**ожу́**, -**о́жишь**;
*impf* **предлага́ть**) *сов перех* to
offer; (*план*, *кандидату́ру*) to
propose ♦ *неперех* to suggest,
propose

**предло́жный** *прил* (*ЛИНГ*)
prepositional

**предме́т** (-**а**) *м* object;
(*обсужде́ния*, *изуче́ния*) subject

**преднаме́ренный** *прил*
(*преступле́ние*) premeditated;
(*обма́н итп*) deliberate

**пре́д|ок** (-**ка**) *м* ancestor

**предоста́в|ить** (-**лю**, -**ишь**) *сов*
*перех*: ~ **что-н кому́-н** to give sb
sth ♦ *неперех*: ~ **кому́-н** +*infin*
(*выбира́ть*, *реша́ть*) to let sb do

**предостереже́ни|е** (-**я**) *ср*
warning

**предостер|е́чь** (-**егу́**, -**ежёшь**
*etc*, -**егу́т**; *pt* -**ёг**, -**егла́**; *impf*
**предостерега́ть**) *сов перех*: ~
**кого́-н** (**от** +*gen*) to warn sb
(against)

**предосторо́жност|ь** (-и) *ж* caution; **ме́ры ~и** precautionary measures, precautions

**предотвра|ти́ть** (-щу́, -ти́шь; *impf* **предотвраща́ть**) *сов перех* to prevent; (*войну́, кри́зис*) to avert

**предохрани́тел|ь** (-я) *м* safety device; (*ЭЛЕК*) fuse (*BRIT*), fuze (*US*)

**предохран|и́ть** (-ю́, -и́шь; *impf* **предохраня́ть**) *сов перех* to protect

**предпола́га|ть** (-ю) *несов от* **предположи́ть** ♦ *перех* (*тре́бовать*) to presuppose ♦ *неперех*: **~ +infin** (*намерева́ться*) to intend to do

**предположе́ни|е** (-я) *ср* (*дога́дка*) supposition

**предположи́тельно** *нареч* supposedly

**предположи́тельный** *прил* anticipated

**предпол|ожи́ть** (-ожу́, -о́жишь; *impf* **предполага́ть**) *сов перех* (*допусти́ть возмо́жность*) to assume, suppose; **~о́жим** (*возмо́жно*) let's assume *or* suppose

**предпосле́дний** *прил* (*но́мер, се́рия*) penultimate; (*в о́череди*) last but one

**предпосы́л|ка** (-ки; *gen pl* -ок) *ж* (*усло́вие*) precondition, prerequisite

**предприи́мчивый** *прил* enterprising

**предпринима́тел|ь** (-я) *м* entrepreneur, businessman

**предпринима́тельств|о** (-а) *ср* enterprise

**предпр|иня́ть** (-иму́, -и́мешь; *pt* -и́нял, -иняла́, *impf* **предпринима́ть**) *сов перех* to undertake

**предприя́ти|е** (-я) *ср* plant; (*КОММ*) enterprise, business

**предрассу́д|ок** (-ка) *м* prejudice

**председа́тел|ь** (-я) *м* chairman

**предсказа́ни|е** (-я) *ср* prediction

**предск|аза́ть** (-ажу́, -а́жешь; *impf* **предска́зывать**) *сов перех* to predict; (*чью-н судьбу́*) to foretell

**предсме́ртный** *прил* (*аго́ния*) death; (*во́ля*) last

**представи́тел|ь** (-я) *м* representative

**представи́тельный** *прил* representative

**представи́тельств|о** (-а) *ср* (*ПОЛИТ*) representation; **дипломати́ческое ~** diplomatic corps

**предста́в|ить** (-лю, -ишь; *impf* **представля́ть**) *сов перех* to present; **представля́ть** (**~** *pf*) **кого́-н кому́-н** (*познако́мить*) to introduce sb to sb; **представля́ть** (**~** *pf*) **(себе́)** to imagine; **~ся** (*impf* **представля́ться**) *несов возв* (*при знако́мстве*) to introduce o.s.; (*возмо́жность*) to present itself

**представле́ни|е** (-я) *ср* presentation; (*ТЕАТР*) performance; (*зна́ние*) idea; **не име́ть** (*impf*) **(никако́го) ~я о +prp** to have no idea about

**представля́|ть** (-ю) *несов от* **предста́вить** ♦ *перех* (*организа́цию, страну́*) to represent; **~** (*impf*) **(себе́) что-н** (*понима́ть*) to understand sth; **~ся** *несов от* **предста́виться**

**предсто|я́ть** (*3sg* -и́т) *несов* to lie ahead

**предстоя́щий** *прил* (*сезо́н*) coming; (*встре́ча*) forthcoming

**предубежде́ни|е** (-я) *ср*

prejudice
**предупре|ди́ть** (-жу́, -ди́шь; *impf* **предупрежда́ть**) *сов перех* to warn; (*остановить*) to prevent
**предупрежде́ни|е** (-я) *ср* warning; (*аварии, заболевания*) prevention
**предусм|отре́ть** (-отрю́, -о́тришь; *impf* **предусма́тривать**) *сов перех* (*учесть*) to foresee; (*приготовиться*) to provide for
**предусмотри́тельный** *прил* prudent
**предчу́встви|е** (-я) *ср* premonition
**предше́ствующий** *прил* previous
**предъяви́тел|ь** (-я) *м* bearer
**предъ|яви́ть** (-явлю́, -я́вишь; *impf* **предъявля́ть**) *сов перех* (*паспорт, билет итп*) to show; (*доказательства*) to produce; (*требования, претензии*) to make; (*иск*) to bring;
**предъявля́ть** (~ *pf*) **права́ на что-н** to lay claim to sth
**предыду́щий** *прил* previous
**предысто́ри|я** (-и) *ж* background
**прее́мник** (-а) *м* successor
**пре́жде** *нареч* (*в прошлом*) formerly; (*сначала*) first ♦ *предл*: ~ +*gen* before; ~ **всего́** first of all; ~ **чем** before
**преждевре́менный** *прил* premature
**пре́жний** *прил* former
**презента́ци|я** (-и) *ж* presentation
**презервати́в** (-а) *м* condom
**президе́нт** (-а) *м* president
**прези́диум** (-а) *м* presidium
**презира́|ть** (-ю) *несов перех* to despise
**презре́ни|е** (-я) *ср* contempt
**презри́тельный** *прил* contemptuous

**преиму́ществ|о** (-а) *ср* advantage
**прейскура́нт** (-а) *м* price list
**преклоне́ни|е** (-я) *ср*: ~ (**пе́ред** +*instr*) admiration (for)
**преклоня́|ться** (-юсь) *несов возв*: ~ **пе́ред** +*instr* to admire
**прекра́сно** *нареч* (*сделать*) brilliantly ♦ *част*: ~! excellent!; **ты ~ зна́ешь, что ты не прав** you know perfectly well that you are wrong
**прекра́сный** *прил* beautiful; (*врач, результат*) excellent
**прекра|ти́ть** (-щу́, -ти́шь; *impf* **прекраща́ть**) *сов перех* to stop ♦ *неперех*: ~ +*infin* to stop doing; ~**ся** (*impf* **прекраща́ться**) *сов возв* (*дождь, занятия*) to stop; (*отношения*) to end
**преле́стный** *прил* charming
**пре́лест|ь** (-и) *ж* charm
**прелю́ди|я** (-и) *ж* prelude
**пре́ми|я** (-и) *ж* (*работнику*) bonus; (*победителю*) prize; (*КОММ*) premium
**премье́р** (-а) *м* premier
**премье́р|а** (-ы) *ж* première
**премье́р-мини́стр** (-а) *м* prime minister, premier
**пренебрега́|ть** (-ю) *несов от* **пренебре́чь**
**пренебреже́ни|е** (-я) *ср* (*законами итп*) disregard; (: *обязанностями*) neglect; (*высокомерие*) contempt
**пренебрежи́тельный** *прил* patronising
**пренебр|е́чь** (-егу́, -ежёшь *etc*, -гу́т; *pt* -ёг, -егла́; *impf* **пренебрега́ть**) *сов*: ~ +*instr* (*опасностью*) to disregard; (*богатством, правилами*) to scorn; (*советом, просьбой*) to ignore

**пре́ни|я (-й)** мн debate ед

**преоблада́|ть** (3sg **-ет**) несов: ~ **(над** +instr) to predominate (over)

**преобразова́ни|е (-я)** ср transformation

**преобраз|ова́ть (-у́ю;** impf **преобразо́вывать)** сов перех to transform

**преодоле́|ть (-ю;** impf **преодолева́ть)** сов перех to overcome; (барьер) to clear

**препара́т (-а)** м (МЕД: также: **медици́нский** ~) drug

**препина́ни|е (-я)** ср: зна́ки ~я punctuation marks мн

**преподава́тел|ь (-я)** м (школы, курсов) teacher; (вуза) lecturer

**преподава́ть (-ю, -ёшь)** несов перех to teach

**преподн|ести́ (-есу́, -есёшь;** pt **-ёс, -есла́;** impf **преподноси́ть)** сов перех: ~ что-н кому́-н to present sb with sth

**препя́тстви|е (-я)** ср obstacle

**препя́тств|овать (-ую;** pf **вос~)** несов: ~ +dat to impede

**прерв|а́ть (-у́, -ёшь;** impf **прерыва́ть)** сов перех (разговор, работу итп) to cut short; (отношения) to break off; (говорящего) to interrupt; **~ся** (impf **прерыва́ться)** сов возв (разговор, игра) to be cut short; (отношения) to be broken off

**прерывистый** прил (звонок) intermittent; (линия) broken

**прес|е́чь (-еку́, -ечёшь** etc, **-еку́т;** pt **-ёк, -екла́;** impf **пресека́ть)** сов перех to suppress

**пресле́довани|е (-я)** ср pursuit; (сексуальное) harassment; (инакомыслия) persecution

**пресле́д|овать (-ую)** несов перех to pursue;

(инакомыслящих) to persecute; (насмешками) to harass

**пресловутый** прил notorious

**пресмыка́ющ|ееся (-егося)** ср reptile

**пресново́дный** прил freshwater

**пре́сный** прил (вода) fresh; (пища) bland

**пресс (-а)** м (ТЕХ) press

**пре́сс|а (-ы)** ж собир the press

**пресс-конфере́нци|я (-и)** ж press conference

**пресс-рели́з (-а)** м press release

**пресс-секрета́р|ь (-я́)** м press secretary

**пресс-центр (-а)** м press office

**престаре́л|ый** прил aged; **дом (для)** ~ых old people's home

**прести́ж (-а)** м prestige

**прести́жный** прил prestigious

**преступле́ни|е (-я)** ср crime

**престу́пник (-а)** м criminal

**престу́пност|ь (-и)** ж (количество) crime

**престу́пный** прил criminal

**претенде́нт (-а)** м (на до́лжность) candidate; (СПОРТ) contender

**претенд|ова́ть (-у́ю)** несов: ~ **на** +acc (стремиться) to aspire to; (заявля́ть права́) to lay claim to

**прете́нзи|я (-и)** ж (обычно мн: на наследство) claim ед; (: на ум, на красоту итп) pretension; (жалоба) complaint

**преткнове́ни|е (-я)** ср: ка́мень ~я stumbling block

**преувели́ч|ить (-у, -ишь;** impf **преувели́чивать)** сов перех to exaggerate

**преуме́ньш|ить (-у, -ишь;** impf **преуменьша́ть)** сов перех to underestimate

**преуспе́|ть (-ю;** impf **преуспева́ть)** сов (в учёбе) to be successful; (в жизни) prosper, thrive

**прецеде́нт** (-а) м precedent

**при** предл: ~ +prp (возле) by, near; (о части) at; (в присутствии) in front of; (о времени) under; (о наличии чего-н у кого-н) on; **он всегда ~ деньга́х** he always has money on him; **я здесь ни ~ чём** it has nothing to do with me

**приба́в|ить** (-лю, -ишь; impf **прибавля́ть**) сов перех to add; (увеличить) to increase; **~ся** (impf **прибавля́ться** сов возв (проблемы, работа итп) to mount up ♦ безл (воды в реке) to rise

**прибежа́ть** (как **бежа́ть**; см. Table 20) сов to come running

**приб|и́ть** (-ью, -ьёшь; imper **-е́й(те)**; impf **прибива́ть**) сов перех (гвоздями) to nail

**приближа́|ть(ся)** (-ю(сь)) несов от **прибли́зить(ся)**

**приближе́ни|е** (-я) ср approach

**приблизи́тельный** прил approximate

**прибли́|зить** (-жу, -зишь; impf **приближа́ть**) сов перех (придвинуть) to move nearer; (ускорить) to bring nearer; **~ся** (impf **приближа́ться**) сов возв to approach

**прибо́|й** (-я) м breakers мн

**прибо́р** (-а) м (измерительный) device; (оптический) instrument; (нагревательный) appliance; (бритвенный) set; **столо́вый ~** setting

**прибре́жный** прил (у моря) coastal; (у реки) riverside

**прибыва́|ть** (-ю) несов от **прибы́ть**

**при́был|ь** (-и) ж profit

**при́быльный** прил profitable

**прибы́ти|е** (-я) ср arrival

**прибы́ть** (как **быть**; см. Table 21; impf **прибыва́ть**) сов to arrive

**приватиза́ци|я** (-и) ж privatization

**приватизи́р|овать** (-ую) (не)сов перех to privatize

**прив|езти́** (-езу́, -езёшь; pt -ёз, -езла́; impf **привози́ть**) сов перех to bring

**прив|ести́** (-еду́, -едёшь; pt -ёл, -ела́) сов от **вести́** ♦ (impf **приводи́ть**) перех (сопроводить) to bring; (подлеж: дорога: к дому) to take; (пример) to give; **~** (pf) **в у́жас** to horrify; **приводи́ть** (**~** pf) **в восто́рг** to delight; **приводи́ть** (**~** pf) **в изумле́ние** to astonish; **приводи́ть** (**~** pf) **в исполне́ние** to put into effect; **приводи́ть** (**~** pf) **в поря́док** to put in order

**приве́т** (-а) м regards мн; (разг: при встрече) hi; (: при расставании) bye; **передава́ть** (**переда́ть** pf) **кому́-н ~** to give sb one's regards

**приве́тливый** прил friendly

**приве́тстви|е** (-я) ср (при встрече) greeting; (делегации) welcome

**приве́тств|овать** (-ую; pf по~) несов перех to welcome

**приви́в|ка** (-ки; gen pl -ок) ж (МЕД) vaccination

**привиде́ни|е** (-я) ср ghost

**привилегиро́ванный** прил privileged

**привиле́ги|я** (-и) ж privilege

**привин|ти́ть** (-чу́, -ти́шь; impf **приви́нчивать**) сов перех to screw on

**при́вкус** (-а) м flavour (BRIT), flavor (US)

**привлека́тельный** прил

attractive

**привлека́|ть (-ю)** *несов от* **привле́чь**

**привлече́ни|е (-я)** *ср* (*покупа́телей*, *внима́ния*) attraction; (*ресу́рсов*) use

**привл|е́чь (-еку́, -ечёшь** *etc*, **-еку́т;** *pt* **-ёк, -екла́;** *impf* **привлека́ть)** *сов перех* to attract; (*ресу́рсы*) to use; **привлека́ть (~ *pf*) кого́-н к** +*dat* (*к рабо́те*, *к уча́стию*) to involve sb in; (*к суду́*) to take sb to; **привлека́ть (~ *pf*) кого́-н к отве́тственности** to call sb to account

**прив|оди́ть (-ожу́, -о́дишь)** *несов от* **привести́**

**прив|ози́ть (-ожу́, -о́зишь)** *несов от* **привезти́**

**привы́к|нуть (-ну;** *pt* **-, -ла;** *impf* **привыка́ть)** *сов:* **~** +*infin* to get into the habit of doing; **привыка́ть (~ *pf*) к** +*dat* (*к но́вому*) to get used to

**привы́ч|ка (-ки;** *gen pl* **-ек)** *ж* habit

**привы́чный** *прил* familiar

**привя́занност|ь (-и)** *ж* attachment

**прив|яза́ть (-яжу́, -я́жешь;** *impf* **привя́зывать)** *сов перех:* **~ что-н/кого́-н к** +*dat* to tie sth/sb to; **~ся** (*impf* **привя́зываться)** *сов возв:* **~ся к** +*dat* (*к сиде́нью*) to fasten o.s. to; (*полюби́ть*) to become attached to

**пригласи́тельный** *прил:* **~ биле́т** invitation

**пригла|си́ть (-шу́, -си́шь;** *impf* **приглаша́ть)** *сов перех* to invite

**приглаше́ни|е (-я)** *ср* invitation

**пригово́р (-а)** *м* (*ЮР*) sentence; (*перен*) condemnation; **выноси́ть** (**вы́нести** *pf*) **~** to pass sentence

**пригово́р|ить (-ю́, -и́шь;** *impf* **пригова́ривать)** *сов перех:* **~ кого́-н к** +*dat* to sentence sb to

**приго|ди́ться (-жу́сь, -ди́шься)** *сов возв:* **~** +*dat* to be useful to

**приго́дный** *прил* suitable

**пригор|е́ть (3sg** **-и́т;** *impf* **пригора́ть)** *сов* to burn

**при́город (-а)** *м* suburb

**при́городный** *прил* suburban; (*по́езд*) commuter

**пригото́в|ить (-лю, -ишь)** *сов от* **гото́вить ♦** (*impf* **приготавливать)** *перех* to prepare; (*посте́ль*) to make; **~ся** *сов от* **гото́виться ♦** *возв:* **~ся (к** +*dat*) (*к путеше́ствию*) to get ready (for); (*к уро́ку*) to prepare (o.s.)

**приготовле́ни|е (-я)** *ср* preparation

**пригро|зи́ть (-жу́, -зи́шь)** *сов от* **грози́ть**

**прида|ва́ть (-ю́, -ёшь)** *несов от* **прида́ть**

**прида́т|ок (-ка)** *м* appendage

**прида́ть** (*как* **дать;** см. Table 16; *impf* **придава́ть)** *сов:* **~ чего́-н кому́-н** (*уве́ренности*) to instil (*BRIT*) *или* instill (*US*) sth in sb **♦** *перех:* **~ что-н чему́-н** (*вид*, *фо́рму*) to give sth to sth; (*ва́жность*) to attach sth to sth

**прида́ч|а (-и)** *ж:* **в ~у** in addition

**придви́н|уть (-у;** *impf* **придвига́ть)** *сов перех:* **~ (к** +*dat*) to move over *или* up (to)

**приде́ла|ть (-ю;** *impf* **приде́лывать)** *сов перех:* **~ что-н к** +*dat* to attach sth to

**прид|ержа́ть (-ержу́, -е́ржишь;** *impf* **приде́рживать)** *сов перех* (*дверь*) to hold (steady); (*ло́шадь*) to restrain

**приде́ржива|ться (-юсь)** *несов*

*возв:* ~ +*gen* (*взглядов*) to hold

**придира́|ться** (-юсь) *несов от* **придра́ться**

**приди́рчивый** *прил* (*человек*) fussy; (*замечание, взгляд*) critical

**придра́ться** (-еру́сь, -ерёшься; *impf* **придира́ться**) *сов возв:* ~ к +*dat* to find fault with

**приду́** *etc сов см.* **прийти́**

**приду́ма|ть** (-ю; *impf* **приду́мывать**) *сов перех* (*отговорку, причину*) to think of *или* up; (*новый прибор*) to devise; (*песню, стихотворение*) to make up

**прие́ду** *etc сов см.* **прие́хать**

**прие́зд** (-а) *м* arrival

**приезжа́|ть** (-ю) *несов от* **прие́хать**

**прие́зж|ий** (-его) *м* visitor ♦ *прил* visiting

**прие́м** (-а) *м* reception; (*у врача*) surgery (*BRIT*), office (*US*); (*СПОРТ*) technique; (*наказания, воздействия*) means; **в два/в три ~а** in two/three attempts; **запи́сываться** (**записа́ться** *pf*) **на ~ к** +*dat* to make an appointment with

**приёмн|ая** (-ой) *ж* (*также:* ~ **ко́мната**) reception

**приёмник** (-а) *м* receiver; (*радио*) radio

**приёмный** *прил* (*часы*) reception; (*день*) visiting; (*экзамены*) entrance; (*комиссия*) selection; (*родители, дети*) adoptive

**прие́хать** (*как* **е́хать**; *см. Table 19; impf* **приезжа́ть**) *сов* to arrive *или* come (*by transport*)

**прижа́|ть** (-му́, -мёшь; *impf* **прижима́ть**) *сов перех:* ~ **что-н/кого́-н к** +*dat* to press sth/sb to *или* against; ~**ся** (*impf*

**прижима́ться**) *сов возв:* ~**ся к** +*dat* to press o.s. against; (*к груди*) to snuggle up to

**приз** (-а; *nom pl* -**ы**) *м* prize

**призва́ни|е** (-я) *ср* (*к науке итп*) vocation

**приз|ва́ть** (-ову́, -овёшь; *pt* -**ва́л**, -**вала́**; *impf* **призыва́ть**) *сов перех* (*к борьбе, к защите*) to call; **призыва́ть** (~ *pf*) **к ми́ру** to call for peace; **призыва́ть** (~ *pf*) **кого́-н к поря́дку** to call sb to order; **призыва́ть** (~ *pf*) **в а́рмию** to call up (to join the army)

**приземл|и́ть** (-ю́, -и́шь; *impf* **приземля́ть**) *сов перех* to land; ~**ся** (*impf* **приземля́ться**) *сов возв* to land

**призёр** (-а) *м* prizewinner

**при́зм|а** (-ы) *ж* prism

**признава́ть(ся)** (-ю́(сь), -ёшь(ся)) *несов от* **призна́ть(ся)**

**при́знак** (-а) *м* (*кризиса, успеха*) sign; (*отравления*) symptom

**призна́ни|е** (-я) *ср* recognition; (*согласие*) acknowledgment; (*в любви*) declaration; (*в преступлении*) confession

**при́знанный** *прил* recognized

**призна́тельност|ь** (-и) *ж* gratitude

**призна́тельный** *прил* grateful

**призна́|ть** (-ю; *impf* **признава́ть**) *сов перех* to recognize; (*счесть*): ~ **что-н/кого́-н** +*instr* to recognize sth/sb as; ~**ся** (*impf* **признава́ться**) *сов возв:* ~**ся кому́-н в чём-н** (*в преступлении*) to confess sth to sb; **признава́ться** (~**ся** *pf*) **кому́-н в любви́** to make a declaration of love to sb

**при́зрак** (-а) *м* ghost

**призы́в** (-а) *м* call; (*в армию*)

conscription, draft (*US*); (*лозунг*) slogan

**призывá|ть** (-ю) *несов от* **призвáть**

**призывни́к** (-á) *м* conscript

**прийти́** (*как* **идти́**; *см. Table 18*; *impf* **приходи́ть**) *сов* (*идя, достичь*) to come (*on foot*); (*телегрáмма, письмó*) to arrive; (*веснá, час свобóды*) to come; (*достигнуть*): ~ **к** +*dat* (*к влáсти, к вы́воду*) to come to; (*к демокрáтии*) to achieve; **приходи́ть** (~ *pf*) **в у́жас/недоумéние** to be horrified/bewildered; **приходи́ть** (~ *pf*) **в востóрг** to go into raptures; **приходи́ть** (~ *pf*) **комý-н в гóлову** *или* **на ум** to occur to sb; **приходи́ть** (~ *pf*) **в себя́** (*после обмóрока*) to come to *или* round; (*успокóиться*) to come to one's senses; **~сь** (*impf* **приходи́ться**) *сов возв*: **~сь на** +*acc* to fall on; (**нам**) **придётся согласи́ться** we'll have to agree

**прикáз** (-а) *м* order

**приказáни|е** (-я) *ср* = **прикáз**

**прик|азáть** (-ажу́, -áжешь; *impf* **прикáзывать**) *сов*: ~ **комý-н** +*infin* to order sb to do

**прикáлыва|ть** (-ю) *несов от* **приколóть**

**прикасá|ться** (-юсь) *несов от* **прикоснýться**

**приклáд** (-а) *м* (*ружья́*) butt

**прикладнóй** *прил* applied

**приклáдыва|ть** (-ю) *несов от* **приложи́ть**

**приклé|ить** (-ю, -ишь; *impf* **приклéивать**) *сов перех* to glue, stick; **~ся** (*impf* **приклéиваться**) *сов возв* to stick

**приключéни|е** (-я) *ср* adventure

**прик|олóть** (-олю́, -óлешь; *impf*

**прикáлывать**) *сов перех* to fasten

**прикосн|ýться** (-у́сь, -ёшься; *impf* **прикасáться**) *сов возв*: ~**к** +*dat* to touch lightly

**прикреп|и́ть** (-лю́, -и́шь; *impf* **прикрепля́ть**) *сов перех*: ~ **что-н/когó-н к** +*dat* to attach sth/sb to

**прикры́ти|е** (-я) *ср* (*махинáций*) cover-up; (*ВОЕН*) cover; **под ~м** +*gen* under the guise of

**прикр|ы́ть** (-óю, -óешь; *impf* **прикрывáть**) *сов перех* to cover; (*закры́ть*) to close (over)

**прик|ури́ть** (-урю́, -у́ришь; *impf* **прикýривать**) *сов* to get a light (*from a lit cigarette*)

**прилáв|ок** (-ка) *м* (*в магази́не*) counter; (*на ры́нке*) stall

**прилагáтельн|ое** (-ого) *ср* (*ЛИНГ: также*: **и́мя ~**) adjective

**прилагá|ть** (-ю) *несов от* **приложи́ть**

**прилегá|ть** (*3sg* -ет) *несов*: ~ **чему́-н** (*одéжда*) to fit sth tightly

**прилéжный** *прил* diligent

**приле|тéть** (-чу́, -ти́шь; *impf* **прилетáть**) *сов* to arrive (*by air*), fly in

**прил|éчь** (-я́гу, -я́жешь *etc*, -я́гут; *pt* -ёг, -еглá) *сов* to lie down for a while

**прили́в** (-а) *м* (*в мóре*) tide

**прили́п|нуть** (-ну; *pt* -, -ла; *impf* **прилипáть** *или* **ли́пнуть**) *сов*: ~ **к** +*dat* to stick to

**прили́чный** *прил* (*человéк*) decent; (*сýмма, результáт*) fair, decent

**приложéни|е** (-я) *ср* (*знáний, энéргии*) application; (*к журнáлу*) supplement; (*к докумéнту*) addendum

**прил|ожи́ть** (-ожу́, -óжишь;

*impf* **прилага́ть**) *сов перех* (*присоединить*) to attach; (*силу, знания*) to apply; **прикла́дывать** (~ *pf*) **что-н к** +*dat* (*руку: ко лбу*) to put sth to; **ума́ не ~ожу́** (*разг*) I don't have a clue

**примене́ни|е** (-я) *ср* (*оружия, машин*) use; (*лекарств*) application; (*мер, метода*) adoption

**прим|ени́ть** (-еню́, -е́нишь; *impf* **применя́ть**) *сов перех* (*меры*) to implement; (*силу*) to use, apply; **применя́ть** (~ *pf*) **что-н** (**к** +*dat*) (*метод, теорию*) to apply sth (to)

**применя́|ться** (*3sg* -**ется**) *несов* (*использоваться*) to be used

**приме́р** (-а) *м* example

**приме́р|ка** (-ки; *gen pl* -ок) *ж* trying on

**приме́рно** *нареч* in an exemplary fashion; (*около*) approximately

**приме́рный** *прил* (*образцовый*) exemplary; (*цифры*) approximate

**при́мес|ь** (-и) *ж* dash

**приме́т|а** (-ы) *ж* (*признак*) sign; (*суеверная*) omen

**примета́|ть** (-ю; *impf* **примётывать**) *сов перех* to stitch on

**примеча́ни|е** (-я) *ср* note

**примире́ни|е** (-я) *ср* reconciliation

**примити́вный** *прил* primitive

**примо́рский** *прил* seaside

**принадлеж|а́ть** (-у́, -и́шь) *несов*: ~ +*dat* to belong to; (*заслуга*) to go to

**принадле́жност|ь** (-и) *ж* characteristic; (*обычно мн*: *комплект*) tackle *ед*; (: *письменные*) accessories *мн*

**прин|ести́** (-есу́, -есёшь; *pt* -ёс, -есла́; *impf* **приноси́ть**) *сов*

*перех* to bring; (*извинения, благодарность*) to express; (*присягу*) to take; **приноси́ть** (~ *pf*) **по́льзу** +*dat* to be of use to; **приноси́ть** (~ *pf*) **вред** +*dat* to harm

**принима́|ть(ся)** (-ю(сь)) *несов от* **приня́ть(ся)**

**прин|оси́ть** (-ошу́, -о́сишь) *несов от* **принести́**

**при́нтер** (-а) *м* (*КОМП*) printer

**принуди́тельный** *прил* forced

**прину́|дить** (-жу, -дишь; *impf* **принужда́ть**) *сов перех*: ~ **кого́-н/что-н к чему́-н/** +*infin* to force sb/sth to sth/to do

**принц** (-а) *м* prince

**принце́сс|а** (-ы) *ж* princess

**при́нцип** (-а) *м* principle

**принципиа́льный** *прил* (*человек, политика*) uncompromising; (*согласие*) in principle

**при́нятый** *прил* accepted

**при|ня́ть** (-му́, -мешь; *pt* -нял, -няла́; *impf* **принима́ть**) *сов перех* to take; (*подарок, условия*) to accept; (*пост*) to take up; (*гостей, телеграмму*) to receive; (*закон, резолюцию*) to pass; (*отношение, вид*) to take on; (*христианство итп*) to adopt; **принима́ть** (~ *pf*) **в/на** +*acc* (*в университет, на работу*) to accept for; **принима́ть** (~ *pf*) **что-н/кого́-н за** +*acc* to mistake sth/sb for; (*счесть*) to take sth/sb as; ~**ся** (*impf* **принима́ться**) *сов возв*: ~**ся** +*infin* (*приступить*) to get down to doing; **принима́ться** (~**ся** *pf*) **за** +*acc* (*приступить*) to get down to

**приобр|ести́** (-ету́, -етёшь; *pt* -ёл, -ела́; *impf* **приобрета́ть**) *сов перех* to acquire, obtain;

(друзей, врагов) to make

**приобрете́ни|е (-я)** *ср*
acquisition; (*КОММ*) procurement

**приорите́т (-а)** *м* priority

**приостан|ови́ть (-овлю́,
-о́вишь;** *impf*
**приостана́вливать)** *сов перех*
to suspend

**припа́д|ок (-ка)** *м* (*МЕД*) attack

**припа́с|ы (-ов)** *мн* supplies *мн*;
(*ВОЕН*) ammunition *ед*

**припе́в (-а)** *м* (*песни*) chorus,
refrain

**прип|иса́ть (-ишу́, -и́шешь;** *impf*
**припи́сывать)** *сов перех* to add;
**припи́сывать (~** *pf*) **что-н кому́-н**
to attribute sth to sb

**приполз|ти́ (-у́, -ёшь;** *impf* **-а́ть)**
*сов перех* to crawl in

**припо́мн|ить (-ю, - ишь;** *impf*
**припомина́ть)** *сов перех* to
remember

**припра́в|а (-ы)** *ж* seasoning

**приравня́|ть (-ю;** *impf*
**прира́внивать)** *сов перех*: ~
**кого́-н/что-н к** +*dat* to equate sb/
sth with

**приро́д|а (-ы)** *ж* nature; (*места
вне города*) countryside

**приро́дный** *прил* natural

**приро́ст (-а)** *м* (*населения*)
growth; (*доходов, урожая*)
increase

**прируч|и́ть (-у́, -и́шь;** *impf*
**прируча́ть)** *сов перех* to tame

**приса́жива|ться (-юсь)** *несов от*
**присе́сть**

**присво́|ить (-ю, -ишь;** *impf*
**присва́ивать)** *сов перех*
(*чужое*) to appropriate; (*дать*): ~
**что-н кому́-н** (*звание*) to confer
sth on sb

**приседа́ни|е (-я)** *ср* squatting
(*physical exercise*)

**прис|е́сть (-я́ду, -я́дешь;** *impf*

**приседа́ть)** *сов* to squat; (*impf*
**приса́живаться; на стул**) to sit
down (*for a short while*)

**приск|ака́ть (-ачу́, -а́чешь;** *impf*
**приска́кивать)** *сов* to gallop *или*
come galloping up

**при|сла́ть (-шлю́, -шлёшь;** *impf*
**присыла́ть)** *сов перех* to send

**прислон|и́ть (-ю́, -и́шь;** *impf*
**прислоня́ть)** *сов перех*: ~ **что-н
к** +*dat* to lean sth against; ~**ся** (*impf*
**прислоня́ться)** *сов возв*: ~**ся к**
+ *dat* to lean against

**прислу́жива|ть (-ю)** *несов*: ~
+*dat* (*официант*) to wait on

**прислу́ша|ться (-юсь;** *impf*
**прислу́шиваться)** *сов возв*: ~ **к**
+*dat* (*к звуку*) to listen to

**присмо́тр (-а)** *м* care

**присм|отре́ть (-отрю́,
-о́тришь;** *impf* **присма́тривать)**
*сов*: ~ **за** +*instr* to look after;
(*найти*) to spot

**присн|и́ться (3sg -и́тся)** *сов от*
**сни́ться**

**присоедине́ни|е (-я)** *ср*
attachment; (*провода*) connection;
(*территории*) annexation

**присоедин|и́ть (-ю́, -и́шь;** *impf*
**присоединя́ть)** *сов перех*: ~
**что-н к** +*dat* to attach sth to;
(*провод*) to connect sth to;
(*территорию*) to annex sth to; ~**ся**
(*impf* **присоединя́ться)** *сов возв*:
~**ся к** +*dat* to join (*к мнению*) to
support

**приспосо́б|ить (-лю, -ишь;** *impf*
**приспоса́бливать)** *сов перех* to
adapt; ~**ся** (*impf*
**приспоса́бливаться)** *сов возв*
(*делать что-н*) to learn how; (*к
условиям*) to adapt (o.s.)

**приспособле́ни|е (-я)** *ср* (*к
условиям итп*) adaptation;
(*механизм итп*) appliance

приста|ва́ть (-ю́, -ёшь) *несов от*
приста́ть

приста́в|ить (-лю, -ишь; *impf*
приставля́ть) *сов перех*: ~
что-н к +*dat* to put sth against

приста́в|ка (-ки; *gen pl* -ок) ж
(*ЛИНГ*) prefix; (*ТЕХ*) attachment

приставля́|ть (-ю) *несов от*
приста́вить

при́стальный *прил* (взгляд,
внимание) fixed; (*интерес,
наблюдение*) intent

при́стан|ь (-и) ж pier

приста́|ть (-ну, -нешь; *impf*
приставать) *сов*: ~ к +*dat*
(*прилипнуть*) to stick to;
(*присоединиться*) to join; (*разг: с
вопросами*) to pester; (*причалить*)
to moor

пристегн|у́ть (-у́, -ёшь; *impf*
пристёгивать) *сов перех* to
fasten; ~ся (*impf*
пристёгиваться) *сов возв* (в
самолёте итп) to fasten one's seat
belt

пристра́ива|ть (-ю) *несов от*
пристро́ить

пристр|ели́ть (-елю́, -е́лишь;
*impf* пристре́ливать) *сов перех*
(*животное*) to put down

пристро́|ить (-ю, -ишь; *impf*
пристра́ивать) *сов перех*
(*комнату*) to build on

пристро́|йка (-йки; *gen pl* -ек) ж
extension

при́ступ (-а) м (*атака,
сердечный*) attack; (*смеха, гнева,
кашля*) fit

прист|упи́ть (-уплю́, -у́пишь;
*impf* приступа́ть) *сов*: ~ к +*dat*
(*начать*) to commence

прис|уди́ть (-ужу́, -у́дишь; *impf*
присужда́ть) *сов перех*: ~ что-н
кому́-н to award sth to sb;
(*учёную степень*) to confer sth

on sb

прису́тстви|е (-я) *ср* presence

прису́тств|овать (-ую) *несов* to
be present

прису́тствующ|ие (-их) *мн* those
present *мн*

присыла́|ть (-ю) *несов от*
присла́ть

прися́г|а (-и) ж oath

прися́жн|ый (-ого) м (*ЮР:
также*: ~ заседа́тель) juror; суд
~ых jury

прит|ащи́ть (-ащу́, -а́щишь;
*impf* прита́скивать) *сов перех* to
drag

притвор|и́ться (-ю́сь, -и́шься;
*impf* притворя́ться) *сов возв*: ~
+*instr* to pretend to be

прити́х|нуть (-ну, -нешь; *pt* -,
-ла; *impf* притиха́ть) *сов* to grow
quiet

прито́к (-а) м (*река*) tributary; ~
+*gen* (*энергии, средств*) supply of;
(*населения*) influx of

прито́м *союз* and what's more

прито́н (-а) м den

при́торный *прил* sickly sweet

прит|упи́ться (*3sg* -у́пится; *impf*
притупля́ться) *сов возв* (*нож*)
to go blunt; (*перен: внимание
итп*) to diminish; (: *чувства*) to
fade; (: *слух*) to fail

притяже́ни|е (-я) *ср* gravitation

притяза́ни|е (-я) *ср*: ~ на +*acc*
claim to

приуро́ч|ить (-у, -ишь) *сов
перех*: ~ что-н к +*dat* to time sth
to coincide with

при|учи́ть (-учу́, -у́чишь; *impf*
приуча́ть) *сов перех*: ~
кого́-н к +*dat*/ +*infin* to train sb
for/to do; ~ся (*impf*
приуча́ться) *сов возв*: ~ся к
+*dat*/+*infin* to train for/to do

прихв|ати́ть (-ачу́, -а́тишь) *сов*

*перех (разг: взять)* to take

**прихо́д** (**-а**) *м* arrival; (*КОММ*) receipts *мн*; (*РЕЛ*) parish; ~ **и расхо́д** (*КОММ*) credit and debit

**прих|оди́ть** (**-ожу́, -о́дишь**) *несов от* **прийти́**; ~**ся** *несов от* **прийти́сь ♦** *возв:* ~**ся кому́-н ро́дственником** to be sb's relative

**прихо́д|овать** (**-ую**; *pf* **о~**) *несов перех* (*КОММ, су́мму*) to enter (*in receipt book*)

**приходя́щ|ий** *прил* nonresident; ~**ая ня́ня** babysitter

**прихожа́н|ин** (**-ина**; *nom pl* **-е**) *м* (*РЕЛ*) parishioner

**прихо́ж|ая** (**-ей**) *ж* entrance hall

**прихожу́(сь)** *несов см.* **приходи́ть(ся)**

**при́хот|ь** (**-и**) *ж* whim

**прице́л** (**-а**) *м* (*ружья́, пу́шки*) sight

**прице́л|иться** (**-юсь, -ишься**; *impf* **прице́ливаться**) *сов возв* to take aim

**прице́п** (**-а**) *м* trailer

**приц|епи́ть** (**-еплю́, -е́пишь**; *impf* **прицепля́ть**) *сов перех* (*ваго́н*) to couple

**прича́л** (**-а**) *м* mooring; (*пассажи́рский*) quay; (*грузово́й, ремо́нтный*) dock

**прича́л|ить** (**-ю, -ишь**; *impf* **прича́ливать**) *сов (не)перех* to moor

**прича́сти|е** (**-я**) *ср* (*ЛИНГ*) participle; (*РЕЛ*) communion

**прича|сти́ть** (**-щу́, -сти́шь**; *impf* **причаща́ть**) *сов перех* (*РЕЛ*) to give communion to; ~**ся** (*impf* **причаща́ться**) *сов возв* (*РЕЛ*) to receive communion

**прича́стный** *прил* (*свя́занный*): ~ **к** +*dat* connected with

**причаща́|ть(ся)** (**-ю(сь)**) *несов от* **причасти́ть(ся)**

**причём** *союз* moreover

**прич|еса́ть** (**-ешу́, -е́шешь**; *impf* **причёсывать**) (*расчёской*) to comb; (*щёткой*) to brush; **причёсывать** (~ *pf*) **кого́-н** to comb/brush sb's hair; ~**ся** (*impf* **причёсываться**) *сов возв* (*см перех*) to comb one's hair; to brush one's hair

**причёс|ка** (**-ки**; *gen pl* **-ок**) *ж* hairstyle

**причи́н|а** (**-ы**) *ж* (*то, что вызыва́ет*) cause; (*обоснова́ние*) reason; **по** ~**е** +*gen* on account of

**причин|и́ть** (**-ю́, -и́шь**; *impf* **причиня́ть**) *сов перех* to cause

**причу́д|а** (**-ы**) *ж* whim

**пришёл(ся)** *сов см.* **прийти́(сь)**

**приш|и́ть** (**-ью́, -ьёшь**; *imper* **-е́й(те)**; *impf* **пришива́ть**) *сов перех* to sew on

**пришла́** *etc сов см.* **прийти́**

**прищем|и́ть** (**-лю́, -и́шь**; *impf* **прищемля́ть**) *сов перех* to catch

**прищу́р|ить** (**-ю, -ишь**; *impf* **прищу́ривать**) *сов перех* (*глаза́*) to screw up; ~**ся** (*impf* **прищу́риваться**) *сов возв* to screw up one's eyes

**прию́т** (**-а**) *м* shelter; (*для сиро́т*) orphanage

**прию|ти́ть** (**-чу́, -ти́шь**) *сов перех* to shelter; ~**ся** *сов возв* to take shelter

**прия́тел|ь** (**-я**) *м* friend

**прия́тно** *нареч* (*удивлён*) pleasantly **♦** *как сказ* it's nice *или* pleasant; **мне** ~ **э́то слы́шать** I'm glad to hear that; **о́чень** ~ (*при знако́мстве*) pleased to meet you

**прия́тный** *прил* pleasant

**про** *предл:* ~ +*acc* about

**про́б|а** (**-ы**) *ж* (*испыта́ние*) test; (*образе́ц*) sample; (*зо́лота*) standard (*of quality*); (*клеймо*) hallmark

**пробе́г** (**-а**) *м* (*СПОРТ*) race; (*: лыжный*) run; (*АВТ*) mileage

**пробежа́ть** (*как* **бежа́ть**; *см. Table 20*; *impf* **пробега́ть**) *сов перех* (*текст*) to skim; (*5 километров*) to cover ♦ *неперех* (*время*) to pass; (*миновать бегом*): **~ ми́мо** +*gen* to run past; (*появиться и исчезнуть*): **~ по** +*dat* (*шум, дрожь*) to run through; **~ся** *сов возв* to run

**пробе́л** (**-а**) *м* (*также перен*) gap

**пробива́|ть(ся)** (**-ю(сь)**) *несов от* **проби́ть(ся)**

**пробира́|ться** (**-юсь**) *несов от* **пробра́ться**

**проби́р|ка** (**-ки**; *gen pl* **-ок**) *ж* test-tube

**проб|и́ть** (**-ью́, -ьёшь**) *сов от* **бить** ♦ (*impf* **пробива́ть**) *перех* (*дыру*) to knock; (*крышу, стену*) to make a hole in; **~ся** (*impf* **пробива́ться**) *сов возв* (*прорваться*) to fight one's way through; (*растения*) to push through *или* up

**про́б|ка** (**-ки**; *gen pl* **-ок**) *ж* cork; (*перен: на дороге*) jam; (*ЭЛЕК*) fuse (*BRIT*), fuze (*US*)

**пробле́м|а** (**-ы**) *ж* problem

**проблемати́чный** *прил* problematic(al)

**про́бный** *прил* trial

**про́б|овать** (**-ую**; *pf* **по~**) *несов перех* (*пирог, вино*) to taste; (*пытаться*): **~** +*infin* to try to do

**пробо́ин|а** (**-ы**) *ж* hole

**пробо́р** (**-а**) *м* parting (*of hair*)

**проб|ра́ться** (**-еру́сь, -ерёшься**; *impf* **пробира́ться**) *сов возв* (*с трудом пройти*) to fight one's way through; (*тихо пройти*) to steal past *или* through

**пробужде́ни|е** (**-я**) *ср* (*ото сна*) waking up; (*сознания, чувств*) awakening

**пробы́|ть** (*как* **быть**; *см. Table 21*) *сов* (*прожить*) to stay, remain

**прова́л** (**-а**) *м* (*в почве, в стене*) hole; (*перен: неудача*) flop; (*: памяти*) failure

**прова|ли́ть** (**-алю́, -а́лишь**; *impf* **прова́ливать**) *сов перех* (*крышу, пол*) to cause to collapse; (*разг: перен: дело, затею*) to botch up; (*: студента*) to fail; **~ся** (*impf* **прова́ливаться**) *сов возв* (*человек*) to fall; (*крыша*) to collapse; (*разг: перен: студент, попытка*) to fail; **как сквозь зе́млю ~али́лся** he disappeared into thin air

**проведу́** *etc сов см.* **провести́**

**пров|езти́** (**-езу́, -езёшь**; *pt* **-ёз, -езла́**; *impf* **провози́ть**) *сов перех* (*незаконно*) to smuggle; (*везя, доставить*): **~ по** +*dat/* **ми́мо** +*gen/***че́рез** +*acc* to take along/past/across

**прове́р|ить** (**-ю, -ишь**; *impf* **проверя́ть**) *сов перех* to check; (*знание, двигатель*) to test; **~ся** (*impf* **проверя́ться**) *сов возв* (*у врача*) to get a check-up

**прове́р|ка** (**-ки**; *gen pl* **-ок**) *ж* (*см глаг*) check-up; test

**пров|ести́** (**-еду́, -едёшь**; *pt* **-ёл, -ела́**; *impf* **проводи́ть**) *сов перех* (*черту, границу*) to draw; (*дорогу*) to build; (*план, реформу*) to implement; (*урок, репетицию*) to hold; (*операцию*) to carry out; (*детство, день*) to spend; **проводи́ть** (**~** *pf*) **ми́мо** +*gen/***че́рез** +*acc* (*людей*) to take past/across

**прове́тр|ить** (**-ю, -ишь**; *impf* **прове́тривать**) *сов перех* to air;

**~ся** (*impf* **прове́триваться**) *сов возв* (*комната, одежда*) to have an airing

**провин|и́ться** (**-ю́сь, -и́шься**) *сов возв:* ~ (**в** +*prp*) to be guilty (of)

**провинциа́льный** *прил* provincial

**прови́нци|я** (**-и**) *ж* province

**про́вод** (**-а**; *nom pl* **-а́**) *м* cable

**пров|оди́ть** (**-ожу́, -о́дишь**) *несов от* **провести́** ♦ (*impf* **провожа́ть**) *сов перех* to see off; **провожа́ть** (~ *pf*) **глаза́ми/ взгля́дом кого́-н** to follow sb with one's eyes/gaze

**прово́д|ка** (**-ки**; *gen pl* **-ок**) *ж* (ЭЛЕК) wiring

**проводни́к** (**-а́**) *м* (*в горах*) guide; (*в поезде*) steward (*BRIT*), porter (*US*)

**про́вод|ы** (**-ов**) *мн* (*прощание*) send-off *ед*

**провожа́|ть** (**-ю**) *несов от* **проводи́ть**

**провожу́** (*не*)*сов см.* **проводи́ть**

**прово́з** (**-а**) *м* (*багажа*) transport; (*незаконный*) smuggling

**провозгла|си́ть** (**-шу́, -си́шь**; *impf* **провозглаша́ть**) *сов перех* to proclaim

**пров|ози́ть** (**-ожу́, -о́зишь**) *несов от* **провезти́**

**провокацио́нный** *прил* provocative

**провока́ци|я** (**-и**) *ж* provocation

**про́волок|а** (**-и**) *ж* wire

**прово́рный** *прил* agile

**провоци́р|овать** (**-ую**; *pf* **с~**) *несов перех* to provoke

**прогиба́|ть(ся)** (**-ю(сь)**) *несов от* **прогну́ть(ся)**

**прогл|оти́ть** (**-очу́, -о́тишь**; *impf* **прогла́тывать** *или* **глота́ть**) *сов перех* (*также перен*) to swallow

**прог|на́ть** (**-оню́, -о́нишь**; *pt* **-на́л, -нала́**; *impf* **прогоня́ть**) *сов перех* (*заставить уйти*) to turn out

**прогно́з** (**-а**) *м* forecast

**прогн|у́ть** (**-у́, -ёшь**; *impf* **прогиба́ть**) *сов перех:* ~ **что-н** to cause sth to sag; **~ся** (*impf* **прогиба́ться**) *сов возв* to sag

**прогоня́|ть** (**-ю**) *несов от* **прогна́ть**

**програ́мм|а** (**-ы**) *ж* programme (*BRIT*), program (*US*); (ПОЛИТ) manifesto; (*также:* **веща́тельная ~**) channel; (ПРОСВЕЩ) curriculum; (КОМП) program

**программи́р|овать** (**-ую**; *pf* **за~**) *несов перех* (КОМП) to program

**программи́ст** (**-а**) *м* (КОМП) programmer

**програ́ммн|ый** *прил* programmed (*BRIT*), programed (*US*); (*экзамен, зачёт*) set; **~ое обеспе́чение** (КОМП) software

**прогре́сс** (**-а**) *м* progress

**прогресси́вный** *прил* progressive

**прогу́л** (**-а**) *м* (*на работе*) absence; (*в школе*) truancy

**прогу́лива|ть** (**-ю**) *несов от* **прогуля́ть**

**прогу́л|ка** (**-ки**; *gen pl* **-ок**) *ж* walk; (*недалёкая поездка*) trip

**прогу́льщик** (**-а**) *м* (*об ученике*) truant

**прогуля́|ть** (**-ю**; *impf* **прогу́ливать**) *сов перех* (*работу*) to be absent from; (*уроки*) to miss; (*гулять*) to walk

**прода|ва́ть** (**-ю́**) *несов от* **прода́ть**

**продав|е́ц** (**-ца́**) *м* seller; (*в магазине*) (shop-)assistant

**продавщи́ц|а** (**-ы**) *ж см.* **продаве́ц**

**прода́ж|а** (-и) ж (дома, товара) sale; (торговля) trade

**прода́|ть** (как дать; см. Table 16; impf **продава́ть**) сов перех to sell; (перен: друга) to betray

**продвига́|ть(ся)** (-ю(сь)) несов от **продви́нуть(ся)**

**продвиже́ни|е** (-я) ср (войск) advance; (по службе) promotion

**продви́н|уть** (-у; impf **продвига́ть**) сов перех to move; (перен: работника) to promote; **~ся** (impf **продвига́ться**) сов возв to move; (войска) to advance; (перен: работник) to be promoted; (: работа) to progress

**продева́|ть** (-ю) несов от **проде́ть**

**проде́ла|ть** (-ю; impf **проде́лывать**) сов перех (отверстие) to make; (работу) to do

**проде́|ть** (-ну, -нешь; impf **продева́ть**) сов перех to thread

**продлева́|ть** (-ю) несов от **продли́ть**

**продле́ни|е** (-я) ср (см глаг) extension; prolongation

**продл|и́ть** (-ю́, -и́шь; impf **продлева́ть**) сов перех to extend; (жизнь) to prolong

**продл|и́ться** (3sg -и́тся) сов от **дли́ться**

**продово́льственный** прил food; **~ магази́н** grocer's (shop) (BRIT), grocery (US)

**продово́льстви|е** (-я) ср provisions мн

**продолгова́тый** прил elongated

**продолжа́|ть** (-ю; pf **продо́лжить**) несов перех to continue; **~ (продо́лжить** pf) +impf infin to continue или carry on doing; **~ся** (pf **продо́лжиться**) несов возв to continue, carry on

**продолже́ни|е** (-я) ср (борьбы, лекции) continuation; (романа) sequel; **в ~** +gen for the duration of

**продолжи́тельност|ь** (-и) ж duration; (сре́дняя) **~ жи́зни** (average) life expectancy

**продолжи́тельный** прил (болезнь, разговор) prolonged

**продо́лж|ить(ся)** (-у(сь), -ишь(ся)) сов от **продолжа́ть(ся)**

**продо́льный** прил longitudinal

**проду́кт** (-а) м product; см. также **проду́кты**

**продукти́вност|ь** (-и) ж productivity

**продукти́вный** прил productive

**продукто́вый** прил food

**проду́кт|ы** (-ов) мн (также: **~ пита́ния**) foodstuffs мн

**проду́кци|я** (-и) ж produce

**проду́манный** прил well thought-out

**проду́ма|ть** (-ю; impf **проду́мывать**) сов перех (действия) to think out

**прое́зд** (-а) м (в транспорте) journey; (место) passage

**проездно́й** прил (документ) travel; **~ биле́т** travel card

**прое́здом** нареч en route

**проезжа́|ть** (-ю) несов от **прое́хать**

**прое́зж|ий** прил (люди) passing through: **~ая часть (у́лицы)** road

**прое́кт** (-а) м project; (дома) design; (закона, договора) draft

**проекти́р|овать** (-ую; pf с~) несов перех (дом) to design; (дороги) to plan; (pf за~; наме́тить) to plan

**прое́ктор** (-а) м (ОПТИКА) projector

**прое́м** (-а) м (дверно́й) aperture

**прое́хать** (как е́хать; см. Table

19) *сов перех* (*миновать*) to pass; (*пропустить*) to miss ♦ (*impf* **проезжа́ть**) *неперех*: ~ **ми́мо** +*gen*/**по** +*dat*/**че́рез** +*асс итп* to drive past/along/across *итп*; ~**ся** *сов возв* (*на машине*) to go for a drive

**прожёктор** (-а) *м* floodlight

**прож|е́чь** (-гу́, -жёшь *итп*, -гу́т; *pt* -ёг, -гла́; *impf* **прожига́ть**) *сов перех* to burn a hole in

**прожива́ни|е** (-я) *ср* stay

**прожива́|ть** (-ю) *несов от* **прожи́ть** ♦ *неперех* to live

**прожига́|ть** (-ю) *несов от* **прожёчь**

**прожи́|ть** (-ву́, -вёшь) *сов* (*пробыть живым*) to live; (*жить*) to spend

**про́з|а** (-ы) *ж* prose

**про́звищ|е** (-а) *ср* nickname

**прозева́|ть** (-ю) *сов от* **зева́ть**

**прозра́чный** *прил* transparent; (*ткань*) see-through

**проигра́|ть** (-ю; *impf* **прои́грывать**) *сов перех* to lose; (*играть*) to play

**прои́грыватель** (-я) *м* record player

**про́игрыш** (-а) *м* loss

**произведе́ни|е** (-я) *ср* work

**произв|ести́** (-еду́, -едёшь; *pt* -ёл, -ела́; *impf* **производи́ть**) *сов перех* (*операцию*) to carry out; (*впечатление, суматоху*) to create

**производи́тель** (-я) *м* producer

**производи́тельность** (-и) *ж* productivity

**производи́тельный** *прил* (*продуктивный*) productive

**произв|оди́ть** (-ожу́, -о́дишь) *несов от* **произвести́** ♦ *перех* (*изготовлять*) to produce, manufacture

**произво́дственн|ый** *прил* (*процесс, план*) production; ~**ое** **объедине́ние** large production company; *см.* **ПО**

**произво́дств|о** (-а) *ср* (*товаров*) production, manufacture; (*отрасль*) industry; (*завод, фабрика*) factory; **промы́шленное** ~ industrial output; (*отрасль*) industry

**произво́л** (-а) *м* despotism

**произво́льный** *прил* (*свободный*) (*СПОРТ*) freestyle; (*вывод*) arbitrary

**произн|ести́** (-есу́, -есёшь; *pt* -ёс, -есла́; *impf* **произноси́ть**) *сов перех* (*слово*) to pronounce; (*речь*) to make

**произн|оси́ть** (-ошу́, -о́сишь) *несов от* **произнести́**

**произноше́ни|е** (-я) *ср* pronunciation

**произойти́** (*как* **идти́**; *см. Table 18*; *impf* **происходи́ть**) *сов* to occur

**происх|оди́ть** (-ожу́, -о́дишь) *несов от* **произойти́** ♦ *неперех*: ~ **от**/**из** +*gen* to come from

**происхожде́ни|е** (-я) *ср* origin

**происше́стви|е** (-я) *ср* event; **доро́жное** ~ road accident

**пройти́** (*как* **идти́**; *см. Table 18*; *impf* **проходи́ть**) *сов* to pass; (*расстояние*) to cover; (*слух*) to spread; (*дорога, канал итп*) to stretch; (*дождь, снег*) to fall; (*операция, переговоры итп*) to go ♦ *перех* (*практику, службу итп*) to complete; (*изучить: тему итп*) to do; **проходи́ть** (~ *pf*) **в** +*асс* (*в институт итп*) to get into; ~**сь** (*impf* **проха́живаться**) *сов возв* (*по комнате*) to pace; (*по парку*) to stroll

**прока́лыва|ть** (-ю) *несов от*

**проколо́ть**

**прока́т** (**-а**) м (*телевизора*) hire; (*также*: **кино~**) film distribution; **брать** (**взять** *pf*) **что-н на ~** to hire sth

**прок|ати́ть** (**-ачу́, -а́тишь**) *сов перех*: ~ **кого́-н** (*на маши́не итп*) to take sb for a ride; **~ся** *сов возв* (*на маши́не*) to go for a ride

**проки́с|нуть** (*3sg* **-нет**, *pt* **-, -ла**) *сов от* **ки́снуть**

**прокла́д|ка** (**-ки**; *gen pl* **-ок**) ж (*действие*: *труб*) laying out; (: *провода*) laying; (*защи́тная*) padding

**прокла́дыва|ть** (**-ю**) *несов от* **проложи́ть**

**прокл|я́сть** (**-яну́, -янёшь**; *pt* **-ял, -яла́, -я́ло**, *impf* **проклина́ть**) *сов перех* to curse

**прокля́тый** *прил* damned

**проко́л** (**-а**) м (*см глаг*) puncturing; lancing; piercing; (*отве́рстие*: *в шине*) puncture

**прок|оло́ть** (**-олю́, -о́лешь**; *impf* **прока́лывать**) *сов перех* (*ши́ну*) to puncture; (*нары́в*) to lance; (*у́ши*) to pierce

**прокр|а́сться** (**-аду́сь, -адёшься**; *impf* **прокра́дываться**) *сов возв*: ~ **в** +*acc*/**ми́мо** +*gen*/**че́рез** +*acc* итп to creep (*BRIT*) *или* sneak (*US*) in(to)/ past/through итп

**прокрич|а́ть** (**-у́, -и́шь**) *сов перех* (*вы́крикнуть*) to shout out

**прокр|ути́ть** (**-учу́, -у́тишь**; *impf* **прокру́чивать**) *сов перех* (*проверну́ть*) to turn; (*мя́со*) to mince; (*разг*: *де́ньги*) to invest illegally

**прокуро́р** (**-а**) м (*го́рода*) procurator; (*на суде́*) counsel for the prosecution

**пролага́|ть** (**-ю**) *несов от*

**проложи́ть**

**прола́мыва|ть** (**-ю**) *несов от* **проломи́ть**

**прола́|ять** (**-ю**) *сов от* **ла́ять**

**пролеж|а́ть** (**-у́, -и́шь**) *сов* to lie

**проле́з|ть** (**-у, -ешь**; *impf* **пролеза́ть**) *сов* to get through

**проле|те́ть** (**-чу́, -ти́шь**; *impf* **пролета́ть**) *сов* to fly; (*челове́к, по́езд*) to fly past; (*ле́то, о́тпуск*) to fly by

**проли́в** (**-а**) м strait(s) (*мн*)

**пролива́|ть(ся)** (**-ю(сь)**) *несов от* **проли́ть(ся)**

**проливно́й** *прил*: ~ **дождь** downpour

**прол|и́ть** (**-ью, -ьёшь**; *pt* **-и́л, -ила́**, *impf* **пролива́ть**) *сов перех* to spill; **~ся** (*impf* **пролива́ться**) *сов возв* to spill

**прол|ожи́ть** (**-ожу́, -о́жишь**; *impf* **прокла́дывать**) *сов перех* to lay

**прол|оми́ть** (**-омлю́, -о́мишь**; *impf* **прола́мывать**) *сов перех* (*лёд*) to break; (*че́реп*) to fracture

**про́мах** (**-а**) м miss; (*перен*) blunder

**промахн|у́ться** (**-у́сь, -ёшься**; *impf* **прома́хиватся**) *сов возв* to miss

**прома́чива|ть** (**-ю**) *несов от* **промочи́ть**

**промедле́ни|е** (**-я**) *ср* delay

**проме́дл|ить** (**-ю, -ишь**) *сов*: ~ **с** +*instr* to delay

**промежу́т|ок** (**-ка**) м gap

**промелькн|у́ть** (**-у́, -ёшь**) *сов* to flash past; ~ (*pf*) **в** +*prp* (*в голове́*) to flash through; (*перед глаза́ми*) to flash past

**промока́|ть** (**-ю**) *несов от* **промо́кнуть, промокну́ть**

♦ *неперех* to let water through

**промока́|ка** (**-ки**; *gen pl* **-ек**) ж

(*разг*) blotting paper

**промо́кн|уть (-у;** *impf* **промока́ть)** *сов* to get soaked

**промокн|у́ть (-у́, -ёшь;** *impf* **промока́ть)** *сов перех* to blot

**промолч|а́ть (-у́, -и́шь)** *сов* to say nothing

**пром|очи́ть (-очу́, -о́чишь;** *impf* **прома́чивать)** *сов перех* to get wet

**промтова́рный** *прил*: ~ **магази́н** small department store

**промтова́р|ы (-ов)** *мн* = **промы́шленные това́ры**

**промч|а́ться (-у́сь, -и́шься)** *сов возв* (*год, жизнь*) to fly by; ~ (*pf*) **ми́мо** +*gen*/**че́рез** +*acc* (*поезд, человек*) to fly past/through

**промыва́ни|е (-я)** *ср* (*желудка*) pumping; (*гла́за, раны*) bathing

**пром|ы́ть (-о́ю, -о́ешь;** *impf* **промыва́ть)** *сов перех* (*желудок*) to pump; (*рану, глаз*) to bathe

**промы́шленник (-а)** *м* industrialist

**промы́шленност|ь (-и)** *ж* industry

**промы́шленн|ый** *прил* industrial; ~**ые това́ры** manufactured goods

**прон|ести́ (-есу́, -есёшь;** *pt* **-ёс, -есла́;** *impf* **проноси́ть)** *сов перех* to carry; (*секретно*) to sneak in; ~**сь** (*impf* **проноси́ться)** *сов возв* (*машина, пуля, бегун*) to shoot by; (*время*) to fly by; (*буря*) to whirl past

**пронзи́тельный** *прил* piercing

**прони́к|нуть (-ну;** *pt* **-, -ла;** *impf* **проника́ть)** *сов перех*: ~ **в** +*acc* to penetrate; (*залезть*) to break into; ~**ся** (*impf* **проника́ться)** *сов возв*: ~**ся** +*instr* to be filled with

**проница́тельный** *прил* (*человек, ум*) shrewd; (*взгляд*) penetrating

**прон|оси́ть(ся) (-ошу́(сь), -о́сишь(ся))** *несов от* **пронести́(сь)**

**пропага́нд|а (-ы)** *ж* propaganda; (*спорта*) promotion

**пропаганди́р|овать (-ую)** *несов перех* (*политику*) to spread propaganda about; (*знания, спорт*) to promote

**пропада́|ть (-ю)** *несов от* **пропа́сть**

**пропа́ж|а (-и)** *ж* (*денег, документов*) loss

**про́паст|ь (-и)** *ж* precipice

**проп|а́сть (-аду́, -адёшь;** *impf* **пропада́ть)** *сов* to disappear; (*деньги, письмо*) to go missing; (*аппетит, голос, слух*) to go; (*усилия, билет в театр*) to be wasted; **пропада́ть (~** *pf*) **без вести** (*человек*) to go missing

**пропе́ллер (-а)** *м* (*АВИА*) propeller

**проп|е́ть (-ою́, -оёшь)** *сов от* **петь**

**проп|иса́ть (-ишу́, -и́шешь;** *impf* **пропи́сывать)** *сов перех* (*человека*) to register; (*лекарство*) to prescribe; ~**ся** *сов возв* to register

**пропи́с|ка (-ки)** *ж* registration

**пропи́ска** - registration. By law every Russian citizen is required to register at his or her place of residence. A stamp confirming the registration is displayed in the passport. This registration stamp is as essential as having the passport itself. See also note at **па́спорт**.

**прописн|о́й** *прил*: ~**а́я бу́ква** capital letter

**пропи́сыва|ть (-ю)** *несов от* **прописа́ть**

**пропита́ни|е (-я)** *ср* food

**пропл|ы́ть (-ыву́, -ывёшь;** *impf* **проплыва́ть)** *сов (человек)* to swim; *(: минова́ть)* to swim past; *(су́дно)* to sail; *(: минова́ть)* to sail past

**пропове́дник (-а)** *м (РЕЛ)* preacher; *(перен: тео́рии)* advocate

**пропове́д|овать (-ую)** *несов перех (РЕЛ)* to preach; *(тео́рию)* to advocate

**про́поведь (-и)** *ж (РЕЛ)* preaching

**прополз|ти́ (-у́, -ёшь;** *pt* **-, -ла́)** *сов:* ~ **по** +*dat*/**в** +*acc итп (насеко́мое, челове́к)* to crawl along/in(to) *итп; (змея́)* to slither along/in(to) *итп*

**прополоска́|ть (-ю)** *сов от* **полоска́ть**

**проп|оло́ть (-олю́, -о́лешь)** *сов от* **поло́ть**

**пропорциона́льный** *прил (фигу́ра)* well-proportioned; *(разви́тие, распределе́ние)* proportional

**пропо́рци|я (-и)** *ж* proportion

**про́пуск (-а)** *м (де́йствие: в зал, че́рез грани́цу итп)* admission; *(в те́ксте, в изложе́нии)* gap; *(нея́вка: на рабо́ту, в шко́лу)* absence; *(nom pl* **-а́;** *докуме́нт)* pass

**пропуска́|ть (-ю)** *несов от* **пропусти́ть** ♦ *перех (свет итп)* to let through; *(во́ду, хо́лод)* to let in

**проп|усти́ть (-ущу́, -у́стишь;** *impf* **пропуска́ть)** *сов перех* to miss; *(разреши́ть)* to allow; **пропуска́ть** *(~ pf)* **кого́-н вперёд** to let sb by

**прораб́ота|ть (-ю;** *impf* **прораба́тывать)** *сов* to work

**прор|асти́ (***3sg* **-астёт,** *pt* **-о́с, -осла́, -осло́;** *impf* **прораста́ть)** *сов (семена́)* to germinate; *(трава́)* to sprout

**прорв|а́ть (-у́, -ёшь;** *pt* **-а́л, -ала́;** *impf* **прорыва́ть)** *сов перех (плоти́ну)* to burst; *(оборо́ну, фронт)* to break through; **~ся** *(impf* **прорыва́ться)** *сов возв (плоти́на, ша́рик)* to burst; **прорыва́ться** *(~ся pf)* **в** +*acc* to burst in(to)

**проре́|зать (-жу, -жешь;** *impf* **проре́зывать)** *сов перех* to cut through; **~ся** *сов от* **ре́заться**

**проре́ктор (-а)** *м* vice-principal

**проро́к (-а)** *м (РЕЛ, перен)* prophet

**проро́ч|ить (-у, -ишь;** *pf* **на~)** *несов перех* to predict

**прор|уби́ть (-ублю́, -у́бишь;** *impf* **~уба́ть)** *сов перех* to make a hole in

**про́руб|ь (-и)** *ж* ice-hole

**проры́в (-а)** *м (фро́нта)* break-through; *(плоти́ны)* bursting; *(про́рванное ме́сто)* breach

**прорыва́|ть(ся) (-ю(сь))** *несов от* **прорва́ть(ся)**

**прор|ы́ть (-о́ю, -о́ешь;** *impf* **прорыва́ть)** *сов перех* to dig

**проса́чива|ться (***3sg* **-ется)** *несов от* **просочи́ться**

**просверл|и́ть (-ю́, -и́шь;** *impf* **просве́рливать** *или* **сверли́ть)** *сов перех* to bore, drill

**просве́т (-а)** *м (в ту́чах)* break; *(перен: в кри́зисе)* light at the end of the tunnel

**просв|ети́ть (-ещу́, -ети́шь;** *impf* **просвеща́ть)** *сов перех* to enlighten

**просветле́ни|е (-я)** *ср (я́сность)* lucidity

**просве́чива|ть (-ю)** *несов от*

**просвети́ть** ♦ *неперех (солнце, луна)* to shine through; *(ткань)* to let light through

**просвеща́|ть (-ю)** *несов от* **просвети́ть**

**просвеще́ни|е (-я)** *ср* education

**просви|сте́ть (-щу́, -сти́шь)** *сов от* **свисте́ть** ♦ *неперех (пуля)* to whistle past

**просе́|ять (-ю)** *impf* **~ивать)** *сов перех (муку, песок)* to sift

**проси|де́ть (-жу́, -ди́шь)** *impf* **проси́живать)** *сов (сиде́ть)* to sit; *(пробыть)* to stay

**проси́тельный** *прил* pleading

**про|си́ть (-шу́, -сишь)** *pf* **по~)** *несов перех* to ask; **~шу́ Вас!** if you please!; **~ (по~** *pf)* **кого́-н о чём-н** / +*infin* to ask sb for sth/to do; **~ (по~** *pf)* **кого́-н за кого́-н** to ask sb a favour (*BRIT*) *или* favor (*US*) on behalf of sb; **~ся (***pf* **по~ся)** *несов возв (о про́сьбе)* to ask permission

**проск|ака́ть (-ачу́, -а́чешь)** *сов:* **~ че́рез/сквозь** +*acc (ло́шадь)* to gallop across/through

**проскользн|у́ть (-у́, -ёшь)** *impf* **проска́льзывать)** *сов (моне́та)* to slide in; *(челове́к)* to slip in; *(перен: сомне́ние)* to creep in

**просла́в|ить (-лю, -ишь)** *impf* **прославля́ть)** *сов перех (сде́лать изве́стным)* to make famous; *(impf* **прославля́ть** *или* **сла́вить; восхвали́ть)** to glorify; **~ся (***impf* **прославля́ться)** *сов возв* to become famous

**просла́вленный** *прил* renowned

**просле|ди́ть (-жу́, -ди́шь)** *impf* **просле́живать)** *сов перех (глаза́ми)* to follow; *(иссле́довать)* to trace ♦ *неперех:* **~ за** +*instr* to follow; *(контроли́ровать)* to monitor

**просмо́тр (-а)** *м (фи́льма)*

viewing; *(докуме́нтов)* inspection

**просм|отре́ть (-отрю́, -о́тришь)** *impf* **просма́тривать)** *сов перех (ознако́миться: чита́я)* to look through; *(: смотря́)* to view; *(пропусти́ть)* to overlook

**просн|у́ться (-у́сь, -ёшься;** *impf* **просыпа́ться)** *сов возв* to wake up; *(перен: любо́вь, страх итп)* to be awakened

**просоч|и́ться (***3sg* **-и́тся;** *impf* **проса́чиваться)** *сов возв (та́кже перен)* to filter through

**просп|а́ть (-лю́, -и́шь;** *pt* **-а́л, -ала́)** *сов (спать)* to sleep; *(impf* **просыпа́ть; встать по́здно)* to oversleep, sleep in

**проспе́кт (-а)** *м (в го́роде)* avenue; *(изда́ние)* brochure

**просро́ч|ить (-у, -ишь)** *impf* **просро́чивать)** *сов перех (платёж)* to be late with; *(па́спорт, биле́т)* to let expire

**проста́ива|ть (-ю)** *несов от* **простоя́ть**

**простира́|ться (-юсь;** *pf* **простере́ться)** *несов возв* to extend

**проститу́т|ка (-ки;** *gen pl* **-ок)** *ж* prostitute

**прости́|ть (прощу́, прости́шь;** *impf* **проща́ть)** *сов перех* to forgive; **проща́ть (~** *pf)* **что-н кому́-н** to excuse *или* forgive sb (for) sth; **~те, как пройти́ на ста́нцию?** excuse me, how do I get to the station?; **~ся (***impf* **проща́ться)** *сов возв:* **~ся с** +*instr* to say goodbye to

**про́сто** *нареч (де́лать)* easily; *(объясня́ть)* simply ♦ *част* just; **всё э́то ~ недоразуме́ние** all this is just a misunderstanding; **~ (так)** for no particular reason

**прост|о́й** *прил* simple; *(оде́жда)*

plain; (*задача*) easy, simple; (*человек, манеры*) unaffected; (*обыкновенный*) ordinary ♦ (**-о́й**) *м* downtime; (*рабочих*) stoppage; ~ каранда́ш lead pencil

**прост|она́ть** (**-ону́, -о́нешь**) *сов* (*не)перех* to groan

**просто́р** (**-а**) *м* expanse; (*свобода*) scope

**просто́рный** *прил* spacious

**простот|а́** (**-ы́**) *ж* (*см прил*) simplicity; plainness; easiness, simplicity; unaffectedness

**просто|я́ть** (**-ю́, -и́шь**; *impf* **проста́ивать**) *сов* to stand; (*бездействуя*) to stand idle

**простра́нств|о** (**-а**) *ср* space; (*территория*) expanse

**простр|ели́ть** (**-елю́, -е́лишь**; *impf* **простре́ливать**) *сов перех* to shoot through

**просту́д|а** (**-ы**) *ж* (*МЕД*) cold

**прост|уди́ть** (**-ужу́, -у́дишь**; *impf* **простужа́ть**) *сов перех*: ~ кого́-н to give sb a cold; **~ся** (*impf* **простужа́ться**) *сов возв* to catch a cold

**просту́женный** *прил*: ребёнок просту́жен the child has got a cold

**прост|упи́ть** (*3sg* **-у́пит**; *impf* **проступа́ть**) *сов* (*пот, пятна*) to come through; (*очертания*) to appear

**просту́п|ок** (**-ка**) *м* misconduct

**простын|я́** (**-и́**; *nom pl* **про́стыни**, *gen pl* **просты́нь**, *dat pl* **-я́м**) *ж* sheet

**просу́н|уть** (**-у, -ешь**; *impf* **просо́вывать**) *сов перех*: ~ в +*acc* to push in

**просчёт** (**-а**) *м* (*счёт*) counting; (*ошибка: в подсчёте*) error; (: *в действиях*) miscalculation

**просчита́|ть** (**-ю**; *impf*

**просчи́тывать**) *сов перех* (*считать*) to count; (*ошибиться*) to miscount; **~ся** (*impf* **просчи́тываться**) *сов возв* (*при счёте*) to miscount; (*в планах*) to miscalculate

**просы́п|ать** (**-лю, -лешь**; *impf* **просыпа́ть**) *сов перех* to spill; **~ся** (*impf* **просыпа́ться**) *сов возв* to spill

**просыпа́|ть** (**-ю**) *несов от* **проспа́ть, просы́пать**; **~ся** *несов от* **просну́ться, просы́паться**

**про́сьб|а** (**-ы**) *ж* request

**прота́лкива|ть** (**-ю**) *несов от* **протолкну́ть**

**прот|ащи́ть** (**-ащу́, -а́щишь**; *impf* **прота́скивать**) *сов перех* to drag

**проте́з** (**-а**) *м* artificial *или* prosthetic limb; зубно́й ~ denture

**протека́|ть** (*3sg* **-ет**) *несов от* **проте́чь** ♦ *неперех* (*вода*) to flow; (*болезнь, явление*) to progress

**протекци|я** (**-и**) *ж* patronage

**прот|ере́ть** (**-ру́, -рёшь**; *pt* **-ёр, -ёрла**; *impf* **протира́ть**) *сов перех* (*износить*) to wear a hole in; (*очистить*) to wipe; **~ся** (*impf* **протира́ться**) *сов возв* (*износиться*) to wear through

**проте́ст** (**-а**) *м* protest; (*ЮР*) objection

**протеста́нт** (**-а**) *м* Protestant

**протеста́нтский** *прил* Protestant

**протест|ова́ть** (**-у́ю**) *несов*: ~ (**про́тив** +*gen*) to protest (against)

**проте́ч|ка** (**-ки**; *gen pl* **-ек**) *ж* leak

**прот|е́чь** (*3sg* **-ечёт**, *pt* **-ёк, -екла́**; *impf* **протека́ть**) *сов* (*вода*) to seep; (*крыша*) to leak

**про́тив** *предл*: ~ +*gen* against; (*прямо перед*) opposite ♦ *как* *сказ*: **я ~ э́того** I am against this

**про́тив|ень (-ня)** *м* baking tray

**проти́в|иться (-люсь, -ишься;**
*pf* **вос~)** *несов возв*: **~** +*dat* to
oppose

**проти́вник (-а)** *м* opponent
♦ *собир* (*ВОЕН*) the enemy

**проти́вно** *нареч* offensively ♦ *как*
*сказ безл* it's disgusting

**проти́вный** *прил* (*мнение*)
opposite; (*неприятный*) disgusting

**противовозду́шный** *прил* anti-
aircraft

**противога́з (-а)** *м* gas mask

**противоде́йств|овать (-ую)**
*несов*: **~** +*dat* to oppose

**противозако́нный** *прил*
unlawful

**противозача́точн|ый** *прил*
contraceptive; **~ое сре́дство**
contraceptive

**противопожа́рный** *прил*
(*меры*) fire-prevention; (*техника*)
fire-fighting

**противополо́жный** *прил*
(*берег*) opposite; (*мнение*)
opposing

**противопоста́в|ить (-лю, -ишь;**
*impf* **противопоставля́ть)** *сов*
*перех*: **~ кого́-н/что́-н** +*dat* to
contrast sb/sth with

**противоречи́вый** *прил*
contradictory

**противоре́чи|е (-я)** *ср*
contradiction; (*классовое*) conflict

**противоре́ч|ить (-у, -ишь)**
*несов*: **~** +*dat* (*человеку*) to
contradict; (*логике, закону итп*)
to defy

**противосто|я́ть (-ю́, -и́шь)**
*несов*: **~** +*dat* (*ветру*) to
withstand; (*уговорам*) to resist

**противоя́ди|е (-я)** *ср* antidote

**протира́|ть(ся) (-ю(сь))** *несов*
*от* **протере́ть(ся)**

**проткн|у́ть (-у́, -ёшь;** *impf*
**протыка́ть)** *сов перех* to pierce

**прото́к (-а)** *м* (*рукав реки*)
tributary; (*соединяющая река*)
channel

**протоко́л (-а)** *м* (*собрания*)
minutes *мн*; (*допроса*) transcript;
(*соглашения*) protocol

**протолкн|у́ть (-у́, -ёшь;** *impf*
**прота́лкивать)** *сов перех* to
push through

**прото́чный** *прил* (*вода*) running

**проту́хн|уть (3sg -ет;** *impf*
**протуха́ть** *или* **ту́хнуть)** *сов* to
go bad *или* off

**протыка́|ть (-ю)** *несов от*
**проткну́ть**

**протя́гива|ть(ся) (-ю(сь))** *несов*
*от* **протяну́ть(ся)**

**протяже́ни|е (-я)** *ср*: **на ~и двух**
**неде́ль/ме́сяцев** over a period of
two weeks/months

**протяже́нност|ь (-и)** *ж* length

**протяже́нный** *прил* prolonged

**протян|у́ть (-у́, -ешь)** *сов от*
**тяну́ть** ♦ (*impf* **протя́гивать**)
*перех* (*верёвку*) to stretch;
(*провод*) to extend; (*руки, ноги*)
to stretch (out); (*предмет*) to hold
out; **~ся** (*impf* **протя́гиваться**)
*сов возв* (*дорога*) to stretch;
(*провод*) to extend; (*рука*) to
stretch out

**про|учи́ть (-учу́, -у́чишь;** *impf*
**проу́чивать)** *сов перех* (*разг*:
*наказать*) to teach a lesson; **~ся**
*сов возв* to study

**проф.** *сокр* (= **профе́ссор**) Prof.

**профессиона́л (-а)** *м* professional

**профессиона́льный** *прил*
professional; (*болезнь, привычка,*
*обучение*) occupational;
(*обучение*) vocational; **~ сою́з**
trade (*BRIT*) *или* labor (*US*) union

**профе́сси|я (-и)** *ж* profession

**профéссор** (-а; *nom pl* **-á**) *м*
professor

**профилáктик|а** (-и) *ж* prevention

**профилакти́ческий** *прил*
(*меры*) prevent(at)ive; (*прививка*)
prophylactic

**про́филь** (-я) *м* profile

**профсою́з** (-а) *м сокр* =
**профессионáльный сою́з**

**профсою́зный** *прил* trade-union

**проха́жива|ться** (-юсь) *несов*
*от* **пройти́сь**

**прохла́д|а** (-ы) *ж* cool

**прохлади́тельный** *прил*: ~
**напи́ток** cool soft drink

**прохла́дно** *нареч* (*встретить*)
coolly ♦ *как сказ* it's cool

**прохла́дный** *прил* cool

**прохо́д** (-а) *м* passage

**прох|оди́ть** (-ожу́, -о́дишь)
*несов от* **пройти́**

**проходн|áя** (-о́й) *ж* checkpoint
(*at entrance to factory etc*)

**проходно́й** *прил*: ~ **балл** pass
mark

> **проходно́й балл** - pass mark.
> This is the score which the student
> has to achieve to be admitted into
> a higher education institution. The
> score is calculated using the marks
> attained during the four entrance
> exams and the average mark in
> the Certificate of Secondary
> Education. The score varies from
> year to year and depends on the
> number and standard of the
> applicants. The score required by
> popular departments can be as
> high as 25. See also notes at
> **аттеста́т зре́лости** and
> **вступи́тельные экза́мены**.

**прохо́ж|ий** (-его) *м* passer-by

**процвета́|ть** (-ю) *несов* (*фирма,*

*бизнесме́н*) to prosper; (*театр,*
*наука*) to flourish; (*хорошо́ жить*)
to thrive

**проц|еди́ть** (-ежу́, -е́дишь) *сов*
**отцеди́ть** ♦ (*impf* **проце́живать**)
*перех* (*бульо́н, сок*) to strain

**процеду́р|а** (-ы) *ж* procedure;
(*МЕД, обычно мн*) course *ед* of
treatment

**процеду́рный** *прил* procedural; ~
**кабине́т** treatment room

**проце́жива|ть** (-ю) *несов от*
**процеди́ть**

**проце́нт** (-а) *м* percentage; **в**
**разме́ре 5 ~ов годовы́х** at a
yearly rate of 5 percent; *см. также*
**проце́нты**

**проце́нтн|ый** *прил* percentage;
~**ая ста́вка** interest rate

**проце́нт|ы** (-ов) *мн* (*КОММ*)
interest *ед*; (*плата*) commission *ед*

**проце́сс** (-а) *м* process; (*ЮР,*
*поря́док*) proceedings *мн*;
(: *также*: **суде́бный ~**) trial;
**воспали́тельный ~** inflammation;
**в ~е** +*gen* in the course of

**проце́ссор** (-а) *м* (*КОМП*)
processor

**прочёл** *сов см.* **проче́сть**

**проч|е́сть** (-ту́, -тёшь; *pt* -ёл,
-ла́) *сов от* **чита́ть**

**про́ч|ий** *прил* other; **поми́мо**
**всего́ ~его** apart from anything
else

**прочита́|ть** (-ю) *сов от* **чита́ть**

**прочла́** *etc сов см.* **проче́сть**

**про́чно** *нареч* (*закрепи́ть*) firmly

**про́чный** *прил* (*материа́л итп*)
durable; (*постро́йка*) solid;
(*зна́ния*) sound; (*отноше́ние,*
*семья́*) stable; (*мир, сча́стье*)
lasting

**прочту́** *etc сов см.* **проче́сть**

**прочь** *нареч* (*в сто́рону*) away;
**ру́ки ~!** hands off!

**прошедш|ий** *прил* (*прошлый*)
past; **~ее время** past tense
**прошёл(ся)** *сов см.* **пройти(сь)**
**прошени|е** (**-я**) *ср* plea;
(*ходатайство*) petition
**прош|ептать** (**-епчу́, -е́пчешь**)
*сов перех* to whisper
**прошла́** *итп сов см.* **пройти́**
**прошлого́дний** *прил* last year's
**про́шл|ое** (**-ого**) *ср* the past
**про́шл|ый** *прил* last; (*прежний*)
past; **в ~ раз** last time; **на ~ой
неде́ле** last week; **в ~ом ме́сяце/
году́** last month/year
**прошу́(сь)** *несов см.*
**проси́ть(ся)**
**проща́йте** *част* goodbye, farewell
**проща́льный** *прил* parting;
(*вечер*) farewell
**проща́ни|е** (**-я**) *ср* (*действие*)
parting; **на ~** on parting
**проща́|ть(ся)** (**-ю(сь)**) *несов от*
**прости́ть(ся)**
**про́ще** *сравн нареч от* **про́сто**
♦ *сравн прил от* **просто́й**
**проще́ни|е** (**-я**) *ср* (*ребёнка,
друга итп*) forgiveness;
(*преступника*) pardon; **проси́ть
(попроси́ть** *pf*) **~я** to say sorry;
**прошу́ ~я!** (I'm) sorry!
**прояви́тел|ь** (**-я**) *м* (*ФОТО*)
developer
**про|яви́ть** (**-явлю́, -я́вишь**; *impf*
**проявля́ть**) *сов перех* to display;
(*ФОТО*) to develop; **~ся** (*impf*
**проявля́ться**) *сов возв* (*талант,
потенциал итп*) to reveal itself;
(*ФОТО*) to be developed
**проявле́ни|е** (**-я**) *ср* display
**проявля́|ть(ся)** (**-ю(сь)**) *несов
от* **прояви́ть(ся)**
**проясн|и́ть** (**-ю́, -и́шь**; *impf*
**проясня́ть**) *сов перех*
(*обстановку*) to clarify; **~ся** (*impf*
**проясня́ться**) *сов возв* (*погода,*

*небо*) to brighten *или* clear up;
(*обстановка*) to be clarified;
(*мысли*) to become lucid
**пруд** (**-а́**; *loc sg* **-у́**) *м* pond
**пружи́н|а** (**-ы**) *ж* (*ТЕХ*) spring
**прут** (**-а́**; *nom pl* **-ья**) *м* twig
**пры́гал|ка** (**-ки**; *gen pl* **-ок**) *ж*
skipping-rope (*BRIT*), skip rope (*US*)
**пры́га|ть** (**-ю**) *несов* to jump;
(*мяч*) to bounce
**пры́гн|уть** (**-у**) *сов* to jump; (*мяч*)
to bounce
**прыгу́н** (**-а́**) *м* (*СПОРТ*) jumper
**прыж|о́к** (**-ка́**) *м* jump; (*в воду*)
dive; **~ки́ в высоту́/длину́** high/
long jump
**прыщ** (**-а́**) *м* spot
**пряд|ь** (**-и**) *ж* lock (*of hair*)
**пря́ж|а** (**-и**) *ж* yarn
**пря́ж|ка** (**-ки**; *gen pl* **-ек**) *ж* (*на
ремне*) buckle; (*на юбке*) clasp
**прям|а́я** (**-о́й**) *ж* straight line
**пря́мо** *нареч* (*о направлении*)
straight ahead; (*ровно*) upright;
(*непосредственно*) straight;
(*откровенно*) directly ♦ *част*
(*действительно*) really
**прям|о́й** *прил* straight; (*путь,
слова, человек*) direct; (*ответ,
политика*) open; (*вызов, обман*)
obvious; (*улики*) hard;
(*сообщение, обязанность итп*)
direct; (*выгода, смысл*) real;
(*значение слова*) literal; **~а́я
трансля́ция** live broadcast; **~о́е
дополне́ние** direct object
**прямоуго́льник** (**-а**) *м* rectangle
**пря́ник** (**-а**) *м* ≈ gingerbread
**пря́ность** (**-и**) *ж* spice
**пря́ный** *прил* spicy
**пря́|тать** (**-чу, -чешь**; *pf* **с~**)
*несов перех* to hide; **~ся** (*pf*
**с~ся**) *несов возв* to hide;
(*человек: от холода*) to shelter
**пря́т|ки** (**-ок**) *мн* hide-and-seek *ед*

(*BRIT*), hide-and-go-seek *ед* (*US*)
**псал|о́м** (**-ма́**) *м* psalm
**псалты́р|ь** (**-и**) *ж* Psalter
**псевдони́м** (**-а**) *м* pseudonym
**псих** (**-а**) *м* (*разг*) nut
**психиа́тр** (**-а**) *м* psychiatrist
**психиатри́ческий** *прил*
psychiatric
**психиатри́|я** (**-и**) *ж* psychiatry
**пси́хик|а** (**-и**) *ж* psyche
**психи́ческий** *прил*
(*заболевание*) mental
**психо́з** (**-а**) *м* (*МЕД*) psychosis
**психо́лог** (**-а**) *м* psychologist
**психологи́ческий** *прил*
psychological
**психоло́ги|я** (**-и**) *ж* psychology
**психотерапе́вт** (**-а**) *м*
psychotherapist
**птен|е́ц** (**-ца́**) *м* chick
**пти́ц|а** (**-ы**) *ж* bird ♦ *собир*:
(*дома́шняя*) ~ poultry
**пти́чий** *прил* (*корм, клетка*) bird
**пу́блик|а** (**-и**) *ж собир* audience;
(*общество*) public
**публика́ци|я** (**-и**) *ж* publication
**публик|ова́ть** (**-у́ю**); *pf* **о~**) *несов*
*перех* to publish
**публици́ст** (**-а**) *м* social
*commentator*
**публици́стик|а** (**-и**) *ж собир*
sociopolitical journalism
**публицисти́ческий** *прил*
sociopolitical
**публи́чный** *прил* public; ~ **дом**
brothel
**пу́гал|о** (**-а**) *ср* scarecrow; (*перен*:
*о человеке*) fright
**пуга́|ть** (**-ю**; *pf* **ис~** *или* **на~**)
*несов перех* to frighten, scare;
~**ся** (*pf* **ис~ся** *или* **на~ся**) *несов*
*возв* to be frightened *или* scared
**пу́говиц|а** (**-ы**) *ж* button
**пу́дел|ь** (**-я**) *м* poodle
**пу́динг** (**-а**) *м* ≈ pudding

**пу́др|а** (**-ы**) *ж* powder; **са́харная ~**
icing sugar
**пу́дрениц|а** (**-ы**) *ж* powder
compact
**пу́др|ить** (**-ю, -ишь**; *pf* **на~**)
*несов перех* to powder; ~**ся** (*pf*
**на~ся**) *несов возв* to powder
one's face
**пузыр|ёк** (**-ька́**) *м уменьш от*
**пузы́рь**; (*для лекарства,*
*чернил*) vial
**пузыр|и́ться** (*3sg* **-и́тся**) *несов*
*возв* (*жидкость*) to bubble;
(*краска*) to blister
**пузы́р|ь** (**-я́**) *м* (*мыльный*)
bubble; (*на коже*) blister
**пулемёт** (**-а**) *м* machine gun
**пуленепробива́емый** *прил*
bullet-proof
**пуло́вер** (**-а**) *м* pullover
**пульвериза́тор** (**-а**) *м* atomizer
**пульс** (**-а**) *м* (*МЕД, перен*) pulse
**пульси́р|овать** (*3sg* **-ует**) *несов*
(*артерии*) to pulsate; (*кровь*) to
pulse
**пульт** (**-а**) *м* panel
**пу́л|я** (**-и**) *ж* bullet
**пункт** (**-а**) *м* point; (*документа*)
clause; (*медицинский*) centre
(*BRIT*), center (*US*);
(*наблюдательный, командный*)
post; **населённый ~** small
settlement
**пункти́р** (**-а**) *м* dotted line
**пунктуа́льный** *прил* (*человек*)
punctual
**пунктуа́ци|я** (**-и**) *ж* punctuation
**пуп|о́к** (**-ка́**) *м* (*АНАТ*) navel
**пург|а́** (**-и́**) *ж* snowstorm
**пуск** (**-а**) *м* (*завода итп*) launch
**пуска́|ть(ся)** (**-ю(сь)**) *несов от*
**пусти́ть(ся)**
**пусте́|ть** (*3sg* **-ет**; *pf* **о~**) *несов* to
become empty; (*улицы*) to
become deserted

пу|сти́ть (-щу́, -стишь; *impf*
пуска́ть) *сов перех* (*руку,
человека*) to let go of; (*лошадь,
санки итп*) to send off; (*станок*) to
start; (*в вагон, в зал*) to let in;
(*пар, дым*) to give off; (*камень,
снаряд*) to throw; (*корни*) to put
out; **пуска́ть** (~ *pf*) **что-н на** +*acc*/
**под** +*acc* (*использовать*) to use
sth as/for; **пуска́ть** (~ *pf*) **кого́-н
куда́-нибудь** to let sb go
somewhere; ~**ся** (*impf* **пуска́ться**)
*сов возв*: ~**ся в** +*acc* (*в
объясне́ния*) to go into;
**пуска́ться** (~**ся** *pf*) **в** ~**ть** to set off
пу́сто *нареч* empty ♦ *как сказ*
(*ничего нет*) it's empty; (*никого
нет*) there's no-one there
пусто́й *прил* empty
пуст|ота́ (-оты́; *nom pl* -о́ты) *ж*
emptiness; (*полое место*) cavity
пусты́|нный *прил* desert;
(*безлюдный*) deserted
пусты́н|я (-и; *gen pl* -ь) *ж* desert
пусты́р|ь (-я́) *м* wasteland
пусты́ш|ка (-ки; *gen pl* -ек) *ж*
(*разг: соска*) dummy (*BRIT*),
pacifier (*US*)

**KEYWORD**

пусть *част*, +*3sg/pl* **1** (*выражает
приказ, угрозу*): **пусть он
придёт у́тром** let him come in the
morning; **пусть она́ то́лько
попро́бует отказа́ться** let her just
try to refuse
**2** (*выражает согласие*): **пусть
бу́дет так** so be it; **пусть бу́дет
по-тво́ему** have it your way
**3** (*всё равно*) OK, all right

пустя́к (-а́) *м* trifle; (*неценный
предмет*) trinket ♦ *как сказ*: э́то ~
it's nothing
пу́таниц|а (-ы) *ж* muddle

пу́таный *прил* muddled
пу́та|ть (-ю; *pf* за~ или с~) *несов
перех* (*нитки, волосы*) to tangle;
(*сбить с толку*) to confuse; (*pf* с~
или пере~; *бумаги, факты итп*)
to mix up; (*pf* в~; *разг*): ~ **кого́-н
в** +*acc* to get sb mixed up in; **я его́
с кем-то** ~**ю** I'm confusing him
with somebody else; **он всегда́** ~**л
на́ши имена́** he always got our
names mixed up; ~**ся** (*pf* за~**ся**
или с~**ся**) *несов возв* to get
tangled; (*в рассказе, в
объясне́нии*) to get mixed up
путёв|ка (-ки; *gen pl* -ок) *ж*
holiday voucher; (*водителя*)
manifest (*of cargo drivers*)
путеводи́тел|ь (-я) *м* guidebook
путём *предл*: ~ +*gen* by means of
путеше́ственник (-а) *м* traveller
(*BRIT*), traveler (*US*)
путеше́стви|е (-я) *ср* journey,
trip; (*морское*) voyage
путеше́ств|овать (-ую) *несов* to
travel
пу́тник (-а) *м* traveller (*BRIT*),
traveler (*US*)
путч (-а) *м* (*ПОЛИТ*) putsch
пут|ь (-и́; *см* Table 3) *м* (*также
перен*) way; (*платформа*)
platform; (*рельсы*) track;
(*путеше́ствие*) journey; **во́дные
~и** waterways; **возду́шные ~и** air
lanes; **нам с Ва́ми не по ~и** we're
not going the same way;
**счастли́вого ~и!** have a good
trip!; ~**и сообще́ния** transport
network
пух (-а; *loc sg* -у́) *м* (*у живо́тных*)
fluff; (*у птиц, у человека*) down;
**ни пу́ха ни пера́!** good luck!
пу́хлый *прил* (*щёки, человек*)
chubby; (*портфель*) bulging
пу́х|нуть (-ну; *pt* -, -ла; *pf* вс~
или о~) *несов* to swell (up)

**пухо́вый** прил (подушка) feather; (платок) angora

**пуч|о́к** (-ка́) м bunch; (света) beam

**пуши́стый** прил (мех, ковёр итп) fluffy; (волосы) fuzzy; (кот) furry

**пу́ш|ка** (-ки; gen pl -ек) ж cannon; (на танке) artillery gun

**пчел|а́** (-ы́; nom pl пчёлы) ж bee

**пчели́ный** прил (мёд) bee's

**пчелово́д** (-а) м bee-keeper

**пшени́ц|а** (-ы) ж wheat

**пшени́чный** прил wheat

**пшённ|ый** прил: ~ая ка́ша millet porridge

**пшен|о́** (-а́) ср millet

**пыла́|ть** (-ю) несов (костёр) to blaze; (перен: лицо) to burn

**пылесо́с** (-а) м vacuum cleaner, hoover ®

**пылесо́с|ить** (-ишь; pf про~) сов перех to vacuum, hoover ®

**пыли́н|ка** (-ки; gen pl -ок) ж speck of dust

**пыл|и́ть** (-ю́, -и́шь; pf на~) несов to raise dust; ~ся (pf за~ся) несов возв to get dusty

**пы́лкий** прил ardent

**пыл|ь** (-и; loc sg -и́) ж dust; вытира́ть (вы́тереть pf) ~ to dust

**пы́льный** прил dusty

**пыльц|а́** (-ы́) ж pollen

**пыта́|ть** (-ю) несов перех to torture; ~ся (pf по~ся) несов возв: ~ся +infin to try to do

**пы́т|ка** (-ки; gen pl -ок) ж torture

**пы́шный** прил (волосы) bushy; (обстановка, приём) splendid

**пьедеста́л** (-а) м (основание) pedestal; (для победителей) rostrum

**пье́с|а** (-ы) ж (ЛИТЕРАТУРА) play; (МУЗ) piece

**пью** etc несов см. **пить**

**пью́щ|ий** (-его) м heavy drinker

**пьяне́|ть** (-ю; pf о~) несов to get drunk

**пья́ниц|а** (-ы) м/ж drunkard

**пья́нств|о** (-а) ср heavy drinking

**пья́нств|овать** (-ую) несов to drink heavily

**пья́н|ый** прил (человек) drunk; (крики, песни итп) drunken ♦ (-ого) м drunk

**пюре́** ср нескл (фрукто́вое) purée; карто́фельное ~ mashed potato

**пя́т|ая** (-ой) ж: одна́ ~ one fifth

**пятёр|ка** (-ки; gen pl -ок) ж (цифра, карта) five; (ПРОСВЕЩ) ≈ A (school mark); (группа из пяти) group of five

**пя́тер|о** (-ы́х; как че́тверо; см. Table 30b) чис five

**пятибо́рь|е** (-я) ср pentathlon

**пяти́десяти** чис см. **пятьдеся́т**

**пятидесятиле́ти|е** (-я) ср fifty years мн; (годовщина) fiftieth anniversary

**пятидесятиле́тний** прил (период) fifty-year; (человек) fifty-year-old

**пятидеся́тый** чис fiftieth

**пя́|титься** (-чусь, -тишься; pf по~) несов возв to move backwards

**пятиуго́льник** (-а) м pentagon

**пятичасово́й** прил (рабочий день) five-hour; (поезд) five-o'clock

**пятиэта́жный** прил five-storey (BRIT), five-story (US)

**пя́т|ка** (-ки; gen pl -ок) ж heel

**пятна́дцатый** чис fifteenth

**пятна́дцат|ь** (-и; как пять; см. Table 26) чис fifteen

**пятни́стый** прил spotted

**пя́тниц|а** (-ы) ж Friday

**пят|но́** (-на́; nom pl пя́тна, gen pl -ен) ср (также перен) stain;

(*другого цвета*) spot

**пя́тый** *чис* fifth

**пят|ь** (-**и́**; *см. Table 26*) *чис* five; (*ПРОСВЕЩ*) ≈ A (*school mark*)

**пятьдеся́т** (-**и́десяти**; *см. Table 26*) *чис* fifty

**пятьсо́т** (-**исо́т**; *см. Table 28*) *чис* five hundred

# Р, р

**р.** *сокр* (= **река́**) R., r.; (= *роди́лся*) b.; (= **рубль**) R., r.

**раб** (-**а́**) *м* slave

**рабо́т|а** (-**ы**) *ж* work; (*источник заработка*) job; **сме́нная ~** shiftwork

**рабо́та|ть** (-**ю**) *несов* to work; (*магазин*) to be open; ~ (*impf*) **на кого́-н/что-н** to work for sb/sth; **кем Вы ~ете?** what do you do for a living?

**рабо́тник** (-**а**) *м* worker; (*учреждения*) employee

**работода́тел|ь** (-**я**) *м* employer

**работоспосо́бный** *прил* (*человек*) able to work hard

**рабо́ч|ий** *прил* worker's; (*человек, одежда*) working ♦ (-**его**) *м* worker; ~**ая си́ла** workforce; ~ **день** working day (*BRIT*), workday (*US*)

**ра́бский** *прил* (*жизнь*) slave-like

**ра́бств|о** (-**а**) *ср* slavery

**рабы́н|я** (-**и**) *ж* slave

**равви́н** (-**а**) *м* rabbi

**ра́венств|о** (-**а**) *ср* equality; **знак ~а** (*МАТ*) equals sign

**равни́н|а** (-**ы**) *ж* plain

**равно́** *нареч* equally ♦ *союз*: ~ (**как**) **и** as well as ♦ *как сказ*: **э́то всё ~** it doesn't make any difference; **мне всё ~** I don't mind;

**я всё ~ приду́** I'll come anyway

**равнове́си|е** (-**я**) *ср* equilibrium; ~ **сил** balance of power

**равноду́шный** *прил*: ~ (**к** +*dat*) indifferent (to)

**равноме́рный** *прил* even

**равнопра́ви|е** (-**я**) *ср* equality

**равноси́льн|ый** *прил*: ~ +*dat* equal to; **э́то ~о отка́зу** this amounts to a refusal

**равноце́нный** *прил* of equal value *или* worth

**ра́вн|ый** *прил* equal; ~**ым о́бразом** equally

**равня́|ть** (-**ю**; *pf* **с~**) *несов перех*: ~ (**с** +*instr*) (*делать равным*) to make equal (with); ~**ся** *несов возв*: ~**ся по** +*dat* to draw level with; (*считать себя равным*): ~**ся с** +*instr* to compare o.s. with; (*быть равносильным*): ~**ся** +*dat* to be equal to

**рагу́** *ср нескл* ragout

**рад** *как сказ*: ~ (+*dat*) glad (of); ~ +*infin* glad *или* pleased to do; ~ **познако́миться с Ва́ми** pleased to meet you

**ра́ди** *предл*: ~ +*gen* for the sake of; ~ **Бо́га!** (*разг*) for God's sake!

**радиа́ци|я** (-**и**) *ж* radiation

**радика́льный** *прил* radical

**радикули́т** (-**а**) *м* lower back pain

**ра́дио** *ср нескл* radio

**радиоакти́вный** *прил* radioactive

**радиовеща́ни|е** (-**я**) *ср* (radio) broadcasting

**радиопереда́ч|а** (-**и**) *ж* radio programme (*BRIT*) *или* program (*US*)

**радиоприёмник** (-**а**) *м* radio (set)

**радиослу́шател|ь** (-**я**) *м* (radio) listener

**радиоста́нци|я** (-**и**) *ж* radio station

**ра́диус** (-**а**) *м* radius

**ра́д|овать** (**-ую**; *pf* **об~**) *несов перех*: ~ **кого́-н** to make sb happy, please sb; **~ся** *несов возв* (*перен: душа*) to rejoice; **~ся** (**об~ся** *pf*) +*dat* (*успехам*) to take pleasure in; **он всегда́ ~уется гостя́м** he is always happy to have visitors

**ра́достный** *прил* joyful

**ра́дост|ь** (**-и**) *ж* joy; **с ~ю** gladly

**ра́дуг|а** (**-и**) *ж* rainbow

**ра́дужн|ый** *прил* (*перен: приятный*) bright; **~ая оболо́чка** (*АНАТ*) iris

**раду́шный** *прил* warm

**раз** (**-а**; *nom pl* **-ы́**, *gen pl* **-**) *м* time ♦ *нескл* (*один*) one ♦ *нареч* (*разг: однажды*) once ♦ *союз* (*разг: если*) if; **в тот/про́шлый ~** that/last time; **на э́тот ~** this time; **ещё ~** (once) again; **~ и навсегда́** once and for all; **ни ра́зу** not once; (**оди́н**) **~ в день** once a day; **~... то ...** (*разг*) if ... then ...

**разба́в|ить** (**-лю, -ишь**; *impf* **разбавля́ть**) *сов перех* to dilute

**разбе́г** (**-а**) *м* (*атлета*) run-up

**разбежа́ться** (*как* **бежа́ть**; *см. Table 20*; *impf* **разбега́ться**) *сов возв* to run off, scatter; (*перед прыжком*) to take a run-up; **у меня́ глаза́ разбега́ются** (*разг*) I'm spoilt for choice

**разбива́|ть(ся)** (**-ю(сь)**) *несов от* **разби́ть(ся)**

**разбира́|ть** (**-ю**) *несов от* **разобра́ть**; **~ся** *несов от* **разобра́ться** ♦ *возв* (*разг: понимать*): **~ся в** +*prp* to be an expert in

**раз|би́ть** (**-обью́, -обьёшь**; *imper* **-бе́й(те)**; *impf* **разбива́ть**) *сов перех* to break; (*машину*) to smash up; (*армию*) to crush; (*аллею*) to lay; **~ся** (*impf*

**разбива́ться**) *сов возв* to break, smash; (*в ава́рии*) to be badly hurt; (*на гру́ппы, на уча́стки*) to break up

**разбогате́|ть** (**-ю**) *сов от* **богате́ть**

**разбо́|й** (**-я**) *м* robbery

**разбо́йник** (**-а**) *м* robber

**разбо́р** (**-а**) *м* (*статьи́, вопро́са*) analysis; **без ~а** indiscriminately

**разбо́рк|а** (**-и**) *ж* in-fighting

**разбо́рный** *прил* (*ме́бель*) flat-pack

**разбо́рчивый** *прил* (*челове́к, вкус*) discerning; (*по́черк*) legible

**разбра́сыва|ть** (**-ю**) *несов от* **разброса́ть**; **~ся** *несов возв*: **~ся** +*instr* (*деньга́ми*) to waste; (*друзья́ми*) to underrate

**разброса́|ть** (**-ю**; *impf* **разбра́сывать**) *сов перех* to scatter

**разб|уди́ть** (**-ужу́, -у́дишь**) *сов от* **буди́ть**

**разва́л** (**-а**) *м* chaos

**разва́лин|а** (**-ы**) *ж* ruins *мн*

**разв|али́ть** (**-алю́, -а́лишь**; *impf* **разва́ливать**) *сов перех* to ruin; **~ся** (*impf* **разва́ливаться**) *сов возв* to collapse

**разв|ари́ться** (*3sg* **-а́рится**; *impf* **разва́риваться**) *сов возв* to be overcooked

**ра́зве** *част* really; **~ он согласи́лся/не знал?** did he really agree/not know?; **~ то́лько** *или* **что** except that

**развева́|ться** (*3sg* **-ется**) *несов возв* (*флаг*) to flutter

**разведе́ни|е** (**-я**) *ср* (*живо́тных*) breeding; (*расте́ний*) cultivation

**разведённый** *прил* (*в разво́де*) divorced

**разве́д|ка** (**-ки**; *gen pl* **-ок**) *ж* (*ГЕО*) prospecting; (*шпиона́ж*) intelligence; (ВОЕН) reconnaissance

**разве́дчик** (-а) м (ГЕО)
prospector; (шпион) intelligence
agent; (ВОЕН) scout

**разв|езти́** (-езу́, -езёшь; pt -ёз,
-езла́, -езло́; impf **развози́ть**)
сов перех (товар) to take

**разверн|у́ть** (-у́, -ёшь; impf
**развёртывать** или
**развора́чивать**) сов перех
(бума́гу) to unfold; (торго́влю
итп) to launch; (кора́бль,
самолёт) to turn around;
(батальо́н) to deploy; **~ся** (impf
**развёртываться** или
**развора́чиваться**) сов возв
(кампа́ния, рабо́та) to get under
way; (автомоби́ль) to turn
around; (вид) to open up

**развесел|и́ть** (-ю́, -и́шь) сов от
**весели́ть**

**разве́|сить** (-шу, -сишь; impf
**разве́шивать**) сов перех to
hang

**разв|ести́** (-еду́, -едёшь; pt -ёл,
-ела́; impf **разводи́ть**) сов перех
(доста́вить) to take; (порошо́к) to
dissolve; (сок) to dilute;
(живо́тных) to breed; (цветы́,
сад) to grow; (мост) to raise; **~сь**
(impf **разводи́ться**) сов возв:
**~сь** (с +instr) to divorce, get
divorced (from)

**разветвле́ни|е** (-я) ср (доро́ги)
fork

**разве́|ять** (-ю; impf **разве́ивать**)
сов перех (облака́) to disperse;
(сомне́ния, грусть) to dispel; **~ся**
(impf **разве́иваться**) сов возв
(облака́) to disperse; (челове́к) to
relax

**развива́|ть(ся)** (-ю(сь)) несов от
**разви́ть(ся)**

**развива́ющ|ийся** прил: **~аяся
страна́** developing country

**разви́л|ка** (-ки; gen pl -ок) ж fork
(in road)

**разви́ти|е** (-я) ср development

**развито́й** прил developed

**раз|ви́ть** (-овью́, -овьёшь; imper
-ве́й(те); impf **развива́ть**) сов
перех to develop; **~ся** (impf
**развива́ться**) сов возв to
develop

**развлека́тельный** прил
entertaining

**развлече́ни|е** (-я) ср entertaining

**развл|е́чь** (-еку́, -ечёшь etc,
-еку́т; pt -ёк, -екла́; impf
**развлека́ть**) сов перех to
entertain; **~ся** (impf
**развлека́ться**) сов возв to have
fun

**разво́д** (-а) м (супру́гов) divorce

**разв|оди́ть(ся)** (-ожу́(сь),
-о́дишь(ся)) несов от
**развести́(сь)**

**разводно́й** прил: **~ мост**
drawbridge

**развора́чива|ть(ся)** (-ю(сь))
несов от **разверну́ть(ся)**

**разворо́т** (-а) м (маши́ны) U-
turn; (в кни́ге) double page

**развра́т** (-а) м promiscuity;
(ни́зкие нра́вы) depravity

**развра|ти́ть** (-щу́, -ти́шь; impf
**развраща́ть**) сов перех to
pervert; (деньга́ми) to deprave,
corrupt; **~ся** (impf **развраща́ться**)
сов возв (см перех) to become
promiscuous; to become corrupted

**разв|яза́ть** (-яжу́, -я́жешь; impf
**развя́зывать**) сов перех
(шну́рки) to untie; (: войну́) to
unleash; **~ся** (impf
**развя́зываться**) сов возв
(шну́рки) to come untied

**развя́з|ка** (-ки; gen pl -ок) ж
(коне́ц) finale; (АВТ) junction

**разгада́|ть** (-ю; impf

**разга́дывать)** *сов перех* (*загадку*) to solve; (*замыслы, тайну*) to guess

**разга́р** (**-а**) *м*: в ~е +*gen* (*сезона*) at the height of; (*боя*) in the heart of; **кани́кулы в (по́лном) ~е** the holidays are in full swing

**разгиба́|ть(ся)** (**-ю(сь)**) *несов от* **разогну́ть(ся)**

**разгла́|дить** (**-жу, -дишь**; *impf* **разгла́живать**) *сов перех* to smooth out

**разгла|си́ть** (**-шу́, -си́шь**; *impf* **разглаша́ть**) *сов перех* to divulge, disclose

**разгова́рива|ть** (**-ю**) *несов*: ~ **(с** +*instr*) to talk (to)

**разгово́р** (**-а**) *м* conversation

**разгово́рник** (**-а**) *м* phrase book

**разгово́рный** *прил* colloquial

**разгово́рчивый** *прил* talkative

**разго́н** (**-а**) *м* (*демонстрации*) breaking up; (*автомобиля*) acceleration

**разгоня́|ть(ся)** (**-ю(сь)**) *несов от* **разогна́ть(ся)**

**разгор|е́ться** (*3sg* **-и́тся**; *impf* **разгора́ться**) *сов возв* to flare up

**разгоряч|и́ться** (**-у́сь, -и́шься**) *сов возв* (*от волнения*) to get het up; (*от бега*) to be hot

**разграни́ч|ить** (**-у, -ишь**; *impf* **разграни́чивать**) *сов перех* to demarcate

**разгро́м** (**-а**) *м* rout; (*разг: беспорядок*) mayhem

**разгром|и́ть** (**-лю́, -и́шь**) *сов перех* (*врага*) to crush; (*книгу*) to slam

**разгр|узи́ть** (**-ужу́, -у́зишь**; *impf* **разгружа́ть**) *сов перех* to unload

**разгры́з|ть** (**-у, -ёшь**) *сов от* **грызть**

**разгу́л** (**-а**) *м* revelry; ~ +*gen* (*реакции*) rule of

**разда|ва́ть(ся)** (**-ю́, -ёшь(ся)**) *несов от* **разда́ть(ся)**

**разд|ави́ть** (**-авлю́, -а́вишь**) *сов от* **дави́ть**

**разда́ть** (*как* **дать**; *см. Table 16*; *impf* **раздава́ть**) *сов перех* to give out, distribute; ~**ся** (*impf* **раздава́ться**) *сов возв* (*звук*) to be heard

**раздва́ива|ться** (**-юсь**) *несов от* **раздво́иться**

**раздви́н|уть** (**-у**; *impf* **раздвига́ть**) *сов перех* to move apart

**раздво|и́ться** (**-ю́сь, -и́шься**; *impf* **раздва́иваться**) *сов возв* (*дорога, река*) to divide into two; (*перен: мнение*) to be divided

**раздева́л|ка** (**-ки**; *gen pl* **-ок**) *ж* changing room

**раздева́|ть(ся)** (**-ю(сь)**) *несов от* **разде́ть(ся)**

**разде́л** (**-а**) *м* (*имущества*) division; (*часть*) section

**разде́ла|ть** (**-ю**; *impf* **разде́лывать**) *сов перех* (*тушу*) to cut up; ~**ся** (*impf* **разде́лываться**) *сов возв* (*разг*): ~**ся с** +*instr* (*с делами*) to finish; (*с долгами*) to settle

**раздел|и́ть** (**-елю́, -е́лишь**) *сов от* **дели́ть** ♦ (*impf* **разделя́ть**) *перех* (*мнение*) to share; ~**ся** *сов от* **дели́ться** ♦ (*impf* **разделя́ться**) *возв* (*мнения, общество*) to become divided

**разде́|ть** (**-ну, -нешь**; *impf* **раздева́ть**) *сов перех* to undress; ~**ся** (*impf* **раздева́ться**) *сов возв* to get undressed

**раздира́|ть** (**-ю**) *несов перех* (*душу, общество*) to tear apart

**раздраже́ни|е** (**-я**) *ср* irritation

**раздражённый** *прил* irritated

**раздражи́тельный** *прил* irritable

**раздраж|и́ть** (-у́, -и́шь; *impf* **раздража́ть**) *сов перех* to irritate, annoy; (*нервы*) to agitate; ~**ся** (*impf* **раздража́ться**) *сов возв* (*кожа, глаза*) to become irritated; (*человек*): ~**ся** (+*instr*) to be irritated (by)

**раздува́|ть(ся)** (-ю(сь)) *несов от* **разду́ть(ся)**

**разду́ма|ть** (-ю; *impf* **разду́мывать**) *сов*: ~ +*infin* to decide not to do

**разду́мыва|ть** (-ю) *несов от* **разду́мать ♦** *неперех*: ~ (*о* +*prp*) (*долго думать*) to contemplate

**разду́мь|е** (-я) *ср* contemplation

**разд|у́ть** (-у́ю; *impf* **раздува́ть**) *сов перех* (*огонь*) to fan; **у неё** ~**у́ло щёку** her cheek has swollen up; ~**ся** (*impf* **раздува́ться**) *сов возв* (*щека*) to swell up

**раз|жа́ть** (-ожму́, -ожмёшь; *impf* **разжима́ть**) *сов перех* (*пальцы, губы*) to relax; ~**ся** (*impf* **разжима́ться**) *сов возв* to relax

**раз|жева́ть** (-ую́; *impf* **разжёвывать**) *сов перех* to chew

**раз|же́чь** (-жгу́, -жжёшь *итп*, -жгу́т; *pt* -жёг, -жгла́; *impf* **разжига́ть**) *сов перех* to kindle

**разлага́|ть(ся)** (-ю(сь)) *несов от* **разложи́ть(ся)**

**разла́д** (-а) *м* (*в делах*) disorder; (*с женой*) discord

**разла́мыва|ть** (-ю) *несов от* **разлома́ть, разломи́ть**

**разле|те́ться** (-чу́сь, -ти́шься; *impf* **разлета́ться**) *сов возв* to fly off (*in different directions*)

**разли́в** (-а) *м* flooding

**раз|ли́ть** (-олью́, -ольёшь; *impf* **разлива́ть**) *сов перех* (*пролить*) to spill; ~**ся** (*impf* **разлива́ться**) *сов возв* (*пролиться*) to spill; (*река*) to overflow

**различа́|ть** (-ю) *несов от* **различи́ть**; ~**ся** *несов возв*; ~**ся по** +*dat* to differ in

**разли́чи|е** (-я) *ср* difference

**различ|и́ть** (-у́, -и́шь; *impf* **различа́ть**) *сов перех* (*увидеть, услышать*) to make out; (*отличить*): ~ (**по** +*dat*) to distinguish (by)

**разли́чный** *прил* different

**разложе́ни|е** (-я) *ср* decomposition; (*общества итп*) disintegration

**разл|ожи́ть** (-ожу́, -о́жишь; *impf* **раскла́дывать**) *сов перех* (*карты*) to arrange; (*диван*) to open out; (*impf* **разлага́ть**; *хим, био*) to decompose; ~**ся** (*impf* **разлага́ться**) *сов возв* (*хим, био*) to decompose; (*общество*) to disintegrate

**разл|оми́ть** (-омлю́, -о́мишь; *impf* **разла́мывать**) *сов перех* (*на части*) to break up

**разлу́к|а** (-и) *ж* separation

**разлуч|и́ть** (-у́, -и́шь; *impf* **разлуча́ть**) *сов перех*: ~ **кого́-н с** +*instr* to separate sb from; ~**ся** (*impf* **разлуча́ться**) *сов возв*: ~**ся** (**с** +*instr*) to be separated (from)

**разл|юби́ть** (-юблю́, -ю́бишь) *сов перех*: ~ +*infin* (*читать, гуля́ть итп*) to lose one's enthusiasm for doing; **он меня́** ~**юби́л** he doesn't love me any more

**разма́|зать** (-жу, -жешь; *impf* **разма́зывать**) *сов перех* to smear

**разма́тыва|ть** (-ю) *несов от* **размота́ть**

**разма́х** (-а) *м* (*рук*) span; (*перен*:

*деятельности*) scope; (: *проекта*) scale; ~ **крýльев** wingspan

**размáхива|ть** (**-ю**) *несов*: ~ +*instr* to wave; (*оружием*) to brandish

**размахн|ýться** (**-ýсь, -ёшься**; *impf* **размáхиваться**) *сов возв* to bring one's arm back; (*перен: разг: разг: в делах итп*) to go to town

**размéн** (**-а**) *м* (*денег, пленных*) exchange; ~ **квартúры** flat swap (*of one large flat for two smaller ones*)

**размéнн|ый** *прил*: ~ **автомáт** change machine; ~**ая монéта** (small) change

**разменя́|ть** (**-ю**; *impf* **размéнивать**) *сов перех* (*деньги*) to change; (*квартиру*) to exchange; ~**ся** (*impf* **размéниваться**) *сов возв* (*перен: разг: обменять жилплощадь*) to do a flat swap (*of one large flat for two smaller ones*)

**размéр** (**-а**) *м* size

**размéренный** *прил* measured

**размести́|ть** (**-щý, -сти́шь**; *impf* **размещáть**) *сов перех* (*в отеле*) to place; (*на столе*) to arrange; ~**ся** (*impf* **размещáться**) *сов возв* (*по комнатам*) to settle o.s.

**размé|тить** (**-чу, -тишь**; *impf* **размечáть**) *сов перех* to mark out

**размеша́|ть** (**-ю**; *impf* **размéшивать**) *сов перех* to stir

**размещá|ть(ся)** (**-ю(сь)**) *несов от* **размести́ть(ся)**

**размина́|ть(ся)** (**-ю(сь)**) *несов от* **размя́ть(ся)**

**размини́р|овать** (**-ую**) (*не*)*сов перех*: ~ **пóле** to clear a field of mines

**размúн|ка** (**-ки**; *gen pl* **-ок**) *ж* (*спортсменов*) warm-up

**размин|ýться** (**-ýсь, -ёшься**) *сов возв* (*не встретиться*) to miss

each other; (*дать пройти*) to pass

**размнóж|ить** (**-у, -ишь**; *impf* **размножáть**) *сов перех* to make (multiple) copies of; ~**ся** (*pf* **размножáться**) *сов возв* (*БИО*) to reproduce

**размóк|нуть** (**-ну**; *pt* **-, -ла**; *impf* **размокáть**) *сов* (*хлеб, картон*) to go soggy; (*почва*) to become sodden

**размóлв|ка** (**-ки**) *ж* quarrel

**разморó|зить** (**-жу, -зишь**; *impf* **разморáживать**) *сов перех* to defrost; ~**ся** (*impf* **разморáживаться**) *сов возв* to defrost

**размотá|ть** (**-ю**; *impf* **размáтывать**) *сов перех* to unwind

**разм|ы́ть** (*3sg* **-óет**; *impf* **размывáть**) *сов перех* to wash away

**размышля́|ть** (**-ю**) *несов*: ~ (**о** +*prp*) to contemplate, reflect (on)

**размягч|ить** (**ý, -и́шь**; *impf* **размягчáть**) *сов перех* to soften

**размя́к|нуть** (**-ну**; *pt* **-, -ла**; *impf* **размякáть**) *сов* to soften

**раз|мя́ть** (**-омнý, -омнёшь**; *impf* **разминáть**) *сов перех* to loosen up; ~**ся** (*impf* **разминáться**) *сов возв* to warm up

**разнáшива|ть(ся)** (**-ю**) *несов от* **разноси́ть(ся)**

**разн|ести́** (**-есý, -есёшь**; *pt* **-ёс, -еслá**; *impf* **разноси́ть**) *сов перех* (*письма*) to deliver; (*тарелки*) to put out; (*тучи*) to disperse; (*заразу, слухи*) to spread; (*раскритиковать*) to slam; ~**сь** (*impf* **разноси́ться**) *сов возв* (*слух, запах*) to spread; (*звук*) to resound

**разнимá|ть** (**-ю**) *несов от* **разня́ть**

**ра́зниц|а (-ы)** ж difference; **кака́я ~?** what difference does it make?

**разви́дность|ь (-и)** ж (*БИО*) variety; (*людей*) type, kind

**разногла́си|е (-я)** ср disagreement

**разнообра́зи|е (-я)** ср variety

**разнообра́зный** прил various

**разноро́дный** прил heterogeneous

**разно́с (-а)** м delivery; (*разг: выговор*) battering

**разн|оси́ть (-ошу́, -о́сишь)** несов от **разнести́** ♦ (*impf* **разна́шивать**) сов перех (*обувь*) to break in; **~ся** несов от **разнести́сь** ♦ (*impf* **разна́шиваться**) сов возв (*обувь*) to be broken in

**разносторо́нний** прил (*деятельность*) wide-ranging; (*ум, личность*) multifaceted

**ра́зность|ь (-и)** ж difference

**разноцве́тный** прил multicoloured (*BRIT*), multicolored (*US*)

**ра́зный** прил different

**разн|я́ть (-иму́, -и́мешь;** *impf* **разнима́ть**) сов перех (*руки*) to unclench; (*дерущихся*) to separate

**разоблач|и́ть (-у́, -и́шь;** *impf* **разоблача́ть**) сов перех to expose

**раз|обра́ть (-беру́, -берёшь;** *impf* **разбира́ть**) сов перех (*бумаги*) to sort out; (*текст*) to analyse (*BRIT*), analyze (*US*); (*вкус, подпись итп*) to make out; **разбира́ть (~ pf) (на ча́сти)** to take apart; **~ся** (*impf* **разбира́ться**) сов возв: **~ся в** +*prp* (*в вопросе, в деле*) to sort out

**разобщённый** прил divided

**ра́зовый** прил: **~ биле́т** single

(*BRIT*) *или* one-way ticket

**раз|огна́ть (-гоню́, -го́нишь;** *impf* **разгоня́ть**) сов перех (*толпу*) to break up; (*тучи*) to disperse; (*машину*) to increase the speed of; **~ся** (*impf* **разгоня́ться**) сов возв to build up speed, accelerate

**разогн|у́ть (-у́, -ёшь;** *impf* **разгиба́ть**) сов перех (*проволоку*) to straighten out; **~ся** (*impf* **разгиба́ться**) сов возв to straighten up

**разогре́|ть (-ю;** *impf* **разогрева́ть**) сов перех (*чайник, суп*) to heat; **~ся** (*impf* **разогрева́ться**) сов возв (*суп*) to heat up

**разозл|и́ть(ся) (-ю́(сь), -и́шь(ся))** сов от **зли́ть(ся)**

**разойти́сь** (как **идти́**; см. *Table 18; impf* **расходи́ться**) сов возв (*гости*) to leave; (*толпа*) to disperse; (*тираж*) to sell out; (*не встретиться*) to miss each other; (*супруги*) to split up; (*шов, крепления*) to come apart; (*перен: мнения*) to diverge; (*разг: дать волю себе*) to get going

**ра́зом** нареч (*разг: все вместе*) all at once; (: *в один приём*) all in one go

**разомкн|у́ть (-у́, -ёшь;** *impf* **размыка́ть**) сов перех (*цепь*) to unfasten; **~ся** (*impf* **размыка́ться**) сов возв to come unfastened

**разорв|а́ть (-у́, -ёшь)** сов от **рвать** ♦ (*impf* **разрыва́ть**) перех to tear *или* rip up; (*перен: связь*) to sever; (: *договор*) to break; **~ся** сов от **рва́ться** ♦ (*impf* **разрыва́ться**) возв (*одежда*) to tear, rip; (*верёвка, цепь*) to break; (*связь*) to be severed; (*снаряд*) to explode

**разоре́ни|е (-я)** *ср (человека)*
impoverishment; *(компании)*
(financial) ruin

**разор|и́ть (-ю́, -и́шь;** *impf*
**разоря́ть) сов перех (деревню,
гнездо)** to plunder; *(население)*
to impoverish; (: *компанию,
страну*) to ruin; **~ся** (*impf*
**разоря́ться) сов возв (человек)**
to become impoverished;
*(компания)* to go bust *или*
bankrupt

**разоруже́ни|е (-я)** *ср* disarming;
*(ПОЛИТ)* disarmament

**разоруж|и́ть (-у́, -и́шь;** *impf*
**разоружа́ть) сов перех** to
disarm; **~ся** (*impf* **разоружа́ться)**
*сов возв* to disarm

**разоря́|ть(ся) (-ю(сь))** *несов от*
**разори́ть(ся)**

**разо|сла́ть (-шлю́, -шлёшь;** *impf*
**рассыла́ть) сов перех** to send
out

**разостла́ть (расстелю́,
рассте́лешь)** *несов* =
**расстели́ть**

**разочарова́ни|е (-я)** *ср* disap-
pointment; *(потеря веры)*: **~ в**
*+prp (в идее)* disenchantment with

**разочаро́ванный** *прил*
disappointed: **~ в** *+prp (в идее)*
disenchanted with

**разочар|ова́ть (-у́ю;** *impf*
**разочаро́вывать) сов перех** to
disappoint; **~ся** (*impf*
**разочаро́вываться) сов возв:**
**~ся в** *+prp* to become
disenchanted with

**разрабо́та|ть (-ю;** *impf*
**разраба́тывать) сов перех** to
develop

**разрабо́т|ка (-ки)** *ж*
development; **га́зовые ~ки** gas
fields *мн*; **нефтяны́е ~ки** oilfields
*мн*

**разра|зи́ться (-жу́сь, -зи́шься;**
*impf* **разража́ться) сов возв** to
break out

**разр|асти́сь** (*3sg* **-асти́тся,** *pt*
**-о́сся, -осла́сь;** *impf*
**разраста́ться) сов возв (лес)** to
spread

**разре́з (-а)** *м (на ю́бке)* slit;
*(ГЕОМ)* section

**разре́|зать (-жу, -жешь)** *сов от*
**ре́зать**

**разреша́|ть (-ю)** *несов от*
**разреши́ть; ~ся** *несов от*
**разреши́ться ♦ неперех**
*(допускаться)* to be allowed *или*
permitted

**разреше́ни|е (-я)** *ср (действие)*
authorization; *(родителей)*
permission; *(проблемы)* resolution;
*(документ)* permit

**разреш|и́ть (-у́, -и́шь;** *impf*
**разреша́ть) сов перех (решить)**
to resolve; *(позволить)*: **~ кому́-н**
*+infin* to allow *или* permit sb to do;
**~и́те?** may I come in?; **~и́те
пройти́** may I pass; **~ся** (*impf*
**разреша́ться) сов возв** to be
resolved

**разровня́|ть (-ю)** *сов от*
**ровня́ть**

**разр|уби́ть (-ублю́, -у́бишь;**
*impf* **разруба́ть) сов перех** to
chop in two

**разру́х|а (-и)** *ж* devastation

**разруши́тельный** *прил*
*(война)* devastating; *(действие)*
destructive

**разру́ш|ить (-у, -ишь;** *impf*
**разруша́ть) сов перех** to
destroy; **~ся** (*impf* **разруша́ться)**
*сов возв* to be destroyed

**разры́в (-а)** *м (отношений)*
severance; *(снаряда)* explosion;
*(во времени, в цифрах)* gap

**разрыва́|ть(ся) (-ю(сь))** *несов*

от **разорва́ть(ся)**

**разря́д** (-а) м (тип) category; (квалифика́ция) grade

**разря|ди́ть** (-жу́, -ди́шь; impf **разряжа́ть**) сов перех (ружьё) to discharge; **разряжа́ть** (~ pf) **обстано́вку** to diffuse the situation

**разря́д|ка** (-ки; gen pl -ок) ж escape; (в те́ксте) spacing; **разря́дка (междунаро́дной напряжённости)** détente

**разряжа́ть** (-ю) несов от **разряди́ть**

**разубе|ди́ть** (-жу́, -ди́шь; impf **разубежда́ть**) сов перех: ~ **кого́-н (в** +prp) to dissuade sb (from)

**разува́|ть(ся)** (-ю(сь)) несов от **разу́ть(ся)**

**ра́зум** (-а) м reason

**разуме́|ться** (3sg -ется) сов возв: **под э́тим ~ется, что ...** by this is meant that ...; **(само́ собо́й) ~ется** that goes without saying
♦ вводн сл: **он, ~ется, не знал об э́том** naturally, he knew nothing about it

**разу́мный** прил (существо́) intelligent; (посту́пок, реше́ние) reasonable

**разу́тый** прил (без о́буви) barefoot

**раз|у́ть** (-у́ю; impf **разува́ть**) сов перех: ~ **кого́-н** to take sb's shoes off; ~**ся** (impf **разува́ться**) сов возв to take one's shoes off

**раз|учи́ть** (-учу́, -у́чишь; impf **разу́чивать**) сов перех to learn; ~**ся** (impf **разу́чиваться**) сов возв: ~**ся** +infin to forget how to do

**разъеда́|ть** (3sg -ет) несов от **разъе́сть**

**разъедини́|ть** (-ю, -и́шь; impf **разъединя́ть**) сов перех (провода́, телефо́н) to disconnect

**разъезжа́|ть** (-ю) несов (по дела́м) to travel; (ката́ться) to ride about; ~**ся** несов от **разъе́хаться**

**разъе́сть** (как **есть**; см. Table 15; impf **разъеда́ть**) сов перех to corrode

**разъе́хаться** (как **е́хать**; см. Table 19; impf **разъезжа́ться**) сов возв (го́сти) to leave

**разъярённый** прил furious

**разъясне́ни|е** (-я) ср clarification

**разъясни́|ть** (-ю, -и́шь; impf **разъясня́ть**) сов перех to clarify

**разыгра́|ть** (-ю; impf **разы́грывать**) сов перех (МУЗ, СПОРТ) to play; (сце́ну) to act out; (в лотере́ю) to raffle; (разг: подшути́ть) to play a joke или trick on

**раз|ыска́ть** (-ыщу́, -ы́щешь; impf **разы́скивать**) сов перех to find

**РАИС** ср сокр (= Росси́йское аге́нтство интеллектуа́льной со́бственности) copyright protection agency

**ра|й** (-я; loc sg -ю́) м paradise

**райо́н** (-а) м (страны́) region; (го́рода) district

**райо́нный** прил district

**ра́йский** прил heavenly

**рак** (-а) м (ЗООЛ, речно́й) crayfish; (: морско́й) crab; (МЕД) cancer; (созве́здие): **Рак** Cancer

**раке́т|а** (-ы) ж rocket; (ВОЕН) missile; (су́дно) hydrofoil

**раке́т|ка** (-ки; gen pl -ок) ж (СПОРТ) racket

**ра́ковин|а** (-ы) ж (ЗООЛ) shell; (для умыва́ния) sink

**ра́ковый** прил (ЗООЛ, КУЛИН) crab; (МЕД) cancer

**ра́м|а** (-ы) ж frame; (АВТ) chassis

**ра́м|ка** (-ки; gen pl -ок) ж frame;

см. также **ра́мки**

**ра́м|ки (-ок)** мн: ~ +gen (*рассказа, обязанностей*) framework ед of; (*закона*) limits мн of; **в ~ках** +gen (*закона, прили́чия*) within the bounds of; (*переговоров*) within the framework of; **за ~ками** +gen beyond the bounds of

**РАН** м сокр (= Росси́йская акаде́мия нау́к) Russian Academy of Sciences

**ра́н|а (-ы)** ж wound

**ра́неный** прил injured; (*ВОЕН*) wounded

**ра́н|ец (-ца)** м (*школьный*) satchel

**ра́н|ить (-ю, -ишь)** (не)сов перех to wound

**ра́нний** прил early

**ра́но** нареч early ♦ как сказ it's early; **~ и́ли по́здно** sooner or later

**ра́ньше** сравн нареч от **ра́но** ♦ нареч (*пре́жде*) before ♦ предл: ~ +gen before; **~ вре́мени** (*ра́доваться итп*) too soon

**ра́порт (-а)** м report

**рапорт|ова́ть (-у́ю)** (не)сов: ~ (кому́-н о чём-н) to report back (to sb on sth)

**ра́с|а (-ы)** ж race

**раси́зм (-а)** м racism

**раси́ст (-а)** м racist

**раска́ива|ться (-юсь)** несов от **раска́яться**

**раскал|и́ть (-ю́, -и́шь**; impf **раска́лять)** сов перех to bring to a high temperature; **~ся** (impf **раскаля́ться**) сов возв to get very hot

**раска́лыва|ть(ся) (-ю(сь))** несов от **расколо́ть(ся)**

**раска́пыва|ть (-ю)** несов от **раскопа́ть**

**раска́т (-а)** м (*гро́ма*) peal

**раската́|ть (-ю**; impf **раска́тывать)** сов перех (*ковёр*) to unroll; (*те́сто*) to roll out; (*доро́гу*) to flatten (out)

**раска́яни|е (-я)** ср repentance

**раска́|яться (-юсь**; impf **раска́иваться)** сов возв: ~ (**в** +prp) to repent (of)

**раскида́|ть (-ю**; impf **раски́дывать)** сов перех to scatter

**раски́н|уть (-у**; impf **раски́дывать)** сов перех (*ру́ки*) to throw open; (*се́ти*) to spread out; (*ла́герь*) to set up; **~ся** (impf **раски́дываться**) сов возв to stretch out

**раскладно́й** прил folding

**раскладу́ш|ка (-ки**; gen pl **-ек)** ж (*разг*) camp bed (*BRIT*), cot (*US*)

**раскла́дыва|ть (-ю)** несов от **разложи́ть**

**раскле́|ить (-ю, -ишь**; impf **раскле́ивать)** сов перех (*закле́енное*) to unstick; (*плака́ты*) to paste up

**раско́ванный** прил relaxed

**раско́л (-а)** м (*организа́ции*) split; (*РЕЛ*) schism

**раск|оло́ть (-олю́, -о́лешь**; impf **раска́лывать)** сов перех to split; (*лёд, оре́х*) to crack; **~ся** (impf **раска́лываться**) сов возв (*поле́но, оре́х*) to split open; (*перен: организа́ция*) to be split

**раскопа́|ть (-ю**; impf **раска́пывать)** сов перех to dig up

**раско́п|ки (-ок)** мн (*рабо́ты*) excavations мн; (*ме́сто*) (archaeological) dig ед

**раскра́|сить (-шу, -сишь**; impf **раскра́шивать)** сов перех to colour (*BRIT*) или color (*US*) (in)

**раскро|и́ть (-ю́, -и́шь)** сов

*перех* to cut

**раскр|ути́ть** (-учу́, -у́тишь; *impf* **раскру́чивать**) *сов перех* (*винт*) to unscrew; (*рекламировать*) to hype up; (*дело*) to set in motion

**раскру́т|ка** (-ки; *gen pl* -ок) ж (*разг*) hyping up

**раскр|ы́ть** (-о́ю, -о́ешь; *impf* **раскрыва́ть**) *сов перех* to open; (*перен: чью-нибудь тайну, план*) to discover; (: *свою тайну, план*) to disclose; ~**ся** (*impf* **раскрыва́ться**) *сов возв* to open

**раск|упи́ть** (-уплю́, -у́пишь; *impf* **раскупа́ть**) *сов перех* to buy up

**ра́совый** *прил* racial

**распа́д** (-а) *м* break-up; (*хим*) decomposition

**распада́|ться** (*3sg* -ется) *несов от* **распа́сться** ♦ *возв* (*состоять из частей*): ~ **на** +*acc* to be divided into

**распа́|сться** (*3sg* -дётся; *impf* **распада́ться**) *сов возв* to break up; (*молекула*) to decompose

**распахн|у́ть** (-у́, -ёшь; *impf* **распа́хивать**) *сов перех* to throw open; ~**ся** (*impf* **распа́хиваться**) *сов возв* to fly open

**распашо́н|ка** (-ки; *gen pl* -ок) ж cotton baby top without buttons

**распеча́та|ть** (-ю; *impf* **распеча́тывать**) *сов перех* (*письмо, пакет*) to open; (*размножить*) to print off

**распеча́т|ка** (-ки; *gen pl* -ок) ж (*доклада*) print-out

**расп|или́ть** (-илю́, -и́лишь; *impf* **распи́ливать**) *сов перех* to saw up

**распина́|ть** (-ю) *несов от* **распя́ть**

**расписа́ни|е** (-я) *ср* timetable, schedule

**расп|иса́ть** (-ишу́, -и́шешь; *impf* **распи́сывать**) *сов перех* (*дела*) to arrange; (*стены, шкату́лку*) to paint; (*разг: женить*) to marry (*in registry office*); ~**ся** (*impf* **распи́сываться**) *сов возв* (*поставить подпись*) to sign one's name; **распи́сываться** (~**ся** *pf*) **с** +*instr* to marry (*in registry office*)

**распи́с|ка** (-ки; *gen pl* -ок) ж (*о получении денег*) receipt; (*о невыезде*) warrant

**распла́т|а** (-ы) ж payment; (*перен: за преступление*) retribution

**распл|ати́ться** (-ачу́сь, -а́тишься; *impf* **распла́чиваться**) *сов возв*: ~ (**с** +*instr*) to pay; (*перен: с предателем*) to revenge o.s. on

**распл|еска́ть** (-ещу́, -е́щешь; *impf* **расплёскивать**) *сов перех* to spill; ~**ся** (*impf* **расплёскиваться**) *сов возв* to spill

**распл́ы́вчатый** *прил* (*рисунок, очертания*) blurred; (*перен: ответ, намёк*) vague

**распл|ы́ться** (-ву́сь, -вёшься; *impf* **расплыва́ться**) *сов возв* (*краски*) to run; (*перен: фигуры*) to be blurred

**распого́д|иться** (*3sg* -ится) *сов возв* (*о погоде*) to clear up

**распозна́|ть** (-ю; *impf* **распознава́ть**) *сов перех* to identify

**располага́|ть** (-ю) *несов от* **расположи́ть** ♦ *непрех*: ~ +*instr* (*временем*) to have available; ~**ся** *несов от* **расположи́ться** ♦ *возв* (*находиться*) to be situated *или* located

**расположе́ни|е** (-я) *ср* (*место: лагеря*) location; (*комнат*) layout; (*симпатия*) disposition

**располо́женный** *прил*: ~ **к** +*dat* (*к человеку*) well-disposed towards; (*к болезни*) susceptible to

**распол|ожи́ть** (**-ожу́, -о́жишь**; *impf* **располага́ть**) *сов перех* (*мебель, вещи итп*) to arrange; (*отряд*) to station; **распола́гать** (~ *pf*) **кого́-н к себе́** to win sb over; **~ся** (*impf* **располага́ться**) *сов возв* (*человек*) to settle down; (*отряд*) to position itself

**распоряди́тел|ь** (**-я**) *м* (*КОММ*) manager

**распоряди́тельный** *прил*: ~ **дире́ктор** managing director

**распоря|ди́ться** (**-жу́сь, -ди́шься**; *impf* **распоряжа́ться**) *сов возв* to give out instructions

**распоря́д|ок** (**-ка**) *м* routine

**распоряжа́|ться** (**-юсь**) *несов от* **распоряди́ться** ♦ *возв*: ~ (+*instr*) to be in charge (of)

**распоряже́ни|е** (**-я**) *ср* (*управление*) management; (*указ*) enactment; **ба́нковское ~** banker's order; **в ~ кого́-н/чего́-н** at sb's/ sth's disposal

**распра́в|ить** (**-лю, -ишь**; *impf* **расправля́ть**) *сов перех* to straighten out; (*крылья*) to spread; **~ся** (*impf* **расправля́ться**) *сов возв* (*см перех*) to be straightened out; to spread

**распределе́ни|е** (**-я**) *ср* distribution; (*после института*) work placement

**распредел|и́ть** (**-ю́, -и́шь**; *impf* **распределя́ть**) *сов перех* to distribute; **~ся** (*impf* **распределя́ться**) *сов возв*: **~ся** (**по** +*dat*) (*по группам*) to divide up (into)

**распрода́ж|а** (**-и**) *ж* sale

**распрода́ть** (*как* **дать**; *см. Table 16*; *impf* **распродава́ть**) *сов*

*перех* to sell off; (*билеты*) to sell out of

**распростране́ни|е** (**-я**) *ср* spreading; (*оружия*) proliferation; (*приказа*) application

**распространённый** *прил* widespread

**распростран|и́ть** (**-ю́, -и́шь**; *impf* **распространя́ть**) *сов перех* to spread; (*правило, приказ*) to apply; (*газеты*) to distribute; (*запах*) to emit; **~ся** (*impf* **распространя́ться**) *сов возв* to spread; **~ся** (*pf*) **на** +*acc* to extend to; (*приказ*) to apply to

**распрям|и́ть** (**-лю́, -и́шь**; *impf* **распрямля́ть**) *сов перех* (*проволоку*) to straighten (out); (*плечи*) to straighten

**расп|усти́ть** (**-ущу́, -у́стишь**; *impf* **распуска́ть**) *сов перех* (*армию*) to disband; (*волосы*) to let down; (*парламент*) to dissolve; (*слухи*) to spread; (*перен*: *ребёнка итп*) to spoil; **~ся** (*impf* **распуска́ться**) *сов возв* (*цветы, почки*) to open out; (*дети, люди*) to get out of hand

**распу́та|ть** (**-ю**; *impf* **распу́тывать**) *сов перех* (*узел*) to untangle; (*перен*: *преступление, загадку*) to unravel; **~ся** (*impf* **распу́тываться**) *сов возв* (*см перех*) to come untangled; to unravel itself

**распу́хн|уть** (**-у**; *impf* **распуха́ть**) *сов* to swell up

**распу́щенный** *прил* unruly; (*безнравственный*) dissolute

**распыл|и́ть** (**-ю́, -и́шь**; *impf* **распыля́ть**) *сов перех* to spray

**распя́ти|е** (**-я**) *ср* crucifixion

**расп|я́ть** (**-ну́, -нёшь**; *impf* **распина́ть**) *сов перех* to crucify

**рассáд|а (-ы)** ж собир (БОТ) seedlings мн

**расс|адúть (-ажý, -áдишь;** impf **рассáживать)** сов перех (гостей, публику) to seat; (цветы) to thin out

**рассве|стú (**3sg **-тёт,** pt **-лó;** impf **рассветáть)** сов безл: **~лó** dawn was breaking

**рассвéт (-а)** м daybreak

**рассéива|ть(ся) (-ю(сь))** несов от **рассéять(ся)**

**рассека|ть (-ю)** несов от **рассéчь**

**расс|елúть (-елю́, -éлишь;** impf **расселя́ть)** сов перех (по комнатам) to accommodate

**расс|ердúть(ся) (-ержý(сь), -éрдишь(ся))** сов от **сердúть(ся)**

**расс|éсться (-я́дусь, -я́дешься;** pt **-éлся, -éлась)** сов возв (по столам, в зале) to take one's seat

**расс|éчь (-екý, -ечёшь** etc, **-екýт;** pt **-ёк, -еклá;** impf **рассекáть)** сов перех to cut in two; (губу, лоб) to cut

**рассéянный** прил absent-minded

**рассé|ять (-ю;** impf **рассéивать)** сов перех (семена, людей) to scatter; (перен: сомнения) to dispel; **~ся** (impf **рассéиваться)** сов возв (люди) to be scattered; (тучи, дым) to disperse

**расскáз (-а)** м story; (свидетеля) account

**расск|азáть (-ажý, -áжешь;** impf **расскáзывать)** сов перех to tell

**расскáзчик (-а)** м storyteller; (автор) narrator

**расслáб|ить (-лю, -ишь;** impf **расслабля́ть)** сов перех to relax; **~ся** (impf **расслабля́ться)** сов возв to relax

**расслéд|овать (-ую)** (не)сов перех to investigate

**рассмáтрива|ть (-ю)** несов от **рассмотрéть ♦** перех: **~ что-н как** to regard sth as

**рассмеш|úть (-ý, -úшь)** сов от **смешúть**

**рассме|я́ться (-ю́сь, -ёшься)** сов возв to start laughing

**рассм|отрéть (-отрю́, -óтришь;** impf **рассмáтривать)** сов перех (изучить) to examine; (различить) to discern

**рассóл (-а)** м brine

**расспр|осúть (-ошý, -óсишь;** impf **расспрáшивать)** сов перех: **~ (о** +prp) to question (about)

**рассрóч|ка (-ки;** gen pl **-ек)** ж installment (BRIT), instalment (US); **в ~ку** on hire purchase (BRIT), on the installment plan (US)

**расставáни|е (-я)** ср parting

**расста|вáться (-ю́сь, -ёшься)** сов от **расстáться**

**расстáв|ить (-лю, -ишь;** impf **расставля́ть)** сов перех to arrange

**расстанóв|ка (-ки;** gen pl **-ок)** ж (мебели, книг) arrangement

**расстá|ться (-нусь, -нешься;** impf **расставáться)** сов возв: **~ с** +instr to part with

**расстегн|ýть (-ý, -ёшь;** impf **расстёгивать)** сов перех to undo; **~ся** (impf **расстёгиваться)** сов возв (человек) to unbutton o.s.; (рубашка, пуговица) to come undone

**расст|елúть (-елю́, -éлешь;** impf **расстилáть)** сов перех to spread out

**расстоя́ни|е (-я)** ср distance

**расстрáива|ть(ся) (-ю(сь))** несов от **расстрóить(ся)**

**расстрéл (-а)** м: **~** +gen shooting или firing at; (казнь) execution (by firing squad)

**расстреля́|ть** (-ю; *impf* **расстре́ливать**) *сов перех* (*демонстра́цию*) to open fire on; (*казни́ть*) to shoot

**расстро́енный** *прил* (*здоро́вье, не́рвы*) weak; (*челове́к, вид*) upset; (*роя́ль*) out of tune

**расстро́|ить** (-ю, -ишь; *impf* **расстра́ивать**) *сов перех* (*пла́ны*) to disrupt; (*челове́ка, желу́док*) to upset; (*здоро́вье*) to damage; (*МУЗ*) to put out of tune; **~ся** (*impf* **расстра́иваться**) *сов возв* (*пла́ны*) to fall through; (*челове́к*) to get upset; (*не́рвы*) to weaken; (*здоро́вье*) to be damaged; (*МУЗ*) to go out of tune

**расстро́йств|о** (-а) *ср* (*огорче́ние*) upset; (*ре́чи*) dysfunction; **~ желу́дка** stomach upset

**расст|упи́ться** (*3sg* -у́пится; *impf* **расступа́ться**) *сов возв* (*толпа́*) to make way

**расс|уди́ть** (-ужу́, -у́дишь) *сов*: **она́ ~уди́ла пра́вильно** her judgement was correct

**рассу́д|ок** (-ка) *м* reason

**рассужда́|ть** (-ю) *несов* to reason; **~** (*impf*) **о** +*prp* to debate

**рассужде́ни|е** (-я) *ср* judg(e)ment

**рассчита́|ть** (-ю; *impf* **рассчи́тывать**) *сов перех* to calculate; **~ся** (*impf* **рассчи́тываться**) *сов возв*: **~ся** (**с** +*instr*) (*с продавцо́м*) to settle up (with)

**рассчи́тыва|ть** (-ю) *несов от* **рассчита́ть ♦** *неперех*: **~ на** +*acc* (*наде́яться*) to count *или* rely on; **~ся** *несов от* **рассчита́ться**

**рассыла́|ть** (-ю) *несов от* **разосла́ть**

**рассы́п|ать** (-лю, -лешь; *impf* **рассыпа́ть**) *сов перех* to spill; **~ся** (*impf* **рассыпа́ться**) *сов возв* (*са́хар, бу́сы*) to spill; (*толпа́*) to scatter

**раста́плива|ть** (-ю) *несов от* **растопи́ть**

**раста́птыва|ть** (-ю) *несов от* **растопта́ть**

**раста́|ять** (-ю) *сов от* **та́ять**

**раство́р** (-а) *м* (*ХИМ*) solution; (*строи́тельный*) mortar

**раствори́мый** *прил* soluble; **~ ко́фе** instant coffee

**раствори́тел|ь** (-я) *м* solvent

**раствор|и́ть** (-ю́, -и́шь; *impf* **растворя́ть**) *сов перех* (*порошо́к*) to dissolve; (*окно́, дверь*) to open; **~ся** (*impf* **растворя́ться**) *сов возв* (*см перех*) to dissolve; to open

**расте́ни|е** (-я) *ср* plant

**растениево́дств|о** (-а) *ср* horticulture

**раст|ере́ть** (**разотру́, разотрёшь**; *pt* -ёр, -ёрла; *impf* **растира́ть**) *сов перех* (*ра́ну, те́ло*) to massage

**расте́рянный** *прил* confused

**растеря́|ться** (-юсь) *сов возв* (*челове́к*) to be at a loss, be confused; (*пи́сьма*) to disappear

**раст|е́чься** (*3sg* -ечётся, *pt* -ёкся, -екла́сь; *impf* **растека́ться**) *сов возв* (*вода́*) to spill

**раст|и́** (-у́, -ёшь; *pt* рос, росла́, росло́; *pf* **вы́~и**) *несов* to grow

**растира́|ть** (-ю) *несов от* **растере́ть**

**расти́тельн|ый** *прил* (*БОТ*) plant; **~ое ма́сло** vegetable oil

**ра|сти́ть** (-щу́, -сти́шь; *pf* **вы́растить**) *несов перех* (*дете́й*) to raise; (*цветы́*) to grow

**раст|опи́ть** (-оплю́, -о́пишь;

*impf* **раста́пливать**) *сов перех*
(*печку*) to light; (*воск, жир, лёд*)
to melt; **~ся** *сов от* **топи́ться**

раст|опта́ть (-опчу́, -о́пчешь;
*impf* **раста́птывать**) *сов перех* to
trample on

расто́рг|нуть (-ну; *pt* -, -ла; *impf*
**расторга́ть**) *сов перех* to annul

растра́т|а (-ы) *ж* (*времени,
денег*) waste; (*хищение*)
embezzlement

растра́|тить (-чу, -тишь; *impf*
**растра́чивать**) *сов перех* to
waste; (*расхитить*) to embezzle

растро́ганный *прил* (*человек*)
touched, moved; (*голос*) emotional

растро́га|ть (-ю) *сов перех*:
**~ кого́-н** (+*instr*) to touch *или* move
sb (by); **~ся** *сов возв* to be
touched *или* moved

раст|яну́ть (-яну́, -я́нешь; *impf*
**растя́гивать**) *сов перех* to
stretch; (*связки*) to strain; **~ся**
(*impf* **растя́гиваться**) *сов возв* to
stretch; (*человек, обоз*) to stretch
out; (*связки*) to be strained

расха́жива|ть (-ю) *несов* to
saunter

расхвата́|ть (-ю; *impf*
**расхва́тывать**) *сов перех* (*разг*)
to snatch up

расхи́|тить (-щу, -тишь; *impf*
**расхища́ть**) *сов перех* to
embezzle

расхо́д (-а) *м* (*энергии*)
consumption; (*обычно мн*:
*затраты*) expense; (: **КОММ, в
бухгалтери**) expenditure *ед*

расх|оди́ться (-ожу́сь,
-о́дишься) *несов от* **разойти́сь**

расхо́дн|ый *прил*: **~ о́рдер**
(*КОММ*) expenses form; **~ые
материа́лы** consumables

расхо́д|овать (-ую; *pf* из~)
*несов перех* (*деньги*) to spend;

(*материалы*) to use up

расхожде́ни|е (-я) *ср*
discrepancy; (*во взгля́дах*)
divergence

расхоте́ть (*как* **хоте́ть**; *см. Table
14*) *сов*: **~** +*infin* (*спать, гуля́ть
итп*) to no longer want to do; **~ся**
*сов безл*: (*мне*) **расхоте́лось
спать** I don't feel sleepy any more

расцв|ести́ (-ету́, -ете́шь; *pt*
-ёл, -ела́, -ело́; *impf*
**расцвета́ть**) *сов* to blossom

расцве́т (-а) *м* (*науки*) heyday;
(*таланта*) height; **он в ~е сил** he
is in the prime of life

расцве́т|ка (-ки; *gen pl* -ок) *ж*
colour (*BRIT*) *или* color (*US*)
scheme

расце́нива|ться (*3sg* -ется)
*несов*: **~ как** to be regarded as

расц|ени́ть (-еню́, -е́нишь; *impf*
**расце́нивать**) *сов перех* to
judge

расце́н|ка (-ки; *gen pl* -ок) *ж*
(*работы*) rate; (*цена*) tariff

расч|еса́ть (-ешу́, -е́шешь; *impf*
**расчёсывать**) *сов перех*
(*волосы*) to comb; **расчёсывать
(~ pf) кого́-н** to comb sb's hair

расчёс|ка (-ки; *gen pl* -ок) *ж*
comb

расчёт (-а) *м* (*стоимости*)
calculation; (*выгода*) advantage;
(*бережливость*) economy; **из ~а**
+*gen* on the basis of; **брать (взять**
*pf*) *или* **принима́ть (приня́ть** *pf*)
**что-н в ~** to take sth into account;
**я с Ва́ми в ~е** we are all even

расчётливый *прил* (*экономный*)
thrifty; (*политик*) calculating

расчётный *прил*: **~ день** payday;
**~ счёт** debit account

расчи́|стить (-щу, -стишь; *impf*
**расчища́ть**) *сов перех* to clear

расшата́|ть (-ю; *impf*
**расша́тывать**) *сов перех* (*стул*)

to make wobbly; (*здоровье*) to damage; **~ся** (*impf* **расша́тываться**) *сов возв* (*стул*) to become wobbly; (*здоровье*) to be damaged

**расшире́ни|е** (**-я**) *ср* widening; (*связей, дела*) expansion; (*зна́ний*) broadening

**расши́р|ить** (**-ю, -ишь**; *impf* **расширя́ть**) *сов перех* to widen; (*де́ло*) to expand; **~ся** (*impf* **расширя́ться**) *сов возв* (*см перех*) to widen; to expand

**расщеп|и́ть** (**-лю́, -и́шь**; *impf* **расщепля́ть**) *сов перех* (*также ФИЗ*) to split; (*ХИМ*) to decompose; **~ся** (*impf* **расщепля́ться**) *сов возв* to splinter; (*ФИЗ*) to split; (*ХИМ*) to decompose

**ратифика́ци|я** (**-и**) *ж* ratification

**ратифици́р|овать** (**-ую**) *(не)сов перех* to ratify

**ра́унд** (**-а**) *м* (*СПОРТ, ПОЛИТ*) round

**рафина́д** (**-а**) *м* sugar cubes *мн*

**рахи́т** (**-а**) *м* (*МЕД*) rickets

**рацио́н** (**-а**) *м* ration

**рационализи́р|овать** (**-ую**) *(не)сов перех* to rationalize

**рациона́льн|ый** *прил* rational; **~ое пита́ние** well-balanced diet

**ра́ци|я** (**-и**) *ж* walkie-talkie; (*ВОЕН*) radio set

**рва́ный** *прил* torn; (*боти́нки*) worn

**рв|ать** (**-у, -ёшь**; *pf* **по~а́ть** *или* **разорва́ть**) *несов перех* to tear, rip; (*перен: дру́жбу*) to break off; (*pf* **вы́~**; *предме́т из рук*) to snatch; (*pf* **сорва́ть**; *цветы́, тра́ву*) to pick ♦ (*pf* **вы~**) *безл*: **его́ ~ёт** he is vomiting *или* being sick; **рва́ться** (*pf* **порва́ться** *или* **разорва́ться**) *несов возв* to tear, rip; (*о́бувь*) to become worn; (*pf* **разорва́ться**; *снаря́д*) to

explode; **рва́ться** (*impf*) **к вла́сти** to be hungry for power

**рве́ни|е** (**-я**) *ср* enthusiasm

**рво́т|а** (**-ы**) *ж* vomiting

**реабилити́р|овать** (**-ую**) *(не)сов перех* to rehabilitate

**реаги́р|овать** (**-ую**) *несов*: **~** (**на** +*acc*) (*на свет*) to react (to); (*pf* **от~** *или* **про~**; *на кри́тику, на слова́*) to react *или* respond (to)

**реакти́вный** *прил*: **~ дви́гатель** jet engine; **~ самолёт** jet (plane)

**реа́ктор** (**-а**) *м* reactor

**реакцио́нный** *прил* reactionary

**реа́кци|я** (**-и**) *ж* reaction

**реализа́ци|я** (**-и**) *ж* (*см глаг*) implementation; disposal

**реали́зм** (**-а**) *м* realism

**реализ|ова́ть** (**-у́ю**) *(не)сов перех* to implement; (*това́р*) to sell

**реали́ст** (**-а**) *м* realist

**реалисти́ческий** *прил* realistic; (*иску́сство*) realist

**реа́льност|ь** (**-и**) *ж* reality; (*пла́на*) feasibility

**реа́льный** *прил* real; (*поли́тика*) realistic; (*план*) feasible

**реанима́ци|я** (**-и**) *ж* resuscitation; **отделе́ние ~и** intensive care unit

**ребён|ок** (**-ка**; *nom pl* **де́ти** *или* **ребя́та**) *м* child; (*грудно́й*) baby

**ребр|о́** (**-а́**; *nom pl* **рёбра**) *ср* (*АНАТ*) rib; (*ку́бика итп*) edge

**ребя́т|а** (**-**) *мн от* **ребёнок**; (*разг: па́рни*) guys *мн*

**рёв** (**-а**) *м* roar

**рева́нш** (**-а**) *м* revenge

**реве́н|ь** (**-я́**) *м* rhubarb

**рев|е́ть** (**-у́, -ёшь**) *несов* to roar

**ревизио́нн|ый** *прил*: **~ая коми́ссия** audit commission

**реви́зи|я** (**-и**) *ж* (*КОММ*) audit; (*тео́рии*) revision

**ревиз|ова́ть** (**-у́ю**) *(не)сов перех*

(*КОММ*) to audit

**ревизо́р** (-а) *м* (*КОММ*) auditor

**ревмати́зм** (-а) *м* rheumatism

**ревни́вый** *прил* jealous

**ревн|ова́ть** (-у́ю) *несов перех*: ~ (**кого́-н**) to be jealous (of sb)

**ре́вностный** *прил* ardent, zealous

**ре́вность** (-и) *ж* jealousy

**революционе́р** (-а) *м* revolutionary

**револю́ци|я** (-и) *ж* revolution

**ре́гби** *ср нескл* rugby

**регби́ст** (-а) *м* rugby player

**регио́н** (-а) *м* region

**региона́льный** *прил* regional

**реги́стр** (-а) *м* register; (*на пишущей машинке*): **ве́рхний/ ни́жний** ~ upper/lower case

**регистра́тор** (-а) *м* receptionist

**регистрату́р|а** (-ы) *ж* reception

**регистри́р|овать** (-ую; *pf* **за~**) *несов перех* to register; ~**ся** (*pf* **за~ся**) *несов возв* to register; (*оформлять брак*) to get married (*at a registry office*)

**регла́мент** (-а) *м* (*порядок*) order of business; (*время*) speaking time

**регули́р|овать** (-ую) *несов перех* to regulate; (*pf* **от~**; *мотор*) to adjust

**регулиро́вщик** (-а) *м*: ~ **у́личного движе́ния** traffic policeman

**регуля́рный** *прил* regular

**редакти́р|овать** (-ую; *pf* **от~**) *несов перех* to edit

**реда́ктор** (-а) *м* editor; (*КОМП*) spellchecker

**редакцио́нн|ый** *прил* editorial; ~**ая колле́гия** editorial board; ~**ая статья́** editorial

**реда́кци|я** (-и) *ж* (*действие*: *текста*) editing; (*формулировка*: *статьи закона*) wording; (*учреждение*) editorial offices *мн*;

(*на радио*) desk; (*на телевидении*) division; **под ~ей** +*gen* edited by

**реде́|ть** (*3sg* -**ет**; *pf* **по~**) *несов* to thin out

**реди́с** (-а) *м* radish

**ре́дкий** *прил* rare; (*волосы*) thin

**ре́дко** *нареч* rarely, seldom

**редколле́ги|я** (-и) *ж сокр* = **редакцио́нная колле́гия**

**ре́дкость** (-и) *ж* rarity; **на ~** unusually

**режи́м** (-а) *ж* regime; (*больничный*) routine; (*КОМП*) mode

**режиссёр** (-а) *м* director (*of film, play etc*); ~-**постано́вщик** (stage) director

**ре́|зать** (-жу, -жешь; *pf* **раз~**) *несов перех* (*металл, кожу*) to cut; (*хлеб*) to slice; (*pf* **за~**; *разг*: *свинью*) to slaughter; (*no pf*; *фигурки итп*) to carve; ~**ся** (*pf* **про~ся**) *несов возв* (*зубы, рога*) to come through

**ре́звый** *прил* agile

**резе́рв** (-а) *м* reserve

**резе́рвный** *прил* reserve; (*КОМП*) backup

**рез|е́ц** (-ца́) *м* (*инструмент*) cutting tool; (*АНАТ*) incisor

**резиде́нци|я** (-и) *ж* residence

**рези́н|а** (-ы) *ж* rubber

**рези́н|ка** (-ки; *gen pl* -**ок**) *ж* (*ластик*) rubber (*BRIT*), eraser (*esp US*); (*тесёмка*) elastic

**рези́новый** *прил* rubber

**ре́зкий** *прил* sharp; (*свет, голос*) harsh; (*запах*) pungent

**ре́зко** *нареч* sharply

**резн|я́** (-и́) *ж* slaughter

**резолю́ци|я** (-и) *ж* (*съезда*) resolution; (*распоряжение*) directive

**резона́нс** (-а) *м* (*ФИЗ*) resonance;

(*перен, реакция*) response
**результа́т (-а)** *м* result
**результати́вный** *прил* productive
**резьб|а́ (-ы́)** *ж* carving; (*винта*) thread
**резюме́** *ср нескл* resumé, summary
**рейд (-а)** *м* raid; (*МОР*) anchorage
**рейс (-а)** *м* (*самолёта*) flight; (*автобуса*) run; (*парохода*) sailing
**ре́йсовый** *прил* regular
**ре́йтинг (-а)** *м* popularity rating
**рейту́з|ы (-)** *мн* thermal pants *мн*
**рек|а́ (-и́;** *acc sg* **-у,** *dat sg* **-е́,** *nom pl* **-и)** *ж* river
**рекла́м|а (-ы)** *ж* (*действие: торговая*) advertising; (*средство*) advert (*BRIT*), advertisement
**реклами́р|овать (-ую)** (*не)сов перех* to advertise
**рекла́мный** *прил* (*отдел, колонка*) advertising; (*статья, фильм*) publicity; **~ ро́лик** advertisement; (*фильма*) trailer
**рекламода́тел|ь (-я)** *м* advertiser
**рекоменда́тельн|ый** *прил*: **~ое письмо́** letter of recommendation
**рекоменд|ова́ть (-у́ю)** (*не)сов перех* to recommend
**реконструи́р|овать (-ую)** (*не)сов перех* to rebuild; (*здание*) to reconstruct
**реко́рд (-а)** *м* record
**реко́рдный** *прил* record(-breaking)
**рекордсме́н (-а)** *м* recordholder
**ре́ктор (-а)** *м* ≈ principal
**ректора́т (-а)** *м* principal's office
**религио́зный** *прил* religious
**рели́ги|я (-и)** *ж* religion
**рельс (-а)** *м* (*обычно мн*) rail
**рем|е́нь (-ня́)** *м* belt; (*сумки*) strap; **привязны́е ~ни** seat belt
**ремесл|о́ (-а́;** *nom pl* **ремёсла,**

*gen pl* **ремёсел**) *ср* trade
**ремеш|о́к (-ка́)** *м* strap
**ремо́нт (-а)** *м* repair; (*здания: крупный*) refurbishment; (: *мелкий*) redecoration; **теку́щий ~** maintenance
**ремонти́р|овать (-ую;** *pf* **от~**) *несов перех* to repair; (*здание*) to renovate
**ремо́нтн|ый** *прил*: **~ые рабо́ты** repairs *мн*; **~ая мастерска́я** repair workshop
**рента́бельный** *прил* profitable
**рентге́н (-а)** *м* (*МЕД*) X-ray
**рентгено́лог (-а)** *м* radiologist
**реорганиз|ова́ть (-у́ю)** (*не)сов перех* to reorganize
**репертуа́р (-а)** *м* repertoire
**репети́р|овать (-ую;** *pf* **от~**) *несов* (*не)перех* to rehearse
**репети́тор (-а)** *м* private tutor
**репети́ци|я (-и)** *ж* rehearsal
**ре́плик|а (-и)** *ж* remark
**репорта́ж (-а)** *м* report
**репортёр (-а)** *м* reporter
**репре́сси|я (-и)** *ж* repression *ед*
**репроду́ктор (-а)** *м* loudspeaker
**репроду́кци|я (-и)** *ж* reproduction (*of painting etc*)
**репута́ци|я (-и)** *ж* reputation
**ресни́ц|а (-ы)** *ж* (*обычно мн*) eyelash
**респонде́нт (-а)** *м* respondent
**респу́блик|а (-и)** *ж* republic
**рессо́р|а (-ы)** *ж* spring
**реставра́тор (-а)** *м* restorer
**реставра́ци|я (-и)** *ж* restoration
**реставри́р|овать (-ую;** *pf* **~ или от~**) *несов перех* to restore
**рестора́н (-а)** *м* restaurant
**ресу́рс (-а)** *м* (*обычно мн*) resource
**рефера́т (-а)** *м* synopsis
**рефере́ндум (-а)** *м* referendum
**рефле́кс (-а)** *м* reflex

**рефо́рм|а (-ы)** *ж* reform

**реформа́тор (-а)** *м* reformer

**рецензи́р|овать (-ую)**; *pf* **про~**) *несов перех* to review

**рецензи|я (-и)** *ж*: **реце́нзия (на** +*acc*) review (of)

**реце́пт (-а)** *м* (*МЕД*) prescription; (*КУЛИН, перен*) recipe

**речево́й** *прил* speech

**речно́й** *прил* river

**реч|ь (-и)** *ж* speech; (*разговорная итп*) language; ~ **идёт о том, как/где/кто** ... the matter in question is how/where/who ...; **об э́том не мо́жет быть и ре́чи** there can be absolutely no question of this; **о чём ~!** (*разг*) sure!, of course!

**реша́|ть(ся) (-ю(сь))** *несов от* **реши́ть(ся)**

**реша́ющий** *прил* decisive; (*слово, матч*) deciding

**реше́ни|е (-я)** *ср* decision; (*проблемы*) solution

**решёт|ка (-ки**; *gen pl* **-ок)** *ж* (*садовая*) trellis; (*оконная*) grille; **за ~кой** behind bars

**реши́мост|ь (-и)** *ж* resolve

**реши́тельно** *нареч* resolutely; (*действовать*) decisively

**реши́тельный** *прил* (*человек, взгляд*) resolute; (*меры*) drastic

**реш|и́ть (-у́, -и́шь**; *impf* **реша́ть)** *сов перех* to decide; (*проблему*) to solve; **~ся** (*impf* **реша́ться)** *сов возв* (*вопрос, судьба*) to be decided; **реша́ться (~ся** *pf*) +*infin* to resolve to do; **реша́ться (~ся** *pf*) **на** +*acc* to decide on

**ре́шк|а (-и)** *ж* (*на монете*) tails; **орёл или ~?** heads or tails?

**ре́|ять (**3*sg* **-ет)** *сов* (*флаг*) to fly

**ржа́ве|ть (**3*sg* **-ет**; *pf* **за~)** *несов* to rust

**ржа́вчин|а (-ы)** *ж* rust

**ржа́вый** *прил* rusty

**ржано́й** *прил* rye

**рж|а́ть (-у, -ёшь)** *несов* to neigh

**ржи** *итп сущ см.* **рожь**

**РИА** *ср сокр* (= **Росси́йское информацио́нное аге́нтство**) Russian News Agency

**Рим (-а)** *м* Rome

**ринг (-а)** *м* (boxing) ring

**ри́н|уться (-усь)** *сов возв* to charge

**рис (-а)** *м* rice

**риск (-а)** *no pl м* risk

**риско́ванный** *прил* risky

**риск|ова́ть (-у́ю)**; *pf* **рискну́ть)** *несов* to take risks; ~ (**рискну́ть** *pf*) +*instr* (*жи́знью, рабо́той*) to risk

**рисова́ни|е (-я)** *ср* (*карандашо́м*) drawing; (*кра́сками*) painting

**рис|ова́ть (-у́ю**; *pf* **на~)** *несов перех* (*карандашо́м*) to draw; (*кра́сками*) to paint

**ри́совый** *прил* rice

**рису́н|ок (-ка)** *м* drawing; (*на ткани*) pattern

**ритм (-а)** *м* rhythm

**ритми́ческий** *прил* rhythmic(al)

**ритуа́л (-а)** *м* ritual

**риф (-а)** *м* reef

**ри́фм|а (-ы)** *ж* rhyme

**р-н** *сокр* = **райо́н**

**робе́|ть (-ю**; *pf* **о~)** *несов* to go shy

**ро́бкий** *прил* shy

**ро́бот (-а)** *м* robot

**р|ов (-ва**; *loc sg* **-ву́)** *м* ditch

**рове́сник (-а)** *м*: **он мой ~** he is the same age as me

**ро́вно** *нареч* (*писа́ть*) evenly; (*черти́ть*) straight; (*через год*) exactly; ~ **в два часа́** at two o'clock sharp

**ро́вный** *прил* even; (*ли́ния*) straight

**ровня́ть** (-ю; *pf* с~ *или* **вы́ровнять**) *несов перех* (*строй*) to straighten; (*pf* раз~ *или* с~; *дорожку*) to level

**рог** (-а; *nom pl* -а́) *м* (*также* МУЗ) horn; **оле́ний ~** antler; **у чёрта на ~а́х** (*разг*) in the middle of nowhere

**рога́тый** *прил* horned; **кру́пный ~ скот** cattle

**род** (-а; *loc sg* -у́, *nom pl* -ы́) *м* clan; (*о семье*) clan, family; (*растений, животных*) genus; (*вид*) type; (*ЛИНГ*) gender; **своего́ ро́да** a kind of; **в не́котором ро́де** to some extent; **что-то в э́том** *или* **тако́м ро́де** something like that

**род.** *сокр* (= *роди́лся*) b.

**роддо́м** (-а) *м сокр* = **роди́льный дом**

**роди́льный** *прил*: **~ дом** maternity hospital

**роди́м|ый** *прил*: **~ое пятно́** birthmark

**ро́дин|а** (-ы) *ж* homeland

**ро́дин|ка** (-ки; *gen pl* -ок) *ж* birthmark

**роди́тел|и** (-ей) *мн* parents *мн*

**роди́тельный** *прил*: **~ паде́ж** the genitive (case)

**роди́тельск|ий** *прил* parental; **~ое собра́ние** parents' meeting

**ро|ди́ть** (-жу́, -ди́шь; *impf* **рожа́ть** *или* **рожда́ть**) (*не*)*сов перех* to give birth to; **~ся** (*impf* **рожда́ться**) (*не*)*сов возв* to be born

**родни́к** (-а́) *м* spring (*water*)

**родно́й** *прил* (*брат, мать итп*) natural; (*город, страна*) native; (*в обращении*) dear; **~ язы́к** mother tongue; *см. также* **родны́е**

**родны́|е** (-х) *мн* relatives *мн*

**родово́й** *прил* (*понятие, признак*) generic; (*ЛИНГ*) gender;

(*имение*) family; (*МЕД, судороги, травма*) birth

**родосло́вн|ая** (-ой) *ж* (*семьи*) ancestry; (*собаки*) pedigree

**родосло́вн|ый** *прил*: **~ое де́рево** family tree

**ро́дственник** (-а) *м* relation, relative

**ро́дственный** *прил* family; (*языки, науки*) related

**родств|о́** (-а́) *ср* relationship; (*душ, идей*) affinity

**ро́д|ы** (-ов) *мн* labour *ед* (*BRIT*), labor *ед* (*US*); **принима́ть** (**приня́ть** *pf*) **~** to deliver a baby

**рожа́|ть** (-ю) *несов от* **роди́ть**

**рожда́емост|ь** (-и) *ж* birth rate

**рожда́|ть(ся)** (-ю(сь)) *несов от* **роди́ть(ся)**

**рожде́ни|е** (-я) *ср* birth; **день ~я** birthday

**рожде́ственский** *прил* Christmas

**Рождеств|о́** (-а́) *ср* (*РЕЛ*) Nativity; (*праздник*) Christmas; **С ~м!** Happy *или* Merry Christmas!

**роже́ниц|а** (-ы) *ж woman in labour*; (*только что родившая*) *woman who has given birth*

**рож|о́к** (-ка́) *м* (*МУЗ*) horn; (*для обуви*) shoehorn

**рожь** (ржи) *ж* rye

**ро́з|а** (-ы) *ж* (*растение*) rose(bush); (*цветок*) rose

**розе́т|ка** (-ки; *gen pl* -ок) *ж* power point

**ро́зниц|а** (-ы) *ж* retail goods *мн*; **продава́ть** (**прода́ть** *pf*) **в ~у** to retail

**ро́зничный** *прил* retail

**ро́зовый** *прил* rose; (*цвет*) pink; (*мечты*) rosy

**ро́зыгрыш** (-а) *м* (*лотереи*) draw; (*шутка*) prank

**ро́зыск** (-а) *м* search; **Уголо́вный ~** Criminal Investigation

Department (*BRIT*), Federal Bureau of Investigation (*US*)

**ро́|й** (**-я**; *nom pl* **-и́**) м (*пчёл*) swarm

**рок** (**-а**) м (*судьба*) fate; (*также:* **~-му́зыка**) rock

**роково́й** *прил* fatal

**ро́лик** (**-а**) м (*валик*) roller; (*колесо*) caster; (*фотоплёнки, бумаги*) roll; (*обычно мн: коньки на колесиках*) roller skate

**рол|ь** (**-и**; *gen pl* **-е́й**) ж role

**ром** (**-а**) м rum

**рома́н** (**-а**) м novel; (*любовная связь*) affair

**романи́ст** (**-а**) м novelist

**рома́нс** (**-а**) м (*МУЗ*) romance

**рома́нтик** (**-а**) м (*мечтатель*) romantic; (*писатель*) romanticist

**рома́ш|ка** (**-ки**; *gen pl* **-ек**) ж camomile

**ромб** (**-а**) м rhombus

**роня́|ть** (**-ю**; *pf* **урони́ть**) *несов перех* to drop; (*авторитет*) to lose

**рос** *итп несов см.* **расти́**

**рос|а́** (**-ы́**; *nom pl* **-ы**) ж dew

**роси́н|ка** (**-ки**; *gen pl* **-ок**) ж dewdrop

**роско́шный** *прил* luxurious, glamorous

**ро́скош|ь** (**-и**) ж luxury

**ро́спис|ь** (**-и**) ж (*узор: на шкатулке*) design; (*: на стенах*) mural; (*подпись*) signature

**ро́спуск** (**-а**) м (*армии*) disbandment; (*парламента*) dissolution

**росси́йск|ий** *прил* Russian; **Росси́йская Федера́ция** the Russian Federation

**Росси́|я** (**-и**) ж Russia

**россия́н|ин** (**-ина**; *nom pl* **-е**, *gen pl* **-**) м Russian

**рост** (**-а**) м growth; (*увеличение*) increase; (*размер: человека*) height; (*nom pl* **-а́**; *длина: пальто, платья*) length

**ро́стбиф** (**-а**) м roast beef

**рост|о́к** (**-ка́**) м (*БОТ*) shoot

**рот** (**рта**; *loc sg* **рту́**) м mouth

**ро́т|а** (**-ы**) ж (*ВОЕН*) company

**ротапри́нт** (**-а**) м offset duplicator

**ро́щ|а** (**-и**) ж grove

**роя́л|ь** (**-я**) м grand piano

**РПЦ** ж *сокр* (= **Ру́сская правосла́вная це́рковь**) Russian Orthodox Church

**р/с** *сокр* = **расчётный счёт**

**рта** *etc сущ см.* **рот**

**ртут|ь** (**-и**) ж mercury

**руб.** *сокр* (= **рубль**) R., r.

**руба́ш|ка** (**-ки**; *gen pl* **-ек**) ж (*мужская*) shirt; **ни́жняя ~** (*женская*) slip; **ночна́я ~** nightshirt

**рубе́ж** (**-а́**) м (*государства*) border; (*: водный, лесной*) boundary; **он живёт за рубежо́м** he lives abroad

**руби́н** (**-а**) м ruby

**руб|и́ть** (**-лю́**, **-ишь**; *pf* **с~**) *сов перех* (*дерево*) to fell; (*ветку*) to chop off

**рубл|ь** (**-я́**) м rouble

**ру́брик|а** (**-и**) ж (*раздел*) column; (*заголовок*) heading

**руга́тельн|ый** *прил*: **~ое сло́во** swearword

**руга́тельств|о** (**-а**) *ср* swearword

**руга́|ть** (**-ю**; *pf* **вы́ругать** *или* **от~**) *несов перех* to scold; **~ся** *несов возв* (*браниться*): **~ся с** +*instr* to scold; (*pf* **вы́ругаться**) to swear; **~ся** (**по~ся** *pf*) **с** +*instr* (*с мужем, с другом*) to fall out with

**руд|а́** (**-ы́**; *nom pl* **-ы**) ж ore

**рудни́к** (**-а́**) м mine

**руж|ьё** (**-ья́**; *nom pl* **-ья**, *gen pl* **-ей**) *ср* rifle

**руи́н|ы** (**-**) *мн* ruins

**рук|а́** (*acc sg* **-у**, *gen sg* **-и́**, *nom pl* **-и**, *gen pl* **-**, *dat pl* **-а́м**) ж hand;

(*верхняя конечность*) arm; **из пе́рвых ~** first hand; **под ~о́й, под ~ми** to hand, handy; **отсю́да до го́рода ~о́й пода́ть** it's a stone's throw from here to the town; **э́то ему́ на́ ~у** that suits him

**рука́в** (-а́) *м* (*одежды*) sleeve

**рукави́ц|а** (-ы) *ж* mitten

**руководи́тел|ь** (-я) *м* leader; (*кафедры, предприятия*) head

**руково|ди́ть** (-жу́, -ди́шь) *несов*: ~ +*instr* to lead; (*учреждением*) to be in charge of; (*страной*) to govern; (*аспирантами*) to supervise

**руково́дств|о** (-а) *м* leadership; (*заводом, институтом*) management; (*пособие*) manual; (*по эксплуатации, по уходу*) instructions мн

**руководя́щий** *прил* (*работник*) managerial; (*орган*) governing

**рукоде́ли|е** (-я) *ср* needlework

**рукопи́сный** *прил* (*текст*) handwritten

**ру́копис|ь** (-и) *ж* manuscript

**рукопожа́ти|е** (-я) *ср* handshake

**рукоя́т|ка** (-ки; *gen pl* -ок) *ж* handle

**рулев|о́й** *прил*: ~о́е колесо́ steering wheel

**руле́т** (-а) *м* (*с джемом*) ≈ swiss roll

**руле́т|ка** (-ки; *gen pl* -ок) *ж* (*для измерения*) tape measure; (*в казино*) roulette

**рул|и́ть** (-ю́, -и́шь) *несов перех* to steer

**руло́н** (-а) *м* roll

**рул|ь** (-я́) *м* steering wheel

**румя́н|а** (-) *мн* blusher *ед*

**румя́н|ец** (-ца) *м* glow

**румя́н|ить** (-ю, -ишь; *pf* на~) *несов перех* (*щёки*) to apply blusher to; ~**ся** (*pf* раз~ся) *несов*

*возв* to flush; (*pf* на~ся; *женщина*) to apply blusher; (*pf* под~ся; *пирог*) to brown

**румя́ный** *прил* rosy; (*пирог*) browned

**РУОП** (-а) *ср сокр* (= Региона́льное управле́ние по борьбе́ с организо́ванной престу́пностью) department fighting organized crime

**руо́пов|ец** (-ца) *м* member of the department fighting organized crime

**ру́пор** (-а) *м* megaphone

**руса́л|ка** (-ки; *gen pl* -ок) *ж* mermaid

**ру́сл|о** (-ла; *gen pl* -ел) *ср* bed (of river); (*перен: направление*) course

**ру́сск|ий** *прил* Russian ♦ (-ого) *м* Russian; ~ язы́к Russian

**ру́сый** *прил* (*волосы*) light brown

**ру́хн|уть** (-у) *сов* to collapse

**руча́тельств|о** (-а) *ср* guarantee

**руча́|ться** (-юсь; *pf* поручи́ться) *несов возв*: ~ за +*acc* to guarantee

**руч|е́й** (-ья́) *м* stream

**ру́ч|ка** (-ки; *gen pl* -ек) *ж уменьш от* рука́; (*двери, чемодана итп*) handle; (*кресла, дивана*) arm; (*для письма*) pen

**ручн|о́й** *прил* hand; (*животное*) tame; ~**я́я кладь, ~ бага́ж** hand luggage; ~**ы́е часы́** (wrist)watch

**РФ** *ж сокр* = Росси́йская Федера́ция

**ры́б|а** (-ы) *ж* fish; **ни ~ ни мя́со** neither here nor there

**рыба́к** (-а́) *м* fisherman

**рыба́л|ка** (-ки; *gen pl* -ок) *ж* fishing

**рыба́цкий** *прил* fishing

**ры́бий** *прил* fish; ~ **жир** cod-liver oil

**ры́бный** *прил* (*магазин*) fish;

(*промышленность*) fishing

**рыболо́в** (-а) *м* angler, fisherman

**Ры́б|ы** (-) *мн* (*созвездие*) Pisces *ед*

**рыв|о́к** (-ка́) *м* jerk; (*в работе*) push

**рыда́|ть** (-ю) *несов* to sob

**ры́жий** *прил* (*волосы*) ginger; (*человек*) red-haired

**ры́н|ок** (-ка) *м* market

**ры́ночник** (-а) *м* marketer

**ры́ночный** *прил* (*КОММ*) market

**ры́|скать** (-щу, -щешь) *несов* to roam, rove

**рысц|а́** (-ы́) *ж* jog trot

**рыс|ь** (-и) *ж* (*ЗООЛ*) lynx; (*бег лошади*) trot

**рыть** (ро́ю, ро́ешь; *pf* вы́~) *несов перех* to dig; **ры́ться** *несов возв* (*в земле, в песке*) to dig; (*искать*) to rummage

**ры́хлый** *прил* (*земля*) loose; (*кирпич*) crumbly

**ры́цар|ь** (-я) *м* knight

**рыча́г** (-а́) *м* (*управления*) lever; (*перен: реформ*) instrument

**рыч|а́ть** (-у́, -и́шь) *несов* to growl

**рья́ный** *прил* zealous

**рэ́кет** (-а) *м* racket

**рэкети́р** (-а) *м* racketeer

**рюкза́к** (-а́) *м* rucksack

**рю́м|ка** (-ки; *gen pl* -ок) *ж* ≈ liqueur glass

**ряби́н|а** (-ы) *ж* (*дерево*) rowan, mountain ash ♦ *собир* (*ягоды*) rowan berries *мн*

**ряд** (-а; *loc sg* -у́, *nom pl* -ы́) *м* row; (*явлений*) sequence; (*prp sg* -е; *несколько*): ~ +*gen* (*вопросов, причин*) a number of; **из ря́да вон выходя́щий** extraordinary; *см. также* **ряды́**

**рядов|о́й** *прил* (*обычный*) ordinary; (*член партии*) rank-and-

file ♦ (-о́го) *м* (*ВОЕН*) private

**ря́дом** *нареч* side by side; (*близко*) nearby; ~ **с** +*instr* next to; **э́то совсе́м** ~ it's really near

**ряд|ы́** (-о́в) *мн* (*армии*) ranks *мн*

**ря́женк|а** (-и) *ж* natural set yoghurt

**ря́с|а** (-ы) *ж* cassock

# С, с

**с** *сокр* (= **се́вер**) N; (= **секу́нда**) s

<hr>
KEYWORD
<hr>

**с** *предл*; +*instr* **1** (*указывает на объект, от которого что-н отделяется*) off; **лист упа́л с де́рева** a leaf fell off the tree; **с рабо́ты/ле́кции** from work/a lecture

**2** (*следуя чему-н*) from; **перево́д с ру́сского** a translation from Russian

**3** (*об источнике*) from; **де́ньги с зака́зчика** money from a customer

**4** (*начиная с*) since; **жду тебя́ с утра́** I've been waiting for you since morning; **с января́ по май** from January to May

**5** (*на основании чего-н*) with; **с одобре́ния парла́мента** with the approval of parliament

**6** (*по причине*): **с го́лоду/ хо́лода/го́ря** of hunger/cold/grief; **я уста́л с доро́ги** I was tired from the journey

♦ *предл*; (+*acc*; *приблизительно*) about; **с киломе́тр/то́нну** about a kilometre (*BRIT*) *или* kilometer (*US*)/ton(ne)

♦ *предл*; +*instr* **1** (*совместно*) with; **я иду́ гуля́ть с дру́гом** I am going for a walk with a friend; **он познако́мился с де́вушкой** he

has met a girl; **мы с ним** he and I
**2** (*о наличии чего-н в чём-н*):
**пиро́г с мя́сом** a meat pie; **хлеб с
ма́слом** bread and butter;
**челове́к с ю́мором** a man with a
sense of humour (*BRIT*) *или* humor
(*US*)
**3** (*при указании на образ
де́йствия*) with; **слу́шать** (*impf*) **с
удивле́нием** to listen with *или* in
surprise; **ждём с нетерпе́нием
встре́чи с Ва́ми** we look forward
to meeting you
**4** (*при посре́дстве*): **с курье́ром**
by courier
**5** (*при наступле́нии чего-н*): **с
во́зрастом** with age; **мы вы́ехали
с рассве́том** we left at dawn
**6** (*об объе́кте воздействия*) with;
**поко́нчить** (*pf*) **с
несправедли́востью** to do away
with injustice; **спеши́ть
(поспеши́ть** *pf*) **с вы́водами** to
draw hasty conclusions; **что с
тобо́й**? what's the matter with
you?

**с.** *сокр* (= **страни́ца**) p.; = **село́**
**са́б|ля (-ли**; *gen pl* **-ель**) *ж* sabre
(*BRIT*), saber (*US*)
**сад (-а**; *loc sg* **-у́**, *nom pl* **-ы́**) *м*
garden; (*фрукто́вый*) orchard;
(*та́кже*: **де́тский ~**) nursery
(school) (*BRIT*), kindergarten
**са|ди́ться (-жу́сь, -ди́шься)**
*несов от* **сесть**
**садо́вник (-а)** *м* (professional)
gardener
**садово́д (-а)** *м* (*специали́ст*)
horticulturalist
**садо́вый** *прил* garden
**са́ж|а (-и)** *ж* soot
**сажа́|ть (-ю**; *pf* **посади́ть**) *несов
перех* to seat; (*де́рево*) to plant;
(*самолёт*) to land; **~ (посади́ть** *pf*)

**кого́-н в тюрьму́** to put sb in
prison
**сайт (-а)** *м* (*КОМП*) site
**саксофо́н (-а)** *м* saxophone
**сала́т (-а)** *м* (*КУЛИН*) salad
**сала́тниц|а (-ы)** *ж* salad bowl
**са́л|о (-а)** *ср* (*живо́тного*) fat;
(*КУЛИН*) lard
**сало́н (-а)** *м* salon; (*авто́буса,
самолёта итп*) passenger section
**салфе́т|ка (-ки**; *gen pl* **-ок**) *ж*
napkin
**са́льто** *ср нескл* mid-air
somersault
**салю́т (-а)** *м* salute
**сам (-ого́**; *f* **~а́**, *nt* **~о́**, *pl* **са́ми**)
*мест* (*я*) myself; (*ты*) yourself; (*он*)
himself; (*как таково́й*) itself; **~ по
себе́** (*отде́льно*) by itself
**сам|а́ (-о́й)** *мест* (*я*) myself; (*ты*)
yourself; (*она́*) herself; *см. также*
**сам**
**сам|е́ц (-ца́)** *м* male (*ZOOL*)
**са́м|и (-их)** *мест* (*мы*) ourselves;
(*они́*) themselves; *см. также* **сам**
**са́м|ка (-ки**; *gen pl* **-ок**) *ж* female
(*ZOOL*)
**са́ммит (-а)** *м* summit
**сам|о́ (-ого́)** *мест* itself; **~ собо́й
(разуме́ется)** it goes without
saying; *см. также* **сам**
**самова́р (-а)** *м* samovar
**самоде́льный** *прил* home-made
**самоде́ятельност|ь (-и)** *ж*
initiative; (*та́кже*:
**худо́жественная ~**) amateur
performing arts
**самоде́ятельный** *прил* (*теа́тр*)
amateur
**самока́т (-а)** *м* scooter
**самолёт (-а)** *м* (aero)plane (*BRIT*),
(air)plane (*US*)
**самолюби́вый** *прил* self-centred
(*BRIT*), self-centred (*US*)
**самооблада́ни|е (-я)** *ср* self-

possession

**самообслу́живани|е (-я)** *ср* self-service

**самоокупа́емост|ь (-и)** *ж* (ЭКОН) self-sufficiency

**самоотве́рженный** *прил* self-sacrificing

**самостоя́тельный** *прил* independent

**самоуби́йств|о (-а)** *ср* suicide; **поко́нчить** *(pf)* **жизнь ~м** to commit suicide

**самоуби́йц|а (-ы)** *м/ж* suicide (victim)

**самоуве́ренный** *прил* self-confident, self-assured

**самоучи́тел|ь (-я)** *м* teach-yourself book

**самочу́встви|е (-я)** *ср*: **как Ва́ше ~?** how are you feeling?

**са́м|ый** *мест* (+n) the very; (+adj; вкусный, красивый итп) the most; **в ~ом нача́ле/конце́** right at the beginning/end; **в ~ом де́ле** really; **на ~ом де́ле** in actual fact

**санато́ри|й (-я)** *м* sanatorium (BRIT), sanitarium (US)

**санда́ли|я (-и)** *ж* (обычно мн) sandal

**са́н|и (-ей)** *мн* sledge *ед* (BRIT), sled *ед* (US); (спортивные) toboggan *ед*

**санита́р|ка (-ки**; *gen pl* **-ок**) *ж* nursing auxiliary

**санита́рн|ый** *прил* sanitary; (ВОЕН) medical; **~ая те́хника** *collective term for plumbing equipment and bathroom accessories*

**са́н|ки (-ок)** *мн* sledge *ед* (BRIT), sled *ед* (US)

**санкциони́р|овать (-ую)** *(не)сов перех* to sanction

**са́нкци|я (-и)** *ж* sanction

**санте́хник (-а)** *м сокр* (= санита́рный те́хник) plumber

**санте́хник|а (-и)** *ж сокр* = **санита́рная те́хника**

**сантиме́тр (-а)** *м* centimetre (BRIT), centimeter (US); (линейка) tape measure

**сапо́г (-а́**; *nom pl* **-и́**, *gen pl* **-**) *м* boot

**сапо́жник (-а)** *м* shoemaker

**сапфи́р (-а)** *м* sapphire

**сара́|й (-я)** *м* shed; (для сена) barn

**сарафа́н (-а)** *м* (платье) pinafore (dress) (BRIT), jumper (US)

**сати́н (-а)** *м* sateen

**сати́р|а (-ы)** *ж* satire

**сати́рик (-а)** *м* satirist

**сау́довск|ий** *прил*: **Сау́довская Ара́вия** Saudi Arabia

**са́ун|а (-ы)** *ж* sauna

**са́хар (-а**; *part gen* **-у**) *м* sugar

**са́харниц|а (-ы)** *ж* sugar bowl

**са́харный** *прил* sugary; **~ диабе́т** diabetes; **~ песо́к** granulated sugar

**сач|о́к (-ка́)** *м* (для ловли рыб) landing net; (для бабочек) butterfly net

**сба́в|ить (-лю, -ишь**; *impf* **сбавля́ть)** *сов перех* to reduce

**сбе́га|ть (-ю)** *сов* (разг): **~ в магази́н** to run to the shop

**сбежа́ть** (как бежа́ть; *см. Table 20*; *impf* **сбега́ть)** *сов* (убежать) to run away; **сбега́ть (~ pf) с** +gen (с горы итп) to run down; **~ся** (*impf* **сбега́ться)** *сов возв* to come running

**сберба́нк (-а)** *м сокр* (= сберега́тельный банк) savings bank

**сберега́тельн|ый** *прил*: **~ банк** savings bank; **~ая ка́сса** savings bank; **~ая кни́жка** savings book

**сберега́|ть (-ю)** *несов от* **сбере́чь**

**сбереже́ни|е (-я)** *ср* (действие)

saving; **~я** savings *мн*

**сбер|е́чь** (**-егу́, -ежёшь** *итп*, **-егу́т**; *pt* **-ёг, -егла́**; *impf* **сберега́ть**) *сов перех* (*здоровье, любовь, отноше́ние*) to preserve; (*де́ньги*) to save (up)

**сберка́сс|а** (**-ы**) *ж сокр* = **сберега́тельная ка́сса**

**сберкни́ж|ка** (**-ки**; *gen pl* **-ек**) *ж сокр* = **сберега́тельная кни́жка**

**сбить** (**собью́, собьёшь**; *imper* **сбе́й(те)**; *impf* **сбива́ть**) *сов перех* to knock down; (*пти́цу, самолёт*) to shoot down; (*сли́вки, я́йца*) to beat; **сби́ться** (*impf* **сбива́ться**) *сов возв* (*ша́пка, повя́зка итп*) to slip; **сбива́ться** (**сби́ться** *pf*) **с пути́** (*также перен*) to lose one's way

**сбли|зить** (**-жу, -зишь**; *impf* **сближа́ть**) *сов перех* to bring closer together; **~ся** (*impf* **сближа́ться**) *сов возв* (*лю́ди, госуда́рства*) to become closer

**сбо́ку** *нареч* at the side

**сбор** (**-а**) *м* (*урожа́я, да́нных*) gathering; (*нало́гов*) collection; (*пла́та: страхово́й итп*) fee; (*при́быль*) takings *мн*, receipts *мн*; (*собра́ние*) assembly, gathering; **тамо́женный/ге́рбовый ~** customs/stamp duty; **все в сбо́ре** everyone is present

**сбо́р|ка** (**-ки**; *gen pl* **-ок**) *ж* (*изде́лия*) assembly

**сбо́рн|ая** (**-ой**) *ж* (*разг*) = **сбо́рная кома́нда**

**сбо́рник** (**-а**) *м* collection (*of stories, articles*)

**сбо́рн|ый** *прил*: **~ пункт** assembly point; **~ая ме́бель** kit furniture; **~ая кома́нда (страны́)** national team

**сбо́рочный** *прил* assembly

**сбра́сыва|ть(ся)** (**-ю(сь)**) *несов*

от **сбро́сить(ся)**

**сбр|ить** (**-е́ю, -е́ешь**; *impf* **сбрива́ть**) *сов перех* to shave off

**сбро́|сить** (**-шу, -сишь**; *impf* **сбра́сывать**) *сов перех* (*предме́т*) to throw down; (*све́ргнуть*) to overthrow; (*ско́рость, давле́ние*) to reduce; **~ся** (*impf* **сбра́сываться**) *сов возв*: **сбра́сываться (~ся** *pf*) **с** +*gen* to throw o.s. from

**сбру́|я** (**-и**) *ж* harness

**СБСЕ** *ср сокр* (= Совеща́ние по безопа́сности и сотру́дничеству в Евро́пе) CSCE

**сбыт** (**-а**) *м* sale

**сбыть** (*как* **быть**; *см. Table 21*; *impf* **сбыва́ть**) *сов перех* (*това́р*) to sell; **сбы́ться** (*impf* **сбыва́ться**) *сов возв* (*наде́жды*) to come true

**СВ** *сокр* (= сре́дние во́лны) MW

**св.** *сокр* (= свято́й) St

**сва́д|ьба** (**-ьбы**; *gen pl* **-еб**) *ж* wedding

**св|али́ть** (**-алю́, -а́лишь**) *сов от* **вали́ть ♦** (*impf* **сва́ливать**) *перех* to throw down; **~ся** *сов от* **вали́ться**

**сва́л|ка** (**-ки**; *gen pl* **-ок**) *ж* (*ме́сто*) rubbish dump

**сваля́|ть** (**-ю**) *сов от* **валя́ть**

**св|ари́ть(ся)** (**-арю́(сь), -а́ришь(ся)**) *сов от* **вари́ть(ся)**

**сва́р|ка** (**-и**) *ж* welding

**сва́рщик** (**-а**) *м* welder

**сва́та|ть** (**-ю**; *pf* **по~** *или* **со~**) *несов перех*: **~ кого́-н (за** +*acc*) to try to marry sb off (to); **~ся** (*pf* **по~ся**) *несов возв*: **~ся к** +*dat* *или* **за** +*acc* to court

**сва́|я** (**-и**) *ж* (*СТРОИТ*) pile

**све́дени|е** (**-я**) *ср* information *ед*; **доводи́ть (довести́** *pf*) **что-н до ~я кого́-н** to bring sth to sb's attention

**сведе́ни|е** (-я) *ср* (*пятна́*) removal; (*в таблицу, в график итп*) arrangement

**све́жий** *прил* fresh; (*журнал*) recent

**свёкл|а** (-ы) *ж* beetroot

**свёк|ор** (-ра) *м* father-in-law, husband's father

**свекро́в|ь** (-и) *ж* mother-in-law, husband's mother

**сверг|ну́ть** (-у; *impf* **сверга́ть**) *сов перех* to overthrow

**свержё́ни|е** (-я) *ср* overthrow

**све́р|ить** (-ю, -ишь; *impf* **сверя́ть**) *сов перех*: ~ **(с** +*instr*) to check (against)

**сверка́|ть** (-ю) *несов* (*звезда, глаза*) to twinkle; (*огни*) to flicker; ~ (*impf*) **умо́м/красото́й** to sparkle with intelligence/beauty

**сверкн|у́ть** (-у́, -ёшь) *сов* to flash

**сверл|и́ть** (-ю́, -и́шь; *pf* **про~**) *несов перех* to drill, bore

**св|ерло́** (-ерла́; *nom pl* ~**ёрла**) *ср* drill

**сверн|у́ть** (-у́, -ёшь; *impf* **свора́чивать**) *сов перех* (*скатать: карту*) to roll up ♦ (*impf* **свора́чивать**) (*повернуть*) to turn; ~**ся** (*impf* **свора́чиваться**) *сов возв* (*человек, животное*) to curl up; (*молоко*) to curdle; (*кровь*) to clot

**све́рстни|к** (-а) *м* peer; **мы с ней** ~**и** she and I are the same age

**свёрт|ок** (-ка) *м* package

**сверх** *предл*: ~ +*gen* (*нормы*) over and above

**сверхзвуково́й** *прил* supersonic

**све́рху** *нареч* (*о направлении*) from the top; (*в верхней части*) on the surface

**сверхуро́чн|ые** (-ых) *мн* (*плата*) overtime pay *ед*

**сверхуро́чн|ый** *прил*: ~**ая**

**рабо́та** overtime

**сверхъесте́ственный** *прил* supernatural

**сверч|о́к** (-ка́) *м* (*ЗООЛ*) cricket

**сверя́|ть** (-ю) *несов от* **све́рить**

**све́с|иться** (*3sg* -ится; *impf* **све́шиваться**) *сов возв* (*ветви*) to overhang

**св|ести́** (-еду́, -едёшь; *pt* -ёл, -ела́; *impf* **своди́ть**) *сов перех*: ~ **с** +*gen* to lead down; (*пятно*) to shift; (*собрать*) to arrange; **своди́ть** (~ *pf*) **кого́-н с ума́** to drive sb mad; ~**сь** (*impf* **своди́ться**) *сов возв*: ~**сь к** +*dat* to be reduced to

**свет** (-а) *м* light; (*Земля*) the world; **ни** ~ **ни заря́** at the crack of dawn; **выходи́ть** (**вы́йти** *pf*) **в** ~ (*книга*) to be published; **ни за что на све́те не сде́лал бы э́того** (*разг*) I wouldn't do it for the world

**света́|ть** (*3sg* -ет) *несов безл* to get *или* grow light

**свети́льник** (-а) *м* lamp

**св|ети́ть** (-ечу́, -е́тишь) *несов* to shine; ~ (**по~** *pf*) **кому́-н** (*фонарём итп*) to light the way for sb; ~**ся** *несов возв* to shine

**светле́|ть** (-ю; *pf* **по~** *или* **про~**) *несов* to lighten

**све́тлый** *прил* light; (*комната, день*) bright; (*ум*) lucid

**светофо́р** (-а) *м* traffic light

**свеч|а́** (-и́; *nom pl* -и, *gen pl* -е́й) *ж* candle; (*МЕД*) suppository; (*ТЕХ*) spark(ing) plug; (*СПОРТ*) lob

**све́чк|а** (-ки; *gen pl* -ек) *ж* candle

**све́ша|ть** (-ю) *сов от* **ве́шать**

**све́шива|ться** (-юсь) *несов от* **све́ситься**

**свива́|ть** (-ю; *pf* **свить**) *несов перех* to weave

**свида́ни|е** (-я) *ср* rendezvous;

(*деловое*) appointment; (*с заключённым, с больным*) visit; (*влюблённых*) date; **до ~я** goodbye; **до ско́рого ~я** see you soon

**свиде́тел|ь** (-я) *м* witness

**свиде́тельств|о** (-а) *ср* evidence; (*документ*) certificate; ~ **о бра́ке/рожде́нии** marriage/birth certificate

**свиде́тельств|овать** (-ую) *несов*: ~ **о** +*prp* to testify to

**свин|е́ц** (-ца́) *м* lead (*metal*)

**свини́н|а** (-ы) *ж* pork

**сви́нк|а** (-и) *ж* (*МЕД*) mumps

**свино́й** *прил* (*сало, корм*) pig; (*из свинины*) pork

**свин|ья́** (-ьи́; *nom pl* **-ьи**, *gen pl* **-е́й**) *ж* pig

**свиса́|ть** (*3sg* -ет) *несов* to hang

**свист** (-а) *м* whistle

**сви|сте́ть** (-щу́, -сти́шь; *pf* **про**~) *несов* to whistle

**сви́стн|уть** (-у) *сов* to give a whistle

**свист|о́к** (-ка́) *м* whistle

**сви́тер** (-а) *м* sweater

**свить** (**совью́, совьёшь**) *сов от* **вить, свива́ть**

**свобо́д|а** (-ы) *ж* freedom; **лише́ние ~ы** imprisonment

**свобо́дный** *прил* free; (*незанятый: место*) vacant; (*движение, речь*) fluent; **вход ~** free admission; ~ **уда́р** (*в футболе*) free kick

**свод** (-а) *м* (*правил итп*) set; (*здания*) vaulting

**св|оди́ть(ся)** (-ожу́(сь), -о́дишь(ся)) *несов от* **свести́(сь)**

**сво́д|ка** (-ки; *gen pl* **-ок**) *ж*: ~ **пого́ды/новосте́й** weather/news summary

**сво́дн|ый** *прил* (*таблица*)

summary; ~ **брат** stepbrother; **~ая сестра́** stepsister

**сво|ё** (-его́) *мест см.* **свой**

**своево́льный** *прил* self-willed

**своевре́менный** *прил* timely

**своеобра́зный** *прил* original; (*необычный*) peculiar

---

KEYWORD

**сво|й** (-его́; *f* **своя́**, *nt* **своё**, *pl* **свои́**; *как мой; см.* Table 8) *мест*

1 (*я*) my; (*ты*) your; (*он*) his; (*она*) her; (*оно*) its; (*мы*) our; (*вы*) your; (*они*) their; **я люблю́ свою́ рабо́ту** I love my work; **мы собра́ли свои́ ве́щи** we collected our things

2 (*собственный*) one's own; **у неё свой компью́тер** she has her own computer

3 (*своеобразный*) its; **э́тот план име́ет свои́ недоста́тки** this plan has its shortcomings

4 (*близкий*): **свой челове́к** one of us

---

**сво́йственный** *прил*: ~ +*dat* characteristic of

**сво́йств|о** (-а) *ср* characteristic, feature

**свора́чива|ть(ся)** (-ю(сь)) *несов от* **сверну́ть(ся)**

**сво|я́** (-е́й) *мест см.* **свой**

**СВЧ** *сокр* (= **сверхвысо́кая частота́**) SHF

**свы́ше** *предл*: ~ +*gen* (*выше*) beyond; (*больше*) over, more than

**свя́занный** *прил*: ~ (**с** +*instr*) connected (to или with); (*имеющий связи*): ~ **с** +*instr* (*с деловыми кругами*) associated with; (*несвободный*) restricted

**свя|за́ть** (-жу́, -жешь) *сов от* **вяза́ть** ♦ (*impf* **свя́зывать**) *перех* (*верёвку итп*) to tie; (*вещи,* человека) to tie up; (*установить сообщение, зависимость*): ~ **что-н с** +*instr* to connect *или* link sth to; ~**ся** (*impf* **свя́зываться**) *сов возв*: ~**ся с** +*instr* to contact; (*разг: с невыгодным делом*) to get (o.s.) caught up in

**свя́з|ка** (**-ки**; *gen pl* **-ок**) *ж* (*ключей*) bunch; (*бумаг, дров*) bundle; (*АНАТ*) ligament; (*ЛИНГ*) copula

**связ|ь** (**-и**) *ж* tie; (*причинная*) connection, link; (*почтовая итп*) communications *мн*; **в ~и́ с** +*instr* (*вследствие*) due to; (*по поводу*) in connection with; **свя́зи с обще́ственностью** public relations

**свя|ти́ть** (**-щу́, -ти́шь**; *pf* **о~**) *несов перех* (*РЕЛ*) to sanctify

**свят|о́й** *прил* holy; (*дело, истина*) sacred ♦ (**-о́го**) *м* (*РЕЛ*) saint

**свяще́нник** (**-а**) *м* priest

**свяще́нный** *прил* holy, sacred; (*долг*) sacred

**с.г.** *сокр* = **сего́ го́да**

**сгиб** (**-а**) *м* bend

**сгиба́|ть** (**-ю**; *pf* **согну́ть**) *несов перех* to bend; ~**ся** (*pf* **согну́ться**) *несов возв* to bend down

**сгни|ть** (**-ю́, -ёшь**) *сов от* **гнить**

**сгно|и́ть** (**-ю́, -и́шь**) *сов от* **гнои́ть**

**сгора́|ть** (**-ю**) *несов от* **сгоре́ть** ♦ *неперех*: ~ **от любопы́тства** to be burning with curiosity

**сгор|е́ть** (**-ю́, -и́шь**; *impf* **сгора́ть** *или* **горе́ть**) *сов* to burn; (*impf* **сгора́ть**; *ЭЛЕК*) to fuse; (*на солнце*) to get burnt

**сгр|ести́** (**-ебу́, -ебёшь**; *pt* **-ёб, -ебла́**; *impf* **сгреба́ть**) *сов перех* (*собрать*) to rake up

**сгр|узи́ть** (**-ужу́, -у́зишь**; *impf* **сгружа́ть**) *сов перех*: ~ (**с** +*gen*)

to unload (from)

**сгусти́|ться** (*impf* **сгуща́ться**) *сов возв* to thicken

**сгущённ|ый** *прил*: ~**ое молоко́** condensed milk

**сда|ва́ть** (**-ю́, -ёшь**; *imper* **-ва́й(те)**) *несов от* **сдать** ♦ *перех*: ~ **экза́мен** to sit an exam; ~**ся** *несов от* **сда́ться** ♦ *возв* (*помещение*) to be leased out; "~**ётся внаём**" "to let"

**сд|ави́ть** (**-авлю́, -а́вишь**; *impf* **сда́вливать**) *сов перех* to squeeze

**сда|ть** (*как* **дать**; *см. Table 16*; *impf* **сдава́ть**) *сов перех* (*пальто, багаж, работу*) to hand in; (*дом, комнату итп*) to rent out, let; (*город, позицию*) to surrender; (*no impf; экзамен, зачёт итп*) to pass; ~**ся** (*impf* **сдава́ться**) *сов возв* to give up; (*солдат, город*) to surrender

**сда́ч|а** (**-и**) *ж* (*деньги*) change; (*экзамена*) passing; (*города*) surrender

**сдвиг** (**-а**) *м* (*в работе*) progress

**сдви́н|уть** (**-у**; *impf* **сдвига́ть**) *сов перех* (*переместить*) to move; (*сблизить*) to move together; ~**ся** (*impf* **сдвига́ться**) *сов возв*: ~**ся** (**с ме́ста**) to move

**сде́ла|ть(ся)** (**-ю(сь)**) *сов от* **де́лать(ся)**

**сде́л|ка** (**-ки**; *gen pl* **-ок**) *ж* deal

**сде́ржанный** *прил* (*человек*) reserved

**сд|ержа́ть** (**-ержу́, -е́ржишь**; *impf* **сде́рживать**) *сов перех* to contain, hold back; **сде́рживать** (~ *pf*) **сло́во/обеща́ние** to keep one's word/promise; ~**ся** (*impf* **сде́рживаться**) *сов возв* to restrain o.s.

**сдёрн|уть** (**-у**; *impf* **сдёргивать**)

сов перех to pull off

**сдира́|ть (-ю)** несов от **содра́ть**

**сдо́бный** прил (тесто) rich

**сду́|ть (-ю;** impf **сдува́ть)** сов перех to blow away

**сеа́нс (-а)** м (КИНО) show; (терапии) session

**себе́** мест см. **себя́** ♦ част (разг): **так ~** so-so; **ничего́ ~** (сносно) not bad; (ирония) well, I never!

**себесто́имост|ь (-и)** ж cost price

| KEYWORD |

**себя́** мест (я) myself; (ты) yourself; (он) himself; (она) herself; (оно) itself; (мы) ourselves; (вы) yourselves; (они) themselves; **он тре́бователен к себе́** he asks a lot of himself; **она́ вини́т себя́** she blames herself; **к себе́** (домой) home; (в свою комнату) to one's room; **"к себе́"** (на двери) "pull"; **"от себя́"** (на двери) "push"; **по себе́** (по своим вкусам) to one's taste; **говори́ть** (impf)/**чита́ть** (impf) **про себя́** to talk/read to o.s.; **она́ себе́ на уме́** (разг) she is secretive; **он у себя́** (в своём доме) he is at home; (в своём кабинете) he is in the office

**се́вер (-а)** м north; **Се́вер** (Арктика) the Arctic North

**се́верн|ый** прил north; (ветер, направление) northerly; (климат, полушарие) northern; **Се́верный Ледови́тый океа́н** Arctic Ocean; **~ое сия́ние** the northern lights мн

**се́веро-восто́к (-а)** м northeast

**се́веро-за́пад (-а)** м northwest

**сего́** мест см. **сей**

**сего́дня** нареч, сущ нескл today; **~ у́тром/днём/ве́чером** this morning/afternoon/evening

**сего́дняшний** прил today's

**седе́|ть (-ю;** pf **по~)** несов to go grey (BRIT) или gray (US)

**сед|ина́ (-ины́;** nom pl **-и́ны)** ж grey (BRIT) или gray (US) hair

**седл|о́ (-а́)** ср saddle

**седо́й** прил (волосы) grey (BRIT), gray (US)

**седьмо́й** чис seventh; **сейча́с ~ час** it's after six

**сезо́н (-а)** м season

**сезо́нный** прил seasonal

**сей (сего́;** см. Table 12) мест this

**сейсми́ческий** прил seismic; (прибор) seismological

**сейф (-а)** м (ящик) safe

**сейча́с** нареч (теперь) now; (скоро) just now; **~ же!** right now!

**секре́т (-а)** м secret

**секрета́рш|а (-и)** ж (разг) secretary

**секрета́р|ь (-я́)** м secretary; **~-машини́стка** secretary

**секре́тный** прил secret

**секс (-а)** м sex

**сексуа́льн|ый** прил sexual; (жизнь, образование) sex; **~ое пресле́дование** или **домога́тельство** sexual harassment

**се́кт|а (-ы)** ж sect

**секта́нт (-а)** м sect member

**се́ктор (-а)** м sector

**секу́нд|а (-ы)** ж second

**секу́ндн|ый** прил (пауза) second's; **~ая стре́лка** second hand (on clock)

**секундоме́р (-а)** м stopwatch

**се́кци|я (-и)** ж section

**сел** итп сов см. **сесть**

**селёд|ка (-ки;** gen pl **-ок)** ж herring

**селезёнк|а (-и)** ж spleen

**селе́ктор (-а)** м (ТЕЛ) intercom

**селе́кци|я (-и)** ж (БИО) selective

breeding

**селе́ни|е** (**-я**) *ср* village

**сел|и́ть** (**-ю́, -ишь**; *pf* **по~**) *несов перех* (*в местности*) to settle; (*в доме*) to house; **~ся** (*pf* **по~ся**) *несов возв* to settle

**сел|о́** (**-а́**; *nom pl* **сёла**) *ср* village

**сельдере́|й** (**-я**) *м* celery

**сельд|ь** (**-и**; *gen pl* **-е́й**) *ж* herring

**се́льск|ий** *прил* (*см сущ*) village; country, rural; **~ое хозя́йство** agriculture

**сельскохозя́йственный** *прил* agricultural

**сёмг|а** (**-и**) *ж* salmon

**семе́йный** *прил* family

**семе́йств|о** (**-а**) *ср* family

**семёр|ка** (**-ки**; *gen pl* **-ок**) *ж* (*цифра, карта*) seven

**се́мер|о** (**-ых**; *как* **че́тверо**; *см. Table 30b*) *чис* seven

**семе́стр** (**-а**) *м* term (*BRIT*), semester (*US*)

**се́меч|ко** (**-ка**; *gen pl* **-ек**) *ср* seed; **~ки** sunflower seeds

**семидеся́тый** *чис* seventieth

**семина́р** (**-а**) *м* seminar

**семина́ри|я** (**-и**) *ж* seminary

**семна́дцатый** *чис* seventeenth

**семна́дцат|ь** (**-и**; *как* **пять**; *см. Table 26*) *чис* seventeen

**сем|ь** (**-и́**; *как* **пять**; *см. Table 26*) *чис* seven

**се́м|ьдесят** (**-и́десяти**; *как* **пятьдеся́т**; *см. Table 26*) *чис* seventy

**сем|ьсо́т** (**-исо́т**; *как* **пятьсо́т**; *см. Table 28*) *чис* seven hundred

**семь|я́** (**-и́**; *nom pl* **-и**) *ж* family

**сём|я** (**-ени**; *как* **вре́мя**; *см. Table 4*) *ср* seed; *no pl* БИО) semen

**сена́тор** (**-а**) *м* senator

**сенн|о́й** *прил*: **~а́я лихора́дка** hay fever

**се́н|о** (**-а**) *м* hay

**сенса́ци|я** (**-и**) *ж* sensation

**сентимента́льный** *прил* sentimental

**сентя́бр|ь** (**-я́**) *м* September

**се́р|а** (**-ы**) *ж* sulphur (*BRIT*), sulfur (*US*); (*в ушах*) (ear)wax

**серва́нт** (**-а**) *м* buffet unit

**се́рвер** (**-а**) *м* (*КОМП*) server

**серви́з** (**-а**) *м*: **столо́вый/ча́йный ~** dinner/tea service

**се́рвис** (**-а**) *м* service (*in shop, restaurant etc*)

**серде́чный** *прил* heart, cardiac; (*челове́к*) warm-hearted; (*приём, разгово́р*) cordial; **~ при́ступ** heart attack

**серди́тый** *прил* angry

**сер|ди́ть** (**-жу́, -дишь**; *pf* **рас~**) *несов перех* to anger, make angry; **~ся** (*pf* **рас~ся**) *несов возв*: **серди́ться (на кого́-н/что-н)** to be angry (with sb/about sth)

**се́рд|це** (**-ца**; *nom pl* **-ца́**) *ср* heart; **в глубине́ ~ца** in one's heart of hearts; **от всего́ ~ца** from the bottom of one's heart

**сердцебие́ни|е** (**-я**) *ср* heartbeat

**серебр|о́** (**-а́**) *ср, собир* silver

**сере́бряный** *прил* silver

**середи́н|а** (**-ы**) *ж* middle

**серёж|ка** (**-ки**; *gen pl* **-ек**) *ж* уменьш от **серьга́**

**сержа́нт** (**-а**) *м* sergeant

**сериа́л** (**-а**) *м* (*ТЕЛ*) series

**се́ри|я** (**-и**) *ж* series; (*кинофи́льма*) part

**се́рн|ый** *прил*: **~ая кислота́** sulphuric (*BRIT*) *или* sulfuric (*US*) acid

**серп** (**-а́**) *м* sickle

**сертифика́т** (**-а**) *м* certificate; (*това́ра*) guarantee (certificate)

**се́рый** *прил* grey (*BRIT*), gray (*US*); **~ хлеб** brown bread

**сер|ьга́ (-ьги́**; *nom pl* **-ьги**, *gen pl* **-ёг**, *dat pl* **-ьга́м**) *ж* earring

**серьёзно** *нареч, вводн сл* seriously

**серьёзный** *прил* serious

**се́сси|я (-и)** *ж* (*суда, парламента*) session; (*также*: **экзаменацио́нная ~**) examinations *мн*

**сестр|а́ (-ы́**; *nom pl* **сёстры**, *gen pl* **сестёр**) *ж* sister; (*также*: **медици́нская ~**) nurse

**сесть (ся́ду, ся́дешь**; *pt* **сел, се́ла**; *impf* **сади́ться**) *сов* to sit down; (*птица, самолёт*) to land; (*солнце, луна*) to go down; (*одежда*) to shrink; (*батаре́йка*) to run down; **сади́ться (~ pf) в по́езд/на самолёт** to get on a train/plane; **сади́ться (~ pf) в тюрьму́** to go to prison

**сетево́й** *прил* (*КОМП*) net; (*магазин*) chain

**се́т|ка (-ки**; *gen pl* **-ок**) *ж* net; (*сумка*) net bag

**сет|ь (-и**; *prp sg* **-и́**, *gen pl* **-е́й**) *ж* (*для ловли рыб итп*) net; (*дорог*) network; (*магазинов*) chain; (*КОМП*) the Net

**сече́ни|е (-я)** *ср* section; **ке́сарево ~** Caesarean (*BRIT*) *или* Cesarean (*US*) (section)

**сечь (секу́, сечёшь** итп, **секу́т**; *pt* **сёк, секла́**) *несов перех* (*рубить*) to cut up

**се́|ять (-ю**; *pf* **по~**) *несов перех* to sow

**сжа́л|иться (-юсь, -ишься)** *сов возв*: **~ (над** +*instr*) to take pity (on)

**сжа́т|ый** *прил* (*воздух, газ*) compressed; (*рассказ*) condensed; **в ~ые сро́ки** in a short space of time

**сжать (сожму́, сожмёшь**; *impf*

**сжима́ть)** *сов перех* to squeeze; (*воздух, газ*) to compress;

**сжа́ться (**impf **сжима́ться)** *сов возв* (*пружина*) to contract; (*человек: от боли, от испуга*) to tense up; (*перен: сердце*) to seize up

**сжечь (сожгу́, сожжёшь** итп, **сожгу́т**; *pt* **сжёг, сожгла́**; *impf* **сжига́ть** *или* **жечь**) *сов перех* to burn

**сжима́|ть(ся) (-ю(сь))** *несов от* **сжа́ть(ся)**

**сза́ди** *нареч* (*подойти*) from behind; (*находиться*) behind
♦ *предл*: **~ +**gen behind

**сзыва́|ть (-ю)** *несов от* **созва́ть**

**сиби́рский** *прил* Siberian

**Сиби́р|ь (-и)** *ж* Siberia

**сибиря́к (-а́)** *м* Siberian

**сигаре́т|а (-ы)** *ж* cigarette

**сигна́л (-а)** *м* signal

**сигнализа́ци|я (-и)** *ж* (*в квартире*) burglar alarm

**сигна́л|ить (-ю, -ишь**; *pf* **про~**) *несов* to signal; (*АВТ*) to honk

**сиде́нь|е (-я)** *ср* seat

**си|де́ть (-жу́, -ди́шь)** *несов* to sit; (*одежда*) to fit

**си́дя** *нареч*: **рабо́тать/есть ~** to work/eat sitting down

**сидя́ч|ий** *прил* (*положение*) sitting; **~ие места́** seats *мн*

**си́л|а (-ы)** *ж* strength; (*тока, ветра, закона*) force; (*воли, слова*) power; (*обычно мн: душевные, творческие*) energy; **в ~у того́ что ...** owing to the fact that ...; **от ~ы** (*разг*) at (the) most; **вступа́ть (вступи́ть** pf) *или* **входи́ть (войти́** pf) **в ~у** to come into *или* take effect; *см. также* **си́лы**

**си́лой** *нареч* by force

**силуэ́т (-а)** *м* (*контур*) silhouette

**сИл|ы** (-) *мн* forces *мн*; **~ами**
**кого́-н** through the efforts of sb;
**свои́ми ~ами** by oneself

**сИльно** *нареч* strongly; (*уда́рить*)
hard; (*хоте́ть, понра́виться итп*)
very much

**сИльный** *прил* strong; (*моро́з*)
hard; (*впечатле́ние*) powerful;
(*дождь*) heavy

**сИмвол** (-а) *м* symbol; (*КОМП*)
character

**символизИр|овать** (-ую) *несов*
*перех* to symbolize

**симметрИ́ческий** *прил*
symmetrical

**симметрИ́|я** (-и) *ж* symmetry

**симпатизИр|овать** (-ую) *несов*:
**~ кому́-н** to like *или* be fond of sb

**симпати́чный** *прил* nice, pleasant

**симпа́ти|я** (-и) *ж* liking, fondness

**симпто́м** (-а) *м* symptom

**симфони́ческий** *прил*
symphonic; **~ орке́стр** symphony
orchestra

**симфо́ни|я** (-и) *ж* (*МУЗ*)
symphony

**синаго́г|а** (-и) *ж* synagogue

**синдро́м** (-а) *м* (*МЕД*) syndrome

**сине́|ть** (-ю; *pf* **по~**) *несов* to turn
blue

**сИний** *прил* blue

**синИ́ц|а** (-ы) *ж* tit (*ZOOL*)

**сино́д** (-а) *м* synod

**сино́ним** (-а) *м* synonym

**сино́птик** (-а) *м* weather forecaster

**сИнтаксис** (-а) *м* syntax

**сИнтез** (-а) *м* (*также ХИМ*)
synthesis

**синтети́ческий** *прил* synthetic

**синхро́нный** *прил* synchronous;
(*перево́д*) simultaneous

**синя́к** (-а́) *м* bruise

**сире́н|а** (-ы) *ж* (*гудо́к*) siren

**сире́невый** *прил* lilac

**сире́н|ь** (-и) *ж* (*куста́рник*) lilac
bush ♦ *собир* (*цветы́*) lilac

**сиро́п** (-а) *м* syrup

**сир|ота́** (-оты́; *nom pl* **-о́ты**) *м/ж*
orphan

**систе́м|а** (-ы) *ж* system

**системати́ческий** *прил* regular

**сИт|ец** (-ца) *м* cotton

**сИтеч|ко** (-ка; *gen pl* **-ек**) *ср* (*для
ча́я*) (tea) strainer

**сИт|о** (-а) *ср* sieve

**ситуа́ци|я** (-и) *ж* situation

**сИтцевый** *прил* (*ткань*) cotton

**СИФ** *м сокр* c.i.f.

**сия́|ть** (-ю) *несов* (*со́лнце,
звезда́*) to shine; (*ого́нь*) to glow

**сия́ющий** *прил* (*глаза́*) shining;
(*лицо́, улы́бка*) beaming

**ск|аза́ть** (-ажу́, -а́жешь) *сов от*
**говори́ть** ♦ *перех*: **-а́жем** (*разг*)
let's say; **~ажи́те!** (*разг*) I say!; **так
~** so to speak; **~ся** (*impf*
**ска́зываться**) *сов возв* (*ум,
о́пыт итп*) to show; (*отрази́ться*):
**~ся на** +*prp* to take its toll on

**ска́з|ка** (-ки; *gen pl* **-ок**) *ж* fairy
tale

**ска́зочный** *прил* fairy-tale

**сказу́ем|ое** (-ого) *ср* (*ЛИНГ*)
predicate

**скака́л|ка** (-ки; *gen pl* **-ок**) *ж*
skipping rope

**ск|ака́ть** (-ачу́, -а́чешь) *несов*
(*челове́к*) to skip; (*мяч*) to
bounce; (*ло́шадь, вса́дник*) to
gallop

**скаков|о́й** *прил*: **~а́я ло́шадь**
racehorse

**скаку́н** (-а́) *м* racehorse

**ск|ала́** (-алы́; *nom pl* **-а́лы**) *ж* cliff

**скали́стый** *прил* rocky

**скалола́з** (-а) *м* rock-climber

**скаме́|йка** (-йки; *gen pl* **-ек**) *ж*
bench

**скам|ья́** (-ьи́; *gen pl* **-е́й**) *ж* bench;
**~ подсуди́мых** (*ЮР*) the dock

**сканда́л** (-а) м scandal; (*ссора*) quarrel

**сканда́л|ить** (-ю, -ишь; *pf* по~) несов to quarrel

**сканда́льный** прил scandalous

**ска́нер** (-а) м (*КОМП*) scanner

**ска́плива|ться** (-юсь) несов от **скопи́ться**

**скарлати́н|а** (-ы) ж scarlet fever

**скат** (-а) м slope; (*АВТ, колесо*) wheel

**ската́|ть** (-ю; *impf* **ска́тывать**) сов перех to roll up

**ска́терт|ь** (-и) ж tablecloth

**ск|ати́ть** (-ачу́, -а́тишь; *impf* **ска́тывать**) сов перех to roll down; **~ся** (*impf* **ска́тываться**) сов возв (*слеза*) to roll down; (*перен*): **~ся к** +*dat*/**на** +*acc* to slide towards/into

**скафа́ндр** (-а) м (*водолаза*) diving suit; (*космонавта*) spacesuit

**ска́ч|ки** (-ек) мн the races мн

**скач|о́к** (-ка́) м leap

**СКВ** ж сокр (= свобо́дно конверти́руемая валю́та) convertible currency

**сква́жин|а** (-ы) ж (*нефтяная, газовая*) well; **замо́чная ~** keyhole

**сквер** (-а) м small public garden

**скве́рный** прил foul

**сквоз|и́ть** (*3sg* -**и́т**) несов безл: **здесь ~и́т** it's draughty here

**сквозня́к** (-а́) м (*в комнате*) draught (*BRIT*), draft (*US*)

**сквозь** предл: **~** +*acc* through

**скво́р|е́ц** (-ца́) м starling

**скворе́чник** (-а) м nesting box

**скеле́т** (-а) м skeleton

**скепти́ческий** прил sceptical

**ски́д|ка** (-ки; *gen pl* -ок) ж (*с цены*) discount, reduction

**ски́н|уть** (-у; *impf* **ски́дывать**) сов перех (*сбросить*) to throw down

**ски́с|нуть** (-ну, -нешь; *pt* -, -ла, -ло; *impf* **скиса́ть**) сов (*молоко*) to turn sour

**склад** (-а) м (*товарный*) store; (*оружия итп*) cache; (*образ: мыслей*) way

**скла́д|ка** (-ки; *gen pl* -ок) ж (*на одежде*) pleat

**складно́й** прил folding

**скла́дыва|ть(ся)** (-ю(сь)) несов от **сложи́ть(ся)**

**скле́|ить** (-ю, -ишь) сов от **кле́ить ♦** (*impf* **скле́ивать**) перех to glue together

**склеро́з** (-а) м sclerosis; **рассе́янный ~** multiple sclerosis

**склон** (-а) м slope

**склоне́ни|е** (-я) ср (*ЛИНГ*) declension

**скл|они́ть** (-оню́, -о́нишь; *impf* **склоня́ть**) сов перех (*опустить*) to lower; **склоня́ть** (**~** *pf*) **кого́-н к побе́гу/на преступле́ние** to persuade sb to escape/commit a crime; **~ся** (*impf* **склоня́ться** сов возв (*нагнуться*) to bend; (*перен*): **~ся к** +*dat* to come round to

**скло́нност|ь** (-и) ж: **~ к** +*dat* (*к музыке*) aptitude for (*к меланхолии, к полноте*) tendency to

**скло́нный** прил: **~ к** +*dat* (*к простудам*) prone или susceptible to; **~** +*infin* (*помири́ться*) inclined to do

**склоня́емый** прил declinable

**склоня́|ть** (-ю) несов от **склони́ть ♦** (*pf* **про~**) перех (*ЛИНГ*) to decline; **~ся** несов от **склони́ться ♦** возв (*ЛИНГ*) to decline

**ск|оба́** (-обы́; *nom pl* -о́бы) ж (*для опоры*) clamp; (*для крепления*) staple

**ско́б|ка** (**-ки**; *gen pl* **-ок**) *ж* уменьш от **скоба́**; (*обычно мн*: *в тексте*) bracket, parentheses *мн*

**ско́ванный** *прил* inhibited

**ск|ова́ть** (**-у́ю**; *impf* **ско́вывать**) *сов перех* (*человека*) to paralyse

**сковород|а́** (**-ы́**; *nom pl* **ско́вороды**) *ж* frying-pan (*BRIT*), skillet (*US*)

**сколь** *нареч* (*как*) how; (*возможно*) as much as; ~ ... **столь (же)** ... as much ... as ...

**сколь|зи́ть** (**-жу́**, **-зи́шь**) *несов* to glide; (*падая*) to slide

**ско́льзкий** *прил* slippery; (*ситуация, вопрос*) sensitive

**скользн|у́ть** (**-у́**, **-ёшь**) *сов* to glide; (*быстро пройти*) to slip

---

KEYWORD

---

**ско́льк|о** (**-их**) *местоимённое нареч* 1; (*+gen*: *книг, часов, дней итп*) how many; (*сахара, сил, работы итп*) how much; **ско́лько люде́й пришло́?** how many people came?; **ско́лько де́нег тебе́ на́до?** how much money do you need?; **ско́лько э́то сто́ит?** how much is it?; **ско́лько тебе́ лет?** how old are you?

2 (*относительное*) as much; **бери́, ско́лько хо́чешь** take as much as you want; **ско́лько уго́дно** as much as you like

♦ *нареч* 1 (*насколько*) as far as; **ско́лько по́мню, он всегда́ был агресси́вный** as far as I remember, he was always aggressive

2 (*много*): **ско́лько люде́й!** what a lot of people!; **не сто́лько ... ско́лько** ... not so much ... as ...

---

**ско́мка|ть** (**-ю**) *сов от* **ко́мкать**

**сконча́|ться** (**-юсь**) *сов возв* to pass away

**скоп|и́ть** (**-лю́**, **-ишь**) *сов от* **копи́ть**; **~ся** *сов от* **копи́ться** ♦ (*impf* **ска́пливаться**) *возв* (*люди*) to gather; (*работа*) to mount up

**ско́р|ая** (**-ой**) *ж* (*разг*: *также*: ~ **по́мощь**) ambulance

**скорб|ь** (**-и**; *gen pl* **-е́й**) *ж* grief

**скоре́е** *сравн прил от* **ско́рый** ♦ *сравн нареч от* **ско́ро** ♦ *част* rather; ~...**чем** *или* **нежели** (*в большей степени*) more likely ... than; (*лучше, охотнее*) rather ... than; ~ **всего́ они́ до́ма** it's most likely they'll be (at) home; ~ **бы он верну́лся** I wish he would come back soon

**скорл|упа́** (**-упы́**; *nom pl* **-у́пы**) *ж* shell

**ско́ро** *нареч* soon ♦ *как сказ* it's soon; ~ **зима́** it will soon be winter

**скоропости́жн|ый** *прил*: ~**ая смерть** sudden death

**скоростно́й** *прил* (*поезд*) high-speed

**ско́рост|ь** (**-и**; *gen pl* **-е́й**) *ж* speed

**скоросшива́тел|ь** (**-я**) *м* (loose-leaf) binder

**скорпио́н** (**-а**) *м* scorpion; (*созвездие*): **Скорпио́н** Scorpio

**ско́р|ый** *прил* (*движение*) fast; (*разлука, визит*) impending; **в ~ом вре́мени** shortly; ~**ая по́мощь** (*учреждение*) ambulance service; (*автомашина*) ambulance; ~ **по́езд** express (train)

**скот** (**-а́**) *м собир* livestock; **моло́чный/мясно́й** ~ dairy/beef cattle

**скреп|и́ть** (**-лю́**, **-и́шь**; *impf* **скрепля́ть**) *сов перех* (*соединить*) to fasten together

**скре́п|ка** (**-ки**; *gen pl* **-ок**) *ж* paperclip

**скре|сти́ть** (**-щу́**, **-сти́шь**; *impf*

**скрéщивать**) *сов перех* to cross; (*животных*) to cross-breed; **~ся** (*impf* **скрéщиваться**) *сов возв* to cross

**скрип** (**-а**) *м* (*двери, пола*) creak; (*металла*) grate

**скрипáч** (**-á**) *м* violinist

**скрип|éть** (**-лю́, -и́шь**) *несов* to creak

**скрип|ка** (**-ки**; *gen pl* **-ок**) *ж* violin

**скрóмност|ь** (**-и**) *ж* modesty

**скрóмный** *прил* modest; (*служащий, должность*) humble

**скр|ути́ть** (**-учу́, -у́тишь**) *сов от* **крути́ть** ♦ (*impf* **скру́чивать**) *перех* (*провода, волосы*) to twist together; **~ся** *сов возв* to twist together

**скрыва́|ть** (**-ю**) *несов от* **скрыть**; **~ся** *несов от* **скры́ться** ♦ *возв* (*от полиции*) to hide

**скры́тный** *прил* secretive

**скры́тый** *прил* (*возможности*) potent; (*тайный*) hidden

**скр|ы́ть** (**-о́ю, -о́ешь**; *impf* **скрыва́ть**) *сов перех* (*спрятать*) to hide; (*факты*) to conceal; **скры́ться** (*impf* **скрыва́ться**) *сов возв* (*от дождя, от погони*) to take cover; (*стать невидимым*) to disappear

**скýдный** *прил* (*запасы*) meagre (*BRIT*), meager (*US*)

**скýк|а** (**-и**) *ж* boredom

**ск|улá** (**-улы́**; *nom pl* **-у́лы**) *ж* (*обычно мн*) cheekbone

**скул|и́ть** (**-ю́, -и́шь**) *несов* to whine

**скýльптор** (**-а**) *м* sculptor

**скульптýр|а** (**-ы**) *ж* sculpture

**скýмбри|я** (**-и**) *ж* mackerel

**ск|упи́ть** (**-уплю́, -у́пишь**; *impf* **скупа́ть**) *сов перех* to buy up

**скупóй** *прил* mean

**скуча́|ть** (**-ю**) *несов* to be bored;

(*тосковáть*): **~ по** +*dat* или **о** +*prp* to miss

**скýчно** *нареч* (*жить, рассказывать итп*) boringly ♦ *как сказ*: **здесь ~** it's boring here; **мне ~** I'm bored

**скýчный** *прил* boring, dreary

**слабé|ть** (**-ю**; *pf* **о~**) *несов* to grow weak; (*дисциплина*) to slacken

**слаби́тельн|ое** (**-ого**) *ср* laxative

**слáбо** *нареч* (*вскри́кнуть*) weakly; (*нажать*) lightly; (*знать*) badly

**слáбост|ь** (**-и**) *ж* weakness

**слáбый** *прил* weak; (*ветер*) light; (*знания, доказáтельство итп*) poor; (*дисциплина итп*) slack

**слáв|а** (**-ы**) *ж* (*героя*) glory; (*писáтеля, актёра итп*) fame; **~ Бóгу!** thank God!

**слав|яни́н** (**-яни́на**; *nom pl* **-я́не**, *gen pl* **-я́н**) *м* Slav

**славя́нский** *прил* Slavonic

**слага́|ть** (**-ю**) *несов от* **сложи́ть**

**слáдкий** *прил* sweet

**слáдко** *нареч* (*пáхнуть*) sweet; (*спать*) deeply

**слáдк|ое** (**-ого**) *ср* sweet things *мн*; (*разг: десéрт*) afters (*BRIT*), dessert (*US*)

**слайд** (**-а**) *м* (*ФОТО*) slide

**слáлом** (**-а**) *м* slalom

**слать** (**шлю, шлёшь**) *несов перех* to send

**слáще** *сравн прил от* **слáдкий** ♦ *сравн нареч от* **слáдко**

**слéва** *нареч* on the left

**слегка́** *нареч* slightly

**след** (**-а**; *nom pl* **-ы**) *м* trace; (*ноги*) footprint

**сле|ди́ть** (**-жу́, -ди́шь**) *несов*: **~ за** +*instr* to follow; (*забóтиться*) to take care of; (*за шпиóном*) to watch

**слéдовани|е** (**-я**) *ср* (*мóде*)

following; **по́езд/авто́бус да́льнего ~я** long-distance train/bus

**сле́довател|ь (-я)** м detective

**сле́довательно** вводн сл consequently ♦ союз therefore

**сле́д|овать (-ую;** pf **по~)** несов (вывод, неприятность) to follow ♦ безл: **Вам ~ует поду́мать об э́том** you should think about it; **как ~ует** properly

**сле́дом** предл: **~ за** +instr following

**сле́дственный** прил investigative

**сле́дстви|е (-я)** ср (последствие) consequence; (ЮР) investigation

**сле́дующий** прил next ♦ мест following; **на ~ день** the next day

**сл|еза́ (-езы́;** nom pl **-ёзы,** dat pl **-еза́м)** ж tear

**слеза́|ть (-ю)** несов от **слезть**

**слез|и́ться (3sg -и́тся)** несов возв (глаза) to water

**слезоточи́вый** прил: **~ газ** tear gas

**слез|ть (-у, -ешь;** pt **-, ла;** impf **слеза́ть)** сов (кожа, краска) to peel off; **слеза́ть (~** pf**) (с** +gen**) (с** дерева) to climb down

**слеп|и́ть (3sg -и́т)** сов перех: **~ глаза́ кому́-н** to blind sb

**сл|епи́ть (-еплю́, -е́пишь)** сов от **лепи́ть**

**слеп|ну́ть (-у;** pf **о~)** несов to go blind

**слеп|о́й** прил blind ♦ **(-о́го)** м blind person

**сле́сар|ь (-я;** nom pl **-я́,** gen pl **-е́й)** м maintenance man

**сле|те́ть (-чу́, -ти́шь;** impf **слета́ть)** сов: **~ (с** +gen**) (птица)** to fly down (from); **~ся (**impf **слета́ться)** сов возв (птицы) to flock

**сли́в|а (-ы)** ж (дерево) plum

(tree); (плод) plum

**слива́|ть(ся) (-ю(сь))** несов от **сли́ть(ся)**

**сли́в|ки (-ок)** мн cream ед

**сли́вочн|ый** прил made with cream; **~ое ма́сло** butter

**сли́зист|ый** прил: **~ая оболо́чка** mucous membrane

**слиз|ь (-и)** ж mucus; (от грязи) slime

**сли́п|нуться (3sg -нется,** pt **-ся, -лась;** impf **слипа́ться)** сов возв to stick together

**сли́т|ок (-ка)** м (металлический) bar; (золота, серебра) ingot

**сли|ть (солью́, сольёшь;** pt **-л, -ла́,** imper **сле́й(те);** impf **слива́ть)** сов перех to pour; (перен: соединить) to merge; **сли́ться** (impf **слива́ться)** сов возв to merge

**сли́шком** нареч too; **э́то уже́ ~** (разг) that's just too much

**слова́рный** прил (работа, статья) dictionary, lexicographic(al); **~ запа́с** vocabulary

**словар|ь (-я́)** м (книга) dictionary; (запас слов) vocabulary

**слове́сный** прил oral; (протест) verbal

**сло́вно** союз (как) like; (как будто) as if

**сло́в|о (-а;** nom pl **-а́)** ср word

**сло́вом** вводн сл in a word

**словосочета́ни|е (-я)** ср word combination

**слог (-а;** nom pl **-и,** gen pl **-о́в)** м syllable

**слоёный** прил: **~ое те́сто** puff pastry

**сложе́ни|е (-я)** ср (в математике) addition; (фигура) build

**сл|ожи́ть (-ожу́, -о́жишь;** impf

**скла́дывать**) *сов перех* (*вещи*) to put; (*чемодан итп*) to pack; (*придавая форму*) to fold (up); (*impf* **скла́дывать** *или* **слага́ть**; *числа*) to add (up); (*песню, стихи*) to make up; **сиде́ть** (*impf*) **~ожа́ ру́ки** to sit back and do nothing; **~ся** (*impf*

**скла́дываться**) *сов возв* (*ситуация*) to arise; (*характер*) to form; (*зонт, пала́тка*) to fold up; (*впечатле́ние*) to be formed

**сло́жно** *нареч* (*де́лать*) in a complicated way ♦ *как сказ* it's difficult

**сло́жность** (**-и**) *ж* (*многообра́зие*) complexity; (*обы́чно мн: тру́дность*) difficulty; **в о́бщей ~и** all in all

**сло́жный** *прил* complex; (*узо́р*) intricate; (*тру́дный*) difficult

**сло|й** (**-я**; *nom pl* **-и́**) *м* layer

**слома́|ть(ся)** (**-ю(сь)**) *сов от* **лома́ть(ся)**

**слом|и́ть** (**-лю́, -ишь**) *сов перех* to break; **~я́ го́лову** (*разг*) at breakneck speed; **~ся** *сов возв* (*перен: челове́к*) to crack

**слон** (**-а́**) *м* elephant; (*ШАХМАТЫ*) bishop

**слон|ёнок** (**-ёнка**; *nom pl* **-я́та**, *gen pl* **-я́т**) *м* elephant calf

**слони́х|а** (**-и**) *ж* cow (*elephant*)

**слоно́в|ый** *прил* elephant; **~ая кость** ivory

**слуг|а́** (**-и́**; *nom pl* **-и**) *м* servant

**служа́н|ка** (**-ки**; *gen pl* **-ок**) *ж* maid

**слу́жащ|ий** (**-его**) *м* white collar worker; **госуда́рственный ~** civil servant; **конто́рский ~** clerk

**слу́жб|а** (**-ы**) *ж* service; (*рабо́та*) work; (*о́рган*) agency; **срок ~ы** durability; **Слу́жба бы́та** consumer services; **Слу́жба**

**за́нятости** ≈ Employment Agency

**служе́бный** *прил* (*дела́ итп*) official

**служи́тел|ь** (**-я**) *м* (*в музе́е, в зоопа́рке*) keeper; (*на автозапра́вке*) attendant; **~ це́ркви** clergyman

**служи́тельниц|а** (**-ы**) *ж* keeper

**сл|ужи́ть** (**-ужу́, -у́жишь**) *несов* to serve; (*в ба́нке*) to work; **чем могу́ ~?** what can I do for you?

**слух** (**-а**) *м* hearing; (*музыка́льный*) ear; (*изве́стие*) rumour (*BRIT*), rumor (*US*)

**слухово́й** *прил* (*нерв, о́рган*) auditory; **~ аппара́т** hearing aid

**случа́|й** (**-я**) *м* occasion; (*случа́йность*) chance; **в ~е** *+gen* in the event of; **во вся́ком ~е** in any case; **на вся́кий ~** just in case

**случа́йно** *нареч* by chance ♦ *вводн сл* by any chance

**случа́йность** (**-и**) *ж* chance

**случа́йный** *прил* (*встре́ча*) chance

**случ|и́ться** (**-у́сь, -и́шься**; *impf* **случа́ться**) *сов возв* to happen

**слу́шани|я** (**-й**) *мн* hearing *ед*

**слу́шател|ь** (**-я**) *м* listener; (*ПРОСВЕЩ*) student

**слу́ша|ть** (**-ю**) *несов перех* (*му́зыку, речь*) to listen to; (*ЮР*) to hear; (*pf* **по~**; *сове́т*) to listen to; **~ся** (*pf* **по~ся**) *несов возв*: **~ся** *+gen* to obey; (*сове́та*) to follow

**слы́ш|ать** (**-у, -ишь**) *несов* to hear ♦ (*pf* **у~**) *перех* to hear; **~** (*impf*) **о** *+prp* to hear about; **он пло́хо ~ит** he's hard of hearing; **~ся** *несов возв* to be heard

**слы́шно** *как сказ* it can be heard; **мне ничего́ не ~** I can't hear a thing; **о ней ничего́ не ~** there's no news of her

**слы́шный** *прил* audible

**слюн|а́** (-ы́) *ж* saliva

**слю́н|ки** (-ок) *мн*: **у меня́ ~ теку́т** my mouth's watering

**сля́кот|ь** (-и) *ж* slush

**см** *сокр* (= **сантиме́тр**) cm

**см.** *сокр* (= **смотри́**) v., qv

**сма́|зать** (-жу, -жешь; *impf* **сма́зывать**) *сов перех* (*ма́слом*) to lubricate

**сма́зк|а** (-и) *ж* lubrication; (*вещество́*) lubricant

**сма́тыва|ть** (-ю) *несов от* **смота́ть**

**смахн|у́ть** (-у́, -ёшь; *impf* **сма́хивать**) *сов перех* to brush off

**сме́жный** *прил* (*ко́мната*) adjoining, adjacent; (*предприя́тие*) affiliated

**смеле́|ть** (-ю; *pf* **о~**) *несов* to grow bolder

**сме́лост|ь** (-и) *ж* (*хра́брость*) courage, bravery

**сме́лый** *прил* courageous, brave; (*иде́я, прое́кт*) ambitious

**сме́н|а** (-ы) *ж* (*руково́дства*) change; (*на произво́дстве*) shift

**см|ени́ть** (-еню́, -е́нишь; *impf* **сменя́ть**) *сов перех* to change; (*колле́гу*) to relieve; **~ся** (*impf* **сменя́ться**) *сов возв* (*руково́дство*) to change

**сме́рте́льный** *прил* mortal; (*ску́ка*) deadly; ~ **слу́чай** fatality

**сме́ртност|ь** (-и) *ж* death *или* mortality (*US*) rate, mortality

**сме́ртн|ый** *прил* mortal; (*разг: ску́ка*) deadly; ~ **пригово́р** death sentence; **~ая казнь** the death penalty, capital punishment

**смерт|ь** (-и) *ж* death; **я уста́л до ~и** I am dead tired

**смеси́тел|ь** (-я) *м* mixer

**сме́|си́ть** (-шу́, -сишь) *сов от* **меси́ть**

**сме|сти́** (-ту́, -тёшь; *pt* -ёл, -ела́, -ело́; *impf* **смета́ть**) *сов перех* to sweep

**сме|сти́ть** (-щу́, -сти́шь; *impf* **смеща́ть**) *сов перех* (*уво́лить*) to remove; **~ся** (*impf* **смеща́ться**) *сов возв* to shift

**смес|ь** (-и) *ж* mixture; **моло́чная ~** powdered baby milk

**сме́т|а** (-ы) *ж* (*ЭКОН*) estimate

**смета́н|а** (-ы) *ж* sour cream

**смета́|ть** (-ю) *несов от* **смести́**

**сме́|ть** (-ю; *pf* **посме́ть**) *несов*: ~ +*infin* to dare to do

**смех** (-а) *м* laughter

**смехотво́рный** *прил* ludicrous

**смеша́|ть** (-ю) *сов от* **меша́ть** ♦ (*impf* **сме́шивать**) *перех* (*спу́тать*) to mix up; **~ся** *сов от* **меша́ться** ♦ (*impf* **сме́шиваться**) *возв* (*сли́ться*) to mingle; (*кра́ски, цвета́*) to blend

**смеш|и́ть** (-у́, -и́шь; *pf* **на~** *или* **рас~**) *несов перех*: ~ **кого́-н** to make sb laugh

**смешно́** *нареч* (*смотре́ться*) funny ♦ *как сказ* it's funny; (*глу́по*) it's ludicrous

**смешно́й** *прил* funny

**смеща́|ть(ся)** (-ю(сь)) *несов от* **смести́ть(ся)**

**смеще́ни|е** (-я) *ср* (*руково́дства*) removal; (*поня́тий, крите́риев*) shift

**сме|я́ться** (-ю́сь) *несов возв* to laugh

**СМИ** *сокр* (= **сре́дства ма́ссовой информа́ции**) mass media

**смир|и́ть** (-ю́, -и́шь; *impf* **смиря́ть**) *сов перех* to suppress; **~ся** (*impf* **смиря́ться**) *сов возв* (*покори́ться*) to submit; (*примири́ться*): **~ся с** +*instr* to resign o.s. to

**сми́рно** *нареч* (сидеть, вести себя) quietly; (ВОЕН): ~! attention!

**сми́рный** *прил* docile

**смог** *etc см см.* **смочь**

**смо́жешь** *etc сов см.* **смочь**

**смол|а́ (-ы́;** *nom pl* **-ы)** *ж* (дерево) resin; (дёготь) tar

**смо́лк|нуть (-ну;** *pt* **-ла;** *impf* **смолка́ть)** *сов* (звуки) to fade away

**сморка|ть (-ю;** *pf* **вы́сморкать)** *несов перех:* ~ **нос** to blow one's nose; **~ся** (*pf* **вы́сморкаться)** *несов возв* to blow one's nose

**сморо́дин|а (-ы)** *ж:* **кра́сная ~** (ягоды) redcurrants *мн;* **чёрная ~** (ягоды) blackcurrants *мн*

**смо́рщ|ить(ся) (-у(сь), -ишь(ся))** *сов от* **мо́рщить(ся)**

**смота́|ть (-ю;** *impf* **сма́тывать)** *сов перех* to wind

**см|отре́ть (-отрю́, -о́тришь;** *pf* **по~)** *несов* to look ♦ *перех* (фильм, игру) to watch; (картину) to look at; (музей, выставку) to look round; (следить): ~ **за** +*instr* to look after; ~ (*impf*) **в/на** +*acc* to look onto; **~отря́ по** +*dat* depending on; **~ся** (*pf* **по~ся)** *несов возв:* **~ся в** +*acc* (в зеркало) to look at o.s. in

**смотри́тел|ь (-я)** *м* attendant

**смо|чь (-гу́, -жешь** *etc,* **-гут;** *pt* **-г, -гла́, -гло́)** *сов от* **мочь**

**сму́глый** *прил* swarthy

**сму́т|а (-ы)** *ж* unrest

**сму|ти́ть (-щу́, -ти́шь;** *impf* **смуща́ть)** *сов перех* to embarrass; **~ся** (*impf* **смуща́ться)** *сов возв* to get embarrassed

**сму́тный** *прил* vague; (время) troubled

**смуще́ни|е (-я)** *ср* embarrassment

**смущённый** *прил* embarrassed

**смысл (-а)** *м* sense; (назначение) point

**см|ыть (-о́ю, -о́ешь;** *impf* **смыва́ть)** *сов перех* to wash off; (подлеж: волна) to wash away; **смы́ться** (*impf* **смыва́ться)** *сов возв* to wash off

**смыч|о́к (-ка́)** *м* (МУЗ) bow

**смягч|и́ть (-у́, -и́шь;** *impf* **смягча́ть)** *сов перех* (кожу, удар) to soften; (боль) to ease; (наказание) to mitigate; (человека) to appease; **~ся** (*impf* **смягча́ться)** *сов возв* to soften

**смя́ть(ся) (сомну́(сь), сомнёшь(ся))** *сов от* **мя́ть(ся)**

**сна** *etc сущ см.* **сон**

**снаб|ди́ть (-жу́, -ди́шь;** *impf* **снабжа́ть)** *сов перех:* ~ **кого́-н/ что-н чем-н** to supply sb/sth with sth

**снабже́ни|е (-я)** *ср* supply

**сна́йпер (-а)** *м* sniper

**снару́жи** *нареч* on the outside; (закрыть) from the outside

**снаря́д (-а)** *м* (ВОЕН) shell; (СПОРТ) apparatus

**снаря|ди́ть (-жу́, -ди́шь;** *impf* **снаряжа́ть)** *сов перех* to equip

**снаряже́ни|е (-я)** *ср* equipment

**снача́ла** *нареч* at first; (ещё раз) all over again

**СНГ** *м сокр* (= Содру́жество Незави́симых Госуда́рств) CIS

**снег (-а;** *loc sg* **-у́,** *nom pl* **-а́)** *м* snow; **идёт ~** it's snowing

**снеги́р|ь (-я́)** *м* bullfinch

**снегови́к (-а́)** *м* snowman

**снегопа́д (-а)** *м* snowfall

**Снегу́роч|ка (-ки;** *gen pl* **-ек)** *ж* Snow Maiden

**Снегу́рочка** - Snow Maiden. She accompanies Father Christmas on his visits to children's New Year parties, where she organizes games and helps to give out the presents.

**снежи́н|ка** (-ки; *gen pl* -ок) ж snowflake
**сне́жный** *прил* snow; (*зима*) snowy
**снеж|о́к** (-ка́) м snowball
**сн|ести́** (-есу́, -есёшь; *pt* -ёс, -есла́, -есло́; *impf* **сноси́ть**) *сов перех* (*отнести*) to take; (*подлеж: буря*) to tear down; (*перен*) to take; (*дом*) to demolish
**снижа́|ть(ся)** (-ю(сь)) *несов от* **сни́зить(ся)**
**сниже́ни|е** (-я) *ср* (*цен итп*) lowering; (*самолёта*) descent; (*выдачи*) reduction
**сни́|зить** (-жу, -зишь; *impf* **снижа́ть**) *сов перех* (*цены, давление итп*) to lower; (*скорость*) to reduce; **~ся** (*impf* **снижа́ться**) *сов возв* to fall; (*самолёт*) to descend
**сни́зу** *нареч* (*внизу*) at the bottom; (*о направлении*) from the bottom
**снима́|ть(ся)** (-ю(сь)) *несов от* **снять(ся)**
**сни́м|ок** (-ка) м (*ФОТО*) snap(shot)
**снисходи́тельный** *прил* lenient; (*высокомерный*) condescending
**сн|и́ться** (-ю́сь, -и́шься; *pf* **при~**) *несов безл*: мне ~и́лся стра́шный сон I was having a terrible dream; мне ~и́лось, что я в гора́х I dreamt I was in the mountains; ты ча́сто ~и́шься мне I often dream about you
**сно́ва** *нареч* again

**снос** (-а) м demolition
**сно́с|ка** (-ки; *gen pl* -ок) ж footnote
**снотво́рн|ое** (-ого) *ср* sleeping pill
**снох|а́** (-и́) ж daughter-in-law (*of husband's father*)
**сн|ять** (-иму́, -и́мешь; *impf* **снима́ть**) *сов перех* to take down; (*плод*) to pick; (*одежду*) to take off; (*запрет, ответственность*) to remove; (*фотографировать*) to photograph; (*копию*) to make; (*нанять*) to rent; (*уволить*) to dismiss; **снима́ть** (*~ pf*) **фотогра́фию** to take a picture; **снима́ть** (*~ pf*) **фильм** to shoot a film; **сня́ться** (*impf* **снима́ться**) *сов возв* (*сфотографироваться*) to have one's photograph taken; (*в фильме*) to appear
**со** *предл* = **с**
**соа́втор** (-а) м coauthor
**соба́к|а** (-и) ж dog
**собаково́д** (-а) м dog-breeder
**соба́чий** *прил* dog's
**собе́с** (-а) м social security; (*орган*) social security department
**собесе́дник** (-а) м: мой ~ замолча́л the person I was talking to fell silent
**собесе́довани|е** (-я) *ср* interview
**собира́тел|ь** (-я) м collector
**собира́|ть** (-ю) *несов от* **собра́ть**; **~ся** *несов от* **собра́ться** ♦ *возв*: я ~ю́сь пойти́ туда́ I'm going to go there
**соблазн|и́ть** (-ю́, -и́шь; *impf* **соблазня́ть**) *сов перех* to seduce; (*прельстить*): ~ **кого́-н чем-н** to tempt sb with sth; **~ся** (*impf* **соблазня́ться**) *сов возв*: ~**ся** +*instr*/ +*infin* to be tempted by/to do

**соблюда́|ть (-ю)** *несов от* **соблюсти́** ♦ *перех* (дисциплину, порядок) to maintain

**соблю|сти́ (-ду́, -дёшь)** *сов от* **блюсти́** ♦ (*impf* **соблюда́ть**) *перех* (закон, правила) to observe

**соболе́зновани|е (-я)** *ср* condolences *мн*

**со́б|оль (-оля;** *nom pl* **-оля́)** *м* sable

**собо́р (-а)** *м* cathedral

**СОБР (-а)** *м сокр* (= Сво́дный отря́д бы́строго реаги́рования) flying squad

**собра́ни|е (-я)** *ср* meeting; (*полит*) assembly; (*картин итп*) collection; ~ **сочине́ний** collected works

**соб|ра́ть (-еру́, -ерёшь;** *pt* **-ра́л, -рала́, -ра́ло;** *impf* **собира́ть**) *сов перех* to gather (together); (*ягоды, грибы*) to pick; (*механизм*) to assemble; (*налоги, подписи*) to collect; ~**ся** (*impf* **собира́ться**) *сов возв* (*гости*) to assemble, gather; (*приготовиться*): ~**ся** +*infin* to get ready to do; **собира́ться (~ся** *pf*) **c** +*instr* (*с силами, с мыслями*) to gather

**собро́в|ец (-ца)** *м* member of the flying squad

**со́бственник (-а)** *м* owner

**со́бственно** *част* actually ♦ *вводн сл*: ~ **(говоря́)** as a matter of fact

**со́бственност|ь (-и)** *ж* property

**со́бственный** *прил* (one's) own

**собы́ти|е (-я)** *ср* event

**сов|а́ (-ы́;** *nom pl* **-ы)** *ж* owl

**соверша́|ть(ся) (-ю)** *несов от* **соверши́ть(ся)**

**соверше́ни|е (-я)** *ср* (*сделки*) conclusion; (*преступления*) committing

**соверше́нно** *нареч* (*очень хорошо*) perfectly; (*совсем*) absolutely, completely

**совершенноле́тн|ий** *прил*: **стать ~им** to come of age

**соверше́нный** *прил* (*хороший*) perfect; (*абсолютный*) absolute, complete; ~ **вид** (*линг*) perfective (aspect)

**соверше́нств|о (-а)** *ср* perfection

**соверше́нств|овать (-ую;** *pf* **y~)** *несов перех* to perfect; ~**ся** (*pf* **y~ся**) *несов возв*: ~**ся в** +*prp* to perfect

**соверш|и́ть (-у́, -и́шь;** *impf* **соверша́ть**) *сов перех* to make; (*сделку*) to conclude; (*преступление*) to commit; (*обряд, подвиг*) to perform; ~**ся** (*impf* **соверша́ться**) *сов возв* (*событие*) to take place

**со́вест|ь (-и)** *ж* conscience; **на ~** (*сделанный*) very well

**сове́т (-а)** *м* advice *только ед*; (*военный*) council

**сове́тник (-а)** *м* (*юстиции итп*) councillor; (*президента*) adviser

**сове́т|овать (-ую;** *pf* **по~)** *несов*: ~ **кому́-н** +*infin* to advise sb to do; ~**ся** (*pf* **по~ся**) *несов возв*: ~**ся с кем-н** (*с другом*) to ask sb's advice; (*с юристом*) to consult sb

**сове́тский** *прил* Soviet

**совеща́ни|е (-я)** *ср* (*собрание*) meeting; (*конгресс*) conference

**совеща́тельный** *прил* (*орган, голос*) consultative

**совеща́|ться (-юсь)** *несов возв* to deliberate

**совмести́мый** *прил* compatible

**совме|сти́ть (-щу́, -сти́шь;** *impf* **совмеща́ть**) *сов перех* to combine

**совме́стн|ый** *прил* (*общий*) joint; ~**ое предприя́тие** joint venture

**сов|о́к** (**-ка́**) м (*для мусора*) dustpan; (*для муки*) scoop

**совоку́пность** (**-и**) ж combination; **в ~и** in total

**совоку́пный** прил (*усилия*) joint

**совпаде́ни|е** (**-я**) ср coincidence; (*данных, цифр*) tallying

**совпа́|сть** (*3sg* **-дёт**; *impf* **совпада́ть**) сов (*события*) to coincide; (*данные, цифры итп*) to tally; (*интересы, мнения*) to meet

**совр|а́ть** (**-у́, -ёшь**) сов от **врать**

**совреме́нник** (**-а**) м contemporary

**совреме́нност|ь** (**-и**) ж the present day; (*идей*) modernity

**совреме́нный** прил contemporary; (*техника*) up-to-date; (*человек, идеи*) modern

**совсе́м** нареч (*новый*) completely; (*молодой*) very; (*нисколько: не пригодный, не нужный*) totally; **не** ~ not quite

**согла́си|е** (**-я**) ср consent; (*в семье*) harmony, accord

**согла|си́ться** (**-шу́сь, -си́шься**; *impf* **соглаша́ться**) сов возв to agree

**согла́сно** предл ~ +*dat* или **с** +*instr* in accordance with

**согла́сн|ый** (**-ого**) м (*также:* ~ **звук**) consonant ♦ прил: ~ **на** +*acc* (*на условия*) agreeable to; **Вы ~ы (со мной)**? do you agree (with me)?

**соглас|ова́ть** (**-у́ю**; *impf* **согласо́вывать**) сов перех (*действия*) to coordinate; (*обговорить*): ~ **что-н с** +*instr* (*план, цену*) to agree sth with; ~**ся** (*не*)*сов возв*: ~**ся с** +*instr* to correspond with

**соглаша́|ться** (**-юсь**) несов от **согласи́ться**

**соглаше́ни|е** (**-я**) ср agreement

**согн|у́ть** (**-у́, -ёшь**) сов от **гнуть, сгиба́ть**

**согре́|ть** (**-ю**; *impf* **согрева́ть**) сов перех (*воду*) to heat up; (*ноги, руки*) to warm up; ~**ся** (*impf* **согрева́ться**) сов возв to warm up; (*вода*) to heat up

**со́д|а** (**-ы**) ж soda

**соде́йстви|е** (**-я**) ср assistance

**соде́йств|овать** (**-ую**) (*не*)*сов*: ~ +*dat* to assist

**содержа́ни|е** (**-я**) ср (*семьи, детей*) upkeep; (*магазина, фермы*) keeping; (*книги*) contents мн; (*сахара, витаминов*) content; (*оглавление*) (table of) contents мн

**содержа́тельный** прил (*статья, доклад*) informative

**сод|ержа́ть** (**-ержу́, -е́ржишь**) несов перех (*детей, родителей, магазин*) to keep; (*ресторан*) to own; (*сахар, ошибки, информацию итп*) to contain; ~**ся** несов возв (*под арестом*) to be held

**содр|а́ть** (**сдеру́, сдерёшь**; *pt* **-а́л, -ала́**; *impf* **сдира́ть**) сов перех (*слой, одежду*) to tear off

**содру́жеств|о** (**-а**) ср (*дружба*) co-operation; (*союз*) commonwealth; **Содру́жество Незави́симых Госуда́рств** the Commonwealth of Independent States

**со́евый** прил soya

**соедин|и́ть** (**-ю́, -и́шь**; *impf* **соединя́ть**) сов перех (*силы, детали*) to join; (*людей*) to unite; (*провода, трубы, по телефону*) to connect; (*города*) to link; ~**ся** (*impf* **соединя́ться**) сов возв (*люди, отряды*) to join together

**сожале́ни|е** (**-я**) ср (*сострадание*) pity; ~ (**о** +*prp*) (*о*

*прошлом, о потере*) regret
(about); **к ~ю** unfortunately
**сожале́|ть (-ю)** *несов:* ~ **о
чём-н/, что** to regret sth/that
**соз|ва́ть (-ову́, -ове́шь;** *pt* **-ва́л,
-вала́;** *impf* **созыва́ть**) *сов перех*
(*пригласить*) to summon; (*impf*
**созыва́ть**; *съезд*) to convene
**созве́зди|е (-я)** *ср* constellation
**созвон|и́ться (-ю́сь, -и́шься;**
*impf* **созва́ниваться**) *сов возв:* ~
**с** +*instr* to phone (*BRIT*) *или* call
(*US*)
**созда|ва́ть(ся) (-ю́, -ёшь)** *несов
от* **созда́ть(ся)**
**созда́ни|е (-я)** *ср* creation;
(*существо*) creature
**созда́тел|ь (-я)** *м* creator
**созда́ть** (*как* **дать**; *см.* Table 16;
*impf* **создава́ть**) *сов перех* to
create; **~ся** (*impf* **создава́ться**)
*сов возв* (*обстановка*) to emerge;
(*впечатление*) to be created
**созна|ва́ть (-ю́, -ёшь)** *несов от*
**созна́ть ♦** *перех* to be aware of;
**~ся** *несов от* **созна́ться**
**созна́ни|е (-я)** *ср* consciousness;
(*вины, долга*) awareness;
**приходи́ть** (**прийти́** *pf*) **в ~** to
come round
**созна́тельност|ь (-и)** *ж*
awareness
**созна́тельный** *прил* (*человек,
возраст*) mature; (*жизнь*) adult;
(*обман, поступок*) intentional
**созна́|ть (-ю;** *impf* **сознава́ть**)
*сов перех* (*вину, долг*) to realize;
**~ся** (*impf* **сознава́ться**) *сов возв:*
**~ся (в** +*prp*) (*в ошибке*) to admit
(to); (*в преступлении*) to confess
(to)
**созре́|ть (-ю)** *сов от* **зреть**
**созыва́|ть (-ю)** *несов от* **созва́ть**
**сойти́** (*как* **идти́**; *см.* Table 18; *impf*
**сходи́ть**) *сов* (*с горы, с*

*лестницы*) to go down; (*с
дороги*) to leave; (*разг*): ~ **с** +*instr*
(*с поезда, с автобуса*) to get off;
**сходи́ть** (~ *pf*) **с ума́** to go mad;
**~сь** (*impf* **сходи́ться**) *сов возв*
(*собраться*) to gather; (*цифры,
показания*) to tally
**сок (-а)** *м* juice
**со́кол (-а)** *м* falcon
**сокра|ти́ть (-щу́, -ти́шь;** *impf*
**сокраща́ть**) *сов перех* to
shorten; (*расходы*) to reduce; **~ся**
(*impf* **сокраща́ться**) *сов возв*
(*расстояние, сроки*) to be
shortened; (*расходы, снабжение*)
to be reduced
**сокраще́ни|е (-я)** *ср* (*см глаг*)
shortening; reduction;
(*сокращённое название*)
abbreviation; (*также:* ~ **шта́тов**)
staff reduction
**сокро́вищ|е (-а)** *ср* treasure
**соку́рсник (-а)** *м:* **он мой ~** he is
in my year
**сол|га́ть (-гу́, -жёшь** *etc,* -**гу́т**)
*сов от* **лгать**
**солда́т (-а;** *gen pl* -) *м* soldier
**солда́тик (-а)** *м* (*игрушка*) toy
soldier
**солёный** *прил* (*пища*) salty;
(*овощи*) pickled in brine; (*вода*)
salt
**солида́рност|ь (-и)** *ж* solidarity
**соли́дный** *прил* (*постройка*)
solid; (*фирма*) established
**соли́ст (-а)** *м* soloist
**сол|и́ть (-ю́, -ишь;** *pf* **по~**) *несов
перех* to salt; (*засаливать*) to
preserve in brine
**со́лнечн|ый** *прил* solar; (*день,
погода*) sunny; ~ **уда́р** sunstroke;
**~ые очки́** sunglasses
**со́лнц|е (-а)** *ср* sun
**со́ло** *ср нескл, нареч* solo
**солове́|й (-ья́)** *м* nightingale

**соло́м|а** (**-ы**) *ж* straw
**соло́менный** *прил* (*шляпа*) straw
**соло́н|ка** (**-ки**; *gen pl* **-ок**) *ж* saltcellar
**соль** (**-и**) *ж* salt
**со́льный** *прил* solo
**сомнева́|ться** (**-юсь**) *несов возв*: ~ **в чём-н/, что** to doubt sth/that
**сомне́ни|е** (**-я**) *ср* doubt
**сомни́тельный** *прил* (*дело, личность*) shady; (*предложение, знакомство*) dubious
**сон** (**сна**) *м* sleep; (*сновидение*) dream
**сона́т|а** (**-ы**) *ж* sonata
**со́нный** *прил* (*заспанный*) sleepy
**соображ|а́ть** (**-ю**) *несов от* **сообрази́ть**
**соображе́ни|е** (**-я**) *ср* (*мысль*) idea; (*обычно мн: мотивы*) reasoning
**сообрази́тельный** *прил* smart
**сообра|зи́ть** (**-жу́, -зи́шь**; *impf* **сообража́ть**) *сов* to work out
**сообща́** *нареч* together
**сообща́|ть** (**-ю**) *несов от* **сообщи́ть**
**сообще́ни|е** (**-я**) *ср* (*информация*) report; (*правительственное*) announcement; (*связь*) communications *мн*
**сообще́ств|о** (**-а**) *ср* association; **мирово́е** *или* **междунаро́дное** ~ international community
**сообщ|и́ть** (**-у́, -и́шь**; *impf* **сообща́ть**) *сов*: ~ **кому́-н о** +*prp* to inform sb of ♦ *перех* (*новости, тайну*) to tell
**сообщник** (**-а**) *м* accomplice
**соотве́тственно** *предл*: ~ +*dat* (*обстановке*) according to
**соотве́тственный** *прил* (*оплата*) appropriate; (*результаты*) fitting
**соотве́тстви|е** (**-я**) *ср*

(*интересов, стилей итп*) correspondence; **в ~и с** +*instr* in accordance with
**соотве́тств|овать** (**-ую**) *несов*: ~ +*dat* to correspond to; (*требованиям*) to meet
**соотве́тствующий** *прил* appropriate
**сооте́чественник** (**-а**) *м* compatriot
**соотноше́ни|е** (**-я**) *ср* correlation
**сопе́рник** (**-а**) *м* rival; (*в спорте*) competitor
**сопе́рнича|ть** (**-ю**) *несов*: ~ **с кем-н в чём-н** to rival sb in sth
**сопра́но** *ср нескл* soprano
**сопровожда́|ть** (**-ю**; *pf* **сопроводи́ть**) *несов перех* to accompany
**сопровожде́ни|е** (**-я**) *ср*: **в ~и** +*gen* accompanied by
**сопротивле́ни|е** (**-я**) *ср* resistance
**сопротивля́|ться** (**-юсь**) *несов возв*: ~ +*dat* to resist
**сор** (**-а**) *м* rubbish
**сорв|а́ть** (**-у́, -ёшь**; *impf* **срыва́ть**) *сов перех* (*цветок, яблоко*) to pick; (*дверь, крышу, одежду*) to tear off; (*лекцию, переговоры*) to sabotage; (*планы*) to frustrate; ~**ся** (*impf* **срыва́ться**) *сов возв* (*человек*) to lose one's temper; (*планы*) to be frustrated; **срыва́ться** (~**ся** *pf*) **с** +*gen* (*с петель*) to come away from
**соревнова́ни|е** (**-я**) *ср* competition
**соревн|ова́ться** (**-у́юсь**) *несов возв* to compete
**сор|и́ть** (**-ю́, -и́шь**; *pf* **на~**) *несов* to make a mess
**сорня́к** (**-а́**) *м* weed
**со́рок** (**-а́**; *см. Table 27*) *чис* forty

**сорóк|а (-и)** ж magpie

**сороковóй** чис fortieth

**сорóч|ка (-ки;** gen pl **-ек)** ж (мужская) shirt; **ночнáя ~** nightgown

**сорт (-а;** nom pl **-á)** м sort; (пшеницы) grade

**сортир|овáть (-ýю;** pf **рас~)** несов перех to sort; (по качеству) to grade

**сос|áть (-ý, -ёшь)** несов перех to suck; (младенец, детёныш) to suckle

**сосéд (-а;** nom pl **-и,** gen pl **-ей)** м neighbour (BRIT), neighbor (US)

**сосéдний** прил neighbouring (BRIT), neighboring (US)

**сосéдств|о (-а)** ср: **жить по ~у** to live nearby; **в ~е с** +instr near

**сосúс|ка (-ки;** gen pl **-ок)** ж sausage

**сóс|ка (-ки;** gen pl **-ок)** ж (на бутылке) teat; (пустышка) dummy (BRIT), pacifier (US)

**соск|очúть (-очý, -óчишь;** impf **соскáкивать)** сов to jump off

**соскýч|иться (-усь, -ишься)** сов возв to be bored; **~ (pf) по** +dat (по детям) to miss

**сослагáтельн|ый** прил: **~ое наклонéние** subjunctive mood

**со|слáть (-шлю, -шлёшь;** impf **ссылáть)** сов перех to exile; **~ся** (impf **ссылáться)** сов возв: **~ся на** +acc to refer to

**сослужúв|ец (-ца)** м colleague

**сос|нá (-ны;** nom pl **-ны,** gen pl **-ен)** ж pine (tree)

**соснóвый** прил pine

**сос|óк (-кá)** м nipple

**сосредотóч|ить (-у, -ишь;** impf **сосредотáчивать)** сов перех to concentrate; **~ся** (impf **сосредотáчиваться)** сов возв (войска) to be concentrated; (внимание): **~ся на** +acc to focus on

**состáв (-а)** м (классовый) structure; **~** +gen (комитета) members мн of; (вещества) composition of

**состáв|ить (-лю, -ишь;** impf **составлять)** сов перех (словарь, список) to compile; (план) to draw up; (сумму) to constitute; (команду) to put together; **~ся** (impf **составляться)** сов возв to be formed

**составн|óй** прил: **~áя часть** component

**состáр|ить (-ю, -ишь)** сов от **стáрить; ~ся** сов возв (человек) to grow old

**состоя́ни|е (-я)** ср state; (больного) condition; (собственность) fortune; **быть** (impf) **в ~и** +infin to be able to do

**состоя́тельный** прил (богатый) well-off

**состо|я́ть (-ю́, -и́шь)** несов: **~ из** +gen (книга) to consist of; (заключаться): **~ в** +prp to be (в партии) to be a member of; **~** (impf) +instr (директором итп) to be; **~ся** несов возв (собрание) to take place

**сострадáни|е (-я)** ср compassion

**состязáни|е (-я)** ср contest

**состязá|ться (-юсь)** несов возв to compete

**сосýд (-а)** м vessel

**сосýл|ька (-ьки;** gen pl **-ек)** ж icicle

**сосуществовáни|е (-я)** ср coexistence

**сот** чис см. **сто**

**сотворéни|е (-я)** ср: **~ мúра** Creation

**сóт|ня (-ни;** gen pl **-ен)** ж (сто) a hundred

**со́тов|ый** *прил*: ~ **телефо́н** mobile phone; **~ая связь** network

**сотру́дник** (**-а**) *м* (*служащий*) employee; **нау́чный ~** research worker

**сотру́дniча|ть** (**-ю**) *несов* to cooperate; (*работать*) to work

**сотру́дничеств|о** (**-а**) *ср* (*см глаг*) cooperation; work

**сотрясе́ни|е** (**-я**) *ср* (*от взрыва*) shaking; (*также*: **~ мо́зга**) concussion

**сотряс|ти́** (**-у́, -ёшь**; *impf* **сотряса́ть**) *сов перех* to shake; **~сь** (*impf* **сотряса́ться**) *сов возв* to shake

**со́т|ы** (**-ов**) *мн*: (**пчели́ные**) ~ honeycomb *ед*

**со́тый** *чис* hundredth

**со́ус** (**-а**) *м* sauce

**соуча́стник** (**-а**) *м* accomplice

**соф|а́** (**-ы́**; *nom pl* **-ы**) *ж* sofa

**со́х|нуть** (**-ну**; *pt* **-, -ла**; *pf* **вы́сохнуть**) *несов* to dry; (*растения*) to wither

**сохран|и́ть** (**-ю́, -и́шь**; *impf* **сохраня́ть**) *сов перех* to preserve; (*КОМП*) to save; **~ся** (*impf* **сохраня́ться**) *сов возв* to be preserved

**сохра́нност|ь** (**-и**) *ж* (*вкладов, документов*) security; **в (по́лной) ~и** (fully) intact

**социа́л-демокра́т** (**-а**) *м* social democrat

**социали́зм** (**-а**) *м* socialism

**социалисти́ческий** *прил* socialist

**социа́льн|ый** *прил* social; **~ая защищённость** social security

**социо́лог** (**-а**) *м* sociologist

**социоло́ги|я** (**-и**) *ж* sociology

**сочета́ни|е** (**-я**) *ср* combination

**сочета́|ть** (**-ю**) (*не*)*сов перех* to combine; **~ся** (*не*)*сов возв* (*соедини́ться*) to combine;

(*гармони́ровать*) to match

**сочине́ни|е** (**-я**) *ср* (*литерату́рное*) work; (*музыка́льное*) composition; (*ПРОСВЕЩ*) essay

**сочин|и́ть** (**-ю́, -и́шь**; *impf* **сочиня́ть**) *сов перех* (*му́зыку*) to compose; (*стихи́, пе́сню*) to write

**со́чный** *прил* (*плод*) juicy; (*трава́*) lush; (*кра́ски*) vibrant

**сочу́встви|е** (**-я**) *ср* sympathy

**сочу́ств|овать** (**-ую**) *несов*: ~ +*dat* to sympathize with

**сошёл(ся)** *etc сов см.* **сойти́(сь)**

**сошью́** *итп сов см.* **сшить**

**сою́з** (**-а**) *м* union; (*вое́нный*) alliance; (*линг*) conjunction

**сою́зник** (**-а**) *м* ally

**сою́зный** *прил* (*а́рмия*) allied; (*сло́во*) conjunctive

**со́|я** (**-и**) *ж* собир soya beans *мн*

**спад** (**-а**) *м* drop; **экономи́ческий ~** recession

**спада́|ть** (*3sg* **-ет**) *несов от* **спасть**

**спазм** (**-а**) *м* spasm

**спа́льный** *прил* (*ме́сто*) sleeping; **~ ваго́н** sleeping car; **~ мешо́к** sleeping bag

**спа́л|ьня** (**-ьни**; *gen pl* **-ен**) *ж* (*ко́мната*) bedroom; (*ме́бель*) bedroom suite

**Спас** (**-а**) *м* (*РЕЛ*) the Day of the Saviour (*in Orthodox Church*)

**спаса́тел|ь** (**-я**) *м* rescuer

**спаса́тельн|ый** *прил* (*ста́нция*) rescue; **~ая ло́дка** lifeboat; **~ жиле́т** lifejacket; **~ по́яс** lifebelt

**спаса́|ть(ся)** (**-ю(сь)**) *несов от* **спасти́(сь)**

**спасе́ни|е** (**-я**) *ср* rescue; (*РЕЛ*) Salvation

**спаси́бо** *част*: ~ (**Вам**) thank you; **большо́е ~!** thank you very much!;

~ **за по́мощь** thanks for the help

**спаси́тел|ь (-я)** м saviour; (РЕЛ) the Saviour

**спас|ти́ (-у́, -ёшь;** impf **спаса́ть)** сов перех to save; ~**сь** (impf **спаса́ться)** сов возв: ~**сь (от** +gen) to escape

**спа|сть (**3sg **-дёт;** impf **спада́ть)** сов (вода) to drop

**сп|ать (-лю, -ишь)** несов to sleep; **ложи́ться (лечь** pf) ~ to go to bed; **спа́ться** несов возв: **мне не ~ится** I can't (get to) sleep

**СПБ** сокр (= **Санкт-Петербу́рг)** St Petersburg

**спекта́кл|ь (-я)** м performance

**спектр (-а)** м spectrum

**спекули́р|овать (-ую)** несов (дефици́том) to profiteer; (КОММ): ~ +instr **(на бирже)** to speculate in

**спекуля́нт (-а)** м (биржевой) speculator; (дефици́том) profiteer

**спекуля́ци|я (-и)** ж (дефицитом) profiteering; (на бирже) speculation

**спе́лый** прил ripe

**спе́реди** нареч in front

**спе́рм|а (-ы)** ж sperm

**сп|еть (**3sg **-е́ет;** pf **поспе́ть)** несов (фрукты, овощи) to ripen
♦ **(-ою́, -оёшь)** сов от **петь**

**спех (-а)** м: **мне не к спе́ху** (разг) I'm in no hurry

**специализи́р|оваться (-уюсь)** (не)сов возв: ~ **в** +prp или **по** +dat to specialize in

**специали́ст (-а)** м specialist

**специа́льност|ь (-и)** ж (профессия) profession

**специа́льный** прил special

**специ́фик|а (-и)** ж specific nature

**специфи́ческий** прил specific

**спе́ци|я (-и)** ж spice

**спецко́р (-а)** м сокр (= специа́льный корреспонде́нт)

special correspondent

**спецку́рс (-а)** м сокр (в вузе: = специа́льный курс) course of lectures in a specialist field

**спецна́з (-а)** м special task force

**спецна́зов|ец (-ца)** м member of the special task force

**спецоде́жд|а (-ы)** ж сокр (= специа́льная оде́жда) work clothes мн

**спецслу́жб|а (-ы)** ж сокр (обычно мн: = специа́льная слу́жба) special service

**спеш|и́ть (-у́, -и́шь)** несов (часы) to be fast; (человек) to be in a rush; ~ **(по~** pf) +infin/**с** +instr to be in a hurry to do/with; ~ (impf) **на по́езд** to rush for the train

**спе́шк|а (-и)** ж (разг) hurry, rush

**спе́шно** нареч hurriedly

**спе́шный** прил urgent

**СПИД (-а)** м сокр (= синдро́м приобретённого иммунодефици́та) AIDS

**спидо́метр (-а)** м speedometer

**спи́кер (-а)** м speaker

**спин|а́ (-ы́;** acc sg **-у,** dat sg **-е́,** nom pl **-ы)** ж (человека, животного) back

**спи́н|ка (-ки;** gen pl **-ок)** ж уменьш от **спина́;** (дивана, стула итп) back; (кровати: верхняя) headboard; (: нижняя) foot

**спинно́й** прил (позвонок) spinal; ~ **мозг** spinal cord

**спира́л|ь (-и)** ж (линия) spiral; (также: **внутрима́точная ~**) coil (contraceptive)

**спирт (-а)** м (ХИМ) spirit

**спиртн|о́е (-о́го)** ср alcohol

**спиртно́й** прил: ~ **напи́ток** alcoholic drink

**сп|иса́ть (-ишу́, -и́шешь;** impf **спи́сывать)** сов перех to copy;

(*КОММ*) to write off

**спи́с|ок** (**-ка**) м list

**спи́ц|а** (**-ы**) ж (*для вязания*) knitting needle; (*колеса*) spoke

**спи́чечн|ый** прил: ~**ая коро́бка** matchbox; ~**ая голо́вка** matchhead

**спи́ч|ка** (**-ки**; *gen pl* **-ек**) ж match

**сплав** (**-а**) м alloy

**спла́в|ить** (**-лю, -ишь**; *impf* **сплавля́ть**) *сов перех* (*металлы*) to alloy

**спла́чива|ть(ся)** (**-ю**) *несов от* **сплоти́ть(ся)**

**спл|ести́** (**-ету́, -етёшь**; *pt* **-ёл, -ела́**) *сов от* **плести́** ♦ (*impf* **сплета́ть**) *перех* to plait; (*пальцы*) to intertwine

**сплетнича|ть** (**-ю**) *несов* to gossip

**спле́т|ня** (**-ни**; *gen pl* **-ен**) ж gossip

**спло|ти́ть** (**-чу́, -ти́шь**; *impf* **спла́чивать**) *сов перех* to unite; ~**ся** (*impf* **спла́чиваться**) *сов возв* to unite

**сплошно́й** прил (*степь*) continuous; (*перепись*) universal; (*разг: неудачи*) utter

**сплошь** нареч (*по всей поверхности*) all over; (*без исключения*) completely; ~ **и ря́дом** (*разг*) everywhere

**сплю** *несов см.* **спать**

**споко́йный** прил (*улица, жизнь*) quiet; (*море, взгляд*) calm

**споко́стви|е** (**-я**) *ср* calm, tranquillity

**сполз|ти́** (**-у́, -ёшь**; *pt* **-, -ла́**; *impf* **сполза́ть**) *сов* to climb down

**спонси́р|овать** (**-ую**) (*не*)*сов* to sponsor

**спо́нсор** (**-а**) м sponsor

**спор** (**-а**) м debate; (*ЮР*) dispute; **на́** ~ (*разг*) as a bet

**спо́р|ить** (**-ю, -ишь**; *pf* **по~**) *несов* (*вести спор*) to argue; (*держать пари*) to bet; ~ (*impf*) **с кем-н о чём-н** или **за что-н** (*о наследстве*) to dispute sth with sb

**спо́рный** прил (*дело*) disputed; (*победа*) doubtful; ~ **вопро́с** moot point

**спорт** (**-а**) м sport

**спортза́л** (**-а**) м *сокр* (= *спорти́вный зал*) sports hall

**спорти́вный** прил sports; (*фигура, человек*) sporty; ~ **костю́м** tracksuit

**спортсме́н** (**-а**) м sportsman

**спо́соб** (**-а**) м way

**спосо́бност|ь** (**-и**) ж ability

**спосо́бный** прил capable; (*талантливый*) able

**спосо́бств|овать** (**-ую**) *сов*: ~ +*dat* (*успеху, развитию*) to encourage

**споткн|у́ться** (**-у́сь, -ёшься**; *impf* **спотыка́ться**) *сов возв* to trip

**спою́** *итп несов см.* **спеть**

**спра́ва** нареч to the right; ~ **от** +*gen* to the right of

**справедли́вост|ь** (**-и**) ж justice

**справедли́вый** прил fair, just; (*вывод*) correct

**спра́виться** (*impf* **справля́ться**) *сов возв*: ~**ся с** +*instr* (*с работой*) to cope with, manage; (*с противником*) to deal with; (*узнавать*); ~**ся о** +*prp* to enquire или ask about

**спра́в|ка** (**-ки**; *gen pl* **-ок**) ж (*сведения*) information; (*документ*) certificate

**спра́вочник** (**-а**) м directory; (*граммати́ческий*) reference book

**спра́вочн|ый** прил (*литерату́ра*) reference; ~**ое бюро́** information office или bureau

**спра́шива|ть(ся)** (**-ю(сь)**) *несов от* **спроси́ть(ся)**

**спрос** (-а) м: ~ **на** +acc (на товары) demand for; (требование): ~ **с** +gen (с родителей) demands мн on; **без спро́са** или **спро́су** without permission

**спр|оси́ть** (-ошу́, -о́сишь; impf **спра́шивать**) сов перех (дорогу, время) to ask; (совета, денег) to ask for; (взыскать): ~ **что-н с** +gen to call sb to account for sth; (осведомиться): ~ **кого́-н о чём-н** to ask sb about sth; **спра́шивать** (~ pf) **ученика́** to question или test a pupil; ~**ся** (impf **спра́шиваться**) сов возв: ~**ся** +gen или **у** +gen (у учителя итп) to ask permission of

**спры́г|нуть** (-ну; impf **спры́гивать**) сов: ~ **с** +gen to jump off

**спряга́|ть** (-ю; pf **про~**) несов перех (линг) to conjugate

**спряже́ни|е** (-я) ср (линг) conjugation

**спря́|тать(ся)** (-чу(сь), -чешь(ся)) сов от **пря́тать(ся)**

**спуск** (-а) м (флага) lowering; (корабля) launch; (воды, газа) draining; (с горы) descent

**спуска́|ть** (-ю) несов от **спусти́ть** ♦ перех: **я не ~л глаз с неё** I didn't take my eyes off her; ~**ся** несов от **спусти́ться**

**спу|сти́ть** (-щу́, -стишь; impf **спуска́ть**) сов перех to lower; (собаку) to let loose; (газ, воду) to drain; ~**ся** (impf **спуска́ться**) сов возв to go down

**спустя́** нареч: ~ **три дня/год** three days/a year later

**спу́та|ть(ся)** (-ю(сь)) сов от **пу́тать(ся)**

**спу́тник** (-а) м (в пути) travelling (BRIT) или traveling (US) companion; (АСТРОНОМИЯ) satellite; (КОСМОС: также: **иску́сственный** ~) sputnik, satellite

**спя́чк|а** (-и) ж hibernation

**сравне́ни|е** (-я) ср comparison; **в ~и** или **по ~ю с** +instr compared with

**сра́внива|ть** (-ю) несов от **сравни́ть, сравня́ть**

**сравни́тельный** прил comparative

**сравн|и́ть** (-ю́, -и́шь; impf **сра́внивать**) сов перех: ~ **что-н/кого́-н (с** +instr) to compare sth/sb (with); ~**ся** сов возв: ~**ся с** +instr to compare with

**сравня́|ть** (-ю) сов от **равня́ть** ♦ (impf **сра́внивать**) перех: ~ **счёт** to equalize

**сраже́ни|е** (-я) ср battle

**сра|зи́ть** (-жу́, -зи́шь; impf **сража́ть**) сов перех (пулей, ударом) to slay; ~**ся** (impf **сража́ться**) сов возв: ~**ся с (с** +instr) to join battle with; (с недостатками) to combat

**сра́зу** нареч (немедленно) straight away; (в один приём) (all) at once

**срас|ти́сь** (3sg -ётся; impf **сраста́ться**) сов возв (кости) to knit (together)

**сред|а́** (-ы́; nom pl -ы) ж medium; (no pl; природная, социальная) environment; (acc sg -у; день недели) Wednesday; **окружа́ющая** ~ environment; **охра́на окружа́ющей** ~**ы** conservation

**среди́** предл: ~ +gen in the middle of; (в числе) among

**средизе́мн|ый** прил: **Средизе́мное мо́ре** the Mediterranean (Sea)

**среднеазиа́тский** *прил* Central Asian

**средневеко́вый** *прил* medieval

**среднегодово́й** *прил* average annual

**сре́дний** *прил* average; (*размер*) medium; (*в середине*) middle; (*школа*) secondary

---

**сре́дняя шко́ла** . Children in Russia start school at the age of six or seven. They stay in the same school throughout their education. They can leave school after eight years if they plan to continue into further education. Those who stay on study for a further two or three years before sitting their final exams. On completing the final exams they receive the Certificate of Secondary Education. See also note at **аттеста́т зре́лости**.

---

**сре́дство** (**-а**) *ср* means *мн*; (*лекарство*) remedy

**срез** (**-а**) *м* (*место*) cut; (*тонкий слой*) section

**сре́|зать** (**-жу, -жешь**; *impf* **среза́ть**) *сов перех* to cut

**срок** (**-а**) *м* (*длительность*) time, period; (*дата*) date; **в ~** (*во время*) in time; **после́дний** или **преде́льный ~** deadline; **~ го́дности** (*товара*) sell-by date; **~ де́йствия** period of validity

**сро́чный** *прил* urgent

**срыв** (**-а**) *м* disruption; (*на экзамене итп*) failure

**срыва́|ть(ся)** (**-ю(сь)**) *несов от* **сорва́ть(ся)**

**сса́дин|а** (**-ы**) *ж* scratch

**ссо́р|а** (**-ы**) *ж* quarrel

**ссо́р|ить** (**-ю, -ишь**; *pf* **по~**) *несов перех* (*друзей*) to cause to quarrel; **~ся** (*pf* **по~ся**) *несов*

**возв** to quarrel

**СССР** *м сокр* (*ИСТ*: = *Сою́з Сове́тских Социалисти́ческих Респу́блик*) USSR

**ссу́д|а** (**-ы**) *ж* loan

**ссу́|дить** (**-жу́, -дишь**; *impf* **ссужа́ть**) *сов перех* (*деньги*) to lend

**ссыла́|ть** (**-ю**) *несов от* **сосла́ть**; **~ся** *несов от* **сосла́ться** ♦ *возв*: **~я́сь на** +*acc* with reference to

**ссы́л|ка** (**-ки**; *gen pl* **-ок**) *ж* exile; (*цитата*) quotation

**ст.** *сокр* (= **ста́нция**) sta.

**ста** *чис см.* **сто**

**стабилизи́р|овать** (**-ую**) (*не*)*сов перех* to stabilize

**стаби́льный** *прил* stable

**ста́в|ить** (**-лю, -ишь**; *pf* **по~**) *несов перех* to put; (*назначать*: *министром*) to appoint; (*оперу*) to stage; **~ (по~** *pf*) **часы́** to set a clock

**ста́в|ка** (**-ки**; *gen pl* **-ок**) *ж* (*также* **КОММ**) rate; (*ВОЕН*) headquarters *мн*; (*в картах*) stake; (*перен*): **~ на** +*acc* (*расчёт*) reliance on

**ставри́д|а** (**-ы**) *ж* (*ЗООЛ*) horse mackerel, scad

**стадио́н** (**-а**) *м* stadium

**ста́ди|я** (**-и**) *ж* stage

**ста́д|о** (**-а**; *nom pl* **-а́**) *ср* (*коров*) herd; (*овец*) flock

**стаж** (**-а**) *м* (*рабочий*) experience

**стажёр** (**-а**) *м* probationer

**стажир|ова́ться** (**-у́юсь**) *несов возв* to work on probation

**стажиро́в|ка** (**-ки**; *gen pl* **-ок**) *ж* probationary period

**стака́н** (**-а**) *м* glass; **бума́жный ~** paper cup

**стал** *сов от* **стать**

**сталева́р** (**-а**) *м* steel-maker

**ста́лкива|ть(ся)** (**-ю(сь)**) *несов от* **столкну́ть(ся)**

**стал|ь (-и)** ж steel

**стам** итп чис см. **сто**

**станда́рт (-а)** м standard

**стан|ови́ться (-овлю́сь, -о́вишься)** несов от **стать**

**становле́ни|е (-я)** ср formation

**стан|о́к (-ка́)** м machine (tool)

**ста́ну** итп сов см. **стать**

**ста́нци|я (-и)** ж station; **телефо́нная ~** telephone exchange

**стара́ни|е (-я)** ср effort

**стара́тельный** прил diligent; (работа) painstaking

**стара́|ться (-юсь;** pf **по~)** несов возв: **~** +infin to try to do

**старе́|ть (-ю;** pf **по~)** несов (человек) to grow old(er), age; (pf **у~;** оборудование) to become out of date

**стари́к (-а́)** м old man

**стари́нный** прил ancient

**ста́р|ить (-ю, -ишь;** pf **со~)** несов перех to age

**старомо́дный** прил old-fashioned

**ста́рост|а (-ы)** м (курса) senior student; (класса: мальчик) head boy; (: девочка) head girl; (клуба) head, president

**ста́рост|ь (-и)** ж old age

**старт (-а)** м (СПОРТ) start; (ракеты) takeoff; (место) takeoff point

**старт|ова́ть (-у́ю)** (не)сов (СПОРТ) to start; (ракета) to take off

**стару́х|а (-и)** ж old woman

**стару́ш|ка (-ки;** gen pl **-ек)** ж = **стару́ха**

**ста́рше** сравн прил от **ста́рый** ♦ как сказ: **я ~ сестры́ на́ год** I am a year older than my sister

**старшекла́ссник (-а)** м senior pupil

**старшеку́рсник (-а)** м senior student

**ста́рший** прил senior; (сестра, брат) elder

**ста́рый** прил old

**стати́стик|а (-и)** ж statistics

**статисти́ческ|ий** прил statistical; **Центра́льное ~ое управле́ние** central statistics office

**ста́тус (-а)** м status

**стату́эт|ка (-ки)** ж statuette

**ста́ту|я (-и)** ж statue

**ста|ть (-ти)** ж: **под ~ кому́-н/ чему́-н** like sb/sth ♦ **(-ну, -нешь;** impf **станови́ться)** сов to stand; (no impf; остановиться) to stop; (начать): **~** +infin to begin или start doing ♦ безл (наличествовать): **нас ста́ло бо́льше/тро́е** there are more/three of us; **с како́й ста́ти?** (разг) why?; **станови́ться (~** pf**)** +instr (учителем) to become; **не ста́ло де́нег/сил** I have no more money/ energy left; **ста́ло быть** (значит) so; **во что бы то ни ста́ло** no matter what

**стат|ья́ (-ьи́;** gen pl **-е́й)** ж (в газете) article; (в законе, в догово́ре) paragraph, clause

**ста́|я (-и)** ж (птиц) flock; (волков) pack; (рыб) shoal

**ствол (-а́)** м (дерева) trunk; (ружья, пушки) barrel

**стеб|ель (-ля)** м (цветка) stem

**стёган|ый** прил quilted; **~ое одея́ло** quilt

**стега́|ть (-ю;** pf **про~)** несов перех (одеяло) to quilt; (no pf; хлыстом) to lash

**стеж|о́к (-ка́)** м stitch

**стека́|ть(ся) (3sg** **-ет(ся))** несов от **сте́чь(ся)**

**стекл|и́ть (-ю́, -и́шь;** pf **о~)** несов перех (окно) to glaze

**стекл|о́ (-а́;** nom pl **стёкла,** gen pl

**стёкол)** *ср* glass; (*также*:
**оконное ~)** (window) pane; (*для
очков*) lenses *мн ♦ собир
(изделия)* glassware

**стёклыш|ко (-ка;** *gen pl* **-ек)** *ср
(осколок)* piece of glass

**стеклянный** *прил* glass

**стел|ить (-ю, -ишь;** *pf* **по~)**
*несов перех (скатерть,
подстилку)* to spread out; (*pf* **на~;**
*паркет*) to lay; **~ (по~** *pf*) **постель**
to make up a bed

**стемне|ть** (*3sg* **-ет**) *сов от*
**темнеть**

**стен|а (-ы;** *acc sg* **-у,** *dat sg* **-е,** *nom
pl* **-ы,** *dat pl* **-ам)** *ж* wall

**стенд (-а)** *м (выставочный)*
display stand; (*испытательный*)
test-bed; (*для стрельбы*) rifle
range

**стен|ка (-ки;** *gen pl* **-ок)** *ж
уменьш от* **стена;** (*желудка,
также ФУТБОЛ*) wall; (*разг:
мебель*) wall unit

**стенн|ой** *прил* wall; **~ая роспись**
mural

**стенографир|овать (-ую;** *pf*
**за~)** *несов перех:* **~ что-н** to take
sth down in shorthand (*BRIT*) *или*
stenography (*US*)

**стенографист (-а)** *м* shorthand
typist (*BRIT*), stenographer (*US*)

**степень (-и;** *gen pl* **-ей)** *ж (также
ПРОСВЕЩ)* degree; (*МАТ*) power

**степь (-и;** *gen pl* **-ей)** *ж* the steppe

**стереосистем|а (-ы)** *ж* stereo

**стереотип (-а)** *м* stereotype

**стер|еть (сотру, сотрёшь;** *pt*
**стёр, стёрла;** *impf* **стирать)** *сов
перех* to wipe off; **~ся** (*impf*
**стираться**) *сов возв (надпись,
краска*) to be worn away;
(*подошвы*) to wear down

**стер|ечь (-егу, -ежёшь** *итп*,
**-егут;** *pt* **-ёг, -егла)** *несов перех*
to watch over

**стерж|ень (-ня)** *м* rod;
(*шариковой ручки*) (ink) cartridge

**стерилиз|овать (-ую)** (*не)сов
перех* to sterilize

**стерильный** *прил* sterile, sterilized

**стерлинг (-а)** *м (ЭКОН)* sterling; **10
фунтов ~ов** 10 pounds sterling

**стеснени|е (-я)** *ср* constraints *мн;*
(*смущение*) shyness

**стеснительный** *прил* shy

**стесн|ить (-ю, -ишь;** *impf*
**стеснять**) *сов перех (хозяев)* to
inconvenience; (*дыхание*) to
constrict

**стесня|ться (-юсь;** *pf* **по~)** *несов
возв:* **~** (*+gen*) to be shy (of)

**стечени|е (-я)** *ср (народа)*
gathering; (*случайностей*)
combination

**ст|ечь** (*3sg* **-ечёт,** *pt* **-ёк, -екла;**
*impf* **стекать**) *сов:* **~ (с** *+gen*) to
run down (from); **стечься** (*impf*
**стекаться**) *сов возв (реки)* to
flow; (*люди*) to congregate

**стилист (-а)** *м* stylist

**стилистический** *прил* stylistic

**стиль (-я)** *м* style

**стимул (-а)** *м* incentive, stimulus

**стимулир|овать (-ую)** (*не)сов
перех* to stimulate; (*работу,
прогресс*) to encourage

**стипенди|я (-и)** *ж* grant

**стиральный** *прил* washing

**стира|ть (-ю)** *несов от* **стереть**
**♦** (*pf* **выстирать** *или* **по~**) *перех*
to wash; **~ся** *несов от* **стереться**

**стир|ка (-ки)** *ж* washing

**стисн|уть (-у;** *impf* **стискивать**)
*сов перех (в руке)* to clench

**стиха|ть (-ю)** *несов от* **стихнуть**

**стих|и (-ов)** *мн (поэзия)* poetry
*ед*

**стихийн|ый** *прил (развитие)*
unrestrained; (*протест*)

spontaneous; **~ое бéдствие** natural disaster

**стихи́|я (-и)** ж (вода, огонь итп) element; (рынка) natural force

**сти́х|нуть (-ну;** pt **-, -ла;** impf **стиха́ть)** сов to die down

**стихотворéни|е (-я)** ср poem

**сто (ста;** см. Table 27) чис one hundred

**стог (-а;** nom pl **-á)** м: **~ céна** haystack

**сто́имост|ь (-и)** ж (затраты) cost; (ценность) value

**сто́|ить (-ю, -ишь)** несов (не)перех; (+асс или +gen; денег) to cost ♦ непéрех: **~** +gen (внимания, любви) to be worth ♦ безл: **~** +infin to be worth doing; **мне ничегó не ~ит сдéлать э́то** it's no trouble for me to do it; **спаси́бо! - не ~ит** thank you! - don't mention it; **~ит (то́лько) захотéть** you only have to wish

**сто́|йка (-йки;** gen pl **-ек)** ж (положение тела) stance; (прилавок) counter

**сто́йкий** прил (человек) steadfast, resilient; (краска) durable, hard-wearing; (запах) stubborn

**стол (-á)** м table; (письменный) desk

**столб (-á)** м (пограничный) post; (телеграфный) pole; (перен: пыли) cloud

**сто́лбик (-а)** м уменьш от **столб;** (цифр) column

**столбня́к (-á)** м tetanus

**столéти|е (-я)** ср (срок) century; (годовщина): **~** +gen centenary of

**сто́лик (-а)** м уменьш от **стол**

**столи́ц|а (-ы)** ж capital (city)

**столи́чн|ый** прил: **~ые теáтры** the capital's theatres

**столкновéни|е (-я)** ср clash; (машин) collision

**столкн|у́ть (-у́, -ёшь;** impf **стáлкивать)** сов перех: **~ (с** +gen) to push off; (подлеж: случай) to bring together; **~ся** (impf **стáлкиваться)** сов возв (машины) to collide; (интересы, характеры) to clash; (встрéтиться); **~ся с** +instr to come into contact with; (случайно) to bump или run into; (с трудностями) to encounter

**столóв|ая (-ой)** ж (заведение) canteen; (комната) dining room

**столóв|ый** прил (мебель) dining-room; **~ая лóжка** tablespoon; **~ая соль** table salt; **~ сервúз** dinner service

**столп|и́ться (**3sg **-и́тся)** сов возв to crowd

**столь** нареч so; **~ же ... скóлько ... as ... as ...**

**стóльк|о** нареч (книг) so many; (сахара) so much ♦ (**-их)** мест (см нареч) this many; this much

**стóлько-то** нареч (книг) X number of; (сахара) X amount of

**столя́р (-á)** м joiner

**стоматóлог (-а)** м dental surgeon

**стоматологи́ческий** прил dental

**стометрóв|ый** прил: **~ая дистáнция** one hundred metres (BRIT) или meters (US)

**стон (-а)** м groan

**стон|áть (-у́, -ешь)** несов to groan

**стоп** межд stop

**стоп|á (-ы́;** nom pl **-ы́)** ж (АНАТ) sole

**стóп|ка (-ки;** gen pl **-ок)** ж (бумаг) pile

**стоп-крáн (-а)** м emergency handle (on train)

**стóпор (-а)** м (ТЕХ) lock

**стоп|тáть (-чу́, -чешь;** impf **стáптывать)** сов перех to wear out; **~ся** (*impf* **ста́птываться**) *сов возв* to wear out

**сто́рож** (**-а**; *nom pl* **-а́**) *м* watchman

**сторожев|о́й** *прил*: **~а́я вы́шка** watchtower

**сторож|и́ть** (**-у́, -и́шь**) *несов перех* = **стере́чь**

**стор|она́** (**-оны́**; *acc sg* **-ону**, *dat sg* **-оне́**, *nom pl* **-оны**, *gen pl* **-о́н**, *dat pl* **-она́м**) *ж* side; (*направление*): **ле́вая/пра́вая ~** the left/right; **в ~оне́** a little way off; **в сто́рону** +*gen* towards; **э́то о́чень любе́зно с Ва́шей ~оны́** that is very kind of you; **с одно́й ~оны́ ... с друго́й ~оны́ ...** on the one hand ... on the other hand ...

**сторо́нник** (**-а**) *м* supporter

**сто́чн|ый** *прил*: **~ая кана́ва** gutter (*in street*); **~ая труба́** drainpipe

**сто́я** *нареч* standing up

**стоя́н|ка** (**-ки**; *gen pl* **-ок**) *ж* (*остановка*) stop; (*автомобилей*) car park (*BRIT*), parking lot (*US*); (*геологов*) camp; **~ такси́** taxi rank

**сто|я́ть** (**-ю́, -и́шь**; *imper* **сто́й(те)**) *несов* to stand; (*бездействовать*) to stand idle; (*pf* **по~**; *защищать*): **~ за** +*acc* to stand up for

**сто́ящий** *прил* (*дело*) worthwhile; (*человек*) worthy

**стр.** *сокр* (= **страни́ца**) pg.

**страда́ни|е** (**-я**) *ср* suffering

**страда́тельный** *прил* (*линг*): **~ зало́г** passive voice

**страда́|ть** (**-ю**) *несов* to suffer

**стра́ж|а** (**-и**) *ж собир* guard; **под ~ей** in custody

**стран|а́** (**-ы́**; *nom pl* **-ы**) *ж* country

**страни́ц|а** (**-ы**) *ж* page

**стра́нно** *нареч* strangely ♦ *как*

*сказ* that is strange *или* odd; **мне ~, что ...** I find it strange that ...

**стра́нный** *прил* strange

**стра́стный** *прил* passionate

**страст|ь** (**-и**) *ж* passion

**стратеги|я** (**-и**) *ж* strategy

**страх** (**-а**) *м* fear

**страхова́ни|е** (**-я**) *ср* insurance; **госуда́рственное ~** national insurance (*BRIT*); **~ жи́зни** life insurance

**страхова́тел|ь** (**-я**) *м person taking out insurance*

**страх|ова́ть** (**-у́ю**; *pf* **за~**) *несов перех*: **~ от** +*gen* (*имущество*) to insure (against); (*принимать меры*) to protect (against); **~ся** (*pf* **за~ся**) *несов возв*: **~ся (от** +*gen*) to insure o.s. (against); (*принимать меры*) to protect o.s. (from)

**страхо́в|ка** (**-ки**; *gen pl* **-ок**) *ж* insurance

**страхов|о́й** *прил* (*фирма, агент*) insurance; **~ взнос** *или* **~а́я пре́мия** insurance premium

**страхо́вщик** (**-а**) *м* insurer

**стра́шно** *нареч* (*кричать*) in a frightening way; (*разг: усталый, довольный*) terribly ♦ *как сказ* it's frightening; **мне ~** I'm frightened *или* scared

**стра́шн|ый** *прил* (*фильм, сон*) terrifying; (*холод итп*) terrible, awful; **ничего́ ~ого** it doesn't matter

**стрек|оза́** (**-озы́**; *nom pl* **-о́зы**) *ж* dragonfly

**стрел|а́** (**-ы́**; *nom pl* **-ы**) *ж* (*для стрельбы́*) arrow; (*поезд*) express (train)

**стрел|е́ц** (**-ьца́**) *м* (*созвездие*): **Стреле́ц** Sagittarius

**стре́л|ка** (**-ки**; *gen pl* **-ок**) *ж* *уменьш от* **стрела́**; (*часов*) hand;

(*компаса*) needle; (*знак*) arrow

**стре́лочник** (-а) *м* signalman

**стрельб**|**а́** (-**ы́**) *ж* shooting, firing

**стреля́**|**ть** (-**ю**) *несов*: ~ (**в** +*acc*) to shoot (at) ♦ *перех* (*убивать*) to shoot; **~ся** *несов возв* to shoot o.s.

**стреми́тельный** *прил* (*движение, атака*) swift; (*изменения*) rapid

**стрем**|**и́ться** (-**лю́сь, -и́шься**) *несов возв*: ~ **в** +*acc* (*в университет*) to aspire to go to; (*на родину*) to long to go to; (*добиваться*): ~ **к** +*dat* (*к славе*) to strive for

**стремле́ни**|**е** (-**я**) *ср*: ~ (**к** +*dat*) striving (for), aspiration (to)

**стре́м**|**я** (-**ени**; *как* **вре́мя**; *см. Table 4*) *ср* stirrup

**стремя́н**|**ка** (-**ки**; *gen pl* -**ок**) *ж* stepladder

**стресс** (-а) *м* stress

**стриж** (-**а́**) *м* swift

**стри́ж**|**ка** (-**ки**; *gen pl* -**ек**) *ж* (*см глаг*) cutting; mowing; pruning; (*причёска*) haircut

**стри**|**чь** (-**гу́, -жёшь** *итп*, -**гу́т**; *pt* -**г, -гла**; *pf* **постри́чь**) *несов перех* (*волосы, траву*) to cut; (*газон*) to mow; (*кусты*) to prune; ~ (**постри́чь** *pf*) **кого́-н** to cut sb's hair; **стри́чься** (*pf* **постри́чься**) *несов возв* (*в парикмахерской*) to have one's hair cut

**стро́гий** *прил* strict; (*причёска, наказание*) severe

**стро́го** *нареч* (*воспитывать*) strictly; (*наказать, сказать*) severely

**строе́ни**|**е** (-**я**) *ср* (*здание*) building; (*организации, вещества*) structure

**стро́же** *сравн прил от* **стро́гий** ♦ *сравн нареч от* **стро́го**

**стро́тел**|**ь** (-**я**) *м* builder

**строи́тельный** *прил* building, construction

**строи́тельств**|**о** (-**а**) *ср* (*зданий*) building, construction

**стро́**|**ить** (-**ю, -ишь**; *pf* **вы́строить** *или* **по~**) *несов перех* to build, construct; (*pf* **по~**; *общество, семью*) to create; (*план*) to make; (*отряд*) to draw up; **~ся** (*pf* **вы́строиться**) *несов возв* (*солдаты*) to form up

**стро́й** (-**я**) *м* (*социальный*) system; (*языка*) structure; (*loc sg* -**ю́**; *ВОЕН, шеренга*) line

**стро́йка** (-**йки**; *gen pl* -**ек**) *ж* (*место*) building *или* construction site

**стро́йный** *прил* (*фигура*) shapely; (*человек*) well-built

**строк**|**а́** (-**и́**; *nom pl* -**и**, *dat pl* -**а́м**) *ж* (*в тексте*) line

**стропти́вый** *прил* headstrong

**стро́ч**|**ка** (-**ки**; *gen pl* -**ек**) *ж* *уменьш от* **строка́**; (*шов*) stitch

**строчн**|**о́й** *прил*: ~**а́я бу́ква** lower case *или* small letter

**структу́р**|**а** (-**ы**) *ж* structure

**струн**|**а́** (-**ы́**; *nom pl* -**ы**) *ж* string

**стру́нный** *прил* (*инструмент*) stringed; ~ **кварте́т** string quartet

**стручко́в**|**ый** *прил*: ~ **пе́рец** chilli; ~**ая фасо́ль** runner beans *мн*

**стру́**|**я** (-**й**; *nom pl* -**и**) *ж* stream

**стряхн**|**у́ть** (-**у́, -ёшь**; *impf* **стря́хивать**) *сов перех* to shake off

**студе́нт** (-а) *м* student

**студе́нческий** *прил* student; ~ **биле́т** student card

**сту́д**|**ень** (-**ня**) *м* jellied meat

**сту́ди**|**я** (-**и**) *ж* studio; (*школа*) school (*for actors, dancers, artists etc*); (*мастерская*) workshop

**сту́ж**|**а** (-**и**) *ж* severe cold

**стук** (-а) м (в дверь) knock; (сердца) thump; (падающего предмета) thud

**стýкн|уть** (-у) сов (в дверь, в окно) to knock; (по столу) to bang; **~ся** (impf **стýкаться**) сов возв to bang o.s.

**стул** (-а; nom pl **-ья**, gen pl **-ьев**) м chair

**ступéн|ь** (-и) ж step; (gen pl **-éй**; процесса) stage

**ступéн|ька** (-ьки; gen pl **-ек**) ж step

**стýп|ка** (-ки; gen pl **-ок**) ж mortar

**ступн|я** (-й) ж (стопа) foot

**стуч|áть** (-ý, -и́шь; pf **по~**) несов (в дверь, в окно) to knock; (по столу) to bang; (сердце) to thump; (зубы) to chatter; **~ся** (pf **по~ся**) несов возв: **~ся** (в +acc) to knock (at); **~ся** (**по~ся** pf) **к** кому-н to knock at sb's door

**стыд** (-á) м shame

**сты|ди́ть** (-жý, -ди́шь; pf **при~**) несов перех to (put to) shame; **~ся** (pf **по~ся**) несов возв: **~ся** +gen/ +infin to be ashamed of/to do

**сты́дно** как сказ it's a shame; **мне ~** I am ashamed; **как тебé не ~!** you ought to be ashamed of yourself!

**сты́|ть** (-ну, -нешь; pf **осты́ть**) несов to go cold; (pf **просты́ть**; мёрзнуть) to freeze

**стюардéсс|а** (-ы) ж air hostess

**стян|ýть** (-ý, -ешь; impf **стя́гивать**) сов перех (пояс, шнуровку) to tighten; (войска) to round up

**суббóт|а** (-ы) ж Saturday

**субподря́д** (-а) м subcontract

**субподря́дчик** (-а) м subcontractor

**субсиди́р|овать** (-ую) (не)сов перех to subsidize

**субси́ди|я** (-и) ж subsidy

**субти́тр** (-а) м subtitle

**субъекти́вный** прил subjective

**сувени́р** (-а) м souvenir

**суверенитéт** (-а) м sovereignty

**суверéнный** прил sovereign

**сугрóб** (-а) м snowdrift

**суд** (-á) м (орган) court; (заседание) court session; (процесс) trial; (мнение) judgement, verdict; **отдава́ть** (**отда́ть** pf) кого-н **под ~** to prosecute sb; **подава́ть** (**пода́ть** pf) **на** кого-н **в ~** to take sb to court

**судéбно-медици́нск|ий** прил: **~ая экспертиза** forensics

**судéбн|ый** прил (заседание, органы) court; (издержки, практика) legal; **~ое решéние** adjudication; **~ое дéло** court case

**судéйск|ий** прил (ЮР) judge's; **~ая коллéгия** (ЮР) the bench; (СПОРТ) panel of judges

**су|ди́ть** (-жý, -дишь) несов перех (преступника) to try; (матч) to referee; (укорять) to judge; **судя́ по** +dat judging by; **~ся** несов возв: **~ся с** кем-н to be involved in a legal wrangle with sb

**сýд|но** (-на; nom pl **-á**, gen pl **-óв**) ср vessel

**судовéрф|ь** (-и) ж сокр (= **судострои́тельная верфь**) shipyard

**судовладéл|ец** (-ьца) м shipowner

**судов|óй** прил: **~áя комáнда** ship's crew; **~ журнáл** ship's log

**судопроизвóдств|о** (-а) ср legal proceedings мн

**сýдорог|а** (-и) ж (от боли) spasm

**сýдорожный** прил convulsive; (перен: приготовления) feverish

**судостро́ени|е** (**-я**) *ср* ship building

**судохо́дный** *прил* navigable; ~ **кана́л** shipping canal

**судохо́дств|о** (**-а**) *ср* navigation

**суд|ьба́** (**-ьбы́**; *nom pl* **-ьбы**, *gen pl* **-еб**) *ж* fate; (*будущее*) destiny; **каки́ми ~ми!** what brought you here!

**суд|ья́** (**-ьи́**; *nom pl* **-ьи**, *gen pl* **-е́й**) *ж* judge; (*СПОРТ*) referee

**суеве́ри|е** (**-я**) *ср* superstition

**суеве́рный** *прил* superstitious

**сует|а́** (**-ы́**) *ж* vanity; (*хлопоты*) commotion

**суе|ти́ться** (**-чу́сь, -ти́шься**) *несов возв* to fuss (about)

**суетли́вый** *прил* fussy; (*жизнь, работа*) busy

**су́етный** *прил* futile; (*хлопотный*) busy; (*человек*) vain

**сужа́|ть** (**-ю**) *несов от* **су́зить**

**сужде́ни|е** (**-я**) *ср* (*мнение*) opinion

**суждено́** *как сказ*: (**нам**) **не ~ бы́ло встре́титься** we weren't fated to meet

**су́|зить** (**-жу, -зишь**; *impf* **сужа́ть**) *сов перех* to narrow

**су|к** (**-ка́**; *loc sg* **-ку́**, *nom pl* **-чья**, *gen pl* **-чьев**) *м* (*дерева*) bough

**су́к|а** (**-и**) *ж* bitch; **~ин сын** (*разг*) son of a bitch (!)

**сук|но́** (**-на́**; *nom pl* **-на**, *gen pl* **-он**) *ср* (*шерстяное*) baize

**сумасше́дш|ий** *прил* mad; (*разг*: *успех*) amazing ♦ (**-его**) *м* madman

**сумасше́стви|е** (**-я**) *ср* madness, lunacy

**сумато́х|а** (**-и**) *ж* chaos

**су́мер|ки** (**-ек**) *мн* twilight *ед*, dusk *ед*

**суме́|ть** (**-ю**) *сов*: ~ +*infin* to manage to do

**су́м|ка** (**-ки**; *gen pl* **-ок**) *ж* bag

**су́мм|а** (**-ы**) *ж* sum

**сумми́р|овать** (**-ую**) (*не*)*сов перех* (*затраты итп*) to add up; (*информацию*) to summarize

**су́моч|ка** (**-ки**; *gen pl* **-ек**) *ж* уменьш от **су́мка**; (*дамская, вечерняя*) handbag

**су́мрак** (**-а**) *м* gloom

**су́мрачный** *прил* gloomy

**сунду́к** (**-а́**) *м* trunk, chest

**суп** (**-а**; *nom pl* **-ы́**) *м* soup

**суперма́ркет** (**-а**) *м* supermarket

**суперобло́ж|ка** (**-ки**; *gen pl* **-ек**) *ж* (dust) jacket

**супру́г** (**-а**; *nom pl* **-и**) *м* spouse; **~и** husband and wife

**супру́г|а** (**-и**) *ж* spouse

**супру́жеский** *прил* marital

**сургу́ч** (**-а́**) *м* sealing wax

**суро́вый** *прил* harsh

**су́слик** (**-а**) *м* ground squirrel (*BRIT*), gopher (*US*)

**суста́в** (**-а**) *м* (*АНАТ*) joint

**су́т|ки** (**-ок**) *мн* twenty four hours *мн*; **кру́глые ~** round the clock

**су́точный** *прил* twenty-four-hour

**суту́л|ить** (**-ю, -ишь**; *pf* **с~**) *несов перех* to hunch; **~ся** (*pf* **с~ся**) *несов возв* to stoop

**сут|ь** (**-и**) *ж* essence; ~ **де́ла** the crux of the matter; **по су́ти (де́ла)** as a matter of fact

**суфле́** *ср нескл* soufflé

**су́ффикс** (**-а**) *м* suffix

**суха́р|ь** (**-я́**) *м* cracker

**сухожи́ли|е** (**-я**) *ср* tendon

**сухо́й** *прил* dry; (*засушенный*) dried; ~ **зако́н** prohibition

**сухопу́тн|ый** *прил* land; **~ые войска́** ground forces *мн*

**сухофру́кт|ы** (**-ов**) *мн* dried fruit *ед*

**су́ш|а** (**-и**) *ж* (dry) land

**су́ше** *сравн прил от* **сухо́й**

**сушёный** *прил* dried
**суш|и́ть** (-ý, -ишь; *pf* **вы́сушить**) *несов перех* to dry; **~ся** *возв* to dry
**суще́ственный** *прил* essential; (*изменения*) substantial
**существи́тельн|ое** (-ого) *ср* (*также*: **и́мя** ~) noun
**существ|ó** (-á) *ср* (*вопроса, дела итп*) essence; (*nom pl* -á; *животное*) creature; **по** ~ý (*говорить*) to the point; (*вводн сл*) essentially
**существовáни|е** (-я) *ср* existence; **срéдства к** ~ю livelihood
**существ|овáть** (-ýю) *несов* to exist
**су́щност|ь** (-и) *ж* essence
**СФ** *м сокр* (= **Совéт Федерáций**) *upper chamber of Russian parliament*
**сфéр|а** (-ы) *ж* sphere; (*производства, науки*) area; **в** ~е +*gen* in the field of; ~ обслу́живания *или* услýг service industry
**схва|ти́ть** (-чý, -тишь) *сов от* **хватáть** ♦ (*impf* **схвáтывать**) *перех* (*мысль, смысл*) to grasp; **~ся** *сов от* **хватáться**
**схвáт|ка** (-ки; *gen pl* -ок) *ж* fight; *см. также* **схвáтки**
**схвáт|ки** (-ок) *мн* (*МЕД*) contractions *мн*
**схéм|а** (-ы) *ж* (*метро, улиц*) plan; (*ЭЛЕК, радио итп*) circuit board
**схо|ди́ть** (-жý, -дишь) *сов* (*разг*: *в театр, на прогýлку*) to go ♦ *несов от* **сойти́**; **~ся** *несов от* **сойти́сь**
**схо́дный** *прил* similar
**схо́дств|о** (-а) *ср* similarity
**сцéн|а** (-ы) *ж* (*подмостки*) stage; (*в пьéсе, на улице*) scene
**сценáри|й** (-я) *м* (*фильма*) script

**сценари́ст** (-а) *м* scriptwriter
**сцеп|и́ть** (-лю́, -ишь; *impf* **сцеплять**) *сов перех* to couple; (*пáльцы*) to clasp
**счáстливо** *нареч* (*жить, рассмеяться*) happily; ~ отдéлаться (*pf*) to have a lucky escape
**счастли́во** *нареч* ~! all the best!; ~ остáвáться! good luck!
**счастли́в|ый** *прил* happy; (*удáчный*) lucky; ~**ого** путú! have a good journey!
**счáсть|е** (-я) *ср* happiness; (*удáча*) luck; **к** ~ю luckily, fortunately; **на нáше** ~ luckily for us
**счесть** (**сочтý, сочтёшь**; *pt* **счёл, сочлá**) *сов от* **считáть**
**счёт** (-а; *loc sg* -ý, *nom pl* -á) *м* (*дéйствие*) counting; (*КОММ, в бáнке*) account; (: *накладнáя*) invoice; (*рестораный, телефóнный*) bill; (*no pl; СПОРТ*) score; **в** +*gen* in lieu of; **за** ~ +*gen* (*фирмы*) at the expense of; (*внедрéний итп*) due to; **на** ~ когó-н at sb's expense; **на э́тот** ~ in this respect; **э́то не в** ~ that doesn't count; **лицевóй** ~ (*КОММ*) personal account; **текýщий** ~ (*КОММ*) current (*BRIT*) *или* checking (*US*) account
**счётн|ый** *прил*: ~**ая машúна** calculator
**счётчик** (-а) *м* meter
**счёт|ы** (-ов) *мн* (*приспособлéние*) abacus *ед*; (*деловые*) dealings *мн*
**счи́танн|ый** *прил*: ~**ые дни**/**минýты** only a few days/minutes; ~**ое колúчество** very few
**счита́|ть** (-ю) *несов* to count ♦ (*pf* **по**~ *или* **со**~) *перех* (*дéньги итп*) to count; (*pf* **по**~ *или*

**счесть**): ~ кого́-н/что-н +*instr* to regard sb/sth as; **я ~ю, что ...** I believe *или* think that ...; **~ся** *несов возв*: **~ся** +*instr* to be considered to be; (*уважать*): **~ся с** +*instr* to respect

**США** *мн сокр* (= *Соединённые Шта́ты Аме́рики*) USA

**сшить** (**сошью́, сошьёшь**; *imper* **сше́й(те)**) *сов от* **шить** ♦ (*impf* **сшива́ть**) *перех* (*соедини́ть шитьём*) to sew together

**съеда́|ть** (**-ю**) *несов от* **съесть**

**съедо́бный** *прил* edible

**съезд** (**-а**) *м* (*парти́йный*) congress

**съе́з|дить** (**-жу, -дишь**) *сов* to go

**съезжа́|ть(ся)** (**-ю(сь)**) *несов от* **съе́хать(ся)**

**съём** *сов см.* **съесть**

**съём|ка** (**-ки**; *gen pl* **-ок**) *ж* (*обычно мн: фи́льма*) shooting *ед*

**съёмочн|ый** *прил*: **~ая площа́дка** film set; **~ая гру́ппа** film crew

**съёмщик** (**-а**) *м* tennant

**съесть** (*как* **есть**; *см. Table 15*; *impf* **есть** *или* **съеда́ть**) *сов перех* (*хлеб, ка́шу*) to eat; (*подлеж: моль, тоска́*) to eat away at

**съе́хать** (*как* **е́хать**; *см. Table 19*; *impf* **съезжа́ть**) *сов*: **~** (**с** +*gen*) (*спусти́ться*) to go down; **съезжа́ть** (**~** *pf*) (**с кварти́ры**) to move out (of one's flat); **~ся** (*impf* **съезжа́ться**) *сов возв* (*делега́ты*) to gather

**съешь** *сов см.* **съесть**

**сы́ворот|ка** (**-ки**; *gen pl* **-ок**) *ж* (*моло́чная*) whey; (*МЕД*) serum

**сыгра́|ть** (**-ю**) *сов от* **игра́ть**

**сын** (**-а**; *nom pl* **-овья́**, *gen pl* **-ове́й**, *dat pl* **-овья́м**) *м* son

**сы́п|ать** (**-лю, -лешь**; *imper* **~ь(те)**) *несов перех* to pour; **~ся** (*pf* **по~ся**) *несов возв* to pour

**сыпу́чий** *прил* crumbly

**сыпь** (**-и**) *ж* rash

**сыр** (**-а**; *nom pl* **-ы́**) *м* cheese

**сыре́|ть** (*3sg* **-ет**) *несов* to get damp

**сырое́ж|ка** (**-ки**; *gen pl* **-ек**) *ж* russula

**сыро́й** *прил* damp; (*мя́со, о́вощи*) raw

**сыр|о́к** (**-ка́**) *м*: **творо́жный ~** sweet curd cheese; **пла́вленный ~** processed cheese

**сы́рост|ь** (**-и**) *ж* dampness

**сырь|ё** (**-я́**) *ср собир* raw materials *мн*

**сыск** (**-а**) *м* criminal detection

**сы́тный** *прил* filling

**сы́тый** *прил* (*не голо́дный*) full

**сэконо́м|ить** (**-лю, -ишь**) *сов от* **эконо́мить**

**сы́щик** (**-а**) *м* detective

**сюда́** *нареч* here

**сюже́т** (**-а**) *м* plot

**сюрпри́з** (**-а**) *м* surprise

**ся́ду** *итп сов см.* **сесть**

# Т, т

**т** *сокр* (= *то́нна*) t

**т.** *сокр* (= *том*) v., vol.; = **ты́сяча**

**та** (**той**) *мест см.* **тот**

**таба́к** (**-а́**) *м* tobacco

**та́бел|ь** (**-я**) *м* (*ПРОСВЕЩ*) school report (*BRIT*), report card (*US, SCOTTISH*); (*гра́фик*) chart

**табле́т|ка** (**-ки**; *gen pl* **-ок**) *ж* tablet

**табли́ц|а** (**-ы**) *ж* table; (*СПОРТ*) (league) table; **~ умноже́ния**

multiplication table

**табло́** *ср нескл* (information) board; (*на стадионе*) scoreboard

**табу́н** (**-á**) *м* herd

**таёжный** *прил* taiga

**таз** (**-а**; *nom pl* **-ы́**) *м* (*сосуд*) basin; (*АНАТ*) pelvis

**таи́нственный** *прил* mysterious

**та́инств|о** (**-а**) *ср* (*РЕЛ*) sacrament

**та|и́ть** (**-ю́, -и́шь**) *несов перех* to conceal; **~ся** *несов возв* (*скрываться*) to hide; (*опасность*) to lurk

**тайг|á** (**-и́**) *ж* the taiga

**тайко́м** *нареч* in secret, secretly

**тайм** (**-а**) *м* (*СПОРТ*) period; **пе́рвый/второ́й ~** (*ФУТБОЛ*) the first/second half

**та́йн|а** (**-ы**) *ж* (*личная*) secret; (*события*) mystery

**тайни́к** (**-á**) *м* hiding place

**та́йный** *прил* secret

---

KEYWORD

---

**так** *нареч* 1 (*указательное: таким образом*) like this, this way; **пусть бу́дет так** so be it

2 (*настолько*) so

3 (*разг: без какого-н намерения*) for no (special) reason; **почему́ ты пла́чешь? - да так** why are you crying? - for no reason

♦ *част* 1 (*разг: ничего*) nothing; **что с тобо́й? - так** what's wrong? - nothing

2 (*разг: приблизительно*) about; **дня так че́рез два** in about two days

3 (*например*) for example

4 (*да*) OK; **так, всё хорошо́** OK, that's fine

♦ *союз* 1 (*в таком случае*) then; **éхать, так éхать** if we are going, (then) let's go

2 (*таким образом*) so; **так ты поéдешь?** so, you are going?

3 (*в разделительных вопросах*): **э́то поле́зная кни́га, не так ли?** it's a useful book, isn't it?; **он хоро́ший челове́к, не так ли?** he's a good person, isn't he?

4 (*во фразах*): **и так** (*и без того́ уже*) anyway; **éсли** *или* **раз так** in that case; **так и бы́ть!** so be it!; **так и есть** (*разг*) sure enough; **так ему́!** serves him right!; **та́к себе** (*разг*) so-so; **так как** since; **так что** so; **так что́бы** so that

**та́кже** *союз, нареч* also; **С Но́вым Го́дом! - И Вас ~** Happy New Year! - the same to you

**тако́в** (**-á, -ó, -ы́**) *как сказ* such

**таково́й** *мест*: **как ~** as such

**так|о́е** (**-о́го**) *ср* (*о чём-н интересном, важном итп*) something; **что тут ~о́го?** what is so special about that?

**так|о́й** *мест* such; **что ~о́е?** what is it?

**та́кс|а** (**-ы**) *ж* (*КОММ*) (fixed) rate

**такси́** *ср нескл* taxi

**такси́ст** (**-а**) *м* taxi driver

**таксопа́рк** (**-а**) *м сокр* (= **таксомото́рный парк**) taxi depot

**такт** (**-а**) *м* (*тактичность*) tact; (*МУЗ*) bar (*BRIT*), measure (*US*)

**та́ктик|а** (**-и**) *ж* tactic; (*ВОЕН*) tactics *мн*

**такти́чный** *прил* tactful

**тала́нт** (**-а**) *м* talent

**тала́нтливый** *прил* talented

**та́ли|я** (**-и**) *ж* waist

**тало́н** (**-а**) *м* ticket; (*на продукты итп*) coupon

**там** *нареч* there; **~ посмо́трим** (*разг*) we'll see

**тамо́женник** (**-а**) *м* customs officer

**тамо́женн|ый** *прил* (*досмотр*)

customs; **~ая пóшлина** customs (duty)

**тамóж|ня** (**-ни**; *gen pl* **-ен**) *ж* customs

**тампóн** (**-а**) *м* tampon

**тá|нец** (**-ца**) *м* dance

**танк** (**-а**) *м* tank

**тá|нкер** (**-а**) *м* tanker (*ship*)

**танц|евáть** (**-ýю**) *несов (не)перех* to dance

**танцóвщик** (**-а**) *м* dancer

**танцóр** (**-а**) *м* dancer

**тáпоч|ка** (**-ки**; *gen pl* **-ек**) *ж* (*обычно мн: домáшняя*) slipper; (*: спортúвная*) plimsoll (*BRIT*), sneaker (*US*)

**тáр|а** (**-ы**) *ж собир* containers *мн*

**таракáн** (**-а**) *м* cockroach

**тарéл|ка** (**-ки**; *gen pl* **-ок**) *ж* plate; **я здесь не в своéй ~ке** (*разг*) I feel out of place here

**тарúф** (**-а**) *м* tariff

**таск|áть** (**-ю**) *несов перех* to lug; **~ся** *несов возв*: **~ся по** +*dat* (*по магазúнам итп*) to trail around; **~ся** (*impf*) **за кем-н** to trail around after sb

**тас|овáть** (**-ýю**; *pf* **с~**) *несов перех* to shuffle

**ТАСС** *м сокр* (= Телегрáфное агéнтство Совéтского Сою́за) Tass (*news agency*)

**татуирóв|ка** (**-ки**; *gen pl* **-ок**) *ж* tattoo

**тáч|ка** (**-ки**; *gen pl* **-ек**) *ж* wheelbarrow

**тащ|úть** (**-ý, -ишь**) *несов перех* to drag; (*тянýть*) to pull; (*нестú*) to haul; (*pf* **вы́тащить**; *перен: в теáтр, на прогýлку*) to drag out; **~ся** *несов возв* (*мéдленно éхать*) to trundle along

**тá|ять** (**-ю**; *pf* **рас~**) *несов* to melt

**ТВ** *м сокр* (= телевúдение) TV

**тверде́|ть** (*3sg* **-ет**; *pf* **за~**) *несов* to harden

**твёрдо** *нареч* (*вéрить, сказáть*) firmly; (*запóмнить*) properly; **я ~ знáю, что ...** I know for sure that ...

**твёрдый** *прил* (*фúз*) solid; (*земля́, предмéт*) hard; (*решéние, сторóнник, тон*) firm; (*цéны, стáвки*) stable; (*знáния*) solid; (*харáктер*) tough; **~ знак** (*лúнг*) hard sign

**твёрже** *сравн прил от* **твёрдый** ♦ *сравн нареч от* **твёрдо**

**тво|й** (**-егó**; *f* **-я́**, *nt* **-ё**, *pl* **-и́**; *как* **мой**; *см. Table 8*) *притяж мест* your; **как по-твоéму?** what is your opinion?; **давáй сдéлаем по-твоéму** let's do it your way

**творéни|е** (**-я**) *ср* creation

**творúтельный** *прил*: **~ падéж** (*лúнг*) the instrumental (case)

**твор|úть** (**-ю́, -úшь**) *несов* to create ♦ (*pf* **со~**) *перех* to create; (*pf* **на~**) *разг* to get up to; **~ся** *несов возв*: **что тут ~ится?** what's going on here?

**творóг** (**-á**) *м* ≈ curd cheese

**творóжный** *прил* curd-cheese

**твóрческий** *прил* creative

**твóрчеств|о** (**-а**) *ср* creative work; (*писáтеля*) work

**тво|я́** (**-éй**) *притяж мест см.* **твой**

**те** (**тех**) *мест см.* **тот**

**т.е.** *сокр* (= **то есть**) i.e.

**теáтр** (**-а**) *м* theatre (*BRIT*), theater (*US*)

**театрáльный** *прил* (*афúша, сезóн*) theatre (*BRIT*), theater (*US*); (*дéятельность*) theatrical; **~ институ́т** drama school

**тебя́** *итп мест см.* **ты**

**тёз|ка** (**-ки**; *gen pl* **-ок**) *м/ж* namesake

**текст** (**-а**) *м* text; (*пéсни*) words *мн*, lyrics *мн*

**тексти́льн|ый** *прил* textile; **~ые изде́лия** textiles *мн*

**теку́чий** *прил* fluid

**теку́щий** *прил* (*год*) current; ~ **счёт** (*КОММ*) current (*BRIT*) *или* checking (*US*) account

**тел.** *сокр* (= **телефо́н**) tel.

**телеви́дени|е** (**-я**) *ср* television

**телевизио́нный** *прил* television; ~ **фильм** television drama

**телеви́зор** (**-а**) *м* television (set)

**телегра́мм|а** (**-ы**) *ж* telegram

**телегра́ф** (**-а**) *м* (*способ связи*) telegraph; (*учреждение*) telegraph office

**телеграфи́р|овать** (**-ую**) (*не*)*сов перех* to wire

**телегра́фн|ый** *прил* telegraphic; **~ое аге́нтство** news agency

**теле́ж|ка** (**-ки**; *gen pl* **-ек**) *ж* (*для багажа, в супермаркете*) trolley

**телезри́тел|ь** (**-я**) *м* viewer

**телека́мер|а** (**-ы**) *ж* television camera

**те́лекс** (**-а**) *м* telex

**тел|ёнок** (**-ёнка**; *nom pl* **-я́та**) *м* calf

**телепереда́ч|а** (**-и**) *ж* TV programme (*BRIT*) *или* program (*US*)

**телеско́п** (**-а**) *м* telescope

**телесту́ди|я** (**-и**) *ж* television studio

**телета́йп** (**-а**) *м* teleprinter (*BRIT*), teletypewriter (*US*), Teletype ®

**телефо́н** (**-а**) *м* telephone

**телефо́нн|ый** *прил* telephone; **~ая кни́га** telephone book *или* directory

**Тел|е́ц** (**-ьца́**) *м* (*созвездие*) Taurus

**телеце́нтр** (**-а**) *м* television centre (*BRIT*) *или* center (*US*)

**те́л|о** (**-а**; *nom pl* **-а́**) *ср* body

**телогре́|йка** (**-йки**; *gen pl* **-ек**) *ж* body warmer

**телохрани́тел|ь** (**-я**) *м* bodyguard

**теля́тин|а** (**-ы**) *ж* veal

**тем** *мест см.* **тот**; **то** ♦ *союз* (*+comparative*): **чем бо́льше**, ~ **лу́чше** the more the better; ~ **бо́лее!** all the more so!; ~ **бо́лее что ...** especially as ...; ~ **не ме́нее** nevertheless; ~ **са́мым** thus

**те́м|а** (**-ы**) *ж* topic; (*МУЗ, ЛИТЕРАТУРА*) theme

**те́ми** *мест см.* **тот**; **то**

**темне́|ть** (*3sg* **-ет**; *pf* **по~**) *несов* to darken ♦ (*pf* **с~**) *безл* to get dark

**темно́** *как сказ*: **на у́лице** ~ it's dark outside

**темнот|а́** (**-ы́**) *ж* darkness

**тёмный** *прил* dark

**темп** (**-а**) *м* speed; **в те́мпе** (*разг*) quickly

**темпера́мент** (**-а**) *м* temperament

**темпера́ментный** *прил* spirited

**температу́р|а** (**-ы**) *ж* temperature

**тенде́нци|я** (**-и**) *ж* tendency; (*предвзятость*) bias

**те́ндер** (**-а**) *м* (*КОММ*) tender

**тенев|о́й** *прил* shady; (*перен: стороны жизни*) shadowy; **~áя эконо́мика** shadow economy; ~ **кабине́т** (*ПОЛИТ*) shadow cabinet

**те́н|и** (**-ей**) *мн* (*также*: ~ **для век**) eye shadow *ед*

**те́ннис** (**-а**) *м* tennis

**тенниси́ст** (**-а**) *м* tennis player

**тен|ь** (**-и**; *prp sg* **-и́**, *gen pl* **-е́й**) *ж* (*место*) shade; (*предмета, человека*) shadow; (*перен*): ~ **+gen** (*волнения, печали*) flicker of; *см. также* **те́ни**

**теорети́ческий** *прил* theoretical

**тео́ри|я** (**-и**) *ж* theory

**тепе́рь** *нареч* now

**тепле́|ть** (*3sg* **-ет**; *pf* **по~**) *несов*

to get warmer

**тепли́ц|а (-ы)** ж hothouse

**тепли́чный** прил (растение) hothouse

**тепл|ó** нареч warmly ♦ **(-á)** ср (также перен) warmth ♦ как сказ it's warm; **мне ~** I'm warm

**теплово́й** прил thermal

**теплохо́д (-а)** м motor ship или vessel

**тепло(электро)центра́л|ь (-и)** ж generator plant (supplying central heating systems)

**тёплый** прил warm

**терапе́вт (-а)** м ≈ general practitioner

**тера́кт (-а)** м сокр (= террористи́ческий акт) terrorist attack

**терапи́|я (-и)** ж (МЕД, наука) (internal) medicine; (лечение) therapy

**тере́ть (тру, трёшь,** pt **тёр, тёрла, тёрло)** несов перех to rub; (овощи) to grate

**терза́|ть (-ю);** pf **рас~** несов перех (добычу) to savage; (pf **ис~;** перен: упрёками, ревностью) to torment; **~ся** несов возв: **~ся** +instr (сомнениями) to be racked by

**тёр|ка (-ки;** gen pl **-ок)** ж grater

**те́рмин (-а)** м term

**термина́л (-а)** м terminal

**термо́метр (-а)** м thermometer

**те́рмос (-а)** м Thermos ®

**термоя́дерный** прил thermonuclear

**терпели́вый** прил patient

**терпе́ни|е (-я)** ср patience

**терп|е́ть (-лю́, -ишь)** несов перех (боль, холод) to suffer, endure; (pf **по~;** неудачу) to suffer; (грубость) to tolerate; **~ (по~** pf) **круше́ние** (корабль) to

be wrecked; (поезд) to crash; **~ не могу́ таки́х люде́й** (разг) I can't stand people like that; **~ не могу́ спо́рить** (разг) I hate arguing; **~ся** несов безл: **мне не те́рпится** +infin I can't wait to do

**терпи́мост|ь (-и)** ж: **~ (к** +dat) tolerance (of)

**терпи́мый** прил tolerant

**терра́с|а (-ы)** ж terrace

**террито́ри|я (-и)** ж territory

**терроризи́р|овать (-ую)** (не)сов перех to terrorize

**террори́зм (-а)** м terrorism

**террори́ст (-а)** м terrorist

**террористи́ческий** прил terrorist

**теря́|ть (-ю;** pf **по~)** несов перех to lose; **~ся** (pf **по~ся)** несов возв to get lost; (робеть) to lose one's nerve

**тесн|и́ть (-ю́, -и́шь;** pf **по~)** несов перех (в толпе) to squeeze; (к стене) to press

**те́сно** нареч (располагать(ся)) close together; (сотрудничать) closely ♦ как сказ: **в кварти́ре о́чень ~** the flat is very cramped; **мы с ним ~ знако́мы** he and I know each other very well

**те́сный** прил (проход) narrow; (помещение) cramped; (одежда) tight; (дружба) close; **мир те́сен** it's a small world

**тест (-а)** м test

**тести́р|овать (-ую)** (не)сов to test

**те́ст|о (-а)** ср (дрожжевое) dough; (слоёное, песочное) pastry (BRIT), paste (US)

**тест|ь (-я)** м father-in-law, wife's father

**тесьм|а́ (-ы́)** ж tape

**тёт|ка (-ки;** gen pl **-ок)** ж auntie

**тетра́д|ь (-и)** ж exercise book

**тёт|я (-и;** gen pl **-ь)** ж aunt; (разг:

*женщина*) lady
**тéфтел|и (-ей)** *мн* meatballs *мн*
**тех** *мест см.* **те**
**тéхник|а (-и)** *ж* technology;
(*приёмы*) technique ♦ *собир*
(*машины*) machinery; (*разг: муз*)
hi-fi; ~ **безопáсности** industrial
health and safety
**тéхникум (-а)** *м* technical college
**технúческ|ий** *прил* technical; ~
**осмóтр** (*АВТ*) ≈ MOT (*BRIT*)
(*annual roadworthiness check*); **~ое**
**обслýживание** maintenance,
servicing
**технологúческий** *прил* technical
**технолóги|я (-и)** *ж* technology
**течéни|е (-я)** *ср* (*поток*) current;
(*в искусстве*) trend; **в ~** +*gen*
during
**те|чь** (*3sg* **-чёт**, *pt* **тёк, ~клá**)
*несов* to flow; (*крыша, лодка*
*итп*) to leak ♦ (**-чи**) *ж* leak
**тёщ|а (-и)** *ж* mother-in-law, wife's
mother
**тигр (-а)** *м* tiger
**тúка|ть** (*3sg* **-ет**) *несов* to tick
**тúн|а (-ы)** *ж* slime
**тип (-а)** *м* type; **тúпа** +*gen* (*разг*)
sort of
**типúчный** *прил*: ~ (**для** +*gen*)
typical (of)
**типовóй** *прил* standard-type
**типогрáфи|я (-и)** *ж* press,
printing house
**типогрáфский** *прил*
typographical; ~ **станóк** printing
press
**тир (-а)** *м* shooting gallery
**тирáж (-á)** *м* (*газеты*) circulation;
(*книги*) printing; (*лотереи*)
drawing
**тирáн (-а)** *м* tyrant
**тирани|я (-и)** *ж* tyranny
**тирé** *ср нескл* dash
**тиск|ú (-óв)** *мн*: **в ~áх** +*gen*

(*перен*) in the grip of
**титáн (-а)** *м* (*хим*) titanium; (*для*
*нагрева воды*) urn; (*о человеке*)
giant
**титр (-а)** *м* (*обычно мн*) credit (*of*
*film*)
**тúтул (-а)** *м* title
**тúтульный** *прил*: ~ **лист** title
page
**тиф (-а)** *м* typhus
**тúхий** *прил* quiet; **Тúхий океáн**
the Pacific (Ocean); ~ **ýжас!** (*разг*)
what a nightmare!
**тúхо** *нареч* (*говорить, жить*)
quietly ♦ *как сказ*: **в дóме** ~ the
house is quiet; ~! (be) quiet!
**тúше** *сравн прил от* **тúхий**
♦ *сравн нареч от* **тúхо** ♦ *как*
*сказ*: ~! quiet!, hush!
**тишин|á (-ы)** *ж* quiet
**т.к.** *сокр* = **так как**
**ткан|ь (-и)** *ж* fabric, material;
(*АНАТ*) tissue
**тк|áть (-у, -ёшь**; *pf* **соткáть**)
*несов перех* to weave
**ткáцк|ий** *прил*: **~ая фáбрика** mill
(*for fabric production*); ~ **станóк**
loom
**тле|ть** (*3sg* **-ет**) *несов* (*дрова,*
*угли*) to smoulder (*BRIT*), smolder
(*US*)
**тмин (-а)** *м* (*кулин*) caraway seeds
*мн*
**т.н.** *сокр* = **так называемый**
**то** *союз* (*условный*): **éсли ... ~ ...**
if ... then ... (*разделительный*): ~
... ~ ... sometimes ... sometimes ...;
**и ~** even; ~ **есть** that is
**то (тогó)** *мест см.* **тот**
**т.о.** *сокр* = **такúм óбразом**
**-то** *част* (*для выделения*):
**письмó-то ты получúл**? did you
(at least) receive the letter?
**тобóй** *мест см.* **ты**
**товáр (-а)** *м* product; (*экон*)

commodity

**това́рищ (-а)** *м* (*приятель*) friend; (*по партии*) comrade

**това́рищеский** *прил* comradely; **~ матч** (*СПОРТ*) friendly (match)

**това́риществ|о (-а)** *ср* (*КОММ*) partnership

**това́рн|ый** *прил* (*производство*) goods; (*рынок*) commodity; **~ая би́ржа** commodity exchange; **~ знак** trademark

**товарообме́н (-а)** *м* barter

**товарооборо́т (-а)** *м* turnover

**тогда́** *нареч* then; **~ как** (*хотя*) while; (*при противопоставлении*) whereas

**того́** *мест см.* **тот**; **то**

**то́же** *нареч* (*также*) too, as well, also

**той** *мест см.* **та**

**ток (-а)** *м* (*ЭЛЕК*) current

**тока́рный** *прил*: **~ стано́к** lathe

**то́кар|ь (-я;** *nom pl* **-я́)** *м* turner

**толк (-а)** *м* (*в рассуждениях*) sense; (*разг: польза*) use; **сбива́ть (сбить** *pf*) **кого́-н с то́лку** to confuse sb

**толка́|ть (-ю;** *pf* **толкну́ть)** *несов перех* to push; (*перен*): **~ кого́-н на** +*acc* to force sb into; **~ся** *несов возв* (*в толпе*) to push (one's way)

**толк|ова́ть (-у́ю)** *несов перех* to interpret

**толко́вый** *прил* intelligent

**толп|а́ (-ы́;** *nom pl* **-ы)** *ж* crowd

**толп|и́ться (3sg** **-и́тся)** *несов возв* to crowd around

**толсте́|ть (-ю;** *pf* **по~)** *несов* to get fatter

**то́лстый** *прил* thick; (*человек*) fat

**толч|о́к (-ка́)** *м* (*в спину*) shove; (*при торможении*) jolt; (*при землетрясении*) tremor; (*перен: к работе*) incentive

**то́лще** *сравн прил от* **то́лстый**

**толщин|а́ (-ы́)** *ж* thickness

KEYWORD

**то́лько** *част* **1** only

**2** (+*pron*/+*adv*; *усиливает выразительность*): **попро́буй то́лько отказа́ться!** just try to refuse!; **поду́май то́лько!** imagine that!

♦ *союз* **1** (*сразу после*) as soon as

**2** (*однако, но*) only; **позвони́, то́лько разгова́ривай недо́лго** phone (*BRIT*) или call (*US*), only don't talk for long

♦ *нареч* **1** (*недавно*) (only) just; **ты давно́ здесь?- нет, то́лько вошла́** have you been here long? - no, I've (only) just come in

**2** (*во фразах*): **то́лько лишь** (*разг*) only; **то́лько и всего́** (*разг*) that's all; **как** или **лишь** или **едва́ то́лько** as soon as; **не то́лько ..., но и ...** not only ... but also ...; **то́лько бы** if only; **то́лько что** only just

**том** *мест см.* **тот**; **то** ♦ **(-а;** *nom pl* **-а́)** *м* volume

**тома́тный** *прил*: **~ сок** tomato juice

**тому́** *мест см.* **тот**; **то**

**тон (-а)** *м* tone

**тонзилли́т (-а)** *м* tonsillitis

**тонизи́рующ|ий** *прил* (*напиток*) refreshing; **~ее сре́дство** tonic

**то́нкий** *прил* thin; (*фигура*) slender; (*черты лица, работа, ум*) fine; (*различия, намёк*) subtle

**то́нн|а (-ы)** *ж* tonne

**тонне́л|ь (-я)** *м* tunnel

**тон|у́ть (-у́, -ешь;** *pf* **у~)** *несов* (*человек*) to drown; (*pf* **за~**; *корабль*) to sink

**то́ньше** *сравн прил от* **то́нкий**

**то́па|ть (-ю)** *несов*: **~ нога́ми** to

stamp one's feet

**топ|и́ть** (**-лю́, -ишь**) *несов перех* (*печь*) to stoke (up); (*масло, воск*) to melt; (*pf* **у~** *или* **по~**; *корабль*) to sink; (*человека*) to drown; **~ся** *несов возв* (*печь*) to burn; (*pf* **у~ся**; *человек*) to drown o.s.

**топлёный** *прил* (*масло*) melted

**то́плив|о** (**-а**) *ср* fuel

**то́пол|ь** (**-я**) *м* poplar

**топо́р** (**-а́**) *м* axe (*BRIT*), ax (*US*)

**то́пот** (**-а**) *м* clatter

**топ|та́ть** (**-чу́, -чешь**; *pf* **по~**) *несов перех* (*траву*) to trample; **~ся** *несов возв* to shift from one foot to the other

**торг** (**-а**) *м* trading

**торг|и́** (**-о́в**) *мн* (*аукцион*) auction *ед*; (*состязание*) tender *ед*

**торг|ова́ть** (**-у́ю**) *несов* (*магазин*) to trade; **~** (*impf*) **+instr** (*мясом, мебелью*) to trade in; **~ся** (*pf* **с~ся**) *несов возв* to haggle

**торго́в|ец** (**-ца**) *м* merchant; (*мелкий*) trader

**торго́вл|я** (**-и**) *ж* trade

**торго́в|ый** *прил* trade; (*судно, флот*) merchant; **~ая сеть** retail network; **~ая то́чка** retail outlet; **~ое представи́тельство** trade mission; **~ центр** shopping centre (*BRIT*), mall (*US*)

**торгпре́д** (**-а**) *м сокр* (= *торго́вый представи́тель*) head of the trade mission

**торгпре́дств|о** (**-а**) *ср сокр* = **торго́вое представи́тельство**

**торже́ственный** *прил* (*день, случай*) special; (*собрание*) celebratory; (*вид, обстановка*) festive; (*обещание*) solemn

**торжеств|о́** (**-а́**) *ср* celebration; (*в голосе, в словах*) triumph

**торжеств|ова́ть** (**-у́ю**; *pf* **вос~**) *несов*: **~** (**над +instr**) to triumph (over)

**то́рмоз** (**-а**; *nom pl* **-а́**) *м* brake

**тормо|зи́ть** (**-жу́, -зи́шь**; *pf* **за~**) *несов перех* (*машину*) to slow down ♦ *неперех* (*машина*) to brake; **~ся** (*pf* **за~ся**) *несов возв* (*работа итп*) to be hindered

**тор|опи́ть** (**-оплю́, -о́пишь**; *pf* **по~**) *несов перех* to hurry; **~ся** (*pf* **по~ся**) *несов возв* to hurry

**торопли́вый** *прил* (*человек*) hasty

**торпе́д|а** (**-ы**) *ж* torpedo

**торт** (**-а**) *м* cake

**торф** (**-а**) *м* peat

**торч|а́ть** (**-у́, -и́шь**) *несов* (*вверх*) to stick up; (*в стороны*) to stick out; (*разг: на улице*) to hang around

**торше́р** (**-а**) *м* standard lamp

**тоск|а́** (**-и́**) *ж* (*на сердце*) anguish; (*скука*) boredom; **~ по ро́дине** homesickness

**тоскли́вый** *прил* gloomy

**тоск|ова́ть** (**-у́ю**) *несов* to pine away; **~** (*impf*) **по +dat** *или* **о +prp** to miss

**тост** (**-а**) *м* toast

KEYWORD

**то|т** (**-го́**; *f* **та**, *nt* **то**, *pl* **те**; *см. Table 11*) *мест* **1** that; **тот дом** that house

**2** (*о ранее упомянутом*) that; **в тот раз/день** that time/day

**3** (*в главных предложениях*): **э́то тот челове́к, кото́рый приходи́л вчера́** it's the man who came yesterday

**4** (*о последнем из названных лиц*): **я посмотре́л на дру́га, тот стоя́л мо́лча** I looked at my friend, who stood silently

**5** (*обычно с отрицанием*): **зашёл не в тот дом** I called at the wrong house

**6** (*об одном из перечисляемых предметов*): **ни тот ни друго́й** neither one nor the other; **тем и́ли ины́м спо́собом** by some means or other; **тот же** the same

**7** (*во фразах*): **до того́** so; **мне не до того́** I have no time for that; **к тому́ же** moreover; **ни с того́ ни с сего́** (*разг*) out of the blue; **тому́ наза́д** ago; **и тому́ подо́бное** et cetera, and so on

**тоталита́рный** *прил* totalitarian
**тота́льный** *прил* total; (*война*) all-out
**то-то** *част* (*разг: вот именно*) exactly, that's just it; (*вот почему*) that's why; (*выражает удовлетворение*): **~ же** pleased to hear it; **~ он удиви́тся!** he WILL be surprised!
**то́тчас** *нареч* immediately
**точи́л|ка** (**-ки**; *gen pl* **-ок**) *ж* pencil sharpener
**точ|и́ть** (**-у́, -ишь**; *pf* **на~**) *несов перех* to sharpen; (*no pf*; *подлеж: червь, ржавчина*) to eat away at
**то́ч|ка** (**-ки**; *gen pl* **-ек**) *ж* point; (*пятнышко*) dot; (*линг*) full stop (*BRIT*), period (*esp US*); **~ зре́ния** point of view; **~ с запято́й** semicolon
**точне́е** *вводн сл* to be exact *или* precise
**то́чно** *нареч* exactly; (*объясни́ть*) exactly, precisely; (*подсчита́ть, перевести́*) accurately ♦ *част* (*разг: действительно*) exactly, precisely
**то́чност|ь** (**-и**) *ж* accuracy
**то́чный** *прил* exact; (*часы, перевод, попадание*) accurate
**точь-в-точь** *нареч* (*разг*) just like
**тошн|и́ть** (*3sg* **-и́т**; *pf* **с~**) *несов*

*безл*: **меня́ ~и́т** I feel sick
**тошнот|а́** (**-ы́**) *ж* (*чувство*) nausea
**то́щий** *прил* (*человек*) skinny
**т.п.** *сокр* (= тому́ подо́бное) etc.
**трав|а́** (**-ы́**; *nom pl* **-ы**) *ж* grass; (*лекарственная*) herb
**трав|и́ть** (**-лю́, -ишь**) *несов перех* (*также перен*) to poison; (*pf* **за~**; *дичь*) to hunt; (*перен: разг: притесня́ть*) to harass, hound; **~ся** (*pf* **о~ся**) *несов возв* to poison o.s.
**тра́вл|я** (**-и**) *ж* hunting; (*демократов*) hounding
**тра́вм|а** (**-ы**) *ж* (*физическая*) injury; (*психическая*) trauma
**травмато́лог** (**-а**) *м* doctor working in a casualty department
**травматологи́ческий** *прил*: **~ отде́л** casualty; **~ пункт** first-aid room
**травми́р|овать** (**-ую**) *(не)сов перех* to injure; (*перен: психически*) to traumatize
**травяно́й** *прил* (*настойка*) herbal
**траге́ди|я** (**-и**) *ж* tragedy
**траги́ческий** *прил* tragic
**традицио́нный** *прил* traditional
**тради́ци|я** (**-и**) *ж* tradition
**тра́ктор** (**-а**) *м* tractor
**тракторист** (**-а**) *м* tractor driver
**трамва́|й** (**-я**) *м* tram (*BRIT*), streetcar (*US*)
**трампли́н** (**-а**) *м* springboard; **лы́жный ~** ski jump
**транзи́стор** (**-а**) *м* (*приёмник*) transistor (radio)
**транзи́т** (**-а**) *м* transit
**транс** (**-а**) *м* (*документ*) transport document
**трансге́нный** *прил* (*овощи*) genetically modified
**трансли́р|овать** (**-ую**) *(не)сов перех* to broadcast
**трансля́ци|я** (**-и**) *ж* (*передача*)

broadcast
**транспарáнт** (-а) м banner
**транспланта́ци|я** (-и) ж
transplant
**тра́нспорт** (-а) м transport
**транспортёр** (-а) м (конвейер)
conveyor belt; (ВОЕН) army
personnel carrier
**транспорти́р** (-а) м protractor
**транспорти́р|овать** (-ую)
(не)сов перех to transport
**тра́нспортный** прил transport
**транше́|я** (-и) ж trench
**трап** (-а) м gangway
**тра́сс|а** (-ы) ж (лыжная) run;
(трубопровода) line;
**автомоби́льная ~** motorway
(BRIT), expressway (US)
**тра́т|а** (-ы) ж spending; **пустáя ~
вре́мени/де́нег** a waste of time/
money
**тра́|тить** (-чу, -тишь; pf ис~ или
по~) несов перех to spend
**тра́ур** (-а) м mourning
**трафаре́т** (-а) м stencil
**тре́бовани|е** (-я) ср demand;
(правило) requirement
**тре́бовательный** прил
demanding
**тре́б|овать** (-ую; pf по~) несов
перех: ~ что-н/ +infin to demand
sth/to do; **~ся** (pf по~ся) несов
возв to be needed или required
**трево́г|а** (-и) ж (волнение)
anxiety; **возду́шная ~** air-raid
warning
**трево́ж|ить** (-у, -ишь; pf вс~)
несов перех to alarm; (pf по~;
мешать) to disturb; **~ся** (pf вс~ся)
несов возв (за детей) to be
concerned
**трево́жный** прил (голос, взгляд)
anxious; (сведения) alarming
**трезве́|ть** (-ю; pf о~) несов to
sober up

**тре́звый** прил (человек) sober;
(перен: идея) sensible
**трём** etc чис см. **три**
**трёмста́м** etc чис см. **три́ста**
**тренажёр** (-а) м equipment used for
physical training
**тре́нер** (-а) м coach
**тре́ни|е** (-я) ср friction
**трениp|ова́ть** (-у́ю; pf на~)
несов перех to train;
(спортсменов) to coach; **~ся** (pf
на~ся) несов возв (спортсмен)
to train
**трениро́в|ка** (-ки; gen pl -ок) ж
training; (отдельное занятие)
training (session)
**трениро́вочный** прил training; ~
**костю́м** tracksuit
**треп|а́ть** (-лю́, -лешь; pf по~)
несов перех (подлеж: ветер) to
blow about; (человека: по плечу)
to pat; (pf ис~ или по~; разг.
обувь, книги) to wear out; **~ся** (pf
ис~ся или по~ся) несов возв
(одежда) to wear out
**тре́пет** (-а) м (волнение) tremor;
(страх) trepidation
**треп|ета́ть** (-ещу́, -е́щешь)
несов (флаги) to quiver; (от
ужаса) to quake, tremble
**треск** (-а) м (сучьев) snapping;
(выстрелов) crackling
**треск|а́** (-и́) ж cod
**треска́|ться** (3sg -ется; pf по~)
несов возв to crack
**тре́сн|уть** (3sg -ет) сов (ветка) to
snap; (стакан, кожа) to crack
**трест** (-а) м (ЭКОН) trust
**тре́т|ий** чис third; **~ье лицо́**
(ЛИНГ) the third person
**тре́т|ь** (-и; nom pl -и, gen pl -ей) ж
third
**тре́ть|е** (-его) ср (КУЛИН) sweet
(BRIT), dessert
**треуго́льник** (-а) м triangle

**треуго́льный** *прил* triangular

**тре́ф|ы** (**-**) *мн* (*КАРТЫ*) clubs *мн*

**трёх** *чис см.* **три**

**трёхкра́тн|ый** *прил*: ~ **чемпио́н** three-times champion; **в ~ом разме́ре** threefold

**трёхме́рный** *прил* 3-D, three-dimensional

**трёхсо́т** *чис см.* **три́ста**

**трёхсо́тый** *чис* three hundredth

**треща́ть** (**-у́**, **-и́шь**) *несов* (*лёд, доски*) to crack; (*кузнечики*) to chip

**тре́щин|а** (**-ы**) *ж* crack

**тр|и** (**-ёх**; *см. Table 24*) *чис* three
♦ *нескл* (*ПРОСВЕЩ*) ≈ C (*school mark*)

**трибу́н|а** (**-ы**) *ж* platform; (*стадиона*) stand

**трибуна́л** (**-а**) *м* tribunal; **вое́нный** ~ military court

**тридца́тый** *чис* thirtieth

**три́дцат|ь** (**-и**; *как* **пять**; *см. Table 26*) *чис* thirty

**три́жды** *нареч* three times

**трико́** *ср нескл* leotard

**трикота́ж** (**-а**) *м* (*ткань*) knitted fabric ♦ *собир* (*одежда*) knitwear

**трикота́жный** *прил* knitted

**трило́ги|я** (**-и**) *ж* trilogy

**трина́дцатый** *чис* thirteenth

**трина́дцат|ь** (**-и**; *как* **пять**; *см. Table 26*) *чис* thirteen

**три́о** *ср нескл* trio

**три́ста** (**трёхсо́т**; *как* **сто**; *см. Table 28*) *чис* three hundred

**триу́мф** (**-а**) *м* triumph

**тро́гательный** *прил* touching

**тро́га|ть** (**-ю**; *pf* **тро́нуть**) *несов перех* to touch; (*подлеж: рассказ, событие*) to move; ~**ся** (*pf* **тро́нуться**) *несов возв* (*поезд*) to move off

**тр|о́е** (**-ои́х**; *см. Table 30а*) *чис* three

**троебо́рь|е** (**-я**) *ср* triathlon

**тро́иц|а** (**-ы**) *ж* (*также*: **Свята́я** ~) the Holy Trinity; (*праздник*) ≈ Trinity Sunday

**Тро́ицын** *прил*: ~ **день** ≈ Trinity Sunday

**тро́|йка** (**-йки**; *gen pl* **-ек**) *ж* (*цифра, карта*) three; (*ПРОСВЕЩ*) ≈ C (*school mark*); (*лошадей*) troika; (*костюм*) three-piece suit

**тройни́к** (**-а́**) *м* (*ЭЛЕК*) (three-way) adaptor

**тройно́й** *прил* triple

**тролле́йбус** (**-а**) *м* trolleybus

**тромбо́н** (**-а**) *м* trombone

**трон** (**-а**) *м* throne

**тро́н|уть(ся)** (**-у(сь)**) *сов от* **тро́гать(ся)**

**троп|а́** (**-ы́**; *nom pl* **-ы**) *ж* pathway

**тро́пик** (**-а**) *м*: **се́верный/ю́жный** ~ the tropic of Cancer/Capricorn

**тропи́н|ка** (**-ки**; *gen pl* **-ок**) *ж* footpath

**тропи́ческий** *прил* tropical

**трос** (**-а**) *м* cable

**тростни́к** (**-а́**) *м* reed; **са́харный** ~ sugar cane

**трост|ь** (**-и**) *ж* walking stick

**тротуа́р** (**-а**) *м* pavement (*BRIT*), sidewalk (*US*)

**трофе́|й** (**-я**) *м* trophy

**трою́родн|ый** *прил*: ~ **брат** second cousin (*male*); ~**ая сестра́** second cousin (*female*)

**троя́кий** *прил* triple

**труб|а́** (**-ы́**; *nom pl* **-ы**) *ж* pipe; (*дымовая*) chimney; (*МУЗ*) trumpet

**труба́ч** (**-а́**) *м* trumpeter

**труб|и́ть** (**-лю́**, **-и́шь**; *pf* **про~**) *несов* (*труба*) to sound; (*МУЗ*): ~ **в** +*acc* to blow

**тру́б|ка** (**-ки**; *gen pl* **-ок**) *ж* tube; (*курительная*) pipe; (*телефона*) receiver

**трубопрово́д** (-а) *м* pipeline

**труд** (-а́) *м* work; (*ЭКОН*) labour (*BRIT*), labor (*US*); **без ~а́** without any difficulty; **с (больши́м) ~о́м** with (great) difficulty

**тру|ди́ться** (-жу́сь, -дишься) *несов возв* to work hard

**тру́дно** *как сказ* it's hard *или* difficult; **у меня́ ~ с деньга́ми** I've got money problems; **мне ~ поня́ть э́то** I find it hard to understand; **(мне) ~ бе́гать/стоя́ть** I have trouble running/standing up; **~ сказа́ть** it's hard to say

**тру́дност|ь** (-и) *ж* difficulty

**тру́дный** *прил* difficult

**трудово́й** *прил* working

**трудова́я кни́жка** - employment record book. This is a booklet in which all employment details are recorded e.g. employment dates, position and any merits or reprimands received in the course of service. This is an extremely important document, the absence of which can make employment almost impossible.

**трудоёмкий** *прил* labour-intensive (*BRIT*), labor-intensive (*US*)

**трудолюби́вый** *прил* hard-working, industrious

**трудя́щ|ийся** *прил* working ♦ (**-егося**) *м* worker

**труп** (-а) *м* corpse

**тру́пп|а** (-ы) *ж* (*ТЕАТР*) company

**трус** (-а) *м* coward

**тру́сик|и** (-ов) *мн* (*детские*) knickers *мн* (*BRIT*), panties *мн* (*US*)

**тру́|сить** (-шу, -сишь; *pf* с~) *несов* to get scared

**трусли́вый** *прил* cowardly

**трус|ы́** (-о́в) *мн* (*бельё: обычно мужские*) (under)pants *мн*;

(*спортивные*) shorts *мн*

**трущо́б|а** (-ы) *ж* slum

**трюк** (-а) *м* trick; (*акробатический*) stunt

**трюм** (-а) *м* hold (*of ship*)

**трюмо́** *ср нескл* (*мебель*) dresser

**трю́фел|ь** (-я; *nom pl* -**я́**) *м* truffle

**тря́п|ка** (-ки; *gen pl* -**ок**) *ж* (*половая*) cloth; (*лоскут*) rag; **~ки** (*разг*) clothes *мн*

**тряс|ти́** (-у́, -ёшь) *несов перех* to shake; **~сь** *несов возв*: **~сь пе́ред** +*instr* (*перед нача́льством*) to tremble before; **~сь** (*impf*) **над** +*instr* (*разг: над ребёнком*) to fret over *или* about

**трях|ну́ть** (-у́, -ёшь) *сов перех* to shake

**т/с** *сокр* (= **теку́щий счёт**) С/А

**ТУ** *м сокр* = **самолёт констру́кции А.Н.Ту́полева**

**туале́т** (-а) *м* toilet; (*одежда*) outfit

**туале́тн|ый** *прил*: **~ая бума́га** toilet paper; **~ое мы́ло** toilet soap; **~ые принадле́жности** toiletries; **~ сто́лик** dressing table

**туберкулёз** (-а) *м* ТВ, tuberculosis

**туго́й** *прил* (*струна, пружина*) taut; (*узел, одежда*) tight; **он туг на́ ухо** (*разг*) he's a bit hard of hearing

**туда́** *нареч* there; **~ и обра́тно** there and back; **биле́т ~ и обра́тно** return (*BRIT*) *или* round-trip (*US*) ticket

**туда́-сюда́** *нареч* all over the place; (*раскачиваться*) backwards and forwards

**ту́же** *сравн прил от* **туго́й**

**туз** (-а́) *м* (*КАРТЫ*) ace

**тузе́м|ец** (-ца) *м* native

**ту́ловищ|е** (-а) *ср* torso

**тума́н** (-а) *м* mist

**тума́нный** *прил* misty; (*идеи*)

nebulous

**тýмб|а** (-ы) ж (*причальная, уличная*) bollard; (*для скульптуры*) pedestal

**тýмбоч|ка** (-ки; *gen pl* -ек) ж *уменьш от* **тýмба**; (*мебель*) bedside cabinet

**тýндр|а** (-ы) ж tundra

**тун|éц** (-цá) м tuna (fish)

**тунея́д|ец** (-ца) м parasite (*fig*)

**туннéл|ь** (-я) м = **тоннéль**

**тупи́к** (-á) м (*улица*) dead end, cul-de-sac; (*для поездов*) siding; (*перен: в переговорах итп*) deadlock

**туп|и́ть** (-лю́, -ишь; *pf* за~) *несов перех* to blunt; ~**ся** (*pf* за~**ся**) *несов возв* to become blunt

**тупóй** *прил* (*нож, карандаш*) blunt; (*человек*) stupid; (*боль, ум*) dull; (*покорность*) blind

**тур** (-а) м (*этап*) round; (*в танце*) turn

**турби́н|а** (-ы) ж turbine

**тури́зм** (-а) м tourism

**тури́ст** (-а) м tourist; (*в походе*) hiker

**туристи́ческий** *прил* tourist

**турнé** *ср нескл* (*ТЕАТР, СПОРТ*) tour

**турни́р** (-а) м tournament

**Тýрци|я** (-и) ж Turkey

**тýсклый** *прил* (*стекло*) opaque; (*краска*) mat(t); (*свет, взгляд*) dull

**тускнé|ть** (*3sg* -ет; *pf* по~) *несов* (*краска, талант*) to fade; (*серебро, позолота*) to tarnish

**тус|овáться** (-ýюсь; *pf* по~) *несов* (*разг*) to hang out

**тусóвк|а** (-и) ж (*разг: на улице*) hanging about; (*вечеринка*) party

**тут** *нареч* here; **и всё ~** (*разг*) and that's that; **не ~-то бы́ло** (*разг*) it

wasn't to be

**тýф|ля** (-ли; *gen pl* -ель) ж shoe

**тýхлый** *прил* (*еда*) rotten; (*запах*) putrid

**тýх|нуть** (*3sg* -нет, *pt* -, -ла, *pf* по~) *несов* (*костёр, свет*) to go out; (*pf* про~; *мясо*) to go off

**тýч|а** (-и) ж rain cloud

**тýш|а** (-и) ж carcass

**тушён|ка** (-ки; *gen pl* -ок) ж (*разг*) tinned (*BRIT*) или canned meat

**тушёный** *прил* (*КУЛИН*) braised

**туш|и́ть** (-ý, -ишь; *pf* за~ или по~) *несов перех* (*огонь*) to put out, extinguish; (*КУЛИН*) to braise

**тýш|ь** (-и) ж (*для рисования*) Indian ink; (*для ресниц*) mascara

**т/ф** м *сокр* = **телевизио́нный фильм**

**ТЦ** м *сокр* (= *телевизио́нный центр*) television centre (*BRIT*) или center (*US*)

**тщáтельный** *прил* thorough

**тщеслáви|е** (-я) *ср* vanity

**тщеслáвный** *прил* vain

**тщéтный** *прил* futile

**ты** (**тебя́**; *см. Table 6a*) *мест* you; **быть** (*impf*) **с кем-н на ~** to be on familiar terms with sb

**ты́|кать** (-чу, -чешь; *pf* ткнуть) *несов перех* (*разг: ударять*): ~ **что-н/кого́-н чем-н** to poke sth/sb with sth

**ты́кв|а** (-ы) ж pumpkin

**тыл** (-а; *loc sg* -ý, *nom pl* -ы́) м (*ВОЕН, территория*) the rear

**ты́льный** *прил* back

**ты́с.** *сокр* = **ты́сяча**

**ты́сяч|а** (-и; *см. Table 29*) ж *чис* thousand

**ты́сячный** *чис* thousandth; (*толпа, армия*) of thousands

**тьм|а** (-ы) ж (*мрак*) darkness, gloom

**ТЭЦ** *ж сокр* = **те́пло(электро)-центра́ль**

**тю́бик** (**-а**) *м* tube

**ТЮЗ** (**-а**) *м сокр* (= **теа́тр ю́ного зри́теля**) children's theatre (BRIT) *или* theater (US)

**тюле́н|ь** (**-я**) *м* (ЗООЛ) seal

**тюльпа́н** (**-а**) *м* tulip

**тюре́мн|ый** *прил* prison; **~ое заключе́ние** imprisonment

**тюрьм|а́** (**-ы́**) *ж* prison

**тя́г|а** (**-и**) *ж* (*в печи*) draught (BRIT), draft (US); (*насоса, пылесоса*) suction; **~ к** +dat (*перен*) attraction to

**тя́гостный** *прил* burdensome; (*впечатления*) depressing

**тяготе́ни|е** (**-я**) *ср* (ФИЗ) gravity

**тя́гот|ы** (**-**) *мн* hardships *мн*

**тя́жб|а** (**-ы**) *ж* dispute

**тяжеле́|ть** (**-ю**; *pf* **о~** *или* **по~**) *несов* to get heavier

**тяжело́** *нареч* heavily; (*больной*) seriously ♦ *как сказ* (*нести*) it's heavy; (*понять*) it's hard; **мне ~ здесь** I find it hard here; **больно́му ~** the patient is suffering

**тяжелоатле́т** (**-а**) *м* weightlifter

**тяжёл|ый** *прил* heavy; (*труд, день*) hard; (*сон*) restless; (*запах*) strong; (*воздух*) stale; (*преступление, болезнь, рана*) serious; (*зрелище, мысли, настроение*) grim; (*трудный: человек, характер*) difficult; **~ая атле́тика** weightlifting; **~ая промы́шленность** heavy industry

**тя́жест|ь** (**-и**) *ж* weight, heaviness; (*работы*) difficulty; (*болезни, преступления*) seriousness, severity; (*обычно мн: тяжёлый предмет*) weight

**тя́жкий** *прил* (*труд*) arduous; (*преступление*) grave

**тян|у́ть** (**-у́, -ешь**) *несов перех* (*канат, сеть итп*) to pull; (*шею, руку*) to stretch out; (*дело*) to drag out; (*pf* **про~**; *кабель*) to lay; (*pf* **вы́тянуть**; *жребий*) to draw ♦ *неперех*: **~ с** +instr (*с ответом, с решением*) to delay; **меня́ тя́нет в Петербу́рг** I want to go to Petersburg; **~ся** *несов возв* to stretch; (*дело, время*) to drag on; (*дым, запах*) to waft; **~ся** (*impf*) **к** +dat to be attracted *или* drawn to

**тя́п|ка** (**-ки**; *gen pl* **-ок**) *ж* hoe

# У, у

**у** *предл*; +gen **1** (*около*) by; **у окна́** by the window

**2** (*обозначает обладателя чего-н*): **у меня́ есть дом/де́ти** I have a house/children

**3** (*обозначает объект, с которым соотносится действие*): **я живу́ у друзе́й** I live with friends; **я учи́лся у него́** I was taught by him

**4** (*указывает на источник получения чего-н*) from; **я попроси́л у дру́га де́нег** I asked for money from a friend ♦ *межд* (*выражает испуг, восторг*) oh

**убега́|ть** (**-ю**) *несов от* **убежа́ть**

**убеди́тельный** *прил* (*пример*) convincing; (*просьба*) urgent

**убед|и́ть** (*2sg* **-и́шь**, *3sg* **-и́т**; *impf* **убежда́ть**) *сов перех*: **~ кого́-н** +infin to persuade sb to do; **убежда́ть** (**~** *pf*) **кого́-н в чём-н** to convince sb of sth; **~ся** (*impf*

**убежда́ться)** *сов возв*: ~**ся в чём-н** to be convinced of sth
**убежа́|ть** (*как* **бежа́ть**; *см.* Table 20; *impf* **убега́ть**) *сов* to run away
**убежде́ни|е (-я)** *ср* (*взгляд*) conviction
**убе́жищ|е (-а)** *ср* (*от дождя, от бомб*) shelter; **полити́ческое ~** political asylum
**убер|е́чь (-егу́, -ежёшь** *итп,* **-егу́т;** *pt* **-ёг, -егла́;** *impf* **убере́гать**) *сов перех* to protect; **~ся** (*impf* **уберега́ться**) *сов возв* (*от опасности итп*) to protect o.s.
**убива́|ть (-ю)** *несов от* **уби́ть**
**уби́йств|о (-а)** *ср* murder
**уби́йц|а (-ы)** *м/ж* murderer
**убира́|ть (-ю)** *несов от* **убра́ть**
**уби́т|ый (-ого)** *м* dead man
**уб|и́ть (-ью, -ьёшь;** *impf* **убива́ть**) *сов перех* to kill; (*о преступлении*) to murder
**убо́гий** *прил* wretched
**убо́|й (-я)** *м* slaughter
**убо́р (-а)** *м*: **головно́й ~** hat
**убо́рк|а (-и)** *ж* (*помещения*) cleaning; **~ урожа́я** harvest
**убо́рн|ая (-ой)** *ж* (*артиста*) dressing room; (*туалет*) lavatory
**убо́рщиц|а (-ы)** *ж* cleaner
**убр|а́ть (уберу́, уберёшь;** *impf* **убира́ть**) *сов перех* (*унести: вещи*) to take away; (*комнату*) to tidy; (*урожай*) to gather (in); **убира́ть (~** *pf*) **со стола́** to clear the table
**у́был|ь (-и)** *ж* decrease; **идти́** (*impf*) **на ~** to decrease
**убы́т|ок (-ка)** *м* loss
**убы́точный** *прил* loss-making
**убью́** *итп сов см.* **уби́ть**
**уважа́ем|ый** *прил* respected, esteemed; **~ господи́н** Dear Sir; **~ая госпожа́** Dear Madam
**уважа́|ть (-ю)** *несов перех* to

respect
**уваже́ни|е (-я)** *ср* respect
**УВД** *ср сокр* (= **Управле́ние вну́тренних дел**) administration of internal affairs within a town or region
**уве́дом|ить (-лю, -ишь;** *impf* **уведомля́ть**) *сов перех* to notify
**уведомле́ни|е (-я)** *ср* notification
**увез|ти́ (-у́, -ёшь;** *pt* **увёз, -ла́;** *impf* **увози́ть**) *сов перех* to take away
**увеличи́тельн|ый** *прил*: ~**ое стекло́** magnifying glass
**увели́ч|ить (-у, -ишь;** *impf* **увели́чивать**) *сов перех* to increase; (*фотографию*) to enlarge; **~ся** (*impf* **увели́чиваться**) *сов возв* to increase
**уве́ренност|ь (-и)** *ж* confidence
**уве́ренный** *прил* confident
**увертю́р|а (-ы)** *ж* overture
**уверя́|ть (-ю)** *несов перех*: **~ кого́-н/что́-н (в чём-н)** to assure sb/sth (of sth)
**ув|ести́ (-еду́, -едёшь;** *pt* **-ёл, -ела́;** *impf* **уводи́ть**) *сов перех* to lead off
**уви́|деть(ся) (-жу(сь), -дишь(ся))** *сов от* **ви́деть(ся)**
**увлека́тельный** *прил* (*рассказ*) absorbing; (*поездка*) entertaining
**увлече́ни|е (-я)** *ср* passion
**увл|е́чь (-еку́, -ечёшь** *итп,* **-еку́т;** *pt* **-ёк, -екла́;** *impf* **увлека́ть**) *сов перех* to lead away; (*перен: захватить*) to captivate; **~ся** (*impf* **увлека́ться**) *сов возв*: **~ся** +*instr* to get carried away with; (*влюбиться*) to fall for; (*шахматами итп*) to become keen on
**ув|оди́ть (-ожу́, -о́дишь)** *несов от* **увести́**
**ув|ози́ть (-ожу́, -о́зишь)** *несов*

от **увезти́**

**уво́л|ить (-ю, -ишь;** *impf*
**увольня́ть)** *сов перех (с
рабо́ты)* to dismiss, sack; **~ся** *(impf
**увольня́ться)** сов возв*: **~ся (с
рабо́ты)** to leave one's job

**увольне́ни|е (-я)** *ср (со слу́жбы)*
dismissal; *(ВОЕН)* leave

**увы́** *межд* alas

**ува́н|уть (-у)** *сов от* **вя́нуть**

**угада́|ть (-ю;** *impf* **уга́дывать)**
*сов перех* to guess

**уга́рный** *прил*: **~ газ** carbon
monoxide

**угаса́|ть (-ю;** *pf* **уга́снуть)** *несов
(ого́нь)* to die down

**угла́** *итп сущ см.* **у́гол**

**углево́д (-а)** *м* carbohydrate

**углеки́слый** *прил*: **~ газ** carbon
dioxide

**углеро́д (-а)** *м (ХИМ)* carbon

**углово́й** *прил* corner; *(также*: **~
уда́р** *СПОРТ)* corner

**углуб|и́ть (-лю́, -и́шь;** *impf*
**углубля́ть)** *сов перех* to deepen;
**~ся** *(impf* **углубля́ться)** *сов возв*
to deepen

**угля́** *итп сущ см.* **у́голь**

**угн|а́ть (угоню́, уго́нишь;** *impf*
**угоня́ть)** *сов перех* to drive off;
*(самолёт)* to hijack

**угнета́|ть (-ю)** *несов перех* to
oppress; *(тяготи́ть)* to depress

**угнете́ни|е (-я)** *ср* oppression

**угово́р|и́ть (-ю́, -и́шь;** *impf*
**угова́ривать)** *сов перех* to
persuade

**уго|ди́ть (-жу́, -ди́шь;** *impf*
**угожда́ть)** *сов (попа́сть)* to end
up; **угожда́ть** *(~ pf)* +dat to please

**уго́дно** *част*: **что ~** whatever you
like ♦ *как сказ*: **что Вам ~?** what
can I do for you?; **кто ~** anyone;
**когда́/како́й ~** whenever/
whichever you like; **от них мо́жно**

**ожида́ть чего́ ~** they might do
anything

**уго́дный** *прил*: **~** +dat pleasing to

**угожда́|ть (-ю)** *несов от*
**угоди́ть**

**у́г|ол (-ла́;** *loc sg* **-лу́)** *м* corner;
*(ГЕОМ)* angle; **~ зре́ния** perspective

**уголо́вник (-а)** *м* criminal

**уголо́вн|ый** *прил* criminal; **~ое
преступле́ние** felony; **~
престу́пник** criminal; **~ ро́зыск**
Criminal Investigation Department

**у́г|оль (-ля́)** *м* coal

**уго́н (-а)** *м (самолёта)* hijacking;
*(кра́жа)* theft

**уго́нщик (-а)** *м (самолёта)*
hijacker

**угоня́|ть (-ю)** *несов от* **угна́ть**

**у́г|орь (-ря́;** *nom pl* **-ри́)** *м (ЗООЛ)*
eel; *(на лице́)* blackhead

**уго|сти́ть (-щу́, -сти́шь;** *impf*
**угоща́ть)** *сов перех*: **~ кого́-н
чем-н** *(пирого́м, вино́м)* to offer
sb sth

**угоща́|ться (-юсь)** *несов возв*:
**~йтесь!** help yourself!

**угрожа́|ть (-ю)** *несов*: **~ кому́-н
(чем-н)** to threaten sb (with sth)

**угро́з|а (-ы)** *ж (обы́чно мн)* threat

**угрызе́ни|е (-я)** *ср*: **~я со́вести**
pangs *мн* of conscience

**угрю́мый** *прил* gloomy

**уда|ва́ться (3sg -ётся)** *несов от*
**уда́ться**

**удал|и́ть (-ю́, -и́шь;** *impf*
**удаля́ть)** *сов перех (отосла́ть)*
to send away; *(игрока́)* to send off;
*(пятно́, занозу, о́рган)* to remove

**уда́р (-а)** *м* blow; *(ного́й)* kick;
*(инсу́льт)* stroke; *(се́рдца)* beat

**ударе́ни|е (-я)** *ср* stress

**уда́р|ить (-ю, -ишь;** *impf*
**ударя́ть)** *сов перех* to hit;
*(ного́й)* to kick; *(подлеж: часы́)* to
strike; **~ся** *(impf* **ударя́ться)** *сов*

*возв*: **~ся о** +*acc* to bang (o.s.) against

**уда́рный** *прил* (*инструмент*) percussion; (*слог*) stressed

**уда́ться** (*как* дать; *см.* Table 16; *impf* **удава́ться**) *сов возв* (*опыт, дело*) to be successful, work; (*пирог*) to turn out well; **нам удало́сь поговори́ть/зако́нчить рабо́ту** we managed to talk to each other/finish the work

**уда́ч**|**а** (-**и**) *ж* (good) luck; **жела́ю ~!** good luck!

**уда́чный** *прил* successful; (*слова*) apt

**удво́**|**ить** (-**ю, -ишь**; *impf* **удва́ивать**) *сов перех* to double

**удел**|**и́ть** (-**ю́, -и́шь**; *impf* **уделя́ть**) *сов перех*: **~ что-н кому́-н/ чему́-н** to devote sth to sb/sth

**уд**|**ержа́ть** (-**ержу́, -е́ржишь**; *impf* **уде́рживать**) *сов перех* to restrain; (*деньги*) to deduct; **уде́рживать** (**~** *pf*) (**за собо́й**) to retain; **уде́рживать** (**~** *pf*) **кого́-н от пое́здки** to keep sb from going on a journey; **~ся** (*impf* **уде́рживаться**) *сов возв* to stop *или* restrain o.s.

**удиви́тельный** *прил* amazing

**удив**|**и́ть** (-**лю́, -и́шь**; *impf* **удивля́ть**) *сов перех* to surprise; **~ся** (*impf* **удивля́ться**) *сов возв*: **~ся** +*dat* to be surprised at *или* by

**удивле́ни**|**е** (-**я**) *ср* surprise

**уди́ть** (**ужу́, у́дишь**) *несов* to angle

**удлин**|**и́ть** (-**ю́, -и́шь**; *impf* **удлиня́ть**) *сов перех* to lengthen; (*срок*) to extend

**удо́бно** *нареч* (*сесть*) comfortably ♦ *как сказ* it's comfortable; (*прилично*) it's proper; **не ~ так говори́ть/де́лать** it is not proper to say so/do so; **мне не ~** I feel

awkward; **мне здесь ~** I'm comfortable here; **мне ~ прийти́ ве́чером** it's convenient for me to come in the evening

**удо́бный** *прил* comfortable; (*время, место*) convenient

**удобре́ни**|**е** (-**я**) *ср* fertilizer

**удо́бств**|**о** (-**а**) *ср* comfort; **кварти́ра со все́ми ~ами** a flat with all (modern) conveniences

**удовлетворе́ни**|**е** (-**я**) *ср* satisfaction; (*требований*) fulfilment

**удовлетвори́тельный** *прил* satisfactory

**удовлетвор**|**и́ть** (-**ю́, -и́шь**; *impf* **удовлетворя́ть**) *сов перех* to satisfy; (*потребности, про́сьбу*) to meet; (*жалобу*) to respond to; **~ся** (*impf* **удовлетворя́ться**) *сов возв*: **~ся** +*instr* to be satisfied with

**удово́льстви**|**е** (-**я**) *ср* pleasure

**удостовере́ни**|**е** (-**я**) *ср* identification (card); **~ ли́чности** identity card

**удочер**|**и́ть** (-**ю́, -и́шь**; *impf* **удочеря́ть**) *сов перех* to adopt (*daughter*)

**у́доч**|**ка** (-**ки**; *gen pl* -**ек**) *ж* (fishing-)rod

**уду́шь**|**е** (-**я**) *ср* suffocation

**уе́хать** (*как* е́хать; *см.* Table 19; *impf* **уезжа́ть**) *сов* to leave, go away

**уж** (-**а́**) *м* (*ЗООЛ*) grass snake ♦ *част* (*при усилении*): **здесь не так ~ пло́хо** it's not as bad as all that here

**ужа́л**|**ить** (-**ю, -ишь**) *сов от* **жа́лить**

**у́жас** (-**а**) *м* horror; (*страх*) terror ♦ *как сказ* (*разг*): (**э́то**) **~!** it's awful *или* terrible!; **ти́хий ~!** (*разг*) what a nightmare!; **до ~а** (*разг*) terribly

**ужасн|у́ть** (-у́, -ёшь; *impf*
**ужаса́ть**) *сов перех* to horrify;
**~ся** (*impf* **ужаса́ться**) *сов возв* to
be horrified

**ужа́сно** *нареч* (*разг: очень*)
awfully, terribly ♦ *как сказ*: **э́то ~**
it's awful *или* terrible

**ужа́сный** *прил* terrible, horrible,
awful

**у́же** *сравн прил от* **у́зкий**

**уже́** *нареч, част* already; **ты же ~
не ма́ленький** you're not a child
any more

**ужива́|ться** (-юсь) *несов от*
**ужи́ться**

**у́жин** (-а) *м* supper

**у́жина|ть** (-ю; *pf* **по~**) *несов* to
have supper

**ужи́|ться** (-ву́сь, -вёшься; *impf*
**ужива́ться**) *сов возв*: **~ с кем-н**
to get on with sb

**узако́н|ить** (-ю, -ишь; *impf*
**узако́нивать**) *сов перех* to
legalize

**у́з|ел** (-ла́) *м* knot; (*мешок*)
bundle; **телефо́нный ~** telephone
exchange; **железнодоро́жный ~**
railway junction; **санита́рный ~**
bathroom and toilet

**у́зкий** *прил* narrow; (*тесный*)
tight; (*перен: человек*) narrow-
minded

**узна́|ть** (-ю; *impf* **узнава́ть**) *сов
перех* to recognize; (*новости*) to
learn

**у́зок** *прил см.* **у́зкий**

**узо́р** (-а) *м* pattern

**узо́рный** *прил* patterned

**уйти́** (*как* **идти́**; *см.* Table 18; *impf*
**уходи́ть**) *сов* (*человек*) to go
away, leave; (*автобус, поезд*) to
go, leave; (*избежать*): **~ от** +*gen*
(*от опасности итп*) to get away
from; (*потребоваться*): **~ на** +*acc*
(*деньги, время*) to be spent on

**ука́з** (-а) *м* (*президента*) decree

**указа́ни|е** (-я) *ср* indication;
(*разъяснение*) instruction;
(*приказ*) directive

**указа́тел|ь** (-я) *м* (*дорожный*)
sign; (*книга*) guide; (*список в
книге*) index; (*прибор*) indicator

**указа́тельн|ый** *прил* **~ое
местоиме́ние** demonstrative
pronoun; **~ па́лец** index finger

**ук|аза́ть** (-ажу́, -а́жешь; *impf*
**ука́зывать**) *сов перех* to point
out; (*сообщить*) to indicate

**ука́з|ка** (-ки; *gen pl* -ок) *ж* pointer

**укача́|ть** (-ю; *impf* **ука́чивать**)
*сов перех* (*усыпить*) to rock to
sleep; **его́ ~ло (в маши́не/на
парохо́де)** he got (car-/sea-)sick

**укла́дыва|ть** (-ю) *несов от*
**уложи́ть**; **~ся** *несов от*
**уложи́ться** ♦ *возв*: **э́то не ~ется
в обы́чные ра́мки** this is out of
the ordinary; **э́то не ~ется в
голове́** *или* **в созна́нии** it's
beyond me

**укло́н** (-а) *м* slant; **под ~** downhill

**укл|они́ться** (-оню́сь,
-о́нишься; *impf* **уклоня́ться**) *сов
возв* (*от удара*) to swerve;
**уклоня́ться** (**~** *pf*) **от** +*gen* to
dodge; (*от темы, от предмета*) to
digress from

**укло́нчивый** *прил* evasive

**уко́л** (-а) *м* prick; (*МЕД*) injection

**ук|оло́ть** (-олю́, -о́лешь) *сов от*
**коло́ть**

**уко́р** (-а) *м* (*упрёк*) reproach; **~ы
со́вести** pangs of conscience

**укоро́|ти́ть** (-чу́, -ти́шь; *impf*
**укора́чивать**) *сов перех* to
shorten; **~ся** (*impf*
**укора́чиваться**) *сов возв* to be
shortened

**укра́дкой** *нареч* furtively

**укра́|сить** (-шу, -сишь; *impf*

**украша́ть)** *сов перех* to decorate; (*жизнь итп*) to brighten (up)

**укра́|сть (-ду́, -дёшь)** *сов от* **красть**

**украша́|ть (-ю)** *несов от* **укра́сить**

**украше́ни|е (-я)** *ср* decoration; (*коллекции*) jewel; (*также*: **ювели́рное ~**) jewellery (*BRIT*), jewelry (*US*)

**укреп|и́ть (-лю́, -и́шь;** *impf* **укрепля́ть)** *сов перех* to strengthen; (*стену*) to reinforce; **~ся** (*impf* **укрепля́ться**) *сов возв* to become stronger

**укрепле́ни|е (-я)** *ср* strengthening

**укро́п (-а)** *м*, *собир* dill

**укро|ти́ть (-щу́, -ти́шь;** *impf* **укроща́ть)** *сов перех* to tame

**укры́ти|е (-я)** *ср* shelter

**укр|ы́ть (-о́ю, -о́ешь;** *impf* **укрыва́ть)** *сов перех* (*закрыть*) to cover; (*беженца*) to shelter; **~ся** (*impf* **укрыва́ться**) *сов возв* to cover o.s.; (*от дождя*) to take cover

**у́ксус (-а)** *м* vinegar

**уку́с (-а)** *м* bite

**ук|уси́ть (-ушу́, -у́сишь)** *сов перех* to bite

**уку́та|ть (-ю;** *impf* **уку́тывать)** *сов перех* to wrap up; **~ся** (*impf* **уку́тываться**) *сов возв* to wrap o.s. up

**ул.** *сокр* (= **у́лица**) St

**ула́влива|ть (-ю)** *несов от* **улови́ть**

**ула́|дить (-жу, -дишь;** *impf* **ула́живать)** *сов перех* to settle

**у́л|ей (-ья)** *м* (bee-)hive

**уле|те́ть (-чу́, -ти́шь;** *impf* **улета́ть)** *сов* (*птица*) to fly away; (*самолёт*) to leave

**улету́ч|иться (-усь, -ишься;** *impf* **улету́чиваться)** *сов возв* to evaporate

**ули́к|а (-и)** *ж* (piece of) evidence

**ули́т|ка (-ки;** *gen pl* **-ок)** *ж* snail

**у́лиц|а (-ы)** *ж* street; **на ~е** outside

**у́личн|ый** *прил* street; **~ое движе́ние** traffic

**уло́в (-а)** *м* catch (of fish)

**улови́мый** *прил*: **едва́** *или* **чуть** *или* **е́ле ~** barely perceptible

**ул|ови́ть (-овлю́, -о́вишь;** *impf* **ула́вливать)** *сов перех* to detect; (*мысль, связь*) to grasp

**ул|ожи́ть (-ожу́, -о́жишь;** *impf* **укла́дывать)** *сов перех* (*ребёнка*) to put to bed; (*вещи, чемодан*) to pack; **~ся** (*impf* **укла́дываться**) *сов возв* to pack; **укла́дываться (~ся** *pf*) **в сро́ки** to keep to the time limit

**улу́чш|ить (-у, -ишь;** *impf* **улучша́ть)** *сов перех* to improve

**улыба́|ться (-юсь;** *pf* **улыбну́ться)** *несов возв*: **~** (*+dat*) to smile (at)

**улы́б|ка (-ки;** *gen pl* **-ок)** *ж* smile

**ультразву́к (-а)** *м* ultrasound

**ультрафиоле́тов|ый** *прил*: **~ые лучи́** ultraviolet rays *мн*

**ум (-а́)** *м* mind; **быть** (*impf*) **без ~а́ от кого́-н/чего́-н** to be wild about sb/sth; **в ~е́** (*считать*) in one's head; **бра́ться (взя́ться** *pf*) **за ~** to see sense; **сходи́ть (сойти́** *pf*) **с ~а́** to go mad; **своди́ть (свести́** *pf*) **кого́-н с ~а** to drive sb mad; (*перен: увлечь*) to drive sb wild; **~а́ не приложу́, куда́/ско́лько/ кто ...** I can't think where/how much/who ...

**ума́лчива|ть (-ю)** *несов от* **умолча́ть**

**уме́лый** *прил* skilful (*BRIT*), skillful (*US*)

уме́ни|е (-я) *ср* ability, skill

уме́ньш|ить (-у, -ишь; *impf* уменьша́ть) *сов перех* to reduce; ~ся (*impf* уменьша́ться) *сов возв* to diminish

уме́ренный *прил* moderate; (*климат, характер*) temperate

ум|ере́ть (-ру́, -рёшь; *impf* умира́ть) *сов* to die

умер|ить (-ю, -ишь; *impf* умеря́ть) *сов перех* to moderate

уме|сти́ть (-щу́, -сти́шь; *impf* умеща́ть) *сов перех* to fit; ~ся (*impf* умеща́ться) *сов возв* to fit

уме́|ть (-ю) *несов* can, to be able to; (*иметь способность*) to know how to; он ~ет пла́вать/чита́ть he can swim/read

умеща́|ть(ся) (-ю(сь)) *несов от* умести́ть(ся)

умира́|ть (-ю) *несов от* умере́ть
♦ *неперех* (*перен*): ~ю, как хочу́ есть/спать I'm dying for something to eat/to go to sleep; я ~ю от ску́ки I'm bored to death

умиротвор|и́ть (-ю́, -и́шь; *impf* умиротворя́ть) *сов перех* (*враждующих*) to pacify; (*агрессора*) to appease

умне́|ть (-ю; *pf* по~) *несов* (*человек*) to grow wiser

у́мниц|а (-ы) *м/ж*: он/она́ ~ he's/she's a clever one; (*разг*): вот ~! good for you!, well done!

у́мно *нареч* (*сделанный*) cleverly; (*вести себя*) sensibly; (*говорить*) intelligently

умножа́|ть (-ю) *несов от* умно́жить

умноже́ни|е (-я) *ср* multiplication

умно́ж|ить (-у, -ишь; *impf* мно́жить *или* умножа́ть) *сов перех* (*МАТ*) to multiply

у́мный *прил* clever, intelligent

умозаключе́ни|е (-я) *ср* (*вывод*) deduction

умол|и́ть (-ю́, -и́шь; *impf* умоля́ть) *сов перех*: ~ кого́-н (+*infin*) to prevail upon sb (to do)

у́молк *м*: без ~у incessantly

умо́лкн|уть (-у; *impf* умолка́ть) *сов* to fall silent

умолч|а́ть (-у́, -и́шь; *impf* ума́лчивать) *сов*: ~ о чём-н to keep quiet about sth

умоля́|ть (-ю) *несов от* умоли́ть
♦ *перех* to implore

умру́ *итп сов см.* умере́ть

умо́ю(сь) *сов см.* умы́ть(ся)

у́мственно *нареч*: ~ отста́лый mentally retarded

у́мственный *прил* (*способности*) mental; ~ труд intellectual work

умудр|и́ться (-ю́сь, -и́шься; *impf* умудря́ться) *сов возв* to manage

умч|а́ть (-у́, -и́шь) *сов перех* to whisk off *или* away; ~ся *сов возв* to dash off

умыва́льник (-а) *м* washstand

умы́|ть (-о́ю, -о́ешь; *impf* умыва́ть) *сов перех* to wash; ~ся (*impf* умыва́ться) *сов возв* to wash

умы́шленный *прил* deliberate, intentional; (*преступление*) premeditated

ун|ести́ (-есу́, -есёшь; *pt* -ёс, -есла́; *impf* уноси́ть) *сов перех* to take away; ~сь (*impf* уноси́ться) *сов возв* to speed off

универма́г (-а) *м* = универса́льный магази́н

универса́льный *прил* universal; (*образование*) all-round; (*человек, машина*) versatile; ~ магази́н department store

универса́м (-а) *м* supermarket

университе́т (-а) *м* university

**унижа́|ть(ся)** (-**ю**(сь)) *несов от* **уни́зить(ся)**

**униже́ни|е** (-я) *ср* humiliation

**уни́женный** *прил* (*человек*) humiliated; (*взгляд, просьба*) humble

**унизи́тельный** *прил* humiliating

**уни́|зить** (-**жу**, -**зишь**; *impf* **унижа́ть**) *сов перех* to humiliate; **унижа́ть** (~ *pf*) **себя́** to abase o.s.; ~**ся** (*impf* **унижа́ться**) *сов возв*: ~**ся** (**пе́ред** +*instr*) to abase o.s. (before)

**уника́льный** *прил* unique

**унита́з** (-а) *м* toilet

**уничто́ж|ить** (-у, -ишь; *impf* **уничтожа́ть**) *сов перех* to destroy

**ун|оси́ть(ся)** (-**ошу́**(сь), -**о́сишь**(ся)) *несов от* **унести́(сь)**

**уныва́|ть** (-ю) *несов* (*человек*) to be downcast *или* despondent

**уны́лый** *прил* despondent

**уны́ни|е** (-я) *ср* despondency

**уня́|ть** (**уйму́**, **уймёшь**; *pt* -**л**, -**ла́**, -**ло**; *impf* **унима́ть**) *сов перех* (*волнение*) to suppress

**упа́д|ок** (-ка) *м* decline

**упак|ова́ть** (-**у́ю**) *сов от* **пакова́ть**

**упако́вк|а** (-и) *ж* packing; (*материал*) packaging

**упасти́** *сов перех*: **упаси́ Бог** *или* **Бо́же** *или* **Го́споди!** God forbid!

**упа́|сть** (-**ду́**, -**дёшь**) *сов от* **па́дать**

**упере́ть** (**упру́**, **упрёшь**; *pt* **упёр**, **упёрла**, **упёрло**; *impf* **упира́ть**) *сов перех*: ~ **что-н в** +*acc* (*в сте́ну итп*) to prop sth against; ~**ся** (*impf* **упира́ться**) *сов возв*: ~**ся чем-н в** +*acc* (*в зе́млю*) to dig sth into; (*натолкну́ться*): ~**ся в** +*acc* (*в сте́ну*) to come up

against

**упива́|ться** (-**юсь**) *несов возв* (*перен*): ~ +*instr* (*сча́стьем*) to be intoxicated by

**упира́|ть** (-ю) *несов от* **упере́ть**; ~**ся** *несов от* **упере́ться** ♦ *возв* (*име́ть причи́ной*): ~**ся в** +*prp* to be down to

**упла́т|а** (-ы) *ж* payment

**упл|ати́ть** (-**ачу́**, -**а́тишь**) *сов от* **плати́ть**

**уплы́|ть** (-**ву́**, -**вёшь**; *impf* **уплыва́ть**) *сов* (*человек, ры́ба итп*) to swim away *или* off; (*кора́бль*) to sail away *или* off

**уподо́б|ить** (-**лю**, -**ишь**; *impf* **уподобля́ть**) *сов перех*: ~ **что-н/кого́-н** +*dat* to compare sth/ sb to; ~**ся** (*impf* **уподобля́ться**) *сов возв*: ~**ся** +*dat* to become like

**уполз|ти́** (-**у́**, -**ёшь**; *pt* -, -**ла́**) *сов* (*змея́*) to slither away

**уполномо́чи|е** (-я) *ср*: **по** ~**ю** +*gen* on behalf of

**уполномо́ч|ить** (-**у**, -**ишь**; *impf* **уполномо́чивать**) *сов перех*: ~ **кого́-н** +*infin* to authorize sb to do

**упом|яну́ть** (-**яну́**, -**я́нешь**; *impf* **упомина́ть**) *сов* (*не*)*перех* (*назва́ть*): ~ +*acc* или (**о** +*prp*) to mention

**упо́р** (-а) *м* (*для ног*) rest; **в** ~ (*стреля́ть*) point-blank; (*смотре́ть*) intently; **де́лать** (**сде́лать** *pf*) ~ **на** +*prp* to put emphasis on

**упо́рный** *прил* persistent

**упо́рств|о** (-а) *ср* persistence

**употреби́тельный** *прил* frequently used

**употреб|и́ть** (-**лю́**, -**и́шь**; *impf* **употребля́ть**) *сов перех* to use

**употребле́ни|е** (-я) *ср* (*слова*) usage; (*лека́рства*) taking; (*алкого́ля, пи́щи*) consumption

**упр.** *сокр* (= **управле́ние**) admin

**управле́ни|е** (**-я**) *ср* (*дела́ми*) administration; (*фи́рмой*) management; (*учрежде́ние*) office; (*систе́ма прибо́ров*) controls *мн*

**управля́|ть** (**-ю**) *несов*: ~ +*instr* (*автомоби́лем*) to drive; (*су́дном*) to navigate; (*госуда́рством*) to govern; (*учрежде́нием, фи́рмой*) to manage; (*орке́стром*) to conduct

**управля́ющ|ий** (**-его**) *м* (*хозя́йством*) manager; (*име́нием*) bailiff

**упражне́ни|е** (**-я**) *ср* exercise

**упражня́|ть** (**-ю**) *несов перех* to exercise; **~ся** *несов возв* to practise

**упраздн|и́ть** (**-ю́, -и́шь**; *impf* **упраздня́ть**) *сов перех* to abolish

**упра́шива|ть** (**-ю**) *несов от* **упроси́ть**

**упрёк** (**-а**) *м* reproach

**упрека́|ть** (**-ю**; *pf* **упрекну́ть**) *несов перех*: ~ **кого́-н** (**в** +*prp*) to reproach sb (for)

**упр|оси́ть** (**-ошу́, -о́сишь**; *impf* **упра́шивать**) *сов перех*: ~ **кого́-н** +*infin* to persuade sb to do

**упро|сти́ть** (**-щу́, -сти́шь**; *impf* **упроща́ть**) *сов перех* to simplify

**упро́ч|ить** (**-у, -ишь**; *impf* **упро́чивать**) *сов перех* to consolidate; **~ся** (*impf* **упро́чиваться**) *сов возв* (*положе́ние, пози́ции*) to be consolidated

**упроща́|ть** (**-ю**) *несов от* **упрости́ть**

**упроще́ни|е** (**-я**) *ср* simplification

**упру́гий** *прил* (*пружи́на, те́ло*) elastic; (*движе́ния*) springy

**упря́ж|ка** (**-ки**; *gen pl* **-ек**) *ж* team (*of horses, dogs etc*); (*упря́жь*) harness

**у́пряж|ь** (**-и**) *ж*; *no pl* harness

**упря́мый** *прил* obstinate, stubborn

**упуска́|ть** (**-ю**; *pf* **упусти́ть**) *несов перех* (*мяч*) to let go of; (*моме́нт*) to miss; ~ (**упусти́ть** *pf*) **из ви́ду** to overlook

**упуще́ни|е** (**-я**) *ср* error, mistake

**ура́** *межд* hooray, hurrah

**уравне́ни|е** (**-я**) *ср* (*МАТ*) equation

**ура́внива|ть** (**-ю**) *несов от* **уравня́ть**

**уравнове́|сить** (**-шу, -сишь**; *impf* **уравнове́шивать**) *сов перех* to balance; **~ся** (*impf* **уравнове́шиваться**) *сов возв* (*си́лы*) to be counterbalanced

**уравнове́шенный** *прил* balanced

**уравня́|ть** (**-ю**; *impf* **ура́внивать**) *сов перех* to make equal

**урага́н** (**-а**) *м* hurricane

**урага́нный** *прил*: ~ **ве́тер** gale

**ура́н** (**-а**) *м* uranium

**урегули́р|овать** (**-ую**) *сов перех* to settle

**у́рн|а** (**-ы**) *ж* (*погреба́льная*) urn; (*для му́сора*) bin; **избира́тельная ~** ballot box

**у́ров|ень** (**-ня**) *м* level; (*те́хники*) standard; (*зарпла́ты*) rate; **встре́ча на вы́сшем ~не** summit meeting; ~ **жи́зни** standard of living

**уро́д** (**-а**) *м person with a deformity*

**уро́дливый** *прил* (*с уро́дством*) deformed; (*некраси́вый*) ugly

**урожа́|й** (**-я**) *м* harvest

**уро́к** (**-а**) *м* lesson; (*зада́ние*) task; (*обы́чно мн: дома́шняя рабо́та*) homework *ед*; **де́лать** (**сде́лать** *pf*) **~и** to do one's homework

**ур|они́ть** (**-оню́, -о́нишь**) *сов от* **роня́ть**

**ус** (-а) *м* whisker; *см. также* **усы́**

**ус|ади́ть** (-ажу́, -а́дишь; *impf* **уса́живать**) *сов перех* (*заставить делать*): ~ **кого́-н за что-н** / +*infin* to sit sb down to sth/ to do

**уса́дьб|а** (-ы) *ж* (*помещичья*) country estate; (*крестьянская*) farmstead

**уса́жива|ть** (-ю) *несов от* **усади́ть**; ~**ся** *несов от* **усе́сться**

**уса́тый** *прил*: ~ **мужчи́на** man with a moustache (*BRIT*) *или* mustache (*US*)

**усво́|ить** (-ю, -ишь; *impf* **усва́ивать**) *сов перех* (*пищу, лекарство*) to assimilate; (*привычку*) to acquire; (*урок*) to master

**усе́рдный** *прил* diligent

**усе́|сться** (-я́дусь, -я́дешься; *pt* -е́лся, -е́лась; *impf* **уса́живаться**) *сов возв* to settle down; **уса́живаться** (~ *pf*) **за** +*acc* (*за работу*) to sit down to

**уси́ленный** *прил* (*охрана*) heightened; (*внимание*) increased

**уси́лива|ть** (-ю) *несов от* **уси́лить**

**уси́ли|е** (-я) *ср* effort

**уси́л|ить** (-ю, -ишь; *impf* **уси́ливать**) *сов перех* to intensify; (*охрану*) to heighten; (*внимание*) to increase; ~**ся** (*impf* **уси́ливаться**) *сов возв* (*ветер*) to get stronger; (*волнение*) to increase

**ускользн|у́ть** (-у́, -ёшь; *impf* **ускольза́ть**) *сов* to slip away

**ускор|ить** (-ю, -ишь; *impf* **ускоря́ть**) *сов перех* (*шаги*) to quicken; (*отъезд*) to speed up; ~**ся** (*impf* **ускоря́ться**) *сов возв* (*шаги*) to quicken; (*решение*) to be speeded up

**усло́ви|е** (-я) *ср* condition; (*договора*) term; (*обычно мн: правила*) requirement; *см. также* **усло́вия**

**усло́в|иться** (-люсь, -ишься; *impf* **усла́вливаться**) *сов возв*: ~ **о** +*prp* (*договориться*) to agree on

**усло́ви|я** (-й) *мн* (*природные*) conditions *мн*; (*задачи*) factors *мн*; **жили́щные** ~ housing; ~ **труда́** working conditions; **в** ~**х** +*gen* in an atmosphere of; **по** ~**м догово́ра** on the terms of the agreement; **на льго́тных** ~**х** on special terms

**усло́вный** *прил* conditional; (*сигнал*) code

**усложн|и́ть** (-ю́, -и́шь; *impf* **усложня́ть**) *сов перех* to complicate; ~**ся** (*impf* **усложня́ться**) *сов возв* to get more complicated

**услу́г|а** (-и) *ж* (*одолжение*) favour (*BRIT*), favor (*US*); (*обычно мн: облуживание*) service; **к Ва́шим** ~**м!** at your service!

**услы́ш|ать** (-у, -ишь) *сов от* **слы́шать**

**усма́трива|ть** (-ю) *несов от* **усмотре́ть**

**усмехн|у́ться** (-у́сь, -ёшься; *impf* **усмеха́ться**) *сов возв* to smile slightly

**усме́шк|а** (-и) *ж* slight smile; **зла́я** ~ sneer

**усмир|и́ть** (-ю́, -и́шь; *impf* ~**я́ть**) *сов перех* (*зверя*) to tame

**усмотре́ни|е** (-я) *ср* discretion

**усм|отре́ть** (-отрю́, -о́тришь; *impf* **усма́тривать**) *сов перех* (*счесть*): ~ **что-н в** +*prp* to see sth in

**усн|у́ть** (-у́, -ёшь) *сов* to fall asleep, go to sleep

**усоверше́нствовани|е** (-я) *ср* improvement

**усомн|и́ться** (-**ю́сь**, -**и́шься**) *сов возв*: ~ **в** +*prp* to doubt

**успева́емост|ь** (-**и**) *ж* performance (*in studies*)

**успе́|ть** (-**ю**; *impf* **успева́ть**) *сов* (*о работе*) to manage; (*прийти вовремя*) to be *или* make it in time

**успе́х** (-**а**) *м* success; (*обычно мн: в спорте, в учёбе*) achievement; **как Ва́ши ~и?** how are you getting on?

**успе́шный** *прил* successful

**успоко́|ить** (-**ю**, -**ишь**; *impf* **успока́ивать**) *сов перех* to calm (down); ~**ся** (*impf* **успока́иваться**) *сов возв* (*человек*) to calm down

**уста́в** (-**а**) *м* (*партийный*) rules *мн*; (*воинский*) regulations *мн*; (*фирмы*) statute

**уста|ва́ть** (-**ю́**, -**ёшь**) *несов от* **уста́ть**

**уста́в|ить** (-**лю**, -**ишь**; *impf* **уставля́ть**) *сов перех* (*занять*): ~ **что-н чем-н** to cover sth with sth; (*разг: устремить*): ~ **что-н в** +*acc* to fix sth on; ~**ся** (*impf* **уставля́ться**) *сов возв* (*разг*): ~**ся на/в** +*acc* to stare at

**уста́лост|ь** (-**и**) *ж* tiredness, fatigue

**уста́лый** *прил* tired

**у́стал|ь** (-**и**) *ж*: **без** *или* **не зна́я ~и** tirelessly

**устан|ови́ть** (-**овлю́**, -**о́вишь**; *impf* **устана́вливать**) *сов перех* to establish; (*сроки*) to set; (*прибор*) to install; ~**ся** (*impf* **устана́вливаться**) *сов возв* to be established

**устано́вк|а** (-**и**) *ж* installation

**устаре́|ть** (-**ю**) *сов от* **старе́ть** ♦ (*impf* **устарева́ть**) *неперех* (*оборудование*) to become

obsolete

**уста́|ть** (-**ну**, -**нешь**; *impf* **уства́ть**) *сов* to get tired

**у́стн|ый** *прил* (*экзамен*) oral; (*обещание, приказ*) verbal; ~**ая речь** spoken language

**усто́йчив|ый** *прил* stable; ~**ое (сло́во)сочета́ние** set phrase

**усто|я́ть** (-**ю́**, -**и́шь**) *сов* (*не упасть*) to remain standing; (*в борьбе итп*) to stand one's ground; (*перед соблазном*) to resist

**устра́ива|ть(ся)** (-**ю(сь)**) *несов от* **устро́ить(ся)**

**устран|и́ть** (-**ю́**, -**и́шь**; *impf* **устраня́ть**) *сов перех* to remove

**устрем|и́ть** (-**лю́**, -**и́шь**; *impf* **устремля́ть**) *сов перех* to direct; ~**ся** (*impf* **устремля́ться**) *сов возв*: ~**ся на** +*acc* (*толпа*) to charge at

**устремле́ни|е** (-**я**) *ср* aspiration

**у́стриц|а** (-**ы**) *ж* oyster

**устро́йтел|ь** (-**я**) *м* organizer

**устро́|ить** (-**ю**, -**ишь**; *impf* **устра́ивать**) *сов перех* to organize; (*подлеж: цена*) to suit; **э́то меня́ ~ит** that suits me; ~**ся** (*impf* **устра́иваться**) *сов возв* (*расположиться*) to settle down; (*прийти в порядок*) to work out; **устра́иваться** (~**ся** *pf*) **на рабо́ту** to get a job

**устро́йств|о** (-**а**) *ср* (*прибора*) construction; (*техническое*) device, mechanism

**усту́п** (-**а**) *м* foothold

**уст|упи́ть** (-**уплю́**, -**у́пишь**; *impf* **уступа́ть**) *сов перех*: ~ **что-н кому́-н** to give sth up for sb; (*победу*) to concede sth to sb ♦ *неперех*: ~ **кому́-н/чему́-н** (*силе, желанию*) to yield to sb/ sth; **уступа́ть** (~ *pf*) **в** +*prp* (*в силе,* *в уме*) to be inferior in

**уступ|ка** (**-ки**; *gen pl* **-ок**) ж
conciliation; (*скидка*) discount;
**пойти** (*pf*) **на ~ку** to compromise

**усть|е** (**-я**) *ср* (*реки*) mouth

**усугуб|и́ть** (**-лю́, -и́шь**; *impf*
**усугубля́ть**) *сов перех* to
aggravate

**ус|ы́** (**-о́в**) *мн* (*у человека*)
moustache *ед* (*BRIT*), mustache *ед*
(*US*); (*у животных*) whiskers *мн*

**усынов|и́ть** (**-лю́, -и́шь**; *impf*
**усыновля́ть**) *сов перех* to adopt
(*son*)

**усып|и́ть** (**-лю́, -и́шь**; *impf*
**усыпля́ть**) *сов перех*
(*больного*) to anaesthetize (*BRIT*),
anesthetize (*US*); (*ребёнка*) to lull
to sleep

**ут|ащи́ть** (**-ащу́, -а́щишь**; *impf*
**ута́скивать**) *сов перех* (*унести*)
to drag away *или* off

**утверди́тельный** *прил* (*также*
*линг*) affirmative

**утвер|ди́ть** (**-жу́, -ди́шь**; *impf*
**утвержда́ть**) *сов перех* (*закон*)
to pass; (*договор*) to ratify; (*план*)
to approve; (*порядок*) to establish;
**~ся** (*impf* **утвержда́ться**) *сов*
*возв* to be established

**утвержда́|ть** (**-ю**) *несов от*
**утверди́ть** ♦ *перех* (*настаивать*)
to maintain; **~ся** *несов от*
**утверди́ться**

**утвержде́ни|е** (**-я**) *ср* (*см глаг*)
passing; ratification; approval;
establishment; (*мысль*) statement

**ут|ёнок** (**-ёнка**; *nom pl* **-я́та**, *gen pl*
**-я́т**) *м* duckling

**утепл|и́ть** (**-ю́, -и́шь**; *impf*
**утепля́ть**) *сов перех* to insulate

**утёс** (**-а**) *м* cliff

**уте́чк|а** (**-и**) *ж* (*также перен*) leak;
(*кадров*) turnover; **~ мозго́в** brain
drain

**ут|е́чь** (*3sg* **-ечёт**, *pt* **-ёк, -екла́,**
**-екло́**; *impf* **утека́ть**) *сов* (*вода*)
to leak out

**уте́ш|ить** (**-у, -ишь**; *impf* **утеша́ть**)
*сов перех* to comfort, console

**ути́хн|уть** (**-у**; *impf* **утиха́ть**) *сов*
(*спор*) to calm down; (*звук*) to die
away; (*вьюга*) to die down

**у́т|ка** (**-ки**; *gen pl* **-ок**) *ж* duck

**уткн|у́ть** (**-у́, -ёшь**) *сов перех*
(*разг: лицо*) to bury; **~ся** *сов*
*возв* (*разг*): **~ся в** +*acc* (*в книгу*)
to bury one's nose in

**утол|и́ть** (**-ю́, -и́шь**; *impf*
**утоля́ть**) *сов перех* to satisfy;
(*жажду*) to quench

**утоми́тельный** *прил* tiring

**утом|и́ть** (**-лю́, -и́шь**; *impf*
**утомля́ть**) *сов перех* to tire; **~ся**
(*impf* **утомля́ться**) *сов возв* to
get tired

**утомле́ни|е** (**-я**) *ср* tiredness

**ут|ону́ть** (**-ону́, -о́нешь**) *сов от*
**тону́ть**

**утопа́|ть** (**-ю**) *несов* (*тонуть*) to
drown

**ут|опи́ть(ся)** (**-оплю́(сь),**
**-о́пишь(ся)**) *сов от* **топи́ть(ся)**

**уточн|и́ть** (**-ю́, -и́шь**; *impf*
**уточня́ть**) *сов перех* to clarify

**утра́т|а** (**-ы**) *ж* loss

**утра́|тить** (**-чу, -тишь**; *impf*
**утра́чивать**) *сов перех*
(*потерять*) to lose; **утра́чивать** (**~**
*pf*) **си́лу** (*документ*) to become
invalid

**у́тренний** *прил* morning;
(*событие*) this morning's

**у́тренник** (**-а**) *м* matinée; (*для*
*детей*) children's party

**у́тр|о** (**-á**; *nom pl* **-á**, *gen pl* **-**, *dat pl*
**-áм**) *ср* morning; **до́брое ~!, с**
**до́брым ~м!** good morning!; **на ~**
next morning; **под ~, к утру́** in the
early hours of the morning

**утро́б**|**а** (-**ы**) ж (*матери*) womb

**утро́**|**ить** (-**ю**, -**ишь**) *сов перех* to treble, triple; **~ся** *сов возв* to treble, triple

**у́тром** *нареч* in the morning

**утружда́**|**ть** (-**ю**) *несов перех*: **~ кого́-н чем-н** to trouble sb with sth; **~ся** *несов возв* to trouble o.s.

**утю́г** (-**а́**) *м* iron (*appliance*)

**утю́ж**|**ить** (-**у**, -**ишь**; *pf* **вы́утюжить** *или* **от~**) *несов перех* to iron

**уф** *межд*: **~!** phew!

**ух** *межд*: **~!** ooh!

**ух**|**а́** (-**и́**) ж fish broth

**уха́жива**|**ть** (-**ю**) *несов*: **~ за** +*instr* (*за больным*) to nurse (*за садом*) to tend (*за женщиной*) to court

**ухв**|**ати́ть** (-**ачу́**, -**а́тишь**; *impf* **ухва́тывать**) *сов перех* (*человека*: *за руку*) to get hold of; (*перен*: *идею, смысл*) to grasp; **~ся** (*impf* **ухва́тываться**) *сов возв*: **~ся за** +*acc* to grab hold of; (*за идею*) to jump at

**у́х**|**о** (-**а**; *nom pl* **у́ши**, *gen pl* **уше́й**) *ср* ear; (*у шапки*) flap

**ухо́д** (-**а**) *м* departure; (*из семьи*) desertion; (*со сцены*) exit; (*за больным, за ребёнком*) care; **~ в отста́вку** resignation; **~ на пе́нсию** retirement

**ух**|**оди́ть** (-**ожу́**, -**о́дишь**) *несов от* **уйти́**

**ухо́женный** *прил* (*ребёнок*) well-looked-after; (*сад*) well-kept

**уху́дш**|**ить** (-**у**, -**ишь**; *impf* **ухудша́ть**) *сов перех* to make worse; **~ся** (*impf* **ухудша́ться**) *сов возв* to deteriorate

**уцеле́**|**ть** (-**ю**) *сов* to survive

**уцене́нный** *прил* reduced

**уцен**|**и́ть** (-**ю́**, -**ишь**; *impf* **уце́нивать**) *сов перех* to reduce (the price of)

**уце́н**|**ка** (-**ки**; *gen pl* -**ок**) ж reduction

**уча́ств**|**овать** (-**ую**) *сов*: **~ в** +*prp* to take part in

**уча́сти**|**е** (-**я**) *ср* participation; (*сочувствие*) concern

**уча**|**сти́ть** (-**щу́**, -**сти́шь**; *impf* **учаща́ть**) *сов перех* to quicken; (*контакты*) to make more frequent; **~ся** (*impf* **учаща́ться**) *сов возв* to quicken; (*контакты*) to become more frequent

**участко́в**|**ый** *прил* local ♦ (-**ого**) *м* (*разг: также*: **~ инспе́ктор**) local policeman; (: *также*: **~ врач**) local GP *или* doctor

**уча́стник** (-**а**) *м* participant; (*экспедиции*) member

**уча́ст**|**ок** (-**ка**) *м* (*земли, кожи итп*) area; (*реки, фронта*) stretch; (*враче́бный*) catchment area; (*земельный*) plot; (*строительный*) site; (*работы*) field; **садо́вый ~** allotment

**у́част**|**ь** (-**и**) ж lot

**учаща́**|**ть(ся)** (-**ю**) *несов от* **участи́ть(ся)**

**уча́щ**|**ийся** (-**егося**) *м* (*школы*) pupil; (*училища*) student

**учёб**|**а** (-**ы**) ж studies *мн*

**уче́бник** (-**а**) *м* textbook

**уче́бн**|**ый** *прил* (*работа*) academic; (*фильм*) educational; (*бой*) mock; (*судно*) training; (*методы*) teaching; **~ая програ́мма** curriculum; **~ое заведе́ние** educational establishment; **~ год** academic year

**уче́ни**|**е** (-**я**) *ср* (*теория*) teachings *мн*; *см. также* **уче́ния**

**учени́к** (-**а́**) *м* (*школы*) pupil; (*училища*) student; (*мастера*) apprentice

**учени́ческий** *прил* (*тетради*)

school

**уче́ни|я (-й)** мн exercises мн

**учён|ый** прил academic; (труды) scholarly; (человек) learned, scholarly ♦ **(-ого)** м academic, scholar; (в области точных и естественных наук) scientist

**уч|е́сть (-ту́, -тёшь;** pt **-ёл, -ла́;** impf **учи́тывать)** сов перех to take into account; **~ти́те, что** ... bear in mind that ...

**учёт (-а)** м (факторов) consideration; (военный, медицинский) registration; (затрат) record; **брать (взять** pf**) на ~** to register; **вести́** (impf) **~** to keep a record

**учётн|ый** прил: **~ая ка́рточка** registration form

**учи́лищ|е (-а)** ср college

**учи́тел|ь (-я;** nom pl **-я́)** м teacher

**учи́тельск|ая (-ой)** ж staffroom

**учи́тыва|ть (-ю)** несов от **уче́сть**

**уч|и́ть (-у́, -ишь;** pf **вы́учить)** несов перех (урок, роль) to learn; (pf **на~** или **об~**): **~ кого́-н чему́-н**/ +infin to teach sb sth/to do; **~ся** несов возв (в школе, в училище) to study; (pf **вы́учиться** или **на~ся**): **~ся чему́-н**/ +infin to learn sth/to do

**учреди́тел|ь (-я)** м founder

**учреди́тельн|ый** прил: **~ое собра́ние** inaugural meeting

**учре|ди́ть (-жу́, -ди́шь;** impf **учрежда́ть)** сов перех (организацию) to set up; (контроль, порядок) to introduce

**учрежде́ни|е (-я)** ср (организации итп) setting up; (научное) establishment; (финансовое, общественное) institution

**учти́вый** прил courteous

**уша́н|ка (-ки;** gen pl **-ок)** ж cap with ear-flaps

**ушёл** etc сов см. **уйти́**

**у́ши** etc сущ см. **у́хо**

**уши́б (-а)** м bruise

**ушиб|и́ть (-у́, -ёшь;** pt **-, -ла;** impf **ушиба́ть)** сов перех to bang; **~ся** сов возв to bruise

**уш|и́ть (-ью́, -ьёшь;** impf **ушива́ть)** сов перех (одежду) to take in

**у́ш|ко (-ка;** nom pl **-ки,** gen pl **-ек)** ср уменьш от **у́хо**; (иголки) eye

**ушла́** etc сов см. **уйти́**

**ушн|о́й** прил ear; **~а́я боль** earache

**уще́л|ье (-ья;** gen pl **-ий)** ср gorge, ravine

**ущем|и́ть (-лю́, -и́шь;** impf **ущемля́ть)** сов перех (палец) to trap; (права) to limit

**ущемле́ни|е (-я)** ср (прав) limitation

**уще́рб (-а)** м (материальный) damage; (здоровью) detriment

**ущипн|у́ть (-у́, -ёшь)** сов перех to nip, pinch

**ую́т (-а)** м comfort, cosiness

**ую́тно** нареч (расположиться) comfortably ♦ как сказ: **здесь ~** it's cosy here; **мне здесь ~** I feel comfortable here

**ую́тный** прил cosy

**уязви́мый** прил vulnerable

**уязв|и́ть (-лю́, -и́шь)** сов перех to wound, hurt

**уясн|и́ть (-ю́, -и́шь;** impf **уясня́ть)** сов перех (значение) to comprehend

# Ф, ф

**фа́брик|а (-и)** ж factory; (*ткацкая, бумажная*) mill
**фабри́чный** прил factory
**фа́з|а (-ы)** ж phase
**фаза́н (-а)** м pheasant
**файл (-а)** м (*КОМП*) file
**фа́кел (-а)** м torch
**факс (-а)** м fax
**факт (-а)** м fact
**факти́чески** нареч actually, in fact
**факти́ческий** прил factual
**фа́ктор (-а)** м factor
**факту́р|а (-ы)** ж texture; (*КОММ*) invoice
**факультати́вный** прил optional
**факульте́т (-а)** м faculty
**фальши́вый** прил false; (*деньги*) counterfeit; (*пение*) out of tune
**фами́ли|я (-и)** ж surname; **де́вичья ~** maiden name
**фамилья́рный** прил over(ly)-familiar
**фан (-а)** м fan
**фана́тик (-а)** м fanatic
**фанати́чный** прил fanatical
**фане́р|а (-ы)** ж plywood; (*для облицовки*) veneer
**фантази́р|овать (-ую)** несов (*мечтать*) to dream; (*выдумывать*) to make up stories
**фанта́зи|я (-и)** ж fantasy; (*выдумка*) fib
**фанта́ст (-а)** м writer of fantasy; (*научный*) science-fiction writer
**фанта́стик|а (-и)** ж, собир (*ЛИТЕРАТУРА*) fantasy; **нау́чная ~** science fiction
**фантасти́ческий** прил fantastic
**фа́р|а (-ы)** ж (*АВТ, АВИА*) light

**фармаце́вт (-а)** м chemist, pharmacist
**фа́ртук (-а)** м apron
**фарфо́р (-а)** м, собир porcelain, bone china
**фарш (-а)** м stuffing, forcemeat; (*мясной*) mince
**фарши́р|ова́ть (-у́ю**; pf **за~) несов перех** to stuff
**фаса́д (-а)** м (*передняя сторона*) facade, front; **за́дний ~** back
**фас|ова́ть (-у́ю**; pf **рас~) несов перех** to prepack
**фасо́л|ь (-и)** ж (*растение*) bean plant ♦ собир (*семена*) beans мн
**фасо́н (-а)** м style
**фат|а́ (-ы́)** ж veil
**фаши́зм (-а)** м fascism
**фаши́ст (-а)** м fascist
**ФБР** ср сокр (= Федера́льное бюро́ рассле́дований (США)) FBI
**февра́л|ь (-я́)** м February

---

**23 Февраля́: День защи́тника оте́чества** - This is an official celebration of the Russian army, though various sections of the armed forces have their own special holidays. Men of all ages and walks of life receive gifts, mainly from women.

---

**федера́льный** прил federal
**федерати́вный** прил federal
**федера́ци|я (-и)** ж federation
**фейерве́рк (-а)** м firework
**фе́льдшер (-а)** м (*в поликлинике*) ≈ practice nurse; **~ ско́рой по́мощи** ≈ paramedic
**фельето́н (-а)** м satirical article
**фемини́зм (-а)** м feminism
**фемини́ст|ка (-ки**; gen pl **-ок)** ж feminist
**фен (-а)** м hairdryer
**феода́льный** прил feudal

**ферз|ь** (**-я́**) м (ШАХМАТЫ) queen
**фе́рм|а** (**-ы**) ж farm
**фе́рмер** (**-а**) м farmer
**фе́рмерск|ий** прил: ~ое
хозя́йство farm
**фестива́л|ь** (**-я**) м festival
**фетр** (**-а**) м felt
**фехтова́ни|е** (**-я**) ср (СПОРТ)
fencing
**фе́|я** (**-и**) ж fairy
**фиа́л|ка** (**-ки**; gen pl **-ок**) ж violet
**фиа́ско** ср нескл fiasco
**фи́г|а** (**-и**) ж (БОТ) fig; (разг) fig
(gesture of refusal); **иди́ на́ фиг!** get
lost!; **ни фига́** nothing at all
**фигу́р|а** (**-ы**) ж figure; (ШАХМАТЫ)
(chess)piece
**фигури́р|овать** (**-ую**) несов to
be present; (имя, тема) to feature
**фигури́ст** (**-а**) м figure skater
**фигу́рн|ый** прил (резьба)
figured; **~ое ката́ние** figure
skating; **~ые ско́бки** curly или
brace brackets
**фи́зик** (**-а**) м physicist
**фи́зик|а** (**-и**) ж physics
**физиологи́ческий** прил
physiological
**физиотерапи́|я** (**-и**) ж
physiotherapy
**физи́ческ|ий** прил physical;
(труд) manual; **~ая культу́ра**
physical education
**физкульту́р|а** (**-ы**) ж сокр (=
физи́ческая культу́ра) PE
**фикс** м: иде́я ~ idée fixe
**фикси́р|овать** (**-ую**; pf **за~**)
несов перех to fix; (отмечать) to
record
**фикти́вный** прил fictitious; ~
**брак** (ЮР) marriage of
convenience
**фи́кус** (**-а**) м ficus
**филармо́ни|я** (**-и**) ж (зал)
concert hall; (организация)
philharmonic society
**филатели́ст** (**-а**) м philatelist
**филе́** ср нескл fillet
**фи́лин** (**-а**) м eagle owl
**фило́лог** (**-а**) м specialist in
language and literature
**филоло́ги|я** (**-и**) ж language and
literature
**филологи́ческий** прил
philological; ~ **факульте́т**
department of language and
literature
**фило́соф** (**-а**) м philosopher
**филосо́фи|я** (**-и**) ж philosophy
**фильм** (**-а**) м film
**фильтр** (**-а**) м filter
**фильтр|ова́ть** (**-у́ю**; pf **про~**)
несов перех to filter
**фина́л** (**-а**) м finale; (СПОРТ) final
**фина́льный** прил final
**финанси́р|овать** (**-ую**) несов
перех to finance
**финанси́ст** (**-а**) м financier;
(специалист) specialist in financial
matters
**фина́нсовый** прил financial; (год)
fiscal; (отдел, инспектор) finance
**фина́нс|ы** (**-ов**) мн finances мн;
**Министе́рство ~ов** ≈ the Treasury
(BRIT), ≈ the Treasury Department
или Department of the Treasury
(US)
**фи́ник** (**-а**) м (плод) date
**фи́ниш** (**-а**) м (СПОРТ) finish
**финиши́р|овать** (**-ую**) (не)сов to
finish
**Финля́нди|я** (**-и**) ж Finland
**финн** (**-а**) м Finn
**фи́нский** прил Finnish; ~ **язы́к**
Finnish; ~ **зали́в** Gulf of Finland
**Ф.И.О.** сокр (= фами́лия, и́мя,
о́тчество) surname, first name,
patronymic
**фиоле́товый** прил purple
**фи́рм|а** (**-ы**) ж firm

**фи́рменный** *прил* (*магазин*) chain; (*разг: товар*) quality; ~ **знак** brand name

**фити́л**|**ь** (**-я́**) *м* wick; (*бомбы*) fuse

**ФИ́ФА** *ж сокр* (= Междунаро́дная федера́ция футбо́ла) FIFA

**фи́ш**|**ка** (**-ки**; *gen pl* **-ек**) *ж* counter, chip

**флаг** (**-а**) *м* flag

**флако́н** (**-а**) *м* bottle

**фланг** (**-а**) *м* flank

**флане́л**|**ь** (**-и**) *ж* flannel

**флейт**|**а** (**-ы**) *ж* flute

**флейти́ст** (**-а**) *м* flautist

**фли́гел**|**ь** (**-я**) *м* (*АРХИТ*) wing

**флома́стер** (**-а**) *м* felt-tip (pen)

**флот** (**-а**) *м* (*ВОЕН*) navy; (*МОР*) fleet; **возду́шный** ~ air force

**флюс** (**-а**) *м* (dental) abscess, gumboil

**фля́г**|**а** (**-и**) *ж* (*бутылка*) flask; (*канистра*) churn

**фойе́** *ср нескл* foyer

**фокстерье́р** (**-а**) *м* fox terrier

**фо́кус** (**-а**) *м* trick; (*ТЕХ, перен*) focus

**фо́кусник** (**-а**) *м* conjurer

**фольг**|**а́** (**-и́**) *ж* foil

**фолькло́р** (**-а**) *м* folklore

**фон** (**-а**) *м* background

**фона́р**|**ь** (**-я́**) *м* (*уличный*) lamp; (*карманный*) torch

**фонд** (**-а**) *м* (*организация*) foundation; (*деньги*) fund; (*жилищный, земельный*) resources *мн*; **фо́нды** (*ценные бумаги*) stocks

**фо́ндов**|**ый** *прил*: ~**ая би́ржа** stock exchange

**фоне́тик**|**а** (**-и**) *ж* phonetics

**фоноте́к**|**а** (**-и**) *ж* record and tape collection

**фонта́н** (**-а**) *м* fountain

**форе́л**|**ь** (**-и**) *ж* trout

**фо́рм**|**а** (**-ы**) *ж* form; (*одежда*) uniform; (*ТЕХ*) mould (*BRIT*), mold (*US*); (*КУЛИН*) (cake) tin (*BRIT*) *или* pan (*US*)

**форма́льност**|**ь** (**-и**) *ж* formality

**форма́льный** *прил* formal; (*подход*) bureaucratic

**форма́т** (**-а**) *м* format

**форма́ци**|**я** (**-и**) *ж* (*общественная*) system

**фо́рменн**|**ый** *прил*: ~ **бланк** standard form; ~**ая оде́жда** uniform

**формирова́ни**|**е** (**-я**) *ср* formation; **вое́нное** ~ military unit

**формир**|**ова́ть** (**-у́ю**; *pf* **с~**) *несов перех* to form; ~**ся** (*pf* **с~ся**) *несов возв* to form

**фо́рмул**|**а** (**-ы**) *ж* formula

**формули́р**|**овать** (**-ую**; *pf* **с~**) *несов перех* to formulate

**формулиро́в**|**ка** (**-ки**; *gen pl* **-ок**) *ж* (*определение*) definition

**фортепья́но** *ср нескл* (grand) piano

**фо́рточ**|**ка** (**-ки**; *gen pl* **-ек**) *ж* hinged, upper pane in window for ventilation

**фо́рум** (**-а**) *м* forum

**фо́сфор** (**-а**) *м* phosphorous

**фотоаппара́т** (**-а**) *м* camera

**фото́граф** (**-а**) *м* photographer

**фотографи́р**|**овать** (**-ую**; *pf* **с~**) *несов перех* to photograph; ~**ся** (*pf* **с~ся**) *несов возв* to have one's photo(graph) taken

**фотогра́фи**|**я** (**-и**) *ж* photography; (*снимок*) photograph

**фотока́рточ**|**ка** (**-ки**; *gen pl* **-ек**) *ж* photo

**фрагме́нт** (**-а**) *м* (*отрывок*) excerpt; (*обломок*) fragment

**фра́з**|**а** (**-ы**) *ж* phrase

**фрак** (**-а**) *м* tail coat, tails *мн*

**фра́кци**|**я** (**-и**) *ж* faction

**Фра́нци|я (-и)** ж France
**францу́жен|ка (-ки)** ж Frenchwoman
**францу́з (-а)** м Frenchman
**францу́зский** прил French; **~ язы́к** French
**фрахт (-а)** м freight
**фрахт|ова́ть (-у́ю;** pf **за~)** несов перех to charter
**фре́с|ка (-ки;** gen pl **-ок)** ж fresco
**фрикаде́л|ька (-ьки;** gen pl **-ек)** ж meatball
**фронт (-а;** nom pl **-ы́)** м front
**фронтови́к (-а́)** м front line soldier; (ветеран) war veteran
**фрукт (-а)** м (БОТ) fruit
**фрукто́вый** прил fruit
**ФСБ** ж нескл сокр (= Федера́льная слу́жба безопа́сности) Department of State Security
**ФСК** ж нескл сокр (= Федера́льная слу́жба контрразве́дки) counterespionage intelligence service
**фтор (-а)** м fluorin(e)
**фу** межд: ~! ugh!
**фуже́р (-а)** м wineglass; (для шампа́нского) flute
**фунда́мент (-а)** м (СТРОИТ) foundations мн, base; (перен: семьи, науки) foundation, basis
**фундамента́льный** прил (здание) sound, solid; (перен: зна́ния) profound
**фунду́к (-а́)** м (плод) hazelnut
**функционе́р (-а)** м official
**функциони́р|овать (-ую)** несов to function
**фу́нкци|я (-и)** ж function
**фунт (-а)** м pound
**фура́ж (-а́)** м fodder
**фура́ж|ка (-ки;** gen pl **-ек)** ж cap; (ВОЕН) forage cap
**фурго́н (-а)** м (АВТ) van; (повозка) (covered) wagon
**фуро́р (-а)** м furore
**фуру́нкул (-а)** м boil
**футбо́л (-а)** м football (BRIT), soccer
**футболи́ст (-а)** м football (BRIT) или soccer player
**футбо́л|ка (-ки;** gen pl **-ок)** ж T-shirt, tee shirt
**футбо́льный** прил football (BRIT), soccer; ~ **мяч** football
**футля́р (-а)** м case
**фы́рка|ть (-ю)** несов (животное) to snort
**фы́ркн|уть (-у)** сов (животное) to give a snort
**фюзеля́ж (-а)** м (АВИА) fuselage

## X, x

**ха́кер (-а)** м (КОМП) hacker
**хала́т (-а)** м (домашний) dressing gown; (врача) gown
**хала́тный** прил negligent
**хам (-а)** м (разг) lout
**ха́мств|о (-а)** ср rudeness
**ха́нжеств|о (-а)** ср prudishness
**ха́ос (-а)** м chaos
**хаоти́чный** прил chaotic
**хара́ктер (-а)** м character, nature; (человека) personality
**характериз|ова́ть (-у́ю)** несов перех to be typical of; (pf **о~**; человека, ситуацию) to characterize
**характери́стик|а (-и)** ж (документ) (character) reference; (описание) description
**характе́рный** прил (свойственный): ~ **(для** +gen) characteristic (of); (случай) typical
**х/б** сокр = **хлопчатобума́жный**
**хвале́бный** прил complimentary

**хвал|и́ть** (-ю́, -ишь; pf **по~**) несов перех to praise

**хва́ста|ться** (-юсь; pf **по~**) несов возв: ~ (+instr) to boast (about)

**хвастли́вый** прил boastful

**хвасту́н** (-а́) м (разг) show-off

**хвата́|ть** (-ю; pf **схвати́ть**) несов перех to grab (hold of), snatch; (престу́пника) to arrest; ♦ (pf **хвати́ть**) безл: ~ +gen (де́нег, вре́мени) to have enough; **мне ~ет де́нег на еду́** I've got enough to buy food; **э́того ещё не ~ло!** (разг) I'm not having this!; **не ~ет то́лько, что́бы он отказа́лся** (разг) now all we need is for him to refuse; **~ся** (pf **схвати́ться**) несов возв: ~ся за +acc (за ру́чку, за ору́жие) to grab

**хва|ти́ть** (-чу́, -тишь) сов от **хвата́ть** ♦ безл (разг): **хва́тит!** that's enough!; **с меня́ хва́тит!** I've had enough!

**хва́т|ка** (-ки; gen pl **-ок**) ж grip; **делова́я ~** business acumen

**хво́йн|ый** прил coniferous; **~ое де́рево** conifer

**хво́рост** (-а) м собир firewood

**хвост** (-а́) м tail; (по́езда) tail end; (причёска) ponytail

**хво́стик** (-а) м (мы́ши, реди́ски) tail; (причёска) pigtail

**хво́|я** (-и) ж собир needles мн (of conifer)

**хек** (-а) м whiting

**хе́рес** (-а) м sherry

**хи́жин|а** (-ы) ж hut

**хи́лый** прил sickly

**хи́мик** (-а) м chemist

**химика́т** (-а) м chemical

**химиотерапи́|я** (-и) ж chemotherapy

**хими́ческ|ий** прил chemical; (факульте́т, кабине́т) chemistry; **~ая чи́стка** (проце́сс) dry-cleaning; (пункт приёма) dry-cleaner's

**хи́ми|я** (-и) ж chemistry

**химчи́ст|ка** (-ки; gen pl **-ок**) ж сокр = **хими́ческая чи́стка**

**хи́ппи** м нескл hippie

**хиру́рг** (-а) м surgeon

**хирурги́ческий** прил surgical; (кли́ника) surgery

**хирурги́|я** (-и) ж surgery

**хитре́ц** (-а́) м cunning devil

**хитр|и́ть** (-ю́, -и́шь; pf **с~**) несов to act slyly

**хи́трост|ь** (-и) ж cunning

**хи́трый** прил cunning

**хихи́ка|ть** (-ю) несов (разг) to giggle

**хище́ни|е** (-я) ср misappropriation

**хи́щник** (-а) м predator

**хи́щн|ый** прил predatory; **~ая пти́ца** bird of prey

**хладнокро́вный** прил composed; (уби́йство) cold-blooded

**хлам** (-а) м собир junk

**хлеб** (-а) м bread; (зерно́) grain

**хле́бниц|а** (-ы) ж bread basket; (для хране́ния) breadbin (BRIT), breadbox (US)

**хлебн|у́ть** (-у́, -ёшь) сов перех (разг: чай итп) to take a gulp of

**хлебозаво́д** (-а) м bakery

**хлев** (-а; nom pl **-а́**) м cowshed

**хл|еста́ть** (-ещу́, -е́щешь) несов перех (ремнём) to whip; (по щека́м) to slap ♦ непере́х (вода́, кровь) to gush

**хлестн|у́ть** (-у́, -ёшь) сов перех to whip; (по щеке́) to slap

**хло́па|ть** (-ю) несов перех (ладо́нью) to slap ♦ непере́х: ~ +instr (две́рью, кры́шкой) to slam; ~ (impf) +dat (арти́сту) to clap

**хло́пковый** прил cotton

**хло́пн|уть** (-у) сов перех (по спине́) to slap ♦ непере́х (в

ладони) to clap; (дверь) to slam
shut

**хло́п|ок** (-ка) м cotton

**хлоп|о́к** (-ка́) м (удар в ладоши)
clap

**хлоп|ота́ть** (-очу́, -о́чешь)
несов (по дому) to busy o.s.; ~
(impf) о +prp (о разрешении) to
request

**хлопотли́вый** прил (человек)
busy; (работа) troublesome

**хло́п|оты** (-о́т; dat pl -отам) мн
(по дому итп) chores мн; (прося
чего-н) efforts мн

**хлопу́ш|ка** (-ки; gen pl -ек) ж
(игрушка) (Christmas) cracker

**хлопчатобума́жный** прил
cotton

**хло́пь|я** (-ев) мн (снега, мыла)
flakes мн; **кукуру́зные ~** cornflakes

**хлор** (-а) м chlorine

**хло́рк|а** (-и) ж (разг) bleaching
powder

**хло́рн|ый** прил: **~ая и́звесть**
bleaching powder

**хлы́н|уть** (3sg -ет) сов to flood

**хмеле́|ть** (-ю; pf за~) несов to be
drunk

**хму́р|ить** (-ю, -ишь; pf на~)
несов перех (лоб, брови) to
furrow; **~ся** (pf на~ся) несов возв
to frown

**хму́рый** прил gloomy

**хны́ка|ть** (-ю) несов (разг:
плакать) to whimper

**хо́бби** ср нескл hobby

**хо́бот** (-а) м (слона) trunk

**ход** (-а; part gen -у, loc sg -у́) м
(машины, поршня) movement;
(событий, дела) course; (часов,
двигателя) working; (КАРТЫ) go;
(манёвр, также ШАХМАТЫ) move;
(возможность) chance; (вход)
entrance; **в хо́де** +gen in the course
of; **~ мы́слей** train of thought;

идти́ (пойти́ pf) в ~ to come into
use; **быть** (impf) **в (большо́м)** ~у́
to be (very) popular; **на ~у́** (есть,
разгова́ривать) on the move;
(пошути́ть) in passing; **с хо́ду**
straight off; **дава́ть (дать** pf) ~
де́лу to set things in motion

**хода́тайств|о** (-а) ср petition

**хода́тайств|овать** (-ую; pf по~)
несов: ~ о чём-н/за кого́-н to
petition for sth/on sb's behalf

**хо|ди́ть** (-жу́, -дишь) несов to
walk; (по магазинам, в гости) to
go (on foot); (поезд, автобус итп)
to go; (слухи) to go round; (часы)
to work; (носить): ~ **в** +prp (в
пальто́, в сапога́х итп) to wear; ~
(impf) +instr (тузом итп) to play;
(конём, пешкой итп) to move

**ходьб|а́** (-ы́) ж walking

**хожу́** несов см. **ходи́ть**

**хоздогово́р** (-а) м сокр (=
хозя́йственный догово́р)
business deal (between companies)

**хозрасчёт** (-а) м (=
хозя́йственный расчёт) system of
management based on self-financing
and self-governing principles

**хозрасчётн|ый** прил: **~ое
предприя́тие** self-financing, self-
governing enterprise

**хозя́|ин** (-ина; nom pl -ева, gen pl
-ев) м (владелец) owner;
(сдающий жильё) landlord;
(принимающий гостей) host;
(перен: распорядитель) master

**хозя́|йка** (-йки; gen pl -ек) ж
(владелица) owner; (сдающая
жильё) landlady; (принимающая
гостей) hostess; (в доме)
housewife

**хозя́йнича|ть** (-ю) несов (в
доме, на кухне) to be in charge;
(командовать) to be bossy

**хозя́йственн|ый** прил

(*деятельность*) economic; (*постройка, инвентарь*) domestic; (*человек*) thrifty; **~ые товáры** hardware; **~ магазúн** hardware shop

**хозя́йств|о** (-а) *ср* (*ЭКОН*) economy; (*фермерское*) enterprise; (*предметы быта*) household goods *мн*; (**домáшнее**) **~** housekeeping

**хозя́йств|овать** (-ую) *несов*: **~ на предприя́тии** to manage an enterprise

**хоккеúст** (-а) *м* hockey player

**хокке́|й** (-я) *м* hockey

**холе́р|а** (-ы) *ж* cholera

**холл** (-а) *м* (*театра, гостиницы*) lobby; (*в квартире, в доме*) hall

**холм** (-á) *м* hill

**холмúстый** *прил* hilly

**хóлод** (-а; *nom pl* -á) *м* cold; (*погода*) cold weather *ед*

**холодá|ть** (*3sg* -ет; *pf* по~) *несов безл* to turn cold

**холоде́|ть** (-ю; *pf* по~) *несов* to get cold; (*от страха*) to go cold

**холодúльник** (-а) *м* (*домашний*) fridge; (*промышленный*) refrigerator

**хóлодно** *нареч* coldly ♦ *как сказ* it's cold; **мне/ей ~** I'm/she's cold

**холóдный** *прил* cold

**холостóй** *прил* (*мужчина*) single, unmarried; (*выстрел, патрон*) blank

**холостя́к** (-á) *м* bachelor

**холст** (-á) *м* canvas

**хомя́к** (-á) *м* hamster

**хор** (-а) *м* choir; (*насмешек*) chorus

**Хорвáти|я** (-и) *ж* Croatia

**хореóграф** (-а) *м* choreographer

**хореогрáфи|я** (-и) *ж* choreography

**хóром** *нареч* in unison

**хор|онúть** (-оню́, -óнишь; *pf* по~) *несов перех* to bury

**хорóшенький** *прил* (*лицо*) cute

**хорóшенько** *нареч* (*разг*) properly

**хороше́|ть** (-ю; *pf* по~) *несов* to become more attractive

**хорóш|ий** *прил* good; **он ~ (собóю)** he's good-looking; **всегó ~его!** all the best!

**хорошó** *нареч* well ♦ *как сказ* it's good; **мне ~** I feel good ♦ *част, вводн сл* okay, all right ♦ *ср нескл* (*ПРОСВЕЩ*) ≈ good (*school mark*); **мне здесь ~** I like it here; **ну, ~!** (*разг: угроза*) right then!; **~ бы поéсть/поспáть** (*разг*) I wouldn't mind a bite to eat/getting some sleep

**хо|тéть** (*см. Table 14*) *несов перех*: **~ +infin** to want to do; **как ~тúте** (*как вам угодно*) as you wish; (*а всё-таки*) no matter what you say; **хóчешь не хóчешь** whether you like it or not; **~** (*impf*) **есть/пить** to be hungry/thirsty; **~ся** *несов безл*: **мне хóчется плáкать/есть** I feel like crying/something to eat

---

KEYWORD

---

**хоть** *союз* 1 (*несмотря на то, что*) (al)though; **хоть я и обúжен, я помогу́ тебé** although I am hurt, I will help you

2 (*до такой степени, что*) even if; **не соглашáется, хоть до утрá просú** he won't agree, even if you ask all night; **хоть убéй, не могу́ пойтú на э́то** I couldn't do that to save my life; **хоть..., хоть...** either..., or...; **езжáй хоть сегóдня, хоть чéрез мéсяц** go either today, or in a month's time ♦ *част* 1 (*служит для усиления*)

at least; **подвези́ его́ хоть до
ста́нции** take him to the station at
least; **пойми́ хоть ты** you of all
people should understand
**2** (*во фра́зах*): **хоть бы** at least;
**хоть бы ты ему́ позвони́л** you
could at least phone him!; **хоть бы
зако́нчить сего́дня!** if only we
could get finished today!; **хоть кто**
anyone; **хоть како́й** any; **ему́
хоть бы что** it doesn't bother him;
**хоть куда́!** (*разг*) excellent!; **хоть
бы и так!** so what!

**хотя́** *союз* although; ~ **и** even
though; ~ **бы** at least
**хо́хот** (**-а**) *м* loud laughter
**хох|ота́ть** (**-очу́, -о́чешь**) *несов*
to guffaw; ~ (*impf*) (**над** +*instr*) to
laugh (at)
**хочу́** *etc несов см.* **хоте́ть**
**хра́брост|ь** (**-и**) *ж* courage,
bravery
**хра́брый** *прил* courageous, brave
**храм** (**-а**) *м* (*РЕЛ*) temple
**хране́ни|е** (**-я**) *ср* (*де́нег*)
keeping; ~ **ору́жия** possession of
firearms; **ка́мера ~я** (*на вокза́ле*)
left-luggage office (*BRIT*) *или*
checkroom (*US*)
**храни́лищ|е** (**-а**) *ср* store
**храни́тел|ь** (**-я**) *м* keeper
**хран|и́ть** (**-ю́, -и́шь**) *несов
перех* to keep; (*досто́инство*) to
protect; (*тради́ции*) to preserve;
**~ся** *несов возв* to be kept
**храп** (**-а**) *м* (*во сне*) snoring
**храп|е́ть** (**-лю́, -и́шь**) *несов* to
snore
**хреб|е́т** (**-та́**) *м* (*АНАТ*) spine; (*ГЕО*)
ridge; **го́рный ~** mountain range
**хрен** (**-а**) *м* horseradish
**хризанте́м|а** (**-ы**) *ж*
chrysanthemum
**хрип** (**-а**) *м* wheezing

**хрип|е́ть** (**-лю́, -и́шь**) *несов* to
wheeze
**хри́плый** *прил* (*го́лос*) hoarse
**хри́пн|уть** (**-у**) *pf* **о~**) *несов* to
become *или* grow hoarse
**христиа|ни́н** (**-ни́на**; *nom pl*
**-а́не**, *gen pl* **-а́н**) *м* Christian
**христиа́нский** *прил* Christian
**христиа́нств|о** (**-а**) *ср* Christianity
**Христ|о́с** (**-а́**) *м* Christ
**хром** (**-а**) *м* (*ХИМ*) chrome
**хрома́|ть** (**-ю**) *несов* to limp
**хромо́й** *прил* lame
**хромосо́м|а** (**-ы**) *ж* chromosome
**хро́ник|а** (**-и**) *ж* chronicle; (*в
газе́ты*) news items
**хрони́ческий** *прил* chronic
**хронологи́ческий** *прил*
chronological
**хру́пкий** *прил* fragile; (*пече́нье,
ко́сти*) brittle; (*перен: фигу́ра*)
delicate; (*: здоро́вье, органи́зм*)
frail
**хруст** (**-а**) *м* crunch
**хруста́лик** (**-а**) *м* (*АНАТ*) lens
**хруста́л|ь** (**-я́**) *м*, *собир* crystal
**хруста́льный** *прил* crystal
**хру|сте́ть** (**-щу́, -сти́шь**) *несов*
to crunch
**хрустя́щий** *прил* crunchy, crisp
**хрю́ка|ть** (**-ю**) *несов* to grunt
**худе́|ть** (**-ю**) *несов* to grow thin;
(*быть на дие́те*) to slim
**худо́жественн|ый** *прил* artistic;
(*шко́ла, вы́ставка*) art; **~ая
литерату́ра** fiction; **~ая
самоде́ятельность** amateur
performing arts; ~ **сало́н** (*вы́ставка*)
art exhibition; (*магази́н*) art gallery
and craft shop; **~ фильм** feature
film
**худо́жник** (**-а**) *м* artist
**худо́й** *прил* thin
**ху́дший** *превос прил* the worst
**ху́же** *сравн прил*, *нареч* worse

**хулига́н** (**-а**) *м* hooligan

**хулига́н|ить** (**-ю, -ишь**; *pf* **на~**) *несов* to act like a hooligan

**хулига́нств|о** (**-а**) *ср* hooliganism

**ху́тор** (**-а**; *nom pl* **-á**) *м* (*фе́рма*) croft; (*село́*) village

# Ц, ц

**ца́п|ля** (**-ли**; *gen pl* **-ель**) *ж* heron

**цара́па|ть** (**-ю**; *pf* **о~**) *несов перех* (*ру́ку*) to scratch; **~ся** (*pf* **о~ся**) *несов возв* to scratch

**цара́пин|а** (**-ы**) *ж* scratch

**цари́ц|а** (**-ы**) *ж* tsarina (*wife of tsar*)

**ца́рский** *прил* tsar's, royal; (*режи́м, прави́тельство*) tsarist

**ца́рств|о** (**-а**) *ср* reign

**ца́рств|овать** (**-ую**) *несов* to reign

**цар|ь** (**-я́**) *м* tsar

**цве|сти́** (**-ту́, -тёшь**) *несов* (*БОТ*) to blossom, flower

**цвет** (**-а**; *nom pl* **-á**) *м* (*окра́ска*) colour (*BRIT*), color (*US*); (*prep sg* **-ý**; *БОТ*) blossom

**цветно́й** *прил* (*каранда́ш*) coloured (*BRIT*), colored (*US*); (*фо́то, фильм*) colour (*BRIT*), color (*US*)

**цвет|о́к** (**-ка́**; *nom pl* **-ы́**) *м* flower (*bloom*); (*ко́мнатный*) plant

**цвето́чный** *прил* flower

**цвету́щий** *прил* blooming

**це|ди́ть** (**-жу́, -дишь**; *pf* **про~**) *несов перех* (*жи́дкость*) to strain; (*перен: слова́*) to force out

**це́др|а** (**-ы**) *ж* (dried) peel *ед*

**целе́бный** *прил* medicinal; (*во́здух*) healthy

**целево́й** *прил* (*финанси́рование*) targeted

**целенапра́вленный** *прил* single-minded; (*поли́тика*) consistent

**целесообра́зный** *прил* expedient

**целеустремлённый** *прил* purposeful

**целико́м** *нареч* (*без ограниче́ний*) wholly, entirely; (*свари́ть*) whole

**целин|а́** (**-ы́**) *ж* virgin territory

**це́л|иться** (**-юсь, -ишься**; *pf* **на~**) *несов возв*: **~ в** +*acc* to (take) aim at

**целлофа́н** (**-а**) *м* cellophane ®

**цел|ова́ть** (**-у́ю**; *pf* **по~**) *несов перех* to kiss; **~ся** (*pf* **по~ся**) *несов возв* to kiss (each other)

**це́л|ое** (**-ого**) *ср* whole

**це́л|ый** *прил* whole, entire; (*неповреждённый*) intact; **в ~ом** (*по́лностью*) as a whole; (*в о́бщем*) on the whole

**цел|ь** (**-и**) *ж* (*при стрельбе́*) target; (*перен*) aim, goal; **с це́лью** +*infin* with the object *или* aim of doing; **с це́лью** +*gen* for; **в це́лях** +*gen* for the purpose of

**це́льный** *прил* (*кусо́к*) solid; (*хара́ктер*) complete

**цеме́нт** (**-а**) *м* cement

**цементи́р|овать** (**-ую**; *pf* **за~**) *несов перех* to cement

**цен|а́** (**-ы́**; *acc sg* **-у**, *dat sg* **-е́**, *nom pl* **-ы**) *ж* price; (*перен: челове́ка*) value; **~о́ю** +*gen* at the expense of

**цензу́р|а** (**-ы**) *ж* censorship

**цен|и́ть** (**-ю́, -ишь**) *несов перех* (*вещь*) to value; (*по́мощь*) to appreciate

**це́нник** (**-а**) *м* (*би́рка*) price tag

**це́нност|ь** (**-и**) *ж* value; **~и** valuables; **материа́льные ~и** commodities

**це́нный** *прил* valuable; (*письмо́*) registered; **~ые бума́ги** securities

**це́нтнер** (**-а**) *м* centner (*100kg*)

**центр** (-а) м centre (*BRIT*), center (*US*); **в це́нтре внима́ния** in the limelight; **торго́вый ~** shopping centre (*BRIT*) *или* mall (*US*)
**централизова́ть** (-у́ю) (*не)сов перех* to centralize
**центра́льный** *прил* central

---

**центра́льное отопле́ние** - central heating. The vast majority of Russians live in flats for which hot water and central heating are provided by huge communal boiler systems. Each city borough has a boiler system of its own. These systems distribute hot water for domestic use all year round and radiators are heated during the cold months. The heating is controlled centrally and individual home owners do not have any say over it. See also note at **отопи́тельный сезо́н**.

---

**Центроба́нк** м *сокр* = Центра́льный банк (Росси́и)
**центрово́й** *прил*: ~ **напада́ющий** centre (*BRIT*) *или* center (*US*) forward ♦ (-**о́го**) м (*в баскетбо́ле*) centre (*BRIT*), center (*US*); (*в футбо́ле*) midfielder
**цепля́ться** (-юсь) *несов возв*: ~ **за** +*acc* to cling *или* hang on to
**цепно́й** *прил* chain
**цепо́чка** (-ки; *gen pl* -ек) ж (*тонкая цепь*) chain; (*машин, людей*) line
**цеп|ь** (-и; *loc sg* -и́) ж chain; (*ЭЛЕК*) circuit; **го́рная ~** mountain range
**церемо́ни|я** (-и) ж ceremony
**церко́вный** *прил* church
**це́рк|овь** (-ви; *instr sg* -овью, *nom pl* -ви, *gen pl* -ве́й) ж church
**цех** (-а; *loc sg* -у́, *nom pl* -а́) м (work)shop (*in factory*)

**цивилиза́ци|я** (-и) ж civilization
**цивилизо́ванный** *прил* civilized
**цикл** (-а) м cycle; (*лекций*) series
**цикл|ева́ть** (-ю́ю; *pf* **от~**) *несов перех* to sand
**цикло́н** (-а) м cyclone
**цили́ндр** (-а) м cylinder; (*шляпа*) top hat
**цини́чный** *прил* cynical
**цинк** (-а) м zinc
**цирк** (-а) м circus
**циркули́р|овать** (*3sg* -ует) *несов* to circulate
**ци́ркул|ь** (-я) м (a pair of) compasses *мн*
**циркуля́р** (-а) м decree
**цисте́рн|а** (-ы) ж cistern
**цита́т|а** (-ы) ж quote, quotation
**цити́р|овать** (-ую; *pf* **про~**) *несов перех* to quote
**ци́трусовый** *прил* citrus
**цифербла́т** (-а) м dial; (*на часа́х*) face
**ци́фр|а** (-ы) ж number; (*арабские, римские*) numeral; (*обычно мн: расчёт*) figure
**ЦРУ** *ср сокр* (= Центра́льное разве́дывательное управле́ние (США)) CIA
**ЦСУ** *ср сокр* = Центра́льное статисти́ческое управле́ние
**ЦТ** *ср сокр* = Центра́льное телеви́дение
**цыга́н** (-а; *nom pl* -е) м gypsy
**цыплёнок** (-ёнка; *nom pl* -я́та, *gen pl* -я́т) м chick
**цы́почк|и** (-ек) *мн*: **на ~ках** on tiptoe

# Ч, ч

**ча|ди́ть (-жу́, -ди́шь;** *pf* **на~)** *несов* to give off fumes

**чаеву́е (-ых)** *мн* tip *ед*

**ча|й (-я;** *part gen* **-ю,** *nom pl* **-и́)** *м* tea; **зава́ривать (завари́ть** *pf*) ~ to make tea; **дава́ть (дать** *pf*) **кому́-н на** ~ to give sb a tip

**ча́|йка (-йки;** *gen pl* **-ек)** *ж* (sea)gull

**ча́йн|ая (-ой)** *ж* tearoom

**ча́йник (-а)** *м* kettle; (*для заварки*) teapot

**ча́йн|ый** *прил*: ~ая ло́жка teaspoon

**ча́ртер (-а)** *м* (*КОММ*) charter

**час (-а;** *nom pl* **-ы́)** *м* hour; **академи́ческий** ~ (*ПРОСВЕЩ*) ≈ period; **кото́рый** ~? what time is it?; **сейча́с 3** ~**а́ но́чи/дня** it's 3 o'clock in the morning/afternoon; *см. также* **часы́**

**часо́в|ня (-ни;** *gen pl* **-ен)** *ж* chapel

**часов|о́й** *прил* (*лекция*) one-hour; (*механизм: ручны́х часо́в*) watch; (: *стенны́х часо́в*) clock ♦ **(-о́го)** *м* sentry; ~**ая стре́лка** the small hand; ~ **по́яс** time zone

**части́ц|а (-ы)** *ж* (*стекла́*) fragment; (*жела́ния*) bit; (*коли́чества*) fraction; (*ФИЗ, ЛИНГ*) particle

**части́чный** *прил* partial

**ча́стник (-а)** *м* (*со́бственник*) (private) owner

**ча́стност|ь (-и)** *ж* (*дета́ль*) detail; (*подро́бность*) particular; **в** ~и for instance

**ча́стн|ый** *прил* private; (*слу́чай*) isolated; ~**ая со́бственность** private property

**ча́сто** *нареч* (*мно́го раз*) often; (*те́сно*) close together

**част|ота́ (-оты́;** *nom pl* **-о́ты)** *ж* (*ТЕХ*) frequency

**ча́стый** *прил* frequent

**част|ь (-и;** *gen pl* **-е́й)** *ж* part; (*симфо́нии*) movement; (*отде́л*) department; (*ВОЕН*) unit; ~ **ре́чи** part of speech; ~ **све́та** continent

**час|ы́ (-о́в)** *мн* (*карма́нные*) watch *ед*; (*стенны́е*) clock *ед*

**ча́ш|ка (-ки;** *gen pl* **-ек)** *ж* cup

**ча́щ|а (-и)** *ж* (*лес*) thick forest; (*за́росль*) thicket

**ча́ще** *сравн прил от* **ча́стый** ♦ *сравн нареч от* **ча́сто**

**чего́** *мест см.* **что**

**чей (чьего́;** *см. Table 5)* (*f* **чья,** *nt* **чьё,** *pl* **чьи)** *мест* whose; ~ **бы то ни́ был** no matter whose it is

**чей-либо (чьего́-либо;** *как* **чей;** *см. Table 5)* (*f* **чья-либо,** *nt* **чьё-либо,** *pl* **чьи-либо)** *мест* = **че́й-нибудь**

**че́й-нибудь (чьего́-нибудь;** *как* **чей;** *см. Table 5)* (*f* **чья-нибудь,** *nt* **чьё-нибудь,** *pl* **чьи-нибудь)** *мест* anyone's

**че́й-то (чьего́-то;** *как чей; см. Table 5)* (*f* **чья́-то,** *nt* **чьё-то,** *pl* **чьи́-то)** *мест* someone's, somebody's

**чек (-а)** *м* (*ба́нковский*) cheque (*BRIT*), check (*US*); (*това́рный, ка́ссовый*) receipt

**че́ковый** *прил* cheque (*BRIT*), check (*US*)

**чёл|ка (-ки;** *gen pl* **-ок)** *ж* (*челове́ка*) fringe (*BRIT*), bangs *мн* (*US*)

**челн|о́к (-ка́)** *м* shuttle; (*торго́вец*) small trader buying goods abroad and selling them on local markets

**челове́к** (**-a**; nom pl **лю́ди**, gen pl **люде́й**) м human (being); (некто, личность) person

**челове́ческий** прил human; (человечный) humane

**челове́честв**|**о** (**-a**) ср humanity, mankind

**челове́чный** прил humane

**че́люст**|**ь** (**-и**) ж (АНАТ) jaw

**чем** мест см. **что** ♦ союз than; (разг: вместо того чтобы) instead of; **~ бо́льше/ра́ньше, тем лу́чше** the bigger/earlier, the better

**чемода́н** (**-a**) м suitcase

**чемпио́н** (**-a**) м champion

**чемпиона́т** (**-a**) м championship

**чему́** мест см. **что**

**чепух**|**а́** (**-и́**) ж nonsense

**че́рв**|**и** (**-е́й**) мн (КАРТЫ) hearts мн

**черви́вый** прил maggoty

**черв**|**ь** (**-я́**; nom pl **-и**, gen pl **-е́й**) м worm; (личинка) maggot

**червя́к** (**-а́**) м worm

**черда́к** (**-а́**) м attic, loft

**черед**|**ова́ть** (**-у́ю**) несов перех: **~ что-н с** +instr to alternate sth with

KEYWORD

**че́рез** предл; +acc **1** (поперёк) across, over; **переходи́ть (перейти́** pf) **че́рез доро́гу** to cross the road

**2** (сквозь) through; **че́рез окно́** through the window

**3** (поверх) over; **че́рез забо́р** over the fence

**4** (спустя) in; **че́рез час** in an hour('s time)

**5** (минуя какое-н пространство): **че́рез три кварта́ла - ста́нция** the station is three blocks away

**6** (при помощи) via; **он переда́л письмо́ че́рез знако́мого** he sent the letter via a friend

**7** (при повторении действия) every; **принима́йте табле́тки че́рез ка́ждый час** take the tablets every hour

**че́реп** (**-a**) м skull

**черепа́х**|**а** (**-и**) ж tortoise; (морская) turtle

**черепи́ц**|**а** (**-ы**) ж собир tiles мн

**чере́ш**|**ня** (**-ни**; gen pl **-ен**) ж cherry

**черне́**|**ть** (**-ю**; pf **по~**) несов (становиться чёрным) to turn black

**черни́к**|**а** (**-и**) ж bilberry

**черни́л**|**а** (**-**) мн ink ед

**черн**|**и́ть** (**-ю́**, **-и́шь**; pf **о~**) несов перех (имя) to tarnish

**чёрно-бе́лый** прил black-and-white

**черновиќ** (**-а́**) м draft

**чёрный** (**-ен**, **-на́**, **-но́**) прил black; (ход) back

**чёрпа**|**ть** (**-ю**) несов перех (жидкость) to ladle

**черстве́**|**ть** (**-ю**; pf **за~**) несов (хлеб) to go stale

**чёрствый** прил (хлеб) stale; (человек) callous

**чёрт** (**-a**; nom pl **че́рти**, gen pl **черте́й**) м (дьявол) devil; **иди́ к ~у!** (разг) go to hell!

**черт**|**а́** (**-ы́**) ж (линия) line; (признак) trait; **в о́бщих ~х** in general terms; см. также **черты́**

**чертёж** (**-а́**) м draft

**чер**|**ти́ть** (**-чу́**, **-тишь**; pf **на~**) несов перех (линию) to draw; (график) to draw up

**чёрточ**|**ка** (**-ки**; gen pl **-ек**) ж (дефис) hyphen

**черт**|**ы́** (**-**) мн (также: **лица́**) features мн

**че**|**са́ть** (**-шу́**, **-шешь**; pf **по~**) несов перех (спину) to scratch;

**~ся** (*pf* **по~ся**) *несов возв* to scratch o.s.; (*no pf*; зудеть) to itch

**чесно́к** (**-á**) *м* garlic

**че́стно** *нареч* (сказать) honestly; (решить) fairly ♦ **как сказ: так бу́дет ~** that'll be fair

**че́стность** (**-и**) *ж* honesty

**че́стный** *прил* honest; **~ое сло́во** honestly

**честолюби́вый** *прил* ambitious

**честь** (**-и**) *ж* honour (*BRIT*), honor (*US*); (*loc sg* **-и́**; почёт) glory; **к че́сти кого́-н** to sb's credit; **отдава́ть (отда́ть** *pf*) **кому́-н ~** to salute sb

**четве́рг** (**-á**) *м* Thursday

**четвере́ньки** (**-ек**) *мн:* **на ~ьках** on all fours

**четвёрка** (**-ки**; *gen pl* **-ок**) *ж* (цифра, карта) four; (*ПРОСВЕЩ*) ≈ В (*school mark*)

**че́тверо** (*см. Table 30a;* **-ы́х**) *чис* four

**четвёртый** *чис* fourth; **сейча́с ~ час** it's after three

**че́тверть** (**-и**) *ж* quarter; (*ПРОСВЕЩ*) term

**четвертьфина́л** (**-а**) *м* (*СПОРТ*) quarter final

**чёткий** *прил* clear; (движения) precise

**чётный** *прил* (число) even

**четы́ре** (**-ёх**; *instr sg* **-ьмя́;** *см. Table 24*) *чис* (цифра, число) four; (*ПРОСВЕЩ*) ≈ В (*school mark*)

**четы́реста** (**-ёхсо́т;** *см. Table 28*) *чис* four hundred

**четырёхуго́льник** (**-а**) *м* quadrangle

**четы́рнадцатый** *чис* fourteenth

**четы́рнадцать** (**-и;** *как* **пять;** *см. Table 26*) *чис* fourteen

**Че́хия** (**-и**) *ж* the Czech Republic

**чехо́л** (**-ла́**) *м* (для мебели) cover; (для гитары, для оружия)

case

**чешу́я** (**-и́**) *ж собир* scales *мн*

**чин** (**-а;** *nom pl* **-ы́**) *м* rank

**чини́ть** (**-ю́, -ишь;** *pf* **по~**) *несов перех* to mend, repair; (*pf* **о~;** карандаш) to sharpen

**чино́вник** (**-а**) *м* (служащий) official

**чи́псы** (**-ов**) *мн* crisps *мн*

**чири́кать** (**-ю**) *несов* to twitter

**чи́сленность** (**-и**) *ж* (армии) numbers *мн*; (учащихся) number; **~ населе́ния** population

**числи́тельное** (**-ого**) *ср* numeral

**число́** (**-ла́;** *nom pl* **-ла,** *gen pl* **-ел**) *ср* number; (день месяца) date; **быть** (*impf*) **в ~ле́** *+gen* to be among(st)

**чи́стить** (**-щу, -стишь;** *pf* **вы́чистить** *или* **по~**) *несов перех* to clean; (зубы) to brush, clean; (*pf* **по~;** яблоко, картошку) to peel; (рыбу) to scale

**чи́сто** *нареч* (только) purely; (убранный, сделанный) neatly ♦ **как сказ: в до́ме ~** the house is clean

**чистови́к** (**-á**) *м* fair copy

**чистосерде́чный** *прил* sincere

**чистота́** (**-ы́**) *ж* purity; **у него́ в до́ме всегда́ ~** his house is always clean

**чи́стый** *прил* (одежда, комната) clean; (совесть, небо) clear; (золото, спирт) pure; (прибыль, вес) net; (случайность) pure; **экологи́чески ~** organic

**чита́льный** *прил:* **~ зал** reading room

**чита́тель** (**-я**) *м* reader

**чита́ть** (**-ю;** *pf* **проче́сть** *или* **про~**) *несов перех* to read; (лекцию) to give

**чиха́ть** (**-ю;** *pf* **чихну́ть**) *несов* to sneeze

**член** (-а) *м* member; (*обычно мн:
конечности*) limb; **полово́й ~**
penis; **~ предложе́ния** part of a
sentence

**чо́ка|ться** (-юсь; *pf* **чо́кнуться**)
*несов возв* to clink glasses (*during
toast*)

**чрева́тый** *прил*: **~** +*instr* fraught
with

**чрезвыча́йно** *нареч* extremely

**чрезвыча́йн|ый** *прил*
(*исключи́тельный*) extraordinary;
(*экстренный*) emergency; **~ое
положе́ние** state of emergency

**чрезме́рный** *прил* excessive

**чте́ни|е** (-я) *ср* reading

KEYWORD

**что** (**чего́**; *см. Table 7*) *мест* 1
(*вопроси́тельное*) what; **что ты
сказа́л?** what did you say?; **что
Вы говори́те!** you don't say!
2 (*относительное*) which; **она́ не
поздоро́валась, что мне бы́ло
неприя́тно** she did not say hello,
which wasn't nice for me; **что ни
говори́ ...** whatever you say ...
3 (*столько сколько*): **она́
закрича́ла что бы́ло сил** she
shouted with all her might
4 (*разг: что-нибудь*) anything;
**е́сли что случи́тся** if anything
happens, should anything happen;
**в слу́чае чего́** if anything happens;
**чуть что - сра́зу скажи́ мне** get
in touch at the slightest thing
♦ *нареч* (*почему*) why; **что ты
грусти́шь?** why are you sad?
♦ *союз* 1 (*при сообщении,
высказывании*): **я зна́ю, что
на́до де́лать** I know what must be
done; **я зна́ю, что он прие́дет** I
know that he will come
2 (*во фразах*): **а что?** (*разг*) why
(do you ask)?; **к чему́** (*зачем*)

why; **не́ за что!** not at all! (*BRIT*),
you're welcome! (*US*); **ни за что!**
(*разг*) no way!; **ни за что ни про
что** (*разг*) for no (good) reason at
all; **что ты!** (*при возражении*)
what!; **я здесь ни при чём** it has
nothing to do with me; **что к чему**
(*разг*) what's what

**чтоб** *союз* = **чтобы**

KEYWORD

**что́бы** *союз*: **что́бы** +*infin*
(*выражает цель*) in order *или* so
as to do
♦ *союз*; +*pt* 1 (*выражает цель*) so
that
2 (*выражает желательность*): **я
хочу́, что́бы она́ пришла́** I want
her to come
3 (*выражает возможность*): **не
мо́жет быть, что́бы он так
поступи́л** it can't be possible that
he could have acted like that
♦ *част* 1 (*выражает пожелание*):
**что́бы она́ заболе́ла!** I hope she
gets ill!
2 (*выражает требование*): **что́бы
я его́ здесь бо́льше не ви́дел!** I
hope (that) I never see him here
again!

**что́-либо** (**чего́-либо**; *как что;
см. Table 7*) *мест* = **что́-нибудь**

**что́-нибудь** (**чего́-нибудь**; *как
что; см. Table 7*) *мест* (*в
утверждении*) something; (*в
вопросе*) anything

**что́-то** (**чего́-то**; *как что; см.
Table 7*) *мест* something;
(*приблизительно*) something like
♦ *нареч* (*разг: почему-то*)
somehow

**чувстви́тельный** *прил* sensitive

**чу́вств|о** (-а) *ср* feeling; **~** +*gen*

(*юмора, долга*) sense of
**чу́вств|овать** (**-ую**; *pf* **по~**) *несов*
*перех* to feel; (*присутствие,
опасность*) to sense; **~** (*impf*) **себя́
хорошо́/нело́вко** to feel good/
awkward; **~ся** *несов возв* (*жара,
усталость*) to be felt
**чугу́н** (**-á**) *м* cast iron
**чуда́к** (**-á**) *м* eccentric
**чудеса́** *итп сущ см.* **чу́до**
**чуде́сный** *прил* (*очень
хороший*) marvellous (*BRIT*),
marvelous (*US*), wonderful;
(*необычный*) miraculous
**чу́д|о** (**-а**; *nom pl* **-еса́**, *gen pl* **-éс**,
*dat pl* **-еса́м**) *ср* miracle
**чудо́вищ|е** (**-а**) *ср* monster
**чудо́вищный** *прил* monstrous
**чу́дом** *нареч* by a miracle
**чу́ждый** *прил* alien
**чужо́й** *прил* (*вещь*) someone *или*
somebody else's; (*речь, обычай*)
foreign; (*человек*) strange
**чул|о́к** (**-ка́**; *gen pl* **-óк**, *dat pl* **-ка́м**)
*м* (*обычно мн*) stocking
**чум|á** (**-ы́**) *ж* plague
**чу́ткий** *прил* sensitive; (*добрый*)
sympathetic
**чу́точку** *нареч* (*разг*) a tiny
bit
**чуть** *нареч* (*разг: едва*) hardly;
(*немного*) a little ♦ *союз* (*как
только*) as soon as; **~ (бы́ло) не**
almost, nearly; **~ что** (*разг*) at the
slightest thing
**чуть-чу́ть** *нареч* (*разг*) a little
**чу́чел|о** (**-а**) *ср* scarecrow
**чушь** (**-и**) *ж* (*разг*) rubbish (*BRIT*),
garbage (*US*), nonsense
**чу́|ять** (**-ю**) *несов перех*
(*собака*) to scent; (*предвидеть*)
to sense
**чьё** (**чьего́**) *мест см.* **чей**
**чьи** (**чьих**) *мест см.* **чей**
**чья** (**чьей**) *мест см.* **чей**

# Ш, ш

**шаг** (**-а**; *nom pl* **-и́**) *м* step
**шага́|ть** (**-ю**) *несов* to march
**шагн|у́ть** (**-у́, -ёшь**) *сов* to step,
take a step
**ша́йб|а** (**-ы**) *ж* (*СПОРТ*) puck
**ша́|йка** (**-йки**; *gen pl* **-ек**) *ж* gang
**шака́л** (**-а**) *м* jackal
**шал|ь** (**-и**) *ж* shawl
**шампа́нск|ое** (**-ого**) *ср*
champagne
**шампиньо́н** (**-а**) *м* (*БОТ*) (field)
mushroom
**шампу́н|ь** (**-я**) *м* shampoo
**шанс** (**-а**) *м* chance
**шанта́ж** (**-á**) *м* blackmail
**шантажи́р|овать** (**-ую**) *несов
перех* to blackmail
**ша́п|ка** (**-ки**; *gen pl* **-ок**) *ж* hat
**шар** (**-а**; *nom pl* **-ы́**) *м* (*ГЕОМ*)
sphere; (*gen sg* **-á**; *бильярдный
итп*) ball; **возду́шный ~** balloon
**ша́рик** (**-а**) *м* (*детский*) balloon
**ша́риков|ый** *прил*: **~ая ру́чка**
ballpoint pen
**ша́р|ить** (**-ю, -ишь**) *несов* (*разг*):
**~ (рука́ми)** to grope
**ша́рка|ть** (**-ю**) *несов*: **~** +*instr* to
shuffle
**шарф** (**-а**) *м* scarf
**шасси́** *ср нескл* (*самолёта*)
landing gear; (*автомобиля*) chassis
**шата́|ть** (**-ю**) *несов перех*
(*раскачивать*) to rock; **~ся** *несов
возв* (*зуб*) to be loose *или*
wobbly; (*стол*) to be wobbly; (*от
ветра*) to shake; (*от усталости*) to
reel; (*по улицам*) to hang around
**шах** (**-а**) *м* (*монарх*) shah; (*в
шахматах*) check
**ша́хматный** *прил* chess

**ша́хмат|ы** (-) *мн* (*игра*) chess *ед*; (*фигуры*) chessmen *мн*

**ша́хт|а** (-ы) *ж* mine; (*лифта*) shaft

**шахтёр** (-а) *м* miner

**ша́ш|ки** (-ек) *мн* (*игра*) draughts *ед* (*BRIT*), checkers *ед* (*US*)

**шашлы́к** (-á) *м* shashlik, kebab

**шва́бр|а** (-ы) *ж* mop

**шварт|ова́ть** (-у́ю; *pf* **при~**) *несов перех* to moor

**швед** (-а) *м* Swede

**шве́дский** *прил* Swedish

**шве́йный** *прил* sewing

**швейца́р** (-а) *м* doorman

**швейца́р|ец** (-ца) *м* Swiss

**Швейца́ри|я** (-и) *ж* Switzerland

**швейца́рский** *прил* Swiss

**Шве́ци|я** (-и) *ж* Sweden

**шве|я́** (-й) *ж* seamstress

**швыря́|ть** (-ю) *несов перех* to hurl

**шевел|и́ть** (-ю́, -и́шь; *pf* **по~**) *несов перех* (*сено*) to turn over; (*подлеж: ветер*) to stir ♦ *неперех*: ~ +*instr* (*пальцами, губами*) to move; **~ся** (*pf* **по~ся**) *несов возв* to stir

**шеде́вр** (-а) *м* masterpiece

**шёл** *несов см.* **идти́**

**шелест|е́ть** (-и́шь) *несов* to rustle

**шёлк** (-а; *nom pl* -á) *м* silk

**шёлковый** *прил* silk

**шелуш|и́ться** (-у́сь, -и́шься) *несов возв* to peel

**шепн|у́ть** (-у́, -ёшь) *сов перех* to whisper

**шёпот** (-а) *м* whisper

**шёпотом** *нареч* in a whisper

**шеп|та́ть** (-чу́, -чешь) *несов перех* to whisper; **~ся** *несов возв* to whisper to each other

**шере́нг|а** (-и) *ж* (*солдат*) rank

**шерст|ь** (-и) *ж* (*животного*) hair; (*пряжа, ткань*) wool

**шерстяно́й** *прил* (*пряжа, ткань*) woollen (*BRIT*), woolen (*US*)

**шерша́вый** *прил* rough

**шесте́р|о** (-ы́х; *см. Table 30b*) *чис* six

**шестидеся́тый** *чис* sixtieth

**шестна́дцатый** *чис* sixteenth

**шестна́дцат|ь** (-и; *как* **пять**; *см. Table 26*) *чис* sixteen

**шесто́й** *чис* sixth

**шест|ь** (-и́; *как* **пять**; *см. Table 26*) *чис* six

**шест|ьдеся́т** (-и́десяти; *как* **пятьдеся́т**; *см. Table 26*) *чис* sixty

**шест|ьсо́т** (-исо́т; *как* **пятьсо́т**; *см. Table 28*) *чис* six hundred

**шеф** (-а) *м* (*полиции*) chief; (*разг: начальник*) boss; (*благотворитель: лицо*) patron; (*организация*) sponsor

**ше́фств|о** (-а) *ср*: ~ **над** +*instr* (*лица*) patronage of; (*организация*) sponsorship of

**ше́фств|овать** (-ую) *несов*: ~ **над** +*instr* (*лицо*) to be patron of; (*организация*) to sponsor

**ше́|я** (-и) *ж* (*АНАТ*) neck

**ши́ворот** (-а) *м* (*разг*): **за** ~ by the collar

**шизофре́ник** (-а) *м* schizophrenic

**шизофрени́|я** (-и) *ж* schizophrenia

**шика́рный** *прил* (*разг*) glamorous, chic

**шимпанзе́** *м нескл* chimpanzee

**ши́н|а** (-ы) *ж* (*АВТ*) tyre (*BRIT*), tire (*US*)

**шине́л|ь** (-и) *ж* greatcoat

**шинк|ова́ть** (-у́ю; *pf* **на~**) *несов перех* (*овощи*) to shred

**шип** (-á) *м* (*растения*) thorn; (*на колесе*) stud; (*на ботинке*) spike

**шип|е́ть** (-лю́, -и́шь) *несов* to hiss; (*шампанское*) to fizz

**шипу́чий** *прил* fizzy

ши́ре *сравн прил от* широ́кий
♦ *сравн нареч от* широко́

ширин|а́ (-ы́) *ж* width; доро́жка
метр ~о́й *или* в ~у́ a path a metre
(*BRIT*) *или* meter (*US*) wide

ши́рм|а (-ы) *ж* screen

широ́к|ий *прил* wide; (*степи,
планы*) extensive; (*перен:
общественность*) general;
(*: смысл*) broad; (*: натура, жест*)
generous; това́ры ~ого
потребле́ния (*ЭКОН*) consumer
goods

широко́ *нареч* (*раскинуться*)
widely; (*улыбаться*) broadly

широкоэкра́нный *прил* (*фильм*)
wide-screen

шир|ота́ (-оты́) *ж* breadth; (*nom pl
-о́ты*, *ГЕО*) latitude

ширпотре́б (-а) *м сокр* (=
широ́кое потребле́ние) (*разг: о
товарах*) consumer goods *мн*; (*: о
плохом товаре*) shoddy goods *мн*

шить (шью, шьёшь; *pf* с~)
*несов перех* (*платье итп*) to sew

ши́фер (-а) *м* slate

шифр (-а) *м* code, cipher

шиш (-а́) *м* (*разг*) gesture of refusal;
(ни) ~а́ (*разг: ничего*) nothing at
all

ши́ш|ка (-ки; *gen pl* -ек) *ж* (*БОТ*)
cone; (*на лбу*) bump, lump

шкал|а́ (-ы́; *nom pl* -ы) *ж* scale

шкату́л|ка (-ки; *gen pl* -ок) *ж*
casket

шкаф (-а; *loc sg* -у́, *nom pl* -ы́) *м*
(*для одежды*) wardrobe; (*для
посуды*) cupboard; кни́жный ~
bookcase

шки́пер (-а) *м* (*МОР*) skipper

шко́л|а (-ы) *ж* school; (*милиции*)
academy; сре́дняя ~ secondary
(*BRIT*) *или* high (*US*) school

шко́л|а-интерна́т (-ы, -а)
boarding school

шко́льник (-а) *м* schoolboy

шко́льниц|а (-ы) *ж* schoolgirl

шко́льный *прил* (*здание*) school

шку́р|а (-ы) *ж* (*животного*) fur;
(*убитого животного*) skin;
(*: обработанная*) hide

шла *несов см.* идти́

шлагба́ум (-а) *м* barrier

шланг (-а) *м* hose

шлем (-а) *м* helmet

шли *несов см.* идти́

шлиф|ова́ть (-у́ю; *pf* от~) *несов
перех* (*ТЕХ*) to grind

шло *несов см.* идти́

шлю́п|ка (-ки; *gen pl* -ок) *ж* (*МОР*)
dinghy; спаса́тельная ~ lifeboat

шля́п|а (-ы) *ж* hat

шля́п|ка (-ки; *gen pl* -ок) *ж* hat;
(*гвоздя*) head; (*гриба*) cap

шмел|ь (-я́) *м* bumblebee

шмы́га|ть (-ю) *несов*: ~ но́сом to
sniff

шнур (-а́) *м* (*верёвка*) cord;
(*телефонный, лампы*) cable

шнур|ова́ть (-у́ю; *pf* за~) *несов
перех* (*ботинки*) to lace up

шнур|о́к (-ка́) *м* (*ботинка*) lace

шов (шва) *м* (*швейный*) seam;
(*хирургический*) stitch, suture;
(*намёточный итп*) stitch

шовини́зм (-а) *м* chauvinism

шок (-а) *м* (*МЕД, перен*) shock

шоки́р|овать (-ую) (*не)сов
перех* to shock

шокола́д (-а) *м* chocolate

шокола́дный *прил* chocolate

шо́рох (-а) *м* rustle

шо́рт|ы (-) *мн* shorts *мн*

шоссе́ *ср нескл* highway

шотла́нд|ец (-ца) *м* Scotsman

Шотла́нди|я (-и) *ж* Scotland

шотла́ндский *прил* Scottish,
Scots

шо́у *ср нескл* (*также перен*) show

шофёр (-а) *м* driver

**шпа́г|а** (-и) ж sword

**шпага́т** (-а) м (бечёвка) string, twine

**шпакл|ева́ть** (-ю́ю; pf за~) несов перех to fill

**шпаклёвк|а** (-и) ж (замазка) filler

**шпа́л|а** (-ы) ж sleeper (RAIL)

**шпил|ь** (-я) м spire

**шпи́л|ька** (-ьки; gen pl -ек) ж (для волос) hairpin; (каблук) stiletto (heel)

**шпина́т** (-а) м spinach

**шпингале́т** (-а) м (на окне) catch

**шпио́н** (-а) м spy

**шпиона́ж** (-а) м espionage

**шпио́н|ить** (-ю, -ишь) несов (разг) to spy

**шприц** (-а) м syringe

**шпро́т|ы** (-ов) мн sprats мн

**шрам** (-а) м (на теле) scar

**шрифт** (-а; nom pl -ы́) м type

**штаб** (-а) м headquarters мн

**штамп** (-а) м (печать) stamp

**штамп|ова́ть** (-у́ю; pf про~) несов перех (документы) to stamp; (pf от~; детали) to punch, press

**шта́нг|а** (-и) ж (СПОРТ, в тяжёлой атлетике) weight; (: ворот) post

**штан|ы́** (-о́в) мн trousers мн

**штат** (-а) м (государства) state; (работники) staff

**шта́тный** прил (сотрудник) permanent

**шта́тск|ий** прил (одежда) civilian ♦ (-ого) м civilian

**штемпел|ь** (-я) м: почто́вый ~ postmark

**штепсел|ь** (-я) м (ЭЛЕК) plug

**што́па|ть** (-ю; pf за~) несов перех to darn

**што́пор** (-а) м corkscrew

**што́р|а** (-ы) ж drape

**шторм** (-а) м gale

**штормов|о́й** прил stormy; ~о́е

**предупрежде́ние** storm warning

**штраф** (-а) м (денежный) fine; (СПОРТ) punishment

**штрафн|о́й** прил penal ♦ (-о́го) м (СПОРТ: также: ~ уда́р) penalty (kick)

**штраф|ова́ть** (-у́ю; pf о~) несов перех to fine; (СПОРТ) to penalize

**штрих** (-а́) м (черта) stroke

**штрихово́й** прил: ~ код bar code

**шту́к|а** (-и) ж (предмет) item

**штукату́р|ить** (-ю, -ишь; pf от~ или о~) несов перех to plaster

**штукату́рк|а** (-и) ж plaster

**штурм** (-а) м (ВОЕН) storm

**шту́рман** (-а) м navigator

**штурм|ова́ть** (-у́ю) несов перех (ВОЕН) to storm

**штык** (-а́) м (ВОЕН) bayonet

**шу́б|а** (-ы) ж (меховая) fur coat

**шум** (-а; part gen -у) м (звук) noise

**шум|е́ть** (-лю́, -и́шь) несов to make a noise

**шу́мный** прил noisy; (разговор, компания) loud; (оживлённый: улица) bustling

**шу́рин** (-а) м brother-in-law (wife's brother)

**шуру́п** (-а) м (ТЕХ) screw

**шурш|а́ть** (-у́, -и́шь) несов to rustle

**шу|ти́ть** (-чу́, -тишь; pf по~) несов to joke; (смеяться): ~ над +instr to make fun of; (no pf; пренебрегать): ~ +instr (здоровьем) to disregard

**шу́т|ка** (-ки; gen pl -ок) ж joke; без ~ок joking apart, seriously

**шутли́вый** прил humourous (BRIT), humorous (US)

**шу́точный** прил (рассказ) comic, funny

**шучу́** несов см. шути́ть

**шху́н|а** (-ы) ж schooner

**шью** итп несов см. шить

# Щ, щ

**щаве́л**|**ь** (**-я́**) *м* sorrel

**ща**|**ди́ть** (**-жу́**, **-ди́шь**; *pf* **по~**) *несов перех* to spare

**щеб**|**ета́ть** (**-ечу́**, **-е́чешь**) *несов* to twitter

**ще́дрост**|**ь** (**-и**) *ж* generosity

**ще́дрый** *прил* generous

**щека́** (**щеки́**; *nom pl* **щёки**, *gen pl* **щёк**, *dat pl* **~м**) *ж* cheek

**щек**|**ота́ть** (**-очу́**, **-о́чешь**; *pf* **по~**) *несов перех* to tickle

**щекотли́вый** *прил* (*вопро́с итп*) delicate

**щёлк**|**а** (**-и**) *ж* small hole

**щёлка**|**ть** (**-ю**) *несов*: **~** +*instr* (*языко́м*) to click; (*кнуто́м*) to crack

**щёлкн**|**уть** (**-у**) *сов* to click; **~** (*pf*) +*instr* (*хлысто́м*) to crack

**щёлоч**|**ь** (**-и**) *ж* alkali

**щелч**|**о́к** (**-ка́**) *м* flick; (*звук*) click

**щел**|**ь** (**-и**; *loc sg* **-и́**, *gen pl* **-е́й**) *ж* (*в полу́*) crack; **смотрова́я ~** peephole

**щен**|**о́к** (**-ка́**; *nom pl* **-я́та**, *gen pl* **-я́т**) *м* (*соба́ки*) pup; (*лисы́*, *волчи́цы*) cub

**щепети́льный** *прил* scrupulous

**ще́п**|**ка** (**-ки**; *gen pl* **-ок**) *ж* splinter; (*для расто́пки*): **~ки** chippings

**щепо́т**|**ка** (**-ки**; *gen pl* **-ок**) *ж* pinch

**щети́н**|**а** (**-ы**) *ж* (*живо́тных*, *щёток*) bristle; (*у мужчи́ны*) stubble

**щети́н**|**иться** (*3sg* **-ится**; *pf* **о~**) *несов возв* to bristle

**щёт**|**ка** (**-ки**; *gen pl* **-ок**) *ж* brush; **~ для воло́с** hairbrush

**щи** (**щей**; *dat pl* **щам**) *мн* cabbage soup *ед*

**щи́колот**|**ка** (**-ки**; *gen pl* **-ок**) *ж* ankle

**щип**|**а́ть** (**-лю́**, **-лешь**) *несов перех* (*до бо́ли*) to nip, pinch; (*no pf*; *подлеж*: *моро́з*) to bite; (*pf* **о~**; *во́лосы*, *ку́рицу*) to pluck; **~ся** *несов возв* (*разг*) to nip, pinch

**щипц**|**ы́** (**-о́в**) *мн*: **хирурги́ческие ~** forceps; **~ для са́хара** sugar-tongs

**щи́пчик**|**и** (**-ов**) *мн* (*для ногте́й*) tweezers *мн*

**щит** (**-а́**) *м* shield; (*рекла́мный*, *баскетбо́льный*) board; (*ТЕХ*) panel

**щитови́дн**|**ый** *прил*: **~ая железа́** thyroid gland

**щу́к**|**а** (**-и**) *ж* pike

**щу́пал**|**ьце** (**-ьца**; *nom pl* **-ьца**, *gen pl* **-ец**) *ср* (*осьмино́га*) tentacle; (*насеко́мых*) feeler

**щу́па**|**ть** (**-ю**; *pf* **по~**) *несов перех* to feel for

**щу́р**|**ить** (**-ю**, **-ишь**; *pf* **со~**) *несов перех*: **~ глаза́** to screw up one's eyes; **~ся** (*pf* **со~ся**) *несов возв* (*от со́лнца*) to squint

# Э, э

**эвакуа́ци**|**я** (**-и**) *ж* evacuation

**эваку́р**|**овать** (**-ую**) (*не)сов* *перех* to evacuate

**ЭВМ** *ж сокр* (= электро́нная вычисли́тельная маши́на) computer

**эволю́ци**|**я** (**-и**) *ж* evolution

**эгои́ст** (**-а**) *м* egoist

**эгоисти́чный** *прил* egotistic(al)

**эква́тор** (**-а**) *м* equator

**эквивале́нт** (**-а**) *м* equivalent

**экза́мен** (**-а**) *м*: **~ (по** +*dat*) (*по исто́рии*) exam(ination) (in);

**выпускны́|е ~ы** Finals; **сдавáть** (*impf*) ~ to sit (*BRIT*) *или* take an exam(ination); **сдать** (*pf*) ~ to pass an exam(ination)

**экзаменáтор (-а)** *м* examiner

**экзаменацио́нный** *прил* examination; (*вопрос*) exam

**экземпля́р (-а)** *м* copy

**экипа́ж (-а)** *м* crew

**экологи́ческий** *прил* ecological

**эколо́ги|я (-и)** *ж* ecology

**экономик|а (-и)** *ж* economy; (*наука*) economics

**экономи́ст (-а)** *м* economist

**эконо́м|ить (-лю, -ишь**; *pf* **с~**) *несов перех* (*энергию, деньги*) to save; (*выгадывать*): ~ **на** +*prp* to economize *или* save on

**экономи́ческий** *прил* economic

**эконо́ми|я (-и)** *ж* economy

**эконо́мный** *прил* (*хозяин*) thrifty; (*метод*) economical

**экра́н (-а)** *м* screen

**экскава́тор (-а)** *м* excavator, digger

**экску́рси|я (-и)** *ж* excursion

**экскурсово́д (-а)** *м* guide

**экспеди́ци|я (-и)** *ж* (*научная*) field work; (*группа людей*) expedition

**эксперимéнт (-а)** *м* experiment

**эксперименти́р|овать (-ую)** *несов*: ~ (**над** *или* **с** +*instr*) to experiment (on *или* with)

**экспéрт (-а)** *м* expert

**эксплуатáци|я (-и)** *ж* exploitation; (*машин*) utilization

**эксплуати́р|овать (-ую)** *несов перех* to exploit; (*машины*) to use

**экспонáт (-а)** *м* exhibit

**э́кспорт (-а)** *м* export

**экспортёр (-а)** *м* exporter

**экспорти́р|овать (-ую)** *несов перех* to export

**экстремáльный** *прил* extreme

**э́кстренный** *прил* urgent; (*заседание*) emergency

**эласти́чный** *прил* stretchy

**элевáтор (-а)** *м* (*С.-Х.*) grain store *или* elevator (*US*)

**элегáнтный** *прил* elegant

**элéктрик (-а)** *м* electrician

**электри́ческий** *прил* electric

**электри́честв|о (-а)** *ср* electricity

**электри́ч|ка (-ки**; *gen pl* **-ек**) *ж* (*разг*) electric train

**электробытов|óй** *прил*: **~ы́е прибóры** electrical appliances *мн*

**элéктрогитáр|а (-ы)** *ж* electric guitar

**электромонтёр (-а)** *м* electrician

**электрóн (-а)** *м* electron

**электрóник|а (-и)** *ж* electronics

**электрóнн|ый** *прил* electronic; ~ **микроскóп** electron microscope; **~ая пóчта** (*КОМП*) e-mail, electronic mail; ~ **áдрес** e-mail address; **~ая страни́ца** webpage

**электропередáч|а (-и)** *ж* power transmission; **ли́ния ~и** power line

**электропóезд (-а)** *м* electric train

**электроприбóр (-а)** *м* electrical device

**электропровóдк|а (-и)** *ж* (electrical) wiring

**электростáнци|я (-и)** *ж* (electric) power station

**электротéхник (-а)** *м* electrical engineer

**электроэнéрги|я (-и)** *ж* electric power

**элемéнт (-а)** *м* element

**элементáрный** *прил* elementary; (*правила*) basic

**эли́т|а (-ы)** *ж собир* élite

**эли́тный** *прил* (*лучший*) élite; (*дом, школа*) exclusive

**эмáлевый** *прил* enamel

**эмалирóванный** *прил* enamelled

**эма́л|ь** (-и) ж enamel

**эмба́рго** ср нескл embargo

**эмбле́м|а** (-ы) ж emblem

**эмбрио́н** (-а) м embryo

**эмигра́нт** (-а) м emigrant

**эмиграцио́нный** прил emigration

**эмигра́ци|я** (-и) ж emigration

**эмигри́р|овать** (-ую) (не)сов to emigrate

**эмоциона́льный** прил emotional

**эмо́ци|я** (-и) ж emotion

**эму́льси|я** (-и) ж emulsion

**энерге́тик|а** (-и) ж power industry

**энергети́ческий** прил energy

**энерги́чный** прил energetic

**эне́рги|я** (-и) ж energy

**э́нн|ый** прил: **~ое число́/коли́чество** X number/amount; **в ~ раз** yet again

**энтузиа́зм** (-а) м enthusiasm

**энциклопе́ди|я** (-и) ж encyclopaedia (BRIT), encyclopedia (US)

**эпи́граф** (-а) м epigraph

**эпиде́ми|я** (-и) ж epidemic

**эпизо́д** (-а) м episode

**эпизоди́ческий** прил (явление) random

**эпиле́пси|я** (-и) ж epilepsy

**эпило́г** (-а) м epilogue (BRIT), epilog (US)

**эпице́нтр** (-а) м epicentre (BRIT), epicenter (US)

**эпопе́|я** (-и) ж epic

**э́пос** (-а) м epic literature

**эпо́х|а** (-и) ж epoch

**э́р|а** (-ы) ж era; **пе́рвый век на́шей ~ы/до на́шей ~ы** the first century AD/BC

**эро́зи|я** (-и) ж erosion

**эроти́ческий** прил erotic

**эскала́тор** (-а) м escalator

**эскала́ци|я** (-и) ж escalation

**эски́з** (-а) м (к карти́не) sketch; (к прое́кту) draft

**эскимо́** ср нескл choc-ice, Eskimo (US)

**эско́рт** (-а) м escort

**эссе́нци|я** (-и) ж (КУЛИН) essence

**эстака́д|а** (-ы) ж (на доро́ге) flyover (BRIT), overpass

**эстафе́т|а** (-ы) ж (СПОРТ) relay (race)

**эсте́тик|а** (-и) ж aesthetics (BRIT), esthetics (US)

**эстети́ческий** прил aesthetic (BRIT), esthetic (US)

**эсто́н|ец** (-ца) м Estonian

**Эсто́ни|я** (-и) ж Estonia

**эстра́д|а** (-ы) ж (для орке́стра) platform; (вид иску́сства) variety

**эстра́дный** прил: **~ конце́рт** variety show

**э́т|а** (-ой) мест см. **э́тот**

**эта́ж** (-а́) м floor, storey (BRIT), story (US); **пе́рвый/второ́й/тре́тий ~** ground/first/second floor (BRIT), first/second/third floor (US)

**этаже́р|ка** (-ки; gen pl **-ок**) ж stack of shelves

**этало́н** (-а) м (ме́ры) standard; (перен: красоты́) model

**эта́п** (-а) м (рабо́ты) stage; (го́нки) lap

**э́т|и** (-их) мест см. **э́тот**

**э́тик|а** (-и) ж ethics

**этике́т** (-а) м etiquette

**этике́т|ка** (-ки; gen pl **-ок**) ж label

**э́тим** мест см. **э́тот**

**э́тими** мест см. **э́ти**

**этимоло́ги|я** (-и) ж etymology

**эти́чный** прил ethical

---
KEYWORD
---

**э́т|о** (-ого; см. Table 10) мест **1** (указа́тельное) this; **э́то бу́дет тру́дно** this will be difficult; **он на всё соглаша́ется - э́то о́чень стра́нно** he is agreeing to everything, this is most strange

**2** (*связка в сказуемом*): **любо́вь
- э́то проще́ние** love is forgiveness
**3** (*как подлежащее*): **с кем ты
разгова́ривал? - э́то была́ моя́
сестра́** who were you talking to? -
that was my sister; **как э́то
произошло́?** how did it happen?
**4** (*для усиления*): **э́то он во
всём винова́т** he is the one who is
to blame for everything

♦ *част* **1** (*служит для усиления*):
**кто э́то звони́л?** who was it who
phoned (*BRIT*) *или* called (*US*)?

---

KEYWORD

**э́т|от** (**-ого**; *f* **э́та**, *nt* **э́то**, *pl* **э́ти**)
(*см.* Table 10) *мест* **1**
(*указательное: о близком
предмете*) this; (: *о близких
предметах*) these; **э́тот дом** this
house; **э́ти кни́ги** these books
**2** (*о данном времени*) this; **э́тот
год осо́бенно тру́дный** this year
is particularly hard; **в э́ти дни я
при́нял реше́ние** in the last few
days I have come to a decision;
**э́тот са́мый** that very
**3** (*о чём-то только что
упомянутом*) this; **он ложи́лся в
10 часо́в ве́чера - э́та привы́чка
меня́ всегда́ удивля́ла** he used to
go to bed at 10 p.m., this habit
always amazed me

♦ *ср* (*как сущ: об одном
предмете*) this one; (: *о многих
предметах*) these ones; **дай мне
вот э́ти** give me these ones; **э́тот
на всё спосо́бен** this one is
capable of anything; **при э́том** at
that

**этю́д** (**-а**) *м* sketch
**эфи́р** (**-а**) *м* (*ХИМ*) ether;
(*воздушное пространство*) air;

**выходи́ть (вы́йти** *pf*) **в ~** to go on
the air; **прямо́й ~** live broadcast
**эффе́кт** (**-а**) *м* effect
**эффекти́вный** *прил* effective
**эффе́ктный** *прил* (*одежда*)
striking; (*речь*) impressive
**э́х|о** (**-а**) *ср* echo
**эшело́н** (**-а**) *м* echelon; (*поезд*)
special train

# Ю, ю

**ю.** *сокр* (= **юг**) S; (= **ю́жный**) S
**юбиле́|й** (**-я**) *м* (*годовщина*)
anniversary; (*празднование*)
jubilee
**ю́б|ка** (**-ки**; *gen pl* **-ок**) *ж* skirt
**ювели́р** (**-а**) *м* jeweller (*BRIT*),
jeweler (*US*)
**ювели́рный** *прил* jewellery (*BRIT*),
jewelery (*US*)
**юг** (**-а**) *м* south
**южа́нин** (**-а**) *м* southerner
**ю́жный** *прил* southern
**ю́мор** (**-а**) *м* humour (*BRIT*), humor
(*US*)
**юмори́ст** (**-а**) *м* comedian
**юмористи́ческий** *прил*
humorous
**ЮНЕ́СКО** *ср сокр* UNESCO
**юнио́р** (**-а**) *м* (*СПОРТ*) junior
**ю́ность** (**-и**) *ж* youth
**ю́нош|а** (**-и**; *nom pl* **-и**, *gen pl* **-ей**)
*м* young man
**ю́ношеский** *прил* youthful;
(*организация*) youth
**ю́ный** *прил* (*молодой*) young
**юриди́ческ|ий** *прил* (*сила*)
juridical; (*образование*) legal; **~
факульте́т** law faculty; **~ая
консульта́ция** ≈ legal advice
office
**юрисди́кци|я** (**-и**) *ж* jurisdiction

**юрисконсульт** (-а) м ≈ solicitor, ≈ lawyer
**юри́ст** (-а) м lawyer
**юсти́ци|я** (-и) ж judiciary; **Министе́рство ~и** Ministry of Justice

# Я, я

**я** (меня́; см. *Table 6a*) мест I ♦ сущ нескл (*личность*) the self, the ego
**я́бед|а** (-ы) м/ж sneak
**я́бедничаｔ|ть** (-ю; *pf* на~) несов: ~ **на** +*acc* (*разг*) to tell tales about
**я́блок|о** (-а; *nom pl* -**и**) *ср* apple
**я́блон|я** (-и) ж apple tree
**я́блочный** *прил* apple
**яв|и́ться** (-лю́сь, -ишься; *impf* **явля́ться**) *сов возв* to appear; (*домой, в гости*) to arrive; **явля́ться** (~ *pf*) +*instr* (*причиной*) to be
**я́в|ка** (-ки; *gen pl* -**ок**) ж appearance
**явле́ни|е** (-я) *ср* phenomenon; (*РЕЛ*) manifestation
**явля́|ться** (-юсь) *несов от* **яви́ться** ♦ *возв*: ~ +*instr* to be
**я́вно** *нареч* (*очевидно*) obviously
**я́вный** *прил* (*вражда*) overt; (*ложь*) obvious
**яв|ь** (-и) ж reality
**ягн|ёнок** (-ёнка; *nom pl* -**я́та**, *gen pl* -**я́т**) м lamb
**я́год|а** (-ы) ж berry
**ягоди́ц|а** (-ы) ж (*обычно мн*) buttock
**яд** (-а) м poison
**я́дерный** *прил* nuclear
**ядови́тый** *прил* poisonous
**яд|ро́** (-ра́; *nom pl* -**ра**, *gen pl* -**ер**) *ср* nucleus; (*Земли, древесины*) core; (*СПОРТ*) shot

**я́зв|а** (-ы) ж (*МЕД*) ulcer
**язви́тельн|ый** *прил* scathing
**язв|и́ть** (-лю́, -и́шь; *pf* съ~) *несов*: ~ +*dat* to sneer at
**язы́к** (-á) м tongue; (*русский, разговорный*) language; **владе́ть** (*impf*) **языко́м** to speak a language
**языково́й** *прил* language
**язы́ческий** *прил* pagan
**язы́ч|ок** (-кá) м (*ботинка*) tongue
**яи́чниц|а** (-ы) ж fried eggs *мн*
**яи́чн|ый** *прил*: ~ **бело́к** egg white; **~ая скорлупá** eggshell
**яйц|о́** (яйцá; *nom pl* **я́йца**, *gen pl* **яиц**, *dat pl* **я́йцам**) *ср* egg; ~ **всмя́тку/вкруту́ю** soft-boiled/hard-boiled egg
**ЯК** (-а) м *сокр* = **самолёт констру́кции А.С. Я́ковлева**
**я́кобы** *союз* (*будто бы*) that ♦ *част* supposedly
**я́кор|ь** (-я; *nom pl* -**я́**) м (*МОР*) anchor
**я́м|а** (-ы) ж (*в земле*) pit
**я́моч|ка** (-ки; *gen pl* -**ек**) ж dimple
**янва́р|ь** (-я́) м January
**янта́р|ь** (-я́) м amber
**Япо́ни|я** (-и) ж Japan
**я́ркий** *прил* bright; (*перен: человек, речь*) brilliant
**ярлы́к** (-á) м label
**я́рмар|ка** (-ки; *gen pl* -**ок**) ж fair; **междунаро́дная ~** international trade fair
**я́ростный** *прил* (*взгляд, слова*) furious; (*атака, критика*) fierce
**я́рост|ь** (-и) ж fury
**я́рус** (-а) м (*в театре*) circle
**я́сл|и** (-ей) *мн* (*также: де́тские ~*) crèche *ед*, day nursery *ед* (*BRIT*)
**я́сно** *нареч* clearly ♦ *как сказ* (*о погоде*) it's fine; (*понятно*) it's clear
**я́сност|ь** (-и) ж clarity
**я́сный** *прил* clear

**я́стреб** (**-а**) м hawk
**я́хт|а** (**-ы**) ж yacht
**яхтсме́н** (**-а**) м yachtsman
**яче́|йка** (**-йки**; *gen pl* **-ек**) ж
  (*сотовая*) cell; (*профсоюзная*)
  branch; (*для почты*) pigeonhole
**ячме́нный** *прил* barley
**ячме́н|ь** (**-я́**) м barley
**я́щериц|а** (**-ы**) ж lizard

**я́щик** (**-а**) м (*вместилище*:
  *большой*) chest; (: *маленький*)
  box; (*в письменном столе итп*)
  drawer; **му́сорный** ~ dustbin
  (*BRIT*), garbage can (*US*); **почто́вый**
  ~ (*на улице*) postbox; (*дома*)
  letterbox
**я́щур** (**-а**) м foot-and-mouth
  disease

А, а
Б, б
В, в
Г, г
Д, д
Е, е
Ж, ж
З, з
И, и
Й, й
К, к
Л, л
М, м
Н, н
О, о
П, п
Р, р
С, с
Т, т
У, у
Ф, ф
Х, х
Ц, ц
Ч, ч
Ш, ш
Щ, щ
Ъ, ъ
Ы, ы
Ь, ь
Э, э
Ю, ю
Я, я

A, a
B, b
C, c
D, d
E, e
F, f
G, g
H, h
I, i
J, j
K, k
L, l
M, m
N, n
O, o
P, p
Q, q
R, r
S, s
T, t
U, u
V, v
W, w
X, x
Y, y
Z, z

## A, a

**A** [eɪ] n (MUS) ля nt ind

KEYWORD

**a** [ə] (before vowel or silent h: **an**) indef art 1: **a book** кни́га; **an apple** я́блоко; **she's a student** она́ студе́нтка
2 (instead of the number "one"): **a week ago** неде́лю наза́д; **a hundred pounds** сто фу́нтов
3 (in expressing time) в +acc; **3 a day** 3 в день; **10 km an hour** 10 км в час
4 (in expressing prices): **30p a kilo** 30 пе́нсов килогра́мм; **£5 a person** £5 с ка́ждого

**AA** n abbr (BRIT) (= Automobile Association) автомоби́льная ассоциа́ция
**AAA** n abbr (= American Automobile Association) америка́нская автомоби́льная ассоциа́ция
**aback** [ə'bæk] adv: **I was taken ~** я был поражён
**abandon** [ə'bændən] vt (person) покида́ть (поки́нуть pf); (search) прекраща́ть (прекрати́ть pf); (hope) оставля́ть (оста́вить pf); (idea) отка́зываться (отказа́ться pf) от +gen
**abbey** ['æbɪ] n абба́тство
**abbreviation** [əbriːvɪ'eɪʃən] n сокраще́ние
**abdomen** ['æbdəmɛn] n брюшна́я по́лость f, живо́т
**abide** [ə'baɪd] vt: **I can't ~ it/him** я э́того/его́ не выношу́; **~ by** vt fus соблюда́ть (соблюсти́ pf)
**ability** [ə'bɪlɪtɪ] n (capacity) спосо́бность f; (talent, skill) спосо́бности fpl

**ablaze** [ə'bleɪz] adj: **to be ~** (on fire) быть (impf) в огне́
**able** ['eɪbl] adj (capable) спосо́бный; (skilled) уме́лый; **he is ~ to ...** он спосо́бен +infin ...
**abnormal** [æb'nɔːml] adj ненорма́льный
**aboard** [ə'bɔːd] prep (position, NAUT, AVIAT) на борту́ +gen; (: train, bus) в +prp; (motion, NAUT, AVIAT) на борт +gen; (: train, bus) в +acc
♦ adv: **to climb ~** (train) сади́ться (сесть pf) в по́езд
**abolish** [ə'bɔlɪʃ] vt отменя́ть (отмени́ть pf)
**abolition** [æbə'lɪʃən] n отме́на
**abortion** [ə'bɔːʃən] n або́рт; **to have an ~** де́лать (сде́лать pf) або́рт

KEYWORD

**about** [ə'baut] adv 1 (approximately: referring to time, price etc) о́коло +gen, приме́рно +acc; **at about two (o'clock)** приме́рно в два (часа́), о́коло двух (часо́в); **I've just about finished** я почти́ зако́нчил
2 (approximately: referring to height, size etc) о́коло +gen, приме́рно +nom; **the room is about 10 metres wide** ко́мната приме́рно 10 ме́тров в ширину́; **she is about your age** она́ приме́рно Ва́шего во́зраста
3 (referring to place) повсю́ду; **to leave things lying about** разбра́сывать (разброса́ть pf) ве́щи повсю́ду; **to run/walk about** бе́гать (impf)/ходи́ть (impf) вокру́г
4: **to be about to do** собира́ться

(собра́ться *pf*) +*infin*; **he was about to go to bed** он собра́лся лечь спать
♦ *prep* 1 (*relating to*) о(б) +*prp*; **a book about London** кни́га о Ло́ндоне; **what is it about?** о чём э́то?; **what** *or* **how about doing ...?** как насчёт того́, что́бы +*infin* ...? 2 (*referring to place*) по +*dat*; **to walk about the town** ходи́ть (*impf*) по го́роду; **her clothes were scattered about the room** её оде́жда была́ разбро́сана по ко́мнате

**above** [ə'bʌv] *adv* (*higher up*) наверху́ ♦ *prep* (*higher than*) над +*instr*; (: *in rank etc*) вы́ше +*gen*; **from ~** све́рху; **mentioned ~** вышеупомя́нутый; **~ all** пре́жде всего́

**abrasive** [ə'breɪzɪv] *adj* (*manner*) жёсткий

**abroad** [ə'brɔːd] *adv* (*to be*) за грани́цей *or* рубежо́м; (*to go*) за грани́цу *or* рубе́ж; (*to come from*) из-за грани́цы *or* рубежа́

**abrupt** [ə'brʌpt] *adj* (*action, ending*) внеза́пный; (*person, manner*) ре́зкий; **~ly** (*leave, end*) внеза́пно; (*speak*) ре́зко

**absence** ['æbsəns] *n* отсу́тствие

**absent** ['æbsənt] *adj* (*person*) отсу́тствующий

**absolute** ['æbsəluːt] *adj* абсолю́тный; **~ly** [æbsə'luːtlɪ] *adv* абсолю́тно, соверше́нно; (*certainly*) безусло́вно

**absorb** [əb'zɔːb] *vt* (*liquid, information*) впи́тывать (впита́ть *pf*); (*light, firm*) поглоща́ть (поглоти́ть *pf*); **he is ~ed in a book** он поглощён кни́гой; **~ent cotton** *n* (*US*) гигроскопи́ческая ва́та; **~ing** *adj* увлека́тельный

**absorption** [əb'sɔːpʃən] *n* (*see vt*)

впи́тывание; поглоще́ние; (*interest*) увлечённость *f*

**abstract** ['æbstrækt] *adj* абстра́ктный

**absurd** [əb'səːd] *adj* абсу́рдный, неле́пый

**abundant** [ə'bʌndənt] *adj* оби́льный

**abuse** *n* [ə'bjuːs] *vb* [ə'bjuːz] *n* (*insults*) брань *f*; (*ill-treatment*) жесто́кое обраще́ние (*misuse*) злоупотребле́ние ♦ *vt* (*see n*) оскорбля́ть (оскорби́ть *pf*); жесто́ко обраща́ться (*impf*) с +*instr*; злоупотребля́ть (злоупотреби́ть *pf*) +*instr*

**abusive** [ə'bjuːsɪv] *adj* (*person*) гру́бый, жесто́кий

**AC** *abbr* (= *alternating current*) переме́нный ток

**academic** [ækə'dɛmɪk] *adj* (*system*) академи́ческий (*qualifications*) учёный; (*work, books*) нау́чный; (*person*) интеллектуа́льный ♦ *n* учёный(ая) *m(f) adj*

**academy** [ə'kædəmɪ] *n* (*learned body*) акаде́мия; (*college*) учи́лище; (*in Scotland*) сре́дняя шко́ла; **~ of music** консервато́рия

**accelerate** [æk'sɛləreɪt] *vi* (*AUT*) разгоня́ться (разгна́ться *pf*)

**acceleration** [æksɛlə'reɪʃən] *n* (*AUT*) разго́н

**accelerator** [æk'sɛləreɪtər] *n* акселера́тор

**accent** ['æksɛnt] *n* акце́нт; (*stress mark*) знак ударе́ния

**accept** [ək'sɛpt] *vt* принима́ть (приня́ть *pf*); (*fact, situation*) мири́ться (примири́ться *pf*) с +*instr*; (*responsibility, blame*) принима́ть (приня́ть *pf*) на себя́; **~able** *adj* прие́млемый; **~ance** *n* приня́тие; (*of fact*) прия́тие

**access** ['æksɛs] *n* до́ступ; **~ible**

[æk'sɛsəbl] *adj* досту́пный

**accessory** [æk'sɛsərɪ] *n*
принадле́жность *f*; **accessories**
*npl* (*DRESS*) аксессуа́ры *mpl*

**accident** ['æksɪdənt] *n* (*disaster*)
несча́стный слу́чай; (*in car etc*)
ава́рия; **by ~** случа́йно; **~al**
[æksɪ'dɛntl] *adj* случа́йный; **~ally**
[æksɪ'dɛntəlɪ] *adv* случа́йно

**acclaim** [ə'kleɪm] *n* призна́ние

**accommodate** [ə'kɔmədeɪt] *vt*
(*subj: person*) предоставля́ть
(предоста́вить *pf*) жильё +*dat*;
(*: car, hotel etc*) вмеща́ть
(вмести́ть *pf*)

**accommodation** [əkɔmə'deɪʃən] *n*
(*to live in*) жильё (*to work in*)
помеще́ние; **~s** *npl* (*US: lodgings*)
жильё *ntsg*

**accompaniment** [ə'kʌmpənɪmənt]
*n* сопровожде́ние; (*MUS*)
аккомпанеме́нт

**accompany** [ə'kʌmpənɪ] *vt*
сопровожда́ть (сопроводи́ть *pf*);
(*MUS*) аккомпани́ровать (*impf*)
+*dat*

**accomplice** [ə'kʌmplɪs] *n*
соо́бщник(ица)

**accomplish** [ə'kʌmplɪʃ] *vt* (*task*)
заверша́ть (заверши́ть *pf*); (*goal*)
достига́ть (дости́гнуть *or*
дости́чь *pf*) +*gen*; **~ed** *adj* (*person*)
тала́нтливый

**accord** [ə'kɔːd] *n*: **of his own ~** по
со́бственному жела́нию; **of its
own ~** сам по себе́; **~ance** *n*: **in
~ance with** в согла́сии *or*
соотве́тствии с +*instr*; **~ing** *prep*:
**~ing to** согла́сно +*dat*; **~ingly** *adv*
соотве́тствующим о́бразом; (*as
a result*) соотве́тственно

**account** [ə'kaunt] *n* (*bill*) счёт; (*in
bank*) (расчётный) счёт; (*report*)
отчёт; **~s** *npl* (*COMM*) счета́ *mpl*;
(*books*) бухга́лтерские кни́ги *fpl*;
**to keep an ~ of** вести́ (*impf*) счёт

+*gen or* +*dat*; **to bring sb to ~ for
sth** призыва́ть (призва́ть *pf*)
кого́-н к отве́ту за что-н; **by all
~s** по всем све́дениям; **it is of no
~** э́то не ва́жно; **on ~** в креди́т;
**on no ~** ни в ко́ем слу́чае; **on ~
of** по причи́не +*gen*; **to take
into~, take ~ of** принима́ть
(приня́ть *pf*) в расчёт; **~ for** *vt fus*
(*expenses*) отчи́тываться
(отчита́ться *pf*) за +*acc*; (*absence,
failure*) объясня́ть (объясни́ть *pf*);
**~able** *adj* отчётный; **to be ~able
to sb for sth** отвеча́ть (*impf*) за
что-н пе́ред кем-н; **~ancy** *n*
бухгалте́рия, бухга́лтерское
де́ло; **~ant** *n* бухга́лтер

**accumulate** [ə'kju:mjuleɪt] *vt*
нака́пливать (накопи́ть *pf*) ♦ *vi*
нака́пливаться (накопи́ться *pf*)

**accuracy** ['ækjurəsɪ] *n* то́чность *f*

**accurate** ['ækjurɪt] *adj* то́чный;
(*person, device*) аккура́тный; **~ly**
*adv* то́чно

**accusation** [ækju'zeɪʃən] *n*
обвине́ние

**accuse** [ə'kju:z] *vt*: **to ~ sb (of sth)**
обвиня́ть (обвини́ть *pf*) кого́-н (в
чём-н); **~d** *n* (*LAW*): **the ~d**
обвиня́емый(ая) *m(f) adj*

**accustomed** [ə'kʌstəmd] *adj*: **I'm ~
to working late/to the heat** я
привы́к рабо́тать по́здно/к жаре́

**ace** [eɪs] *n* (*CARDS*) туз; (*TENNIS*)
вы́игрыш с пода́чи,

**ache** [eɪk] *n* боль *f* ♦ *vi* боле́ть
(*impf*); **my head ~s** у меня́ боли́т
голова́

**achieve** [ə'tʃi:v] *vt* (*result*)
достига́ть (дости́гнуть *or*
дости́чь *pf*) +*gen*; (*success*)
добива́ться (доби́ться *pf*) +*gen*;
**~ment** *n* достиже́ние

**acid** ['æsɪd] *adj* (*CHEM*) кисло́тный;
(*taste*) ки́слый ♦ *n* (*CHEM*)
кислота́; **~ rain** *n* кисло́тный

дождь m

**acknowledge** [ək'nɔlɪdʒ] vt (letter etc: also: ~ **receipt of**) подтверждáть (подтвердúть pf) получéние +gen; (fact) признавáть (признáть pf); ~**ment** n (of letter etc) подтверждéние получéния

**acne** ['æknɪ] n угрú mpl, прыщú mpl

**acorn** ['eɪkɔ:n] n жёлудь m

**acquaintance** n знакóмый(ая) m(f) adj

**acquire** [ə'kwaɪər] vt приобретáть (приобрестú pf)

**acquisition** [ækwɪ'zɪʃən] n приобретéние

**acre** ['eɪkər] n акр

**across** [ə'krɔs] prep (over) чéрез +acc; (on the other side of) на другóй сторонé +gen, по ту стóрону+gen; (crosswise over) чéрез +acc, поперёк +gen ♦ adv на ту или другýю стóрону; (measurement: width) ширинóй; to **walk ~ the road** переходúть (перейтú pf) дорóгу; to **take sb ~ the road** переводúть (перевестú pf) когó-н чéрез дорóгу; the lake **is 12 km ~** ширинá óзера - 12 км; ~ **from** напрóтив +gen

**act** [ækt] n (also LAW) акт; (deed) постýпок; (of play) дéйствие, акт ♦ vi (do sth) поступáть (поступúть pf), дéйствовать (impf); (behave) вестú (повестú pf) себя; (have effect) дéйствовать (подéйствовать pf); (THEAT) игрáть (сыгрáть pf); in the ~ **of** в процéссе +gen; to ~ **as** дéйствовать (impf) в кáчестве +gen; ~**ing** adj: ~**ing director** исполняющий обязанности дирéктора ♦ n (profession) актёрская профéссия

**action** ['ækʃən] n (deed) постýпок,

дéйствие; (motion) движéние (MIL) воéнные дéйствия ntpl; (LAW) иск; the machine was out of ~ машúна вышла из строя; to **take ~** принимáть (принять pf) мéры

**active** ['æktɪv] adj актúвный; (volcano) дéйствующий; ~**ly** adv (participate) актúвно; (discourage, dislike) сúльно

**activist** ['æktɪvɪst] n активúст(ка)

**activity** [æk'tɪvɪtɪ] n (being active) актúвность f; (action) дéятельность f; (pastime) занятие

**actor** ['æktər] n актёр

**actress** ['æktrɪs] n актрúса

**actual** ['æktjuəl] adj (real) действúтельный; the ~ **work hasn't begun yet** самá рабóта ещё не началáсь; ~**ly** adv (really) действúтельно; (in fact) на сáмом дéле, фактúчески; (even) дáже

**acupuncture** ['ækjupʌŋktʃər] n иглоукáлывание, акупунктýра

**acute** [ə'kju:t] adj óстрый; (anxiety) сúльный; ~ **accent** акýт

**AD** adv abbr (= Anno Domini) н.э.

**ad** [æd] n abbr (inf) = **advertisement**

**adamant** ['ædəmənt] adj непреклóнный

**adapt** [ə'dæpt] vt (alter) приспосáбливать (приспосóбить pf) ♦ vi: to ~ (to) приспосáбливаться (приспосóбиться pf) (к +dat), адаптúроваться (impf/pf) (к +dat)

**add** [æd] vt (to collection etc) прибавлять (прибáвить pf); (comment) добавлять (добáвить pf); (figures: also: ~ **up**) склáдывать (сложúть pf) ♦ vi: to ~ **to** (workload) увелúчивать (увелúчить pf); (problems) усугублять (усугубúть pf)

**adder** ['ædə<sup>r</sup>] *n* гадю́ка
**addict** ['ædɪkt] *n* (*also*: **drug ~**)
наркома́н; **~ed** [ə'dɪktɪd] *adj*: **to be
~ed to** (*drugs etc*) пристрасти́ться
(*pf*) к +*dat*; (*fig*): **he's ~ed to
football** он зая́длый люби́тель
футбо́ла; **~ion** [ə'dɪkʃən] *n*
пристра́стие; **drug ~ion**
наркома́ния; **~ive** [ə'dɪktɪv] *adj*
(*drug*) вызыва́ющий привыка́ние
**addition** [ə'dɪʃən] *n* (*sum*)
сложе́ние; (*thing added*)
добавле́ние; (*to collection*)
пополне́ние; **in ~** вдоба́вок,
дополни́тельно; **in ~ to** в
дополне́ние к +*dat*; **~al** *adj*
дополни́тельный
**address** [ə'drɛs] *n* а́дрес; (*speech*)
речь *f* ♦ *vt* адресова́ть (*impf/pf*);
(*person*) обраща́ться (обрати́ться
*pf*) к +*dat*; (*problem*) занима́ться
(заня́ться *pf*) +*instr*; **~ book** *n*
записна́я кни́жка
**adept** ['ædɛpt] *adj*: **~ at** иску́сный в
+*prp*
**adequate** ['ædɪkwɪt] *adj* (*sufficient*)
доста́точный; (*satisfactory*)
адеква́тный
**adhere** [əd'hɪə<sup>r</sup>] *vi*: **to ~ to** (*fig*)
приде́рживаться (*impf*) +*gen*
**adhesive** [əd'hi:zɪv] *adj* кле́йкий
♦ *n* клей
**ad hoc** [æd'hɔk] *adj* (*committee*)
со́зданный на ме́сте
**adjacent** [ə'dʒeɪsənt] *adj*: **~ (to)**
сме́жный (с +*instr*)
**adjective** ['ædʒɛktɪv] *n*
прилага́тельное *nt adj*
**adjust** [ə'dʒʌst] *vt* (*plans, views*)
приспоса́бливать (приспосо́бить
*pf*); (*clothing*) поправля́ть
(попра́вить *pf*); (*mechanism*)
регули́ровать (отрегули́ровать
*pf*) ♦ *vi*: **to ~ (to)**
приспоса́бливаться
(приспосо́биться *pf*) (к +*dat*);

**~able** *adj* регули́руемый; **~ment**
*n* (*to surroundings*) адапта́ция; (*of
prices, wages*) регули́рование; **to
make ~ments to** вноси́ть (внести́
*pf*) измене́ния в +*acc*
**administer** [əd'mɪnɪstə<sup>r</sup>] *vt* (*country,
department*) управля́ть (*impf*)
+*instr*, руководи́ть (*impf*) +*instr*;
(*justice*) отправля́ть (*impf*); (*test*)
проводи́ть (провести́ *pf*)
**administration** [ədmɪnɪs'treɪʃən] *n*
(*management*) администра́ция
**administrative** [əd'mɪnɪstrətɪv] *adj*
администрати́вный
**admiration** [ædmə'reɪʃən] *n*
восхище́ние
**admire** [əd'maɪə<sup>r</sup>] *vt* восхища́ться
(восхити́ться *pf*) +*instr*; (*gaze at*)
любова́ться (*impf*) +*instr*; **~r** *n*
покло́нник(ица)
**admission** [əd'mɪʃən] *n*
(*admittance*) до́пуск; (*entry fee*)
входна́я пла́та; **"~ free", "free ~"**
"вход свобо́дный"
**admit** [əd'mɪt] *vt* (*confess, accept*)
признава́ть (призна́ть *pf*); (*permit
to enter*) впуска́ть (впусти́ть *pf*);
(*to hospital*) госпитализи́ровать
(*impf/pf*); **~ to** *vt fus* (*crime*)
сознава́ться (созна́ться *pf*) в
+*prp*; **~tedly** [əd'mɪtɪdlɪ] *adv*:
**~tedly it is not easy** призна́ться,
э́то не легко́
**adolescence** [ædəu'lɛsns] *n*
подростко́вый во́зраст
**adolescent** [ædəu'lɛsnt] *adj*
подростко́вый ♦ *n* подро́сток
**adopt** [ə'dɔpt] *vt* (*son*) усыновля́ть
(усынови́ть *pf*); (*daughter*)
удочеря́ть (удочери́ть *pf*); (*policy*)
принима́ть (приня́ть *pf*); **~ed** *adj*
(*child*) приёмный; **~ion** [ə'dɔpʃən]
*n* (*see vt*) усыновле́ние;
удочере́ние; приня́тие
**adore** [ə'dɔ:<sup>r</sup>] *vt* обожа́ть (*impf*)
**adrenalin** [ə'drɛnəlɪn] *n* адренали́н

**Adriatic** [ˌeɪdrɪˈætɪk] n: **the ~**
Адриа́тика

**adult** [ˈædʌlt] n взро́слый(ая) m(f)
adj ♦ adj (grown-up) взро́слый; **~
film** фильм для взро́слых

**adultery** [əˈdʌltərɪ] n супру́жеская
неве́рность f

**advance** [ədˈvɑːns] n (progress)
успе́х; (MIL) наступле́ние;
(money) ава́нс ♦ adj (booking)
предвари́тельный ♦ vt (theory,
idea) выдвига́ть (вы́двинуть pf)
♦ vi продвига́ться (продви́нуться
pf) вперёд; (MIL) наступа́ть (impf);
**in ~** зара́нее, предвари́тельно;
**to ~ sb money** плати́ть
(заплати́ть pf) кому́-н ава́нсом;
**~d** adj (studies) для продви́нутого
у́ровня; (course) продви́нутый;
(child, country) разви́той; **~d
maths** вы́сшая матема́тика

**advantage** [ədˈvɑːntɪdʒ] n
преиму́щество; **to take ~ of**
(person) испо́льзовать (pf); **to our
~** в на́ших интере́сах; **~ous**
[ˌædvənˈteɪdʒəs] adj (situation)
вы́годный; **it's ~ous to us** нам
э́то вы́годно

**adventure** [ədˈventʃər] n
приключе́ние

**adventurous** [ədˈventʃərəs] adj
(person) сме́лый

**adverb** [ˈædvəːb] n наре́чие

**adversary** [ˈædvəsərɪ] n
проти́вник(ница)

**adverse** [ˈædvəːs] adj
неблагоприя́тный

**adversity** [ədˈvəːsɪtɪ] n беда́,
несча́стие

**advert** [ˈædvəːt] n abbr (BRIT) =
**advertisement**

**advertise** [ˈædvətaɪz] vti
реклами́ровать (impf); **to ~ on
television/in a newspaper** дава́ть
(дать pf) объявле́ние по
телеви́дению/в газе́ту; **to ~ a job**

объявля́ть (объяви́ть pf) ко́нкурс
на ме́сто; **to ~ for staff** дава́ть
(дать pf) объявле́ние, что
тре́буются рабо́тники; **~ment**
[ədˈvəːtɪsmənt] n рекла́ма;
(classified) объявле́ние

**advice** [ədˈvaɪs] n сове́т; **a piece of
~** сове́т; **to take legal ~**
обраща́ться (обрати́ться pf) (за
сове́том) к юри́сту

**advisable** [ədˈvaɪzəbl] adj
целесообра́зный

**advise** [ədˈvaɪz] vt сове́товать
(посове́товать pf) +dat;
(professionally) консульти́ровать
(проконсульти́ровать pf) +gen; **to
~ sb of sth** извеща́ть (извести́ть
pf) кого́-н о чём-н; **to ~ (sb)
against doing** отсове́товать (pf)
(кому́-н) +impf infin; **~r** n
сове́тник, консульта́нт; **legal ~r**
юрискон́сульт

**advisor** [ədˈvaɪzər] n = **adviser**; **~y**
[ədˈvaɪzərɪ] adj

**advocate** vb [ˈædvəkeɪt] n [ˈædvəkɪt]
vt выступа́ть (вы́ступить pf) за
+acc ♦ n (LAW) защи́тник,
адвока́т; (supporter): **~ of**
сторо́нник(ица) +gen

**Aegean** [iːˈdʒiːən] n: **the ~**
Эге́йское мо́ре

**aerial** [ˈɛərɪəl] n анте́нна ♦ adj
возду́шный; **~ photography**
аэрофотосъёмка

**aerobics** [ɛəˈrəubɪks] n аэро́бика

**aeroplane** [ˈɛərəpleɪn] n (BRIT)
самолёт

**aerosol** [ˈɛərəsɔl] n аэрозо́ль m

**aesthetic** [iːsˈθetɪk] adj
эстети́ческий

**affair** [əˈfɛər] n (matter) де́ло; (also:
**love ~**) рома́н

**affect** [əˈfekt] vt (influence)
де́йствовать (поде́йствовать pf)
or влия́ть (повлия́ть pf) на +acc;
(afflict) поража́ть (порази́ть pf);

(*move deeply*) тро́гать (тро́нуть *pf*)

**affection** [ə'fɛkʃən] *n*
привя́занность *f*; **~ate** *adj*
не́жный

**affluent** ['æfluənt] *adj*
благополу́чный

**afford** [ə'fɔːd] *vt* позволя́ть
(позво́лить *pf*) себе́; **I can't ~ it**
мне э́то не по карма́ну; **I can't ~
the time** мне вре́мя не
позволя́ет; **~able** *adj* досту́пный

**Afghanistan** [æf'gænɪstæn] *n*
Афганиста́н

**afloat** [ə'fləut] *adv* (*floating*) на
плаву́

**afraid** [ə'freɪd] *adj* испу́ганный; **to
be ~ of sth/sb/of doing** боя́ться
(*impf*) чего́-н/кого́-н/+*infin*; **to be ~
to** боя́ться (побоя́ться *pf*) +*infin*; **I
am ~ that** (*apology*) бою́сь, что; **I
am ~ so/not** бою́сь, что да/
нет

**Africa** ['æfrɪkə] *n* А́фрика; **African**
*adj* африка́нский

**after** ['ɑːftə'] *prep* (*time*) по́сле +*gen*,
спустя́ +*acc*, че́рез +*acc*; (*place,
order*) за +*instr* ♦ *adv* пото́м, по́сле
♦ *conj* по́сле того́ как; **~ three
years they divorced** спустя́ *or*
че́рез три го́да они́ развели́сь;
**who are you ~?** кто Вам ну́жен?;
**to name sb ~ sb** называ́ть
(назва́ть *pf*) кого́-н в честь кого́-н;
**it's twenty ~ five** (*US*) сейча́с
два́дцать мину́т деся́того; **to ask
~ sb** справля́ться (спра́виться *pf*)
о ком-н; **~ all** в конце́ концо́в; **~
he left** по́сле того́ как он ушёл; **~
having done this** сде́лав э́то;
**~math** *n* после́дствия *ntpl*;
**~noon** *n* втора́я полови́на дня;
**in the ~** днём; **~-shave (lotion)**
*n* одеколо́н по́сле бритья́;
**~wards** (*US* **~ward**) *adv*
впосле́дствии, пото́м

**again** [ə'gɛn] *adv* (*once more*) ещё

раз, сно́ва; (*repeatedly*) опя́ть; **I
won't go there ~** я бо́льше не
пойду́ туда́; **~ and ~** сно́ва и
сно́ва

**against** [ə'gɛnst] *prep* (*lean*) к +*dat*;
(*hit, rub*) о +*acc*; (*stand*) у +*gen*; (*in
opposition to*) про́тив +*gen*; (*at odds
with*) вопреки́ +*dat*; (*compared to*)
по сравне́нию с +*instr*

**age** [eɪdʒ] *n* во́зраст; (*period in
history*) век

**aged¹** ['eɪdʒd] *adj*: **a boy ~ ten**
ма́льчик десяти́ лет

**aged²** ['eɪdʒɪd] *npl*: **the ~**
престаре́лые *pl adj*

**agency** ['eɪdʒənsɪ] *n* (*COMM*) бюро́
*nt ind*, аге́нтство; (*POL*)
управле́ние

**agenda** [ə'dʒɛndə] *n* (*of meeting*)
пове́стка (дня)

**agent** ['eɪdʒənt] *n* аге́нт; (*COMM*)
посре́дник; (*CHEM*) реакти́в

**aggression** [ə'grɛʃən] *n* агре́ссия

**aggressive** [ə'grɛsɪv] *adj* (*belligerent*)
агресси́вный

**agility** [ə'dʒɪlɪtɪ] *n* прово́рство;
**mental agility** жи́вость *f* ума́

**AGM** *n abbr* = **annual general
meeting**

**ago** [ə'gəu] *adv*: **two days ~** два
дня наза́д; **not long ~** неда́вно;
**how long ~?** как давно́?

**agony** ['ægənɪ] *n* мучи́тельная
боль *f*; **to be in ~** му́читься (*impf*)
от бо́ли

**agree** [ə'griː] *vt* согласо́вывать
(согласова́ть *pf*) ♦ *vi*: **to ~ with**
(*have same opinion*) соглаша́ться
(согласи́ться *pf*) с +*instr*;
(*correspond*) согласова́ться (*impf/
pf*) с +*instr*; **to ~ that** соглаша́ться
(согласи́ться *pf*), что; **garlic
doesn't ~ with me** я не
переношу́ чеснока́; **to ~ to sth/to
do** соглаша́ться (согласи́ться *pf*)
на что-н/+*infin*; **~able** *adj*

(*pleasant*) прия́тный; (*willing*): **I am ~able** я согла́сен; **~ment** n (*consent*) согла́сие; (*arrangement*) соглаше́ние, догово́р; **in ~ment with** в согла́сии с +*instr*; **we are in complete ~ment** ме́жду на́ми по́лное согла́сие

**agricultural** [ægrɪ'kʌltʃərəl] *adj* сельскохозя́йственный; **~ land** земе́льные уго́дья

**agriculture** ['ægrɪkʌltʃər] *n* се́льское хозя́йство

**ahead** [ə'hɛd] *adv* впереди́; (*direction*) вперёд; **~ of** впереди́ +*gen* (*earlier than*) ра́ньше +*gen*; **~ of time** *or* **schedule** досро́чно; **go right** *or* **straight ~** иди́те вперёд *or* пря́мо; **go ~!** (*giving permission*) приступа́йте!, дава́йте!

**aid** [eɪd] *n* (*assistance*) по́мощь f; (*device*) приспособле́ние ♦ *vt* помога́ть (помо́чь *pf*) +*dat*; **in ~ of** в по́мощь +*dat*; *see also* **hearing**

**aide** [eɪd] *n* помо́щник

**AIDS** [eɪdz] *n abbr* (= *acquired immune deficiency syndrome*) СПИД

**aim** [eɪm] *n* (*objective*) цель f ♦ *vi* (*also*: **take ~**) це́литься (наце́литься *pf*) ♦ *vt*: **to ~** (*at*) (*gun, camera*) наводи́ть (навести́ *pf*) (на +*acc*); (*missile, blow*) це́лить (наце́лить *pf*) (на +*acc*); (*remark*) направля́ть (напра́вить *pf*) (на +*acc*); **to ~ to do** ста́вить (поста́вить *pf*) свое́й це́лью +*infin*; **he has a good ~** он ме́ткий стрело́к

**ain't** [eɪnt] (*inf*) = **am not, are not, is not**

**air** [ɛər] *n* во́здух; (*appearance*) вид ♦ *vt* (*room, bedclothes*) прове́тривать (прове́трить *pf*); (*views*) обнаро́довать (*pf*) ♦ *cpd* возду́шный; **by ~** по во́здуху; **on the ~** (*be*) в эфи́ре; (*go*) в эфи́р; **~borne** *adj* (*attack*) возду́шный;

**~ conditioning** *n* кондициони́рование; **~craft** *n inv* самолёт; **Air Force** *n* Вое́нно-Возду́шные Си́лы *fpl*; **~ hostess** *n* (*BRIT*) бортпроводни́ца, стюарде́сса; **~line** *n* авиакомпа́ния; **~ mail** *n*: **by ~ mail** авиапо́чтой; **~plane** *n* (*US*) самолёт; **~port** *n* аэропо́рт; **~ rage** *n* хулига́нское поведе́ние на борту́ самолёта; **~ raid** *n* возду́шный налёт

**airy** ['ɛərɪ] *adj* (*room*) просто́рный

**aisle** [aɪl] *n* прохо́д

**alarm** [ə'lɑːm] *n* (*anxiety*) трево́га; (*device*) сигнализа́ция ♦ *vt* трево́жить (встрево́жить *pf*); **~ clock** *n* буди́льник

**Albania** [æl'beɪnɪə] *n* Алба́ния

**album** ['ælbəm] *n* альбо́м

**alcohol** ['ælkəhɔl] *n* алкого́ль *m*; **~ic** [ælkə'hɔlɪk] *adj* алкого́льный ♦ *n* алкого́лик(и́чка)

**alcove** ['ælkəuv] *n* алько́в

**alert** [ə'lɜːt] *adj* внима́тельный; (*to danger*) бди́тельный ♦ *vt* (*police etc*) предупрежда́ть (предупреди́ть *pf*); **to be on the ~** (*also MIL*) быть (*impf*) начеку́

**A levels** - квалификацио́нные экза́мены. Шко́льники сдаю́т их в во́зрасте 17-18 лет. Полу́ченные результа́ты определя́ют приём в университе́т. Экза́мены сдаю́тся по трём предме́там. Вы́бор предме́тов дикту́ется специа́льностью, кото́рую выпускники́ плани́руют изуча́ть в университе́те.

**Algeria** [æl'dʒɪərɪə] *n* Алжи́р

**alias** ['eɪlɪəs] *n* вы́мышленное и́мя *nt* ♦ *adv*: **~ John** он же Джон

**alibi** ['ælɪbaɪ] *n* а́либи *nt ind*

**alien** ['eɪlɪən] n (extraterrestrial) инопланетя́нин(-я́нка) ♦ adj: ~ (to) чу́ждый (+dat)

**~ate** ['eɪlɪəneɪt] vt отчужда́ть (impf), отта́лкивать (оттолкну́ть pf)

**alight** [ə'laɪt] adj: **to be** ~ горе́ть (impf); (eyes, face) сия́ть (impf)

**alike** [ə'laɪk] adj одина́ковый ♦ adv одина́ково; **they look** ~ они́ похо́жи друг на дру́га

**alive** [ə'laɪv] adj (place) оживлённый; **he is** ~ он жив

KEYWORD

**all** [ɔːl] adj весь (f вся, nt всё, pl все); **all day** весь день; **all night** всю ночь; **all five stayed** все пя́теро оста́лись; **all the books** все кни́ги; **all the time** всё вре́мя ♦ pron **1** всё; **I ate it all, I ate all of it** я всё съел; **all of us stayed** мы все оста́лись; **we all sat down** мы все се́ли; **is that all?** э́то всё? **2** (in phrases): **above all** пре́жде всего́; **after all** в конце́ концо́в; **all in all** в це́лом or о́бщем; **not at all** (in answer to question) совсе́м or во́все нет; (in answer to thanks) не́ за что; **I'm not at all tired** я совсе́м не уста́л ♦ adv совсе́м; **I am all alone** я совсе́м оди́н; **I did it all by myself** я всё сде́лал сам; **it's not as hard as all that** э́то во́все не так уж тру́дно; **all the more/better** тем бо́лее/лу́чше; **I have all but finished** я почти́ (что) зако́нчил; **the score is two all** счёт 2:2

**all clear** n отбо́й

**allegation** [ælɪ'ɡeɪʃən] n обвине́ние

**allege** [ə'ledʒ] vt (claim) утвержда́ть (impf); **~dly** [ə'ledʒɪdlɪ] adv я́кобы

**allegiance** [ə'liːdʒəns] n ве́рность

f; (to idea) приве́рженность f

**allergic** [ə'ləːdʒɪk] adj: **he is** ~ **to ...** у него́ аллерги́я на +acc ...

**allergy** ['ælədʒɪ] n (MED) аллерги́я

**alleviate** [ə'liːvɪeɪt] vt облегча́ть (облегчи́ть pf)

**alley** ['ælɪ] n переу́лок

**alliance** [ə'laɪəns] n сою́з; (POL) алья́нс

**allied** ['ælaɪd] adj сою́зный

**alligator** ['ælɪɡeɪtə'] n аллига́тор

**all-in** ['ɔːlɪn] adj (BRIT): **it cost me £100** ~ в о́бщей сло́жности мне э́то сто́ило £100

**all-night** ['ɔːl'naɪt] adj ночно́й

**allocate** ['æləkeɪt] vt выделя́ть (вы́делить pf); (tasks) поруча́ть (поручи́ть pf)

**all-out** ['ɔːlaut] adj (effort) максима́льный; (attack) масси́рованный

**allow** [ə'lau] vt (permit) разреша́ть (разреши́ть pf); (: claim, goal) признава́ть (призна́ть pf) действи́тельным; (set aside: sum) выделя́ть (вы́делить pf); (concede): **to** ~ **that** допуска́ть (допусти́ть pf), что; **to** ~ **sb to do** разреша́ть (разреши́ть pf) or позволя́ть (позво́лить pf) кому́-н +infin; ~ **for** vt fus учи́тывать (уче́сть pf), принима́ть (приня́ть pf) в расчёт; **~ance** n (COMM) де́ньги pl на расхо́ды; (pocket money) карма́нные де́ньги; (welfare payment) посо́бие; **to make ~ances for** де́лать (сде́лать pf) ски́дку для +gen

**all right** adv хорошо́, норма́льно; (positive response) хорошо́, ла́дно ♦ adj неплохо́й, норма́льный; **is everything ~?** всё норма́льно or в поря́дке?; **are you ~?** как ты?, ты в поря́дке? (разг); **do you like him? - he's ~** он Вам нра́вится? - ничего́

**all-time** ['ɔːl'taɪm] *adj* (*record*) непревзойдённый; **inflation is at an ~ low** инфляция на небывало низком уровне

**ally** *n* ['ælaɪ] *n* союзник

**almighty** [ɔːl'maɪtɪ] *adj* (*tremendous*) колоссальный

**almond** ['ɑːmənd] *n* миндаль *m*

**almost** ['ɔːlməust] *adv* почти; (*all but*) чуть *or* едва не

**alone** [ə'ləun] *adj, adv* один; **to leave sb/sth ~** оставлять (оставить *pf*) кого-н/что-н в покое; **let ~ ...** не говоря уже о +*prp* ...

**along** [ə'lɒŋ] *prep* (*motion*) по +*dat*, вдоль +*gen*; (*position*) вдоль +*gen* ♦ *adv*: **is he coming ~ (with us)?** он идёт с нами?; **he was limping ~** он шёл хромая; **~ with** вместе с +*instr*; **all ~** с самого начала; **~side** *prep* (*position*) рядом с +*instr*, вдоль +*gen*; (*motion*) к +*dat* ♦ *adv* рядом

**aloud** [ə'laud] *adv* (*read, speak*) вслух

**alphabet** ['ælfəbɛt] *n* алфавит

**alpine** ['ælpaɪn] *adj* высокогорный, альпийский

**Alps** [ælps] *npl*: **the ~** Альпы *pl*

**already** [ɔːl'rɛdɪ] *adv* уже

**alright** ['ɔːl'raɪt] *adv* (*BRIT*) = **all right**

**also** ['ɔːlsəu] *adv* (*about subject*) также, тоже; (*about object*) также; (*moreover*) кроме того, к тому же; **he ~ likes apples** он также *or* тоже любит яблоки; **he likes apples ~** он любит также яблоки

**altar** ['ɔltər] *n* алтарь *m*

**alter** ['ɔltər] *vt* изменять (изменить *pf*) ♦ *vi* изменяться (измениться *pf*); **~ation** [ɔltə'reɪʃən] *n* изменение

**alternate** *adj* [ɔl'təːnɪt] *vb* ['ɔltəːneɪt] *adj* чередующийся; (*US:*

*alternative*) альтернативный ♦ *vi*: **to ~ (with)** чередоваться (*impf*) (с +*instr*); **on ~ days** через день

**alternative** [ɔl'təːnətɪv] *adj* альтернативный ♦ *n* альтернатива; **~ly** *adv*: **~ly one could ...** кроме того можно ...

**although** [ɔːl'ðəu] *conj* хотя

**altitude** ['æltɪtjuːd] *n* (*of plane*) высота; (*of place*) высота над уровнем моря

**altogether** [ɔːltə'gɛðər] *adv* (*completely*) совершенно; (*in all*) в общем, в общей сложности

**aluminium** [ælju'mɪnɪəm] *n* (*BRIT*) алюминий

**aluminum** [ə'luːmɪnəm] *n* (*US*) = **aluminium**

**always** ['ɔːlweɪz] *adv* всегда

**am** [æm] *vb see* **be**

**A.M.** *n abbr* (= *Assembly Member*) член ассамблеи

**a.m.** *adv abbr* (= *ante meridiem*) до полудня

**AMA** *n abbr* = *American Medical Association*

**amateur** ['æmətər] *n* любитель *m*; **~ dramatics** любительский театр; **~ photographer** фотограф-любитель *m*

**amazement** [ə'meɪzmənt] *n* изумление

**amazing** [ə'meɪzɪŋ] *adj* (*surprising*) поразительный; (*fantastic*) изумительный, замечательный

**ambassador** [æm'bæsədər] *n* посол

**ambiguity** [æmbɪ'gjuɪtɪ] *n* неясность *f*, двусмысленность *f*

**ambiguous** [æm'bɪgjuəs] *adj* неясный, двусмысленный

**ambition** [æm'bɪʃən] *n* (*see adj*) честолюбие; амбиция; (*aim*) цель *f*

**ambitious** [æm'bɪʃəs] *adj* (*positive*) честолюбивый; (*negative*) амбициозный

**ambivalent** [æm'bɪvələnt] *adj*
(*attitude*) двойственный; (*person*)
противоречивый

**ambulance** ['æmbjuləns] *n* скорая
помощь *f*

**ambush** ['æmbuʃ] *n* засада ♦ *vt*
устраивать (устроить *pf*) засаду
+*dat*

**amend** [ə'mend] *vt* (*law, text*)
пересматривать (пересмотреть
*pf*) ♦ *n*: **to make ~s** заглаживать
(загладить *pf*) (свою) вину;
**~ment** *n* поправка

**amenities** [ə'mi:nɪtɪz] *npl* удобства
*ntpl*

**America** [ə'merɪkə] *n* Америка; **~n**
*adj* американский ♦ *n*
американец(нка)

**amicable** ['æmɪkəbl] *adj*
(*relationship*) дружеский

**amid(st)** [ə'mɪd(st)] *prep* посреди
+*gen*

**amiss** [ə'mɪs] *adj, adv*: **there's
something ~** здесь что-то
неладно

**ammunition** [æmju'nɪʃən] *n* (*for
gun*) патроны *mpl*

**amnesty** ['æmnɪstɪ] *n* амнистия

**among(st)** [ə'mʌŋ(st)] *prep* среди
+*gen*

**amount** [ə'maunt] *n* количество
♦ *vi*: **to amount to** (*total*)
составлять (составить *pf*)

**amp(ère)** ['æmp(ɛər)] *n* ампер

**ample** ['æmpl] *adj* (*large*)
солидный; (*abundant*) обильный;
(*enough*) достаточный; **to have ~
time/room** иметь (*impf*)
достаточно времени/места

**amuse** [ə'mju:z] *vt* развлекать
(развлечь *pf*); **~ment** *n* (*mirth*)
удовольствие; (*pastime*)
развлечение; **~ment arcade** *n*
павильон с игровыми
аппаратами

**an** [æn] *indef art see* **a**

**anaemia** [ə'ni:mɪə] (*US* **anemia**) *n*
анемия, малокровие

**anaesthetic** [ænɪs'θetɪk] (*US*
**anesthetic**) *n* наркоз

**analyse** ['ænəlaɪz] (*US* **analyze**) *vt*
анализировать
(проанализировать *pf*)

**analysis** [ə'næləsɪs] (*pl* **analyses**) *n*
анализ

**analyst** ['ænəlɪst] *n* (*political*)
аналитик, комментатор;
(*financial, economic*) эксперт; (*US:
psychiatrist*) психиатр

**analytic(al)** [ænə'lɪtɪk(l)] *adj*
аналитический

**analyze** ['ænəlaɪz] *vt* (*US*) = **analyse**

**anarchy** ['ænəkɪ] *n* анархия

**anatomy** [ə'nætəmɪ] *n* анатомия;
(*body*) организм

**ancestor** ['ænsɪstər] *n* предок

**anchor** ['æŋkər] *n* якорь *m*

**anchovy** ['æntʃəvɪ] *n* анчоус

**ancient** ['eɪnʃənt] *adj* (*civilization,
person*) древний; (*monument*)
старинный

**and** [ænd] *conj* и; **my father ~ I** я и
мой отец, мы с отцом; **bread ~
butter** хлеб с маслом; **~ so on** и
так далее; **try ~ come**
постарайтесь прийти; **he talked
~ talked** он всё говорил и
говорил

**Andes** ['ændi:z] *npl*: **the ~** Анды *pl*

**anecdote** ['ænɪkdəut] *n*
любопытная история

**anemia** [ə'ni:mɪə] *n* (*US*) =
**anaemia**

**anesthetic** [ænɪs'θetɪk] *n* (*US*) =
**anaesthetic**

**angel** ['eɪndʒəl] *n* ангел

**anger** ['æŋɡər] *n* гнев,
возмущение

**angle** ['æŋɡl] *n* (*corner*) угол

**angler** ['æŋɡlər] *n* рыболов

**Anglican** ['æŋɡlɪkən] *adj*
англиканский ♦ *n*

англика́нец(а́нка)

**angling** ['æŋglɪŋ] n ры́бная ло́вля

**angrily** ['æŋgrɪlɪ] adv серди́то, гне́вно

**angry** ['æŋgrɪ] adj серди́тый, гне́вный; (wound) воспалённый; **to be ~ with sb/at sth** серди́ться (impf) на кого́-н/что-н; **to get ~** серди́ться (рассерди́ться pf)

**anguish** ['æŋgwɪʃ] n му́ка

**animal** ['ænɪməl] n живо́тное nt adj; (wild animal) зверь m (pej: person) зверь, живо́тное ♦ adj живо́тный

**animated** adj оживлённый, живо́й; (film) мультипликацио́нный

**animation** [ænɪ'meɪʃən] n (enthusiasm) оживле́ние

**ankle** ['æŋkl] n лоды́жка

**anniversary** [ænɪ'vɔ:sərɪ] n годовщи́на

**announce** [ə'nauns] vt (engagement, decision) объявля́ть (объяви́ть pf) (о +prp); (birth, death) извеща́ть (извести́ть pf) о +prp; **~ment** n объявле́ние; (in newspaper etc) сообще́ние

**annoy** [ə'nɔɪ] vt раздража́ть (раздражи́ть pf); **~ed** adj раздражённый; **~ing** adj (noise) раздража́ющий; (mistake, event) доса́дный; **he is ~ing** он меня́ раздража́ет

**annual** ['ænjuəl] adj (meeting) ежего́дный; (income) годово́й; **~ly** adv ежего́дно

**annum** ['ænəm] n see **per**

**anonymity** [ænə'nɪmɪtɪ] n анони́мность f

**anonymous** [ə'nɔnɪməs] adj анони́мный

**anorak** ['ænəræk] n ку́ртка

**anorexia** [ænə'rɛksɪə] n аноре́ксия

**another** [ə'nʌðər] pron друго́й ♦ adj: **~ book** (additional) ещё

одна́ кни́га; (different) друга́я кни́га; see also **one**

**answer** ['ɑ:nsər] n отве́т; (to problem) реше́ние ♦ vi отвеча́ть (отве́тить pf) ♦ vt (letter, question) отвеча́ть (отве́тить pf) на +acc; (person) отвеча́ть (отве́тить pf) +dat; **in ~ to your letter** в отве́т на Ва́ше письмо́; **to ~ the phone** подходи́ть (подойти́ pf) к телефо́ну; **to ~ the bell** or **the door** открыва́ть (откры́ть pf) дверь; **~ to** vt fus (description) соотве́тствовать (impf) +dat; **~ing machine** n автоотве́тчик

**ant** [ænt] n мураве́й

**antagonism** [æn'tægənɪzəm] n антагони́зм

**Antarctic** [ænt'ɑ:ktɪk] n: **the ~** Анта́рктика

**antelope** ['æntɪləup] n антило́па

**anthem** ['ænθəm] n: **national ~** госуда́рственный гимн

**antibiotic** ['æntɪbaɪ'ɔtɪk] n антибио́тик

**antibody** ['æntɪbɔdɪ] n антите́ло

**anticipate** [æn'tɪsɪpeɪt] vt (expect) ожида́ть (impf) +gen; (foresee) предуга́дывать (предугада́ть pf); (forestall) предвосхища́ть (предвосхи́тить pf)

**anticipation** [æntɪsɪ'peɪʃən] n (expectation) ожида́ние; (eagerness) предвкуше́ние

**antics** ['æntɪks] npl (of child) ша́лости fpl

**antidepressant** ['æntɪdɪ'prɛsnt] n антидепресса́нт

**antidote** ['æntɪdəut] n противоя́дие

**antifreeze** ['æntɪfri:z] n антифри́з

**antique** [æn'ti:k] n антиква́рная вещь f, предме́т старины́ ♦ adj антиква́рный

**antiquity** [æn'tɪkwɪtɪ] n анти́чность f

**anti-Semitism** ['æntɪ'sɛmɪtɪzəm] *n*
антисемити́зм

**antiseptic** [æntɪ'sɛptɪk] *n*
антисе́птик

**anxiety** [æŋ'zaɪətɪ] *n* трево́га

**anxious** ['æŋkʃəs] *adj* (*person, look*)
беспоко́йный, озабо́ченный
(*time*) трево́жный; **she is ~ to do**
она́ о́чень хо́чет +*infin*; **to be ~**
**about** беспоко́иться (*impf*) о +*prp*

KEYWORD

**any** ['ɛnɪ] *adj* 1 (*in questions etc*):
**have you any butter/children?** у
Вас есть ма́сло/де́ти?; **do you**
**have any questions?** у Вас есть
каки́е-нибудь вопро́сы?; **if there**
**are any tickets left** е́сли ещё
оста́лись биле́ты
2 (*with negative*): **I haven't any**
**bread/books** у меня́ нет хле́ба/
книг; **I didn't buy any newspapers**
я не купи́л газе́т
3 (*no matter which*) любо́й; **any**
**colour will do** любо́й цвет
подойдёт
4 (*in phrases*): **in any case** в
любо́м слу́чае; **any day now** в
любо́й день; **at any moment** в
любо́й моме́нт; **at any rate** во
вся́ком слу́чае; (*anyhow*) так и́ли
ина́че; **any time** (*at any moment*) в
любо́й моме́нт; (*whenever*) в
любо́е вре́мя; (*as response*) не́ за
что
♦ *pron* 1 (*in questions etc*): **I need**
**some money, have you got any?**
мне нужны́ де́ньги, у Вас есть?;
**can any of you sing?** кто-нибудь
из вас уме́ет петь?
2 (*with negative*) ни оди́н (*f* одна́,
*nt* одно́, *pl* одни́); **I haven't any**
(**of those**) у меня́ таки́х нет
3 (*no matter which one(s)*) любо́й;
**take any you like** возьми́те то,
что Вам нра́вится

♦ *adv* 1 (*in questions etc*): **do you**
**want any more soup?** хоти́те
ещё су́пу?; **are you feeling any**
**better?** Вам лу́чше?
2 (*with negative*): **I can't hear him**
**any more** я бо́льше его́ не
слы́шу; **don't wait any longer** не
жди́те бо́льше; **he isn't any**
**better** ему́ не лу́чше

**anybody** ['ɛnɪbɔdɪ] *pron* = **anyone**

**anyhow** ['ɛnɪhau] *adv* (*at any rate*)
так и́ли ина́че; **the work is done**
~ (*haphazardly*) рабо́та сде́лана
ко́е-как; **I shall go** ~ я так и́ли
ина́че пойду́

**anyone** ['ɛnɪwʌn] *pron* (*in questions*
*etc*) кто-нибудь; (*with negative*)
никто́; (*no matter who*) любо́й,
вся́кий; **can you see** ~? Вы
ви́дите кого́-нибудь?; **I can't see**
~ я никого́ не ви́жу; ~ **could do it**
любо́й *or* вся́кий мо́жет э́то
сде́лать; **you can invite** ~ Вы
мо́жете пригласи́ть кого́ уго́дно

**anything** ['ɛnɪθɪŋ] *pron* (*in questions*
*etc*) что-нибудь; (*with negative*)
ничего́; (*no matter what*) (всё,)
что уго́дно; **can you see** ~? Вы
ви́дите что-нибудь?; **I can't see** ~
я ничего́ не ви́жу; ~ (**at all**) **will**
**do** всё, что уго́дно подойдёт

**anyway** ['ɛnɪweɪ] *adv* всё равно́;
(*in brief*): ~, **I didn't want to go** в
о́бщем, я не хоте́л идти́; **I will be**
**there** ~ я всё равно́ там бу́ду; ~,
**I couldn't stay even if I wanted to**
в любо́м слу́чае, я не мог
оста́ться, да́же е́сли бы я хоте́л;
**why are you phoning,** ~? а всё-
таки, почему́ Вы звони́те?

KEYWORD

**anywhere** ['ɛnɪwɛər] *adv* 1 (*in*
*questions etc*: *position*) где-нибудь;
(: *motion*) куда́-нибудь; **can you**

**see him anywhere?** Вы его где-нибудь видите?; **did you go anywhere yesterday?** Вы вчера куда-нибудь ходили?
**2** (*with negative: position*) нигде; (*: motion*) никуда; **I can't see him anywhere** я нигде его не вижу; **I'm not going anywhere today** сегодня я никуда не иду
**3** (*no matter where: position*) где угодно; (*: motion*) куда угодно; **anywhere in the world** где угодно в мире; **put the books down anywhere** положите книги куда угодно

**apart** [ə'pɑːt] *adv* (*position*) в стороне; (*motion*) в сторону; (*separately*) раздельно, врозь; **they are ten miles ~** они находятся на расстоянии десяти миль друг от друга; **to take ~** разбирать (разобрать *pf*) (на части); **~ from** кроме +*gen*
**apartheid** [ə'pɑːteɪt] *n* апартеид
**apartment** [ə'pɑːtmənt] *n* (*US*) квартира; (*room*) комната
**apathy** ['æpəθɪ] *n* апатия
**ape** [eɪp] *n* человекообразная обезьяна ♦ *vt* копировать (скопировать *pf*)
**aperitif** [ə'pɛrɪtiːf] *n* аперитив
**apex** ['eɪpɛks] *n* (*also fig*) вершина
**apiece** [ə'piːs] *adv* (*each person*) на каждого; (*each thing*) за штуку
**apologize** [ə'pɒlədʒaɪz] *vi*: **to ~** (**for sth to sb**) извиняться (извиниться *pf*) (за что-н перед кем-н)
**apology** [ə'pɒlədʒɪ] *n* извинение
**appalling** [ə'pɔːlɪŋ] *adj* (*awful*) ужасный; (*shocking*) возмутительный
**apparatus** [æpə'reɪtəs] *n* аппаратура; (*in gym*) (гимнастический) снаряд; (*of*

*organization*) аппарат
**apparent** [ə'pærənt] *adj* (*seeming*) видимый; (*obvious*) очевидный; **~ly** *adv* по всей видимости
**appeal** [ə'piːl] *vi* (*LAW*) апеллировать (*impf/pf*), подавать (подать *pf*) апелляцию ♦ *n* (*attraction*) привлекательность *f*; (*plea*) призыв; (*LAW*) апелляция, обжалование; **to ~ (to sb) for** (*help, funds*) обращаться (обратиться *pf*) (к кому-н) за +*instr*; (*calm, order*) призывать (призвать *pf*) (кого-н) к +*dat*; **to ~ to** (*attract*) привлекать (привлечь *pf*), нравиться (понравиться *pf*) +*dat*; **~ing** *adj* привлекательный; (*pleading*) умоляющий
**appear** [ə'pɪər] *vi* появляться (появиться *pf*); (*seem*) казаться (показаться *pf*); **to ~ in court** представать (предстать *pf*) перед судом; **to ~ on TV** выступать (выступить *pf*) по телевидению; **it would ~ that ...** похоже (на то), что ...; **~ance** (*arrival*) появление; (*look, aspect*) внешность *f*; (*in public, on TV*) выступление
**appendices** [ə'pɛndɪsiːz] *npl of* **appendix**
**appendicitis** [əpɛndɪ'saɪtɪs] *n* аппендицит
**appendix** [ə'pɛndɪks] (*pl* **appendices**) *n* приложение; (*ANAT*) аппендикс
**appetite** ['æpɪtaɪt] *n* аппетит
**applaud** [ə'plɔːd] *vi* аплодировать (*impf*), рукоплескать (*impf*) ♦ *vt* аплодировать (*impf*) +*dat*, рукоплескать (*impf*) +*dat*; (*praise*) одобрять (одобрить *pf*)
**applause** [ə'plɔːz] *n* аплодисменты *pl*
**apple** ['æpl] *n* яблоко
**applicable** [ə'plɪkəbl] *adj*: **~ (to)**

примени́мый (к +dat)

**applicant** ['æplɪkənt] n ( for job, scholarship) кандида́т; ( for college) абитурие́нт

**application** [æplɪ'keɪʃən] n ( for job, grant etc) заявле́ние; ~ **form** n заявле́ние-анке́та

**applied** [ə'plaɪd] adj прикладно́й

**apply** [ə'plaɪ] vt (paint, make-up) наноси́ть (нанести́ pf) ♦ vi: **to ~ to** применя́ться (impf) к +dat; (ask) обраща́ться (обрати́ться pf) (с про́сьбой) к +dat; **to ~ o.s. to** сосредота́чиваться (сосредото́читься pf) на +prp; **to ~ for a grant/job** подава́ть (пода́ть pf) заявле́ние на стипе́ндию/о прие́ме на рабо́ту

**appoint** [ə'pɔɪnt] vt назнача́ть (назна́чить pf); **~ed** adj: **at the ~ed time** в назна́ченное вре́мя; **~ment** n (of person) назначе́ние; (post) до́лжность f; (arranged meeting) приём; **to make an ~ment (with sb)** назнача́ть (назна́чить pf) (кому́-н) встре́чу; **I have an ~ment with the doctor** я записа́лся (на приём) к врачу́

**appraisal** [ə'preɪzl] n оце́нка

**appreciate** [ə'priːʃɪeɪt] vt (value) цени́ть (impf); (understand) оце́нивать (оцени́ть pf) ♦ vi (COMM) повыша́ться (повы́ситься pf) в цене́

**appreciation** [əpriːʃɪ'eɪʃən] n (understanding) понима́ние; (gratitude) призна́тельность f

**apprehensive** [æprɪ'hɛnsɪv] adj (glance etc) опа́сливый

**apprentice** [ə'prɛntɪs] n учени́к, подмасте́рье; **~ship** n учени́чество

**approach** [ə'prəʊtʃ] vi приближа́ться (прибли́зиться pf) ♦ vt (ask, apply to) обраща́ться (обрати́ться pf) к +dat; (come to)

приближа́ться (прибли́зиться pf) к +dat; (consider) подходи́ть (подойти́ pf) к +dat ♦ n подхо́д; (advance: also fig) приближе́ние

**appropriate** [ə'prəʊprɪeɪt] adj (behaviour) подоба́ющий; (remarks) уме́стный; (tools) подходя́щий

**approval** [ə'pruːvəl] n одобре́ние; (permission) согла́сие; **on ~** (COMM) на про́бу

**approve** [ə'pruːv] vt (motion, decision) одобря́ть (одо́брить pf); (product, publication) утвержда́ть (утверди́ть pf); **~ of** vt fus одобря́ть (одо́брить pf)

**approximate** [ə'prɔksɪmɪt] adj приблизи́тельный; **~ly** adv приблизи́тельно

**apricot** ['eɪprɪkɔt] n абрико́с

**April** ['eɪprəl] n апре́ль m

**apron** ['eɪprən] n фа́ртук

**apt** [æpt] adj уда́чный, уме́стный; **~ to do** скло́нный +infin

**aquarium** [ə'kwɛərɪəm] n аква́риум

**Aquarius** [ə'kwɛərɪəs] n Водоле́й

**Arab** ['ærəb] adj ара́бский ♦ n ара́б(ка); **~ian** [ə'reɪbɪən] adj ара́бский; **~ic** adj ара́бский

**arbitrary** ['ɑːbɪtrərɪ] adj произво́льный

**arbitration** [ɑːbɪ'treɪʃən] n трете́йский суд; (INDUSTRY) арбитра́ж; **the dispute went to ~** спо́р пе́редан в арбитра́ж

**arc** [ɑːk] n (also MATH) дуга́

**arch** [ɑːtʃ] n а́рка, свод; (of foot) свод ♦ vt (back) выгиба́ть (вы́гнуть pf)

**archaeology** [ɑːkɪ'ɔlədʒɪ] (US **archeology**) n археоло́гия

**archaic** [ɑː'keɪɪk] adj архаи́ческий

**archbishop** [ɑːtʃ'bɪʃəp] n архиепи́скоп

**archeology** [ɑːkɪ'ɔlədʒɪ] n (US) = **archaeology**

**architect** [ˈɑːkɪtɛkt] n (of building)
архите́ктор; **~ure** n архитекту́ра

**archive** [ˈɑːkaɪvz] n архи́в; **~s** npl
(documents) архи́в msg

**Arctic** [ˈɑːktɪk] adj аркти́ческий ♦ n:
**the ~** Аркти́ка

**ardent** [ˈɑːdənt] adj пы́лкий

**arduous** [ˈɑːdjʊəs] adj тяжёлый,
тя́жкий

**are** [ɑː] vb see **be**

**area** [ˈɛərɪə] n о́бласть f (part of
place) уча́сток f; (: of room) часть f

**arena** [əˈriːnə] n (also fig) аре́на

**aren't** [ɑːnt] = **are not**; see **be**

**Argentina** [ɑːdʒənˈtiːnə] n
Аргенти́на

**arguably** [ˈɑːgjʊəblɪ] adv возмо́жно

**argue** [ˈɑːgjuː] vi (quarrel)
ссо́риться (поссо́риться pf);
(reason) дока́зывать (доказа́ть pf)

**argument** [ˈɑːgjʊmənt] n (quarrel)
ссо́ра; (reasons) аргуме́нт, до́вод

**Aries** [ˈɛəriz] n Ове́н

**arise** [əˈraɪz] (pt **arose**, pp **~n**) vi
(occur) возника́ть (возни́кнуть
pf); **~n** [əˈrɪzn] pp of **arise**

**aristocracy** [ærɪsˈtɔkrəsɪ] n
аристокра́тия

**arithmetic** [əˈrɪθmətɪk] n (MATH)
арифме́тика; (calculation) подсчёт

**arm** [ɑːm] n рука́; (of chair) ру́чка;
(of clothing) рука́в ♦ vt вооружа́ть
(вооружи́ть pf); **~s** npl (MIL)
вооруже́ние ntsg; (HERALDRY)
герб; **~ in ~** по́д руку; **~chair** n
кре́сло; **~ed** adj вооружённый

**armour** [ˈɑːmər] (US **armor**) n (also:
**suit of ~**) доспе́хи mpl

**army** [ˈɑːmɪ] n (also fig) а́рмия

**aroma** [əˈrəʊmə] n арома́т;
**~therapy** [ərəʊməˈθɛrəpɪ] n
аромотерапия

**arose** [əˈrəʊz] pt of **arise**

**around** [əˈraʊnd] adv вокру́г ♦ prep
(encircling) вокру́г +gen; (near,
about) о́коло +gen

**arouse** [əˈraʊz] vt (interest, passions)
возбужда́ть (возбуди́ть pf)

**arrange** [əˈreɪndʒ] vt (organize)
устра́ивать (устро́ить pf); (put in
order) расставля́ть (расста́вить
pf) ♦ vi: **we have ~d for a car to
pick you up** мы договори́лись,
что́бы за Ва́ми зае́хала маши́на;
**to ~ to do** догова́риваться
(договори́ться pf) +infin; **~ment** n
(agreement) договорённость f;
(order, layout) расположе́ние;
**~ments** npl (plans)
приготовле́ния ntpl

**array** [əˈreɪ] n: **~ of** ряд +gen

**arrears** [əˈrɪəz] npl задо́лженность
fsg; **to be in ~ with one's rent**
име́ть (impf) задо́лженность по
квартпла́те

**arrest** [əˈrɛst] vt (LAW: person)
аресто́вывать (арестова́ть pf) ♦ n
аре́ст; **under ~** под аре́стом

**arrival** [əˈraɪvl] n (of person, vehicle)
прибы́тие; **new ~** новичо́к;;
(baby) новорождённый(ая) m(f)
adj

**arrive** [əˈraɪv] vi (traveller)
прибыва́ть (прибы́ть pf); (letter,
news) приходи́ть (прийти́ pf);
(baby) рожда́ться (роди́ться pf)

**arrogance** [ˈærəgəns] n
высокоме́рие

**arrogant** [ˈærəgənt] adj
высокоме́рный

**arrow** [ˈærəʊ] n (weapon) стрела́;
(sign) стре́лка

**arse** [ɑːs] n (BRIT : inf!) жо́па (!)

**arsenal** [ˈɑːsɪnl] n арсена́л

**arson** [ˈɑːsn] n поджо́г

**art** [ɑːt] n иску́сство; **Arts** npl
(SCOL) гуманита́рные нау́ки fpl

**artery** [ˈɑːtərɪ] n (also fig) арте́рия

**art gallery** n (national) карти́нная
галере́я; (private) (арт-)галере́я

**arthritis** [ɑːˈθraɪtɪs] n артри́т

**artichoke** [ˈɑːtɪtʃəʊk] n (also: **globe**

~) артишо́к; (*also*: **Jerusalem** ~) земляна́я гру́ша

**article** ['ɑːtɪkl] *n* (*object*) предме́т; (*LING*) арти́кль *m*; (*in newspaper, document*) статья́

**articulate** *vb* [ɑː'tɪkjuleɪt] *adj* [ɑː'tɪkjulɪt] *vt* (*ideas*) выража́ть (вы́разить *pf*) ♦ *adj*: **she is very ~** она́ чётко выража́ет свои́ мы́сли

**artificial** [ɑːtɪ'fɪʃəl] *adj* иску́сственный (*affected*) неесте́ственный

**artillery** [ɑː'tɪlərɪ] *n* (*corps*) артилле́рия

**artist** ['ɑːtɪst] *n* худо́жник(ица) (*performer*) арти́ст(ка); **~ic** [ɑː'tɪstɪk] *adj* худо́жественный

KEYWORD

**as** [æz, əz] *conj* **1** (*referring to time*) когда́; **he came in as I was leaving** он вошёл, когда́ я уходи́л; **as the years went by** с года́ми; **as from tomorrow** с за́втрашнего дня

**2** (*in comparisons*): **as big as** тако́й же большо́й, как; **twice as big as** в два ра́за бо́льше, чем; **as white as snow** бе́лый, как снег; **as much money/many books as** сто́лько же де́нег/книг, ско́лько; **as soon as** как то́лько; **as soon as possible** как мо́жно скоре́е

**3** (*since, because*) поско́льку, так как

**4** (*referring to manner, way*) как; **do as you wish** де́лайте, как хоти́те; **as she said** как она́ сказа́ла

**5** (*concerning*): **as for** *or* **to** что каса́ется +*gen*

**6**: **as if** *or* **though** как бу́дто; **he looked as if he had been ill** он вы́глядел так, как бу́дто он был бо́лен

♦ *prep* (*in the capacity of*): **he works as a waiter** он рабо́тает

официа́нтом; **as chairman of the company, he ...** как глава́ компа́нии он ...; *see also* **long**; **same**; **such**; **well**

**a.s.a.p.** *adv abbr* = **as soon as possible**

**ascent** [ə'sɛnt] *n* (*slope*) подъём; (*climb*) восхожде́ние

**ash** [æʃ] *n* (*of fire*) зола́, пе́пел; (*of cigarette*) пе́пел; (*wood, tree*) я́сень *m*

**ashamed** [ə'ʃeɪmd] *adj*: **to be ~ (of)** стыди́ться (*impf*) (+*gen*); **I'm ~ of ...** мне сты́дно за +*acc* ...

**ashore** [ə'ʃɔːʳ] *adv* (*be*) на берегу́; (*swim, go*) на бе́рег

**ashtray** ['æʃtreɪ] *n* пе́пельница

**Asia** ['eɪʃə] *n* А́зия; **~n** *adj* азиа́тский ♦ *n* азиа́т(ка)

**aside** [ə'saɪd] *adv* в сто́рону ♦ *n* ре́плика

**ask** [ɑːsk] *vt* (*inquire*) спра́шивать (спроси́ть *pf*); (*invite*) звать (позва́ть *pf*); **to ~ sb for sth/sb to do** проси́ть (попроси́ть *pf*) что-н у кого́-н/кого́-н +*infin*; **to ~ sb about** спра́шивать (спроси́ть *pf*) кого́-н о +*prp*; **to ~ (sb) a question** задава́ть (зада́ть *pf*) (кому́-н) вопро́с; **to ~ sb out to dinner** приглаша́ть (пригласи́ть *pf*) кого́-н в рестора́н; **~ for** *vt fus* проси́ть (попроси́ть *pf*) (*trouble*) напра́шиваться (напроси́ться *pf*) на +*acc*

**asleep** [ə'sliːp] *adj*: **to be ~** спать (*impf*); **to fall ~** засыпа́ть (засну́ть *pf*)

**asparagus** [əs'pærəgəs] *n* спа́ржа

**aspect** ['æspɛkt] *n* (*element*) аспе́кт, сторона́; (*quality, air*) вид

**aspirin** ['æsprɪn] *n* аспири́н

**ass** [æs] *n* (*also fig*) осёл; (*US* : *inf!*) жо́па (!)

**assassin** [ə'sæsɪn] *n*

(полити́ческий) уби́йца *m/f*;
**~ation** [əsæsɪ'neɪʃən] *n*
(полити́ческое) уби́йство
**assault** [ə'sɔːlt] *n* нападе́ние; (*MIL,*
*fig*) ата́ка ♦ *vt* напада́ть (напа́сть
*pf*) на +*acc*; (*sexually*) наси́ловать
(изнаси́ловать *pf*)
**assemble** [ə'sɛmbl] *vt* собира́ть
(собра́ть *pf*) ♦ *vi* собира́ться
(собра́ться *pf*)
**assembly** [ə'sɛmblɪ] *n* (*meeting*)
собра́ние; (*institution*) ассамбле́я,
законода́тельное собра́ние;
(*construction*) сбо́рка
**assert** [ə'səːt] *vt* (*opinion, authority*)
утвержда́ть (утверди́ть *pf*);
(*rights, innocence*) отста́ивать
(отстоя́ть *pf*); **~ion** [ə'səːʃən] *n*
(*claim*) утвержде́ние
**assess** [ə'sɛs] *vt* оце́нивать
(оцени́ть *pf*); **~ment** *n*: **~ment**
**(of)** оце́нка (+*gen*)
**asset** ['æsɛt] *n* (*quality*)
досто́инство; **~s** *npl* (*property,*
*funds*) акти́вы *mpl*; (*COMM*) акти́в
*msg*бала́нса
**assignment** [ə'saɪnmənt] *n*
зада́ние
**assist** [ə'sɪst] *vt* помога́ть (помо́чь
*pf*) +*dat*; (*financially*)
соде́йствовать
(посоде́йствовать *pf*) +*dat*; **~ance**
*n* (*see vt*) по́мощь *f*; соде́йствие;
**~ant** *n* помо́щник(ица); (*in office*
*etc*) ассисте́нт(ка); (*BRIT : also*:
**shop ~ant**) продаве́ц(вщи́ца)
**associate** *n* [ə'səuʃɪɪt] *vb* [ə'səuʃɪeɪt]
*n* (*colleague*) колле́га *m/f* ♦ *adj*
(*member, professor*)
ассоции́рованный ♦ *vt* (*mentally*)
ассоции́ровать (*impf/pf*); **to ~ with**
**sb** обща́ться (*impf*) с кем-н
**association** [əsəusɪ'eɪʃən] *n*
ассоциа́ция; (*involvement*) связь *f*
**assorted** [ə'sɔːtɪd] *adj*
разнообра́зный

**assortment** [ə'sɔːtmənt] *n* (*of*
*clothes, colours*) ассортиме́нт; (*of*
*books, people*) подбо́р
**assume** [ə'sjuːm] *vt* (*suppose*)
предполага́ть (предположи́ть
*pf*), допуска́ть (допусти́ть *pf*);
(*responsibility*) принима́ть
(приня́ть *pf*) (на себя́); (*air*)
напуска́ть (напусти́ть *pf*) на
себя́; (*power*) брать (взять *pf*)
**assumption** [ə'sʌmpʃən] *n*
предположе́ние; (*of responsibility*)
приня́тие на себя́; **~ of power**
прихо́д к вла́сти
**assurance** [ə'ʃuərəns] *n* (*promise*)
завере́ние; (*confidence*)
уве́ренность *f*; (*insurance*)
страхова́ние
**assure** [ə'ʃuər] *vt* (*reassure*)
заверя́ть (заве́рить *pf*);
(*guarantee*) обеспе́чивать
(обеспе́чить *pf*)
**asthma** ['æsmə] *n* а́стма
**astonishment** [ə'stɔnɪʃmənt] *n*
изумле́ние
**astrology** [əs'trɔlədʒɪ] *n*
астроло́гия
**astronomical** [æstrə'nɔmɪkl] *adj*
(*also fig*) астрономи́ческий
**astronomy** [əs'trɔnəmɪ] *n*
астроно́мия
**astute** [əs'tjuːt] *adj* (*person*)
проница́тельный

---
KEYWORD
---

**at** [æt] *prep* **1** (*referring to position*)
в/на +*prp*; **at school** в шко́ле; **at**
**the theatre** в теа́тре; **at a concert**
на конце́рте; **at the station** на
ста́нции; **at the top** наверху́; **at**
**home** до́ма; **they are sitting at**
**the table** они́ сидя́т за столо́м;
**at my friend's (house)** у моего́
дру́га; **at the doctor's** у врача́
**2** (*referring to direction*) в/на +*acc*;
**to look at** смотре́ть (посмотре́ть

*pf*) на +*acc*; **to throw sth at sb**
(*stone*) броса́ть (бро́сить *pf*) что-н
or чем-н в кого́-н
**3** (*referring to time*): **at four o'clock**
в четы́ре часа́; **at half past two** в
полови́не тре́тьего; **at a quarter
to two** без че́тверти два; **at a
quarter past two** в че́тверть
тре́тьего; **at dawn** на заре́; **at
night** но́чью; **at Christmas** на
Рождество́; **at lunch** за обе́дом;
**at times** времена́ми
**4** (*referring to rates*): **at one pound
a kilo** по фу́нту за килогра́мм;
**two at a time** по дво́е; **at fifty
km/h** со ско́ростью пятьдеся́т
км/ч; **at full speed** на по́лной
ско́рости
**5** (*referring to manner*): **at a stroke**
одни́м ма́хом; **at peace** в ми́ре
**6** (*referring to activity*): **to be at
home/work** быть (*impf*) до́ма/на
рабо́те; **to play at cowboys**
игра́ть (*impf*) в ковбо́и; **to be
good at doing** хорошо́ уме́ть
(*impf*) +*infin*
**7** (*referring to cause*): **he is
surprised/annoyed at sth** он
удивлён/раздражён чем-н; **I am
surprised at you** Вы меня́
удивля́ете; **I stayed at his
suggestion** я оста́лся по его́
предложе́нию

**ate** [eɪt] *pt of* **eat**
**atheist** ['eɪθɪɪst] *n* атеи́ст(ка)
**Athens** ['æθɪnz] *n* Афи́ны *pl*
**athlete** ['æθliːt] *n* спортсме́н(ка)
**athletic** [æθ'letɪk] *adj* спорти́вный;
**~s** [æθ'letɪks] *n* лёгкая атле́тика
**Atlantic** [ət'læntɪk] *n*: **the ~ (Ocean)**
Атланти́ческий океа́н
**atlas** ['ætləs] *n* а́тлас
**atmosphere** ['ætməsfɪər] *n*
атмосфе́ра
**atom** ['ætəm] *n* а́том; **~ic** [ə'tɔmɪk]

*adj* а́томный
**attach** [ə'tætʃ] *vt* прикрепля́ть
(прикрепи́ть *pf*); (*document, letter*)
прилага́ть (приложи́ть *pf*); **he is
~ed to** (*fond of*) он привя́зан к
+*dat*; **to ~ importance to**
придава́ть (прида́ть *pf*) значе́ние
+*dat*; **~ment** *n* (*device*)
приспособле́ние, наса́дка;
**~ment (to sb)** (*love*)
привя́занность *f* (к кому́-н)
**attack** [ə'tæk] *vt* (*MIL, fig*) атакова́ть
(*impf/pf*); (*assault*) напада́ть
(напа́сть *pf*) на +*acc* ♦ *n* (*MIL, fig*)
ата́ка; (*assault*) нападе́ние; (*of
illness*) при́ступ; **~er** *n*: **his/her
~er** напа́вший(ая) *m(f) adj* на
него́/неё
**attain** [ə'teɪn] *vt* (*happiness, success*)
достига́ть (дости́гнуть or
дости́чь *pf*) +*gen*, добива́ться
(доби́ться *pf*) +*gen*
**attempt** [ə'tempt] *n* попы́тка ♦ *vt*:
**to ~ to do** пыта́ться (попыта́ться
*pf*) +*infin*; **to make an ~ on sb's life**
соверша́ть (соверши́ть *pf*)
покуше́ние на кого́-н; **~ed** *adj*:
**~ed murder** покуше́ние на
жизнь; **~ed suicide/burglary**
попы́тка самоуби́йства/
ограбле́ния
**attend** [ə'tend] *vt* (*school, church*)
посеща́ть (*impf*); **~ to** *vt fus* (*needs,
patient*) занима́ться (заня́ться *pf*)
+*instr*; (*customer*) обслу́живать
(обслужи́ть *pf*); **~ance** *n*
прису́тствие; (*SCOL*)
посеща́емость *f*; **~ant** *n*
сопровожда́ющий(ая) *m(f) adj*; (*in
garage*) служи́тель(ница) *m(f)*
**attention** [ə'tenʃən] *n* внима́ние;
(*care*) ухо́д; **for the ~ of ...** (*ADMIN*)
к све́дению +*gen* ...
**attentive** [ə'tentɪv] *adj* (*audience*)
внима́тельный; (*polite*)
предупреди́тельный

**attic** ['ætɪk] n (living space) мансáрда; (storage space) чердáк

**attitude** ['ætɪtjuːd] n: ~ **(to** or **towards)** отношéние (к +dat)

**attorney** [ə'təːnɪ] n (US: lawyer) юрúст; **Attorney General** n (BRIT) минúстр юстúции; (US) Генерáльный прокурóр

**attract** [ə'trækt] vt привлекáть (привлéчь pf); ~**ion** [ə'trækʃən] n (appeal) привлекáтельность f; ~**ive** adj привлекáтельный

**attribute** n ['ætrɪbjuːt] vb [ə'trɪbjuːt] n прúзнак, атрибýт ♦ vt: **to ~ sth to** (cause) относúть (отнестú pf) что-н за счёт +gen; (painting, quality) припúсывать (приписáть pf) что-н +dat

**aubergine** ['əubəʒiːn] n баклажáн

**auction** ['ɔːkʃən] n (also: **sale by ~**) аукцóн ♦ vt продавáть (продáть pf) на аукцóне

**audible** ['ɔːdɪbl] adj слышный

**audience** ['ɔːdɪəns] n аудитóрия, пýблика

**audit** ['ɔːdɪt] vt (COMM) проводúть (провестú pf) ревúзию +gen

**audition** [ɔː'dɪʃən] n прослýшивание

**auditor** ['ɔːdɪtəʳ] n ревúзия, аудúтор

**auditorium** [ɔːdɪ'tɔːrɪəm] n зал

**August** ['ɔːgəst] n áвгуст

**aunt** [ɑːnt] n тётя; ~**ie** ['ɑːntɪ] n dimin of **aunt**

**au pair** ['əu'pɛəʳ] n (also: ~ **girl**) молодáя нáня-инострáнка, живýщая в семьé

**aura** ['ɔːrə] n (fig: air) ореóл

**austere** [ɔs'tɪəʳ] adj стрóгий; (person, manner) сурóвый

**Australia** [ɔs'treɪlɪə] n Австрáлия

**Austria** ['ɔstrɪə] n Áвстрия

**authentic** [ɔː'θɛntɪk] adj пóдлинный

**author** ['ɔːθəʳ] n (of text, plan)

áвтор; (profession) писáтель(ница) m(f)

**authoritarian** [ɔːθɔrɪ'tɛərɪən] adj (conduct) авторитáрный

**authoritative** [ɔː'θɔrɪtətɪv] adj авторитéтный

**authority** [ɔː'θɔrɪtɪ] n (power) власть f; (POL) управлéние; (expert) авторитéт; (official permission) полномóчие; **the authorities** npl (ruling body) влáсти fpl

**autobiography** [ɔːtəbaɪ'ɔgrəfɪ] n автобиогрáфия

**autograph** ['ɔːtəgrɑːf] n автóграф ♦ vt надпúсывать (надписáть pf)

**automatic** [ɔːtə'mætɪk] adj автоматúческий ♦ n (US: gun) (самозарáдный) пистолéт; (car) автомобúль m с автоматúческим переключéнием скоростéй; ~**ally** adv автоматúчески

**automobile** ['ɔːtəməbiːl] n (US) автомобúль m

**autonomous** [ɔː'tɔnəməs] adj (region) автонóмный; (person, organization) самостоáтельный

**autonomy** [ɔː'tɔnəmɪ] n автонóмия, самостоáтельность f

**autumn** ['ɔːtəm] n óсень f; **in ~** óсенью

**auxiliary** [ɔːg'zɪlɪərɪ] adj вспомогáтельный ♦ n помóщник

**avail** [ə'veɪl] n: **to no ~** напрáсно

**availability** [əveɪlə'bɪlɪtɪ] n налúчие

**available** [ə'veɪləbl] adj достýпный; (person) свобóдный

**avalanche** ['ævəlɑːnʃ] n лавúна

**avenue** ['ævənjuː] n (street) ýлица; (drive) аллéя

**average** ['ævərɪdʒ] n срéднее nt adj ♦ adj срéдний ♦ vt достигáть (достúчь pf) в срéднем +gen; (sum) составлáть (состáвить pf) в срéднем; **on ~** в срéднем

**avert** [ə'vəːt] vt предотвращáть

(предотврати́ть *pf*); (*blow, eyes*)
отводи́ть (отвести́ *pf*)
**aviary** ['eɪvɪərɪ] *n* пти́чий вольéр
**aviation** [eɪvɪ'eɪʃən] *n* авиа́ция
**avid** ['ævɪd] *adj* (*keen*) стра́стный
**avocado** [ævə'kɑːdəu] *n* (*also*: ~
**pear**: *BRIT*) авока́до *nt ind*
**avoid** [ə'vɔɪd] *vt* избега́ть
(избежа́ть *pf*)
**await** [ə'weɪt] *vt* ожида́ть (*impf*)
+*gen*
**awake** [ə'weɪk] (*pt* **awoke**, *pp*
**awoken** *or* ~**d**) *adj*: **he is** ~ он
просну́лся; **he was still** ~ он ещё
не спал
**award** [ə'wɔːd] *n* награ́да ♦ *vt*
награжда́ть (награди́ть *pf*);
(*LAW*) присужда́ть (присуди́ть *pf*)
**aware** [ə'wɛər] *adj*: **to be** ~ (**of**)
(*realize*) сознава́ть (*impf*) (+*acc*); **to**
**become** ~ **of sth/that** осознава́ть
(осозна́ть *pf*) что-н/, что; ~**ness** *n*
осозна́ние
**away** [ə'weɪ] *adv* (*movement*) в
сто́рону; (*position*) в стороне́; (*far
away*) далеко́; **the holidays are**
**two weeks** ~ до кани́кул
(оста́лось) две неде́ли; ~ **from**
(*movement*) от +*gen*; (*position*) в
стороне́ от +*gen*; **two kilometres**
~ **from the town** в двух
киломе́трах от го́рода; **two**
**hours** ~ **by car** в двух часа́х езды́
на маши́не; **he's** ~ **for a week** он
в отъе́зде на неде́лю; **to take** ~
(**from**) (*remove*) забира́ть
(забра́ть *pf*) (у +*gen*); (*subtract*)
отнима́ть (отня́ть *pf*) (от +*gen*);
**he is working** ~ (*continuously*) он
продолжа́ет рабо́тать
**awe** [ɔː] *n* благогове́ние
**awful** ['ɔːfəl] *adj* ужа́сный; **an** ~ **lot**
(**of**) ужа́сно мно́го (+*gen*); ~**ly** *adv*
ужа́сно
**awkward** ['ɔːkwəd] *adj* (*clumsy*)
неуклю́жий; (*inconvenient*)

неудо́бный; (*embarrassing*)
нело́вкий
**awoke** [ə'wəuk] *pt of* **awake**; ~**n** *pp*
*of* **awake**
**axe** [æks] (*US* **ax**) *n* топо́р ♦ *vt*
(*project*) отменя́ть (отмени́ть *pf*);
(*jobs*) сокраща́ть (сократи́ть *pf*)
**axis** ['æksɪs] (*pl* **axes**) *n* ось *f*

# B, b

**B** [biː] *n* (*MUS*) си *nt ind*
**BA** *n abbr* = **Bachelor of Arts**
**baby** ['beɪbɪ] *n* ребёнок; (*newborn*)
младе́нец; ~ **carriage** (*US*)
коля́ска; ~**-sit** *vi* смотре́ть (*impf*)
за детьми́; ~**-sitter** *n*
приходя́щая ня́ня
**bachelor** ['bætʃələr] *n* холостя́к;
**Bachelor of Arts/Science**
≈бакала́вр гуманита́рных/
есте́ственных нау́к

КEYWORD

**back** [bæk] *n* **1** (*of person, animal*)
спина́; **the back of the hand**
ты́льная сторона́ ладо́ни
**2** (*of house, car etc*) за́дняя часть
*f*; (*of chair*) спи́нка; (*of page, book*)
оборо́т
**3** (*FOOTBALL*) защи́тник
♦ *vt* **1** (*candidate*: *also*: **back up**)
подде́рживать (поддержа́ть *pf*)
**2** (*financially*: *horse*) ста́вить
(поста́вить *pf*) на +*acc*; (*: person*)
финанси́ровать (*impf*)
**3**: **he backed the car into the**
**garage** он дал за́дний ход и
поста́вил маши́ну в гара́ж
♦ *vi* (*car etc*: *also*: **back up**)
дава́ть (дать *pf*) за́дний ход
♦ *adv* **1** (*not forward*) обра́тно,
наза́д; **he ran back** он побежа́л
обра́тно *or* наза́д
**2** (*returned*): **he's back** он

вернýлся
3 (*restitution*): **to throw the ball back** кидáть (кинуть *pf*) мяч обрáтно
4 (*again*): **to call back** (*visit again*) заходить (зайти *pf*) ещё раз; (*TEL*) перезвáнивать (перезвонить *pf*)
♦ *cpd* 1 (*payment*) зáдним числóм 2 (*AUT, seat, wheels*) зáдний
**back down** *vi* отступáть (отступить *pf*)
**back out** *vi* (*of promise*) отступáться (отступиться *pf*)
**back up** *vt* (*person, theory etc*) поддéрживать (поддержáть *pf*)

**back**: ~**ache** *n* прострéл, боль *f* в поясни́це; ~**bencher** *n* (*BRIT*) заднескамéечник; ~**bone** *n* позвонóчник; **he's the ~bone of the organization** на нём дéржится вся организáция; ~**ground** *n* (*of picture*) зáдний план; (*of events*) предысто́рия; (*experience*) óпыт; **he's from a working class ~ground** он из рабóчей семьи́; **against a ~ground of ...** на фóне +*gen* ...; ~**hand** *n* (*TENNIS*) удáр слéва; ~**ing** *n* (*support*) поддéржка; ~**lash** *n* (*fig*) обрáтная реáкция; ~**log** *n*: ~**log of work** невы́полненная рабóта; ~**pack** *n* рюкзáк; ~**side** *n* (*inf*) зад; ~**stage** *adv* за кули́сами; ~**ward** *adj* (*movement*) обрáтный; (*person, country*) отстáлый; ~**wards** *adv* назáд; (*list*) наоборóт; (*fall*) нáвзничь; **to walk ~wards** пя́титься (попя́титься *pf*); ~**yard** *n* (*of house*) зáдний двор
**bacon** ['beɪkən] *n* бекóн
**bacteria** [bæk'tɪərɪə] *npl* бактéрии *fpl*
**bad** [bæd] *adj* плохóй; (*mistake*)

серьёзный; (*injury, crash*) тяжёлый; (*food*) ту́хлый; **his ~ leg** его́ больнáя ногá; **to go ~** (*food*) ту́хнуть (проту́хнуть *pf*), пóртиться (испóртиться *pf*)
**badge** [bædʒ] *n* значóк
**badger** ['bædʒə] *n* барсу́к
**badly** ['bædlɪ] *adv* плóхо; ~ **wounded** тяжелó рáненый; **he needs it ~** он си́льно в э́том нуждáется; **to be ~ off (for money)** нуждáться (*impf*) (в деньгáх)
**badminton** ['bædmɪntən] *n* бадминтóн
**bad-tempered** ['bæd'tɛmpəd] *adj* вспы́льчивый; (*now*) раздражённый
**bag** [bæg] *n* су́мка; (*paper, plastic*) пакéт; (*handbag*) су́мочка; (*satchel*) рáнец; (*case*) портфéль *m*; ~**s of** (*inf*) у́йма +*gen*
**baggage** ['bægɪdʒ] *n* (*US*) багáж
**baggy** ['bægɪ] *adj* мешковáтый
**Bahamas** [bə'hɑːməz] *npl*: **the ~** Багáмские островá *mpl*
**bail** [beɪl] *n* (*money*) залóг ♦ *vt* (*also*: **to grant ~ to**) выпускáть (вы́пустить *pf*) под залóг; **he was released on ~** он был вы́пущен под залóг; ~ **out** *vt* (*LAW*) плати́ть (заплати́ть *pf*) залóговую су́мму за +*acc*; (*boat*) вычéрпывать (вы́черпать *pf*) вóду из +*gen*
**bailiff** ['beɪlɪf] *n* (*LAW, BRIT*) судéбный исполни́тель *m*; (: *US*) помóщник шери́фа
**bait** [beɪt] *n* (*for fish*) нажи́вка; (*for animal, criminal*) примáнка ♦ *vt* (*hook, trap*) наживля́ть (наживи́ть *pf*)
**bake** [beɪk] *vt* печь (испéчь *pf*) ♦ *vi* (*bread etc*) пéчься (испéчься *pf*); (*make cakes etc*) печь (*impf*); ~**d beans** *npl* консерви́рованная

фасо́ль *fsg* (*в тома́те*); **~r** *n*
пе́карь *m*; (*also:* **the baker's**)
бу́лочная *f adj*; **~ry** *n* пека́рня;
(*shop*) бу́лочная *f adj*
**baking** ['beɪkɪŋ] *n* вы́печка; **she
does her ~ once a week** она́
печёт раз в неде́лю; **~ powder**
*n* разрыхли́тель *m*
**balance** ['bæləns] *n* (*equilibrium*)
равнове́сие; (*COMM, in account*)
бала́нс; (*: remainder*) оста́ток;
(*scales*) весы́ *pl* ♦ *vt* (*budget,
account*) баланси́ровать
(сбаланси́ровать *pf*); (*make equal*)
уравнове́шивать (уравнове́сить
*pf*); **~ of payments/trade**
платёжный/торго́вый бала́нс; **~d**
*adj* (*diet*) сбаланси́рованный
**balcony** ['bælkənɪ] *n* балко́н
**bald** [bɔːld] *adj* (*head*) лы́сый; (*tyre*)
стёртый
**bale** [beɪl] *n* (*of hay etc*) тюк
**ball** [bɔːl] *n* (*for football, tennis*) мяч;
(*for golf*) мя́чик; (*of wool, string*)
клубо́к; (*dance*) бал
**ballerina** [bælə'riːnə] *n* балери́на
**ballet** ['bæleɪ] *n* бале́т
**balloon** [bə'luːn] *n* возду́шный
шар; (*also:* **hot air ~**) аэроста́т
**ballot** ['bælət] *n* голосова́ние,
баллотиро́вка
**ballroom** ['bɔːlrum] *n* ба́льный зал
**Baltic** ['bɔːltɪk] *n*: **the ~**
Балти́йское мо́ре ♦ *adj*: **the ~
States** стра́ны *fpl* Ба́лтии,
прибалти́йские госуда́рства *ntpl*
**bamboo** [bæm'buː] *n* бамбу́к
**ban** [bæn] *vt* (*prohibit*) запреща́ть
(запрети́ть *pf*); (*suspend, exclude*)
отстраня́ть (отстрани́ть *pf*) ♦ *n*
(*prohibition*) запре́т
**banal** [bə'nɑːl] *adj* бана́льный
**banana** [bə'nɑːnə] *n* бана́н
**band** [bænd] *n* (*group: of people,
rock musicians*) гру́ппа; (*: of jazz,
military musicians*) орке́стр

**bandage** ['bændɪdʒ] *n* повя́зка ♦ *vt*
бинтова́ть (забинтова́ть *pf*)
**bandwagon** ['bændwægən] *n*: **to
jump on the ~** эксплуати́ровать
(*impf/pf*) ситуа́цию
**bang** [bæŋ] *n* стук; (*explosion*)
вы́стрел; (*blow*) уда́р ♦ *excl* бах
♦ *vt* (*door*) хло́пать (хло́пнуть *pf*)
+*instr*; (*head etc*) ударя́ть (уда́рить
*pf*) ♦ *vi* (*door*) захло́пываться
(захло́пнуться *pf*)
**bangs** [bæŋz] *npl* (*US*) чёлка *fsg*
**banish** ['bænɪʃ] *vt* высыла́ть
(вы́слать *pf*)
**bank** [bæŋk] *n* банк; (*of river, lake*)
бе́рег; (*of earth*) на́сыпь *f*; **~ on** *vt
fus* полага́ться (положи́ться *pf*)
на +*acc*; **~ account** *n* ба́нковский
счёт; **~ card** *n* ба́нковская
ка́рточка; **~ holiday** *n* (*BRIT*)
нерабо́чий день *m* (*обычно
понеде́льник*); **~ note** *n* банкно́т
**bankrupt** ['bæŋkrʌpt] *adj*
обанкро́тившийся; **to go ~**
обанкро́титься (*pf*); **I am ~** я -
банкро́т, я обанкро́тился; **~cy** *n*
банкро́тство, несостоя́тельность
*f*
**bank statement** *n* вы́писка с
ба́нковского счёта
**banner** ['bænər] *n* транспара́нт
**bannister** ['bænɪstər] *n* (*usu pl*)
пери́ла *pl*
**banquet** ['bæŋkwɪt] *n* банке́т
**baptism** ['bæptɪzəm] *n* креще́ние
**bar** [bɑːr] *n* (*pub*) бар; (*counter*)
сто́йка; (*rod*) прут; (*of soap*)
брусо́к; (*of chocolate*) пли́тка;
(*MUS*) такт ♦ *vt* (*door, way*)
загора́живать (загороди́ть *pf*);
(*person*) не допуска́ть (допусти́ть
*pf*); **~s** *npl* (*on window*) решётка
*fsg*; **behind ~s** за решёткой; **the
Bar** адвокату́ра; **~ none** без
исключе́ния
**barbaric** [bɑː'bærɪk] *adj*

ва́рварский
**barbecue** ['bɑːbɪkjuː] *n* барбекю́ *nt ind*
**barbed wire** ['bɑːbd-] *n* колю́чая про́волока
**barber** ['bɑːbər] *n* парикма́хер
**bar code** *n* штрихово́й код
**bare** [bɛər] *adj* (*body*) го́лый, обнажённый; (*trees*) оголённый ♦ *vt* (*one's body*) оголи́ть (оголя́ть *pf*), обнажа́ть (обнажи́ть *pf*); (*teeth*) ска́лить (оска́лить *pf*); **in** or **with ~ feet** босико́м; **~foot** *adj* босо́й ♦ *adv* босико́м; **~ly** *adv* едва́
**bargain** ['bɑːgɪn] *n* сде́лка; (*good buy*) вы́годная поку́пка
**barge** [bɑːdʒ] *n* ба́ржа
**bark** [bɑːk] *n* (*of tree*) кора́ ♦ *vi* (*dog*) ла́ять (*impf*)
**barley** ['bɑːlɪ] *n* ячме́нь *m*
**barman** ['bɑːmən] (*irreg*) *n* ба́рмен
**barn** [bɑːn] *n* амба́р
**barometer** [bəˈrɒmɪtər] *n* баро́метр
**baron** ['bærən] *n* баро́н; (*of press, industry*) магна́т
**barracks** ['bærəks] *npl* каза́рма *fsg*
**barrage** ['bærɑːʒ] *n* (*fig*) лави́на
**barrel** ['bærəl] *n* (*of wine, beer*) бо́чка; (*of oil*) барре́ль *m*; (*of gun*) ствол
**barren** ['bærən] *adj* (*land*) беспло́дный
**barricade** [bærɪˈkeɪd] *n* баррика́да ♦ *vt* баррикади́ровать (забаррикади́ровать *pf*); **to ~ o.s. in** баррикади́роваться (забаррикади́роваться *pf*)
**barrier** ['bærɪər] *n* (*at entrance*) барье́р; (*at frontier*) шлагба́ум; (*fig: to progress*) препя́тствие
**barring** ['bɑːrɪŋ] *prep* за исключе́нием +*gen*
**barrister** ['bærɪstər] *n* (*BRIT*) адвока́т
**barrow** ['bærəu] *n* (*also*: **wheel~**)

та́чка
**barter** ['bɑːtər] *vi* производи́ть (произвести́ *pf*) ба́ртерный обме́н
**base** [beɪs] *n* основа́ние; (*of monument etc*) ба́за, постаме́нт; (*MIL*) ба́за; (*for organization*) местонахожде́ние ♦ *adj* ни́зкий ♦ *vt*: **to ~ sth on** (*opinion*) осно́вывать (*impf*) что-н на +*prp*; **~ball** *n* бейсбо́л; **~ment** *n* подва́л;
**bases**[1] *npl of* **base**
**bases**[2] ['beɪsɪz] *npl of* **basis**
**basic** ['beɪsɪk] *adj* (*fundamental*) фундамента́льный; (*elementary*) нача́льный; (*primitive*) элемента́рный; **~ally** *adv* по существу́; (*on the whole*) в основно́м; **~s** *npl*: **the ~s** осно́вы *fpl*
**basil** ['bæzl] *n* базили́к
**basin** ['beɪsn] *n* (*also*: **wash~**) ра́ковина; (*GEO*) бассе́йн
**basis** ['beɪsɪs] (*pl* **bases**) *n* основа́ние; **on a part-time ~** на непо́лной ста́вке; **on a trial ~** на испыта́тельный срок
**basket** ['bɑːskɪt] *n* корзи́на; **~ball** *n* баскетбо́л
**bass** [beɪs] *n* бас ♦ *adj* бассо́вый
**bastard** ['bɑːstəd] *n* внебра́чный ребёнок; (*infl*) ублю́док (!)
**bat** [bæt] *n* (*ZOOL*) лету́чая мышь *f*; (*SPORT*) бита́; (*BRIT : TABLE TENNIS*) раке́тка
**batch** [bætʃ] *n* (*of bread*) вы́печка; (*of papers*) па́чка
**bath** [bɑːθ] *n* ва́нна ♦ *vt* купа́ть (вы́купать *pf*); **to have a ~** принима́ть (приня́ть *pf*) ва́нну; *see also* **baths**
**bathe** [beɪð] *vi* (*swim*) купа́ться (*impf*); (*US: have a bath*) принима́ть (приня́ть *pf*) ва́нну ♦ *vt* (*wound*) промыва́ть (промы́ть *pf*)

**bathroom** ['bɑːθrum] n ва́нная f adj

**baths** [bɑːðz] npl (also: **swimming ~**) пла́вательный бассе́йн msg

**bath towel** n ба́нное полоте́нце

**baton** ['bætən] n (MUS) дирижёрская па́лочка; (POLICE) дуби́нка; (SPORT) эстафе́тная па́лочка

**battalion** [bə'tæliən] n батальо́н

**batter** ['bætər] vt (person) бить (изби́ть pf); (subj: wind, rain) бить (поби́ть pf) ♦ n жи́дкое те́сто

**battery** ['bætəri] n (of torch etc) батаре́йка; (AUT) аккумуля́тор

**battle** ['bætl] n би́тва, бой

**bay** [beɪ] n зали́в; (smaller) бу́хта; **loading ~** погру́зочная площа́дка; **to hold sb at ~** держа́ть (impf) кого́-н на расстоя́нии

**bazaar** [bə'zɑːr] n база́р, ры́нок; (fete) благотвори́тельный база́р

**B & B** n abbr = **bed and breakfast**

**BBC** n abbr (= British Broadcasting Corporation) Би-Би-Си nt ind

**BC** adv abbr (= before Christ) до рождества́ Христо́ва

---

KEYWORD

**be** [biː] (pt **was, were**, pp **been**) aux vb 1 (with present participle: forming continuous tenses): **what are you doing?** что Вы де́лаете?; **it is raining** идёт дождь; **they're working tomorrow** они́ рабо́тают за́втра; **the house is being built** дом стро́ится; **I've been waiting for you for ages** я жду Вас уже́ це́лую ве́чность

2 (with pp: forming passives): **he was killed** он был уби́т; **the box had been opened** я́щик откры́ли; **the thief was nowhere to be seen** во́ра нигде́ не́ было ви́дно

3 (in tag questions) не так or

пра́вда ли, да; **she's back again, is she?** она́ верну́лась, да or не так or пра́вда ли?; **she is pretty, isn't she?** она́ хоро́шенькая, не пра́вда ли or да?

4 (to +infin): **the house is to be sold** дом до́лжны прода́ть; **you're to be congratulated for all your work** Вас сле́дует поздра́вить за всю Ва́шу рабо́ту; **he's not to open it** он не до́лжен открыва́ть э́то

♦ vb 1 (+ complement: in present tense): **he is English** он англича́нин; (in past/future tense) быть (impf) +instr; **he was a doctor** он был врачо́м; **she is going to be very tall** она́ бу́дет о́чень высо́кой; **I'm tired** я уста́л; **I was hot/cold** мне бы́ло жа́рко/ хо́лодно; **two and two are four** два́жды два - четы́ре; **she's tall** она́ высо́кая; **be careful!** бу́дьте осторо́жны!; **be quiet!** ти́хо!, ти́ше!

2 (of health): **how are you feeling?** как Вы себя́ чу́вствуете?; **he's very ill** он о́чень бо́лен; **I'm better now** мне сейча́с лу́чше

3 (of age): **how old are you?** ско́лько Вам лет?; **I'm sixteen (years old)** мне шестна́дцать (лет)

4 (cost): **how much is the wine?** ско́лько сто́ит вино́?; **that'll be £5.75, please** с Вас £5.75, пожа́луйста

♦ vi 1 (exist) быть (impf); **there are people who ...** есть лю́ди, кото́рые ...; **there is one drug that ...** есть одно́ лека́рство, кото́рое ...; **is there a God?** Бог есть?

2 (occur) быва́ть (impf); **there are frequent accidents on this road** на э́той доро́ге ча́сто быва́ют

ава́рии; **be that as it may** как бы то ни́ было; **so be it** так и быть, быть по сему́

3 (*referring to place*): **I won't be here tomorrow** меня́ здесь за́втра не бу́дет; **the book is on the table** кни́га на столе́; **there are pictures on the wall** на стене́ карти́ны; **Edinburgh is in Scotland** Эдинбу́рг нахо́дится в Шотла́ндии; **there is someone in the house** в до́ме кто-то есть; **we've been here for ages** мы здесь уже́ це́лую ве́чность

4 (*referring to movement*) быть (*impf*); **where have you been?** где Вы бы́ли?; **I've been to the post office** я был на по́чте

♦ *impers vb* 1 (*referring to time*): **it's five o'clock (now)** сейча́с пять часо́в; **it's the 28th of April (today)** сего́дня 28-ое апре́ля

2 (*referring to distance, weather: in present tense*): **it's 10 km to the village** до дере́вни 10 км; (: *in past/future tense*) быть (*impf*); **it's hot/cold (today)** сего́дня жа́рко/хо́лодно; **it was very windy yesterday** вчера́ бы́ло о́чень ве́трено; **it will be sunny tomorrow** за́втра бу́дет со́лнечно

3 (*emphatic*): **it's (only) me/the postman** э́то я/почтальо́н; **it was Maria who paid the bill** и́менно Мари́я оплати́ла счёт

**beach** [bi:tʃ] *n* пляж
**beacon** ['bi:kən] *n* (*marker*) сигна́льный ого́нь *m*
**bead** [bi:d] *n* бу́сина; (*of sweat*) ка́пля
**beak** [bi:k] *n* клюв
**beam** [bi:m] *n* (*ARCHIT*) ба́лка, стропи́ло; (*of light*) луч
**bean** [bi:n] *n* боб; **French ~**

фасо́ль *f no pl*; **runner ~** фасо́ль о́гненная; **coffee ~** кофе́йное зерно́
**bear** [bɛəʳ] (*pt* **bore**, *pp* **borne**) *n* медве́дь(е́дица) *m(f)* ♦ *vt* (*cost, responsibility*) нести́ (понести́ *pf*); (*weight*) нести́ (*impf*) ♦ *vi*: **to ~ right/left** (*AUT*) держа́ться (*impf*) пра́вого/ле́вого поворо́та; **~ out** *vt* подде́рживать (поддержа́ть *pf*)
**beard** [bɪəd] *n* борода́; **~ed** *adj* борода́тый
**bearing** ['bɛərɪŋ] *n* (*connection*) отноше́ние; **~s** *npl* (*also*: **ball ~s**) ша́рики *mpl* подши́пника; **to take a ~** ориенти́роваться (*impf/pf*)
**beast** [bi:st] *n* (*also inf*) зверь *m*
**beat** [bi:t] (*pt* **~**, *pp* **~en**) *n* (*of heart*) бие́ние; (*MUS, rhythm*) ритм; (*POLICE*) уча́сток ♦ *vt* (*wife, child*) бить (поби́ть *pf*); (*eggs etc*) взбива́ть (взби́ть *pf*); (*opponent, record*) побива́ть (поби́ть *pf*); (*drum*) бить (*impf*) в +*acc* ♦ *vi* (*heart*) би́ться (*impf*); (*rain, wind*) стуча́ть (*impf*); **~ it!** (*inf*) кати́сь!; **off the ~en track** по непроторённому пути́; **~ up** *vt* (*person*) избива́ть (изби́ть *pf*); **~ing** *n* избие́ние; (*thrashing*) по́рка
**beautiful** ['bju:tɪful] *adj* краси́вый; (*day, experience*) прекра́сный; **~ly** ['bju:tɪflɪ] *adv* (*play, sing etc*) краси́во, прекра́сно
**beauty** ['bju:tɪ] *n* красота́; (*woman*) краса́вица
**beaver** ['bi:vəʳ] *n* (*ZOOL*) бобр
**became** [bɪ'keɪm] *pt of* **become**
**because** [bɪ'kɔz] *conj* потому́ что; (*since*) так как; **~ of** из-за +*gen*
**become** [bɪ'kʌm] (*irreg: like* **come**) *vi* станови́ться (стать *pf*) +*instr*; **to ~ fat** толсте́ть (потолсте́ть *pf*); **to ~ thin** худе́ть (похуде́ть *pf*)

**bed** [bɛd] *n* кровáть *f*; (*of river, sea*) дно; (*of flowers*) клýмба; **to go to ~** ложúться (лечь *pf*) спать; **~ and breakfast** *n* мáленькая чáстная гостúница с зáвтраком; (*terms*) ночлéг и зáвтрак; **~clothes** *npl* постéльное бельё *ntsg*; **~ding** *n* постéльные принадлéжности *fpl*; **~room** *n* спáльня; **~side** *n*: **at sb's ~side** у постéли когó-н; **~spread** *n* покрывáло; **~time** *n* врéмя *nt* ложúться спать

**bee** [biː] *n* пчелá

**beech** [biːtʃ] *n* бук

**beef** [biːf] *n* говя́дина; **roast ~** рóстбиф

**been** [biːn] *pp of* **be**

**beer** [bɪər] *n* пúво

**beet** [biːt] *n* (*vegetable*) кормовáя свёкла; (*US* : *also*: **red ~**) свёкла

**beetle** ['biːtl] *n* жук

**beetroot** ['biːtruːt] *n* (*BRIT*) свёкла

**before** [bɪ'fɔːr] *prep* пéред +*instr*, до +*gen* ♦ *conj* до тогó *or* пéред тем, как ♦ *adv* (*time*) рáньше, прéжде; **the day ~ yesterday** позавчерá; **do this ~ you forget** сдéлайте э́то, покá Вы не забы́ли; **~ going** пéред ухóдом; **~ she goes** до тогó *or* пéред тем, как онá уйдёт; **the week ~** недéлю назáд, на прóшлой недéле; **I've never seen it ~** я никогдá э́того рáньше не вúдел; **~hand** *adv* зарáнее

**beg** [bɛg] *vi* попрошáйничать (*impf*), нúщенствовать (*impf*) ♦ *vt* (*also*: **~ for**: *food, money*) просúть (*impf*); (: *mercy, forgiveness*) умоля́ть (умолúть *pf*) о +*prp*; **to ~ sb to do** умоля́ть (умолúть *pf*) когó-н +*infin*

**began** [bɪ'gæn] *pt of* **begin**

**beggar** ['bɛgər] *n* попрошáйка, нúщий(ая) *m(f) adj*

**begin** [bɪ'gɪn] (*pt* **began**, *pp* **begun**) *vt* начинáть (начáть *pf*) ♦ *vi* начинáться (начáться *pf*); **to ~ doing** *or* **to do** начинáть (начáть *pf*) +*impf infin*; **~ner** *n* начинáющий(ая) *m(f) adj*; **~ning** *n* начáло

**begun** [bɪ'gʌn] *pp of* **begin**

**behalf** [bɪ'hɑːf] *n*: **on** *or* (*US*) **in ~ of** от úмени +*gen*; (*for benefit of* ) в пóльзу +*gen*, в интерéсах +*gen*; **on my/his ~** от моегó/егó úмени

**behave** [bɪ'heɪv] *vi* вестú (*impf*) себя́; (*also*: **~ o.s.**) вестú (*impf*) себя́ хорошó

**behaviour** [bɪ'heɪvjər] (*US* **behavior**) *n* поведéние

**behind** [bɪ'haɪnd] *prep* (*at the back of* ) за +*instr*, позадú +*gen*; (*supporting*) за +*instr*, (*lower in rank etc*) нúже +*gen* ♦ *adv* сзáди, позадú ♦ *n* (*buttocks*) зад; **to be ~ schedule** отставáть (отстáть *pf*) от грáфика

**beige** [beɪʒ] *adj* бéжевый

**Beijing** ['beɪ'dʒɪŋ] *n* Пекúн

**Beirut** [beɪ'ruːt] *n* Бейрýт

**Belarus** [bɛlə'rus] *n* Белорýсь *f*

**belated** [bɪ'leɪtɪd] *adj* запоздáлый

**belfry** ['bɛlfrɪ] *n* колокóльня

**Belgian** ['bɛldʒən] *n* бельгúец(úйка)

**Belgium** ['bɛldʒəm] *n* Бéльгия

**belief** [bɪ'liːf] *n* (*conviction*) убеждéние; (*trust, faith*) вéра; **it's beyond ~** э́то невероя́тно; **in the ~ that** полагáя, что

**believe** [bɪ'liːv] *vt* вéрить (повéрить *pf*) +*dat or* в +*acc* ♦ *vi* вéрить (*impf*); **to ~ in** вéрить (повéрить *pf*) в +*acc*

**bell** [bɛl] *n* кóлокол; (*small*) колокóльчик; (*on door*) звонóк

**belligerent** [bɪ'lɪdʒərənt] *adj* воúнственный

**belly** ['bɛlɪ] *n* (*of animal*) брю́хо; (*of*

*person*) живо́т

**belong** [bɪˈlɔŋ] *vi*: **to ~ to** принадлежа́ть (*impf*) +*dat*; (*club*) состоя́ть (*impf*) в +*prp*; **this book ~s here** ме́сто э́той кни́ги здесь; **~ings** *npl* ве́щи *fpl*

**beloved** [bɪˈlʌvɪd] *adj* люби́мый

**below** [bɪˈləu] *prep* (*position*) под +*instr*; (*motion*) под +*acc*; (*less than*) ни́же +*gen* ♦ *adv* (*position*) внизу́; (*motion*) вниз; **see ~** смотри́ ни́же

**belt** [bɛlt] *n* (*leather*) реме́нь *m*; (*cloth*) по́яс; (*of land*) по́яс, зо́на; (*TECH*) приводно́й реме́нь

**bemused** [bɪˈmjuːzd] *adj* озада́ченный

**bench** [bɛntʃ] *n* скамья́; (*BRIT : POL*) места́ *ntpl* па́ртий в парла́менте; (*in workshop*) верста́к; (*in laboratory*) лаборато́рный стол; **the Bench** (*LAW*) суде́йская колле́гия

**bend** [bɛnd] (*pt, pp* **bent**) *vt* гнуть (согну́ть *pf*), сгиба́ть (*impf*) ♦ *vi* (*person*) гну́ться (согну́ться *pf*) ♦ *n* (*BRIT: in road*) поворо́т; (*in pipe*) изги́б; (*in river*) излу́чина; **~ down** *vi* наклоня́ться (наклони́ться *pf*), нагиба́ться (нагну́ться *pf*)

**beneath** [bɪˈniːθ] *prep* (*position*) под +*instr*; (*motion*) под +*acc*; (*unworthy of*) ни́же +*gen* ♦ *adv* внизу́

**beneficial** [bɛnɪˈfɪʃəl] *adj*: **~ (to)** благотво́рный (для +*gen*)

**benefit** [ˈbɛnɪfɪt] *n* (*advantage*) вы́года; (*money*) посо́бие ♦ *vt* приноси́ть (принести́ *pf*) по́льзу +*dat* ♦ *vi*: **he'll ~ from it** он полу́чит от э́того вы́году

**benevolent** [bɪˈnɛvələnt] *adj* (*person*) доброжела́тельный

**benign** [bɪˈnaɪn] *adj* добросерде́чный; (*MED*) доброка́чественный

**bent** [bɛnt] *pt, pp of* **bend** ♦ *adj*

(*wire, pipe*) по́гнутый; **he is ~ on doing** он настро́ился +*infin*

**bereaved** [bɪˈriːvd] *adj* понёсший тяжёлую утра́ту ♦ *n*: **the ~** друзья́ *mpl* и ро́дственники *mpl* поко́йного

**Berlin** [bəːˈlɪn] *n* Берли́н

**Bermuda** [bəːˈmjuːdə] *n* Берму́дские острова́ *mpl*

**berry** [ˈbɛrɪ] *n* я́года

**berserk** [bəˈsəːk] *adj*: **to go ~** чуме́ть (очуме́ть *pf*)

**berth** [bəːθ] *n* (*in caravan, on ship*) ко́йка; (*on train*) по́лка; (*mooring*) прича́л

**beset** [bɪˈsɛt] (*pt, pp* **~**) *vt*: **we have been ~ by problems** нас одолева́ли пробле́мы

**beside** [bɪˈsaɪd] *prep* ря́дом с +*instr*, о́коло +*gen*, у +*gen*; **to be ~ o.s. (with)** быть (*impf*) вне себя́ (от +*gen*); **that's ~ the point** э́то к де́лу не отно́сится

**besides** [bɪˈsaɪdz] *adv* кро́ме того́ ♦ *prep* кро́ме +*gen*, помимо +*gen*

**best** [bɛst] *adj* лу́чший ♦ *adv* лу́чше всего́; **the ~ part of** (*quantity*) бо́льшая часть +*gen*; **at ~** в лу́чшем слу́чае; **to make the ~ of sth** испо́льзовать (*impf*) что-н наилу́чшим о́бразом; **to do one's ~** де́лать (сде́лать *pf*) всё возмо́жное; **to the ~ of my knowledge** наско́лько мне изве́стно; **to the ~ of my ability** в ме́ру мои́х спосо́бностей; **~ man** *n* ша́фер; **~seller** *n* бестсе́ллер

**bet** [bɛt] (*pt, pp* **~** or **~ted**) *n* (*wager*) пари́ *nt ind*; (*in gambling*) ста́вка ♦ *vi* (*wager*) держа́ть (*impf*) пари́; (*expect, guess*) би́ться (*impf*) об закла́д ♦ *vt*: **to ~ sb sth** спо́рить (поспо́рить *pf*) с кем-н на что-н; **to ~ money on sth** ста́вить (поста́вить *pf*) де́ньги на что-н

**betray** [bɪ'treɪ] vt (friends)
предава́ть (преда́ть pf); (trust)
обма́нывать (обману́ть pf); **~al** n
преда́тельство

**better** ['betər] adj лу́чший ♦ adv
лу́чше ♦ vt (score) улучша́ть
(улу́чшить pf) ♦ n: **to get the ~ of**
брать (взять pf) верх над +instr; **I
feel ~** я чу́вствую себя́ лу́чше; **to
get ~** (MED) поправля́ться
(попра́виться pf); **I had ~ go** мне
лу́чше уйти́; **he thought ~ of it** он
переду́мал; **~ off** adj (wealthier)
бо́лее состоя́тельный

**betting** ['betɪŋ] n пари́ nt ind

**between** [bɪ'twi:n] prep ме́жду
+instr ♦ adv: **in ~** ме́жду тем

**beware** [bɪ'weər] vi: **to ~ (of)**
остерега́ться (остере́чься pf)
(+gen)

**bewildered** [bɪ'wɪldəd] adj
изумлённый

**beyond** [bɪ'jɔnd] prep (position) за
+instr; (motion) за +acc;
(understanding) вы́ше +gen;
(expectations) сверх +gen; (doubt)
вне +gen; (age) бо́льше +gen;
(date) по́сле +gen ♦ adv (position)
вдали́; (motion) вдаль; **it's ~
repair** э́то невозмо́жно почини́ть

**bias** ['baɪəs] n (against)
предубежде́ние; (towards)
пристра́стие

**bib** [bɪb] n (child's) нагру́дник

**Bible** ['baɪbl] n Би́блия

**biblical** ['bɪblɪkl] adj библе́йский

**bicycle** ['baɪsɪkl] n велосипе́д

**bid** [bɪd] (pt **bade** or ~, pp **~(den)**) n
(at auction) предложе́ние цены́;
(attempt) попы́тка ♦ vt (offer)
предлага́ть (предложи́ть pf) ♦ vi:
**to ~ for** (at auction) предлага́ть
(предложи́ть pf) це́ну за +acc;
**~der** n: **the highest ~der** лицо́,
предлага́ющее наивы́сшую це́ну

**big** [bɪg] adj большо́й; (important)

ва́жный; (bulky) кру́пный; (older:
brother, sister) ста́рший

**bigotry** ['bɪgətrɪ] n фанати́зм

**bike** [baɪk] n (inf: bicycle) ве́лик

**bikini** [bɪ'ki:nɪ] n бики́ни nt ind

**bilateral** [baɪ'lætərl] adj
двусторо́нний

**bilingual** [baɪ'lɪŋgwəl] adj
двуязы́чный

**bill** [bɪl] n (invoice) счёт; (POL)
законопрое́кт; (US: banknote)
казначе́йский биле́т, банкно́т;
(beak) клюв; **~board** n доска́
объявле́ний

**billion** ['bɪljən] n (BRIT) биллио́н;
(US) миллиа́рд

**bin** [bɪn] n (BRIT : also: **rubbish ~**)
му́сорное ведро́; (container)
я́щик

**bind** [baɪnd] (pt, pp **bound**) vt (tie)
привя́зывать (привяза́ть pf);
(hands, feet) свя́зывать (связа́ть
pf); (oblige) обя́зывать (обяза́ть
pf); (book) переплета́ть
(переплести́ pf); **~ing** adj
обя́зывающий

**bingo** ['bɪŋgəʊ] n лото́ nt ind

**binoculars** [bɪ'nɔkjʊləz] npl
бино́кль msg

**biography** [baɪ'ɔgrəfɪ] n
биогра́фия

**biological** [baɪə'lɔdʒɪkl] adj (science)
биологи́ческий; (warfare)
бактериологи́ческий; (washing
powder) содержа́щий
биопрепара́ты

**biology** [baɪ'ɔlədʒɪ] n биоло́гия

**birch** [bə:tʃ] n берёза

**bird** [bə:d] n пти́ца

**Biro** ® ['baɪərəʊ] n ша́риковая
ру́чка

**birth** [bə:θ] n рожде́ние; **to give ~
to** рожа́ть (роди́ть pf); **~
certificate** n свиде́тельство о
рожде́нии; **~ control** n (policy)
контро́ль m рожда́емости;

(*methods*) противозача́точные ме́ры *fpl*; **~day** *n* день *m* рожде́ния ♦ *cpd*: **~day card** откры́тка ко дню рожде́ния; *see also* **happy**; **~place** *n* ро́дина

**biscuit** ['bɪskɪt] *n* (*BRIT*) пече́нье; (*US*) ≈ кекс

**bisexual** ['baɪ'sɛksjuəl] *adj* бисексуа́льный

**bishop** ['bɪʃəp] *n* (*REL*) епи́скоп; (*CHESS*) слон

**bit** [bɪt] *pt of* **bite** ♦ *n* (*piece*) кусо́к, кусо́чек; (*COMPUT*) бит; **a ~ of** немно́го +*gen*; **a ~ dangerous** слегка́ опа́сный; **~ by ~** ма́ло-пома́лу, понемно́гу

**bitch** [bɪtʃ] *n* (*also inf!*) су́ка (*also !*)

**bite** [baɪt] (*pt* **bit**, *pp* **bitten**) *vt* куса́ть (укуси́ть *pf*) ♦ *vi* куса́ться (*impf*) ♦ *n* (*insect bite*) уку́с; **to ~ one's nails** куса́ть (*impf*) но́гти; **let's have a ~ (to eat)** (*inf*) дава́йте переку́сим; **he had a ~ of cake** он откуси́л кусо́к пирога́

**bitter** ['bɪtər] *adj* го́рький; (*wind*) пронизывающий; (*struggle*) ожесточённый; **~ness** *n* (*anger, of taste*) го́речь *f*, ожесточённость *f*

**bizarre** [bɪ'zɑːr] *adj* стра́нный, причу́дливый

**black** [blæk] *adj* чёрный; (*tea*) без молока́; (*person*) чернокожий ♦ *n* (*colour*) чёрный цвет, чёрное *nt adj*; (*person*): **Black** негр(итя́нка); **~ and blue** в синяка́х; **to be in the ~** име́ть (*impf*) де́ньги в ба́нке; **~berry** *n* ежеви́ка *f no pl*; **~bird** *n* (чёрный) дрозд; **~board** *n* кла́ссная доска́; **~ coffee** *n* чёрный ко́фе *m ind*; **~currant** *n* чёрная сморо́дина; **~ eye** *n* синя́к под гла́зом; **to give sb a ~ eye** подбива́ть (подби́ть *pf*) кому́-н глаз; **~mail** *n* шанта́ж ♦ *vt* шантажи́ровать (*impf*); **~**

**market** *n* чёрный ры́нок; **~out** *n* (*ELEC*) обесто́чка; (*TV, RADIO*) приостановле́ние переда́ч; (*MED*) о́бморок; **~ pepper** *n* чёрный пе́рец; **Black Sea** *n*: **the Black Sea** Чёрное мо́ре; **~smith** *n* кузне́ц

**bladder** ['blædər] *n* мочево́й пузы́рь *m*

**blade** [bleɪd] *n* ле́звие; (*of propeller, oar*) ло́пасть *f*; **a ~ of grass** трави́нка

**blame** [bleɪm] *n* вина́ ♦ *vt*: **to ~ sb for sth** вини́ть (*impf*) кого́-н в чём-н; **he is to ~ (for sth)** он винова́т (в чём-н)

**bland** [blænd] *adj* (*food*) пре́сный

**blank** [blæŋk] *adj* (*paper*) чи́стый; (*look*) пусто́й ♦ *n* (*of memory*) прова́л; (*on form*) про́пуск; (*for gun*) холосто́й патро́н

**blanket** ['blæŋkɪt] *n* одея́ло; (*of snow*) покро́в; (*of fog*) пелена́

**blasé** ['blɑːzeɪ] *adj* валья́жный

**blasphemy** ['blæsfɪmɪ] *n* богоху́льство

**blast** [blɑːst] *n* (*explosion*) взрыв ♦ *vt* (*blow up*) взрыва́ть (взорва́ть *pf*)

**blatant** ['bleɪtənt] *adj* я́вный

**blaze** [bleɪz] *n* (*fire*) пла́мя *nt*; (*of colour*) полыха́ние

**blazer** ['bleɪzər] *n* фо́рменный пиджа́к

**bleach** [bliːtʃ] *n* (*also:* **household ~**) отбе́ливатель *m* ♦ *vt* (*fabric*) отбе́ливать (отбели́ть *pf*)

**bleak** [bliːk] *adj* (*day, face*) уны́лый; (*prospect*) мра́чный

**bleed** [bliːd] (*pt, pp* **bled**) *vi* кровото́чить (*impf*); **my nose is ~ing** у меня́ из но́са идёт кровь

**blend** [blɛnd] *n* (*of tea, whisky*) буке́т ♦ *vt* (*CULIN*) сме́шивать (смеша́ть *pf*) ♦ *vi* (*also:* **~ in**) сочета́ться (*impf*)

**bless** [bles] (*pt, pp* **~ed** *or* **blest**) *vt* благословля́ть (благослови́ть *pf*); **~ you!** бу́дьте здоро́вы!; **~ing** *n* благослове́ние; (*godsend*) Бо́жий дар

**blew** [blu:] *pt of* **blow**

**blind** [blaɪnd] *adj* слепо́й ♦ *n* што́ра; (*also:* **Venetian ~**) жалюзи́ *pl ind* ♦ *vt* ослепля́ть (ослепи́ть *pf*); **the ~** *npl* (*blind people*) слепы́е *pl adj*; **to be ~ (to)** (*fig*) не ви́деть (*impf*) (+*acc*); **~ly** *adv* (*without thinking*) сле́по; **~ness** *n* (*physical*) слепота́

**blink** [blɪŋk] *vi* морга́ть (*impf*); (*light*) мига́ть (*impf*)

**bliss** [blɪs] *n* блаже́нство

**blithely** ['blaɪðlɪ] *adv* беспе́чно

**blizzard** ['blɪzəd] *n* вьюга

**bloated** ['bləʊtɪd] *adj* (*face, stomach*) взду́тый; **I feel ~** я весь разду́лся

**blob** [blɔb] *n* (*of glue, paint*) сгу́сток; (*shape*) сму́тное очерта́ние

**bloc** [blɔk] *n* блок

**block** [blɔk] *n* (*of buildings*) кварта́л; (*of stone etc*) плита́ ♦ *vt* (*barricade*) блоки́ровать (заблоки́ровать *pf*), загора́живать (загороди́ть *pf*); (*progress*) препя́тствовать (*impf*); **~ of flats** (*BRIT*) многокварти́рный дом; **mental ~** прова́л па́мяти; **~ade** [blɔ'keɪd] *n* блока́да; **~age** ['blɔkɪdʒ] *n* блоки́рование

**bloke** [bləʊk] *n* (*BRIT : inf*) па́рень *m*

**blond(e)** [blɔnd] *adj* белоку́рый ♦ *n*: **~e** (*woman*) блонди́нка

**blood** [blʌd] *n* кровь *f*; **~ donor** *n* до́нор; **~ pressure** *n* кровяно́е давле́ние; **~shed** *n* кровопроли́тие; **~stream** *n* кровообраще́ние; **~ test** *n* ана́лиз кро́ви; **~y** *adj* (*battle*) крова́вый; (*BRIT : inf!*): **this ~y weather** э́та прокля́тая пого́да; **~y good** (*inf!*) черто́вски хоро́ший

**blossom** ['blɔsəm] *n* цвет, цвете́ние

**blot** [blɔt] *n* (*on text*) кля́кса

**blow** [bləʊ] (*pt* **blew**, *pp* **~n**) *n* уда́р ♦ *vi* (*wind, person*) дуть (поду́ть *pf*); (*fuse*) перегора́ть (перегоре́ть *pf*) ♦ *vt* (*subj: wind*) гнать (*impf*); (*instrument*) дуть (*impf*) в +*acc*; **to ~ one's nose** сморка́ться (вы́сморкаться *pf*); **~ away** *vt* сдува́ть (сдуть *pf*); **~ up** *vi* (*storm, crisis*) разража́ться (разрази́ться *pf*) ♦ *vt* (*bridge*) взрыва́ть (взорва́ть *pf*); (*tyre*) надува́ть (наду́ть *pf*)

**blue** [blu:] *adj* (*colour: light*) голубо́й; (*: dark*) си́ний; (*unhappy*) гру́стный; **the ~s** *npl* (*MUS*) блюз *msg*; **out of the ~** (*fig*) как гром среди́ я́сного не́ба; **~bell** *n* колоко́льчик; **~print** *n* (*fig*): **a ~print (for)** прое́кт (+*gen*)

**bluff** [blʌf] *n*: **to call sb's ~** заставля́ть (заста́вить *pf*) кого́-н раскры́ть ка́рты

**blunder** ['blʌndər] *n* гру́бая оши́бка

**blunt** [blʌnt] *adj* тупо́й; (*person*) прямолине́йный

**blur** [blə:r] *n* (*shape*) сму́тное очерта́ние ♦ *vt* (*vision*) затума́нивать (затума́нить *pf*); (*distinction*) стира́ть (стере́ть *pf*)

**blush** [blʌʃ] *vi* красне́ть (покрасне́ть *pf*)

**BNP** *n abbr* = **British National Party**

**boar** [bɔ:r] *n* бо́ров; (*wild pig*) каба́н

**board** [bɔ:d] *n* доска́; (*card*) карто́н; (*committee*) комите́т; (*in firm*) правле́ние ♦ *vt* (*ship, train*) сади́ться (сесть *pf*) на +*acc*; **on ~**

(*NAUT, AVIAT*) на борту́; **full ~**
(*BRIT*) по́лный пансио́н; **half ~**
(*BRIT*) пансио́н с за́втраком и
у́жином; **~ and lodging**
прожива́ние и пита́ние; **~ing
card** n (*AVIAT, NAUT*) поса́дочный
тало́н; **~ing school** n шко́ла-
интерна́т

**boast** [bəust] vi: **to ~ (about** or **of)**
хва́статься (похва́статься pf)
(+*instr*)

**boat** [bəut] n (*small*) ло́дка; (*large*)
кора́бль m

**bob** [bɔb] vi (*boat : also:* **~ up and
down**) пока́чиваться (*impf*)

**bodily** [ˈbɔdɪlɪ] adj физи́ческий
♦ adv целико́м

**body** [ˈbɔdɪ] n те́ло; (*of car*)
ко́рпус; (*torso*) ту́ловище; (*fig:
group*) гру́ппа; (*: organization*)
о́рган; **~guard** n телохрани́тель
m; **~ language** n язы́к же́стов;
**~work** n ко́рпус

**bog** [bɔg] n (*GEO*) боло́то, тряси́на

**bogus** [ˈbəugəs] adj (*claim*)
фикти́вный

**boil** [bɔɪl] vt (*water*) кипяти́ть
(вскипяти́ть pf); (*eggs, potatoes*)
вари́ть (свари́ть pf) ♦ vi кипе́ть
(вскипе́ть pf) ♦ n фуру́нкул; **to
come to the** (*BRIT*) or **a** (*US*) **~**
вскипе́ть (*pf*); **~ed egg** n
варёное яйцо́; **~er** n (*device*)
парово́й котёл, бо́йлер

**boisterous** [ˈbɔɪstərəs] adj
разбитно́й

**bold** [bəuld] adj (*brave*) сме́лый;
(*pej: cheeky*) на́глый; (*pattern,
colours*) бро́ский

**bolt** [bəult] n (*lock*) засо́в; (*with nut*)
болт ♦ adv: **~ upright**
вы́тянувшись в стру́нку

**bomb** [bɔm] n бо́мба ♦ vt бомби́ть
(*impf*)

**bombardment** [bɔmˈbɑːdmənt] n
бомбардиро́вка

**bomber** [ˈbɔmər] n (*AVIAT*)
бомбардиро́вщик

**bombshell** [ˈbɔmʃɛl] n (*fig*): **the
news was a real ~** э́то изве́стие
произвело́ эффе́кт
разорва́вшейся бо́мбы

**bond** [bɔnd] n у́зы pl; (*FINANCE*)
облига́ция

**bone** [bəun] n кость f ♦ vt
отделя́ть (отдели́ть pf) от
косте́й; **~ marrow** n ко́стный
мозг

**bonfire** [ˈbɔnfaɪər] n костёр

**bonnet** [ˈbɔnɪt] n (*hat*) ка́пор;
(*BRIT: of car*) капо́т

**bonus** [ˈbəunəs] n (*payment*)
пре́мия; (*fig*) дополни́тельное
преиму́щество

**bony** [ˈbəunɪ] adj (*person, fingers*)
костля́вый; (*meat, fish*) кости́стый

**boo** [buː] excl фу ♦ vt освисты́вать
(освиста́ть pf)

**book** [buk] n кни́га; (*of stamps,
tickets*) кни́жечка ♦ vt (*ticket, table*)
зака́зывать (заказа́ть pf); (*seat,
room*) брони́ровать
(заброни́ровать pf); (*subj:
policeman, referee*) штрафова́ть
(оштрафова́ть pf); **~s** npl
(*accounts*) бухга́лтерские кни́ги
fpl; **~case** n кни́жный шкаф; **~let**
n брошю́ра; **~mark** n закла́дка;
**~shop** n кни́жный магази́н

**boom** [buːm] n (*noise*) ро́кот;
(*growth*) бум

**boon** [buːn] n бла́го

**boost** [buːst] n (*to confidence*)
сти́мул ♦ vt стимули́ровать (*impf*)

**boot** [buːt] n (*for winter*) сапо́г; (*for
football*) бу́тса; (*for walking*)
боти́нок; (*BRIT: of car*) бага́жник

**booth** [buːð] n (*at fair*) ларёк;;
(*TEL, for voting*) бу́дка

**booze** [buːz] (*inf*) n вы́пивка

**border** [ˈbɔːdər] n (*of country*)
грани́ца; (*for flowers*) бордю́р; (*on

*cloth etc*) кайма́ ♦ *vt* (*road, river etc*)
окаймля́ть (окайми́ть *pf*);
(*country: also:* ~ **on**) грани́чить
(*impf*) с +*instr*; **~line** *n*: on the ~line
на гра́ни

**bore** [bɔːʳ] *pt of* **bear** ♦ *vt* (*hole*)
сверли́ть (просверли́ть *pf*);
(*person*) наску́чить (*pf*) +*dat* ♦ *n*
(*person*) зану́да *m/f*; **to be** ~**d**
скуча́ть (*impf*); **~dom** *n* (*condition*)
ску́ка; (*boring quality*) зану́дство

**boring** [ˈbɔːrɪŋ] *adj* ску́чный

**born** [bɔːn] *adj* рождённый; **to be**
~ рожда́ться (роди́ться *pf*)

**borne** [bɔːn] *pp of* **bear**

**borough** [ˈbʌrə] *n*
администрати́вный о́круг

**borrow** [ˈbɔrəu] *vt*: **to** ~ **sth from
sb** занима́ть (заня́ть *pf*) что-н у
кого́-н

**Bosnia** [ˈbɔznɪə] *n* Бо́сния;
**~-Herzegovina** [-,hɜːtsəgəuˈviːnə]
*n* Бо́сния-Герцегови́на

**bosom** [ˈbuzəm] *n* (*ANAT*) грудь *f*

**boss** [bɔs] *n* (*employer*)
хозя́ин(я́йка), босс ♦ *vt* (*also:* ~
**around,** ~ **about**)
распоряжа́ться (*impf*),
кома́ндовать (*impf*) +*instr*; **~y** *adj*
вла́стный

**both** [bəuθ] *adj, pron* о́ба *f* (о́бе)
♦ *adv*: ~ **A and B** и А, и Б; **~ of us
went, we ~ went** мы о́ба пошли́

**bother** [ˈbɔðəʳ] *vt* (*worry*)
беспоко́ить (обеспоко́ить *pf*);
(*disturb*) беспоко́ить
(побеспоко́ить *pf*) ♦ *vi* (*also:* ~
**o.s.**) беспоко́иться (*impf*) ♦ *n*
(*trouble*) беспоко́йство; (*nuisance*)
хло́поты *pl*; **to** ~ **doing** брать
(взять *pf*) на себя́ труд +*infin*

**bottle** [ˈbɔtl] *n* буты́лка; **~-opener**
*n* што́пор

**bottom** [ˈbɔtəm] *n* (*of container,
sea*) дно; (*ANAT*) зад; (*of page, list*)
низ; (*of class*) отстаю́щий(ая) *m(f)*

*adj* ♦ *adj* (*lowest*) ни́жний; (*last*)
после́дний

**bough** [bau] *n* сук

**bought** [bɔːt] *pt, pp of* **buy**

**boulder** [ˈbəuldəʳ] *n* валу́н

**bounce** [bauns] *vi* (*ball*)
отска́кивать (отскочи́ть *pf*);
(*cheque*) верну́ться (*pf*) (ввиду́
отсу́тствия де́нег на счету́) ♦ *vt*
(*ball*) ударя́ть (уда́рить *pf*); **~r** *n*
(*inf*) вышиба́ла *m*

**bound** [baund] *pt, pp of* **bind** ♦ *vi*
(*leap*) пры́гать (пры́гнуть *pf*)
♦ *adj*: **he is** ~ **by law to ...** его́
обя́зывает зако́н +*infin* ... ♦ *npl*: ~**s**
(*limits*) преде́лы *mpl*

**boundary** [ˈbaundrı] *n* грани́ца

**boundless** [ˈbaundlıs] *adj*
безграни́чный

**bouquet** [ˈbukeı] *n* буке́т

**bourgeois** [ˈbuəʒwɑː] *adj*
буржуа́зный

**bout** [baut] *n* (*of illness*) при́ступ;
(*of activity*) всплеск

**boutique** [buːˈtiːk] *n* ла́вка

**bow¹** [bəu] *n* (*knot*) бант; (*weapon*)
лук; (*MUS*) смычо́к

**bow²** [bau] *n* (*of head, body*)
покло́н; (*NAUT: also:* ~**s**) нос ♦ *vi*
(*with head, body*) кла́няться
(поклони́ться *pf*); (*yield*): **to** ~ **to**
*or* **before** поддава́ться
(подда́ться *pf*) +*dat or* на +*acc*

**bowels** [ˈbauəlz] *npl* кише́чник
*msg*

**bowl** [bəul] *n* (*plate, food*) ми́ска,
ча́ша; (*ball*) шар

**bowling** [ˈbəulıŋ] *n* (*game*)
кегельба́н

**bowls** [bəulz] *n* (*game*) игра́ в
шары́

**bow tie** [bəu-] *n* ба́бочка

**box** [bɔks] *n* я́щик, коро́бка; (*also:*
**cardboard** ~) карто́нная
коро́бка; (*THEAT*) ло́жа; (*inf: TV*)
я́щик; **~er** *n* боксёр; **~ing** *n* бокс;

**Boxing Day** n (BRIT) день после Рождества

**Boxing Day** - пе́рвый день по́сле Рождества́. Буква́льно "День коро́бок". Этот день явля́ется пра́здничным. Его́ назва́ние свя́зано с обы́чаем де́лать пода́рки, упако́ванные в рожде́ственские коро́бки, почтальо́нам, разно́счикам газе́т и други́м рабо́тникам, ока́зывающим услу́ги по до́му.

**box office** n театра́льная ка́сса
**boy** [bɔɪ] n ма́льчик; (son) сыно́к
**boycott** ['bɔɪkɔt] n бойко́т ♦ vt бойкоти́ровать (impf/pf)
**boyfriend** ['bɔɪfrɛnd] n друг
**BR** abbr (formerly) = **British Rail**
**bra** [brɑː] n ли́фчик
**brace** [breɪs] n (on leg) ши́на; (on teeth) пласти́нка ♦ vt (knees, shoulders) напряга́ть (напря́чь pf); ~s npl (BRIT: for trousers) подтя́жки pl; **to ~ o.s.** (for shock) собира́ться (собра́ться pf) с ду́хом
**bracelet** ['breɪslɪt] n брасле́т
**bracing** ['breɪsɪŋ] adj бодря́щий
**bracken** ['brækən] n (BOT) орля́к
**bracket** ['brækɪt] n (TECH) кронште́йн; (group, range) катего́рия; (also: **brace ~**) ско́бка; (also: **round ~**) кру́глая ско́бка; (also: **square ~**) квадра́тная ско́бка ♦ vt (word, phrase) заключа́ть (заключи́ть pf) в ско́бки
**brain** [breɪn] n мозг; ~s npl (also CULIN) мозги́ mpl; ~**wave** n: **he had a ~wave** на него́ нашло́ озаре́ние; ~**y** adj мозгови́тый
**brake** [breɪk] n то́рмоз ♦ vi тормози́ть (затормози́ть pf)
**bramble** ['bræmbl] n ежеви́ка
**bran** [bræn] n о́труби pl

**branch** [brɑːntʃ] n (of tree) ве́тка, ветвь f; (of bank, firm etc) филиа́л
**brand** [brænd] n (also: ~ **name**) фи́рменная ма́рка ♦ vt (cattle) клейми́ть (заклейми́ть pf)
**brand-new** ['brænd'njuː] adj соверше́нно но́вый
**brandy** ['brændɪ] n бре́нди nt ind, конья́к
**brash** [bræʃ] adj наха́льный
**brass** [brɑːs] n (metal) лату́нь f; **the ~** духовы́е инструме́нты mpl
**brat** [bræt] n (pej) озорни́к
**brave** [breɪv] adj сме́лый, хра́брый ♦ vt сме́ло or хра́бро встреча́ть (встре́тить pf); ~**ry** ['breɪvərɪ] n сме́лость f, хра́брость f
**brawl** [brɔːl] n дра́ка
**brazen** ['breɪzn] adj (woman) бессты́жий ♦ vt: **to ~ it out** выкру́чиваться (вы́крутиться pf)
**Brazil** [brə'zɪl] n Брази́лия
**breach** [briːtʃ] vt (defence, wall) пробива́ть (проби́ть pf) ♦ n (gap) брешь f; **~ of contract/of the peace** наруше́ние догово́ра/ обще́ственного поря́дка
**bread** [brɛd] n (food) хлеб; ~ **and butter** n хлеб с ма́слом; ~**bin** n (BRIT) хле́бница; ~**box** n (US) = **breadbin**; ~**crumbs** npl (CULIN) паниро́вочные сухари́ mpl
**breadth** [brɛtθ] n ширина́; (fig: of knowledge, subject) широта́
**break** [breɪk] (pt **broke**, pp **broken**) vt (crockery) разбива́ть (разби́ть pf); (leg, arm) лома́ть (слома́ть pf); (law, promise) наруша́ть (нару́шить pf); (record) побива́ть (поби́ть pf) ♦ vi (crockery) разбива́ться (разби́ться pf); (storm) разража́ться (разрази́ться pf); (weather) по́ртиться (испо́ртиться pf); (dawn) бре́зжить (забре́зжить pf); (story, news) сообща́ть (сообщи́ть

*pf*) ♦ *n* (*gap*) пробе́л; (*chance*) шанс; (*fracture*) перело́м; (*playtime*) переме́на; **to ~ even** (*COMM*) зака́нчивать (зако́нчить *pf*) без убы́тка; **to ~ free** or **loose** вырыва́ться (вы́рваться *pf*) на свобо́ду; **~ down** *vt* (*figures etc*) разбива́ть (разби́ть *pf*) по статья́м ♦ *vi* (*machine, car*) лома́ться (слома́ться *pf*); (*person*) сломи́ться (*pf*); (*talks*) срыва́ться (сорва́ться *pf*)

**~ in** *vi* (*burglar*) вла́мываться (вломи́ться *pf*); (*interrupt*) вме́шиваться (вмеша́ться *pf*)

**~ into** *vt fus* (*house*) вла́мываться (вломи́ться *pf*) в +*acc*

**~ off** *vi* (*branch*) отла́мываться (отломи́ться *pf*); (*speaker*) прерыва́ться (прерва́ть *pf*) речь ♦ *vt* (*engagement*) расторга́ть (расто́ргнуть *pf*)

**~ out** *vi* (*begin*) разража́ться (разрази́ться *pf*); (*escape*) сбега́ть (сбежа́ть *pf*); **to ~ out in spots/a rash** покрыва́ться (покры́ться *pf*) прыща́ми/сы́пью

**~ up** *vi* (*ship*) разбива́ться (разби́ться *pf*); (*crowd, meeting*) расходи́ться (разойти́сь *pf*); (*marriage, partnership*) распада́ться (распа́сться *pf*); (*SCOL*) закрыва́ться (закры́ться *pf*) на кани́кулы ♦ *vt* разла́мывать (разломи́ть *pf*); (*journey*) прерыва́ть (прерва́ть *pf*); (*fight*) прекраща́ть (прекрати́ть *pf*)

**breakdown** ['breɪkdaun] *n* (*in communications*) наруше́ние, срыв; (*of marriage*) распа́д; (*also:* **nervous ~**) не́рвный срыв

**breaker** ['breɪkə<sup>r</sup>] *n* вал

**breakfast** ['brɛkfəst] *n* за́втрак

**break-in** ['breɪkɪn] *n* взлом

**breakthrough** ['breɪkθruː] *n* (*in*

*technology*) перело́мное откры́тие

**breakwater** ['breɪkwɔːtə<sup>r</sup>] *n* мол, волноре́з

**breast** [brɛst] *n* грудь *f*; (*of meat*) груди́нка; (*of poultry*) бе́лое мя́со; **~-feed** (*irreg: like* **feed**) *vt* корми́ть (покорми́ть *pf*) гру́дью ♦ *vi* корми́ть (*impf*) (гру́дью)

**breath** [brɛθ] *n* вдох; (*breathing*) дыха́ние; **to be out of ~** запыха́ться (запыха́ться *pf*)

**breathe** [briːð] *vi* дыша́ть (*impf*); **~ in** *vt* вдыха́ть (вдохну́ть *pf*) ♦ *vi* де́лать (сде́лать *pf*) вдох

**~ out** *vi* де́лать (сде́лать *pf*) вы́дох

**breathing** ['briːðɪŋ] *n* дыха́ние; **~ space** *n* (*fig*) переды́шка

**breathless** ['brɛθlɪs] *adj* (*from exertion*) запыха́вшийся

**breathtaking** ['brɛθteɪkɪŋ] *adj* захва́тывающий дух

**bred** [brɛd] *pt, pp of* **breed**

**breed** [briːd] (*pt, pp* **bred**) *vt* (*animals, plants*) разводи́ть (развести́ *pf*) ♦ *vi* размножа́ться (*impf*) ♦ *n* (*ZOOL*) поро́да; **~ing** *n* (*of dogs*) разведе́ние

**breeze** [briːz] *n* бриз

**breezy** ['briːzɪ] *adj* (*manner, tone*) оживлённый; (*weather*) прохла́дный

**brew** [bruː] *vt* (*tea*) зава́ривать (завари́ть *pf*); (*beer*) вари́ть (свари́ть *pf*) ♦ *vi* (*storm*) надвига́ться (надви́нуться *pf*); (*fig: trouble*) назрева́ть (назре́ть *pf*); **~ery** *n* пивова́ренный заво́д

**bribe** [braɪb] *n* взя́тка, по́дкуп ♦ *vt* (*person*) подкупа́ть (подкупи́ть *pf*), дава́ть (дать *pf*) взя́тку; **~ry** ['braɪbərɪ] *n* по́дкуп

**brick** [brɪk] *n* (*for building*) кирпи́ч

**bridal** ['braɪdl] *adj* подвене́чный, сва́дебный

**bride** [braɪd] n неве́ста; **~groom** n
жени́х; **~smaid** n подру́жка
неве́сты

**bridge** [brɪdʒ] n мост; (NAUT)
капита́нский мо́стик; (CARDS)
бридж; (of nose) перено́сица ♦ vt
(fig: gap) преодолева́ть
(преодоле́ть pf)

**bridle** ['braɪdl] n узде́чка, узда́

**brief** [briːf] adj (period of time)
коро́ткий; (description) кра́ткий
♦ n (task) зада́ние ♦ vt знако́мить
(ознако́мить pf) с +instr; **~s** npl
(for men) трусы́ pl; (for women)
тру́сики pl; **~case** n портфе́ль m;
(attaché case) диплома́т; **~ing** n
инструкта́ж; (PRESS) бри́финг; **~ly**
adv (glance, smile) бе́гло; (explain)
вкра́тце

**bright** [braɪt] adj (light, colour)
я́ркий; (room, future) све́тлый;
(clever: person, idea) блестя́щий;
(lively: person) живо́й, весёлый;
**~en** vt (also: **~en up**: room, event)
оживля́ть (оживи́ть pf) ♦ vi
(weather) проясня́ться
(проясни́ться pf); (person)
оживля́ться (оживи́ться pf);
(face) светле́ть (просветле́ть pf)

**brilliance** ['brɪljəns] n я́ркость f,
блеск; (of person) гениа́льность f

**brilliant** ['brɪljənt] adj блестя́щий;
(sunshine) я́ркий; (inf: holiday etc)
великоле́пный

**brim** [brɪm] n (of cup) край; (of hat)
поля́ pl

**bring** [brɪŋ] (pt, pp **brought**) vt
(thing) приноси́ть (принести́ pf);
(person: on foot) приводи́ть
(привести́ pf); (: by transport)
привози́ть (привезти́ pf);
(satisfaction, trouble) доставля́ть
(доста́вить pf); **~ about** vt (cause:
unintentionally) вызыва́ть
(вы́звать pf); (: intentionally)
осуществля́ть (осуществи́ть pf);

**~ back** vt (restore) возрожда́ть
(возроди́ть pf); (return)
возвраща́ть (возврати́ть pf),
верну́ть (pf); **~ down** vt
(government) сверга́ть (све́ргнуть
pf); (plane) сбива́ть (сбить pf); **~**
(price) снижа́ть (сни́зить pf); **~
forward** vt (meeting) переноси́ть
(перенести́ pf) на бо́лее ра́нний
срок; **~ out** vt вынима́ть (вы́нуть
pf); (publish) выпуска́ть
(вы́пустить pf); **~ up** vt (carry up)
приноси́ть (принести́ pf) наве́рх;
(child) воспи́тывать (воспита́ть
pf); (subject)
поднима́ть (подня́ть pf); **he
brought up his food** его́
стошни́ло

**brink** [brɪŋk] n: **on the ~ of** (fig) на
гра́ни +gen

**brisk** [brɪsk] adj (tone) отры́вистый;
(person, trade) оживлённый;
**business is ~** дела́ иду́т по́лным
хо́дом

**Britain** ['brɪtən] n (also: **Great ~**)
Брита́ния

**British** ['brɪtɪʃ] adj брита́нский; **the
~** npl брита́нцы mpl; **~ Isles** npl:
**the ~ Isles** Брита́нские острова́
mpl; **~ Rail** n (formerly)
Брита́нская желе́зная доро́га

**Briton** ['brɪtən] n брита́нец(нка)

**brittle** ['brɪtl] adj хру́пкий, ло́мкий

**broad** [brɔːd] adj (wide, general)
широ́кий; (strong) си́льный; **in ~
daylight** средь бе́ла дня; **~cast**
(pt, pp **~cast**) n (ра́дио)переда́ча;
(TV) (теле)переда́ча ♦ vt
трансли́ровать (impf) ♦ vi веща́ть
(impf); **~en** vt расширя́ть
(расши́рить pf) ♦ vi расширя́ться
(расши́риться pf); **~ly** adv
вообще́

**broccoli** ['brɔkəlɪ] n бро́кколи nt
ind

**brochure** ['brəʊʃjuər] n брошю́ра

**broke** [brəuk] *pt of* **break** ♦ *adj*: **I am** ~ (*inf*) я на мели; ~**n** *pp of* **break** ♦ *adj* (*window, cup etc*) разбитый; (*machine, leg*) сломанный; **in** ~**n Russian** на ломаном русском

**broker** ['brəukər] *n* (*in shares*) брокер; (*in insurance*) страховой агент

**brolly** ['brɒlɪ] *n* (*BRIT : inf*) зонт

**bronchitis** [brɒŋ'kaɪtɪs] *n* бронхит

**bronze** [brɒnz] *n* (*metal*) бронза; (*sculpture*) бронзовая скульптура

**brooch** [brəutʃ] *n* брошь *f*

**Bros.** *abbr* (*COMM*: = *brothers*) братья *mpl*

**broth** [brɒθ] *n* похлёбка

**brothel** ['brɒθl] *n* публичный дом, бордель *m*

**brother** ['brʌðər] *n* брат; ~**-in-law** *n* (*sister's husband*) зять *m*; (*wife's brother*) шурин; (*husband's brother*) деверь *m*

**brought** [brɔːt] *pt, pp of* **bring**

**brow** [brau] *n* лоб, чело; (*also*: **eye~**) бровь *f*; (*of hill*) гребень *m*

**brown** [braun] *adj* коричневый; (*hair*) тёмно-русый; (*eyes*) карий; (*tanned*) загорелый ♦ *n* (*colour*) коричневый цвет ♦ *vt* (*CULIN*) подрумянивать (подрумянить *pf*); ~ **bread** *n* чёрный хлеб; ~ **sugar** *n* неочищенный сахар

**browse** [brauz] *vi* осматриваться (осмотреться *pf*); **to** ~ **through a book** пролистывать (пролистать *pf*) книгу; ~**r** *n* (*COMPUT*) броузер

**bruise** [bruːz] *n* (*on face etc*) синяк ♦ *vt* ушибать (ушибить *pf*)

**brunette** [bruː'net] *n* брюнетка

**brunt** [brʌnt] *n*: **to bear the** ~ **of** принимать (принять *pf*) на себя основной удар +*gen*

**brush** [brʌʃ] *n* (*for cleaning*) щётка; (*for painting*) кисть *f*; (*for shaving*) помазок ♦ *vt* (*sweep*) подметать

(подмести *pf*); (*groom*) чистить (почистить *pf*); (*also*: ~ **against**) задевать (задеть *pf*)

**Brussels** ['brʌslz] *n* Брюссель *m*; ~ **sprout** *n* брюссельская капуста

**brutal** ['bruːtl] *adj* жестокий, зверский; (*honesty*) жёсткий; ~**ity** [bruː'tælɪtɪ] *n* (*of person, action*) жестокость *f*, зверство

**brute** [bruːt] *n* зверь *m* ♦ *adj*: **by** ~ **force** грубой силой

**bubble** ['bʌbl] *n* пузырь *m*; ~ **bath** *n* пенистая ванна

**buck** [bʌk] *n* (*US : inf*) бакс

**bucket** ['bʌkɪt] *n* ведро

**buckle** ['bʌkl] *n* пряжка

**bud** [bʌd] *n* (*of tree*) почка; (*of flower*) бутон

**Buddhism** ['budɪzəm] *n* буддизм

**buddy** ['bʌdɪ] *n* (*US*) приятель *m*, дружок

**budge** [bʌdʒ] *vt* (*fig: person*) заставлять (заставить *pf*) уступить ♦ *vi* сдвигаться (сдвинуться *pf*) (с места)

**budgerigar** ['bʌdʒərɪgɑːr] *n* волнистый попугайчик

**budget** ['bʌdʒɪt] *n* бюджет

**budgie** ['bʌdʒɪ] *n* = **budgerigar**

**buff** [bʌf] *adj* коричневый ♦ *n* (*inf: enthusiast*) спец, знаток

**buffalo** ['bʌfələu] (*pl* ~ *or* ~**es**) *n* (*BRIT*) буйвол; (*US: bison*) бизон

**buffer** ['bʌfər] *n* буфер

**buffet** ['bufeɪ] *n* (*BRIT: in station*) буфет; (*food*) шведский стол

**bug** [bʌg] *n* (*insect*) насекомое *nt adj*; (*COMPUT*) ошибка; (*fig: germ*) вирус; (*hidden microphone*) подслушивающее устройство ♦ *vt* (*room etc*) прослушивать (*impf*); (*inf: annoy*): **to** ~ **sb** действовать (*impf*) кому-н на нервы

**buggy** ['bʌgɪ] *n* (*also*: **baby** ~) складная (детская) коляска

**build** [bɪld] (pt, pp **built**) n (of person) (тело)сложе́ние ♦ vt стро́ить (постро́ить pf); ~ **up** vt (forces, production) нара́щивать (impf); (stocks) нака́пливать (накопи́ть pf); ~**er** n строи́тель m; ~**ing** n строе́ние; ~**ing society** n (BRIT) ≈ "строи́тельное о́бщество"

building society - строи́тельное о́бщество или ипоте́чный ба́нк. Они́ бы́ли со́зданы для предоставле́ния ипоте́чного жили́щного кредитова́ния. Одновреме́нно строи́тельные о́бщества функциони́ровали как сберега́тельные ба́нки. В после́дние го́ды они́ ста́ли предоставля́ть бо́лее широ́кий объём ба́нковских услу́г.

**built** [bɪlt] pt, pp of **build** ♦ adj: ~**-in** встро́енный
**bulb** [bʌlb] n (BOT) лу́ковица; (ELEC) ла́мпа, ла́мпочка
**Bulgaria** [bʌlˈɡɛərɪə] n Болга́рия
**bulimia** [bəˈlɪmɪə] n булими́я
**bulk** [bʌlk] n грома́да; **in** ~ о́птом; **the** ~ **of** бо́льшая часть +gen; ~**y** adj громо́здкий
**bull** [bul] n (ZOOL) бык
**bulldozer** [ˈbuldəuzəʳ] n бульдо́зер
**bullet** [ˈbulɪt] n пу́ля
**bulletin** [ˈbulɪtɪn] n (journal) бюллете́нь m; **news** ~ сво́дка новосте́й; ~ **board** n (COMPUT) доска́ объявле́ний
**bullock** [ˈbulək] n вол
**bully** [ˈbulɪ] n задира m/f, пресле́дователь m ♦ vt трави́ть (затрави́ть pf)
**bum** [bʌm] n (inf: backside) за́дница; (esp US: tramp) бродя́га m/f; (: good-for-nothing) безде́льник

**bumblebee** [ˈbʌmblbiː] n шмель m
**bump** [bʌmp] n (minor accident) столкнове́ние; (jolt) толчо́к; (swelling) ши́шка ♦ vt (strike) ударя́ть (уда́рить pf); ~ **into** vt fus ната́лкиваться (натолкну́ться pf) на +acc; ~**er** n (AUT) ба́мпер ♦ adj: ~**er crop** or **harvest** небыва́лый урожа́й; ~**y** adj (road) уха́бистый
**bun** [bʌn] n (CULIN) сдо́бная бу́лка; (of hair) у́зел
**bunch** [bʌntʃ] n (of flowers) буке́т; (of keys) свя́зка; (of bananas) гроздь f; (of people) компа́ния; ~**es** npl (in hair) хво́стики mpl
**bundle** [ˈbʌndl] n (of clothes) у́зел; (of sticks) вяза́нка; (of papers) па́чка ♦ vt (also: ~ **up**) свя́зывать (связа́ть pf) в у́зел; **to** ~ **sth/sb into** зата́лкивать (затолкну́ть pf) что-н/кого́-н в +acc
**bungalow** [ˈbʌŋɡələu] n бунга́ло nt ind
**bunk** [bʌŋk] n (bed) ко́йка; ~ **beds** npl двухъя́русная крова́ть fsg
**bunker** [ˈbʌŋkəʳ] n бу́нкер
**bunny** [ˈbʌnɪ] n (also: ~ **rabbit**) за́йчик
**buoy** [bɔɪ] n буй, ба́кен
**buoyant** [ˈbɔɪənt] adj (fig: economy, market) оживлённый; (: person) жизнера́достный
**burden** [ˈbəːdn] n (responsibility) бре́мя nt; (load) но́ша ♦ vt: **to** ~ **sb with** обременя́ть (обремени́ть pf) кого́-н +instr
**bureau** [ˈbjuərəu] (pl ~**x**) n (BRIT) бюро́ nt ind; (US) комо́д
**bureaucracy** [bjuəˈrɔkrəsɪ] n (POL, COMM) бюрокра́тия; (system) бюрократи́зм
**bureaucrat** [ˈbjuərəkræt] n бюрокра́т
**bureaux** [ˈbjuərəuz] npl of **bureau**
**burger** [ˈbəːɡəʳ] n бу́ргер

**burglar** ['bə:glər] n взло́мщик; ~
**alarm** n сигнализа́ция; ~**y** n
(crime) кра́жа со взло́мом,
кварти́рный разбо́й
**burial** ['bɛrɪəl] n погребе́ние,
по́хороны pl
**burly** ['bə:lɪ] adj дю́жий
**burn** [bə:n] (pt, pp ~**ed** or ~**t**) vt
жечь (сжечь pf), сжига́ть (сжечь
pf); (intentionally) поджига́ть
(подже́чь pf) ♦ vi (house, wood)
горе́ть (сгоре́ть pf), сгора́ть
(сгоре́ть pf); (cakes) подгора́ть
(подгоре́ть pf) ♦ n ожо́г; ~**er** n
горе́лка; ~**ing** adj (building, forest)
горя́щий; (issue, ambition) жгу́чий
**burst** [bə:st] (pt, pp ~) vt разрыва́ть (разорва́ть pf) ♦ vi
(tyre, balloon, pipe) ло́паться
(ло́пнуть pf) ♦ n (of gunfire) залп;
(of energy) прили́в; (also: ~ **pipe**)
проры́в; **to ~ into flames**
вспы́хивать (вспы́хнуть pf); **to ~
into tears** распла́каться (pf); **to ~
out laughing** расхохота́ться (pf);
**to be ~ing with** (pride, anger)
раздува́ться (разду́ться pf) от
+gen; ~ **into** vt fus (room)
врыва́ться (ворва́ться pf)
**bury** ['bɛrɪ] vt (object) зарыва́ть
(зары́ть pf), зака́пывать
(закопа́ть pf); (person) хорони́ть
(похорони́ть pf); **many people
were buried in the rubble** мно́го
люде́й бы́ло погребено́ под
обло́мками
**bus** [bʌs] n авто́бус; (double decker)
(двухэта́жный) авто́бус
**bush** [buʃ] n куст; **to beat about
the ~** ходи́ть (impf) вокру́г да
о́коло
**bushy** ['buʃɪ] adj пуши́стый
**busily** ['bɪzɪlɪ] adv делови́то,
энерги́чно
**business** ['bɪznɪs] n (matter) де́ло;
(trading) би́знес, де́ло; (firm)

предприя́тие; (occupation)
заня́тие; **to be away on ~** быть
(impf) в командиро́вке; **it's none
of my ~** э́то не моё де́ло; **he
means ~** он настро́ен серьёзно;
~**like** adj делови́тый; ~**man** (irreg)
n бизнесме́н; ~ **trip** n делова́я
пое́здка; ~**woman** (irreg) n
бизнесме́нка
**bus stop** n авто́бусная остано́вка
**bust** [bʌst] n бюст, грудь f;
(measurement) объём груди́;
(sculpture) бюст ♦ adj: **to go ~**
(firm) прогора́ть (прогоре́ть pf)
**bustle** ['bʌsl] n сумато́ха, суета́
**bustling** ['bʌslɪŋ] adj оживлённый,
шу́мный
**busy** ['bɪzɪ] adj (person) занято́й;
(street) оживлённый, шу́мный;
(TEL): **the line is ~** ли́ния занята́
♦ vt: **to ~ o.s. with** занима́ться
(заня́ться pf) +instr

---
KEYWORD
---

**but** [bʌt] conj **1** (yet) но; (: in
contrast) а; **he's not very bright,
but he's hard-working** он не
о́чень умён, но усе́рден; **I'm
tired but Paul isn't** я уста́л, а
Па́вел нет
**2** (however) но; **I'd love to
come, but I'm busy** я бы с
удово́льствием пришёл, но я
за́нят
**3** (showing disagreement, surprise
etc) но; **but that's fantastic!** но
э́то же потряса́юще!
♦ prep (apart from, except): **no-one
but him can do it** никто́, кро́ме
него́, не мо́жет э́то сде́лать;
**nothing but trouble** сплошны́е or
одни́ неприя́тности; **but for
you/your help** е́сли бы не Вы/
Ва́ша по́мощь; **I'll do anything
but that** я сде́лаю всё, что
уго́дно, но то́лько не э́то

♦ *adv* ( *just, only*): **she's but a child** она́ всего́ лишь ребёнок; **I can but try** коне́чно, я могу́ попро́бовать; **the work is all but finished** рабо́та почти́ зако́нчена

**butcher** ['butʃər] *n* мясни́к; (*also*: ~**'s (shop)**) мясно́й магази́н

**butt** [bʌt] *n* (*large barrel*) бо́чка; (*of rifle*) прикла́д; (*of pistol*) рукоя́тка; (*of cigarette*) оку́рок; (*BRIT*: *of teasing*) предме́т

**butter** ['bʌtər] *n* (сли́вочное) ма́сло ♦ *vt* нама́зывать (нама́зать *pf*) (сли́вочным) ма́слом; ~**cup** *n* лю́тик

**butterfly** ['bʌtəflaɪ] *n* ба́бочка; (*also*: ~ **stroke**) баттерфля́й

**buttocks** ['bʌtəks] *npl* я́годицы *fpl*

**button** ['bʌtn] *n* (*on clothes*) пу́говица; (*on machine*) кно́пка; (*US*: *badge*) значо́к ♦ *vt* (*also*: ~ **up**) застёгивать (застегну́ть *pf*)

**buy** [baɪ] (*pt, pp* **bought**) *vt* покупа́ть (купи́ть *pf*) ♦ *n* поку́пка; **to ~ sb sth/sth from sb** покупа́ть (купи́ть *pf*) кому́-н что-н/что-н у кого́-н; **to ~ sb a drink** покупа́ть (купи́ть *pf*) кому́-н вы́пить; ~**er** *n* покупа́тель(ница) *m(f)*

**buzz** [bʌz] *n* жужжа́ние; ~**er** *n* зу́ммер, звоно́к

KEYWORD

**by** [baɪ] *prep* **1** (*referring to cause, agent*): **he was killed by lightning** его́ уби́ло мо́лнией; **a painting by Van Gogh** карти́на Ван Го́га; **it's by Shakespeare** э́то Шекспи́р **2** (*referring to manner, means*): **by bus/train** авто́бусом/по́ездом; **by car** на маши́не; **by phone** по телефо́ну; **to pay by cheque** плати́ть (заплати́ть *pf*) че́ком; **by moonlight** при све́те луны́; **by**

**candlelight** при свеча́х; **by working constantly, he ...** благодаря́ тому́, что он рабо́тал без остано́вки, он ...

**3** (*via, through*) че́рез +*acc*; **by the back door** че́рез за́днюю дверь; **by land/sea** по су́ше/мо́рю

**4** (*close to*) у +*gen*, о́коло +*gen*; **the house is by the river** дом нахо́дится у *or* о́коло реки́; **a holiday by the sea** о́тпуск на мо́ре

**5** (*past*) ми́мо +*gen*; **she rushed by me** она́ пронесла́сь ми́мо меня́

**6** (*not later than*) к +*dat*; **by four o'clock** к четырём часа́м; **by the time I got here ...** к тому́ вре́мени, когда́ я добра́лся сюда́ ...

**7** (*during*): **by day** днём; **by night** но́чью

**8** (*amount*): **to sell by the metre/ kilo** продава́ть (прода́ть *pf*) ме́трами/килогра́ммами; **she is paid by the hour** у неё почасова́я опла́та

**9** (*MATH, measure*) на +*acc*; **to multiply/divide by three** умножа́ть (умно́жить *pf*)/дели́ть (раздели́ть *pf*) на три; **a room three metres by four** ко́мната разме́ром три ме́тра на четы́ре

**10** (*according to*) по +*dat*; **to play by the rules** игра́ть (*impf*) по пра́вилам; **it's all right by me** я не возража́ю; **by law** по зако́ну

**11**: **(all) by oneself** (*alone*) (соверше́нно) оди́н (*f* одна́, *pl* одни́); (*unaided*) сам (*f* сама́, *pl* са́ми); **I did it all by myself** я сде́лал всё оди́н *or* сам; **he was standing by himself** он стоя́л оди́н

**12**: **by the way** кста́ти, ме́жду про́чим

♦ *adv* **1** *see* **pass** *etc*

2: **by and by** вско́ре; **by and large** в це́лом

---

**bye(-bye)** ['baɪ('baɪ)] *excl* пока́
**by-election** ['baɪɪlekʃən] *n* (*BRIT*) дополни́тельные вы́боры *mpl*
**bygone** ['baɪɡɔn] *n*: **let ~s be ~s** что бы́ло, то прошло́
**bypass** ['baɪpɑːs] *n* (*AUT*) объе́зд, окружна́я доро́га; (*MED*) обходно́е шунти́рование ♦ *vt* (*town*) объезжа́ть (объе́хать *pf*)
**by-product** ['baɪprɔdʌkt] *n* (*INDUSTRY*) побо́чный проду́кт
**bystander** ['baɪstændər] *n* свиде́тель(ница) *m(f)*, прохо́жий(ая) *m(f) adj*
**byte** [baɪt] *n* (*COMPUT*) байт

# C, c

**C** [siː] *n* (*MUS*) до *nt ind*
**C.** *abbr* = **Celsius**, **centigrade**
**CA** *n abbr* (*BRIT*) = **chartered accountant**
**cab** [kæb] *n* такси́ *nt ind*; (*of truck etc*) каби́на
**cabaret** ['kæbəreɪ] *n* кабаре́ *nt ind*
**cabbage** ['kæbɪdʒ] *n* капу́ста
**cabin** ['kæbɪn] *n* (*on ship*) каю́та; (*on plane*) каби́на
**cabinet** ['kæbɪnɪt] *n* шкаф; (*also:* **display ~**) го́рка; (*POL*) кабине́т (мини́стров)
**cable** ['keɪbl] *n* ка́бель *m*; (*rope*) кана́т; (*metal*) трос ♦ *vt* (*message*) телеграфи́ровать (*impf/pf*); ~ **television** *n* ка́бельное телеви́дение
**cacti** ['kæktaɪ] *npl of* **cactus**
**cactus** ['kæktəs] (*pl* **cacti**) *n* ка́ктус
**cadet** [kə'dɛt] *n* курса́нт
**Caesarean** [sɪ'zɛərɪən] *n* (*also:* ~ **section**) ке́сарево сече́ние
**café** ['kæfeɪ] *n* кафе́ *nt ind*

**caffein(e)** ['kæfiːn] *n* кофеи́н
**cage** [keɪdʒ] *n* ( *for animal*) кле́тка
**cagoule** [kə'ɡuːl] *n* дождеви́к
**cake** [keɪk] *n* (*large*) торт; (*small*) пиро́жное *nt adj*
**calcium** ['kælsɪəm] *n* ка́льций
**calculate** ['kælkjuleɪt] *vt* ( *figures, cost*) подсчи́тывать (подсчита́ть *pf*); (*distance*) вычисля́ть (вы́числить *pf*); (*estimate*) рассчи́тывать (рассчита́ть *pf*)
**calculating** ['kælkjuleɪtɪŋ] *adj* расчётливый
**calculation** [kælkju'leɪʃən] *n* (*see vb*) подсчёт; вычисле́ние; расчёт
**calculator** ['kælkjuleɪtər] *n* калькуля́тор
**calendar** ['kæləndər] *n* календа́рь *m*
**calf** [kɑːf] (*pl* **calves**) *n* (*of cow*) телёнок; (*ANAT*) икра́
**calibre** ['kælɪbər] (*US* **caliber**) *n* кали́бр
**call** [kɔːl] *vt* называ́ть (назва́ть *pf*); (*TEL*) звони́ть (позвони́ть *pf*) +*dat*; (*summon*) вызыва́ть (вы́звать *pf*); (*arrange*) созыва́ть (созва́ть *pf*) ♦ *vi* (*shout*) крича́ть (кри́кнуть *pf*); (*TEL*) звони́ть (позвони́ть *pf*); (*visit : also:* ~ **in**, ~ **round**) заходи́ть (зайти́ *pf*) ♦ *n* (*shout*) крик; (*TEL*) звоно́к; **she is ~ed Suzanne** её зову́т Сюза́нна; **the mountain is ~ed Ben Nevis** гора́ называ́ется Бен Не́вис; **to be on** ~ дежу́рить (*impf*); ~ **back** *vi* (*return*) заходи́ть (зайти́ *pf*) опя́ть; (*TEL*) перезва́нивать (перезвони́ть *pf*) ♦ *vt* (*TEL*) перезва́нивать (перезвони́ть *pf*) +*dat*; ~ **for** *vt fus* (*demand*) призыва́ть (призва́ть *pf*) к +*dat*; ( *fetch*) заходи́ть (зайти́ *pf*) за +*instr*; ~ **off** *vt* отменя́ть (отмени́ть *pf*); ~ **on** *vt fus* (*visit*) заходи́ть (зайти́ *pf*) к +*dat*; (*appeal to*) призыва́ть (призва́ть *pf*) к

+*dat*; ~ **out** *vi* крича́ть (кри́кнуть *pf*); ~ **centre** *n* (*BRIT*) центр приёма комме́рческих итп звонко́в в большо́м объёме

**callous** ['kæləs] *adj* безду́шный

**calm** [kɑːm] *adj* споко́йный; (*place*) ти́хий; (*weather*) безве́тренный ♦ *n* тишина́, поко́й ♦ *vt* успока́ивать (успоко́ить *pf*); ~ **down** *vt* успока́ивать (успоко́ить *pf*) ♦ *vi* успока́иваться (успоко́иться *pf*)

**calorie** ['kælərɪ] *n* кало́рия

**calves** [kɑːvz] *npl of* **calf**

**Cambodia** [kæm'bəudɪə] *n* Камбо́джа

**camcorder** ['kæmkɔːdər] *n* видеока́мера

**came** [keɪm] *pt of* **come**

**camel** ['kæməl] *n* верблю́д

**camera** ['kæmərə] *n* фотоаппара́т; (*also*: **cine~, movie ~**) кинока́мера; (*TV*) телека́мера; **~man** (*irreg*) *n* (*CINEMA*) (кино)опера́тор; (*TV*) (теле)опера́тор

**camouflage** ['kæməflɑːʒ] *n* (*MIL*) камуфля́ж, маскиро́вка ♦ *vt* маскирова́ть (замаскирова́ть *pf*)

**camp** [kæmp] *n* ла́герь *m*; (*MIL*) вое́нный городо́к ♦ *vi* разбива́ть (разби́ть *pf*) ла́герь; (*go camping*) жить (*impf*) в пала́тках

**campaign** [kæm'peɪn] *n* кампа́ния ♦ *vi*: **to ~ (for/against)** вести́ (*impf*) кампа́нию (за +*acc*/про́тив +*gen*)

**camping** ['kæmpɪŋ] *n* ке́мпинг; **to go ~** отправля́ться (отпра́виться *pf*) в похо́д

**camp site** *n* ке́мпинг

**campus** ['kæmpəs] *n* студе́нческий городо́к

**can¹** [kæn] *n* (*for food*) консе́рвная ба́нка ♦ *vt* консерви́ровать (законсерви́ровать *pf*)

---

KEYWORD

**can²** [kæn] (*negative* **cannot, can't**, *conditional*, *pt* **could**) *aux vb* **1** (*be able to*) мочь (смочь *pf*); **you can do it** Вы смо́жете э́то сде́лать; **I'll help you all I can** я помогу́ Вам всем, чем смогу́; **I can't go on any longer** я бо́льше не могу́; **I can't see you** я не ви́жу Вас; **she couldn't sleep that night** в ту ночь она́ не могла́ спать

**2** (*know how to*) уме́ть (*impf*); **I can swim** я уме́ю пла́вать; **can you speak Russian?** Вы уме́ете говори́ть по-ру́сски?

**3** (*may*) мо́жно; **can I use your phone?** мо́жно от Вас позвони́ть?; **could I have a word with you?** мо́жно с Ва́ми поговори́ть?; **you can smoke if you like** Вы мо́жете кури́ть, е́сли хоти́те; **can I help you with that?** я могу́ Вам в э́том помо́чь?

**4** (*expressing disbelief, puzzlement*): **it can't be true!** (э́того) не мо́жет быть!; **what CAN he want?** что же ему́ ну́жно?

**5** (*expressing possibility, suggestion*): **he could be in the library** он, мо́жет быть *or* возмо́жно, в библиоте́ке; **she could have been delayed** возмо́жно, что её задержа́ли

---

**Canada** ['kænədə] *n* Кана́да

**canal** [kə'næl] *n* кана́л

**canary** [kə'nɛərɪ] *n* канаре́йка

**cancel** ['kænsəl] *vt* отменя́ть (отмени́ть *pf*); (*contract, cheque, visa*) аннули́ровать (*impf/pf*); **~lation** [kænsə'leɪʃən] *n* (*see vb*) отме́на; аннули́рование

**cancer** ['kænsər] *n* (*MED*) рак; **Cancer** Рак

**candid** ['kændɪd] *adj* и́скренний

**candidate** [ˈkændɪdeɪt] *n* претенде́нт; (*in exam*) экзамену́емый(ая) *m(f) adj*; (*POL*) кандида́т

**candle** [ˈkændl] *n* свеча́; **~stick** *n* подсве́чник

**candour** [ˈkændəʳ] (*US* **candor**) *n* и́скренность *f*

**candy** [ˈkændɪ] *n* (*US*) конфе́та

**cane** [keɪn] *n* (*BOT*) тростни́к; (*stick*) ро́зга ♦ *vt* (*BRIT*) нака́зывать (наказа́ть *pf*) ро́згами

**cannabis** [ˈkænəbɪs] *n* гаши́ш

**canned** [kænd] *adj* (*fruit etc*) консерви́рованный

**cannon** [ˈkænən] (*pl* **~** *or* **~s**) *n* пу́шка

**cannot** [ˈkænɔt] = **can not**; *see* **can²**

**canoe** [kəˈnuː] *n* кано́э *nt ind*

**can't** [kænt] = **cannot**; *see* **can²**

**canteen** [kænˈtiːn] *n* столо́вая *f adj*

**canter** [ˈkæntəʳ] *vi* галопи́ровать (*impf*)

**canvas** [ˈkænvəs] *n* (*also ART*) холст; (*for tents*) брезе́нт; (*NAUT*) паруси́на ♦ *adj* паруси́новый

**canyon** [ˈkænjən] *n* каньо́н

**cap** [kæp] *n* ке́пка; (*of uniform*) фура́жка; (*of pen*) колпачо́к; (*of bottle*) кры́шка ♦ *vt* (*outdo*) превосходи́ть (превзойти́ *pf*)

**capability** [keɪpəˈbɪlɪtɪ] *n* спосо́бность *f*

**capable** [ˈkeɪpəbl] *adj* (*person*) спосо́бный; **~ of sth/doing** спосо́бный на что-н/+*infin*

**capacity** [kəˈpæsɪtɪ] *n* ёмкость *f*; (*of ship, theatre etc*) вмести́тельность *f*; (*of person: capability*) спосо́бность *f*; (: *role*) роль *f*

**cape** [keɪp] *n* (*GEO*) мыс; (*cloak*) плащ

**capital** [ˈkæpɪtl] *n* (*also:* **~ city**) столи́ца; (*money*) капита́л; (*also:* **~ letter**) загла́вная бу́ква; **~ism**

*n* капитали́зм; **~ist** *adj* капиталисти́ческий ♦ *n* капитали́ст; **~ punishment** *n* сме́ртная казнь *f*

**Capricorn** [ˈkæprɪkɔːn] *n* Козеро́г

**capsule** [ˈkæpsjuːl] *n* ка́псула

**captain** [ˈkæptɪn] *n* команди́р; (*of team, in army*) капита́н

**caption** [ˈkæpʃən] *n* по́дпись *f*

**captive** [ˈkæptɪv] *n* у́зник(ица), пле́нник(ица)

**captivity** [kæpˈtɪvɪtɪ] *n* плен

**capture** [ˈkæptʃəʳ] *vt* захва́тывать (захвати́ть *pf*); (*animal*) лови́ть (пойма́ть *pf*); (*attention*) прико́вывать (прикова́ть *pf*) ♦ *n* (*of person, town*) захва́т; (*of animal*) пойма́

**car** [kɑːʳ] *n* автомоби́ль *m*, маши́на; (*RAIL*) ваго́н

**caramel** [ˈkærəməl] *n* (*sweet*) караме́ль *f*

**carat** [ˈkærət] *n* кара́т

**caravan** [ˈkærəvæn] *n* (*BRIT*) жило́й автоприце́п; **~ site** *n* (*BRIT*) площа́дка для стоя́нки жилы́х автоприце́пов

**carbohydrate** [kɑːbəʊˈhaɪdreɪt] *n* углево́д

**car bomb** *n* бо́мба, подло́женная в маши́ну

**carbon** [ˈkɑːbən] *n* углеро́д; **~ dioxide** [-daɪˈɔksaɪd] *n* дву́окись *f* углеро́да

**car boot sale** - буква́льно "прода́жа с бага́жника". Э́тим поня́тием обознача́ется прода́жа поде́ржанных веще́й. Това́ры выставля́ются в бага́жниках маши́н и́ли на стола́х. Прода́жи прово́дятся на автостоя́нках, в поля́х и́ли любы́х други́х откры́тых простра́нствах.

**card** [kɑ:d] *n* картóн; (*also*: **playing ~**) (игрáльная) кáрта; (*also*: **greetings ~**) открытка; (*also*: **visiting~, business ~**) визи́тная кáрточка; **~board** *n* картóн

**cardiac** ['kɑ:dıæk] *adj* сердéчный; (*unit*) кардиологи́ческий

**cardigan** ['kɑ:dıgən] *n* жакéт (*вязаный*)

**cardinal** ['kɑ:dınl] *adj* (*importance, principle*) кардинáльный; (*number*) коли́чественный ♦ *n* кардинáл

**care** [kɛəʳ] *n* (*worry*) забóта; (*of patient*) ухóд; (*attention*) внимáние ♦ *vi*: **to ~ about** люби́ть (*impf*); **in sb's ~** на чьём-н попечéнии; **to take ~ (to do)** позабóтиться (*pf*) (+*infin*); **to take ~ of** забóтиться (позабóтиться *pf*) о +*prp*; (*problem*) занимáться (заня́ться *pf*) +*instr*; **~ of** для передáчи +*dat*; **I don't ~** мне всё равнó; **I couldn't ~ less** мне наплевáть; **~ for** *vt fus* забóтиться (позабóтиться *pf*) о +*prp*; **he ~s for her** (*like*) он неравнодýшен к ней

**career** [kə'rıəʳ] *n* карьéра; **~ woman** (*irreg*) *n* деловáя жéнщина

**carefree** ['kɛəfri:] *adj* беззабóтный

**careful** ['kɛəful] *adj* осторóжный; (*thorough*) тщáтельный; **(be) ~!** осторóжно!, береги́сь!; **~ly** ['kɛəfəlı] *adv* (*see adj*) осторóжно; тщáтельно

**careless** ['kɛəlıs] *adj* (*clumsy*) невнимáтельный; (*casual*) небрéжный; (*untroubled*) беззабóтный

**caretaker** ['kɛəteıkəʳ] *n* завхóз

**cargo** ['kɑ:gəu] *n* (*pl* **~es**) *n* груз

**car hire** *n* (*BRIT*) прокáт автомоби́лей

**Caribbean** [kærı'bi:ən] *n*: **the ~ (Sea)** Кари́бское мóре

**caricature** ['kærıkətjuəʳ] *n* карикатýра

**caring** ['kɛərıŋ] *adj* (*person etc*) забóтливый

**carnation** [kɑ:'neıʃən] *n* гвозди́ка

**carnival** ['kɑ:nıvl] *n* карнавáл; (*US: funfair*) аттракциóнный городóк

**carol** ['kærəl] *n* (*also*: **Christmas ~**) рождéственский гимн

**car park** *n* (*BRIT*) автостоя́нка

**carpenter** ['kɑ:pıntəʳ] *n* плóтник

**carpet** ['kɑ:pıt] *n* ковёр ♦ *vt* устилáть (устлáть *pf*) коврáми

**carriage** ['kærıdʒ] *n* (*BRIT : RAIL*) (пассажи́рский) вагóн *m*, (*horse-drawn*) экипáж; (*costs*) стóимость *f* перевóзки; **~way** *n* (*BRIT*) проéзжая часть *f* дорóги

**carrier** ['kærıəʳ] *n* (*MED*) носи́тель *m*; (*COMM*) транспортирóвщик; **~ bag** *n* (*BRIT*) пакéт (*для покýпок*)

**carrot** ['kærət] *n* (*BOT*) моркóвь *f*

**carry** ['kærı] *vt* (*take*) носи́ть/нести́ (*impf*); (*transport*) вози́ть/везти́ (*impf*); (*involve*) влечь (повлéчь *pf*) (за собóй); (*MED*) переноси́ть (*impf*) ♦ *vi* (*sound*) передавáться (*impf*); **to get carried away (by)** (*fig*) увлекáться (увлéчься *pf*) (+*instr*); **~ on** *vi* продолжáться (продóлжиться *pf*) ♦ *vt* продолжáть (продóлжить *pf*); **~ out** *vt* (*orders*) выполня́ть (вы́полнить *pf*); (*investigation*) проводи́ть (провести́ *pf*); **~cot** *n* (*BRIT*) переноснáя колыбéль *f*; **~-on** *n* (*inf*) суматóха

**cart** [kɑ:t] *n* телéга, повóзка ♦ *vt* (*inf*) таскáть/тащи́ть (*impf*)

**carton** ['kɑ:tən] *n* картóнная корóбка; (*container*) пакéт

**cartoon** [kɑ:'tu:n] *n* (*drawing*) карикатýра; (*BRIT: comic strip*) кóмикс; (*TV*) мультфи́льм

**cartridge** ['kɑ:trɪdʒ] n (in gun)
ги́льза; (of pen) (черни́льный)
балло́нчик

**carve** [kɑ:v] vt (meat) нареза́ть
(наре́зать pf); (wood, stone)
ре́зать (impf) по +dat

**carving** ['kɑ:vɪŋ] n резно́е
изде́лие

**car wash** n мо́йка автомоби́лей

**case** [keɪs] n слу́чай; (MED, patient)
больно́й(а́я) m(f) adj; (LAW)
(суде́бное) де́ло; (investigation)
рассле́дование; (for spectacles)
футля́р; (BRIT : also: **suit~**)
чемода́н; (of wine) я́щик
(содержа́щий 12 буты́лок); **in ~
(of)** в слу́чае (+gen); **in any ~** во
вся́ком слу́чае; **just in ~** на
вся́кий слу́чай

**cash** [kæʃ] n нали́чные pl adj
(де́ньги) ♦ vt: **to ~ a cheque**
обнали́чивать (обнали́чить pf);
**to pay (in) ~** плати́ть (заплати́ть
pf) нали́чными; **~ on delivery**
нало́женный платёж; **~ card** n
банкома́тная ка́рточка; **~ desk** n
(BRIT) ка́сса; **~ dispenser** n (BRIT)
банкома́т; **~ flow** n движе́ние
де́нежной нали́чности; **~ier**
[kæ'ʃɪər] n касси́р

**cashmere** ['kæʃmɪər] n кашеми́р

**casino** [kə'si:nəu] n казино́ nt ind

**casserole** ['kæsərəul] n рагу́ nt ind;
(also: **~ dish**) ла́тка

**cassette** [kæ'sɛt] n кассе́та

**cast** [kɑ:st] (pt, pp ~) vt (light,
shadow, glance) броса́ть (бро́сить
pf); (FISHING) забра́сывать
(забро́сить pf); (doubts) се́ять
(посе́ять pf) ♦ n (THEAT) соста́в
(исполни́телей); (MED : also:
**plaster ~**) гипс; **to ~ one's vote**
отдава́ть (отда́ть pf) свой го́лос

**caster sugar** ['kɑ:stə-] n (BRIT)
са́харная пу́дра

**castle** ['kɑ:sl] n за́мок; (fortified)

кре́пость f; (CHESS) ладья́, тура́

**casual** ['kæʒjul] adj (meeting)
случа́йный; (attitude)
небре́жный; (clothes)
повседне́вный; **~ly** adv (behave)
небре́жно; (dress) про́сто

**casualty** ['kæʒjultɪ] n (sb injured)
пострада́вший(ая) m(f) adj; (sb
killed) же́ртва; (department)
травматоло́гия

**cat** [kæt] n (pet) ко́шка; (tomcat)
кот; **big ~s** (ZOOL) коша́чьи pl adj

**catalogue** ['kætələg] (US **catalog**) n
катало́г

**catalyst** ['kætəlɪst] n катализа́тор

**catapult** ['kætəpʌlt] n (BRIT)
рога́тка

**catarrh** [kə'tɑ:r] n ката́р

**catastrophe** [kə'tæstrəfɪ] n
катастро́фа

**catastrophic** [kætə'strɔfɪk] adj
катастрофи́ческий

**catch** [kætʃ] (pt, pp **caught**) vt
лови́ть (пойма́ть pf); (bus etc)
сади́ться (сесть pf) на +acc;
(breath: in shock) затаи́ть
(затаи́ть pf); (: after running)
передохну́ть (pf); (attention)
привлека́ть (привле́чь pf); (hear)
ула́вливать (улови́ть pf); (illness)
подхва́тывать (подхвати́ть pf)
♦ vi (become trapped) застрева́ть
(застря́ть pf) ♦ n (of fish) уло́в; (of
ball) захва́т; (hidden problem)
подво́х; (of lock) защёлка; **to ~
sight of** уви́деть (pf); **to ~ fire**
загора́ться (загоре́ться pf); **~ on**
vi (become popular) приживаться (прижи́ться pf); **~
up** vi (fig) нагоня́ть (нагна́ть pf)
♦ vt (also: **~ up with**) догоня́ть
(догна́ть pf); **~ing** adj (MED)
зара́зный

**category** ['kætɪgərɪ] n катего́рия

**cater** ['keɪtər] vi: **to ~ (for)**
организова́ть (impf/pf) пита́ние
(для +gen); **~ for** vt fus (BRIT: needs,

*tastes*) удовлетворя́ть (удовлетвори́ть *pf*); (: *readers etc*) обслу́живать (обслужи́ть *pf*)
**cathedral** [kə'θi:drəl] *n* собо́р
**Catholic** ['kæθəlɪk] *adj* католи́ческий ♦ *n* като́лик(и́чка)
**cattle** ['kætl] *npl* скот *msg*
**catwalk** ['kætwɔ:k] *n* помо́ст (*для пока́за мод*)
**caught** [kɔ:t] *pt, pp of* **catch**
**cauliflower** ['kɔlɪflauər] *n* цветна́я капу́ста
**cause** [kɔ:z] *n* (*reason*) причи́на; (*aim*) де́ло ♦ *vt* явля́ться (яви́ться *pf*) причи́ной +*gen*
**caution** ['kɔ:ʃən] *n* осторо́жность *f*; (*warning*) предупрежде́ние, предостереже́ние ♦ *vt* предупрежда́ть (предупреди́ть *pf*)
**cautious** ['kɔ:ʃəs] *adj* осторо́жный; **~ly** *adv* осторо́жно
**cavalry** ['kævəlrɪ] *n* кавале́рия; (*mechanized*) мотопехо́та
**cave** [keɪv] *n* пеще́ра; **~ in** *vi* (*roof*) обва́ливаться (обвали́ться *pf*)
**caviar(e)** ['kævɪɑːr] *n* икра́
**cavity** ['kævɪtɪ] *n* (*in tooth*) дупло́
**CBI** *n abbr* (= *Confederation of British Industries*) Конфедера́ция брита́нской промы́шленности
**cc** *abbr* (= *cubic centimetre*) куби́ческий сантиме́тр
**CCTV** *n abbr* (= *closed-circuit television*) за́мкнутая телевизио́нная систе́ма
**CD** *n abbr* = **compact disc**; **~ player** прои́грыватель *m* для компа́кт-ди́сков **~-ROM** *n* компа́кт-диск ПЗУ
**cease** [si:s] *vi* прекраща́ться (прекрати́ться *pf*); **~-fire** *n* прекраще́ние огня́
**cedar** ['si:dər] *n* кедр
**ceiling** ['si:lɪŋ] *n* (*also fig*) потоло́к
**celebrate** ['selɪbreɪt] *vt*

пра́здновать (отпра́здновать *pf*) ♦ *vi* весели́ться (повесели́ться *pf*); **to ~ Mass** соверша́ть (соверши́ть *pf*) прича́стие; **~d** *adj* знамени́тый
**celebration** [selɪ'breɪʃən] *n* (*event*) пра́здник; (*of anniversary etc*) пра́зднование
**celebrity** [sɪ'lebrɪtɪ] *n* знамени́тость *f*
**celery** ['selərɪ] *n* сельдере́й
**cell** [sel] *n* (*in prison*) ка́мера; (*BIO*) кле́тка
**cellar** ['selər] *n* подва́л; (*also*: **wine ~**) ви́нный по́греб
**cello** ['tʃeləu] *n* виолонче́ль *f*
**cellulose** ['seljuləus] *n* клетча́тка, целлюло́за
**Celsius** ['selsɪəs] *adj*: **30 degrees ~** 30 гра́дусов по Це́льсию
**Celtic** ['keltɪk] *adj* ке́льтский
**cement** [sə'ment] *n* цеме́нт
**cemetery** ['semɪtrɪ] *n* кла́дбище
**censor** ['sensər] *n* це́нзор ♦ *vt* подверга́ть (подве́ргнуть *pf*) цензу́ре; **~ship** *n* цензу́ра
**census** ['sensəs] *n* пе́репись *f*
**cent** [sent] *n* цент; *see also* **per cent**
**centenary** [sen'ti:nərɪ] *n* столе́тие
**center** *etc* (*US*) *see* **centre** *etc*
**centigrade** ['sentɪɡreɪd] *adj*: **30 degrees ~** 30 гра́дусов по Це́льсию
**centimetre** ['sentɪmi:tər] (*US* **centimeter**) *n* сантиме́тр
**centipede** ['sentɪpi:d] *n* многоно́жка
**central** ['sentrəl] *adj* центра́льный; **this flat is very ~** э́та кварти́ра располо́жена бли́зко к це́нтру; **Central America** *n* Центра́льная Аме́рика; **~ heating** *n* центра́льное отопле́ние
**centre** ['sentər] (*US* **center**) *n* центр ♦ *vt* (*PHOT, TYP*) центри́ровать (*impf/pf*); **~ forward** *n*

центра́льный напада́ющий *m adj*,
центр-фо́рвард
**century** ['sɛntjuri] *n* век
**ceramic** [sɪ'ræmɪk] *adj*
керами́ческий; **~s** *npl* кера́мика
*fsg*
**cereal** ['sɪːrɪəl] *n*: **~s** зерновы́е *pl*
*adj*; (*also*: **breakfast ~**) хло́пья *pl*
к за́втраку
**ceremony** ['sɛrɪmənɪ] *n*
церемо́ния; (*behaviour*)
церемо́нии *fpl*; **with ~** со все́ми
форма́льностями
**certain** ['səːtən] *adj*
определённый; **I'm ~ (that)** я
уве́рен(, что); **~ days**
определённые дни; **a ~ pleasure**
не́которое удово́льствие; **it's ~
(that)** несомне́нно(, что); **in ~
circumstances** при
определённых обстоя́тельствах;
**a ~ Mr Smith** не́кий Ми́стер
Смит; **for ~** наверняка́; **~ly** *adv*
(*undoubtedly*) несомне́нно; (*of
course*) коне́чно; **~ty** *n* (*assurance*)
уве́ренность *f*; (*inevitability*)
несомне́нность *f*
**certificate** [sə'tɪfɪkɪt] *n*
свиде́тельство; (*doctor's etc*)
спра́вка; (*diploma*) дипло́м
**cervix** ['səːvɪks] *n* ше́йка ма́тки
**cf.** *abbr* = **compare**
**CFC** *n abbr* (= *chlorofluorocarbon*)
хлорфтороуглеро́д
**ch.** *abbr* = **chapter** гл.
**chain** [tʃeɪn] *n* цепь *f*; (*decorative,
on bicycle*) цепо́чка; (*of shops,
hotels*) сеть *f*; (*of events, ideas*)
версни́ца ♦ *vt* (*also*: **~ up**: *person*)
прико́вывать (прикова́ть *pf*);
(: *dog*) сажа́ть (посади́ть *pf*) на
цепь; **a ~ of mountains** го́рная
цепь
**chair** [tʃɛər] *n* стул; (*also*: **arm~**)
кре́сло; (*of university*) ка́федра;
(*also*: **~person**) председа́тель *m*

♦ *vt* председа́тельствовать (*impf*)
на +*prp*; **~ lift** *n* кана́тный
подъёмник; **~man** (*irreg*) *n*
председа́тель *m*; (*BRIT*: *COMM*)
президе́нт
**chalet** ['ʃæleɪ] *n* шале́ *m ind*
**chalk** [tʃɔːk] *n* мел
**challenge** ['tʃælɪndʒ] *n* вы́зов;
(*task*) испыта́ние ♦ *vt* (*also SPORT*)
броса́ть (бро́сить *pf*) вы́зов +*dat*;
(*authority, right etc*) оспа́ривать
(оспо́рить *pf*); **to ~ sb to**
вызыва́ть (вы́звать *pf*) кого́-н на
+*acc*
**challenging** ['tʃælɪndʒɪŋ] *adj* (*tone,
look*) вызыва́ющий; (*task*)
тру́дный
**chamber** ['tʃeɪmbər] *n* ка́мера;
(*POL*) пала́та; **~ of commerce**
Торго́вая Пала́та
**champagne** [ʃæm'peɪn] *n*
шампа́нское *nt adj*
**champion** ['tʃæmpɪən] *n* чемпио́н;
(*of cause*) побо́рник(ица); (*of
person*) защи́тник(ица); **~ship** *n*
(*contest*) чемпиона́т; (*title*) зва́ние
чемпио́на
**chance** [tʃɑːns] *n* шанс;
(*opportunity*) возмо́жность *f*; (*risk*)
риск ♦ *vt* рискова́ть (*impf*) +*instr*
♦ *adj* случа́йный; **to take a ~**
рискну́ть (*pf*); **by ~** случа́йно; **to
leave to ~** оставля́ть (оста́вить
*pf*) на во́лю слу́чая
**chancellor** ['tʃɑːnsələr] *n* (*POL*)
ка́нцлер; **Chancellor of the
Exchequer** *n* (*BRIT*) Ка́нцлер
казначе́йства

**Chancellor of the Exchequer** -
ка́нцлер казначе́йства. В
Великобрита́нии он выполня́ет
фу́нкции мини́стра фина́нсов.

**chandelier** [ʃændə'lɪər] *n* лю́стра
**change** [tʃeɪndʒ] *vt* меня́ть

(поменя́ть *pf*); (*money: to other currency*) обме́нивать (обменя́ть *pf*); (: *for smaller currency*) разме́нивать (разменя́ть *pf*) ♦ *vi* (*alter*) меня́ться (*impf*), изменя́ться (измени́ться *pf*); (*one's clothes*) переодева́ться (переоде́ться *pf*); (*change trains etc*) де́лать (сде́лать *pf*) переса́дку ♦ *n* (*alteration*) измене́ние; (*difference*) переме́на; (*replacement*) сме́на; (*also*: **small** *or* **loose ~**) ме́лочь *f*; (*money returned*) сда́ча; **to ~ sb into** превраща́ть (преврати́ть *pf*) кого́-н в +*acc*; **to ~ one's mind** переду́мывать (переду́мать *pf*); **to ~ gear** переключа́ть (переключи́ть *pf*) ско́рость; **for a ~** для разнообра́зия

**channel** ['tʃænl] *n* кана́л; (*NAUT*) тра́сса ♦ *vt*: **to ~ into** направля́ть (напра́вить *pf*) на +*acc* ♦ *adj*: **the C~ Islands** Норма́ндские острова́ *mpl*; **the (English) C~** Ла-Ма́нш; **the C~ Tunnel** тунне́ль *m* под Ла-Ма́ншем

**chant** [tʃɑ:nt] *n* сканди́рование; (*REL*) пе́ние

**chaos** ['keɪɔs] *n* ха́ос

**chaotic** [keɪˈɔtɪk] *adj* хаоти́чный

**chap** [tʃæp] *n* (*BRIT*: *inf*) па́рень *m*

**chapel** ['tʃæpl] *n* (*in church*) приде́л; (*in prison etc*) часо́вня; (*BRIT*: *also*: **non-conformist ~**) протеста́нтская нон-конформи́стская це́рковь

**chaplain** ['tʃæplɪn] *n* капелла́н

**chapter** ['tʃæptə*] *n* глава́; (*in life, history*) страни́ца

**character** ['kærɪktə*] *n* (*personality*) ли́чность *f*; (*nature*) хара́ктер; (*in novel, film*) геро́й; (*letter, symbol*) знак; **~istic** ['kærɪktə'rɪstɪk] *n* характе́рная черта́ ♦ *adj*: **~istic (of)** характе́рный (для +*gen*)

**charcoal** ['tʃɑ:kəul] *n* (*fuel*) древе́сный у́голь *m*

**charge** [tʃɑ:dʒ] *n* (*fee*) пла́та; (*LAW*) обвине́ние; (*responsibility*) отве́тственность *f*; (*MIL*) ата́ка ♦ *vi* атакова́ть (*impf/pf*) ♦ *vt* (*battery, gun*) заряжа́ть (заряди́ть *pf*); (*LAW*): **to ~ sb with** предъявля́ть (предъяви́ть *pf*) кому́-н обвине́ние в +*prp*; **~s** *npl* (*COMM*) де́нежный сбор *msg*; (*TEL*) телефо́нный тари́ф *msg*; **to reverse the ~s** (*BRIT*) звони́ть (позвони́ть *pf*) по колле́кту; **to take ~ of** (*child*) брать (взять *pf*) на попече́ние; (*company*) брать (взять *pf*) на себя́ руково́дство +*instr*; **to be in ~ of** отвеча́ть (*impf*) за +*acc*; **who's in ~ here?** кто здесь гла́вный?; **to ~ (sb) (for)** проси́ть (попроси́ть *pf*) (у кого́-н) пла́ту (за +*acc*); **how much do you ~ for?** ско́лько Вы про́сите за +*acc*?; **~ card** *n* креди́тная ка́рточка (*определённого магази́на*)

**charisma** [kæˈrɪzmə] *n* обая́ние, хари́зма

**charitable** ['tʃærɪtəbl] *adj* благотвори́тельный

**charity** ['tʃærɪtɪ] *n* (*organization*) благотвори́тельная организа́ция; (*kindness*) мило-се́рдие; (*money, gifts*) ми́лостыня

---

**charity shop** - благотвори́тельный магази́н. В э́тих магази́нах рабо́тают волонтёры, продаю́щие поде́ржанную оде́жду, ста́рые кни́ги, предме́ты дома́шнего обихо́да. Получа́емая при́быль направля́ется в благотвори́тельные о́бщества, кото́рые э́ти магази́ны подде́рживают.

**charm** [tʃɑːm] n очарова́ние, обая́ние; (on bracelet etc) брело́к ♦ vt очаро́вывать (очарова́ть pf); **~ing** adj очарова́тельный

**chart** [tʃɑːt] n гра́фик; (of sea) навигацио́нная ка́рта; (of stars) ка́рта звёздного не́ба ♦ vt наноси́ть (нанести́ pf) на ка́рту; (progress) следи́ть (impf) за +instr; **~s** npl (MUS) хит-пара́д msg

**charter** ['tʃɑːtər] vt фрахтова́ть (зафрахтова́ть pf) ♦ n ха́ртия; (COMM) уста́в; **~ed accountant** n (BRIT) бухга́лтер вы́сшей квалифика́ции; **~ flight** n ча́ртерный рейс

**chase** [tʃeɪs] vt гоня́ться (impf) or гна́ться (impf) за +instr ♦ n пого́ня; **to ~ away** or **off** прогоня́ть (прогна́ть pf)

**chasm** ['kæzəm] n (GEO) про́пасть f

**chassis** ['ʃæsɪ] n шасси́ nt ind

**chat** [tʃæt] vi болта́ть (поболта́ть pf) ♦ n бесе́да; **~ show** n (BRIT) шо́у с уча́стием знамени́тостей

**chatter** ['tʃætər] n (gossip) болтовня́

**chauffeur** ['ʃəʊfər] n (персона́льный) шофёр

**cheap** [tʃiːp] adj дешёвый ♦ adv дёшево; **~er** adj деше́вле; **~ly** adv дёшево

**cheat** [tʃiːt] vi (at cards) жу́льничать (impf); (in exam) спи́сывать (списа́ть pf) ♦ n жу́лик ♦ vt: **to ~ sb (out of £10)** надува́ть (наду́ть pf) кого́-н (на £10)

**check** [tʃɛk] vt проверя́ть (прове́рить pf); (halt) уде́рживать (удержа́ть pf); (curb) сде́рживать (сдержа́ть pf); (US: items) отмеча́ть (отме́тить pf) ♦ n (inspection) прове́рка; (US: bill) счёт; (: COMM) = **cheque**; (pattern)

кле́тка ♦ adj кле́тчатый; **~ in** vi (at hotel etc) регистри́роваться (зарегистри́роваться pf) ♦ vt (luggage) сдава́ть (сдать pf); **~ out** vi выпи́сываться (вы́писаться pf); **~ up** vi: **to ~ up on** наводи́ть (навести́ pf) спра́вки о +prp; **~ing account** n (US) теку́щий счёт; **~out** n контро́ль m, ка́сса; **~room** n (US) ка́мера хране́ния; **~up** n осмо́тр

**cheek** [tʃiːk] n щека́; (impudence) на́глость f; (nerve) де́рзость f; **~y** adj наха́льный, на́глый

**cheer** [tʃɪər] vt приве́тствовать (поприве́тствовать pf) ♦ vi одобри́тельно восклица́ть (impf); **~s** npl (of welcome) приве́тственные во́згласы mpl; (of approval) одобри́тельные во́згласы mpl; **~s!** (за) Ва́ше здоро́вье!; **~ up** vi развесели́ться (pf), повеселе́ть (pf) ♦ vt развесели́ть (pf); **~ up!** не грусти́те!; **~ful** adj весёлый

**cheese** [tʃiːz] n сыр

**cheetah** ['tʃiːtə] n гепа́рд

**chef** [ʃɛf] n шеф-по́вар

**chemical** ['kɛmɪkl] adj хими́ческий ♦ n химика́т; (in laboratory) реакти́в

**chemist** ['kɛmɪst] n (BRIT: pharmacist) фармаце́вт; (scientist) хи́мик; **~ry** n хи́мия

**chemotherapy** [kiːməʊ'θɛrəpɪ] n химиотерапи́я

**cheque** [tʃɛk] n (BRIT) чек; **~book** n (BRIT) че́ковая кни́жка; **~ card** n (BRIT) ка́рточка, подтвержда́ющая платёжеспосо́бность владе́льца

**cherish** ['tʃɛrɪʃ] vt леле́ять (взлеле́ять pf)

**cherry** ['tʃɛrɪ] n чере́шня; (sour variety) ви́шня

**chess** [tʃɛs] n ша́хматы pl
**chest** [tʃest] n грудь f; (box) сунду́к
**chestnut** ['tʃesnʌt] n кашта́н
**chest of drawers** n комо́д
**chew** [tʃuː] vt жева́ть (impf); ~**ing gum** n жева́тельная рези́нка
**chic** [ʃiːk] adj шика́рный, элега́нтный
**chick** [tʃɪk] n цыплёнок; (of wild bird) птене́ц
**chicken** ['tʃɪkɪn] n ку́рица; (inf: coward) труси́шка m/f; ~**pox** n ветря́нка
**chief** [tʃiːf] n (of organization etc) нача́льник ♦ adj гла́вный, основно́й; ~ **executive** (US ~ **executive officer**) n гла́вный исполни́тельный дире́ктор; ~**ly** adv гла́вным о́бразом
**child** [tʃaɪld] (pl ~**ren**) n ребёнок; **do you have any** ~**ren?** у Вас есть де́ти?; ~**birth** n ро́ды pl; ~**hood** n де́тство; ~**ish** adj (games, attitude) ребя́ческий; (person) ребя́чливый; ~**like** adj де́тский; ~**minder** n (BRIT) ня́ня; ~**ren** ['tʃɪldrən] npl of **child**
**Chile** ['tʃɪlɪ] n Чи́ли ind
**chili** ['tʃɪlɪ] n (US) = **chilli**
**chill** [tʃɪl] n (MED) просту́да ♦ vt охлажда́ть (охлади́ть pf); **to catch a** ~ простужа́ться (простуди́ться pf)
**chilli** ['tʃɪlɪ] (US **chili**) n кра́сный стручко́вый пе́рец
**chilly** ['tʃɪlɪ] adj холо́дный
**chimney** ['tʃɪmnɪ] n (дымова́я) труба́
**chimpanzee** [tʃɪmpæn'ziː] n шимпанзе́ m ind
**chin** [tʃɪn] n подборо́док
**China** ['tʃaɪnə] n Кита́й
**china** ['tʃaɪnə] n фарфо́р
**Chinese** [tʃaɪ'niːz] adj кита́йский ♦ n inv кита́ец(а́янка)
**chip** [tʃɪp] n (of wood) ще́пка; (of

stone) оско́лок; (also: **micro~**) микросхе́ма, чип ♦ vt отбива́ть (отби́ть pf); ~**s** npl (BRIT) карто́фель msg-фри; (US: also: **potato ~s**) чи́псы mpl
**chiropodist** [kɪ'rɔpədɪst] n (BRIT) мозо́льный опера́тор m/f
**chisel** ['tʃɪzl] n (for wood) долото́; (for stone) зуби́ло
**chives** [tʃaɪvz] npl лук-ре́занец msg
**chlorine** ['klɔːriːn] n хлор
**chocolate** ['tʃɔklɪt] n шокола́д; (sweet) шокола́дная конфе́та
**choice** [tʃɔɪs] n вы́бор
**choir** ['kwaɪər] n хор; (area) хо́ры pl
**choke** [tʃəuk] vi дави́ться (подави́ться pf); (with smoke, anger) задыха́ться (задохну́ться pf) ♦ vt (strangle) души́ть (задуши́ть or удуши́ть pf)
**cholesterol** [kə'lɛstərɔl] n холестери́н; **high** ~ с высо́ким содержа́нием холестери́на
**choose** [tʃuːz] (pt **chose**, pp **chosen**) vt выбира́ть (вы́брать pf); **to** ~ **to do** реша́ть (реши́ть pf) +infin
**chop** [tʃɔp] vt (wood) руби́ть (наруби́ть pf); (also: ~ **up**: vegetables, meat) ре́зать (наре́зать or поре́зать pf) ♦ n (CULIN) ≈ отбивна́я (котле́та)
**chord** [kɔːd] n (MUS) акко́рд
**chore** [tʃɔːr] n (burden) повседне́вная обя́занность f; **household** ~**s** дома́шние хло́поты
**choreographer** [kɔrɪ'ɔgrəfər] n хорео́граф; (of ballet) балетме́йстер
**chorus** ['kɔːrəs] n хор; (refrain) припе́в
**chose** [tʃəuz] pt of **choose**; ~**n** ['tʃəuzn] pp of **choose**
**Christ** [kraɪst] n Христо́с
**Christian** ['krɪstɪən] adj

христиа́нский ♦ *n* христиани́н(а́нка); **~ity** [krɪstɪ'ænɪtɪ] *n* христиа́нство; **~ name** *n* и́мя *nt*

**Christmas** ['krɪsməs] *n* Рождество́; **Happy** *or* **Merry ~**! Счастли́вого Рождества́!; **~ card** *n* рожде́ственская откры́тка

**Christmas cracker** - рожде́ственская хлопу́шка. В отли́чие от обы́чной хлопу́шки в неё завора́чиваются бума́жная коро́на, шу́тка и ма́ленький пода́рок. Механи́зм хлопу́шки приво́дится в де́йствие, е́сли дёрнуть за о́ба её конца́ одновре́менно. Раздаётся хлопо́к и из хдопу́шки выпада́ет пода́рок.

**Christmas Day** *n* день *m* Рождества́
**Christmas Eve** *n* Соче́льник

**Christmas pudding** - рожде́ственский пу́динг. Кекс, пригото́вленный на пару́ и содержа́щий большо́е коли́чество сушёных фру́ктов.

**Christmas tree** *n* (рожде́ственская) ёлка
**chrome** [krəum] *n* хром
**chronic** ['krɒnɪk] *adj* хрони́ческий
**chronological** [krɒnə'lɒdʒɪkl] *adj* (order) хронологи́ческий
**chubby** ['tʃʌbɪ] *adj* пу́хлый
**chuck** [tʃʌk] *vt* (inf) швыря́ть (швырну́ть *pf*)
**chuckle** ['tʃʌkl] *vi* посме́иваться (impf)
**chunk** [tʃʌŋk] *n* (of meat) кусо́к
**church** [tʃə:tʃ] *n* це́рковь *f*; **~yard** *n* пого́ст
**CIA** *n abbr* (US) (= Central Intelligence Agency) ЦРУ
**CID** *n abbr* (BRIT: = Criminal Investigation Department) уголо́вный ро́зыск
**cider** ['saɪdər] *n* сидр
**cigar** [sɪ'gɑ:r] *n* сига́ра
**cigarette** [sɪgə'rɛt] *n* сигаре́та
**cinema** ['sɪnəmə] *n* кинотеа́тр
**cinnamon** ['sɪnəmən] *n* кори́ца
**circle** ['sə:kl] *n* круг; (THEAT) балко́н
**circuit** ['sə:kɪt] *n* (ELEC) цепь *f*; (tour) турне́ *nt ind*; (track) трек
**circular** ['sə:kjulər] *adj* (plate, pond etc) кру́глый ♦ *n* циркуля́р
**circulate** ['sə:kjuleɪt] *vi* циркули́ровать (impf) ♦ *vt* передава́ть (переда́ть *pf*)
**circulation** [sə:kju'leɪʃən] *n* (PRESS) тира́ж; (MED) кровообраще́ние; (COMM) обраще́ние; (of air, traffic) циркуля́ция
**circumstances** ['sə:kəmstənsɪz] *npl* обстоя́тельства *ntpl*
**circus** ['sə:kəs] *n* (show) цирк
**cite** [saɪt] *vt* цити́ровать (процити́ровать *pf*); (LAW) вызыва́ть (вы́звать *pf*) в суд
**citizen** ['sɪtɪzn] *n* (of country) граждани́н(а́нка); (of town) жи́тель(ница) *m(f)*; **~ship** *n* гражда́нство
**city** ['sɪtɪ] *n* го́род; **the City** Си́ти *nt ind*

**the City** - Си́ти. Э́тот райо́н Ло́ндона явля́ется его́ фина́нсовым це́нтром.

**civic** ['sɪvɪk] *adj* муниципа́льный; (duties, pride) гражда́нский
**civil** ['sɪvɪl] *adj* гражда́нский; (authorities) госуда́рственный; (polite) учти́вый; **~ian** [sɪ'vɪlɪən] *adj* (life) обще́ственный ♦ *n*

ми́рный(ая) жи́тель(ница) m(f);
~**ian casualties** же́ртвы среди́
ми́рного населе́ния

**civilization** [sɪvɪlaɪ'zeɪʃən] n
цивилиза́ция

**civilized** ['sɪvɪlaɪzd] adj
культу́рный; (society)
цивилизо́ванный

**civil**: ~ **liberties** npl гражда́нские
свобо́ды fpl; ~ **servant** n
госуда́рственный слу́жащий m
adj; **Civil Service** n
госуда́рственная слу́жба; ~ **war**
n гражда́нская война́

**clad** [klæd] adj: ~ **(in)** облачённый
(в +acc)

**claim** [kleɪm] vt (responsibility)
брать (взять pf) на себя́; (credit)
припи́сывать (приписа́ть pf)
себе́; (rights, inheritance)
претендова́ть (impf) or притяза́ть
(impf) на +acc ♦ vi (for insurance)
де́лать (сде́лать pf) страхову́ю
заявку ♦ n (assertion)
утвержде́ние; (for compensation)
заявка; (to inheritance, land)
прете́нзия, притяза́ние; **to ~**
**(that)** or **to be** утвержда́ть (impf),
что

**clamour** ['klæmər] (US **clamor**) vi:
**to ~ for** шу́мно тре́бовать (impf)
+gen

**clamp** [klæmp] n зажи́м ♦ vt
зажима́ть (зажа́ть pf)

**clan** [klæn] n клан

**clandestine** [klæn'dɛstɪn] adj
подпо́льный

**clap** [klæp] vi хло́пать (impf)

**claret** ['klærət] n бордо́ nt ind

**clarify** ['klærɪfaɪ] vt (fig)
разъясня́ть (разъясни́ть pf)

**clarinet** [klærɪ'nɛt] n кларне́т

**clarity** ['klærɪtɪ] n (fig) я́сность f

**clash** [klæʃ] n столкнове́ние; (of
events etc) совпаде́ние; (of metal
objects) зва́канье ♦ vi

ста́лкиваться (столкну́ться pf);
(colours) не совмеща́ться (impf);
(events etc) совпада́ть (совпа́сть
pf) (по вре́мени); (metal objects)
зва́кать (impf)

**class** [klɑːs] n класс; (lesson) уро́к;
(of goods: type) разря́д; (: quality)
сорт ♦ vt классифици́ровать
(impf/pf)

**classic** ['klæsɪk] adj класси́ческий
♦ n класси́ческое произведе́ние;
~**al** adj класси́ческий

**classification** [klæsɪfɪ'keɪʃən] n
классифика́ция; (category)
разря́д

**classified** ['klæsɪfaɪd] adj
засекре́ченный

**classless** ['klɑːslɪs] adj
бескла́ссовый

**classroom** ['klɑːsrum] n класс

**clatter** ['klætər] n зва́канье; (of
hooves) цо́канье

**clause** [klɔːz] n (LAW) пункт

**claustrophobic** [klɔːstrə'fəubɪk] adj:
**she is ~** она́ страда́ет
клаустрофо́бией

**claw** [klɔː] n ко́готь m; (of lobster)
клешня́

**clay** [kleɪ] n гли́на

**clean** [kliːn] adj чи́стый; (edge,
fracture) ро́вный ♦ vt (hands, face)
мыть (вы́мыть pf); (car, cooker)
чи́стить (почи́стить pf); ~ **out** vt
(tidy) вычища́ть (вы́чистить pf); ~
**up** vt (room) убира́ть (убра́ть pf);
(child) мыть (помы́ть pf); ~**er** n
убо́рщик(ица); (substance)
мо́ющее сре́дство; ~**liness**
['klɛnlɪnɪs] n чистопло́тность f

**cleanse** [klɛnz] vt очища́ть
(очи́стить pf); (face) мыть
(вы́мыть pf); (cut) промыва́ть
(промы́ть pf); ~**r** n очища́ющий
лосьо́н

**clean-shaven** ['kliːn'ʃeɪvn] adj
чи́сто вы́бритый

**clear** [klɪəʳ] adj ясный; (footprint, writing) чёткий; (glass, water) прозрачный; (road) свободный; (conscience, profit) чистый ♦ vt (space, room) освобождать (освободить pf); (suspect) оправдывать (оправдать pf); (fence etc) брать (взять pf) ♦ vi (sky) проясняться (проясниться pf); (fog, smoke) рассеиваться (рассеяться pf) ♦ adv: ~ of подальше от +gen; to make it ~ to sb that ... давать (дать pf) кому-н понять, что ...; to ~ the table убирать (убрать pf) со стола; ~ up vt убирать (убрать pf); (mystery, problem) разрешать (разрешить pf); ~ance n расчистка; (permission) разрешение; ~-cut adj ясный, чёткий; ~ing n поляна; ~ly adv ясно; (obviously) явно, очевидно

**cleft** [klɛft] n расселина

**clergy** ['klə:dʒɪ] n духовенство; ~man (irreg) n священник

**clerical** ['klɛrɪkl] adj канцелярский; (REL) церковный

**clerk** [klɑːk, (US) klə:rk] n (BRIT) клерк, делопроизводитель(ница) m(f); (US: sales person) продавец(вщица)

**clever** ['klɛvəʳ] adj (intelligent) умный

**cliché** ['kliːʃeɪ] n клише nt ind, штамп

**click** [klɪk] vt (tongue, heels) щёлкать (щёлкнуть pf) +instr ♦ vi (device, switch) щёлкать (щёлкнуть pf) ~ on vt fus (COMPUT) щёлкать (щёлкнуть pf)

**client** ['klaɪənt] n клиент

**cliff** [klɪf] n скала, утёс

**climate** ['klaɪmɪt] n климат

**climax** ['klaɪmæks] n кульминация

**climb** [klaɪm] vi подниматься (подняться pf); (plant) ползти (impf); (plane) набирать (набрать pf) высоту ♦ vt (stairs) взбираться (взобраться pf) по +prp; (tree, hill) взбираться (взобраться pf)+acc ♦ n подъём; to ~ over a wall перелезать (перелезть pf) через стену; ~er n альпинист(ка)

**clinch** [klɪntʃ] vt (deal) заключать (заключить pf); (argument) разрешать (разрешить pf)

**cling** [klɪŋ] (pt, pp **clung**) vi (clothes) прилегать (impf); to ~ to вцепляться (вцепиться pf) в +acc; (fig) цепляться (impf) за +acc

**clinic** ['klɪnɪk] n клиника; ~al adj клинический; (fig: attitude) бесстрастный

**clip** [klɪp] n (also: **paper ~**) скрепка; (for hair) заколка; (TV, CINEMA) клип ♦ vt (fasten) прикреплять (прикрепить pf); (cut) подстригать (подстричь pf); ~ping n (PRESS) вырезка

**clique** [kliːk] n клика

**cloak** [kləuk] n (cape) плащ; ~room n гардероб; (BRIT: WC) уборная f adj

**clock** [klɔk] n (timepiece) часы pl; ~wise adv по часовой стрелке; ~work adj (toy) заводной

**clone** [kləun] n (BIO) клон

**close¹** [kləus] adj близкий; (writing) убористый; (contact, ties) тесный; (watch, attention) пристальный; (weather, room) душный ♦ adv близко; ~ to (near) близкий к +dat; ~ to or on (almost) близко к +dat; ~ by or at hand рядом

**close²** [kləuz] vt закрывать (закрыть pf); (finalize) заключать (заключить pf); (end) завершать (завершить pf) ♦ vi закрываться (закрыться pf); (end)

завершáться (заверши́ться pf)
♦ n конéц; ~ **down** vt
закрывáть (закры́ть pf) ♦ vi
закрывáться (закры́ться pf); ~**d**
adj закры́тый

**closely** ['kləuslɪ] adv при́стально;
(connected, related) тéсно

**closet** ['klɔzɪt] n (cupboard) шкаф

**close-up** ['kləusʌp] n крýпный
план

**closure** ['kləuʒər] n (of factory, road)
закры́тие

**clot** [klɔt] n сгýсток; (in vein)
тромб

**cloth** [klɔθ] n ткань f; (for cleaning
etc) тря́пка

**clothes** [kləuðz] npl одéжда fsg; ~
**brush** n одёжная щётка; ~ **peg**
(US ~ **pin**) n прищéпка

**clothing** ['kləuðɪŋ] n = **clothes**

**cloud** [klaud] n óблако; ~**y** adj (sky)
óблачный; (liquid) мýтный

**clout** [klaut] vt (inf) долбанýть (pf)

**clove** [kləuv] n гвозди́ка; ~ **of**
**garlic** дóлька чеснокá

**clover** ['kləuvər] n клéвер

**clown** [klaun] n клóун

**club** [klʌb] n клуб; (weapon)
дуби́нка; (also: **golf** ~) клю́шка;
~**s** npl (CARDS) трéфы fpl

**clue** [klu:] n ключ; (for police)
ули́ка; **I haven't a** ~ (я) поня́тия
не имéю

**clump** [klʌmp] n зáросли fpl

**clumsy** ['klʌmzɪ] adj неуклю́жий;
(object) неудóбный

**clung** [klʌŋ] pt, pp of **cling**

**cluster** ['klʌstər] n скоплéние

**clutch** [klʌtʃ] n хвáтка; (AUT)
сцеплéние ♦ vt сжимáть (сжать
pf)

**clutter** ['klʌtər] vt (also: ~ **up**)
захламля́ть (захлами́ть pf)

**cm** abbr (= centimetre) см

**CND** n abbr = Campaign for Nuclear
Disarmament

**Co.** abbr = **company**, **county**

**coach** [kəutʃ] n (bus) автóбус;
(horse-drawn) экипáж; (of train)
вагóн; (SPORT) трéнер; (SCOL)
репети́тор ♦ vt (SPORT)
тренировáть (натренировáть pf);
(SCOL): **to** ~ **sb for** готóвить
(подготóвить pf) когó-н к +dat

**coal** [kəul] n ýголь m

**coalition** [kəuə'lɪʃən] n коали́ция

**coarse** [kɔ:s] adj грýбый

**coast** [kəust] n бéрег; (area)
побережье; ~**al** adj прибрéжный;
~**guard** n офицéр береговóй
слýжбы; ~**line** n береговáя
ли́ния

**coat** [kəut] n пальтó nt ind; (on
animal: fur) мех; (: wool) шерсть
f; (of paint) слой ♦ vt покрывáть
(покры́ть pf); ~ **hanger** n
вéшалка

**cobweb** ['kɔbwɛb] n паути́на

**cocaine** [kə'keɪn] n кокаи́н

**cock** [kɔk] n петýх ♦ vt (gun)
взводи́ть (взвести́ pf); ~**erel**
['kɔkərəl] n петýх

**cockney** - кóкни. Так называ́ют
выхóдцев из востóчного
райóна Лóндона. Они́ говоря́т
на осóбом диалéкте
англи́йского языкá. Кóкни
тáкже обознача́ет э́тот
диалéкт.

**cockpit** ['kɔkpɪt] n каби́на

**cockroach** ['kɔkrəutʃ] n таракáн

**cocktail** ['kɔkteɪl] n коктéйль m;
(with fruit, prawns) салáт

**cocoa** ['kəukəu] n какáо nt ind

**coconut** ['kəukənʌt] n кокóсовый
орéх; (flesh) кокóс

**COD** abbr = **cash on delivery**; (US:
= collect on delivery) налóженный
платёж

**cod** [kɔd] n трескá f no pl

**code** [kəud] n код; (of behaviour)
ко́декс; **post ~** (BRIT) почто́вый
и́ндекс

**coffee** ['kɔfɪ] n ко́фе m ind; **~ table**
n кофе́йный сто́лик

**coffin** ['kɔfɪn] n гроб

**cognac** ['kɔnjæk] n конья́к

**coherent** [kəu'hɪərənt] adj
свя́зный, стро́йный; **she was
very ~** её речь была́ о́чень
связно́й

**coil** [kɔɪl] n мото́к ♦ vt сма́тывать
(смота́ть pf)

**coin** [kɔɪn] n моне́та ♦ vt
приду́мывать (приду́мать pf)

**coincide** [kəuɪn'saɪd] vi совпада́ть
(совпа́сть pf); **~nce** [kəu'ɪnsɪdəns]
n совпаде́ние

**coke** [kəuk] n кокс

**colander** ['kɔləndər] n дуршла́г

**cold** [kəuld] adj холо́дный ♦ n
хо́лод; (MED) просту́да; **it's ~**
хо́лодно; **I am** or **feel ~** мне
хо́лодно; **to catch ~** or **a ~**
простужа́ться (простуди́ться pf);
**in ~ blood** хладнокро́вно; **~ly** adv
хо́лодно; **~ sore** n лихора́дка
(на губе́ и́ли носу́)

**colic** ['kɔlɪk] n ко́лики pl

**collaboration** [kəlæbə'reɪʃən] n
сотру́дничество

**collapse** [kə'læps] vi (building,
system, plans) ру́шиться (ру́хнуть
pf); (table etc) скла́дываться
(сложи́ться pf); (company)
разоря́ться (разори́ться pf);
(government) разва́ливаться
(развали́ться pf); (MED, person)
свали́ться (pf) ♦ n (of building)
обва́л; (of system, plans)
круше́ние; (of company)
разоре́ние; (of government)
паде́ние; (MED) упа́док сил,
колла́пс

**collar** ['kɔlər] n воротни́к; (for dog
etc) оше́йник; **~bone** n ключи́ца

**colleague** ['kɔliːg] n колле́га m/f

**collect** [kə'lɛkt] vt собира́ть
(собра́ть pf); (stamps etc)
коллекциони́ровать (impf); (BRIT:
fetch) забира́ть (забра́ть pf);
(debts etc) взы́скивать (взыска́ть
pf) ♦ vi (crowd) собира́ться
(собра́ться pf); **to call ~** (US)
звони́ть (impf) по колле́кту; **~ion**
[kə'lɛkʃən] n (of stamps etc)
колле́кция; (for charity, also REL)
поже́ртвования ntpl; (of mail)
вы́емка; **~ive** adj коллекти́вный;
**~or** n коллекционе́р; (of taxes etc)
сбо́рщик

**college** ['kɔlɪdʒ] n учи́лище; (of
university) ко́лледж; (of technology
etc) институ́т

**colliery** ['kɔlɪərɪ] n (BRIT) у́гольная
ша́хта

**collision** [kə'lɪʒən] n столкнове́ние

**colon** ['kəulən] n (LING) двоето́чие;
(ANAT) пряма́я кишка́

**colonel** ['kə:nl] n полко́вник

**colony** ['kɔlənɪ] n коло́ния

**color** etc (US) = **colour** etc

**colossal** [kə'lɔsl] adj колосса́льный

**colour** ['kʌlər] (US **color**) n цвет
♦ vt раскра́шивать (раскра́сить
pf); (dye) кра́сить (покра́сить pf);
(fig: opinion) окра́шивать
(окра́сить pf) ♦ vi красне́ть
(покрасне́ть pf); **skin ~** цвет
ко́жи; **in ~** в цве́те; **~ in** vt
раскра́шивать (раскра́сить pf);
**~ed** adj цветно́й; **~ film** n
цветна́я плёнка; **~ful** adj
кра́сочный; (character) я́ркий;
**~ing** n (of skin) цвет лица́; (in
food) краси́тель m; **~ scheme** n
цветова́я га́мма; **~ television** n
цветно́й телеви́зор

**column** ['kɔləm] n коло́нна; (of
smoke) столб; (PRESS) ру́брика

**coma** ['kəumə] n: **to be in a ~**
находи́ться (impf) в ко́ме

**comb** [kəum] *n* расчёска;
(*ornamental*) гребень *m* ♦ *vt*
расчёсывать (расчеса́ть *pf*); (*fig*)
прочёсывать (прочеса́ть *pf*)
**combat** [kɒm'bæt] *n* бой; (*battle*)
би́тва ♦ *vt* боро́ться (*impf*) про́тив
+*gen*
**combination** [kɒmbɪ'neɪʃən] *n*
сочета́ние, комбина́ция; (*code*)
код
**combine** [kəm'baɪn] *vt*
комбини́ровать
(скомбини́ровать *pf*) ♦ *vi* (*groups*)
объединя́ться (объедини́ться *pf*)

KEYWORD

**come** [kʌm] (*pt* **came**, *pp* **come**) *vi*
**1** (*move towards: on foot*)
подходи́ть (подойти́ *pf*); (: *by
transport*) подъезжа́ть
(подъе́хать *pf*); **to come running**
подбега́ть (подбежа́ть *pf*)
**2** (*arrive: on foot*) приходи́ть
(прийти́ *pf*); (: *by transport*)
приезжа́ть (прие́хать *pf*); **he
came running to tell us** он
прибежа́л, сказа́ть нам; **are you
coming to my party?** Вы придёте
ко мне на вечери́нку?; **I've only
come for an hour** я зашёл то́лько
на час
**3** (*reach*) доходи́ть (дойти́ *pf*) до
+*gen*; **to come to** (*power, decision*)
приходи́ть (прийти́ *pf*) к +*dat*
**4** (*occur*): **an idea came to me** мне
в го́лову пришла́ иде́я
**5** (*be, become*): **to come into being**
возника́ть (возни́кнуть *pf*); **to
come loose** отходи́ть (отойти́ *pf*);
**I've come to like him** он стал мне
нра́виться
**come about** *vi*: **how did it come
about?** каки́м о́бразом э́то
произошло́?, как э́то
получи́лось?; **it came about
through** ... э́то получи́лось из-за

+*gen* ...
**come across** *vt fus*
ната́лкиваться (натолкну́ться *pf*)
на +*acc*
**come away** *vi* уходи́ть (уйти́ *pf*);
(*come off*) отходи́ть (отойти́ *pf*)
**come back** *vi* возвраща́ться
(возврати́ться *pf*), верну́ться (*pf*)
**come by** *vt fus* достава́ть
(доста́ть *pf*)
**come down** *vi* (*price*)
понижа́ться (пони́зиться *pf*); **the
tree came down in the storm**
де́рево снесло́ бу́рей; **the
building will have to come down
soon** зда́ние должны́ ско́ро
снести́ **come forward** *vi*
(*volunteer*) вызыва́ться
(вы́зваться *pf*)
**come from** *vt fus*: **she comes
from India** она́ из Индии
**come in** *vi* (*person*) входи́ть
(войти́ *pf*); **to come in on** (*deal*)
вступа́ть (вступи́ть *pf*) в +*acc*;
**where does he come in?** в чём
его́ роль?
**come in for** *vt fus* подверга́ться
(подве́ргнуться *pf*) +*dat*
**come into** *vt fus* (*fashion*)
входи́ть (войти́ *pf*) в +*acc*; (*money*)
насле́довать (унасле́довать *pf*)
**come off** *vi* (*button*) отрыва́ться
(оторва́ться *pf*); (*handle*)
отла́мываться (отлома́ться *pf*);
(*can be removed*) снима́ться (*impf*);
(*attempt*) удава́ться (уда́ться *pf*)
**come on** *vi* (*pupil*) де́лать
(сде́лать *pf*) успе́хи; (*work*)
продвига́ться (продви́нуться *pf*);
(*lights etc*) включа́ться
(включи́ться *pf*); **come on!** ну!,
дава́йте!
**come out** *vi* выходи́ть (вы́йти
*pf*); (*stain*) сходи́ть (сойти́ *pf*)
**come round** *vi* очну́ться (*pf*),
приходи́ть (прийти́ *pf*) в себя́

**come to** vi = **come round**
**come up** vi (sun) всходи́ть
(взойти́ pf); (event) приближа́ться
(прибли́зиться pf); (questions)
возника́ть (возни́кнуть pf);
**something important has come
up** случи́лось что-то ва́жное
**come up against** vt fus
ста́лкиваться (столкну́ться pf) с
+instr
**come up with** vt fus (idea,
solution) предлага́ть
(предложи́ть pf)
**come upon** vt fus ната́лкиваться
(натолкну́ться pf) на +acc

**comeback** ['kʌmbæk] n: **to make a
~** (actor etc) обрета́ть (обрести́ pf)
но́вую популя́рность
**comedian** [kə'mi:dɪən] n ко́мик
**comedy** ['kɔmɪdɪ] n коме́дия
**comet** ['kɔmɪt] n коме́та
**comfort** ['kʌmfət] n комфо́рт;
(relief) утеше́ние ♦ vt утеша́ть
(уте́шить pf); **~s** npl (luxuries)
удо́бства ntpl; **~able** adj
комфорта́бельный, удо́бный; **to
be ~able** (physically) чу́вствовать
(impf) себя́ удо́бно; (financially)
жить (impf) в доста́тке; (patient)
чу́вствовать (impf) себя́
норма́льно; **~ably** adv удо́бно
**comic** ['kɔmɪk] adj коми́ческий,
смешно́й ♦ n (comedian) ко́мик;
(BRIT: magazine) ко́микс
**coming** ['kʌmɪŋ] adj
приближа́ющийся
**comma** ['kɔmə] n запята́я f adj
**command** [kə'mɑ:nd] n кома́нда;
(control) контро́ль m; (mastery)
владе́ние ♦ vt (MIL) кома́ндовать
(impf) +instr
**commemorate** [kə'mɛməreɪt] vt
(with statue etc) увекове́чивать
(увекове́чить pf); (with event etc)
отмеча́ть (отме́тить pf)

**commence** [kə'mɛns] vt
приступа́ть (приступи́ть pf)
к +dat ♦ vi начина́ться (нача́ться
pf)
**commend** [kə'mɛnd] vt хвали́ть
(похвали́ть pf); (recommend): **to ~
sth to sb** рекомендова́ть
(порекомендова́ть pf) что-н
кому́-н
**comment** ['kɔmɛnt] n замеча́ние
♦ vi: **to ~ (on)** комменти́ровать
(прокомменти́ровать pf); **"no ~"**
"возде́рживаюсь от
коммента́риев"; **~ary** ['kɔməntərɪ]
n (SPORT) репорта́ж; **~ator**
['kɔmənteɪtə<sup>r</sup>] n коммента́тор
**commerce** ['kɔmə:s] n комме́рция
**commercial** [kə'mə:ʃəl] adj
комме́рческий ♦ n рекла́ма
**commission** [kə'mɪʃən] n зака́з;
(COMM) комиссио́нные pl adj;
(committee) коми́ссия ♦ vt
зака́зывать (заказа́ть pf); **out of ~**
неиспра́вный
**commit** [kə'mɪt] vt (crime)
соверша́ть (соверши́ть pf);
(money) выделя́ть (вы́делить pf);
(entrust) вверя́ть (вве́рить pf); **to
~ o.s.** принима́ть (приня́ть pf) на
себя́ обяза́тельства; **to ~ suicide**
поко́нчить (pf) жизнь
самоуби́йством; **~ment** n (belief)
пре́данность f; (obligation)
обяза́тельство
**committee** [kə'mɪtɪ] n комите́т
**commodity** [kə'mɔdɪtɪ] n това́р
**common** ['kɔmən] adj о́бщий;
(usual) обы́чный; (vulgar)
вульга́рный ♦ npl: **the Commons**
(also: **the House of Commons**:
BRIT) Пала́та fsg о́бщин; **to have
sth in ~ (with sb)** име́ть (impf)
что-н о́бщее (с кем-н); **it's ~
knowledge that** общеизве́стно,
что; **to** or **for the ~ good** для
всео́бщего бла́га; **~ law** n

обы́чное пра́во; **~ly** adv обы́чно;
**Common Market** n: the
**Common Market** О́бщий ры́нок;
**~place** adj обы́чный, обы́денный

**House of Commons** - Пала́та
о́бщин. Одна́ из пала́т
брита́нского парла́мента. В
ней заседа́ет 650 вы́борных
чле́нов парла́мента.

**common sense** n здра́вый
смысл
**Commonwealth** n (BRIT): the
**Commonwealth** Содру́жество
**commotion** [kə'məuʃən] n
сумато́ха
**communal** ['kɔmju:nl] adj (shared)
о́бщий; (flat) коммуна́льный
**commune** ['kɔmju:n] n комму́на
**communicate** [kə'mju:nɪkeɪt] vt
передава́ть (переда́ть pf) ♦ vi: to
~ **(with)** обща́ться (impf) (с +instr)
**communication** [kəmju:nɪ'keɪʃən]
n коммуника́ция
**communion** [kə'mju:nɪən] n (also:
**Holy Communion**) Свято́е
Прича́стие
**communism** ['kɔmjunɪzəm] n
коммуни́зм
**communist** ['kɔmjunɪst] adj
коммунисти́ческий ♦ n
коммуни́ст(ка)
**community** [kə'mju:nɪtɪ] n
о́бщественность f; (within larger
group) о́бщина; **the business ~**
деловы́е круги́; ~ **centre** (BRIT) n
≈ обще́ственный центр

**community service** - трудова́я
пови́нность. Для не́которых
наруши́телей зако́на така́я
фо́рма наказа́ния заменя́ет
тюре́мное заключе́ние.

**commuter** [kə'mju:tə<sup>r</sup>] n челове́к,

кото́рый е́здит на рабо́ту из
при́города в го́род
**compact** [kəm'pækt] adj компа́кт-
ный; ~ **disc** n компа́кт-диск
**companion** [kəm'pænjən] n
спу́тник(ица)
**company** ['kʌmpənɪ] n компа́ния;
(THEAT) тру́ппа; (companionship)
компа́ния, о́бщество; **to keep sb**
~ составля́ть (соста́вить pf)
кому́-н компа́нию
**comparable** ['kɔmpərəbl] adj (size)
сопостави́мый
**comparative** [kəm'pærətɪv] adj (also
LING) сравни́тельный; **~ly** adv
сравни́тельно
**compare** [kəm'pɛə<sup>r</sup>] vt: to ~ **sb/sth**
**with** or **to** сра́внивать (сравни́ть
pf) кого́-н/что-н с +instr (set side by
side) сопоставля́ть (сопоста́вить
pf) кого́-н/что-н с +instr ♦ vi: to ~
**(with)** соотноси́ться (impf) (с
+instr)
**comparison** [kəm'pærɪsn] n (see vt)
сравне́ние; сопоставле́ние; **in ~**
**(with)** по сравне́нию or в
сравне́нии (с +instr)
**compartment** [kəm'pɑ:tmənt] n
купе́ nt ind; (section) отделе́ние
**compass** ['kʌmpəs] n ко́мпас; **~es**
npl (also: **pair of ~es**) ци́ркуль
msg
**compassion** [kəm'pæʃən] n
сострада́ние; **~ate** adj
сострада́тельный
**compatible** [kəm'pætɪbl] adj
совмести́мый
**compel** [kəm'pɛl] vt вынужда́ть
(вы́нудить pf); **~ling** adj
(argument) убеди́тельный;
(reason) настоя́тельный
**compensate** ['kɔmpənseɪt] vt: to ~
**sb for sth** компенси́ровать (impf/
pf) кому́-н что-н ♦ vi: to ~ **for**
(distress, loss) компенси́ровать
(impf/pf)

**compensation** [kɔmpən'seɪʃən] *n* компенсация

**compete** [kəm'pi:t] *vi* (*in contest etc*) соревноваться (*impf*); **to ~ (with)** (*companies*) конкурировать (*impf*) (с +*instr*); (*rivals*) соперничать (*impf*) (с +*instr*)

**competence** ['kɔmpɪtəns] *n* компетенция

**competent** ['kɔmpɪtənt] *adj* (*person*) компетентный

**competing** [kəm'pi:tɪŋ] *adj* (*claims, explanations*) противоположный

**competition** [kɔmpɪ'tɪʃən] *n* соревнование; (*between firms*) конкуренция; (*between rivals*) соперничество

**competitive** [kəm'pɛtɪtɪv] *adj* (*person*) честолюбивый; (*price*) конкурентноспособный

**competitor** [kəm'pɛtɪtər] *n* (*rival*) соперник, конкурент; (*participant*) участник(ица) соревнования

**compile** [kəm'paɪl] *vt* составлять (составить *pf*)

**complacent** [kəm'pleɪsnt] *adj* безразличие

**complain** [kəm'pleɪn] *vi*: **to ~ (about)** жаловаться (пожаловаться *pf*) (на +*acc*); **~t** *n* жалоба; **to make a ~t against** подавать (подать *pf*) жалобу на +*acc*

**complement** [kɔmplɪmənt] *vt* дополнять (дополнить *pf*)

**complete** [kəm'pli:t] *adj* полный; (*finished*) завершённый ♦ *vt* (*building, task*) завершать (завершить *pf*); (*set*) комплектовать (укомплектовать *pf*); (*form*) заполнять (заполнить *pf*); **~ly** *adv* полностью, совершенно

**completion** [kəm'pli:ʃən] *n* (*of building, task*) завершение

**complex** ['kɔmplɛks] *adj* сложный

♦ *n* комплекс

**complexion** [kəm'plɛkʃən] *n* (*of face*) цвет лица

**complexity** [kəm'plɛksɪtɪ] *n* сложность *f*

**compliance** [kəm'plaɪəns] *n* (*submission*) послушание; **~ with** следование +*dat*

**complicate** ['kɔmplɪkeɪt] *vt* усложнять (усложнить *pf*); **~d** *adj* сложный

**complication** [kɔmplɪ'keɪʃən] *n* осложнение

**compliment** *n* ['kɔmplɪmənt] *vb* ['kɔmplɪmɛnt] *n* комплимент, хвала ♦ *vt* хвалить (похвалить *pf*); **~s** *npl* (*regards*) наилучшие пожелания *ntpl*; **to ~ sb, pay sb a ~** делать (сделать *pf*) кому-н комплимент; **~ary** [kɔmplɪ'mɛntərɪ] *adj* (*remark*) лестный; (*ticket etc*) дарственный

**comply** [kəm'plaɪ] *vi*: **to ~ (with)** подчиняться (подчиниться *pf*) (+*dat*)

**component** [kəm'pəʊnənt] *adj* составной ♦ *n* компонент

**compose** [kəm'pəʊz] *vt* сочинять (сочинить *pf*); **to be ~d of** состоять (*impf*) из +*gen*; **to ~ o.s.** успокаиваться (успокоиться *pf*); **~d** *adj* спокойный; **~r** *n* композитор

**composition** [kɔmpə'zɪʃən] *n* (*structure*) состав; (*essay*) сочинение; (*MUS*) композиция

**compost** ['kɔmpɔst] *n* компост

**composure** [kəm'pəʊzər] *n* самообладание

**compound** ['kɔmpaʊnd] *n* (*CHEM*) соединение; (*LING*) сложное слово; (*enclosure*) комплекс

**comprehend** [kɔmprɪ'hɛnd] *vt* постигать (постигнуть *or* постичь *pf*)

**comprehension** [kɔmprɪ'hɛnʃən] *n*

понима́ние

**comprehensive** [kɔmprɪ'hɛnsɪv] adj
исче́рпывающий ♦ n (BRIT: also:
~ **school**)
общеобразова́тельная шко́ла

**comprehensive school** -
общеобразова́тельная шко́ла.
В Великобрита́нии э́то
госуда́рственная шко́ла для
дете́й в во́зрасте 11-18 лет.

**comprise** [kəm'praɪz] vt (also: **be
~d of**) включа́ть (impf) в себя́,
состоя́ть (impf) из +gen; (constitute)
составля́ть (соста́вить pf)
**compromise** ['kɔmprəmaɪz] n
компроми́сс ♦ vt
компромети́ровать
(скомпромети́ровать pf) ♦ vi идти́
(пойти́ pf) на компроми́сс
**compulsion** [kəm'pʌlʃən] n (desire)
влече́ние; (force) принужде́ние
**compulsive** [kəm'pʌlsɪv] adj
патологи́ческий; (reading etc)
захва́тывающий
**compulsory** [kəm'pʌlsərɪ] adj
(attendance) обяза́тельный;
(redundancy) принуди́тельный
**computer** [kəm'pju:tər] n
компью́тер; ~ **game** n
компью́терная игра́
**computing** [kəm'pju:tɪŋ] n (as
subject) компью́терное де́ло
**comrade** ['kɔmrɪd] n това́рищ
**con** [kɔn] vt надува́ть (наду́ть pf)
♦ n (trick) обма́н, надува́тельство
**conceal** [kən'si:l] vt укрыва́ть
(укры́ть pf); (keep back) скрыва́ть
(скрыть pf)
**concede** [kən'si:d] vt признава́ть
(призна́ть pf)
**conceited** [kən'si:tɪd] adj
высокоме́рный
**conceivable** [kən'si:vəbl] adj
мы́слимый

**conceive** [kən'si:v] vt (idea)
заду́мывать (заду́мать pf) ♦ vi
забере́менеть (pf)
**concentrate** ['kɔnsəntreɪt] vi
сосредото́чиваться
(сосредото́читься pf),
концентри́роваться
(сконцентри́роваться pf) ♦ vt: **to
~ (on)** (energies) сосредото́чивать
(сосредото́чить pf) or
концентри́ровать
(сконцентри́ровать pf) (на +prp)
**concentration** [kɔnsən'treɪʃən] n
сосредото́чение, концентра́ция;
(attention) сосредото́ченность f;
(CHEM) концентра́ция
**concept** ['kɔnsɛpt] n поня́тие;
**~ion** [kən'sɛpʃən] n (idea)
конце́пция; (BIO) зача́тие
**concern** [kən'sə:n] n (affair) де́ло;
(worry) трево́га, озабо́ченность f;
(care) уча́стие; (COMM)
предприя́тие ♦ vt (worry)
беспоко́ить (impf), трево́жить
(impf); (involve) вовлека́ть
(вовле́чь pf); **to be ~ed (about)**
беспоко́иться (impf) (о +prp); **~ing**
prep относи́тельно +gen
**concert** ['kɔnsət] n конце́рт
**concerted** [kən'sə:tɪd] adj
совме́стный
**concession** [kən'sɛʃən] n
(compromise) усту́пка; (right)
конце́ссия; (reduction) льго́та
**concise** [kən'saɪs] adj кра́ткий
**conclude** [kən'klu:d] vt
зака́нчивать (зако́нчить pf);
(treaty, deal etc) заключа́ть
(заключи́ть pf); (decide)
приходи́ть (прийти́ pf) к
заключе́нию or вы́воду
**concluding** [kən'klu:dɪŋ] adj
заключи́тельный
**conclusion** [kən'klu:ʒən] n
заключе́ние; (of speech)
оконча́ние; (of events)

завершéние

**conclusive** [kən'klu:sıv] *adj*
(*evidence*) неопровержи́мый

**concrete** ['kɔnkri:t] *n* бетóн ♦ *adj*
бетóнный; (*fig*) конкрéтный

**concussion** [kən'kʌʃən] *n*
сотрясéние мóзга

**condemn** [kən'dɛm] *vt* осуждáть
(осуди́ть *pf*); (*building*) бракова́ть
(забракова́ть *pf*); **~ation**
[kɔndɛm'neıʃən] *n* осуждéние

**condensation** [kɔndɛn'seıʃən] *n*
конденсáция

**condition** [kən'dıʃən] *n* состоя́ние;
(*requirement*) усло́вие ♦ *vt*
формирова́ть (сформирова́ть
*pf*); (*hair, skin*) обрабáтывать
(обрабóтать *pf*); **~s** *npl*
(*circumstances*) усло́вия *ntpl*; **on ~
that** при усло́вии, что; **~al** *adj*
усло́вный; **~er** *n* (*for hair*)
бальзáм; (*for fabrics*)
смягчáющий раство́р

**condom** ['kɔndəm] *n* презервати́в

**condone** [kən'dəun] *vt*
потвóрствовать (*impf*) +*dat*

**conduct** *n* ['kɔndʌkt] *vb* [kən'dʌkt] *n*
(*of person*) поведéние ♦ *vt* (*survey
etc*) проводи́ть (провести́ *pf*);
(*MUS*) дирижи́ровать (*impf*); (*PHYS*)
проводи́ть (*impf*); **to ~ o.s.** вести́
(повести́ *pf*) себя́; **~or** [kən'dʌktər]
*n* (*MUS*) дирижёр; (*US : RAIL*)
контролёр; (*on bus*) конду́ктор

**cone** [kəun] *n* кóнус; (*also*: **traffic
~**) *конусообрáзное дорóжное
заграждéние*; (*BOT*) ши́шка; (*ice-
cream*) морóженое *nt adj*
(*трубóчка*)

**confectionery** [kən'fɛkʃənər] *n*
конди́терские изделия *ntpl*

**confederation** [kənfɛdə'reıʃən] *n*
конфедерáция

**confer** [kən'fə:r] *vi* совещáться
(*impf*) ♦ *vt*: **to ~ sth (on sb)**
(*honour*) окáзывать (оказáть *pf*)

что-н (комý-н); (*degree*)
присуждáть (присуди́ть *pf*) что-н
(комý-н)

**conference** ['kɔnfərəns] *n*
конферéнция

**confess** [kən'fɛs] *vt* (*guilt,
ignorance*) признавáть (призна́ть
*pf*); (*sin*) испóведоваться
(испóведаться *pf*) в +*prp* ♦ *vi* (*to
crime*) признавáться (призна́ться
*pf*); **~ion** [kən'fɛʃən] *n* призна́ние;
(*REL*) и́споведь *f*

**confide** [kən'faıd] *vi*: **to ~ in**
доверя́ться (довéриться *pf*) +*dat*

**confidence** ['kɔnfıdns] *n*
увéренность *f*; (*in self*)
увéренность в себé; **in ~**
конфиденциáльно

**confident** ['kɔnfıdənt] *adj* (*see n*)
увéренный; увéренный в себé

**confidential** [kɔnfı'dɛnʃəl] *adj*
конфиденциáльный; (*tone*)
довери́тельный

**confine** [kən'faın] *vt* (*lock up*)
запирáть (запере́ть *pf*); (*limit*): **to
~ (to)** ограни́чивать (ограни́чить
*pf*) (+*instr*); **~d** *adj* закры́тый;
**~ment** *n* (*in jail*) (тюрéмное)
заключéние; **~s** ['kɔnfaınz] *npl*
предéлы *mpl*

**confirm** [kən'fə:m] *vt*
подтверждáть (подтверди́ть *pf*);
**~ation** [kɔnfə'meıʃən] *n*
подтверждéние; **~ed** *adj*
убеждённый

**conflict** ['kɔnflıkt] *n* конфли́кт; (*of
interests*) столкновéние; **~ing** *adj*
противорéчивый; (*interests*)
противополóжный

**conform** [kən'fə:m] *vi*: **to ~ (to)**
подчиня́ться (подчини́ться *pf*)
(+*dat*)

**confront** [kən'frʌnt] *vt* (*problems*)
стáлкиваться (столкну́ться *pf*) с
+*instr*; (*enemy*) противостоя́ть
(*impf*) +*dat*; **~ation** [kɔnfrən'teıʃən]

*n* конфронта́ция

**confuse** [kən'fjuːz] *vt* запу́тывать (запу́тать *pf*); (*mix up*) пу́тать (спу́тать *pf*); **~d** *adj* (*person*) озада́ченный

**confusing** [kən'fjuːzɪŋ] *adj* запу́танный

**confusion** [kən'fjuːʒən] *n* (*perplexity*) замеша́тельство; (*mix-up*) пу́таница; (*disorder*) беспоря́док

**congested** [kən'dʒɛstɪd] *adj* (*see n*) перегру́женный; перенаселённый

**congestion** [kən'dʒɛstʃən] *n* (*on road*) перегру́женность *f*; (*in area*) перенаселённость *f*

**congratulate** [kən'grætjuleɪt] *vt*: **to ~ sb (on)** поздравля́ть (поздра́вить *pf*) кого́-н (с +*instr*)

**congratulations** [kəngrætjuˈleɪʃənz] *npl* поздравле́ния *ntpl*; **~ (on)** (*from one person*) поздравля́ю (с +*instr*); (*from several people*) поздравля́ем (с +*instr*)

**congregation** [kɔŋgrɪˈgeɪʃən] *n* прихожа́не *mpl*, прихо́д

**congress** ['kɔŋgrɛs] *n* конгре́сс; (*US*): **Congress** конгре́сс США; **~man** (*irreg*) (*US*) конгрессме́н

**conjunctivitis** [kəndʒʌŋktɪ'vaɪtɪs] *n* конъюнктиви́т

**conjunction** [kən'dʒʌŋkʃən] *n* (*LING*) сою́з

**conjure** ['kʌndʒəʳ] *vt* (*fig*) сообража́ть (сообрази́ть *pf*); **~ up** *vt* (*memories*) пробужда́ть (пробуди́ть *pf*)

**connect** [kə'nɛkt] *vt* (*ELEC*) подсоединя́ть (подсоедини́ть *pf*), подключа́ть (подключи́ть *pf*); (*fig: associate*) свя́зывать (связа́ть *pf*) ♦ *vi*: **to ~ with** согласо́вываться (согласова́ться *pf*) по расписа́нию с +*instr*; **to ~ sb/sth (to)** соединя́ть (соедини́ть

*pf*) кого́-н/что-н (с +*instr*); **he is ~ed with ...** он свя́зан с +*instr* ...; **I am trying to ~ you** (*TEL*) я пыта́юсь подключи́ть Вас; **~ion** [kə'nɛkʃən] *n* связь *f*; (*train etc*) переса́дка

**connoisseur** [kɔnɪ'səːʳ] *n* знато́к

**conquer** ['kɔŋkəʳ] *vt* (*MIL*) завоёвывать (завоева́ть *pf*); (*overcome*) поборо́ть (*pf*)

**conquest** ['kɔŋkwɛst] *n* (*MIL*) завоева́ние

**cons** [kɔnz] *npl see* **convenience**; **pro**

**conscience** ['kɔnʃəns] *n* со́весть *f*

**conscientious** [kɔnʃɪ'ɛnʃəs] *adj* добросо́вестный

**conscious** ['kɔnʃəs] *adj* (*deliberate*) созна́тельный; (*aware*): **to be ~ of sth/that** сознава́ть (*impf*) что-н/, что; **the patient was ~** пацие́нт находи́лся в созна́нии; **~ness** *n* созна́ние; (*of group*) самосозна́ние

**consecutive** [kən'sɛkjutɪv] *adj*: **on three ~ occasions** в трёх слу́чаях подря́д; **on three ~ days** три дня подря́д

**consensus** [kən'sɛnsəs] *n* еди́ное мне́ние; **~ (of opinion)** консе́нсус

**consent** [kən'sɛnt] *n* согла́сие

**consequence** ['kɔnsɪkwəns] *n* сле́дствие; **of ~** (*significant*) значи́тельный; **it's of little ~** э́то не име́ет большо́го значе́ния; **in ~** (*consequently*) сле́довательно, всле́дствие э́того

**consequently** ['kɔnsɪkwəntlɪ] *adv* сле́довательно

**conservation** [kɔnsə'veɪʃən] *n* (*also*: **nature ~**) охра́на приро́ды, природоохра́на

**conservative** [kən'səːvətɪv] *adj* консервати́вный; (*estimate*) скро́мный; (*BRIT : POL*): **Conservative** консервати́вный

♦ n (BRIT): **Conservative** консерва́тор

**conservatory** [kən'sə:vətrı] n застеклённая вера́нда

**conserve** [kən'sə:v] vt сохраня́ть (сохрани́ть pf); (energy) сберега́ть (сбере́чь pf) ♦ n варе́нье

**consider** [kən'sıdə'] vt (believe) счита́ть (посчита́ть pf); (study) рассма́тривать (рассмотре́ть pf); (take into account) учи́тывать (уче́сть pf); (regard): **to ~ that ...** полага́ть (impf) или счита́ть (impf), что ...; **to ~ sth** (think about) ду́мать (impf) о чём-н; **~able** adj значи́тельный; **~ably** adv значи́тельно; **~ate** adj (person) забо́тливый; (action) внима́тельный; **~ation** [kənsıdə'reıʃən] n рассмотре́ние, обду́мывание; (factor) соображе́ние; (thoughtfulness) внима́ние; **~ing** prep учи́тывая +acc

**consignment** [kən'saınmənt] n (COMM) па́ртия

**consist** [kən'sıst] vi: **to ~ of** состоя́ть (impf) из +gen

**consistency** [kən'sıstənsı] n после́довательность f; (of yoghurt etc) консисте́нция

**consistent** [kən'sıstənt] adj после́довательный

**consolation** [kənsə'leıʃən] n утеше́ние

**console** [kən'səul] vt утеша́ть (уте́шить pf)

**consolidate** [kən'sɔlıdeıt] vt (position, power) укрепля́ть (укрепи́ть pf)

**consonant** ['kənsənənt] n согла́сный m adj

**consortium** [kən'sɔ:tıəm] n консо́рциум

**conspicuous** [kən'spıkjuəs] adj заме́тный

**conspiracy** [kən'spırəsı] n за́говор

**constable** ['kʌnstəbl] (BRIT : also: **police ~**) n (участко́вый) полице́йский m adj

**constant** ['kɔnstənt] adj постоя́нный; (fixed) неизме́нный; **~ly** adv постоя́нно

**constipation** [kɔnstı'peıʃən] n запо́р

**constituency** [kən'stıtjuənsı] n (area) избира́тельный о́круг

**constituent** [kən'stıtjuənt] n избира́тель(ница) m(f); (component) составна́я часть f

**constitute** ['kɔnstıtju:t] vt (represent) явля́ться (яви́ться pf) +instr, (make up) составля́ть (соста́вить pf)

**constitution** [kɔnstı'tju:ʃən] n (of country, person) конститу́ция; (of organization) уста́в; **~al** adj конституцио́нный

**constraint** [kən'streınt] n (restriction) ограниче́ние

**construct** [kən'strʌkt] vt сооружа́ть (сооруди́ть pf); **~ion** [kən'strʌkʃən] n (of building etc) сооруже́ние; (structure) констру́кция; **~ive** adj конструкти́вный

**consul** ['kɔnsl] n ко́нсул; **~ate** ['kɔnsjulıt] n ко́нсульство

**consult** [kən'sʌlt] vt (friend) сове́товаться (посове́товаться pf) с +instr, (book, map) справля́ться (спра́виться pf) в +prp; **to ~ sb (about)** (expert) консульти́роваться (проконсульти́роваться pf) с кем-н (о +prp); **~ant** n консульта́нт; (MED) врач-консульта́нт; **~ation** [kɔnsəl'teıʃən] n (MED) консульта́ция; (discussion) совеща́ние

**consume** [kən'sju:m] vt

потребля́ть (потреби́ть *pf*); ~**r** *n* потреби́тель *m*; ~**r goods** *npl* потреби́тельские това́ры *mpl*

**consumption** [kənˈsʌmpʃən] *n* потребле́ние; (*amount*) расхо́д

**cont.** *abbr* = **continued**: ~ **on** продолже́ние на +*prp*

**contact** [ˈkɒntækt] *n* (*communication*) конта́кт; (*touch*) соприкоснове́ние; (*person*) делово́й(а́я) знако́мый(ая) *m(f)* *adj* ♦ *vt* свя́зываться (связа́ться *pf*) с +*instr*; ~ **lenses** *npl* конта́ктные ли́нзы *fpl*

**contagious** [kənˈteɪdʒəs] *adj* зара́зный; (*fig*) зарази́тельный

**contain** [kənˈteɪn] *vt* (*hold*) вмеща́ть (вмести́ть *pf*); (*include*) содержа́ть (*impf*); (*curb*) сде́рживать (сдержа́ть *pf*); **to** ~ **o.s.** сде́рживаться (сдержа́ться *pf*); ~**er** *n* конте́йнер

**contamination** [kəntæmɪˈneɪʃən] *n* загрязне́ние

**contemplate** [ˈkɒntəmpleɪt] *vt* (*consider*) размышля́ть (*impf*) о +*prp*; (*look at*) созерца́ть (*impf*)

**contemporary** [kənˈtɛmpərərɪ] *adj* совреме́нный ♦ *n* совреме́нник(ица)

**contempt** [kənˈtɛmpt] *n* презре́ние; ~ **of court** оскорбле́ние суда́; ~**uous** *adj* презри́тельный

**contend** [kənˈtɛnd] *vt*: **to** ~ **that** утвержда́ть (*impf*), что ♦ *vi*: **to** ~ **with** (*problem etc*) боро́ться (*impf*) с +*instr*; **to** ~ **for** (*power*) боро́ться (*impf*) за +*acc*; ~**er** *n* претенде́нт(ка)

**content** *n* [ˈkɒntɛnt] *adj, vb* [kənˈtɛnt] *n* содержа́ние ♦ *adj* дово́льный ♦ *vt* (*satisfy*) удовлетворя́ть (удовлетвори́ть *pf*); ~**s** *npl* (*of bottle etc*) содержи́мое *ntsg adj*; (*of book*)

содержа́ние *ntsg*; (**table of**) ~**s** оглавле́ние; ~**ed** *adj* дово́льный

**contention** [kənˈtɛnʃən] *n* (*assertion*) утвержде́ние; (*argument*) разногла́сие

**contest** *n* [ˈkɒntɛst] *vb* [kənˈtɛst] *n* (*sport*) соревнова́ние; (*beauty*) ко́нкурс; (*for power etc*) борьба́ ♦ *vt* оспа́ривать (оспо́рить *pf*); (*election, competition*) боро́ться (*impf*) на +*prp*; ~**ant** [kənˈtɛstənt] *n* уча́стник(ница)

**context** [ˈkɒntɛkst] *n* конте́кст

**continent** [ˈkɒntɪnənt] *n* контине́нт, матери́к; **the Continent** (*BRIT*) Евро́па (*кроме брита́нских острово́в*)

**continental** [kɒntɪˈnɛntl] *adj* (*BRIT*) европе́йский

**continental breakfast** - европе́йский за́втрак. В европе́йский за́втрак вхо́дят хлеб, ма́сло и джем. Его́ подаю́т в гости́ницах вме́сто традицио́нного за́втрака из беко́на и яи́чницы.

**continental quilt** *n* (*BRIT*) стёганое одея́ло

**contingency** [kənˈtɪndʒənsɪ] *n* возмо́жность *f*

**contingent** [kənˈtɪndʒənt] *n* (*also MIL*) континге́нт

**continual** [kənˈtɪnjuəl] *adj* непреры́вный, постоя́нный; ~**ly** *adv* (*constantly*) непреры́вно, постоя́нно

**continuation** [kəntɪnjuˈeɪʃən] *n* продолже́ние

**continue** [kənˈtɪnjuː] *vi* (*carry on*) продолжа́ться (*impf*); (*after interruption: talk*) продолжа́ться (продо́лжиться *pf*); (: *person*) продолжа́ть (продо́лжить *pf*) ♦ *vt* (*carry on*) продолжа́ть

(продо́лжить *pf*)

**continuity** [kɔntɪˈnjuːɪtɪ] *n*
прее́мственность *f*

**continuous** [kənˈtɪnjuəs] *adj*
непреры́вный; (*line*) сплошно́й

**contraception** [kɔntrəˈsɛpʃən] *n*
предупрежде́ние бере́мен-
ности

**contraceptive** [kɔntrəˈsɛptɪv] *n*
противозача́точное сре́дство,
контрацепти́в

**contract** *n* [ˈkɔntrækt] *vb* [kənˈtrækt]
*n* догово́р, контра́кт ♦ *vi*
сжима́ться (сжа́ться *pf*) ♦ *vt* (*MED*)
заболева́ть (заболе́ть *pf*) +*instr*;
**~ion** [kənˈtrækʃən] *n* (*MED*)
родова́я поту́га; **~or** [kənˈtræktər]
*n* подря́дчик

**contradict** [kɔntrəˈdɪkt] *vt* (*person*)
возража́ть (возрази́ть *pf*) +*dat*;
(*statement*) возража́ть (возрази́ть
*pf*) на +*acc*; **~ion** [kɔntrəˈdɪkʃən] *n*
противоре́чие; **~ory** *adj*
противоречи́вый

**contrary** [ˈkɔntrərɪ] *adj*
противополо́жный ♦ *n*
противополо́жность *f*; **on the ~**
напро́тив, наоборо́т; **unless you
hear to the ~** е́сли не бу́дет
други́х инстру́кций

**contrast** *n* [ˈkɔntrɑːst] *vb* [kənˈtrɑːst]
*n* контра́ст ♦ *vt* сопоставля́ть
(сопоста́вить *pf*); **in ~ to** or **with**
по контра́сту с +*instr*; **~ing**
[kənˈtrɑːstɪŋ] *adj* (*colours*)
контрасти́рующий; (*views*)
противополо́жный

**contribute** [kənˈtrɪbjuːt] *vi* (*give*)
де́лать (сде́лать *pf*) вклад ♦ *vt*
(*money, an article*) вноси́ть
(внести́ *pf*); **to ~ to** (*to charity*)
же́ртвовать (поже́ртвовать *pf*)
на +*acc* или для +*gen*; (*to paper*)
писа́ть (написа́ть *pf*) для +*gen*; (*to
discussion*) вноси́ть (внести́ *pf*)
вклад в +*prp*; (*to problem*)

усугубля́ть (усугуби́ть *pf*)

**contribution** [kɔntrɪˈbjuːʃən] *n*
(*donation*) поже́ртвование,
вклад; (*to debate, campaign*)
вклад; (*to journal*) публика́ция

**contributor** [kənˈtrɪbjutər] *n* (*to
appeal*) же́ртвователь *m*; (*to
newspaper*) а́втор

**control** [kənˈtrəul] *vt*
контроли́ровать (*impf*) ♦ *n* (*of
country, organization*) контро́ль *m*;
(*of o.s.*) самооблада́ние; **~s** *npl* (*of
vehicle*) управле́ние; (*on radio etc*)
ру́чки *fpl* настро́йки; **to ~ o.s.**
сохраня́ть (сохрани́ть *pf*)
самооблада́ние; **to be in ~ of**
контроли́ровать (*impf*);
**everything is under ~** всё под
контро́лем; **out of ~**
неуправля́емый

**controversial** [kɔntrəˈvəːʃl] *adj*
спо́рный; (*person, writer*)
неоднозна́чный

**controversy** [ˈkɔntrəvəːsɪ] *n*
диску́ссия, спор

**convene** [kənˈviːn] *vt* созыва́ть
(созва́ть *pf*) ♦ *vi* собира́ться
(собра́ться *pf*)

**convenience** [kənˈviːnɪəns] *n*
удо́бство; **at your ~** когда́ Вам
бу́дет удо́бно; **a flat with all
modern ~s** or (*BRIT*) **all mod cons**
кварти́ра со все́ми удо́бствами

**convenient** [kənˈviːnɪənt] *adj*
удо́бный

**convent** [ˈkɔnvənt] *n* (*REL*)
(же́нский) монасты́рь *m*

**convention** [kənˈvɛnʃən] *n* (*custom*)
усло́вность *f*; (*conference*)
конфере́нция; (*agreement*)
конве́нция; **~al** *adj*
традицио́нный; (*methods,
weapons*) обы́чный

**converge** [kənˈvəːdʒ] *vi* (*people*)
съезжа́ться (съе́хаться *pf*)

**conversation** [kɔnvəˈseɪʃən] *n*

беседа, разговор; **to have a ~ with sb** разговаривать (impf) or беседовать (побеседовать pf) с кем-н

**conversely** [kən'və:slɪ] adv наоборот

**conversion** [kən'və:ʃən] n обращение; (of weights) перевод; (of substances) превращение

**convert** vb [kən'və:t] n ['kɔnvə:t] vt (person) обращать (обратить pf) ♦ n новообращённ(ая)m(f) adj; **to ~ sth into** превращать (превратить pf) что-н в +acc

**convey** [kən'veɪ] vt передавать (передать pf); (cargo, person) перевозить (перевезти pf)

**convict** vb [kən'vɪkt] n ['kɔnvɪkt] vt осуждать (осудить pf) ♦ n каторжник; **~ion** [kən'vɪkʃən] n (belief) убеждение; (certainty) убеждённость f; (LAW) осуждение; (: previous) судимость f

**convince** [kən'vɪns] vt (assure) уверять (уверить pf); (persuade) убеждать (убедить pf); **~d** adj: **~d of/that** убеждённый в +prp/, что

**convincing** [kən'vɪnsɪŋ] adj убедительный

**convoy** ['kɔnvɔɪ] n (of trucks) колонна; (of ships) конвой

**cook** [kuk] vt готовить (приготовить pf) ♦ vi (person) готовить (impf); (food) готовиться (impf) ♦ n повар; **~er** n плита; **~ery** n кулинария; **~ery book** n (BRIT) поваренная or кулинарная книга; **~ie** n (esp US) печенье; **~ing** n готовка; **I like ~ing** я люблю готовить

**cool** [ku:l] adj прохладный; (dress, clothes) лёгкий; (person: calm) невозмутимый; (: hostile) холодный; (inf: great) крутой ♦ vi (water, air) остывать (остыть pf);

**~!** (inf) здорово!

**cooperate** [kəu'ɔpəreɪt] vi (collaborate) сотрудничать (impf); (assist) содействовать (impf)

**cooperation** [kəuɔpə'reɪʃən] n (see vi) кооперация, сотрудничество; содействие

**cooperative** [kəu'ɔpərətɪv] n кооператив ♦ adj: **he is very ~** он всегда готов оказать помощь

**coordinate** vb [kəu'ɔ:dɪneɪt] n [kəu'ɔ:dɪnət] vt (activity, attack) согласовывать (согласовать pf), координировать (impf/pf) ♦ n (MATH) координата

**coordination** [kəuɔ:dɪ'neɪʃən] n координация

**cop** [kɔp] n (BRIT: inf) мент

**cope** [kəup] vi: **to ~ with** справляться (справиться pf) с +instr

**copper** ['kɔpər] n (metal) медь f

**copy** ['kɔpɪ] n (duplicate) копия; (of book etc) экземпляр ♦ vt копировать (скопировать pf); **~right** n авторское право, копирайт

**coral** ['kɔrəl] n коралл

**cord** [kɔ:d] n (string) верёвка; (ELEC) шнур; (fabric) вельвет

**cordial** ['kɔ:dɪəl] adj сердечный

**cordon** ['kɔ:dn] n кордон, оцепление

**corduroy** ['kɔ:dərɔɪ] n вельвет

**core** [kɔ:r] n (of fruit) сердцевина; (of problem) суть f ♦ vt вырезать (вырезать pf) сердцевину +gen

**coriander** [kɔrɪ'ændər] n (spice) кинза, кориандр

**cork** [kɔ:k] n пробка; **~screw** n штопор

**corn** [kɔ:n] n (BRIT) зерно; (US: maize) кукуруза; (on foot) мозоль f; **~ on the cob** початок кукурузы

**corner** ['kɔ:nər] n угол; (SPORT: also: ~ **kick**) угловой m adj (удар)

**cornflour** ['kɔːnflauəʳ] n (BRIT)
кукурузная мука

**coronary** ['kɔrənəri] n (also: ~
**thrombosis**) коронарный
тромбоз

**coronation** [kɔrə'neɪʃən] n
коронация

**coroner** ['kɔrənəʳ] n (LAW)
коронер (судья, расследующий
причины смерти, происшедшей
при подозрительных
обстоятельствах)

**corporal** ['kɔːpərl] adj: ~
**punishment** телесное наказание

**corporate** ['kɔːpərɪt] adj
корпорационный; (ownership)
общий; (identity) корпоративный

**corporation** [kɔːpə'reɪʃən] n (COMM)
корпорация

**corps** [kɔːʳ] (pl ~) n (also MIL)
корпус

**corpse** [kɔːps] n труп

**correct** [kə'rekt] adj правильный;
(proper) соответствующий ♦ vt
исправлять (исправить pf);
(exam) проверять (проверить pf);
**~ion** [kə'rekʃən] n исправление;
(mistake corrected) поправка

**correspond** [kɔrɪs'pɔnd] vi: to ~
(with) (write) переписываться
(impf) (с +instr); (tally)
согласовываться (impf) (с +instr);
(equate): to ~ (to)
соответствовать (impf) (+dat);
**~ence** n (letters) переписка; (: in
business) корреспонденция;
(relationship) соотношение; **~ent**
n (PRESS) корреспондент(ка)

**corridor** ['kɔrɪdɔːʳ] n коридор; (in
train) проход

**corrosion** [kə'rəuʒən] n (damage)
ржавчина

**corrugated** ['kɔrəgeɪtɪd] adj
рифлёный

**corrupt** [kə'rʌpt] adj продажный,
коррумпированный ♦ vt

развращать (развратить pf);
**~ion** [kə'rʌpʃən] n коррупция,
продажность f

**cosmetic** [kɔz'metɪk] n (usu pl)
косметика

**cosmopolitan** [kɔzmə'pɔlɪtn] adj
(place) космополитический

**cost** [kɔst] (pt, pp ~) n (price)
стоимость f ♦ vt стоить (impf); (pt,
pp **~ed**; find out cost of )
рассчитывать (рассчитать pf)
стоимость +gen; **~s** npl (COMM)
расходы mpl; (LAW) судебные
издержки fpl; **how much does it
~?** сколько это стоит?; **to ~ sb
sth** (time, job) стоить (impf) кому-н
чего-н; **at all ~s** любой ценой;
**~ly** adj (expensive)
дорогостоящий; **~ of living** n
стоимость f жизни

**costume** ['kɔstjuːm] n костюм;
(BRIT : also: **swimming ~**)
купальник, купальный костюм

**cosy** ['kəuzi] (US **cozy**) adj (room,
atmosphere) уютный

**cot** [kɔt] n (BRIT) детская кроватка;
(US: camp bed) койка; **~ death** n
внезапная смерть здорового
младенца во сне

**cottage** ['kɔtɪdʒ] n коттедж

**cotton** ['kɔtn] n (fabric) хлопок,
хлопчатобумажная ткань f;
(thread) (швейная) нитка; **~
wool** n (BRIT) вата

**couch** [kautʃ] n тахта, диван

**cough** [kɔf] vi кашлять (impf) ♦ n
кашель m

**could** [kud] pt of **can²**; **~n't**
['kudnt] = **could not**; see **can²**

**council** ['kaunsl] n совет; **city or
town ~** муниципалитет,
городской совет; **~ house** n
(BRIT) дом, принадлежащий
муниципалитету; **~lor** n член
муниципалитета; **~ tax** n (BRIT)
муниципальный налог

**council estate** - муниципа́льный жило́й микрорайо́н. Дома́ в таки́х райо́нах стро́ятся на сре́дства муниципалите́та. Типовы́е постро́йки включа́ют многоэта́жные дома́ и́ли ряд одноти́пных примыка́ющих друг к дру́гу домо́в с сада́ми.

**counsel** ['kaunsl] n (advice) сове́т; (lawyer) адвока́т ♦ vt: **to ~ sth/sb to do** сове́товать (посове́товать pf) что-н/кому́-н +infin; **~lor** n сове́тник; (US: lawyer) адвока́т

**count** [kaunt] vt счита́ть (посчита́ть pf); (include) счита́ть (impf) ♦ vi счита́ть (сосчита́ть pf); (qualify) счита́ться (impf); (matter) име́ть (impf) значе́ние ♦ n подсчёт; (level) у́ровень m; **~ on** vt fus рассчи́тывать (impf) на +acc; **~down** n обра́тный счёт

**counter** ['kauntər] n (in shop, café) прила́вок; (in bank, post office) сто́йка; (in game) фи́шка ♦ vt опроверга́ть (опрове́ргнуть pf) ♦ adv: **~ to** в противове́с +dat

**counterpart** ['kauntəpa:t] n (of person) колле́га m/f

**countless** ['kauntlis] adj несчётный, бесчи́сленный

**country** ['kʌntri] n страна́; (native land) ро́дина; (rural area) дере́вня; **~side** n дере́вня, се́льская ме́стность f

**county** ['kaunti] n гра́фство

**county** - гра́фство. В Великобрита́нии, Ирла́ндии и США э́то - администрати́вно-территориа́льная едини́ца эквивале́нтная о́бласти и управля́емая ме́стным прави́тельством.

**coup** [ku:] (pl **~s**) n (also: **~ d'état**) госуда́рственный переворо́т

**couple** ['kʌpl] n (married couple) (супру́жеская) па́ра; (of people, things) па́ра; **a ~ of** (some) па́ра +gen

**coupon** ['ku:pɔn] n (voucher) купо́н; (form) тало́н

**courage** ['kʌrɪdʒ] n сме́лость f, хра́брость f; **~ous** [kə'reɪdʒəs] adj сме́лый, хра́брый

**courgette** [kuə'ʒɛt] n (BRIT) молодо́й кабачо́к

**courier** ['kurɪər] n курье́р; (for tourists) руководи́тель m гру́ппы

**course** [kɔ:s] n курс; (of events, time) ход; (of action) направле́ние; (of river) тече́ние; **first/last ~** пе́рвое/сла́дкое блю́до; **of ~** коне́чно

**court** [kɔ:t] n (LAW) суд; (SPORT) корт; (royal) двор; **to take sb to ~** подава́ть (пода́ть pf) на кого́-н в суд

**courteous** ['kə:tɪəs] adj ве́жливый

**courtesy** ['kə:təsi] n ве́жливость f; **(by) ~ of** благодаря́ любе́зности +gen

**courtroom** ['kɔ:trum] n зал суда́

**courtyard** ['kɔ:tja:d] n вну́тренний двор

**cousin** ['kʌzn] n (also: **first ~**: male) двою́родный брат; (: female) двою́родная сестра́

**cove** [kəuv] n (bay) бу́хта

**cover** ['kʌvər] vt закрыва́ть (закры́ть pf); (with cloth) укрыва́ть (укры́ть pf); (distance) покрыва́ть (покры́ть pf); (topic) рассма́тривать (рассмотре́ть pf); (include) охва́тывать (охвати́ть pf); (PRESS) освеща́ть (освети́ть pf) ♦ n (for furniture, machinery) чехо́л; (of book etc) обло́жка; (shelter)

укры́тие; **~s** npl ( for bed)
постельное бельё ntsg; **he was
~ed in** or **with** (mud) он был
покры́т +instr; **to take ~**
укрыва́ться (укры́ться pf); **under
~** в укры́тии; **under ~ of darkness**
под покро́вом темноты́; **~ up** vt
закрыва́ть (закры́ть pf) ♦ vi (fig):
**to ~ up for sb** покрыва́ть
(покры́ть pf) кого́-н; **~age** n
освеще́ние; **~ing** n пласт; (of
snow, dust etc) слой; (on floor)
насти́л; **~-up** n ши́рма,
прикры́тие

**cow** [kau] n (also inf!) коро́ва (also !)
**coward** ['kauəd] n трус(и́ха); **~ice**
['kauədɪs] n тру́сость f; **~ly** adj
трусли́вый
**cowboy** ['kaubɔɪ] n ковбо́й
**coy** [kɔɪ] adj (shy) засте́нчивый
**cozy** ['kəuzɪ] adj (US) = **cosy**
**crab** [kræb] n краб
**crack** [kræk] n (noise) треск; (gap)
щель f; (in dish, wall) тре́щина ♦ vt
(whip, twig) щёлкать (щёлкнуть
pf) +instr; (dish etc) раска́лывать
(расколо́ть pf); (nut) коло́ть
(расколо́ть pf); (problem) реша́ть
(реши́ть pf); (code) разга́дывать
(разгада́ть pf); (joke) отпуска́ть
(отпусти́ть pf)
**crackle** ['krækl] vi потре́скивать
(impf)
**cradle** ['kreɪdl] n (crib) колыбе́ль
f
**craft** [krɑːft] n (trade) ремесло́;
(boat: pl inv) кора́бль f; **~sman**
(irreg) n реме́сленник;
**~smanship** n (quality) вы́делка;
(skill) мастерство́; **~y** adj лука́вый
**cram** [kræm] vt: **to ~ sth with**
набива́ть (наби́ть pf) что-н +instr;
**to ~ sth into** вти́скивать
(вти́снуть pf) что-н в +acc
**cramp** [kræmp] n су́дорога; **~ed**
adj те́сный

**crane** [kreɪn] n (TECH)
(подъёмный) кран
**crank** [kræŋk] n (person) чуда́к;
(handle) заводна́я рукоя́тка
**crash** [kræʃ] n (noise) гро́хот; (of
car) ава́рия; (of plane, train)
круше́ние ♦ vt разбива́ть
(разби́ть pf) ♦ vi разбива́ться
(разби́ться pf); (two cars)
ста́лкиваться (столкну́ться pf); **~
course** n интенси́вный курс; **~
helmet** n защи́тный шлем
**crass** [kræs] adj тупо́й
**crate** [kreɪt] n деревя́нный я́щик;
( for bottles) упако́вочный я́щик
**crater** ['kreɪtəʳ] n (of volcano)
кра́тер; (of bomb) воро́нка
**crave** [kreɪv] vti: **to ~ sth** or **for sth**
жа́ждать (impf) чего́-н
**crawl** [krɔːl] vi (move) по́лзать/
ползти́ (impf); (SPORT) кроль f
**craze** [kreɪz] n пова́льное
увлече́ние
**crazy** ['kreɪzɪ] adj сумасше́дший;
**he's ~ about skiing** (inf) он
поме́шан на лы́жах; **to go ~**
помеша́ться (pf)
**cream** [kriːm] n сли́вки pl;
(cosmetic) крем ♦ adj (colour)
кре́мовый; **~y** adj (taste)
сли́вочный
**crease** [kriːs] n (fold) скла́дка; (: in
trousers) стре́лка; (in dress, on
brow) морщи́на
**create** [kriː'eɪt] vt (impression)
создава́ть (созда́ть pf); (invent)
твори́ть (impf), создава́ть
(созда́ть pf)
**creation** [kriː'eɪʃən] n созда́ние;
(REL) сотворе́ние
**creative** [kriː'eɪtɪv] adj тво́рческий
**creature** ['kriːtʃəʳ] n (animal)
существо́; (person) созда́ние
**crèche** [krɛʃ] n (де́тские) я́сли pl
**credentials** [krɪ'dɛnʃlz] npl
(references) квалифика́ция fsg; ( for

*identity*) рекоменда́тельное письмо́ *ntsg*, рекоменда́ция *fsg*

**credibility** [krɛdɪˈbɪlɪtɪ] *n* (*see adj*) правдоподо́бность *f*; авторите́т

**credible** [ˈkrɛdɪbl] *adj* вероя́тный, правдоподо́бный; (*person*) авторите́тный

**credit** [ˈkrɛdɪt] *n* (*COMM*) креди́т; (*recognition*) до́лжное *nt adj* ♦ *vt* (*COMM*) кредитова́ть (*impf/pf*); **to ~ sb with sth** (*sense*) припи́сывать (приписа́ть *pf*) кому́-н что-н; **~s** *npl* (*CINEMA, TV*) ти́тры *mpl*; ~ **card** *n* креди́тная ка́рточка; **~or** *n* кредито́р

**creed** [kriːd] *n* (*REL*) (веро)уче́ние

**creek** [kriːk] *n* у́зкий зали́в; (*US: stream*) руче́й

**creep** [kriːp] (*pt, pp* **crept**) *vi* (*person, animal*) кра́сться (*impf*) ♦ *n* (*inf*) подхали́м(ка); ~**y** *adj* жу́ткий

**crept** [krɛpt] *pt, pp of* **creep**

**crescent** [ˈkrɛsnt] *n* полуме́сяц

**cress** [krɛs] *n* кресс-сала́т

**crest** [krɛst] *n* (*of hill*) гре́бень *m*; (*of bird*) хохоло́к, гребешо́к; (*coat of arms*) герб

**crew** [kruː] *n* экипа́ж; (*TV, CINEMA*) съёмочная гру́ппа

**cricket** [ˈkrɪkɪt] *n* (*game*) кри́кет; (*insect*) сверчо́к

**crime** [kraɪm] *n* преступле́ние; (*illegal activity*) престу́пность *f*

**criminal** [ˈkrɪmɪnl] *n* престу́пник(ица) ♦ *adj* (*illegal*) престу́пный

**crimson** [ˈkrɪmzn] *adj* мали́новый, тёмно-кра́сный

**cripple** [ˈkrɪpl] *n* кале́ка *m/f* ♦ *vt* (*person*) кале́чить (искале́чить *pf*)

**crisis** [ˈkraɪsɪs] (*pl* **crises**) *n* кри́зис

**crisp** [krɪsp] *adj* (*food*) хрустя́щий; (*weather*) све́жий; (*reply*) чёткий; ~**s** *npl* (*BRIT*) чи́псы *pl*

**criterion** [kraɪˈtɪərɪən] (*pl* **criteria**) *n* крите́рий

**critic** [ˈkrɪtɪk] *n* кри́тик; ~**al** *adj* крити́ческий; (*person, opinion*) крити́чный; **he is ~al** (*MED*) он в крити́ческом состоя́нии; ~**ally** *adv* (*speak, look*) крити́чески; ~**ism** [ˈkrɪtɪsɪzəm] *n* кри́тика; (*of book, play*) крити́ческий разбо́р; ~**ize** [ˈkrɪtɪsaɪz] *vt* критикова́ть (*impf*)

**Croatia** [krəʊˈeɪʃə] *n* Хорва́тия

**crockery** [ˈkrɔkərɪ] *n* посу́да

**crocodile** [ˈkrɔkədaɪl] *n* (*ZOOL*) крокоди́л

**crocus** [ˈkrəʊkəs] *n* шафра́н

**crook** [krʊk] *n* (*criminal*) жу́лик; ~**ed** [ˈkrʊkɪd] *adj* криво́й; (*dishonest*) жуликова́тый; (*business*) жу́льнический

**crop** [krɔp] *n* (*сельско-хозя́йственная*) культу́ра; (*harvest*) урожа́й; (*also*: **riding ~**) плеть *f*

**cross** [krɔs] *n* крест; (*mark*) кре́стик; (*BIO*) по́месь *f* ♦ *vt* пересека́ть (пересе́чь *pf*), переходи́ть (перейти́ *pf*); (*cheque*) кросси́ровать (*impf/pf*); (*arms etc*) скре́щивать (скрести́ть *pf*) ♦ *adj* серди́тый; ~ **out** *vt* вычёркивать (вы́черкнуть *pf*); ~**ing** *n* перепра́ва; (*also*: **pedestrian crossing**) перехо́д; ~**roads** *n* перекрёсток; ~ **section** *n* (*of population*) про́филь *m*; (*of object*) попере́чное сече́ние; ~**word** *n* кроссво́рд

**crotch** [krɔtʃ] *n* проме́жность *f*; **the trousers are tight in the ~** брю́ки жмут в шагу́

**crouch** [krautʃ] *vi* приседа́ть (присе́сть *pf*)

**crow** [krəʊ] *n* (*bird*) воро́на

**crowd** [kraud] *n* толпа́; ~**ed** *adj* (*area*) перенаселённый; **the room**

**was ~ed** комната была полна людей

**crown** [kraun] n корона; (of head) макушка; (of hill) вершина; (of tooth) коронка ♦ vt короновать (impf/pf); **the Crown** (Британская) Корона

**crucial** ['kru:ʃl] adj решающий; (work) важный

**crucifixion** [kru:sɪ'fɪkʃən] n распятие (на кресте)

**crude** [kru:d] adj (materials) сырой; (fig: basic) примитивный; (: vulgar) грубый

**cruel** ['kruəl] adj жестокий; **~ty** n жестокость f

**cruise** [kru:z] n круиз ♦ vi крейсировать (impf)

**crumb** [krʌm] n (of cake etc) крошка

**crumble** ['krʌmbl] vt крошить (раскрошить pf) ♦ vi осыпаться (осыпаться pf); (fig) рушиться (рухнуть pf)

**crunch** [krʌntʃ] vt (food etc) грызть (разгрызть pf) ♦ n (fig): **the ~** критический or решающий момент; **~y** adj хрустящий

**crusade** [kru:'seɪd] n (campaign) крестовый поход

**crush** [krʌʃ] vt (squash) выжимать (выжать pf); (crumple) мять (смять pf); (defeat) сокрушать (сокрушить pf); (upset) уничтожать (уничтожить pf) ♦ n (crowd) давка; **to have a ~ on sb** сходить (impf) с ума по кому-н

**crust** [krʌst] n корка; (of earth) кора

**crutch** [krʌtʃ] n (MED) костыль m

**crux** [krʌks] n суть f

**cry** [kraɪ] vi плакать (impf); (also: ~ **out**) кричать (крикнуть pf) ♦ n крик

**crypt** [krɪpt] n склеп

**cryptic** ['krɪptɪk] adj загадочный

**crystal** ['krɪstl] n (glass) хрусталь; (CHEM) кристалл

**cub** [kʌb] n детёныш

**Cuba** ['kju:bə] n Куба

**cube** [kju:b] n (also MATH) куб ♦ vt возводить (возвести pf) в куб

**cubic** ['kju:bɪk] adj кубический

**cubicle** ['kju:bɪkl] n (at pool) кабинка

**cuckoo** ['kuku:] n кукушка

**cucumber** ['kju:kʌmbər] n огурец

**cuddle** ['kʌdl] vt обнимать (обнять pf) ♦ vi обниматься (обняться pf) ♦ n ласка

**cue** [kju:] n кий; (THEAT) реплика

**cuff** [kʌf] n (of sleeve) манжета; (US: of trousers) отворот; (blow) шлепок; **off the ~** экспромтом

**cuisine** [kwɪ'zi:n] n кухня (кушанья)

**cul-de-sac** ['kʌldəsæk] n тупик

**culinary** ['kʌlɪnərɪ] adj кулинарный

**culmination** [kʌlmɪ'neɪʃən] n кульминация

**culprit** ['kʌlprɪt] n (person) виновник(ница)

**cult** [kʌlt] n (also REL) культ

**cultivate** ['kʌltɪveɪt] vt (crop, feeling) культивировать (impf); (land) возделывать (impf)

**cultural** ['kʌltʃərəl] adj культурный

**culture** ['kʌltʃər] n культура; **~d** adj культурный

**cumbersome** ['kʌmbəsəm] adj громоздкий

**cumulative** ['kju:mjulətɪv] adj (effect, result) суммарный; (process) нарастающий

**cunning** ['kʌnɪŋ] n хитрость f ♦ adj (crafty) хитрый

**cup** [kʌp] n чашка; (as prize) кубок; (of bra) чашечка

**cupboard** ['kʌbəd] n шкаф

**curate** ['kjuərɪt] n викарий

**curator** [kjuə'reɪtər] n хранитель m

**curb** [kə:b] vt (powers etc)

обуздывать (обуздать *pf*) ♦ *n* (*US: kerb*) бордюр

**cure** [kjuə⁺] *vt* вылечивать (вылечить *pf*); (*CULIN*) обрабатывать (обработать *pf*) ♦ *n* лекарство; (*solution*) средство

**curfew** ['kə:fju:] *n* комендантский час

**curiosity** [kjuərɪ'ɔsɪtɪ] *n* (*see adj*) любопытство; любознательность *f*

**curious** ['kjuərɪəs] *adj* любопытный; (*interested*) любознательный

**curl** [kə:l] *n* (*of hair*) локон, завиток ♦ *vt* (*hair*) завивать (завить *pf*); (: *tightly*) закручивать (закрутить *pf*) ♦ *vi* (*hair*) виться (*impf*); ~**y** *adj* вьющийся

**currant** ['kʌrnt] *n* (*dried grape*) изюминка; ~**s** (*dried grapes*) кишмиш

**currency** ['kʌrnsɪ] *n* валюта

**current** ['kʌrnt] *n* (*of air, water*) поток; (*ELEC*) ток ♦ *adj* (*present*) текущий, современный; (*accepted*) общепринятый; ~ **account** *n* (*BRIT*) текущий счёт; ~ **affairs** *npl* текущие события *ntpl*; ~**ly** *adv* в данный *or* настоящий момент

**curriculum** [kə'rɪkjuləm] (*pl* ~**s** *or* **curricula**) *n* (*SCOL*) (учебная) программа

**curriculum vitae** [kərɪkjuləm'vi:taɪ] *n* (*BRIT*) автобиография

**curry** ['kʌrɪ] *n* блюдо с кэрри

**curse** [kə:s] *n* проклятие; (*swearword*) ругательство

**curt** [kə:t] *adj* резкий

**curtain** ['kə:tn] *n* занавес; (*light*) занавеска

**curve** [kə:v] *n* изгиб

**cushion** ['kuʃən] *n* подушка ♦ *vt* смягчать (смягчить *pf*)

**custard** ['kʌstəd] *n* заварной крем

**custody** ['kʌstədɪ] *n* опека; **to take into ~** брать (взять *pf*) под стражу

**custom** ['kʌstəm] *n* (*traditional*) традиция; (*convention*) обычай; (*habit*) привычка; ~**ary** *adj* обычный, традиционный

**customer** ['kʌstəmə⁺] *n* (*of shop*) покупатель(ница) *m(f)*; (*of business*) клиент, заказчик

**customs** ['kʌstəmz] *npl* таможня *fsg*

**cut** [kʌt] (*pt, pp* ~) *vt* (*bread, meat*) резать (разрезать *pf*); (*hand, knee*) резать (порезать *pf*); (*grass, hair*) стричь (постричь *pf*); (*text*) сокращать (сократить *pf*); (*spending, supply*) урезывать (урезать *pf*); (*prices*) снижать (снизить *pf*) ♦ *vi* резать (*impf*) ♦ *n* (*in skin*) порез; (*in salary, spending*) снижение; (*of meat*) кусок; ~ **down** *vt* (*tree*) срубать (срубить *pf*); (*consumption*) сокращать (сократить *pf*); ~ **off** *vt* отрезать (отрезать *pf*); (*electricity, water*) отключать (отключить *pf*); (*TEL*) разъединять (разъединить *pf*); ~ **out** *vt* (*remove*) вырезать (вырезать *pf*); (*stop*) прекращать (прекратить *pf*); ~ **up** *vt* разрезать (разрезать *pf*)

**cute** [kju:t] *adj* (*sweet*) милый, прелестный

**cutlery** ['kʌtlərɪ] *n* столовый прибор

**cut-price** (*US* **cut-rate**) *adj* по сниженной цене

**cut-rate** *adj* (*US*) = **cut-price**

**cutting** ['kʌtɪŋ] *adj* (*edge*) острый; (*remark etc*) язвительный ♦ *n* (*BRIT : PRESS*) вырезка; (*from plant*) черенок

**CV** *n abbr* (*BRIT*) = **curriculum vitae**

**cybercafé** ['saɪbəkæfeɪ] *n*

интернет-кафе́ nt ind
**cyberspace** ['saɪbəspeɪs] n
киберпростра́нство
**cycle** ['saɪkl] n цикл; (bicycle)
велосипе́д
**cyclone** ['saɪkləʊn] n цикло́н
**cylinder** ['sɪlɪndər] n цили́ндр; (of
gas) балло́н
**cymbals** ['sɪmblz] npl таре́лки fpl
**cynical** ['sɪnɪkl] adj цини́чный
**cynicism** ['sɪnɪsɪzəm] n цини́зм
**Cyprus** ['saɪprəs] n Кипр
**cystitis** [sɪs'taɪtɪs] n цисти́т
**Czech** [tʃɛk] adj че́шский ♦ n чех
(че́шка); **~ Republic** n: **the ~**
**Republic** Че́шская Респу́блика

# D, d

**D** [diː] n (MUS) ре
**dab** [dæb] vt (eyes, wound)
промокну́ть (pf); (paint, cream)
наноси́ть (нанести́ pf)
**dad** [dæd] n (inf) па́па m, па́почка
m; **~dy** n (inf) = **dad**
**daffodil** ['dæfədɪl] n нарци́сс
**daft** [dɑːft] adj (ideas) дура́цкий;
(person) чо́кнутый
**dagger** ['dægər] n кинжа́л
**daily** ['deɪlɪ] adj (dose) су́точный;
(routine) повседне́вный; (wages)
дневно́й ♦ n (also: **~ paper**)
ежедне́вная газе́та ♦ adv
ежедне́вно
**dainty** ['deɪntɪ] adj изя́щный
**dairy** ['dɛərɪ] n (BRIT: shop)
моло́чный магази́н; (for making
butter) маслоде́льня; (for making
cheese) сырова́рня; **~ farm**
моло́чная фе́рма; **~ products**
моло́чные проду́кты mpl
**daisy** ['deɪzɪ] n маргари́тка
**dam** [dæm] n да́мба ♦ vt
перекрыва́ть (перекры́ть pf)
да́мбой

**damage** ['dæmɪdʒ] n (harm)
уще́рб; (dents etc) поврежде́ние;
(fig) вред ♦ vt поврежда́ть
(повреди́ть pf); (fig) вреди́ть
(повреди́ть pf) +dat; **~s** npl (LAW)
компенса́ция fsg
**damn** [dæm] vt осужда́ть (осуди́ть
pf) ♦ adj (inf: also: **~ed**)
прокля́тый ♦ n (inf): **I don't give**
**a ~** мне плева́ть; **~ (it)!** чёрт
возьми́ or побери́!; **~ing** adj
обличи́тельный
**damp** [dæmp] adj (building, wall)
сыро́й; (cloth) вла́жный ♦ n
сы́рость f ♦ vt (also: **~en**)
сма́чивать (смочи́ть pf); (: fig)
охлажда́ть (охлади́ть pf)
**damson** ['dæmzən] n терносли́ва
**dance** [dɑːns] n та́нец; (social event)
та́нцы mpl ♦ vi танцева́ть (impf);
**~r** n танцо́вщик(ица); (for fun)
танцо́р
**dandelion** ['dændɪlaɪən] n
одува́нчик
**danger** ['deɪndʒər] n опа́сность f;
**"~!"** "опа́сно!"; **in/out of ~** в/вне
опа́сности; **he is in ~ of losing his**
**job** ему́ грози́т поте́ря рабо́ты;
**~ous** adj опа́сный
**Danish** ['deɪnɪʃ] adj да́тский ♦ npl:
**the ~** датча́не
**dare** [dɛər] vt: **to ~ sb to do**
вызыва́ть (вы́звать pf) кого́-н
+infin ♦ vi: **to ~ (to) do** сметь
(посме́ть pf) +infin; **I ~ say** сме́ю
заме́тить
**daring** ['dɛərɪŋ] adj (audacious)
де́рзкий; (bold) сме́лый
**dark** [dɑːk] adj тёмный;
(complexion) сму́глый ♦ n: **in the ~**
в темноте́; **~ blue** etc тёмно-
си́ний etc; **after ~** по́сле
наступле́ния темноты́; **~ness** n
темнота́, **~room** n тёмная
ко́мната, прояви́тельная
лаборато́рия

**darling** ['dɑːlɪŋ] *adj* дорого́й(а́я) *m(f) adj*

**dart** [dɑːt] *n (in game)* дро́тик *(для игры́ в дарт); (in sewing)* вы́тачка; **~s** *n* дарт

**dash** [dæʃ] *n (drop)* ка́пелька; *(sign)* тире́ *nt ind* ♦ *vt (throw)* швыря́ть (швырну́ть *pf); (shatter: hopes)* разруша́ть (разру́шить *pf*), разбива́ть (разби́ть *pf*) ♦ *vi:* **to ~ towards** рвану́ться *(pf)* к +*dat*

**dashboard** ['dæʃbɔːd] *n (AUT)* прибо́рная пане́ль *f*

**data** ['deɪtə] *npl* да́нные *pl adj;* **~base** *n* ба́за да́нных

**date** [deɪt] *n (day)* число́, да́та; *(with friend)* свида́ние; *(fruit)* фи́ник ♦ *vt* дати́ровать *(impf/pf); (person)* встреча́ться *(impf)* с +*instr;* **~ of birth** да́та рожде́ния; **to ~** на сего́дняшний день; **out of ~** устаре́лый; *(expired)* просро́ченный; **up to ~** совреме́нный; **~d** *adj* устаре́лый

**daughter** ['dɔːtər] *n* дочь *f;* **~-in-law** *n* сноха́

**daunting** ['dɔːntɪŋ] *adj* устраша́ющий

**dawn** [dɔːn] *n (of day)* рассве́т

**day** [deɪ] *n (period)* су́тки *pl,* день *m; (daylight)* день *m; (heyday)* вре́мя *nt;* **the ~ before** накану́не; **the ~ after** на сле́дующий день; **the ~ after tomorrow** послеза́втра; **the ~ before yesterday** позавчера́; **the following ~** на сле́дующий день; **by ~** днём; **~light** *n* дневно́й свет; **~ return** *n (BRIT)* обра́тный биле́т *(действи́тельный в тече́ние одного́ дня);* **~time** *n* день *m*

**daze** [deɪz] *vt (stun)* ошеломля́ть (ошеломи́ть *pf*) ♦ *n:* **in a ~** в тума́не

**dazzle** ['dæzl] *vt (blind)* ослепля́ть (ослепи́ть *pf*)

**DC** *abbr (= direct current)* постоя́нный ток

**dead** [dɛd] *adj* мёртвый; *(arm, leg)* онеме́лый ♦ *adv (inf: completely)* абсолю́тно; *(inf: directly)* пря́мо ♦ *npl:* **the ~** мёртвые *pl adj; (in accident, war)* поги́бшие *pl adj;* **the battery is ~** батаре́йка се́ла; **the telephone is ~** телефо́н отключи́лся; **to shoot sb ~** застрели́ть *(pf)* кого́-н; **~ tired** сме́ртельно уста́лый *or* уста́вший; **~ end** *n* тупи́к; **~line** *n* после́дний *or* преде́льный срок; **~lock** *n* тупи́к; **~ly** *adj (lethal)* смертоно́сный; **Dead Sea** *n:* **the Dead Sea** Мёртвое мо́ре

**deaf** [dɛf] *adj (totally)* глухо́й

**deal** [diːl] *(pt, pp* **~t***) n (agreement)* сде́лка ♦ *vt (blow)* наноси́ть (нанести́ *pf); (cards)* сдава́ть (сдать *pf*); **a great ~ (of)** о́чень мно́го (+*gen*); **~ in** *vt fus (COMM, drugs)* торгова́ть *(impf)* +*instr;* **~ with** *vt fus* име́ть *(impf)* де́ло с +*instr; (problem)* реша́ть (реши́ть *pf); (subject)* занима́ться (заня́ться *pf*) +*instr;* **~t** [dɛlt] *pt, pp of* **deal**

**dean** [diːn] *n (SCOL)* дека́н

**dear** [dɪər] *adj* дорого́й ♦ *n:* **(my) ~** *(to man, boy)* дорого́й (мой); *(to woman, girl)* дорога́я (моя́) ♦ *excl:* **~ me!** о, Го́споди!; **Dear Sir** уважа́емый господи́н; **Dear Mrs Smith** дорога́я *or* уважа́емая ми́ссис Смит; **~ly** *adv (love)* о́чень; *(pay)* до́рого

**death** [dɛθ] *n* смерть *f;* **~ penalty** *n* сме́ртная казнь *f;* **~ toll** *n* число́ поги́бших

**debatable** [dɪ'beɪtəbl] *adj* спо́рный

**debate** [dɪ'beɪt] *n* деба́ты *pl* ♦ *vt (topic)* обсужда́ть (обсуди́ть *pf*)

**debit** ['dɛbɪt] *vt:* **to ~ a sum to sb** *or*

**to sb's account** дебетовáть *(impf/ pf)* сýмму с когó-н *or* с чьегó-н счёта; *see also* **direct debit**

**debris** ['dɛbriː] *n* облóмки *mpl*, развáлины *fpl*

**debt** [dɛt] *n (sum)* долг; **to be in ~** быть *(impf)* в долгý; **~or** *n* должни́к

**decade** ['dɛkeɪd] *n* десятилéтие

**decaffeinated** [dɪ'kæfɪneɪtɪd] *adj:* **~ coffee** кóфе без кофеи́на

**decay** [dɪ'keɪ] *n* разрушéние

**deceased** [dɪ'siːst] *n:* **the ~** покóйный(ая) *m(f) adj*

**deceit** [dɪ'siːt] *n* обмáн

**deceive** [dɪ'siːv] *vt* обмáнывать (обманýть *pf*)

**December** [dɪ'sɛmbər] *n* декáбрь *m*

**decency** ['diːsənsɪ] *n (propriety)* благопристóйность *f*

**decent** ['diːsənt] *adj (wages, meal)* прили́чный; *(behaviour, person)* порядочный

**deception** [dɪ'sɛpʃən] *n* обмáн

**deceptive** [dɪ'sɛptɪv] *adj* обмáнчивый

**decide** [dɪ'saɪd] *vt (settle)* решáть (реши́ть *pf*) ♦ *vi:* **to ~ to do/that** решáть (реши́ть *pf*) +*infin/*, что; **to ~ on** останáвливаться (останови́ться *pf*) на +*prp*; **~dly** *adv (distinctly)* несомнéнно; *(emphatically)* реши́тельно

**deciduous** [dɪ'sɪdjuəs] *adj* ли́ственный, листопáдный

**decision** [dɪ'sɪʒən] *n* решéние

**decisive** [dɪ'saɪsɪv] *adj* реши́тельный

**deck** [dɛk] *n (NAUT)* пáлуба; *(of cards)* колóда; *(also:* **record ~)** прои́грыватель *m*; **top ~** *(of bus)* вéрхний этáж; **~ chair** *n* шезлóнг

**declaration** [dɛklə'reɪʃən] *n (statement)* декларáция; *(of war)* объявлéние

**declare** [dɪ'klɛər] *vt (state)* объявлять (объяви́ть *pf*); *(for tax)* деклари́ровать *(impf/pf)*

**decline** [dɪ'klaɪn] *n (drop)* падéние; *(in strength)* упáдок; *(lessening)* уменьшéние; **to be in** *or* **on the ~** быть *(impf)* в упáдке

**décor** ['deɪkɔːr] *n* отдéлка

**decorate** ['dɛkəreɪt] *vt (room etc)* отдéлывать (отдéлать *pf*); *(adorn):* **to ~ (with)** украшáть (украсить *pf*) +*instr*

**decoration** [dɛkə'reɪʃən] *n (on tree, dress)* украшéние; *(medal)* нагрáда

**decorative** ['dɛkərətɪv] *adj* декорати́вный

**decorator** ['dɛkəreɪtər] *n* обóйщик

**decrease** ['diːkriːs] *vt* уменьшáть (умéньшить *pf*) ♦ *vi* уменьшáться (умéньшиться *pf*) ♦ *n:* **~ (in)** уменьшéние (+*gen*)

**decree** [dɪ'kriː] *n* постановлéние

**dedicate** ['dɛdɪkeɪt] *vt:* **to ~ to** посвящáть (посвяти́ть *pf*) +*dat*

**dedication** [dɛdɪ'keɪʃən] *n (devotion)* прéданность *f*; *(in book etc)* посвящéние

**deduction** [dɪ'dʌkʃən] *n (conclusion)* умозаключéние; *(subtraction)* вычитáние; *(amount)* вы́чет

**deed** [diːd] *n (feat)* деяние, постýпок; *(LAW)* акт

**deep** [diːp] *adj* глубóкий; *(voice)* ни́зкий ♦ *adv:* **the spectators stood 20 ~** зри́тели стояли в 20 рядóв; **the lake is 4 metres ~** глубинá óзера - 4 мéтра; **~ blue** *etc* тёмно-си́ний *etc*; **~en** *vi (crisis, mystery)* углубляться (углуби́ться *pf*); **~ly** *adv* глубокó; **~-sea** *cpd (fishing)* глубоковóдный; **~-sea diver** водолáз; **~-seated** *adj* закоренéлый

**deer** [dɪər] *n inv* олéнь *m*

**defeat** [dɪ'fiːt] *n* поражéние ♦ *vt*

наноси́ть (нанести́ pf)
пораже́ние +dat

**defect** ['di:fɛkt] n (in product)
дефе́кт; (of plan) недоста́ток;
**~ive** [dɪ'fɛktɪv] adj (goods)
дефе́ктный

**defence** [dɪ'fɛns] (US **defense**) n
защи́та; (MIL) оборо́на; **~less** adj
беззащи́тный

**defend** [dɪ'fɛnd] vt защища́ть
(защити́ть pf); (LAW) защища́ть
(impf); **~ant** n подсуди́мый(ая)
m(f) adj, обвиня́емый(ая) m(f) adj;
(in civil case) отве́тчик(ица); **~er** n
защи́тник

**defense** etc (US) = **defence** etc

**defensive** [dɪ'fɛnsɪv] adj (weapons,
measures) оборони́тельный;
(behaviour, manner) вызыва́ющий
♦ n: **he was on the ~** он был
гото́в к оборо́не

**defer** [dɪ'fə:ʳ] vt отсро́чивать
(отсро́чить pf)

**deference** ['dɛfərəns] n почте́ние

**defiance** [dɪ'faɪəns] n вы́зов; **in ~
of** вопреки́ +dat

**defiant** [dɪ'faɪənt] adj (person, reply)
де́рзкий; (tone) вызыва́ющий

**deficiency** [dɪ'fɪʃənsɪ] n (lack)
нехва́тка

**deficient** [dɪ'fɪʃənt] adj: **to be ~ in**
(lack) испы́тывать (impf)
недоста́ток в +prp

**deficit** ['dɛfɪsɪt] n (COMM) дефици́т

**define** [dɪ'faɪn] vt определя́ть
(определи́ть pf); (word etc) дава́ть
(дать pf) определе́ние +dat

**definite** ['dɛfɪnɪt] adj
определённый; **he was ~ about it**
его́ мне́ние на э́тот счёт бы́ло
определённым; **~ly** adv
определённо; (certainly)
несомне́нно

**definition** [dɛfɪ'nɪʃən] n (of word)
определе́ние

**definitive** [dɪ'fɪnɪtɪv] adj

оконча́тельный

**deflate** [di:'fleɪt] vt (tyre, balloon)
спуска́ть (спусти́ть pf)

**deflect** [dɪ'flɛkt] vt (shot) отража́ть
(отрази́ть pf); (criticism)
отклоня́ть (отклони́ть pf);
(attention) отвлека́ть (отвле́чь pf)

**deformed** [dɪ'fɔ:md] adj
деформи́рованный

**deft** [dɛft] adj ло́вкий

**defuse** [di:'fju:z] vt разряжа́ть
(разряди́ть pf)

**defy** [dɪ'faɪ] vt (resist) оспа́ривать
(оспо́рить pf); (fig: description etc)
не поддава́ться (impf) +dat; **to ~
sb to do** (challenge) призыва́ть
(призва́ть pf) кого́-н +infin

**degenerate** vb [dɪ'dʒɛnəreɪt] adj
[dɪ'dʒɛnərɪt] vi вырожда́ться
(вы́родиться pf) ♦ adj
вы́родившийся

**degrading** [dɪ'greɪdɪŋ] adj
унизи́тельный

**degree** [dɪ'gri:] n (extent) сте́пень f;
(unit of measurement) гра́дус;
(SCOL) (учёная) сте́пень; **by ~s**
постепе́нно; **to some~, to a
certain ~** до не́которой сте́пени

**delay** [dɪ'leɪ] vt (decision, event)
откла́дывать (отложи́ть pf);
(person, plane etc) заде́рживать
(задержа́ть pf) ♦ vi ме́длить (impf)
♦ n заде́ржка; **to be ~ed**
заде́рживаться (impf); **without ~**
незамедли́тельно

**delegate** n ['dɛlɪgɪt] vb ['dɛlɪgeɪt] n
делега́т ♦ vt (task) поруча́ть
(поручи́ть pf)

**delegation** [dɛlɪ'geɪʃən] n (group)
делега́ция; (of task) переда́ча

**deliberate** adj [dɪ'lɪbərɪt] vb
[dɪ'lɪbəreɪt] adj (intentional)
наме́ренный; (slow)
нетороплѝвый ♦ vi совеща́ться
(impf); (person) разду́мывать
(impf); **~ly** adv (see adj)

намеренно, нарочно;
неторопливо

**delicacy** ['delɪkəsɪ] *n* тонкость *f*;
( *food* ) деликатес

**delicate** ['delɪkɪt] *adj* тонкий;
( *problem* ) деликатный; ( *health* )
хрупкий

**delicatessen** [delɪkə'tɛsn] *n*
гастрономия, магазин
деликатесов

**delicious** [dɪ'lɪʃəs] *adj* очень
вкусный; ( *smell* ) восхитительный

**delight** [dɪ'laɪt] *n* ( *feeling* ) восторг
♦ *vt* радовать (порадовать *pf*); **to
take (a) ~ in** находить ( *impf* )
удовольствие в +*prp*; **~ed** *adj*: ( **to
be** ) **~ed (at** *or* **with)** (быть ( *impf* ) в
восторге (от +*gen*); **he was ~ed to
see her** он был рад видеть её;
**~ful** ♦ *adj* восхитительный

**delinquent** [dɪ'lɪŋkwənt] *adj*
преступный

**delirious** [dɪ'lɪrɪəs] *adj*: **to be ~** ( *with
fever* ) быть ( *impf* ) в бреду; ( *with
excitement* ) быть ( *impf* ) в упоении

**deliver** [dɪ'lɪvəʳ] *vt* ( *goods* )
доставлять (доставить *pf*); ( *letter* )
вручать (вручить *pf*); ( *message* )
передавать (передать *pf*);
( *speech* ) произносить
(произнести *pf*); ( *baby* )
принимать (принять *pf*); **~y** *n* ( *of
goods* ) доставка; ( *of baby* ) роды
*pl*; **to take ~y of** получать
(получить *pf*)

**deluge** ['dɛljuːdʒ] *n* ( *fig* ) лавина

**delusion** [dɪ'luːʒən] *n*
заблуждение

**demand** [dɪ'mɑːnd] *vt* требовать
(потребовать *pf*) +*gen* ♦ *n* ( *request,
claim* ) требование; ( *ECON*): **~ (for)**
спрос (на +*acc*); **to be in ~**
( *commodity* ) пользоваться ( *impf* )
спросом; **on ~** по требованию;
**~ing** *adj* ( *boss* ) требовательный;
( *child* ) трудный; ( *work: requiring*

*effort* ) тяжёлый

**demeanour** [dɪ'miːnəʳ] ( *US*
**demeanor**) *n* манера поведения

**demented** [dɪ'mɛntɪd] *adj*
помешанный

**demise** [dɪ'maɪz] *n* ( *fig* ) упадок

**demo** ['dɛməu] *n abbr* ( *inf* ) =
**demonstration**

**democracy** [dɪ'mɔkrəsɪ] *n* ( *system* )
демократия; ( *country* )
демократическая страна

**democrat** ['dɛməkræt] *n* демократ;
**Democrat** ( *US* ) член партии
демократов; **~ic** [dɛmə'krætɪk] *adj*
демократический; **Democratic
Party** ( *US* ) партия демократов

**demolish** [dɪ'mɔlɪʃ] *vt* сносить
(снести *pf*); ( *argument* )
разгромить ( *pf* )

**demolition** [dɛmə'lɪʃən] *n* ( *see vb* )
снос; разгром

**demon** ['diːmən] *n* демон

**demonstrate** ['dɛmənstreɪt] *vt*
демонстрировать
(продемонстрировать *pf*) ♦ *vi*: **to
~ (for/against)** демонстрировать
( *impf* ) (за +*acc*/против +*gen*)

**demonstration** [dɛmən'streɪʃən] *n*
демонстрация

**den** [dɛn] *n* ( *of animal, person* )
логово

**denial** [dɪ'naɪəl] *n* отрицание;
( *refusal* ) отказ

**denim** ['dɛnɪm] *n* джинсовая
ткань *f*; **~s** *npl* ( *jeans* ) джинсы *pl*

**Denmark** ['dɛnmɑːk] *n* Дания

**denote** [dɪ'nəut] *vt* ( *indicate* )
указывать (указать *pf*) на +*acc*

**denounce** [dɪ'nauns] *vt* ( *condemn* )
осуждать (осудить *pf*); ( *inform on* )
доносить (донести *pf*) на +*acc*

**dense** [dɛns] *adj* ( *smoke, foliage etc* )
густой; ( *inf: person* ) тупой; **~ly**
*adv*: **~ly populated** густо
населённый

**density** ['dɛnsɪtɪ] *n* плотность *f*;

**single/double-~ disk** диск с одина́рной/двойно́й пло́тностью

**dent** [dɛnt] n (in metal) вмя́тина ♦ vt (also: **make a ~ in:** car etc) оставля́ть (оста́вить pf) вмя́тину на +acc

**dental** ['dɛntl] adj зубно́й

**dentist** ['dɛntɪst] n зубно́й врач, стомато́лог

**dentures** ['dɛntʃəz] npl зубно́й проте́з msg

**denunciation** [dɪnʌnsɪ'eɪʃən] n осужде́ние

**deny** [dɪ'naɪ] vt отрица́ть (impf); (allegation) отверга́ть (отве́ргнуть pf); (refuse): **to ~ sb sth** отка́зывать (отказа́ть pf) кому́-н в чём-н

**deodorant** [di:'əudərənt] n дезодора́нт

**depart** [dɪ'pɑ:t] vi (person) отбыва́ть (отбы́ть pf); (bus, train) отправля́ться (отпра́виться pf); (plane) улета́ть (улете́ть pf); **to ~ from** (fig) отклоня́ться (отклони́ться pf) от +gen

**department** [dɪ'pɑ:tmənt] n (in shop) отде́л; (SCOL) отделе́ние; (POL) ве́домство, департа́мент; **~ store** n универса́льный магази́н, универма́г

**departure** [dɪ'pɑ:tʃər] n (see vb) отъе́зд; отправле́ние; вы́лет; **~ lounge** n зал вы́лета

**depend** [dɪ'pɛnd] vi: **to ~ on** зави́сеть (impf) от +gen; (trust) полага́ться (положи́ться pf) на +acc; **it ~s** смотря́ по обстоя́тельствам, как полу́чится; **~ing on ...** в зави́симости от +gen ...; **~able** adj надёжный; **~ence** n зави́симость f; **~ent** adj: **~ent (on)** зави́симый (от +gen) ♦ n иждиве́нец(нка)

**depict** [dɪ'pɪkt] vt изобража́ть

(изобрази́ть pf)

**deplorable** [dɪ'plɔ:rəbl] adj (behaviour) возмути́тельный; (conditions) плаче́вный

**deploy** [dɪ'plɔɪ] vt дислоци́ровать (impf/pf)

**deport** [dɪ'pɔ:t] vt депорти́ровать (impf/pf), высыла́ть (вы́слать pf)

**deposit** [dɪ'pɔzɪt] n (in account) депози́т, вклад; (down payment) пе́рвый взнос, зада́ток; (of ore, oil) за́лежь f ♦ vt (money) помеща́ть (помести́ть pf); (bag) сдава́ть (сдать pf); **~ account** n депози́тный счёт

**depot** ['dɛpəu] n (storehouse) склад; (for buses) парк; (for trains) депо́ nt ind; (US: station) ста́нция

**depreciation** [dɪpri:ʃɪ'eɪʃən] n обесце́нивание

**depress** [dɪ'prɛs] vt (PSYCH) подавля́ть (impf), угнета́ть (impf); **~ed** adj (person) пода́вленный, угнетённый; (prices) сни́женный; **~ed area** райо́н, пережива́ющий экономи́ческий упа́док; **~ing** adj (news, outlook) удруча́ющий; **~ion** [dɪ'prɛʃən] n депре́ссия; (METEOROLOGY) о́бласть f ни́зкого давле́ния

**deprivation** [dɛprɪ'veɪʃən] n (poverty) нужда́

**deprive** [dɪ'praɪv] vt: **to ~ sb of** лиша́ть (лиши́ть pf) кого́-н +gen; **~d** adj бе́дный; (family, child) обездо́ленный

**depth** [dɛpθ] n глубина́; **in the ~s of despair** в глубо́ком отча́янии; **to be out of one's ~** (in water) не достава́ть (impf) до дна

**deputy** ['dɛpjutɪ] n замести́тель m; (POL) депута́т ♦ cpd: **~ chairman** замести́тель председа́теля; **~ head** (BRIT: SCOL) замести́тель дире́ктора

**deranged** [dɪ'reɪndʒd] adj

психически расстроенный; **he is ~** у него расстроена психика

**derelict** ['derılıkt] *adj* заброшенный

**derive** [dı'raıv] *vt*: **to ~ (from)** (*pleasure*) получать (получить *pf*) (от +*gen*); (*benefit*) извлекать (извлечь *pf*) (из +*gen*)

**descend** [dı'sɛnd] *vt* (*stairs*) спускаться (спуститься *pf*) по +*dat*; (*hill*) спускаться (спуститься *pf*) с +*gen* ♦ *vi* (*go down*) спускаться (спуститься *pf*); **~ant** *n* потомок

**descent** [dı'sɛnt] *n* спуск; (*AVIAT*) снижение; (*origin*) происхождение

**describe** [dıs'kraıb] *vt* описывать (описать *pf*)

**description** [dıs'krıpʃən] *n* описание; (*sort*) род

**descriptive** [dıs'krıptıv] *adj* (*writing*) описательный

**desert** *n* ['dɛzət] *vb* [dı'zə:t] *n* пустыня ♦ *vt* покидать (покинуть *pf*) ♦ *vi* (*MIL*) дезертировать (*impf/pf*); **~ island** *n* необитаемый остров

**deserve** [dı'zə:v] *vt* заслуживать (заслужить *pf*)

**deserving** [dı'zə:vıŋ] *adj* достойный

**design** [dı'zaın] *n* дизайн; (*process: of dress*) моделирование; (*sketch: of building*) проект; (*pattern*) рисунок ♦ *vt* (*house, kitchen*) проектировать (спроектировать *pf*); (*product, test*) разрабатывать (разработать *pf*)

**designate** ['dɛzıgneıt] *vt* (*nominate*) назначать (назначить *pf*); (*indicate*) обозначать (обозначить *pf*)

**designer** [dı'zaınər] *n* (*also*: **fashion ~**) модельер; (*ART*) дизайнер; (*of machine*) конструктор

**desirable** [dı'zaıərəbl] *adj* (*proper*) желательный

**desire** [dı'zaıər] *n* желание ♦ *vt* (*want*) желать (*impf*)

**desk** [dɛsk] *n* (*in office, study*) (письменный) стол; (*for pupil*) парта; (*in hotel, at airport*) стойка; (*BRIT*: *also*: **cash-~**) касса; **~top** *adj* настольный

**desolate** ['dɛsəlıt] *adj* (*place*) заброшенный; (*person*) покинутый

**despair** [dıs'pɛər] *n* отчаяние ♦ *vi*: **to ~ of sth/doing** (отчаяться *pf*) в чём-н/+*infin*

**despatch** [dıs'pætʃ] *n, vt* = **dispatch**

**desperate** ['dɛspərıt] *adj* (*action, situation*) отчаянный; (*criminal*) отъявленный; **to be ~** (*person*) быть (*impf*) в отчаянии; **to be ~ to do** жаждать (*impf*) +*infin*; **to be ~ for money** крайне нуждаться (*impf*) в деньгах; **~ly** *adv* отчаянно; (*very*) чрезвычайно

**desperation** [dɛspə'reıʃən] *n* отчаяние

**despicable** [dıs'pıkəbl] *adj* презренный

**despise** [dıs'paız] *vt* презирать (*impf*)

**despite** [dıs'paıt] *prep* несмотря на +*acc*

**dessert** [dı'zə:t] *n* десерт

**destination** [dɛstı'neıʃən] *n* (*of person*) цель *f*; (*of mail*) место назначения

**destined** ['dɛstınd] *adj*: **he is ~ to do** ему суждено +*infin*; **to be ~ for** предназначаться (*impf*) для +*gen*

**destiny** ['dɛstını] *n* судьба

**destitute** ['dɛstıtju:t] *adj* обездоленный

**destroy** [dıs'trɔı] *vt* уничтожать (уничтожить *pf*), разрушать (разрушить *pf*)

**destruction** [dɪs'trʌkʃən] *n*
уничтоже́ние, разруше́ние
**destructive** [dɪs'trʌktɪv] *adj*
(*capacity, force*) разруши́тельный;
(*criticism*) сокруши́тельный;
(*emotion*) губи́тельный
**detached** [dɪ'tætʃt] *adj*
беспристра́стный; ~ **house**
особня́к
**detachment** [dɪ'tætʃmənt] *n*
отстранённость *f*; (*MIL*) отря́д
**detail** ['diːteɪl] *n* подро́бность *f*,
дета́ль *f* ♦ *vt* перечисля́ть
(перечи́слить *pf*); **in** ~ подро́бно,
в деталя́х; ~**ed** *adj* дета́льный,
подро́бный
**detain** [dɪ'teɪn] *vt* заде́рживать
(задержа́ть *pf*); (*in hospital*)
оставля́ть (оста́вить *pf*)
**detect** [dɪ'tekt] *vt* обнару́живать
(обнару́жить *pf*); (*sense*)
чу́вствовать (почу́вствовать *pf*);
~**ion** [dɪ'tekʃən] *n* (*discovery*)
обнаруже́ние; ~**ive** *n* сы́щик,
детекти́в
**detention** [dɪ'tenʃən] *n*
(*imprisonment*) содержа́ние под
стра́жей; (*arrest*) задержа́ние;
(*SCOL*): **to give sb** ~ оставля́ть
(оста́вить *pf*) кого́-н по́сле
уро́ков

**detention** - в брита́нских
шко́лах дете́й, наруша́ющих
дисципли́ну, в ка́честве
наказа́ния мо́гут оста́вить
по́сле уро́ков в шко́ле.

**deter** [dɪ'tə:r] *vt* уде́рживать
(удержа́ть *pf*)
**detergent** [dɪ'tə:dʒənt] *n* мо́ющее
сре́дство
**deteriorate** [dɪ'tɪərɪəreɪt] *vi*
ухудша́ться (уху́дшиться *pf*)
**deterioration** [dɪtɪərɪə'reɪʃən] *n*
ухудше́ние

**determination** [dɪtə:mɪ'neɪʃən] *n*
(*resolve*) реши́мость *f*;
(*establishment*) установле́ние
**determine** [dɪ'tə:mɪn] *vt* (*find out*)
устана́вливать (установи́ть *pf*);
(*establish, dictate*) определя́ть
(определи́ть *pf*); ~**d** *adj*
реши́тельный, волево́й; ~**d to do**
по́лный реши́мости +*infin*
**deterrent** [dɪ'terənt] *n* сре́дство
сде́рживания, сде́рживающее
сре́дство; **nuclear** ~ сре́дство
я́дерного сде́рживания
**detour** ['diːtuər] *n* (*also US*) объе́зд
**detract** [dɪ'trækt] *vi*: **to** ~ **from**
умаля́ть (умали́ть *pf*)
**detriment** ['detrɪmənt] *n*: **to the** ~
**of** в уще́рб +*dat*; ~**al** [detrɪ'mentl]
*adj*: ~**al to** вре́дный для +*gen*
**devaluation** [diːvælju'eɪʃən] *n*
(*ECON*) девальва́ция
**devalue** ['diː'væljuː] *vt* (*ECON*)
обесце́нивать (обесце́нить *pf*);
(*person, work*) недооце́нивать
(недооцени́ть *pf*)
**devastating** ['devəsteɪtɪŋ] *adj*
(*weapon, storm*) разруши́тельный;
(*news, effect*) ошеломля́ющий
**develop** [dɪ'veləp] *vt* (*idea, industry*)
развива́ть (разви́ть *pf*); (*plan,
resource*) разраба́тывать
(разрабо́тать *pf*); (*land*)
застра́ивать (застро́ить *pf*);
(*PHOT*) проявля́ть (прояви́ть *pf*)
♦ *vi* (*evolve, advance*) развива́ться
(разви́ться *pf*); (*appear*)
проявля́ться (прояви́ться *pf*);
~**ment** *n* разви́тие; (*of resources*)
разрабо́тка; (*of land*) застро́йка
**deviation** [diːvɪ'eɪʃən] *n*: ~ **(from)**
отклоне́ние (от +*gen*)
**device** [dɪ'vaɪs] *n* (*apparatus*)
устро́йство, прибо́р
**devil** ['devl] *n* дья́вол, чёрт
**devious** ['diːvɪəs] *adj* (*person*)
лука́вый

**devise** [dɪ'vaɪz] vt разраба́тывать (разрабо́тать pf)

**devoid** [dɪ'vɔɪd] adj: ~ of лишённый +gen

**devolution** [di:və'lu:ʃən] n переда́ча вла́сти (ме́стным о́рганам)

**devote** [dɪ'vəut] vt: to ~ sth to посвяща́ть (посвяти́ть pf) что-н +dat; ~d adj (admirer, partner) пре́данный; his book is ~d to Scotland его́ кни́га посвящена́ Шотла́ндии

**devotion** [dɪ'vəuʃən] n пре́данность f; (REL) поклоне́ние

**devout** [dɪ'vaut] adj (REL) благочести́вый

**dew** [dju:] n роса́

**diabetes** [daɪə'bi:ti:z] n диабе́т

**diabetic** [daɪə'bɛtɪk] n диабе́тик

**diabolical** [daɪə'bɔlɪkl] adj (inf) жу́ткий

**diagnose** [daɪəg'nəuz] vt (illness) диагности́ровать (impf/pf); (problem) определя́ть (определи́ть pf)

**diagnosis** [daɪəg'nəusɪs] (pl **diagnoses**) n диа́гноз

**diagonal** [daɪ'ægənl] adj диагона́льный

**diagram** ['daɪəgræm] n схе́ма

**dial** ['daɪəl] n (of clock) цифербла́т; (of radio) регуля́тор настро́йки ♦ vt (number) набира́ть (набра́ть pf)

**dialect** ['daɪəlɛkt] n диале́кт

**dialling tone** ['daɪəlɪŋ-] (US **dial tone**) n непреры́вный гудо́к

**dialogue** ['daɪəlɔg] (US **dialog**) n диало́г

**dial tone** n (US) = **dialling tone**

**diameter** [daɪ'æmɪtər] n диа́метр

**diamond** ['daɪəmənd] n алма́з; (cut diamond) бриллиа́нт; (shape) ромб; ~s npl (CARDS) бу́бны fpl

**diaper** ['daɪəpər] n (US) подгу́зник

**diaphragm** ['daɪəfræm] n диафра́гма

**diarrhoea** [daɪə'ri:ə] (US **diarrhea**) n поно́с

**diary** ['daɪərɪ] n (journal) дневни́к; (engagements book) ежедне́вник

**dice** [daɪs] npl of **die**; (in game) ку́бик ♦ vt ре́зать (наре́зать pf) ку́биками

**dictate** [dɪk'teɪt] vt диктова́ть (продиктова́ть pf)

**dictator** [dɪk'teɪtər] n дикта́тор; ~ship n диктату́ра

**dictionary** ['dɪkʃənrɪ] n слова́рь m

**did** [dɪd] pt of **do**

**didn't** ['dɪdnt] = **did not**

**die** [daɪ] vi (person, emotion) умира́ть (умере́ть pf); (smile, light) угаса́ть (уга́снуть pf); to be dying for sth/to do до сме́рти хоте́ть (impf) чего́-н/+infin

**diesel** ['di:zl] n ди́зель m; (also: ~ oil) ди́зельное то́пливо

**diet** ['daɪət] n дие́та

**differ** ['dɪfər] vi: to ~ (from) отлича́ться (impf) (от +gen); (disagree): to ~ about расходи́ться (разойти́сь pf) в вопро́се +gen; ~ence n разли́чие; (in size, age) ра́зница; (disagreement) разногла́сие; ~ent adj друго́й, ино́й; (various) разли́чный, ра́зный; to be ~ent from отлича́ться (impf) от +gen; ~entiate [dɪfə'rɛnʃɪeɪt] vi: to ~entiate (between) проводи́ть (провести́ pf) разли́чие (ме́жду +instr); ~ently adv (otherwise) ина́че, по-друго́му; (in different ways) по-ра́зному

**difficult** ['dɪfɪkəlt] adj тру́дный, тяжёлый; ~y n тру́дность f, затрудне́ние

**diffuse** [dɪ'fju:s] vt (information) распространя́ть (распространи́ть pf)

**dig** [dɪg] (*pt, pp* **dug**) *vt* (*hole*) копа́ть (вы́копать *pf*), рыть (вы́рыть *pf*); (*garden*) копа́ть (вскопа́ть *pf*) ♦ *n* (*prod*) толчо́к; (*excavation*) раско́пки *fpl*; **to ~ one's nails into** впива́ться (впи́ться *pf*) ногтя́ми в +*acc*; **~ up** *vt* (*plant*) выка́пывать (вы́копать *pf*); (*information*) раска́пывать (раскопа́ть *pf*)

**digest** [daɪˈdʒɛst] *vt* (*food*) перева́ривать (перевари́ть *pf*); (*facts*) усва́ивать (усво́ить *pf*); **~ion** [dɪˈdʒɛstʃən] *n* пищеваре́ние

**digit** [ˈdɪdʒɪt] *n* (*number*) ци́фра; **~al** *adj*: **~al watch** электро́нные часы́ *mpl*; **~al camera** цифрова́я ка́мера; **~al TV** цифрово́е телеви́дение

**dignified** [ˈdɪgnɪfaɪd] *adj* по́лный досто́инства

**dignity** [ˈdɪgnɪtɪ] *n* досто́инство

**dilapidated** [dɪˈlæpɪdeɪtɪd] *adj* ве́тхий

**dilemma** [daɪˈlɛmə] *n* диле́мма

**diligent** [ˈdɪlɪdʒənt] *adj* (*worker*) усе́рдный, приле́жный

**dilute** [daɪˈluːt] *vt* (*liquid*) разбавля́ть (разба́вить *pf*)

**dim** [dɪm] *adj* (*outline, memory*) сму́тный; (*light*) ту́склый; (*room*) пло́хо освещённый ♦ *vt* (*light*) приглуша́ть (приглуши́ть *pf*)

**dimension** [daɪˈmɛnʃən] *n* (*measurement*) измере́ние; (*also pl: scale, size*) разме́ры *mpl*; (*aspect*) аспе́кт

**diminish** [dɪˈmɪnɪʃ] *vi* уменьша́ться (уме́ньшиться *pf*)

**din** [dɪn] *n* гро́хот

**dine** [daɪn] *vi* обе́дать (пообе́дать *pf*); **~r** *n* (*person*) обе́дающий(ая) *m(f) adj*; (*US*) дешёвый рестора́н

**dinghy** [ˈdɪŋgɪ] *n* (*also:* **sailing ~**) шлю́пка; (*also:* **rubber ~**) надувна́я ло́дка

**dingy** [ˈdɪndʒɪ] *adj* (*streets, room*) мра́чный; (*clothes, curtains etc*) замы́зганный

**dining room** [ˈdaɪnɪŋ-] *n* столо́вая *f adj*

**dinner** [ˈdɪnəʳ] *n* (*evening meal*) у́жин; (*lunch, banquet*) обе́д; **~ jacket** *n* смо́кинг; **~ party** *n* зва́ный обе́д

**dinosaur** [ˈdaɪnəsɔːʳ] *n* диноза́вр

**dip** [dɪp] *n* (*depression*) впа́дина; (*CULIN*) со́ус ♦ *vt* (*immerse*) погружа́ть (погрузи́ть *pf*), окуна́ть (окуну́ть *pf*); (: *in liquid*) мака́ть (макну́ть *pf*), обма́кивать (обмакну́ть *pf*); (*BRIT : AUT, lights*) приглуша́ть (приглуши́ть *pf*) ♦ *vi* (*ground, road*) идти́ (пойти́ *pf*) под укло́н; **to go for a ~** окуна́ться (окуну́ться *pf*)

**diploma** [dɪˈpləʊmə] *n* дипло́м

**diplomacy** [dɪˈpləʊməsɪ] *n* дипломати́я

**diplomat** [ˈdɪpləmæt] *n* диплома́т; **~ic** [dɪpləˈmætɪk] *adj* (*POL*) дипломати́ческий; (*tactful*) дипломати́чный

**dire** [daɪəʳ] *adj* (*consequences*) злове́щий; (*poverty, situation*) жу́ткий

**direct** [daɪˈrɛkt] *adj* прямо́й ♦ *adv* пря́мо ♦ *vt* (*company, project etc*) руководи́ть (*impf*) +*instr*; (*play, film*) ста́вить (поста́вить *pf*); **to ~ (towards** *or* **at)** (*attention, remark*) направля́ть (напра́вить *pf*) (на +*acc*); **to ~ sb to do** (*order*) веле́ть (*impf*) кому́-н +*infin*; **can you ~ me to ...?** Вы не ука́жете, где нахо́дится ...?; **~ debit** *n* (*BRIT : COMM*) прямо́е дебетова́ние; **~ion** [dɪˈrɛkʃən] *n* (*way*) направле́ние; **~ions** *npl* (*instructions*) указа́ния *ntpl*; **to have a good sense of ~ion** хорошо́ ориенти́роваться (*pf*);

~ions for use инстру́кция; ~ly [dɪˈrɛktlɪ] adv пря́мо; (at once) сейча́с же; (as soon as) как то́лько; ~or [dɪˈrɛktə<sup>r</sup>] n (COMM) дире́ктор; (of project) руководи́тель m; (TV, CINEMA) режиссёр; ~ory [dɪˈrɛktərɪ] n спра́вочник

**dirt** [dəːt] n грязь f; ~**y** adj гря́зный ♦ vt па́чкать (испа́чкать pf)

**disability** [dɪsəˈbɪlɪtɪ] n: (**physical**) ~ инвали́дность f no pl; **mental** ~ у́мственная неполноце́нность f

**disabled** [dɪsˈeɪbld] adj (mentally) у́мственно неполноце́нный; (physically): ~ **person** инвали́д ♦ npl: **the** ~ инвали́ды mpl

**disadvantage** [dɪsədˈvɑːntɪdʒ] n недоста́ток

**disagree** [dɪsəˈɡriː] vi (differ) расходи́ться (разойти́сь pf); **to** ~ (**with**) (oppose) не соглаша́ться (согласи́ться pf) (с +instr); **I** ~ **with you** я с Ва́ми не согла́сен; ~**ment** n разногла́сие; (opposition): ~**ment with** несогла́сие с +instr

**disappear** [dɪsəˈpɪə<sup>r</sup>] vi исчеза́ть (исче́знуть pf); ~**ance** n исчезнове́ние

**disappoint** [dɪsəˈpɔɪnt] vt разочаро́вывать (разочарова́ть pf); ~**ed** adj разочаро́ванный; ~**ing** adj: **the film is rather** ~**ing** э́тот фильм не́сколько разочаро́вывает; ~**ment** n разочарова́ние

**disapproval** [dɪsəˈpruːvəl] n неодобре́ние

**disapprove** [dɪsəˈpruːv] vi: **to** ~ (**of**) не одобря́ть (impf) (+acc)

**disarm** [dɪsˈɑːm] vt (MIL) разоружа́ть (разоружи́ть pf); ~**ament** n разоруже́ние

**disarray** [dɪsəˈreɪ] n: **in** ~ в смяте́нии (hair, clothes) в

беспоря́дке

**disaster** [dɪˈzɑːstə<sup>r</sup>] n (natural) бе́дствие; (man-made, also fig) катастро́фа

**disastrous** [dɪˈzɑːstrəs] adj губи́тельный

**disband** [dɪsˈbænd] vt распуска́ть (распусти́ть pf) ♦ vi расформиро́вываться (расформирова́ться pf)

**disbelief** [ˈdɪsbəˈliːf] n неве́рие

**disc** [dɪsk] n (ANAT) межпозвоно́чный хрящ; (COMPUT) = **disk**

**discard** [dɪsˈkɑːd] vt (object) выбра́сывать (вы́бросить pf); (idea, plan) отбра́сывать (отбро́сить pf)

**discern** [dɪˈsəːn] vt (see) различа́ть (различи́ть pf); (identify) определя́ть (определи́ть pf); ~**ing** adj разбо́рчивый

**discharge** vb [dɪsˈtʃɑːdʒ] n [ˈdɪstʃɑːdʒ] vt (waste) выбра́сывать (вы́бросить pf); (patient) выпи́сывать (вы́писать pf); (employee) увольня́ть (уво́лить pf); (soldier) демобилизова́ть (impf/pf) ♦ n (MED) выделе́ние; (of patient) вы́писка; (of employee) увольне́ние; (of soldier) демобилиза́ция

**disciple** [dɪˈsaɪpl] n (REL) апо́стол; (fig) учени́к(и́ца)

**discipline** [ˈdɪsɪplɪn] n дисципли́на ♦ vt дисциплини́ровать (impf/pf); (punish) налага́ть (наложи́ть pf) дисциплина́рное взыска́ние на +acc

**disclose** [dɪsˈkləuz] vt раскрыва́ть (раскры́ть pf)

**disclosure** [dɪsˈkləuʒə<sup>r</sup>] n раскры́тие

**disco** [ˈdɪskəu] n abbr (= discotheque) дискоте́ка

**discomfort** [dɪsˈkʌmfət] n (unease)

нело́вкость f; (pain) недомога́ние

**discontent** [dɪskən'tent] n
недово́льство

**discord** ['dɪskɔːd] n разла́д

**discount** n ['dɪskaunt] vb [dɪs'kaunt]
n ски́дка ♦ vt (COMM) снижа́ть
(сни́зить pf) це́ну на +acc; (idea,
fact) не принима́ть (приня́ть pf) в
расчёт

**discourage** [dɪs'kʌrɪdʒ] vt
(dishearten) препя́тствовать
(воспрепя́тствовать pf); **to ~ sb
from doing** отгова́ривать
(отговори́ть pf) кого́-н +infin

**discover** [dɪs'kʌvər] vt
обнару́живать (обнару́жить pf);
**~y** n откры́тие

**discredit** [dɪs'krɛdɪt] vt
дискредити́ровать (impf/pf)

**discreet** [dɪs'kriːt] adj (tactful)
такти́чный; (careful)
осмотри́тельный; (barely
noticeable) непримéтный

**discrepancy** [dɪs'krɛpənsɪ] n
расхожде́ние

**discretion** [dɪs'krɛʃən] n (tact)
такти́чность f; **use your (own) ~**
поступа́йте по своему́
усмотре́нию

**discriminate** [dɪs'krɪmɪneɪt] vi: **to ~
between** различа́ть (различи́ть
pf); **to ~ against**
дискримини́ровать (impf/pf)

**discrimination** [dɪskrɪmɪ'neɪʃən] n
(bias) дискримина́ция;
(discernment) разбо́рчивость f

**discuss** [dɪs'kʌs] vt обсужда́ть
(обсуди́ть pf); **~ion** [dɪs'kʌʃən] n
(talk) обсужде́ние; (debate)
диску́ссия

**disdain** [dɪs'deɪn] n презре́ние

**disease** [dɪ'ziːz] n боле́знь f

**disgrace** [dɪs'greɪs] n позо́р ♦ vt
позо́рить (опозо́рить pf); **~ful** adj
позо́рный

**disgruntled** [dɪs'grʌntld] adj
недово́льный

**disguise** [dɪs'gaɪz] n маскиро́вка
♦ vt (object) маскирова́ть
(замаскирова́ть pf); **to ~ (as)**
(dress up) переодева́ть
(переоде́ть pf) (+instr); (make up)
гримирова́ть (загримирова́ть pf)
(под +acc); **in ~** (person)
переоде́тый

**disgust** [dɪs'gʌst] n отвраще́ние
♦ vt внуша́ть (внуши́ть pf)
отвраще́ние +dat; **~ing** adj
отврати́тельный

**dish** [dɪʃ] n блю́до; **to do** or **wash
the ~es** мыть (вы́мыть pf) посу́ду

**dishevelled** [dɪ'ʃɛvəld] (US
**disheveled**) adj растрёпанный

**dishonest** [dɪs'ɔnɪst] adj
нече́стный; **~y** n нече́стность f

**dishwasher** ['dɪʃwɔʃər] n
посудомо́ечная маши́на

**disillusion** [dɪsɪ'luːʒən] vt
разочаро́вывать (разочарова́ть
pf)

**disinfectant** [dɪsɪn'fɛktənt] n
дезинфици́рующее сре́дство

**disintegrate** [dɪs'ɪntɪgreɪt] vi (break
up) распада́ться (распа́сться pf)

**disinterested** [dɪs'ɪntrəstɪd] adj
(impartial) бескоры́стный

**disk** [dɪsk] n диск

**dislike** [dɪs'laɪk] n (feeling)
неприя́знь f ♦ vt не люби́ть (impf);
**I ~ the idea** мне не нра́вится э́та
иде́я; **he ~s cooking** он не лю́бит
гото́вить

**dislodge** [dɪs'lɔdʒ] vt смеща́ть
(смести́ть pf)

**dismal** ['dɪzml] adj уны́лый,
мра́чный; (failure, performance)
жа́лкий

**dismantle** [dɪs'mæntl] vt
разбира́ть (разобра́ть pf)

**dismay** [dɪs'meɪ] n трево́га,
смяте́ние ♦ vt приводи́ть
(привести́ pf) в смяте́ние

**dismiss** [dɪs'mɪs] vt (worker)
увольня́ть (уво́лить pf); (pupils,
soldiers) распуска́ть (распусти́ть
pf); (LAW) прекраща́ть
(прекрати́ть pf); (possibility, idea)
отбра́сывать (отбро́сить pf); ~al
n (sacking) увольне́ние

**disobedience** [dɪsə'bi:dɪəns] n
непослуша́ние

**disorder** [dɪs'ɔ:dəʳ] n беспоря́док;
(MED) расстро́йство; **civil ~**
социа́льные беспоря́дки

**dispatch** [dɪs'pætʃ] vt (send)
отправля́ть (отпра́вить pf) ♦ n
(sending) отпра́вка; (PRESS)
сообще́ние; (MIL) донесе́ние

**dispel** [dɪs'pɛl] vt рассе́ивать
(рассе́ять pf)

**dispense** [dɪs'pɛns] vt (medicines)
приготовля́ть (пригото́вить pf);
**~ with** vt fus обходи́ться
(обойти́сь pf) без +gen; **~r** n
торго́вый автома́т

**disperse** [dɪs'pə:s] vt (objects)
рассе́ивать (рассе́ять pf); (crowd)
разгоня́ть (разогна́ть pf) ♦ vi
рассе́иваться (рассе́яться pf)

**display** [dɪs'pleɪ] n демонстра́ция;
(exhibition) вы́ставка ♦ vt (emotion,
quality) выка́зывать (вы́казать pf);
(goods, exhibits) выставля́ть
(вы́ставить pf)

**displeasure** [dɪs'plɛʒəʳ] n
неудово́льствие

**disposable** [dɪs'pəuzəbl] adj
одноразо́вый

**disposal** [dɪs'pəuzl] n (of goods)
реализа́ция; (of rubbish)
удале́ние; **to have sth at one's ~**
располага́ть (impf) чем-н

**dispose** [dɪs'pəuz] vi: **~ of**
избавля́ться (изба́виться pf) от
+gen; (problem, task) справля́ться
(спра́виться pf) с +instr

**disposed** [dɪs'pəuzd] adj: **to be well
~ towards sb** хорошо́ относи́ться

(impf) к кому́-н

**disposition** [dɪspə'zɪʃən] n (nature)
нрав

**disproportionate** [dɪsprə'pɔ:ʃənət]
adj (excessive) неопра́вданно
большо́й; **~ to** несоизмери́мый с
+instr

**dispute** [dɪs'pju:t] n спор;
(domestic) ссо́ра; (LAW) тя́жба ♦ vt
оспа́ривать (оспо́рить pf)

**disregard** [dɪsrɪ'gɑ:d] vt
пренебрега́ть (пренебре́чь pf)

**disrupt** [dɪs'rʌpt] vt наруша́ть
(нару́шить pf); **~ion** [dɪs'rʌpʃən] n
(interruption) наруше́ние

**dissatisfaction** [dɪssætɪs'fækʃən] n
неудовлетворённость f,
недово́льство

**dissatisfied** [dɪs'sætɪsfaɪd] adj
неудовлетворённый; **~ (with)**
недово́льный (+instr)

**dissent** [dɪ'sɛnt] n инакомы́слие

**dissident** ['dɪsɪdnt] n диссиде́нт
♦ adj диссиде́нтский

**dissolve** [dɪ'zɔlv] vt (substance)
растворя́ть (раствори́ть pf);
(organization, parliament)
распуска́ть (распусти́ть pf);
(marriage) расторга́ть
(расто́ргнуть pf) ♦ vi
растворя́ться (раствори́ться pf);
**to ~ in(to) tears** залива́ться
(зали́ться pf) слеза́ми

**dissuade** [dɪ'sweɪd] vt: **to ~ sb
(from sth)** отгова́ривать
(отговори́ть pf) кого́-н (от
чего́-н)

**distance** ['dɪstns] n (in space)
расстоя́ние; (in sport) диста́нция;
(in time) отдалённость f; **in the ~**
вдалеке́, вдали́; **from a ~**
издалека́, и́здали

**distant** ['dɪstnt] adj (place, time)
далёкий; (relative) да́льний;
(manner) отчуждённый

**distaste** [dɪs'teɪst] n неприя́знь f;

**~ful** adj неприя́тный

**distinct** [dɪs'tɪŋkt] adj (clear) отчётливый; (unmistakable) определённый; (different): ~ **(from)** отли́чный (от +gen); **as ~ from** в отли́чие от +gen; **~ion** [dɪs'tɪŋkʃən] n (difference) отли́чие; (honour) честь f; (SCOL) ≈ "отли́чно"; **~ive** adj своеобра́зный, характе́рный; (feature) отличи́тельный

**distinguish** [dɪs'tɪŋgwɪʃ] vt различа́ть (различи́ть pf); **to ~ o.s.** отлича́ться (отличи́ться pf); **~ed** adj ви́дный; **~ing** adj (feature) отличи́тельный

**distort** [dɪs'tɔːt] vt искажа́ть (искази́ть pf); **~ion** [dɪs'tɔːʃən] n искаже́ние

**distract** [dɪs'trækt] vt отвлека́ть (отвле́чь pf); **~ed** adj (dreaming) невнима́тельный; (anxious) встрево́женный; **~ion** [dɪs'trækʃən] n (diversion) отвлече́ние; (amusement) развлече́ние

**distraught** [dɪs'trɔːt] adj: ~ **(with)** обезу́мевший (от +gen)

**distress** [dɪs'trɛs] n отча́яние; (through pain) страда́ние ♦ vt расстра́ивать (расстро́ить pf), приводи́ть (привести́ pf) в отча́яние

**distribute** [dɪs'trɪbjuːt] vt (prizes) раздава́ть (разда́ть pf); (leaflets) распространя́ть (распространи́ть pf); (profits, weight) распределя́ть (распредели́ть pf)

**distribution** [dɪstrɪ'bjuːʃən] n (of goods) распростране́ние; (of profits, weight) распределе́ние

**distributor** [dɪs'trɪbjutər] n (COMM) дистрибью́тер

**district** ['dɪstrɪkt] n райо́н

**distrust** [dɪs'trʌst] n недове́рие

♦ vt не доверя́ть (impf) +dat

**disturb** [dɪs'təːb] vt (person) беспоко́ить (побеспоко́ить pf); (thoughts, peace) меша́ть (помеша́ть pf) +dat; (disorganize) наруша́ть (нару́шить pf); **~ance** n расстро́йство; (violent event) беспоря́дки mpl; **~ed** adj (person: upset) расстро́енный; **emotionally ~ed** психи́чески неуравнове́шенный; **~ing** adj трево́жный

**disused** [dɪs'juːzd] adj забро́шенный

**ditch** [dɪtʃ] n ров, кана́ва; (for irrigation) кана́л ♦ vt (inf: person, car) броса́ть (бро́сить pf); (: plan) забра́сывать (забро́сить pf)

**dive** [daɪv] n (from board) прыжо́к (в во́ду); (underwater) ныря́ние ♦ vi ныря́ть (impf); **to ~ into** (bag, drawer etc) запуска́ть (запусти́ть pf) ру́ку в +acc; (shop, car etc) ныря́ть (нырну́ть pf) в +acc; **~r** n водола́з

**diverse** [daɪ'vəːs] adj разнообра́зный

**diversion** [daɪ'vəːʃən] n (BRIT : AUT) объе́зд; (of attention, funds) отвлече́ние

**diversity** [daɪ'vəːsɪtɪ] n разнообра́зие, многообра́зие

**divert** [daɪ'vəːt] vt (traffic) отводи́ть (отвести́ pf); (funds, attention) отвлека́ть (отвле́чь pf)

**divide** [dɪ'vaɪd] vt (split) разделя́ть (раздели́ть pf); (MATH) дели́ть (раздели́ть pf); (share out) дели́ть (подели́ть pf) ♦ vi дели́ться (раздели́ться pf); (road) разделя́ться (раздели́ться pf); **~d highway** n (US) автотра́сса

**dividend** ['dɪvɪdɛnd] n (COMM) дивиде́нд; (fig): **to pay ~s** приноси́ть (принести́ pf) дивиде́нды

**divine** [dɪ'vaɪn] *adj* боже́ственный
**diving** ['daɪvɪŋ] *n* ныря́ние; (*SPORT*)
прыжки́ *mpl* в во́ду; **~ board** *n*
вы́шка (*для прыжко́в в во́ду*)
**divinity** [dɪ'vɪnɪtɪ] *n* (*SCOL*)
богосло́вие
**division** [dɪ'vɪʒən] *n* (*also MATH*)
деле́ние; (*sharing out*)
разделе́ние; (*disagreement*)
разногла́сие; (*COMM*)
подразделе́ние; (*MIL*) диви́зия;
(*SPORT*) ли́га
**divorce** [dɪ'vɔːs] *n* разво́д ♦ *vt*
(*LAW*) разводи́ться (развести́сь
*pf*) с +*instr*; **~d** *adj* разведённый;
**~e** [dɪvɔː'siː] *n* разведённый(ая)
*m(f) adj*
**divulge** [daɪ'vʌldʒ] *vt* разглаша́ть
(разгласи́ть *pf*)
**DIY** *n abbr* (*BRIT*) (= *do-it-yourself*)
сде́лай сам
**dizzy** ['dɪzɪ] *adj*: **~ turn** *or* **spell**
при́ступ головокруже́ния
**DJ** *n abbr* (= *disc jockey*) диск-жоке́й

KEYWORD

**do** [duː] (*pt* **did**, *pp* **done**) *aux vb* 1
(*in negative constructions and
questions*); **I don't understand** я не
понима́ю; **she doesn't want it**
она́ не хо́чет э́того; **didn't you
know?** ра́зве Вы не зна́ли?; **what
do you think?** что Вы ду́маете?
2 (*for emphasis*) действи́тельно;
**she does look rather pale** она́
действи́тельно вы́глядит о́чень
бле́дной; **oh do shut up!** да,
замолчи́ же!
3 (*in polite expressions*)
пожа́луйста; **do sit down**
пожа́луйста, сади́тесь; **do take
care!** пожа́луйста, береги́ себя́!
4 (*used to avoid repeating vb*): **she
swims better than I do** она́
пла́вает лу́чше меня́ *or*, чем я;
**do you read newspapers? - yes, I**

**do/no, I don't** Вы чита́ете
газе́ту? - да(, чита́ю)/нет(, не
чита́ю); **she lives in Glasgow - so
do I** она́ живёт в Гла́зго - и я
то́же; **he didn't like it and neither
did we** ему́ э́то не понра́вилось,
и нам то́же; **who made this
mess? - I did** кто здесь насори́л?
- я; **he asked me to help him and
I did** он попроси́л меня́ помо́чь
ему́, что я и сде́лал
5 (*in tag questions*) не так *or*
пра́вда ли; **you like him, don't
you?** он Вам нра́вится, не так *or*
пра́вда ли?; **I don't know him, do
I?** я его́ не зна́ю, не так *or*
пра́вда ли?
♦ *vt* 1 де́лать (сде́лать *pf*); **what
are you doing tonight?** что Вы
де́лаете сего́дня ве́чером?; **I've
got nothing to do** мне не́чего
де́лать; **what can I do for you?**
чем могу́ быть поле́зен?; **we're
doing "Othello" at school**
(*studying*) мы прохо́дим
"Оте́лло" в шко́ле; (*performing*)
мы ста́вим "Оте́лло" в шко́ле;
**to do one's teeth** чи́стить
(почи́стить *pf*) зу́бы; **to do one's
hair** причёсываться
(причеса́ться *pf*); **to do the
washing-up** (*BRIT*) мыть (помы́ть
*pf*) посу́ду
2 (*AUT etc*): **the car was doing 100
(km/h)** маши́на шла со
ско́ростью 100 км/ч; **we've done
200 km already** мы уже́
прое́хали 200 км; **he can do 100
km/h in that car** на э́той маши́не
он мо́жет е́хать со ско́ростью
100 км/ч
♦ *vi* 1 (*act, behave*) де́лать
(сде́лать *pf*); **do as I do** де́лайте,
как я; **you did well to react so
quickly** ты молоде́ц, что так
бы́стро среаги́ровал

**2** (*get on, fare*): **he's doing well/ badly at school** он хорошо́/пло́хо у́чится; **the firm is doing well** дела́ в фи́рме иду́т успе́шно; **how do you do?** о́чень прия́тно
**3** (*be suitable*) подходи́ть (подойти́ *pf*); **will it do?** э́то подойдёт?
**4** (*be sufficient*) хвата́ть (хвати́ть *pf*) +*gen*; **will ten pounds do?** десяти́ фу́нтов хва́тит?; **that'll do** э́того доста́точно; **that'll do!** (*in annoyance*) дово́льно!, хва́тит!; **to make do (with)** удовлетворя́ться (удовлетвори́ться *pf*) (+*instr*)
♦ *n* (*inf*): **we're having a bit of a do on Saturday** у нас бу́дет вечери́нка в суббо́ту; **it was a formal do** э́то был официа́льный приём
**do away with** *vt fus* (*abolish*) поко́нчить (*pf*) с +*instr*
**do up** *vt* (*laces*) завя́зывать (завяза́ть *pf*); (*dress, buttons*) застёгивать (застегну́ть *pf*); (*room, house*) ремонти́ровать (отремонти́ровать *pf*)
**do with** *vt fus*: **I could do with a drink** я бы вы́пил чего́-нибудь; **I could do with some help** по́мощь мне бы не помеша́ла; **what has it got to do with you?** како́е э́то име́ет к Вам отноше́ние?; **I won't have anything to do with it** я не жела́ю име́ть к э́тому никако́го отноше́ния; **it has to do with money** э́то каса́ется де́нег
**do without** *vt fus* обходи́ться (обойти́сь *pf*) без +*gen*

**docile** ['dəusaɪl] *adj* кро́ткий
**dock** [dɔk] *n* (*NAUT*) док; (*LAW*) скамья́ подсуди́мых; **~s** *npl* (*NAUT*) док *msg*, верфь *fsg*; **~yard**

*n* док, верфь *f*
**doctor** ['dɔktər] *n* (*MED*) врач; (*SCOL*) до́ктор
**doctrine** ['dɔktrɪn] *n* доктри́на
**document** ['dɔkjumənt] *n* докуме́нт; **~ary** [dɔkju'mɛntərɪ] *adj* документа́льный фильм; **~ation** [dɔkjumən'teɪʃən] *n* документа́ция
**dodge** [dɔdʒ] *vt* увёртываться (увернуться *pf*) от +*gen*
**dodgy** ['dɔdʒɪ] *adj* (*inf*): **~ character** подозри́тельный тип
**does** [dʌz] *vb see* **do**; **~n't** ['dʌznt] = **does not**
**dog** [dɔg] *n* соба́ка ♦ *vt* пресле́довать (*impf*)
**dogged** ['dɔgɪd] *adj* упо́рный
**dogma** ['dɔgmə] *n* до́гма; **~tic** [dɔg'mætɪk] *adj* догмати́ческий
**dole** [dəul] *n* (*BRIT*) посо́бие по безрабо́тице; **to be on the ~** получа́ть (*impf*) посо́бие по безрабо́тице
**doll** [dɔl] *n* (*also US : inf*) ку́кла
**dollar** ['dɔlər] *n* до́ллар
**dolphin** ['dɔlfɪn] *n* дельфи́н
**dome** [dəum] *n* ку́пол
**domestic** [də'mɛstɪk] *adj* дома́шний; (*trade, politics*) вну́тренний; (*happiness*) семе́йный
**dominant** ['dɔmɪnənt] *adj* (*share, role*) преоблада́ющий, домини́рующий; (*partner*) вла́стный
**dominate** ['dɔmɪneɪt] *vt* домини́ровать (*impf*) над +*instr*
**dominoes** ['dɔmɪnəuz] *n* (*game*) домино́ *nt ind*
**donate** [də'neɪt] *vt*: **to ~ (to)** же́ртовать (поже́ртвовать *pf*) (+*dat or* на +*acc*)
**donation** [də'neɪʃən] *n* поже́ртвование
**done** [dʌn] *pp of* **do**
**donkey** ['dɔŋkɪ] *n* осёл

**donor** ['dəunər] n (MED) дóнор; (to charity) жéртвователь(ница) m(f)

**don't** [dəunt] = **do not**

**donut** ['dəunʌt] n (US) = **doughnut**

**doom** [du:m] n рок ♦ vt: **the plan was ~ed to failure** план был обречён на провáл

**door** [dɔːr] n дверь f; ~**bell** n (двернóй) звонóк; ~ **handle** n двернáя рýчка; (of car) рýчка двéри; ~**mat** n половúк; ~**step** n порóг; ~**way** n двернóй проём

**dope** [dəup] n (inf: drug) гашúш; (: person) придýрок ♦ vt вводúть (ввестú pf) наркóтик +dat

**dormitory** ['dɔːmɪtrɪ] n óбщая спáльня n; (US: building) общежúтие

**DOS** [dɔs] n abbr (COMPUT: = disk operating system) ДОС, DOS

**dosage** ['dəusɪdʒ] n дóза

**dose** [dəus] n (of medicine) дóза

**dossier** ['dɔsɪeɪ] n досьé nt ind

**dot** [dɔt] n тóчка; (speck) крáпинка, пятнышко ♦ vt: ~**ted with** усéянный +instr; **on the ~** минýта в минýту

**double** ['dʌbl] adj двойнóй ♦ adv: **to cost ~** стóить (impf) вдвóе дорóже ♦ n двойнúк ♦ vt удвáивать (удвóить pf) ♦ vi (increase) удвáиваться (удвóиться pf); **on the~**, (BRIT) **at the ~** бегóм; ~ **bass** n контрабáс; ~ **bed** n двуспáльная кровáть f; ~**-decker** n (also: ~-**decker bus**) двухэтáжный автóбус; ~ **glazing** n (BRIT) двойны́е рáмы fpl; ~ **room** n (in hotel) двухмéстный нóмер; ~**s** n (TENNIS) пáры fpl

**doubly** ['dʌblɪ] adv вдвойнé

**doubt** [daut] n сомнéние ♦ vt сомневáться (impf); (mistrust) сомневáться (impf) в +prp, не доверять (impf) +dat; **I ~ whether** or **if she'll come** я сомневáюсь,

что онá придёт; ~**ful** adj сомнúтельный; ~**less** adv несомнéнно

**dough** [dəu] n (CULIN) тéсто; ~**nut** (US **donut**) n пóнчик

**dove** [dʌv] n гóлубь m

**down** [daun] n (feathers) пух ♦ adv (motion) вниз; (position) внизý ♦ prep (towards lower level) (вниз) с +gen or по +dat; (along) (вдоль) по +dat ♦ vt (inf: drink) проглáтывать (проглотúть pf); ~ **with the government!** долóй прáвительство! ~**fall** n падéние; (from drinking etc) гúбель f; ~**hill** adv (face, look) вниз; **to go ~hill** (person, business) идтú (пойтú pf) под гору; (road) идтú (пойтú pf) под уклóн; ~**pour** n лúвень m; ~**right** adj я́вный; (refusal) пóлный ♦ adv совершéнно; **Down's syndrome** n синдрóм Дáуна; ~**stairs** adv (position) внизý; (motion) вниз; ~**stream** adv вниз по течéнию; ~**-to-earth** adj (person) простóй; (solution) практúчный; ~**town** adv (position) в цéнтре; (motion) в центр; ~**ward** adj напрáвленный вниз ♦ adv вниз; ~**ward trend** тендéнция на понижéние; ~**wards** adv = **downward**

**dozen** ['dʌzn] n дю́жина; **a ~ books** дю́жина книг; ~**s of** деся́тки +gen

**Dr** abbr = **doctor**

**drab** [dræb] adj уны́лый

**draft** [drɑːft] n (first version) черновúк; (US: MIL) призы́в ♦ vt набрáсывать (набросáть pf); (proposal) составля́ть (состáвить pf); see also **draught**

**drag** [dræg] vt тащúть (impf); (lake, pond) прочёсывать (прочесáть pf) ♦ vi (time, event etc) тянýться (impf)

**dragon** ['drægn] *n* драко́н; **~fly** *n* стрекоза́

**drain** [dreɪn] *n* водосто́к, водоотво́д; ( *fig* ): **~ on** (*on resources*) уте́чка +*gen*; (*on health, energy*) расхо́д +*gen* ♦ *vt* (*land, glass*) осуша́ть (осуши́ть *pf*); (*vegetables*) сливать (слить *pf*); (*wear out*) утомля́ть (утоми́ть *pf*) ♦ *vi* (*liquid*) стека́ть (стечь *pf*); **~age** ['dreɪnɪdʒ] *n* (*system*) канализа́ция; (*process*) дрена́ж, осуше́ние; **~ing board** (*US* **~board**) *n* су́шка

**drama** ['drɑːmə] *n* (*also fig*) дра́ма; **~tic** [drə'mætɪk] *adj* драмати́ческий; (*increase etc*) ре́зкий; (*change*) рази́тельный; **~tist** *n* драмату́рг

**drank** [dræŋk] *pt of* **drink**

**drastic** ['dræstɪk] *adj* (*measure*) реши́тельный; (*change*) коренно́й

**draught** [drɑːft] (*US* **draft**) *n* (*of air*) сквозня́к; **on ~** (*beer*) бочко́вое; **~s** *n* (*BRIT*) ша́шки *pl*

**draw** [drɔː] (*pt* **drew**, *pp* **~n**) *vt* (*ART*) рисова́ть (нарисова́ть *pf*); (*TECH*) черти́ть (начерти́ть *pf*); (*pull: cart*) тащи́ть (*impf*); (: *curtains*) задёргивать (задёрнуть *pf*); (*gun, tooth*) вырыва́ть (вы́рвать *pf*); (*attention*) привлека́ть (привле́чь *pf*); (*crowd*) собира́ть (собра́ть *pf*); (*money*) снима́ть (снять *pf*); (*wages*) получа́ть (получи́ть *pf*) ♦ *vi* (*SPORT*) игра́ть (сыгра́ть *pf*) в ничью́ ♦ *n* (*SPORT*) ничья́; (*lottery*) лотере́я; **to ~ near** приближа́ться (прибли́зиться *pf*); **~ up** *vi* (*train, bus etc*) подъезжа́ть (подъе́хать *pf*) ♦ *vt* (*chair etc*) придвига́ть (придви́нуть *pf*); (*document*) составля́ть (соста́вить *pf*); **~back**

*n* недоста́ток; **~er** *n* я́щик; **~ing** *n* (*picture*) рису́нок; **~ing pin** *n* (*BRIT*) (канцеля́рская) кно́пка; **~ing room** *n* гости́ная *f adj*

**drawl** [drɔːl] *n* протя́жное произноше́ние

**drawn** [drɔːn] *pp of* **draw**

**dread** [drɛd] *n* у́жас ♦ *vt* страши́ться (*impf*) +*gen*; **~ful** *adj* ужа́сный, стра́шный

**dream** [driːm] (*pt, pp* **~ed** or **~t**) *n* сон; (*ambition*) мечта́ ♦ *vt*: **I must have ~t it** мне э́то, наве́рное, присни́лось ♦ *vi* ви́деть (*impf*) сон; (*wish*) мечта́ть (*impf*); **~y** *adj* (*expression, person etc*) мечта́тельный

**dreary** ['drɪərɪ] *adj* тоскли́вый

**dress** [drɛs] *n* ( *frock*) пла́тье; (*no pl: clothing*) оде́жда ♦ *vt* одева́ть (оде́ть *pf*); (*wound*) перевя́зывать (перевяза́ть *pf*) ♦ *vi* одева́ться (оде́ться *pf*); **to get ~ed** одева́ться (оде́ться *pf*); **~ up** *vi* наряжа́ться (наряди́ться *pf*); **~er** *n* (*BRIT*) буфе́т; (*US*: *chest of drawers*) туале́тный сто́лик; **~ing** *n* (*MED*) повя́зка; (*CULIN*) запра́вка; **~ing gown** *n* (*BRIT*) хала́т; **~ing room** *n* (*THEAT*) (артисти́ческая) убо́рная *f adj*; (*SPORT*) раздева́лка; **~ing table** *n* туале́тный сто́лик

**drew** [druː] *pt of* **draw**

**dried** [draɪd] *adj* ( *fruit*) сушёный; (*milk*) сухо́й

**drift** [drɪft] *n* (*of current*) ско́рость *f*; (*of snow*) зано́с, сугро́б; (*meaning*) смысл ♦ *vi* (*boat*) дрейфова́ть (*impf*); **snow had ~ed over the road** доро́гу занесло́ сне́гом

**drill** [drɪl] *n* (*drill bit*) сверло́; (*machine*) дрель *f*; (: *for mining etc*) бура́в; (*MIL*) уче́ние ♦ *vt* (*hole*) сверли́ть (просверли́ть *pf*) ♦ *vi*

( *for oil* ) бури́ть *(impf)*

**drink** [drɪŋk] ( *pt* **drank**, *pp* **drunk**) *n* напи́ток; ( *alcohol* ) (спиртно́й) напи́ток; ( *sip* ) глото́к ♦ *vt* пить (вы́пить *pf* ) ♦ *vi* пить *(impf)*; **to have a ~** попи́ть *(pf)*; ( *alcoholic* ) вы́пить *(pf)*; **I had a ~ of water** я вы́пил воды́; **~-driving** *n* вожде́ние в нетре́звом состоя́нии; **~er** *n* пью́щий(ая) *m(f) adj*; **~ing water** *n* питьева́я вода́

**drip** [drɪp] *n* ка́панье; ( *one drip* ) ка́пля; ( *MED* ) ка́пельница ♦ *vi* ( *water, rain* ) ка́пать *(impf)*; **the tap is ~ping** кран течёт

**drive** [draɪv] ( *pt* **drove**, *pp* **~n**) *n* ( *journey* ) пое́здка; ( *also*: **~way**) подъе́зд; ( *energy* ) напо́р; ( *campaign* ) кампа́ния; ( *COMPUT* : *also*: **disk ~**) дисково́д ♦ *vt* ( *vehicle* ) води́ть/вести́ *(impf)*; ( *motor, wheel* ) приводи́ть (привести́ *pf* ) в движе́ние ♦ *vi* води́ть (вести́ *pf* ) (маши́ну); ( *travel* ) е́здить/е́хать *(impf)*; **right-/left-hand ~** пра́во-/левосторо́нее управле́ние; **to ~ sb to the airport** отвози́ть (отвезти́ *pf* ) кого́-н в аэропо́рт; **to ~ sth into** ( *nail, stake* ) вбива́ть (вбить *pf* ) что-н в +*acc*; **to ~ sb mad** своди́ть (свести́ *pf* ) кого́-н с ума́; **~n** [ˈdrɪvn] *pp of* **drive**; **~r** *n* води́тель *m*; ( *of train* ) машини́ст; **~r's license** *n* ( *US* ) (води́тельские) права́ *ntpl*; **~way** *n* подъе́зд

**driving** [ˈdraɪvɪŋ] *n* вожде́ние; **~ licence** *n* ( *BRIT* ) (води́тельские) права́ *ntpl*

**drizzle** [ˈdrɪzl] *n* и́зморось *f* ♦ *vi* мороси́ть *(impf)*

**drone** [drəun] *n* ( *noise* ) гуде́ние

**drop** [drɔp] *n* ( *of water* ) ка́пля; ( *reduction* ) паде́ние; ( *fall: distance* ) расстоя́ние ( *све́рху вниз* ) ♦ *vt* ( *object* ) роня́ть (урони́ть *pf* ); ( *eyes* ) опуска́ть (опусти́ть *pf* ); ( *voice, price* ) понижа́ть (пони́зить *pf* ); ( *also*: **~ off**: *passenger* ) выса́живать (вы́садить *pf* ) ♦ *vi* па́дать (упа́сть *pf* ); ( *wind* ) стиха́ть (сти́хнуть *pf* ); **~s** *npl* ( *MED* ) ка́пли *fpl*; **~ off** *vi* ( *go to sleep* ) засыпа́ть (засну́ть *pf* ); **~ out** *vi* ( *of game, deal* ) выходи́ть (вы́йти *pf* ); **~-out** *n* ( *from society* ) отщепе́нец(нка); **~pings** *npl* помёт *msg*

**drought** [draut] *n* за́суха

**drove** [drəuv] *pt of* **drive**

**drown** [draun] *vt* топи́ть (утопи́ть *pf* ); ( *also*: **~ out**: *sound* ) заглуша́ть (заглуши́ть *pf* ) ♦ *vi* тону́ть (утону́ть *pf* )

**drug** [drʌg] *n* ( *MED* ) лека́рство; ( *narcotic* ) нарко́тик ♦ *vt* ( *person, animal* ) вводи́ть (ввести́ *pf* ) нарко́тик +*dat*; **to be on ~s** быть *(impf)* на нарко́тиках; **hard/soft ~s** си́льные/сла́бые нарко́тики

**drugstore** - апте́ка.
Америка́нские апте́ки сочета́ют в себе́ апте́ки и кафе́. В них продаю́т не то́лько лека́рства, но и космети́ческие това́ры, напи́тки и заку́ски.

**drum** [drʌm] *n* бараба́н; ( *for oil* ) бо́чка; **~s** *npl* ( *kit* ) уда́рные инструме́нты *mpl*; **~mer** *n* ( *in rock group* ) уда́рник

**drunk** [drʌŋk] *pp of* **drink** ♦ *adj* пья́ный ♦ *n* пья́ный(ая) *m(f) adj*; ( *also*: **~ard** ) пья́ница *m/f*; **~en** *adj* пья́ный

**dry** [draɪ] *adj* сухо́й; ( *lake, riverbed* ) высохший; ( *humour* ) сде́ржанный; ( *lecture, subject* ) ску́чный ♦ *vt* ( *clothes, ground* )

сушить (высушить pf); (surface)
вытирать (вытереть pf) ♦ vi
сохнуть (высохнуть pf);
**~-cleaner's** n химчистка

**DSS** n abbr (BRIT: = Department of
Social Security) Министерство
социального обеспечения

**dual** ['dju:əl] adj двойной; (function)
двойственный; **~ carriageway** n
(BRIT) автотрасса

**dubious** ['dju:bɪəs] adj
сомнительный

**Dublin** ['dʌblɪn] n Дублин

**duchess** ['dʌtʃɪs] n герцогиня

**duck** [dʌk] n утка ♦ vi (also: ~
**down**) пригибаться (пригнуться
pf)

**due** [dju:] adj (expected)
предполагаемый; (attention,
consideration) должный: **I am ~
£20** мне должны or полагается
£20 ♦ n: **to give sb his** (or **her**) ~
отдавать (отдать pf) кому-н
должное ♦ adv: ~ **north** прямо на
север; **~s** npl (for club etc) взносы
mpl; **in ~ course** в своё время; ~
**to** из-за +gen; **he is ~ to go** он
должен идти

**duel** ['djuəl] n дуэль f

**duet** [dju:'ɛt] n дуэт

**dug** [dʌg] pt, pp of **dig**

**duke** [dju:k] n герцог

**dull** [dʌl] adj (light, colour) тусклый,
мрачный; (sound) глухой; (pain,
wit) тупой; (event) скучный ♦ vt
притуплять (притупить pf)

**duly** ['dju:lɪ] adv (properly)
должным образом; (on time)
своевременно

**dumb** [dʌm] adj (mute) немой; (inf:
pej: person) тупой; (: idea)
дурацкий

**dummy** ['dʌmɪ] n (tailor's model)
манекен; (BRIT: for baby) соска,
пустышка ♦ adj (bullet) холостой

**dump** [dʌmp] n (also: **rubbish ~**)

свалка; (inf: pej: place) дыра ♦ vt
(put down) сваливать (свалить
pf), выбрасывать (выбросить pf);
(car) бросать (бросить pf)

**dung** [dʌŋ] n навоз

**dungarees** [dʌŋgə'ri:z] npl
комбинезон msg

**duplicate** n, adj ['dju:plɪkət] vb
['dju:plɪkeɪt] n дубликат, копия
♦ adj запасной ♦ vt копировать
(скопировать pf); (repeat)
дублировать (продублировать
pf); **in ~** в двойном экземпляре

**durable** ['djuərəbl] adj прочный

**duration** [djuə'reɪʃən] n
продолжительность f

**during** ['djuərɪŋ] prep (in the course
of ) во время +gen, в течение
+gen; (from beginning to end) в
течение +gen

**dusk** [dʌsk] n сумерки pl

**dust** [dʌst] n пыль f ♦ vt вытирать
(вытереть pf) пыль с +gen; **to ~
with** (cake etc) посыпать
(посыпать pf) +instr; **~bin** n (BRIT)
мусорное ведро; **~y** adj
пыльный

**Dutch** [dʌtʃ] adj голландский ♦ npl:
**the ~** голландцы mpl; **they
decided to go ~** (inf ) они
решили, что каждый будет
платить за себя

**duty** ['dju:tɪ] n (responsibility)
обязанность f; (obligation) долг;
(tax) пошлина; **on ~** на
дежурстве; **off ~** вне службы;
**~-free** adj (drink etc)
беспошлинный

**duvet** ['du:veɪ] n (BRIT) одеяло

**dwarf** [dwɔ:f] (pl **dwarves**) n
карлик ♦ vt делать (сделать pf)
крохотным; (achievement)
умалять (умалить pf)

**dwarves** [dwɔ:vz] npl of **dwarf**

**dwell** [dwɛl] (pt, pp **dwelt**) vi
проживать (impf); ~ **on** vt fus

заде́рживаться (задержа́ться pf) на +prp

**dye** [daɪ] n краси́тель m, кра́ска ♦ vt кра́сить (покра́сить pf)

**dying** ['daɪɪŋ] adj (person, animal) умира́ющий

**dyke** [daɪk] n (BRIT: wall) да́мба

**dynamic** [daɪ'næmɪk] adj (leader, force) динами́чный

**dynamite** ['daɪnəmaɪt] n динами́т

**dynamo** ['daɪnəməu] n (ELEC) дина́мо-маши́на

# E, e

**E** [iː] n (MUS) ми nt ind

**each** [iːtʃ] adj, pron ка́ждый; ~ **other** друг дру́га; **they hate ~ other** они́ ненави́дят друг дру́га; **they think about ~ other** они́ ду́мают друг о дру́ге; **they have two books ~** у ка́ждого из них по две кни́ги

**eager** ['iːgər] adj (keen) увлечённый; (excited) возбуждённый; **to be ~ for/to do** жа́ждать (impf) +gen/+infin

**eagle** ['iːgl] n орёл

**ear** [ɪər] n (ANAT) у́хо; (of corn) ко́лос; **~ache** n ушна́я боль f; **I have ~ache** у меня́ боли́т у́хо

**earl** [əːl] n (BRIT) граф

**earlier** ['əːlɪər] adj бо́лее ра́нний ♦ adv ра́ньше, ра́нее

**early** ['əːlɪ] adv ра́но ♦ adj ра́нний; (quick: reply) незамедли́тельный; (settlers) пе́рвый; **~ in the morning** ра́но у́тром; **to have an ~ night** ра́но ложи́ться (лечь pf) спать; **in the ~ spring, ~ in the spring** ра́нней весно́й; **in the ~ 19th century, ~ in the 19th century** в нача́ле 19-го ве́ка; **~ retirement** n: **to take ~ retirement** ра́но уходи́ть (уйти́ pf) на пе́нсию

**earn** [əːn] vt (salary) зараба́тывать (зарабо́тать pf); (interest) приноси́ть (принести́ pf); (praise) заслу́живать (заслужи́ть pf)

**earnest** ['əːnɪst] adj (person, manner) серьёзный; (wish, desire) и́скренний; **in ~** всерьёз

**earnings** ['əːnɪŋz] npl за́работок msg

**earring** ['ɪərɪŋ] n серьга́

**earth** [əːθ] n земля́; (BRIT : ELEC) заземле́ние ♦ vt (BRIT : ELEC) заземля́ть (заземли́ть pf); **Earth** (planet) Земля́; **~enware** n кера́мика; **~quake** n землетрясе́ние

**ease** [iːz] n лёгкость f; (comfort) поко́й ♦ vt (pain, problem) облегча́ть (облегчи́ть pf); (tension) ослабля́ть (осла́бить pf); **to ~ sth into** вставля́ть (вста́вить pf) что-н в +acc; **to ~ sth out of** вынима́ть (вы́нуть pf) что-н из +gen; **to ~ o.s. into** опуска́ться (опусти́ться pf) в +acc; **at ~!** (MIL) во́льно!

**easily** ['iːzɪlɪ] adv (see adj) легко́; непринуждённо; (without doubt) несомне́нно

**east** [iːst] n восто́к ♦ adj восто́чный ♦ adv на восто́к; **the East** Восто́к

**Easter** ['iːstər] n Па́сха; **~ egg** n (chocolate) пасха́льное яйцо́

**eastern** ['iːstən] adj восто́чный

**East Germany** n (formerly) Восто́чная Герма́ния

**easy** ['iːzɪ] adj лёгкий; (manner) непринуждённый ♦ adv: **to take it** or **things ~** не напряга́ться (impf); **~-going** adj (person) уживчивый, покла́дистый

**eat** [iːt] (pt **ate**, pp **~en**) vt есть (съесть pf) ♦ vi есть (impf)

**ebony** ['ɛbənɪ] n эбе́новое or чёрное де́рево

**EC** *n abbr* (= *European Community*) ЕС

**ECB** *n abbr* = *European Central Bank*

**eccentric** [ɪkˈsɛntrɪk] *adj* эксцентри́чный

**ecclesiastic(al)** [ɪkliːzɪˈæstɪk(l)] *adj* духо́вный

**echo** [ˈɛkəu] (*pl* **~es**) *n* э́хо ♦ *vt* (*repeat*) вто́рить (*impf*) +*dat* ♦ *vi* (*sound*) отдава́ться (отда́ться *pf*) **the room ~ed with her laughter** в ко́мнате раздава́лся её смех

**eclipse** [ɪˈklɪps] *n* затме́ние

**ecological** [iːkəˈlɔdʒɪkəl] *adj* экологи́ческий

**ecology** [ɪˈkɔlədʒɪ] *n* эколо́гия

**economic** [iːkəˈnɔmɪk] *adj* экономи́ческий; (*profitable*) рента́бельный; **~al** *adj* экономи́чный; (*thrifty*) эконо́мный; **~s** *n* (*SCOL*) эконо́мика

**economist** [ɪˈkɔnəmɪst] *n* экономи́ст

**economy** [ɪˈkɔnəmɪ] *n* эконо́мика, хозя́йство; (*financial prudence*) эконо́мия; **~ class** *n* (*AVIAT*) дешёвые поса́дочные места́

**ecstasy** [ˈɛkstəsɪ] *n* (*rapture*) экста́з

**ecstatic** [ɛksˈtætɪk] *adj* восто́рженный

**eczema** [ˈɛksɪmə] *n* экзе́ма

**edge** [ɛdʒ] *n* край; (*of knife etc*) остриё ♦ *vt* (*trim*) окаймля́ть (окайми́ть *pf*); **on ~** (*fig*) нерво́зный; **to ~ away from** отходи́ть (отойти́ *pf*) бочко́м от +*gen*

**edgy** [ˈɛdʒɪ] *adj* нерво́зный

**edible** [ˈɛdɪbl] *adj* съедо́бный

**Edinburgh** [ˈɛdɪnbərə] *n* Эдинбу́рг

**edit** [ˈɛdɪt] *vt* редакти́ровать (отредакти́ровать *pf*); (*broadcast, film*) монти́ровать (смонти́ровать *pf*); **~ion** [ɪˈdɪʃən] *n* (*of book*) изда́ние; (*of newspaper, programme*) вы́пуск; **~or** *n*

реда́ктор; (*PRESS, TV*) обозрева́тель *m*; **~orial** [ɛdɪˈtɔːrɪəl] *adj* редакцио́нный ♦ *n* редакцио́нная *f adj* (статья́)

**educate** [ˈɛdjukeɪt] *vt* (*teach*) дава́ть (дать *pf*) образова́ние +*dat*; (*instruct*) просвеща́ть (просвети́ть *pf*)

**education** [ɛdjuˈkeɪʃən] *n* (*schooling*) просвеще́ние, образова́ние; (*teaching*) обуче́ние; (*knowledge*) образова́ние; **~al** *adj* (*institution*) уче́бный; (*staff*) преподава́тельский; **~al policy** поли́тика в о́бласти просвеще́ния; **~al system** систе́ма образова́ния *or* просвеще́ния

**EEC** *n abbr* (= *European Economic Community*) ЕЭС

**eel** [iːl] *n* у́горь *m*

**eerie** [ˈɪərɪ] *adj* жу́ткий

**effect** [ɪˈfɛkt] *n* (*result*) эффе́кт; **to take ~** (*drug*) де́йствовать (поде́йствовать *pf*); (*law*) вступа́ть (вступи́ть *pf*) в си́лу; **in ~** в су́щности; **~ive** *adj* (*successful*) эффекти́вный; (*actual*) действи́тельный; **~ively** *adv* (*successfully*) эффекти́вно; (*in reality*) в су́щности, факти́чески; **~iveness** *n* эффекти́вность *f*

**efficiency** [ɪˈfɪʃənsɪ] *n* (*see adj*) эффекти́вность *f*; де́льность *f*

**efficient** [ɪˈfɪʃənt] *adj* эффекти́вный; (*person*) де́льный

**effort** [ˈɛfət] *n* уси́лие; (*attempt*) попы́тка; **~less** *adj* (*achievement*) лёгкий

**e.g.** *adv abbr* (*for example*: = *exempli gratia*) наприме́р

**egg** [ɛg] *n* яйцо́; **hard-boiled/soft-boiled** ~ яйцо́ вкруту́ю/всмя́тку; **~ cup** *n* рю́мка для яйца́; **~plant** *n* (*esp US*) баклажа́н

**ego** ['i:gəu] *n* самолюбие

**Egypt** ['i:dʒɪpt] *n* Египет

**eight** [eɪt] *n* восемь; **~een** *n* восемнадцать; **~eenth** [eɪ'ti:nθ] *adj* восемнадцатый; **~h** [eɪtθ] *adj* восьмой; **~ieth** *adj* восьмидесятый; **~y** *n* восемьдесят

**Eire** ['ɛərə] *n* Эйре *nt ind*

**either** ['aɪðər] *adj* (*one or other*) любой (*из двух*); (*both, each*) каждый ♦ *adv* также ♦ *pron*: **~ (of them)** любой (из них) ♦ *conj*: ~ **yes or no** либо да, либо нет; **on ~ side** на обеих сторонах; **I don't smoke - I don't ~** я не курю - я тоже; **I don't like ~** мне не нравится ни тот, ни другой; **there was no sound from ~ of the flats** ни из одной из квартир не доносилось ни звука

**elaborate** *adj* [ɪ'læbərɪt] *vb* [ɪ'læbəreɪt] *adj* сложный ♦ *vt* (*expand*) развивать (развить *pf*); (*refine*) разрабатывать (разработать *pf*) ♦ *vi*: **to ~ on** (*idea, plan*) рассматривать (рассмотреть *pf*) в деталях

**elastic** [ɪ'læstɪk] *n* резинка ♦ *adj* (*stretchy*) эластичный

**elated** [ɪ'leɪtɪd] *adj*: **to be ~** ликовать (*impf*)

**elation** [ɪ'leɪʃən] *n* ликование

**elbow** ['ɛlbəu] *n* локоть *m*

**elder** ['ɛldər] *adj* старший ♦ *n* (*tree*) бузина; (*older person*): **~s** старшие *pl adj*; **~ly** *adj* пожилой ♦ *npl*: **the ~ly** престарелые *pl adj*

**eldest** ['ɛldɪst] *adj* (*самый*) старший ♦ *n* старший(ая) *m(f) adj*

**elect** [ɪ'lɛkt] *vt* избирать (избрать *pf*) ♦ *adj*: **the president ~** избранный президент; **to ~ to do** предпочитать (предпочесть *pf*) +*infin*; **~oral** *adj* избирательный; **~orate** *n*: **the** **~orate** электорат, избиратели *mpl*

**electric** [ɪ'lɛktrɪk] *adj* электрический; **~al** *adj* электрический; **~ blanket** *n* одеяло-грелка; **~ian** [ɪlɛk'trɪʃən] *n* электромонтёр, электрик; **~ity** [ɪlɛk'trɪsɪtɪ] *n* электричество

**electronic** [ɪlɛk'trɔnɪk] *adj* электронный; **~s** *n* электроника

**elegance** ['ɛlɪgəns] *n* элегантность *f*

**elegant** ['ɛlɪgənt] *adj* элегантный

**element** ['ɛlɪmənt] *n* (*also CHEM*) элемент; (*of heater, kettle etc*) (электронагревательный) элемент; **the ~s** *npl* стихия *fsg*; **he is in his ~** он в своей стихии; **~ary** [ɛlɪ'mɛntərɪ] *adj* элементарный; (*school, education*) начальный

**elephant** ['ɛlɪfənt] *n* слон(иха)

**elevation** [ɛlɪ'veɪʃən] *n* (*height*) возвышенность *f*

**elevator** ['ɛlɪveɪtər] *n* (*US*) лифт

**eleven** [ɪ'lɛvn] *n* одиннадцать; **~th** *adj* одиннадцатый

**eligible** ['ɛlɪdʒəbl] *adj* (*for marriage*) подходящий; **to be ~ for** (*qualified*) иметь (*impf*) право на +*acc*; (*suitable*) подходить (подойти *pf*)

**eliminate** [ɪ'lɪmɪneɪt] *vt* исключать (исключить *pf*); (*team, contestant*) выбивать (выбить *pf*)

**elimination** [ɪlɪmɪ'neɪʃən] *n* (*see vt*) исключение; устранение

**élite** [eɪ'li:t] *n* элита

**elm** [ɛlm] *n* вяз

**eloquent** ['ɛləkwənt] *adj* (*description, person*) красноречивый; (*speech*) яркий

**else** [ɛls] *adv* (*other*) ещё; **nothing ~** больше ничего; **somewhere ~** (*be*) где-нибудь ещё; (*go*) куда-нибудь ещё; (*come from*) откуда-

нибудь ещё; **everywhere ~**
везде; **where ~?** (*position*) где
ещё?; (*motion*) куда ещё?;
**everyone ~** все остальны́е;
**nobody ~ spoke** бо́льше никто́
не говори́л; **or ~ ...** а не то ...;
**~where** *adv* (*be*) в друго́м or
ино́м ме́сте; (*go*) в друго́е or
ино́е ме́сто

**elusive** [ɪ'lu:sɪv] *adj* неулови́мый

**e-mail** ['i:meɪl] *n* электро́нная
по́чта ♦ *vt* (*message*) посыла́ть
(посла́ть *pf*) по электро́нной
по́чте; **to ~ sb** писа́ть (написа́ть
*pf*) кому́-н по электро́нной
по́чте; **~ address** а́дрес
электро́нной по́чты,
электро́нный а́дрес

**emancipation** [ɪmænsɪ'peɪʃən] *n*
освобожде́ние; (*of women*)
эмансипа́ция

**embankment** [ɪm'bæŋkmənt] *n* (*of
road, railway*) на́сыпь *f*; (*of river*)
на́бережная *f adj*

**embargo** [ɪm'bɑ:gəu] (*pl* **~es**) *n*
эмба́рго *nt ind*

**embark** [ɪm'bɑ:k] *vi*: **to ~ on**
(*journey*) отправля́ться
(отпра́виться *pf*) в +*acc*; (*task*)
бра́ться (взя́ться *pf*); (*course of
action*) предпринима́ть
(предприня́ть *pf*)

**embarrass** [ɪm'bærəs] *vt* смуща́ть
(смути́ть *pf*); (*POL*) ста́вить
(поста́вить *pf*) в
затрудни́тельное положе́ние;
**~ed** *adj* смущённый; **~ing** *adj*
(*position*) нело́вкий, неудо́бный;
**~ment** *n* (*feeling*) смуще́ние;
(*problem*) затрудне́ние

**embassy** ['ɛmbəsɪ] *n* посо́льство

**embedded** [ɪm'bɛdɪd] *adj* (*object*)
вде́ланный

**emblem** ['ɛmbləm] *n* эмбле́ма

**embody** [ɪm'bɔdɪ] *vt* (*incarnate*)
воплоща́ть (воплоти́ть *pf*);

(*include*) содержа́ть (*impf*) (в себе́)

**embrace** [ɪm'breɪs] *vt* обнима́ть
(обня́ть *pf*); (*include*) охва́тывать
(охвати́ть *pf*) ♦ *vi* обнима́ться
(*impf*)

**embroidery** *n* (*stitching*) вы́шивка;
(*activity*) выши́вание

**embryo** ['ɛmbrɪəu] *n* (*BIO*) эмбрио́н

**emerald** ['ɛmərəld] *n* изумру́д

**emerge** [ɪ'mə:dʒ] *vi* (*fact*)
всплыва́ть (всплыть *pf*); (*industry,
society*) появля́ться (появи́ться
*pf*); **to ~ from** (*from room,
imprisonment*) выходи́ть (вы́йти
*pf*) из +*gen*

**emergency** [ɪ'mə:dʒənsɪ] *n*
экстрема́льная ситуа́ция; **in an ~**
в экстрема́льной ситуа́ции; **state
of ~** чрезвыча́йное положе́ние; **~
talks** э́кстренные перегово́ры; **~
exit** *n* авари́йный вы́ход

**emigrate** ['ɛmɪgreɪt] *vi*
эмигри́ровать (*impf/pf*)

**emigration** [ɛmɪ'greɪʃən] *n*
эмигра́ция

**eminent** ['ɛmɪnənt] *adj* ви́дный,
зна́тный

**emission** [ɪ'mɪʃən] *n* (*of gas*)
вы́брос; (*of radiation*) излуче́ние

**emotion** [ɪ'məuʃən] *n* (*feeling*)
чу́вство; **~al** *adj* эмоциона́льный;
(*issue*) волну́ющий

**emotive** [ɪ'məutɪv] *adj* волну́ющий

**emphasis** ['ɛmfəsɪs] (*pl* **emphases**)
*n* значе́ние; (*in speaking*)
ударе́ние, акце́нт

**emphasize** ['ɛmfəsaɪz] *vt*
подчёркивать (подчеркну́ть *pf*)

**emphatic** [ɛm'fætɪk] *adj* (*statement,
denial*) категори́ческий,
реши́тельный; (*person*) твёрдый,
категори́чный; **~ally** *adv*
категори́чески; (*certainly*)
реши́тельно

**empire** ['ɛmpaɪər] *n* импе́рия

**empirical** [ɛm'pɪrɪkl] *adj*

эмпири́ческий

**employ** [ɪmˈplɔɪ] vt нанима́ть (наня́ть pf); (tool, weapon) применя́ть (примени́ть pf); **~ee** [ɪmplɔɪˈiː] n рабо́тник; **~er** n работода́тель m; **~ment** n рабо́та; (availability of jobs) за́нятость f

**emptiness** [ˈɛmptɪnɪs] n пустота́

**empty** [ˈɛmptɪ] adj пусто́й ♦ vt (container) опорожня́ть (опорожни́ть pf); (place, house etc) опустоша́ть (опустоши́ть pf) ♦ vi (house) пусте́ть (опусте́ть pf); **~-handed** adj с пусты́ми рука́ми

**EMU** n abbr = economic and monetary union

**emulate** [ˈɛmjuleɪt] vt подража́ть (impf) +dat

**emulsion** [ɪˈmʌlʃən] n (also: ~ **paint**) эму́льсия, эмульсио́нная кра́ска

**enable** [ɪˈneɪbl] vt (make possible) спосо́бствовать (impf) +dat; **to ~ sb to do** (allow) дава́ть (дать pf) возмо́жность кому́-н +infin

**enact** [ɪˈnækt] vt (play) разы́грывать (разыгра́ть pf)

**enamel** [ɪˈnæməl] n эма́ль f

**enchanting** [ɪnˈtʃɑːntɪŋ] adj обворожи́тельный

**encl.** abbr (on letters etc: = enclosed, enclosure) приложе́ние

**enclose** [ɪnˈkləuz] vt (land, space) огора́живать (огороди́ть pf); (object) заключа́ть (заключи́ть pf); **to ~ (with)** (letter) прилага́ть (приложи́ть) (к +dat); **please find ~d a cheque for £100** здесь прилага́ется чек на £100

**enclosure** [ɪnˈkləuʒəʳ] n огоро́женное ме́сто

**encompass** [ɪnˈkʌmpəs] vt (include) охва́тывать (охвати́ть pf)

**encore** [ɔŋˈkɔːʳ] excl бис ♦ n: **as an ~** на бис

**encounter** [ɪnˈkauntəʳ] n встре́ча ♦ vt встреча́ться (встре́титься pf) с +instr; (problem) ста́лкиваться (столкну́ться pf) с +instr

**encourage** [ɪnˈkʌrɪdʒ] vt поощря́ть (поощри́ть pf); (growth) спосо́бствовать (impf) +dat; **to ~ sb to do** убежда́ть (impf) кого́-н +infin; **~ment** n (see vb) поощре́ние; подде́ржка

**encyclop(a)edia** [ɛnsaɪkləuˈpiːdɪə] n энциклопе́дия

**end** [ɛnd] n коне́ц; (aim) цель f ♦ vt (also: **bring to an~, put an ~ to**) класть (положи́ть pf) коне́ц +dat, прекраща́ть (прекрати́ть pf) ♦ vi (situation, activity, period) конча́ться (ко́нчиться pf); **in the ~** в конце́ концо́в; **on ~** (object) стоймя́; **for hours on ~** часа́ми; **~ up** vi: **to ~ up in** (place) ока́зываться (оказа́ться pf) в +prp; (in prison) угожда́ть (угоди́ть pf) в +prp; **we ~ed up taking a taxi** в конце́ концо́в мы взя́ли такси́

**endanger** [ɪnˈdeɪndʒəʳ] vt подверга́ть (подве́ргнуть pf) опа́сности; **an ~ed species** вымира́ющий вид

**endearing** [ɪnˈdɪərɪŋ] adj (smile) покоря́ющий; (person, behaviour) располага́ющий

**endeavour** [ɪnˈdɛvəʳ] (US **endeavor**) n (attempt) попы́тка

**ending** [ˈɛndɪŋ] n (of book etc) коне́ц

**endless** [ˈɛndlɪs] adj бесконе́чный; (forest, beach) бескра́йний

**endorse** [ɪnˈdɔːs] vt (cheque) распи́сываться (расписа́ться pf) на +prp; (document) де́лать (сде́лать pf) отме́тку на +prp; (proposal, candidate) подде́рживать (поддержа́ть pf); **~ment** n (approval) подде́ржка;

(BRIT : AUT) отме́тка

**endurance** [ɪn'djuərəns] n
вынóсливость f

**endure** [ɪn'djuər] vt переносúть
(перенестú pf) ♦ vi вы́стоять (pf)

**enemy** ['ɛnəmɪ] adj вра́жеский,
неприя́тельский ♦ n враг;
(opponent) протúвник

**energetic** [ɛnə'dʒɛtɪk] adj
энергúчный

**energy** ['ɛnədʒɪ] n эне́ргия

**enforce** [ɪn'fɔːs] vt (law) следúть
(impf) or проследúть (pf) за
соблюде́нием +gen

**engage** [ɪn'geɪdʒ] vt (attention,
interest) привле́чь (привле́чь
pf); (person) нанима́ть (наня́ть pf)
♦ vi: **to ~ in** занима́ться (заня́ться
pf) +instr; **~d** adj (couple)
обручённый; (BRIT: busy): **the line
is ~d** лúния занята́; **he is ~d to**
он обручён с +instr; **to get ~d**
обруча́ться (обручúться pf); **~d
tone** n (BRIT : TEL) гудкú pl
"за́нято"; **~ment** n (appointment)
договорённость f; (to marry)
обруче́ние; **~ment ring** n
обруча́льное кольцó

**engine** ['ɛndʒɪn] n (AUT) двúгатель
m, мотóр; (RAIL) локомотúв

**engineer** [ɛndʒɪ'nɪər] n (designer)
инжене́р; (for repairs) меха́ник;
(US : RAIL) машинúст; **~ing** n
(SCOL) инжене́рное де́ло; (design)
технúческий диза́йн

**England** ['ɪŋɡlənd] n Áнглия

**English** ['ɪŋɡlɪʃ] adj англúйский ♦ n
(LING) англúйский язы́к; **the ~** npl
(people) англича́не mpl; **~man**
(irreg) n англича́нин

**enhance** [ɪn'hɑːns] vt (enjoyment,
beauty) усúливать (усúлить pf);
(reputation) повыша́ть (повы́сить
pf)

**enigmatic** [ɛnɪɡ'mætɪk] adj
зага́дочный

**enjoy** [ɪn'dʒɔɪ] vt любúть (impf);
(have benefit of) облада́ть (impf)
+instr; **to ~ o.s.** хорошó
проводúть (провестú pf) вре́мя;
**to ~ doing** любúть (impf) +infin;
**~able** adj прия́тный; **~ment** n
удовóльствие

**enlarge** [ɪn'lɑːdʒ] vt увелúчивать
(увелúчить pf) ♦ vi: **to ~ on**
распространя́ться (impf) о +prp;
**~ment** n (PHOT) увеличе́ние

**enlightened** [ɪn'laɪtnd] adj
просвещённый

**enlist** [ɪn'lɪst] vt (person) вербова́ть
(завербова́ть pf); (support)
заруча́ться (заручúться pf) +instr
♦ vi: **to ~ in** (MIL) вербова́ться
(завербова́ться pf) в +acc

**enormous** [ɪ'nɔːməs] adj
грома́дный

**enough** [ɪ'nʌf] adj доста́точно
+gen ♦ pron доста́точно ♦ adv: **big
~** доста́точно большóй; **I've had
~!** с меня́ доста́точно or хва́тит!;
**have you got ~ work to do?** у Вас
доста́точно рабóты?; **have you
had ~ to eat?** Вы нае́лись?;
**that's~, thanks** доста́точно,
спасúбо; **I've had ~ of him** он
мне надое́л; **~! довóльно!;
strangely** or **oddly ~ ...** как э́то ни
стра́нно ...

**enquire** [ɪn'kwaɪər] vti = **inquire**

**enrich** [ɪn'rɪtʃ] vt обогаща́ть
(обогатúть pf)

**en route** [ɔn'ruːt] adv (to place) по
путú

**ensure** [ɪn'ʃuər] vt обеспе́чивать
(обеспе́чить pf)

**entail** [ɪn'teɪl] vt влечь (повле́чь pf)
за собóй

**enter** ['ɛntər] vt (room, building)
входúть (войтú pf) в +acc;
(university, college) поступа́ть
(поступúть pf) в +acc; (club,
profession, contest) вступа́ть

(вступи́ть pf) в +acc; (in book)
заноси́ть (занести́ pf); (COMPUT)
вводи́ть (ввести́ pf) ♦ vi входи́ть
(войти́ pf); **to ~ sb in** (competition)
запи́сывать (записа́ть pf) кого́-н
в +acc; **~ into** vt fus (discussion, deal)
вступа́ть (вступи́ть pf) в +acc

**enterprise** ['ɛntəpraɪz] n (company,
undertaking) предприя́тие;
(initiative) предприи́мчивость f;
**free/private ~** свобо́дное/ча́стное
предпринима́тельство

**enterprising** ['ɛntəpraɪzɪŋ] adj
(person) предприи́мчивый;
(scheme) предпринима́тельский

**entertain** [ɛntə'teɪn] vt (amuse)
развлека́ть (развле́чь pf); (play
host to) принима́ть (приня́ть pf);
(idea) разду́мывать (impf) над
+instr; **~er** n эстра́дный арти́ст;
**~ing** adj занима́тельный,
развлека́тельный; **~ment** n
развлече́ние; (show)
представле́ние

**enthusiasm** [ɪn'θu:zɪæzəm] n
энтузиа́зм

**enthusiastic** [ɪnθu:zɪ'æstɪk] adj: **~
(about)** по́лный энтузиа́зма (по
по́воду +gen)

**entice** [ɪn'taɪs] vt соблазня́ть
(соблазни́ть pf); (to place)
зама́нивать (замани́ть pf)

**entire** [ɪn'taɪər] adj весь; **~ly** adv
по́лностью; (for emphasis)
соверше́нно

**entitled** adj: **to be ~ to sth/to do**
име́ть (impf) пра́во на что-н/+infin

**entourage** [ɔntu'rɑ:ʒ] n антура́ж,
окруже́ние

**entrance** n ['ɛntrns] vb [ɪn'trɑ:ns] n
(way in) вход; (arrival) появле́ние
♦ vt обвора́живать (обворожи́ть
pf); **to gain ~ to** (university)
поступа́ть (поступи́ть pf) в +acc;
(profession) вступа́ть (вступи́ть pf)
в +acc; **to make an ~** появля́ться

(появи́ться pf)

**entrepreneur** ['ɔntrəprə'nəːr] n
предпринима́тель(ница) m(f)

**entry** ['ɛntrɪ] n вход; (in register,
accounts) за́пись f; (in reference
book) статья́; (arrival: in country)
въезд; **"no ~"** "нет вхо́да"; (AUT)
"нет въе́зда"; **~ form** n зая́вка
на уча́стие

**envelope** ['ɛnvələup] n конве́рт

**envious** ['ɛnvɪəs] adj зави́стливый

**environment** [ɪn'vaɪərnmənt] n
среда́; **the ~** окружа́ющая среда́;
**~al** [ɪnvaɪərn'mɛntl] adj
экологи́ческий

**envisage** [ɪn'vɪzɪdʒ] vt предви́деть
(impf)

**envoy** ['ɛnvɔɪ] n посла́нник

**envy** ['ɛnvɪ] n за́висть f ♦ vt
зави́довать (позави́довать pf)
+dat; **to ~ sb sth** зави́довать
(позави́довать pf) кому́-н из-за
чего́-н

**epic** ['ɛpɪk] n эпопе́я; (poem)
эпи́ческая поэ́ма ♦ adj
эпоха́льный

**epidemic** [ɛpɪ'dɛmɪk] n эпиде́мия

**epilepsy** ['ɛpɪlɛpsɪ] n эпиле́псия

**episode** ['ɛpɪsəud] n эпизо́д

**epitaph** ['ɛpɪtɑ:f] n эпита́фия

**epoch** ['i:pɔk] n эпо́ха

**equal** ['i:kwl] adj ра́вный; (intensity,
quality) одина́ковый ♦ n
ра́вный(ая) m(f) adj ♦ vt (number)
равня́ться (impf) +dat; **he is ~ to**
(task) ему́ по си́лам or по плечу́;
**~ity** [i:'kwɔlɪtɪ] n ра́венство,
равнопра́вие; **~ly** adv
одина́ково; (share) по́ровну

**equate** [ɪ'kweɪt] vt: **to ~ sth with
sth, ~ sth to sth** прира́внивать
(приравня́ть pf) что-н к чему́-н

**equation** [ɪ'kweɪʒən] n (MATH)
уравне́ние

**equator** [ɪ'kweɪtər] n эква́тор

**equilibrium** [i:kwɪ'lɪbrɪəm] n

равнове́сие

**equinox** ['iːkwɪnɔks] *n*
равноде́нствие

**equip** [ɪ'kwɪp] *vt*: **to ~ (with)**
(*person, army*) снаряжа́ть
(снаряди́ть *pf*) (+*instr*); (*room, car*)
обору́довать (*impf/pf*) (+*instr*); **to ~
sb for** (*prepare*) гото́вить
(подгото́вить *pf*) кого́-н к +*dat*;
**~ment** *n* обору́дование

**equivalent** [ɪ'kwɪvələnt] *n*
эквивале́нт ♦ *adj*: **~ (to)**
эквивале́нтный (+*dat* )

**era** ['ɪərə] *n* э́ра

**eradicate** [ɪ'rædɪkeɪt] *vt*
искореня́ть (искорени́ть *pf*)

**erase** [ɪ'reɪz] *vt* стира́ть (стере́ть
*pf*); **~r** *n* рези́нка, ла́стик

**erect** [ɪ'rɛkt] *adj* (*posture*) прямо́й
♦ *vt* (*build*) воздвига́ть
(воздви́гнуть *pf*), возводи́ть
(возвести́ *pf*); (*assemble*) ста́вить
(поста́вить *pf*); **~ion** [ɪ'rɛkʃən] *n*
(*see vb*) возведе́ние; устано́вка;
(*PHYSIOL*) эре́кция

**erosion** [ɪ'rəuʒən] *n* эро́зия

**erotic** [ɪ'rɔtɪk] *adj* эроти́ческий

**erratic** [ɪ'rætɪk] *adj* (*attempts*)
беспоря́дочный; (*behaviour* )
сумасбро́дный

**error** ['ɛrə*] *n* оши́бка

**erupt** [ɪ'rʌpt] *vi* (*war, crisis*)
разража́ться (разрази́ться *pf*);
**the volcano ~ed** произошло́
изверже́ние вулка́на; **~ion**
[ɪ'rʌpʃən] *n* (*of volcano*)
изверже́ние; (*of fighting*) взрыв

**escalator** ['ɛskəleɪtə*] *n* эскала́тор

**escape** [ɪs'keɪp] *n* (*from prison*)
побе́г; (*from person*) бе́гство; (*of
gas*) уте́чка ♦ *vi* убега́ть (убежа́ть
*pf*); (*from jail*) бежа́ть (*impf/pf*);
(*leak*) утека́ть (уте́чь *pf*) ♦ *vt*
(*consequences etc*) избега́ть
(избежа́ть *pf*) +*gen*; **his name ~s
me** его́ и́мя вы́пало у меня́ из

па́мяти; **to ~ from** (*place*) сбега́ть
(сбежа́ть *pf*) из/с +*gen*; (*person*)
сбега́ть (сбежа́ть *pf*) от +*gen*; **he
~d with minor injuries** он
отде́лался лёгкими уши́бами

**escort** *n* ['ɛskɔːt] *vb* [ɪs'kɔːt] *n*
сопровожде́ние; (*MIL, POLICE*)
конво́й; (: *one person*) конвои́р
♦ *vt* сопровожда́ть (сопроводи́ть
*pf*)

**especially** [ɪs'pɛʃlɪ] *adv* осо́бенно

**espionage** ['ɛspɪɑnɑːʒ] *n* шпиона́ж

**essay** ['ɛseɪ] *n* (*SCOL*) сочине́ние

**essence** ['ɛsns] *n* су́щность *f*;
(*CULIN*) эссе́нция

**essential** [ɪ'sɛnʃl] *adj*
обяза́тельный, необходи́мый;
(*basic*) суще́ственный ♦ *n*
необходи́мое *nt adj*; **~s** (*of subject*)
осно́вы; **it is ~ to ...** необходи́мо
+*infin* ...; **~ly** *adv* в су́щности

**establish** [ɪs'tæblɪʃ] *vt* (*organization*)
учрежда́ть (учреди́ть *pf*); (*facts,
contact*) устана́вливать
(установи́ть *pf*); (*reputation*)
утвержда́ть (утверди́ть *pf*) за
собо́й; **~ed** *adj* (*business*)
при́знанный; (*custom, practice*)
установи́вшийся; **~ment** *n* (*see
vb*) учрежде́ние; установле́ние;
утвержде́ние; (*shop etc*)
заведе́ние; **the Establishment**
исте́блишмент

**estate** [ɪs'teɪt] *n* (*land* ) поме́стье;
(*BRIT*: *also*: **housing ~**) жило́й
ко́мплекс; **~ agent** *n* (*BRIT*) аге́нт
по прода́же недви́жимости,
риэ́лтер

**esteem** [ɪs'tiːm] *n*: **to hold sb in
high ~** относи́ться (*impf*) к кому́-н
с больши́м почте́нием, чтить
(*impf*) кого́-н

**estimate** *vb* ['ɛstɪmeɪt] *n* ['ɛstɪmət] *vt*
(*reckon*) предвари́тельно
подсчи́тывать (подсчита́ть *pf*);
(: *cost*) оце́нивать (оцени́ть *pf*)

♦ n (*calculation*) подсчёт; (*assessment*) оценка; (*builder's etc*) смета

**estranged** [ɪs'treɪndʒd] adj (*from spouse, family*) ставший чужим

**estuary** ['estjuərɪ] n устье

**etc.** *abbr* (= *et cetera*) и т.д.

**eternal** [ɪ'tɜ:nl] adj вечный

**eternity** [ɪ'tɜ:nɪtɪ] n вечность f

**ethical** ['ɛθɪkl] adj (*relating to ethics*) этический; (*morally right*) этичный

**ethics** ['ɛθɪks] n, npl этика fsg

**Ethiopia** [i:θɪ'əʊpɪə] n Эфиопия

**ethnic** ['ɛθnɪk] adj этнический

**etiquette** ['ɛtɪkɛt] n этикет

**EU** n abbr (= *European Union*) ЕС, Евросоюз

**euphemism** ['ju:fəmɪzəm] n эвфемизм

**euphoria** [ju:'fɔ:rɪə] n эйфория

**euro** ['jʊərəʊ] n евро m ind

**Europe** ['jʊərəp] n Европа; **~an** [jʊərə'pi:ən] adj европейский; **~an Community** n Европейское сообщество; **~an Union** n Европейский Союз

**euthanasia** [ju:θə'neɪzɪə] n эвтаназия

**evacuate** [ɪ'vækjʊeɪt] vt (*people*) эвакуировать (*impf/pf*); (*place*) освобождать (освободить *pf*)

**evacuation** [ɪvækjʊ'eɪʃən] n (*see vb*) эвакуация; освобождение

**evade** [ɪ'veɪd] vt (*duties, question*) уклоняться (уклониться *pf*) от +*gen*; (*person*) избегать (*impf*) +*gen*

**evaluate** [ɪ'væljʊeɪt] vt оценивать (оценить *pf*)

**evasion** [ɪ'veɪʒən] n (*of responsibility, tax etc*) уклонение

**evasive** [ɪ'veɪsɪv] adj (*reply, action*) уклончивый

**eve** [i:v] n: **on the ~ of** накануне +*gen*

**even** ['i:vn] adj (*level, smooth*) ровный; (*equal*) равный;

(*number*) чётный ♦ adv даже; **~ if** даже если; **~ though** хотя и; **~ more** ещё больше; (+*adj*) ещё более; **~ so** (и) всё же; **not ~** даже не; **I am ~ more likely to leave now** теперь ещё более вероятно, что я уеду; **to break ~** заканчивать (закончить *pf*) без убытка; **to get ~ with sb** (*inf*) расквитаться (*pf*) с кем-н

**evening** ['i:vnɪŋ] n вечер; **in the ~** вечером; **~ dress** n (*no pl: formal clothes*) вечерний туалет

**event** [ɪ'vɛnt] n (*occurrence*) событие; (*SPORT*) вид (соревнования); **in the ~ of** в случае +*gen*

**eventual** [ɪ'vɛntʃʊəl] adj конечный; **~ly** adv в конце концов

**ever** ['ɛvə*] adv (*always*) всегда; (*at any time*) когда-либо, когда-нибудь; **why ~ not?** почему же нет?; **the best ~** самый лучший; **have you ~ been to Russia?** Вы когда-нибудь были в России?; **better than ~** лучше, чем когда-либо; **~ since** с тех пор; **~ since our meeting** со дня нашей встречи; **~ since we met** с тех пор как мы встретились; **~ since that day** с того дня; **~green** adj вечнозелёный

KEYWORD

**every** ['ɛvrɪ] adj 1 (*each*) каждый; (*all*) все; **every one of them** каждый из них; **every shop in the town was closed** все магазины города были закрыты

2 (*all possible*) всякий, всяческий; **we wish you every success** мы желаем Вам всяческих успехов; **I gave you every assistance** я помог Вам всем, чем только возможно; **I tried every option** я испробовал все варианты; **I**

**have every confidence in him** я в
нём совершённо увёрен; **he's
every bit as clever as his brother**
он столь же умён, как и его
брат
3 (*showing recurrence*) ка́ждый;
**every week** ка́ждую неде́лю;
**every other car** ка́ждая втора́я
маши́на; **she visits me every
other/third day** она́ прихо́дит ко
мне че́рез день/ка́ждые два дня;
**every now and then** вре́мя от
вре́мени

**everybody** ['ɛvrɪbɔdɪ] *pron* (*each*)
ка́ждый; (*all*) все *pl*
**everyday** ['ɛvrɪdeɪ] *adj* (*daily*)
ежедне́вный; (*common*)
повседне́вный
**everyone** ['ɛvrɪwʌn] *pron* =
**everybody**
**everything** ['ɛvrɪθɪŋ] *pron* всё
**everywhere** ['ɛvrɪwɛə'] *adv* везде́,
повсю́ду
**eviction** [ɪ'vɪkʃən] *n* выселе́ние
**evidence** ['ɛvɪdns] *n* (*proof* )
доказа́тельство; (*testimony*)
показа́ние; (*indication*) при́знаки
*mpl*; **to give** ~ дава́ть (дать *pf*)
(свиде́тельские) показа́ния
**evident** ['ɛvɪdnt] *adj* очеви́дный;
~**ly** *adv* очеви́дно
**evil** ['iːvl] *adj* (*person, spirit*) злой;
(*influence*) дурно́й; (*system*)
ги́бельный ♦ *n* зло
**evocative** [ɪ'vɔkətɪv] *adj*
*навева́ющий чу́вства и
воспомина́ния*
**evoke** [ɪ'vəuk] *vt* вызыва́ть
(вы́звать *pf*)
**evolution** [iːvə'luːʃən] *n* эволю́ция
**evolve** [ɪ'vɔlv] *vi* (*animal, plant*)
эволюциони́ровать (*impf/pf*);
(*plan, idea*) развива́ться
(разви́ться *pf*)
**ex-** [ɛks] *prefix* (*former*) экс-,

бы́вший
**exacerbate** [ɛks'æsəbeɪt] *vt*
усугубля́ть (усугуби́ть *pf*)
**exact** [ɪg'zækt] *adj* то́чный ♦ *vt*: **to ~
sth from** (*payment*) взы́скивать
(взыска́ть *pf*) что-н с +*gen*; ~**ing**
*adj* (*task*) тру́дный; (*person*)
взыска́тельный; ~**ly** *adv* то́чно
**exaggerate** [ɪg'zædʒəreɪt] *vti*
преувели́чивать (преувели́чить
*pf*)
**exaggeration** [ɪgzædʒə'reɪʃən] *n*
преувеличе́ние
**exam** [ɪg'zæm] *n abbr* =
**examination**
**examination** [ɪgzæmɪ'neɪʃən] *n*
(*inspection*) изуче́ние;
(*consideration*) рассмотре́ние;
(*SCOL*) экза́мен; (*MED*) осмо́тр
**examine** [ɪg'zæmɪn] *vt* (*scrutinize*)
рассма́тривать (рассмотре́ть *pf*),
изуча́ть (изучи́ть *pf*); (*inspect*)
осма́тривать (осмотре́ть *pf*);
(*SCOL*) экзаменова́ть
(проэкзаменова́ть *pf*); (*MED*)
осма́тривать (осмотре́ть *pf*); ~**r** *n*
(*SCOL*) экзамена́тор
**example** [ɪg'zɑːmpl] *n* приме́р; **for
~** наприме́р
**exasperation** [ɪgzɑːspə'reɪʃən] *n*
раздраже́ние
**exceed** [ɪk'siːd] *vt* превыша́ть
(превы́сить *pf*); ~**ingly** *adv*
весьма́, чрезвыча́йно
**excel** [ɪk'sɛl] *vi*: **to ~ (in** or **at)**
отлича́ться (отличи́ться *pf*) (в
+*prp*); ~**lence** ['ɛksələns] *n* (*in sport,
business*) мастерство́; (*superiority*)
превосхо́дство; **Excellency**
['ɛksələnsɪ] *n*: **His Excellency** его́
превосходи́тельство; ~**lent**
['ɛksələnt] *adj* отли́чный,
превосхо́дный
**except** [ɪk'sɛpt] *prep* (*also*: ~ **for**)
кро́ме +*gen* ♦ *vt*: **to ~ sb (from)**
исключа́ть (исключи́ть *pf*) кого́-н

(из +*gen*); ~ **if/when** кро́ме тех
слу́чаев, е́сли/когда́; ~ **that**
кро́ме того́, что; **~ion** [ɪkˈsɛpʃən]
*n* исключе́ние; **to take ~ion to**
обижа́ться (оби́деться *pf*) на
+*acc*; **~ional** [ɪkˈsɛpʃənl] *adj*
исключи́тельный

**excess** [ɪkˈsɛs] *n* избы́ток; ~
**baggage** *n* изли́шек багажа́;
**~ive** *adj* чрезме́рный

**exchange** [ɪksˈtʃeɪndʒ] *n* (*argument*)
перепа́лка ♦ *vt*: **to ~ (for)** (*goods
etc*) обме́нивать (обменя́ть *pf*)
(на +*acc*); **~ (of)** обме́н (+*instr*); **~
rate** *n* (*COMM*) валю́тный *or*
обме́нный курс

**Exchequer** [ɪksˈtʃɛkəᶜ] *n* (*BRIT*): **the
~** казначе́йство

**excise** [ˈɛksaɪz] *n* акци́з, акци́зный
сбор

**excite** [ɪkˈsaɪt] *vt* возбужда́ть
(возбуди́ть *pf*), волнова́ть
(взволнова́ть *pf*); **to get ~d**
возбужда́ться (возбуди́ться *pf*),
волнова́ться (взволнова́ться *pf*);
**~ment** *n* (*agitation*)
возбужде́ние; (*exhilaration*)
волне́ние

**exciting** [ɪkˈsaɪtɪŋ] *adj* (*news,
opportunity*) волну́ющий

**exclude** [ɪksˈkluːd] *vt* исключа́ть
(исключи́ть *pf*)

**exclusion** [ɪksˈkluːʒən] *n*
исключе́ние

**exclusive** [ɪksˈkluːsɪv] *adj* (*hotel,
interview*) эксклюзи́вный; (*use,
right*) исключи́тельный; **~ of**
исключа́я +*acc*; **~ly** *adv*
исключи́тельно

**excruciating** [ɪksˈkruːʃɪeɪtɪŋ] *adj*
мучи́тельный

**excursion** [ɪksˈkəːʃən] *n* экску́рсия

**excuse** *n* [ɪksˈkjuːs] *vb* [ɪksˈkjuːz] *n*
оправда́ние ♦ *vt* (*justify*)
опра́вдывать (оправда́ть *pf*);
(*forgive*) проща́ть (прости́ть *pf*);

**to make ~s for sb** опра́вдываться
(*impf*) за кого́-н; **that's no ~!** э́то
не оправда́ние!; **to ~ sb from sth**
освобожда́ть (освободи́ть *pf*)
кого́-н от чего́-н; **~ me!**
извини́те!, прости́те!; (*as
apology*) извини́те *or* прости́те
(меня́)!; **if you will ~ me, I have
to ...** с Ва́шего разреше́ния я
до́лжен ...

**execute** [ˈɛksɪkjuːt] *vt* (*kill*) казни́ть
(*impf/pf*); (*carry out*) выполня́ть
(вы́полнить *pf*)

**execution** [ɛksɪˈkjuːʃən] *n* (*see vb*)
казнь *f*; выполне́ние

**executive** [ɪgˈzɛkjutɪv] *n* (*person*)
руководи́тель *m*; (*committee*)
исполни́тельный о́рган ♦ *adj*
(*board, role*) руководя́щий

**exemplary** [ɪgˈzɛmplərɪ] *adj*
приме́рный

**exempt** [ɪgˈzɛmpt] *adj*: **~ from**
освобождённый от +*gen* ♦ *vt*: **to ~
sb from** освобожда́ть
(освободи́ть *pf*) кого́-н от +*gen*;
**~ion** [ɪgˈzɛmpʃən] *n*
освобожде́ние

**exercise** [ˈɛksəsaɪz] *n* (*SPORT*)
заря́дка, гимна́стика; (: *for legs,
stomach etc*) (физи́ческое)
упражне́ние; (*also SCOL, MUS*)
упражне́ние; ♦ *vt* (*patience*)
проявля́ть (прояви́ть *pf*);
(*authority, right*) применя́ть
(примени́ть *pf*); (*dog*)
выгу́ливать (*impf*) ♦ *vi* (*also*:
**to take ~**) упражня́ться
(*impf*); **military ~s** вое́нные
уче́ния; **~ bike** *n* велосипе́д-
тренажёр

**exert** [ɪgˈzəːt] *vt* (*influence, pressure*)
ока́зывать (оказа́ть *pf*); (*authority*)
применя́ть (примени́ть *pf*); **to ~
o.s.** напряга́ться (напря́чься *pf*);
**~ion** [ɪgˈzəːʃən] *n* (*effort*) уси́лие

**exhaust** [ɪgˈzɔːst] *n* (*also*: **~ pipe**)

**exhibit** 474 **explain**

выхлопна́я труба́; (*fumes*)
выхлопны́е га́зы *mpl* ♦ *vt* (*person*)
изнуря́ть (изнури́ть *pf*); (*money,
resources*) истоща́ть (истощи́ть
*pf*); (*topic*) исче́рпывать
(исче́рпать *pf*); **~ed** *adj*
изнурённый, изнеможённый;
**~ion** [ɪɡˈzɔːstʃən] *n* изнеможе́ние;
**nervous ~ion** не́рвное
истоще́ние; **~ive** *adj*
исче́рпывающий

**exhibit** [ɪɡˈzɪbɪt] *n* экспона́т ♦ *vt*
(*paintings*) экспони́ровать (*impf/
pf*), выставля́ть (вы́ставить *pf*);
(*quality, emotion*) проявля́ть
(прояви́ть *pf*); **~ion** [ɛksɪˈbɪʃən] *n*
(*of paintings etc*) вы́ставка

**exhilarating** [ɪɡˈzɪləreɪtɪŋ] *adj*
волну́ющий

**exile** [ˈɛksaɪl] *n* (*banishment*)
ссы́лка, изгна́ние; (*person*)
ссы́льный(ая) *m(f) adj*, изгна́нник
♦ *vt* (*abroad*) высыла́ть (вы́слать
*pf*)

**exist** [ɪɡˈzɪst] *vi* существова́ть
(*impf*); **~ence** *n* существова́ние;
**~ing** *adj* существу́ющий

**exit** [ˈɛksɪt] *n* (*way out*) вы́ход; (*on
motorway*) вы́езд; (*departure*) ухо́д

**exodus** [ˈɛksədəs] *n* ма́ссовое
бе́гство, исхо́д

**exotic** [ɪɡˈzɔtɪk] *adj* экзоти́ческий

**expand** [ɪksˈpænd] *vt* (*area, business,
influence*) расширя́ть (расши́рить
*pf*) ♦ *vi* (*gas, metal, business*)
расширя́ться (расши́риться *pf*)

**expanse** [ɪksˈpæns] *n*: **an ~ of sea/
sky** морско́й/небе́сный просто́р

**expansion** [ɪksˈpænʃən] *n*
расшире́ние; (*of economy*) рост

**expatriate** [ɛksˈpætrɪət] *n*
эмигра́нт(ка)

**expect** [ɪksˈpɛkt] *vt* ожида́ть (*impf*);
(*baby*) ждать (*impf*); (*suppose*)
полага́ть (*impf*) ♦ *vi*: **to be ~ing** (*be
pregnant*) ждать (*impf*) ребёнка;

**~ancy** *n* предвкуше́ние; **life
~ancy** продолжи́тельность *f*
жи́зни; **~ation** [ɛkspɛkˈteɪʃən] *n*
(*hope*) ожида́ние

**expedient** [ɪksˈpiːdɪənt] *adj*
целесообра́зный

**expedition** [ɛkspəˈdɪʃən] *n*
экспеди́ция; (*for pleasure*) похо́д

**expel** [ɪksˈpɛl] *vt* (*from school etc*)
исключа́ть (исключи́ть *pf*); (*from
place*) изгоня́ть (изгна́ть *pf*)

**expenditure** [ɪksˈpɛndɪtʃər] *n*
(*money spent*) затра́ты *fpl*; (*of
energy, time, money*) затра́та,
расхо́д

**expense** [ɪksˈpɛns] *n* (*cost*)
сто́имость *f*; **~s** *npl* (*travelling etc
expenses*) расхо́ды *mpl*;
(*expenditure*) затра́ты *fpl*; **at the ~
of** за счёт +*gen*

**expensive** [ɪksˈpɛnsɪv] *adj* дорого́й

**experience** [ɪksˈpɪərɪəns] *n* (*in job,
of situation*) о́пыт; (*event, activity*)
слу́чай; (: *difficult, painful*)
испыта́ние ♦ *vt* испы́тывать
(испыта́ть *pf*), пережива́ть
(пережи́ть *pf*); **~d** *adj* о́пытный

**experiment** [ɪksˈpɛrɪmənt] *n*
экспериме́нт, о́пыт ♦ *vi*: **to ~
(with/on)** эксперименти́ровать
(*impf*) (с +*instr*/на +*prp*); **~al**
[ɪkspɛrɪˈmɛntl] *adj* (*methods, ideas*)
эксперимента́льный; (*tests*)
про́бный

**expert** [ˈɛkspəːt] *n* экспе́рт,
специали́ст; **~ opinion/advice**
мне́ние/сове́т экспе́рта *or*
специали́ста; **~ise** [ɛkspəːˈtiːz] *n*
зна́ния *ntpl* и о́пыт

**expire** [ɪksˈpaɪər] *vi* (*run out*)
истека́ть (исте́чь *pf*); **my passport
~s in January** срок де́йствия
моего́ па́спорта истека́ет в
январе́

**explain** [ɪksˈpleɪn] *vt* объясня́ть
(объясни́ть *pf*)

**explanation** [ɛksplə'neɪʃən] n
объясне́ние
**explanatory** [ɪks'plænətrɪ] adj
объясни́тельный,
поясни́тельный
**explicit** [ɪks'plɪsɪt] adj я́вный,
очеви́дный; (sex, violence)
открове́нный
**explode** [ɪks'pləud] vi (bomb,
person) взрыва́ться (взорва́ться
pf); (population) ре́зко возраста́ть
(возрасти́ pf)
**exploit** vb [ɪks'plɔɪt] n ['ɛksplɔɪt] vt
эксплуати́ровать (impf);
(opportunity) испо́льзовать (impf/
pf) ♦ n дея́ние; **~ation**
[ɛksplɔɪ'teɪʃən] n (see vb)
эксплуата́ция; испо́льзование
**exploratory** [ɪks'plɔrətrɪ] adj
(expedition) иссле́довательский;
(talks) предвари́тельный
**explore** [ɪks'plɔːʳ] vt (place)
иссле́довать (impf/pf); (idea,
suggestion) изуча́ть (изучи́ть pf);
**~r** n иссле́дователь(ница) m(f)
**explosion** [ɪks'pləuʒən] n взрыв;
**population ~** демографи́ческий
взрыв
**explosive** [ɪks'pləusɪv] adj (device,
effect) взрывно́й; (situation)
взрывоопа́сный; (person)
вспы́льчивый ♦ n (substance)
взры́вчатое вещество́; (device)
взрывно́е устро́йство
**exponent** [ɪks'pəunənt] n (of idea,
theory) побо́рник(ица)
**export** n, cpd ['ɛkspɔːt] vb [ɛks'pɔːt] n
(process) э́кспорт, вы́воз; (product)
предме́т э́кспорта ♦ vt
экспорти́ровать (impf/pf),
вывози́ть (вы́везти pf) ♦ cpd (duty,
licence) э́кспортный
**expose** [ɪks'pəuz] vt (object)
обнажа́ть (обнажи́ть pf); (truth,
plot) раскрыва́ть (раскры́ть pf);
(person) разоблача́ть

(разоблачи́ть pf); **to ~ sb to sth**
подверга́ть (подве́ргнуть pf)
кого́-н чему́-н; **~d** adj (place): **~d**
**(to)** откры́тый (+dat)
**exposure** [ɪks'pəuʒəʳ] n (of culprit)
разоблаче́ние; (PHOT) вы́держка,
экспози́ция; **to suffer from ~**
(MED) страда́ть (пострада́ть pf)
от переохлажде́ния
**express** [ɪks'prɛs] adj (clear)
чёткий; (BRIT: service) сро́чный ♦ n
экспре́сс ♦ vt выража́ть
(вы́разить pf); **~ion** [ɪks'prɛʃən] n
выраже́ние; **~ive** adj
вырази́тельный
**expulsion** [ɪks'pʌlʃən] n (from
school etc) исключе́ние; (from
place) изгна́ние
**exquisite** [ɛks'kwɪzɪt] adj (perfect)
изы́сканный
**extend** [ɪks'tɛnd] vt (visit, deadline)
продлева́ть (продли́ть pf);
(building) расширя́ть (расши́рить
pf); (hand) протя́гивать
(протяну́ть pf); (welcome)
ока́зывать (оказа́ть pf) ♦ vi (land,
road) простира́ться (impf);
(period) продолжа́ться
(продо́лжиться pf); **to ~ an**
**invitation to sb** приглаша́ть
(пригласи́ть pf) кого́-н
**extension** [ɪks'tɛnʃən] n (of
building) пристро́йка; (of time)
продле́ние; (ELEC) удлини́тель
m; (TEL, in house) паралле́льный
телефо́н; (: in office) доба́вочный
телефо́н
**extensive** [ɪks'tɛnsɪv] adj
обши́рный; (damage)
значи́тельный; **~ly** adv: **he has**
**travelled ~ly** он мно́го
путеше́ствовал
**extent** [ɪks'tɛnt] n (of area etc)
протяжённость f; (of problem etc)
масшта́б; **to some ~** до
не́которой сте́пени; **to go to the**

~ **of** ... доходи́ть (дойти́ *pf*) до
того́, что ...; **to such an ~ that** ...
до тако́й сте́пени, что ...
**exterior** [ɛksˈtɪərɪəʳ] *adj* нару́жный
♦ *n* (*outside*) вне́шняя сторона́
**external** [ɛksˈtəːnl] *adj* вне́шний
**extinct** [ɪksˈtɪŋkt] *adj* (*animal*)
вы́мерший; (*plant*) исче́знувший;
**to become ~** (*animal*) вымира́ть
(вы́мереть *pf*); (*plant*) исчеза́ть
(исче́знуть *pf*); **~ion** [ɪksˈtɪŋkʃən] *n*
(*of animal*) вымира́ние; (*of plant*)
исчезнове́ние
**extortion** [ɪksˈtɔːʃən] *n*
вымога́тельство
**extortionate** [ɪksˈtɔːʃnɪt] *adj* (*price*)
граби́тельский; (*demands*)
вымога́тельский
**extra** [ˈɛkstrə] *adj* (*additional*)
дополни́тельный; (*spare*) ли́шний
♦ *adv* (*in addition*) дополни́тельно;
(*especially*) осо́бенно ♦ *n* (*luxury*)
изли́шество; (*surcharge*) допла́та
**extract** *vb* [ɪksˈtrækt] *n* [ˈɛkstrækt] *vt*
извлека́ть (извле́чь *pf*); (*tooth*)
удаля́ть (удали́ть *pf*); (*mineral*)
добыва́ть (добы́ть *pf*); (*money,
promise*) вытя́гивать (вы́тянуть *pf*)
♦ *n* (*from novel, recording*)
отры́вок
**extradition** [ɛkstrəˈdɪʃən] *n* вы́дача
(*престу́пника*)
**extraordinary** [ɪksˈtrɔːdnrɪ] *adj*
незауря́дный, необыча́йный
**extravagance** [ɪksˈtrævəgəns] *n*
(*with money*) расточи́тельство
**extravagant** [ɪksˈtrævəgənt] *adj*
(*lavish*) экстравага́нтный;
(*wasteful: person*) расточи́тельный
**extreme** [ɪksˈtriːm] *adj* кра́йний;
(*situation*) экстрема́льный; (*heat,
cold*) сильне́йший ♦ *n* (*of
behaviour*) кра́йность *f*; **~ly** *adv*
кра́йне
**extrovert** [ˈɛkstrəvəːt] *n* экстрове́рт
**exuberant** [ɪɡˈzjuːbərnt] *adj* (*person,*

*behaviour*) экспанси́вный
**eye** [aɪ] *n* (*ANAT*) глаз; (*of needle*)
у́шко ♦ *vt* разгля́дывать
(разгляде́ть *pf*); **to keep an ~ on**
(*person, object*) присма́тривать
(присмотре́ть *pf*) за +*instr*; (*time*)
следи́ть (*impf*) за +*instr*; **~brow** *n*
бровь *f*; **~lash** *n* ресни́ца; **~lid** *n*
ве́ко; **~liner** *n* каранда́ш для век;
**~ shadow** *n* те́ни *fpl* (для век);
**~sight** *n* зре́ние; **~witness** *n*
очеви́дец

# F, f

**F** [ɛf] *n* (*MUS*) фа
**F** *abbr* = **Fahrenheit**
**fabric** [ˈfæbrɪk] *n* (*cloth*) ткань
*f*
**fabulous** [ˈfæbjuləs] *adj* (*inf*)
ска́зочный; (*extraordinary*)
невероя́тный
**façade** [fəˈsɑːd] *n* фаса́д; (*pretence*)
ви́димость *f*
**face** [feɪs] *n* (*of person, organization*)
лицо́; (*of clock*) цифербла́т; (*of
mountain, cliff*) склон ♦ *vt* (*fact*)
признава́ть (призна́ть *pf*); **the
house ~s the sea** дом обращён к
мо́рю; **he was facing the door** он
был обращён лицо́м к две́ри;
**we are facing difficulties** нам
предстоя́т тру́дности; **~ down**
лицо́м вниз; **to lose/save ~**
теря́ть (потеря́ть *pf*)/спаса́ть
(спасти́ *pf*) репута́цию *or* лицо́; **to
make** *or* **pull a ~** де́лать (сде́лать
*pf*) грима́су; **in the ~ of** (*difficulties
etc*) пе́ред лицо́м +*gen*; **on the ~
of it** на пе́рвый взгляд; **~ to ~
(with)** лицо́м к лицу́ (с +*instr*); **~
up to** *vt fus* признава́ть
(призна́ть *pf*); (*difficulties*)
справля́ться (спра́виться *pf*) с
+*instr*; **~ cloth** *n* (*BRIT*) махро́вая

салфётка (для лица́); ~ **value** n номина́льная сто́имость f; **to take sth at** ~ **value** принима́ть (приня́ть pf) что-н за чи́стую моне́ту

**facial** ['feɪʃl] adj: ~ **expression** выраже́ние лица́; ~ **hair** во́лосы, расту́щие на лице́

**facilitate** [fə'sɪlɪteɪt] vt спосо́бствовать (impf/pf) +dat

**facilities** [fə'sɪlɪtɪz] npl усло́вия ntpl; (buildings) помеще́ние ntsg; (equipment) обору́дование ntsg; **cooking** ~ усло́вия для приготовле́ния пи́щи

**facing** ['feɪsɪŋ] prep напро́тив +gen

**fact** [fækt] n факт; **in** ~ факти́чески

**faction** ['fækʃən] n (group) фра́кция

**factor** ['fæktər] n (of problem) фа́ктор

**factory** ['fæktərɪ] n (for textiles) фа́брика; (for machinery) заво́д

**factual** ['fæktjuəl] adj факти́ческий

**faculty** ['fækəltɪ] n спосо́бность f; (of university) факульте́т

**fad** [fæd] n причу́да

**fade** [feɪd] vi (colour) выцвета́ть (вы́цвести pf); (light, hope, smile) угаса́ть (уга́снуть pf); (sound) замира́ть (замере́ть pf); (memory) тускне́ть (потускне́ть pf)

**fag** [fæg] n (BRIT : inf) сигаре́та

**Fahrenheit** ['færənhaɪt] n Фаренге́йт

**fail** [feɪl] vt (exam, candidate) прова́ливать (провали́ть pf); (subj: memory) изменя́ть (измени́ть pf) +dat; (: person) подводи́ть (подвести́ pf); (: courage) покида́ть (поки́нуть pf) ♦ vi (candidate, attempt) прова́ливаться (провали́ться pf); (brakes) отка́зывать (отказа́ть pf); **my eyesight/health is** ~**ing** у меня́ слабе́ет зре́ние/здоро́вье;

**to** ~ **to do** (be unable) не мочь (смочь pf) +infin; **without** ~ обяза́тельно, непреме́нно; ~**ing** n недоста́ток ♦ prep за неиме́нием +gen; ~**ure** n прова́л, неуда́ча; (TECH) ава́рия, вы́ход из стро́я; (person) неуда́чник(ица)

**faint** [feɪnt] adj сла́бый; (recollection) сму́тный; (mark) едва́ заме́тный ♦ vi (MED) па́дать (упа́сть pf) в о́бморок; **to feel** ~ чу́вствовать (почу́вствовать pf) сла́бость; ~**est** adj: **I haven't the** ~**est idea** я не име́ю ни мале́йшего поня́тия

**fair** [fɛər] adj (person, decision) справедли́вый; (size, number) изря́дный; (chance, guess) хоро́ший; (skin, hair) све́тлый; (weather) хоро́ший, я́сный ♦ n (also: **trade** ~) я́рмарка; (BRIT : also: **fun**~) аттракцио́ны mpl ♦ adv: **to play** ~ вести́ (impf) дела́ че́стно; ~**ground** n я́рмарочная пло́щадь f; ~**ly** adv (justly) справедли́во; (quite) дово́льно; ~ **play** n че́стная игра́

**fairy** ['fɛərɪ] n фе́я; ~ **tale** n ска́зка

**faith** [feɪθ] n (also REL) ве́ра; ~**ful** adj: ~**ful (to)** ве́рный (+dat); ~**fully** adv ве́рно

**fake** [feɪk] n (painting, document) подде́лка ♦ adj фальши́вый, подде́льный ♦ vt (forge) подде́лывать (подде́лать pf); (feign) симули́ровать (impf)

**fall** [fɔːl] (pt fell, pp ~en) n паде́ние; (US: autumn) о́сень f ♦ vi па́дать (упа́сть pf); (government) пасть (pf); (rain, snow) па́дать (impf), выпада́ть (вы́пасть pf); ~**s** npl (waterfall) водопа́д msg; **a** ~ **of snow** снегопа́д; **to** ~ **flat** (plan) прова́ливаться (провали́ться pf); **to** ~ **flat (on one's face)** па́дать

(упа́сть pf) ничко́м; ~ **back on** vt
fus прибега́ть (прибе́гнуть pf) к
+dat; ~ **down** vi (person) па́дать
(упа́сть pf); (building) ру́шиться
(ру́хнуть pf); ~ **for** vt fus (trick,
story) ве́рить (пове́рить pf) +dat;
(person) влюбля́ться (влюби́ться
pf) в +acc; ~ **in** vi (roof)
обва́ливаться (обвали́ться pf); ~
**off** vi па́дать (упа́сть pf); (handle,
button) отва́ливаться
(отвали́ться pf); ~ **out** vi (hair,
teeth) выпада́ть (вы́пасть pf); **to ~
out with sb** ссо́риться
(поссо́риться pf) с кем-н
**fallacy** ['fæləsɪ] n заблужде́ние
**fallen** ['fɔːlən] pp of **fall**
**false** [fɔːls] adj (untrue, wrong)
ло́жный; (insincere, artificial)
фальши́вый; ~ **teeth** npl (BRIT)
иску́сственные зу́бы mpl
**fame** [feɪm] n сла́ва
**familiar** [fə'mɪlɪəʳ] adj (well-known)
знако́мый; (intimate) дру́жеский;
**he is ~ with** (subject) он знако́м с
+instr
**family** ['fæmɪlɪ] n семья́; (children)
де́ти pl
**famine** ['fæmɪn] n го́лод
**famous** ['feɪməs] adj знамени́тый
**fan** [fæn] n (folding) ве́ер; (ELEC)
вентиля́тор; (of famous person)
покло́нник(ица); (of sports team)
боле́льщик(ица); ( : inf ) фан ♦ vt
(face) обма́хивать (обмахну́ть
pf); (fire) раздува́ть (разду́ть pf)
**fanatic** [fə'nætɪk] n (extremist)
фана́тик
**fanciful** ['fænsɪful] adj
причу́дливый
**fan club** n клуб покло́нников,
фан-клуб (разг)
**fancy** ['fænsɪ] n (whim) при́хоть f
♦ adj шика́рный ♦ vt (want)
хоте́ть (захоте́ть pf); (imagine)
вообража́ть (вообрази́ть pf); **to**

**take a ~ to** увлека́ться (увле́чься
pf) +instr; **he fancies her** (inf ) она́
ему́ нра́вится; ~ **that!**
представля́ете!; ~ **dress** n
маскара́дный костю́м
**fanfare** ['fænfeəʳ] n фанфа́ра
**fang** [fæŋ] n (of wolf ) клык
**fantastic** [fæn'tæstɪk] adj
фантасти́ческий; **that's ~!**
замеча́тельно!, потряса́юще!
**fantasy** ['fæntəsɪ] n фанта́зия
**far** [fɑːʳ] adj (distant) да́льний ♦ adv
(a long way) далеко́; (much)
гора́здо; **at the ~ end** в да́льнем
конце́; **at the ~ side** на друго́й
стороне́; ~ **left/right** (POL)
кра́йне ле́вый/пра́вый; ~ **away**, ~
**off** далеко́; **he was ~ from poor**
он был далеко́ or отню́дь не
бе́ден; **by** ~ намно́го; **go as ~ as
the post office** дойди́те до
по́чты; **as ~ as I know** наско́лько
мне изве́стно; **how ~?** (distance)
как далеко́?; ~**away** adj (place)
да́льний, далёкий; (look)
отсу́тствующий
**farce** [fɑːs] n фарс
**farcical** ['fɑːsɪkl] adj ( fig) неле́пый
**fare** [feəʳ] n (in taxi, train, bus)
сто́имость f прое́зда; **half/full** ~
полсто́имости/по́лная сто́имость
прое́зда
**Far East** n: **the ~** Да́льний Восто́к
**farm** [fɑːm] n фе́рма ♦ vt (land)
обраба́тывать (обрабо́тать pf);
~**er** n фе́рмер; ~**house** n
фе́рмерская уса́дьба; ~**ing** n
(agriculture) се́льское хозя́йство;
(of crops) выра́щивание; (of
animals) разведе́ние; ~**land** n
земе́льные уго́дья ntpl; ~**yard** n
фе́рмерский двор
**far-reaching** ['fɑː'riːtʃɪŋ] adj (reform)
далеко́ иду́щий; (effect) глубо́кий
**farther** ['fɑːðəʳ] adv да́лее
**fascinating** ['fæsɪneɪtɪŋ] adj (story)

захва́тывающий; (*person*)
очарова́тельный
**fascination** [fæsɪ'neɪʃən] *n*
очарова́ние
**fascism** ['fæʃɪzəm] *n* (*POL*) фаши́зм
**fashion** ['fæʃən] *n* (*trend*) мо́да;
**in/out of ~** в/не в мо́де; **in a
friendly ~** по-дру́жески; **~able** *adj*
мо́дный; **~ show** *n* пока́з *or*
демонстра́ция мод
**fast** [fɑ:st] *adv* (*quickly*) бы́стро;
(*firmly: stick*) про́чно; (: *hold*)
кре́пко ♦ *n* (*REL*) пост ♦ *adj*
бы́стрый; (*progress*)
стреми́тельный; (*car*)
скоростно́й; (*colour*) про́чный; **to
be ~** (*clock*) спеши́ть (*impf*); **he is ~
asleep** он кре́пко спит
**fasten** ['fɑ:sn] *vt* закрепля́ть
(закрепи́ть *pf*); (*door*) запира́ть
(запере́ть *pf*); (*shoe*) завя́зывать
(завяза́ть *pf*); (*coat, dress*)
застёгивать (застегну́ть *pf*); (*seat
belt*) пристёгивать (пристегну́ть
*pf*) ♦ *vi* (*coat, belt*) застёгиваться
(застегну́ться *pf*); (*door*)
запира́ться (запере́ться *pf*)
**fast food** *n* бы́стро
пригото́вленная еда́
**fat** [fæt] *adj* то́лстый ♦ *n* жир
**fatal** ['feɪtl] *adj* (*mistake*)
фата́льный, роково́й; (*injury,
illness*) смерте́льный; **~ly** *adv*
(*injured*) смерте́льно
**fate** [feɪt] *n* судьба́, рок; **~ful** *adj*
роково́й
**father** ['fɑ:ðəʳ] *n* оте́ц; **~-in-law** *n*
(*wife's father*) свёкор; (*husband's
father*) тесть *m*
**fathom** ['fæðəm] *n* фа́том,
морска́я са́жень *f* ♦ *vt* (*also: ~
out*) постига́ть (пости́чь *pf*)
**fatigue** [fə'ti:g] *n* утомле́ние
**fatty** ['fætɪ] *adj* (*food*) жи́рный
**fault** [fɔ:lt] *n* (*blame*) вина́; (*defect:
in person*) недоста́ток; (: *in*

*machine*) дефе́кт; (*GEO*) разло́м
♦ *vt* (*criticize*) придира́ться (*impf*) к
+*dat*; **it's my ~** э́то моя́ вина́; **to
find ~ with** придира́ться
(придра́ться *pf*) к +*dat*; **I am at ~** я
винова́т; **~y** *adj* (*goods*)
испо́рченный; (*machine*)
повреждённый
**fauna** ['fɔ:nə] *n* фа́уна
**favour** ['feɪvəʳ] (*US* **favor**) *n*
(*approval*) расположе́ние; (*help*)
одолже́ние ♦ *vt* (*prefer: solution*)
ока́зывать (оказа́ть *pf*)
предпочте́ние +*dat*; (: *pupil etc*)
выделя́ть (вы́делить *pf*); (*assist*)
благоприя́тствовать (*impf*) +*dat*;
**to do sb a ~** ока́зывать (оказа́ть
*pf*) кому́-н услу́гу; **in ~ of** в
по́льзу +*gen*; **~able** (*US
favorable*) *adj* благоприя́тный;
**~ite** (*US* **favorite**) *adj* люби́мый
♦ *n* люби́мец; (*SPORT*) фавори́т
**fawn** [fɔ:n] *n* молодо́й оле́нь *m*
**fax** [fæks] *n* факс ♦ *vt* посыла́ть
(посла́ть *pf*) фа́ксом
**FBI** *n abbr* (*US*) (= *Federal Bureau of
Investigation*) ФБР
**FE** *abbr* (= *Further Education*) ≈
профессиона́льно-техни́ческое
образова́ние
**fear** [fɪəʳ] *n* страх; (*less strong*)
боя́знь *f*; (*worry*) опасе́ние ♦ *vt*
боя́ться (*impf*) +*gen*; **for ~ of
missing my flight** боя́сь
опозда́ть на самолёт; **~ful** *adj*
(*person*): **to be ~ful of** боя́ться
(*impf*) *or* страши́ться (*impf*) +*gen*;
**~less** *adj* бесстра́шный
**feasible** ['fi:zəbl] *adj*
осуществи́мый
**feast** [fi:st] *n* (*banquet*) пир; (*REL :
also: ~ day*) пра́здник
**feat** [fi:t] *n* по́двиг
**feather** ['fɛðəʳ] *n* перо́
**feature** ['fi:tʃəʳ] *n* осо́бенность *f*,
черта́; (*PRESS*) о́черк; (*TV, RADIO*)

переда́ча ♦ vi: **to ~ in**
фигури́ровать (impf) в +prp; **~s** npl
(of face) черты́ fpl (лица́); **~ film** n
худо́жественный фильм
**February** ['fɛbruərɪ] n февра́ль m
**fed** [fɛd] pt, pp of **feed**
**federal** ['fɛdərəl] adj федера́льный
**federation** [fɛdə'reɪʃən] n
федера́ция
**fed up** adj: **he is ~** он сыт по
го́рло, ему́ надое́ло
**fee** [fiː] n пла́та; **school ~s** пла́та
за обуче́ние
**feeble** ['fiːbl] adj хи́лый; (excuse)
сла́бый
**feed** [fiːd] (pt, pp **fed**) n (fodder)
корм ♦ vt корми́ть (накорми́ть
pf); **to ~ sth into** (data) загружа́ть
(загрузи́ть pf) что-н в +acc;
(paper) подава́ть (пода́ть pf)
что-н в +acc; **~ on** vt fus пита́ться
(impf) +instr
**feel** [fiːl] (pt, pp **felt**) vt (touch)
тро́гать (потро́гать pf);
(experience) чу́вствовать (impf),
ощуща́ть (ощути́ть pf); **to ~ (that)**
(believe) счита́ть (impf), что; **he ~s**
**hungry** он го́лоден; **she ~s cold**
ей хо́лодно; **to ~ lonely/better**
чу́вствовать (impf) себя́
одино́ко/лу́чше; **I don't ~ well** я
пло́хо себя́ чу́вствую; **the**
**material ~s like velvet** э́тот
материа́л на о́щупь как ба́рхат; **I**
**~ like ...** (want) мне хо́чется ...; **~**
**about** vi: **to ~ about for sth**
иска́ть (impf) что-н о́щупью; **~ing**
n чу́вство; (physical) ощуще́ние
**feet** [fiːt] npl of **foot**
**fell** [fɛl] pt of **fall**
**fellow** ['fɛləu] n (man) па́рень m;
(of society) действи́тельный член
♦ cpd: **their ~ prisoners/students**
их сока́мерники/соку́рсники;
**~ship** n (SCOL) стипе́ндия (для
иссле́довательской рабо́ты)

**felt** [fɛlt] pt, pp of **feel** ♦ n фетр
**female** ['fiːmeɪl] n са́мка ♦ adj
же́нский; (child) же́нского по́ла
**feminine** ['fɛmɪnɪn] adj (clothes,
behaviour) же́нственный; (LING)
же́нского ро́да
**feminist** ['fɛmɪnɪst] n
фемини́ст(ка)
**fence** [fɛns] n (barrier) забо́р,
и́згородь f
**fencing** ['fɛnsɪŋ] n (SPORT)
фехтова́ние
**fend** [fɛnd] vi: **to ~ for o.s.**
забо́титься (позабо́титься pf) о
себе́; **~ off** vt отража́ть
(отрази́ть pf)
**fender** ['fɛndər] n (US: of car) крыло́
**fern** [fəːn] n па́поротник
**ferocious** [fə'rəuʃəs] adj (animal,
attack) свире́пый; (behaviour, heat)
ди́кий
**ferocity** [fə'rɔsɪtɪ] n свире́пость f,
жесто́кость f
**ferry** ['fɛrɪ] n (also: **~boat**) паро́м
♦ vt перевози́ть (перевезти́ pf)
**fertile** ['fəːtaɪl] adj (land, soil)
плодоро́дный; (imagination)
бога́тый; (woman) спосо́бный к
зача́тию
**fertility** [fə'tɪlɪtɪ] n (of land, soil)
плодоро́дие; (of woman)
спосо́бность f к зача́тию
**fertilizer** ['fəːtɪlaɪzər] n удобре́ние
**fervent** ['fəːvənt] adj пы́лкий
**fervour** ['fəːvər] (US **fervor**) n пыл
**festival** ['fɛstɪvəl] n (REL) пра́здник;
(ART, MUS) фестива́ль m
**festive** ['fɛstɪv] adj (mood)
пра́здничный; **the ~ season** (BRIT)
≈ Свя́тки pl
**festivities** [fɛs'tɪvɪtɪz] npl
пра́зднества ntpl
**fetch** [fɛtʃ] vt (object) приноси́ть
(принести́ pf); (person) приводи́ть
(привести́ pf); (by car) привози́ть
(привезти́ pf)

**fête** [feɪt] n благотворительный базар

**fetus** ['fi:təs] n (US) = **foetus**

**feud** [fju:d] n вражда

**fever** ['fi:vəʳ] n (temperature) жар; (disease) лихорадка; ~**ish** adj лихорадочный; (person: with excitement) возбуждённый; **he is** ~**ish** у него жар, его лихорадит

**few** [fju:] adj (not many) немногие (some) некоторые pl adj ♦ pron: (a) ~ немногие pl adj; **a** ~ (several) несколько +gen; ~**er** adj меньше +gen

**fiancé** [fɪ'ɑ:ŋseɪ] n жених; ~**e** n невеста

**fiasco** [fɪ'æskəu] n фиаско nt ind

**fibre** ['faɪbəʳ] (US **fiber**) n волокно; (dietary) клетчатка

**fickle** ['fɪkl] adj непостоянный

**fiction** ['fɪkʃən] n (LITERATURE) художественная литература; ~**al** adj (event, character) вымышленный

**fictitious** [fɪk'tɪʃəs] adj (invented) фиктивный; (imaginary) вымышленный

**fiddle** ['fɪdl] n (MUS) скрипка; (swindle) надувательство ♦ vt (BRIT: accounts) подделывать (подделать pf)

**fidelity** [fɪ'delɪtɪ] n (loyalty) верность f

**field** [fi:ld] n в поле; (fig) область f

**fierce** [fɪəs] adj свирепый; (fighting) яростный

**fiery** ['faɪərɪ] adj (sunset) огненный; (temperament) горячий

**fifteen** [fɪf'ti:n] n пятнадцать; ~**th** adj пятнадцатый

**fifth** [fɪfθ] adj пятый ♦ n (fraction) пятая f adj; (AUT: also: ~ **gear**) пятая скорость f

**fiftieth** ['fɪftɪɪθ] adj пятидесятый

**fifty** ['fɪftɪ] n пятьдесят

**fig** [fɪg] n инжир

**fight** [faɪt] (pt, pp **fought**) n драка; (campaign, struggle) борьба ♦ vt (person) драться (подраться pf) с +instr; (MIL) воевать (impf) с +instr; (illness, problem, emotion) бороться (impf) с +instr ♦ vi (people) драться (impf); (MIL) воевать (impf); **to** ~ **an election** участвовать (impf) в предвыборной борьбе; ~**er** n (also fig) борец; ~**ing** n (battle) бой; (brawl) драка

**figure** ['fɪgəʳ] n фигура; (number) цифра ♦ vt (think) считать (impf) ♦ vi (appear) фигурировать (impf); ~ **out** vt понимать (понять pf); ~**head** n (fig, pej) номинальный глава m

**file** [faɪl] n (dossier) дело; (folder) скоросшиватель m; (COMPUT) файл ♦ vt (papers, document) подшивать (подшить pf); (LAW, claim) подавать (подать pf); (wood, fingernails) шлифовать (отшлифовать pf) ♦ vi: **to** ~ **in/ past** входить (войти pf)/ проходить (пройти pf) колонной; **in single** ~ в колонну по одному

**fill** [fɪl] vi (room etc) наполняться (наполниться pf) ♦ vt (vacancy) заполнять (заполнить pf); (need) удовлетворять (удовлетворить pf) ♦ n: **to eat one's** ~ наедаться (наесться pf); **to** ~ **(with)** (container) наполнять (наполнить pf) (+instr); (space, area) заполнять (заполнить pf) (+instr); ~ **in** vt заполнять (заполнить pf); ~ **up** vt (container) наполнять (наполнить pf); (space) заполнять (заполнить pf) ♦ vi (AUT) заправляться (заправиться pf)

**fillet** ['fɪlɪt] n филе nt ind

**filling** ['fɪlɪŋ] n (for tooth) пломба; (of pie) начинка; (of cake) прослойка

**film** [fɪlm] n (CINEMA) фильм;
(PHOT) плёнка; (of powder, liquid
etc) тóнкий слой ♦ vti снимáть
(снять pf); ~ **star** n кинозвездá
m/f

**Filofax** ® ['faɪləʊfæks] n ≈
ежеднéвник

**filter** ['fɪltə<sup>r</sup>] n фильтр ♦ vt
фильтровáть (профильтровáть
pf)

**filth** [fɪlθ] n грязь f; ~**y** adj
грязный

**fin** [fɪn] n (of fish) плавнúк

**final** ['faɪnl] adj (last) послéдний;
(SPORT) финáльный; (ultimate)
заключúтельный; (definitive)
окончáтельный ♦ n (SPORT)
финáл; ~**s** npl (SCOL) выпускнúе
экзáмены mpl; ~**e** [fɪ'nɑːlɪ] n
финáл; ~**ist** n финалúст; ~**ly** adv
(eventually) в концé концóв;
(lastly) наконéц

**finance** [faɪ'næns] n финáнсы pl
♦ vt финансúровать (impf/pf); ~**s**
npl (personal) финáнсы pl

**financial** [faɪ'nænʃəl] adj
финáнсовый

**find** [faɪnd] (pt, pp **found**) vt
находúть (найтú pf); (discover)
обнарýживать (обнарýжить pf)
♦ n нахóдка; **to ~ sb at home**
заставáть (застáть pf) когó-н
дóма; **to ~ sb guilty** (LAW)
признавáть (признáть pf) когó-н
винóвным(ой); ~ **out** vt (fact,
truth) узнавáть (узнáть pf);
(person) разоблачáть
(разоблачúть pf) ♦ vi: **to ~ out
about** узнавáть (узнáть pf) о +prp;
~**ings** npl (LAW) заключéние ntsg;
(in research) результáты mpl

**fine** [faɪn] adj прекрáсный;
(delicate: hair, features) тóнкий;
(sand, powder, detail) мéлкий;
(adjustment) тóчный ♦ adv (well)

прекрáсно ♦ n штраф ♦ vt
штрафовáть (оштрафовáть pf);
**he's ~** (well) он чýвствует себя́
хорошó; (happy) у негó всё в
порядке; **the weather is ~** погóда
хорóшая; **to cut it ~** (of time)
оставлять (остáвить pf) слúшком
мáло врéмени

**finger** ['fɪŋgə<sup>r</sup>] n пáлец ♦ vt (touch)
трóгать (потрóгать pf); **little ~**
мизúнец

**finish** ['fɪnɪʃ] n конéц; (SPORT)
фúниш; (polish etc) отдéлка ♦ vt
закáнчивать (закóнчить pf),
кончáть (кóнчить pf) ♦ vi
закáнчиваться (закóнчиться pf);
(person) закáнчивать (закóнчить
pf); **to ~ doing** кончáть (кóнчить
pf) +infin; **he ~ed third** (in race etc)
он закóнчил трéтьим; ~ **off** vt
закáнчивать (закóнчить pf); (kill)
прикáнчивать (прикóнчить pf); ~
**up** vt (food) доедáть (доéсть pf);
(drink) допивáть (допúть pf) ♦ vi
(end up) кончáть (кóнчить pf)

**Finland** ['fɪnlənd] n Финляндия;
**Gulf of ~** Фúнский залúв

**Finn** [fɪn] n финн; ~**ish** adj
фúнский

**fir** [fəː<sup>r</sup>] n ель f

**fire** ['faɪə<sup>r</sup>] n (flames) огóнь m,
плáмя nt; (in hearth) огóнь m;
(accidental) пожáр; (bonfire)
костёр ♦ vt (gun etc) выстрелить
(pf) из +gen; (arrow) выпускáть
(выпустить pf); (stimulate)
разжигáть (разжéчь pf); (inf:
dismiss) увольнять (увóлить pf)
♦ vi (shoot) выстрелить (pf); **the
house is on ~** дом горúт or в
огнé; ~ **alarm** n пожáрная
сигнализáция; ~**arm** n
огнестрéльное орýжие nt no pl; ~
**brigade** n пожáрная комáнда; ~
**engine** n пожáрная машúна; ~
**escape** n пожáрная лéстница;

**~-extinguisher** n огнетуши́тель m; **~man** (irreg) n пожа́рный m adj, пожа́рник; **~place** n ками́н; **~ station** n пожа́рное депо́ nt ind; **~wood** n дрова́ pl; **~works** npl фейерве́рк msg

**firm** [fə:m] adj (ground, decision, faith) твёрдый; (mattress) жёсткий; (grasp, body, muscles) кре́пкий ♦ n фи́рма; **~ly** adv (believe, stand) твёрдо; (grasp, shake hands) кре́пко

**first** [fə:st] adj пе́рвый ♦ adv (before all others) пе́рвый; (firstly) во-пе́рвых ♦ n (AUT : also: **~ gear**) пе́рвая ско́рость f; (BRIT : SCOL, degree) дипло́м пе́рвой сте́пени; **at ~** снача́ла; **~ of all** пре́жде всего́; **~ aid** n пе́рвая по́мощь f; **~-aid kit** n паке́т пе́рвой по́мощи; **~-class** adj (excellent) первокла́ссный; **~-class ticket** биле́т пе́рвого кла́сса; **~-class stamp** ма́рка пе́рвого кла́сса

**first-class postage** - в Великобрита́нии мо́жно приобрести́ почто́вые ма́рки пе́рвого и второ́го кла́сса. Пи́сьма с ма́ркой пе́рвого кла́сса доставля́ются по ме́сту назначе́ния на сле́дующий день.

**first-hand** adj непосре́дственный; **a ~ account** расска́з очеви́дца
**first lady** n (US) пе́рвая ле́ди f ind
**firstly** adv во-пе́рвых
**first name** n и́мя nt
**first-rate** adj первокла́ссный
**fiscal** ['fɪskl] adj фиска́льный
**fish** [fɪʃ] n inv ры́ба ♦ vt (river, area) лови́ть (impf) ры́бу в +prp, рыба́чить (impf) в +prp ♦ vi (commercially) занима́ться (impf)

рыболо́вством; (as sport, hobby) занима́ться (impf) рыбно́й ло́влей; **to go ~ing** ходи́ть/идти́ (пойти́ pf) на рыба́лку; **~erman** (irreg) n рыба́к; **~ing rod** n у́дочка; **~ slice** n рыбный нож

**fish and chips** - жа́реная ры́ба и карто́фель фри. Эта традицио́нная брита́нская бы́страя еда́ продаётся в специа́льных магази́нах. Её мо́жно съесть тут же в магази́не или купи́ть на вы́нос.

**fist** [fɪst] n кула́к
**fit** [fɪt] adj (suitable) приго́дный; (healthy) в хоро́шей фо́рме ♦ vt (subj: clothes etc) подходи́ть (подойти́ pf) по разме́ру +dat, быть (impf) впо́ру +dat ♦ vi (clothes) подходи́ть (подойти́ pf) по разме́ру, быть (impf) впо́ру; (parts) подходи́ть (подойти́ pf) ♦ n (MED) припа́док; (of coughing, giggles) при́ступ; **~ to do** (ready) гото́вый +infin; **~ for** (suitable for) приго́дный для +gen; **a ~ of anger** при́ступ гне́ва; **this dress is a good ~** э́то пла́тье хорошо́ сиди́т; **by ~s and starts** уры́вками; **~ in** vi (person, object) впи́сываться (вписа́ться pf); **~ness** n (MED) состоя́ние здоро́вья; **~ting** adj (thanks) надлежа́щий; **~tings** npl: **fixtures and ~tings** обору́дование ntsg
**five** [faɪv] n пять; **~r** n (inf: BRIT) пять фу́нтов; (: US) пять до́лларов
**fix** [fɪks] vt (arrange: date) назнача́ть (назна́чить pf); (: amount) устана́вливать (установи́ть pf); (mend) нала́живать (нала́дить pf) ♦ n (inf): **to be in a ~** влипа́ть

(вли́пнуть *pf*); **~ed** *adj* (*price*) твёрдый; (*ideas*) навя́зчивый; (*smile*) засты́вший

**fixture** ['fɪkstʃəʳ] *n see* **fittings**

**fizzy** ['fɪzɪ] *adj* шипу́чий, газиро́ванный

**flabby** ['flæbɪ] *adj* дря́блый

**flag** [flæg] *n* флаг; **~ship** *n* фла́гман

**flair** [flɛəʳ] *n* (*style*) стиль *m*; **a ~ for** (*talent*) дар *or* тала́нт к +*dat*; **political ~** полити́ческий тала́нт

**flak** [flæk] *n* (*inf*) нахлобу́чка

**flake** [fleɪk] *n* (*of snow, soap powder*) хло́пья *pl*; (*of rust, paint*) слой

**flamboyant** [flæm'bɔɪənt] *adj* я́ркий, бро́ский; (*person*) колори́тный

**flame** [fleɪm] *n* (*of fire*) пла́мя *nt*

**flank** [flæŋk] *n* (*of animal*) бок; (*MIL*) фланг ♦ *vt*: **~ed by** ме́жду +*instr*

**flannel** ['flænl] *n* (*fabric*) фланéль *f*; (*BRIT*: *also*: **face ~**) махро́вая салфе́тка (*для лица́*)

**flap** [flæp] *n* (*of envelope*) отворо́т; (*of pocket*) кла́пан ♦ *vt* (*wings*) хло́пать (*impf*) +*instr*

**flare** [flɛəʳ] *n* (*signal*) сигна́льная раке́та; **~ up** *vi* вспы́хивать (вспы́хнуть *pf*)

**flash** [flæʃ] *n* вспы́шка; (*also*: **news ~**) "мо́лния" ♦ *vt* (*light*) (внеза́пно) освеща́ть (освети́ть *pf*); (*news, message*) посыла́ть (посла́ть *pf*) мо́лнией; (*look*) мета́ть (метну́ть *pf*) ♦ *vi* (*lightning, light, eyes*) сверка́ть (сверкну́ть *pf*); (*light on ambulance etc*) мига́ть (*impf*); **in a ~** мгнове́нно; **to ~ by** *or* **past (sth)** (*person*) мча́ться (промча́ться *pf*) ми́мо (чего́-н); **~light** *n* фона́рь *m*, прожéктор; **~y** *adj* (*pej*) крича́щий

**flask** [flɑːsk] *n* (*also*: **vacuum ~**) те́рмос

**flat** [flæt] *adj* (*surface*) пло́ский; (*tyre*) спу́щенный; (*battery*) сéвший; (*beer*) выдохшийся; (*refusal, denial*) категори́ческий; (*MUS, note*) бемо́льный; (*rate, fee*) еди́ный ♦ *n* (*BRIT*: *apartment*) кварти́ра; (*AUT*: *also*: **~ tyre**) спу́щенная ши́на; (*MUS*) бемо́ль *m*; **to work ~ out** выкла́дываться (вы́ложиться *pf*) по́лностью; **~ly** *adv* (*deny*) на́чисто; (*refuse*) наотре́з

**flatter** ['flætəʳ] *vt* льсти́ть (польсти́ть *pf*) +*dat*

**flavour** ['fleɪvəʳ] (*US* **flavor**) *vt* (*soup*) приправля́ть (припра́вить *pf*) ♦ *n* (*taste*) вкус; (*of ice-cream etc*) при́вкус; **strawberry-~ed** с клубни́чным при́вкусом

**flaw** [flɔː] *n* (*in argument, character*) недоста́ток, изъя́н; (*in cloth, glass*) дефéкт; **~less** *adj* безупре́чный

**flea** [fliː] *n* блоха́

**fleck** [flɛk] *n* (*mark*) кра́пинка

**flee** [fliː] (*pt, pp* **fled**) *vt* (*danger, famine*) бежа́ть (*impf*) от +*gen*; (*country*) бежа́ть (*impf/pf*) из +*gen* ♦ *vi* спаса́ться (*impf*) бе́гством

**fleece** [fliːs] *n* (*sheep's coat*) (овéчья) шку́ра; (*sheep's wool*) овéчья шерсть *f*

**fleet** [fliːt] *n* (*of ships*) флот; (*of lorries, cars*) парк

**fleeting** ['fliːtɪŋ] *adj* мимолётный

**Flemish** ['flɛmɪʃ] *adj* флама́ндский

**flesh** [flɛʃ] *n* (*ANAT*) плоть *f*; (*of fruit*) мя́коть *f*

**flew** [fluː] *pt of* **fly**

**flex** [flɛks] *n* ги́бкий шнур ♦ *vt* (*leg, muscles*) размина́ть (размя́ть *pf*); **~ibility** *n* ги́бкость *f*; **~ible** *adj* ги́бкий

**flick** [flɪk] *vt* (*with finger*) сма́хивать (смахну́ть *pf*); (*ash*) стря́хивать (стряхну́ть *pf*); (*whip*) хлестнуть (pf) +instr; (switch) щёлкать (щёлкнуть pf) +instr

**flicker** ['flɪkər] vi (light, flame) мерцать (impf)

**flight** [flaɪt] n полёт; (of steps) пролёт (лестницы)

**flimsy** ['flɪmzɪ] adj (shoes, clothes) лёгкий; (structure) непрочный; (excuse, evidence) слабый

**fling** [flɪŋ] (pt, pp **flung**) vt (throw) швырять (швырнуть pf)

**flip** [flɪp] vt (coin) подбрасывать (подбросить pf) щелчком

**float** [fləʊt] n (for fishing) поплавок; (for swimming) пенопластовая доска для обучающихся плавать; (money) размéнные деньги pl ♦ vi (object, person: on water) плавать (impf); (sound, cloud) плыть (impf) ♦ vt (idea, plan) пускать (пустить pf) в ход; **to ~ a company** выпускать (выпустить pf) акции компании на рынок

**flock** [flɒk] n (of sheep) стадо; (of birds) стая ♦ vi: **to ~ to** стекаться (стечься pf) в +prp

**flood** [flʌd] n (of water) наводнение; (of letters, imports etc) поток ♦ vt (subj: water) заливать (залить pf); (: people) наводнять (наводнить pf) ♦ vi (place) наполняться (наполниться pf) водой; **to ~ into** (people, goods) хлынуть (pf) в/на +acc; **~ing** n наводнение

**floor** [flɔːr] n (of room) пол; (storey) этаж; (of sea, valley) дно ♦ vt (subj: question, remark) сражать (сразить pf); **ground** or (US) **first ~** первый этаж; **~board** n половица

**flop** [flɒp] n (failure) провал

**floppy** ['flɒpɪ] adj, n (also: **~ disk**) дискета, гибкий диск

**flora** ['flɔːrə] n флора; **~l** ['flɔːrl] adj (pattern) цветистый

**flour** ['flaʊər] n мука

**flourish** ['flʌrɪʃ] vi (business) процветать (impf); (plant) пышно расти (impf) ♦ n (bold gesture): **with a ~** демонстративно; **~ing** adj (company, trade) процветающий

**flow** [fləʊ] n (also ELEC) поток; (of blood, river) течение ♦ vi течь (impf)

**flower** ['flaʊər] n цветок ♦ vi (plant, tree) цвести (impf); **~s** цветы; **~bed** n клумба; **~pot** n цветочный горшок; **~y** adj цветистый; (perfume) цветочный

**flown** [fləʊn] pp of **fly**

**flu** [fluː] n (MED) грипп

**fluent** ['fluːənt] adj (linguist) свободно говорящий; (speech) бéглый; (writing) свободный; **he speaks ~ Russian, he's ~ in Russian** он свободно говорит по-русски

**fluff** [flʌf] n (on jacket, carpet) ворс; **~y** adj (soft) пушистый

**fluid** ['fluːɪd] adj (movement) текучий; (situation) переменчивый ♦ n жидкость f

**fluke** [fluːk] n (inf) удача, везéние

**flung** [flʌŋ] pt, pp of **fling**

**fluorescent** [fluəˈresnt] adj (dial, light) флюоресцирующий

**fluoride** ['fluəraɪd] n фторид

**flurry** ['flʌrɪ] n (of snow) вихрь m; **a ~ of activity** бурная деятельность f

**flush** [flʌʃ] n (on face) румянец ♦ vt (drains, pipe) промывать (промыть pf) ♦ vi (redden) зардéться (pf) ♦ adj: **~ with** (level) на одном уровне с +instr; **to ~ the toilet** спускать (спустить pf) воду в туалете; **~ed** adj раскраснéвшийся

**flustered** ['flʌstəd] adj смущённый

**flute** [fluːt] n флéйта

**flutter** ['flʌtər] n (of wings) взмах

**flux** [flʌks] n: **in a state of** ~ в состоянии непрерывного изменения

**fly** [flaɪ] (pt **flew**, pp **flown**) n (insect) муха; (on trousers : also: **flies**) ширинка ♦ vt (plane) летать (impf) на +prp; (passengers, cargo) перевозить (перевезти pf); (distances) пролетать (пролететь pf), преодолевать (преодолеть pf) ♦ vi (also fig) летать/лететь (impf); (flag) развеваться (impf); **~ing** n (activity) лётное дело ♦ adj: **a ~ing visit** краткий визит; **with ~ing colours** блестяще

**foal** [fəul] n жеребёнок

**foam** [fəum] n пена; (also: ~ **rubber**) поролон

**focal point** ['fəukl-] n средоточие

**focus** ['fəukəs] (pl **~es**) n (PHOT) фокус; (of attention, argument) средоточие ♦ vt (camera) настраивать (настроить pf) ♦ vi: **to ~ (on)** (PHOT) настраиваться (настроиться pf) (на +acc); **to ~ on** (fig) сосредотачиваться (сосредоточиться pf) на +prp; **in ~** в фокусе; **out of ~** не в фокусе

**fodder** ['fɒdər] n корм, фураж

**foetus** ['fiːtəs] (US **fetus**) n плод, зародыш

**fog** [fɒg] n туман; **~gy** adj туманный; **it's ~gy** туманно

**foil** [fɔɪl] vt срывать (сорвать pf) ♦ n (metal) фольга

**fold** [fəuld] n (crease) складка; (: in paper) сгиб ♦ vt (clothes, paper) складывать (сложить pf); (arms) скрещивать (скрестить pf); **~er** n папка; (ring-binder) скоросшиватель m; **~ing** adj складной

**foliage** ['fəulɪdʒ] n (of tree etc) листва

**folk** [fəuk] npl люди pl, народ msg ♦ cpd (art, music) народный; **~s** npl (inf: relatives) близкие pl adj; **~lore** n фольклор

**follow** ['fɒləu] vt (leader, person) следовать (последовать pf) за +instr; (example, advice) следовать (последовать pf) +dat; (event, story) следить (impf) за +instr; (route, path) держаться (impf) +gen ♦ vi следовать (последовать pf); **to ~ suit** (fig) следовать (последовать pf) примеру; **~ up** vt (letter, offer) рассматривать (рассмотреть pf); (case) расследовать (impf); **~er** n (of person, belief, cause) последователь(ница) m(f); **~ing** adj следующий ♦ n (followers) последователи mpl

**fond** [fɒnd] adj (smile, look, parents) ласковый; (memory) приятный; **to be ~ of** любить (impf)

**food** [fuːd] n еда, пища; **~ poisoning** n пищевое отравление; **~ processor** n кухонный комбайн

**fool** [fuːl] n дурак ♦ vt (deceive) обманывать (обмануть pf), одурачивать (одурачить pf); **~ish** adj (stupid) глупый; (rash) неосмотрительный

**foot** [fut] (pl **feet**) n (of person) нога, ступня; (of animal) нога; (of bed) конец; (of cliff) подножие; (measure) фут ♦ vt: **to ~ the bill** платить (заплатить pf); **on ~** пешком

**foot** - фут. Мера длины равная 30.4 см.

**footage** ['futɪdʒ] n (CINEMA, material) кадры mpl

**foot: ~ball** n футбольный мяч; (game: BRIT) футбол; (: US) американский футбол; **~baller** n

(BRIT) футболи́ст; **~hills** npl
предго́рья ntpl; **~hold** n (on rock
etc) опо́ра; **~ing** n ( fig) осно́ва;
**to lose one's ~ing** ( fall) теря́ть
(потеря́ть pf) опо́ру; **~note** n
сно́ска; **~path** n тропи́нка,
доро́жка; **~print** n след; **~wear**
n о́бувь f

KEYWORD

**for** [fɔːʳ] prep 1 (indicating
destination) в/на +acc; (indicating
intention) за +instr; **the train for
London** по́езд в or на Ло́ндон; **he
left for work** он уе́хал на рабо́ту;
**he went for the paper/the doctor**
он пошёл за газе́той/врачо́м; **is
this for me?** э́то мне or для
меня́?; **there's a letter for you**
Вам письмо́; **it's time for lunch/
bed** пора́ обе́дать/спать
2 (indicating purpose) для +gen;
**what's it for?** для чего́ э́то?; **give
it to me - what for?** да́йте мне
э́то - заче́м or для чего́?; **to
pray for peace** моли́ться (impf) за
мир
3 (on behalf of, representing): **to
speak for sb** говори́ть (impf) от
лица́ кого́-н; **MP for Brighton**
член парла́мента от Бра́йтона;
**he works for the government** он
на госуда́рственной слу́жбе; **he
works for a local firm** он
рабо́тает на ме́стную фи́рму; **I'll
ask him for you** я спрошу́ его́ от
Ва́шего и́мени; **to do sth for sb**
(on behalf of ) де́лать (сде́лать pf)
что-н за кого́-н
4 (because of ) из-за +gen; **for
lack of funds** из-за отсу́тствия
средств; **for this reason** по э́той
причи́не; **for some reason, for
whatever reason** по како́й-то
причи́не; **for fear of being
criticized** боя́сь кри́тики; **to be**

**famous for sth** быть (impf)
изве́стным чем-н
5 (with regard to) для +gen; **it's
cold for July** для ию́ля сейча́с
хо́лодно; **he's tall for his age** для
своего́ во́зраста он высо́кий; **a
gift for languages** спосо́бность к
языка́м; **for everyone who voted
yes, 50 voted no** на ка́ждый
го́лос "за", прихо́дится 50
голосо́в "про́тив"
6 (in exchange for, in favour of ) за
+acc; **I sold it for £5** я прода́л э́то
за £5; **I'm all for it** я целико́м и
по́лностью за э́то
7 (referring to distance): **there are
roadworks for five miles** на
протяже́нии пяти́ миль
произво́дятся доро́жные
рабо́ты; **to stretch for miles**
простира́ться (impf) на мно́го
миль; **we walked for miles/for
ten miles** мы прошли́ мно́го
миль/де́сять миль
8 (referring to time) на +acc; (: in
past): **he was away for 2 years** он
был в отъе́зде 2 го́да, его́ не́
бы́ло 2 го́да; (: in future): **she will
be away for a month** она́
уезжа́ет на ме́сяц; **can you do it
for tomorrow?** Вы мо́жете
сде́лать э́то к за́втрашнему
дню?; **it hasn't rained for 3 weeks**
уже́ 3 неде́ли не́ было дождя́;
**for hours** часа́ми
9 (with infinite clause): **it is not for
me to decide** не мне реша́ть;
**there is still time for you to do it**
у Вас ещё есть вре́мя сде́лать
э́то; **for this to be possible ...**
что́бы э́то осуществи́ть, ...
10 (in spite of ) несмотря́ на +acc;
**for all his complaints** несмотря́
на все его́ жа́лобы
11 (in phrases): **for the first/last
time** в пе́рвый/после́дний раз;

**for the time being** пока́
♦ *conj* (*rather formal*) и́бо

**forbid** [fə'bɪd] (*pt* **forbad(e)**, *pp*
**forbidden**) *vt* запреща́ть
(запрети́ть *pf*); **to ~sb to do**
запреща́ть (запрети́ть *pf*) кому́-н
+*infin*; **~ding** *adj* вражде́бный

**force** [fɔ:s] *n* (*also PHYS*) си́ла ♦ *vt*
(*compel*) вынужда́ть (вы́нудить
*pf*), принужда́ть (прину́дить *pf*);
(*push*) толка́ть (толкну́ть *pf*);
(*break open*) взла́мывать
(взлома́ть *pf*); **the Forces** *npl*
(*BRIT : MIL*) вооружённые си́лы
*fpl*; **in ~** в большо́м коли́честве;
**to ~ o.s. to do** заставля́ть
(заста́вить *pf*) себя́ +*infin*; **~d** *adj*
(*landing*) вы́нужденный; (*smile*)
принуждённый; **~ful** *adj*
си́льный

**forcibly** ['fɔ:səblɪ] *adv* наси́льно

**fore** [fɔ:ʳ] *n*: **to come to the ~**
выдвига́ться (вы́двинуться *pf*)

**forecast** ['fɔ:ka:st] (*irreg: like* **cast**) *n*
прогно́з ♦ *vt* предска́зывать
(предсказа́ть *pf*)

**forecourt** ['fɔ:kɔ:t] *n* (*of garage*)
пере́дняя площа́дка

**forefinger** ['fɔ:fɪŋɡəʳ] *n*
указа́тельный па́лец

**forefront** ['fɔ:frʌnt] *n*: **in** or **at the ~**
**of** (*movement*) в аванга́рде +*gen*

**foreground** ['fɔ:ɡraund] *n*
пере́дний план

**forehead** ['fɔrɪd] *n* лоб

**foreign** ['fɔrɪn] *adj* (*language, tourist,
firm*) иностра́нный; (*trade*)
вне́шний; (*country*) зарубе́жный;
**~ person** иностра́нец(нка); **~er** *n*
иностра́нец(нка); **~ exchange** *n*
(*system*) обме́н валю́ты; **Foreign
Office** *n* (*BRIT*) министе́рство
иностра́нных дел; **Foreign
Secretary** *n* (*BRIT*) мини́стр
иностра́нных дел

**foreman** ['fɔ:mən] (*irreg*) *n*
(*INDUSTRY*) ма́стер

**foremost** ['fɔ:məust] *adj* (*most
important*) важне́йший ♦ *adv*: **first
and ~** в пе́рвую о́чередь,
пре́жде всего́

**forensic** [fə'rensɪk] *adj* (*medicine,
test*) суде́бный

**forerunner** ['fɔ:rʌnəʳ] *n*
предше́ственник(нница)

**foresee** [fɔ:'si:] (*irreg: like* **see**) *vt*
предви́деть (*impf/pf*); **~able** *adj*: **in
the ~able future** в обозри́мом
бу́дущем

**foresight** ['fɔ:saɪt] *n*
предусмотри́тельность *f*

**forest** ['fɔrɪst] *n* лес; **~ry** *n*
лесово́дство, лесни́чество

**forever** [fə'revəʳ] *adv* (*for good*)
навсегда́, наве́чно; (*endlessly*)
ве́чно

**foreword** ['fɔ:wə:d] *n* предисло́вие

**forgave** [fə'ɡeɪv] *pt of* **forgive**

**forge** [fɔ:dʒ] *vt* (*signature, money*)
подде́лывать (подде́лать *pf*); **~ry**
*n* подде́лка

**forget** [fə'ɡet] (*pt* **forgot**, *pp*
**forgotten**) *vt* забыва́ть (забы́ть
*pf*); (*appointment*) забыва́ть
(забы́ть *pf*) о +*prp* ♦ *vi* забыва́ть
(забы́ть *pf*); **~ful** *adj* забы́вчивый;
**~-me-not** *n* незабу́дка

**forgive** [fə'ɡɪv] (*pt* **forgave**, *pp* **~n**)
*vt* (*pardon*) проща́ть (прости́ть
*pf*); **to ~ sb sth** проща́ть
(прости́ть *pf*) кому́-н что-н; **to ~
sb for sth** (*excuse*) проща́ть
(прости́ть *pf*) кого́-н за что-н; **I
forgave him for doing it** я
прости́л его́ за то, что он
сде́лал э́то; **~ness** *n* проще́ние

**forgot** [fə'ɡɔt] *pt of* **forget**; **~ten** *pp*
*of* **forget**

**fork** [fɔ:k] *n* ви́лка; (*for gardening*)
ви́лы *pl*; (*in road etc*)
разветвле́ние

**forlorn** [fə'lɔːn] *adj* поки́нутый; (*hope, attempt*) тще́тный

**form** [fɔːm] *n* (*type*) вид; (*shape*) фо́рма; (*SCOL*) класс; (*questionnaire*) анке́та; (*also*: **booking ~**) бланк ♦ *vt* (*make*) образо́вывать (образова́ть *pf*); (*organization, group*) формирова́ть (сформирова́ть *pf*); (*idea, habit*) выраба́тывать (вы́работать *pf*); **in top ~** в прекра́сной фо́рме

**formal** ['fɔːməl] *adj* форма́льный; (*person, behaviour*) церемо́нный; (*occasion*) официа́льный; **~ clothes** официа́льная фо́рма оде́жды; **~ities** [fɔː'mælɪtɪz] *npl* форма́льности *fpl*; **~ity** [fɔː'mælɪtɪ] *n* форма́льность *f*; (*of person, behaviour*) церемо́нность *f*; (*of occasion*) официа́льность *f*; **~ly** *adv* форма́льно; (*behave*) церемо́нно

**format** ['fɔːmæt] *n* форма́т

**formation** [fɔː'meɪʃən] *n* формирова́ние

**formative** ['fɔːmətɪv] *adj*: **in his ~ years** в го́ды становле́ния его́ ли́чности

**former** ['fɔːmər] *adj* бы́вший; (*earlier*) пре́жний ♦ *n*: **the ~ ... the latter ...** пе́рвый ... после́дний ...; **~ly** *adv* ра́нее, ра́ньше

**formidable** ['fɔːmɪdəbl] *adj* (*opponent*) гро́зный; (*task*) серьёзнейший

**formula** ['fɔːmjulə] (*pl* **~e** *or* **~s**) *n* (*MATH, CHEM*) фо́рмула; (*plan*) схе́ма; **~te** ['fɔːmjuleɪt] *vt* (*plan, strategy*) выраба́тывать (вы́работать *pf*); (*opinion, thought*) формули́ровать (сформули́ровать *pf*)

**fort** [fɔːt] *n* кре́пость *f*, форт

**forte** ['fɔːtɪ] *n* си́льная сторона́

**forth** [fɔːθ] *adv*: **to go back and ~** ходи́ть (*impf*) взад и вперёд; **and**

**so ~** и так да́лее; **~coming** *adj* предстоя́щий; (*person*) общи́тельный; **~right** *adj* (*condemnation, opposition*) откры́тый

**fortieth** ['fɔːtɪɪθ] *adj* сороково́й

**fortnight** ['fɔːtnaɪt] (*BRIT*) *n* две неде́ли; **~ly** *adv* раз в две неде́ли ♦ *adj*: **~ly magazine** журна́л, выходя́щий раз в две неде́ли

**fortress** ['fɔːtrɪs] *n* кре́пость *f*

**fortunate** ['fɔːtʃənɪt] *adj* (*event, choice*) счастли́вый; (*person*) уда́чливый; **he was ~ to get a job** на его́ сча́стье, он получи́л рабо́ту; **it is ~ that ...** к сча́стью ...; **~ly** *adv* к сча́стью; **~ly for him** на его́ сча́стье

**fortune** ['fɔːtʃən] *n* (*wealth*) состоя́ние; (*also*: **good ~**) сча́стье, уда́ча; **ill ~** невезе́ние, неуда́ча

**forty** ['fɔːtɪ] *n* со́рок

**forum** ['fɔːrəm] *n* фо́рум

**forward** ['fɔːwəd] *adv* вперёд ♦ *n* (*SPORT*) напада́ющий(ая) *m(f) adj*, фо́рвард ♦ *vt* (*letter, parcel*) пересыла́ть (пересла́ть *pf*) ♦ *adj* (*position*) пере́дний; (*not shy*) де́рзкий; **to move ~** (*progress*) продвига́ться (продви́нуться *pf*); **~s** *adv* вперёд

**fossil** ['fɔsl] *n* окамене́лость *f*, ископа́емое *nt adj*

**foster** ['fɔstər] *vt* (*child*) брать (взять *pf*) на воспита́ние

**fought** [fɔːt] *pt, pp of* **fight**

**foul** [faul] *adj* га́дкий, ме́рзкий; (*language*) непристо́йный; (*temper*) жу́ткий ♦ *n* (*SPORT*) наруше́ние ♦ *vt* (*dirty*) га́дить (зага́дить *pf*)

**found** [faund] *pt, pp of* **find** ♦ *vt* (*establish*) осно́вывать (основа́ть *pf*); **~ation** *n* (*base*) осно́ва;

(*organization*) о́бщество, фонд;
(*also*: **~ation cream**) крем под
макия́ж; **~ations** *npl* (*of building*)
фунда́мент *msg*; **~er** *n*
основа́тель(ница) *m(f)*

**fountain** ['fauntɪn] *n* фонта́н

**four** [fɔːʳ] *n* четы́ре; **on all ~s** на
четвере́ньках

**fourteen** ['fɔː'tiːn] *n*
четы́рнадцать; **~th** *adj*
четы́рнадцатый

**fourth** ['fɔːθ] *adj* четвёртый ♦ *n*
(*AUT*: *also*: **~ gear**) четвёртая
ско́рость *f*

**fowl** [faul] *n* пти́ца

**fox** [fɔks] *n* лиса́ ♦ *vt* озада́чивать
(озада́чить *pf*)

**foyer** ['fɔɪeɪ] *n* (*in hotel etc*) фойе́ *nt
ind*

**fraction** ['frækʃən] *n* (*portion*)
части́ца; (*MATH*) дробь *f*; **a ~ of a
second** до́ля секу́нды

**fracture** ['fræktʃəʳ] *n* перело́м ♦ *vt*
(*bone*) лома́ть (слома́ть *pf*)

**fragile** ['frædʒaɪl] *adj* хру́пкий

**fragment** ['frægmənt] *n* фрагме́нт;
(*of glass*) оско́лок, обло́мок

**fragrance** ['freɪgrəns] *n*
благоуха́ние

**fragrant** ['freɪgrənt] *adj* души́стый

**frail** [freɪl] *adj* (*person*) сла́бый,
не́мощный; (*structure*) хру́пкий

**frame** [freɪm] *n* (*of building,
structure*) карка́с, о́стов; (*of
person*) сложе́ние; (*of picture,
window*) ра́ма; (*of spectacles*: *also*:
**~s**) опра́ва ♦ *vt* обрамля́ть
(обра́мить *pf*); **~ of mind**
настрое́ние; **~work** *n* карка́с;
(*fig*) ра́мки *fpl*

**France** [frɑːns] *n* Фра́нция

**franchise** ['fræntʃaɪz] *n* (*POL*) пра́во
го́лоса; (*COMM*) франши́за

**frank** [fræŋk] *adj* (*discussion, person*)
открове́нный; (*look*) откры́тый;
**~ly** *adv* открове́нно

**frantic** ['fræntɪk] *adj* иступлённый;
(*hectic*) лихора́дочный

**fraternity** [frə'təːnɪtɪ] *n* (*club*)
содру́жество

**fraud** [frɔːd] *n* (*person*) моше́нник;
(*crime*) моше́нничество; **~ulent**
*adj* (*scheme, claim*)
моше́ннический

**fraught** [frɔːt] *adj*: **~ with**
чрева́тый +*instr*

**fray** [freɪ] *vi* трепа́ться
(истрепа́ться *pf*); **tempers were
~ed** все бы́ли на гра́ни срыва

**freak** [friːk] *adj* стра́нный,
ненорма́льный ♦ *n*: **he is a ~** он
ненорма́льный

**freckle** ['frɛkl] *n* (*usu pl*) весну́шка

**free** [friː] *adj* свобо́дный; (*costing
nothing*) беспла́тный ♦ *vt* (*prisoner
etc*) освобожда́ть (освободи́ть
*pf*), выпуска́ть (вы́пустить *pf*) (на
свобо́ду); (*object*) высвобожда́ть
(вы́свободить *pf*); **~ (of charge),
for ~** беспла́тно; **~dom** *n*
свобо́да; **~ kick** (*FOOTBALL*)
свобо́дный уда́р; **~lance** *adj*
внешта́тный, рабо́тающий по
договора́м; **~ly** *adv* (*without
restriction*) свобо́дно; (*liberally*)
оби́льно; **~-range** *adj*: **~-range
eggs** я́йца от кур на свобо́дном
вы́гуле; **~ will** *n*: **of one's own ~
will** по (свое́й) до́брой во́ле

**freeze** [friːz] (*pt* **froze**, *pp* **frozen**) *vi*
(*weather*) холода́ть (похолода́ть
*pf*); (*liquid, pipe, person*) замерза́ть
(замёрзнуть *pf*); (*person: stop
moving*) застыва́ть (засты́ть *pf*)
♦ *vt* замора́живать (заморо́зить
*pf*) ♦ *n* (*on arms, wages*)
замора́живание; **~r** *n*
морози́льник

**freezing** ['friːzɪŋ] *adj*: **~ (cold)**
ледяно́й ♦ *n*: **3 degrees below ~** 3
гра́дуса моро́за *or* ни́же нуля́;
**I'm ~** я замёрз; **it's ~** о́чень

хо́лодно

**freight** [freɪt] n фрахт

**French** [frentʃ] adj францу́зский;
**the ~** npl (people) францу́зы mpl;
**~ fries** npl (US) карто́фель msg-
фри; **~man** (irreg) n францу́з

**frenzy** ['frenzɪ] n (of violence)
остервене́ние, бе́шенство

**frequency** ['fri:kwənsɪ] n частота́

**frequent** adj ['fri:kwənt] vb
[frɪ'kwɛnt] adj ча́стый ♦ vt
посеща́ть (impf); **~ly** adv ча́сто

**fresh** [freʃ] adj све́жий; (instructions,
approach) но́вый; **to make a ~
start** начина́ть (нача́ть pf)
за́ново; **~ in one's mind** свежо́ в
па́мяти; **~er** n (BRIT : inf)
первоку́рсник; **~ly** adv: **~ly made**
свежепригото́вленный; **~ly
painted** свежевы́крашенный;
**~water** adj (lake) пре́сный; (fish)
пресново́дный

**fret** [frɛt] vi волнова́ться (impf)

**friction** ['frɪkʃən] n тре́ние; (fig)
тре́ния ntpl

**Friday** ['fraɪdɪ] n пя́тница

**fridge** [frɪdʒ] n (BRIT) холоди́льник

**fried** [fraɪd] pt, pp of **fry** ♦ adj
жа́реный

**friend** [frɛnd] n (male) друг;
(female) подру́га; **~ly** adj (person,
smile etc) дружелю́бный;
(government, country)
дру́жественный; (place,
restaurant) прия́тный ♦ n (also: **~ly
match**) това́рищеский матч; **to
be ~ly with** дружи́ть (impf) с
+instr; **to be ~ly to sb** относи́ться
(отнести́сь pf) к кому́-н
дружелю́бно; **~ship** n дру́жба

**fright** [fraɪt] n испу́г; **to take ~**
испуга́ться (pf); **~en** vt пуга́ть
(испуга́ть pf); **~ened** adj
испу́ганный; **to be ~ened (of)**
боя́ться (impf) (+gen); **he is ~ened
by change** его́ пуга́ют

измене́ния; **~ening** adj
стра́шный, устраша́ющий

**frilly** adj: **~ dress** пла́тье с
обо́рками

**fringe** [frɪndʒ] n (BRIT : of hair)
чёлка; (on shawl, lampshade etc)
бахрома́; (of forest etc) край,
окра́ина

**frivolous** ['frɪvələs] adj (conduct,
person) легкомы́сленный; (object,
activity) пустя́чный

**fro** [frəu] adv: **to and ~** туда́-сюда́

**frog** [frɔg] n лягу́шка

---

KEYWORD

---

**from** [frɔm] prep 1 (indicating
starting place, origin etc) из +gen, с
+gen; (from a person) от +gen; **he is
from Cyprus** он с Ки́пра; **from
London to Glasgow** из Ло́ндона
в Гла́зго; **a letter from my sister**
письмо́ от мое́й сестры́; **a
quotation from Dickens** цита́та из
Ди́ккенса; **to drink from the
bottle** пить (impf) из буты́лки;
**where do you come from?** Вы
отку́да?

2 (indicating movement: from inside)
из +gen; (: away from) от +gen;
(: off) с +gen; (: from behind) из-за
+gen; **she ran from the house** она́
вы́бежала из до́ма; **the car drove
away from the house** маши́на
отъе́хала от до́ма; **he took the
magazine from the table** он взял
журна́л со стола́; **they got up
from the table** они́ вста́ли из-за
стола́

3 (indicating time) с +gen; **from two
o'clock to** or **until** or **till three
(o'clock)** с двух часо́в до трёх
(часо́в); **from January (to August)**
с января́ (по а́вгуст)

4 (indicating distance: position) от
+gen; (: motion) до +gen; **the hotel
is one kilometre from the beach**

гости́ница нахо́дится в киломе́тре от пля́жа; **we're still a long way from home** мы ещё далеко́ от до́ма
5 (*indicating price, number etc*: *range*) от +*gen*; (: *change*) с +*gen*; **prices range from £10 to £50** це́ны колеблются с £10 до £50; **the interest rate was increased from nine per cent to ten per cent** проце́нтные ста́вки повы́сились с девяти́ до десяти́ проце́нтов
6 (*indicating difference*) от +*gen*; **to be different from sb/sth** отлича́ться (*impf*) от кого́-н/ чего́-н
7 (*because of, on the basis of* ): **from what he says** су́дя по тому́, что он говори́т; **from what I understand** как я понима́ю; **to act from conviction** де́йствовать (*impf*) по убежде́нию; **he is weak from hunger** он слаб от го́лода

**front** [frʌnt] *n* (*of house, also fig*) фаса́д; (*of dress*) пе́ред; (*of train, car*) пере́дняя часть *f*; (*also*: **sea ~**) на́бережная *f adj*; (*MIL, METEOROLOGY*) фронт ♦ *adj* передний; **in ~** вперёд; **in ~ of** перед +*instr*; **~ door** *n* входна́я дверь *f*; **~ier** ['frʌntɪəʳ] *n* грани́ца; **~ page** *n* пе́рвая страни́ца (*газе́ты*)
**frost** [frɔst] *n* моро́з; (*also*: **hoar~**) и́ней; **~bite** *n* обмороже́ние; **~y** *adj* (*weather, night*) моро́зный; (*welcome, look*) ледяно́й
**froth** ['frɔθ] *n* (*on liquid*) пе́на
**frown** [fraun] *n* нахму́ренный взгляд
**froze** [frəuz] *pt of* **freeze**; **~n** *pp of* **freeze**
**fruit** [fru:t] *n inv* фрукт; (*fig*) плод; **~ful** *adj* плодотво́рный; **~ion** [fru:'ɪʃən] *n*: **to come to ~ion**

дава́ть (дать *pf*) плоды́; **~ machine** *n* (*BRIT*) игрово́й автома́т
**frustrate** [frʌs'treɪt] *vt* (*person, plan*) расстра́ивать (расстро́ить *pf*)
**frustration** [frʌs'treɪʃən] *n* доса́да
**fry** [fraɪ] (*pt, pp* **fried**) *vt* жа́рить (пожа́рить *pf*); **~ing pan** (*US*) **~-pan**) *n* сковорода́
**ft.** *abbr* = **feet**, **foot**
**fudge** [fʌdʒ] *n* ≈ сли́вочная пома́дка
**fuel** ['fjuəl] *n* (*for heating*) то́пливо; (*for plane, car etc*) горю́чее *nt adj*
**fugitive** ['fju:dʒɪtɪv] *n* бегле́ц(ля́нка)
**fulfil** [ful'fɪl] (*US* **fulfill**) *vt* (*function, desire, promise*) исполня́ть (испо́лнить *pf*); (*ambition*) осуществля́ть (осуществи́ть *pf*); **~ment** (*US* **~lment**) *n* (*of promise, desire*) исполне́ние; (*satisfaction*) удовлетворе́ние; (*of ambitions*) осуществле́ние
**full** [ful] *adj* по́лный; (*skirt*) широ́кий ♦ *adv*: **to know ~ well that** прекра́сно знать (*impf*), что; **at ~ volume/power** на по́лную гро́мкость/мо́щность; **I'm ~ (up)** я сыт; **he is ~ of enthusiasm/hope** он по́лон энтузиа́зма/наде́жды; **~ details** все дета́ли; **at ~ speed** на по́лной ско́рости; **a ~ two hours** це́лых два часа́; **in ~** по́лностью; **~-length** *adj* (*film, novel*) полнометра́жный; (*coat*) дли́нный; (*mirror*) высо́кий; **~ moon** *n* по́лная луна́; **~-scale** *adj* (*attack, war, search etc*) широкомасшта́бный; **~-time** *adj, adv* (*study*) на дневно́м отделе́нии; (*work*) на по́лной ста́вке; **~y** *adv* (*completely*) по́лностью, вполне́; **~y as big as** по кра́йней ме́ре тако́й же величины́, как; **~y fledged** *adj*

(*teacher, barrister*) вполне́ сложи́вшийся

**fumes** [fju:mz] *npl* испаре́ния *ntpl*, пары́ *mpl*

**fun** [fʌn] *n*: **what ~!** как ве́село!; **to have ~** весели́ться (повесели́ться *pf*); **he's good ~ (to be with)** с ним ве́село; **for ~** для заба́вы; **to make ~ of** подшу́чивать (подшути́ть *pf*) над +*instr*

**function** ['fʌŋkʃən] *n* фу́нкция; (*product*) произво́дная *f adj*; (*social occasion*) прие́м ♦ *vi* (*operate*) функциони́ровать (*impf*); **~al** *adj* (*operational*) де́йствующий; (*practical*) функциона́льный

**fund** [fʌnd] *n* фонд; (*of knowledge etc*) запа́с; **~s** *npl* (*money*) (де́нежные) сре́дства *ntpl*, фо́нды *mpl*

**fundamental** [fʌndə'mentl] *adj* фундамента́льный

**funding** ['fʌndɪŋ] *n* финанси́рование

**funeral** ['fju:nərəl] *n* по́хороны *pl*

**fungus** ['fʌŋgəs] (*pl* **fungi**) *n* (*plant*) гриб; (*mould*) пле́сень *f*

**funnel** ['fʌnl] *n* (*for pouring*) воро́нка; (*of ship*) труба́

**funny** ['fʌnɪ] *adj* (*amusing*) заба́вный; (*strange*) стра́нный, чудно́й

**fur** [fəːʳ] *n* мех

**furious** ['fjuərɪəs] *adj* (*person*) взбешённый; (*exchange, argument*) бу́рный; (*effort, speed*) неисто́вый

**furnace** ['fəːnɪs] *n* печь *f*

**furnish** ['fəːnɪʃ] *vt* (*room, building*) обставля́ть (обста́вить *pf*); **to ~ sb with sth** (*supply*) предоставля́ть (предоста́вить *pf*) что-н кому́-н; **~ings** *npl* обстано́вка *fsg*

**furniture** ['fəːnɪtʃəʳ] *n* ме́бель *f*; **piece of ~** предме́т ме́бели

**furry** ['fəːrɪ] *adj* пуши́стый

**further** ['fəːðəʳ] *adj* дополни́тельный ♦ *adv* (*farther*) да́льше; (*moreover*) бо́лее того́ ♦ *vt* (*career, project*) продвига́ть (продви́нуть *pf*), соде́йствовать (*impf/pf*) +*dat*; **~ education** *n* (*BRIT*) сре́днее специа́льное образова́ние

**further education** - сре́днее специа́льное образова́ние. Его́ мо́жно получи́ть в ко́лледжах. Обуче́ние прово́дится на осно́ве по́лного дневно́го ку́рса, почасово́го или вече́рнего ку́рса.

**furthermore** *adv* бо́лее того́

**furthest** ['fəːðɪst] *superl of* **far**

**furtive** ['fəːtɪv] *adj*: **~ movement/ glance** движе́ние/взгляд укра́дкой

**fury** ['fjuərɪ] *n* я́рость *f*, бе́шенство

**fuse** [fju:z] (*US* **fuze**) *n* (*ELEC*) предохрани́тель *m*; (*on bomb*) фити́ль *m*

**fusion** ['fju:ʒən] *n* (*of ideas, qualities*) слия́ние; (*also*: **nuclear ~**) я́дерный си́нтез

**fuss** [fʌs] *n* (*excitement*) сумато́ха; (*anxiety*) суета́; (*trouble*) шум; **to make** *or* **kick up a ~** поднима́ть (подня́ть *pf*) шум; **to make a ~ of sb** носи́ться (*impf*) с кем-н; **~y** *adj* (*nervous*) суетли́вый; (*choosy*) ме́лочный, су́етный; (*elaborate*) вы́чурный

**future** ['fju:tʃəʳ] *adj* бу́дущий ♦ *n* бу́дущее *nt*; (*LING*: *also*: **~ tense**) бу́дущее вре́мя *nt*; **in (the) ~** в бу́дущем; **in the near/**

**immediate ~** в недалёком/
ближа́йшем бу́дущем
**fuze** [fju:z] n (US) = **fuse**
**fuzzy** ['fʌzɪ] adj (thoughts, picture)
расплы́вчатый; (hair) пуши́стый

# G, g

**g.** abbr = **gram** г
**gadget** ['gædʒɪt] n
приспособле́ние
**Gaelic** ['geɪlɪk] n (LING) га́льский
язы́к
**gag** [gæg] n (on mouth) кляп ♦ vt
вставля́ть (вста́вить pf) кляп +dat
**gain** [geɪn] n (increase) приро́ст ♦ vt
(confidence, experience)
приобрета́ть (приобрести́ pf);
(speed) набира́ть (набра́ть pf) ♦ vi
(benefit): **to ~ from sth** извлека́ть
(извле́чь pf) вы́году из чего́-н; **to
~ 3 pounds (in weight)**
поправля́ться (попра́виться pf)
на 3 фу́нта; **to ~ on sb** догоня́ть
(догна́ть pf) кого́-н
**gala** ['gɑːlə] n (festival)
пра́зднество
**galaxy** ['gæləksɪ] n гала́ктика
**gale** [geɪl] n (wind) си́льный ве́тер;
(at sea) штормово́й ве́тер
**gallery** ['gælərɪ] n (also: **art ~**)
галере́я; (in hall, church) балко́н;
(in theatre) галёрка
**gallon** ['gælɪn] n галло́н (4,5 ли́тра)
**gallop** ['gæləp] vi (horse) скака́ть
(impf) (гало́пом), галопи́ровать
(impf)
**galore** [gə'lɔːʳ] adv в изоби́лии
**gamble** ['gæmbl] n риско́ванное
предприя́тие, риск ♦ vt (money)
ста́вить (поста́вить pf) ♦ vi (take a
risk) рискова́ть (рискну́ть pf);
(bet) игра́ть (impf) в аза́ртные
и́гры; **to ~ on sth** (also fig) де́лать
(сде́лать pf) ста́вку на что-н; **~r** n

игро́к
**gambling** ['gæmblɪŋ] n аза́ртные
и́гры fpl
**game** [geɪm] n игра́; (match) матч;
(esp TENNIS) гейм; (also: **board ~**)
насто́льная игра́; (CULIN) дичь f
♦ adj (willing): **~ (for)** гото́вый (на
+acc); **big ~** кру́пный зверь
**gammon** ['gæmən] n (bacon)
о́корок; (ham) ветчина́
**gang** [gæŋ] n ба́нда; (of friends)
компа́ния
**gangster** ['gæŋstəʳ] n га́нгстер
**gap** [gæp] n (space) промежу́ток;
(: between teeth) щерби́на; (: in
time) интерва́л; (difference)
расхожде́ние; **generation ~**
разногла́сия ме́жду
поколе́ниями
**gaping** ['geɪpɪŋ] adj (hole)
зия́ющий
**garage** ['gærɑːʒ] n гара́ж; (petrol
station) запра́вочная ста́нция,
бензоколо́нка
**garbage** ['gɑːbɪdʒ] n (US: rubbish)
му́сор; (inf: nonsense) ерунда́; **~
can** n (US) помо́йный я́щик
**garden** ['gɑːdn] n сад; **~s** npl (park)
парк msg; **~er** n садово́д;
(employee) садо́вник(ица); **~ing** n
садово́дство
**garish** ['gɛərɪʃ] adj (light) ре́зкий;
(dress, colour) крича́щий
**garland** ['gɑːlənd] n гирля́нда
**garlic** ['gɑːlɪk] n чесно́к
**garment** ['gɑːmənt] n наря́д
**garnish** ['gɑːnɪʃ] vt украша́ть
(укра́сить pf)
**garrison** ['gærɪsn] n гарнизо́н
**gas** [gæs] n газ; (US: gasoline)
бензи́н ♦ vt (kill) удуша́ть
(удуши́ть pf) (га́зом)
**gash** [gæʃ] n (wound) глубо́кая
ра́на; (cut) глубо́кий поре́з ♦ vt
распа́рывать (распоро́ть pf)
**gasoline** ['gæsəliːn] n (US) бензи́н

**gasp** [gɑːsp] n (breath) вдох
**gas station** n (US) запрáвочная стáнция, бензоколóнка
**gastric** ['gæstrɪk] adj (MED) желýдочный
**gate** [geɪt] n калѝтка; (at airport) вы́ход; **~s** ворóта pl; **~way** n ворóта pl
**gather** ['gæðəʳ] vt собирáть (собрáть pf); (understand) полагáть (impf) ♦ vi собирáться (собрáться pf); **to ~ speed** набирáть (набрáть pf) скóрость; **~ing** n собрáние
**gaudy** ['gɔːdɪ] adj пёстрый
**gauge** [geɪdʒ] n (instrument) измерѝтельный прибóр ♦ vt (amount, quantity) измеря́ть (измéрить pf); (fig) оцéнивать (оценѝть pf)
**gaunt** [gɔːnt] adj измождённый
**gauntlet** ['gɔːntlɪt] n (fig): **to run the ~** подвергáться (подвéргнуться pf) напáдкам; **to throw down the ~** бросáть (брóсить pf) перчáтку
**gauze** [gɔːz] n (fabric) мáрля
**gave** [geɪv] pt of **give**
**gay** [geɪ] adj (cheerful) весёлый; (homosexual): **~ bar** бар для голубы́х or гомосексуалѝстов ♦ n гомосексуалѝст, голубóй m adj; **he is ~** он гомосексуалѝст or голубóй
**gaze** [geɪz] n (прѝстальный) взгляд ♦ vi: **to ~ at sth** разгля́дывать (impf) что-н
**GB** abbr = **Great Britain**
**GCSE** n abbr (BRIT) (= General Certificate of Secondary Education)

GCSE - аттестáт о срéднем образовáнии. Шкóльники сдаю́т экзáмены для получéния э́того аттестáта в вóзрасте 15-16 лет.

Часть предмéтов, по котóрым сдаю́тся экзáмены, обязáтельна, часть - по вы́бору. Однáко э́того аттестáта не достáточно для поступлéния в университéт.

**gear** [gɪəʳ] n (equipment, belongings etc) принадлéжности fpl; (AUT) скóрость f; (: mechanism) передáча f ♦ vt (fig): **to ~ sth to** приспосáбливать (приспосóбить pf) что-н к +dat; **top** or (US) **high/low ~** вы́сшая/нѝзкая скóрость; **in ~** в зацеплéнии; **~box** n корóбка передáч or скоростéй; **~ lever** (US **~ shift**) n переключáтель m скоростéй
**geese** [giːs] npl of **goose**
**gelatin(e)** ['dʒɛlətiːn] n желатѝн
**gem** [dʒɛm] n (stone) драгоцéнный кáмень m, самоцвéт
**Gemini** ['dʒɛmɪnaɪ] n Близнецы́ mpl
**gender** ['dʒɛndəʳ] n (sex) пол; (LING) род
**gene** [dʒiːn] n ген
**general** ['dʒɛnərl] n (MIL) генерáл ♦ adj óбщий; (movement, interest) всеóбщий; **in ~** в óбщем; **~ election** n всеóбщие вы́боры mpl; **~ly** adv вообщé; (+vb) обы́чно; **to become ~ly available** становѝться (стать pf) общедостýпным(ой); **it is ~ly accepted that ...** общепрѝзнанно, что ...
**generate** ['dʒɛnəreɪt] vt (power, electricity) генерѝровать (impf), выраба́тывать (вы́работать pf); (excitement, interest) вызывáть (вы́звать pf); (jobs) создавáть (создáть pf)
**generation** [dʒɛnəˈreɪʃən] n поколéние; (of power) генерѝрование; **for ~s** из

поколе́ния в поколе́ние

**generator** ['dʒɛnəreɪtəʳ] n
генера́тор

**generosity** [dʒɛnə'rɔsɪtɪ] n
ще́дрость f

**generous** ['dʒɛnərəs] adj (person:
lavish) ще́дрый; (: unselfish)
великоду́шный; (amount of
money) значи́тельный

**genetics** [dʒɪ'nɛtɪks] n гене́тика

**Geneva** [dʒɪ'niːvə] n Жене́ва

**genial** ['dʒiːnɪəl] adj (smile,
expression) приве́тливый; (host)
раду́шный

**genitals** ['dʒɛnɪtlz] npl половы́е
о́рганы mpl

**genius** ['dʒiːnɪəs] n (skill) тала́нт;
(person) ге́ний

**gent** [dʒɛnt] n abbr (BRIT : inf ) =
**gentleman**

**gentle** ['dʒɛntl] adj не́жный,
ла́сковый; (nature, movement,
landscape) мя́гкий

**gentleman** ['dʒɛntlmən] (irreg) n
(man) джентльме́н

**gently** ['dʒɛntlɪ] adv (smile, treat,
speak) не́жно, ла́сково; (curve,
slope, move) мя́гко

**gentry** ['dʒɛntrɪ] n inv: **the ~**
дворя́нство

**gents** [dʒɛnts] n: **the ~** мужско́й
туале́т

**genuine** ['dʒɛnjuɪn] adj (sincere)
и́скренний; (real) по́длинный

**geographic(al)** [dʒɪə'græfɪk(l)] adj
географи́ческий

**geography** [dʒɪ'ɔgrəfɪ] n
геогра́фия

**geology** [dʒɪ'ɔlədʒɪ] n геоло́гия

**geometry** [dʒɪ'ɔmətrɪ] n геоме́трия

**Georgia** ['dʒɔːdʒə] n Гру́зия; **~n** adj
грузи́нский

**geranium** [dʒɪ'reɪnɪəm] n гера́нь f

**geriatric** [dʒɛrɪ'ætrɪk] adj
гериатри́ческий

**germ** [dʒəːm] n (MED) микро́б

**German** ['dʒəːmən] adj неме́цкий
♦ n не́мец(мка); **~ measles** n
(BRIT) красну́ха

**Germany** ['dʒəːmənɪ] n Герма́ния

**gesture** ['dʒɛstjəʳ] n жест

---
KEYWORD
---

**get** [gɛt] (pt, pp **got**; US pp **gotten**)
vi 1 (become) станови́ться (стать
pf); **it's getting late** стано́вится
по́здно; **to get old** старе́ть
(постаре́ть pf); **to get tired**
устава́ть (уста́ть pf); **to get cold**
мёрзнуть (замёрзнуть pf); **to get
annoyed easily** легко́
раздража́ться (impf); **he was
getting bored** ему́ ста́ло ску́чно;
**he gets drunk every weekend** он
напива́ется ка́ждый выходно́й
2 (be): **he got killed** его́ уби́ли;
**when do I get paid?** когда́ мне
запла́тят?
3 ( go): **to get to/from**
добира́ться (добра́ться pf) до
+gen/из +gen/с +gen; **how did you
get here?** как Вы сюда́
добрали́сь?
4 (begin): **to get to know sb**
узнава́ть (узна́ть pf) кого́-н; **I'm
getting to like him** он начина́ет
мне нра́виться; **let's get started**
дава́йте начнём
♦ modal aux vb: **you've got to do it**
Вы должны́ э́то сде́лать
♦ vt 1: **to get sth done** сде́лать
(pf) что-н; **to get the washing
done** стира́ть (постира́ть pf); **to
get the dishes done** мыть
(помы́ть or вы́мыть pf) посу́ду; **to
get the car started** or **to start**
заводи́ть (завести́ pf) маши́ну; **to
get sb to do** заставля́ть
(заста́вить pf) кого́-н +infin; **to get
sb ready** собира́ть (собра́ть pf)
кого́-н; **to get sth ready** гото́вить
(пригото́вить pf) что-н; **to get sb**

**drunk** напа́ивать (напои́ть pf) кого́-н; **she got me into trouble** она́ вовлекла́ меня́ в неприя́тности

**2** (obtain: permission, results) получа́ть (получи́ть pf); (find: job, flat) находи́ть (найти́ pf); (person: call) звать (позва́ть pf); (: pick up) забира́ть (забра́ть pf); (call out: doctor, plumber etc) вызыва́ть (вы́звать pf); (object: carry) приноси́ть (принести́ pf); (: buy) покупа́ть (купи́ть pf); (: deliver) доставля́ть (доста́вить pf); **we must get him to hospital** мы должны́ доста́вить его́ в больни́цу; **do you think we'll get the piano through the door?** как Вы ду́маете, мы прота́щим пиани́но че́рез дверь?; **I'll get the car** я схожу́ за маши́ной; **can I get you something to drink?** Позво́льте предложи́ть Вам что-нибудь вы́пить?

**3** (receive) получа́ть (получи́ть pf); **to get a reputation for** приобрета́ть (приобрести́ pf) дурну́ю репута́цию +instr; **what did you get for your birthday?** что Вам подари́ли на день рожде́ния?

**4** (grab) хвата́ть (схвати́ть pf); (hit): **the bullet got him in the leg** пу́ля попа́ла ему́ в но́гу

**5** (catch, take): **we got a taxi** мы взя́ли такси́; **did she get her plane?** она́ успе́ла на самолёт?; **what train are you getting?** каки́м по́ездом Вы е́дете?; **where do I get the train?** где мне сесть на по́езд?

**6** (understand) понима́ть (поня́ть pf); (hear) рассли́шать (pf); (do you) get it? (inf) (тебе́) поня́тно?; **I've got it!** тепе́рь поня́тно!; **I'm sorry, I didn't get**

**your name** прости́те, я не рассли́шал Ва́ше и́мя

**7** (have, possess): **how many children have you got?** ско́лько у Вас дете́й?; **I've got very little time** у меня́ о́чень ма́ло вре́мени

**get about** vi (news) распространя́ться (распространи́ть-ся pf); **I don't get about much now** (go places) тепе́рь я ма́ло где быва́ю

**get along** vi: **get along with** ла́дить (impf) с +instr; (manage) = **get by**; **I'd better be getting along** мне, пожа́луй, пора́ (идти́)

**get at** vt fus (criticize) придира́ться (придра́ться pf) к +dat; (reach) дотя́гиваться (дотяну́ться pf) до +gen

**get away** vi (leave) уходи́ть (уйти́ pf); (escape) убега́ть (убежа́ть pf)

**get away with** vt fus: **he gets away with everything** ему́ всё схо́дит с рук

**get back** vi (return) возвраща́ться (возврати́ться pf), верну́ться (pf) ♦ vt получа́ть (получи́ть pf) наза́д or обра́тно

**get by** vi (pass) проходи́ть (пройти́ pf); (manage): **to get by without** обходи́ться (обойти́сь pf) без +gen; **I will get by** (manage) я спра́влюсь

**get down** vt (depress) угнета́ть (impf) ♦ vi: **to get down from** слеза́ть (слезть pf) с +gen

**get down to** vt fus сади́ться (сесть pf) or бра́ться (взя́ться pf) за +acc

**get in** vi (train) прибыва́ть (прибы́ть pf), приходи́ть (прийти́ pf); (arrive home) приходи́ть (прийти́ pf); (to concert, building) попада́ть (попа́сть pf), проходи́ть (пройти́ pf); **he got in by ten votes** он прошёл с большинство́м в де́сять голосо́в; **as soon as the bus arrived we all got in** как то́лько авто́бус подошёл, мы се́ли в него́

**get into** vt fus (building) входи́ть (войти́ pf) в +acc; (vehicle) сади́ться (сесть pf) в +acc; (clothes) влеза́ть (влезть pf) в +acc; (fight, argument) вступа́ть (вступи́ть pf) в +acc; (university, college) поступа́ть (поступи́ть pf) в +acc; (subj: train) прибыва́ть (прибы́ть pf) в/на +acc; **to get into bed** ложи́ться (лечь pf) в посте́ль

**get off** vi (escape): **to get off lightly/with sth** отде́лываться (отде́латься pf) легко́/чем-н ♦ vt (clothes) снима́ть (снять pf) ♦ vt fus (train, bus) сходи́ть (сойти́ pf) с +gen; (horse, bicycle) слеза́ть (слезть pf) с +gen

**get on** vi (age) старе́ть (impf); **how are you getting on?** как Ва́ши успе́хи?

**get out** vi (leave) выбира́ться (вы́браться pf); (socialize) выбира́ться (вы́браться pf) из до́ма

**get out of** vt fus (duty) отде́лываться (отде́латься pf) от +gen

**get over** vt fus (illness) преодолева́ть (преодоле́ть pf)

**get round** vt fus (law, rule) обходи́ть (обойти́ pf); (fig: person) угова́ривать (уговори́ть pf)

**get through** vi (TEL) дозва́ниваться (дозвони́ться pf)

**get through to** vt fus (TEL) дозва́ниваться (дозвони́ться pf) до +gen

**get together** vi (several people) собира́ться (собра́ться pf) ♦ vt

(people) собира́ть (собра́ть pf)

**get up** vi встава́ть (встать pf)

**get up to** vt fus (BRIT) затева́ть (зате́ять pf); **they're always getting up to mischief** они́ всегда́ прока́зничают

**ghastly** ['gɑːstlɪ] adj ме́рзкий, омерзи́тельный

**gherkin** ['gəːkɪn] n марино́ванный огуре́ц

**ghetto** ['gɛtəu] n ге́тто nt ind

**ghost** [gəust] n (spirit) привиде́ние, при́зрак

**giant** ['dʒaɪənt] n (in myths) велика́н; (fig, COMM) гига́нт ♦ adj огро́мный

**Gibraltar** [dʒɪ'brɔːltəʳ] n Гибралта́р

**giddy** ['gɪdɪ] adj: **I feel ~** (dizzy) у меня́ кру́жится голова́

**gift** [gɪft] n (present) пода́рок; (ability) дар, тала́нт; **~ed** adj одарённый

**gigantic** [dʒaɪ'gæntɪk] adj гига́нтский

**giggle** ['gɪgl] vi хихи́кать (impf)

**gills** [gɪlz] npl (of fish) жа́бры fpl

**gilt** [gɪlt] adj позоло́ченный

**gimmick** ['gɪmɪk] n уло́вка, трюк

**gin** [dʒɪn] n джин

**ginger** ['dʒɪndʒəʳ] n (spice) имби́рь m; **~bread** n (cake) имби́рный пиро́г; (biscuit) имби́рное пече́нье

**gingerly** ['dʒɪndʒəlɪ] adv опа́сливо

**giraffe** [dʒɪ'rɑːf] n жира́ф

**girl** [gəːl] n (child) де́вочка; (young unmarried woman) де́вушка; (daughter) до́чка; **an English ~** молода́я англича́нка; **~friend** n подру́га

**giro** ['dʒaɪrəu] n (BRIT: welfare cheque) чек, по кото́рому получа́ют посо́бия по безрабо́тице

**gist** [dʒɪst] n суть f

KEYWORD

**give** [gɪv] (pt **gave**, pt **given**) vt **1**
(hand over): **to give sb sth** or **sth
to sb** дава́ть (дать pf) кому́-н
что-н; **they gave her a book for
her birthday** они́ подари́ли ей
кни́гу на день рожде́ния
**2** (used with noun to replace verb):
**to give a sigh** вздыха́ть
(вздохну́ть pf); **to give a shrug**
передёргивать (передёрнуть pf)
плеча́ми; **to give a speech**
выступа́ть (вы́ступить pf) с
ре́чью; **to give a lecture** чита́ть
(прочита́ть pf) ле́кцию; **to give
three cheers** три́жды прокрича́ть
(pf) "ура́"
**3** (tell: news) сообща́ть
(сообщи́ть pf); (advice) дава́ть
(дать pf); **could you give him a
message for me please? tell him
that ...** переда́йте ему́,
пожа́луйста, от меня́, что ...; **I've
got a message to give you from
your brother** я до́лжен переда́ть
тебе́ что-то от твоего́ бра́та
**4**: **to give sb sth** (clothing, food,
right) дава́ть (дать pf) кому́-н
что-н; (title) присва́ивать
(присво́ить pf) кому́-н что-н;
(honour, responsibility) возлага́ть
(возложи́ть pf) на кого́-н что-н;
**to give sb a surprise** удивля́ть
(удиви́ть pf) кого́-н; **that's given
me an idea** э́то навело́ меня́ на
мысль
**5** (dedicate: one's life) отдава́ть
(отда́ть pf); **you'll need to give
me more time** Вы должны́ дать
мне бо́льше вре́мени; **she gave
it all her attention** она́ отнесла́сь
к э́тому с больши́м внима́нием
**6** (organize: dinner etc) дава́ть
(дать pf)
♦ vi **1** (stretch: fabric)

растя́гиваться (растяну́ться pf)
**2** (break, collapse) = **give way**
**give away** vt (money, object)
отдава́ть (отда́ть pf); (bride)
отдава́ть (отда́ть pf) за́муж
**give back** vt отдава́ть (отда́ть
pf) обра́тно
**give in** vi (yield) сдава́ться
(сда́ться pf)
♦ vt (essay etc) сдава́ть (сдать pf)
**give off** vt fus (smoke, heat)
выделя́ть (impf)
**give out** vt (distribute) раздава́ть
(разда́ть pf)
**give up** vi (stop trying) сдава́ться
(сда́ться pf)
♦ vt (job, boyfriend) броса́ть
(бро́сить pf); (idea, hope)
оставля́ть (оста́вить pf); **to give
up smoking** броса́ть (бро́сить pf)
кури́ть; **to give o.s. up** сдава́ться
(сда́ться pf)
**give way** vi (rope, ladder) не
выде́рживать (вы́держать pf);
(wall, roof) обва́ливаться
(обвали́ться pf); (floor)
прова́ливаться (провали́ться pf);
(chair) ру́хнуть (pf); (BRIT : AUT)
уступа́ть (уступи́ть pf) доро́гу;
**his legs gave way beneath him** у
него́ подкоси́лись но́ги

**glacier** ['glæsɪə'] n ледни́к
**glad** [glæd] adj: **I am ~** я рад; **~ly**
adv (willingly) с ра́достью
**glamorous** ['glæmərəs] adj
шика́рный, роско́шный
**glance** [glɑːns] n (look) взгляд ♦ vi:
**to ~ at** взгля́дывать (взгляну́ть
pf) на +acc
**glancing** ['glɑːnsɪŋ] adj боково́й
**gland** [glænd] n железа́
**glare** [glɛə'] n взгляд; (of light)
сия́ние
**glaring** ['glɛərɪŋ] adj я́вный,
вопию́щий

**glass** [glɑːs] n (substance) стекло́; (container, contents) стака́н; ~**es** npl (spectacles) очки́ ntpl

**glaze** [gleɪz] n (on pottery) глазу́рь f; ~**d** adj (eyes) му́тный, ту́склый

**gleam** [gliːm] vi мерца́ть (impf)

**glee** [gliː] n (joy) ликова́ние

**glen** [glɛn] n речна́я доли́на

**glib** [glɪb] adj (promise, response) бо́йкий

**glide** [glaɪd] vi скользи́ть (impf); (AVIAT) плани́ровать (impf); (bird) пари́ть (impf); ~**r** n планёр

**gliding** ['glaɪdɪŋ] n плани́рование

**glimmer** ['glɪmər] n (of interest, hope) про́блеск; (of light) мерца́ние

**glimpse** [glɪmps] n: ~ **of** взгляд на +acc ♦ vt ви́деть (уви́деть pf) ме́льком, взгляну́ть (pf) на +acc

**glint** [glɪnt] vi блесте́ть (блесну́ть pf), мерца́ть (impf)

**glitter** ['glɪtər] vi сверка́ть (сверкну́ть pf)

**global** ['gləʊbl] adj (interest, attention) глоба́льный; ~ **warming** n глоба́льное потепле́ние

**globe** [gləʊb] n (world) земно́й шар; (model of world) гло́бус

**gloom** [gluːm] n мрак; (fig) уны́ние

**glorified** ['glɔːrɪfaɪd] adj несча́стный; **she is merely a ~ secretary** она́ всего́-на́всего несча́стная секрета́рша

**glorious** ['glɔːrɪəs] adj (sunshine, flowers) великоле́пный

**glory** ['glɔːrɪ] n (prestige) сла́ва

**gloss** [glɔs] n гля́нец, лоск; (also: ~ **paint**) гля́нцевая кра́ска

**glossary** ['glɔsərɪ] n глосса́рий

**glossy** ['glɔsɪ] adj (photograph, magazine) гля́нцевый; (hair) блестя́щий

**glove** [glʌv] n перча́тка; ~ **compartment** n перча́точный я́щик, бардачо́к (разг)

**glow** [gləʊ] vi свети́ться (impf)

**glucose** ['gluːkəʊs] n глюко́за

**glue** [gluː] n клей ♦ vt: **to ~ sth onto sth** прикле́ивать (прикле́ить pf) что-н на что-н

**glum** [glʌm] adj мра́чный

**glut** [glʌt] n избы́ток

**gnarled** [nɑːld] adj (tree) сучкова́тый; (hand) скрю́ченный

**gnat** [næt] n мо́шка

KEYWORD

**go** [gəʊ] (pt **went**, pp **gone**, pl **goes**) vi 1 (move: on foot) ходи́ть/ идти́ (пойти́ pf); (travel: by transport) е́здить/е́хать (пое́хать pf); **she went into the kitchen** она́ пошла́ на ку́хню; **he often goes to China** он ча́сто е́здит в Кита́й; **they are going to the theatre tonight** сего́дня ве́чером они́ иду́т в теа́тр

2 (depart: on foot) уходи́ть (уйти́ pf); (: by plane) улета́ть (улете́ть pf); (: by train, car) уезжа́ть (уе́хать pf); **the plane goes at 6am** самолёт улета́ет в 6 часо́в утра́; **the train/bus goes at 6pm** по́езд/ авто́бус ухо́дит в 6 часо́в; **I must go now** мне на́до идти́

3 (attend): **to go to** ходи́ть (impf) в/на +acc; **she doesn't go to lectures/school** она́ не хо́дит на ле́кции/в шко́лу; **she went to university** она́ учи́лась в университе́те

4 (take part in activity): **to go dancing** ходи́ть/идти́ (пойти́ pf) танцева́ть

5 (work): **is your watch going?** Ва́ши часы́ иду́т?; **the bell went** прозвене́л звоно́к; **the tape recorder was still going** магнитофо́н всё ещё рабо́тал

6 (*become*): **to go pale** бледне́ть (побледне́ть *pf*); **to go mouldy** пле́сневеть (запле́сневеть *pf*)
7 (*be sold*) расходи́ться (разойти́сь *pf*); **the books went for £10** кни́ги разошли́сь по £10
8 (*fit, suit*): **to go with** подходи́ть (подойти́ *pf*) к +*dat*
9 (*be about to, intend to*): **to go to do** собира́ться (собра́ться *pf*) +*infin*
10 (*time*) идти́ (*impf*)
11 (*event, activity*) проходи́ть (пройти́ *pf*); **how did it go?** как всё прошло́?
12 (*be given*) идти́ (пойти́ *pf*); **the proceeds will go to charity** при́быль пойдёт на благотвори́тельные це́ли; **the job is to go to someone else** рабо́ту даду́т кому́-то друго́му
13 (*break etc*): **the fuse went** предохрани́тель перегоре́л; **the leg of the chair went** но́жка сту́ла слома́лась
14 (*be placed*): **the milk goes in the fridge** молоко́ быва́ет в холоди́льнике
♦ *n* 1 (*try*) попы́тка; **to have a go (at doing)** де́лать (сде́лать *pf*) попы́тку (+*infin*)
2 (*turn*): **whose go is it?** (*in board games*) чей ход?
3 (*move*): **to be on the go** быть (*impf*) на нога́х
**go about** *vi* (*also*: **go around**: *rumour*) ходи́ть (*impf*)
**go ahead** *vi* (*event*) продолжа́ться (продо́лжиться *pf*); **to go ahead with** (*project*) приступа́ть (приступи́ть *pf*) к +*dat*; **may I begin? - yes, go ahead!** мо́жно начина́ть? - да, дава́йте!
**go along** *vi* идти́ (пойти́ *pf*); **to go along with sb** (*accompany*)

идти́ (пойти́ *pf*) с кем-н; (*agree*) соглаша́ться (согласи́ться *pf*) с кем-н
**go away** *vi* (*leave: on foot*) уходи́ть (уйти́ *pf*); (: *by transport*) уезжа́ть (уе́хать *pf*); **go away and think about it for a while** иди́ и поду́май об э́том
**go back** *vi* (*return, go again*) возвраща́ться (возврати́ться *pf*), верну́ться (*pf*); **we went back into the house** мы верну́лись в дом; **I am never going back to her house again** я никогда́ бо́льше не пойду́ к ней
**go for** *vt fus* (*fetch: paper, doctor*) идти́ (пойти́ *pf*) за +*instr*; (*choose, like*) выбира́ть (вы́брать *pf*); (*attack*) набра́сываться (набро́ситься *pf*) на +*acc*; **that goes for me too** ко мне э́то то́же отно́сится
**go in** *vi* (*enter*) входи́ть (войти́ *pf*), заходи́ть (зайти́ *pf*)
**go in for** *vt fus* (*enter*) принима́ть (приня́ть *pf*) уча́стие в +*prp*; (*take up*) заня́ться (*pf*) +*instr*
**go into** *vt fus* (*enter*) входи́ть (войти́ *pf*) в +*acc*; (*take up*) заня́ться (*pf*) +*instr*; **to go into details** входи́ть (*impf*) or вдава́ться (*impf*) в подро́бности
**go off** *vi* (*leave: on foot*) уходи́ть (уйти́ *pf*); (: *by transport*) уезжа́ть (уе́хать *pf*); (*food*) по́ртиться (испо́ртиться *pf*); (*bomb*) взрыва́ться (взорва́ться *pf*); (*gun*) выстре́ливать (вы́стрелить *pf*); (*alarm*) звони́ть (зазвони́ть *pf*); (*event*) проходи́ть (пройти́ *pf*); (*lights*) выключа́ться (вы́ключиться *pf*)
♦ *vt fus* разлюби́ть (*pf*)
**go on** *vi* (*discussion*) продолжа́ться (*impf*); (*continue*): **to go on (doing)** продолжа́ть

*(impf)* *(+infin)*; **life goes on** жизнь продолжа́ется; **what's going on here?** что здесь происхо́дит?; **we don't have enough information to go on** у нас недоста́точно информа́ции
**go on with** *vt fus* продолжа́ть (продо́лжить *pf*)
**go out** *vi* (*fire, light*) га́снуть (пога́снуть *pf*); (*leave*): **to go out of** выходи́ть (вы́йти *pf*) из *+gen*; **are you going out tonight?** Вы сего́дня ве́чером куда́-нибудь идёте?
**go over** *vi* идти́ (пойти́ *pf*) ♦ *vt fus* просма́тривать (просмотре́ть *pf*)
**go through** *vt fus* (*town etc: by transport*) проезжа́ть (прое́хать *pf*) че́рез *+acc*; (*files, papers*) просма́тривать (просмотре́ть *pf*)
**go up** *vi* (*ascend*) поднима́ться (подня́ться *pf*); (*price, level, buildings*) расти́ (вы́расти *pf*)
**go without** *vt fus* обходи́ться (обойти́сь *pf*) без *+gen*

**go-ahead** ['gəuəhɛd] *n* добро́
**goal** [gəul] *n* (*SPORT*) гол; (*aim*) цель *f*; ~**keeper** *n* врата́рь *m*, голки́пер; ~ **post** *n* боковая́ шта́нга, сто́йка воро́т
**goat** [gəut] *n* (*billy*) козёл; (*nanny*) коза́
**go-between** ['gəubɪtwiːn] *n* посре́дник(ица)
**god** [gɔd] *n* (*fig*) божество́, бог; **God** Бог; ~**child** *n* кре́стник(ица); ~**daughter** *n* кре́стница; ~**dess** *n* боги́ня; ~**father** *n* крёстный оте́ц; ~**mother** *n* крёстная мать *f*; ~**son** *n* кре́стник
**goggles** ['gɔglz] *npl* защи́тные очки́ *ntpl*
**going** ['gəuɪŋ] *adj*: **the ~ rate** теку́щие расце́нки *fpl*

**gold** [gəuld] *n* (*metal*) зо́лото ♦ *adj* золото́й; ~ **reserves** золото́й запа́с; ~**fish** *n* сере́бряный кара́сь *m*
**golf** [gɔlf] *n* гольф; ~ **club** *n* (*stick*) клю́шка (в го́льфе); ~ **course** *n* по́ле для игры́ в гольф
**gone** [gɔn] *pp of* **go**
**gong** [gɔŋ] *n* гонг
**good** [gud] *adj* хоро́ший; (*pleasant*) прия́тный; (*kind*) до́брый ♦ *n* (*virtue*) добро́; (*benefit*) по́льза; ~**s** *npl* (*COMM*) това́ры *mpl*; ~! хорошо́!; **to be ~ at** име́ть (*impf*) спосо́бности к *+dat*; **it's ~ for you** э́то поле́зно (для здоро́вья); **would you be ~ enough to ...?** не бу́дете ли Вы так добры́ *+pf infin* ...?; **a ~ deal (of)** большо́е коли́чество (*+gen*); **a ~ many** мно́го *+gen*; ~ **afternoon/evening!** до́брый день/ве́чер!; ~ **morning!** до́брое у́тро!; ~ **night!** (*on leaving*) до свида́ния!; (*on going to bed*) споко́йной *or* до́брой но́чи!; **it's no ~ complaining** жа́ловаться бесполе́зно; **for ~** навсегда́; ~**bye** *excl* до свида́ния; **to say ~bye (to)** проща́ться (попроща́ться *pf*) (с *+instr*); **Good Friday** *n* Страстна́я пя́тница; ~**-looking** *adj* краси́вый; ~**-natured** *adj* доброду́шный; (*pet*) послу́шный; ~**ness** *n* доброта́; **for ~ness sake!** ра́ди Бо́га!; ~**ness gracious!** Бо́же!, Го́споди!; ~**will** *n* (*of person*) до́брая во́ля
**goose** [guːs] (*pl* **geese**) *n* гусь(сы́ня) *m(f)*
**gooseberry** ['guzbərɪ] *n* крыжо́вник *m no pl*
**goose pimples** *npl* гуси́ная ко́жа *fsg*
**gore** [gɔːr] *vt* бода́ть (заборда́ть *pf*)
**gorge** [gɔːdʒ] *n* тесни́на, (у́зкое)

ущéлье ♦ vt: **to ~ o.s. (on)**
наедáться (наéсться pf) (+gen)
**gorgeous** ['gɔːdʒəs] adj
прелéстный
**gorilla** [gə'rɪlə] n горúлла
**gorse** [gɔːs] n (BOT) утёсник
**gospel** ['gɔspl] n (REL) Евáнгелие
**gossip** ['gɔsɪp] n (rumours) сплéтня;
(chat) разговóры mpl; (person)
сплéтник(ица)
**got** [gɔt] pt, pp of **get**; **~ten** pp (US)
of **get**
**gout** [gaut] n (MED) подáгра
**govern** ['gʌvən] vt (country)
управлáть (impf) +instr; (event,
conduct) руковóдить (impf) +instr
**governess** ['gʌvənɪs] n
гувернáнтка
**government** ['gʌvnmənt] n
прави́тельство; (act) управлéние
**governor** ['gʌvənər] n (of state,
colony) губернáтор; (of school etc)
член правлéния
**gown** [gaun] n (dress) плáтье; (of
teacher, judge) мáнтия
**GP** n abbr (= general practitioner)
участкóвый терапéвт
**grab** [græb] vt хватáть (схвати́ть
pf) ♦ vi: **to ~ at** хватáться
(схвати́ться pf) за +acc
**grace** [greɪs] n грáция, изящество;
(REL) моли́тва (пéред едóй); **5
days' ~** 5 дней отсрóчки; **~ful** adj
(animal, person) грацио́зный
**gracious** ['greɪʃəs] adj (person, smile)
любéзный ♦ excl: **(good) ~!** Бóже
прáвый!
**grade** [greɪd] n (COMM, quality)
сорт; (SCOL, mark) оцéнка; (US:
school year) класс ♦ vt (rank, class)
распределáть (распредели́ть pf);
(products) сортировáть
(рассортировáть pf); **~ crossing**
n (US) железнодорóжный
переéзд; **~ school** n (US)
начáльная шкóла

**gradient** ['greɪdɪənt] n (of hill)
уклóн
**gradual** ['grædjuəl] adj
постепéнный; **~ly** adv
постепéнно
**graduate** n ['grædjuɪt] vb
['grædjueɪt] n выпускни́к(и́ца) ♦ vi:
**to ~ from** закáнчивать
(закóнчить pf); **I ~d last year** я
закóнчил университéт в
прóшлом годý
**graduation** [grædju'eɪʃən] n
(ceremony) выпускнóй вéчер
**graffiti** [grə'fiːtɪ] n, npl графи́ти nt
ind
**grain** [greɪn] n (seed) зернó; (no pl:
cereals) хлéбные злáки mpl; (of
sand) песчи́нка; (of salt)
крупи́нка; (of wood) волокнó
**gram** [græm] n грамм
**grammar** ['græmər] n граммáтика;
**~ school** n (BRIT) ≈ гимнáзия

**grammar school** - гимнáзия. В
Великобритáнии гимнáзии
даю́т срéднее образовáние.
Ученики́ поступáют в них на
кóнкурсной оснóве. Числó их
невеликó. Однáко в США
**grammar school** называ́ются
начáльные шкóлы.

**grammatical** [grə'mætɪkl] adj
граммати́ческий
**gramme** [græm] n = **gram**
**grand** [grænd] adj грандиóзный;
(gesture) вели́чественный; **~child**
(pl **~children**) n внук(у́чка); **~dad**
n (inf) дéдушка m; **~daughter** n
внýчка; **~eur** ['grændjər] n
великолéпие; **~father** n дед;
**~iose** ['grændɪəus] adj
грандиóзный; **~ma** n (inf)
бабýля, бáбушка; **~mother** n
бáбушка; **~parents** npl дéдушка
m и бáбушка; **~ piano** n роя́ль

m; ~**son** n внук; ~**stand** n (SPORT) центра́льная трибу́на
**granite** ['grænɪt] n грани́т
**granny** ['grænɪ] n (inf) = **grandma**
**grant** [grɑ:nt] vt (money, visa) выдава́ть (вы́дать pf); (request) удовлетворя́ть (удовлетвори́ть pf); (admit) признава́ть (призна́ть pf) ♦ n (SCOL) стипе́ндия; (ADMIN) грант; **to take sb/sth for ~ed** принима́ть (приня́ть pf) кого́-н/ что-н как до́лжное
**grape** [greɪp] n виногра́д m no pl; ~**fruit** (pl ~**fruit** or ~**fruits**) n грейпфру́т
**graph** [grɑ:f] n (diagram) гра́фик; ~**ic** adj (explicit) вырази́тельный; (design) изобрази́тельный; ~**ics** n гра́фика
**grapple** ['græpl] vi: **to ~ with sb** схва́тываться (схвати́ться pf) с кем-н
**grasp** [grɑ:sp] vt хвата́ть (схвати́ть pf) ♦ n (grip) хва́тка; (understanding) понима́ние; ~**ing** adj (greedy) а́лчный
**grass** [grɑ:s] n трава́; (lawn) газо́н; ~**hopper** n кузне́чик; ~-**roots** adj (support, organization) низово́й
**grate** [greɪt] n ками́нная решётка ♦ vt (CULIN) тере́ть (натере́ть pf) ♦ vi (metal, chalk): **to ~ (on)** скрежета́ть (impf) (по +dat)
**grateful** ['greɪtful] adj благода́рный
**grater** ['greɪtə'] n тёрка
**gratifying** ['grætɪfaɪɪŋ] adj прия́тный
**grating** ['greɪtɪŋ] n решётка ♦ adj скрипу́чий
**gratitude** ['grætɪtju:d] n благода́рность f
**grave** [greɪv] n моги́ла ♦ adj серьёзный
**gravel** ['grævl] n гра́вий
**gravestone** ['greɪvstəun] n

надгро́бие
**graveyard** ['greɪvjɑ:d] n кла́дбище
**gravity** ['grævɪtɪ] n тяготе́ние, притяже́ние; (seriousness) серьёзность f
**gravy** ['greɪvɪ] n (sauce) со́ус
**gray** [greɪ] adj (US) = **grey**
**graze** [greɪz] vi пасти́сь (impf) ♦ vt (scrape) цара́пать (оцара́пать pf)
**grease** [gri:s] n (lubricant) сма́зка; (fat) жир ♦ vt сма́зывать (сма́зать pf); ~**proof paper** n (BRIT) жиронепроница́емая бума́га
**greasy** ['gri:sɪ] adj жи́рный
**great** [greɪt] adj (large) большо́й; (heat, pain) си́льный; (city, man) вели́кий; (inf: terrific) замеча́тельный; **Great Britain** n Великобрита́ния

**Great Britain** - Великобрита́ния. В Великобрита́нию вхо́дят А́нглия, Шотла́ндия и Уэ́льс. Эти стра́ны вме́сте с Се́верной Ирла́ндией образу́ют **United Kingdom** - Соединённое Короле́вство (Великобрита́нии).

**great-** prefix пра-
**greatly** adv о́чень; (influenced) весьма́, в значи́тельной сте́пени
**Greece** [gri:s] n Гре́ция
**greed** [gri:d] n жа́дность f; (for power, wealth) жа́жда; ~**y** adj жа́дный
**Greek** [gri:k] adj гре́ческий
**green** [gri:n] adj зелёный ♦ n (colour) зелёный цвет; (grass) лужа́йка; ~**s** npl (vegetables) зе́лень fsg; ~ **belt** n зелёная зо́на, зелёный по́яс; ~**ery** n зе́лень f; ~**grocer** n (BRIT) зеленщи́к; (shop) овощно́й магази́н; ~**house** n тепли́ца;

**~house effect** n: the ~**house effect** парнико́вый эффе́кт

**Greenland** ['gri:nlənd] n Гренла́ндия

**greet** [gri:t] vt приве́тствовать (поприве́тствовать pf), здоро́ваться (поздоро́ваться pf); (news) встреча́ть (встре́тить pf); **~ing** n приве́тствие

**gregarious** [grə'gɛərɪəs] adj общи́тельный

**grenade** [grə'neɪd] n (also: **hand ~**) (ручна́я) грана́та

**grew** [gru:] pt of **grow**

**grey** [greɪ] (US **gray**) adj се́рый; (hair) седо́й; **~hound** n борза́я f adj

**grid** [grɪd] n (pattern) се́тка; (grating) решётка; (ELEC) еди́ная энергосисте́ма

**grief** [gri:f] n го́ре

**grievance** ['gri:vəns] n жа́лоба

**grieve** [gri:v] vi горева́ть (impf); **to ~ for** горева́ть (impf) о +prp

**grievous** ['gri:vəs] adj: **~ bodily harm** тяжёлые теле́сные повреждения ntpl

**grill** [grɪl] n (on cooker) гриль m; (grilled food : also: **mixed ~**) жа́ренные на гри́ле проду́кты mpl ♦ vt (BRIT) жа́рить (пожа́рить pf) (на гри́ле)

**grim** [grɪm] adj (place, person) мра́чный, угрю́мый; (situation) тяжёлый

**grimace** [grɪ'meɪs] n грима́са

**grime** [graɪm] n (from soot, smoke) ко́поть f; (from mud) грязь f

**grin** [grɪn] n широ́кая улы́бка ♦ vi: **to ~ (at)** широко́ улыба́ться (улыбну́ться pf) (+dat)

**grind** [graɪnd] (pt, pp **ground**) vt (coffee, pepper) моло́ть (смоло́ть pf); (US: meat) прокру́чивать (прокрути́ть pf); (knife) точи́ть (наточи́ть pf)

**grip** [grɪp] n хва́тка; (of tyre) сцепле́ние ♦ vt (object) схва́тывать (схвати́ть pf); (audience, attention) захва́тывать (захвати́ть pf); **to come to ~s with** занима́ться (заня́ться pf) +instr; **~ping** adj захва́тывающий

**grisly** ['grɪzlɪ] adj жу́ткий

**grit** [grɪt] n (stone) щебень m ♦ vt (road) посыпа́ть (посы́пать pf) щебнем; **to ~ one's teeth** сти́скивать (сти́снуть pf) зу́бы

**groan** [grəun] n (of person) стон

**grocer** ['grəusər] n бакале́йщик; **~ies** npl бакале́я fsg; **~'s (shop)** n бакале́йный магази́н, бакале́я

**groin** [grɔɪn] n пах

**groom** [gru:m] n (for horse) ко́нюх; (also: **bride~**) жени́х ♦ vt (horse) уха́живать (impf) за +instr; **to ~ sb for** (job) гото́вить (подгото́вить pf) кого́-н к +dat

**groove** [gru:v] n кана́вка

**gross** [grəus] adj вульга́рный; (neglect, injustice) вопию́щий; (COMM, income) валово́й; **~ly** adv чрезме́рно

**grotesque** [grə'tɛsk] adj гроте́скный

**ground** [graund] pt, pp of **grind** ♦ n (earth, land) земля́; (floor) пол; (US : also: **~ wire**) заземле́ние; (usu pl: reason) основа́ние ♦ vt (US : ELEC) заземля́ть (заземли́ть pf); **~s** npl (of coffee) гу́ща fsg; **school ~s** шко́льная площа́дка; **sports ~** спорти́вная площа́дка; **on the ~** на земле́; **to the ~** (burnt) дотла́; **the plane was ~ed by the fog** самолёт не мог подня́ться в во́здух из-за тума́на; **~ing** n (in education) подгото́вка; **~work** n (preparation) фунда́мент, осно́ва; **to do the ~work** закла́дывать (заложи́ть pf) фунда́мент

**group** [gru:p] n гру́ппа

**grouse** [graus] n inv (bird) (шотла́ндская) куропа́тка

**grow** [grəu] (pt **grew**, pp **~n**) vi расти́ (вы́расти pf); (become) станови́ться (стать pf) ♦ vt (roses, vegetables) выра́щивать (вы́растить pf); (beard, hair) отра́щивать (отрасти́ть pf); **~ up** vi (child) расти́ (вы́расти pf), взросле́ть (повзросле́ть pf)

**growl** [graul] vi (dog) рыча́ть (impf)

**grown** [grəun] pp of **grow**; **~-up** n (adult) взро́слый(ая) m(f) adj ♦ adj (son, daughter) взро́слый

**growth** [grəuθ] n рост; (increase) приро́ст; (MED) о́пухоль f

**grub** [grʌb] n (larva) личи́нка; (inf: food) жратва́

**grubby** ['grʌbɪ] adj гря́зный

**grudge** [grʌdʒ] n недово́льство; **to bear sb a ~** зата́ивать (затаи́ть pf) на кого́-н оби́ду

**gruelling** ['gruəlɪŋ] (US **grueling**) adj изнури́тельный, тя́жкий

**gruesome** ['gru:səm] adj жу́ткий

**gruff** [grʌf] adj (voice) хри́плый; (manner) ре́зкий

**grumble** ['grʌmbl] vi ворча́ть (impf)

**grumpy** ['grʌmpɪ] adj сварли́вый

**grunt** [grʌnt] vi (pig) хрю́кать (хрю́кнуть pf); (person) бурча́ть (бу́ркнуть pf)

**guarantee** [gærən'ti:] n (assurance) поручи́тельство; (warranty) гара́нтия ♦ vt гаранти́ровать (impf/pf); **he can't ~ (that) he'll come** он не мо́жет поручи́ться, что он придёт

**guard** [gɑːd] n (one person) охра́нник; (squad) охра́на; (BRIT: RAIL) конду́ктор; (TECH) предохрани́тельное устро́йство; (also: **fire~**) предохрани́тельная решётка (пе́ред ками́ном) ♦ vt (prisoner) охраня́ть (impf); (secret) храни́ть (impf); **to ~ (against)** (protect) охраня́ть (impf) (от +gen); **to be on one's ~** быть (impf) насторо́же or начеку́; **~ against** vt fus (prevent) предохраня́ть (impf) от +gen; **~ed** adj (statement, reply) осторо́жный; **~ian** n (LAW) опеку́н

**guerrilla** [gə'rɪlə] n партиза́н(ка)

**guess** [gɛs] vt (estimate) счита́ть (сосчита́ть pf) приблизи́тельно; (correct answer) уга́дывать (угада́ть pf) ♦ vi дога́дываться (догада́ться pf) ♦ n дога́дка; **to take** or **have a ~** отга́дывать (отгада́ть pf)

**guest** [gɛst] n (visitor) гость(я) m(f); (in hotel) постоя́лец(лица); **~house** n гости́ница

**guidance** ['gaɪdəns] n (advice) сове́т

**guide** [gaɪd] n (in museum, on tour) гид, экскурсово́д; (also: **~book**) путеводи́тель m; (handbook) руково́дство ♦ vt (show around) води́ть (impf); (direct) направля́ть (напра́вить pf); **~book** n путеводи́тель m; **~ dog** n соба́ка-поводы́рь f; **~lines** npl руково́дство ntsg

**guild** [gɪld] n ги́льдия

**guilt** [gɪlt] n (remorse) вина́; (culpability) вино́вность f; **~y** adj (person, expression) винова́тый; (of crime) вино́вный

**guinea pig** ['gɪnɪ-] n морска́я сви́нка; (fig) подо́пытный кро́лик

**guise** [gaɪz] n: **in** or **under the ~ of** под ви́дом or личи́ной +gen

**guitar** [gɪ'tɑ:r] n гита́ра

**gulf** [gʌlf] n (GEO) зали́в; (fig) про́пасть f

**gull** [gʌl] n ча́йка

**gullible** ['gʌlɪbl] adj легкове́рный

**gully** ['gʌlɪ] n (ravine) лощи́на

**gulp** [gʌlp] vi нéрвно сглáтывать (сглотнýть pf) ♦ vt (also: ~ **down**) проглáтывать (проглотить pf)

**gum** [gʌm] n (ANAT) деснá; (glue) клей; (also: **chewing-~**) жвáчка (разг), жевáтельная резинка

**gun** [gʌn] n пистолéт; (rifle, airgun) ружьё; **~fire** n стрельбá; **~man** (irreg) n вооружённый бандит; **~point** n: **at ~point** под дýлом пистолéта; **~shot** n выстрел

**guru** ['guru:] n гурý m ind

**gust** [gʌst] n (of wind) порыв

**gusto** ['gʌstəu] n: **with ~** (eat) с удовóльствием; (work) с жáром

**gut** [gʌt] n (ANAT) кишкá; **~s** npl (ANAT) кишки fpl, внýтренности fpl; (inf: courage) мýжество ntsg

**gutter** ['gʌtər] n (in street) стóчная канáва; (of roof) водостóчный жёлоб

**guy** [gaɪ] n (inf: man) пáрень m; (also: **~rope**) палáточный шнур

**gym** [dʒɪm] n (also: **~nasium**) гимнастический зал; (also: **~nastics**) гимнáстика; **~nastics** [dʒɪm'næstɪks] n гимнáстика

**gynaecologist** [gaɪnɪ'kɔlədʒɪst] (US **gynecologist**) n гинекóлог

**gypsy** ['dʒɪpsɪ] n цыгáн(ка)

# H, h

**habit** ['hæbɪt] n (custom) привычка; (addiction) пристрáстие; (REL) облачéние

**habitat** ['hæbɪtæt] n средá обитáния

**habitual** [hə'bɪtjuəl] adj (action) привычный; (liar, drinker) отъявленный

**hack** [hæk] vt отрубáть (отрубить pf) ♦ n (pej: writer) писáка m/f

**had** [hæd] pt, pp of **have**

**haddock** ['hædək] (pl ~ or **~s**) n трескá

**hadn't** ['hædnt] = **had not**

**haemorrhage** ['hɛmərɪdʒ] (US **hemorrhage**) n кровотечéние; **brain ~** кровоизлияние (в мозг)

**haggard** ['hægəd] adj (face, look) измождённый

**Hague** [heɪg] n: **The ~** Гаáга

**hail** [heɪl] n град ♦ vt (flag down) подзывáть (подозвáть pf) ♦ vi: **it's ~ing** идёт град; **~stone** n грáдина

**hair** [hɛər] n вóлосы pl; (of animal) волосянóй покрóв; **to do one's ~** причёсываться (причесáться pf); **~brush** n щётка для волóс; **~cut** n стрижка; **~dresser** n парикмáхер; **~ dryer** n фен; **~ spray** n лак для волóс; **~style** n причёска; **~y** adj (person) волосáтый; (animal) мохнáтый

**half** [hɑ:f] (pl **halves**) n половина; (also: **~ pint**: of beer etc) полпинты f; (on train, bus) билéт за полценý ♦ adv наполовину; **one and a ~** (with m/nt nouns) полторá +gen sg; (with f nouns) полторы +gen sg; **three and a ~** три с половиной; **a dozen** (of) полдюжины f (+gen); **a pound** (of) полфýнта m (+gen); **a week and a ~** полторы недéли; **~ (of)** половина (+gen); **~ the amount of** половина +gen; **to cut sth in ~** разрезáть (разрéзать pf) что-н пополáм; **~-hearted** adj ленивый; **~-hour** n полчасá m; **~-price** adj, adv за полцены; **~-time** n перерыв мéжду тáймами; **~way** adv на полпути

---

**half-term** - корóткие каникулы. В середине тримéстров шкóльникам даю́т корóткий перерыв в 3-4 дня.

**hall** [hɔːl] *n* (*in house*) прихо́жая *f
adj*, холл; (*for concerts, meetings
etc*) зал

**hallmark** ['hɔːlmɑːk] *n* про́ба; (*fig*)
отличи́тельная черта́

**Hallowe'en** ['hæləu'iːn] *n* кану́н
Дня всех святы́х

**Hallowe'en** - кану́н Дня всех
святы́х. Этот пра́здник
отмеча́ют ве́чером 31 октября́.
По тради́ции э́то день ведьм и
ду́хов. Де́ти наряжа́ются в
костю́мы ведьм и вампи́ров,
де́лают ла́мпы из тыкв. С
наступле́нием темноты́ они́
хо́дят по дома́м, игра́я в игру́
подо́бную ру́сским
Коробе́йникам. Е́сли хозя́ева
не даю́т де́тям конфе́т, они́
мо́гут сыгра́ть над ни́ми шу́тку.

**hallucination** [həluːsɪ'neɪʃən] *n*
галлюцина́ция

**hallway** ['hɔːlweɪ] *n* прихо́жая *f
adj*, холл

**halo** ['heɪləu] *n* (*REL*) нимб

**halt** [hɔːlt] *n* остано́вка ♦ *vt*
остана́вливать (останови́ть *pf*)
♦ *vi* остана́вливаться
(останови́ться *pf*)

**halve** [hɑːv] *vt* (*reduce*) сокраща́ть
(сократи́ть *pf*) наполови́ну;
(*divide*) дели́ть (раздели́ть *pf*)
попола́м

**halves** [hɑːvz] *pl of* **half**

**ham** [hæm] *n* (*meat*) ветчина́;
**~burger** *n* га́мбургер

**hammer** ['hæmər] *n* молото́к ♦ *vi*
(*on door etc*) колоти́ть (*impf*) ♦ *vt*
(*nail*): **to ~ in** забива́ть (заби́ть
*pf*), вбива́ть (вбить *pf*); **to ~ sth
into sb** (*fig*) вда́лбливать
(вдолби́ть *pf*) что-н кому́-н

**hamper** ['hæmpər] *vt* меша́ть
(помеша́ть *pf*) +*dat* ♦ *n* (*basket*)

больша́я корзи́на с кры́шкой

**hamster** ['hæmstər] *n* хомя́к

**hand** [hænd] *n* (*ANAT*) рука́, кисть
*f*; (*of clock*) стре́лка; (*worker*)
рабо́чий *m adj* ♦ *vt* (*give*) вруча́ть
(вручи́ть *pf*); **to give** *or* **lend sb a ~**
протя́гивать (протяну́ть *pf*)
кому́-н ру́ку (по́мощи); **at ~** под
руко́й; **in ~** (*situation*) под
контро́лем; (*time*) в
распоряже́нии; **on ~** (*person,
services etc*) в распоряже́нии; **I
have the information to ~** я
располага́ю информа́цией; **on
the one ~..., on the other ~...** с
одно́й стороны́ ..., с друго́й
стороны́ ...; **~ in** *vt* (*work*)
сдава́ть (сдать *pf*); **~ out** *vt*
раздава́ть (разда́ть *pf*); **~ over** *vt*
передава́ть (переда́ть *pf*),
вруча́ть (вручи́ть *pf*); **~bag** *n*
(да́мская) су́мочка; **~brake** *n*
ручно́й то́рмоз; **~cuffs** *npl*
нару́чники *mpl*; **~ful** *n* (*fig: of
people*) го́рстка; **~-held** *adj*
ручно́й

**handicap** ['hændɪkæp] *n* (*disability*)
физи́ческая неполноце́нность *f*;
(*disadvantage*) препя́тствие ♦ *vt*
препя́тствовать (воспрепя́тст-
вовать *pf*) +*dat*; **mentally/
physically ~ped** у́мственно/
физи́чески неполноце́нный

**handkerchief** ['hæŋkətʃɪf] *n*
носово́й плато́к

**handle** ['hændl] *n* ру́чка ♦ *vt*
(*touch*) держа́ть (*impf*) в рука́х;
(*deal with*) занима́ться (*impf*)
+*instr*; (*: successfully*) справля́ться
(спра́виться *pf*) с +*instr*; (*treat:
people*) обраща́ться (*impf*) с +*instr*;
**to fly off the ~** (*inf*) срыва́ться
(сорва́ться *pf*); **"~ with care"**
"обраща́ться осторо́жно"

**hand luggage** *n* ручна́я кладь *f*

**handmade** ['hænd'meɪd] *adj*

ручно́й рабо́ты; **it's ~** э́то ручна́я рабо́та

**hand-out** ['hændaut] *n* благотвори́тельная по́мощь *f*; (*summary: of lecture*) кра́ткое изложе́ние

**handshake** ['hændʃeɪk] *n* рукопожа́тие

**handsome** ['hænsəm] *adj* (*man*) краси́вый; (*woman*) интере́сный; (*building, profit*) внуши́тельный

**handwriting** ['hændraɪtɪŋ] *n* по́черк

**handy** ['hændɪ] *adj* (*useful*) удо́бный; (*close at hand*) побли́зости

**hang** [hæŋ] (*pt, pp* **hung**) *vt* ве́шать (пове́сить *pf*); (*pt, pp* **~ed**; *execute*) ве́шать (пове́сить *pf*) ♦ *vi* висе́ть (*impf*) ♦ *n*: **to get the ~ of sth** (*inf*) разбира́ться (разобра́ться *pf*) в чём-н; **~ around** *vi* слоня́ться (*impf*), болта́ться (*impf*); **~ on** *vi* (*wait*) подожда́ть (*impf*); **~ up** *vi* (*TEL*) ве́шать (пове́сить *pf*) тру́бку ♦ *vt* ве́шать (пове́сить *pf*)

**hangar** ['hæŋəʳ] *n* анга́р

**hangover** ['hæŋəuvəʳ] *n* (*after drinking*) похме́лье

**hanky** ['hæŋkɪ] *n abbr* = **handkerchief**

**haphazard** [hæp'hæzəd] *adj* бессисте́мный

**happen** ['hæpən] *vi* случа́ться (случи́ться *pf*), происходи́ть (произойти́ *pf*); **I ~ed to meet him in the park** я случа́йно встре́тил его́ в па́рке; **as it ~s** кста́ти

**happily** ['hæpɪlɪ] *adv* (*luckily*) к сча́стью; (*cheerfully*) ра́достно

**happiness** ['hæpɪnɪs] *n* сча́стье

**happy** ['hæpɪ] *adj* (*pleased*) счастли́вый; (*cheerful*) весёлый; **I am ~ (with it)** (*content*) я дово́лен (э́тим); **he is always ~ to help** он

всегда́ рад помо́чь; **~ birthday!** с днём рожде́ния!

**harassment** ['hærəsmənt] *n* пресле́дование

**harbour** ['hɑːbəʳ] (*US* **harbor**) *n* га́вань *f* ♦ *vt* (*hope, fear*) зата́ивать (затаи́ть *pf*); (*criminal, fugitive*) укрыва́ть (укры́ть *pf*)

**hard** [hɑːd] *adj* (*surface, object*) твёрдый; (*question, problem*) тру́дный; (*work, life*) тяжёлый; (*person*) суро́вый; (*facts, evidence*) неопровержи́мый ♦ *adv*: **to work ~** мно́го и усе́рдно рабо́тать (*impf*); **I don't have any ~ feelings** я не держу́ зла; **he is ~ of hearing** он туг на́ ухо; **to think ~** хорошо́ поду́мать (*pf*); **to try ~ to win** упо́рно добива́ться (*impf*) побе́ды; **to look ~ at** смотре́ть (посмотре́ть *pf*) при́стально на +*acc*; **~back** *n* кни́га в твёрдом переплёте; **~ disc** *n* жёсткий диск; **~en** *vt* (*substance*) де́лать (сде́лать *pf*) твёрдым(ой); (*attitude, person*) ожесточа́ть (ожесточи́ть *pf*) ♦ *vi* (*see vt*) твёрде́ть (затверде́ть *pf*); ожесточа́ться (ожесточи́ться *pf*)

**hardly** ['hɑːdlɪ] *adv* едва́; **~ ever/ anywhere** почти́ никогда́/нигде́

**hardship** ['hɑːdʃɪp] *n* тя́готы *pl*, тру́дности *fpl*

**hard up** *adj* (*inf*) нужда́ющийся; **I am ~** я нужда́

**hardware** ['hɑːdwɛəʳ] *n* (*tools*) скобяны́е изде́лия *ntpl*

**hard-working** [hɑːd'wəːkɪŋ] *adj* усе́рдный

**hardy** ['hɑːdɪ] *adj* выно́сливый; (*plant*) морозоусто́йчивый

**hare** [hɛəʳ] *n* за́яц

**harm** [hɑːm] *n* (*injury*) теле́сное повреждение, тра́вма; (*damage*) уще́рб ♦ *vt* (*thing*) поврежда́ть (повреди́ть *pf*); (*person*) наноси́ть

(нанести *pf*) вред +*dat*; **~ful** *adj*
вре́дный; **~less** *adj* безоби́дный
**harmonica** [hɑː'mɔnɪkə] *n* губна́я
гармо́ника
**harmonious** [hɑː'məunɪəs] *adj*
гармони́чный
**harmony** ['hɑːmənɪ] *n* гармо́ния
**harness** ['hɑːnɪs] *n* ( *for horse*)
у́пряжь *f*; ( *for child* ) постро́мки
*fpl*; (*safety harness*) привязны́е
ремни́ *mpl* ♦ *vt* (*horse*) запряга́ть
(запря́чь *pf*); (*resources, energy*)
ста́вить (поста́вить *pf*) себе́ на
слу́жбу
**harp** [hɑːp] *n* а́рфа
**harrowing** ['hærəuɪŋ] *adj*
душераздира́ющий
**harsh** [hɑːʃ] *adj* (*sound, light,
criticism*) ре́зкий; (*person, remark*)
жёсткий; (*life, winter*) суро́вый
**harvest** ['hɑːvɪst] *n* (*time*) жа́тва;
(*of barley, fruit*) урожа́й ♦ *vt*
собира́ть (собра́ть *pf*) урожа́й
+*gen*
**has** [hæz] *vb see* **have**
**hash** [hæʃ] *n*: **to make a ~ of sth**
запа́рывать (запоро́ть *pf*) что-н
**hasn't** ['hæznt] = **has not**
**hassle** ['hæsl] (*inf* ) *n* моро́ка
**haste** [heɪst] *n* спе́шка; **~n** ['heɪsn]
*vt* торопи́ть (поторопи́ть *pf*) ♦ *vi*:
**to ~n to do** торопи́ться
(поторопи́ться *pf*) +*infin*
**hastily** ['heɪstɪlɪ] *adv* (*see adj*)
поспе́шно; опроме́тчиво
**hasty** ['heɪstɪ] *adj* поспе́шный;
(*rash*) опроме́тчивый
**hat** [hæt] *n* шля́па; (*woolly*) ша́пка
**hatch** [hætʃ] *n* (*NAUT : also*: **~way**)
люк; (*also*: **service ~**)
разда́точное окно́ ♦ *vi* (*also*: **~
out**) вылупля́ться (вы́лупиться
*pf*)
**hatchet** ['hætʃɪt] *n* (*axe*) топо́рик
**hate** [heɪt] *vt* ненави́деть (*impf*)
**hatred** ['heɪtrɪd] *n* не́нависть *f*

**haul** [hɔːl] *vt* (*pull*) таска́ть/тащи́ть
(*impf*) ♦ *n* (*of stolen goods etc*)
добы́ча; (*also*: **перево́зка**
**haunt** [hɔːnt] *vt* ( *fig*)
пресле́довать (*impf*); **to ~ sb/a
house** явля́ться (яви́ться *pf*)
кому́-н/в до́ме; **~ed** *adj*: **this
house is ~ed** в э́том дом есть
привиде́ния

┌─ KEYWORD ─────────────────────┐

**have** [hæv] (*pt, pp* **had**) *aux vb* **1**: **to
have arrived** прие́хать (*pf*); **have
you already eaten?** ты уже́ поέл?;
**he has been kind to me** он был
добр ко мне; **he has been
promoted** он получи́л
повыше́ние по слу́жбе; **has he
told you?** он Вам сказа́л?; **having**
*or* **when he had finished ...**
зако́нчив *or* когда́ он зако́нчил ...
**2** (*in tag questions*) не так ли;
**you've done it, haven't you?** Вы
сде́лали э́то, не так ли?
**3** (*in short answers and questions*):
**you've made a mistake - no I
haven't/so I have** Вы оши́блись -
нет, не оши́бся/да, оши́бся; **we
haven't paid - yes we have!** мы
не заплати́ли - нет, заплати́ли!;
**I've been there before, have you?**
я там уже́ был, а Вы?
♦ *modal aux vb* (*be obliged* ): **I have
(got) to finish this work** я до́лжен
зако́нчить э́ту рабо́ту; **I haven't
got** *or* **I don't have to wear
glasses** мне не на́до носи́ть
очки́; **this has to be a mistake**
э́то, наверняка́, оши́бка
♦ *vt* **1** (*possess*): **I etc have** у меня́
(есть) *etc* +*nom*; **he has (got) blue
eyes/dark hair** у него́ голубы́е
глаза́/тёмные во́лосы; **do you
have** *or* **have you got a car?** у Вас
есть маши́на?
**2** (*referring to meals etc*): **to have**

**dinner** обéдать (пообéдать pf); **to have breakfast** зáвтракать (позáвтракать pf); **to have a cigarette** выкýривать (выкурить pf) сигарéту; **to have a glass of wine** выпивáть (выпить pf) бокáл винá

3 (receive, obtain etc): **may I have your address?** Вы мóжете дать мне свой áдрес?; **you can have the book for £5** берите книгу за £5; **I must have the report by tomorrow** доклáд дóлжен быть у меня к зáвтрашнему дню; **she is having a baby in March** онá бýдет рожáть в мáрте

4 (allow) допускáть (допустить pf); **I won't have it!** я этого не допущý!

5: **I am having my television repaired** мне должны починить телевизор; **to have sb do** просить (попросить pf) когó-н +infin; **he soon had them all laughing** вскóре он застáвил всех смеяться

6 (experience, suffer): **I have flu/a headache** у меня грипп/болит головá; **to have a cold** простужáться (простудиться pf); **she had her bag stolen** у неё укрáли сýмку; **he had an operation** емý сдéлали операцию

7 (+n): **to have a swim** плáвать (поплáвать pf); **to have a rest** отдыхáть (отдохнýть pf); **let's have a look** давáйте посмóтрим; **we are having a meeting tomorrow** зáвтра у нас бýдет собрáние; **let me have a try** дáйте мне попрóбовать

**have out** vt: **to have it out with sb** объясняться (объясниться pf) с кем-н; **she had her tooth out** ей удалили зуб; **she had her tonsils out** ей вырезали глáнды

**haven** ['heɪvn] n (fig) убéжище
**haven't** ['hævnt] = **have not**
**havoc** ['hævək] n (chaos) хáос
**hawk** [hɔːk] n ястреб
**hay** [heɪ] n сéно; **~ fever** n сеннáя лихорáдка; **~stack** n стог сéна
**hazard** ['hæzəd] n опáсность f ♦ vt: **to ~ a guess** осмéливаться (осмéлиться pf) предположить; **~ous** adj опáсный
**haze** [heɪz] n дымка; **heat ~** мáрево
**hazy** ['heɪzɪ] adj тумáнный
**he** [hiː] pron он
**head** [hed] n (ANAT) головá; (mind) ум; (of list, queue) начáло; (of table) главá; (COMM) руководитель(ница) m(f); (SCOL) дирéктор ♦ vt возглавлять (возглáвить pf); **~s or tails** ≈ орёл или рéшка; **he is ~ over heels in love** он влюблён пó уши; **~ for** vt fus (place) направляться (напрáвиться pf) в/на +acc or к +dat; (disaster) обрекáть (обрéчь pf) себя на +acc; **~ache** n (MED) головнáя боль f; **~ing** n заголóвок; **~land** n мыс; **~light** n фáра; **~line** n заголóвок; **~long** adv (headfirst) головóй вперёд; (hastily) опромéтчиво; **~master** n дирéктор шкóлы; **~mistress** n дирéктор шкóлы; **~ office** n управлéние; **~-on** adj лобовóй ♦ adv нос к нóсу; **~phones** npl наýшники mpl; **~quarters** npl штаб-квартира fsg; **~scarf** n косынка, (головнóй) платóк; **~ teacher** n дирéктор шкóлы; **~way** n: **to make ~way** продвигáться (продвинуться pf) вперёд; **~y** adj (experience) головокружительный;

(*atmosphere*) пьяня́щий

**heal** [hi:l] *vt* вылéчивать
(вы́лечить *pf*); (*damage*)
поправля́ть (попра́вить *pf*) ♦ *vi*
(*injury*) заживáть (зажи́ть *pf*);
(*damage*) восстана́вливаться
(восстанови́ться *pf*)

**health** [hɛlθ] *n* здоро́вье; ~ **care** *n*
здравоохранéние; **Health
Service** *n* (*BRIT*): **the Health
Service** здравоохранéния; ~**y** *adj*
здоро́вый; (*pursuit*) поле́зный;
(*profit*) доста́точно хоро́ший

**heap** [hi:p] *n* (*small*) ку́ча; (*large*)
гру́да ♦ *vt*: **to ~ (up)** (*stones, sand*)
сва́ливать (свали́ть *pf*) в ку́чу; **to
~ with sth** (*plate, sink*) наполня́ть
(напо́лнить *pf*) чем-н; ~**s of** (*inf*)
ку́ча *fsg +gen*

**hear** [hɪə<sup>r</sup>] (*pt, pp* ~**d**) *vt* слы́шать
(услы́шать *pf*); (*lecture, concert,
case*) слу́шать (*impf*); **to ~ about**
слы́шать (услы́шать *pf*) о +*prp*; **to
~ from sb** слы́шать (услы́шать *pf*)
от кого́-н; **I can't ~ you** Вас не
слы́шно; ~**d** [hə:d] *pt, pp of* **hear**;
~**ing** *n* (*sense*) слух; (*LAW, POL*)
слу́шание; ~**ing aid** *n* слуховóй
аппара́т

**heart** [hɑ:t] *n* сéрдце; (*of problem,
matter*) суть *f*; ~**s** *npl* (*CARDS*)
чéрви *fpl*; **to lose/take ~** пасть
(*pf*)/не па́дать (*impf*) ду́хом; **at ~** в
глубинé души́; (**off**) **by ~**
наизу́сть; ~**ache** *n* сердéчная
боль *f*; ~ **attack** *n* сердéчный
при́ступ, инфа́ркт; ~**beat** *n*
(*rhythm*) сердцебиéние; ~**broken**
*adj*: **he is** ~**broken** он уби́т го́рем;
~ **failure** *n* (*fatal*) остано́вка
сéрдца; ~**felt** *adj* и́скренний

**hearth** [hɑ:θ] *n* очáг

**heartless** ['hɑ:tlɪs] *adj*
бессердéчный

**hearty** ['hɑ:tɪ] *adj* (*person, laugh*)

задо́рный, весёлый; (*welcome,
support*) сердéчный; (*appetite*)
здоро́вый

**heat** [hi:t] *n* тепло́; (*extreme*) жар;
(*of weather*) жарá; (*excitement*)
пыл; (*also*: **qualifying ~**: *in race*)
забéг; (: *in swimming*) заплы́в ♦ *vt*
(*water, food*) греть (нагрéть *pf*);
(*house*) отáпливать (отопи́ть *pf*);
~ **up** *vi* (*water, house*) согревáться
(согрéться *pf*) ♦ *vt* (*food, water*)
подогревáть (подогрéть *pf*);
(*room*) обогревáть (обогрéть *pf*);
~**ed** *adj* (*argument*) горя́чий;
(*pool*) обогревáемый; ~**er** *n*
обогревáтель *m*

**heath** [hi:θ] *n* (*BRIT*) (вéресковая)
пу́стошь *f*

**heather** ['hɛðə<sup>r</sup>] *n* вéреск

**heating** ['hi:tɪŋ] *n* отоплéние

**heat wave** *n* перио́д си́льной
жары́

**heaven** ['hɛvn] *n* рай; ~**ly** *adj* (*fig*)
ра́йский

**heavily** ['hɛvɪlɪ] *adv* (*fall, sigh*)
тяжело́; (*drink, smoke, depend*)
си́льно; (*sleep*) крéпко

**heavy** ['hɛvɪ] *adj* тяжёлый; (*rain,
blow, fall*) си́льный; (*build: of
person*) грýзный; **he is a ~
drinker/smoker** он мно́го пьёт/
ку́рит

**Hebrew** ['hi:bru:] *adj*
древнеевре́йский

**Hebrides** ['hɛbrɪdi:z] *npl*: **the ~**
Гебри́дские островá *mpl*

**hectic** ['hɛktɪk] *adj* (*day*)
суматóшный; (*activities*)
лихора́дочный

**he'd** [hi:d] = **he would**, **he had**

**hedge** [hɛdʒ] *n* живáя и́згородь *f*

**hedgehog** ['hɛdʒhɔg] *n* ёж

**heed** [hi:d] *vt* (*also*: **take ~ of**)
принимáть (приня́ть *pf*) во
внимáние

**heel** [hi:l] *n* (*of foot*) пя́тка; (*of shoe*)

каблук

**hefty** ['hɛftɪ] adj (person, object) здоровённый; (profit, fine) изрядный

**height** [haɪt] n (of tree, of plane) высота; (of person) рост; (of power) вершина; (of season) разгар; (of luxury, taste) верх; **~en** vt усиливать (усилить pf)

**heir** [ɛəʳ] n наследник; **~ess** n наследница

**held** [hɛld] pt, pp of **hold**

**helicopter** ['hɛlɪkɔptəʳ] n вертолёт

**helium** ['hiːlɪəm] n гелий

**hell** [hɛl] n (also fig) ад; **~!** (inf) чёрт!

**he'll** [hiːl] = **he will, he shall**; see **will**

**hello** [hə'ləu] excl здравствуйте; (informal) привет; (TEL) алло

**helmet** ['hɛlmɪt] n (of policeman, miner) каска; (also: **crash ~**) шлем

**help** [hɛlp] n помощь f ♦ vt помогать (помочь pf) +dat; **~!** на помощь!, помогите!; **~ yourself** угощайтесь; **he can't ~ it** он ничего не может поделать с этим; **~er** n помощник(ица); **~ful** adj полезный; **~less** adj беспомощный; **~line** n телефон доверия

**hem** [hɛm] n (of dress) подол

**hemorrhage** ['hɛmərɪdʒ] n (US) = **haemorrhage**

**hen** [hɛn] n (chicken) курица

**hence** [hɛns] adv (therefore) следовательно, вследствие этого; **2 years ~** (from now) по истечении двух лет

**hepatitis** [hɛpə'taɪtɪs] n гепатит, болезнь f Боткина

**her** [həːʳ] pron (direct) её; (indirect) ей; (after prep: +gen) неё; (: +instr, +dat, +prp) ней; see also **me** ♦ adj её; (referring to subject of sentence)

свой; see also **my**

**herald** ['hɛrəld] vt (event) предвещать (impf)

**herb** [həːb] n трава; (as medicine) лекарственная трава; **~s** npl (CULIN) зелень fsg

**herd** [həːd] n стадо

**here** [hɪəʳ] adv (location) здесь; (destination) сюда; (at this point: in past) тут; **from ~** отсюда; **"~!"** (present) "здесь!"; **~ is..., ~ are ...** вот ...

**hereditary** [hɪ'rɛdɪtrɪ] adj наследственный

**heresy** ['hɛrəsɪ] n ересь f

**heritage** ['hɛrɪtɪdʒ] n наследие

**hermit** ['həːmɪt] n отшельник(ица)

**hernia** ['həːnɪə] n грыжа

**hero** ['hɪərəu] (pl **~es**) n герой; **~ic** [hɪ'rəuɪk] adj героический

**heroin** ['hɛrəuɪn] n героин

**heroine** ['hɛrəuɪn] n героиня

**heron** ['hɛrən] n цапля

**herring** ['hɛrɪŋ] n (ZOOL) сельдь f; (CULIN) селёдка

**hers** [həːz] pron её; (referring to subject of sentence) свой; see also **mine**[1]

**herself** [həː'sɛlf] pron (reflexive, after prep: +acc, +gen) себя; (: +dat, +prp) себе; (: +instr) собой; (emphatic) сама; (alone): **by ~** одна; see also **myself**

**he's** [hiːz] = **he is, he has**

**hesitant** ['hɛzɪtənt] adj нерешительный; **to be ~ to do** не решаться (impf) +infin

**hesitate** ['hɛzɪteɪt] vi колебаться (поколебаться pf); (be unwilling) не решаться (impf)

**hesitation** [hɛzɪ'teɪʃən] n колебание

**heterosexual** ['hɛtərəu'sɛksjuəl] adj гетеросексуальный

**heyday** ['heɪdeɪ] n: **the ~ of** расцвет +gen

**hi** [haɪ] *excl* (*as greeting*) приве́т
**hiccoughs** ['hɪkʌps] *npl* = **hiccups**
**hiccups** ['hɪkʌps] *npl*: **she's got (the) ~** у неё икота́
**hide** [haɪd] (*pt* **hid**, *pp* **hidden**) *n* (*skin*) шку́ра ♦ *vt* (*object, person*) пря́тать (спря́тать *pf*); (*feeling, information*) скрыва́ть (скрыть *pf*); (*sun, view*) закрыва́ть (закры́ть *pf*) ♦ *vi*: **to ~ (from sb)** пря́таться (спря́таться *pf*) (от кого́-н); **~away** *n* убе́жище
**hideous** ['hɪdɪəs] *adj* жу́ткий; (*face*) омерзи́тельный
**hiding** ['haɪdɪŋ] *n* (*beating*) по́рка; **to be in ~** скрыва́ться (*impf*)
**hierarchy** ['haɪərɑːkɪ] *n* иера́рхия
**hi-fi** ['haɪfaɪ] *n* (*system*) стерео-систе́ма
**high** [haɪ] *adj* высо́кий; (*wind*) си́льный ♦ *adv* высоко́; **the building is 20 m ~** высота́ зда́ния - 20 м; **to be ~** (*inf: on drugs etc*) кайфова́ть (*impf*); **~ risk** высо́кая сте́пень ри́ска; **~ in the air** (*position*) высоко́ в во́здухе; **~chair** *n* высо́кий сту́льчик (*для ма́леньких дете́й*); **~er education** *n* вы́сшее образова́ние; **~ jump** *n* прыжо́к в высоту́; **Highlands** *npl*: **the Highlands** Высокого́рья *ntpl* (*Шотла́ндии*); **~light** *n* (*of event*) кульмина́ция ♦ *vt* (*problem, need*) выявля́ть (вы́явить *pf*); **~ly** *adv* о́чень; (*paid*) высоко́; **to speak ~ly of** высо́ко отзыва́ться (отозва́ться *pf*) о +*prp*; **to think ~ly of** быть (*impf*) высо́кого мне́ния о +*prp*; **~ness** *n*: **Her/His Highness** Её/Его́ Высо́чество; **~-pitched** *adj* пронзи́тельный; **~-rise** *adj* высо́тный; **~ school** *n* (*BRIT*) сре́дняя шко́ла (*для 11-18ти ле́тних*); (*US*) сре́дняя шко́ла (*для 14-18ти ле́тних*)

**high school** - сре́дняя шко́ла. В Брита́нии де́ти посеща́ют сре́днюю шко́лу в во́зрасте от 11 до 18 лет. В США шко́льники внача́ле посеща́ют мла́дшую сре́днюю шко́лу, а зате́м, в во́зрасте от 14 до 18 лет, сре́днюю шко́лу. Шко́льное образова́ние обяза́тельно до 16 лет.

**high**: **~ season** *n* (*BRIT*) разга́р сезо́на; **~ street** *n* (*BRIT*) центра́льная у́лица; **~way** *n* (*US*) тра́сса, автостра́да; (*main road*) автостра́да
**hijack** ['haɪdʒæk] *vt* (*plane, bus*) угоня́ть (угна́ть *pf*)
**hike** [haɪk] *n*: **to go for a ~** идти́ (пойти́ *pf*) в похо́д
**hilarious** [hɪ'lɛərɪəs] *adj* чрезвыча́йно смешно́й
**hill** [hɪl] *n* (*small*) холм; (*fairly high*) гора́; (*slope*) склон; **~side** *n* склон; **~y** *adj* холми́стый
**him** [hɪm] *pron* (*direct*) его́; (*indirect*) ему́; (*after prep: +gen*) него́; (: +*dat*) нему́; (: +*instr*) ним; (: +*prp*) нём; *see also* **me**; **~self** *pron* (*reflexive, after prep: +acc, +gen*) себя́; (: +*dat*, +*prp*) себе́; (: +*instr*) собо́й; (*emphatic*) сам; (*alone*) **by ~self** оди́н; *see also* **myself**
**hinder** ['hɪndər] *vt* препя́тствовать (воспрепя́тствовать *pf*) *or* меша́ть (помеша́ть *pf*) +*dat*
**hindrance** ['hɪndrəns] *n* поме́ха
**hindsight** ['haɪndsaɪt] *n*: **with ~** ретроспекти́вным взгля́дом
**Hindu** ['hɪnduː] *adj* инду́сский
**hinge** [hɪndʒ] *n* (*on door*) петля́
**hint** [hɪnt] *n* (*suggestion*) намёк; (*tip*) сове́т; (*sign, glimmer*) подо́бие

**hip** [hɪp] n бедро́
**hippopotami** [hɪpə'pɔtəmaɪ] npl of
**hippopotamus**
**hippopotamus** [hɪpə'pɔtəməs] (pl
~es or **hippopotami**) n
гиппопота́м
**hire** ['haɪə\*] vt (BRIT: car, equipment)
брать (взять pf) напрока́т;
(venue) снима́ть (снять pf),
арендова́ть (impf/pf); (worker)
нанима́ть (наня́ть pf) ♦ n (BRIT: of
car) прока́т; **for ~** напрока́т;
**~-purchase** n (BRIT): **to buy sth
on ~-purchase** покупа́ть (купи́ть
pf) что-н в рассро́чку
**his** [hɪz] adj его́; (referring to subject
of sentence) свой; see also **my**
♦ pron его́; see also **mine¹**
**hiss** [hɪs] vi (snake, gas) шипе́ть
(impf)
**historian** [hɪ'stɔːrɪən] n исто́рик
**historic** [hɪ'stɔrɪk] adj (agreement,
achievement) истори́ческий; **~al**
adj (event, film) истори́ческий
**history** ['hɪstərɪ] n (of town, country)
исто́рия
**hit** [hɪt] (pt ~) vt ударя́ть (уда́рить
pf); (target) попада́ть (попа́сть pf)
в +acc; (collide with: car)
ста́лкиваться (столкну́ться pf) с
+instr; (affect: person, services)
ударя́ть (уда́рить pf) по +dat ♦ n
(COMPUT) посеще́ние; (success):
**the play was a big ~** пье́са
по́льзовалась больши́м
успе́хом; **to ~ it off (with sb)** (inf)
находи́ть (найти́ pf) о́бщий язы́к
(с кем-н)
**hitch** [hɪtʃ] vt (also: ~ **up**: trousers,
skirt) подтя́гивать (подтяну́ть pf)
♦ n (difficulty) поме́ха; **to ~ sth to**
(fasten) привя́зывать (привяза́ть
pf) что-н к +dat; (hook)
прицепля́ть (прицепи́ть pf) что-н
к +dat; **to ~ (a lift)** лови́ть
(пойма́ть pf) попу́тку

**hi-tech** ['haɪtɛk] adj
высокотехни́ческий
**hitherto** [hɪðə'tuː] adv (formal) до
настоя́щего вре́мени
**HIV** n abbr (= human immuno-
deficiency virus) ВИЧ; **~-negative/
positive** с отрица́тельной/
положи́тельной реа́кцией на
ВИЧ
**hive** [haɪv] n (of bees) у́лей
**HMS** abbr (BRIT) = His (or Her)
Majesty's Ship
**hoard** [hɔːd] n (of food) (та́йный)
запа́с; (of treasure) клад ♦ vt
(provisions) запаса́ть (запасти́ pf);
(money) копи́ть (скопи́ть pf)
**hoarse** [hɔːs] adj (voice) хри́плый
**hoax** [həuks] n (false alarm)
ло́жная трево́га
**hob** [hɔb] n ве́рхняя часть плиты́
с конфо́рками
**hobby** ['hɔbɪ] n хо́бби nt ind
**hockey** ['hɔkɪ] n хокке́й (на траве́)
**hog** [hɔg] vt (inf) завладева́ть
(завладе́ть pf) +instr
**hoist** [hɔɪst] n подъёмник,
лебёдка ♦ vt поднима́ть
(подня́ть pf); **to ~ sth on to one's
shoulders** взва́ливать (взвали́ть
pf) что-н на пле́чи
**hold** [həuld] (pt, pp **held**) vt (grip)
держа́ть (impf); (contain) вмеща́ть
(impf); (detain) содержа́ть (impf);
(power, qualification) облада́ть
(impf) +instr; (post) занима́ть
(заня́ть pf); (conversation, meeting)
вести́ (провести́ pf); (party)
устра́ивать (устро́ить pf) ♦ vi
(withstand pressure) выде́рживать
(вы́держать pf); (be valid)
остава́ться (оста́ться pf) в си́ле
♦ n (grasp) захва́т; (NAUT) трюм;
(AVIAT) грузово́й отсе́к; **to ~
one's head up** высоко́ держа́ть
(impf) го́лову; **to ~ sb hostage**
держа́ть (impf) кого́-н в ка́честве

заложника; ~ **the line!** (*TEL*) не
клади́те *or* ве́шайте тру́бку!; **he
~s you responsible for her death**
он счита́ет Вас вино́вным в её
сме́рти; **to catch** *or* **grab ~ of**
хвата́ться (схвати́ться *pf*) за *+acc*;
**to have a ~ over sb** держа́ть
(*impf*) кого́-н в рука́х; ~ **back** *vt*
(*thing*) приде́рживать
(придержа́ть *pf*); (*person*)
уде́рживать (удержа́ть *pf*);
(*information*) скрыва́ть (скрыть
*pf*); ~ **down** *vt* (*person*)
уде́рживать (удержа́ть *pf*); **to ~
down a job** уде́рживаться
(удержа́ться *pf*) на рабо́те; ~ **on**
*vi* (*grip*) держа́ться (*impf*); (*wait*)
ждать (подожда́ть *pf*); ~ **on!** (*TEL*)
не клади́те *or* ве́шайте тру́бку!;
~ **on to** *vt fus* (*for support*)
держа́ться (*impf*) за *+acc*; (*keep*:
*object*) приде́рживать
(придержа́ть *pf*); (: *beliefs*)
сохраня́ть (сохрани́ть *pf*); ~ **out**
*vt* (*hand*) протя́гивать
(протяну́ть *pf*); (*hope, prospect*)
сохраня́ть (сохрани́ть *pf*) ♦ *vi*
(*resist*) держа́ться (продержа́ться
*pf*); ~ **up** *vt* (*raise*) поднима́ть
(подня́ть *pf*); (*support*)
подде́рживать (поддержа́ть *pf*);
(*delay*) заде́рживать (задержа́ть
*pf*); (*rob*) гра́бить (огра́бить *pf*);
~**er** *n* (*container*) держа́тель *m*; (*of
ticket, record*) облада́тель(ница)
*m(f)*; **title ~er** нося́щий(ая) *m(f) adj*
ти́тул; ~**-up** *n* (*robbery*)
ограбле́ние; (*delay*) заде́ржка;
(*BRIT: in traffic*) про́бка
**hole** [həʊl] *n* (*in wall*) дыра́; (*in
road*) я́ма; (*burrow*) нора́; (*in
clothing*) ды́рка; (*in argument*)
брешь *f*
**holiday** [ˈhɒlɪdeɪ] *n* (*BRIT*: *from
school*) кани́кулы *pl*; (: *from work*)
о́тпуск; (*day off*) выходно́й день

*m*; (*also*: **public ~**) пра́здник; **on ~**
(*from school*) на кани́кулах; (*from
work*) в о́тпуске
**Holland** [ˈhɒlənd] *n* Голла́ндия
**hollow** [ˈhɒləʊ] *adj* (*container*)
по́лый; (*log, tree*) дупли́стый;
(*cheeks*) впа́лый; (*laugh*)
нейскре́нний; (*claim, sound*)
пусто́й ♦ *n* (*in ground*) впа́дина;
(*in tree*) дупло́ ♦ *vt*: **to ~ out**
выка́пывать (вы́копать *pf*)
**holly** [ˈhɒlɪ] *n* остроли́ст
**holocaust** [ˈhɒləkɔːst] *n* (*nuclear*)
истребле́ние; (*Jewish*) холоко́ст
**holy** [ˈhəʊlɪ] *adj* свято́й
**homage** [ˈhɒmɪdʒ] *n*: **to pay ~ to**
воздава́ть (возда́ть *pf*) по́чести
*+dat*
**home** [həʊm] *n* дом; (*area, country*)
ро́дина ♦ *cpd* дома́шний; (*ECON,
POL*) вну́тренний; (*SPORT*): **~ team**
хозя́ева *mpl* по́ля ♦ *adv* (*go, come*)
домо́й; (*hammer etc*) в то́чку; **at ~**
до́ма; (*in country*) на ро́дине; (*in
situation*) как у себя́ до́ма; **make
yourself at ~** чу́вствуйте себя́ как
до́ма; ~**land** *n* ро́дина; ~**less** *adj*
бездо́мный ♦ *npl*: **the ~less**
бездо́мные *pl adj*; ~**ly** *adj*
ую́тный; ~**-made** *adj* (*food*)
дома́шний; (*bomb*)
самоде́льный; **Home Office** *n*
(*BRIT*): **the Home Office** ≈
Министе́рство вну́тренних дел
**homeopathy** [həʊmɪˈɒpəθɪ] *n* (*US*)
= **homoeopathy**
**home**: ~ **page** *n* электро́нная
страни́ца *or* страни́чка; **Home
Secretary** *n* (*BRIT*) = мини́стр
вну́тренних дел; ~**sick** *adj*: **to be
~sick** (*for family*) скуча́ть (*impf*) по
до́му; (*for country*) скуча́ть (*impf*)
по ро́дине; ~ **town** *n* родно́й
го́род; ~**work** *n* дома́шняя
рабо́та, дома́шнее зада́ние
**homicide** [ˈhɒmɪsaɪd] *n* (*esp US*)

убийство

**homoeopathy** [həʊmɪˈɔpəθɪ] (*US* **homeopathy**) *n* гомеопа́тия

**homogeneous** [hɔməʊˈdʒiːnɪəs] *adj* одноро́дный

**homosexual** [hɔməʊˈsɛksjuəl] *adj* гомосексуа́льный ♦ *n* гомосексуали́ст(ка)

**honest** [ˈɔnɪst] *adj* че́стный; **~ly** *adv* че́стно; **~y** *n* че́стность *f*

**honey** [ˈhʌnɪ] *n* (*food*) мёд; **~moon** *n* медо́вый ме́сяц; **~suckle** *n* жи́молость *f*

**honorary** [ˈɔnərərɪ] *adj* почётный

**honour** [ˈɔnər] (*US* **honor**) *vt* (*person*) почита́ть (*impf*), чтить (*impf*); (*commitment*) выполня́ть (вы́полнить *pf*) ♦ *n* (*pride*) честь *f*; (*tribute, distinction*) по́честь *f*; **~able** *adj* (*person, action*) благоро́дный

**honours degree** - (учёная) сте́пень. Студе́нты университе́тов получа́ют учёную сте́пень. Така́я сте́пень вы́ше по у́ровню, чем так называ́емая "обы́чная сте́пень" или "зачёт".

**hood** [hud] *n* капюшо́н; (*US : AUT*) капо́т; (*of cooker*) вытяжно́й колпа́к

**hoof** [huːf] (*pl* **hooves**) *n* копы́то

**hook** [huk] *n* крючо́к ♦ *vt* прицепля́ть (прицепи́ть *pf*)

**hooligan** [ˈhuːlɪgən] *n* хулига́н

**hoop** [huːp] *n* о́бруч

**hoover** ® [ˈhuːvər] (*BRIT*) *n* пылесо́с ♦ *vt* пылесо́сить (пропылесо́сить *pf*)

**hooves** [huːvz] *npl* of **hoof**

**hop** [hɔp] *vi* скака́ть (*impf*) на одно́й ноге́

**hope** [həʊp] *vti* наде́яться (*impf*) ♦ *n* наде́жда; **to ~ that/to do** наде́яться (*impf*), что/+*infin*; **I ~ so/not** наде́юсь, что да/нет; **~ful** *adj* (*person*) по́лный наде́жд; (*situation*) обнадёживающий; **to be ~ful of sth** наде́яться (*impf*) на что-н; **~fully** *adv* (*expectantly*) с наде́ждой; **~fully, he'll come back** бу́дем наде́яться, что он вернётся; **~less** *adj* (*situation, person*) безнадёжный; **I'm ~less at names** я не в состоя́нии запомина́ть имена́

**hops** [hɔps] *npl* хмель *msg*

**horizon** [həˈraɪzn] *n* горизо́нт; **~tal** [hɔrɪˈzɔntl] *adj* горизонта́льный

**hormone** [ˈhɔːməʊn] *n* гормо́н

**horn** [hɔːn] *n* (*of animal*) рог; (*also*: **French ~**) валто́рна; (*AUT*) гудо́к

**horoscope** [ˈhɔrəskəʊp] *n* гороско́п

**horrendous** [həˈrɛndəs] *adj* ужаса́ющий

**horrible** [ˈhɔrɪbl] *adj* ужа́сный

**horrid** [ˈhɔrɪd] *adj* проти́вный, ме́рзкий

**horror** [ˈhɔrər] *n* (*alarm*) у́жас; (*dislike*) отвраще́ние; (*of war*) у́жасы *mpl*

**horse** [hɔːs] *n* ло́шадь *f*; **~back** *adv*: **on ~back** верхо́м; **~power** *n* лошади́ная си́ла; **~ racing** *n* ска́чки *fpl*; **~radish** *n* хрен; **~shoe** *n* подко́ва

**horticulture** [ˈhɔːtɪkʌltʃər] *n* растениево́дство

**hose** [həʊz] *n* (*also*: **~pipe**) шланг

**hospice** [ˈhɔspɪs] *n* больни́ца (*для безнадёжно больны́х*)

**hospitable** [ˈhɔspɪtəbl] *adj* (*person, behaviour*) гостеприи́мный

**hospital** [ˈhɔspɪtl] *n* больни́ца

**hospitality** [hɔspɪˈtælɪtɪ] *n* гостеприи́мство

**host** [həʊst] *n* (*at party, dinner*)

хозя́ин; (*TV, RADIO*) веду́щий *m adj*; **a ~ of** ма́сса +*gen*, мно́жество +*gen*

**hostage** ['hɔstɪdʒ] *n* зало́жник(ица)

**hostel** ['hɔstl] *n* общежи́тие; (*for homeless*) прию́т; (*also*: **youth ~**) молодёжная гости́ница

**hostess** ['həustɪs] *n* (*at party, dinner etc*) хозя́йка; (*TV, RADIO*) веду́щая *f adj*; (*BRIT*: *also*: **air ~**) стюарде́сса

**hostile** ['hɔstaɪl] *adj* (*person, attitude*) враждебный; (*conditions, environment*) неблагоприя́тный; (*troops*) вра́жеский

**hostility** [hɔ'stɪlɪtɪ] *n* враждебность *f*

**hot** [hɔt] *adj* (*object, temper, argument*) горя́чий; (*weather*) жа́ркий; (*spicy: food*) о́стрый; **she is ~** ей жа́рко; **it's ~** (*weather*) жа́рко

**hotel** [həu'tɛl] *n* гости́ница, оте́ль *m*

**hotly** ['hɔtlɪ] *adv* горячо́

**hot-water bottle** [hɔt'wɔːtə-] *n* гре́лка

**hound** [haund] *vt* трави́ть (затрави́ть *pf*) ♦ *n* го́нчая *f adj*

**hour** ['auər] *n* час; **~ly** *adj* (*rate*) почасово́й; (*service*) ежеча́сный

**house** *n* [haus] *vb* [hauz] *n* дом; (*THEAT*) зал ♦ *vt* (*person*) сели́ть (посели́ть *pf*); (*collection*) размеща́ть (размести́ть *pf*); **at my ~** у меня́ до́ма; **the House of Commons/Lords** (*BRIT*) Пала́та о́бщин/ло́рдов; **on the ~** (*inf*) беспла́тно; **~hold** *n* (*inhabitants*) домоча́дцы *mpl*; (*home*) дом; **~keeper** *n* эконо́мка; **~wife** (*irreg*) *n* дома́шняя хозя́йка, домохозя́йка; **~work** *n* дома́шние дела́ *ntpl*

**House of Lords** - Пала́та ло́рдов. Брита́нский парла́мент состои́т из двух пала́т: из Пала́ты о́бщин, чле́ны кото́рой избира́ются, и Пала́ты ло́рдов, кото́рая в настоя́щее вре́мя пережива́ет пери́од рефо́рм. До неда́внего вре́мени её чле́ны не избира́лись.

**housing** ['hauzɪŋ] *n* жильё; **~ estate** (*US* **~ project**) *n* жили́щный ко́мплекс; (*larger*) жило́й масси́в

**hover** ['hɔvər] *vi* (*bird, insect*) пари́ть (*impf*); **~craft** *n* су́дно на возду́шной поду́шке

┌─────────────┐
│ KEYWORD │
└─────────────┘

**how** [hau] *adv* **1** (*in what way*) как; **to know how to do** уме́ть (*impf*) +*infin*, знать (*impf*), как +*infin*; **how did you like the film?** как Вам понра́вился фильм?; **how are you?** как дела́ *or* Вы?

**2** ско́лько; **how much milk/many people?** ско́лько молока́/челове́к?; **how long?** как до́лго?, ско́лько вре́мени?; **how old are you?** ско́лько Вам лет?; **how tall is he?** како́го он ро́ста?; **how lovely/awful!** как чуде́сно/ужа́сно!

**howl** [haul] *vi* (*animal, wind*) выть (*impf*); (*baby, person*) реве́ть (*impf*)

**HP** *n abbr* (*BRIT*) = **hire-purchase**

**h.p.** *abbr* (*AUT*: = **horsepower**) л.с.

**HQ** *abbr* = **headquarters**

**HTML** *abbr* (= *hypertext markup language*) ри́пертекст

**hub** [hʌb] *n* (*of wheel*) сту́пица; (*fig*) средото́чие

**hue** [hjuː] *n* тон, отте́нок

**hug** [hʌg] *vt* обнима́ть (обня́ть *pf*);

(*object*) обхва́тывать (обхвати́ть *pf*)

**huge** [hju:dʒ] *adj* огро́мный, грома́дный; **~ly** *adv* чрезвыча́йно

**hull** [hʌl] *n* (*NAUT*) ко́рпус

**hum** [hʌm] *vt* напева́ть (*impf*) (*без слов*) ♦ *vi* (*person*) напева́ть (*impf*); (*machine*) гуде́ть (прогуде́ть *pf*)

**human** ['hju:mən] *adj* челове́ческий ♦ *n* (*also*: **~ being**) челове́к

**humane** [hju:'meɪn] *adj* (*treatment*) челове́чный

**humanitarian** [hju:mænɪ'tɛərɪən] *adj* (*aid*) гуманита́рный; (*principles*) гума́нный

**humanity** [hju:'mænɪtɪ] *n* (*mankind*) челове́чество; (*humaneness*) челове́чность *f*, гума́нность *f*

**human rights** *npl* права́ *ntpl* челове́ка

**humble** ['hʌmbl] *adj* скро́мный ♦ *vt* сбива́ть (сбить *pf*) спесь с +*gen*

**humidity** [hju:'mɪdɪtɪ] *n* вла́жность *f*

**humiliate** [hju:'mɪlɪeɪt] *vt* унижа́ть (уни́зить *pf*)

**humiliation** [hju:mɪlɪ'eɪʃən] *n* униже́ние

**humility** [hju:'mɪlɪtɪ] *n* (*modesty*) скро́мность *f*

**humming bird** *n* коли́бри *m/f ind*

**humor** ['hju:mər] (*US*) = **humour**

**humorous** ['hju:mərəs] *adj* (*book*) юмористи́ческий; (*remark*) шутли́вый; **~ person** челове́к с ю́мором

**humour** ['hju:mər] (*US* **humor**) *n* ю́мор; (*mood*) настрое́ние ♦ *vt* ублажа́ть (ублажи́ть *pf*)

**hump** [hʌmp] *n* (*in ground*) буго́р; (*on back*) горб

**hunch** [hʌntʃ] *n* дога́дка

**hundred** ['hʌndrəd] *n* сто; **~th** *adj* со́тый

**hung** [hʌŋ] *pt, pp of* **hang**

**Hungarian** [hʌŋ'gɛərɪən] *adj* венге́рский

**Hungary** ['hʌŋgərɪ] *n* Ве́нгрия

**hunger** ['hʌŋgər] *n* го́лод; **~ strike** *n* голодо́вка

**hungry** ['hʌŋgrɪ] *adj* голо́дный; (*keen*): **~ for** жа́ждущий +*gen*; **he is ~** он го́лоден

**hunk** [hʌŋk] *n* (большо́й) кусо́к

**hunt** [hʌnt] *vt* (*animal*) охо́титься (*impf*) на +*acc*; (*criminal*) охо́титься (*impf*) за +*instr* ♦ *vi* (*SPORT*) охо́титься (*impf*) ♦ *n* охо́та; (*for criminal*) ро́зыск; **to ~ (for)** (*search*) иска́ть (*impf*); **~er** *n* охо́тник(ица); **~ing** *n* охо́та

**hurdle** ['hə:dl] *n* препя́тствие; (*SPORT*) барье́р

**hurricane** ['hʌrɪkən] *n* урага́н

**hurried** ['hʌrɪd] *adj* (*departure*) поспе́шный; (*action*) торопли́вый

**hurry** ['hʌrɪ] *n* спе́шка ♦ *vi* спеши́ть (поспеши́ть *pf*), торопи́ться (поторопи́ться *pf*) ♦ *vt* (*person*) подгоня́ть (подогна́ть *pf*), торопи́ть (поторопи́ть *pf*); **to be in a ~** спеши́ть (*impf*), торопи́ться (*impf*); **~ up** *vt* (*person*) подгоня́ть (подогна́ть *pf*), торопи́ть (поторопи́ть *pf*); (*process*) ускоря́ть (уско́рить *pf*) ♦ *vi* торопи́ться (поторопи́ться *pf*); **~ up!** поторопи́сь!, скоре́е!

**hurt** [hə:t] (*pt, pp* **~**) *vt* причиня́ть (причини́ть *pf*) боль +*dat*; (*injure*) ушиба́ть (ушиби́ть *pf*); (*feelings*) задева́ть (заде́ть *pf*) ♦ *vi* (*be painful*) боле́ть (*impf*) ♦ *adj* (*offended*) оби́женный; (*injured*) уши́бленный; **to ~ o.s.** ушиба́ться (ушиби́ться *pf*); **~ful** *adj* оби́дный

**husband** ['hʌzbənd] n муж

**hush** [hʌʃ] n тишина; ~! тихо!, тише!

**husky** ['hʌskɪ] adj (voice) хриплый
♦ n ездовая собака

**hut** [hʌt] n (house) избушка, хижина; (shed) сарай

**hyacinth** ['haɪəsɪnθ] n гиацинт

**hydraulic** [haɪ'drɔːlɪk] adj гидравлический

**hydrogen** ['haɪdrədʒən] n водород

**hyena** [haɪ'iːnə] n гиена

**hygiene** ['haɪdʒiːn] n гигиена

**hygienic** [haɪ'dʒiːnɪk] adj (product) гигиенический

**hymn** [hɪm] n церковный гимн

**hype** [haɪp] n (inf) ажиотаж

**hypnosis** [hɪp'nəʊsɪs] n гипноз

**hypocrisy** [hɪ'pɔkrɪsɪ] n лицемерие

**hypocritical** [hɪpə'krɪtɪkl] adj лицемерный

**hypothermia** [haɪpə'θəːmɪə] n гипотермия

**hypotheses** [haɪ'pɔθɪsiːz] npl of **hypothesis**

**hypothesis** [haɪ'pɔθɪsɪs] (pl **hypotheses**) n гипотеза

**hypothetic(al)** [haɪpəʊ'θɛtɪk(l)] adj гипотетический

**hysteria** [hɪ'stɪərɪə] n истерия

## I, i

**I** [aɪ] pron я

**ice** [aɪs] n лёд; (ice cream) мороженое nt adj ♦ vt покрывать (покрыть pf) глазурью; **~berg** n айсберг; **~ cream** n мороженое nt adj; **~ hockey** n хоккей (на льду)

**Iceland** ['aɪslənd] n Исландия

**icicle** ['aɪsɪkl] n сосулька

**icing** ['aɪsɪŋ] n глазурь f; **~ sugar** n (BRIT) сахарная пудра (для приготовления глазури)

**icon** ['aɪkɔn] n (REL) икона; (COMPUT) иконка

**icy** ['aɪsɪ] adj (cold) ледяной; (road) обледенелый

**I'd** [aɪd] = **I would**, **I had**

**idea** [aɪ'dɪə] n идея

**ideal** [aɪ'dɪəl] n идеал ♦ adj идеальный; **~ist** n идеалист(ка)

**identical** [aɪ'dɛntɪkl] adj идентичный

**identification** [aɪdɛntɪfɪ'keɪʃən] n определение, идентификация; (of person, body) опознание; **(means of)** ~ удостоверение личности

**identify** [aɪ'dɛntɪfaɪ] vt определять (определить pf); (person) узнавать (узнать pf); (body) опознавать (опознать pf); (distinguish) выявлять (выявить pf)

**identity** [aɪ'dɛntɪtɪ] n (of person) личность f; (of group, nation) самосознание

**ideology** [aɪdɪ'ɔlədʒɪ] n идеология

**idiom** ['ɪdɪəm] n (phrase) идиома

**idiot** ['ɪdɪət] n идиот(ка)

**idle** ['aɪdl] adj праздный; (lazy) ленивый; (unemployed) безработный; (machinery, factory) бездействующий; **to be** ~ бездействовать (impf)

**idol** ['aɪdl] n кумир; (REL) идол

**idyllic** [ɪ'dɪlɪk] adj идиллический

**i.e.** abbr (that is: = id est) т.е.

KEYWORD

**if** [ɪf] conj 1 (conditional use) если; **if I finish early, I will ring you** если я закончу рано, я тебе позвоню; **if I were you (I would ...)** на Вашем месте (я бы ...)
2 (whenever) когда
3 (although): **(even) if** даже если; **I'll get it done, (even) if it takes all night** я сделаю это, даже

если э́то займёт у меня́ всю
ночь
4 (*whether*) ли; **I don't know if he
is here** я не зна́ю, здесь ли он;
**ask him if he can stay** спроси́те,
смо́жет ли он оста́ться
5: **if so/not** е́сли да/нет; **if only**
е́сли бы то́лько; **if only I could**
е́сли бы я то́лько мог; *see also* **as**

**ignite** [ɪɡ'naɪt] *vt* (*set fire to*)
зажига́ть (заже́чь *pf*) ♦ *vi*
загора́ться (загоре́ться *pf*)
**ignition** [ɪɡ'nɪʃən] *n* (*AUT*)
зажига́ние
**ignorance** ['ɪɡnərəns] *n*
неве́жество
**ignorant** ['ɪɡnərənt] *adj*
неве́жественный; **~ of** (*a subject*)
несве́дущий в +*prp*; **he is ~ of
that fact** (*unaware of*) он не зна́ет
об э́том
**ignore** [ɪɡ'nɔːr] *vt* игнори́ровать
(*impf/pf*); (*disregard*) пренебрега́ть
(пренебре́чь *pf*)
**I'll** [aɪl] = **I will**, **I shall**
**ill** [ɪl] *adj* больно́й; (*effects*) дурно́й
♦ *adv*: **to speak ~ (of sb)** ду́рно
говори́ть (*impf*) (о ком-н); **he is ~**
он бо́лен; **to be taken ~**
заболева́ть (заболе́ть *pf*)
**illegal** [ɪ'liːɡl] *adj* незако́нный;
(*organization*) нелега́льный
**illegible** [ɪ'lɛdʒɪbl] *adj*
неразбо́рчивый
**illegitimate** [ɪlɪ'dʒɪtɪmət] *adj* (*child*)
внебра́чный; (*activities*)
незако́нный, нелегити́мный
**ill-fated** [ɪl'feɪtɪd] *adj* злополу́чный
**ill-health** [ɪl'hɛlθ] *n* плохо́е
здоро́вье
**illicit** [ɪ'lɪsɪt] *adj* (*substance*)
незако́нный; (*affair*)
предосуди́тельный
**illiterate** [ɪ'lɪtərət] *adj*
негра́мотный

**illness** ['ɪlnɪs] *n* боле́знь *f*
**illogical** [ɪ'lɔdʒɪkl] *adj* нелоги́чный
**illuminate** [ɪ'luːmɪneɪt] *vt* (*light up*)
освеща́ть (освети́ть *pf*)
**illusion** [ɪ'luːʒən] *n* (*false idea*)
иллю́зия; (*trick*) фо́кус
**illustrate** ['ɪləstreɪt] *vt*
иллюстри́ровать
(проиллюстри́ровать *pf*)
**illustration** [ɪlə'streɪʃən] *n*
иллюстра́ция
**illustrious** [ɪ'lʌstrɪəs] *adj* (*person*)
просла́вленный; (*career*)
блестя́щий
**I'm** [aɪm] = **I am**
**image** ['ɪmɪdʒ] *n* (*picture*) о́браз;
(*public face*) и́мидж; (*reflection*)
изображе́ние
**imaginary** [ɪ'mædʒɪnərɪ] *adj*
(*creature, land*) вообража́емый
**imagination** [ɪmædʒɪ'neɪʃən] *n*
воображе́ние
**imaginative** [ɪ'mædʒɪnətɪv] *adj*
(*solution*) хитроу́мный; **he is very
~** он облада́ет бога́тым
воображе́нием
**imagine** [ɪ'mædʒɪn] *vt* (*visualize*)
представля́ть (предста́вить *pf*)
(себе́), вообража́ть (вообрази́ть
*pf*); (*dream*) вообража́ть
(вообрази́ть *pf*); (*suppose*)
предполага́ть (предположи́ть *pf*)
**imitate** ['ɪmɪteɪt] *vt* подража́ть
(*impf*) +*dat*, имити́ровать (*impf*)
**imitation** [ɪmɪ'teɪʃən] *n*
подража́ние, имита́ция
**immaculate** [ɪ'mækjulət] *adj*
безупре́чный
**immaterial** [ɪmə'tɪərɪəl] *adj*
несуще́ственный
**immature** [ɪmə'tjuər] *adj* незре́лый
**immediate** [ɪ'miːdɪət] *adj* (*reaction,
answer*) неме́дленный; (*need*)
безотлага́тельный; (*family*)
ближа́йший; **~ly** *adv* (*at once*)
неме́дленно; (*directly*) сра́зу

**immense** [ɪ'mɛns] *adj* огро́мный, грома́дный

**immigrant** ['ɪmɪgrənt] *n* иммигра́нт(ка)

**immigration** [ɪmɪ'greɪʃən] *n* иммигра́ция; (*also*: ~ **control**) иммиграцио́нный контро́ль

**imminent** ['ɪmɪnənt] *adj* (*arrival, departure*) неминýемый

**immobile** [ɪ'məubaɪl] *adj* неподви́жный

**immoral** [ɪ'mɔrl] *adj* амора́льный, безнра́вственный

**immortal** [ɪ'mɔ:tl] *adj* бессме́ртный

**immune** [ɪ'mju:n] *adj*: **he is ~ to** (*disease*) у него́ иммуните́т про́тив +*gen*; (*flattery, criticism etc*) он невоспри́имчив к +*dat*; ~ **system** *n* имму́нная систе́ма

**immunity** [ɪ'mju:nɪtɪ] *n* (*to disease*) иммуните́т; (*to criticism*) невоспри́имчивость f; (*from prosecution*) неприкоснове́нность f

**immunize** ['ɪmjunaɪz] *vt*: **to ~ sb (against)** де́лать (сде́лать *pf*) кому́-н приви́вку (про́тив +*gen*)

**impact** ['ɪmpækt] *n* (*of crash*) уда́р; (*force*) уда́рная си́ла; (*of law, measure*) возде́йствие

**impaired** *adj* (*hearing, speech*) затруднённый

**impart** [ɪm'pɑ:t] *vt*: **to ~ (to)** (*skills*) передава́ть (переда́ть *pf*) (+*dat*); (*news*) ве́дать (пове́дать *pf*) (+*dat*); (*flavour*) придава́ть (прида́ть *pf*) (+*dat*)

**impartial** [ɪm'pɑ:ʃl] *adj* беспристра́стный

**impatience** [ɪm'peɪʃəns] *n* нетерпе́ние

**impatient** [ɪm'peɪʃənt] *adj* нетерпели́вый; **to get** *or* **grow ~** теря́ть (потеря́ть *pf*) терпе́ние; **she was ~ to leave** ей не терпе́лось уйти́

**impeccable** [ɪm'pɛkəbl] *adj* безупре́чный

**impediment** [ɪm'pɛdɪmənt] *n*: **speech ~** дефе́кт ре́чи

**impending** [ɪm'pɛndɪŋ] *adj* граду́щий

**imperative** [ɪm'pɛrətɪv] *adj*: **it is ~ that ...** необходи́мо, что́бы ...

**imperceptible** [ɪmpə'sɛptɪbl] *adj* неощути́мый

**imperfect** [ɪm'pə:fɪkt] *adj* (*system*) несоверше́нный; (*goods*) дефе́ктный

**imperial** [ɪm'pɪərɪəl] *adj* (*history, power*) импе́рский; (*BRIT: measure*): ~ **system** брита́нская систе́ма едини́ц измере́ния и ве́са

**impersonal** [ɪm'pə:sənl] *adj* (*organization, place*) безли́кий

**impersonate** [ɪm'pə:səneɪt] *vt* выдава́ть (вы́дать *pf*) себя́ за +*acc*

**impertinent** [ɪm'pə:tɪnənt] *adj* де́рзкий

**impetuous** [ɪm'pɛtjuəs] *adj* поры́вистый

**implement** *vb* ['ɪmplɪmənt] *n* ['ɪmplɪmənt] *vt* проводи́ть (провести́ *pf*) в жизнь ♦ *n* (*for gardening*) ору́дие

**implication** [ɪmplɪ'keɪʃən] *n* (*inference*) сле́дствие

**implicit** [ɪm'plɪsɪt] *adj* (*inferred*) невы́раженный, имплици́тный; (*unquestioning*) безоговоро́чный

**implore** [ɪm'plɔ:ʳ] *vt* умоля́ть (умоли́ть *pf*)

**imply** [ɪm'plaɪ] *vt* (*hint*) намека́ть (намекну́ть *pf*); (*mean*) означа́ть (*impf*)

**import** *vb* [ɪm'pɔ:t] *n, cpd* ['ɪmpɔ:t] *vt* импорти́ровать (*impf/pf*), ввози́ть (ввезти́ *pf*) ♦ *n* (*article*) импорти́руемый това́р;

(*importation*) и́мпорт ♦ *cpd*: ~
**duty/licence** по́шлина/лице́нзия
на ввоз

**importance** [ɪm'pɔːtns] *n*
ва́жность *f*

**important** [ɪm'pɔːtnt] *adj* ва́жный;
**it's not** ~ э́то нева́жно

**impose** [ɪm'pəuz] *vt* (*restrictions,
fine*) налага́ть (наложи́ть *pf*);
(*discipline, rules*) вводи́ть (ввести́
*pf*) ♦ *vi* навя́зываться (навяза́ться
*pf*)

**imposing** [ɪm'pəuzɪŋ] *adj*
вели́чественный

**impossible** [ɪm'pɔsɪbl] *adj* (*task,
demand*) невыполни́мый;
(*situation, person*) невыноси́мый

**impotent** ['ɪmpətnt] *adj*
бесси́льный

**impractical** [ɪm'præktɪkl] *adj* (*plan
etc*) нереа́льный; (*person*)
непракти́чный

**impress** [ɪm'pres] *vt* (*person*)
производи́ть (произвести́ *pf*)
впечатле́ние на +*acc*; **to ~ sth on
sb** внуша́ть (внуши́ть *pf*) что-н
кому́-н

**impression** [ɪm'preʃən] *n*
впечатле́ние; (*of stamp, seal*)
отпеча́ток; (*imitation*) имита́ция;
**he is under the ~ that ...** у него́
создало́сь впечатле́ние, что ...;
**~able** *adj* впечатли́тельный

**impressive** [ɪm'presɪv] *adj*
впечатля́ющий

**imprint** ['ɪmprɪnt] *n* отпеча́ток

**imprison** [ɪm'prɪzn] *vt* заключа́ть
(заключи́ть *pf*) в тюрьму́; **~ment**
*n* (тюре́мное) заключе́ние

**improbable** [ɪm'prɔbəbl] *adj*
невероя́тный

**impromptu** [ɪm'prɔmptjuː] *adj*
(*party*) импровизи́рованный

**improve** [ɪm'pruːv] *vt* улучша́ть
(улу́чшить *pf*) ♦ *vi* улучша́ться
(улу́чшиться *pf*); (*pupil*)

становиться (стать *pf*) лу́чше;
**the patient ~d** больно́му ста́ло
лу́чше; **~ment** *n*: **~ment (in)**
улучше́ние (+*gen*)

**improvise** ['ɪmprəvaɪz] *vti*
импровизи́ровать (*impf/pf*)

**impudent** ['ɪmpjudnt] *adj*
бессты́дный

**impulse** ['ɪmpʌls] *n* (*urge*) поры́в;
**to act on ~** поддава́ться
(подда́ться *pf*) поры́ву

**impulsive** [ɪm'pʌlsɪv] *adj* (*person*)
импульси́вный; (*gesture*)
поры́вистый

KEYWORD

**in** [ɪn] *prep* **1** (*indicating position*) в/
на +*prp*; **in the house/garden** в
до́ме/саду́; **in the street/Ukraine**
на у́лице/Украи́не; **in London/
Canada** в Ло́ндоне/Кана́де; **in the
country** в дере́вне; **in town** в
го́роде; **in here** здесь; **in there**
там

**2** (*indicating motion*) в/на +*acc*; **in
the house/room** в дом/ко́мнату

**3** (*indicating time: during*): **in
spring/summer/autumn/winter**
весно́й/ле́том/о́сенью/зимо́й; **in
the morning/afternoon/evening**
у́тром/днём/ве́чером; **in the
evenings** по вечера́м; **at 4 o'clock
in the afternoon** в 4 часа́ дня

**4** (*indicating time: in the space of*)
за +*acc*; (: *after a period of*) че́рез
+*acc*; **I did it in 3 hours** я сде́лал
э́то за 3 часа́; **I'll see you in 2
weeks** уви́димся че́рез 2 неде́ли

**5** (*indicating manner etc*): **in a
loud/quiet voice** гро́мким/ти́хим
го́лосом; **in English/Russian** по-
англи́йски/по-ру́сски, на
англи́йском/ру́сском языке́

**6** (*wearing*) в +*prp*; **the boy in the
blue shirt** ма́льчик в голубо́й
руба́шке

**7** (*indicating circumstances*): **in the sun** на со́лнце; **in the rain** под дождём; **in the shade** в тени́; **a rise in prices** повыше́ние цен
**8** (*indicating mood, state*) в +*prp*; **in despair** в отча́янии
**9** (*with ratios, numbers*): **one in ten households** одна́ из десяти́ семе́й; **20 pence in the pound** 20 пе́нсов с ка́ждого фу́нта; **they lined up in twos** они́ вы́строились по́ двое; **a gradient of one in five** укло́н оди́н к пяти́
**10** (*referring to people, works*) у +*gen*; **the disease is common in children** э́то заболева́ние ча́сто встреча́ется у дете́й; **in Dickens** у Ди́ккенса; **you have a good friend in him** он тебе́ хоро́ший друг
**11** (*indicating profession etc*): **to be in publishing/advertising** занима́ться (*impf*) изда́тельским де́лом/рекла́мным би́знесом; **to be in teaching** рабо́тать (*impf*) учи́телем; **to be in the army** быть (*impf*) в а́рмии
**12** (*with present participle*): **in saying this** говоря́ э́то; **in behaving like this, she ...** поступа́я таки́м о́бразом, она́ ...
♦ *adv*: **to be in** (*train, ship, plane*) прибыва́ть (прибы́ть *pf*); (*in fashion*) быть (*impf*) в мо́де; **is he in today?** он сего́дня здесь?; **he is not in today** его́ сего́дня нет; **he wasn't in yesterday** его́ вчера́ не́ было; **he'll be in later today** он бу́дет по́зже сего́дня; **to ask sb in** предлага́ть (предложи́ть *pf*) кому́-н войти́; **to walk in** входи́ть (войти́ *pf*)
♦ *n*: **to know all the ins and outs** знать (*impf*) все ходы́ и вы́ходы

**in.** *abbr* = **inch**

**inability** [ɪnə'bɪlɪtɪ] *n*: ~ **(to do)** неспосо́бность *f* (+*infin*)
**inaccessible** [ɪnək'sesɪbl] *adj* (*also fig*) недосту́пный
**inaccurate** [ɪn'ækjurət] *adj* нето́чный
**inactivity** [ɪnæk'tɪvɪtɪ] *n* безде́ятельность *f*
**inadequate** [ɪn'ædɪkwət] *adj* недоста́точный; (*work*) неудовлетвори́тельный; (*person*) некомпете́нтный; **to feel** ~ чу́вствовать (*impf*) себя́ не на у́ровне
**inadvertently** [ɪnəd'və:tntlɪ] *adv* неча́янно, неумы́шленно
**inanimate** [ɪn'ænɪmət] *adj* (*object*) неодушевлённый
**inappropriate** [ɪnə'prəuprɪət] *adj* (*unsuitable*) неподходя́щий; (*improper*) неуме́стный
**inarticulate** [ɪnɑ:'tɪkjulət] *adj* (*person*) косноязы́чный
**inasmuch as** [ɪnəz'mʌtʃ-] *adv* (*in that*) поско́льку; (*insofar as*) наско́лько
**inaudible** [ɪn'ɔ:dɪbl] *adj* невня́тный
**inauguration** [ɪnɔ:gju'reɪʃən] *n* (*of person*) вступле́ние в до́лжность; (*of a president*) инаугура́ция
**Inc.** *abbr* = **incorporated**
**incapable** [ɪn'keɪpəbl] *adj* (*helpless*) беспо́мощный; ~ **of sth/doing** неспосо́бный на что-н/+*infin*
**incense** *n* ['ɪnsɛns] *vb* [ɪn'sɛns] *n* ла́дан ♦ *vt* приводи́ть (привести́ *pf*) в я́рость
**incentive** [ɪn'sɛntɪv] *n* сти́мул
**incessant** [ɪn'sɛsnt] *adj* бесконе́чный, постоя́нный
**incest** ['ɪnsɛst] *n* кровосмеше́ние
**inch** [ɪntʃ] *n* (*measurement*) дюйм

---

**inch** - дюйм. Ме́ра длины́ ра́вная 2.54 см.

**incidence** ['ɪnsɪdns] n число; **high ~** высо́кий у́ровень

**incident** ['ɪnsɪdnt] n (event) слу́чай; **without ~** без происше́ствий; **~ally** [ɪnsɪ'dentəlɪ] adv (by the way) кста́ти, ме́жду про́чим

**incite** [ɪn'saɪt] vt (violence, hatred) возбужда́ть (возбуди́ть pf); (people) подстрека́ть (impf)

**inclination** [ɪnklɪ'neɪʃən] n (desire) расположенность f; (tendency) скло́нность f

**incline** n ['ɪnklaɪn] vb [ɪn'klaɪn] n (slope) укло́н, накло́н ♦ vi: **he is ~d to ...** он скло́нен +infin ....; **he is ~d to depression** он скло́нен к депре́ссиям

**include** [ɪn'kluːd] vt включа́ть (включи́ть pf)

**including** [ɪn'kluːdɪŋ] prep включа́я +acc

**inclusion** [ɪn'kluːʒən] n включе́ние

**inclusive** [ɪn'kluːsɪv] adj: **~ of** включа́я +acc; **the price is fully ~** цена́ включа́ет в себя́ всё; **from March 1st to 5th** с 1-ого до 5-ого ма́рта включи́тельно

**incoherent** [ɪnkəu'hɪərənt] adj (argument) непосле́довательный; (speech) несвя́зный; (person) косноязы́чный

**income** ['ɪnkʌm] n дохо́д; **~ support** n де́нежное посо́бие (се́мьям с ни́зким дохо́дом); **~ tax** n подохо́дный нало́г

**incomparable** [ɪn'kɔmpərəbl] adj несравне́нный

**incompatible** [ɪnkəm'pætɪbl] adj несовмести́мый

**incompetence** [ɪn'kɔmpɪtns] n некомпете́нтность f

**incompetent** [ɪn'kɔmpɪtnt] adj (person) некомпете́нтный; (work) неуме́лый

**incomplete** [ɪnkəm'pliːt] adj (unfinished) незавершённый; (partial) непо́лный

**incomprehensible** [ɪnkɔmprɪ-'hensɪbl] adj непоня́тный

**inconceivable** [ɪnkən'siːvəbl] adj немы́слимый

**inconsistency** [ɪnkən'sɪstənsɪ] n (of actions) непосле́довательность f; (of statement) противоре́чивость f

**inconsistent** [ɪnkən'sɪstnt] adj (see n) непосле́довательный; противоре́чивый; (work) неро́вный; **~ with** (beliefs, values) несовмести́мый с +instr

**inconvenience** [ɪnkən'viːnjəns] n (problem) неудо́бство ♦ vt причиня́ть (причини́ть pf) беспоко́йство +dat

**inconvenient** [ɪnkən'viːnjənt] adj неудо́бный

**incorporate** [ɪn'kɔːpəreɪt] vt (contain) включа́ть (impf) в себя́, содержа́ть (impf); **to ~ (into)** включа́ть (включи́ть pf) (в +acc)

**incorrect** [ɪnkə'rekt] adj неве́рный, непра́вильный

**increase** n ['ɪnkriːs] vb [ɪn'kriːs] n: **~ (in), ~ (of)** увеличе́ние (+gen) ♦ vi увели́чиваться (увели́читься pf) ♦ vt увели́чивать (увели́чить pf); (price) поднима́ть (подня́ть pf)

**increasingly** adv (with comparative) всё; (more intensely) всё бо́лее; (more often) всё ча́ще

**incredible** [ɪn'kredɪbl] adj невероя́тный

**incredulous** [ɪn'kredjuləs] adj недове́рчивый

**incur** [ɪn'kəːr] vt (expenses, loss) нести́ (понести́ pf); (debt) нака́пливать (накопи́ть pf); (disapproval, anger) навлека́ть (навле́чь pf) на себя́

**incurable** [ɪn'kjuərəbl] adj (disease) неизлечи́мый

**indebted** [ɪn'detɪd] adj: **I am ~ to you** (grateful) я Вам обя́зан

**indecent** [ɪn'diːsnt] *adj*
непристойный

**indecisive** [ɪndɪ'saɪsɪv] *adj*
нерешительный

**indeed** [ɪn'diːd] *adv* (*certainly*)
действительно, в самом деле;
(*in fact, furthermore*) более того;
**this book is very interesting ~** эта
книга весьма интересная; **thank
you very much ~** большое Вам
спасибо; **he is ~ very talented** он
на самом деле очень талантлив;
**yes ~!** да, действительно *or*
конечно!

**indefinite** [ɪn'dɛfɪnɪt] *adj* (*answer,
view*) неопределённый; (*period,
number*) неограниченный; **~ly**
*adv* (*continue, wait*) бесконечно;
(*be closed, delayed*) на
неопределённое время

**independence** [ɪndɪ'pɛndns] *n*
независимость *f*

**independent** [ɪndɪ'pɛndnt] *adj*
независимый

**in-depth** ['ɪndɛpθ] *adj* глубокий

**indestructible** [ɪndɪs'trʌktəbl] *adj*
(*object*) прочный; (*friendship,
alliance*) нерушимый

**index** ['ɪndɛks] (*pl* ~**es**) *n* (*in book*)
указатель *m*; (*in library etc*)
каталог; **price ~** индекс цен; ~
**finger** *n* указательный палец

**India** ['ɪndɪə] *n* Индия; ~**n** *adj*
индийский ♦ *n* индиец; **Red ~n**
индеец

**indicate** ['ɪndɪkeɪt] *vt* указывать
(указать *pf*) на +*acc*; (*mention*)
указывать (указать *pf*)

**indication** [ɪndɪ'keɪʃən] *n* знак; **all
the ~s are that ...** всё указывает
на то, что ...

**indicative** [ɪn'dɪkətɪv] *adj*: **to be ~
of** свидетельствовать (*impf*) о
+*prp*, указывать (*impf*) на +*acc*

**indicator** ['ɪndɪkeɪtər] *n* (*AUT*)
указатель *m* поворота; (*fig*)

показатель *m*

**indifference** [ɪn'dɪfrəns] *n*
безразличие, равнодушие

**indifferent** [ɪn'dɪfrənt] *adj*
безразличный, равнодушный;
(*mediocre*) посредственный

**indigestion** [ɪndɪ'dʒɛstʃən] *n*
несварение желудка

**indignant** [ɪn'dɪgnənt] *adj*: ~ **at
sth/with sb** возмущённый
чем-н/кем-н

**indignation** [ɪndɪg'neɪʃən] *n*
возмущение, негодование

**indirect** [ɪndɪ'rɛkt] *adj* (*way*)
окольный, обходный; (*answer*)
уклончивый; (*effect*) побочный; ~
**object** (*LING*) косвенное
дополнение

**indiscriminate** [ɪndɪs'krɪmɪnət] *adj*
(*bombing*) беспорядочный

**indispensable** [ɪndɪs'pɛnsəbl] *adj*
(*object*) необходимый; (*person*)
незаменимый

**indisputable** [ɪndɪs'pjuːtəbl] *adj*
(*undeniable*) неоспоримый

**individual** [ɪndɪ'vɪdjuəl] *n*
личность *f*, индивидуум ♦ *adj*
индивидуальный; **certain ~s**
отдельные личности; **~ly** *adv* в
отдельности; (*responsible*) лично

**indoctrination** [ɪndɔktrɪ'neɪʃən] *n*
идеологическая обработка

**indoor** ['ɪndɔːr] *adj* (*plant*)
комнатный; (*pool*) закрытый; ~**s**
*adv* (*go*) в помещение; (*be*) в
помещении; **he stayed ~s all
morning** он просидел дома всё
утро

**induce** [ɪn'djuːs] *vt* (*cause*)
вызывать (вызвать *pf*); (*persuade*)
побуждать (побудить *pf*); (*MED,
birth*) стимулировать (*impf/pf*)

**indulge** [ɪn'dʌldʒ] *vt* (*desire, whim
etc*) потворствовать (*impf*) +*dat*,
потакать (*impf*) +*dat*; (*person, child*)
баловать (избаловать *pf*) ♦ *vi*: **to**

~ **in** ба́ловаться (поба́ловаться
pf) +instr; **~nce** n (pleasure)
при́хоть f; (leniency) потво́рство
**industrial** [ɪn'dʌstrɪəl] adj
индустриа́льный,
промы́шленный; ~ **accident**
несча́стный слу́чай на
произво́дстве; ~ **action** n
забасто́вка; ~ **estate** n (BRIT)
индустриа́льный парк
**industry** ['ɪndəstrɪ] n
(manufacturing) индустри́я,
промы́шленность f no pl;
**industries** о́трасли pl
промы́шленности; **tourist/**
**fashion** ~ индустри́я тури́зма/
мо́ды
**inedible** [ɪn'ɛdɪbl] adj
несъедо́бный
**ineffective** [ɪnɪ'fɛktɪv] adj
неэффекти́вный
**inefficiency** [ɪnɪ'fɪʃənsɪ] n (see adj)
неэффекти́вность f;
непроизводи́тельность f
**inefficient** [ɪnɪ'fɪʃənt] adj
неэффекти́вный; (machine)
непроизводи́тельный
**inept** [ɪ'nɛpt] adj неуме́лый
**inequality** [ɪnɪ'kwɔlɪtɪ] n (of system)
нера́венство
**inert** [ɪ'nəːt] adj (still)
неподви́жный
**inescapable** [ɪnɪ'skeɪpəbl] adj
неизбе́жный
**inevitable** [ɪn'ɛvɪtəbl] adj
неизбе́жный, неотврати́мый
**inevitably** [ɪn'ɛvɪtəblɪ] adv
неизбе́жно
**inexcusable** [ɪnɪks'kjuːzəbl] adj
непрости́тельный
**inexpensive** [ɪnɪk'spɛnsɪv] adj
недорого́й
**inexperienced** [ɪnɪk'spɪərɪənst] adj
нео́пытный
**inexplicable** [ɪnɪk'splɪkəbl] adj
необъясни́мый

**infamous** ['ɪnfəməs] adj (person)
бесче́стный
**infant** ['ɪnfənt] n (baby) младе́нец;
(young child) ребёнок
**infantry** ['ɪnfəntrɪ] n пехо́та

**infant school** -
подготови́тельная шко́ла. В
Великобрита́нии таку́ю шко́лу
посеща́ют де́ти в во́зрасте от 5
(иногда́ 4) до 7 лет.

**infatuation** [ɪnfætju'eɪʃən] n
страсть f
**infect** [ɪn'fɛkt] vt заража́ть
(зарази́ть pf); **~ion** [ɪn'fɛkʃən] n
зара́за, инфе́кция; **~ious**
[ɪn'fɛkʃəs] adj (disease)
инфекцио́нный; (fig)
зарази́тельный
**inference** ['ɪnfərəns] n заключе́ние
**inferior** [ɪn'fɪərɪər] adj (position,
status) подчинённый; (goods)
ни́зкого ка́чества
**infertile** [ɪn'fəːtaɪl] adj беспло́дный
**infertility** [ɪnfəː'tɪlɪtɪ] n беспло́дие
**infested** [ɪn'fɛstɪd] adj: **the house is**
~ **with rats** дом киши́т кры́сами
**infidelity** [ɪnfɪ'dɛlɪtɪ] n неве́рность
f
**infinite** ['ɪnfɪnɪt] adj бесконе́чный
**infinitive** [ɪn'fɪnɪtɪv] n инфинити́в,
неопределённая фо́рма глаго́ла
**infinity** [ɪn'fɪnɪtɪ] n бесконе́чность
f
**infirm** [ɪn'fəːm] adj не́мощный;
**~ary** n больни́ца
**inflammable** [ɪn'flæməbl] adj
(fabric) легко́
воспламеня́ющийся; (chemical)
горю́чий
**inflammation** [ɪnflə'meɪʃən] n
воспале́ние
**inflation** [ɪn'fleɪʃən] n инфля́ция
**inflexible** [ɪn'flɛksɪbl] adj (rule,
timetable) жёсткий; (person)

негибкий

**inflict** [ɪnˈflɪkt] vt: **to ~ sth on sb**
причинять (причинить pf) что-н
кому-н

**influence** [ˈɪnfluəns] n (power)
влияние; (effect) воздействие ♦ vt
влиять (повлиять pf) на +acc;
**under the ~ of alcohol** под
воздействием алкоголя

**influential** [ɪnfluˈɛnʃl] adj
влиятельный

**influx** [ˈɪnflʌks] n приток

**inform** [ɪnˈfɔːm] vt: **to ~ sb of sth**
сообщать (сообщить pf) кому-н
о чём-н ♦ vi: **to ~ on sb** доносить
(донести pf) на кого-н

**informal** [ɪnˈfɔːml] adj (visit,
invitation) неофициальный;
(discussion, manner)
непринуждённый; (clothes)
будничный

**information** [ɪnfəˈmeɪʃən] n
информация, сообщение; **a
piece of ~** сообщение

**informative** [ɪnˈfɔːmətɪv] adj
содержательный

**informer** [ɪnˈfɔːməʳ] n (also: **police
~**) осведомитель(ница) m(f)

**infrastructure** [ˈɪnfrəstrʌktʃəʳ] n
инфраструктура

**infringe** [ɪnˈfrɪndʒ] vt (law)
преступать (преступить pf) ♦ vi:
**to ~ on** ущемлять (ущемить pf),
посягать (посягнуть pf) на +acc

**infuriating** [ɪnˈfjuərɪeɪtɪŋ] adj
возмутительный

**ingenious** [ɪnˈdʒiːnjəs] adj
хитроумный; (person)
изобретательный

**ingenuity** [ɪndʒɪˈnjuːɪtɪ] n (see adj)
хитроумность f;
изобретательность f

**ingredient** [ɪnˈɡriːdɪənt] n
ингредиент; (fig) составная
часть f

**inhabit** [ɪnˈhæbɪt] vt населять

(impf); **~ant** n житель(ница) m(f)

**inhale** [ɪnˈheɪl] vt вдыхать
(вдохнуть pf) ♦ vi делать
(сделать pf) вдох; (when smoking)
затягиваться (затянуться pf)

**inherent** [ɪnˈhɪərənt] adj: **~ in** or **to**
присущий +dat

**inherit** [ɪnˈhɛrɪt] vt наследовать
(impf/pf), унаследовать (pf);
**~ance** n наследство

**inhibit** [ɪnˈhɪbɪt] vt сковывать
(сковать pf); (growth)
задерживать (задержать pf); **~ed**
adj скованный; **~ion** n [ɪnhɪˈbɪʃən] n
скованность f no pl

**inhospitable** [ɪnhɔsˈpɪtəbl] adj
(person, place) неприветливый

**inhuman** [ɪnˈhjuːmən] adj
(behaviour) бесчеловечный

**initial** [ɪˈnɪʃl] adj первоначальный,
начальный ♦ n (also: **~ letter**)
начальная буква ♦ vt ставить
(поставить pf) инициалы на +prp;
**~s** npl (of name) инициалы mpl;
**~ly** adv (at first) вначале, сначала

**initiate** [ɪˈnɪʃɪeɪt] vt (talks etc)
класть (положить pf) начало
+dat, зачинать (impf); (new
member) посвящать (посвятить
pf)

**initiation** [ɪnɪʃɪˈeɪʃən] n начало;
(into secret etc) посвящение

**initiative** [ɪˈnɪʃətɪv] n инициатива,
начинание; (enterprise)
инициативность f; **to take the ~**
брать (взять pf) на себя
инициативу

**inject** [ɪnˈdʒɛkt] vt (drugs, poison)
вводить (ввести pf); (patient): **to ~
sb with sth** делать (сделать pf)
укол чего-н кому-н; **to ~ into**
(money) вливать (влить pf) в +acc;
**~ion** [ɪnˈdʒɛkʃən] n укол; (of
money) вливание

**injunction** [ɪnˈdʒʌŋkʃən] n (LAW)
судебный запрет

**injure** ['ɪndʒər] vt (person, limb, feelings) ра́нить (impf/pf); **~d** adj ра́неный

**injury** ['ɪndʒərɪ] n ра́на; (industrial, sports) тра́вма

**injustice** [ɪn'dʒʌstɪs] n несправедли́вость f

**ink** [ɪŋk] n (in pen) черни́ла pl

**inland** ['ɪnlənd] adv (travel) вглубь; **Inland Revenue** n (BRIT) ≈ (Гла́вное) нало́говое управле́ние

**in-laws** ['ɪnlɔːz] npl (of woman) родня́ со стороны́ му́жа; (of man) родня́ со стороны́ жены́

**inlet** ['ɪnlɛt] n (ýзкий) зали́в

**inmate** ['ɪnmeɪt] n (of prison) заключённый(ая) m(f) adj; (of asylum) пацие́нт(ка)

**inn** [ɪn] n тракти́р

**inner** ['ɪnər] adj вну́тренний; ~ **city** n центра́льная часть f го́рода

**innocence** ['ɪnəsns] n неви́нность f; (naivety) неви́нность f

**innocent** ['ɪnəsnt] adj невино́вный; (naive) неви́нный

**innovation** [ɪnəu'veɪʃən] n но́вшество

**innumerable** [ɪ'njuːmrəbl] adj бесчи́сленный

**inoculation** [ɪnɔkju'leɪʃən] n приви́вка

**input** ['ɪnput] n (resources, money) вложе́ние

**inquest** ['ɪnkwɛst] n (into death) (суде́бное) рассле́дование

**inquire** [ɪn'kwaɪər] vi: to ~ (about) наводи́ть (навести́ pf) спра́вки (о +prp); (health) справля́ться (спра́виться pf) о +prp; to ~ when/where осведомля́ться (осве́домиться pf) когда/где; ~ **into** vt fus рассле́довать (impf/pf)

**inquisitive** [ɪn'kwɪzɪtɪv] adj любопы́тный

**ins** abbr = **inches**

**insane** [ɪn'seɪn] adj безу́мный, сумасше́дший

**insatiable** [ɪn'seɪʃəbl] adj ненасы́тный

**inscription** [ɪn'skrɪpʃən] n на́дпись f

**insect** ['ɪnsɛkt] n насеко́мое nt adj; **~icide** [ɪn'sɛktɪsaɪd] n инсектици́д

**insecure** [ɪnsɪ'kjuər] adj (person) неуве́ренный в себе́

**insecurity** [ɪnsɪ'kjuərɪtɪ] n неуве́ренность f в себе́

**insensitive** [ɪn'sɛnsɪtɪv] adj бесчу́вственный

**inseparable** [ɪn'sɛprəbl] adj (ideas, elements) нераздели́мый; (friends) неразлу́чный

**insert** [ɪn'səːt] vt: to ~ (into) вставля́ть (вста́вить pf) (в +acc); (piece of paper) вкла́дывать (вложи́ть pf) (в +acc); ~**ion** [ɪn'səːʃən] n (in book, file) вста́вка; (of needle) введе́ние

**inside** ['ɪn'saɪd] n вну́тренняя часть f ♦ adj вну́тренний ♦ adv (be) внутри́; (go) внутрь ♦ prep (position) внутри́ +gen; (motion) внутрь +gen; ~ **ten minutes** в преде́лах десяти́ мину́т; **~s** npl (inf: stomach) вну́тренности fpl; ~ **out** adv наизна́нку; (know) вдоль и поперёк

**insight** ['ɪnsaɪt] n: ~ **(into)** понима́ние (+gen)

**insignificant** [ɪnsɪg'nɪfɪknt] adj незначи́тельный

**insist** [ɪn'sɪst] vi: to ~ **(on)** наста́ивать (настоя́ть pf) (на +prp); **he ~ed that I came** он настоя́л на том, что́бы я пришёл; **he ~ed that all was well** он утвержда́л, что всё в поря́дке; **~ence** n настоя́ние; **~ent** ♦ adj насто́йчивый

**insofar as** [ɪnsəuˈfɑːˁ-] *adv* поско́льку

**insolent** [ˈɪnsələnt] *adj* (*attitude, remark*) на́глый

**insomnia** [ɪnˈsɔmnɪə] *n* бессо́нница

**inspect** [ɪnˈspɛkt] *vt* (*equipment, premises*) осма́тривать (осмотре́ть *pf*); **~ion** [ɪnˈspɛkʃən] *n* осмо́тр; **~or** *n* (*ADMIN, POLICE*) инспе́ктор; (*BRIT: on buses, trains*) контролёр

**inspiration** [ɪnspəˈreɪʃən] *n* вдохнове́ние

**inspire** [ɪnˈspaɪəˁ] *vt* (*workers, troops*) вдохновля́ть (вдохнови́ть *pf*); **to ~ sth (in sb)** внуша́ть (внуши́ть *pf*) что-н (кому́-н)

**instability** [ɪnstəˈbɪlɪtɪ] *n* нестаби́льность *f*

**install** [ɪnˈstɔːl] *vt* (*machine*) устана́вливать (установи́ть *pf*); (*official*) ста́вить (поста́вить *pf*); **~ation** [ɪnstəˈleɪʃən] *n* (*of machine, plant*) устано́вка

**instalment** [ɪnˈstɔːlmənt] (*US* **installment**) *n* (*of payment*) взнос; (*of story*) часть *f*; **to pay in ~s** плати́ть (заплати́ть *pf*) в рассро́чку

**instance** [ˈɪnstəns] *n* приме́р; **for ~** наприме́р; **in the first ~** в пе́рвую о́чередь

**instant** [ˈɪnstənt] *n* мгнове́ние, миг ♦ *adj* (*reaction, success*) мгнове́нный; (*coffee*) раствори́мый; **come here this ~!** иди́ сюда́ сию́ же мину́ту!; **~ly** *adv* неме́дленно, сра́зу

**instead** [ɪnˈstɛd] *adv* взаме́н ♦ *prep*: **~ of** вме́сто *or* взаме́н +*gen*

**instep** [ˈɪnstɛp] *n* подъём (*ноги́, ту́фли*)

**instil** [ɪnˈstɪl] *vt*: **to ~ sth in(to) sb** вселя́ть (всели́ть *pf*) что-н в кого́-н

**instinct** [ˈɪnstɪŋkt] *n* инсти́нкт; **by ~** инстинкти́вно; **~ive** [ɪnˈstɪŋktɪv] *adj* инстинкти́вный

**institute** [ˈɪnstɪtjuːt] *n* (*for research, teaching*) институ́т; (*professional body*) ассоциа́ция ♦ *vt* (*system, rule*) учрежда́ть (учреди́ть *pf*)

**institution** [ɪnstɪˈtjuːʃən] *n* учрежде́ние; (*custom, tradition*) институ́т

**instruct** [ɪnˈstrʌkt] *vt*: **to ~ sb in sth** обуча́ть (обучи́ть *pf*) кого́-н чему́-н; **to ~ sb to do** поруча́ть (поручи́ть *pf*) кому́-н +*infin*; **~ion** [ɪnˈstrʌkʃən] *n* (*teaching*) обуче́ние; **~ions** *npl* (*orders*) указа́ния *ntpl*; **~ions (for use)** инстру́кция *or* руково́дство (по примене́нию); **~or** *n* (*for driving etc*) инстру́ктор

**instrument** [ˈɪnstrumənt] *n* инструме́нт; **~al** [ɪnstruˈmɛntl] *adj*: **to be ~al in** игра́ть (сыгра́ть *pf*) суще́ственную роль в +*prp*

**insufficient** [ɪnsəˈfɪʃənt] *adj* недоста́точный

**insulation** [ɪnsjuˈleɪʃən] *n* (*against cold*) (тепло)изоля́ция

**insulin** [ˈɪnsjulɪn] *n* инсули́н

**insult** *vb* [ɪnˈsʌlt] *n* [ˈɪnsʌlt] *vt* оскорбля́ть (оскорби́ть *pf*) ♦ *n* оскорбле́ние; **~ing** [ɪnˈsʌltɪŋ] *adj* оскорби́тельный

**insurance** [ɪnˈʃuərəns] *n* страхова́ние; **~ policy** *n* страхово́й по́лис

**insure** [ɪnˈʃuəˁ] *vt*: **to ~ (against)** страхова́ть (застрахова́ть *pf*) (от +*gen*); **to ~ (o.s.) against** страхова́ться (застрахова́ться *pf*) от +*gen*

**intact** [ɪnˈtækt] *adj* (*unharmed*) неповреждённый; (*whole*) нетро́нутый

**intake** [ˈɪnteɪk] *n* (*of food, drink*) потребле́ние; (*BRIT: of pupils, recruits*) набо́р

**integral** ['ɪntɪgrəl] adj
неотъе́млемый

**integrate** ['ɪntɪgreɪt] vt
интегри́ровать (impf/pf) ♦ vi
(groups, individuals) объединя́ться
(объедини́ться pf)

**integrity** [ɪn'tɛgrɪtɪ] n (morality)
че́стность f, поря́дочность f

**intellect** ['ɪntəlɛkt] n интелле́кт;
**~ual** [ɪntə'lɛktjuəl] adj
интеллектуа́льный ♦ n
интеллектуа́л

**intelligence** [ɪn'tɛlɪdʒəns] n ум;
(thinking power) у́мственные
спосо́бности fpl; (MIL etc)
разве́дка; ~ **service** n
разве́дывательная слу́жба

**intelligent** [ɪn'tɛlɪdʒənt] adj у́мный;
(animal) разу́мный

**intend** [ɪn'tɛnd] vt: to ~ sth for
предназнача́ть (предназна́чить
pf) что-н для +gen; to ~ to do
намерева́ться (impf) +infin; **~ed**
adj (effect) заплани́рованный;
(victim) предполага́емый

**intense** [ɪn'tɛns] adj (heat, emotion)
си́льный; (noise, activity)
интенси́вный; **~ly** adv си́льно,
интенси́вно

**intensify** [ɪn'tɛnsɪfaɪ] vt уси́ливать
(уси́лить pf)

**intensity** [ɪn'tɛnsɪtɪ] n (of effort, sun)
интенси́вность f

**intensive** [ɪn'tɛnsɪv] adj
интенси́вный; ~ **care**
интенси́вная терапи́я

**intent** [ɪn'tɛnt] adj: ~ **(on)**
сосредото́ченный (на +prp); to
**be ~ on doing** (determined)
стреми́ться (impf) +infin

**intention** [ɪn'tɛnʃən] n наме́рение;
**~al** adj наме́ренный

**interact** [ɪntər'ækt] vi: to ~ **(with)**
взаимоде́йствовать (impf) (с
+instr); **~ion** [ɪntər'ækʃən] n
взаимоде́йствие

**interchangeable** [ɪntə'tʃeɪndʒəbl]
adj взаимозаменя́емый

**intercom** ['ɪntəkɔm] n селе́ктор

**intercourse** ['ɪntəkɔːs] n (sexual)
полово́е сноше́ние

**interest** ['ɪntrɪst] n: ~ **(in)** интере́с
(к +dat); (COMM, sum of money)
проце́нты mpl ♦ vt интересова́ть
(impf); to ~ sb in sth
заинтересо́вывать
(заинтересова́ть pf) кого́-н в
чём-н; **~ed** adj
заинтересо́ванный; to be ~ed **(in
sth)** (music etc) интересова́ться
(impf) (чем-н); **~ing** adj
интере́сный; ~ **rate** n
проце́нтная ста́вка

**interfere** [ɪntə'fɪər] vi: to ~ **in**
вме́шиваться (вмеша́ться pf) в
+acc; to ~ **with** (hinder) меша́ть
(помеша́ть pf) +dat; **~nce** n
вмеша́тельство

**interim** ['ɪntərɪm] adj (government)
вре́менный; (report)
промежу́точный ♦ n: **in the** ~ тем
вре́менем

**interior** [ɪn'tɪərɪər] n (of building)
интерье́р; (of car, box etc)
вну́тренность f ♦ adj (door, room
etc) вну́тренний; ~ **department/
minister** департа́мент/мини́стр
вну́тренних дел

**intermediate** [ɪntə'miːdɪət] adj
(stage) промежу́точный

**internal** [ɪn'təːnl] adj вну́тренний

**international** [ɪntə'næʃənl] adj
междунаро́дный

**Internet** ['ɪntənɛt] n Интерне́т; ~
**café** n интерне́т-кафе́ nt ind; ~
**Service Provider** n интерне́т-
прова́йдер

**interpret** [ɪn'təːprɪt] vt (explain)
интерпрети́ровать (impf/pf),
толкова́ть (impf); (translate)
переводи́ть (перевести́ pf)
(у́стно) ♦ vi переводи́ть

(перевести *pf*) (*устно*); **~ation**
[ɪntə:prɪ'teɪʃən] *n* интерпрета́ция,
толкова́ние; **~er** *n*
перево́дчик(ица) (*устный*)

**interrogation** [ɪntɛrəu'geɪʃən] *n*
допро́с

**interrupt** [ɪntə'rʌpt] *vti* прерыва́ть
(прерва́ть *pf*); **~ion** [ɪntə'rʌpʃən] *n*
(*act*) прерыва́ние

**interval** ['ɪntəvl] *n* интерва́л;
(*BRIT : SPORT*) переры́в; (: *THEAT*)
антра́кт; **at ~s** вре́мя от вре́мени

**intervene** [ɪntə'vi:n] *vi* (*in
conversation, situation*)
вме́шиваться (вмеша́ться *pf*);
(*event*) меша́ть (помеша́ть *pf*)

**intervention** [ɪntə'vɛnʃən] *n*
(*interference*) вмеша́тельство;
(*mediation*) посре́дничество

**interview** ['ɪntəvju:] *n* (*see vt*)
собесе́дование; интервью́ *nt ind*
♦ *vt* ( *for job*) проводи́ть
(провести́ *pf*) собесе́дование с
+*instr*; (*RADIO, TV etc*)
интервью́ировать (*impf/pf*), брать
(взять *pf*) интервью́ у +*gen*

**intestine** [ɪn'tɛstɪn] *n* кишка́; **~s**
кише́чник *msg*

**intimacy** ['ɪntɪməsɪ] *n* инти́мность
*f*, бли́зость *f*

**intimate** ['ɪntɪmət] *adj* ( *friend,
relationship*) бли́зкий; (*conversation,
atmosphere*) инти́мный;
(*knowledge*) глубо́кий,
непосре́дственный

**intimidate** [ɪn'tɪmɪdeɪt] *vt*
запу́гивать (запуга́ть *pf*)

**intimidation** [ɪntɪmɪ'deɪʃən] *n*
запу́гивание

---
KEYWORD
---

**into** ['ɪntu] *prep* **1** (*indicating motion*)
в/на +*acc*; **into the house/garden**
в дом/сад; **into the post office/
factory** на по́чту/фа́брику;
**research into cancer**

иссле́дования в о́бласти
ра́ковых заболева́ний; **he
worked late into the night** он
рабо́тал до по́здней но́чи
**2** (*indicating change of condition,
result*): **she has translated the
letter into Russian** она́ перевела́
письмо́ на ру́сский язы́к; **the
vase broke into pieces** ва́за
разби́лась на ме́лкие кусо́чки;
**they got into trouble for it** им
попа́ло за э́то; **he lapsed into
silence** он погрузи́лся в
молча́ние; **to burst into tears**
распла́каться (*pf*); **to burst into
flames** вспы́хивать (вспы́хнуть
*pf*)

**intolerable** [ɪn'tɔlərəbl] *adj*
невыноси́мый

**intolerance** [ɪn'tɔlərns] *n*
нетерпи́мость *f*

**intolerant** [ɪn'tɔlərnt] *adj*
нетерпи́мый

**intranet** ['ɪntrənɛt] *n* интране́т,
лока́льная вычисли́тельная сеть

**intricate** ['ɪntrɪkət] *adj* (*pattern*)
замыслова́тый; (*relationship*)
сло́жный

**intriguing** [ɪn'tri:gɪŋ] *adj*
( *fascinating*) интригу́ющий

**introduce** [ɪntrə'dju:s] *vt* (*new idea,
measure etc*) вводи́ть (ввести́ *pf*);
(*speaker, programme*)
представля́ть (предста́вить *pf*);
**to ~ sb (to sb)** представля́ть
(предста́вить *pf*) кого́-н (кому́-н);
**to ~ sb to** (*pastime etc*) знако́мить
(познако́мить *pf*) кого́-н с
+*instr*

**introduction** [ɪntrə'dʌkʃən] *n*
введе́ние; (*to person, new
experience*) знако́мство

**introductory** [ɪntrə'dʌktərɪ] *adj*
(*lesson*) вступи́тельный

**introvert** ['ɪntrəuvə:t] *n* интрове́рт

**intrude** [ɪn'truːd] vi: **to ~ (on)** вторга́ться (вто́ргнуться pf) (в/на +acc); **~r** n: **there is an ~r in our house** к нам в дом кто-то вто́ргся

**intrusion** [ɪn'truːʒən] n вторже́ние

**intuition** [ɪntjuː'ɪʃən] n интуи́ция

**intuitive** [ɪn'tjuːɪtɪv] adj интуити́вный

**inundate** ['ɪnʌndeɪt] vt: **to ~ with** (calls etc) засыпа́ть (засы́пать pf) +instr

**invade** [ɪn'veɪd] vt (MIL) вторга́ться (вто́ргнуться pf) в +acc

**invalid** n ['ɪnvəlɪd] adj [ɪn'vælɪd] n инвали́д ♦ adj недействи́тельный

**invaluable** [ɪn'væljuəbl] adj неоцени́мый

**invariably** [ɪn'vɛərɪəblɪ] adv неизме́нно

**invasion** [ɪn'veɪʒən] n (MIL) вторже́ние

**invent** [ɪn'vɛnt] vt изобрета́ть (изобрести́ pf); (fabricate) выду́мывать (вы́думать pf); **~ion** [ɪn'vɛnʃən] n (see vt) изобрете́ние; вы́думка; **~ive** adj изобрета́тельный; **~or** n изобрета́тель m

**inventory** ['ɪnvəntrɪ] n (of house etc) (инвентаризацио́нная) о́пись f

**invertebrate** [ɪn'vəːtɪbrət] n беспозвоно́чное nt adj

**inverted commas** [ɪn'vəːtɪd-] npl (BRIT : LING) кавы́чки fpl

**invest** [ɪn'vɛst] vt вкла́дывать (вложи́ть pf) ♦ vi: **to ~ in** вкла́дывать (вложи́ть pf) де́ньги в +acc

**investigate** [ɪn'vɛstɪgeɪt] vt (accident, crime) рассле́довать (impf/pf)

**investigation** [ɪnvɛstɪ'geɪʃən] n рассле́дование

**investment** [ɪn'vɛstmənt] n

(activity) инвести́рование; (amount of money) инвести́ция, вклад

**investor** [ɪn'vɛstər] n инве́стор, вкла́дчик

**invigilator** - экзаменацио́нный наблюда́тель. Он раздаёт экзаменацио́нные листы́ и следя́т за тем, что́бы студе́нты не спи́сывали.

**invigorating** [ɪn'vɪgəreɪtɪŋ] adj (air) бодря́щий

**invincible** [ɪn'vɪnsɪbl] adj (army, team) непобеди́мый

**invisible** [ɪn'vɪzɪbl] adj неви́димый

**invitation** [ɪnvɪ'teɪʃən] n приглаше́ние

**invite** [ɪn'vaɪt] vt приглаша́ть (пригласи́ть pf); (discussion, criticism) побужда́ть (побуди́ть pf) к +dat; **to ~ sb to do** предлага́ть (предложи́ть pf) кому́-н +infin

**inviting** [ɪn'vaɪtɪŋ] adj соблазни́тельный

**invoice** ['ɪnvɔɪs] n счёт, факту́ра ♦ vt выпи́сывать (вы́писать pf) счёт or факту́ру +dat

**involuntary** [ɪn'vɔləntrɪ] adj (action, reflex) непроизво́льный

**involve** [ɪn'vɔlv] vt (include) вовлека́ть (вовле́чь pf); (concern, affect) каса́ться (impf) +gen; **to ~ sb (in sth)** вовлека́ть (вовле́чь pf) кого́-н (во что-н); **~ment** n (participation) прича́стность f; (enthusiasm) увлече́ние

**iodine** ['aɪəudiːn] n йод

**ion** ['aɪən] n (ELEC) ио́н

**IOU** n abbr (= I owe you) долгова́я распи́ска

**IQ** n abbr (= intelligence quotient) коэффицие́нт у́мственного разви́тия

**IRA** n abbr (= Irish Republican Army)
ИРА

**Iran** [ɪˈrɑːn] n Ира́н; **~ian** [ɪˈreɪnɪən]
adj ира́нский

**Iraq** [ɪˈrɑːk] n Ира́к; **~i** [ɪˈrɑːkɪ] adj
ира́кский

**Ireland** [ˈaɪələnd] n Ирла́ндия

**iris** [ˈaɪrɪs] (pl **~es**) n (ANAT)
ра́дужная оболо́чка (гла́за)

**Irish** [ˈaɪrɪʃ] adj ирла́ндский ♦ npl:
**the ~** ирла́ндцы; **~man** (irreg) n
ирла́ндец

**iron** [ˈaɪən] n (metal) желе́зо; (for
clothes) утю́г ♦ cpd желе́зный ♦ vt
(clothes) гла́дить (погла́дить pf);
**~ out** vt (fig: problems) ула́живать
(ула́дить pf)

**ironic(al)** [aɪˈrɔnɪk(l)] adj
ирони́ческий

**ironing board** n гла́дильная
доска́

**ironmonger** [ˈaɪənmʌŋɡər] n (BRIT)
торго́вец скобяны́ми изде́лиями

**irony** [ˈaɪrənɪ] n иро́ния

**irrational** [ɪˈræʃənl] adj
неразу́мный, нерациона́льный

**irreconcilable** [ɪrɛkənˈsaɪləbl] adj
(ideas, conflict) непримири́мый

**irregular** [ɪˈrɛɡjʊlər] adj (pattern)
непра́вильной фо́рмы; (surface)
неро́вный; (LING) непра́вильный

**irrelevant** [ɪˈrɛləvənt] adj: **this fact
is ~** э́тот факт к де́лу не
отно́сится

**irreparable** [ɪˈrɛprəbl] adj (damage)
непоправи́мый

**irreplaceable** [ɪrɪˈpleɪsəbl] adj
незамени́мый

**irrepressible** [ɪrɪˈprɛsəbl] adj
неудержи́мый

**irresistible** [ɪrɪˈzɪstɪbl] adj (urge,
desire) непреодоли́мый; (person,
thing) неотрази́мый

**irrespective** [ɪrɪˈspɛktɪv] prep: **~ of**
незави́симо от +gen

**irresponsible** [ɪrɪˈspɔnsɪbl] adj
безотве́тственный

**irreverent** [ɪˈrɛvərnt] adj (person,
behaviour) непочти́тельный

**irrevocable** [ɪˈrɛvəkəbl] adj (action,
decision) бесповоро́тный

**irrigation** [ɪrɪˈɡeɪʃən] n ороше́ние,
иррига́ция

**irritable** [ˈɪrɪtəbl] adj
раздражи́тельный

**irritate** [ˈɪrɪteɪt] vt раздража́ть
(раздражи́ть pf)

**irritating** [ˈɪrɪteɪtɪŋ] adj (sound etc)
доса́дный; (person) неприя́тный

**irritation** [ɪrɪˈteɪʃən] n
раздраже́ние

**is** [ɪz] vb see **be**

**ISA** n abbr (= individual savings
account) индивидуа́льный
сберега́тельный счёт (вид
вкла́да)

**Islam** [ˈɪzlɑːm] n (REL) исла́м; **~ic**
[ɪzˈlæmɪk] adj исла́мский,
мусульма́нский

**island** [ˈaɪlənd] n (GEO) о́стров

**isn't** [ˈɪznt] = **is not**

**isolate** [ˈaɪsəleɪt] vt (set apart)
изоли́ровать (impf/pf); **~d** adj
(place, person) изоли́рованный;
(incident) отде́льный

**isolation** [aɪsəˈleɪʃən] n изоля́ция

**ISP** n abbr = **Internet Service
Provider**

**Israel** [ˈɪzreɪl] n Изра́иль m; **~i**
[ɪzˈreɪlɪ] adj изра́ильский

**issue** [ˈɪʃuː] n (problem, subject)
вопро́с, пробле́ма; (of book,
stamps etc) вы́пуск; (most
important part): **the ~** суть f ♦ vt
(newspaper) выпуска́ть
(вы́пустить pf); (statement)
де́лать (сде́лать pf); (equipment,
documents) выдава́ть (вы́дать pf);
**to be at ~** быть (impf) предме́том
обсужде́ния; **to make an ~ of sth**
де́лать (сде́лать pf) пробле́му из
чего́-н

KEYWORD

**it** [ɪt] pron 1 (specific subject) он (f
она, nt оно); (direct object) его (f
её); (indirect object) ему (f ей);
(after prep: +gen) него (f неё);
(: +dat) нему (f ней); (: +instr)
ним (f ней); (: +prp) нём (f ней);
**where is your car? - it's in the
garage** где Ваша машина? - она
в гараже; **I like this hat, whose is
it?** мне нравится эта шляпа, чья
она?
2 это; (: indirect object) этому; **what
kind of car is it? - it's a Lada** какая
это машина? - это Лада; **who is
it? - it's me** кто это? - это я
3 (after prep: +gen) этого; (: +dat)
этому; (: +instr) этим; (: +prp)
этом; **I spoke to him about it** я
говорил с ним об этом; **why is it
that ...?** отчего ...?; **what is it?**
(what's wrong) что такое?
4 (impersonal): **it's raining** идёт
дождь; **it's cold today** сегодня
холодно; **it's interesting that ...**
интересно, что ...; **it's 6 o'clock**
сейчас 6 часов; **it's the 10th of
August** сегодня 10-ое августа

**Italian** [ɪ'tæljən] adj итальянский
**italics** [ɪ'tælɪks] npl (TYP) курсив
msg
**Italy** ['ɪtəlɪ] n Италия
**itch** [ɪtʃ] vi чесаться (impf); **he was
~ing to know our secret** ему не
терпелось узнать наш секрет;
**~y** adj: **I feel all ~y** у меня всё
чешется
**it'd** ['ɪtd] = **it had**, **it would**
**item** ['aɪtəm] n предмет; (on
agenda) пункт; (also: **news ~**)
сообщение
**itinerary** [aɪ'tɪnərərɪ] n маршрут
**it'll** ['ɪtl] = **it shall**, **it will**
**its** [ɪts] adj, pron его (f её); (referring
to subject of sentence) свой (f своя,
nt своё) see also **my**; **mine¹**
**it's** [ɪts] = **it has**, **it is**
**itself** [ɪt'sɛlf] pron (reflexive) себя;
(emphatic: masculine) сам по себе;
(: feminine) сама по себе;
(: neuter) само по себе
**ITV** n abbr (BRIT : TV) = Independent
Television
**I've** [aɪv] = **I have**
**ivory** ['aɪvərɪ] n (substance)
слоновая кость f
**ivy** ['aɪvɪ] n (BOT) плющ

# J, j

**jab** [dʒæb] n (BRIT : inf : MED) укол
**jack** [dʒæk] n (AUT) домкрат;
(CARDS) валет
**jackal** ['dʒækl] n шакал
**jackdaw** ['dʒækdɔː] n галка
**jacket** ['dʒækɪt] n куртка; (of suit)
пиджак; (of book) суперобложка
**jackpot** ['dʒækpɔt] n джэк-пот, куш
**jaded** ['dʒeɪdɪd] adj утомлённый
**jagged** ['dʒægɪd] adj зубчатый
**jail** [dʒeɪl] n тюрьма ♦ vt сажать
(посадить pf) (в тюрьму)
**jam** [dʒæm] n (preserve) джем; (also:
**traffic ~**) пробка ♦ vt (passage)
забивать (забить pf); (mechanism)
заклинивать (заклинить pf) ♦ vi
(drawer) застревать (застрять pf);
**to ~ sth into** запихивать
(запихнуть pf) что-н в +acc
**janitor** ['dʒænɪtər] n вахтёр
**January** ['dʒænjuərɪ] n январь m
**Japan** [dʒə'pæn] n Япония
**Japanese** [dʒæpə'niːz] n
японец(нка)
**jar** [dʒɑːr] n банка
**jargon** ['dʒɑːgən] n жаргон
**jasmine** ['dʒæzmɪn] n жасмин
**jaunt** [dʒɔːnt] n вылазка; **~y** adj
(tone, step) бойкий

**javelin** ['dʒævlɪn] n копьё

**jaw** [dʒɔː] n чéлюсть f

**jazz** [dʒæz] n джаз

**jealous** ['dʒɛləs] adj ревни́вый; **to be ~ of** (possessive) ревнова́ть (impf) к +dat; (envious) зави́довать (impf) +dat; **~y** n (resentment) рéвность f; (envy) зáвисть f

**jeans** [dʒiːnz] npl джи́нсы pl

**jelly** ['dʒɛlɪ] n желé nt ind; (US) джем; **~fish** n медýза

**jeopardy** ['dʒɛpədɪ] n: **to be in ~** быть (impf) в опáсности

**jerk** [dʒəːk] n (jolt) рывóк ♦ vt дёргать (дёрнуть pf), рванýть (pf) ♦ vi дёргаться (дёрнуться pf); **the car ~ed to a halt** маши́на рéзко затормози́ла

**jersey** ['dʒəːzɪ] n (pullover) сви́тер

**Jesus** ['dʒiːzəs] n (REL) Иисýс

**jet** [dʒɛt] n (of gas, liquid) струя́; (AVIAT) реакти́вный самолёт; **~ lag** n наруше́ние сýточного режи́ма органи́зма пóсле дли́тельного полёта

**jetty** ['dʒɛtɪ] n прича́л

**Jew** [dʒuː] n евре́й(ка)

**jewel** ['dʒuːəl] n драгоце́нный кáмень m; **~ler** (US **~er**) n ювели́р; **~lery** (US **~ry**) n драгоце́нности fpl, ювели́рные изде́лия ntpl

**Jewess** ['dʒuːɪs] n евре́йка

**Jewish** ['dʒuːɪʃ] adj евре́йский

**jibe** [dʒaɪb] n насме́шка

**jiffy** ['dʒɪfɪ] n (inf): **in a ~** ми́гом

**jig** [dʒɪg] n джи́га

**jigsaw** ['dʒɪgsɔː] n (also: **~ puzzle**) головолóмка

**job** [dʒɔb] n рабóта; (task) де́ло; (inf: difficulty): **I had a ~ getting here!** я с трудóм добра́лся сюда́!; **it's not my ~** это не моё де́ло; **it's a good ~ that ...** хорошó ещё, что ...; **Jobcentre** n (BRIT) би́ржа труда́; **~less** adj

безрабóтный

**jockey** ['dʒɔkɪ] n жоке́й

**jog** [dʒɔg] vt толка́ть (толкнýть pf) ♦ vi бéгать (impf) труcцóй; **to ~ sb's memory** подстёгивать (подстегнýть pf) чью-н пáмять; **~ging** n бег труcцóй

**join** [dʒɔɪn] vt (organization) вступа́ть (вступи́ть pf) в +acc; (put together) соединя́ть (соедини́ть pf); (group, queue) присоединя́ться (присоедини́ться pf) к +dat ♦ vi (rivers) слива́ться (сли́ться pf); (roads) сходи́ться (сойти́сь pf); **~ in** vi присоединя́ться (присоедини́ться pf) ♦ vt fus (work, discussion etc) принима́ть (приня́ть pf) уча́стие в +prp; **~ up** vi (meet) соединя́ться (соедини́ться pf); (MIL) поступа́ть (поступи́ть pf) на вое́нную слýжбу

**joiner** ['dʒɔɪnəʳ] n (BRIT) столя́р

**joint** [dʒɔɪnt] n (TECH) стык; (ANAT) суста́в; (BRIT : CULIN) куcóк (мя́са); (inf: place) притóн; (: of cannabis) скрýтка с марихуа́ной, кося́к ♦ adj совме́стный

**joke** [dʒəuk] n (gag) шýтка, анекдóт; (also: **practical ~**) рóзыгрыш ♦ vi шути́ть (пошути́ть pf); **to play a ~ on** шути́ть (пошути́ть pf) над +instr, сыгра́ть (pf) шýтку с +instr; **~r** n шутни́к; (CARDS) джóкер

**jolly** ['dʒɔlɪ] adj весёлый ♦ adv (BRIT : inf) óчень

**jolt** [dʒəult] n (jerk) рывóк ♦ vt встрáхивать (встряхнýть pf); (emotionally) потряса́ть (потрясти́ pf)

**journal** ['dʒəːnl] n журна́л; (diary) дневни́к; **~ism** n журнали́стика; **~ist** n журнали́ст(ка)

**journey** ['dʒəːnɪ] n поéздка;

(*distance covered*) путь m, доро́га

**jovial** ['dʒəuvɪəl] *adj* бо́дрый, жизнера́достный

**joy** [dʒɔɪ] *n* ра́дость f; **~ful** *adj* ра́достный; **~rider** *n* челове́к, угоня́ющий маши́ны ра́ди развлече́ния

**JP** *n abbr* (= *Justice of the Peace*) мирово́й судья́ m

**Jr.** *abbr* (*in names*) = **junior**

**jubilant** ['dʒu:bɪlnt] *adj* лику́ющий

**jubilee** ['dʒu:bɪli:] *n* юбиле́й

**judge** [dʒʌdʒ] *n* судья́ m ♦ *vt* (*competition, person etc*) суди́ть (*impf*); (*consider, estimate*) оце́нивать (оцени́ть *pf*); **~ment** *n* (*LAW*) верди́кт, реше́ние суда́; (*view*) сужде́ние; (*discernment*) рассуди́тельность f

**judicial** [dʒu:'dɪʃl] *adj* суде́бный

**judiciary** [dʒu:'dɪʃɪərɪ] *n*: **the ~** суде́бные о́рганы *mpl*

**judo** ['dʒu:dəu] *n* дзюдо́ *nt ind*

**jug** [dʒʌg] *n* кувши́н

**juggle** ['dʒʌgl] *vi* жонгли́ровать (*impf*) ♦ *vt* (*fig*) жонгли́ровать (*impf*) +*instr*

**juice** [dʒu:s] *n* сок

**juicy** ['dʒu:sɪ] *adj* со́чный

**jukebox** ['dʒu:kbɔks] *n* музыка́льный автома́т

**July** [dʒu:'laɪ] *n* ию́ль m

**jumble** ['dʒʌmbl] *n* (*muddle*) нагроможде́ние ♦ *vt* (*also*: **~ up**) переме́шивать (перемеша́ть *pf*); **~ sale** *n* (*BRIT*) благотвори́тельная распрода́жа поде́ржанных веще́й

**jumbo** ['dʒʌmbəu] *n* (*also*: **~ jet**) реакти́вный аэро́бус

**jump** [dʒʌmp] *vi* пры́гать (пры́гнуть *pf*); (*start*) подпры́гивать (подпры́гнуть *pf*); (*increase*) подска́кивать (подскочи́ть *pf*) ♦ *vt* (*fence*) перепры́гивать (перепры́гнуть

*pf*) (че́рез +*acc*), переска́кивать (перескочи́ть *pf*) (че́рез +*acc*) ♦ *n* прыжо́к; (*increase*) скачо́к; **to ~ the queue** (*BRIT*) идти́ (пойти́ *pf*) без о́череди

**jumper** ['dʒʌmpər] *n* (*BRIT*) сви́тер, дже́мпер; (*US: dress*) сарафа́н

**junction** ['dʒʌŋkʃən] *n* (*BRIT: of roads*) перекрёсток; (: *RAIL*) у́зел

**June** [dʒu:n] *n* ию́нь m

**jungle** ['dʒʌŋgl] *n* джу́нгли *pl*

**junior** ['dʒu:nɪər] *adj* мла́дший ♦ *n* мла́дший(ая) *m(f) adj*; **he's ~ to me (by 2 years), he's my ~ (by 2 years)** он мла́дше меня́ (на 2 го́да)

**junk** [dʒʌŋk] *n* барахло́, хлам; **~ food** *n* еда́, содержа́щая ма́ло пита́тельных веще́ств; **~ie** *n* (*inf*) наркома́н; **~ mail** *n* незапро́шенная почто́вая рекла́ма

**jurisdiction** [dʒuərɪs'dɪkʃən] *n* (*LAW*) юрисди́кция; (*ADMIN*) сфе́ра полномо́чий

**juror** ['dʒuərər] *n* прися́жный заседа́тель m

**jury** ['dʒuərɪ] *n* прися́жные *pl adj* (заседа́тели)

**just** [dʒʌst] *adj* справедли́вый ♦ *adv* (*exactly*) как раз, и́менно; (*only*) то́лько; (*barely*) едва́; **he's ~ left** он то́лько что ушёл; **it's ~ right** э́то как раз то, что на́до; **~ two o'clock** ро́вно два часа́; **she's ~ as clever as you** она́ столь же умна́, как и ты; **it's ~ as well (that)** ... и хорошо́, (что) ...; **~ as he was leaving** как раз когда́ он собра́лся уходи́ть; **~ before Christmas** пе́ред са́мым Рождество́м; **there was ~ enough petrol** бензи́на едва́ хвати́ло; **~ here** вот здесь; **he (only) ~ missed** он чуть не попа́л; **~ listen!** ты то́лько послу́шай!

**justice** ['dʒʌstɪs] n (LAW, system) правосу́дие; (fairness) справедли́вость f; (US: judge) судья́ m; **to do ~ to** (fig) отдава́ть (отда́ть pf) до́лжное +dat

**justification** [dʒʌstɪfɪ'keɪʃən] n основа́ние; (of action) оправда́ние

**justify** ['dʒʌstɪfaɪ] vt опра́вдывать (оправда́ть pf); **to ~ o.s.** опра́вдываться (оправда́ться pf)

**juvenile** ['dʒuːvənaɪl] n несовершенноле́тний(яя) m(f) adj, подро́сток ♦ adj де́тский

# K, k

**K** abbr = one thousand; (COMPUT: = kilobyte) K

**kangaroo** [kæŋgə'ruː] n кенгуру́ m ind

**karaoke** [kɑːrə'əʊki] n карио́ки ind

**karate** [kə'rɑːtɪ] n карате́ nt ind

**kebab** [kə'bæb] n ≈ шашлы́к

**keel** [kiːl] n киль m

**keen** [kiːn] adj о́стрый; (eager) стра́стный, увлечённый; (competition) напряжённый; **to be ~ to do** or **on doing** о́чень хоте́ть (impf) +infin; **to be ~ on sth** увлека́ться (impf) чем-н

**keep** [kiːp] (pt, pp **kept**) vt (receipt, money) оставля́ть (оста́вить pf) себе́; (store) храни́ть (impf); (preserve) сохраня́ть (сохрани́ть pf); (house, shop, family) содержа́ть (impf); (prisoner, chickens) держа́ть (impf); (accounts, diary) вести́ (impf); (promise) сде́рживать (сдержа́ть pf) ♦ vi (in certain state or place) остава́ться (оста́ться pf); (food) сохраня́ться (impf); (continue): **to ~ doing** продолжа́ть (impf) +impf infin ♦ n:

he has enough for his ~ ему́ доста́точно на прожи́тие; **where do you ~ the salt?** где у вас соль?; **he tries to ~ her happy** он де́лает всё для того́, что́бы она́ была́ дово́льна; **to ~ the house tidy** содержа́ть (impf) дом в поря́дке; **to ~ sth to o.s.** держа́ть (impf) что-н при себе́; **to ~ sth (back) from sb** скрыва́ть (скрыть pf) что-н от кого́-н; **to ~ sth from happening** не дава́ть (дать pf) чему́-н случи́ться; **to ~ time** (clock) идти́ (impf) то́чно; **~ on** vi: **to ~ on doing** продолжа́ть (impf) +impf infin; **to ~ on (about)** не переставая говори́ть (impf) (о +prp); **~ out** vt не впуска́ть (впусти́ть pf); **"~ out"** "посторо́нним вход воспрещён"; **~ up** vt (payments, standards) подде́рживать (impf) ♦ vi: **to ~ up (with)** поспева́ть (поспе́ть pf) (за +instr), идти́ (impf) в но́гу (с +instr); **~ fit** n аэро́бика

**kennel** ['kɛnl] n конура́; **~s** npl гости́ница fsg для соба́к

**Kenya** ['kɛnjə] n Ке́ния

**kept** [kɛpt] pt, pp of **keep**

**kerb** [kəːb] n (BRIT) бордю́р

**kettle** ['kɛtl] n ча́йник

**key** [kiː] n ключ; (of piano, computer) кла́виша ♦ cpd ключево́й ♦ vt (also: ~ **in**) набира́ть (набра́ть pf) (на клавиату́ре); **~board** n клавиату́ра; **~ring** n брело́к

**khaki** ['kɑːkɪ] n, adj ха́ки nt, adj ind

**kick** [kɪk] vt (person, table) ударя́ть (уда́рить pf) ного́й; (ball) ударя́ть (уда́рить pf) ного́й по +dat; (inf: habit, addiction) поборо́ть (pf) ♦ vi (horse) ляга́ться (impf) ♦ **~ off** vi: **the match ~s off at 3pm** матч начина́ется в 3 часа́ (в футбо́ле)

**kid** [kɪd] n (inf: child) ребёнок; (goat) козлёнок
**kidnap** ['kɪdnæp] vt похищать (похитить pf)
**kidney** ['kɪdnɪ] n (MED) почка; (CULIN) почки fpl
**kill** [kɪl] vt убивать (убить pf); to ~ o.s. покончить (pf) с собой; to be ~ed (in war, accident) погибать (погибнуть pf); ~er n убийца m/f
**kilo** ['kiːləu] n килограмм, кило nt ind (разг); ~gram(me) ['kɪləugræm] n килограмм; ~metre ['kɪləmiːtər] (US ~meter) n километр
**kind** [kaɪnd] adj добрый ♦ n тип, род; in ~ (COMM) натурой; a ~ of род +gen; two of a ~ две вещи одного типа; what ~ of ...? какой ...?
**kindergarten** ['kɪndəgɑːtn] n детский сад
**kind-hearted** [kaɪnd'hɑːtɪd] adj добрый, добросердечный
**kindly** ['kaɪndlɪ] adj (smile) добрый; (person, tone) доброжелательный ♦ adv (smile, behave) любезно, доброжелательно; will you ~ give me his address будьте добры, дайте мне его адрес
**kindness** ['kaɪndnɪs] n (quality) доброта
**king** [kɪŋ] n король m; ~dom n королевство; the animal/plant ~dom животное/растительное царство; ~fisher n зимородок
**kiosk** ['kiːɔsk] n киоск; (BRIT : TEL) телефонная будка
**kipper** ['kɪpər] n ≈ копчёная селёдка
**kiss** [kɪs] n поцелуй ♦ vt целовать (поцеловать pf) ♦ vi целоваться (поцеловаться pf)
**kit** [kɪt] n (also: sports ~) (спортивный) костюм; (equipment) снаряжение; (set of tools) набор; (for assembly) комплект
**kitchen** ['kɪtʃɪn] n кухня
**kite** [kaɪt] n (toy) воздушный змей
**kitten** ['kɪtn] n котёнок
**kitty** ['kɪtɪ] n (pool of money) общая касса
**kiwi** ['kiːwiː] n киви f ind
**km** abbr (= kilometre) км
**knack** [næk] n способность f
**knee** [niː] n колено
**kneel** [niːl] (pt, pp knelt) vi (also: ~ down: action) вставать (встать pf) на колени; (: state) стоять (impf) на коленях
**knew** [njuː] pt of **know**
**knickers** ['nɪkəz] npl (BRIT) (женские) трусики mpl
**knife** [naɪf] (pl **knives**) n нож ♦ vt ранить (impf) ножом
**knight** [naɪt] n рыцарь m; (CHESS) конь m
**knit** [nɪt] vt (garment) вязать (связать pf) ♦ vi вязать (impf); (bones) срастаться (срастись pf); to ~ one's brows хмурить (нахмурить pf) брови; ~ting n вязанье; ~ting needle n вязальная спица
**knives** [naɪvz] npl of **knife**
**knob** [nɔb] n (on door) ручка; (on radio etc) кнопка
**knock** [nɔk] vt (strike) ударять (ударить pf); (bump into) сталкиваться (столкнуться pf) с +instr; (inf: criticize) критиковать (impf) ♦ n (blow, bump) удар, толчок; (on door) стук; to ~ some sense into sb учить (научить pf) кого-н уму-разуму; he ~ed at or on the door он постучал в дверь; ~ down vt (person, price) сбивать (сбить pf); ~ out vt (subj: person, drug) оглушать (оглушить pf); (BOXING) нокаутировать (pf); (defeat)

выбива́ть (вы́бить *pf*); ~ **over** *vt* сбива́ть (сбить *pf*)

**knot** [nɔt] *n* (*also NAUT*) у́зел; (*in wood*) сучо́к ♦ *vt* завя́зывать (завяза́ть *pf*) узло́м

**know** [nəu] (*pt* **knew**, *pp* ~**n**) (*facts, people*) знать (*impf*); **to ~ how to do** уме́ть (*impf*) +*infin*; **to ~ about** *or* **of** знать (*impf*) о +*prp*; ~**-all** *n* (*BRIT : inf: pej*) всезна́йка *m/f*; ~**-how** *n* но́у-ха́у *nt ind*; ~**ingly** *adv* (*purposely*) созна́тельно; (*smile, look*) понима́юще

**knowledge** ['nɔlɪdʒ] *n* зна́ние; (*things learnt*) зна́ния *ntpl*; (*awareness*) представле́ние; ~**able** *adj* зна́ющий; **he is very** ~**able about art** он большо́й знато́к иску́сства

**known** [nəun] *pp of* **know**

**knuckle** ['nʌkl] *n* костя́шка

**KO** *n abbr* (= **knockout**) нока́ут

**Korea** [kə'rɪə] *n* Коре́я

**Kosovan** ['kɔsəvən] *n* косова́р

**Kosovar** ['kɔsəvɑːr] *n* косова́р

**Kosovo** ['kɔsəvəu] *n* Ко́сово

# L, l

**L** *abbr* (*BRIT : AUT*: = **learner**) учени́к

**l.** *abbr* (= **litre**) л

**lab** [læb] *n abbr* = **laboratory**

**label** ['leɪbl] *n* этике́тка, ярлы́к; (*on suitcase*) би́рка ♦ *vt* (*see n*) прикрепля́ть (прикрепи́ть *pf*) ярлы́к на +*acc*; прикрепля́ть (прикрепи́ть *pf*) би́рку к +*dat*

**labor** ['leɪbər] *n* (*US*) = **labour**

**laboratory** [lə'bɔrətərɪ] *n* лаборато́рия

**labour** ['leɪbər] (*US* **labor**) *n* (*work*) труд; (*workforce*) рабо́чая си́ла; (*MED*) ро́ды *mpl*; **to be in ~** рожа́ть (*impf*); ~**er** *n* неквалифици́рованный рабо́чий

*m adj*

**lace** [leɪs] *n* (*fabric*) кру́жево; (*of shoe*) шнуро́к ♦ *vt* (*shoe : also*: ~ **up**) шнурова́ть (зашнурова́ть *pf*)

**lack** [læk] *n* (*absence*) отсу́тствие; (*shortage*) недоста́ток, нехва́тка ♦ *vt*: **she ~ed self-confidence** ей не хвата́ло *or* не достава́ло уве́ренности в себе́; **through** *or* **for ~ of** из-за недоста́тка +*gen*

**lacquer** ['lækər] *n* лак

**lad** [læd] *n* па́рень *m*

**ladder** ['lædər] *n* ле́стница; (*BRIT : in tights*) спусти́вшиеся пе́тли *fpl*

**laden** ['leɪdn] *adj*: **to be ~ (with)** ломи́ться (*impf*) от +*gen*; (*person*): ~ **(with)** нагру́женный (+*instr*)

**ladle** ['leɪdl] *n* поло́вник

**lady** ['leɪdɪ] *n* (*woman*) да́ма; **ladies and gentlemen ...** да́мы и господа́ ...; **young/old ~** молода́я/пожила́я же́нщина; **the ladies' (room)** же́нский туале́т; ~**bird** *n* бо́жья коро́вка; ~**bug** *n* (*US*) = **ladybird**

**lag** [læg] *n* (*period of time*) заде́ржка

**lager** ['lɑːgər] *n* све́тлое пи́во

**laid** [leɪd] *pt, pp of* **lay**

**lain** [leɪn] *pp of* **lie**

**lake** [leɪk] *n* о́зеро

**lamb** [læm] *n* (*ZOOL*) ягнёнок; (*CULIN*) (молода́я) бара́нина

**lame** [leɪm] *adj* (*person, animal*) хромо́й; (*excuse, argument*) сла́бый

**lament** [lə'mɛnt] *n* плач ♦ *vt* опла́кивать (опла́кать *pf*)

**lamp** [læmp] *n* ла́мпа; (*street lamp*) фона́рь *m*; ~**post** *n* (*BRIT*) фона́рный столб; ~**shade** *n* абажу́р

**land** [lænd] *n* земля́ ♦ *vi* (*from ship*) выса́живаться (вы́садиться *pf*); (*AVIAT*) приземля́ться (приземли́ться *pf*) ♦ *vt* (*plane*) сажа́ть (посади́ть pf); (goods) выгружа́ть (вы́грузить pf); **to ~ sb with sth** (inf) нава́ливать (навали́ть pf) что-н на кого́-н; **~ing** n (of house) ле́стничная площа́дка; (of plane) поса́дка, приземле́ние; **~lady** n (of house, flat) домовладе́лица, хозя́йка; (of pub) хозя́йка; **~lord** n (of house, flat) домовладе́лец, хозя́ин; (of pub) хозя́ин; **~mark** n (назе́мный) ориенти́р; (fig) ве́ха; **~owner** n землевладе́лец(лица); **~scape** n (view, painting) пейза́ж; (terrain) ландша́фт; **~slide** n (GEO) о́ползень m; (POL : also: **landslide victory**) реши́тельная побе́да

**lane** [leɪn] n (in country) тропи́нка; (of road) полоса́; (SPORT) доро́жка

**language** ['læŋgwɪdʒ] n язы́к; **bad ~** скверносло́вие

**lantern** ['læntən] n фона́рь m

**lap** [læp] n коле́ни ntpl; (SPORT) круг

**lapel** [lə'pɛl] n ла́цкан

**lapse** [læps] n (bad behaviour) про́мах; (of time) промежу́ток; (of concentration) поте́ря

**laptop** ['læptɔp] n лапто́п, лэпто́п

**larch** [lɑːtʃ] n ли́ственница

**lard** [lɑːd] n свино́й жир

**larder** ['lɑːdər] n кладова́я f adj

**large** [lɑːdʒ] adj большо́й; (major) кру́пный; **at ~** (as a whole) в це́лом; (at liberty) на во́ле; **~ly** adv по бо́льшей ча́сти; **~ly because ...** в основно́м, потому́ что ...; **~-scale** adj крупномасшта́бный

**lark** [lɑːk] n (bird) жа́воронок

**larva** ['lɑːvə] (pl **~e**) n личи́нка

**laryngitis** [lærɪn'dʒaɪtɪs] n ларинги́т

**laser** ['leɪzər] n ла́зер; **~ printer** n ла́зерный при́нтер

**lash** [læʃ] n (eyelash) ресни́ца; (of whip) уда́р (хлыста́) ♦ vt (also: ~ against: subj: rain, wind) хлеста́ть (impf) о +acc; (tie): **to ~ to** привя́зывать (привяза́ть pf) к +dat

**last** [lɑːst] adj (most recent) про́шлый; (final) после́дний ♦ adv в после́дний раз; (finally) в конце́ ♦ vi (continue) дли́ться (продли́ться pf), продолжа́ться (impf); (keep: thing) сохраня́ться (сохрани́ться pf); (person) держа́ться (продержа́ться pf); (suffice): **we had enough money to ~ us** нам хвати́ло де́нег; **~ year** в про́шлом году́; **~ week** на про́шлой неде́ле; **~ night** (early) вчера́ ве́чером; (late) про́шлой но́чью; **at ~** наконе́ц; **~ but one** предпосле́дний; **~ing** adj (friendship) продолжи́тельный, дли́тельный; (solution) долговре́менный; **~ly** adv наконе́ц; **~-minute** adj после́дний

**latch** [lætʃ] n (on gate) задви́жка; (on front door) замо́к m

**late** [leɪt] adj по́здний; (dead) поко́йный ♦ adv по́здно; (behind time) с опозда́нием; **to be ~** опа́здывать (опозда́ть pf); **of ~** в после́днее вре́мя; **in ~ May** в конце́ ма́я; **~comer** n опозда́вший(ая)m(f) adj; **~ly** adv в после́днее вре́мя

**later** ['leɪtər] adj (time, date) бо́лее по́здний; (meeting, version) после́дующий ♦ adv по́зже, поздне́е; **~ on** впосле́дствии, по́зже; **he arrived ~ than me** он пришёл по́зже меня́

**latest** ['leɪtɪst] adj са́мый по́здний; (most recent) (са́мый) после́дний; (news) после́дний; **at the ~** са́мое по́зднее

**lathe** [leɪð] n тока́рный стано́к

**lather** [ˈlɑːðə<sup>r</sup>] n (мы́льная) пе́на

**Latin** [ˈlætɪn] n (LING) лати́нский язы́к ♦ adj: ~ **languages** рома́нские языки́; ~ **countries** стра́ны Южной Евро́пы; ~ **America** n Лати́нская Аме́рика

**latitude** [ˈlætɪtjuːd] n (GEO) широта́

**latter** [ˈlætə<sup>r</sup>] adj после́дний ♦ n: **the ~** после́дний(яя) m(f) adj

**Latvia** [ˈlætvɪə] n Ла́твия; ~**n** adj латви́йский ♦ n (LING) латы́шский язы́к

**laugh** [lɑːf] n смех ♦ vi смея́ться (impf); **for a ~** (inf) для сме́ха; ~ **at** vt fus смея́ться (посмея́ться pf) над +instr; ~**able** adj смехотво́рный; ~**ing stock** n: **to be the ~ing stock of** служи́ть (impf) посме́шищем для +gen; ~**ter** n смех

**launch** [lɔːntʃ] n (of rocket, product) за́пуск ♦ vt (ship) спуска́ть (спусти́ть pf) на́ воду; (rocket) запуска́ть (запусти́ть pf); (attack, campaign) начина́ть (нача́ть pf); (product) пуска́ть (пусти́ть pf) в прода́жу, запуска́ть (запусти́ть pf)

**Laundrette**® [lɔːnˈdrɛt] n (BRIT) пра́чечная f adj самообслу́живания

**laundry** [ˈlɔːndrɪ] n (washing) сти́рка

**laurel** [ˈlɔrl] n лавр, ла́вровое де́рево

**lava** [ˈlɑːvə] n ла́ва

**lavatory** [ˈlævətərɪ] n туале́т

**lavender** [ˈlævəndə<sup>r</sup>] n лава́нда

**lavish** [ˈlævɪʃ] adj (amount, hospitality) ще́дрый ♦ vt: **to ~ sth on sb** осыпа́ть (осы́пать pf) кого́-н чем-н

**law** [lɔː] n зако́н; (professions): **(the) ~** юриспруде́нция; (SCOL) пра́во; **it's against the ~** э́то противозако́нно; ~**-abiding** adj

законопослу́шный; ~ **and order** n правопоря́док; ~**ful** adj зако́нный

**lawn** [lɔːn] n газо́н; ~ **mower** n газонокоси́лка

**lawsuit** [ˈlɔːsuːt] n суде́бный иск

**lawyer** [ˈlɔːjə<sup>r</sup>] n (solicitor, barrister) юри́ст

**lax** [læks] adj (discipline) сла́бый; (standards) ни́зкий; (morals, behaviour) распу́щенный

**laxative** [ˈlæksətɪv] n слаби́тельное nt adj

**lay** [leɪ] (pt, pp **laid**) pt of **lie** ♦ adj (not expert) непрофессиона́льный; (REL) мирско́й ♦ vt (place) класть (положи́ть pf); (table) накрыва́ть (накры́ть pf) (на +acc); (carpet) стлать (постели́ть pf); (cable) прокла́дывать (проложи́ть pf); (egg) откла́дывать (отложи́ть pf); ~ **down** vt (object) класть (положи́ть pf); (rules etc) устана́вливать (установи́ть pf); (weapons) скла́дывать (сложи́ть pf); **to ~ down the law** прика́зывать (приказа́ть pf); ~ **off** vt (workers) увольня́ть (уво́лить pf); ~ **on** vt (meal etc) устра́ивать (устро́ить pf); ~ **out** vt раскла́дывать (разложи́ть pf); ~**-by** (BRIT) площа́дка для вре́менной стоя́нки (на автодоро́ге)

**layer** [ˈleɪə<sup>r</sup>] n слой

**layout** [ˈleɪaut] n (of garden, building) плани́ровка

**laziness** [ˈleɪzɪnɪs] n лень f

**lazy** [ˈleɪzɪ] adj лени́вый

**lb.** abbr (= pound (weight)) фунт

---

**lb.** - фунт. Ме́ра ве́са ра́вная 0.454 кг.

---

**lead**[1] [liːd] (pt, pp **led**) n (front

*position*) пе́рвенство, ли́дерство; (*clue*) нить f; (*in play, film*) гла́вная роль f; (*for dog*) поводо́к; (*ELEC*) про́вод ♦ vt (*competition, market*) лиди́ровать (*impf*) в +prp; (*opponent*) опережа́ть (*impf*); (*person, group: guide*) вести́ (повести́ pf); (*activity, organization etc*) руководи́ть (*impf*) +instr ♦ vi (*road, pipe*) вести́ (*impf*); (*SPORT*) лиди́ровать (*impf*); **to ~ the way** ука́зывать (указа́ть pf) путь; ~ **away** vt уводи́ть (увести́ pf); ~ **on** vt води́ть (*impf*) за́ нос; ~ **to** vt *fus* вести́ (привести́ pf) к +dat; ~ **up to** vt fus (*events*) приводи́ть (привести́ pf) к +dat; (*topic*) подводи́ть (подвести́ pf) к +dat

**lead²** [lɛd] n (*metal*) свине́ц; (*in pencil*) графи́т

**leader** ['li:dər] n (*of group, SPORT*) ли́дер; ~**ship** n руково́дство; (*quality*) ли́дерские ка́чества ntpl

**lead-free** ['lɛdfri:] adj не содержа́щий свинца́

**leading** ['li:dɪŋ] adj (*most important*) веду́щий; (*first, front*) пере́дний

**lead singer** [li:d-] n соли́ст(ка)

**leaf** [li:f] (pl **leaves**) n лист

**leaflet** ['li:flɪt] n листо́вка

**league** [li:g] n ли́га; **to be in ~ with sb** быть (*impf*) в сго́воре с кем-н

**leak** [li:k] n уте́чка; (*hole*) течь f ♦ vi протека́ть (проте́чь pf); (*liquid, gas*) проса́чиваться (просочи́ться pf) ♦ vt (*information*) разглаша́ть (разгласи́ть pf)

**lean** [li:n] (pt, pp ~**ed** or ~**t**) adj (*person*) сухоща́вый; (*meat*) по́стный ♦ vt: **to ~ sth on** or **against** прислони́ть (прислони́ть pf) что-н к +dat ♦ vi: **to ~ forward/ back** наклоня́ться (наклони́ться pf) вперёд/наза́д; **to ~ against** (*wall*) прислоня́ться

(прислони́ться pf) к +dat; (*person*) опира́ться (опере́ться pf) на +acc; **to ~ on** (*chair*) опира́ться (опере́ться pf) о +acc; (*rely on*) опира́ться (опере́ться pf) на +acc; ~**t** [lɛnt] pt, pp of **lean**

**leap** [li:p] (pt, pp ~**ed** or ~**t**) n скачо́к ♦ vi пры́гать (пры́гнуть pf); (*price, number*) подска́кивать (подскочи́ть pf); ~ **year** n високо́сный год

**learn** [lə:n] (pt, pp ~**ed** or ~**t**) vt (*skill*) учи́ться (научи́ться pf) +dat; (*facts, poem*) учи́ть (вы́учить pf) ♦ vi учи́ться (*impf*); **to ~ about** or **of/that ...** (*hear, read*) узнава́ть (узна́ть pf) о +prp/, что ...; **to ~ about sth** (*study*) изуча́ть (изучи́ть pf) что-н; **to ~ (how) to do** учи́ться (научи́ться pf) +impf infin; ~**ed** ['lə:nɪd] adj учёный; ~**t** [lə:nt] pt, pp of **learn**

**lease** [li:s] n аре́ндный догово́р, аре́нда ♦ vt: **to ~ sth (to sb)** сдава́ть (сдать pf) что-н в аре́нду (кому́-н); **to ~ sth from sb** арендова́ть (*impf/pf*) обра́ть (взять pf) в аре́нду у кого́-н

**leash** [li:ʃ] n поводо́к

**least** [li:st] adj: **the ~** (+noun (*smallest*) наиме́ньший ( (*slightest*): *difficulty*) мале́йший ♦ adv (+vb) ме́ньше всего́; (+adj): наиме́нее; **at ~** по кра́йней ме́ре; **not in the ~** (*as response*) отню́дь нет; (+vb, +adj) ниско́лько or во́все не

**leather** ['lɛðər] n ко́жа

**leave** [li:v] (pt, pp **left**) vt оставля́ть (оста́вить pf), покида́ть (поки́нуть pf); (*go away from: on foot*) уходи́ть (уйти́ pf) из +gen; (: by transport*) уезжа́ть (уе́хать pf) из +gen; (*party, committee*) выходи́ть (вы́йти pf) из +gen ♦ vi (*on foot*) уходи́ть (уйти́ pf); (*by*

*transport)* уезжа́ть (уе́хать *pf*);
*(bus, train)* уходи́ть (уйти́ *pf*) ♦ *n*
о́тпуск; **to ~ sth to sb** *(money,
property)* оставля́ть (оста́вить *pf*)
что-н кому́-н; **to be left (over)**
оставля́ться (оста́ться *pf*); **on ~** в
о́тпуске; **~ behind** *vt* оставля́ть
(оста́вить *pf*); **~ out** *vt (omit)*
пропуска́ть (пропусти́ть *pf*); **he
was left out** его́ пропусти́ли
**leaves** [liːvz] *npl of* **leaf**
**lecture** ['lɛktʃər] *n* ле́кция ♦ *vi*
чита́ть *(impf)* ле́кции ♦ *vt (scold)*:
**to ~ sb on** *or* **about** чита́ть
(прочита́ть *pf*) кому́-н ле́кцию по
по́воду +*gen*; **to give a ~ on**
чита́ть (прочита́ть *pf*) ле́кцию о
+*prp*; **~r** *n (BRIT : SCOL)*
преподава́тель(ница) *m(f)*
**led** [lɛd] *pt, pp of* **lead**[1]
**ledge** [lɛdʒ] *n* вы́ступ; *(of window)*
подоко́нник
**leech** [liːtʃ] *n (also fig)* пия́вка
**leek** [liːk] *n* лук-поре́й *no pl*
**left** [lɛft] *pt, pp of* **leave** ♦ *adj (of
direction, position)* ле́вый ♦ *n* ле́вая
сторона́ ♦ *adv (motion)*: **(to the) ~**
нале́во; *(position)*: **(on the) ~**
сле́ва; **the Left** *(POL)* ле́вые *pl adj*;
**~-handed** *adj*: **he/she is ~-handed**
он/она́ левша́; **~-wing** *adj (POL)*
ле́вый
**leg** [lɛg] *n (ANAT)* нога́; *(of insect,
furniture)* но́жка; *(also:* **trouser ~)**
штани́на; *(of journey, race)* эта́п
**legacy** ['lɛgəsɪ] *n (in will)*
насле́дство; *(fig)* насле́дие
**legal** ['liːgl] *adj (advice, requirement)*
юриди́ческий; *(system, action)*
суде́бный; *(lawful)* зако́нный;
**~ity** [lɪˈgælɪtɪ] *n* зако́нность *f*; **~ize**
*vt* узако́нивать (узако́нить *pf*);
**~ly** *adv* юриди́чески; *(by law)* по
зако́ну
**legend** ['lɛdʒənd] *n (story)* леге́нда;
*(person)* легенда́рная ли́чность *f*;

**~ary** *adj* легенда́рный
**legislation** [lɛdʒɪsˈleɪʃən] *n*
законода́тельство
**legislative** ['lɛdʒɪslətɪv] *adj (POL)*
законода́тельный
**legitimate** [lɪˈdʒɪtɪmət] *adj*
зако́нный, легити́мный
**leisure** ['lɛʒər] *n (also:* **~ time)**
досу́г, свобо́дное вре́мя *nt*; **at
(one's) ~** не спеша́; **~ centre** *n*
спорти́вно-оздорови́тельный
ко́мплекс; **~ly** *adj* неторопли́вый
**lemon** ['lɛmən] *n (fruit)* лимо́н;
**~ade** [lɛməˈneɪd] *n* лимона́д
**lend** [lɛnd] *(pt, pp* **lent)** *vt*: **to ~ sth
to sb, ~ sb sth** ода́лживать
(одолжи́ть *pf*) что-н кому́-н
**length** [lɛŋθ] *n (measurement)*
длина́; *(distance)* протяжённость
*f*; *(piece: of wood, cloth etc)*
отре́зок; *(duration)*
продолжи́тельность *f*; **at ~** *(for a
long time)* простра́нно; **~y** *adj
(text)* дли́нный; *(meeting)*
продолжи́тельный; *(explanation)*
простра́нный
**lenient** ['liːnɪənt] *adj* мя́гкий
**lens** [lɛnz] *n (of glasses, camera)*
ли́нза
**Lent** [lɛnt] *n* Вели́кий Пост
**lent** [lɛnt] *pt, pp of* **lend**
**lentil** ['lɛntl] *n* чечеви́ца *no pl*
**Leo** ['liːəu] *n* Лев
**leopard** ['lɛpəd] *n* леопа́рд
**leotard** ['liːətɑːd] *n* трико́ *nt ind*
**lesbian** ['lɛzbɪən] *adj* лесби́йский
♦ *n* лесбия́нка
**less** [lɛs] *adj (attention, money)*
ме́ньше +*gen* ♦ *adv (beautiful,
clever)* ме́нее ♦ *prep* ми́нус +*nom*;
**~ than** ме́ньше *or* ме́нее +*gen*; **~
than half** ме́ньше полови́ны; **~
than ever** ме́ньше, чем когда́-
либо; **~ and ~** всё ме́ньше и
ме́ньше; *(+adj)* всё ме́нее и
ме́нее; **the ~ ... the more ...** чем

ме́ньше ..., тем бо́льше ...; **~er**
adj: **to a ~er extent** в ме́ньшей
сте́пени

**lesson** ['lɛsn] n уро́к; **to teach sb a
~** (fig) проучи́ть (pf) кого́-н

**let** [lɛt] (pt, pp ~) vt (BRIT: lease)
сдава́ть (сдать pf) (внаём);
(allow): **to ~ sb do** разреша́ть
(разреши́ть pf) or позволя́ть
(позво́лить pf) кому́-н +infin; **~ me
try** да́йте я попро́бую; **to ~ sb
know about** ... дава́ть (дать pf)
кому́-н знать о +prp ...; **~'s go
there** дава́й(те) пойдём туда́; **~'s
do it!** дава́й(те) сде́лаем э́то;
**"to ~"** "сдаётся внаём"; **to ~ go
of** отпуска́ть (отпусти́ть pf); **~
down** vt (tyre etc) спуска́ть
(спусти́ть pf); (fig: person)
подводи́ть (подвести́ pf); **~ in** vt
(water, air) пропуска́ть
(пропусти́ть pf); (person) впуска́ть
(впусти́ть pf); **~ off** vt (culprit,
child) отпуска́ть (отпусти́ть pf);
(bomb) взрыва́ть (взорва́ть pf); **~
out** vt выпуска́ть (вы́пустить pf);
(sound) издава́ть (изда́ть pf)

**lethal** ['liːθl] adj (weapon, chemical)
смертоно́сный; (dose)
смерте́льный

**lethargic** [lɛ'θɑːdʒɪk] adj вя́лый,
со́нный

**letter** ['lɛtər] n письмо́; (of
alphabet) бу́ква; **~ box** n (BRIT)
почто́вый я́щик

**letter box** - почто́вый я́щик.
Поми́мо почто́вого я́щика
да́нное сло́во та́кже
обознача́ет про́резь во
входно́й две́ри, в кото́рую
опуска́ется корреспонде́нция.

**lettuce** ['lɛtɪs] n сала́т лату́к
**leukaemia** [luːˈkiːmɪə] (US
**leukemia**) n белокро́вие,
лейкеми́я

**level** ['lɛvl] adj (flat) ро́вный ♦ n
у́ровень m ♦ adv: **to draw ~ with**
(person, vehicle) поравня́ться (pf) с
+instr; **to be ~ with** быть (impf) на
одно́м у́ровне с +instr

**lever** ['liːvər] n рыча́г; (bar) лом;
**~age** n (fig: influence) влия́ние

**levy** ['lɛvɪ] n нало́г ♦ vt налага́ть
(наложи́ть pf)

**liability** [laɪə'bɪlətɪ] n (responsibility)
отве́тственность f; (person, thing)
обу́за m/f; **liabilities** npl (COMM)
обяза́тельства ntpl

**liable** ['laɪəbl] adj: **~ for** (legally
responsible) подсу́дный за +acc; **to
be ~ to** подлежа́ть (impf) +dat;
**he's ~ to take offence** возмо́жно,
что он оби́дится

**liaison** [liːˈeɪzɔn] n (cooperation)
взаимоде́йствие, коопера́ция

**liar** ['laɪər] n лжец, лгун(ья)

**libel** ['laɪbl] n клевета́

**liberal** ['lɪbərl] adj: **~** (large, generous)
ще́дрый; **Liberal Democrat** n
либера́л-демокра́т; **the Liberal
Democrats** (party) па́ртия
либера́л-демокра́тов

**liberate** ['lɪbəreɪt] vt освобожда́ть
(освободи́ть pf)

**liberation** [lɪbə'reɪʃən] n
освобожде́ние

**liberty** ['lɪbətɪ] n свобо́да; **to be at
~** (criminal) быть (impf) на
свобо́де; **I'm not at ~ to
comment** я не во́лен
комменти́ровать; **to take the ~ of
doing** позволя́ть (позво́лить pf)
себе́ +infin

**Libra** ['liːbrə] n Весы́ pl

**librarian** [laɪ'brɛərɪən] n
библиоте́карь m

**library** ['laɪbrərɪ] n библиоте́ка

**lice** [laɪs] npl of **louse**

**licence** ['laɪsns] (US **license**) n

(*permit*) лице́нзия; (*AUT* : *also*:
**driving ~**) (води́тельские) права́
*ntpl*

**license** ['laɪsns] *n* (*US*) = **licence**
♦ *vt* выдава́ть (вы́дать *pf*)
лице́нзию на +*acc*; **~d** *adj*
(*restaurant*) с лице́нзией на
прода́жу спиртны́х напи́тков

**lick** [lɪk] *vt* (*stamp, fingers etc*)
лиза́ть (*impf*), обли́зывать
(облиза́ть *pf*); **to ~ one's lips**
обли́зываться (облиза́ться *pf*)

**lid** [lɪd] *n* кры́шка; (*also*: **eye~**)
ве́ко

**lie** [laɪ] (*pt* **lay**, *pp* **lain**) *vi* (*be
horizontal*) лежа́ть (*impf*); (*be
situated*) лежа́ть (*impf*),
находи́ться (*impf*); (*problem, cause*)
заключа́ться (*impf*); (*pt, pp* **~d**; *be
untruthful*) лгать (солга́ть *pf*),
врать (совра́ть *pf*) ♦ *n* (*untrue
statement*) ложь *f no pl*; **to ~** *or* **be
lying in first/last place** занима́ть
(*impf*) пе́рвое/после́днее ме́сто; **~
down** *vi* (*motion*) ложи́ться (лечь
*pf*); (*position*) лежа́ть (*impf*); **~-in** *n*
(*BRIT*): **to have a ~-in** встава́ть
(встать *pf*) попо́зже

**lieutenant** [lɛf'tɛnənt, (*US*)
luː'tɛnənt] *n* лейтена́нт

**life** [laɪf] (*pl* **lives**) *n* жизнь *f*; **~
belt** *n* (*BRIT*) спаса́тельный круг;
**~boat** *n* спаса́тельное су́дно; (*on
ship*) спаса́тельная шлю́пка;
**~guard** *n* спаса́тель *m*; **~ jacket**
*n* спаса́тельный жиле́т; **~less** *adj*
безжи́зненный; **~line** *n* (*fig*)
сре́дство выжива́ния; **~long**
♦ *adj* (*friend, habit*) неизме́нный;
**it was a ~long ambition of his** э́то
бы́ло мечто́й всей его́ жи́зни; **~
preserver** *n* (*US*) = **life jacket**;
**~style** *n* о́браз жи́зни; **~time** *n*
(*of person*) жизнь *f*; (*of institution*)
вре́мя *nt* существова́ния

**lift** [lɪft] *vt* поднима́ть (подня́ть

*pf*); (*ban, sanctions*) снима́ть
(снять *pf*) ♦ *vi* (*fog*) рассе́иваться
(рассе́яться *pf*) ♦ *n* (*BRIT*) лифт; **to
give sb a ~** (*BRIT* : *AUT*) подвози́ть
(подвезти́ *pf*) кого́-н

**ligament** ['lɪgəmənt] *n* свя́зка

**light** [laɪt] (*pt, pp* **lit**) *n* свет; (*AUT*)
фа́ра ♦ *vt* (*candle, fire*) зажига́ть
(заже́чь *pf*); (*place*) освеща́ть
(освети́ть *pf*) ♦ *adj* (*pale, bright*)
све́тлый; (*not heavy*) лёгкий; **~s**
*npl* (*also*: **traffic ~s**) светофо́р
*msg*; **have you got a ~?** (*for
cigarette*) мо́жно у Вас
прикури́ть?; **to come to ~**
выясня́ться (вы́ясниться *pf*); **in
the ~ of** (*discussions etc*) в све́те
+*gen*; **~ up** *vi* (*face*) светле́ть
(просветле́ть *pf*) ♦ *vt* (*illuminate*)
освеща́ть (освети́ть *pf*);
**~-hearted** *adj* (*person*)
беспе́чный; (*question, remark*)
несерьёзный; **~house** *n* мая́к;
**~ing** *n* освеще́ние; **~ly** *adv* (*touch,
kiss*) слегка́; (*eat, treat*) легко́;
(*sleep*) чу́тко; **to get off ~ly** легко́
отде́лываться (отде́латься *pf*)

**lightning** ['laɪtnɪŋ] *n* мо́лния

**like** [laɪk] *prep* как +*acc*; (*similar to*)
похо́жий на +*acc* ♦ *vt* (*sweets,
reading*) люби́ть (*impf*) ♦ *n*: **and
the ~** и тому́ подо́бное; **he looks
~ his father** он похо́ж на своего́
отца́; **what does she look ~?** как
она́ вы́глядит?; **what's he ~?** что
он за челове́к?; **there's nothing ~
...** ничто́ не мо́жет сравни́ться с
+*instr* ...; **do it ~ this** де́лайте э́то
так; **that's just ~ him** (*typical*) э́то
на него́ похо́же; **it is nothing ~ ...**
э́то совсе́м не то, что ...; **I ~/~d
him** он мне нра́вится/
понра́вился; **I would~, I'd ~** мне
хоте́лось бы, я бы хоте́л; **would
you ~ a coffee?** хоти́те ко́фе?; **his
~s and dislikes** его́ вку́сы; **~able**

*adj* симпати́чный

**likelihood** ['laɪklɪhud] *n*
вероя́тность *f*

**likely** ['laɪklɪ] *adj* вероя́тный; **she is
~ to agree** она́, вероя́тно,
согласи́тся; **not ~!** (*inf*) ни за
что!

**likeness** ['laɪknɪs] *n* схо́дство

**likewise** ['laɪkwaɪz] *adv* та́кже; **to
do ~** поступа́ть (поступи́ть *pf*)
таки́м же о́бразом

**lilac** ['laɪlək] *n* сире́нь *f no pl*

**lily** ['lɪlɪ] *n* ли́лия

**limb** [lɪm] *n* (*ANAT*) коне́чность *f*

**lime** [laɪm] *n* (*fruit*) лайм; (*tree*)
ли́па; (*chemical*) и́звесть *f*

**limelight** ['laɪmlaɪt] *n*: **to be in the
~** быть (*impf*) в це́нтре внима́ния

**limestone** ['laɪmstəun] *n*
известня́к

**limit** ['lɪmɪt] *n* преде́л; (*restriction*)
лими́т, ограниче́ние ♦ *vt*
(*production, expense etc*)
лимити́ровать (*impf/pf*),
ограни́чивать (ограни́чить *pf*);
**~ation** [lɪmɪ'teɪʃən] *n*
ограниче́ние; **~ed** *adj*
ограни́ченный

**limousine** ['lɪməzi:n] *n* лимузи́н

**limp** [lɪmp] *n* хрома́ть (*impf*) ♦ *adj*
(*person, limb*) бесси́льный;
(*material*) мя́гкий

**line** [laɪn] *n* ли́ния; (*row*) ряд; (*of
writing, song*) строка́, стро́чка;
(*wrinkle*) морщи́на; (*wire*) про́вод;
(*fig: of thought*) ход; (*of business,
work*) о́бласть *f* ♦ *vt* (*road*)
выстра́иваться (вы́строиться *pf*)
вдоль +*gen*; (*clothing*) подбива́ть
(подби́ть *pf*); (*container*)
выкла́дывать (вы́ложить *pf*)
изнутри́; **hold the ~ please!** (*TEL*)
пожа́луйста, не кла́дите тру́бку!;
**to cut in ~** (*US*) идти́ (пойти́ *pf*)
без о́череди; **in ~ with** (*in keeping
with*) в соотве́тствии с +*instr*; **~**

**up** *vi* выстра́иваться
(вы́строиться *pf*) ♦ *vt* (*order*)
выстра́ивать (вы́строить *pf*)

**lined** [laɪnd] *adj* (*paper*)
лино́ванный; (*face*)
морщи́нистый

**linen** ['lɪnɪn] *n* (*sheets etc*) бельё

**liner** ['laɪnə'] *n* (*ship*) ла́йнер; (*also:
bin ~*) целофа́новый мешо́к для
му́сорного ведра́

**linesman** ['laɪnzmən] (*irreg*) *n*
судья́ *m* на ли́нии

**linger** ['lɪŋɡə'] *vi* уде́рживаться
(удержа́ться *pf*); (*person*)
заде́рживаться (задержа́ться *pf*)

**lingerie** ['lænʒəri:] *n* же́нское
(ни́жнее) бельё

**linguist** ['lɪŋɡwɪst] *n* (*language
specialist*) лингви́ст; **~ics**
[lɪŋ'ɡwɪstɪks] *n* языкозна́ние,
лингви́стика

**lining** ['laɪnɪŋ] *n* (*cloth*) подкла́дка

**link** [lɪŋk] *n* связь *f*; (*of chain*)
звено́ ♦ *vt* (*join*) соединя́ть
(соедини́ть *pf*); (*associate*): **to ~
with** *or* **to** свя́зывать (связа́ть *pf*)
с +*instr*; **~ up** *vt* (*systems*)
соединя́ть (соедини́ть *pf*) ♦ *vi*
соединя́ться (соедини́ться *pf*)

**lino** ['laɪnəu] *n* = **linoleum**

**linoleum** [lɪ'nəuliəm] *n* лино́леум

**lion** ['laɪən] *n* лев

**lip** [lɪp] *n* (*ANAT*) губа́; **~-read** *vi*
чита́ть (*impf*) с губ; **~stick** *n*
(губна́я) пома́да

**liqueur** [lɪ'kjuə'] *n* ликёр

**liquid** ['lɪkwɪd] *n* жи́дкость *f* ♦ *adj*
жи́дкий

**liquor** ['lɪkə'] *n* (*esp US*) спиртно́е *nt
adj*, спиртно́й напи́ток

**Lisbon** ['lɪzbən] *n* Лиссабо́н

**lisp** [lɪsp] *n* шепеля́вость *f*

**list** [lɪst] *n* спи́сок ♦ *vt* (*enumerate*)
перечисля́ть (перечи́слить *pf*);
(*write down*) составля́ть
(соста́вить *pf*) спи́сок +*gen*

**listen** ['lɪsn] *vi*: **to ~ (to sb/sth)**
слу́шать *(impf)* (кого́-н/что́-н)
**lit** [lɪt] *pt, pp of* **light**
**liter** ['li:tər] *n* (*US*) = **litre**
**literacy** ['lɪtərəsɪ] *n* гра́мотность *f*
**literal** ['lɪtərl] *adj* буква́льный; **~ly**
*adv* буква́льно
**literary** ['lɪtərərɪ] *adj* литерату́рный
**literate** ['lɪtərət] *adj* (*able to read
and write*) гра́мотный
**literature** ['lɪtrɪtʃər] *n* литерату́ра
**Lithuania** [lɪθjuˈeɪnɪə] *n* Литва́; **~n**
*adj* лито́вский
**litre** ['li:tər] (*US* **liter**) *n* литр
**litter** ['lɪtər] *n* (*rubbish*) му́сор;
(*ZOOL*) помёт, вы́водок
**little** ['lɪtl] *adj* ма́ленький;
(*younger*) мла́дший; (*short*)
коро́ткий ♦ *adv* ма́ло; **a ~ (bit)**
немно́го; **~ by ~** понемно́гу;
**~-known** *adj* малоизве́стный
**live** *vb* [lɪv] *adj* [laɪv] *vi* жить *(impf)*
♦ *adj* (*animal, plant*) живо́й;
(*broadcast*) прямо́й; (*performance*)
пе́ред пу́бликой; (*bullet*) боево́й;
(*ELEC*) под напряже́нием; **~**
**with sb** жить *(impf)* с кем-н; **he ~d**
**to (be) a hundred** он дожи́л до
ста лет; **~ on** *vt fus* (*food*) жить
*(impf)* на +*prp*; (*salary*) жить *(impf)*
на +*acc*; **~ up to** *vt fus*
опра́вдывать (оправда́ть *pf*)
**livelihood** ['laɪvlɪhud] *n* сре́дства
*ntpl* к существова́нию
**lively** ['laɪvlɪ] *adj* живо́й; (*place,
event*) оживлённый
**liver** ['lɪvər] *n* (*ANAT*) пе́чень *f*;
(*CULIN*) печёнка
**lives** [laɪvz] *npl of* **life**
**livestock** ['laɪvstɔk] *n* скот
**living** ['lɪvɪŋ] *adj* живо́й ♦ *n*: **to
earn** *or* **make a ~** зараба́тывать
(зарабо́тать *pf*) на жизнь; **~
conditions** *npl* усло́вия *ntpl*
жи́зни; **~ room** *n* гости́ная *f adj*;
**~ standards** *npl* жи́зненный

у́ровень *msg*
**lizard** ['lɪzəd] *n* я́щерица
**load** [ləud] *n* (*of person, animal*)
но́ша; (*of vehicle*) груз; (*weight*)
нагру́зка ♦ *vt* (*also*: **~ up**: *goods*)
грузи́ть (погрузи́ть *pf*); (*gun,
camera*) заряжа́ть (заряди́ть *pf*);
**to ~ (with)** (*also*: **~ up**: *vehicle,
ship*) загружа́ть (загрузи́ть *pf*)
(+*instr*); **~s of, a ~ of** (*inf*) ку́ча
+*gen*; **a ~ of rubbish** (*inf*)
сплошна́я чепуха́; **~ed** *adj* (*gun*)
заря́женный; **~ed question**
вопро́с с подте́кстом *or*
подво́хом
**loaf** [ləuf] (*pl* **loaves**) *n* буха́нка
**loan** [ləun] *n* заём; (*money*) ссу́да
♦ *vt* дава́ть (дать *pf*) взаймы́;
(*money*) ссужа́ть (ссуди́ть *pf*); **to
take sth on ~** брать (взять *pf*)
что-н на вре́мя
**loathe** [ləuð] *vt* ненави́деть *(impf)*
**loaves** [ləuvz] *npl of* **loaf**
**lobby** ['lɔbɪ] *n* (*of building*)
вестибю́ль *m*; (*pressure group*)
ло́бби *nt ind* ♦ *vt* склоня́ть
(склони́ть *pf*) на свою́ сто́рону;
(*POL*) лобби́ровать *(impf)*
**lobster** ['lɔbstər] *n* ома́р
**local** ['ləukl] *adj* ме́стный; **the ~s**
*npl* ме́стные *pl adj* (жи́тели); **~
authorities** *npl* ме́стные вла́сти
*fpl*; **~ government** *n* ме́стное
управле́ние; **~ly** *adv* (*live, work*)
побли́зости
**locate** [ləuˈkeɪt] *vt* определя́ть
(определи́ть *pf*) расположе́ние *or*
местонахожде́ние +*gen*; **to be ~d
in** (*situated*) распола́гаться *(impf)*,
находи́ться *(impf)* в/на +*prp*
**location** [ləuˈkeɪʃən] *n* (*place*)
расположе́ние,
местонахожде́ние; **on ~** (*CINEMA*)
на нату́ре
**loch** [lɔx] *n* (*SCOTTISH*) о́зеро
**lock** [lɔk] *n* (*on door etc*) замо́к; (*on

canal) шлюз; (of hair) ло́кон ♦ vt
запира́ть (запере́ть pf) ♦ vi (door)
запира́ться (запере́ться pf);
(wheels) тормози́ть (затормози́ть
pf); ~ **in** vt: **to ~ sb in** запира́ть
(запере́ть pf) кого́-н; ~ **up** vt
(criminal etc) упря́тывать
(упря́тать pf); (house) запира́ть
(запере́ть pf) ♦ vi запира́ться
(запере́ться pf)

**locker** ['lɔkər] n шка́фчик

**locomotive** [ləukə'məutıv] n
локомоти́в

**locust** ['ləukəst] n саранча́ f no pl

**lodge** [lɔdʒ] n привра́тницкая f adj;
~**r** n квартира́нт(ка)

**lodgings** ['lɔdʒıŋz] npl кварти́ра fsg

**loft** [lɔft] n черда́к

**log** [lɔg] n бревно́; (for fire)
поле́но; (account) журна́л ♦ vt
(event, fact) регистри́ровать
(зарегистри́ровать pf); ~ **off** vi
(COMPUT) выходи́ть (вы́йти pf) из
систе́мы; ~ **on** vi (COMPUT)
входи́ть (войти́ pf) в систе́му

**logic** ['lɔdʒık] n ло́гика; ~**al** adj
(based on logic) логи́ческий;
(reasonable) логи́чный

**logo** ['ləugəu] n эмбле́ма

**London** ['lʌndən] n Ло́ндон

**lone** [ləun] adj (person) одино́кий

**loneliness** ['ləunlınıs] n
одино́чество

**lonely** ['ləunlı] adj (person,
childhood) одино́кий; (place)
уединённый

**long** [lɔŋ] adj дли́нный; (in time)
до́лгий ♦ adv (see adj) дли́нно;
до́лго ♦ vi: ~ **for sth/to do**
жа́ждать (impf) чего́-н/+infin; **so** or
**as ~ as you don't mind** е́сли
то́лько Вы не возража́ете; **don't
be ~**! не заде́рживайтесь!; **how
~ is the street?** какова́ длина́
э́той у́лицы?; **how ~ is the
lesson?** ско́лько дли́тся уро́к?; **6**

metres ~ длино́й в 6 ме́тров; **6
months ~** продолжи́тельностью
в 6 ме́сяцев; **all night (~)** всю
ночь (напролёт); **he no ~er
comes** он бо́льше не прихо́дит;
~ **before** задо́лго до +gen; ~ **after**
до́лгое вре́мя по́сле +gen; **before**
~ вско́ре; **at ~ last** наконе́ц;
~-**distance** adj (travel) да́льний

**longitude** ['lɔŋgıtju:d] n долгота́

**long**: ~ **jump** n прыжо́к в длину́;
~-**life** adj консерви́рованный;
(battery) продлённого де́йствия;
~-**lost** adj (relative etc) давно́
поте́рянный; ~-**standing** adj
долголе́тний; ~-**suffering** adj
многострада́льный; ~-**term** adj
долгосро́чный

**look** [luk] vi (see) смотре́ть
(посмотре́ть pf); (glance)
взгляну́ть (pf); (seem, appear)
вы́глядеть (impf) ♦ n (glance)
взгляд; (appearance) вид;
(expression) выраже́ние; ~**s** npl:
**good ~s** краси́вая вне́шность fsg;
**to ~ south/(out) onto the sea**
(face) выходи́ть (impf) на юг/на
мо́ре; ~ **after** vt fus (care for)
уха́живать (impf) за +instr; (deal
with) забо́титься (impf) о +prp; ~
**around** vt fus = **look round**; ~ **at**
vt fus смотре́ть (посмотре́ть pf)
на +acc; (read quickly)
просма́тривать (просмотре́ть pf);
~ **back** vi (turn around): **to ~ back
(at)** огля́дываться (огляну́ться
pf) (на +acc); ~ **down on** vt fus
(fig) смотре́ть (impf) свысока́ на
+acc; ~ **for** vt fus иска́ть (impf); ~
**forward to** vt fus: **to ~ forward to
sth** ждать (impf) чего́-н с
нетерпе́нием; **we ~ forward to
hearing from you** (с
нетерпе́нием) ждём Ва́шего
отве́та; ~ **into** vt fus
рассле́довать (impf/pf); ~ **on** vi

(watch) наблюда́ть (impf); ~ **out** vi (beware): **to ~ out (for)** остерега́ться (impf) (+gen); **to ~ out (of)** (glance out) выгля́дывать (вы́глянуть pf) (в +acc); **~ out for** vt fus (search for) стара́ться (постара́ться pf) найти́; **~ round** vt fus (museum etc) осма́тривать (осмотре́ть pf); (window) смотре́ть (посмотре́ть pf) в +acc; **~ to** vt fus (rely on) ждать (impf) от +gen; **~ up** vi поднима́ть (подня́ть pf) глаза́; (situation) идти́ (пойти́ pf) к лу́чшему ♦ vt (fact) смотре́ть (посмотре́ть pf); **~out** n (person) наблюда́тель(ница) m(f); (point) наблюда́тельный пункт; **to be on the ~out for sth** присма́тривать (impf) что-н

**loop** [luːp] n пе́тля ♦ vt: **to ~ sth round sth** завя́зывать (завяза́ть pf) что-н пе́тлей вокру́г чего́-н

**loose** [luːs] adj свобо́дный; (knot, grip, connection) сла́бый; (hair) распу́щенный ♦ n: **to be on the ~** быть (impf) в бега́х; **the handle is ~** ру́чка расшата́лась; **to set ~** (prisoner) освобожда́ть (освободи́ть pf); **~n** vt (belt, screw, grip) ослабля́ть (осла́бить pf)

**loot** [luːt] n (inf) награ́бленное nt adj ♦ vt (shops, homes) разграбля́ть (разгра́бить pf)

**lord** [lɔːd] n (BRIT: peer) лорд; (REL): **the Lord** Госпо́дь m; **my Lord** мило́рд; **good Lord!** Бо́же пра́вый!

**lorry** ['lɒrɪ] n (BRIT) грузови́к

**lose** [luːz] (pt, pp **lost**) vt теря́ть (потеря́ть pf); (contest, argument) прои́грывать (проигра́ть pf) ♦ vi (in contest, argument) прои́грывать (проигра́ть pf); **~r** n

(in contest, competition) прои́гравший(ая) m(f) adj

**loss** [lɒs] n поте́ря; (sense of bereavement) утра́та; (COMM) убы́ток; **heavy ~es** тяжёлые поте́ри fpl; **to be at a ~** теря́ться (растеря́ться pf)

**lost** [lɒst] pt, pp of **lose** ♦ adj пропа́вший; **to get ~** заблуди́ться (pf)

**lot** [lɒt] n (of people, goods) па́ртия; (at auction) лот; **a ~ (of)** (many) мно́го (+gen); **the ~** (everything) всё; **~s of ...** мно́го +gen ...; **I see a ~ of him** мы с ним ча́сто ви́димся; **I read/don't read a ~** я мно́го/ма́ло чита́ю; **a ~ bigger/ more expensive** намно́го or гора́здо бо́льше/доро́же; **to draw ~s (for sth)** тяну́ть (impf) жре́бий (для чего́-н)

**lotion** ['ləʊʃən] n лосьо́н

**lottery** ['lɒtərɪ] n лотере́я

**loud** [laʊd] adj (noise, voice, laugh) гро́мкий; (support, condemnation) громогла́сный; (clothes) крича́щий ♦ adv гро́мко; **out ~** вслух; **~ly** adv (speak, laugh) гро́мко; (support) громогла́сно; **~speaker** n громкоговори́тель m

**lounge** [laʊndʒ] n (in house, hotel) гости́ная f adj; (at airport) зал ожида́ния

**louse** [laʊs] (pl **lice**) n (insect) вошь f

**lovable** ['lʌvəbl] adj ми́лый

**love** [lʌv] vt люби́ть (impf) ♦ n: **~ (for)** любо́вь f (к +dat); **to ~ to do** люби́ть (impf) +infin; **I'd ~ to come** я бы с удово́льствием пришёл; **"~ (from) Anne"** "лю́бящая Вас А́нна"; **to fall in ~ with** влюбля́ться (влюби́ться pf) в +acc; **he is in ~ with her** он в неё влюблён; **to make ~** занима́ться (заня́ться pf) любо́вью; **"fifteen**

~" (TENNIS) "пятна́дцать - ноль"; ~ **affair** n рома́н; ~ **life** n инти́мная жизнь f

**lovely** ['lʌvlɪ] adj (beautiful) краси́вый; (delightful) чуде́сный

**lover** ['lʌvəʳ] n (sweetheart) любо́вник(ица); (of art etc) люби́тель(ница) m(f)

**loving** ['lʌvɪŋ] adj не́жный

**low** [ləu] adj ни́зкий; (quiet) ти́хий; (depressed) пода́вленный ♦ adv (fly) ни́зко; (sing: quietly) ти́хо ♦ n (METEOROLOGY) ни́зкое давле́ние; **we are (running) ~ on milk** у нас оста́лось ма́ло молока́; **an all-time ~** небыва́ло ни́зкий у́ровень

**lower** ['ləuəʳ] adj (bottom: of two things) ни́жний; (less important) ни́зший ♦ vt (object) спуска́ть (спусти́ть pf); (level, price) снижа́ть (сни́зить pf); (voice) понижа́ть (пони́зить pf); (eyes) опуска́ть (опусти́ть pf)

**lower sixth** - ни́жняя ступе́нь шко́льного квалификацио́нного ку́рса. Этот курс дли́тся два го́да, в тече́ние кото́рых шко́льники гото́вятся к квалификацио́нным экза́менам, даю́щим пра́во на поступле́ние в университе́т.

**low-fat** ['ləu'fæt] adj (food, drink) обезжи́ренный

**loyal** ['lɔɪəl] adj ве́рный; (POL) лоя́льный; **~ty** n ве́рность f; (POL) лоя́льность f; **~ty card** n ≈ диско́нтная ка́рта

**L-plates** - бе́лая табли́чка, на кото́рую нанесена́ кра́сная бу́ква 'L', обознача́ющая "**Learner**" - Учени́к.

Таки́е табли́чки помеща́ются на за́днем или ветрово́м стекле́ автомоби́лей, води́тели кото́рых прохо́дят курс по вожде́нию.

**Ltd** abbr (COMM: = limited (liability) company) компа́ния с ограни́ченной отве́тственностью

**lucid** ['lu:sɪd] adj (writing, speech) я́сный

**luck** [lʌk] n (also: **good ~**) уда́ча; **bad ~** неуда́ча; **good ~!** уда́чи (Вам)!; **hard** or **tough ~!** не повезло́!; **~ily** adv к сча́стью; **~y** adj (object) счастли́вый; (person) уда́чливый; **he is ~ at cards/ in love** ему́ везёт в ка́ртах/ любви́

**lucrative** ['lu:krətɪv] adj при́быльный, дохо́дный; (job) высокоопла́чиваемый

**ludicrous** ['lu:dɪkrəs] adj смехотво́рный

**luggage** ['lʌgɪdʒ] n бага́ж

**lukewarm** ['lu:kwɔ:m] adj слегка́ тёплый; (fig) прохла́дный

**lull** [lʌl] n зати́шье ♦ vt: **to ~ sb to sleep** убаю́кивать (убаю́кать pf) кого́-н; **to ~ sb into a false sense of security** усыпля́ть (усыпи́ть pf) чью-н бди́тельность

**lullaby** ['lʌləbaɪ] n колыбе́льная f adj

**luminous** ['lu:mɪnəs] adj (digit, star) светя́щийся

**lump** [lʌmp] n (of clay, snow) ком; (of butter, sugar) кусо́к; (bump) ши́шка; (growth) о́пухоль f ♦ vt: **to ~ together** меша́ть (смеша́ть pf) в (одну́) ку́чу; **a ~ sum** единовре́менно выпла́чиваемая су́мма; **~y** adj (sauce) комкова́тый

**lunar** ['lu:nəʳ] adj лу́нный

**lunatic** ['lu:nətɪk] adj безу́мный

**lunch** [lʌntʃ] n обе́д; ~ **time** n
обе́денное вре́мя nt, обе́д
**lung** [lʌŋ] n лёгкое nt adj; ~ **cancer**
рак лёгких
**lurch** [lə:tʃ] vi: **the car ~ed forward**
маши́ну бро́сило вперёд
**lure** [luəʳ] vt зама́нивать
(замани́ть pf); **to ~ sb away from**
отвлека́ть (отвле́чь pf) кого́-н от
+gen
**lush** [lʌʃ] adj (healthy) пы́шный
**lust** [lʌst] n (sexual desire) по́хоть f;
( greed): ~ **(for)** жа́жда (к +dat)
**lustre** ['lʌstəʳ] (US **luster**) n блеск
**Luxembourg** ['lʌksəmbə:g] n
Люксембу́рг
**luxurious** [lʌg'zjuəriəs] adj
роско́шный
**luxury** ['lʌkʃəri] n (great comfort)
ро́скошь f; (treat) роско́шество
**lyrical** ['lirikl] adj (fig)
восто́рженный
**lyrics** ['liriks] npl текст msg (пе́сни)

# M, m

**m.** abbr (= **metre**) м; = **mile**,
**million**
**MA** n abbr = **Master of Arts**
**mac** [mæk] n (BRIT : inf ) макинто́ш
**macabre** [mə'ka:brə] adj жу́ткий
**macaroni** [mækə'rəuni] n
макаро́ны pl
**Macedonia** [mæsi'dəuniə] n
Македо́ния
**machine** [mə'ʃi:n] n маши́на; (also:
**sewing ~**) маши́нка; ~ **gun** n
пулемёт; ~**ry** [mə'ʃi:nəri] n
обору́дование; (POL) механи́зм
**mackerel** ['mækrl] n inv ску́мбрия
**mackintosh** ['mækintɔʃ] n = **mac**
**mad** [mæd] adj сумасше́дший,
поме́шанный; (angry) бе́шеный;
(keen): **he is ~ about** он поме́шан
на +prp

**madam** ['mædəm] n ( form of
address) мада́м f ind, госпожа́
**made** [meid] pt, pp of **make**
**madman** ['mædmən] (irreg) n
сумасше́дший m adj
**madness** ['mædnis] n безу́мие
**Madrid** [mə'drid] n Мадри́д
**Mafia** ['mæfiə] n: **the ~** ма́фия
**magazine** [mægə'zi:n] n журна́л
**maggot** ['mægət] n личи́нка
(насеко́мых)
**magic** ['mædʒik] n ма́гия; ~**al** adj
маги́ческий; (experience, evening)
волше́бный; ~**ian** [mə'dʒiʃən] n
(conjurer) фо́кусник
**magistrate** ['mædʒistreit] n (LAW)
мирово́й судья́ m
**magnet** ['mægnit] n магни́т; ~**ic**
[mæg'netik] adj магни́тный;
(personality) притяга́тельный
**magnificent** [mæg'nifisnt] adj
великоле́пный
**magnify** ['mægnifai] vt
увели́чивать (увели́чить pf);
(sound) уси́ливать (уси́лить pf);
~**ing glass** n увеличи́тельное
стекло́, лу́па
**magnitude** ['mægnitju:d] n (size)
величина́; (importance) масшта́б
**mahogany** [mə'hɔgəni] n кра́сное
де́рево
**maid** [meid] n (in house) служа́нка;
(in hotel) го́рничная f adj
**maiden** ['meidn] adj ( first) пе́рвый;
~ **name** n де́вичья фами́лия
**mail** [meil] n по́чта ♦ vt
отправля́ть (отпра́вить pf) по
по́чте; (COMPUT): **to ~ sb** писа́ть
(написа́ть pf) кому́-н по
электро́нной по́чте; ~**box** n (US:
letter box) почто́вый я́щик; ~
**order** n зака́з това́ров по по́чте
**maim** [meim] vt кале́чить
(искале́чить pf)
**main** [mein] adj гла́вный ♦ n: **gas/
water** ~ газопрово́дная/

водопрово́дная магистра́ль f;
**the ~s** npl сеть fsg; **~ meal** обе́д;
**~land** n: **the ~land** матери́к; **~ly**
adv гла́вным о́бразом; **~stay** n
гла́вная опо́ра; **~stream** n
госпо́дствующее направле́ние

**maintain** [meɪnˈteɪn] vt ( friendship,
system, momentum) подде́рживать
(подержа́ть pf); (building)
обслу́живать (impf) (affirm: belief,
opinion) утвержда́ть (impf)

**maintenance** [ˈmeɪntənəns] n (of
friendship, system) подде́ржка;
(of building) обслу́живание; (LAW,
alimony) алиме́нты pl

**maize** [meɪz] n кукуру́за, маи́с

**majestic** [məˈdʒɛstɪk] adj
велича́ственный

**majesty** [ˈmædʒɪstɪ] n: **Your**
**Majesty** Ва́ше Вели́чество

**major** [ˈmeɪdʒəʳ] adj (important)
суще́ственный

**majority** [məˈdʒɔrɪtɪ] n
большинство́

**make** [meɪk] (pt, pp **made**) vt
де́лать (сде́лать pf); (clothes)
шить (сшить pf); (manufacture)
изготовля́ть (изгото́вить pf);
(meal) гото́вить (пригото́вить pf);
(money) зараба́тывать
(зарабо́тать pf); (profit) получа́ть
(получи́ть pf) ♦ n (brand) ма́рка;
**to ~ sb do** (force) заставля́ть
(заста́вить pf) кого́-н +infin; **2 and**
**2 = 4** (equal) 2 плюс 2 равня́ется
четырём; **to ~ sb unhappy**
расстра́ивать (расстро́ить pf)
кого́-н; **to ~ a noise** шуме́ть
(impf); **to ~ the bed** стели́ть
(постели́ть pf) посте́ль; **to ~ a**
**fool of sb** де́лать (сде́лать pf) из
кого́-н дурака́; **to ~ a profit**
получа́ть (получи́ть pf) при́быль;
**to ~ a loss** нести́ (понести́ pf)
убы́ток; **to ~ it** (arrive) успева́ть
(успе́ть pf); **let's ~ it Monday**

дава́йте договори́мся на
понеде́льник; **to ~ do with/**
**without** обходи́ться (обойти́сь
pf) +instr/без +gen; **~ for** vt fus
(place) направля́ться
(напра́виться pf) к +dat/в +acc; **~**
**out** vt (decipher) разбира́ть
(разобра́ть pf); (see) различа́ть
(различи́ть pf); (write out)
выпи́сывать (вы́писать pf);
(understand) разбира́ться
(разобра́ться pf) в +prp; **~ up** vt
fus (constitute) составля́ть
(соста́вить pf) ♦ vt (invent)
выду́мывать (вы́думать pf) ♦ vi
(after quarrel) мири́ться
(помири́ться pf); (with cosmetics):
**to ~ (o.s.) up** де́лать (сде́лать pf)
макия́ж; **~ up for** vt fus (mistake)
загла́живать (загла́дить pf); (loss)
восполня́ть (воспо́лнить pf); **~r** n
(of goods) изготови́тель m; **~shift**
adj вре́менный; **~-up** n
косме́тика, макия́ж; (THEAT) грим

**making** [ˈmeɪkɪŋ] n (of programme)
созда́ние; **to have the ~s of**
име́ть (impf) зада́тки +gen

**malaria** [məˈlɛərɪə] n маляри́я

**male** [meɪl] n (human) мужчи́на m;
(animal) саме́ц ♦ adj мужско́й;
(child) мужско́го по́ла

**malice** [ˈmælɪs] n зло́ба

**malicious** [məˈlɪʃəs] adj зло́бный,
злой

**malignant** [məˈlɪɡnənt] adj (MED)
злока́чественный

**mall** [mɔːl] n (also: **shopping ~**)
≈ торго́вый центр

**mallet** [ˈmælɪt] n деревя́нный
молото́к

**malnutrition** [mælnjuːˈtrɪʃən] n
недоеда́ние

**malt** [mɔːlt] n ( grain) со́лод; (also:
**~ whisky**) солодо́вое ви́ски nt
ind

**mammal** [ˈmæml] n

млекопита́ющее *nt adj*

**mammoth** ['mæməθ] *adj* (*task*)
колосса́льный

**man** [mæn] (*pl* **men**) *n* мужчи́на *m*;
(*person, mankind*) челове́к ♦ *vt*
(*machine*) обслу́живать (*impf*);
(*post*) занима́ть (заня́ть *pf*); **an
old ~** стари́к; **~ and wife** муж и
жена́

**manage** ['mænɪdʒ] *vi* (*get by*)
обходи́ться (обойти́сь *pf*) ♦ *vt*
(*business, organization*) руководи́ть
(*impf*) +*instr*, управля́ть (*impf*) +*instr*;
(*shop, restaurant*) заве́довать
(*impf*) +*instr*; (*economy*) управля́ть
(*impf*) +*instr*; (*workload, task*)
справля́ться (спра́виться (*impf*)) с
+*instr*; **I ~d to convince him** мне
удало́сь убеди́ть его́; **~ment** *n*
(*body*) руково́дство; (*act*): **~ment
(of)** управле́ние (+*instr*); **~r** ♦ *n* (*of
business, organization*)
управля́ющий *m adj*, ме́неджер;
(*of shop*) заве́дующий *m adj*; (*of
pop star*) ме́неджер; (*SPORT*)
гла́вный тре́нер; **~ress** ['mænɪdʒ]
*n* (*of shop*) заве́дующая *f adj*; **~rial**
[mænɪ'dʒɪərɪəl] *adj* (*role*)
руководя́щий; **~rial staff**
руководя́щий аппара́т

**managing director** ['mænɪdʒɪŋ-]
*n* управля́ющий дире́ктор

**mandarin** ['mændərɪn] *n* (*also:* **~
orange**) мандари́н

**mandate** ['mændeɪt] *n* (*POL*)
полномо́чие

**mandatory** ['mændətərɪ] *adj*
обяза́тельный

**mane** [meɪn] *n* гри́ва

**maneuver** [mə'nu:vər] *n, vb* (*US*) =
**manoeuvre**

**mango** ['mæŋgəu] (*pl* **~es**) *n* ма́нго
*nt ind*

**mania** ['meɪnɪə] *n* (*also PSYCH*)
ма́ния

**maniac** ['meɪnɪæk] *n* манья́к

**manic** ['mænɪk] *adj* безу́мный,
маниака́льный

**manifest** ['mænɪfest] *vt* проявля́ть
(прояви́ть *pf*) ♦ *adj* очеви́дный,
я́вный

**manifesto** [mænɪ'festəu] *n*
манифе́ст

**manipulate** [mə'nɪpjuleɪt] *vt*
манипули́ровать (*impf*) +*instr*

**mankind** [mæn'kaɪnd] *n*
челове́чество

**manly** ['mænlɪ] *adj* му́жественный

**man-made** ['mæn'meɪd] *adj*
иску́сственный

**manner** ['mænər] *n* (*way*) о́браз;
(*behaviour*) мане́ра; **~s** *npl*
(*conduct*) мане́ры *fpl*; **all ~ of
things/people** всевозмо́жные
ве́щи/лю́ди; **in a ~ of speaking** в
не́котором ро́де; **~ism** *n*
мане́ры *fpl*

**manoeuvre** [mə'nu:vər] (*US*
**maneuver**) *vt* передвига́ть
(передви́нуть *pf*); (*manipulate*)
маневри́ровать (*impf*) +*instr* ♦ *vi*
маневри́ровать (*impf*) ♦ *n* манёвр

**manpower** ['mænpauər] *n* рабо́чая
си́ла

**mansion** ['mænʃən] *n* особня́к

**manslaughter** ['mænslɔ:tər] *n*
непредумы́шленное уби́йство

**mantelpiece** ['mæntlpi:s] *n*
ками́нная доска́

**manual** ['mænjuəl] *adj* ручно́й ♦ *n*
посо́бие; **~ worker**
чернорабо́чий(ая) *m(f) adj*

**manufacture** [mænju'fæktʃər] *vt*
(*goods*) изготовля́ть (изгото́вить
*pf*), производи́ть (произвести́ *pf*)
♦ *n* изготовле́ние,
произво́дство; **~r** *n*
изготови́тель *m*, производи́тель
*m*

**manure** [mə'njuər] *n* наво́з

**manuscript** ['mænjuskrɪpt] *n* (*old
text*) манускри́пт; (*before printing*)

ру́копись f

**many** ['mɛnɪ] adj (a lot of ) мно́го +gen ♦ pron (several) мно́гие pl adj; **a great ~** о́чень мно́го +gen, мно́жество +gen; **how ~?** ско́лько?; **~ a time** мно́го раз; **in ~ cases** во мно́гих слу́чаях; **~ of us** мно́гие из нас

**map** [mæp] n ка́рта; (of town) план

**maple** ['meɪpl] n клён

**mar** [mɑːʳ] vt по́ртить (испо́ртить pf)

**marathon** ['mærəθən] n марафо́н

**marble** ['mɑːbl] n (stone) мра́мор

**March** [mɑːtʃ] n март

**march** [mɑːtʃ] vi маршова́ть (промаршова́ть pf) ♦ n марш

**mare** [mɛəʳ] n кобы́ла

**margarine** [mɑːdʒəˈriːn] n маргари́н

**margin** ['mɑːdʒɪn] n (on page) поля́ ntpl; (of victory) преиму́щество; (of defeat) меньшинство́; (also: **profit ~**) ма́ржа, чи́стая при́быль f no pl; **~al** adj незначи́тельный

**marigold** ['mærɪɡəuld] n ноготки́ mpl

**marijuana** [mærɪˈwɑːnə] n марихуа́на

**marina** [məˈriːnə] n мари́на, при́стань f для яхт

**marine** [məˈriːn] adj морско́й; (engineer) судово́й ♦ n (BRIT) слу́жащий m adj вое́нно-морско́го фло́та; (US) морско́й пехоти́нец

**marital** ['mærɪtl] adj супру́жеский; **~ status** семе́йное положе́ние

**maritime** ['mærɪtaɪm] adj морско́й

**mark** [mɑːk] n (symbol) значо́к, поме́тка; (stain) пятно́; (of shoes etc) след; (token) знак; (BRIT : SCOL) отме́тка, оце́нка ♦ vt (occasion) отмеча́ть (отме́тить pf); (with pen) помеча́ть (поме́тить pf); (subj: shoes, tyres) оставля́ть (оста́вить pf) след на +prp; (furniture) повреждá́ть (повреди́ть pf); (clothes, carpet) ста́вить (поста́вить pf) пятно́ на +prp; (place, time) ука́зывать (указа́ть pf); (BRIT : SCOL) проверя́ть (прове́рить pf); **~ed** adj заме́тный; **~er** n (sign) знак; (bookmark) закла́дка; (pen) фломáстер

**market** ['mɑːkɪt] n ры́нок ♦ vt (promote) реклами́ровать (impf); (sell) выпуска́ть (вы́пустить pf) в прода́жу; **~ing** n ма́ркетинг; **~ research** n ма́ркетинговые иссле́дования ntpl

**marmalade** ['mɑːməleɪd] n джем (цитрусовый)

**maroon** [məˈruːn] vt: **we were ~ed** мы бы́ли отре́заны от вне́шнего ми́ра

**marquee** [mɑːˈkiː] n марки́за, пала́точный павильо́н

**marriage** ['mærɪdʒ] n брак; (wedding) сва́дьба; **~ certificate** n свиде́тельство о бра́ке

**married** ['mærɪd] adj (man) жена́тый; (woman) заму́жняя; (couple) жена́тые; (life) супру́жеский

**marrow** ['mærəu] n (BOT) кабачо́к; (also: **bone ~**) ко́стный мозг

**marry** ['mærɪ] vt (subj: man) жени́ться (impf/pf) на +prp; (: woman) выходи́ть (вы́йти pf) за́муж за +acc; (: priest) венча́ть (обвенча́ть pf); (also: **~ off**: son) жени́ть (impf/pf); (: daughter) выдава́ть (вы́дать pf) за́муж ♦ vi: **to get married** (man) жени́ться (impf); (woman) выходи́ть (вы́йти pf) за́муж; (couple) жени́ться (пожени́ться pf)

**Mars** [mɑːz] n Марс

**marsh** [mɑːʃ] n боло́то

**marshal** ['mɑːʃl] n (at public event) распоряди́тель(ница) m(f) ♦ vt (support) упоря́дочивать (упоря́дочить pf); **police ~** (US) нача́льник полице́йского уча́стка

**marshy** ['mɑːʃɪ] adj боло́тистый

**martial law** ['mɑːʃəl-] n вое́нное положе́ние

**martyr** ['mɑːtər] n му́ченик(ица)

**marvellous** (US **marvelous**) ['mɑːvləs] adj восхити́тельный, изуми́тельный

**Marxist** ['mɑːksɪst] adj маркси́стский ♦ n маркси́ст(ка)

**marzipan** ['mɑːzɪpæn] n марципа́н

**mascara** [mæs'kɑːrə] n тушь f для ресни́ц

**mascot** ['mæskət] n талисма́н

**masculine** ['mæskjulɪn] adj мужско́й; (LING) мужско́го ро́да

**mash** [mæʃ] vt де́лать (сде́лать pf) пюре́ из +gen

**mask** [mɑːsk] n ма́ска ♦ vt (feelings) маскирова́ть (impf)

**mason** ['meɪsn] n (also: **stone ~**) ка́менщик; (also: **free~**) масо́н, во́льный ка́менщик; **~ic** [mə'sɔnɪk] adj масо́нский; **~ry** n (ка́менная) кла́дка

**mass** [mæs] n (also PHYS) ма́сса; (REL): **Mass** прича́стие ♦ cpd ма́ссовый; **the ~es** npl (наро́дные) ма́ссы fpl; **~es of** (inf) ма́сса fsg +gen, у́йма fsg +gen

**massacre** ['mæsəkər] n ма́ссовое уби́йство, резня́

**massage** ['mæsɑːʒ] n масса́ж ♦ vt (rub) масси́ровать (impf)

**massive** ['mæsɪv] adj масси́вный; (support, changes) огро́мный

**mass media** n inv сре́дства ntpl ма́ссовой информа́ции

**mast** [mɑːst] n ма́чта

**master** ['mɑːstər] n (also fig) хозя́ин ♦ vt (control) владе́ть (овладе́ть pf) +instr; (learn, understand) овладева́ть (овладе́ть pf) +instr; **Master Smith** (title) господи́н or ма́стер Смит; **Master of Arts/Science** ≈ маги́стр гуманита́рных/ есте́ственных нау́к; **~piece** n шеде́вр

**masturbation** [mæstə'beɪʃən] n мастурба́ция

**mat** [mæt] n ко́врик; (also: **door~**) дверно́й ко́врик; (also: **table ~**) подста́вка ♦ adj = **matt**

**match** [mætʃ] n спи́чка; (SPORT) матч; (equal) ро́вня m/f ♦ vt (subj: colours) сочета́ться (impf) с +instr; (correspond to) соотве́тствовать (impf) +dat ♦ vi (colours, materials) сочета́ться (impf); **to be a good ~** (colours, clothes) хорошо́ сочета́ться (impf); **they make** or **are a good ~** они́ хоро́шая па́ра; **~ing** adj сочета́ющийся

**mate** [meɪt] n (inf: friend) друг; (animal) саме́ц(мка); (NAUT) помо́щник капита́на ♦ vi спа́риваться (спа́риться pf)

**material** [mə'tɪərɪəl] n материа́л ♦ adj материа́льный; **~s** npl (equipment) принадле́жности fpl; **building ~s** строи́тельные материа́лы; **~ize** vi материализова́ться (impf/pf), осуществля́ться (осуществи́ться pf)

**maternal** [mə'təːnl] adj матери́нский

**maternity** [mə'təːnɪtɪ] n матери́нство

**mathematics** [mæθə'mætɪks] n матема́тика

**maths** [mæθs] n abbr = **mathematics**

**matron** ['meɪtrən] n (in hospital) ста́ршая медсестра́; (in school) (шко́льная) медсестра́

**matt** [mæt] *adj* ма́товый
**matter** ['mætəʳ] *n* де́ло, вопро́с;
(*substance, material*) вещество́ ♦ *vi*
име́ть (*impf*) значе́ние; **~s** *npl*
(*affairs, situation*) дела́ *ntpl*; **reading**
**~** (*BRIT*) материа́л для чте́ния;
**what's the ~?** в чём де́ло?; **no ~**
**what** несмотря́ ни на что; **as a ~**
**of course** как само́ собо́й
разуме́ющееся; **as a ~ of fact**
со́бственно говоря́; **it doesn't ~**
э́то не ва́жно; **~-of-fact** *adj* (*tone*)
бесстра́стный
**mattress** ['mætrɪs] *n* матра́с
**mature** [mə'tjuəʳ] *adj* (*person*)
зре́лый; (*cheese, wine*)
вы́держанный ♦ *vi* (*develop*)
развива́ться (разви́ться *pf*);
(*grow up*) взросле́ть
(повзросле́ть *pf*); (*cheese*) зреть *or*
созрева́ть (созре́ть *pf*); (*wine*)
выста́иваться (вы́стояться *pf*)
**maturity** [mə'tjuərɪtɪ] *n* зре́лость
*f*
**maximum** ['mæksɪməm] (*pl*
**maxima** *or* **~s**) *adj*
максима́льный ♦ *n* ма́ксимум
**May** [meɪ] *n* май

May Day - Первома́й. По
тради́ции в э́тот день
пра́зднуется нача́ло весны́.

**may** [meɪ] (*conditional* **might**) *vi* (*to
show possibility*): **I ~ go to Russia** я,
мо́жет быть, пое́ду в Росси́ю; (*to
show permission*): **~ I smoke/come?**
мо́жно закури́ть/мне прийти́?; **it
~ or might rain** мо́жет пойти́
дождь; **you ~ or might as well go
now** Вы, пожа́луй, мо́жете идти́
сейча́с; **come what ~** будь что
бу́дет
**maybe** ['meɪbi:] *adv* (*perhaps*)
мо́жет быть
**mayhem** ['meɪhɛm] *n* погро́м

**mayonnaise** [meɪə'neɪz] *n*
майоне́з
**mayor** [mɛəʳ] *n* мэр

KEYWORD

**me** [mi:] *pron* **1** (*direct*) меня́; **he
loves me** он лю́бит меня́; **it's me**
э́то я
**2** (*indirect*) мне; **give me them** *or*
**them to me** да́йте их мне
**3** (*after prep: +gen*) меня́; (*: +dat,
+prp*) мне; (*: +instr*) мной; **it's for
me** (*on answering phone*) э́то мне
**4** (*referring to subject of sentence:
after prep: +gen*) себя́; (*: +dat*)
себе́; (*: +instr*) собо́й; (*: +prp*)
себе́; **I took him with me** я взял
его́ с собо́й

**meadow** ['mɛdəu] *n* луг
**meagre** ['mi:gəʳ] (*US* **meager**) *adj*
ску́дный
**meal** [mi:l] *n* еда́ *no pl*; (*afternoon*)
обе́д; (*evening*) у́жин; **during ~s**
во вре́мя еды́, за едо́й
**mean** [mi:n] (*pt, pp* **~t**) *adj* (*miserly*)
скупо́й; (*unkind*) вре́дный;
(*vicious*) по́длый ♦ *vt* (*signify*)
зна́чить (*impf*), означа́ть (*impf*);
(*refer to*) име́ть (*impf*) в виду́ ♦ *n*
(*average*) середи́на; **~s** *npl* (*way*)
спо́соб *msg*, сре́дство *ntsg*;
(*money*) сре́дства *ntpl*; **by ~s of**
посре́дством +*gen*, с по́мощью
+*gen*; **by all ~s!** пожа́луйста!; **do
you ~ it?** Вы э́то серьёзно?; **to ~**
**to do** (*intend*) намерева́ться
(*impf*) +*infin*; **to be ~t for**
предназнача́ться (*impf*) для +*gen*;
**~ing** *n* (*purpose, value*) смысл;
(*definition*) значе́ние; **~ingful** *adj*
(*result, occasion*) значи́тельный;
(*glance, remark*) много-
значи́тельный; **~ingless** *adj*
бессмы́сленный; **~t** [mɛnt] *pt, pp*
*of* **mean**; **~time** *adv* (*also:* **in the**

~**time**) тем вре́менем, ме́жду тем; ~**while** adv = **meantime**

**measles** ['mi:zlz] n корь f

**measure** ['meʒər] vt измеря́ть (изме́рить pf) ♦ n ме́ра; (of whisky etc) по́рция; (also: **tape ~**) руле́тка, сантиме́тр ♦ vi: **the room ~s 10 feet by 20** пло́щадь ко́мнаты 10 фу́тов на 20; ~**d** adj (tone) сде́ржанный; (step) разме́ренный; (opinion) взве́шенный; ~**ments** npl ме́рки fpl, разме́ры mpl

**meat** [mi:t] n мя́со; **cold ~s** (BRIT) холо́дные мясны́е заку́ски fpl

**mechanic** [mɪ'kænɪk] n меха́ник; ~**al** adj механи́ческий; ~**s** npl (of government) меха́ника fsg

**mechanism** ['mɛkənɪzəm] n механи́зм

**medal** ['mɛdl] n меда́ль f; ~**list** (US ~**ist**) n медали́ст(ка)

**meddle** ['mɛdl] vi: **to ~ in** вме́шиваться (вмеша́ться pf) в +acc; **to ~ with sth** вторга́ться (вто́ргнуться pf) во что-н

**media** ['mi:dɪə] n or npl: **the ~** сре́дства ntpl ма́ссовой информа́ции, ме́дия ♦ npl see **medium**

**mediaeval** [mɛdɪ'i:vl] adj = **medieval**

**mediate** ['mi:dɪeɪt] vi (arbitrate) посре́дничать (impf)

**mediator** ['mi:dɪeɪtər] n посре́дник(ица)

**medical** ['mɛdɪkl] adj медици́нский ♦ n медосмо́тр

**medication** [mɛdɪ'keɪʃən] n лека́рство, лека́рственный препара́т

**medicinal** [mɛ'dɪsɪnl] adj (substance, qualities) лека́рственный

**medicine** ['mɛdsɪn] n (science) медици́на; (drug) лека́рство

**medieval** [mɛdɪ'i:vl] adj

средневеко́вый

**mediocre** [mi:dɪ'əukər] adj заура́дный, посре́дственный

**meditation** [mɛdɪ'teɪʃən] n (REL) медита́ция

**Mediterranean** [mɛdɪtə'reɪnɪən] adj: **the ~ (Sea)** Средизе́мное мо́ре

**medium** ['mi:dɪəm] (pl **media** or ~**s**) adj сре́дний ♦ n сре́дство

**meek** [mi:k] adj кро́ткий

**meet** [mi:t] (pt, pp **met**) vt встреча́ть (встре́тить pf); (obligations) выполня́ть (вы́полнить pf); (problem) ста́лкиваться (столкну́ться pf) с +instr; (need) удовлетворя́ть (удовлетвори́ть pf) ♦ vi (people) встреча́ться (встре́титься pf); (lines, roads) пересека́ться (пересе́чься pf); ~ **with** vt fus (difficulty) ста́лкиваться (столкну́ться pf) с +instr; (success) по́льзоваться (impf) +instr; (approval) находи́ть (найти́ pf); ~**ing** n встре́ча; (at work, of committee etc) заседа́ние, собра́ние; (POL: also: **mass ~ing**) ми́тинг; **she's at a ~ing** она́ на заседа́нии

**melancholy** ['mɛlənkəlɪ] adj (smile) меланхоли́ческий

**mellow** ['mɛləu] adj (sound) бархати́стый; (taste) мя́гкий ♦ vi смягча́ться (смягчи́ться pf)

**melodrama** ['mɛləudrɑ:mə] n мелодра́ма

**melody** ['mɛlədɪ] n мело́дия

**melon** ['mɛlən] n ды́ня

**melt** [mɛlt] vi та́ять (раста́ять pf) ♦ vt (snow, butter) топи́ть (растопи́ть pf)

**member** ['mɛmbər] n (also ANAT) член; **Member of Parliament** (BRIT) член парла́мента; ~**ship** n (members) чле́ны mpl; (status) члéнство; **~ship card** n члéнский билéт

**membrane** ['mɛmbreɪn] n мембрáна

**memento** [məˈmɛntəu] n сувенúр

**memo** ['mɛməu] n (ADMIN, instruction) дирекτúва

**memoirs** ['mɛmwɑːz] npl мемуáры pl

**memorable** ['mɛmərəbl] adj пáмятный

**memorial** [mɪˈmɔːrɪəl] n пáмятник ♦ cpd (service) мемориáльный

**memorize** ['mɛməraɪz] vt заýчивать (заучúть pf) (наизýсть)

**memory** ['mɛmərɪ] n пáмять f; (recollection) воспоминáние; **in ~ of** в пáмять о +prp

**men** [mɛn] npl of **man**

**menace** ['mɛnɪs] n (threat) угрóза

**menacing** ['mɛnɪsɪŋ] adj угрожáющий

**mend** [mɛnd] vt ремонтúровать (отремонтúровать pf), чинúть (починúть pf); (clothes) чинúть (починúть pf) ♦ n: **to be on the ~** идтú (impf) на попрáвку; **to ~ one's ways** исправлáться (испрáвиться pf)

**menial** ['miːnɪəl] adj чёрный

**meningitis** [mɛnɪnˈdʒaɪtɪs] n менингúт

**menopause** ['mɛnəupɔːz] n: **the ~** климактерúческий перúод, клúмакс

**menstruation** [mɛnstru'eɪʃən] n менструáция

**menswear** ['mɛnzwɛər] n мужскáя одéжда

**mental** ['mɛntl] adj (ability, exhaustion) ýмственный; (image) мýсленный; (illness) душéвный, психúческий; (arithmetic, calculation) в умé; **~ity** [mɛn'tælɪtɪ] n менталитéт, умонастроéние

**mention** ['mɛnʃən] n упоминáние

♦ vt упоминáть (упомянýть pf); **don't ~ it!** нé за что!

**mentor** ['mɛntɔːr] n настáвник

**menu** ['mɛnjuː] n (also COMPUT) меню́ nt ind

**MEP** n abbr (BRIT) (= Member of the European Parliament) член Еврοпéйского парлáмента

**mercenary** ['mɜːsɪnərɪ] adj корýстный ♦ n наёмник

**merchant** ['mɜːtʃənt] n торгóвец

**merciful** ['mɜːsɪful] adj милосéрдный; (fortunate) благóй

**merciless** ['mɜːsɪlɪs] adj беспощáдный

**mercury** ['mɜːkjurɪ] n (metal) ртуть f

**mercy** ['mɜːsɪ] n милосéрдие; **to be at sb's ~** быть (impf) во влáсти когó-н

**mere** [mɪər] adj: **she's a ~ child** онá всегó лишь ребёнок; **his ~ presence irritates her** самó егó присýтствие раздражáет её; **~ly** adv (simply) прóсто; (just) тóлько

**merge** [mɜːdʒ] vt сливáть (слить pf), объединáть (объединúть pf) ♦ vi (also COMM) сливáться (слúться pf); (roads) сходúться (сойтúсь pf); **~r** n (COMM) слияние

**meringue** [məˈræŋ] n безé nt ind

**merit** ['mɛrɪt] n достóинство ♦ vt заслýживать (заслужúть pf)

**merry** ['mɛrɪ] adj весёлый; **Merry Christmas!** С Рождествóм!, Счастлúвого Рождествá!

**mesh** [mɛʃ] n (net) сеть f

**mess** [mɛs] n (in room) беспорáдок; (of situation) неразберúха; (MIL) столóвая f adj; **to be in a ~** (untidy) быть (impf) в беспорáдке; **~ up** vt (spoil) пóртить (испóртить pf)

**message** ['mɛsɪdʒ] n сообщéние; (note) запúска; (of play, book)

идéя; **to leave sb a ~** (*note*)
оставля́ть (оста́вить *pf*) кому́-н
запи́ску; **can I give him a ~?** ему́
что́-нибудь переда́ть?

**messenger** ['mesɪndʒəʳ] *n* курьéр,
посы́льный *m adj*

**Messrs** *abbr* (*on letters:* = *messieurs*)
гг.

**messy** ['mesɪ] *adj* (*untidy*)
неýбранный

**met** [met] *pt, pp of* **meet**

**metabolism** [mɛ'tæbəlɪzəm] *n*
метаболи́зм, обмéн вещéств

**metal** ['metl] *n* метáлл

**metaphor** ['metəfəʳ] *n* метáфора

**meteor** ['mi:tɪəʳ] *n* метеóр

**meteorology** [mi:tɪə'rɔlədʒɪ] *n*
метеороло́гия

**meter** ['mi:təʳ] *n* (*instrument*)
счёт
чик; (*US: unit*) = **metre**

**method** ['meθəd] *n* (*way*) мéтод,
спóсоб; **~ical** [mɪ'θɔdɪkl] *adj*
методи́чный; **Methodist** *n* (*REL*)
методи́ст(ка)

**meticulous** [mɪ'tɪkjuləs] *adj*
тщáтельный

**metre** ['mi:təʳ] (*US* **meter**) *n* метр

**metric** ['metrɪk] *adj* метри́ческий

**metropolitan** [metrə'pɔlɪtn] *adj*
столи́чный

**Mexico** ['meksɪkəu] *n* Мéксика

**mice** [maɪs] *npl of* **mouse**

**micro: ~phone** *n* микрофóн;
**~scope** *n* микроскóп; **~scopic**
*adj* микроскопи́ческий; **~wave** *n*
(*also:* **~wave oven**)
микроволновáя печь *f*

**mid** [mɪd] *adj:* **in ~ May/afternoon**
в середи́не мáя/дня; **in ~ air** в
вóздухе; **~day** *n* пóлдень *m*

**middle** ['mɪdl] *n* середи́на ♦ *adj*
срéдний; **in the ~ of** посреди́
+*gen*; **Middle Ages** *npl:* **the Middle
Ages** срéдние векá *mpl*; **~-class**
*adj:* **~-class people/values** люди/

цéнности срéднего клáсса;
**Middle East** *n:* **the Middle East**
Бли́жний Востóк

**midge** [mɪdʒ] *n* мóшка

**midnight** ['mɪdnaɪt] *n* пóлночь *f*

**midst** [mɪdst] *n:* **in the ~ of**
посреди́ +*gen*

**midway** [mɪd'weɪ] *adv:* **~ (between)**
на полпути́ (мéжду +*instr*); **~
through** в середи́не +*gen*

**midweek** [mɪd'wi:k] *adv* в
середи́не недéли

**midwife** ['mɪdwaɪf] (*pl* **midwives**)
*n* акушéрка

**might** [maɪt] *vb see* **may**; **~y** *adj*
мóщный

**migraine** ['mi:greɪn] *n* мигрéнь *f*

**migrant** ['maɪgrənt] *adj:* **~ worker**
рабóчий-мигрáнт

**migration** [maɪ'greɪʃən] *n*
мигрáция

**mike** [maɪk] *n abbr* = **microphone**

**mild** [maɪld] *adj* мя́гкий; (*interest*)
слáбый; (*infection*) лёгкий

**mildew** ['mɪldju:] *n* (*mould*)
плéсень *f*

**mildly** ['maɪldlɪ] *adv* (*see adj*)
мя́гко; слегкá; легкó; **to put it ~**
мя́гко говоря́

**mile** [maɪl] *n* ми́ля; **~age** *n*
кол`и́чество миль; **~stone** *n*
≈ километрóвый столб; (*fig*)
вéха

mile - ми́ля. В Великобритáнии
и Амéрике расстоя́ние
измеря́ется в ми́лях, а не в
киломéтрах. Однá ми́ля
равня́ется 1,609 мéтрам.

**militant** ['mɪlɪtnt] *adj*
вои́нствующий

**military** ['mɪlɪtərɪ] *adj* воéнный ♦ *n:*
**the ~** воéнные *pl adj*; **~ service** *n*
воéнная слýжба

**militia** [mɪ'lɪʃə] *n* (нарóдное)

ополче́ние

**milk** [mɪlk] *n* молоко́ ♦ *vt* (*cow*) дои́ть (подои́ть *pf*); (*fig*) эксплуати́ровать (*impf*); **~y** *adj* моло́чный

**mill** [mɪl] *n* (*factory*: *making cloth*) фа́брика; (: *making steel*) заво́д; (*for coffee, pepper etc*) ме́льница

**millimetre** (*US* **millimeter**) [ˈmɪlɪmiːtəʳ] *n* миллиме́тр

**million** [ˈmɪljən] *n* миллио́н; **~aire** [mɪljəˈnɛəʳ] *n* миллионе́р

**mime** [maɪm] *n* пантоми́ма ♦ *vt* изобража́ть (изобрази́ть *pf*) же́стами

**mimic** [ˈmɪmɪk] *vt* (*subj*: *comedian*) пароди́ровать (*impf/pf*)

**min.** *abbr* (= **minute**) мин(.)

**mince** [mɪns] *vt* (*meat*) пропуска́ть (пропусти́ть *pf*) че́рез мясору́бку ♦ *n* (*BRIT*) (мясно́й) фарш

**mince pie** - пирожо́к с сухофру́ктами. Хотя́ э́то выраже́ние буква́льно означа́ет "пирожо́к с фа́ршем", начи́нка тако́го пирожка́ состои́т из сухофру́ктов, а не из мя́са.

**mind** [maɪnd] *n* (*intellect*) ум ♦ *vt* (*look after*) смотре́ть (*impf*) за +*instr*; **I don't ~ the noise** шум меня́ не беспоко́ит; **it's always on my ~** э́то не выхо́дит у меня́ из головы́; **to keep** *or* **bear sth in ~** име́ть (*impf*) что-н в виду́; **to make up one's ~** реша́ться (реши́ться *pf*); **to my ~ ...** по моему́ мне́нию ...; **I don't ~** мне всё равно́; **~ you, ...** име́йте в виду́ ...; **never ~!** ничего́!; **~ful** *adj*: **to be ~ful of** име́ть (*impf*) в виду́; **~less** *adj* (*violence*) безду́мный; (*job*) механи́ческий

**mine¹** [maɪn] *pron* **1** мой (*f* моя́, *nt* моё, *pl* мои́); **that book is mine** э́та кни́га моя́; **that house is mine** э́тот дом мой; **this is mine** э́то моё; **an uncle of mine** мой дя́дя

**2** (*referring back to subject*) свой (*f* своя́, *nt* своё, *pl* свои́); **may I borrow your pen? I have forgotten mine** мо́жно взять Ва́шу ру́чку? я забы́л свою́

**mine²** [maɪn] *n* (*for coal*) ша́хта; (*explosive*) ми́на ♦ *vt* (*coal*) добыва́ть (добы́ть *pf*); **~field** *n* ми́нное по́ле; **~r** *n* шахтёр

**mineral** [ˈmɪnərəl] *n* минера́л; (*ore*) поле́зное ископа́емое *nt adj*; **~ water** *n* минера́льная вода́

**miniature** [ˈmɪnətʃəʳ] *adj* миниатю́рный

**minibus** [ˈmɪnɪbʌs] *n* микроавто́бус

**minicab** - такси́. Э́тот тип такси́ регули́руется зако́ном в ме́ньшей сте́пени. В отли́чие от традицио́нного чёрного такси́ его́ вызыва́ют по телефо́ну, а не остана́вливают на у́лице.

**Minidisc**® [ˈmɪnɪdɪsk] *n* ми́ни-диск

**minimal** [ˈmɪnɪml] *adj* минима́льный

**minimize** [ˈmɪnɪmaɪz] *vt* (*reduce*) своди́ть (свести́ *pf*) к ми́нимуму; (*play down*) преуменьша́ть (преуме́ньшить *pf*)

**minimum** [ˈmɪnɪməm] (*pl* **minima**) *n* ми́нимум ♦ *adj* минима́льный

**mining** [ˈmaɪnɪŋ] *n* (*industry*) у́гольная промы́шленность *f*

**minister** [ˈmɪnɪstəʳ] *n* (*BRIT*)

мини́стр; (REL) свяще́нник; **~ial**
[mɪnɪsˈtɪərɪəl] adj (BRIT)
министе́рский

**ministry** [ˈmɪnɪstrɪ] n (BRIT : POL)
министе́рство

**minor** [ˈmaɪnəʳ] adj (injuries)
незначи́тельный; (repairs)
ме́лкий ♦ n (LAW)
несовершенноле́тний(яя) m(f)
adj; **~ity** [maɪˈnɔrɪtɪ] n
меньшинство́

**mint** [mɪnt] n (BOT) мя́та; (sweet)
мя́тная конфе́та ♦ vt чека́нить
(отчека́нить pf); **in ~ condition** в
прекра́сном состоя́нии

**minus** [ˈmaɪnəs] n (also: ~ **sign**)
ми́нус ♦ prep: **12 ~ 6 equals 6** 12
ми́нус 6 равня́ется 6; **~ 24**
**(degrees)** ми́нус 24 гра́дуса

**minute¹** [maɪˈnjuːt] adj (search)
тща́тельный

**minute²** [ˈmɪnɪt] n мину́та; **~s** npl
(of meeting) протоко́л msg; **at the**
**last ~** в после́днюю мину́ту

**miracle** [ˈmɪrəkl] n чу́до

**miraculous** [mɪˈrækjuləs] adj
чуде́сный

**mirror** [ˈmɪrəʳ] n зе́ркало

**misbehave** [mɪsbɪˈheɪv] vi пло́хо
себя́ вести́ (impf)

**miscarriage** [ˈmɪskærɪdʒ] n (MED)
вы́кидыш; **~ of justice** суде́бная
оши́бка

**miscellaneous** [mɪsɪˈleɪnɪəs] adj
(subjects, items) разнообра́зный

**mischief** [ˈmɪstʃɪf] n озорство́;
(maliciousness) зло

**mischievous** [ˈmɪstʃɪvəs] adj
(naughty, playful) озорно́й

**misconception** [ˈmɪskənˈsɛpʃən] n
заблужде́ние, ло́жное
представле́ние

**misconduct** [mɪsˈkɔndʌkt] n
дурно́е поведе́ние; **professional**
**~** наруше́ние служе́бной
дисципли́ны

**miserable** [ˈmɪzərəbl] adj (unhappy)
несча́стный; (unpleasant)
скве́рный; (donation, conditions)
жа́лкий; (failure) позо́рный

**misery** [ˈmɪzərɪ] n (unhappiness)
невзго́да; (wretchedness) жа́лкое
существова́ние

**misfortune** [mɪsˈfɔːtʃən] n
несча́стье

**misguided** [mɪsˈɡaɪdɪd] adj (person)
неве́рно ориенти́рованный;
(ideas) оши́бочный

**misinterpret** [mɪsɪnˈtəːprɪt] vt
неве́рно интерпрети́ровать
(impf/pf) or толкова́ть
(истолкова́ть pf)

**mislead** [mɪsˈliːd] (irreg: like lead¹)
vt вводи́ть (ввести́ pf) в
заблужде́ние; **~ing** adj
обма́нчивый

**misprint** [ˈmɪsprɪnt] n опеча́тка

**Miss** [mɪs] n мисс f ind

**miss** [mɪs] vt (train, bus etc)
пропуска́ть (пропусти́ть pf);
(target) не попада́ть (попа́сть pf)
в +acc; (person, home) скуча́ть
(impf) по +dat; (chance, opportunity)
упуска́ть (упусти́ть pf) ♦ vi
(person) прома́хиваться
(промахну́ться pf) ♦ n про́мах;
**you can't ~ my house** мой дом
невозмо́жно не заме́тить; **~ out**
vt (BRIT) пропуска́ть (пропусти́ть
pf)

**missile** [ˈmɪsaɪl] n (MIL) раке́та

**missing** [ˈmɪsɪŋ] adj пропа́вший;
(tooth, wheel) недостаю́щий; **to**
**be ~** (absent) отсу́тствовать (impf);
**to be~, go ~** пропада́ть
(пропа́сть pf) без вести

**mission** [ˈmɪʃən] n (also POL, REL)
ми́ссия; **~ary** n миссионе́р(ка)

**mist** [mɪst] n (light) ды́мка

**mistake** [mɪsˈteɪk] (irreg: like take) n
оши́бка ♦ vt (be wrong about)
ошиба́ться (ошиби́ться pf) в +prp;

by ~ по оши́бке; **to make a ~** ошиба́ться (ошиби́ться *pf*), де́лать (сде́лать *pf*) оши́бку; **to ~ A for B** принима́ть (приня́ть *pf*) А за Б; **~n** *pp of* **mistake** ♦ *adj*: **to be ~n** ошиба́ться (ошиби́ться *pf*)

> **mistletoe** - оме́ла. В Великобрита́нии и США э́то расте́ние испо́льзуется как рожде́ственское украше́ние. По обы́чаю под оме́лой полага́ется целова́ться.

**mistook** [mɪs'tuk] *pt of* **mistake**
**mistress** ['mɪstrɪs] *n* (*also fig*) хозя́йка; (*lover*) любо́вница
**mistrust** [mɪs'trʌst] *vt* не доверя́ть (*impf*) +*dat* ♦ *n*: **~ (of)** недове́рие (к +*dat*)
**misty** ['mɪstɪ] *adj* (*day*) тума́нный
**misunderstand** [mɪsʌndə'stænd] (*irreg: like* **understand**) *vt* непра́вильно понима́ть (поня́ть *pf*) ♦ *vi* не понима́ть (поня́ть *pf*); **~ing** *n* недоразуме́ние
**misuse** *n* [mɪs'juːs] *vb* [mɪs'juːz] *n* (*of power, funds*) злоупотребле́ние ♦ *vt* злоупотребля́ть (злоупотреби́ть *pf*) +*instr*
**mix** [mɪks] *vt* (*cake, cement*) заме́шивать (замеси́ть *pf*) ♦ *n* смесь *f* ♦ *vi* (*people*): **to ~ (with)** обща́ться (*impf*) (с +*instr*); **to ~ sth (with sth)** сме́шивать (смеша́ть *pf*) что-н (с чем-н); **~ up** *vt* (*combine*) переме́шивать (перемеша́ть *pf*); (*confuse: people*) пу́тать (спу́тать *pf*); (*: things*) пу́тать (перепу́тать *pf*); **~er** *n* (*for food*) ми́ксер; **~ture** ['mɪkstʃər] *n* смесь *f*; **~-up** *n* пу́таница
**mm** *abbr* (= **millimetre**) мм
**moan** [məun] *n* (*cry*) стон ♦ *vi* (*inf: complain*): **to ~ (about)** ныть (*impf*) (о +*prp*)

**moat** [məut] *n* ров
**mob** [mɔb] *n* (*crowd*) толпа́
**mobile** ['məubaɪl] *adj* подви́жный ♦ *n* (*toy*) подвесно́е декорати́вное украше́ние; (*phone*) моби́льный телефо́н, моби́льник (*разг*); **~ phone** *n* моби́льный телефо́н
**mobility** [məu'bɪlɪtɪ] *n* подви́жность *f*
**mobilize** ['məubɪlaɪz] *vt* мобилизова́ть (*impf/pf*)
**mock** [mɔk] *vt* (*ridicule*) издева́ться (*impf*) над +*instr* ♦ *adj* (*fake*) ло́жный; **~ery** *n* издева́тельство; **to make a ~ery of sb/sth** выставля́ть (вы́ставить *pf*) кого́-н/что-н на посме́шище
**mod cons** *npl abbr* (*BRIT*) = **modern conveniences**
**mode** [məud] *n* (*of life*) о́браз; (*of transport*) вид
**model** ['mɔdl] *n* моде́ль *f*, маке́т; (*also:* **fashion ~**) моде́ль, манеке́нщик(ица); (*also:* **artist's ~**) нату́рщик(ица) ♦ *adj* (*ideal*) образцо́вый
**modem** ['məudɛm] *n* (*COMPUT*) моде́м
**moderate** *adj, n* ['mɔdərət] *vb* ['mɔdəreɪt] *adj* (*views, amount*) уме́ренный; (*change*) незначи́тельный ♦ *vt* умеря́ть (уме́рить *pf*)
**moderation** [mɔdə'reɪʃən] *n* уме́ренность *f*
**modern** ['mɔdən] *adj* совреме́нный
**modest** ['mɔdɪst] *adj* скро́мный; **~y** *n* скро́мность *f*
**modification** [mɔdɪfɪ'keɪʃən] *n* (*see vb*) модифика́ция; видоизмене́ние
**modify** ['mɔdɪfaɪ] *vt* (*vehicle, engine*) модифици́ровать (*impf/pf*); (*plan*) видоизменя́ть (видоизмени́ть *pf*)

**moist** [mɔɪst] *adj* вла́жный; **~en** *vt* (*lips*) увлажня́ть (увлажни́ть *pf*); (*sponge*) мочи́ть (смочи́ть *pf*); **~ure** *n* вла́га

**mold** [məuld] *n, vb* (*US*) = **mould**

**mole** [məul] *n* (*spot*) ро́динка; (*ZOOL*) крот

**molecule** [ˈmɔlɪkjuːl] *n* моле́кула

**molt** [məult] *vi* (*US*) = **moult**

**mom** [mɔm] *n* (*US*) = **mum**

**moment** [ˈməumənt] *n* моме́нт, мгнове́ние; **for a ~** на мгнове́ние; **at that ~** в э́тот моме́нт; **at the ~** в настоя́щий моме́нт; **~ary** *adj* мгнове́нный

**momentous** [məuˈmɛntəs] *adj* знамена́тельный

**momentum** [məuˈmɛntəm] *n* (*fig*) дви́жущая си́ла; **to gather** *or* **gain ~** набира́ть (набра́ть *pf*) си́лу

**mommy** [ˈmɔmɪ] *n* (*US*) = **mummy**

**monarch** [ˈmɔnək] *n* мона́рх; **~y** *n* мона́рхия

**monastery** [ˈmɔnəstərɪ] *n* монасты́рь *m*

**Monday** [ˈmʌndɪ] *n* понеде́льник

**monetary** [ˈmʌnɪtərɪ] *adj* де́нежный

**money** **~** [ˈmʌnɪ] *n* де́ньги *pl*; **to make ~** (*person*) зараба́тывать (зарабо́тать *pf*) де́ньги; (*make a profit*) де́лать (сде́лать *pf*) де́ньги

**mongrel** [ˈmʌŋɡrəl] *n* дворня́га

**monitor** [ˈmɔnɪtər] *n* монито́р ♦ *vt* (*broadcasts, pulse*) следи́ть (*impf*) за +*instr*

**monk** [mʌŋk] *n* мона́х

**monkey** [ˈmʌŋkɪ] *n* обезья́на

**monopoly** [məˈnɔpəlɪ] *n* монопо́лия

**monotonous** [məˈnɔtənəs] *adj* однообра́зный, моното́нный

**monster** [ˈmɔnstər] *n* чудо́вище, монстр

**monstrous** [ˈmɔnstrəs] *adj* чудо́вищный

**month** [mʌnθ] *n* ме́сяц; **~ly** *adj* ежеме́сячный; (*ticket*) ме́сячный ♦ *adv* ежеме́сячно

**monument** [ˈmɔnjumənt] *n* (*memorial*) па́мятник, монуме́нт; **~al** [mɔnjuˈmɛntl] *adj* (*important*) монумента́льный; (*terrific*) колосса́льный

**mood** [muːd] *n* настрое́ние; (*of crowd*) настро́й; **to be in a good/ bad ~** быть (*impf*) в хоро́шем/ плохо́м настрое́нии; **~y** *adj* (*temperamental*): **she is a very ~y person** у неё о́чень переме́нчивое настрое́ние

**moon** [muːn] *n* луна́; **~light** *n* лу́нный свет

**moor** [muər] *n* ве́ресковая пу́стошь *f*

**moose** [muːs] *n inv* лось *m*

**mop** [mɔp] *n* (*for floor*) шва́бра; (*of hair*) копна́ ♦ *vt* (*floor*) мыть (вы́мыть *or* помы́ть *pf*) (шва́брой); (*eyes, face*) вытира́ть (вы́тереть *pf*)

**moped** [ˈməupɛd] *n* мопе́д

**moral** [ˈmɔrl] *adj* мора́льный; (*person*) нра́вственный ♦ *n* (*of story*) мора́ль *f*; **~s** *npl* (*values*) нра́вы *mpl*

**morale** [mɔˈrɑːl] *n* мора́льный дух

**morality** [məˈrælɪtɪ] *n* нра́вственность *f*

**morbid** [ˈmɔːbɪd] *adj* (*imagination*) ненорма́льный; (*ideas*) жу́ткий

KEYWORD

**more** [mɔːr] *adj* **1** (*greater in number etc*) бо́льше +*gen*; **I have more friends than enemies** у меня́ бо́льше друзе́й, чем враго́в **2** (*additional*) ещё; **do you want (some) more tea?** хоти́те ещё ча́ю?; **is there any more wine?** вино́ ещё есть?; **I have no** *or* **I don't have any more money** у

меня́ бо́льше нет де́нег; **it'll take a few more weeks** э́то займёт ещё не́сколько неде́ль
♦ *pron* 1 ( *greater amount* ): **more than ten** бо́льше десяти́; **we've sold more than a hundred tickets** мы прода́ли бо́лее ста биле́тов; **it costs more than we expected** э́то сто́ит бо́льше, чем мы ожида́ли
2 ( *further or additional amount* ): **is there any more?** ещё есть?; **there's no more** бо́льше ничего́ нет; **a little more** ещё немно́го *or* чуть-чу́ть; **many/much more** намно́го/гора́здо бо́льше
♦ *adv* 1 (+*vb*) бо́льше; **I like this picture more** э́та карти́на мне нра́вится бо́льше
2: **more dangerous/difficult (than)** бо́лее опа́сный/тру́дный(, чем)
3: **more economically (than)** бо́лее экономи́чно(, чем); **more easily/quickly (than)** ле́гче/быстре́е(, чем); **more and more** ( *excited, friendly* ) всё бо́лее и бо́лее; **he grew to like her more and more** она́ нра́вилась ему́ всё бо́льше и бо́льше; **more or less** бо́лее и́ли ме́нее; **she is more beautiful than ever** она́ прекра́снее, чем когда́-либо; **he loved her more than ever** он люби́л её всё бо́льше, чем когда́-либо; **the more..., the better** чем бо́льше ..., тем лу́чше; **once more** ещё раз; **I'd like to see more of you** мне хоте́лось бы ви́деть тебя́ ча́ще

**moreover** [mɔː'rəʊvəʳ] *adv* бо́лее того́
**morgue** [mɔːg] *n* морг
**morning** ['mɔːnɪŋ] *n* у́тро; ( *between midnight and 3 a.m.* ) ночь *f* ♦ *cpd* у́тренний; **in the ~** у́тром;

**3 o'clock in the ~** 3 часа́ но́чи; **7 o'clock in the ~** 7 часо́в утра́
**Morse** [mɔːs] *n* ( *also:* **~ code** ) а́збука Мо́рзе
**mortal** ['mɔːtl] *adj* ( *man, sin* ) сме́ртный; ( *deadly* ) смерте́льный; **~ity** [mɔː'tælɪtɪ] *n* сме́ртность *f*
**mortar** ['mɔːtəʳ] *n* ( *cement* ) цеме́нтный раство́р
**mortgage** ['mɔːgɪdʒ] *n* ипоте́чный креди́т ♦ *vt* закла́дывать ( *заложи́ть pf* )
**Moscow** ['mɔskəʊ] *n* Москва́
**Moslem** ['mɔzləm] *adj, n* = **Muslim**
**mosque** [mɔsk] *n* мече́ть *f*
**mosquito** [mɔs'kiːtəʊ] ( *pl* **~es** ) *n* кома́р
**moss** [mɔs] *n* мох

KEYWORD

**most** [məʊst] *adj* 1 ( *almost all: countable nouns* ) большинство́ +*gen*; (: *uncountable and collective nouns* ) бо́льшая часть +*gen*; **most cars** большинство́ маши́н; **most milk** бо́льшая часть молока́; **in most cases** в большинстве́ слу́чаев
2 ( *largest, greatest* ): **who has the most money?** у кого́ бо́льше всего́ де́нег?; **this book has attracted the most interest among the critics** э́та кни́га вы́звала наибо́льший интере́с у кри́тиков
♦ *pron* ( *greatest quantity, number: countable nouns* ) большинство́; (: *uncountable and collective nouns* ) бо́льшая часть *f*; **most of the houses** большинство́ домо́в; **most of the cake** бо́льшая часть то́рта; **do the most you can** де́лайте всё, что Вы мо́жете; **I ate the most** я съел бо́льше всех; **to make the most of sth** максима́льно испо́льзовать

(*impf/pf*) что-н; **at the (very) most** са́мое бо́льшее
♦ *adv* (*+vb: with inanimate objects*) бо́льше всего́; (: *with animate objects*) бо́льше всех; (*+adv*) исключи́тельно; (*+adj*) са́мый, наибо́лее; **I liked him the most** он понра́вился мне бо́льше всех; **what do you value most, wealth or health?** что Вы бо́льше всего́ це́ните, бога́тство и́ли здоро́вье?

**mostly** ['məustlɪ] *adv* бо́льшей ча́стью, в основно́м
**MOT** *n abbr* (*BRIT*) = Ministry of Transport; **~ (test)** техосмо́тр

**MOT** - техосмо́тр. По зако́ну автомоби́ли, кото́рым бо́льше трёх лет, должны́ ежего́дно проходи́ть техосмо́тр.

**motel** [məu'tɛl] *n* моте́ль *m*
**moth** [mɔθ] *n* мотылёк
**mother** ['mʌðər] *n* мать *f* ♦ *vt* (*pamper*) ня́нчиться (*impf*) с +*instr*
♦ *adj*: **~ country** ро́дина, родна́я страна́; **~hood** *n* матери́нство; **~-in-law** *n* (*wife's mother*) тёща; (*husband's mother*) свекро́вь *f*; **~ tongue** *n* родно́й язы́к

**Mother's Day** - День Ма́тери. Отмеча́ется в четвёртое воскресе́нье Вели́кого Поста́. В э́тот день поздравле́ния и пода́рки получа́ют то́лько ма́мы.

**motif** [məu'ti:f] *n* (*design*) орна́мент
**motion** ['məuʃən] *n* (*movement, gesture*) движе́ние; (*proposal*) предложе́ние; **~less** *adj* неподви́жный

**motivated** ['məutɪveɪtɪd] *adj* (*inspired*) целеустремлённый; **~ by envy/greed** дви́жимый за́вистью/жа́дностью
**motivation** [məutɪ'veɪʃən] *n* (*drive*) целеустремлённость *f*
**motive** ['məutɪv] *n* моти́в, побужде́ние
**motor** ['məutər] *n* мото́р ♦ *cpd* (*trade*) автомоби́льный; **~bike** *n* мотоци́кл; **~cycle** *n* мотоци́кл; **~ist** *n* автомобили́ст; **~way** *n* (*BRIT*) автомагистра́ль *f*, автостра́да
**motto** ['mɔtəu] *n* (*pl* **~es**) *n* деви́з
**mould** [məuld] (*US* mold) *n* (*cast*) фо́рма; (*mildew*) пле́сень *f* ♦ *vt* (*substance*) лепи́ть (вы́лепить *pf*); (*fig: opinion, character*) формирова́ть (сформирова́ть *pf*); **~y** *adj* (*food*) запле́сневелый
**moult** [məult] (*US* molt) *vi* линя́ть (*impf*)
**mound** [maund] *n* (*heap*) ку́ча
**mount** [maunt] *vt* (*horse*) сади́ться (сесть *pf*) на +*acc*; (*display*) устра́ивать (устро́ить *pf*); (*jewel*) оправля́ть (опра́вить *pf*); (*picture*) обрамля́ть (обра́мить *pf*); (*stair*) всходи́ть (взойти́ *pf*) по +*dat* ♦ *vi* (*increase*) расти́ (*impf*) ♦ *n*: **Mount Ararat** гора́ Арара́т; **~ up** *vi* нака́пливаться (накопи́ться *pf*)
**mountain** ['mauntɪn] *n* гора́ ♦ *cpd* го́рный; **~ bike** *n* велосипе́д, для езды́ по пересечённой ме́стности; **~ous** *adj* го́рный, гори́стый
**mourn** [mɔ:n] *vt* (*death*) опла́кивать (*impf*) ♦ *vi*: **to ~ for** скорбе́ть (*impf*) по +*dat* и́ли о +*prp*; **~ful** *adj* ско́рбный; **~ing** *n* тра́ур; **in ~ing** в тра́уре
**mouse** [maus] (*pl* mice) *n* мышь *f*; **~ mat**, **~ pad** *n* ко́врик для мы́ши

**moustache** [məs'tɑ:ʃ] (US
   **mustache**) n усы́ mpl
**mouth** [mauθ] (pl ~**s**) n рот; (of
   cave, hole) вход; (of river) у́стье;
   ~**ful** n (of food) кусо́чек; (of drink)
   глото́к; ~ **organ** n губна́я
   гармо́шка; ~**piece** n (MUS)
   мундшту́к; (of telephone)
   микрофо́н
**move** [mu:v] n (movement)
   движе́ние; (in game) ход; (of
   house) перее́зд; (of job) перехо́д
   ♦ vt передвига́ть (передви́нуть
   pf); (piece: in game) ходи́ть (пойти́
   pf) +instr; (arm etc) дви́гать
   (дви́нуть pf) +instr; (person:
   emotionally) тро́гать (тро́нуть pf),
   растро́гать (pf) ♦ vi дви́гаться
   (дви́нуться pf); (things) дви́гаться
   (impf); (also: ~ **house**) переезжа́ть
   (перее́хать pf); **get a ~ on!**
   потора́пливайтесь!; ~ **about** vi
   (change position) передвига́ться
   (передви́нуться pf),
   перемеща́ться (перемести́ться
   pf); (travel) переезжа́ть (impf) с
   ме́ста на ме́сто; ~ **around** vi =
   **move about**; ~ **away** vi: **to ~
   away (from)** (leave) уезжа́ть
   (уе́хать pf) (из +gen) (step away)
   отходи́ть (отойти́ pf) (от +gen); ~
   **in** vi (police, soldiers) входи́ть
   (войти́ pf); **to ~ in(to)** (house)
   въезжа́ть (въе́хать pf) (в +acc); ~
   **out** vi (of house) выезжа́ть
   (вы́ехать pf); ~ **over** vi (to make
   room) подвига́ться (подви́нуться
   pf); ~ **up** vi (be promoted)
   продвига́ться (продви́нуться pf)
   по слу́жбе; ~**ment** n движе́ние;
   (between fixed points)
   передвиже́ние; (in attitude, policy)
   сдвиг
**movie** ['mu:vɪ] (esp US) n
   (кино)фи́льм; **to go to the ~s**
   ходи́ть/идти́ (пойти́ pf) в кино́

**moving** ['mu:vɪŋ] adj (emotional)
   тро́гательный; (mobile)
   подви́жный
**mow** [məu] (pt ~**ed**, pp ~**ed** or ~**n**)
   vt (grass) подстрига́ть
   (подстри́чь pf)
**MP** n abbr = **Member of
   Parliament**
**mph** abbr = **miles per hour**
**MP3** abbr MP3
**Mr** ['mɪstər] n: ~ **Smith** (informal)
   ми́стер Смит; (formal) г-н
   Смит
**Mrs** ['mɪsɪz] n: ~ **Smith** (informal)
   ми́ссис Смит; (formal) г-жа Смит,
   госпожа́ Смит

**Ms** - да́нное сокраще́ние
употребля́ется гла́вным
о́бразом в пи́сьменном языке́
и заменя́ет "мисс" и "ми́ссис".
Употребля́я его́, вы не
ука́зываете, за́мужем же́нщина
или нет.

**MSP** n abbr (= Member of the
   Scottish Parliament) член
   шотла́ндского парла́мента

KEYWORD

**much** [mʌtʃ] adj мно́го +gen; **we
   haven't got much time** у нас не
   так мно́го вре́мени; **how much
   money do you need?** ско́лько
   +gen; **how much money
   do you need?** ско́лько де́нег Вам
   ну́жно?; **he's spent so much
   money today** он сего́дня
   потра́тил так мно́го де́нег; **I
   have as much money as you (do)**
   у меня́ сто́лько же де́нег,
   ско́лько у Вас; **I don't have as
   much time as you (do)** у меня́
   нет сто́лько вре́мени, ско́лько у
   Вас
   ♦ pron мно́го, мно́гое; **much is
   still unclear** мно́гое ещё нея́сно;

there isn't much to do here здесь нечего делать; **how much does it cost? - too much** сколько это стоит? - слишком дорого; **how much is it?** сколько это стоит?, почём это? (*разг*)

♦ *adv* 1 (*greatly, a great deal*) очень; **thank you very much** большое спасибо; **we are very much looking forward to your visit** мы очень ждём Вашего приезда; **he is very much a gentleman** он настоящий джентельмен; **however much he tries** сколько бы он ни старался; **I try to help as much as possible** *or* **I can** я стараюсь помогать как можно больше *or* сколько могу; **I read as much as ever** я читаю столько же, сколько прежде; **he is as much a member of the family as you** он такой же член семьи, как и Вы

2 (*by far*) намного, гораздо; **I'm much better now** мне сейчас намного *or* гораздо лучше; **it's much the biggest publishing company in Europe** это самое крупное издательство в Европе

3 (*almost*) почти; **the view today is much as it was 10 years ago** вид сегодня почти такой же, как и 10 лет назад; **how are you feeling? - much the same** как Вы себя чувствуете? - всё так же

**muck** [mʌk] *n* (*dirt*) грязь *f*
**mud** [mʌd] *n* грязь *f*
**muddle** ['mʌdl] *n* (*mix-up*) путаница, неразбериха; (*mess*) беспорядок ♦ *vt* (*also*: ~ **up**: *person*) запутывать (запутать *pf*); (: *things*) перемешивать (перемешать *pf*)
**muddy** ['mʌdɪ] *adj* грязный
**muffled** ['mʌfld] *adj*

приглушённый
**mug** [mʌg] *n* кружка; (*inf*: *face*) морда; (: *fool*) дурень *m* ♦ *vt* грабить (ограбить *pf*) (*на улице*)
**mule** [mju:l] *n* (*ZOOL*) мул
**multilevel** ['mʌltɪlevl] *adj* (*US*) = **multistorey**
**multinational** [mʌltɪ'næʃənl] *adj* международный
**multiple** ['mʌltɪpl] *adj* (*injuries*) многочисленный ♦ *n* (*MATH*) кратное число; ~ **collision** столкновение нескольких автомобилей; ~ **sclerosis** *n* рассеянный склероз
**multiplication** [mʌltɪplɪ'keɪʃən] *n* умножение
**multiply** ['mʌltɪplaɪ] *vt* умножать (умножить *pf*) ♦ *vi* размножаться (размножиться *pf*)
**multistorey** ['mʌltɪ'stɔ:rɪ] *adj* (*BRIT*) многоэтажный
**multitude** ['mʌltɪtju:d] *n* (*large number*): **a** ~ **of** множество +*gen*
**mum** [mʌm] (*BRIT*: *inf*) *n* мама ♦ *adj*: **to keep** ~ **about sth** помалкивать (*impf*) о чём-н
**mumble** ['mʌmbl] *vt* бормотать (пробормотать *pf*) ♦ *vi* бормотать (*impf*)
**mummy** ['mʌmɪ] *n* (*BRIT*: *inf*) мамуля, мама; (*corpse*) мумия
**mumps** [mʌmps] *n* свинка
**munch** [mʌntʃ] *vti* жевать (*impf*)
**mundane** [mʌn'deɪn] *adj* обыденный
**municipal** [mju:'nɪsɪpl] *adj* муниципальный
**mural** ['mjuərl] *n* фреска, настенная роспись *f*
**murder** ['mə:dər] *n* убийство (*умышленное*) ♦ *vt* убивать (убить *pf*) (*умышленно*); ~**er** *n* убийца *m/f*
**murky** ['mə:kɪ] *adj* (*street, night*) мрачный; (*water*) мутный

**murmur** ['məːmər] *n* (*of voices, waves*) ро́пот ♦ *vti* шепта́ть (*impf*)
**muscle** ['mʌsl] *n* мы́шца, му́скул
**muscular** ['mʌskjulər] *adj* (*pain, injury*) мы́шечный; (*person*) му́скулистый
**museum** [mjuː'zɪəm] *n* музе́й
**mushroom** ['mʌʃrum] *n* гриб
**music** ['mjuːzɪk] *n* му́зыка; ~**al** *adj* музыка́льный; (*sound, tune*) мелоди́чный ♦ *n* мюзикл; ~**ian** [mjuː'zɪʃən] *n* музыка́нт
**Muslim** ['mʌzlɪm] *n* мусульма́нин(нка) ♦ *adj* мусульма́нский
**mussel** ['mʌsl] *n* ми́дия
**must** [mʌst] *n* (*need*) необходи́мость *f* ♦ *aux vb* (*necessity*): **I ~ go** мне на́до *or* ну́жно идти́; (*obligation*): **I ~ do it** я до́лжен э́то сде́лать; (*probability*): **he ~ be there by now** он до́лжен уже́ быть там; **you ~ come and see me soon** Вы обяза́тельно должны́ ско́ро ко мне зайти́; **why ~ he behave so badly?** отчего́ он так пло́хо себя́ ведёт?
**mustache** ['mʌstæʃ] *n* (*US*) = **moustache**
**mustard** ['mʌstəd] *n* горчи́ца
**muster** ['mʌstər] *vt* (*support, energy*) собира́ть (собра́ть *pf*); (*troops*) набира́ть (набра́ть *pf*)
**mustn't** ['mʌsnt] = **must not**
**mute** [mjuːt] *adj* (*silent*) безмо́лвный
**mutilate** ['mjuːtɪleɪt] *vt* (*person*) уве́чить (изуве́чить *pf*); (*thing*) уро́довать (изуро́довать *pf*)
**mutiny** ['mjuːtɪnɪ] *n* мяте́ж, бунт
**mutter** ['mʌtər] *vti* бормота́ть (*impf*)
**mutton** ['mʌtn] *n* бара́нина
**mutual** ['mjuːtʃuəl] *adj* (*feeling, help*) взаи́мный; (*friend, interest*)

о́бщий; ~ **understanding** взаимопонима́ние; ~**ly** *adv* взаи́мно
**muzzle** ['mʌzl] *n* (*of dog*) мо́рда; (*of gun*) ду́ло; (*for dog*) намо́рдник ♦ *vt* (*dog*) надева́ть (наде́ть *pf*) намо́рдник на +*acc*

---
KEYWORD
---

**my** [maɪ] *adj* **1** мой; (*referring back to subject of sentence*) свой; **this is my house/car** э́то мой дом/моя́ маши́на; **is this my pen or yours?** э́то моя́ ру́чка или Ва́ша?; **I've lost my key** я потеря́л свой ключ
**2** (*with parts of the body etc*): **I've washed my hair/cut my finger** я помы́л го́лову/поре́зал па́лец

---
KEYWORD
---

**myself** [maɪ'sɛlf] *pron* **1** (*reflexive*): **I've hurt myself** я уши́бся; **I consider myself clever** я счита́ю себя́ у́мным; **I am ashamed of myself** мне сты́дно за моё поведе́ние
**2** (*complement*): **she's the same age as myself** она́ одного́ во́зраста со мной
**3** (*after prep*: +*gen*) себя́; (: +*dat*, +*prp*) себе́; (: +*instr*) собо́й; **I wanted to keep the book for myself** я хоте́л оста́вить кни́гу себе́; **I sometimes talk to myself** иногда́ я сам с собо́й разгова́риваю; **(all) by myself** (*alone*) сам; **I made it all by myself** я всё э́то сде́лал сам
**4** (*emphatic*) сам; **I myself chose the flowers** я сам выбира́л цветы́

**mysterious** [mɪs'tɪərɪəs] *adj* таи́нственный
**mystery** ['mɪstərɪ] *n* (*puzzle*)

загáдка
**mystical** ['mɪstɪkl] *adj* мисти́ческий
**myth** [mɪθ] *n* миф; **~ology** *n* мифолóгия

# N, n

**n/a** *abbr* (= *not applicable*) не применя́ется
**nag** [næg] *vt* (*scold*) пили́ть (*impf*)
**nail** [neɪl] *n* нóготь *m*; (*TECH*) гвоздь *m* ♦ *vt*: **to ~ sth to** прибива́ть (приби́ть *pf*) что-н к +*dat*; **~ polish** *n* лак для ногтéй
**naive** [naɪ'iːv] *adj* наи́вный
**naked** ['neɪkɪd] *adj* гóлый
**name** [neɪm] *n* (*of person*) и́мя *nt*; (*of place, object*) назва́ние; (*of pet*) кли́чка ♦ *vt* называ́ть (назва́ть *pf*); **what's your ~?** как Вас зову́т?; **my ~ is Peter** меня́ зову́т Пи́тер; **what's the ~ of this place?** как называ́ется э́то мéсто?; **by ~** по и́мени; **in the ~ of** (*for the sake of* ) во и́мя +*gen*; (*representing*) от и́мени +*gen*; **~less** *adj* (*unknown*) безымя́нный; (*anonymous*) неизвéстный; **~ly** *adv* а и́менно
**nanny** ['nænɪ] *n* ня́ня
**nap** [næp] *n* (*sleep*) корóткий сон
**napkin** ['næpkɪn] *n* (*also*: **table ~**) салфéтка
**nappy** ['næpɪ] *n* (*BRIT*) подгу́зник
**narrative** ['nærətɪv] *n* истóрия, пóвесть *f*
**narrator** [nə'reɪtər] *n* (*in book*) расскáзчик(ица); (*in film*) ди́ктор
**narrow** ['nærəu] *adj* у́зкий; (*majority, advantage*) незначи́тельный ♦ *vi* (*road*) сужа́ться (су́зиться *pf*); ( *gap, difference*) уменьша́ться (умéньшиться *pf*) ♦ *vt*: **to ~ sth down to** своди́ть (свести́ *pf*) что-н к +*dat*; **to have a ~ escape**

едва́ спасти́сь (*pf*)
**nasal** ['neɪzl] *adj* (*voice*) гнуса́вый
**nasty** ['nɑːstɪ] *adj* (*unpleasant*) проти́вный; (*malicious*) злóбный; (*situation, wound*) сквéрный
**nation** ['neɪʃən] *n* нарóд; (*state*) страна́; (*native population*) на́ция
**national** ['næʃənl] *adj* национа́льный; **National Health Service** *n* (*BRIT*) госуда́рственная слу́жба здравоохранéния; **National Insurance** *n* (*BRIT*) госуда́рственное страхова́ние; **~ism** *n* национали́зм; **~ist** *adj* националисти́ческий; **~ity** [næʃə'nælɪtɪ] *n* (*status*) гражда́нство; (*ethnic group*) нарóдность *f*
**nationwide** ['neɪʃənwaɪd] *adj* общенарóдный ♦ *adv* по всей странé
**native** ['neɪtɪv] *n* (*local inhabitant*) мéстный(ая) жи́тель(ница) *m(f)* ♦ *adj* (*indigenous*) кореннóй, искóнный; (*of one's birth*) роднóй; (*innate*) врождённый; **a ~ of Russia** урожéнец(нка) Росси́и; **a ~ speaker of Russian** носи́тель(ница) *m(f)* ру́сского языка́
**NATO** ['neɪtəu] *n abbr* (= *North Atlantic Treaty Organization*) НА́ТО
**natural** ['nætʃrəl] *adj* (*behaviour*) естéственный; (*aptitude, materials*) прирóдный; (*disaster*) стихи́йный; **~ist** *n* натурали́ст; **~ly** *adv* естéственно; (*innately*) от прирóды; (*in nature*) естéственным óбразом; **~ly, I refused** естéственно, я отказа́лся
**nature** ['neɪtʃər] *n* (*also*: **Nature**) прирóда; (*character*) нату́ра; (*sort*) хара́ктер; **by ~** (*person*) по нату́ре; (*event, thing*) по прирóде
**naughty** ['nɔːtɪ] *adj* (*child*)

непослу́шный, озорно́й

**nausea** ['nɔːsɪə] *n* тошнота́

**nautical** ['nɔːtɪkl] *adj* морско́й

**naval** ['neɪvl] *adj* вое́нно-морско́й

**navel** ['neɪvl] *n* пупо́к

**navigate** ['nævɪgeɪt] *vt* (*NAUT, AVIAT*) управля́ть (*impf*) +*instr* ♦ *vi* определя́ть (определи́ть *pf*) маршру́т

**navigation** [nævɪ'geɪʃən] *n* (*science*) навига́ция; (*of*) управле́ние (+*instr*)

**navigator** ['nævɪgeɪtəʳ] *n* штурма́н

**navy** ['neɪvɪ] *n* вое́нно-морско́й флот; **~(-blue)** *adj* тёмно-си́ний

**Nazi** ['nɑːtsɪ] *n* наци́ст(ка)

**NB** *abbr* (*note well: = nota bene*) NB, нотабе́не

**near** [nɪəʳ] *adj* бли́зкий ♦ *adv* бли́зко ♦ *prep* (*also: ~ **to**: space*) во́зле +*gen*, о́коло +*gen*; (: *time*) к +*dat*, о́коло +*gen*; **~by** *adj* близлежа́щий ♦ *adv* поблизости; **~ly** *adv* почти́; **I ~ly fell** я чуть (бы́ло) не упа́л

**neat** [niːt] *adj* (*person, place*) опря́тный; (*work*) аккура́тный; (*clear: categories*) чёткий; (*esp US : inf*) кла́ссный; **~ly** *adv* (*dress*) опря́тно; (*work*) аккура́тно; (*sum up*) чётко

**necessarily** ['nɛsɪsrɪlɪ] *adv* неизбе́жно

**necessary** ['nɛsɪsrɪ] *adj* необходи́мый; (*inevitable*) обяза́тельный, неизбе́жный; **it's not ~** э́то не обяза́тельно; **it is ~ to/that ...** необходи́мо +*infin* что́бы ...

**necessity** [nɪ'sɛsɪtɪ] *n* необходи́мость *f*; **necessities** *npl* (*essentials*) предме́ты *mpl* пе́рвой необходи́мости

**neck** [nɛk] *n* (*ANAT*) ше́я; (*of garment*) во́рот; (*of bottle*) го́рлышко; **~lace** ['nɛklɪs] *n*

ожере́лье

**need** [niːd] *n* потре́бность *f*; (*deprivation*) нужда́; (*necessity*): **~ (for)** нужда́ (в +*prp*) ♦ *vt*: **I ~ time/ money** мне ну́жно вре́мя/нужны́ де́ньги; **there's no ~ to worry** не́зачем волнова́ться; **I ~ to see him** мне на́до *or* ну́жно с ним уви́деться; **you don't ~ to leave yet** Вам ещё не пора́ уходи́ть

**needle** ['niːdl] *n* игла́, иго́лка; (*for knitting*) спи́ца ♦ *vt* (*fig : inf*) подка́лывать (подколо́ть *pf*)

**needless** ['niːdlɪs] *adj* изли́шний; **~ to say** само́ собо́й разуме́ется

**needn't** ['niːdnt] = **need not**

**needy** ['niːdɪ] *adj* нужда́ющийся

**negative** ['nɛgətɪv] *adj* (*also ELEC*) отрица́тельный ♦ *n* (*PHOT*) негати́в

**neglect** [nɪ'glɛkt] *vt* (*child, work*) забра́сывать (забро́сить *pf*); (*garden, health*) запуска́ть (запусти́ть *pf*); (*duty*) пренебрега́ть (пренебре́чь *pf*) ♦ *n*: **~ (of)** невнима́ние (к +*dat*); **in a state of ~** в запусте́нии

**negligence** ['nɛglɪdʒəns] *n* хала́тность *f*

**negligible** ['nɛglɪdʒɪbl] *adj* ничто́жный

**negotiate** [nɪ'gəuʃɪeɪt] *vt* (*treaty, deal*) заключа́ть (заключи́ть *pf*); (*obstacle*) преодолева́ть (преодоле́ть *pf*); (*corner*) огиба́ть (обогну́ть *pf*) ♦ *vi*: **to ~ (with sb for sth)** вести́ (*impf*) перегово́ры (с кем-н о чём-н)

**negotiation** [nɪgəuʃɪ'eɪʃən] *n* (*of treaty, deal*) заключе́ние; (*of obstacle*) преодоле́ние; **~s** перегово́ры *mpl*

**negotiator** [nɪ'gəuʃɪeɪtəʳ] *n* уча́стник перегово́ров

**neigh** [neɪ] *vi* ржать (*impf*)

**neighbour** ['neɪbəʳ] (*US* **neighbor**)

*n* сосе́д(ка); **~hood** *n* (*place*) райо́н; (*people*) сосе́ди *mpl*; **~ing** *adj* сосе́дний
**neither** ['naɪðər] *adj* ни тот, ни друго́й ♦ *conj*: **I didn't move and ~ did John** ни я, ни Джон не дви́нулись с ме́ста ♦ *pron*: ~ **of them came** ни тот ни друго́й не пришли́, ни оди́н из них не пришёл; ~ **version is true** ни та ни друга́я ве́рсия не верна́; ~ ... **nor** ... ни ..., ни ...; ~ **good nor bad** ни хорошо́, ни пло́хо
**neon** ['ni:ɔn] *n* нео́н
**nephew** ['nevju:] *n* племя́нник
**nerve** [nə:v] *n* (*ANAT*) нерв; (*courage*) вы́держка; (*impudence*) на́глость *f*
**nervous** ['nə:vəs] *adj* не́рвный; **to be** *or* **feel ~** не́рвничать (*impf*); ~ **breakdown** *n* не́рвный срыв; **~ness** *n* не́рвность *f*
**nest** [nest] *n* гнездо́
**nestle** ['nesl] *vi* приюти́ться (*pf*)
**net** [net] *n* (*also fig*) сеть *f*; (*SPORT*) се́тка; (*COMPUT*): **the Net** Сеть *f* ♦ *adj* (*COMM*) чи́стый ♦ *vt* (*fish*) лови́ть (пойма́ть *pf*) в сеть; (*profit*) приноси́ть (принести́ *pf*)
**Netherlands** ['neðələndz] *npl*: **the ~** Нидерла́нды *pl*
**nett** [net] *adj* = **net**
**nettle** ['netl] *n* крапи́ва
**network** ['netwə:k] *n* сеть *f*
**neurotic** [njuə'rɔtɪk] *adj* неврастени́чный
**neutral** ['nju:trəl] *adj* нейтра́льный ♦ *n* (*AUT*) холосто́й ход
**never** ['nevər] *adv* никогда́; ~ **in my life** никогда́ в жи́зни; **~theless** *adv* тем не ме́нее
**new** [nju:] *adj* (*brand new*) но́вый; (*recent*) неда́вний; **~born** *adj* новоро́жденный; **~comer** *n* новичо́к; **~ly** *adv* неда́вно
**news** [nju:z] *n* (*good, bad*)

но́вость *f*, изве́стие; **a piece of ~** но́вость; **the ~** (*RADIO, TV*) но́вости *fpl*; ~ **agency** *n* информацио́нное аге́нтство; **~letter** *n* информацио́нный бюллете́нь *m*; **~reader** *n* ди́ктор (*програ́ммы новосте́й*)
**New Year** *n* Но́вый год; **Happy ~!** С Но́вым го́дом!; **~'s Day** *n* пе́рвое января́; **~'s Eve** *n* кану́н Но́вого го́да
**New Zealand** [nju:'zi:lənd] *n* Но́вая Зела́ндия
**next** [nekst] *adj* сле́дующий; (*adjacent*) сосе́дний ♦ *adv* пото́м, зате́м ♦ *prep*: ~ **to** ря́дом с +*instr*, во́зле +*gen*; ~ **time** в сле́дующий раз; **the ~ day** на сле́дующий день; ~ **year** в бу́дущем *or* сле́дующем году́; **in the ~ 15 minutes** в ближа́йшие 15 мину́т; ~ **to nothing** почти́ ничего́; ~ **please!** сле́дующий, пожа́луйста!; ~ **door** *adv* по сосе́дству, ря́дом ♦ *adj* (*neighbour*) ближа́йший; ~ **of kin** *n* ближа́йший ро́дственник
**NHS** *n abbr* (*BRIT*) = **National Health Service**
**nib** [nɪb] *n* перо́
**nibble** ['nɪbl] *vt* надку́сывать (надкуси́ть *pf*)
**nice** [naɪs] *adj* прия́тный, хоро́ший; (*attractive*) симпати́чный; **to look ~** хорошо́ вы́глядеть (*impf*); **that's very ~ of you** о́чень ми́ло с Ва́шей стороны́
**nick** [nɪk] *n* (*in skin*) поре́з; (*in surface*) зару́бка ♦ *vt* (*inf: steal*) ута́скивать (утащи́ть *pf*); **in the ~ of time** как раз во́время
**nickel** ['nɪkl] *n* ни́кель *m*; (*US: coin*) моне́та в 5 це́нтов
**nickname** ['nɪkneɪm] *n* кли́чка, про́звище ♦ *vt* прозыва́ть

(прозва́ть *pf*)

**nicotine** ['nɪkəti:n] *n* никоти́н

**niece** [ni:s] *n* племя́нница

**niggling** ['nɪglɪŋ] *adj* навя́зчивый

**night** [naɪt] *n* ночь *f*; (*evening*) ве́чер; **at~, by ~** но́чью; **all ~ long** всю ночь напролёт; **in** or **during the ~** но́чью; **last ~** вчера́ но́чью; (*evening*) вчера́ ве́чером; **the ~ before last** позапро́шлой но́чью; (*evening*) позавчера́ ве́чером; **~club** *n* ночно́й клуб; **~dress** *n* ночна́я руба́шка; **~fall** *n* су́мерки *pl*; **~gown** *n* = **nightdress**

**nightingale** ['naɪtɪŋgeɪl] *n* солове́й

**nightlife** ['naɪtlaɪf] *n* ночна́я жизнь *f*

**nightly** ['naɪtlɪ] *adj* (*every night*) ежено́щный ♦ *adv* ежено́щно

**nightmare** ['naɪtmeəʳ] *n* кошма́р

**nil** [nɪl] *n* нуль *m*; (*BRIT: score*) ноль *m*

**nimble** ['nɪmbl] *adj* (*agile*) шу́стрый; (*alert*) сообрази́тельный

**nine** [naɪn] *n* де́вять; **~teen** *n* девятна́дцать; **~teenth** *adj* девятна́дцатый; **~tieth** *adj* девяно́стый; **~ty** *n* девяно́сто

**ninth** [naɪnθ] *adj* девя́тый

**nip** [nɪp] *vt* (*pinch*) щипа́ть (ущипну́ть *pf*); (*bite*) куса́ть (укуси́ть *pf*) ♦ *vi* (*BRIT : inf* ): **to ~ out** выска́кивать (вы́скочить *pf*)

**nipple** ['nɪpl] *n* (*ANAT*) сосо́к

**nitrogen** ['naɪtrədʒən] *n* азо́т

KEYWORD

**no** [nəu] (*pl* **noes**) *adv* (*opposite of "yes"*) нет; **are you coming? - no (I'm not)** Вы придёте? -нет(, не приду́); **no thank you** нет, спаси́бо

♦ *adj* (*not any*): **I have no money/ books** у меня́ нет де́нег/книг; **there is no one here** здесь

никого́ нет; **it is of no importance at all** э́то не име́ет никако́го значе́ния; **no system is totally fair** никака́я систе́ма не явля́ется по́лностью справедли́вой; **"no entry"** "вход воспрещён"; **"no smoking"** "не кури́ть"

♦ *n*: **there were twenty noes** два́дцать голосо́в бы́ли "про́тив"

**nobility** [nəu'bɪlɪtɪ] *n* (*class*) знать *f*, дворя́нство

**noble** ['nəubl] *adj* (*aristocratic*) дворя́нский, зна́тный; (*high-minded*) благоро́дный

**nobody** ['nəubədɪ] *pron* никто́

**nocturnal** [nɔk'tə:nl] *adj* ночно́й

**nod** [nɔd] *vi* кива́ть (*impf*) ♦ *n* киво́к ♦ *vt*: **to ~ one's head** кива́ть (кивну́ть *pf*) голово́й; **~ off** *vi* задрема́ть (*pf*)

**noise** [nɔɪz] *n* шум

**noisy** ['nɔɪzɪ] *adj* шу́мный

**nominal** ['nɔmɪnl] *adj* номина́льный

**nominate** ['nɔmɪneɪt] *vt* (*propose*): **to ~ sb (for)** выставля́ть (вы́ставить *pf*) кандидату́ру кого́-н (на +*acc*); (*appoint*): **to ~ sb (to/as)** назнача́ть (назна́чить *pf*) кого́-н (на +*acc*/+*instr*)

**nomination** [nɔmɪ'neɪʃən] *n* (*see vb*) выставле́ние; назначе́ние

**nominee** [nɔmɪ'ni:] *n* кандида́т

**non-** [nɔn] *prefix* не-

**none** [nʌn] *pron* (*person*) никто́, ни оди́н; (*thing: countable*) ничто́, ни оди́н; (: *uncountable*) ничего́; **~ of you** никто́ or ни оди́н из вас; **I've ~ left** у меня́ ничего́ не оста́лось

**nonetheless** ['nʌnðə'lɛs] *adv* тем не ме́нее, всё же

**nonfiction** [nɔn'fɪkʃən] *n* документа́льная литерату́ра

**nonsense** ['nɔnsəns] *n* ерунда́,

чепуха́

**non-smoker** [nɒn'sməukə<sup>r</sup>] *adj*
некуря́щий *m adj*

**nonstop** *adj* (*conversation*)
беспреры́вный; (*flight*)
беспоса́дочный ♦ *adv* (*speak*)
беспреры́вно; (*fly*) без поса́дки

**noodles** ['nu:dlz] *npl* вермише́ль
*fsg*

**noon** [nu:n] *n* по́лдень *m*

**no-one** ['nəuwʌn] *pron* = **nobody**

**noose** [nu:s] *n* пе́тля

**nor** [nɔ:<sup>r</sup>] *conj* = **neither** ♦ *adv see*
**neither**

**norm** [nɔ:m] *n* но́рма

**normal** ['nɔ:ml] *adj* норма́льный;
**~ly** *adv* (*usually*) обы́чно; (*properly*)
норма́льно

**north** [nɔ:θ] *n* се́вер ♦ *adj*
се́верный ♦ *adv* (*go*) на се́вер;
(*be*) к се́веру; **North Africa** *n*
Се́верная Африка; **North
America** *n* Се́верная Аме́рика;
**~east** *n* се́веро-восто́к; **~erly**
['nɔ:ðəlɪ] *adj* се́верный; **~ern**
['nɔ:ðən] *adj* се́верный; **Northern
Ireland** *n* Се́верная Ирла́ндия;
**North Pole** *n* Се́верный по́люс;
**North Sea** *n* Се́верное мо́ре;
**~west** *n* се́веро-за́пад

**Norway** ['nɔ:weɪ] *n* Норве́гия

**Norwegian** [nɔ:'wi:dʒən] *adj*
норве́жский

**nose** [nəuz] *n* нос; (*sense of smell*)
нюх, чутьё; **~bleed** *n* носово́е
кровотече́ние; **~y** ['nəuzɪ] *adj*
(*inf*) = **nosy**

**nostalgia** [nɒs'tældʒɪə] *n*
ностальги́я

**nostalgic** [nɒs'tældʒɪk] *adj* (*memory,
film*) ностальги́ческий; **to be ~
(for)** испы́тывать (*impf*)
ностальги́ю (по +*dat*), тоскова́ть
(*impf*) по +*dat*

**nostril** ['nɒstrɪl] *n* ноздря́

**nosy** ['nəuzɪ] *adj* (*inf*): **to be ~**

сова́ть (*impf*) нос в чужи́е дела́

**not** [nɒt] *adv* нет; (*before verbs*) не;
**he is ~** *or* **isn't at home** его́ нет
до́ма; **he asked me ~ to do it** он
попроси́л меня́ не де́лать э́того;
**you must ~** *or* **you mustn't do
that** (*forbidden*) э́того нельзя́
де́лать; **it's too late, isn't it?** уже́
сли́шком по́здно, не пра́вда ли?;
**~ that ...** не то, что́бы ...; **~ yet**
нет ещё, ещё нет; **~ now** не
сейча́с; *see also* **all**; **only**

**notably** ['nəutəblɪ] *adv* (*particularly*)
осо́бенно; (*markedly*) заме́тно

**notch** [nɒtʃ] *n* насе́чка

**note** [nəut] *n* (*record*) за́пись *f*;
(*letter*) запи́ска; (*also*: **foot~**)
сно́ска; (*also*: **bank~**) банкно́та;
(*MUS*) но́та; (*tone*) тон ♦ *vt*
(*observe*) замеча́ть (заме́тить *pf*);
(*also*: **~ down**) запи́сывать
(записа́ть *pf*); **~book** *n* записна́я
кни́жка; **~d** *adj* изве́стный; **~pad**
*n* блокно́т; **~paper** *n* пи́счая
бума́га

**nothing** ['nʌθɪŋ] *n* ничто́; (*zero*)
ноль *m*; **he does ~** он ничего́ не
де́лает; **there is ~ to do/be said**
де́лать/сказа́ть не́чего; **~ new/
much/of the sort** ничего́ но́вого/
осо́бенного/подо́бного; **for ~**
да́ром

**notice** ['nəutɪs] *n* (*announcement*)
объявле́ние; (*warning*)
предупрежде́ние ♦ *vt* замеча́ть
(заме́тить *pf*); **to take ~ of**
обраща́ть (обрати́ть *pf*)
внима́ние на +*acc*; **at short ~** без
предупрежде́ния; **until further ~**
впредь до дальне́йшего
уведомле́ния; **~able** *adj*
заме́тный; **~ board** *n* доска́
объявле́ний

**notify** ['nəutɪfaɪ] *vt*: **to ~ sb (of sth)**
уведомля́ть (уве́домить *pf*)
кого́-н (о чём-н)

**notion** ['nəuʃən] n (idea) поня́тие; (opinion) представле́ние

**notorious** [nəu'tɔːrɪəs] adj печа́льно изве́стный

**noun** [naun] n (и́мя nt) существи́тельное nt adj

**nourish** ['nʌrɪʃ] vt пита́ть (impf); (fig) взра́щивать (взрасти́ть pf); **~ing** adj пита́тельный; **~ment** n (food) пита́ние

**novel** ['nɔvl] n рома́н ♦ adj оригина́льный; **~ist** n романи́ст(ка); **~ty** n (newness) новизна́; (object) нови́нка

**November** [nəu'vɛmbər] n ноя́брь m

**novice** ['nɔvɪs] n (in job) новичо́к

**now** [nau] adv тепе́рь, сейча́с ♦ conj: **~ (that)** ... тепе́рь, когда́ ...; **right ~** пря́мо сейча́с; **by ~** к настоя́щему вре́мени; **~ and then** or **again** вре́мя от вре́мени; **from ~ on** отны́не, впредь; **until ~** до сих пор; **~adays** adv в на́ши дни

**nowhere** ['nəuwɛər] adv (be) нигде́; (go) никуда́

**nuclear** ['njuːklɪər] adj я́дерный

**nucleus** ['njuːklɪəs] (pl **nuclei**) n ядро́

**nude** [njuːd] adj обнажённый, наго́й ♦ n: **in the ~** в обнажённом ви́де

**nudge** [nʌdʒ] vt подта́лкивать (подтолкну́ть pf)

**nudity** ['njuːdɪtɪ] n нагота́

**nuisance** ['njuːsns] n доса́да; (person) зану́да; **what a ~!** кака́я доса́да!

**numb** [nʌm] adj: **~ (with)** онеме́вший (от +gen); **to go ~** неме́ть (онеме́ть pf)

**number** ['nʌmbər] n но́мер; (MATH) число́; (written figure) ци́фра; (quantity) коли́чество ♦ vt (pages etc) нумерова́ть (пронумерова́ть pf); (amount to) насчи́тывать (impf); **a ~ of** не́сколько +gen, ряд +gen; **~plate** n (BRIT) номерно́й знак

**numeral** ['njuːmərəl] n ци́фра

**numerical** [njuːˈmɛrɪkl] adj (value) числово́й; **in ~ order** по номера́м

**numerous** ['njuːmərəs] adj многочи́сленный; **on ~ occasions** многокра́тно

**nun** [nʌn] n мона́хиня

**nurse** [nəːs] n медсестра́; (also: **male ~**) медбра́т ♦ vt (patient) уха́живать (impf) за +instr

**nursery** ['nəːsərɪ] n (institution) я́сли pl; (room) де́тская f adj; (for plants) пито́мник; **~ rhyme** n де́тская пе́сенка; **~ school** n де́тский сад

**nursing** ['nəːsɪŋ] n (profession) профе́ссия медсестры́; **~ home** n ча́стный дом для престаре́лых

**nurture** ['nəːtʃər] vt (child, plant) выра́щивать (вы́растить pf)

**nut** [nʌt] n (BOT) оре́х; (TECH) га́йка; **~meg** n муска́тный оре́х

**nutrient** ['njuːtrɪənt] n пита́тельное вещество́

**nutrition** [njuːˈtrɪʃən] n (nourishment) пита́тельность f; (diet) пита́ние

**nutritious** [njuːˈtrɪʃəs] adj пита́тельный

**nylon** ['naɪlɔn] n нейло́н ♦ adj нейло́новый

# O, o

**oak** [əuk] n дуб ♦ adj дубо́вый

**OAP** n abbr (BRIT) = **old age pensioner**

**oar** [ɔːr] n весло́

**oasis** [əu'eɪsɪs] (pl **oases**) n оа́зис

**oath** [əuθ] n (promise) кля́тва; (: LAW) прися́га; (swear word) прокля́тие; **on** (BRIT) or **under ~**

под прися́гой
**oats** [əuts] *npl* овёс *msg*
**obedience** [ə'bi:dɪəns] *n*
повинове́ние, послуша́ние
**obedient** [ə'bi:dɪənt] *adj*
послу́шный
**obese** [əu'bi:s] *adj* ту́чный
**obey** [ə'beɪ] *vt* подчиня́ться
(подчини́ться *pf*) +*dat*,
повинова́ться (*impf/pf*) +*dat*
**obituary** [ə'bɪtjuərɪ] *n* некроло́г
**object** *n* ['ɔbdʒɪkt] *vb* [əb'dʒɛkt] *n*
(*thing*) предме́т; (*aim, purpose*)
цель *f*; (*of affection, desires*)
объе́кт; (*LING*) дополне́ние ♦ *vi*:
**to ~ (to)** возража́ть (возрази́ть
*pf*) (про́тив +*gen*); **money is no ~**
де́ньги - не пробле́ма; **~ion**
[əb'dʒɛkʃən] *n* возраже́ние; **I have
no ~ion to ...** я не име́ю никаки́х
возраже́ний про́тив +*gen* ...;
**~ionable** [əb'dʒɛkʃənəbl] *adj*
(*language, conduct*)
возмути́тельный; (*person*)
гну́сный; **~ive** [əb'dʒɛktɪv] *adj*
объекти́вный ♦ *n* цель *f*
**obligation** [ɔblɪ'geɪʃən] *n*
обяза́тельство
**obligatory** [ə'blɪgətərɪ] *adj*
обяза́тельный
**oblige** [ə'blaɪdʒ] *vt* обя́зывать
(обяза́ть *pf*); (*force*): **to ~ sb to do**
обя́зывать (обяза́ть *pf*) кого́-н
+*infin*; **I'm much ~d to you for
your help** (*grateful*) я о́чень
обя́зан Вам за Ва́шу по́мощь
**obliging** [ə'blaɪdʒɪŋ] *adj* любе́зный
**oblivion** [ə'blɪvɪən] *n* забве́ние
**oblivious** [ə'blɪvɪəs] *adj*: **to be ~ of**
*or* **to** не сознава́ть (*impf*) +*gen*
**obnoxious** [əb'nɔkʃəs] *adj*
отврати́тельный
**oboe** ['əubəu] *n* гобо́й
**obscene** [əb'si:n] *adj*
непристо́йный
**obscure** [əb'skjuə*] *adj* (*little known*)

неприме́тный; (*incomprehensible*)
сму́тный ♦ *vt* (*view etc*)
загора́живать (загороди́ть *pf*);
(*truth etc*) затемня́ть (затемни́ть
*pf*)
**observant** [əb'zə:vnt] *adj*
наблюда́тельный
**observation** [ɔbzə'veɪʃən] *n*
наблюде́ние; (*remark*) замеча́ние
**observe** [əb'zə:v] *vt* (*watch*)
наблюда́ть (*impf*) за +*instr*;
(*comment*) замеча́ть (заме́тить
*pf*); (*abide by*) соблюда́ть
(соблюсти́ *pf*); **~r** *n* наблюда́тель
*m*
**obsession** [əb'sɛʃən] *n* страсть *f*,
одержи́мость *f*
**obsessive** [əb'sɛsɪv] *adj* стра́стный,
одержи́мый
**obsolete** ['ɔbsəli:t] *adj* устаре́вший
**obstacle** ['ɔbstəkl] *n* препя́тствие
**obstinate** ['ɔbstɪnɪt] *adj* упря́мый
**obstruct** [əb'strʌkt] *vt* (*road, path*)
загора́живать (загороди́ть *pf*);
(*traffic, progress*) препя́тствовать
(воспрепя́тствовать *pf*) +*dat*;
**~ion** [əb'strʌkʃən] *n* (*of law*)
обстру́кция; (*object*) препя́тствие
**obtain** [əb'teɪn] *vt* приобрета́ть
(приобрести́ *pf*)
**obvious** ['ɔbvɪəs] *adj* очеви́дный;
**~ly** *adv* очеви́дно; (*of course*)
разуме́ется; **~ly not** разуме́ется,
нет
**occasion** [ə'keɪʒən] *n* (*time*) раз;
(*case, opportunity*) слу́чай; (*event*)
собы́тие; **~al** *adj* ре́дкий,
неча́стый; **~ally** *adv* и́зредка
**occupant** ['ɔkjupənt] *n* (*long-term*)
обита́тель(ница) *m(f)*
**occupation** [ɔkju'peɪʃən] *n*
заня́тие; (*MIL*) оккупа́ция
**occupy** ['ɔkjupaɪ] *vt* занима́ть
(заня́ть *pf*); (*country, attention*)
захва́тывать (захвати́ть *pf*); **to ~
o.s. with sth** занима́ться

(заня́ться pf) чем-н
**occur** [ə'kə:r] vi происходи́ть
(произойти́ pf), случа́ться
(случи́ться pf); (exist) встреча́ться
(встре́титься pf); **to ~ to sb**
приходи́ть (прийти́ pf) кому́-н в
го́лову; **~rence** n (event)
происше́ствие
**ocean** ['əuʃən] n океа́н
**o'clock** [ə'klɔk] adv: **it is five ~**
сейча́с пять часо́в
**October** [ɔk'təubər] n октя́брь m
**octopus** ['ɔktəpəs] n осьмино́г
**odd** [ɔd] adj (strange) стра́нный,
необы́чный; (uneven) нечётный;
(not paired) непа́рный; **60-~**
шестьдеся́т с ли́шним; **at ~ times**
времена́ми; **I was the ~ one out**
я был ли́шний; **~ly** adv (behave,
dress) стра́нно; see also **enough**;
**~s** npl (in betting) ста́вки fpl; **to be
at ~s (with)** быть (impf) не в
лада́х (с +instr )
**odour** ['əudər] (US **odor**) n за́пах

**of** [ɔv, əv] prep 1 (expressing
belonging): **the history of Russia**
исто́рия Росси́и; **a friend of ours**
наш друг; **a boy of 10** ма́льчик
десяти́ лет; **that was kind of you**
э́то бы́ло о́чень любе́зно с
Ва́шей стороны́; **a man of great
ability** челове́к больши́х
спосо́бностей; **the city of New
York** го́род Нью-Йо́рк; **south of
London** к ю́гу от Ло́ндона
2 (expressing quantity, amount,
dates etc): **a kilo of flour**
килогра́мм муки́; **how much of
this material do you need?**
ско́лько тако́й тка́ни Вам
ну́жно?; **there were three of them**
(people) их бы́ло тро́е; (objects) их
бы́ло три; **three of us stayed**
тро́е из нас оста́лись; **the 5th of**

**July** 5-ое ию́ля; **on the 5th of
July** 5-ого ию́ля
3 ( from) из +gen; **the house is
made of wood** дом сде́лан из
де́рева

**off** [ɔf] adv 1 (referring to distance,
time): **it's a long way off** э́то
далеко́ отсю́да; **the city is 5
miles off** до го́рода 5 миль; **the
game is 3 days off** до игры́
оста́лось 3 дня
2 (departure): **to go off to Paris/
Italy** уезжа́ть (уе́хать pf) в
Пари́ж/Ита́лию; **I must be off** мне
пора́ (идти́)
3 (removal): **to take off one's hat/
clothes** снима́ть (снять pf)
шля́пу/оде́жду; **the button came
off** пу́говица оторвала́сь; **ten
percent off** (COMM) ски́дка в
де́сять проце́нтов
4: **to be off** (on holiday) быть (impf)
в о́тпуске; **I'm off on Fridays** (day
off ) у меня́ выходно́й по
пя́тницам; **he was off on Friday**
(absent) в пя́тницу его́ не́ было
на рабо́те; **I have a day off** у
меня́ отгу́л; **to be off sick** не
рабо́тать (impf) по боле́зни
♦ adj (not on) вы́ключенный;
(: tap) закры́тый; (disconnected)
отключённый
2 (cancelled: meeting, match)
отменённый; (: agreement)
расто́ргнутый
3 (BRIT): **to go off** (milk)
прокиса́ть (проки́снуть pf);
(cheese, meat) по́ртиться
(испо́ртиться pf)
4: **on the off chance** на вся́кий
слу́чай; **to have an off day**
встава́ть (встать pf) с ле́вой ноги́
♦ prep 1 (indicating motion) с +gen;

**to fall off a cliff** упа́сть (pf) со скалы́ 2 (distant from) от +gen; **it's just off the M1** э́то недалеко́ от автостра́ды M1; **it's five km off the main road** э́то в пяти́ км от шоссе́; **to be off meat** (dislike) разлюби́ть (pf) мя́со

**offence** [ə'fens] (US **offense**) n (crime) правонаруше́ние; **to take ~ at** обижа́ться (оби́деться pf) на +acc

**offend** [ə'fend] vt (person) обижа́ть (оби́деть pf); **~er** n правонаруши́тель(ница) m(f); **~ing** adj соотве́тствующий

**offense** [ə'fens] n (US) = **offence**

**offensive** [ə'fensɪv] adj (remark, behaviour) оскорби́тельный ♦ n (MIL) наступле́ние ♦ **~ weapon** ору́дие нападе́ния

**offer** ['ɔfər] n предложе́ние ♦ vt предлага́ть (предложи́ть pf)

**office** ['ɔfɪs] n о́фис; (room) кабине́т; **doctor's ~** (US) кабине́т врача́; **to take ~** (person) вступа́ть (вступи́ть pf) в до́лжность

**officer** ['ɔfɪsər] n (MIL) офице́р; (also: **police ~**) полице́йский m adj; (: in Russia) милиционе́р

**official** [ə'fɪʃl] adj официа́льный ♦ n (of organization) должностно́е лицо́; **government ~** официа́льное лицо́

**off-licence** ['ɔflaɪsns] n (BRIT) ви́нный магази́н

**off-line** [ɔf'laɪn] adj (COMPUT) автоно́мный; (switched off) отключённый

**off-peak** ['ɔf'piːk] adj (heating, electricity) непи́ковый

**offset** ['ɔfset] (irreg) vt уравнове́шивать (уравнове́сить pf)

**offshore** [ɔf'ʃɔːr] adj (oilrig, fishing) морско́й; (COMM) оффшо́рный; **~ wind** ве́тер с бе́рега

**offspring** ['ɔfsprɪŋ] n inv о́тпрыск

**often** ['ɔfn] adv ча́сто; **how ~ ...?** как ча́сто ...?; **more ~ than not** ча́ще всего́; **as ~ as not** дово́льно ча́сто; **every so ~** вре́мя от вре́мени

**oil** [ɔɪl] n ма́сло; (petroleum) нефть f; (for heating) печно́е то́пливо ♦ vt сма́зывать (сма́зать pf); **~y** adj (rag) прома́сленный; (skin) жи́рный

**ointment** ['ɔɪntmənt] n мазь f

**O.K.** ['əu'keɪ] excl (inf) хорошо́, ла́дно

**old** [əuld] adj ста́рый; **how ~ are you?** ско́лько Вам лет?; **he's 10 years ~** ему́ 10 лет; **~ man** стари́к; **~ woman** стару́ха; **~er brother** ста́рший брат; **~ age** n ста́рость f; **~-fashioned** adj старомо́дный

**olive** ['ɔlɪv] n (fruit) масли́на, оли́вка ♦ adj оли́вковый; **~ oil** n оли́вковое ма́сло

**Olympic Games** npl: **the ~ Games** (also: **the ~s**) Олимпи́йские и́гры fpl

**omelet(te)** ['ɔmlɪt] n омле́т

**omen** ['əumən] n предзнаменова́ние

**ominous** ['ɔmɪnəs] adj злове́щий

**omission** [əu'mɪʃən] n про́пуск

**omit** [əu'mɪt] vt пропуска́ть (пропусти́ть pf)

---

KEYWORD

**on** [ɔn] prep 1 (position) на +prp; (motion) на +acc; **the book is on the table** кни́га на столе́; **to put the book on the table** класть (положи́ть pf) кни́гу на стол; **on the left** сле́ва; **the house is on the main road** дом стои́т у шоссе́ 2 (indicating means, method, condition etc): **on foot** пешко́м; **on**

**the plane/train** (*go*) на
самолёте/по́езде; (*be*) в
самолёте/по́езде; **on the radio/
television** по ра́дио/телеви́зору;
**she's on the telephone** она́
разгова́ривает по телефо́ну; **to
be on medication** принима́ть
(*impf*) лека́рства; **to be on
holiday/business** быть (*impf*) в
о́тпуске/командиро́вке
3 (*referring to time*): **on Friday** в
пя́тницу; **on Fridays** по
пя́тницам; **on June 20th** 20-ого
ию́ня; **a week on Friday** че́рез
неде́лю, счита́я с пя́тницы; **on
arrival** по прие́зде; **on seeing this**
уви́дев э́то
4 (*about, concerning*) о +*prp*;
**information on train services**
информа́ция о расписа́нии
поездо́в; **a book on physics**
кни́га по фи́зике
♦ *adv* 1 (*referring to dress*) в +*prp*; **to
have one's coat on** быть (*impf*) в
пальто́; **what's she got on?** во
что она́ была́ оде́та?; **she put
her boots/hat on** она́ наде́ла
сапоги́/шля́пу
2 (*further, continuously*) да́льше,
да́лее; **to walk on** идти́ (*impf*)
да́льше
♦ *adj* 1 (*functioning, in operation*)
включённый; (: *tap*) откры́тый; **is
the meeting still on?** (*not
cancelled*) собра́ние состои́тся?;
**there's a good film on at the
cinema** в кинотеа́тре идёт
хоро́ший фильм
2: **that's not on!** (*inf: of behaviour*)
так не пойдёт *or* не годи́тся!

**once** [wʌns] *adv* (оди́н) раз;
(*formerly*) когда́-то, одна́жды
♦ *conj* как то́лько; **at ~** сра́зу же;
(*simultaneously*) вме́сте; **~ a week**
(оди́н) раз в неде́лю; **~ more**

ещё раз; **~ and for all** раз и
навсегда́

**oncoming** [ˈɔnkʌmɪŋ] *adj*
встре́чный

KEYWORD

**one** [wʌn] *n* оди́н (*f* одна́, *nt* одно́,
*pl* одни́); **one hundred and fifty**
сто пятьдеся́т; **one day there
was a knock at the door**
одна́жды разда́лся стук в дверь;
**one by one** оди́н за други́м
♦ *adj* 1 (*sole*) еди́нственный; **the
one book which ...** еди́нственная
кни́га, кото́рая ...
2 (*same*) оди́н; **they all belong to
the one family** они́ все из одно́й
семьи́
♦ *pron* 1: **I'm the one who told
him** э́то я сказа́л ему́; **this one**
э́тот (*f* э́та, *nt* э́то); **that one** тот (*f*
та, *nt* то); **I've already got one** у
меня́ уже́ есть
2: **one another** друг дру́га; **do
you ever see one another?** Вы
когда́-нибудь ви́дитесь?; **they
didn't dare look at one another**
они́ не сме́ли взгляну́ть друг на
дру́га
3 (*impersonal*): **one never knows**
никогда́ не зна́ешь; **one has to
do it** на́до сде́лать э́то; **to cut
one's finger** поре́зать (*pf*) (себе́)
па́лец

**one:** **~-man** *adj* (*business*)
индивидуа́льный; **~-off** *n* (*BRIT*:
*inf*) едини́чный слу́чай; **~'s** *adj*:
**to dry ~'s hands** вытира́ть
(вы́тереть *pf*) ру́ки; **naturally ~
loves ~'s children** челове́ку
сво́йственно люби́ть свои́х
дете́й; **~self** *pron* (*reflexive*) себя́;
(*emphatic*) сам; (*after prep*: +*acc*,
+*gen*) себя́; (: +*dat*) себе́; (: +*instr*)
собо́й; (: +*prp*) себе́; **to hurt ~self**

ушибаться (ушибиться *pf*); **to keep sth for ~self** держать *(impf)* что-н при себе; **to talk to ~self** разговаривать *(impf)* с (самим) собой; **~-sided** *adj* односторонний; (*contest*) неравный; **~-way** *adj*: **~-way street** улица с односторонним движением

**on-line** [ɔn'laɪn] *adj* онлайновый; **to go ~** включаться (включиться *pf*) в сеть

**ongoing** ['ɔngəʊɪŋ] *adj* продолжающийся

**onion** ['ʌnjən] *n* лук

**only** ['əʊnlɪ] *adv* только ♦ *adj* единственный ♦ *conj* только; **not ~ ... but also ...** не только ..., но и ...

**onset** ['ɔnsɛt] *n* наступление

**onshore** ['ɔnʃɔ:r] *adj*: **~ wind** ветер с моря

**onward(s)** ['ɔnwəd(z)] *adv* вперёд, дальше; **from that time ~** с тех пор

**opal** ['əʊpl] *n* опал

**opaque** [əʊ'peɪk] *adj* матовый

**OPEC** *n abbr* (= *Organization of Petroleum-Exporting Countries*) ОПЕК

**open** ['əʊpn] *adj* открытый ♦ *vt* открывать (открыть *pf*) ♦ *vi* открываться (открыться *pf*); (*book, debate etc*) начинаться (начаться *pf*); **in the ~ (air)** на открытом воздухе; **~ up** *vt* открывать (открыть *pf*) ♦ *vi* открываться (открыться *pf*); **~ing** *adj* (*speech, remarks etc*) вступительный ♦ *n* (*gap, hole*) отверстие; (*job*) вакансия; **~ly** *adv* открыто; **~-minded** *adj* (*person*) открытый; **~-plan** *adj*: **~-plan office** офис с открытой планировкой

**opera** ['ɔpərə] *n* опера

**operate** ['ɔpəreɪt] *vt* управлять *(impf)* +*instr* ♦ *vi* действовать *(impf)*; (*MED*): **to ~ (on sb)** оперировать (прооперировать *pf*) (кого-н)

**operation** [ɔpə'reɪʃən] *n* операция; (*of machine: functioning*) работа; (: *controlling*) управление; **to be in ~** действовать *(impf)*; **he had an ~** (*MED*) ему сделали операцию; **~al** [ɔpə'reɪʃənl] *adj*: **the machine was ~al** машина функционировала

**operative** ['ɔpərətɪv] *adj* (*law etc*) действующий

**operator** ['ɔpəreɪtər] *n* (*TEL*) телефонист(ка); (*TECH*) оператор

**opinion** [ə'pɪnjən] *n* мнение; **in my ~** по моему мнению, по-моему; **~ poll** *n* опрос общественного мнения

**opponent** [ə'pəʊnənt] *n* оппонент, противник(ница); (*SPORT*) противник

**opportunity** [ɔpə'tju:nɪtɪ] *n* возможность *f*; **to take the ~ of doing** пользоваться (воспользоваться *pf*) случаем, чтобы +*infin*

**oppose** [ə'pəʊz] *vt* противиться (воспротивиться *pf*) +*dat*; **to be ~d to sth** противиться *(impf)* чему-н; **as ~d to** в противоположность +*dat*

**opposing** [ə'pəʊzɪŋ] *adj* (*ideas, forces*) противоборствующий; **the ~ team** команда противника

**opposite** ['ɔpəzɪt] *adj* противоположный ♦ *adv* напротив ♦ *prep* напротив +*gen* ♦ *n*: **the ~** противоположное *nt adj*

**opposition** [ɔpə'zɪʃən] *n* оппозиция; **the Opposition** (*POL*) оппозиционная партия

**oppress** [ə'prɛs] *vt* угнетать *(impf)*; **~ion** [ə'prɛʃən] *n* угнетение; **~ive**

*adj* (*régime*) угнета́тельский; (*weather, heat*) гнету́щий

**opt** [ɔpt] *vi*: **to ~ for** избира́ть (избра́ть *pf*); **to ~ to do** реша́ть (реши́ть *pf*) +*infin*; **~ out** *vi*: **to ~ out of** выходи́ть (вы́йти *pf*) из +*gen*

**optical** [ˈɔptɪkl] *adj* опти́ческий

**optician** [ɔpˈtɪʃən] *n* окули́ст

**optimism** [ˈɔptɪmɪzəm] *n* оптими́зм

**optimistic** [ɔptɪˈmɪstɪk] *adj* оптимисти́чный

**optimum** [ˈɔptɪməm] *adj* оптима́льный

**option** [ˈɔpʃən] *n* (*choice*) возмо́жность *f*, вариа́нт; **~al** *adj* необяза́тельный

**or** [ɔːr] *conj* и́ли; (*otherwise*): **~ (else)** а то, ина́че; (*with negative*): **he hasn't seen ~ heard anything** он ничего́ не ви́дел и не слы́шал

**oral** [ˈɔːrəl] *adj* у́стный; (*medicine*) ора́льный ♦ *vt* у́стный экза́мен

**orange** [ˈɔrɪndʒ] *n* апельси́н ♦ *adj* (*colour*) ора́нжевый

**orbit** [ˈɔːbɪt] *n* орби́та ♦ *vt* обраща́ться (обрати́ться *pf*) вокру́г +*gen*

**orchard** [ˈɔːtʃəd] *n* сад (*фрукто́вый*)

**orchestra** [ˈɔːkɪstrə] *n* (*MUS*) орке́стр

**orchid** [ˈɔːkɪd] *n* орхиде́я

**ordeal** [ɔːˈdiːl] *n* испыта́ние

**order** [ˈɔːdər] *n* зака́з; (*command*) прика́з; (*sequence, discipline*) поря́док ♦ *vt* зака́зывать (заказа́ть *pf*); (*command*) прика́зывать (приказа́ть *pf*) +*dat*; (*also*: **put in ~**) располага́ть (расположи́ть *pf*) по поря́дку; **in ~** в поря́дке; **in ~ to do** для того́ чтобы +*infin*; **out of ~** (*not in sequence*) не по поря́дку; (*not working*) неиспра́вный; **to ~ sb to**

**do** прика́зывать (приказа́ть *pf*) кому́-н +*infin*; **~ form** *n* бланк зака́за; **~ly** *n* (*MED*) санита́р ♦ *adj* (*room*) опря́тный; (*system*) упоря́доченный

**ordinary** [ˈɔːdnrɪ] *adj* обы́чный, обыкнове́нный; (*mediocre*) зауря́дный; **out of the ~** необыкнове́нный

**ore** [ɔːr] *n* руда́

**organ** [ˈɔːgən] *n* (*ANAT*) о́рган; (*MUS*) орга́н; **~ic** [ɔːˈgænɪk] *adj* (*fertilizer*) органи́ческий; (*food*) экологи́чески чи́стый; **~ism** *n* органи́зм

**organization** [ɔːgənaɪˈzeɪʃən] *n* организа́ция

**organize** [ˈɔːgənaɪz] *vt* организо́вывать (*impf/pf*), устра́ивать (устро́ить *pf*)

**orgasm** [ˈɔːgæzəm] *n* орга́зм

**Orient** [ˈɔːrɪənt] *n*: **the ~** Восто́к

**oriental** [ɔːrɪˈentl] *adj* восто́чный

**origin** [ˈɔrɪdʒɪn] *n* происхожде́ние; **~al** [əˈrɪdʒɪnl] *adj* первонача́льный; (*new*) оригина́льный; (*genuine*) по́длинный; (*imaginative*) самобы́тный ♦ *n* по́длинник, оригина́л; **~ally** [əˈrɪdʒɪnəlɪ] *adv* первонача́льно; **~ate** [əˈrɪdʒɪneɪt] *vi*: **to ~ate from** происходи́ть (произойти́ *pf*) от/из +*gen*; **to ~ate in** зарожда́ться (зароди́ться *pf*) в +*prp*

**ornament** [ˈɔːnəmənt] *n* (*decorative object*) украше́ние; **~al** [ɔːnəˈmentl] *adj* декорати́вный

**ornate** [ɔːˈneɪt] *adj* декорати́вный

**orphan** [ˈɔːfn] *n* сирота́ *m/f*; **~age** *n* де́тский дом

**orthodox** [ˈɔːθədɔks] *adj* ортодокса́льный; **the Russian Orthodox Church** Ру́сская правосла́вная це́рковь

**orthopaedic** [ɔːθəˈpiːdɪk] (*US*

orthopedic) adj ортопеди́ческий
**ostrich** ['ɒstrɪtʃ] n стра́ус
**other** ['ʌðəʳ] adj друго́й ♦ pron: **the
~ (one)** друго́й(а́я) m(f) adj,
друго́е nt adj ♦ adv: **~ than** кро́ме
+gen; **~s** (other people) други́е pl
adj; **the ~s** остальны́е pl adj; **the ~
day** на днях; **~wise** adv
(differently) ина́че, по-друго́му;
(apart from that) в остально́м
♦ conj а то, ина́че
**otter** ['ɒtəʳ] n вы́дра
**ought** [ɔːt] (pt **~**) aux vb: **I ~ to do it**
мне сле́дует э́то сде́лать; **this ~
to have been corrected** э́то
сле́довало испра́вить; **he ~ to
win** он до́лжен вы́играть
**ounce** [auns] n у́нция

---

**ounce** - у́нция. Ме́ра ве́са
ра́вная 28.349 гр.

---

**our** ['auəʳ] adj наш; see also **my**; **~s**
pron наш; (referring to subject of
sentence) свой; see also **mine¹**;
**~selves** pl pron (reflexive,
complement) себя́; (after prep: +acc,
+gen) себя́; (: +dat, +prp) себе́;
(: +instr) собо́й; (emphatic) са́ми;
(alone): **(all) by ~selves** са́ми; **let's
keep it between ~selves** дава́йте
оста́вим э́то ме́жду на́ми; see also
**myself**
**oust** [aust] vt изгоня́ть (изгна́ть pf)

---

KEYWORD

---

**out** [aut] adv 1 (not in): **they're out
in the garden** они́ в саду́; **out in
the rain/snow** под дождём/
сне́гом; **out here** здесь; **out there**
там; **to go out** выходи́ть (вы́йти
pf); **out loud** гро́мко
2 (not at home, absent): **he is out
at the moment** его́ сейча́с нет
(до́ма); **let's have a night out on
Friday** дава́йте пойдём куда́-

нибудь в пя́тницу ве́чером!
3 (indicating distance) в +prp; **the
boat was ten km out (from the
shore)** кора́бль находи́лся в
десяти́ км от бе́рега
4 (SPORT): **the ball is out** мяч за
преде́лами по́ля
♦ adj 1: **to be out** (unconscious)
быть (impf)без созна́ния; (out of
game) выбыва́ть (вы́быть pf);
(flowers) распуска́ться
(распусти́ться pf); (news, secret)
станови́ться (стать pf)
изве́стным(ой); ( fire, light, gas)
ту́хнуть (поту́хнуть pf), га́снуть
(пога́снуть pf); **to go out of
fashion** выходи́ть (вы́йти pf) из
мо́ды
2 ( finished): **before the week was
out** до оконча́ния неде́ли
3: **to be out to do** (intend )
намерева́ться (impf) +infin; **to be
out in one's calculations** (wrong)
ошиба́ться (ошиби́ться pf) в
расчётах
♦ prep 1 (outside, beyond) из +gen;
**to go out of the house** выходи́ть
(вы́йти pf) из до́ма; **to be out of
danger** (safe) быть (impf) вне
опа́сности
2 (cause, motive): **out of curiosity**
из любопы́тства; **out of fear/joy/
boredom** от стра́ха/ра́дости/
ску́ки; **out of grief** с го́ря; **out of
necessity** по необходи́мости
3 ( from, from among) из +gen
4 (without): **we are out of sugar/
petrol** у нас ко́нчился са́хар/
бензи́н

---

**out-and-out** ['autəndaut] adj
(villain) отъя́вленный
**outbreak** ['autbreɪk] n (of disease,
violence) вспы́шка; (of war)
нача́ло
**outburst** ['autbəːst] n взрыв

**outcast** ['autkɑːst] n изгой

**outcome** ['autkʌm] n исход

**outcry** ['autkraı] n негодование, протест

**outdated** [aut'deıtıd] adj (customs, ideas) отживший; (technology) устарелый

**outdo** [aut'duː] (irreg) vt превосходить (превзойти pf)

**outdoor** [aut'dɔːʳ] adj на открытом воздухе; (pool) открытый; **~s** adv на улице, на открытом воздухе

**outer** ['autəʳ] adj наружный; **~ space** n космическое пространство

**outfit** ['autfıt] n (clothes) костюм

**outgoing** ['autɡəuıŋ] adj (extrovert) общительный; (president, mayor etc) уходящий

**outing** ['autıŋ] n поход

**outlandish** [aut'lændıʃ] adj диковинный

**outlaw** ['autlɔː] vt объявлять (объявить pf) вне закона

**outlay** ['autleı] n затраты fpl

**outlet** ['autlɛt] n (hole) выходное отверстие; (pipe) сток; (COMM : also: **retail ~**) торговая точка; (for emotions) выход

**outline** ['autlaın] n (shape) контур, очертания ntpl; (sketch, explanation) набросок ♦ vt (fig) описывать (описать pf)

**outlook** ['autluk] n (attitude) взгляды mpl, воззрения ntpl; (prospects) перспективы fpl

**outlying** ['autlaııŋ] adj отдалённый

**outnumber** [aut'nʌmbəʳ] vt численно превосходить (превзойти pf)

**out-of-date** [autəv'deıt] adj (clothes) немодный; (equipment) устарелый

**out-of-the-way** ['autəvðə'weı] adj (place) глубинный

**outpatient** ['autpeıʃənt] n амбулаторный(ая) пациент(ка)

**output** ['autput] n (emotion) выработка, продукция; (COMPUT) выходные данные pl

**outrage** ['autreıdʒ] n (emotion) возмущение ♦ vt возмущать (возмутить pf); **~ous** [aut'reıdʒəs] adj возмутительный

**outright** [aut'raıt] adv (win, own) абсолютно; (refuse, deny) наотрез; (ask) прямо ♦ adj (winner, victory) абсолютный; (refusal, hostility) открытый; **to be killed ~** погибать (погибнуть pf) сразу

**outset** ['autsɛt] n начало

**outside** [aut'saıd] n наружная сторона ♦ adj наружный, внешний ♦ adv (be) снаружи; (go) наружу ♦ prep вне +gen, за пределами +gen; (building) у +gen; (city) под +instr; **~r** n (stranger) посторонний(яя) m(f) adj

**outskirts** ['autskəːts] npl окраины fpl

**outspoken** [aut'spəukən] adj откровенный

**outstanding** [aut'stændıŋ] adj (exceptional) выдающийся; (unfinished) незаконченный; (unpaid) неоплаченный

**outward** ['autwəd] adj внешний; **the ~ journey** поездка туда

**outweigh** [aut'weı] vt перевешивать (перевесить pf)

**outwit** [aut'wıt] vt перехитрить (pf)

**oval** ['əuvl] adj овальный

**ovary** ['əuvərı] n яичник

**ovation** [əu'veıʃən] n овация

**oven** ['ʌvn] n (domestic) духовка

KEYWORD

**over** ['əuvəʳ] adv 1 (across): **to cross over** переходить (перейти pf); **over here** здесь; **over there** там;

**to ask sb over** (*to one's house*)
приглашáть (приглаcúть *pf*)
когó-н в гóсти *or* к себé
**2** (*indicating movement from
upright*): **to knock/turn sth over**
сбивáть (сбить *pf*)/
перевoрáчивать (перевeрнýть
*pf*) что-н; **to fall over** пáдать
(упáсть *pf*); **to bend over**
нагибáться (нагнýться *pf*)
**3** (*finished*): **the game is over**
игрá окóнчена; **his life is over**
жизнь егó закóнчилась
**4** (*excessively*) слúшком, чересчýр
**5** (*remaining: money, food etc*):
**there are 3 over** остáлось 3
**6**: **all over** (*everywhere*) вездé,
повсюду; **over and over** (*again*)
снóва и снóва
♦ *prep* **1** (*on top of*) на +*prp*;
(*above, in control of*) над +*instr*
**2** (*on(to) the other side of*) чéрез
+*acc*; **the pub over the road** паб
чéрез дорóгу
**3** (*more than*) свúше +*gen*,
бóльше+*gen*; **she is over 40** ей
бóльше 40; **over and above**
намнóго бóльше, чем
**4** (*in the course of*) в течéние
+*gen*, за +*acc*; **over the winter** зá
зиму, в течéние зимú; **let's
discuss it over dinner** давáйте
обсýдим э́то за обéдом; **the
work is spread over two weeks**
рабóта рассчúтана на две
недéли

**overall** ['əuvərɔːl] *adj* óбщий ♦ *adv*
(*in general*) в цéлом *or* óбщем;
(*altogether*) целикóм ♦ *n* (*BRIT*)
халáт; **~s** *npl* (*clothing*)
комбинезóн *msg*; **~ majority**
подавляющее большинство
**overboard** ['əuvəbɔːd] *adv*: **to fall ~**
пáдать (упáсть *pf*) зá борт
**overcast** ['əuvəkɑːst] *adj* хмýрый,

пáсмурный
**overcoat** ['əuvəkəut] *n* пальтó *nt
ind*
**overcome** [əuvə'kʌm] (*irreg*) *vt*
(*problems*) преодолевáть
(преодолéть *pf*)
**overcrowded** [əuvə'kraudɪd] *adj*
перепóлненный
**overdo** [əuvə'duː] (*irreg*) *vt* (*work,
exercise*) перестарáться (*pf*) в +*prp*;
(*interest, concern*) утрúровать
(*impf*)
**overdose** ['əuvədəus] *n*
передозирóвка
**overdraft** ['əuvədrɑːft] *n*
перерасхóд, овердрáфт
**overdrawn** [əuvə'drɔːn] *adj*: **he is ~**
он превúсил кредúт своегó
текýщего счёта
**overdue** [əuvə'djuː] *adj* (*change,
reform etc*) запоздáлый
**overgrown** [əuvə'grəun] *adj*
(*garden*) зарóсший
**overhead** *adv* ['əuvəhɛd] *adj, n*
['əuvəhɛd] *adv* наверхý, над
головóй; (*in the sky*) в нéбе ♦ *adj*
(*lighting*) вéрхний; (*cable, railway*)
надзéмный ♦ *n* (*US*) = **overheads**;
**~s** *npl* (*expenses*) накладнúе
расхóды *mpl*
**overhear** [əuvə'hɪər] (*irreg*) *vt*
(*случáйно*) подслýшать (*pf*)
**overjoyed** [əuvə'dʒɔɪd] *adj*: **to be ~
(at)** óчень рáдоваться
(обрáдоваться *pf*) (+*dat*); **she was
~ to see him** онá былá óчень
рáда вúдеть егó
**overlap** [əuvə'læp] *vi* находúть
(*impf*) одúн на другóй; (*fig*)
частúчно совпадáть (совпáсть
*pf*)
**overleaf** [əuvə'liːf] *adv* на оборóте
**overload** [əuvə'ləud] *vt* (*also ELEC,
fig*) перегружáть (перегрузúть
*pf*)
**overlook** [əuvə'luk] *vt* (*place*)

выходи́ть *(impf)* на +*acc*; *(problem)* упуска́ть (упусти́ть *pf)* из ви́ду; *(behaviour)* закрыва́ть (закры́ть *pf)* глаза́ на +*acc*

**overnight** [əuvə'naɪt] *adv (during the night)* за́ ночь; *(fig)* в одноча́сье, сра́зу; **to stay ~** ночева́ть (переночева́ть *pf)*

**overpowering** [əuvə'pauərɪŋ] *adj (heat, stench)* невыноси́мый

**overriding** [əuvə'raɪdɪŋ] *adj (factor, consideration)* реша́ющий

**overrun** [əuvə'rʌn] *(irreg)* vi *(meeting)* затя́гиваться (затяну́ться *pf)*

**overseas** [əuvə'siːz] *adv (live, work)* за рубежо́м or грани́цей; *(go)* за рубе́ж or грани́цу ♦ *adj (market, trade)* вне́шний; *(student, visitor)* иностра́нный

**oversee** [əuvə'siː] *vt* следи́ть *(impf)* за +*instr*

**overshadow** [əuvə'ʃædəu] *vt (place, building etc)* возвыша́ться *(impf)* над +*instr*; *(fig)* затмева́ть (затми́ть *pf)*

**oversight** ['əuvəsaɪt] *n* недосмо́тр

**overt** [əu'vəːt] *adj* откры́тый

**overtake** [əuvə'teɪk] *(irreg)* vt *(AUT)* обгоня́ть (обогна́ть *pf)*

**overthrow** [əuvə'θrəu] *(irreg)* vt сверга́ть (све́ргнуть *pf)*

**overtime** ['əuvətaɪm] *n* сверхуро́чное вре́мя *nt*

**overture** ['əuvətʃuə] *n (MUS)* увертю́ра; *(fig)* вступле́ние

**overturn** [əuvə'təːn] *vt (car, chair)* перевора́чивать (переверну́ть *pf)*; *(decision, plan)* отверга́ть (отве́ргнуть *pf)*; *(government, system)* сверга́ть (све́ргнуть *pf)*

**overweight** [əuvə'weɪt] *adj* ту́чный

**overwhelm** [əuvə'wɛlm] *vt (subj: feelings, emotions)* переполня́ть (перепо́лнить *pf)*; **~ing** *adj (victory, defeat)* по́лный; *(majority)*

подавля́ющий; *(feeling, desire)* всепобежда́ющий

**owe** [əu] *vt*: **she ~s me £500** она́ должна́ мне £500; **he ~s his life to that man** он обя́зан свое́й жи́знью э́тому челове́ку

**owing to** ['əuɪŋ-] *prep* всле́дствие +*gen*

**owl** [aul] *n* сова́

**own** [əun] *vt* владе́ть *(impf)* +*instr* ♦ *adj* со́бственный; **he lives on his ~** он живёт оди́н; **to get one's ~ back** отыгрыва́ться (отыгра́ться *pf)*; **~ up** *vi*: **to ~ up to sth** признава́ться (призна́ться *pf)* в чём-н; **~er** *n* владе́лец(лица); **~ership** *n*: **~ership (of)** владе́ние (+*instr)*

**ox** [ɔks] *(pl* **~en**) *n* бык

**oxygen** ['ɔksɪdʒən] *n* кислоро́д

**oyster** ['ɔɪstə] *n* у́стрица

**oz.** *abbr* = **ounce**

**ozone** ['əuzəun] *n* озо́н; **~ hole** *n* озо́новая дыра́

# P, p

**p** *abbr (BRIT)* = **penny, pence**

**PA** *n abbr (= personal assistant)* референ́т, ли́чный секрета́рь *m*

**pa** [pɑː] *n (inf)* па́па *m*

**p.a.** *abbr* = **per annum**

**pace** [peɪs] *n (step)* шаг; *(speed)* темп ♦ *vi*: **to ~ up and down** ходи́ть *(impf)* взад вперёд; **to keep ~ with** идти́ *(impf)* в но́гу с +*instr*; **~maker** *n (MED)* ритмиза́тор се́рдца

**Pacific** [pə'sɪfɪk] *n*: **the ~ (Ocean)** Ти́хий океа́н

**pacifist** ['pæsɪfɪst] *n* пацифи́ст(ка)

**pack** [pæk] *n (packet)* па́чка; *(of wolves)* ста́я; *(also*: **back~**) рюкза́к; *(of cards)* коло́да ♦ *vt (fill)* накова́ть (упакова́ть *pf)*;

(*cram*): **to ~ into** набивáть
(набúть *pf*) в +*acc* ♦ *vi*: **to ~ (one's
bags)** уклáдываться (уложúться
*pf*)
**package** ['pækɪdʒ] *n* пакéт; (*also*: **~
deal** : *COMM*) пакéт
предложéний; **~ holiday** *n* (*BRIT*)
организóванный óтдых по
путёвке
**packet** ['pækɪt] *n* (*of cigarettes etc*)
пáчка; (*of crisps*) пакéт
**packing** ['pækɪŋ] *n* проклáдочный
материáл; (*act*) упакóвка
**pact** [pækt] *n* пакт
**pad** [pæd] *n* (*of paper*) блокнóт;
(*soft material*) проклáдка ♦ *vt*
(*cushion, soft toy etc*) набивáть
(набúть *pf*)
**paddle** ['pædl] *n* (*oar*)
байдáрочное веслó; (*US*: *bat*)
ракéтка ♦ *vt* управлять (*impf*)
+*instr* ♦ *vi* (*in sea*) шлёпать (*impf*)
**paddock** ['pædək] *n* (*field*) вы́гон
**padlock** ['pædlɔk] *n* (висячий)
замóк
**paedophile** ['pi:dəufaɪl] (*US*
**pedophile**) *n* педофúл
**pagan** ['peɪgən] *adj* язы́ческий
**page** [peɪdʒ] *n* странúца; (*also*:
**~boy**) паж ♦ *vt* (*in hotel etc*)
вызывáть (вы́звать *pf*) (по
селéктору)
**paid** [peɪd] *pt, pp of* **pay**
**pain** [peɪn] *n* боль *f*; **to be in ~**
страдáть (*impf*) от бóли; **to take
~s to do** старáться (постарáться
*pf*) изо всех сил +*infin*; **~ful** *adj*
мучúтельный; **my back is ~ful** у
меня́ болúт спинá; **~fully** *adv*
(*fig*: *very*) глубокó; (: *aware,
familiar*) до бóли; **~killer** *n*
болеутоля́ющее *nt adj*
(срéдство); **~less** *adj*
безболéзненный; **~staking** *adj*
кропотлúвый
**paint** [peɪnt] *n* крáска ♦ *vt* крáсить

(покрáсить *pf*); (*picture, portrait*)
рисовáть (нарисовáть *pf*), писáть
(написáть *pf*); **to ~ the door blue**
крáсить (покрáсить *pf*) дверь в
голубóй цвет; **~er** *n* (*artist*)
худóжник(ица); (*decorator*)
маля́р; **~ing** *n* картúна; (*activity*:
*of artist*) жúвопись *f*; (: *of
decorator*) маля́рное дéло;
**~work** *n* крáска
**pair** [pɛər] *n* пáра
**pajamas** [pə'dʒɑːməz] *npl* (*US*)
пижáма *fsg*
**pal** [pæl] *n* (*inf*) дружóк
**palace** ['pæləs] *n* дворéц
**pale** [peɪl] *adj* блéдный
**Palestine** ['pælɪstaɪn] *n* Палестúна
**pallet** ['pælɪt] *n* (*for goods etc*)
поддóн
**palm** [pɑːm] *n* (*also*: **~ tree**)
пáльма; (*of hand*) ладóнь *f* ♦ *vt*:
**to ~ sth off on sb** (*inf*)
подсóвывать (подсýнуть *pf*)
что-н комý-н
**palpable** ['pælpəbl] *adj* ощутúмый
**pamphlet** ['pæmflət] *n* брошю́ра;
(*political, literary etc*) памфлéт
**pan** [pæn] *n* (*also*: **sauce~**)
кастрю́ля; (*also*: **frying ~**)
сковородá
**pancake** ['pænkeɪk] *n* (*thin*) блин;
(*thick*) олáдья
**panda** ['pændə] *n* пáнда,
бамбýковый медвéдь *m*
**pane** [peɪn] *n*: **~ (of glass)** (*in
window*) окóнное стеклó
**panel** ['pænl] *n* (*of wood, glass etc*)
панéль *f*; (*of experts*) комúссия; **~
of judges** жюрú *nt ind*; **~ling** (*US
~ing*) *n* деревя́нная обшúвка
**pang** [pæŋ] *n* (*of jealousy*) укóл; **~s
of conscience** укóры сóвести; **~
of regret** мýки сожалéния;
**hunger ~s** голóдные бóли
**panic** ['pænɪk] *n* пáника ♦ *vi*
паниковáть (*impf*)

**panorama** [pænə'rɑːmə] n панорáма

**pansy** ['pænzɪ] n анютины глáзки pl

**panther** ['pænθər] n пантéра

**pantihose** ['pæntɪhəuz] npl (US) колгóтки pl

**pantomime** - рождéственское представлéние. Комéдии с богáтым музыкáльным оформлéнием, напúсанные по мотúвам извéстных скáзок, такúх как "Зóлушка", "Кот в сапогáх" и др. Онú предназнáчены глáвным óбразом для детéй. Теáтры стáвят их в Рождествó.

**pants** [pænts] npl (BRIT: underwear) трусы́ pl; (US: trousers) брю́ки pl

**paper** ['peɪpər] n бумáга; (also: **news~**) газéта; (exam) пúсьменный экзáмен; (essay: at conference) доклáд; (: in journal) статья́; (also: **wall~**) обóи pl ♦ adj бумáжный ♦ vt оклéивать (оклéить pf) обóями; **~s** npl (also: **identity ~s**) докумéнты mpl; **~back** n кнúга в мя́гкой облóжке; **~clip** n (канцеля́рская) скрéпка; **~work** n бумáжная волокúта

**papier-maché** [pæpjeɪ'mæʃeɪ] n папьé-машé nt ind

**paprika** ['pæprɪkə] n крáсный мóлотый пéрец

**par** [pɑːr] n: **to be on a ~ with** быть (impf) на рáвных с +instr

**parachute** ['pærəʃuːt] n парашю́т

**parade** [pə'reɪd] n шéствие; (MIL) парáд ♦ vi (MIL) идтú (impf) стрóем

**paradise** ['pærədaɪs] n (also fig) рай

**paradox** ['pærədɔks] n парадóкс; **~ically** [pærə'dɔksɪklɪ] adv как э́то ни парадоксáльно

**paraffin** ['pærəfɪn] n (BRIT: also: ~ **oil**) керосúн

**paragraph** ['pærəgrɑːf] n абзáц

**parallel** ['pærəlɛl] adj параллéльный; (fig: similar) аналогúчный ♦ n параллéль f

**paralyse** ['pærəlaɪz] vt (BRIT: also fig) парализовáть (impf/pf); **he is ~d** он парализóван

**paralysis** [pə'rælɪsɪs] n (MED) паралúч

**paramilitary** [pærə'mɪlɪtərɪ] adj военизúрованный

**paramount** ['pærəmaunt] adj первостепéнный

**paranoia** [pærə'nɔɪə] n паранóйя

**paranoid** ['pærənɔɪd] adj (person) паранóидный

**paraphrase** ['pærəfreɪz] vt перефразúровать (impf/pf)

**parasite** ['pærəsaɪt] n паразúт

**parcel** ['pɑːsl] n (package) свёрток; (sent by post) посы́лка

**pardon** ['pɑːdn] n (LAW) помúлование ♦ vt (LAW) мúловать (помúловать pf); **~ me!, I beg your ~!** прошу́ прощéния!; **(I beg your) ~?**, (US) **~ me?** (what did you say?) простúте, не расслы́шал

**parent** ['pɛərənt] n родúтель(ница) m(f); **~s** npl (mother and father) родúтели mpl; **~al** [pə'rɛntl] adj родúтельский

**parenthesis** [pə'rɛnθɪsɪs] (pl **parentheses**) n (phrase) ввóдное предложéние

**Paris** ['pærɪs] n Парúж

**parish** ['pærɪʃ] n (REL) прихóд

**parity** ['pærɪtɪ] n (of pay etc) паритéт

**park** [pɑːk] n парк ♦ vt стáвить (постáвить pf), парковáть

(припаркова́ть *pf*) ♦ *vi*
парко́ваться (припаркова́ться *pf*)

**parking** ['pɑːkɪŋ] *n* (*of vehicle*)
парко́вка; (*space to park*) стоя́нка;
**"no ~"** "стоя́нка запрещена́"; **~ lot** *n* (*US*) (а́вто)стоя́нка

**parliament** ['pɑːləmənt] *n*
парла́мент; **~ary** [pɑːlə'mɛntərɪ]
*adj* парла́ментский

**parody** ['pærədɪ] *n* паро́дия

**parole** [pə'rəʊl] *n*: **he was released on ~** (*LAW*) он был освобождён
под че́стное сло́во

**parrot** ['pærət] *n* попуга́й

**parry** ['pærɪ] *vt* (*blow*) отража́ть
(отрази́ть *pf*)

**parsley** ['pɑːslɪ] *n* петру́шка

**parsnip** ['pɑːsnɪp] *n* пастерна́к
(посевно́й)

**part** [pɑːt] *n* (*section, division*) часть
*f*; (*component*) дета́ль *f*; (*role*) роль
*f*; (*episode*) се́рия; (*US: in hair*)
пробо́р ♦ *adv* = **partly** ♦ *vt*
разделя́ть (раздели́ть *pf*); (*hair*)
расчёсывать (расчеса́ть *pf*) на
пробо́р ♦ *vi* (*people*) расстава́ться
(расста́ться *pf*); (*crowd*)
расступа́ться (расступи́ться *pf*);
**to take ~ in** принима́ть (приня́ть
*pf*) уча́стие в +*prp*; **to take sb's ~**
(*support*) станови́ться (стать *pf*)
на чью-н сто́рону; **for my ~** с
мое́й стороны́; **for the most ~**
бо́льшей ча́стью; **~ with** *vt fus*
расстава́ться (расста́ться *pf*) с
+*instr*

**partial** ['pɑːʃl] *adj* (*incomplete*)
части́чный; **I am ~ to chocolate**
(*like*) у меня́ пристра́стие к
шокола́ду

**participant** [pɑː'tɪsɪpənt] *n*
уча́стник(ица)

**participate** [pɑː'tɪsɪpeɪt] *vi*: **to ~ in**
уча́ствовать (*impf*) в +*prp*

**participation** [pɑːtɪsɪ'peɪʃən] *n*
уча́стие

**particle** ['pɑːtɪkl] *n* части́ца

**particular** [pə'tɪkjʊlər] *adj* (*distinct, special*) осо́бый; (*fussy*)
привере́дливый; **~s** *npl* (*personal details*) да́нные *pl adj*; **in ~** в
ча́стности; **~ly** *adv* осо́бенно

**parting** ['pɑːtɪŋ] *n* разделе́ние; (*farewell*) проща́ние; (*BRIT: in hair*) пробо́р ♦ *adj* проща́льный

**partisan** [pɑːtɪ'zæn] *adj* (*politics*)
пристра́стный; (*views*) пы́лкий
♦ *n* (*supporter*) приве́рженец

**partition** [pɑː'tɪʃən] *n* (*wall, screen*)
перегоро́дка

**partly** ['pɑːtlɪ] *adv* части́чно

**partner** ['pɑːtnər] *n* партнёр(ша);
(*spouse*) супру́г(а); (*COMM, SPORT, CARDS*) партнёр; **~ship** *n* (*COMM, company*) това́рищество; (: *with person*) партнёрство; (*POL*) сою́з

**part-time** ['pɑːt'taɪm] *adj* (*work*)
почасово́й; (*staff*) на почасово́й
ста́вке ♦ *adv*: **to work ~** быть
(*impf*) на почасово́й ста́вке; **to study ~** обуча́ться (*impf*) по
непо́лной програ́мме

**party** ['pɑːtɪ] *n* па́ртия; (*celebration: formal*) ве́чер; (: *informal*)
вечери́нка; (*group: rescue*) отря́д;
(: *of tourists etc*) гру́ппа ♦ *cpd* (*POL*)
парти́йный; **birthday ~**
пра́зднование дня рожде́ния,
день рожде́ния

**pass** [pɑːs] *vt* (*time*) проводи́ть
(провести́ *pf*); (*hand over*)
передава́ть (переда́ть *pf*); (*go past: on foot*) проходи́ть (пройти́
*pf*); (: *by transport*) проезжа́ть
(прое́хать *pf*); (*overtake: vehicle*)
обгоня́ть (обогна́ть *pf*); (*exam*)
сдава́ть (сдать *pf*); (*law, proposal*)
принима́ть (приня́ть *pf*) ♦ *vi* (*go past: on foot*) проходи́ть (пройти́
*pf*); (: *by transport*) проезжа́ть
(прое́хать *pf*); (*in exam*) сдава́ть
(сдать *pf*) экза́мен ♦ *n* (*permit*)

пропуск; (*GEO*) перевал; (*SPORT*) пас, передача; (*SCOL*: *also*: ~ **mark**): **to get a ~** получать (получить *pf*) зачёт; **~ by** *vi* (*on foot*) проходить (пройти *pf*); (*by transport*) проезжать (проехать *pf*); **~ on** *vt* передавать (передать *pf*)

**passage** ['pæsɪdʒ] *n* (*also ANAT*) проход; (*in book*) отрывок; (*journey*) путешествие

**passenger** ['pæsɪndʒər] *n* пассажир(ка)

**passer-by** [pɑːsə'baɪ] (*pl* **passers-by**) *n* прохожий(ая) *m(f) adj*

**passing** ['pɑːsɪŋ] *adj* мимолётный ♦ *n*: **in ~** мимоходом

**passion** ['pæʃən] *n* страсть *f*; **~ate** *adj* страстный

**passive** ['pæsɪv] *adj* пассивный

**passport** ['pɑːspɔːt] *n* паспорт

**password** ['pɑːswɜːd] *n* пароль *m*

**past** [pɑːst] *prep* мимо +*gen*; (*beyond*) за +*instr*; (*later than*) после +*gen* ♦ *adj* (*government etc*) прежний; (*week, month etc*) прошлый ♦ *n* прошлое *nt adj*; (*LING*): **the ~ (tense)** прошедшее время ♦ *adv*: **to run ~** пробегать (пробежать *pf*) мимо; **ten/quarter ~ eight** десять минут/четверть девятого; **for the ~ few days** за последние несколько дней

**pasta** ['pæstə] *n* макаронные изделия *ntpl*

**paste** [peɪst] *n* (*wet mixture*) паста; (*glue*) клейстер; (*CULIN*) паштет ♦ *vt* (*paper etc*) наносить (нанести *pf*) клей на +*acc*

**pastel** ['pæstl] *adj* пастельный

**pastime** ['pɑːstaɪm] *n* времяпрепровождение

**pastoral** ['pɑːstərl] *adj* (*REL*) пасторский

**pastry** ['peɪstrɪ] *n* (*dough*) тесто

**pasture** ['pɑːstʃər] *n* пастбище

**pat** [pæt] *vt* (*dog*) ласкать (приласкать *pf*) ♦ *n*: **to give sb/o.s. a ~ on the back** (*fig*) хвалить (похвалить *pf*) кого-н/себя

**patch** [pætʃ] *n* (*of material*) заплата; (*also*: **eye ~**) повязка; (*area*) пятно; (*repair*) заплата ♦ *vt* (*clothes*) латать (залатать *pf*); **to go through a bad ~** переживать (*impf*) трудные времена; **bald ~** лысина; **~work** *n* (*SEWING*) лоскутная работа; **~y** *adj* (*colour*) пятнистый; (*information, knowledge etc*) отрывочный

**pâté** ['pæteɪ] *n* (*CULIN*) паштет

**patent** ['peɪtnt] *n* патент ♦ *vt* (*COMM*) патентовать (запатентовать *pf*)

**paternal** [pə'tɜːnl] *adj* (*love, duty*) отцовский

**path** [pɑːθ] *n* (*trail, track*) тропа, тропинка; (*concrete, gravel etc*) дорожка; (*trajectory*) линия движения

**pathetic** [pə'θetɪk] *adj* жалостный; (*very bad*) жалкий

**pathological** [pæθə'lɔdʒɪkl] *adj* (*liar, hatred*) патологический

**pathology** [pə'θɔlədʒɪ] *n* патология

**patience** ['peɪʃns] *n* (*quality*) терпение

**patient** ['peɪʃnt] *n* пациент(ка) ♦ *adj* терпеливый

**patio** ['pætɪəu] *n* патио *m ind*, внутренний дворик

**patriot** ['peɪtrɪət] *n* патриот(ка); **~ic** [pætrɪ'ɔtɪk] *adj* патриотичный; (*song etc*) патриотический; **~ism** *n* патриотизм

**patrol** [pə'trəul] *n* патруль *m* ♦ *vt* патрулировать (*impf*)

**patron** ['peɪtrən] *n* (*client*) (постоянный) клиент; (*benefactor: of charity*) шеф, покровитель *m*; **~ of the arts** покровитель(ница) *m(f)* иску́сств; **~age** *n* (*of charity*) шéфство, покрови́тельство; **~ize** ['pætrənaɪz] *vt* (*pej: look down on*) трети́ровать (*impf*); **~ saint** *n* (*REL*) засту́пник(ица)

**pattern** ['pætən] *n* (*design*) узóр; (*SEWING*) вы́кройка

**pause** [pɔːz] *n* переры́в; (*in speech*) пáуза ♦ *vi* дéлать (сдéлать *pf*) переры́в; (*in speech*) дéлать (сдéлать *pf*) пáузу

**pave** [peɪv] *vt* мости́ть (вы́мостить *pf*); **to ~ the way for** (*fig*) прокла́дывать (проложи́ть *pf*) путь для +*gen*; **~ment** *n* (*BRIT*) тротуáр

**pavilion** [pə'vɪlɪən] *n* (*SPORT*) павильóн

**paw** [pɔː] *n* (*of animal*) лáпа

**pawn** [pɔːn] *n* (*CHESS, fig*) пéшка ♦ *vt* закла́дывать (заложи́ть *pf*); **~broker** *n* ростовщи́к(и́ца)

**pay** [peɪ] (*pt, pp* **paid**) *n* зарплáта ♦ *vt* (*sum of money, wage*) плати́ть (заплати́ть *pf*); (*debt, bill*) плати́ть (уплати́ть *pf*) ♦ *vi* (*be profitable*) окупáться (окупи́ться *pf*); **to ~ attention (to)** обращáть (обрати́ть *pf*) внимáние (на +*acc*); **to ~ sb a visit** наноси́ть (нанести́ *pf*) комý-н визи́т; **~ back** *vt* возвращáть (возврати́ть *pf*), вернýть (*pf*); (*person*) отпла́чивать (отплати́ть *pf*); **~ for** *vt fus* плати́ть (заплати́ть *pf*) за +*acc*; (*fig*) поплати́ться (*pf*) за +*acc*; **~ in** *vt* вноси́ть (внести́ *pf*); **~ off** *vt* (*debt*) выпла́чивать (вы́платить *pf*); (*creditor*) рассчи́тываться (рассчитáться *pf*) с +*instr*; (*person*) рассчи́тывать (рассчитáть *pf*) ♦ *vi* окупáться (окупи́ться *pf*); **~ up** *vi* рассчи́тываться (рассчитáться *pf*) сполнá); **~able** *adj* (*cheque*): **~able to** подлежáщий уплáте на

*и́мя* +*gen*; **~ment** *n* (*act*) платёж, уплáта; (*amount*) вы́плата

**PC** *n abbr* = **personal computer** ПК; (*BRIT*) = **police constable**; = **politically correct**

**pc** *abbr* = **per cent**

**pea** [piː] *n* (*BOT, CULIN*) горóх *m no pl*

**peace** [piːs] *n* (*not war*) мир; (*calm*) покóй; **~ful** *adj* (*calm*) ми́рный

**peach** [piːtʃ] *n* пéрсик

**peacock** ['piːkɔk] *n* павли́н

**peak** [piːk] *n* верши́на, пик; (*of cap*) козырёк

**peanut** ['piːnʌt] *n* арáхис

**pear** [pɛəʳ] *n* грýша

**pearl** [pɜːl] *n* жемчýжина; **~s** жéмчуг

**peasant** ['pɛznt] *n* крестья́нин(нка)

**peat** [piːt] *n* торф

**pebble** ['pɛbl] *n* гáлька *no pl*

**peck** [pɛk] *vt* (*subj: bird*) клевáть (*impf*); (: *once*) клю́нуть (*pf*) ♦ *n* (*kiss*) поцелýй

**peculiar** [pɪ'kjuːlɪəʳ] *adj* (*strange*) своеобрáзный; (*unique*): **~ to** свóйственный +*dat*

**pedal** ['pɛdl] *n* педáль *f* ♦ *vi* крути́ть (*impf*) педáли

**pedantic** [pɪ'dæntɪk] *adj* педанти́чный

**pedestal** ['pɛdəstl] *n* пьедестáл

**pedestrian** [pɪ'dɛstrɪən] *n* пешехóд

**pedigree** ['pɛdɪɡriː] *n* родослóвная *f adj* ♦ *cpd* порóдистый

**pedophile** ['piːdəfaɪl] *n* (*US*) = **paedophile**

**pee** [piː] *vi* (*inf*) пи́сать (попи́сать *pf*)

**peel** [piːl] *n* кожурá ♦ *vt* (*vegetables, fruit*) чи́стить (почи́стить *pf*) ♦ *vi* (*paint*) лупи́ться (облупи́ться *pf*); (*wallpaper*) отставáть (отстáть *pf*); (*skin*) шелуши́ться (*impf*)

**peep** [piːp] *n* (*look*) взгляд

укра́дкой ♦ *vi* взгля́дывать (взгляну́ть *pf*)

**peer** [pɪəʳ] *n* (*BRIT*: *noble*) пэр; (*equal*) ро́вня *m/f*; (*contemporary*) рове́сник(ица) ♦ *vi*: **to ~ at** всма́триваться (всмотре́ться *pf*) в +*acc*

**peg** [pɛg] *n* (*for coat etc*) крючо́к; (*BRIT*: *also*: **clothes ~**) прище́пка

**pejorative** [pɪ'dʒɔrətɪv] *adj* уничижи́тельный

**pelvis** ['pɛlvɪs] *n* таз

**pen** [pɛn] *n* ру́чка; (*felt-tip*) флома́стер; (*enclosure*) заго́н

**penal** ['piːnl] *adj* (*colony, institution*) исправи́тельный; (*system*) кара́тельный; **~ code** уголо́вный ко́декс; **~ize** *vt* нака́зывать (наказа́ть *pf*); (*SPORT*) штрафова́ть (оштрафова́ть *pf*)

**penalty** ['pɛnltɪ] *n* наказа́ние; (*fine*) штраф; (*SPORT*) пена́льти *m ind*

**pence** [pɛns] *npl of* **penny**

**pencil** ['pɛnsl] *n* каранда́ш

**pending** ['pɛndɪŋ] *prep* впредь до +*gen*, в ожида́нии +*gen* ♦ *adj* (*lawsuit, exam etc*) предстоя́щий

**pendulum** ['pɛndjuləm] *n* ма́ятник

**penetrate** ['pɛnɪtreɪt] *vt* (*subj*: *person, light*) проника́ть (прони́кнуть *pf*) в/на +*acc*

**penetration** [pɛnɪ'treɪʃən] *n* проникнове́ние

**penguin** ['pɛŋgwɪn] *n* пингви́н

**penicillin** [pɛnɪ'sɪlɪn] *n* пеницилли́н

**peninsula** [pə'nɪnsjulə] *n* полуо́стров

**penis** ['piːnɪs] *n* пе́нис, половой член

**penknife** ['pɛnnaɪf] *n* перочи́нный нож

**penniless** ['pɛnɪlɪs] *adj* без гроша́

**penny** ['pɛnɪ] (*pl* **pennies** *or* (*BRIT*) **pence**) *n* (*BRIT*) пе́нни *nt ind*, пенс

**pension** ['pɛnʃən] *n* пе́нсия; **~er** *n* (*BRIT*: *also* **old age ~er**) пенсионе́р(ка)

**pentagon** ['pɛntəgən] *n* (*US*): **the Pentagon** Пентаго́н

**pent-up** ['pɛntʌp] *adj* зада́вленный

**penultimate** [pɛ'nʌltɪmət] *adj* предпосле́дний

**people** ['piːpl] *npl* (*persons*) лю́ди *pl*; (*nation, race*) наро́д; **several ~ came** пришло́ не́сколько челове́к; **~ say that ...** говоря́т, что ...

**pepper** ['pɛpəʳ] *n* пе́рец ♦ *vt* (*fig*): **to ~ with** забра́сывать (заброса́ть *pf*) +*instr*; **~mint** *n* (*sweet*) мя́тная конфе́та

**per** [pəːʳ] *prep* (*of amounts*) на +*acc*; (*of price*) за +*acc*; (*of charge*) с +*gen*; **~ annum/day** в год/день; **~ person** на челове́ка

**perceive** [pə'siːv] *vt* (*realize*) осознава́ть (осозна́ть *pf*)

**per cent** *n* проце́нт

**percentage** [pə'sɛntɪdʒ] *n* проце́нт

**perception** [pə'sɛpʃən] *n* (*insight*) понима́ние

**perceptive** [pə'sɛptɪv] *adj* проница́тельный

**perch** [pəːtʃ] *vi*: **to ~ (on)** (*bird*) сади́ться (сесть *pf*) (на +*acc*); (*person*) приса́живаться (присе́сть *pf*) (на +*acc*)

**percolator** ['pəːkəleɪtəʳ] *n* (*also*: **coffee ~**) кофева́рка

**percussion** [pə'kʌʃən] *n* уда́рные инструме́нты *mpl*

**perennial** [pə'rɛnɪəl] *adj* (*fig*) ве́чный

**perfect** *adj* ['pəːfɪkt] *vb* [pə'fɛkt] *adj* соверше́нный, безупре́чный; (*weather*) прекра́сный; (*utter*: *nonsense etc*) соверше́нный ♦ *vt* (*technique*) соверше́нствовать (усоверше́нствовать *pf*); **~ion** [pə'fɛkʃən] *n* соверше́нство;

**~ionist** [pə'fɛkʃənɪst] n
взыскáтельный человéк; **~ly**
['pə:fɪktlɪ] adv (well, all right)
вполнé
**perform** [pə'fɔ:m] vt (task,
operation) выполнять (выполнить
pf); (piece of music) исполнять
(испóлнить pf); (play) игрáть
(сыгрáть pf) ♦ vi (well, badly)
справляться (спрáвиться pf);
**~ance** n (of actor, athlete etc)
выступлéние; (of musical work)
исполнéние; (of play, show)
представлéние; (of car, engine,
company) рабóта; **~er** n
исполнитель(ница) m(f)
**perfume** ['pə:fju:m] n духи pl
**perhaps** [pə'hæps] adv мóжет
быть, возмóжно
**peril** ['pɛrɪl] n опáсность f
**perimeter** [pə'rɪmɪtər] n периметр
**period** ['pɪərɪəd] n (length of time)
периóд; (SCOL) урóк; (esp US: full
stop) тóчка; (MED) менструáция
♦ adj (costume, furniture)
старинный; **~ic** [pɪərɪ'ɔdɪk] adj
периодический; **~ical** [pɪərɪ'ɔdɪkl]
n (magazine) периодическое
издáние ♦ adj периодический
**periphery** [pə'rɪfərɪ] n периферия
**perish** ['pɛrɪʃ] vi (person) погибáть
(погибнуть pf)
**perk** [pə:k] n (inf)
дополнительное преимущество
**perm** [pə:m] n перманéнт,
химическая завивка
**permanent** ['pə:mənənt] adj
постоянный; (dye, ink) стóйкий
**permissible** [pə'mɪsɪbl] adj
допустимый, позволительный
**permission** [pə'mɪʃən] n
позволéние, разрешéние
**permit** vb [pə'mɪt] n ['pə:mɪt] vt
позволять (позвóлить pf) ♦ n
разрешéние
**perpetual** [pə'pɛtjuəl] adj (motion,

questions) вéчный; (darkness, noise)
постоянный
**persecute** ['pə:sɪkju:t] vt
преслéдовать (impf)
**persecution** [pə:sɪ'kju:ʃən] n
преслéдование
**perseverance** [pə:sɪ'vɪərns] n
настóйчивость f
**persevere** [pə:sɪ'vɪər] vi
упóрствовать (impf)
**persist** [pə'sɪst] vi: **to ~ (in doing)**
настáивать (настоять pf) (на том,
чтобы +infin); **~ence** n упóрство;
**~ent** adj непрекращáющийся;
(smell) стóйкий; (person) упóрный
**person** ['pə:sn] n человéк; **in ~**
лично; **~al** adj личный; **~al
computer** n персонáльный
компьютер; **~ality** [pə:sə'nælɪtɪ] n
харáктер; (famous person)
знаменитость f; **~ally** adv лично;
**to take sth ~ally** принимáть
(принять pf) что-н на свой счёт
**personnel** [pə:sə'nɛl] n персонáл,
штат; (MIL) личный состáв
**perspective** [pə'spɛktɪv] n (ARCHIT,
ART) перспектива; (way of
thinking) видение; **to get sth into
~** (fig) смотрéть (посмотрéть pf)
на что-н в истинном свéте
**perspiration** [pə:spɪ'reɪʃən] n пот
**persuade** [pə'sweɪd] vt: **to ~ sb to
do** убеждáть (убедить pf) or
уговáривать (уговорить pf)
когó-н +infin
**persuasion** [pə'sweɪʒən] n
убеждéние
**persuasive** [pə'sweɪsɪv] adj
(argument) убедительный;
(person) настóйчивый
**pertinent** ['pə:tɪnənt] adj умéстный
**Peru** [pə'ru:] n Перý f ind
**perverse** [pə'və:s] adj (contrary)
врéдный
**perversion** [pə'və:ʃən] n
извращéние

**pervert** vb [pə'vəːt] n ['pəːvəːt] vt (person, mind) развраща́ть (разврати́ть pf), растлева́ть (растли́ть pf); (truth, sb's words) извраща́ть (изврати́ть pf) ♦ n (also: **sexual ~**) (полово́й) извраще́нец

**pessimism** ['pɛsɪmɪzəm] n пессими́зм

**pessimistic** [pɛsɪ'mɪstɪk] adj пессимисти́чный

**pest** [pɛst] n (insect) вреди́тель m; (fig: nuisance) зану́да m/f

**pester** ['pɛstər] vt пристава́ть (приста́ть pf) к +dat

**pesticide** ['pɛstɪsaɪd] n пестици́д

**pet** [pɛt] n дома́шнее живо́тное nt adj

**petal** ['pɛtl] n лепесто́к

**petite** [pə'tiːt] adj миниатю́рный

**petition** [pə'tɪʃən] n (signed document) пети́ция

**petrified** ['pɛtrɪfaɪd] adj (fig) оцепене́вший; **I was ~** я оцепене́л

**petrol** ['pɛtrəl] (BRIT) n бензи́н

**petroleum** [pə'trəulɪəm] n нефть f

**petty** ['pɛtɪ] adj (trivial) ме́лкий; (small-minded) ограни́ченный

**pew** [pjuː] n скамья́ (в це́ркви)

**phantom** ['fæntəm] n (ghost) фанто́м

**pharmaceutical** [fɑːmə'sjuːtɪkl] adj фармацевти́ческий

**pharmacist** ['fɑːməsɪst] n фармаце́вт

**pharmacy** ['fɑːməsɪ] n (shop) апте́ка

**phase** [feɪz] n фа́за ♦ vt: **to ~ sth in** поэта́пно вводи́ть (ввести́ pf) что-н; **to ~ sth out** поэта́пно ликвиди́ровать (impf/pf) что-н

**PhD** n abbr (= Doctor of Philosophy) до́ктор филосо́фии

**pheasant** ['fɛznt] n фаза́н

**phenomena** [fə'nɔmɪnə] npl of **phenomenon**

**phenomenal** [fə'nɔmɪnl] adj феномена́льный

**phenomenon** [fə'nɔmɪnən] (pl **phenomena**) n явле́ние, феноме́н

**philosopher** [fɪ'lɔsəfər] n фило́соф

**philosophical** [fɪlə'sɔfɪkl] adj филосо́фский

**philosophy** [fɪ'lɔsəfɪ] n филосо́фия

**phobia** ['fəubjə] n фо́бия, страх

**phone** [fəun] n телефо́н ♦ vt звони́ть (позвони́ть pf) +dat; **to be on the ~** говори́ть (impf) по телефо́ну; (possess phone) име́ть (impf) телефо́н; **~ back** vt перезва́нивать (перезвони́ть pf) +dat ♦ vi перезва́нивать (перезвони́ть pf); **~ up** vt звони́ть (позвони́ть pf) +dat; **~ book** n телефо́нная кни́га; **~ box** n (BRIT) телефо́нная бу́дка; **~ call** n телефо́нный звоно́к; **~ card** n телефо́нная ка́рта

**phonetics** [fə'nɛtɪks] n фоне́тика

**phoney** ['fəunɪ] adj фальши́вый

**photo** ['fəutəu] n фотогра́фия; **~copier** ['fəutəukɔpɪər] n (machine) ксе́рокс, копирова́льная маши́на; **~copy** n ксероко́пия, фотоко́пия ♦ vt фотокопи́ровать (сфотокопи́ровать pf), ксерокопи́ровать (impf/pf); **~genic** [fəutəu'dʒɛnɪk] adj фотогени́чный; **~graph** n фотогра́фия ♦ vt фотографи́ровать (сфотографи́ровать pf); **~grapher** [fə'tɔgrəfər] n фото́граф; **~graphy** [fə'tɔgrəfɪ] n фотогра́фия

**phrase** [freɪz] n фра́за ♦ vt формули́ровать (сформули́ровать pf)

**physical** ['fɪzɪkl] adj физи́ческий;

(*world, object*) материа́льный; ~ly *adv* физи́чески

**physician** [fɪ'zɪʃən] *n* (*esp US*) врач

**physicist** ['fɪzɪsɪst] *n* фи́зик

**physics** ['fɪzɪks] *n* фи́зика

**physiotherapy** [fɪzɪəu'θɛrəpɪ] *n* физиотерапия

**physique** [fɪ'ziːk] *n* (*of person*) телосложе́ние

**pianist** ['piːənɪst] *n* пиани́ст(ка)

**piano** [pɪ'ænəu] *n* пиани́но, фортепья́но *nt ind*

**pick** [pɪk] *n* (*also:* ~axe) кирка́ ♦ *vt* (*select*) выбира́ть (вы́брать *pf*); (*gather: fruit, flowers*) собира́ть (собра́ть *pf*); (*remove*) рвать (*impf*); (*lock*) взла́мывать (взлома́ть *pf*); **take your ~** выбира́йте; **to ~ one's nose/teeth** ковыря́ть (*impf*) в носу́/зуба́х; **to ~ a quarrel (with sb)** иска́ть (*impf*) по́вод для ссо́ры (с кем-н); **~ out** *vt* (*distinguish*) разгляде́ть (*pf*); (*select*) отбира́ть (отобра́ть *pf*); **~ up** *vi* (*improve*) улучша́ться (улу́чшиться *pf*) ♦ *vt* (*lift*) поднима́ть (подня́ть *pf*); (*arrest*) забира́ть (забра́ть *pf*); (*collect: person: by car*) заезжа́ть (зае́хать *pf*) за +*instr*; (*passenger*) подбира́ть (подобра́ть *pf*); (*language, skill etc*) усва́ивать (усво́ить *pf*); (*RADIO*) лови́ть (пойма́ть *pf*); **to ~ up speed** набира́ть (набра́ть *pf*) ско́рость; **to ~ o.s. up** (*after falling*) поднима́ться (подня́ться *pf*)

**picket** ['pɪkɪt] *n* пике́т ♦ *vt* пикети́ровать (*impf*)

**pickle** ['pɪkl] *n* (*also:* ~s) соле́нья *ntpl* ♦ *vt* (*in vinegar*) маринова́ть (замаринова́ть *pf*); (*in salt water*) соли́ть (засоли́ть *pf*)

**pickpocket** ['pɪkpɔkɪt] *n* вор-карма́нник

**picnic** ['pɪknɪk] *n* пикни́к

**picture** ['pɪktʃər] *n* карти́на; (*photo*) фотогра́фия; (*TV*) изображе́ние ♦ *vt* (*imagine*) рисова́ть (нарисова́ть *pf*) карти́ну +*gen*; **the ~s** *npl* (*BRIT : inf*) кино́ *nt ind*

**picturesque** [pɪktʃə'rɛsk] *adj* живопи́сный

**pie** [paɪ] *n* пиро́г; (*small*) пирожо́к

**piece** [piːs] *n* (*portion, part*) кусо́к; (*component*) дета́ль *f* ♦ *vt*: **to ~ together** (*information*) свя́зывать (связа́ть *pf*); (*object*) соединя́ть (соедини́ть *pf*); **a ~ of clothing** вещь *f*, предме́т оде́жды; **a ~ of advice** сове́т; **to take to ~s** (*dismantle*) разбира́ть (разобра́ть *pf*)

**pier** [pɪər] *n* пирс

**pierce** [pɪəs] *vt* протыка́ть (проткну́ть *pf*), прока́лывать (проколо́ть *pf*)

**pig** [pɪg] *n* (*also fig*) свинья́

**pigeon** ['pɪdʒən] *n* го́лубь *m*; **~hole** *n* (*in office, bureau*) яче́йка (*для корреспонде́нции*)

**pigment** ['pɪgmənt] *n* пигме́нт

**pigtail** ['pɪgteɪl] *n* коси́чка

**pike** [paɪk] *n inv* (*fish*) щу́ка

**pile** [paɪl] *n* (*large heap*) ку́ча, гру́да; (*neat stack*) сто́пка; (*of carpet*) ворс ♦ *vi*: **to ~ into** (*vehicle*) набива́ться (наби́ться *pf*) в +*acc*; **to ~ out of** (*vehicle*) выва́ливаться (вы́валиться *pf*) из +*gen*; **~ up** *vt* (*objects*) сва́ливать (свали́ть *pf*) в ку́чу ♦ *vi* громозди́ться (*impf*); (*problems, work*) нака́пливаться (накопи́ться *pf*)

**piles** [paɪlz] *npl* (*MED*) геморро́й *msg*

**pilgrimage** ['pɪlgrɪmɪdʒ] *n* пало́мничество

**pill** [pɪl] *n* табле́тка; **the ~** (*contraceptive*) противозача́точные *pl adj* (*табле́тки*)

**pillar** ['pɪlər] *n* (*ARCHIT*) столб,

коло́нна

**pillow** ['pɪləu] n поду́шка; **~case** n на́волочка

**pilot** ['paɪlət] n (AVIAT) пило́т, лётчик ♦ cpd (scheme, study etc) эксперимента́льный ♦ vt (aircraft) управля́ть (impf) +instr

**pimple** ['pɪmpl] n прыщ, пры́щик

**PIN** [pɪn] n (= personal identification number; also: **~ number**) персона́льный идентификацио́нный но́мер

**pin** [pɪn] n (for clothes, papers) була́вка ♦ vt прика́лывать (приколо́ть pf); **~s and needles** (fig) колотьё; **to ~ sth on sb** (fig) возлага́ть (возложи́ть pf) что-н на кого́-н; **~ down** vt: **to ~ sb down** (fig) принужда́ть (прину́дить pf) кого́-н

**pinch** [pɪntʃ] n (small amount) щепо́тка ♦ vt щипа́ть (ущипну́ть pf); (inf: steal) стащи́ть (pf); **at a ~** в кра́йнем слу́чае

**pine** [paɪn] n (tree, wood) сосна́

**pineapple** ['paɪnæpl] n анана́с

**pink** [pɪŋk] adj ро́зовый

**pint** [paɪnt] n пи́нта

**pint** - пи́нта. Одна́ пи́нта равна́ 0.568 л.

**pioneer** [paɪə'nɪəʳ] n (of science, method) первооткрыва́тель m, нова́тор

**pious** ['paɪəs] adj на́божный

**pip** [pɪp] n (of grape, melon) ко́сточка; (of apple, orange) зёрнышко

**pipe** [paɪp] n (for water, gas) труба́; (for smoking) тру́бка ♦ vt (water, gas, oil) подава́ть (пода́ть pf); **~s** npl (also: **bag~s**) волы́нка fsg

**pirate** ['paɪərət] n (sailor) пира́т ♦ vt (video tape, cassette) незако́нно распространя́ть (распространи́ть pf)

**Pisces** ['paɪsi:z] n Рыбы fpl

**pistol** ['pɪstl] n пистоле́т

**pit** [pɪt] n (in ground) я́ма; (also: **coal ~**) ша́хта; (quarry) карье́р ♦ vt: **to ~ one's wits against sb** состяза́ться (impf) в уме́ с кем-н

**pitch** [pɪtʃ] n (BRIT : SPORT) по́ле; (MUS) высота́; (level) у́ровень m

**pitiful** ['pɪtɪful] adj жа́лкий

**pitiless** ['pɪtɪlɪs] adj безжа́лостный

**pity** ['pɪtɪ] n жа́лость f ♦ vt жале́ть (пожале́ть pf)

**pivot** ['pɪvət] n (fig) центр

**pizza** ['pi:tsə] n пи́цца

**placard** ['plækɑ:d] n плака́т

**place** [pleɪs] vt (put) помеща́ть (помести́ть pf); (identify: person) вспомина́ть (вспо́мнить pf) ♦ n ме́сто; (home): **at his ~** у него́ (до́ма); **to ~ an order with sb for sth** (COMM) зака́зывать (заказа́ть pf) что-н у кого́-н; **to take ~** происходи́ть (произойти́ pf); **out of ~** (inappropriate) неуме́стный; **in the first ~** (first of all) во-пе́рвых; **to change ~s with sb** меня́ться (поменя́ться pf) места́ми с кем-н

**placid** ['plæsɪd] adj (person) ти́хий

**plague** [pleɪg] n (MED) чума́; (fig: of locusts etc) наше́ствие ♦ vt (fig: subj: problems) осажда́ть (осади́ть pf)

**plaice** [pleɪs] n inv ка́мбала

**plain** [pleɪn] adj просто́й; (unpatterned) гла́дкий; (clear) я́сный, поня́тный ♦ adv (wrong, stupid etc) я́вно ♦ n (GEO) равни́на; **~ly** adv я́сно

**plan** [plæn] n план ♦ vt плани́ровать (запланирова́ть pf); (draw up plans for) плани́ровать (impf) ♦ vi плани́ровать (impf)

**plane** [pleɪn] n (AVIAT) самолёт; (fig: level) план

**planet** ['plænɪt] n планéта

**plank** [plæŋk] n (of wood) доскá

**planner** ['plænər] n (of towns) планирóвщик

**planning** ['plænɪŋ] n (of future, event) плани́рование; (also: **town ~**) планирóвка

**plant** [plɑːnt] n (BOT) растéние; (factory) заво́д; (machinery) устано́вка ♦ vt (seed, garden) сажáть (посади́ть pf); (field) засéивать (засéять pf); (bomb, evidence) подклáдывать (подложи́ть pf); **~ation** [plæn'teɪʃən] n (of tea, sugar etc) плантáция; (of trees) лесонасаждéние

**plaque** [plæk] n (on teeth) налёт; (on building) мемориáльная доскá

**plaster** ['plɑːstər] n (for walls) штукатýрка; (also: **~ of Paris**) гипс; (BRIT: also: **sticking ~**) плáстырь m ♦ vt (wall, ceiling) штукатýрить (оштукатýрить pf); (cover): **to ~ with** заштукатýривать (заштукатýрить pf) +instr

**plastic** ['plæstɪk] n пластмáсса ♦ adj (made of plastic) пластмáссовый

**plate** [pleɪt] n (dish) тарéлка

**plateau** ['plætəu] (pl **~s** or **~x**) n платó nt ind

**platform** ['plætfɔːm] n (at meeting) трибýна; (at concert) помóст; (for landing, loading on etc) площáдка; (RAIL, POL) платфóрма

**platonic** [plə'tɔnɪk] adj платони́ческий

**plausible** ['plɔːzɪbl] adj убеди́тельный

**play** [pleɪ] n пьéса ♦ vt (subj: children: game) игрáть (impf) в +acc; (sport, cards) игрáть (сыгрáть pf) в +acc; (opponent) игрáть (сыгрáть pf) с +instr; (part,

piece of music) игрáть (сыгрáть pf); (instrument) игрáть (impf) на +prp; (tape, record) стáвить (постáвить pf) ♦ vi игрáть (impf); **~ down** vt не заостря́ть (impf) внимáние на +prp; **~er** n (SPORT) игрóк; **~ful** adj (person) игри́вый; **~ground** n (in park) дéтская площáдка; (in school) игровáя площáдка; **~group** n дéтская грýппа; **~pen** n (дéтский) манéж; **~time** n (SCOL) перемéна; **~wright** n драматýрг

**plc** abbr (BRIT) (= public limited company) публи́чная компáния с ограни́ченной отвéтственностью

**plea** [pliː] n (personal request) мольбá; (public request) призы́в; (LAW) заявлéние

**plead** [pliːd] vt (ignorance, ill health etc) ссылáться (сослáться pf) на +acc ♦ vi (LAW): **to ~ guilty/not guilty** признавáть (признáть pf) себя́ вино́вным(ой)/ невино́вным(ой); (beg): **to ~ with sb** умоля́ть (impf) кого́-н

**pleasant** ['plɛznt] adj прия́тный

**please** [pliːz] excl пожáлуйста ♦ vt угождáть (угоди́ть pf) +dat; **~ yourself!** (inf) как Вам угóдно!; **do as you ~** дéлайте как хоти́те; **he is difficult/easy to ~** емý трýдно/легкó угоди́ть; **~d** adj: **~d (with)** довóльный (+instr); **~d to meet you** óчень прия́тно

**pleasure** ['plɛʒər] n удово́льствие; **it's a ~** не сто́ит; **to take ~ in** получáть (получи́ть pf) удово́льствие от +gen

**pleat** [pliːt] n склáдка

**pledge** [plɛdʒ] n обязáтельство ♦ vt (money) обя́зываться (обязáться pf) дать; (support) обя́зываться (обязáться pf) оказáть

**plentiful** ['plɛntɪful] adj обильный

**plenty** ['plɛntɪ] n (enough) изобилие; ~ **of** (food, money etc) много +gen; (jobs, people, houses) множество +gen; **we've got ~ of time to get there** у нас вполне достаточно времени, чтобы туда добраться

**pliable** ['plaɪəbl] adj (material) гибкий

**pliers** ['plaɪəz] npl плоскогубцы pl

**plight** [plaɪt] n муки fpl

**plot** [plɔt] n (conspiracy) заговор; (of story) сюжет; (of land) участок
♦ vt (plan) замышлять (замыслить impf); (MATH) наносить (нанести pf) ♦ vi (conspire) составлять (составить pf) заговор

**plough** [plau] (US **plow**) n плуг ♦ vt пахать (вспахать pf)

**ploy** [plɔɪ] n уловка

**pluck** [plʌk] vt (eyebrows) выщипывать (выщипать pf); (instrument) перебирать (impf) струны +gen; **to ~ up courage** набираться (набраться pf) храбрости or мужества

**plug** [plʌg] n (ELEC) вилка, штепсель m; (in sink, bath) пробка ♦ vt (hole) затыкать (заткнуть pf); (inf: advertise) рекламировать (разрекламировать pf); ~ **in** vt (ELEC) включать (включить pf) в розетку

**plum** [plʌm] n слива

**plumber** ['plʌmər] n водопроводчик, слесарь-сантехник

**plumbing** ['plʌmɪŋ] n (piping) водопровод и канализация; (trade, work) слесарное дело

**plummet** ['plʌmɪt] vi: **to ~ (down)** (price, amount) резко падать (упасть pf)

**plump** [plʌmp] adj полный, пухлый ♦ vi: **to ~ for** (inf) выбирать (выбрать pf)

**plunge** [plʌndʒ] n (fig: of prices etc) резкое падение ♦ vt (knife) метать (метнуть pf); (hand) выбрасывать (выбросить pf) ♦ vi (fall) рухнуть (pf); (dive) бросаться (броситься pf); (fig: prices etc) резко падать (упасть pf); **to take the ~** (fig) отваживаться (отважиться pf)

**plural** ['pluərl] n множественное число

**plus** [plʌs] n, adj плюс ind ♦ prep: **ten ~ ten is twenty** десять плюс десять - двадцать; **ten/twenty ~** (more than) десять/двадцать с лишним

**plush** [plʌʃ] adj шикарный

**plutonium** [pluː'təunɪəm] n плутоний

**plywood** ['plaɪwud] n фанера

**PM** abbr (BRIT) = **Prime Minister**

**p.m.** adv abbr (= post meridiem) после полудня

**pneumonia** [njuː'məunɪə] n воспаление лёгких, пневмония

**PO Box** n abbr (= Post Office Box) абонентский or почтовый ящик

**pocket** ['pɔkɪt] n карман; (fig: small area) уголок ♦ vt класть (положить pf) себе в карман; **to be out of ~** (BRIT) быть (impf) в убытке

**pod** [pɔd] n (BOT) стручок

**poem** ['pəuɪm] n (long) поэма; (short) стихотворение

**poet** ['pəuɪt] n поэт(есса); ~**ic** [pəu'ɛtɪk] adj поэтический; ~**ry** n поэзия

**poignant** ['pɔɪnjənt] adj пронзительный

**point** [pɔɪnt] n (of needle, knife etc) остриё, кончик; (purpose) смысл; (significant part) суть f; (particular

_position_) то́чка; (_detail, moment_)
моме́нт; (_stage in development_)
ста́дия; (_score_) очко́; (ELEC: _also_:
**power ~**) розе́тка ♦ _vt_ (_show,
mark_) ука́зывать (указа́ть _pf_) _vi_:
**to ~ at** ука́зывать (указа́ть _pf_) на
+_acc_; **~s** _npl_ (RAIL) стре́лка _fsg_; **to
be on the ~ of doing** собира́ться
(_impf_) +_infin_; **I made a ~ of visiting
him** я счёл необходи́мым
посети́ть его́; **to get/miss the ~**
понима́ть (поня́ть _pf_)/не
понима́ть (поня́ть _pf_) суть; **to
come to the ~** доходи́ть (дойти́
_pf_) до су́ти; **there's no ~ in doing**
нет смы́сла +_infin_; **to ~ sth at sb**
(_gun etc_) наце́ливать (наце́лить
_pf_) что-н на кого́-н; **~ out** _vt_
ука́зывать (указа́ть _pf_) на +_acc_; **~
to** _vt fus_ ука́зывать (указа́ть _pf_)
на +_acc_; **~-blank** _adv_ (_refuse_)
наотре́з; (_say, ask_) напрями́к
♦ _adj_: **at ~-blank range** в упо́р;
**~ed** _adj_ о́стрый; (_fig: remark_)
язви́тельный; **~less** _adj_
бессмы́сленный; **~ of view** _n_
то́чка зре́ния
**poise** [pɔɪz] _n_ равнове́сие
**poison** ['pɔɪzn] _n_ яд ♦ _vt_ отравля́ть
(отрави́ть _pf_); **~ous** _adj_ (_toxic_)
ядови́тый
**poke** [pəʊk] _vt_ (_with stick etc_)
ты́кать (ткнуть _pf_); **to ~ sth in(to)**
(_put_) втыка́ть (воткну́ть _pf_) что-н
в +_acc_
**poker** ['pəʊkə<sup>r</sup>] _n_ кочерга́; (CARDS)
по́кер
**Poland** ['pəʊlənd] _n_ По́льша
**polar** ['pəʊlə<sup>r</sup>] _adj_ поля́рный; **~
bear** _n_ бе́лый медве́дь _m_
**pole** [pəʊl] _n_ (_stick_) шест; (_telegraph
pole_) столб; (GEO) по́люс; **~ vault**
_n_ прыжки́ _pl_ с шесто́м
**police** [pə'liːs] _npl_ поли́ция _fsg_; (_in
Russia_) мили́ция _fsg_ ♦ _vt_
патрули́ровать (_impf_); **~man**

(_irreg_) _n_ полице́йский _m adj_; **~
station** _n_ полице́йский уча́сток;
(_in Russia_) отделе́ние мили́ции;
**~woman** (_irreg_) _n_
(же́нщина-)полице́йский _m adj_
**policy** ['pɔlɪsɪ] _n_ поли́тика; (_also_:
**insurance ~**) по́лис
**polio** ['pəʊlɪəʊ] _n_ полиомиели́т
**Polish** ['pəʊlɪʃ] _adj_ по́льский
**polish** ['pɔlɪʃ] _n_ (_for furniture_)
(полирова́льная) па́ста; (_for
shoes_) гутали́н; (_for floor_)
масти́ка; (_shine, also fig_) лоск ♦ _vt_
(_furniture etc_) полирова́ть
(отполирова́ть _pf_); (_floors, shoes_)
натира́ть (натере́ть _pf_); **~ed** _adj_
(_style_) отто́ченный
**polite** [pə'laɪt] _adj_ ве́жливый
**political** [pə'lɪtɪkl] _adj_
полити́ческий; (_person_)
полити́чески акти́вный,
политизи́рованный; **~ly** _adv_
полити́чески; **~ly correct**
полити́чески корре́ктный
**politician** [pɔlɪ'tɪʃən] _n_ поли́тик,
полити́ческий де́ятель _m_
**politics** ['pɔlɪtɪks] _n_ поли́тика;
(SCOL) политоло́гия
**poll** [pəʊl] _n_ (_also_: **opinion ~**)
опро́с; (_usu pl: election_) вы́боры
_mpl_ ♦ _vt_ (_number of votes_)
набира́ть (набра́ть _pf_)
**pollen** ['pɔlən] _n_ пыльца́
**pollute** [pə'luːt] _vt_ загрязня́ть
(загрязни́ть _pf_)
**pollution** [pə'luːʃən] _n_
загрязне́ние; (_substances_)
загрязни́тель _m_
**polo neck** ['pəʊləʊ-] _n_ (_also_: **~
sweater** _or_ **jumper**) сви́тер с
кру́глым воротнико́м
**polyester** [pɔlɪ'ɛstə<sup>r</sup>] _n_ (_fabric_)
полиэфи́рное волокно́
**polystyrene** [pɔlɪ'staɪriːn] _n_
пенопла́ст
**polytechnic** [pɔlɪ'tɛknɪk] _n_ (_college_)

≈ политехни́ческий институ́т

**polythene** ['pɔliθiːn] *n* полиэтиле́н

**pomegranate** ['pɔmigrænit] *n*
(*BOT*) грана́т

**pompous** ['pɔmpəs] *adj* (*pej: person,
style*) напы́щенный, чва́нный

**pond** [pɔnd] *n* пруд

**ponder** ['pɔndər] *vt* обду́мывать
(обду́мать *pf*)

**pony** ['pəuni] *n* по́ни *m ind*; **~tail** *n*
(*hairstyle*) хвост, хво́стик

**poodle** ['puːdl] *n* пу́дель *m*

**pool** [puːl] *n* (*puddle*) лу́жа; (*pond*)
пруд; (*also*: **swimming ~**)
бассе́йн; (*fig: of light, paint*)
пятно́; (*SPORT, COMM*) пул ♦ *vt*
объединя́ть (объедини́ть *pf*); **~s**
*npl* (*also*: **football ~s**)
футбо́льный тотализа́тор;
**typing~**, (*US*) **secretary ~**
машинопи́сное бюро́ *nt ind*

**poor** [puər] *adj* (*not rich*) бе́дный;
(*bad*) плохо́й; **the ~** *npl* (*people*)
беднота́ *fsg*, бе́дные *pl adj*; **~ in**
(*resources etc*) бе́дный +*instr*; **~ly**
*adv* пло́хо ♦ *adj*: **she is feeling ~ly**
она́ пло́хо себя́ чу́вствует

**pop** [pɔp] *n* (*also*: **~ music**) поп-
му́зыка; (*inf: US: father*) па́па *m*;
(*sound*) хлопо́к ♦ *vi* (*balloon*)
ло́паться (ло́пнуть *pf*) ♦ *vt* (*put
quickly*): **to ~ sth into/onto**
забра́сывать (забро́сить *pf*)
что-н в +*acc*/на +*acc*; **~ in** *vi*
загля́дывать (загляну́ть *pf*),
заска́кивать (заскочи́ть *pf*); **~ up**
*vi* вылеза́ть (вы́лезти *pf*); **~corn** *n*
возду́шная кукуру́за, попко́рн

**pope** [pəup] *n*: **the Pope** Па́па *m*
ри́мский

**poplar** ['pɔplər] *n* то́поль *m*

**poppy** ['pɔpi] *n* мак

**pop star** *n* поп-звезда́ *m/f*

**populace** ['pɔpjuləs] *n*: **the ~**
наро́д

**popular** ['pɔpjulər] *adj*

популя́рный; **~ity** [pɔpju'læriti] *n*
популя́рность *f*

**population** [pɔpju'leiʃən] *n* (*of
town, country*) населе́ние

**porcelain** ['pɔːslin] *n* фарфо́р

**porch** [pɔːtʃ] *n* крыльцо́; (*US*)
вера́нда

**pore** [pɔːr] *n* по́ра

**pork** [pɔːk] *n* свини́на

**porn** [pɔːn] *n* (*inf*) порногра́фия

**pornographic** [pɔːnə'græfik] *adj*
порнографи́ческий

**pornography** [pɔː'nɔgrəfi] *n*
порногра́фия

**porpoise** ['pɔːpəs] *n* бу́рый
дельфи́н

**porridge** ['pɔridʒ] *n* овся́ная ка́ша

**port** [pɔːt] *n* (*harbour*) порт; (*wine*)
портве́йн; **~ of call** порт захо́да

**portable** ['pɔːtəbl] *adj*
портати́вный

**porter** ['pɔːtər] *n* (*doorkeeper*)
портье́ *m ind*, швейца́р; (*for
luggage*) носи́льщик

**portfolio** [pɔːt'fəuliəu] *n* (*ART*)
па́пка

**portion** ['pɔːʃən] *n* (*part*) часть *f*;
(*equal part*) до́ля; (*of food*) по́рция

**portrait** ['pɔːtreit] *n* портре́т

**portray** [pɔː'trei] *vt* изобража́ть
(изобрази́ть *pf*); **~al** *n*
изображе́ние

**Portugal** ['pɔːtjugl] *n* Португа́лия

**Portuguese** [pɔːtju'giːz] *adj*
португа́льский

**pose** [pəuz] *n* по́за ♦ *vt* (*question*)
ста́вить (поста́вить *pf*); (*problem,
danger*) создава́ть (созда́ть *pf*)
♦ *vi* (*pretend*): **to ~ as** выдава́ть
(вы́дать *pf*) себя́ за +*acc*; **to ~ for**
пози́ровать (*impf*) для +*gen*

**posh** [pɔʃ] *adj* (*inf: hotel etc*)
фешене́бельный; (: *person,
behaviour*) великосве́тский

**position** [pə'ziʃən] *n* положе́ние;
(*of house, thing*) расположе́ние,

**место**; (*job*) до́лжность *f*; (*in competition, race*) ме́сто; (*attitude*) пози́ция ♦ *vt* располага́ть (расположи́ть *pf*)

**positive** ['pɒzɪtɪv] *adj* (*affirmative*) положи́тельный; (*certain*) уве́ренный, убеждённый; (*definite: decision, policy*) определённый

**possess** [pə'zɛs] *vt* владе́ть (*impf*) +*instr*; (*quality, ability*) облада́ть (*impf*) +*instr*; **~ion** [pə'zɛʃən] *n* (*state of possessing*) владе́ние; **~ions** *npl* (*belongings*) ве́щи *fpl*; **to take ~ion of** вступа́ть (вступи́ть *pf*) во владе́ние +*instr*; **~ive** *adj* (*quality*) со́бственнический; (*person*) ревни́вый; (*LING*) притяжа́тельный

**possibility** [pɒsɪ'bɪlɪtɪ] *n* возмо́жность *f*

**possible** ['pɒsɪbl] *adj* возмо́жный; **it's ~** э́то возмо́жно; **as soon as ~** как мо́жно скоре́е

**possibly** ['pɒsɪblɪ] *adv* (*perhaps*) возмо́жно; **if you ~ can** е́сли то́лько Вы мо́жете; **I cannot ~ come** я ника́к не смогу́ прийти́

**post** [pəust] *n* (*BRIT: mail*) по́чта; (*pole*) столб; (*job, situation*) пост ♦ *vt* (*BRIT: mail*) посыла́ть (посла́ть *pf*), отправля́ть (отпра́вить *pf*) (по по́чте); **~age** *n* почто́вые расхо́ды *mpl*; **~al** *adj* почто́вый; **~card** *n* (почто́вая) откры́тка; **~code** *n* (*BRIT*) почто́вый и́ндекс

**poster** ['pəustər] *n* афи́ша, плака́т; (*for advertising*) по́стер

**postgraduate** ['pəust'grædjuət] *n* аспира́нт(ка) ♦ *adj*: **~ study** аспиранту́ра

**posthumous** ['pɒstjuməs] *adj* посме́ртный

**postman** ['pəustmən] (*irreg*) *n* почтальо́н

**post office** *n* почто́вое отделе́ние, отделе́ние свя́зи; (*organization*): **the Post Office** ≈ Министе́рство свя́зи

**postpone** [pəus'pəun] *vt* откла́дывать (отложи́ть *pf*); **~ment** *n* отсро́чка

**postscript** ['pəustskrɪpt] *n* (*in letter*) постскри́птум

**posture** ['pɒstʃər] *n* (*of body*) оса́нка

**postwar** [pəust'wɔːr] *adj* послевое́нный

**posy** ['pəuzɪ] *n* буке́тик

**pot** [pɒt] *n* (*for cooking, flowers*) горшо́к; (*also*: **tea~**) (зава́рочный) ча́йник; (*also*: **coffee~**) кофе́йник; (*bowl, container*) ба́нка ♦ *vt* (*plant*) сажа́ть (посади́ть *pf*); **a ~ of tea** ча́йник ча́я

**potato** [pə'teɪtəu] (*pl* **~es**) *n* карто́фель *m no pl*, карто́шка (*разг*); (*single potato*) карто́фелина

**potent** ['pəutnt] *adj* мо́щный; (*drink*) кре́пкий

**potential** [pə'tɛnʃl] *adj* потенциа́льный ♦ *n* потенциа́л; **~ly** *adv* потенциа́льно

**pottery** ['pɒtərɪ] *n* кера́мика; (*factory*) фа́брика керами́ческих изде́лий; (*small*) керами́ческий цех

**potty** ['pɒtɪ] *adj* (*inf: mad*) чо́кнутый ♦ *n* (*for child*) горшо́к

**pouch** [pautʃ] *n* (*for tobacco*) кисе́т; (*for coins*) кошелёк; (*ZOOL*) су́мка

**poultry** ['pəultrɪ] *n* (*birds*) дома́шняя пти́ца; (*meat*) пти́ца

**pounce** [pauns] *vi*: **to ~ on** набра́сываться (набро́ситься *pf*) на +*acc*

**pound** [paund] *n* (*money, weight*) фунт; **~ sterling** *n* фунт сте́рлингов

**pound** - фунт. Ме́ра ве́са ра́вная 0.454 кг.

**pour** [pɔːʳ] vt (liquid) налива́ть (нали́ть pf); (dry substance) насыпа́ть (насы́пать pf) ♦ vi (water etc) ли́ться (impf); (rain) лить (impf); **to ~ sb some tea** налива́ть (нали́ть pf) кому́-н чай; **~ in** vi (people) вали́ть (повали́ть pf); (news, letters etc) сы́паться (посы́паться pf); **~ out** vi (people) вали́ть (повали́ть pf) ♦ vt (drink) налива́ть (нали́ть pf); (fig: thoughts etc) излива́ть (изли́ть pf)

**pout** [paut] vi надува́ть (наду́ть pf) гу́бы, ду́ться (наду́ться pf)

**poverty** ['pɔvətɪ] n бе́дность f

**powder** ['paudəʳ] n порошо́к; (also: **face ~**) пу́дра

**power** ['pauəʳ] n (authority) власть f; (ability, opportunity) возмо́жность f; (legal right) полномо́чие; (of engine) мо́щность f; (electricity) (электро)эне́ргия; **to be in ~** находи́ться (impf) у вла́сти; **~ful** adj могу́чий; (person, organization) могу́щественный; (argument, engine) мо́щный; **~less** adj бесси́льный; **~ station** n электроста́нция

**pp** abbr = **pages**

**PR** n abbr = **public relations**

**practicable** ['præktɪkəbl] adj осуществи́мый

**practical** ['præktɪkl] adj (not theoretical) практи́ческий; (sensible, viable) практи́чный; (good with hands) уме́лый; **~ity** [præktɪ'kælɪtɪ] n практи́чность f; **~ities** npl (of situation etc) практи́ческая сторона́ fsg; **~ly** adv практи́чески

**practice** ['præktɪs] n пра́ктика;

(custom) привы́чка ♦ vti (US) = **practise**; **in ~** на пра́ктике; **I am out of ~** я разучи́лся

**practise** ['præktɪs] (US **practice**) vt (piano etc) упражня́ться (impf) на +acc; (sport, language) отраба́тывать (отрабо́тать pf); (custom) приде́рживаться (impf) +gen; (craft) занима́ться (impf) +instr; (religion) испове́довать (impf) ♦ vi (MUS) упражня́ться (impf); (SPORT) тренирова́ться (impf); (lawyer, doctor) практикова́ть (impf); **to ~ law/ medicine** занима́ться (impf) адвока́тской/враче́бной пра́ктикой

**practising** ['præktɪsɪŋ] adj (Christian etc) на́божный; (doctor, lawyer) практику́ющий

**practitioner** [præk'tɪʃənəʳ] n терапе́вт

**pragmatic** [præg'mætɪk] adj (reason etc) прагмати́ческий

**praise** [preɪz] n (approval) похвала́ ♦ vt хвали́ть (похвали́ть pf)

**pram** [præm] n (BRIT) де́тская коля́ска

**prawn** [prɔːn] n креве́тка

**pray** [preɪ] vi моли́ться (помоли́ться pf); **to ~ for/that** моли́ться (impf) за +acc/, что́бы; **~er** [preəʳ] n моли́тва

**preach** [priːtʃ] vi пропове́довать (impf) ♦ vt (sermon) произноси́ть (произнести́ pf); **~er** n пропове́дник(ица)

**precarious** [prɪ'kɛərɪəs] adj риско́ванный

**precaution** [prɪ'kɔːʃən] n предосторо́жность f

**precede** [prɪ'siːd] vt предше́ствовать (impf) +dat; **~nce** ['presɪdəns] n (priority) первоочерёдность f; **~nt** ['presɪdənt] n прецеде́нт

**preceding** [prɪ'siːdɪŋ] *adj*
предше́ствующий

**precinct** ['priːsɪŋkt] *n* (*US: in city*)
райо́н, префекту́ра; **pedestrian ~**
(*BRIT*) пешехо́дная зо́на; **shopping ~** (*BRIT*) торго́вый центр

**precious** ['prɛʃəs] *adj* це́нный;
(*stone*) драгоце́нный

**precise** [prɪ'saɪs] *adj* то́чный; **~ly**
*adv* (*accurately*) то́чно; (*exactly*)
ро́вно

**precision** [prɪ'sɪʒən] *n* то́чность *f*

**precocious** [prɪ'kəʊʃəs] *adj*: **a ~
child** не по года́м развито́й
ребёнок

**precondition** ['priːkən'dɪʃən] *n*
предпосы́лка

**predator** ['prɛdətər] *n* хи́щник

**predecessor** ['priːdɪsesər] *n*
предше́ственник(ица)

**predicament** [prɪ'dɪkəmənt] *n*
затрудни́тельное положе́ние

**predict** [prɪ'dɪkt] *vt* предска́зывать
(предсказа́ть *pf*); **~able** *adj*
предсказу́емый; **~ion** [prɪ'dɪkʃən]
*n* предсказа́ние

**predominantly** [prɪ'dɔmɪnəntlɪ] *adv*
преиму́щественно

**preface** ['prɛfəs] *n* предисло́вие

**prefect** - ста́роста шко́лы.
Ста́ростами мо́гут быть то́лько
старшекла́ссники. Они́
помога́ют учителя́м
подде́рживать в шко́ле
дисципли́ну.

**prefer** [prɪ'fəːr] *vt* предпочита́ть
(предпоче́сть *pf*); **~able** *adj*
предпочти́тельный; **~ably** *adv*
предпочти́тельно; **~ence**
['prɛfrəns] *n* (*liking*): **to have a
~ence for** предпочита́ть (*impf*);
**~ential** [prɛfə'rɛnʃəl] *adj*: **~ential
treatment** осо́бое отноше́ние

**prefix** ['priːfɪks] *n* приста́вка

**pregnancy** ['prɛgnənsɪ] *n*
бере́менность *f*

**pregnant** ['prɛgnənt] *adj*
бере́менная; (*remark, pause*)
многозначи́тельный; **she is 3
months ~** она́ на четвёртом
ме́сяце бере́менности

**prehistoric** ['priːhɪs'tɔrɪk] *adj*
доистори́ческий

**prejudice** ['prɛdʒudɪs] *n* (*dislike*)
предрассу́док; (*preference*)
предвзя́тость *f*, предубежде́ние

**preliminary** [prɪ'lɪmɪnərɪ] *adj*
предвари́тельный

**prelude** ['prɛljuːd] *n* прелю́дия

**premature** ['prɛmətʃuər] *adj*
преждевре́менный; (*baby*)
недоно́шенный

**premier** ['prɛmɪər] *adj* лу́чший ♦ *n*
премье́р(-мини́стр)

**première** ['prɛmɪeər] *n* премье́ра

**premise** ['prɛmɪs] *n* предпосы́лка;
**~s** *npl* (*of business*) помеще́ние
*ntsg*; **on the ~s** в помеще́нии

**premium** ['priːmɪəm] *n* пре́мия; **to
be at a ~** по́льзоваться (*impf*)
больши́м спро́сом

**premonition** [prɛmə'nɪʃən] *n*
предчу́вствие

**preoccupation** [priːɔkju'peɪʃən] *n*:
**~ with** озабо́ченность *f* +*instr*

**preoccupied** [priː'ɔkjupaɪd] *adj*
озабо́ченный

**preparation** [prɛpə'reɪʃən] *n*
(*activity*) подгото́вка; (*of food*)
приготовле́ние; **~s** *npl*
(*arrangements*) приготовле́ния *ntpl*

**preparatory** [prɪ'pærətərɪ] *adj*
подготови́тельный

**prepare** [prɪ'pɛər] *vt*
подгота́вливать (подгото́вить
*pf*); (*meal*) гото́вить (пригото́вить
*pf*) ♦ *vi*: **to ~ for** гото́виться
(подгото́виться *pf*) к +*dat*; **~d** *adj*
гото́вый; **~d for** (*ready*) гото́вый к
+*dat*

**preposition** [prepə'zɪʃən] n
предло́г

**preposterous** [prɪ'pɔstərəs] adj
ди́кий

**prescribe** [prɪ'skraɪb] vt (MED)
пропи́сывать (прописа́ть pf)

**prescription** [prɪ'skrɪpʃən] n (MED,
slip of paper) реце́пт; (: medicine)
лека́рство (назна́ченное
врачо́м)

**presence** ['prezns] n прису́тствие;
(fig) нару́жность f; **in sb's ~** в
прису́тствии кого́-н

**present** adj, n ['preznt] vb [prɪ'zent]
adj (current) ны́нешний,
настоя́щий; (in attendance)
прису́тствующий ♦ n (gift)
пода́рок ♦ vt представля́ть
(предста́вить pf); (RADIO, TV)
вести́ (impf); **to ~ sth to sb, ~ sb
with sth** (prize etc) вруча́ть
(вручи́ть pf) что-н кому́-н; (gift)
преподноси́ть (преподнести́ pf)
что-н кому́-н; **to ~ sb (to)**
(introduce) представля́ть
(предста́вить pf) кого́-н (+dat);
**the ~** (time) настоя́щее nt adj; **at ~**
в настоя́щее вре́мя; **to give sb a
~** дари́ть (подари́ть pf) кому́-н
пода́рок; **~ation** [prezn'teɪʃən] n
(of report etc) изложе́ние;
(appearance) вне́шний вид; (also:
**~ation ceremony**) презента́ция;
**~-day** adj сего́дняшний,
ны́нешний; **~er** [prɪ'zentər] n
(RADIO, TV) веду́щий(ая) m(f) adj;
(: of news) ди́ктор; **~ly** adv
вско́ре; (now) в настоя́щее
вре́мя

**preservation** [prezə'veɪʃən] n
(act: of building, democracy)
сохране́ние

**preservative** [prɪ'zə:vətɪv] n (for
food) консерва́нт; (for wood)
пропи́точный соста́в

**preserve** [prɪ'zə:v] vt сохраня́ть

(сохрани́ть pf); (food)
консерви́ровать
(законсерви́ровать pf) ♦ n (usu pl:
jam) варе́нье

**preside** [prɪ'zaɪd] vi: **to ~ (over)**
председа́тельствовать (impf) (на
+prp)

**presidency** ['prezɪdənsɪ] n
президе́нтство

**president** ['prezɪdənt] n (POL,
COMM) президе́нт; **~ial**
[prezɪ'denʃl] adj президе́нтский;
**~ial candidate** кандида́т в
президе́нты; **~ial adviser**
сове́тник президе́нта

**press** [pres] n (also: **printing ~**)
печа́тный стано́к ♦ vt (hold
together) прижима́ть (прижа́ть
pf); (push) нажима́ть (нажа́ть pf);
(iron) гла́дить (погла́дить pf);
(pressurize: person) вынужда́ть
(вы́нудить pf); **the ~** (newspapers,
journalists) пре́сса; **to ~ sth on sb**
(insist) навя́зывать (навяза́ть pf)
что-н кому́-н; **to ~ sb to do or
into doing** вынужда́ть (вы́нудить
pf) кого́-н +infin; **to ~ for** (change
etc) наста́ивать (настоя́ть pf) на
+prp; **~ on** vi продолжа́ть (impf)
**~ ahead** vi: **to ~ ahead with**
продолжа́ть (продо́лжить pf); **~
conference** n пресс-
конфере́нция; **~ing** adj (urgent)
неотло́жный

**pressure** ['preʃər] n давле́ние;
(stress) напряже́ние; **to put ~ on
sb (to do)** ока́зывать (оказа́ть pf)
давле́ние or нажи́м на кого́-н
(+infin); **~ group** n инициати́вная
гру́ппа

**prestige** [pres'ti:ʒ] n прести́ж

**prestigious** [pres'tɪdʒəs] adj
прести́жный

**presumably** [prɪ'zju:məblɪ] adv
на́до полага́ть

**presume** [prɪ'zju:m] vt: **to ~ (that)**

(*suppose*) предполага́ть
(предположи́ть *pf*), что
**presumption** [prɪ'zʌmpʃən] *n*
предположе́ние
**presumptuous** [prɪ'zʌmpʃəs] *adj*
самонаде́янный
**pretence** [prɪ'tɛns] (*US* **pretense**) *n*
притво́рство; **under false ~s** под
ло́жным предло́гом
**pretend** [prɪ'tɛnd] *vi*: **to ~ that**
притворя́ться (притвори́ться *pf*),
что; **he ~ed to help** он сде́лал
вид, что помога́ет; **he ~ed to be
asleep** он притвори́лся, что спит
**pretense** [prɪ'tɛns] *n* (*US*) =
**pretence**
**pretentious** [prɪ'tɛnʃəs] *adj*
претенцио́зный
**pretext** ['pri:tɛkst] *n* предло́г
**pretty** ['prɪtɪ] *adj* (*person*)
хоро́шенький; (*thing*) краси́вый
♦ *adv* (*quite*) дово́льно
**prevail** [prɪ'veɪl] *vi* (*be current*)
преоблада́ть (*impf*),
превали́ровать (*impf*); (*gain
influence*) оде́рживать (одержа́ть
*pf*) верх; **~ing** *adj* (*wind*)
преоблада́ющий
**prevent** [prɪ'vɛnt] *vt* (*accident etc*)
предотвраща́ть (предотврати́ть
*pf*), предупрежда́ть
(предупреди́ть *pf*); **to ~ sb from
doing** меша́ть (помеша́ть *pf*)
кому́-н +*infin*; **~ative** *adj* =
**preventive**; **~ion** [prɪ'vɛnʃən] *n*
предотвраще́ние,
предупрежде́ние; **~ive** *adj* (*POL,
measures*) превенти́вный;
(*medicine*) профилакти́ческий
**preview** ['pri:vju:] *n* (*of film*)
(закры́тый) просмо́тр; (*of
exhibition*) верниса́ж
**previous** ['pri:vɪəs] *adj*
предыду́щий; **~ to** до +*gen*; **~ly**
*adv* (*before*) ра́нее; (*in the past*)
пре́жде

**prey** [preɪ] *n* добы́ча
**price** [praɪs] *n* цена́ ♦ *vt* оце́нивать
(оцени́ть *pf*); **~less** *adj* (*diamond,
painting etc*) бесце́нный; **~ list** *n*
прейскура́нт
**prick** [prɪk] *n* (*pain*) уко́л ♦ *vt* (*make
hole in*) прока́лывать (проколо́ть
*pf*); (*finger*) коло́ть (уколо́ть *pf*);
**to ~ up one's ears** навостри́ть (*pf*)
у́ши
**prickly** ['prɪklɪ] *adj* колю́чий
**pride** [praɪd] *n* го́рдость *f*; (*pej:
arrogance*) горды́ня ♦ *vt*: **to ~ o.s.
on** горди́ться (*impf*) +*instr*
**priest** [pri:st] *n* свяще́нник; **~hood**
*n* свяще́нство
**prim** [prɪm] *adj* чо́порный
**primarily** ['praɪmərɪlɪ] *adv* в
пе́рвую о́чередь
**primary** ['praɪmərɪ] *adj* (*task*)
первостепе́нный,
первоочередно́й ♦ *n* (*US : POL*)
предвари́тельные вы́боры *mpl*; **~
school** *n* (*BRIT*) нача́льная шко́ла
**prime** [praɪm] *adj* (*most important*)
гла́вный, основно́й; (*best quality*)
первосо́ртный; (*example*) я́ркий
♦ *n* расцве́т ♦ *vt* (*fig: person*)
подгота́вливать (подгото́вить
*pf*); **Prime Minister** *n* премье́р-
мини́стр
**primitive** ['prɪmɪtɪv] *adj* (*early*)
первобы́тный; (*unsophisticated*)
примити́вный
**primrose** ['prɪmrəuz] *n* первоцве́т
**prince** [prɪns] *n* принц; (*Russian*)
князь *m*; **~ss** [prɪn'sɛs] *n*
принце́сса; (*Russian: wife*)
княги́ня; (: *daughter*) княжна́
**principal** ['prɪnsɪpl] *adj* гла́вный,
основно́й ♦ *n* (*of school, college*)
дире́ктор; (*of university*) ре́ктор
**principle** ['prɪnsɪpl] *n* при́нцип;
(*scientific law*) зако́н; **in ~** в
при́нципе; **on ~** из при́нципа
**print** [prɪnt] *n* (*TYP*) шрифт; (*ART*)

эстамп, гравюра; (*PHOT, fingerprint*) отпечаток; (*footprint*) след ♦ *vt* (*book etc*) печатать (напечатать *pf*); (*cloth*) набивать (набить *pf*); (*write in capitals*) писать (написать *pf*) печатными буквами; **this book is out of ~** эта книга больше не издаётся; **~er** *n* (*machine*) принтер; (*firm : also :* **~er's**) типография

**prior** ['praɪə<sup>r</sup>] *adj* (*previous*) прежний; (*more important*) главнейший; **to have ~ knowledge of sth** знать (*impf*) о чём-н заранее; **~ to** до +*gen*

**priority** [praɪ'ɔrɪtɪ] *n* (*most urgent task*) первоочередная задача; (*most important thing, task*) приоритет; **to have ~ (over)** иметь (*impf*) преимущество (перед +*instr*)

**prison** ['prɪzn] *n* тюрьма ♦ *cpd* тюремный; **~er** *n* (*in prison*) заключённый(ая) *m(f) adj*; (*captured person*) пленный(ая) *m(f) adj*; **~er of war** военнопленный *m adj*

**privacy** ['prɪvəsɪ] *n* уединение

**private** ['praɪvɪt] *adj* (*property, industry*) частный; (*discussion, club*) закрытый; (*belongings, life*) личный; (*thoughts, plans*) скрытый; (*secluded*) уединённый; (*secretive, reserved*) замкнутый; (*confidential*) конфиденциальный; **"~"** (*on door*) "посторонним вход воспрещён"; **in ~** конфиденциально

**privatize** ['praɪvɪtaɪz] *vt* приватизировать (*impf/pf*)

**privilege** ['prɪvɪlɪdʒ] *n* привилегия; **~d** *adj* привилегированный

**prize** [praɪz] *n* приз ♦ *adj* первоклассный ♦ *vt* (высоко) ценить (*impf*)

**pro** [prəu] *prep* (*in favour of*) за +*acc*

♦ *n*: **the ~s and cons** за и против

**probability** [prɔbə'bɪlɪtɪ] *n*: **~ of/ that** вероятность *f* +*gen*/того, что; **in all ~** по всей вероятности

**probable** ['prɔbəbl] *adj* вероятный

**probably** ['prɔbəblɪ] *adv* вероятно

**probation** [prə'beɪʃən] *n* (*LAW*) условное осуждение; (*employee*) испытательный срок

**probe** [prəub] *vt* (*investigate*) расследовать (*impf/pf*); (*poke*) прощупывать (прощупать *pf*)

**problem** ['prɔbləm] *n* проблема

**procedure** [prə'si:dʒə<sup>r</sup>] *n* процедура

**proceed** [prə'si:d] *vi* (*activity, event, process*) продолжаться (продолжиться *pf*); (*person*) продвигаться (продвинуться *pf*); **to ~ with** (*continue*) продолжать (продолжить *pf*); **to ~ to do** продолжать (продолжить *pf*) +*infin*; **~ings** *npl* (*events*) мероприятия *ntpl*; (*LAW*) судебное разбирательство *ntsg*

**process** ['prəuses] *n* процесс ♦ *vt* обрабатывать (обработать *pf*); **in the ~** в процессе

**procession** [prə'seʃən] *n* процессия

**proclaim** [prə'kleɪm] *vt* провозглашать (провозгласить *pf*)

**proclamation** [prɔklə'meɪʃən] *n* провозглашение

**prod** [prɔd] *vt* (*push*) тыкать (ткнуть *pf*) ♦ *n* тычок

**prodigy** ['prɔdɪdʒɪ] *n*: **child ~** вундеркинд

**produce** *vb* [prə'dju:s] *n* ['prɔdju:s] *vt* производить (произвести *pf*); (*CHEM*) вырабатывать (выработать *pf*); (*evidence, argument*) представлять (представить *pf*); (*bring or take out*) предъявлять (предъявить *pf*); (*play, film*) стáвить (постáвить *pf*) ♦ (*AGR*) (сельскохозя́йственная) продýкция; **~r** *n* (*of film, play*) режиссёр-постанóвщик, продю́сер; (*of record*) продю́сер

**product** [ˈprɔdʌkt] *n* (*thing*) изде́лие; (*food, result*) продýкт

**production** [prəˈdʌkʃən] *n* (*process*) произвóдство; (*amount produced*) продýкция; (*THEAT*) постанóвка

**productive** [prəˈdʌktɪv] *adj* производи́тельный, продукти́вный

**productivity** [prɔdʌkˈtɪvɪtɪ] *n* производи́тельность *f*, продукти́вность *f*

**profess** [prəˈfɛs] *vt* (*claim*) претендовáть (*impf*) на +*acc*

**profession** [prəˈfɛʃən] *n* профéссия; **~al** *adj* профессионáльный

**professor** [prəˈfɛsər] *n* (*BRIT*) профéссор; (*US*) преподавáтель(ница) *m(f)*

**proficient** [prəˈfɪʃənt] *adj* умéлый

**profile** [ˈprəufaɪl] *n* (*of face*) прóфиль *m*; (*article*) óчерк

**profit** [ˈprɔfɪt] *n* при́быль *f*, дохóд ♦ *vi*: **to ~ by** *or* **from** (*fig*) извлекáть (извлéчь *pf*) вы́году из +*gen*; **~ability** [prɔfɪtəˈbɪlɪtɪ] *n* при́быльность *f*; **~able** *adj* при́быльный; (*fig*) вы́годный

**profound** [prəˈfaund] *adj* глубóкий

**prognosis** [prɔgˈnəusɪs] (*pl* **prognoses**) *n* прогнóз

**program(me)** [ˈprəugræm] *n* прогрáмма ♦ *vt* программи́ровать (запрограмми́ровать *pf*); **~r** *n* программи́ст(ка)

**progress** *n* [ˈprəugrɛs] *vb* [prəˈgrɛs] *n* (*advances, changes*) прогрéсс; (*development*) разви́тие ♦ *vi* прогресси́ровать (*impf*); (*continue*)

продолжáться (продóлжиться *pf*); **the match is in ~** матч идёт; **~ion** [prəˈgrɛʃən] *n* (*gradual development*) продвижéние; **~ive** [prəˈgrɛsɪv] *adj* прогресси́вный; (*gradual*) постепéнный

**prohibit** [prəˈhɪbɪt] *vt* запрещáть (запрети́ть *pf*); **~ion** [prəuɪˈbɪʃən] *n* запрещéние, запрéт

**project** *n* [ˈprɔdʒɛkt] *vb* [prəˈdʒɛkt] *n* проéкт ♦ *vt* (*plan, estimate*) проекти́ровать (запроекти́ровать *pf*) ♦ *vi* (*jut out*) выступáть (вы́ступить *pf*)

**projection** [prəˈdʒɛkʃən] *n* (*estimate*) перспекти́вная оцéнка

**projector** [prəˈdʒɛktər] *n* (*CINEMA*) кинопроéктор; (*also*: **slide ~**) проéктор

**prolific** [prəˈlɪfɪk] *adj* плодови́тый

**prologue** [ˈprəulɔg] (*US* **prolog**) *n* пролóг

**prolong** [prəˈlɔŋ] *vt* продлевáть (продли́ть *pf*)

**promenade** [prɔməˈnɑːd] *n* променáд

**prominence** [ˈprɔmɪnəns] *n* (*of person*) ви́дное положéние; (*of issue*) ви́дное мéсто

**prominent** [ˈprɔmɪnənt] *adj* выдаю́щийся

**promiscuous** [prəˈmɪskjuəs] *adj* разврáтный

**promise** [ˈprɔmɪs] *n* (*vow*) обещáние; (*talent*) потенциáл; (*hope*) надéжда ♦ *vi* (*vow*) давáть (дать *pf*) обещáние ♦ *vt*: **to ~ sb sth**, **~ sth to sb** обещáть (пообещáть *pf*) что-н комý-н; **to ~ (sb) to do/that** обещáть (пообещáть *pf*) (комý-н) +*infin*/, что; **to ~ well** подавáть (*impf*) больши́е надéжды

**promising** [ˈprɔmɪsɪŋ] *adj* многообещáющий

**promote** [prəˈməut] *vt* (*employee*)

повыша́ть (повы́сить pf) (в до́лжности); (product, pop-star) реклами́ровать (impf/pf); (ideas) подде́рживать (поддержа́ть pf); **~r** n (of event) аге́нт; (of cause, idea) пропаганди́ст(ка)

**promotion** [prə'məʊʃən] n (at work) повыше́ние (в до́лжности); (of product, event) рекла́ма

**prompt** [prɔmpt] adj незамедли́тельный ♦ vt (cause) побужда́ть (побуди́ть pf); (when talking) подска́зывать (подсказа́ть pf) ♦ adv: at 8 o'clock ~ ро́вно в 8 часо́в; to ~ sb to do побужда́ть (побуди́ть pf) кого́-н +infin; **~ly** adv (immediately) незамедли́тельно; (exactly) то́чно

**prone** [prəʊn] adj: ~ to (inclined to) скло́нный к +dat

**pronoun** ['prəʊnaʊn] n местоиме́ние

**pronounce** [prə'naʊns] vt (word) произноси́ть (произнести́ pf); (declaration, verdict) объявля́ть (объяви́ть pf); (opinion) выска́зывать (вы́сказать pf); **~d** adj отчётливый

**pronunciation** [prənʌnsɪ'eɪʃən] n (of word) произноше́ние

**proof** [pru:f] n (evidence) доказа́тельство ♦ adj: this vodka is 70% ~ э́то семидесятигра́дусная во́дка

**prop** [prɔp] n (support) подпо́рка ♦ vt (also: ~ up) подпира́ть (подпере́ть pf); to ~ sth against прислоня́ть (прислони́ть pf) что-н к +dat; **~s** npl (THEAT) реквизи́т msg

**propaganda** [prɔpə'gændə] n пропага́нда

**propel** [prə'pɛl] vt (vehicle, machine) приводи́ть (привести́ pf) в движе́ние; **~ler** n пропе́ллер

**proper** ['prɔpər] adj (real)

настоя́щий; (correct) до́лжный, надлежа́щий; (socially acceptable) прили́чный; **~ly** adv (eat, study) как сле́дует; (behave) прили́чно, до́лжным о́бразом

**property** ['prɔpətɪ] n (possessions) со́бственность f; (building and land) недви́жимость f; (quality) сво́йство

**prophecy** ['prɔfɪsɪ] n проро́чество

**proportion** [prə'pɔ:ʃən] n (part) часть f, до́ля; (ratio) пропо́рция, соотноше́ние; **~al** adj: **~al (to)** пропорциона́льный (+dat)

**proposal** [prə'pəʊzl] n предложе́ние

**propose** [prə'pəʊz] vt (plan, toast) предлага́ть (предложи́ть pf); (motion) выдвига́ть (вы́двинуть pf) ♦ vi (offer marriage): **to ~ (to sb)** де́лать (сде́лать pf) предложе́ние (кому́-н); **to ~ sth/ to do** or **doing** предполага́ть (impf) что-н/+infin

**proposition** [prɔpə'zɪʃən] n (statement) утвержде́ние; (offer) предложе́ние

**proprietor** [prə'praɪətər] n владе́лец(лица)

**prose** [prəʊz] n (not poetry) про́за

**prosecute** ['prɔsɪkju:t] vt: **to ~ sb** пресле́довать (impf) кого́-н в суде́бном поря́дке

**prosecution** [prɔsɪ'kju:ʃən] n (LAW, action) суде́бное пресле́дование; (: accusing side) обвине́ние

**prosecutor** ['prɔsɪkju:tər] n обвини́тель m

**prospect** ['prɔspɛkt] n перспекти́ва; **~s** npl (for work etc) перспекти́вы fpl; **~ive** [prə'spɛktɪv] adj (future) бу́дущий; (potential) возмо́жный; **~us** [prə'spɛktəs] n проспе́кт

**prosper** ['prɔspər] vi преуспева́ть (преуспе́ть pf); **~ity** [prɔ'spɛrɪtɪ] n

процветáние; **~ous** adj
преуспевáющий
**prostitute** ['prɒstɪtjuːt] n
проститýтка
**protagonist** [prə'tægənɪst] n
(supporter) привéрженец
**protect** [prə'tɛkt] vt защищáть
(защитить pf); **~ion** [prə'tɛkʃən] n
защита; **~ive** adj защитный;
(person) забóтливый, бéрежный
**protein** ['prəutiːn] n белóк,
протеин
**protest** n ['prəutɛst] vb [prə'tɛst] n
протéст ♦ vi: **to ~ about/against**
протестовáть (impf) по повóду
+gen/прóтив +gen ♦ vt (insist): **to ~
that** заявлять (заявить pf), что
**Protestant** ['prɒtɪstənt] n
протестáнт(ка)
**protocol** ['prəutəkɒl] n протокóл
**prototype** ['prəutətaɪp] n прототип
**proud** [praud] adj: **~ (of)** гóрдый
(+instr)
**prove** [pruːv] vt докáзывать
(доказáть pf) ♦ vi: **to ~ (to be)**
оказáться (impf/pf) +instr; **to ~ o.s.**
проявлять (проявить pf) себя
**proverb** ['prɒvəːb] n послóвица;
**~ial** [prə'vəːbɪəl] adj легендáрный
**provide** [prə'vaɪd] vt обеспéчивать
(обеспéчить pf) +instr; **to ~ sb
with sth** обеспéчивать
(обеспéчить pf) когó-н чем-н; **~
for** vt fus (person) обеспéчивать
(обеспéчить pf); **~d (that)** conj
при услóвии, что
**providing** [prə'vaɪdɪŋ] conj =
**provided (that)**
**province** ['prɒvɪns] n óбласть f
**provincial** [prə'vɪnʃəl] adj
провинциáльный
**provision** [prə'vɪʒən] n (supplying)
обеспéчение; (of contract,
agreement) положéние; **~s** npl
(food) провизия fsg; **~al** adj
врéменный

**provocation** [prɒvə'keɪʃən] n
провокáция
**provocative** [prə'vɒkətɪv] adj
(remark, gesture) провокациóнный
**provoke** [prə'vəuk] vt
провоцировать
(спровоцировать pf)
**proximity** [prɒk'sɪmɪtɪ] n блúзость
f
**proxy** ['prɒksɪ] n: **by ~** по
довéренности
**prudent** ['pruːdnt] adj
благоразýмный
**prune** [pruːn] n черносли́в m no pl
♦ vt подрезáть (подрéзать pf)
**PS** abbr = **postscript**
**pseudonym** ['sjuːdənɪm] n
псевдоним
**psychiatric** [saɪkɪ'ætrɪk] adj
психиатрический
**psychiatrist** [saɪ'kaɪətrɪst] n
психиáтр
**psychic** ['saɪkɪk] adj (also: **~al**:
person) яснови́дящий
**psychological** [saɪkə'lɒdʒɪkl] adj
психологи́ческий
**psychologist** [saɪ'kɒlədʒɪst] n
психóлог
**psychology** [saɪ'kɒlədʒɪ] n
психолóгия
**psychopath** ['saɪkəupæθ] n
психопáт(ка)
**psychotic** [saɪ'kɒtɪk] adj
психически больнóй
**PTO** abbr (= please turn over)
смотри́ на оборóте
**pub** [pʌb] n паб, пивнáя f adj
**puberty** ['pjuːbətɪ] n половáя
зрéлость f
**public** ['pʌblɪk] adj обще́ственный;
(statement, action etc) публи́чный
♦ n: **the ~** (everyone)
обще́ственность f, нарóд; **to
make ~** предавáть (предáть pf)
глáсности; **in ~** публи́чно
**publication** [pʌblɪ'keɪʃən] n

публика́ция, изда́ние

**publicity** [pʌb'lɪsɪtɪ] n (information) рекла́ма, па́блисити nt ind; (attention) шуми́ха

**publicize** ['pʌblɪsaɪz] vt предава́ть (преда́ть pf) гла́сности

**public**: **~ly** adv публи́чно; **~ opinion** n обще́ственное мне́ние; **~ relations** npl вне́шние свя́зи fpl, свя́зи с обще́ственностью; **~ school** n (BRIT) ча́стная шко́ла; (US) госуда́рственная шко́ла

**publish** ['pʌblɪʃ] vt издава́ть (изда́ть pf); (PRESS, letter, article) публикова́ть (опубликова́ть pf); **~er** n (company) изда́тельство; **~ing** n (profession) изда́тельское де́ло

**pudding** ['pudɪŋ] n пу́динг; (BRIT: dessert) сла́дкое nt adj; **black~**, (US) **blood ~** кровяна́я колбаса́

**puddle** ['pʌdl] n лу́жа

**puff** [pʌf] n (of wind) дунове́ние; (of cigarette, pipe) затя́жка; (of smoke) клуб

**pull** [pul] vt тяну́ть (потяну́ть pf); (trigger) нажима́ть (нажа́ть pf) на +acc; (curtains etc) заде́ргивать (задёрнуть pf) ♦ vi (tug) тяну́ть (impf) ♦ n: **to give sth a ~** (tug) тяну́ть (потяну́ть pf) что-н; **to ~ to pieces** разрыва́ть (разорва́ть pf) на ча́сти; **to ~ o.s. together** брать (взять pf) себя́ в ру́ки; **to ~ sb's leg** (fig) разы́грывать (разыгра́ть pf) кого́-н; **~ down** vt (building) сноси́ть (снести́ pf); **~ in** vt (crowds, people) привлека́ть (привле́чь pf); **~ out** vt (extract) выта́скивать (вы́тащить pf) ♦ vi: **to ~ out (from)** (AUT: from kerb) отъезжа́ть (отъе́хать pf) (от +gen); **~ up** vi (stop) остана́вливаться (останови́ться pf) ♦ vt (plant) вырыва́ть (вы́рвать

pf) (с ко́рнем)

**pulley** ['pulɪ] n шкив

**pullover** ['puləuvər] n сви́тер, пуло́вер

**pulpit** ['pulpɪt] n ка́федра

**pulse** [pʌls] n (ANAT) пульс

**puma** ['pju:mə] n пу́ма

**pump** [pʌmp] n насо́с; (also: **petrol ~**) бензоколо́нка ♦ vt кача́ть (накача́ть pf); (extract: oil, water, gas) выка́чивать (вы́качать pf)

**pumpkin** ['pʌmpkɪn] n ты́ква

**pun** [pʌn] n каламбу́р

**punch** [pʌntʃ] n уда́р; ( for making holes) дыроко́л; (drink) пунш ♦ vt (hit): **to ~ sb/sth** ударя́ть (уда́рить pf) кого́-н/что-н кулако́м

**punctual** ['pʌŋktjuəl] adj пунктуа́льный

**punctuation** [pʌŋktju'eɪʃən] n пунктуа́ция

**puncture** ['pʌŋktʃər] n (AUT) проко́л ♦ vt прока́лывать (проколо́ть pf)

**punish** ['pʌnɪʃ] vt: **to ~ sb (for sth)** нака́зывать (наказа́ть pf) кого́-н (за что-н); **~ment** n наказа́ние

**punter** ['pʌntər] n (inf: customer) клие́нт(ка)

**pupil** ['pju:pl] n (SCOL) учени́к(и́ца); (of eye) зрачо́к

**puppet** ['pʌpɪt] n марионе́тка

**puppy** ['pʌpɪ] n ( young dog) щено́к

**purchase** ['pə:tʃɪs] n поку́пка ♦ vt покупа́ть (купи́ть pf)

**pure** [pjuər] adj чи́стый; **~ly** adv чи́сто

**purify** ['pjuərɪfaɪ] vt очища́ть (очи́стить pf)

**purity** ['pjuərɪtɪ] n чистота́

**purple** ['pə:pl] adj фиоле́товый

**purpose** ['pə:pəs] n цель f; **on ~** наме́ренно; **~ful** adj целеустремлённый

**purr** [pə:r] *vi* мурлы́кать *(impf)*

**purse** [pə:s] *n (BRIT:* кошелёк; *(US: handbag)* су́мка ♦ *vt:* **to ~ one's lips** поджима́ть (поджа́ть *pf)* гу́бы

**pursue** [pə'sju:] *vt* пресле́довать *(impf)*; *(fig: policy)* проводи́ть *(impf)*; *(: interest)* проявля́ть *(impf)*

**pursuit** [pə'sju:t] *n (of person, thing)* пресле́дование; *(of happiness, wealth etc)* по́иски *mpl*; *(pastime)* заня́тие

**push** [puʃ] *n (shove)* толчо́к ♦ *vt (press)* нажима́ть (нажа́ть *pf)*; *(shove)* толка́ть (толкну́ть *pf)*; *(promote)* прота́лкивать (протолкну́ть *pf)* ♦ *vi (press)* нажима́ть (нажа́ть *pf)*; *(shove)* толка́ться *(impf)*; *(fig):* **to ~ for** тре́бовать (потре́бовать *pf)* +*acc* or +*gen*; **~ through** *vt (measure, scheme)* прота́лкивать (протолкну́ть *pf)*; **~ up** *vt (prices)* повыша́ть (повы́сить *pf)*; **~y** *adj (pej)* насты́рный

**put** [put] *(pt, pp ~)* *vt* ста́вить (поста́вить *pf)*; *(thing: horizontally)* класть (положи́ть *pf)*; *(person: in institution)* помеща́ть (помести́ть *pf)*; *(: in prison)* сажа́ть (посади́ть *pf)*; *(idea, feeling)* выража́ть (вы́разить *pf)*; *(case, view)* излага́ть (изложи́ть *pf)*; **I ~ it to you that ...** я говорю́ Вам, что ...; **~ across** *vt (ideas etc)* объясня́ть (объясни́ть *pf)*; **~ away** *vt (store)* убира́ть (убра́ть *pf)*; **~ back** *vt (replace)* класть (положи́ть *pf)* на ме́сто; *(postpone)* откла́дывать (отложи́ть *pf)*; *(delay)* заде́рживать (задержа́ть *pf)*; **~ by** *vt* откла́дывать (отложи́ть *pf)*; **~ down** *vt (place)* ста́вить (поста́вить *pf)*; *(: horizontally)* класть (положи́ть *pf)*; *(note down)* запи́сывать (записа́ть *pf)*;

*(suppress, humiliate)* подавля́ть (подави́ть *pf)*; *(animal: kill)* умерщвля́ть (умертви́ть *pf)*; **to ~ sth down to** *(attribute)* объясня́ть (объясни́ть *pf)* что-н +*instr*; **~ forward** *vt (ideas)* выдвига́ть (вы́двинуть *pf)*; **~ in** *vt (application, complaint)* подава́ть (пода́ть *pf)*; *(time, effort)* вкла́дывать (вложи́ть *pf)*; **~ off** *vt (delay)* откла́дывать (отложи́ть *pf)*; *(discourage)* отта́лкивать (оттолкну́ть *pf)*; *(switch off)* выключа́ть (вы́ключить *pf)*; **~ on** *vt (clothes)* надева́ть (наде́ть *pf)*; *(make-up, ointment etc)* накла́дывать (наложи́ть *pf)*; *(light etc)* включа́ть (включи́ть *pf)*; *(kettle, record, dinner)* ста́вить (поста́вить *pf)*; *(assume: look)* напуска́ть (напусти́ть *pf)* на себя́; *(behaviour)* принима́ть (приня́ть *pf)*; **to ~ on weight** поправля́ться (попра́виться *pf)*; **~ out** *vt (fire)* туши́ть (потуши́ть *pf)*; *(candle, cigarette, light)* гаси́ть (погаси́ть *pf)*; *(rubbish)* выноси́ть (вы́нести *pf)*; *(one's hand)* вытя́гивать (вы́тянуть *pf)*; **~ through** *vt (person, call)* соединя́ть (соедини́ть *pf)*; *(plan, agreement)* выполня́ть (вы́полнить *pf)*; **~ up** *vt (building, tent)* ста́вить (поста́вить *pf)*; *(umbrella)* раскрыва́ть (раскры́ть *pf)*; *(hood)* надева́ть (наде́ть *pf)*; *(poster, sign)* выве́шивать (вы́весить *pf)*; *(price, cost)* поднима́ть (подня́ть *pf)*; *(guest)* помеща́ть (помести́ть *pf)*; **~ up with** *vt fus* мири́ться *(impf)* с +*instr*

**putty** ['pʌtɪ] *n* зама́зка

**puzzle** ['pʌzl] *n (game, toy)* головоло́мка

**puzzling** ['pʌzlɪŋ] *adj* запу́танный

**pyjamas** [pɪ'dʒɑ:məz] *(US* **pajamas)**

*npl*: **(a pair of) ~** пижа́ма *fsg*
**pylon** ['paɪlən] *n* пило́н, опо́ра
**pyramid** ['pɪrəmɪd] *n (GEOM)*
пирами́да
**python** ['paɪθən] *n* пито́н

# Q, q

**quadruple** [kwɔ'dru:pl] *vt*
увели́чивать (увели́чить *pf*) в
четы́ре ра́за ♦ *vi* увели́чиваться
(увели́читься *pf*) в четы́ре ра́за
**quaint** [kweɪnt] *adj* чудно́й
**quake** [kweɪk] *vi* трепета́ть *(impf)*
**qualification** [kwɔlɪfɪ'keɪʃən] *n (usu
pl: academic, vocational)*
квалифика́ция; *(skill, quality)*
ка́чество; **what are your ~s?**
кака́я у Вас квалифика́ция?
**qualified** ['kwɔlɪfaɪd] *adj (trained)*
квалифици́рованный; **I'm not ~
to judge that** я не компете́нтен
суди́ть об э́том
**qualify** ['kwɔlɪfaɪ] *vt (modify: make
more specific)* уточня́ть (уточни́ть
*pf*); (: *express reservation*)
огова́ривать (оговори́ть *pf*) ♦ *vi*:
**to ~ as an engineer** получа́ть
(получи́ть *pf*) квалифика́цию
инжене́ра; **to ~ (for)** *(benefit etc)*
име́ть *(impf)* пра́во (на +*acc*); (*in
competition*) выходи́ть (вы́йти *pf*)
в +*acc*
**quality** ['kwɔlɪtɪ] *n* ка́чество;
(*property: of wood, stone*) сво́йство
**quantity** ['kwɔntɪtɪ] *n* коли́чество
**quarantine** ['kwɔrntɪ:n] *n*
каранти́н
**quarrel** ['kwɔrl] *n* ссо́ра ♦ *vi*: **to ~
(with)** ссо́риться (поссо́риться
*pf*) (с +*instr*); **~some** *adj* вздо́рный
**quarry** ['kwɔrɪ] *n* карье́р; (*for stone*)
каменоло́мня
**quarter** ['kwɔ:tər] *n* че́тверть *f*; (*of
year, town*) кварта́л; (*US: coin*)

два́дцать пять це́нтов ♦ *vt*
дели́ть (раздели́ть *pf*) на четы́ре
ча́сти; **~s** *npl* (*for living*)
помеще́ние *ntsg*; (: *MIL*) каза́рмы
*fpl*; **a ~ of an hour** че́тверть *f*
ча́са; **~ly** *adj* (*meeting*)
(еже)кварта́льный; (*payment*)
(по)кварта́льный ♦ *adv* (*see adj*)
ежекварта́льно; покварта́льно
**quartz** [kwɔ:ts] *n* кварц
**quash** [kwɔʃ] *vt* (*verdict, judgement*)
отменя́ть (отмени́ть *pf*)
**quay** [ki:] *n* (*also*: **~side**) при́стань
*f*
**queasy** ['kwi:zɪ] *adj*: **I feel a bit ~**
меня́ немно́го мути́т
**queen** [kwi:n] *n* короле́ва; (*CARDS*)
да́ма; (*CHESS*) ферзь *m*
**queer** [kwɪər] *adj* (*odd*) стра́нный
♦ *n* (*pej: homosexual*) го́мик,
голубо́й *m adj*
**quell** [kwɛl] *vt* подавля́ть
(подави́ть *pf*)
**quench** [kwɛntʃ] *vt*: **to ~ one's
thirst** утоля́ть (утоли́ть *pf*)
жа́жду
**query** ['kwɪərɪ] *n* вопро́с ♦ *vt*
подверга́ть (подве́ргнуть *pf*)
сомне́нию
**quest** [kwɛst] *n* по́иск
**question** ['kwɛstʃən] *n* вопро́с;
(*doubt*) сомне́ние ♦ *vt* (*interrogate*)
допра́шивать (допроси́ть *pf*);
(*doubt*) усомни́ться (*pf*) в +*prp*;
**beyond ~** бесспо́рно; **that's out
of the ~** об э́том не мо́жет быть
и ре́чи; **~able** *adj* сомни́тельный;
**~ mark** *n* вопроси́тельный знак;
**~naire** [kwɛstʃə'nɛər] *n* анке́та
**queue** [kju:] *n* (*BRIT*) о́чередь *f* ♦ *vi*
(*also*: **~ up**) стоя́ть *(impf)* в
о́череди
**quibble** ['kwɪbl] *vi*: **to ~ about** or
**over** спо́рить (поспо́рить *pf*) о
+*prp*
**quick** [kwɪk] *adj* бы́стрый; (*clever*:

*person*) сообрази́тельный;
(: *mind*) живо́й; (*brief*) кра́ткий;
**be ~!** бы́стро!; **~ly** *adv* бы́стро;
**~sand** *n* зыбу́чий песо́к;
**~-witted** *adj* сообрази́тельный

**quid** [kwɪd] *n inv* (*BRIT* : *inf*) фунт
(сте́рлингов)

**quiet** ['kwaɪət] *adj* ти́хий; (*peaceful, not busy*) споко́йный; (*without fuss*) сде́ржанный ♦ *n* (*silence*)
тишина́; (*peace*) поко́й; **~en** *vi*
(*also*: **~en down**) затиха́ть
(зати́хнуть *pf*); **~ly** *adv* ти́хо;
(*calmly*) споко́йно

**quilt** [kwɪlt] *n* (*also*: **continental ~**)
стёганое одея́ло

**quirk** [kwəːk] *n* причу́да, при́хоть
*f*

**quit** [kwɪt] (*pt, pp* ~ *or* **~ted**) *vt*
броса́ть (бро́сить *pf*) ♦ *vi* (*give up*)
сдава́ться (сда́ться *pf*); (*resign*)
увольня́ться (уво́литься *pf*)

**quite** [kwaɪt] *adv* (*rather*)
дово́льно; (*entirely*) соверше́нно;
(*almost*): **the flat's not ~ big enough** кварти́ра недоста́точно
больша́я; **~ a few** дово́льно
мно́го; **~ (so)!** ве́рно!, (вот)
и́менно!

**quits** [kwɪts] *adj*: **let's call it ~**
бу́дем кви́ты

**quiver** ['kwɪvəʳ] *vi* (*shake*)
трепета́ть (*impf*)

**quiz** [kwɪz] *n* (*game*) викто́рина
♦ *vt* расспра́шивать
(расспроси́ть *pf*)

**quota** ['kwəʊtə] *n* кво́та

**quotation** [kwəʊ'teɪʃən] *n* цита́та;
(*estimate*) цена́ (продавца́)

**quote** [kwəʊt] *n* цита́та; (*estimate*)
цена́ ♦ *vt* цити́ровать
(процити́ровать *pf*); (*figure, example*) приводи́ть (привести́
*pf*); (*price*) назнача́ть (назна́чить
*pf*); **~s** *npl* (*quotation marks*)
кавы́чки *fpl*

# R, r

**rabbi** ['ræbaɪ] *n* равви́н

**rabbit** ['ræbɪt] *n* (*male*) кро́лик;
(*female*) крольчи́ха

**rabble** ['ræbl] *n* (*pej*) сброд

**rabies** ['reɪbiːz] *n* бе́шенство,
водобоя́знь *f*

**RAC** *n abbr* (*BRIT*: = *Royal Automobile Club*) Короле́вская
автомоби́льная ассоциа́ция

**race** [reɪs] *n* (*species*) ра́са;
(*competition*) го́нки *fpl*; (: *running*)
забе́г; (: *swimming*) заплы́в;
(: *horse race*) ска́чки *fpl*; (*for power, control*) борьба́ ♦ *vt* (*horse*) гнать
(*impf*) ♦ *vi* (*compete*) принима́ть
(приня́ть *pf*) уча́стие в
соревнова́нии; (*hurry*) мча́ться
(*impf*); (*pulse*) учаща́ться
(участи́ться *pf*); **~course** *n*
ипподро́м; **~horse** *n* скакова́я
ло́шадь *f*

**racial** ['reɪʃl] *adj* ра́совый

**racing** ['reɪsɪŋ] *n* (*horse racing*)
ска́чки *fpl*; (*motor racing*) го́нки *fpl*

**racism** ['reɪsɪzəm] *n* раси́зм

**racist** ['reɪsɪst] *adj* раси́стский ♦ *n*
раси́ст(ка)

**rack** [ræk] *n* (*shelf*) по́лка; (*also*:
**luggage ~**) бага́жная по́лка;
(*also*: **roof ~**) бага́жник (*на
кры́ше автомоби́ля*); (*for dishes*)
суши́лка для посу́ды ♦ *vt*: **she
was ~ed by pain** её терза́ла
боль; **to ~ one's brains** лома́ть
(*impf*) го́лову

**racket** ['rækɪt] *n* (*SPORT*) раке́тка;
(*noise*) гвалт; (*con*) жу́льничество;
(*extortion*) рэ́кет

**radar** ['reɪdɑːʳ] *n* рада́р

**radiance** ['reɪdɪəns] *n* (*glow*)
сия́ние

**radiant** ['reɪdɪənt] *adj* (*smile, person*)

сия́ющий

**radiation** [reɪdɪˈeɪʃən] n (radioactive)
радиа́ция, радиоакти́вное
излуче́ние; (of heat, light)
излуче́ние

**radiator** [ˈreɪdɪeɪtəʳ] n радиа́тор,
батаре́я; (AUT) радиа́тор

**radical** [ˈrædɪkl] adj радика́льный

**radii** [ˈreɪdɪaɪ] npl of **radius**

**radio** [ˈreɪdɪəu] n (broadcasting)
ра́дио nt ind; (for transmitting and
receiving) радиопереда́тчик ♦ vt
(person) свя́зываться (связа́ться
pf) по ра́дио с +instr; on the ~ по
ра́дио; **~active** adj
радиоакти́вный; **~ station** n
радиоста́нция

**radish** [ˈrædɪʃ] n реди́ска; **~es**
реди́с msg

**radius** [ˈreɪdɪəs] (pl **radii**) n ра́диус

**RAF** n abbr (BRIT: = **Royal Air
Force**) ≈ ВВС

**raffle** [ˈræfl] n (вещева́я) лотере́я

**raft** [rɑːft] n плот

**rag** [ræg] n тря́пка; (pej: newspaper)
газете́нка; **~s** npl (clothes)
лохмо́тья pl

**rage** [reɪdʒ] n (fury) бе́шенство,
я́рость f ♦ vi (person)
свире́пствовать (impf); (storm,
debate) бушева́ть (impf); it's all
the ~ (in fashion) все помеша́лись
на э́том

**ragged** [ˈrægɪd] adj (edge)
зазу́бренный; (clothes)
потрёпанный

**raid** [reɪd] n (MIL) рейд; (criminal)
налёт; (by police) обла́ва, рейд
♦ vt (see n) соверша́ть
(соверши́ть pf) рейд на +acc;
соверша́ть (соверши́ть pf) налёт
на +acc

**rail** [reɪl] n (on stairs, bridge etc)
пери́ла pl; **~s** npl (RAIL) ре́льсы
mpl; **by ~** по́ездом; **~ing(s)** n(pl)
(iron fence) решётка fsg; **~road** n

(US) = **railway**; **~way** n (BRIT)
желе́зная доро́га ♦ cpd
железнодоро́жный; **~way line** n
(BRIT) железнодоро́жная ли́ния;
**~way station** n (BRIT: large)
железнодоро́жный вокза́л;
(: small) железнодоро́жная
ста́нция

**rain** [reɪn] n дождь m ♦ vi: it's ~ing
идёт дождь; in the ~ под
дождём, в дождь; **~bow** n
ра́дуга; **~coat** n плащ; **~fall** n
(measurement) у́ровень m
оса́дков; **~y** adj (day) дождли́вый

**raise** [reɪz] n (esp US) повыше́ние
♦ vt (lift, produce) поднима́ть
(подня́ть pf); (increase, improve)
повыша́ть (повы́сить pf); (doubts:
subj: person) выска́зывать
(вы́сказать pf); (: results)
вызыва́ть (вы́звать pf); (rear:
family) воспи́тывать (воспита́ть
pf); (get together: army, funds)
собира́ть (собра́ть pf); (: loan)
изы́скивать (изыска́ть pf); **to ~
one's voice** повыша́ть (повы́сить
pf) го́лос

**raisin** [ˈreɪzn] n изю́минка; **~s**
изю́м m no pl

**rake** [reɪk] n (tool) гра́бли pl ♦ vt
(garden) разра́внивать
(разровня́ть pf) (гра́блями);
(leaves, hay) сгреба́ть (сгрести́ pf)

**rally** [ˈrælɪ] n (POL etc)
манифеста́ция; (AUT)
(а́вто)ра́лли nt ind; (TENNIS) ра́лли
nt ind ♦ vt (supporters) спла́чивать
(сплоти́ть pf) ♦ vi (supporters)
спла́чиваться (сплоти́ться pf)

**RAM** n abbr (COMPUT: = random
access memory) ЗУПВ

**ram** [ræm] n бара́н ♦ vt (crash into)
тара́нить (протара́нить pf); (push:
bolt) задвига́ть (задви́нуть pf);
(: fist) дви́нуть (pf) +instr

**ramble** [ˈræmbl] vi (walk) броди́ть

(impf); (talk : also: ~ **on**)
заимствовать (impf)
**rambling** ['ræmblɪŋ] adj (speech)
несвязный
**ramp** [ræmp] n скат, уклон; **on ~**
(US : AUT) въезд на автостраду;
**off ~** (US : AUT) съезд с
автострады
**rampage** [ræm'peɪdʒ] n: **to be on
the ~** буйствовать (impf)
**rampant** ['ræmpənt] adj: **to be ~**
(crime) свирепствовать (impf)
**ramshackle** ['ræmʃækl] adj ветхий
**ran** [ræn] pt of **run**
**ranch** [rɑːntʃ] n ранчо nt ind
**random** ['rændəm] adj случайный
♦ n: **at ~** наугад
**rang** [ræŋ] pt of **ring**
**range** [reɪndʒ] n (series: of proposals)
ряд; (: of products) ассортимент m
no pl; (: of colours) гамма; (of
mountains) цепь f; (of missile)
дальность f, радиус действия;
(of voice) диапазон; (MIL : also:
**shooting ~**) стрельбище ♦ vt
(place in a line) выстраивать
(выстроить pf) ♦ vi: **to ~ over**
(extend ) простираться (impf); **to ~
from ... to ...** колебаться (impf) от
+gen ... до +gen ...
**ranger** ['reɪndʒər] n (in forest)
лесник; (in park)
смотритель(ница) m(f)
**rank** [ræŋk] n (row) ряд; (MIL)
шеренга; (status) чин, ранг;
(BRIT : also: **taxi ~**) стоянка такси
♦ vi: **to ~ among** числиться (impf)
среди +gen ♦ vt: **I ~ him sixth** я
ставлю его на шестое место; **the
~ and file** (fig) рядовые члены
mpl
**ransom** ['rænsəm] n выкуп; **to hold
to ~** (fig) держать (impf) в
заложниках
**rant** [rænt] vi: **to ~ and rave** рвать
(impf) и метать (impf)

**rap** [ræp] vi: **to ~ on a door/table**
стучать (постучать pf) в дверь/
по столу
**rape** [reɪp] n изнасилование ♦ vt
насиловать (изнасиловать pf)
**rapid** ['ræpɪd] adj стремительный;
**~ly** adv стремительно
**rapist** ['reɪpɪst] n насильник
**rapport** [ræ'pɔːr] n
взаимопонимание
**rapturous** ['ræptʃərəs] adj
восторженный
**rare** [reər] adj редкий; (steak)
кровавый; **~ly** adv редко,
нечасто
**rash** [ræʃ] adj опрометчивый ♦ n
(MED) сыпь f no pl
**raspberry** ['rɑːzbərɪ] n малина f no
pl
**rat** [ræt] n (also fig) крыса
**rate** [reɪt] n (speed) скорость f; (: of
change, inflation) темп; (of interest)
ставка; (ratio) уровень m; (price:
at hotel etc) расценка ♦ vt (value)
оценивать (оценить pf); (estimate)
расценивать (расценить pf); **~s**
npl (BRIT: property tax) налог msg
на недвижимость; **to ~ sb as**
считать (impf) кого-н +instr; **to ~
sth as** расценивать (расценить
pf) что-н как
**rather** ['rɑːðər] adv (quite, somewhat)
довольно; (to some extent)
несколько; (more accurately): **or ~**
вернее сказать; **it's ~ expensive**
(quite) это довольно дорого;
**there's ~ a lot** довольно много; **I
would ~ go** я, пожалуй, пойду;
**I'd ~ not leave** я бы не хотел
уходить; **~ than** (+n) а не +nom,
вместо +gen; **~ than go to the
park, I went to the cinema**
вместо того чтобы идти в парк,
я пошёл в кино
**ratify** ['rætɪfaɪ] vt ратифицировать
(impf/pf)

**rating** ['reɪtɪŋ] n оце́нка, ре́йтинг; **~s** npl (RADIO, TV) ре́йтинг msg

**ratio** ['reɪʃɪəu] n соотноше́ние; **in the ~ of one hundred to one** в соотноше́нии сто к одному́

**ration** ['ræʃən] n (allowance: of food) рацио́н, паёк; (: of petrol) но́рма ♦ vt норми́ровать (impf/pf); **~s** npl (MIL) рацио́н msg

**rational** ['ræʃənl] adj разу́мный, рациона́льный; **~ly** adv рациона́льно

**rattle** ['rætl] n дребезжа́ние; (of train, car) громыха́ние; (for baby) погрему́шка ♦ vi (small objects) дребезжа́ть (impf) ♦ vt (shake noisily) сотряса́ть (сотрясти́ pf); (fig: unsettle) нерви́ровать (impf); **to ~ along** (car, bus) прогромыха́ть (impf); **the wind ~d the windows** о́кна дребезжа́ли от ве́тра; **~snake** n грему́чая змея́

**raucous** ['rɔːkəs] adj роко́чущий

**rave** [reɪv] vi (in anger) бесснова́ться (impf), бушева́ть (impf); (MED) бре́дить (impf); (with enthusiasm): **to ~ about** восторга́ться (impf) +instr

**raven** ['reɪvən] n во́рон

**ravine** [rə'viːn] n уще́лье

**raw** [rɔː] adj сыро́й; (unrefined: sugar) нерафини́рованный; (sore) све́жий; (inexperienced) зелёный; (weather, day) промо́зглый; **~ material** n сырьё nt no pl

**ray** [reɪ] n луч; (of heat) пото́к

**razor** ['reɪzər] n бри́тва; **safety ~** безопа́сная бри́тва; **electric ~** электробри́тва

**Rd** abbr = **road**

**re** [riː] prep относи́тельно +gen

**reach** [riːtʃ] vt (place, end, agreement) достига́ть (дости́гнуть or дости́чь pf) +gen; (conclusion, decision) приходи́ть (прийти́ pf) к +dat; (be able to touch) достава́ть (доста́ть pf); (by telephone) свя́зываться (связа́ться pf) с +instr ♦ vi: **to ~ into** запуска́ть (запусти́ть pf) ру́ку в +acc; **out of/within ~** вне/в преде́лах досяга́емости; **within ~ of the shops** недалеко́ от магази́нов; **"keep out of the ~ of children"** "бере́чь от дете́й"; **to ~ for** прота́гивать (протяну́ть pf) ру́ку к +dat; **to ~ up** прота́гивать (протяну́ть pf) ру́ку вверх; **~ out** vt прота́гивать (протяну́ть pf) ♦ vi: **to ~ out for sth** прота́гивать (протяну́ть pf) ру́ку за чем-н

**react** [riː'ækt] vi (CHEM): **to ~ (with)** вступа́ть (вступи́ть pf) в реа́кцию (с +instr); (MED): **to ~ (to)** реаги́ровать (impf) (на +acc); (respond) реаги́ровать (отреаги́ровать pf) (на +acc); (rebel): **to ~ (against)** восстава́ть (восста́ть pf) (про́тив +gen); **~ion** [riː'ækʃən] n (CHEM) реа́кция; (also MED, POL): **~ion (to/against)** реа́кция (на +acc/про́тив +gen); **~ions** npl (reflexes) реа́кция fsg; **~ionary** [riː'ækʃənrɪ] adj реакцио́нный; **~or** n (also: **nuclear ~or**) реа́ктор

**read¹** [red] pt, pp of **read²**

**read²** [riːd] (pt, pp ~) vt чита́ть (прочита́ть or проче́сть pf); (mood) определя́ть (определи́ть pf); (thermometer etc) снима́ть (снять pf) показа́ния с +gen; (SCOL) изуча́ть (impf) ♦ vi (person) чита́ть (impf); (text etc) чита́ться (impf); **~ out** vt зачи́тывать (зачита́ть pf); **~er** n (of book, newspaper etc) чита́тель(ница) m(f); **~ership** n (of newspaper etc) круг чита́телей

**readily** ['redɪlɪ] adv (willingly) с гото́вностью; (easily) легко́

**readiness** ['rɛdɪnɪs] n готóвность f; **in ~** наготóве

**reading** ['riːdɪŋ] n (of books etc) чтéние; (on thermometer etc) показáние

**ready** ['rɛdɪ] adj готóвый ♦ vt: **to get sb/sth ~** готóвить (подготóвить pf) когó-н/что-н; **to get ~** готóвиться (приготóвиться pf)

**real** [rɪəl] adj настоя́щий; (leather) натурáльный; **in ~ terms** реáльно; **~ estate** n недви́жимость f; **~ism** n реали́зм; **~istic** [rɪə'lɪstɪk] adj реалисти́ческий; **~ity** [riː'ælɪtɪ] n реáльность f, действи́тельность f; **in ~ity** на сáмом дéле, в реáльности

**realization** [rɪəlaɪ'zeɪʃən] n (see vt) осознáние; осуществлéние

**realize** ['rɪəlaɪz] vt (understand) осознавáть (осознáть pf); (fulfil) осуществля́ть (осуществи́ть pf)

**really** ['rɪəlɪ] adv (very) óчень; (actually): **what ~ happened?** что произошлó в действи́тельности or на сáмом дéле?; **~?** (with interest) действи́тельно?, прáвда?; (expressing surprise) неужéли?

**realm** [rɛlm] n (fig: of activity, study) óбласть f, сфéра

**reap** [riːp] vt (fig) пожинáть (пожáть pf)

**reappear** [riːə'pɪər] vi снóва появля́ться (появи́ться pf)

**rear** [rɪər] adj зáдний ♦ n (back) зáдняя часть f ♦ vt (cattle, family) вырáщивать (вы́растить pf) ♦ vi (also: ~ **up**) станови́ться (стать pf) на ды́бы

**rearrange** [riːə'reɪndʒ] vt (objects) переставля́ть (перестáвить pf); (order) изменя́ть (измени́ть pf)

**reason** ['riːzn] n (cause) причи́на; (ability to think) рáзум, рассýдок; (sense) смысл ♦ vi: **to ~ with sb** убеждáть (impf) когó-н; **it stands to ~ that ...** разумéется, что ...; **~able** adj разýмный; (quality) неплохóй; (price) умéренный; **~ably** adv (sensibly) разýмно; (fairly) довóльно; **~ing** n рассуждéние

**reassurance** [riːə'ʃuərəns] n (comfort) поддéржка

**reassure** [riːə'ʃuər] vt (comfort) утешáть (утéшить pf); **to ~ sb of** заверя́ть (завéрить pf) когó-н в +prp

**reassuring** [riːə'ʃuərɪŋ] adj ободря́ющий

**rebate** ['riːbeɪt] n обрáтная вы́плата

**rebel** n ['rɛbl] vb [rɪ'bɛl] n бунтáрь(рка) m(f) ♦ vi восставáть (восстáть pf); **~lion** [rɪ'bɛljən] n восстáние; **~lious** [rɪ'bɛljəs] adj (child, behaviour) стропти́вый; (troops) мятéжный

**rebound** vb [rɪ'baund] n ['riːbaund] vi: **to ~ (off)** отскáкивать (отскочи́ть pf) (от +gen) ♦ n: **he married her on the ~** он жени́лся на ней пóсле разочаровáния в любви́ к другóй

**rebuild** [riː'bɪld] (irreg: like **build**) vt (town, building) перестрáивать (перестрóить pf); (fig) восстанáвливать (восстанови́ть pf)

**rebuke** [rɪ'bjuːk] vt дéлать (сдéлать pf) вы́говор +dat

**recall** [rɪ'kɔːl] vt вспоминáть (вспóмнить pf); (parliament, ambassador etc) отзывáть (отозвáть pf)

**recapture** [riː'kæptʃər] vt (town, territory) снóва захвáтывать (захвати́ть pf); (atmosphere etc) воссоздавать (воссоздать *pf*)

**receding** [rɪ'siːdɪŋ] *adj* (*hair*) редеющий

**receipt** [rɪ'siːt] *n* (*document*) квитанция; (*act of receiving*) получение; **~s** *npl* (*COMM*) денежные поступления *ntpl*, платежи *mpl*

**receive** [rɪ'siːv] *vt* получать (получить *pf*); (*criticism*) встречать (встретить *pf*); (*visitor, guest*) принимать (принять *pf*); **~r** *n* (*TEL*) (телефонная) трубка; (*COMM*) ликвидатор (*неплатёжеспособной компании*)

**recent** ['riːsnt] *adj* недавний; **~ly** *adv* недавно

**reception** [rɪ'sɛpʃən] *n* (*in hotel*) регистрация; (*in office, hospital*) приёмная *f adj*; (*in health centre*) регистратура; (*party, also RADIO, TV*) приём; **~ist** *n* (*in hotel, hospital*) регистратор; (*in office*) секретарь *m*

**receptive** [rɪ'sɛptɪv] *adj* восприимчивый

**recess** [rɪ'sɛs] *n* (*POL*) каникулы *pl*

**recession** [rɪ'sɛʃən] *n* (*ECON*) спад

**recipe** ['rɛsɪpɪ] *n* (*also fig*) рецепт

**recipient** [rɪ'sɪpɪənt] *n* получатель *m*

**reciprocal** [rɪ'sɪprəkl] *adj* взаимный, обоюдный

**recital** [rɪ'saɪtl] *n* (*concert*) сольный концерт

**recite** [rɪ'saɪt] *vt* (*poem*) декламировать (продекламировать *pf*)

**reckless** ['rɛkləs] *adj* безответственный

**reckon** ['rɛkən] *vt* (*calculate*) считать (посчитать *or* сосчитать *pf*); (*think*): **I ~ that ...** я считаю, что ...

**reclaim** [rɪ'kleɪm] *vt* (*demand back*)

требовать (потребовать *pf*) обратно; (*land: from sea*) отвоёвывать (отвоевать *pf*)

**recognition** [rɛkəg'nɪʃən] *n* признание; (*of person, place*) узнавание; **he has changed beyond ~** он изменился до неузнаваемости

**recognize** ['rɛkəgnaɪz] *vt* признавать (признать *pf*); (*symptom*) распознавать (распознать *pf*); **to ~ (by)** (*person, place*) узнавать (узнать *pf*) (по +*dat*)

**recollect** [rɛkə'lɛkt] *vt* припоминать (припомнить *pf*), вспоминать (вспомнить *pf*); **~ion** [rɛkə'lɛkʃən] *n* воспоминание, память *f*

**recommend** [rɛkə'mɛnd] *vt* рекомендовать (порекомендовать *pf*); **~ation** [rɛkəmɛn'deɪʃən] *n* рекомендация

**reconcile** ['rɛkənsaɪl] *vt* (*people*) мирить (помирить *pf*); (*facts, beliefs*) примирять (примирить *pf*); **to ~ o.s. to sth** смиряться (смириться *pf*) с чем-н

**reconciliation** [rɛkənsɪlɪ'eɪʃən] *n* примирение

**reconsider** [riːkən'sɪdər] *vt* пересматривать (пересмотреть *pf*)

**reconstruct** [riːkən'strʌkt] *vt* перестраивать (перестроить *pf*); (*event, crime*) воспроизводить (воспроизвести *pf*), реконструировать (*impf/pf*); **~ion** [riːkən'strʌkʃən] *n* (*of building*) перестройка; (*of country*) перестройка; (*of crime*) воспроизведение

**record** *vb* [rɪ'kɔːd] *n, adj* ['rɛkɔːd] *vt* (*in writing, on tape*) записывать (записать *pf*); (*register: temperature, speed etc*)

регистри́ровать
(зарегистри́ровать *pf*) ♦ *n* (*written account*) за́пись *f*; (*of meeting*)
протоко́л; (*of attendance*) учёт;
(*MUS*) пласти́нка; (*history: of person, company*) репута́ция; (*also:*
**criminal ~**) суди́мость *f*; (*SPORT*)
реко́рд ♦ *adj*: **in ~ time** в
реко́рдное вре́мя; **off the ~**
(*speak*) неофициа́льно; **~er**
[rɪ'kɔːdər] *n* (*MUS*) англи́йская
фле́йта; **~ holder** [-'həʊldə]
(*SPORT*) *n* рекордсме́н(ка); **~ing**
[rɪ'kɔːdɪŋ] *n* за́пись *f*; **~ player**
[-'pleɪə] *n* прои́грыватель *m*
**recount** [rɪ'kaunt] *vt* (*story*)
пове́дать (*pf*); (*event*) пове́дать
(*pf*) о +*prp*
**recoup** [rɪ'kuːp] *vt* (*losses*)
компенси́ровать (*impf/pf*)
**recover** [rɪ'kʌvər] *vt* получа́ть
(получи́ть *pf*) обра́тно; (*COMM*)
возмеща́ть (возмести́ть *pf*) ♦ *vi*
(*get better*): **to ~ (from)**
попра́вливаться (попра́виться *pf*)
(по́сле +*gen*); **~y** *n* (*MED*)
выздоровле́ние; (*COMM*) подъём;
(*of stolen items*) возвраще́ние; (*of lost items*) обнаруже́ние
**recreation** [rɛkrɪ'eɪʃən] *n* (*leisure activities*) развлече́ние
**recruit** [rɪ'kruːt] *n* (*MIL*)
новобра́нец, призывни́к ♦ *vt* (*into organization, army*) вербова́ть
(завербова́ть *pf*); (*into company*)
нанима́ть (наня́ть *pf*); (**new**) **~** (*in company*) но́вый сотру́дник; (*in organization*) но́вый член; **~ment**
*n* (*MIL*) вербо́вка; (*by company*)
набо́р (*на рабо́ту*)
**rectangle** ['rɛktæŋgl] *n*
прямоуго́льник
**rectangular** [rɛk'tæŋgjulər] *adj*
прямоуго́льный
**rectify** ['rɛktɪfaɪ] *vt* исправля́ть
(испра́вить *pf*)

**recuperate** [rɪ'kjuːpəreɪt] *vi*
оправля́ться (опра́виться *pf*)
**recur** [rɪ'kɔːr] *vi* повторя́ться
(повтори́ться *pf*); **~rence** *n*
повторе́ние; **~rent** *adj*
повторя́ющийся
**recycle** [riː'saɪkl] *vt*
перераба́тывать (перерабо́тать
*pf*)
**red** [rɛd] *n* кра́сный цвет; (*pej : POL*) кра́сный(ая) *m(f) adj* ♦ *adj*
кра́сный; (*hair*) ры́жий; **to be in the ~** име́ть (*impf*)
задо́лженность; **Red Cross** *n*
Кра́сный Крест; **~currant** *n*
кра́сная сморо́дина *f no pl*
**redeem** [rɪ'diːm] *vt* (*situation, reputation*) спаса́ть (спасти́ *pf*);
(*debt*) выпла́чивать (вы́платить
*pf*)
**redefine** [riːdɪ'faɪn] *vt*
пересма́тривать (пересмотре́ть
*pf*)
**redhead** ['rɛdhɛd] *n* ры́жий(ая) *m(f)*
*adj*
**redress** [rɪ'drɛs] *vt* (*error, wrong*)
исправля́ть (испра́вить *pf*)
**red tape** *n* (*fig*) бюрокра́тия,
волоки́та
**reduce** [rɪ'djuːs] *vt* сокраща́ть
(сократи́ть *pf*); **to ~ sb to tears**
доводи́ть (довести́ *pf*) кого́-н до
слёз; **to ~ sb to silence**
заставля́ть (заста́вить *pf*) кого́-н
замолча́ть; **he was ~d to stealing**
он дошёл до того́, что стал
ворова́ть
**reduction** [rɪ'dʌkʃən] *n* (*in price*)
ски́дка; (*in numbers*) сокраще́ние
**redundancy** [rɪ'dʌndənsɪ] (*BRIT*)
сокраще́ние (шта́тов)
**redundant** [rɪ'dʌndnt] *adj* (*BRIT: unemployed*) уво́ленный; (*useless*)
изли́шний; **he was made ~** его́
сократи́ли
**reed** [riːd] *n* (*BOT*) тростни́к

**reef** [ri:f] n риф
**reel** [ri:l] n катушка; (of film, tape) бобина
**ref** [rɛf] n abbr (SPORT : inf) = **referee**
**refer** [rɪ'fə:r] vt: **to ~ sb to** (book etc) отсылать (отослать pf) кого-н к +dat; (doctor) направлять (направить pf) кого-н к +dat; **~ to** vt fus упоминать (упомянуть pf) о +prp; (relate to) относиться (impf) к +dat; (consult) обращаться (обратиться pf) к +dat
**referee** [rɛfə'ri:] n (SPORT) рефери m ind, судья m; (BRIT: for job) лицо, дающее рекомендацию ♦ vt судить (impf)
**reference** ['rɛfrəns] n (mention) упоминание; (in book, paper) ссылка; (for job: letter) рекомендация; **with ~ to** (in letter) ссылаясь на +acc; **~ book** n справочник
**referendum** [rɛfə'rɛndəm] (pl **referenda**) n референдум
**referral** [rɪ'fə:rəl] n направление
**refine** [rɪ'faɪn] vt (sugar) рафинировать (impf/pf); (oil) очищать (очистить pf); (theory, task) совершенствовать (усовершенствовать pf); **~d** adj (person, taste) утончённый; **~ment** n (of person) утончённость f; (of system) усовершенствование
**reflect** [rɪ'flɛkt] vt отражать (отразить pf) ♦ vi (think) раздумывать (impf); **~ on** vt (discredit) отражаться (отразиться pf) на +acc; **~ion** [rɪ'flɛkʃən] n отражение; (thought) раздумье; (comment): **~ion on** суждение о +prp; **on ~ion** взвесив все обстоятельства
**reflex** ['ri:flɛks] n рефлекс
**reform** [rɪ'fɔ:m] n (of law, system) реформа ♦ vt (character) преобразовать (impf/pf); (system) реформировать (impf/pf)
**refrain** [rɪ'freɪn] n (of song) припев ♦ vi: **to ~ from commenting** воздерживаться (воздержаться pf) от комментариев
**refresh** [rɪ'frɛʃ] vt освежать (освежить pf); **~ing** adj (sleep) освежающий; (drink) тонизирующий; **~ments** npl закуски fpl и напитки mpl
**refrigerator** [rɪ'frɪdʒəreɪtər] n холодильник
**refuge** ['rɛfju:dʒ] n (shelter) убежище, прибежище; **to take ~ in** находить (найти pf) прибежище в +prp
**refugee** [rɛfju'dʒi:] n беженец(нка)
**refund** n ['ri:fʌnd] vb [rɪ'fʌnd] n возмещение ♦ vt возмещать (возместить pf)
**refurbish** [ri:'fə:bɪʃ] vt ремонтировать (отремонтировать pf); **~ment** n ремонт
**refusal** [rɪ'fju:zəl] n отказ
**refuse**[1] [rɪ'fju:z] vt (offer, gift) отказываться (отказаться pf) от +gen; (permission) отказывать (отказать pf) в +prp ♦ vi отказываться (отказаться pf); **to ~ to do** отказываться (отказаться pf) +infin
**refuse**[2] ['rɛfju:s] n мусор
**refute** [rɪ'fju:t] vt опровергать (опровергнуть pf)
**regain** [rɪ'geɪn] vt (power, position) вновь обретать (обрести pf)
**regard** [rɪ'gɑ:d] n (esteem) уважение ♦ vt (consider) считать (impf); (view, look on): **to ~ with** относиться (отнестись pf) с +instr; **to give one's ~s to** передавать (передать pf) поклоны +dat; **as ~s, with ~ to**

что касается +gen, относи́тельно +gen; **~ing** prep относи́тельно +gen; **~less** adv (continue) несмотря́ ни на что; **~less of** несмотря́ на +acc, не счита́ясь с +instr

**reggae** [ˈrɛgeɪ] n ре́гги m ind

**regime** [reɪˈʒiːm] n (POL) режи́м

**regiment** [ˈrɛdʒɪmənt] n полк

**region** [ˈriːdʒən] n (area: of country) регио́н; (: smaller) райо́н; (ADMIN, ANAT) о́бласть f; **in the ~ of** (fig) в райо́не +gen; **~al** adj (organization) областно́й, региона́льный; (accent) ме́стный

**register** [ˈrɛdʒɪstəʳ] n (census, record) за́пись f; (SCOL) журна́л; (also: **electoral ~**) спи́сок избира́телей ♦ vt регистри́ровать (зарегистри́ровать pf); (subj: meter etc) пока́зывать (показа́ть pf) ♦ vi регистри́роваться (зарегистри́роваться pf); (as student) запи́сываться (записа́ться pf); (make impression) запечатлева́ться (запечатле́ться pf) в па́мяти; **~ed** adj (letter) заказно́й; **Registered Trademark** n зарегистри́рованный това́рный знак

**registrar** [ˈrɛdʒɪstrɑːʳ] n регистра́тор

**registration** [rɛdʒɪsˈtreɪʃən] n регистра́ция; (AUT : also: **~ number**) (регистрацио́нный) но́мер автомоби́ля

**registry office** [ˈrɛdʒɪstrɪ-] n (BRIT) ≈ ЗАГС (отде́л за́писей гражда́нского состоя́ния)

**regret** [rɪˈgrɛt] n сожале́ние ♦ vt сожале́ть (impf) о +prp; (death) скорбе́ть (impf) о +prp; **~table** adj приско́рбный, досто́йный сожале́ния

**regular** [ˈrɛgjuləʳ] adj регуля́рный;

(even) ро́вный; (symmetrical) пра́вильный; (usual: time) обы́чный ♦ n (in cafe, restaurant) завсегда́тай; (in shop) клие́нт; **~ly** adv регуля́рно; (symmetrically: shaped etc) пра́вильно

**regulate** [ˈrɛgjuleɪt] vt регули́ровать (отрегули́ровать pf)

**regulation** [rɛgjuˈleɪʃən] n регули́рование; (rule) пра́вило

**rehabilitation** [ˈriːəbɪlɪˈteɪʃən] n (of addict) реабилита́ция; (of criminal) интегра́ция

**rehearsal** [rɪˈhəːsəl] n репети́ция

**rehearse** [rɪˈhəːs] vt репети́ровать (отрепети́ровать pf)

**reign** [reɪn] n ца́рствование ♦ vi (monarch) ца́рствовать (impf); (fig) цари́ть (impf)

**reimburse** [riːɪmˈbəːs] vt возмеща́ть (возмести́ть pf)

**rein** [reɪn] n (for horse) вожжа́

**reincarnation** [ˈriːɪnkɑːˈneɪʃən] n (belief) переселе́ние душ

**reindeer** [ˈreɪndɪəʳ] n inv се́верный оле́нь m

**reinforce** [riːɪnˈfɔːs] vt (strengthen) укрепля́ть (укрепи́ть pf); (back up) подкрепля́ть (подкрепи́ть pf); **~ment** n укрепле́ние; **~ments** npl (MIL) подкрепле́ние ntsg

**reinstate** [riːɪnˈsteɪt] vt восстана́вливать (восстанови́ть pf) в пре́жнем положе́нии

**reject** vb [rɪˈdʒɛkt] n [ˈriːdʒɛkt] vt отклоня́ть (отклони́ть pf), отверга́ть (отве́ргнуть pf); (political system) отверга́ть (отве́ргнуть pf); (candidate) отклоня́ть (отклони́ть pf); (goods) бракова́ть (забракова́ть pf) ♦ n (product) некондицио́нное изде́лие; **~ion** [rɪˈdʒɛkʃən] n отклоне́ние

**rejoice** [rɪˈdʒɔɪs] vi: **to ~ at** or **over**

ликова́ть (impf) по по́воду +gen

**rejuvenate** [rɪ'dʒu:vəneɪt] vt (person) омола́живать (омолоди́ть pf)

**relapse** [rɪ'læps] n (MED) рециди́в

**relate** [rɪ'leɪt] vt (tell) переска́зывать (пересказа́ть pf); (connect): **to ~ sth to** относи́ть (отнести́ pf) что-н к +dat ♦ vi: **to ~ to** (person) сходи́ться (сойти́сь pf) с +instr; (subject, thing) относи́ться (отнести́сь pf) к +dat; **~d** adj: **~d (to)** (person) состоя́щий в родстве́ (с +instr); (animal, language) ро́дственный (с +instr); **they are ~d** они́ состоя́т в родстве́

**relating to** [rɪ'leɪtɪŋ-] prep относи́тельно +gen

**relation** [rɪ'leɪʃən] n (member of family) ро́дственник(ица); (connection) отноше́ние; **~s** npl (dealings) сноше́ния ntpl; (relatives) ро́дственники mpl, родня́ fsg; **~ship** n (between two people, countries) (взаимо-)отноше́ния ntpl; (between two things, affair) связь f

**relative** ['relətɪv] n (family member) ро́дственник(ица) ♦ adj (comparative) относи́тельный; **~ to** (in relation to) относя́щийся к +dat; **~ly** adv относи́тельно

**relax** [rɪ'læks] vi расслабля́ться (рассла́биться pf) ♦ vt (grip, rule, control) ослабля́ть (осла́бить pf); (person) расслабля́ть (рассла́бить pf); **~ation** [ri:læk'seɪʃən] n о́тдых; (of muscle) расслабле́ние; (of grip, rule, control) ослабле́ние; **~ed** adj непринуждённый, рассла́бленный; **~ing** adj (holiday) расслабля́ющий

**relay** n ['ri:leɪ] vb [rɪ'leɪ] n (race) эстафе́та ♦ vt передава́ть (переда́ть pf)

**release** [rɪ'li:s] n (from prison) освобожде́ние; (of gas, book, film) вы́пуск ♦ vt (see n) освобожда́ть (освободи́ть pf); выпуска́ть (вы́пустить pf); (TECH, catch, spring etc) отпуска́ть (отпусти́ть pf)

**relentless** [rɪ'lentlɪs] adj (effort) неосла́бный; (rain) продолжи́тельный; (determined) неуста́нный

**relevance** ['reləvəns] n (of remarks, question) уме́стность f; (of information) актуа́льность f

**relevant** ['reləvənt] adj актуа́льный; **~ to** относя́щийся к +dat

**reliability** [rɪlaɪə'bɪlɪtɪ] n (see adj) надёжность f; достове́рность f

**reliable** [rɪ'laɪəbl] adj надёжный; (information) достове́рный

**reliance** [rɪ'laɪəns] n: **~ (on)** (person, drugs) зави́симость f (от +gen)

**relic** ['relɪk] n (of past etc) рели́квия

**relief** [rɪ'li:f] n облегче́ние; (aid) по́мощь f

**relieve** [rɪ'li:v] vt (pain, suffering) облегча́ть (облегчи́ть pf); (fear, worry) уменьша́ть (уме́ньшить pf); (colleague, guard) сменя́ть (смени́ть pf); **to ~ sb of sth** освобожда́ть (освободи́ть pf) кого́-н от чего́-н

**relieved** adj: **to feel ~** чу́вствовать (почу́вствовать pf) облегче́ние

**religion** [rɪ'lɪdʒən] n рели́гия

**religious** [rɪ'lɪdʒəs] adj религио́зный

**relinquish** [rɪ'lɪŋkwɪʃ] vt (authority) отка́зываться (отказа́ться pf) от +gen

**relish** ['relɪʃ] n (CULIN) припра́ва; (enjoyment) наслажде́ние ♦ vt наслажда́ться (наслади́ться pf) +instr, смакова́ть (impf)

**reluctance** [rɪ'lʌktəns] n нежела́ние

**reluctant** [rɪ'lʌktənt] adj неохо́тный; (person): **he is ~ to go there** он идёт туда́ неохо́тно; **~ly** adv неохо́тно

**rely on** [rɪ'laɪ-] vt fus (count on) рассчи́тывать (impf) на +acc; (trust) полага́ться (положи́ться pf) на +acc

**remain** [rɪ'meɪn] vi остава́ться (оста́ться pf); **~der** n оста́ток; **~ing** adj сохрани́вшийся, оста́вшийся; **~s** npl (of meal) оста́тки mpl; (of building) разва́лины fpl; (of body) оста́нки mpl

**remand** [rɪ'mɑːnd] n: **on ~** взя́тый под стра́жу ♦ vt: **he was ~ed in custody** он был взят под стра́жу

**remark** [rɪ'mɑːk] n замеча́ние ♦ vt замеча́ть (заме́тить pf); **~able** adj замеча́тельный

**remedial** [rɪ'miːdɪəl] adj (classes) исправи́тельный, корректи́вный

**remedy** ['rɛmədɪ] n (cure) сре́дство ♦ vt исправля́ть (испра́вить pf)

**remember** [rɪ'mɛmbər] vt (recall) вспомина́ть (вспо́мнить pf); (bear in mind) по́мнить (impf)

**remembrance** [rɪ'mɛmbrəns] n па́мять f

---

**Remembrance day** - День па́мяти. Отмеча́ется в ближа́йшее к 11 ноября́ воскресе́нье. В э́тот день лю́ди чтят па́мять поги́бших в двух мировы́х во́йнах. Они́ покупа́ют кра́сные бума́жные ма́ки и но́сят их в петли́цах. Де́ньги, вы́рученные от прода́жи ма́ков иду́т на благотвори́тельные це́ли.

---

**remind** [rɪ'maɪnd] vt: **to ~ sb to do** напомина́ть (напо́мнить pf) кому́-н +infin; **to ~ sb of sth**

напомина́ть (напо́мнить pf) кому́-н о чём-н; **she ~s me of her mother** она́ напомина́ет мне свою́ мать; **~er** n напомина́ние

**reminisce** [rɛmɪ'nɪs] vi вспомина́ть (вспо́мнить pf); **~nt** adj: **to be ~nt of sth** напомина́ть (напо́мнить pf) что-н

**remit** [rɪ'mɪt] vt (send) пересыла́ть (пересла́ть pf)

**remnant** ['rɛmnənt] n оста́ток

**remorse** [rɪ'mɔːs] n раска́яние

**remote** [rɪ'məut] adj (place, time) отдалённый; **~ control** n дистанцио́нное управле́ние; **~ly** adv отдалённо; **I'm not ~ly interested** я ниско́лько не заинтересо́ван

**removable** [rɪ'muːvəbl] adj съёмный

**removal** [rɪ'muːvəl] n удале́ние; (BRIT: of furniture) перево́зка

**remove** [rɪ'muːv] vt (take away) убира́ть (убра́ть pf); (clothing, employee) снима́ть (снять pf); (stain) удаля́ть (удали́ть pf); (problem, doubt) устраня́ть (устрани́ть pf)

**Renaissance** [rɪ'neɪsɑːs] n: **the ~** (HISTORY) Возрожде́ние

**render** ['rɛndər] vt (assistance) ока́зывать (оказа́ть pf); (harmless, useless) де́лать (сде́лать pf) +instr

**rendezvous** ['rɒndɪvuː] n (meeting) свида́ние; (place) ме́сто свида́ния

**renew** [rɪ'njuː] vt возобновля́ть (возобнови́ть pf); **~al** n возобновле́ние

**renounce** [rɪ'nauns] vt отка́зываться (отказа́ться pf) от +gen; (belief, throne) отрека́ться (отре́чься pf) от +gen

**renovate** ['rɛnəveɪt] vt модернизи́ровать (impf/pf); (building) де́лать (сде́лать pf) капита́льный ремо́нт в +prp

**renovation** [rɛnə'veɪʃən] n
модерниза́ция; (of work of art)
реставра́ция; (of building)
капита́льный ремо́нт

**renowned** [rɪ'naund] adj
просла́вленный

**rent** [rɛnt] n кварти́рная пла́та ♦ vt
(take for rent: house) снима́ть
(снять pf); (: television, car) брать
(взять pf) напрока́т; (also: ~ out:
house) сдава́ть (сдать pf) (внаём);
(: television, car) дава́ть (дать pf)
напрока́т; ~al n (charge) пла́та за
прока́т

**rep** [rɛp] n abbr (COMM) =
**representative**

**repair** [rɪ'pɛəʳ] n ремо́нт ♦ vt
(clothes, shoes) чини́ть (починить
pf); (car) ремонти́ровать
(отремонти́ровать pf); **in good/
bad ~** в хоро́шем/плохо́м
состоя́нии

**repay** [riː'peɪ] (irreg) vt (money, debt)
выпла́чивать (вы́платить pf);
(person) упла́чивать (уплати́ть pf)
+dat; **to ~ sb (for sth)** (favour)
отпла́чивать (отплати́ть pf)
кому́-н (за что-н); ~**ment** n
вы́плата

**repeat** [rɪ'piːt] vt повторя́ть
(повтори́ть pf) ♦ vi повторя́ться
(повтори́ться pf) ♦ n (RADIO, TV)
повторе́ние; ~**edly** adv
неоднокра́тно

**repel** [rɪ'pɛl] vt (disgust)
отта́лкивать (оттолкну́ть pf);
~**lent** n: insect ~**lent** репелле́нт

**repent** [rɪ'pɛnt] vi: **to ~ (of)** ка́яться
(пока́яться pf) (в +prp); ~**ance** n
покая́ние

**repercussions** [riːpə'kʌʃənz] npl
после́дствия ntpl

**repertoire** ['rɛpətwɑːʳ] n
репертуа́р

**repetition** [rɛpɪ'tɪʃən] n (repeat)
повторе́ние

**repetitive** [rɪ'pɛtɪtɪv] adj
повторя́ющийся

**replace** [rɪ'pleɪs] vt (put back)
класть (положи́ть pf) обра́тно;
(: vertically) ста́вить (поста́вить pf)
обра́тно; (take the place of)
заменя́ть (замени́ть pf); ~**ment** n
заме́на

**replay** n ['riːpleɪ] vb [riː'pleɪ] n (of
match) переигро́вка; (of film)
повто́рный пока́з ♦ vt (match,
game) переи́грывать (переигра́ть
pf); (part of tape) повто́рно
прои́грывать (проигра́ть pf)

**replenish** [rɪ'plɛnɪʃ] vt (stock etc)
пополня́ть (попо́лнить pf)

**replica** ['rɛplɪkə] n (copy) ко́пия

**reply** [rɪ'plaɪ] n отве́т ♦ vi отвеча́ть
(отве́тить pf)

**report** [rɪ'pɔːt] n (account) докла́д,
отчёт; (PRESS, TV etc) репорта́ж;
(statement) сообще́ние; (BRIT:
also: **school ~**) отчёт об
успева́емости ♦ vt сообща́ть
(сообщи́ть pf) о +prp; (event,
meeting) докла́дывать (доложи́ть
pf) о +prp; (person) доноси́ть
(донести́ pf) на +acc ♦ vi (make a
report) докла́дывать (доложи́ть
pf); **to ~ to sb** (present o.s.)
явля́ться (яви́ться pf) к
кому́-н; (be responsible to) быть
(impf) под нача́лом кого́-н; **to ~
that** сообща́ть (сообщи́ть pf),
что; ~**edly** adv как сообща́ют;
~**er** n репортёр

**represent** [rɛprɪ'zɛnt] vt (person,
nation) представля́ть
(предста́вить pf); (view, belief)
излага́ть (изложи́ть pf);
(constitute) представля́ть (impf)
собо́й; (idea, emotion)
символизи́ровать (impf/pf);
(describe): **to ~ sth as** изобража́ть
(изобрази́ть pf) что-н как; ~**ation**

[rɛprɪzɛn'teɪʃən] n (state) представи́тельство; (picture, statue) изображе́ние; **~ative** n представи́тель m ♦ adj представи́тельный

**repress** [rɪ'prɛs] vt подавля́ть (подави́ть pf); **~ion** [rɪ'prɛʃən] n подавле́ние; **~ive** adj репресси́вный

**reprieve** [rɪ'priːv] n (LAW) отсро́чка (в исполне́нии пригово́ра); (fig: delay) переды́шка

**reprimand** ['rɛprɪmɑːnd] n вы́говор ♦ vt де́лать (сде́лать pf) вы́говор +dat

**reprisal** [rɪ'praɪzl] n распра́ва

**reproach** [rɪ'prəʊtʃ] n упрёк ♦ vt: to ~ sb for sth/with sth упрека́ть (упрекну́ть pf) кого́-н за что-н/в чём-н

**reproduce** [riːprə'djuːs] vt воспроизводи́ть (воспроизвести́ pf) ♦ vi размножа́ться (размно́житься pf)

**reproduction** [riːprə'dʌkʃən] n воспроизведе́ние; (ART) репроду́кция

**reptile** ['rɛptaɪl] n пресмыка́ющееся nt adj (живо́тное)

**republic** [rɪ'pʌblɪk] n респу́блика; **~an** n (US: POL): **Republican** республика́нец(нка)

**repulsive** [rɪ'pʌlsɪv] adj отврати́тельный

**reputable** ['rɛpjutəbl] adj (person) уважа́емый; **~ company** компа́ния с хоро́шей репута́цией

**reputation** [rɛpju'teɪʃən] n репута́ция

**reputed** [rɪ'pjuːtɪd] adj (rumoured) предполага́емый; **~ly** adv по о́бщему мне́нию

**request** [rɪ'kwɛst] n (polite demand)

про́сьба; (formal demand) зая́вка ♦ vt: to ~ sth of or from sb проси́ть (попроси́ть pf) что-н у кого́-н

**require** [rɪ'kwaɪər] vt (subj: person) нужда́ться (impf) в +prp; (: thing, situation) тре́бовать (impf); (order): to ~ sth of sb тре́бовать (потре́бовать pf) что-н от кого́-н; **we ~ you to complete the task** мы тре́буем, что́бы Вы заверши́ли рабо́ту; **~ment** n (need, want) потре́бность f

**requisite** ['rɛkwɪzɪt] n тре́бование ♦ adj необходи́мый

**rescue** ['rɛskjuː] n спасе́ние ♦ vt: to ~ (from) спаса́ть (спасти́ pf) (от +gen); **to come to sb's ~** приходи́ть (прийти́ pf) кому́-н на по́мощь

**research** [rɪ'səːtʃ] n иссле́дование ♦ vt иссле́довать (impf/pf); **~er** n иссле́дователь m

**resemblance** [rɪ'zɛmbləns] n схо́дство

**resemble** [rɪ'zɛmbl] vt походи́ть (impf) на +acc

**resent** [rɪ'zɛnt] vt (fact) негодова́ть (impf) про́тив +gen; (person) негодова́ть (impf) на +acc; **~ful** adj негоду́ющий; **I am ~ful of his behaviour** его́ поведе́ние приво́дит меня́ в негодова́ние; **~ment** n негодова́ние

**reservation** [rɛzə'veɪʃən] n (booking) предвари́тельный зака́з; (doubt) сомне́ние; (for tribe) резерва́ция

**reserve** [rɪ'zəːv] n (store) резе́рв, запа́с; (also: **nature ~**) запове́дник; (SPORT) запасно́й игро́к; (restraint) сде́ржанность f ♦ vt (look, tone) сохраня́ть (сохрани́ть pf); (seats, table etc) зака́зывать (заказа́ть pf); **in ~** в резе́рве or запа́се; **~d** adj (*restrained*) сде́ржанный

**reservoir** ['rezəvwɑ:ʳ] n (*of water*) водохрани́лище

**reshuffle** [ri:'ʃʌfl] n: Cabinet ~ перетасо́вка or перестано́вки fpl в кабине́те мини́стров

**reside** [rɪ'zaɪd] vi (*live*) прожива́ть (*impf*); **~nce** ['rezɪdəns] n (*home*) резиде́нция; (*length of stay*) пребыва́ние; **~nt** ['rezɪdənt] n (*of country, town*) (постоя́нный(ая)) жи́тель(ница) m(f); (*in hotel*) прожива́ющий(ая) m(f) adj ♦ adj (*population*) постоя́нный; **~ntial** [rezɪ'denʃəl] adj (*area*) жило́й; (*course, college*) с прожива́нием

**resign** [rɪ'zaɪn] vi (*from post*) уходи́ть (уйти́ pf) в отста́вку ♦ vt (*one's post*) оставля́ть (оста́вить pf) с +gen; **to ~ o.s. to** смиря́ться (смири́ться pf) с +instr; **~ation** [rezɪg'neɪʃən] n отста́вка; (*acceptance*) поко́рность f, смире́ние; **~ed** adj (*to situation etc*) смири́вшийся

**resilience** [rɪ'zɪlɪəns] n сто́йкость f

**resilient** [rɪ'zɪlɪənt] adj сто́йкий

**resin** ['rezɪn] n смола́

**resist** [rɪ'zɪst] vt сопротивля́ться (*impf*) +dat; (*temptation*) устоя́ть (pf) пе́ред +instr; **~ance** n (*opposition*) сопротивле́ние; (*to illness*) сопротивля́емость f

**resolute** ['rezəlu:t] adj (*faith*) твёрдый; (*opposition*) реши́тельный

**resolution** [rezə'lu:ʃən] n (*decision*) реше́ние; (: *formal*) резолю́ция; (*determination*) реши́мость f; (*of problem, difficulty*) разреше́ние

**resolve** [rɪ'zɔlv] n реши́тельность f ♦ vt (*problem, difficulty*) разреша́ть (разреши́ть pf) ♦ vi: **to ~ to do** реша́ть (реши́ть pf) +infin; **~d** adj реши́тельный

**resonant** ['rezənənt] adj зву́чный

**resort** [rɪ'zɔ:t] n (*town*) куро́рт; (*recourse*) прибега́ние ♦ vi: **to ~ to** прибега́ть (прибе́гнуть pf) к +dat; **the last ~** после́дняя наде́жда; **in the last ~** в кра́йнем слу́чае

**resounding** [rɪ'zaundɪŋ] adj (*noise*) зву́чный; (*fig: success*) гро́мкий

**resource** [rɪ'sɔ:s] n ресу́рс; **~ful** adj изобрета́тельный, нахо́дчивый

**respect** [rɪs'pekt] n уваже́ние ♦ vt уважа́ть (*impf*); **~s** npl (*greetings*) почте́ние ntsg; **with ~ to, in ~ of** в отноше́нии +gen; **in this ~** в э́том отноше́нии; **~ability** n респекта́бельность f; **~able** adj прили́чный; (*morally correct*) респекта́бельный; **~ful** adj почти́тельный

**respective** [rɪs'pektɪv] adj: **he drove them to their ~ homes** он отвёз их обо́их по дома́м; **~ly** adv соотве́тственно

**respond** [rɪs'pɔnd] vi (*answer*) отвеча́ть (отве́тить pf); (*react*): **to ~ to** (*pressure, criticism*) реаги́ровать (отреаги́ровать pf) на +acc

**response** [rɪs'pɔns] n (*answer*) отве́т; (*reaction*) резона́нс, о́тклик

**responsibility** [rɪspɔnsɪ'bɪlɪtɪ] n (*liability*) отве́тственность f; (*duty*) обя́занность f

**responsible** [rɪs'pɔnsɪbl] adj: ~ **(for)** отве́тственный (за +acc)

**responsive** [rɪs'pɔnsɪv] adj (*child, nature*) отзы́вчивый; ~ **to** (*demand, treatment*) восприи́мчивый к +dat

**rest** [rest] n (*relaxation, pause*) о́тдых; (*stand, support*) подста́вка ♦ vi (*relax, stop*) отдыха́ть (отдохну́ть pf) ♦ vt (*head, eyes etc*) дава́ть (дать pf) о́тдых +dat; (*lean*): **to ~ sth against** прислоня́ть (прислони́ть pf) что-н к +dat; **the ~** (*remainder*)

остально́е nt adj; **the ~ of them**
остальны́е (из них); **to ~ on**
(person) опира́ться (опере́ться pf)
на +acc; (idea) опира́ться (impf) на
+acc; (object) лежа́ть (impf) на +prp;
**~ assured that ...** бу́дьте
уве́рены, что ...; **it ~s with him
to ...** на нём лежи́т обя́занность
+infin ...; **to ~ one's eyes** or **gaze
on** остана́вливать (останови́ть
pf) (свой) взгляд на +acc

**restaurant** ['rɛstərɔ̃ŋ] n рестора́н
**restful** ['rɛstful] adj ми́рный,
поко́йный
**restless** ['rɛstlɪs] adj беспоко́йный
**restoration** [rɛstə'reɪʃən] n (of
building etc) реставра́ция; (of
order, health) восстановле́ние
**restore** [rɪ'stɔːr] vt (see n)
реставри́ровать
(отреставри́ровать pf);
восстана́вливать (восстанови́ть
pf); (stolen property) возвраща́ть
(возврати́ть pf); (to power)
верну́ть (pf)
**restrain** [rɪs'treɪn] vt сде́рживать
(сдержа́ть pf); (person): **to ~ sb
from doing** не дава́ть (дать pf)
кому́-н +infin; **~ed** adj
сде́ржанный; **~t** n (moderation)
сде́ржанность f; (restriction)
ограниче́ние
**restrict** [rɪs'trɪkt] vt ограни́чивать
(ограни́чить pf); **~ion** [rɪs'trɪkʃən]
n: **~ion (on)** ограниче́ние (на
+acc); **~ive** adj ограничи́тельный;
(clothing) стесня́ющий
**result** [rɪ'zʌlt] n результа́т ♦ vi: **to
~ in** зака́нчиваться (зако́нчиться
pf) +instr; **as a ~ of** в результа́те
+gen
**resume** [rɪ'zjuːm] vt (work, journey)
возобновля́ть (возобнови́ть pf)
♦ vi продолжа́ть (продо́лжить pf)
**résumé** ['reɪzjuːmeɪ] n резюме́ nt
ind; (US: for job) автобиогра́фия

**resumption** [rɪ'zʌmpʃən] n
возобновле́ние
**resurgence** [rɪ'səːdʒəns] n всплеск
**retail** ['riːteɪl] adj ро́зничный ♦ adv
в ро́зницу; **~er** n ро́зничный
торго́вец; **~ price** n ро́зничная
цена́
**retain** [rɪ'teɪn] vt (keep) сохраня́ть
(сохрани́ть pf)
**retaliate** [rɪ'tælɪeɪt] vi: **to ~ (against)**
(attack) наноси́ть (нанести́ pf)
отве́тный уда́р (+dat); (ill-
treatment) отпла́чивать
(отплати́ть pf) (за +acc)
**retaliation** [rɪtælɪ'eɪʃən] n (see vi)
отве́тный уда́р; возме́здие
**retarded** [rɪ'tɑːdɪd] adj (growth,
development) заме́дленный
**reticent** ['rɛtɪsnt] adj сде́ржанный
**retina** ['rɛtɪnə] n сетча́тка
**retire** [rɪ'taɪər] vi (give up work)
уходи́ть (уйти́ pf) на пе́нсию;
(withdraw) удаля́ться (удали́ться
pf); (go to bed) удаля́ться
(удали́ться pf) на поко́й; **~d** adj:
**he is ~d** он на пе́нсии; **~ment** n
вы́ход or ухо́д на пе́нсию
**retiring** [rɪ'taɪərɪŋ] adj (shy)
засте́нчивый
**retreat** [rɪ'triːt] n (place) убе́жище;
(withdrawal) ухо́д; (MIL)
отступле́ние ♦ vi отступа́ть
(отступи́ть pf)
**retribution** [rɛtrɪ'bjuːʃən] n
возме́здие
**retrieval** [rɪ'triːvəl] n
восстановле́ние
**retrieve** [rɪ'triːv] vt (object)
получа́ть (получи́ть pf) обра́тно;
(honour) восстана́вливать
(восстанови́ть pf); (situation)
спаса́ть (спасти́ pf)
**retrospect** ['rɛtrəspɛkt] n: **in ~** в
ретроспе́кции; **~ive** [rɛtrə'spɛktɪv]
adj (law, tax) име́ющий обра́тную
си́лу

**return** [rɪ'tə:n] n ( from, to place)
возвраще́ние; (of sth stolen etc)
возвра́т; (COMM) дохо́д ♦ cpd
( journey, ticket) обра́тный ♦ vi
возвраща́ться (возврати́ться pf),
верну́ться (pf) ♦ vt возвраща́ть
(возврати́ть pf), верну́ть (pf);
(LAW, verdict) выноси́ть (вы́нести
pf); (POL, candidate) избира́ть
(избра́ть pf); (ball) отбива́ть
(отби́ть pf); in ~ (for) в отве́т (на
+acc); many happy ~s (of the day)!
с днём рожде́ния!; to ~ to
(consciousness) приходи́ть
(прийти́ pf) в +acc; (power)
верну́ться (pf) к +dat

**reunion** [ri:'ju:nɪən] n (reuniting)
воссоедине́ние; (party) встре́ча

**rev** [rev] n abbr (AUT) = **revolution**

**Rev.** abbr (REL) = **Reverend**

**revamp** [ri:'væmp] vt обновля́ть
(обнови́ть pf)

**reveal** [rɪ'vi:l] vt (make known)
обнару́живать (обнару́жить pf);
(make visible) открыва́ть (откры́ть
pf); ~ing adj (action, statement)
показа́тельный; (dress) откры́тый

**revel** ['revl] vi: to ~ in sth
упива́ться (impf) чем-н; to ~ in
doing обожа́ть (impf) +infin

**revelation** [revə'leɪʃən] n ( fact)
откры́тие

**revenge** [rɪ'vendʒ] n месть f; to
take ~ on, ~ o.s. on мстить
(отомсти́ть pf) +dat

**revenue** ['revənju:] n дохо́ды
mpl

**reverence** ['revərəns] n почте́ние

**Reverend** ['revərənd] adj: the
Reverend его́ преподо́бие

**reversal** [rɪ'və:sl] n радика́льное
измене́ние; (of roles) переме́на

**reverse** [rɪ'və:s] n (opposite)
противополо́жность f; (of coin,
medal) оборо́тная сторона́; (of
paper) оборо́т; (AUT : also: ~

gear) обра́тный ход ♦ adj
(opposite) обра́тный ♦ vt (order,
position, decision) изменя́ть
(измени́ть pf); (process, policy)
повора́чивать (поверну́ть pf)
вспять ♦ vi (BRIT : AUT) дава́ть
(дать pf) за́дний ход; in ~ order в
обра́тном поря́дке; to ~ a car
дава́ть (дать pf) за́дний ход; to ~
roles меня́ться (поменя́ться pf)
роля́ми

**revert** [rɪ'və:t] vi: to ~ to (to former
state) возвраща́ться
(возврати́ться pf) к +dat; (LAW:
money, property) переходи́ть
(перейти́ pf) к +dat

**review** [rɪ'vju:] n (of situation, policy
etc) пересмо́тр; (of book, film etc)
реце́нзия; (magazine) обозре́ние
♦ vt (situation, policy etc)
пересма́тривать (пересмотре́ть
pf); (book, film etc) рецензи́ровать
(отрецензи́ровать pf)

**revise** [rɪ'vaɪz] vt (manuscript)
перераба́тывать (перерабо́тать
pf); (opinion, law) пересма́тривать
(пересмотре́ть pf) ♦ vi (SCOL)
повторя́ть (повтори́ть pf)

**revision** [rɪ'vɪʒən] n (see vb)
перерабо́тка; пересмо́тр;
повторе́ние

**revival** [rɪ'vaɪvəl] n (recovery)
оживле́ние; (of interest, faith)
возрожде́ние

**revive** [rɪ'vaɪv] vt (person)
возвраща́ть (возврати́ть pf) к
жи́зни; (economy, industry)
оживля́ть (оживи́ть pf); (tradition,
interest etc) возрожда́ть
(возроди́ть pf) ♦ vi (see vt)
приходи́ть (прийти́ pf) в
созна́ние; оживля́ться
(оживи́ться pf); возрожда́ться
(возроди́ться pf)

**revolt** [rɪ'vəult] n (rebellion)
восста́ние ♦ vi (rebel) восстава́ть

(восста́ть *pf*) ♦ *vt* вызыва́ть
(вы́звать *pf*) вращéние у +*gen*;
**~ing** *adj* отврати́тельный
**revolution** [revə'lu:ʃən] *n*
револю́ция; (*of wheel, earth etc*)
оборо́т; **~ary** *adj*
революцио́нный ♦ *n*
революционе́р(ка)
**revolve** [rɪ'vɒlv] *vi* (*turn*)
враща́ться (*impf*); (*fig*): **to ~
(a)round** враща́ться (*impf*) вокру́г
+*gen*
**revolver** [rɪ'vɒlvə<sup>r</sup>] *n* револьве́р
**revulsion** [rɪ'vʌlʃən] *n* отвращéние
**reward** [rɪ'wɔ:d] *n* награ́да ♦ *vt*: **to
~ (for)** (*effort*) вознаграждáть
(вознагради́ть *pf*) (за +*acc*); **~ing**
*adj*: **this work is ~ing** э́та рабо́та
прино́сит удовлетворéние
**rewind** [ri:'waɪnd] (*irreg*) *vt*
перемáтывать (перемотáть *pf*)
**rewrite** [ri:'raɪt] (*irreg*) *vt* (*rework*)
перепи́сывать (переписáть *pf*)
**rhetorical** [rɪ'tɒrɪkl] *adj*
ритори́ческий
**rheumatism** ['ru:mətɪzəm] *n*
ревмати́зм
**rhinoceros** [raɪ'nɒsərəs] *n* носоро́г
**rhubarb** ['ru:bɑ:b] *n* реве́нь *m*
**rhyme** [raɪm] *n* ри́фма; (*in poetry*)
разме́р
**rhythm** ['rɪðm] *n* ритм
**rib** [rɪb] *n* (*ANAT*) ребро́
**ribbon** ['rɪbən] *n* ле́нта; **in ~s** (*torn*)
в кло́чья
**rice** [raɪs] *n* рис
**rich** [rɪtʃ] *adj* бога́тый; (*clothes,
jewels*) роско́шный; (*food, colour,
life*) насы́щенный; (*abundant*): **~ in**
бога́тый +*instr*; **the ~** *npl* (*rich
people*) бога́тые *pl adj*; **~es** *npl*
(*wealth*) бога́тство *ntsg*; **~ly** *adv*
(*dressed, decorated*) бога́то;
(*rewarded*) ще́дро; (*deserved,
earned*) вполнé
**rickets** ['rɪkɪts] *n* (*MED*) рахи́т

**ricochet** ['rɪkəʃeɪ] *vi*
рикошети́ровать (*impf*)
**rid** [rɪd] (*pt, pp* **~**) *vt*: **to ~ sb of sth**
избавля́ть (изба́вить *pf*) кого́-н
от чего́-н; **to get ~ of**
избавля́ться (изба́виться *pf*) or
отде́лываться (отде́латься *pf*) от
+*gen*
**ridden** ['rɪdn] *pp of* **ride**
**riddle** ['rɪdl] *n* (*conundrum*) зага́дка
♦ *vt*: **~d with** (*holes, bullets*)
изрешечённый +*instr*; (*guilt,
doubts*) по́лный +*gen*; (*corruption*)
прони́занный +*instr*
**ride** [raɪd] (*pt* **rode**, *pp* **ridden**) *n*
пое́здка ♦ *vi* (*as sport*) е́здить
(*impf*) верхо́м; (*go somewhere,
travel*) е́здить/е́хать (пое́хать *pf*)
♦ *vt* (*horse*) е́здить/е́хать (*impf*)
верхо́м на +*prp*; (*bicycle,
motorcycle*) е́здить/е́хать (*impf*) на
+*prp*; (*distance*) проезжáть
(прое́хать *pf*); **a 5 mile ~** пое́здка
в 5 миль; **to take sb for a ~** (*fig*)
прокати́ть (*pf*) кого́-н; **~r** *n* (*on
horse*) нае́здник(ица); (*on bicycle*)
велосипеди́ст(ка); (*on motorcycle*)
мотоцикли́ст(ка)
**ridge** [rɪdʒ] *n* (*of hill*) гре́бень *m*
**ridicule** ['rɪdɪkju:l] *vt* высме́ивать
(вы́смеять *pf*)
**ridiculous** [rɪ'dɪkjuləs] *adj*
смехотво́рный; **it's ~** э́то
смешно́
**riding** ['raɪdɪŋ] *n* верхова́я езда́
**rife** [raɪf] *adj*: **to be ~** (*corruption*)
процветáть (*impf*); **to be ~ with**
(*rumours, fears*) изоби́ловать (*impf*)
+*instr*
**rifle** ['raɪfl] *n* (*MIL*) винто́вка; (*for
hunting*) ружьё
**rift** [rɪft] *n* (*also fig*) тре́щина
**rig** [rɪg] *n* (*also*: **oil ~**) бурова́я
устано́вка ♦ *vt* подтасо́вывать
(подтасовáть *pf*) результáты
+*gen*; **~ging** *n* (*NAUT*) такела́ж

**right** [raɪt] adj пра́вильный; (person, time, size) подходя́щий; (fair, just) справедли́вый; (not left) пра́вый ♦ n (entitlement) пра́во; (not left) пра́вая сторона́ ♦ adv (correctly) пра́вильно; (not to the left) напра́во ♦ vt (ship) выра́внивать (вы́ровнять pf); (car) ста́вить (поста́вить pf) на колёса; (fault, situation) исправля́ть (испра́вить pf); (wrong) устраня́ть (устрани́ть pf) ♦ excl так, хорошо́; **she's ~** она́ права́; **that's ~!** (answer) пра́вильно!; **is that clock ~?** э́ти часы́ пра́вильно иду́т?; **on the ~** спра́ва; **you are in the ~** пра́вда за Ва́ми; **by ~s** по справедли́вости; **~ and wrong** хоро́шее и дурно́е; **~ now** сейча́с же; **~ away** сра́зу же; **~eous** [ˈraɪtʃəs] adj пра́ведный; **~ful** adj зако́нный; **~-handed** adj: **he is ~-handed** он правша́; **~ly** adv (with reason) справедли́во; **~ of way** n (path etc) пра́во прохо́да; (AUT) пра́во прое́зда; **~-wing** adj (POL) пра́вый

**rigid** [ˈrɪdʒɪd] adj (structure, control) жёсткий; (fig: attitude etc) ко́сный

**rigor** [ˈrɪɡər] n (US) = **rigour**

**rigorous** [ˈrɪɡərəs] adj жёсткий; (training) серьёзный

**rigour** [ˈrɪɡər] (US **rigor**) n жёсткость f; **~s** npl (severity) тя́готы fpl, тру́дности fpl

**rim** [rɪm] n (of glass, dish) край; (of spectacles) ободо́к; (of wheel) о́бод

**rind** [raɪnd] n (of bacon, cheese) ко́рка; (of lemon, orange etc) кожура́

**ring** [rɪŋ] (pt **rang**, pp **rung**) n (of metal, smoke) кольцо́; (of people, objects, light) круг; (of spies, drug dealers etc) сеть f; (for boxing)

ринг; (of circus) аре́на; (of doorbell, telephone) звоно́к ♦ vi звони́ть (позвони́ть pf); (doorbell) звене́ть (impf); (also: **~ out**: voice, shot) раздава́ться (разда́ться pf) ♦ vt (BRIT : TEL) звони́ть (позвони́ть pf) +dat; **to give sb a ~** (BRIT : TEL) звони́ть (позвони́ть pf) кому́-н; **my ears are ~ing** у меня́ звени́т в уша́х; **to ~ the bell** звони́ть (impf) в звоно́к; **~ up** vt (BRIT) звони́ть (позвони́ть pf) +dat; **~ing** n (of telephone, doorbell) звоно́к; (of church bell, in ears) звон

**rink** [rɪŋk] n (also: **ice~, roller skating ~**) като́к

**rinse** [rɪns] vt полоска́ть (прополоска́ть pf) ♦ n: **to give sth a ~** опола́скивать (ополосну́ть pf) что-н

**riot** [ˈraɪət] n (disturbance) беспоря́дки mpl, бесчи́нства ntpl ♦ vi бесчи́нствовать (impf); **to run ~** бу́йствовать (impf); **~ous** adj (mob, behaviour) бесчи́нствующий; (living) разгу́льный; (welcome) бу́рный

**rip** [rɪp] n разры́в ♦ vt (paper, cloth) разрыва́ть (разорва́ть pf) ♦ vi разрыва́ться (разорва́ться pf)

**ripe** [raɪp] adj спе́лый, зре́лый; **~n** vi спеть (поспе́ть pf), зреть or созрева́ть (созре́ть pf) ♦ vt: **the sun will ~n them** они́ созре́ют на со́лнце

**ripple** [ˈrɪpl] n рябь f no pl, зыбь f no pl; (of laughter, applause) волна́

**rise** [raɪz] (pt **rose**, pp **~n**) n (slope) подъём; (increase) повыше́ние; (fig: of state, leader) возвыше́ние ♦ vi поднима́ться (подня́ться pf); (prices, numbers, voice) повыша́ться (повы́ситься pf); (sun, moon) всходи́ть (взойти́ pf); (also: **~ up**: rebels) восстава́ть (восста́ть pf); (in rank)

продвига́ться (продви́нуться *pf*);
~ **to power** прихо́д к вла́сти; **to
give** ~ **to** вызыва́ть (вы́звать *pf*);
**to** ~ **to the occasion** оказыва́ться
(оказа́ться *pf*) на высоте́
положе́ния; **~n** [rɪzn] *pp of* **rise**
**rising** [ˈraɪzɪŋ] *adj* (*number, prices*)
расту́щий; (*sun, moon*)
восходя́щий
**risk** [rɪsk] *n* риск ♦ *vt* (*endanger*)
рискова́ть (*impf*) +*instr*; (*chance*)
рискова́ть (рискну́ть *pf*) +*instr*; **to
take a** ~ рискова́ть (рискну́ть *pf*),
идти́ (пойти́ *pf*) на риск; **to run
the** ~ **of doing** рискова́ть (*impf*)
+*infin*; **at** ~ в опа́сной ситуа́ции;
**to put sb/sth at** ~ подверга́ть
(подве́ргнуть *pf*) кого́-н/что-н
ри́ску; **at one's own** ~ на свой
(страх и) риск; **~y** *adj*
риско́ванный
**rite** [raɪt] *n* обря́д; **last ~s**
после́днее прича́стие
**ritual** [ˈrɪtjuəl] *adj* ритуа́льный ♦ *n*
(*REL*) обря́д; (*procedure*) ритуа́л
**rival** [ˈraɪvl] *n* сопе́рник(ица); (*in
business*) конкуре́нт ♦ *adj* (*business*)
конкури́рующий ♦ *vt*
сопе́рничать (*impf*) с +*instr*; ~
**team** кома́нда сопе́рника; **~ry** *n*
(*in sport, love*) сопе́рничество; (*in
business*) конкуре́нция
**river** [ˈrɪvər] *n* река́ ♦ *cpd* (*port,
traffic*) речно́й; **up/down** ~
вверх/вниз по реке́
**road** [rəud] *n* доро́га, путь *m*; (*in
town*) доро́га; (*motorway etc*)
доро́га, шоссе́ *nt ind* ♦ *cpd*
(*accident*) доро́жный; **major/
minor** ~ гла́вная/второстепе́нная
доро́га; ~ **sense** чу́вство доро́ги;
~ **junction** пересече́ние доро́г,
перекрёсток; **~block** *n*
доро́жное загражде́ние; ~ **rage**
*n* хулига́нское поведе́ние на
автодоро́ге; **~side** *n* обо́чина

**roam** [rəum] *vi* скита́ться (*impf*)
**roar** [rɔːʳ] *n* рёв; (*of laughter*)
взрыв ♦ *vi* реве́ть (*impf*); **to** ~ **with
laughter** хохота́ть (*impf*)
**roast** [rəust] *n* (*of meat*) жарко́е *nt*
*adj* ♦ *vt* (*meat, potatoes*) жа́рить
(зажа́рить *pf*)
**rob** [rɔb] *vt* гра́бить (огра́бить *pf*);
**to** ~ **sb of sth** красть (укра́сть *pf*)
что-н у кого́-н; (*fig*) лиша́ть
(лиши́ть *pf*) кого́-н чего́-н; **~ber** *n*
граби́тель *m*; **~bery** *n*
ограбле́ние, грабёж
**robe** [rəub] *n* (*for ceremony etc*)
ма́нтия; (*also:* **bath** ~) ба́нный
хала́т; (*US*) плед
**robin** [ˈrɔbɪn] *n* (*ZOOL*: *also:* ~
**redbreast**) заря́нка
**robot** [ˈrəubɔt] *n* ро́бот
**robust** [rəuˈbʌst] *adj* (*person*)
кре́пкий
**rock** [rɔk] *n* (*substance*) (го́рная)
поро́да; (*boulder*) валу́н; (*US:
small stone*) ка́мешек; (*MUS*: *also:*
~ **music**) рок ♦ *vt* (*swing*) кача́ть
(*impf*); (*shake*) шата́ть (*impf*) ♦ *vi*
(*object*) кача́ться (*impf*), шата́ться
(*impf*); (*person*) кача́ться (*impf*); **on
the ~s** (*drink*) со льдом; (*marriage
etc*) на гра́ни распа́да; ~ **and
roll** *n* рок-н-ро́лл
**rocket** [ˈrɔkɪt] *n* раке́та
**rocky** [ˈrɔkɪ] *adj* (*hill*) скали́стый;
(*path, soil*) камени́стый; (*unstable*)
ша́ткий
**rod** [rɔd] *n* прут; (*also:* **fishing** ~)
у́дочка
**rode** [rəud] *pt of* **ride**
**rodent** [ˈrəudnt] *n* грызу́н
**rogue** [rəug] *n* плут
**role** [rəul] *n* роль *f*; ~ **model** *n*
приме́р (для подража́ния)
**roll** [rəul] *n* (*of paper, cloth etc*)
руло́н; (*of banknotes*) сви́ток;
(*also:* **bread** ~) бу́лочка; (*register,
list*) спи́сок; (*of drums*) бой; (*of*

*thunder*) раскат ♦ *vt* (*ball, stone etc*) катать/катить (*impf*); (*also*: ~ **up**: *string*) скручивать (скрутить *pf*); (*: sleeves, eyes*) закатывать (закатать *pf*); (*cigarette*) свёртывать (свернуть *pf*); (*also*: ~ **out**: *pastry*) раскатывать (раскатать *pf*) ♦ *vi* (*also*: ~ **along**: *ball, car etc*) катиться (*impf*); (*ship*) качаться (*impf*); ~ **up** *vt* (*carpet, newspaper*) сворачивать (свернуть *pf*); ~**er** *n* (*for hair*) бигуди *pl ind*; ~**er skates** *npl* ролики *mpl*, роликовые коньки *mpl*; ~**ing pin** *n* скалка; ~**ing stock** *n* (*RAIL*) подвижной состав

**ROM** [rɔm] *n abbr* (*COMPUT*: = *read-only memory*) ПЗУ

**Roman** ['rəumən] *adj* римский; ~ **Catholic** *adj* (римско-)католический ♦ *n* католи́к(ичка)

**romance** [rə'mæns] *n* (*love affair, novel*) роман; (*charm*) романтика

**Romania** [rəu'meɪnɪə] *n* Румыния; ~**n** *adj* румынский

**romantic** [rə'mæntɪk] *adj* романти́чный; (*play, story etc*) романти́ческий

**Rome** [rəum] *n* Рим

**roof** [ruːf] (*pl* ~**s**) *n* крыша; **the** ~ **of the mouth** нёбо

**room** [ruːm] *n* (*in house*) комната; (*in school*) класс; (*in hotel*) номер; (*space*) место; ~**s** *npl* (*lodging*) квартира *fsg*; **"~s to let"**, (*US*) **"~s for rent"** "сдаются комнаты"; **single/double** ~ (*in hotel*) одноместный/двухместный номер

**roost** [ruːst] *vi* усаживаться (усесться *pf*) на ночлег

**root** [ruːt] *n* корень *m*; ~**s** *npl* (*family origins*) корни *mpl*

**rope** [rəup] *n* верёвка ♦ *vt* (*also*: ~ **off**: *area*) отгораживать (отгородить *pf*) верёвкой; **to** ~ **to** привязывать (привязать *pf*) верёвкой к +*dat*; **to** ~ **together** связывать (связать *pf*) верёвкой; **to know the** ~**s** (*fig*) знать (*impf*), что к чему

**rose** [rəuz] *pt of* **rise** ♦ *n* роза

**rosemary** ['rəuzmərɪ] *n* розмарин

**roster** ['rɔstər] *n*: **duty** ~ расписание дежурств

**rosy** ['rəuzɪ] *adj* (*face, cheeks*) румяный; (*situation*) радостный; (*future*) радужный

**rot** [rɔt] *n* (*result*) гниль *f* ♦ *vt* гноить (сгноить *pf*) ♦ *vi* гнить (сгнить *pf*)

**rota** ['rəutə] *n* расписание дежурств

**rotary** ['rəutərɪ] *adj* (*motion*) вращательный; (*engine*) роторно-поршневой

**rotate** [rəu'teɪt] *vt* вращать (*impf*); (*crops, jobs*) чередовать (*impf*) ♦ *vi* вращаться (*impf*)

**rotation** [rəu'teɪʃən] *n* вращение; (*of crops*) севооборот

**rotten** ['rɔtn] *adj* гнилой; (*meat, eggs*) тухлый; (*fig: unpleasant*) мерзкий; (*inf: bad*) поганый; **to feel** ~ (*ill*) чувствовать (*impf*) себя погано

**rouble** ['ruːbl] (*US* **ruble**) *n* рубль *m*

**rough** [rʌf] *adj* грубый; (*surface*) шероховатый; (*terrain*) пересечённый; (*person, manner*) резкий; (*sea*) бурный; (*town, area*) опасный; (*plan, work*) черновой; (*guess*) приблизительный ♦ *vt*: **to** ~ **it** ограничивать (ограничить *pf*) себя ♦ *adv*: **to sleep** ~ (*BRIT*) ночевать (*impf*) где придётся; ~**ly** *adv* грубо; (*approximately*) приблизительно

**Roumania** *etc* = **Romania** *etc*

**round** [raund] *adj* круглый; (*duty: of policeman, doctor*) обход; (*game: of cards, golf*) партия; (*in*

*competition*) тур; (*of ammunition*) комплéкт; (*of talks, also* BOXING) рáунд ♦ *vt* огибáть (обогнýть *pf*)
♦ *prep* (*surrounding*) вокрýг +*gen*; (*approximately*): ~ **about three hundred** гдé-то óколо трёхсот
♦ *adv*: **all** ~ кругóм, вокрýг; **a ~ of applause** взрыв аплодисмéнтов; **a ~ of drinks** по бокáлу на кáждого; ~ **his neck/the table** вокрýг егó шéи/столá; **the shop is just** ~ **the corner** (*fig*) до магазúна рукóй подáть; **to go** ~ **the back** обходúть (обойтú *pf*) сзáди; **to walk** ~ **the room** ходúть (*impf*) по кóмнате; **to go** ~ **to sb's (house)** ходúть/идтú (*impf*) к комý-н; **there's enough to go** ~ хвáтит на всех; ~ **off** *vt* (*speech etc*) завершáть (завершúть *pf*); ~ **up** *vt* (*cattle, people*) сгонять (согнáть *pf*); (*price, figure*) округлять (округлúть *pf*);
~**about** *n* (BRIT : AUT) кольцевáя трáнспортная развязка; (: *at fair*) карусéль *f* ♦ *adj*: **in a** ~**about way** окóльным путём; ~**up** *n* (*of information*) свóдка
**rouse** [rauz] *vt* (*wake up*) будúть (разбудúть *pf*); (*stir up*) возбуждáть (возбудúть *pf*)
**rousing** ['rauzɪŋ] *adj* (*cheer*) бýрный
**route** [ru:t] *n* (*way*) путь *m*, дорóга; (*of bus, train etc*) маршрýт
**routine** [ru:'ti:n] *adj* (*work*) повседнéвный; (*procedure*) обычный ♦ *n* (*habits*) распорядок; (*drudgery*) рутúна; (THEAT) нóмер
**row**[1] [rəu] *n* (*way*) ряд ♦ *vi* грестú (*impf*)
♦ *vt* управлять (*impf*) +*instr*; **in a** ~ (*fig*) подряд
**row**[2] [rau] *n* (*noise*) шум; (*dispute*) скандáл; (*inf*: *scolding*) нагоняй

♦ *vi* скандáлить (посандáлить *pf*)
**rowdy** ['raudɪ] *adj* бýйный
**rowing** ['rəuɪŋ] *n* грéбля
**royal** ['rɔɪəl] *adj* королéвский; **Royal Air Force** *n* (BRIT) ≈ Воéнно-воздýшные сúлы *fpl* Великобритáнии; ~**ty** *n* (*royal persons*) члéны *mpl* королéвской семьú; (*payment*) (áвторский) гонорáр
**rpm** *abbr* (= *revolutions per minute*) оборóты в минýту
**RSVP** *abbr* (= *répondez s'il vous plaît*) прóсим отвéтить на приглашéние
**rub** [rʌb] *vt* (*part of body*) терéть (потерéть *pf*); (*object*: *to clean*) терéть (*impf*); (: *to dry*) вытирáть (вытереть *pf*); (*hands* : *also*: ~ **together**) потирáть (потерéть *pf*)
♦ *n*: **to give sth a** ~ (*polish*) натирáть (натерéть *pf*) что-н; **to** ~ **sb up** *or* (US) ~ **sb the wrong way** раздражáть (раздражúть *pf*) когó-н
**rubber** ['rʌbəʳ] *n* (*substance*) резúна, каучýк; (BRIT: *eraser*) резúнка, лáстик
**rubbish** ['rʌbɪʃ] *n* мýсор; (*junk*) хлам; (*fig* : *pej*: *nonsense*) ерундá, чушь *f*; (: *goods*) дрянь *f*
**rubble** ['rʌbl] *n* облóмки *mpl*
**ruble** ['ru:bl] *n* (US) = **rouble**
**ruby** ['ru:bɪ] *n* рубúн
**rucksack** ['rʌksæk] *n* рюкзáк
**rudder** ['rʌdəʳ] *n* руль *m*
**ruddy** ['rʌdɪ] *adj* (*face*) румяный
**rude** [ru:d] *adj* (*impolite*) грýбый; (*unexpected*) жестóкий
**rudimentary** [ru:dɪ'mɛntərɪ] *adj* элементáрный
**rug** [rʌg] *n* кóврик; (BRIT: *blanket*) плед
**rugby** ['rʌgbɪ] *n* (*also*: ~ **football**) рéгби *nt ind*

**rugged** [ˈrʌgɪd] adj (landscape)
скалистый; (features) грубый;
(character) прямой
**ruin** [ˈruːɪn] n (destruction: of
building, plans) разрушение;
(downfall) гибель f; (bankruptcy)
разорение ♦ vt (building, hopes,
plans) разрушать (разрушить pf);
(future, health, reputation) губить
(погубить pf); (person: financially)
разорять (разорить pf); (spoil:
clothes) портить (испортить pf);
**~s** npl (of building) развалины fpl,
руины fpl
**rule** [ruːl] n (norm, regulation)
правило; (government)
правление ♦ vt (country, people)
править (impf) +instr ♦ vi (leader,
monarch etc) править (impf); **as a ~**
как правило; **~ out** vt (exclude)
исключать (исключить pf); **~d** adj
(paper) линованый; **~r** n
правитель(ница) m(f); (instrument)
линейка
**ruling** [ˈruːlɪŋ] adj (party) правящий
♦ n (LAW) постановление
**rum** [rʌm] n ром
**Rumania** etc = **Romania** etc
**rumble** [ˈrʌmbl] n (of traffic,
thunder) гул
**rumour** [ˈruːməʳ] (US **rumor**) n
слух ♦ vt: **it is ~ed that ...** ходят
слухи, что ...
**rump** [rʌmp] n (of horse) круп; (of
cow) зад
**run** [rʌn] (pt **ran**, pp **~**) n (fast pace)
бег; (journey) поездка; (SKIING)
трасса; (CRICKET, BASEBALL) очко;
(in tights etc) спустившиеся петли
fpl ♦ vi бегать/бежать (impf); (flee)
бежать (impf/pf), сбегать
(сбежать pf); (work: machine)
работать (impf); (bus, train)
ходить (impf); (play, show) идти
(impf); (: contract) длиться (impf);
(in election) баллотироваться (pf)

♦ vt (race, distance) пробегать
(пробежать pf); (business, hotel)
управлять (impf) +instr;
(competition, course) организовать
(impf/pf); (house) вести (impf);
(COMPUT, program) выполнять
(выполнить pf); (water) пускать
(пустить pf); (bath) наполнять
(наполнить pf); (PRESS, feature)
печатать (напечатать pf); **to ~
sth along** or **over** (hand, fingers)
проводить (провести pf) чем-н
по +dat; **in the long ~** в конечном
итоге; **to be on the ~** скрываться
(impf); **I'll ~ you to the station** я
подвезу Вас до станции; **~
about** vi бегать (impf); **~ around**
vi = **run about**; **~ away** vi
убегать (убежать pf); **~ down** vt
(production, industry) сворачивать
(свернуть pf); (AUT, hit) сбивать
(сбить pf); (criticize) поносить
(impf); **to be ~ down** (person)
выбиваться (выбиться pf) из
сил; **~ in** vt (BRIT: car)
обкатывать (обкатать pf); **~ into**
vt fus (meet: person) сталкиваться
(столкнуться pf) с +instr, (: trouble)
наталкиваться (натолкнуться pf)
на +acc; (collide with) врезаться
(врезаться pf) в +acc; **~ off** vt
(copies) делать (сделать pf),
отснять (pf) ♦ vi (person, animal)
сбегать (сбежать pf); **~ out** vi
(person) выбегать (выбежать pf);
(liquid) вытекать (вытечь pf);
(lease, visa) истекать (истечь pf);
(money) иссякать (иссякнуть pf);
**my passport ~s out in July** срок
действия моего паспорта
истекает в июле; **~ out of** vt fus
**I've ~ out of money/petrol** or (US)
**gas** у меня кончились деньги/
кончился бензин; **~ over** vt (AUT)
давить (задавить pf); **~ through**
vt fus пробегать (пробежать pf);

(*rehearse*) прогоня́ть (прогна́ть *pf*); **~ up** *vt*: **to ~ up a debt** аккумули́ровать (*impf/pf*) долги́; **to ~ up against** (*difficulties*) ста́лкиваться (столкну́ться *pf*) с +*instr*; **~away** *adj* (*truck, horse etc*) потеря́вший управле́ние

**rung** [rʌŋ] *pp of* **ring** ♦ *n* (*of ladder*) ступе́нька

**runner** ['rʌnəʳ] *n* (*in race: person*) бегу́н(ья); (*: horse*) скаку́н; (*on sledge, for drawer etc*) по́лоз; **~-up** *n* финали́ст (*заня́вший второ́е ме́сто*)

**running** ['rʌnɪŋ] *n* (*sport*) бег; (*of business*) руково́дство ♦ *adj* (*water: to house*) водопрово́дный; **he is in/out of the ~ for sth** ему́ сули́т/ не сули́т что-н; **6 days ~** 6 дней подря́д; **~ costs** *npl* (*of business*) операцио́нные изде́ржки *fpl*; (*of car*) содержа́ние *ntsg*

**runny** ['rʌnɪ] *adj* (*honey, egg*) жи́дкий; (*nose*) сопли́вый

**run-up** ['rʌnʌp] *n* (*to event*) преддве́рие

**runway** ['rʌnweɪ] *n* взлётно-поса́дочная полоса́

**rupture** ['rʌptʃəʳ] *n* (*MED*) гры́жа

**rural** ['ruərl] *adj* се́льский

**rush** [rʌʃ] *n* (*hurry*) спе́шка; (*COMM, sudden demand*) большо́й спрос; (*of water*) пото́к; (*of emotion*) прили́в ♦ *vt*: **to ~ one's meal/ work** второпя́х съеда́ть (съесть *pf*)/де́лать (сде́лать *pf*) рабо́ту ♦ *vi* (*person*) бежа́ть (*impf*); (*air, water*) хлы́нуть (*pf*); **~es** *npl* (*BOT*) камы́ш *mpl*; **~ hour** *n* час пик

**Russia** ['rʌʃə] *n* Росси́я; **~n** *adj* (*native Russian*) ру́сский; (*belonging to Russian Federation*) росси́йский ♦ *n* ру́сский(ая) *m(f) adj*; (*LING*) ру́сский язы́к

**rust** [rʌst] *n* ржа́вчина ♦ *vi* ржаве́ть (заржаве́ть *pf*)

**rustic** ['rʌstɪk] *adj* дереве́нский

**rusty** ['rʌstɪ] *adj* ржа́вый; (*fig: skill*) подзабы́тый

**rut** [rʌt] *n* (*groove*) колея́, борозда́; **to get into a ~** (*fig*) заходи́ть (зайти́ *pf*) в тупи́к

**ruthless** ['ru:θlɪs] *adj* беспоща́дный

**rye** [raɪ] *n* рожь *f*

# S, s

**Sabbath** ['sæbəθ] *n* (*Christian*) воскресе́нье

**sabotage** ['sæbətɑ:ʒ] *n* сабота́ж ♦ *vt* (*machine, building*) выводи́ть (вы́вести *pf*) из стро́я; (*plan, meeting*) саботи́ровать (*impf/pf*)

**sachet** ['sæʃeɪ] *n* паке́тик

**sack** [sæk] *n* (*bag*) мешо́к ♦ *vt* (*dismiss*) увольня́ть (уво́лить *pf*); **to give sb the ~** увольня́ть (уво́лить *pf*) кого́-н (с рабо́ты); **I got the ~** меня́ уво́лили (с рабо́ты); **~ing** *n* (*dismissal*) увольне́ние

**sacred** ['seɪkrɪd] *adj* свяще́нный; (*place*) свято́й

**sacrifice** ['sækrɪfaɪs] *n* же́ртва; (*REL*) жертвоприноше́ние ♦ *vt* (*fig*) же́ртвовать (поже́ртвовать *pf*) +*instr*

**sad** [sæd] *adj* печа́льный

**saddle** ['sædl] *n* седло́

**sadistic** [sə'dɪstɪk] *adj* сади́стский

**sadly** ['sædlɪ] *adv* (*unhappily*) печа́льно, гру́стно; (*unfortunately*) к сожале́нию; (*seriously: mistaken, neglected*) серьёзно

**sadness** ['sædnɪs] *n* печа́ль *f*, грусть *f*

**sae** *abbr* (*BRIT*: = *stamped addressed envelope*) надпи́санный конве́рт с ма́ркой

**safari** [sə'fɑ:rɪ] *n*: **to go on ~**

проводи́ть (провести́ *pf*) о́тпуск в сафа́ри
**safe** [seɪf] *adj* (*place, subject*) безопа́сный; (*return, journey*) благополу́чный; (*bet*) надёжный ♦ *n* сейф; **to be ~** находи́ться (*impf*) в безопа́сности; **~ from** (*attack*) защищённый от +*gen*; **~ and sound** цел и невреди́м; **(just) to be on the ~ side** на вся́кий слу́чай; **~guard** *n* гара́нтия ♦ *vt* (*life, interests*) охраня́ть (*impf*); **~ly** *adv* (*assume, say*) с уве́ренностью; (*drive, arrive*) благополу́чно; **~ty** *n* безопа́сность *f*; **~ty pin** *n* англи́йская була́вка
**saga** ['sɑ:gə] *n* са́га
**sage** [seɪdʒ] *n* (*herb*) шалфе́й
**Sagittarius** [sædʒɪ'tɛərɪəs] *n* Стреле́ц
**said** [sɛd] *pt, pp of* say
**sail** [seɪl] *n* па́рус ♦ *vt* (*boat*) пла́вать/плыть (*impf*) на +*prp* ♦ *vi* (*passenger, ship*) пла́вать/плыть (*impf*); (*also:* **set ~**) отплыва́ть (отплы́ть *pf*); **to go for a ~** е́хать (пое́хать *pf*) ката́ться на ло́дке; **~ing** *n* (*SPORT*) па́русный спорт; **~or** *n* моря́к, матро́с
**saint** [seɪnt] *n* свято́й(а́я) *m(f) adj*; **~ly** *adj* свято́й
**sake** [seɪk] *n*: **for the ~ of sb/sth, for sb's/sth's ~** ра́ди кого́-н/ чего́-н
**salad** ['sæləd] *n* сала́т
**salami** [sə'lɑ:mɪ] *n* саля́ми *f ind*
**salary** ['sælərɪ] *n* зарпла́та
**sale** [seɪl] *n* (*act*) прода́жа; (*with discount*) распрода́жа; (*auction*) то́рги *mpl*; **~s** *npl* (*amount sold*) объём *msg* прода́жи; **"for ~"** "продаётся"; **on ~** в прода́же; **~sman** (*irreg*) *n* (*also:* **travelling ~sman**) торго́вый аге́нт
**salient** ['seɪlɪənt] *adj* суще́ственный

**saliva** [sə'laɪvə] *n* слюна́
**salmon** ['sæmən] *n inv* (*ZOOL*) лосо́сь *m*; (*CULIN*) лососи́на
**salon** ['sælɒn] *n* сало́н; **beauty ~** космети́ческий сало́н
**salt** [sɔ:lt] *n* соль *f*; **~y** *adj* солёный
**salute** [sə'lu:t] *n* (*MIL*) салю́т ♦ *vt* (*MIL*) отдава́ть (отда́ть *pf*) честь +*dat*; (*fig*) приве́тствовать (*impf*)
**salvage** ['sælvɪdʒ] *n* (*saving*) спасе́ние ♦ *vt* (*also fig*) спаса́ть (спасти́ *pf*)
**salvation** [sæl'veɪʃən] *n* спасе́ние
**same** [seɪm] *adj* тако́й же; (*identical*) одина́ковый ♦ *pron*: **the ~** тот же (са́мый) (*f* та же (са́мая), *nt* то же (са́мое), *pl* те же (са́мые)); **the ~ book as** та же (са́мая) кни́га, что и; **at the ~ time** (*simultaneously*) в то же вре́мя; (*yet*) в то же вре́мя; **all** *or* **just the ~** всё равно́; **to do the ~ (as sb)** де́лать (сде́лать *pf*) то же (са́мое) (, что и кто-н); **Happy New Year! - the ~ to you!** С Но́вым Го́дом! - Вас та́кже!
**sample** ['sɑ:mpl] *n* (*of work, goods*) образе́ц ♦ *vt* (*food, wine*) про́бовать (попро́бовать *pf*); **to take a blood/urine ~** брать (взять *pf*) кровь/мочу́ на ана́лиз
**sanction** ['sæŋkʃən] *n* (*approval*) са́нкция ♦ *vt* (*approve*) санкциони́ровать (*impf/pf*); **~s** *npl* (*severe measures*) са́нкции *fpl*
**sanctuary** ['sæŋktjʊərɪ] *n* (*for animals*) запове́дник; (*for people*) убе́жище
**sand** [sænd] *n* песо́к ♦ *vt* (*also:* **~ down**) ошку́ривать (ошку́рить *pf*)
**sandal** ['sændl] *n* санда́лия
**sandpaper** ['sændpeɪpər] *n* нажда́чная бума́га
**sandstone** ['sændstəʊn] *n* песча́ник

**sandwich** ['sændwɪtʃ] n бутербро́д
♦ vt: ~ed between зажа́тый
ме́жду +instr; cheese/ham ~
бутербро́д с сы́ром/ветчино́й
**sandy** ['sændɪ] adj песча́ный
**sane** [seɪn] adj разу́мный
**sang** [sæŋ] pt of **sing**
**sanitary** ['sænɪtərɪ] adj
санита́рный; (clean) гигиени́чный
**sanitation** [sænɪ'teɪʃən] n
санитари́я
**sanity** ['sænɪtɪ] n (of person)
рассу́док; (sense) разу́мность f
**sank** [sæŋk] pt of **sink**
**Santa Claus** [sæntə'klɔːz] n (in
Britain etc) Са́нта-Кла́ус; (in Russia)
≈ Дед Моро́з
**sap** [sæp] n (BOT) сок ♦ vt (strength)
выса́сывать (вы́сосать pf); (confidence) отбира́ть (отобра́ть pf)
**sapling** ['sæplɪŋ] n молодо́е
де́ревце
**sapphire** ['sæfaɪər] n сапфи́р
**sarcasm** ['sɑːkæzm] n сарка́зм
**sarcastic** [sɑː'kæstɪk] adj
саркасти́чный
**sardine** [sɑː'diːn] n сарди́на
**sash** [sæʃ] n (around waist) куша́к;
(over shoulder) ле́нта
**sat** [sæt] pt, pp of **sit**
**Satan** ['seɪtn] n Сатана́ m
**satellite** ['sætəlaɪt] n спу́тник; (POL,
country) сателли́т; ~ **dish** n
спу́тниковая анте́нна
**satin** ['sætɪn] adj атла́сный
**satire** ['sætaɪər] n сати́ра
**satirical** [sə'tɪrɪkl] adj
сатири́ческий
**satisfaction** [sætɪs'fækʃən] n
(pleasure) удовлетворе́ние;
(refund, apology etc) возмеще́ние
**satisfactory** [sætɪs'fæktərɪ] adj
удовлетвори́тельный
**satisfy** ['sætɪsfaɪ] vt удовлетворя́ть
(удовлетвори́ть pf); (convince)
убежда́ть (убеди́ть pf); **to ~ sb**

**(that)** убежда́ть (убеди́ть pf)
кого́-н (в том, что); ~**ing** adj
прия́тный
**saturation** [sætʃə'reɪʃən] n (process)
насыще́ние; (state)
насы́щенность f
**Saturday** ['sætədɪ] n суббо́та

**Saturday job** - суббо́тняя
рабо́та. Брита́нские шко́льники
в суббо́ту не у́чатся, поэ́тому
мно́гие подро́стки
устра́иваются на суббо́тнюю
рабо́ту в кафе́ и́ли магази́н.

**sauce** [sɔːs] n со́ус; ~**pan** n
кастрю́ля
**saucer** ['sɔːsər] n блю́дце
**Saudi Arabia** [saudɪə'reɪbɪə] n
Сау́довская Ара́вия
**sauna** ['sɔːnə] n са́уна, фи́нская
ба́ня
**sausage** ['sɔsɪdʒ] n (for cooking)
санде́лька, соси́ска
**savage** ['sævɪdʒ] adj свире́пый
**save** [seɪv] vt (rescue) спаса́ть
(спасти́ pf); (economize on)
эконо́мить (сэконо́мить pf); (put
by) сберега́ть (сбере́чь pf); (keep:
receipts, file) сохраня́ть
(сохрани́ть pf); (: seat, place)
занима́ть (заня́ть pf); (work,
trouble) избавля́ть (изба́вить pf)
от +gen; (SPORT) отбива́ть (отби́ть
pf), отража́ть (отрази́ть pf) ♦ vi
(also: ~ up) копи́ть (скопи́ть pf)
де́ньги ♦ prep поми́мо +gen
**saving** ['seɪvɪŋ] n ♦ adj:
**the ~ grace of** спасе́ние +gen; ~**s**
npl (money) сбереже́ния ntpl
**saviour** ['seɪvjər] (US **savior**) n
спаси́тель(ница) m(f); (REL)
Спаси́тель m
**savour** ['seɪvər] (US **savor**) vt (food,
drink) смакова́ть (impf);
(experience) наслажда́ться

(наслади́ться *pf*) +*instr*; **~y** (*US* savory) *adj* несла́дкий

**saw** [sɔ:] (*pt* **~ed**, *pp* **~ed** or **~n**) *vt* пили́ть (*impf*) ♦ *n* пила́ ♦ *pt of* see; **~dust** *n* опи́лки *pl*; **~mill** *n* лесопи́льный заво́д

**saxophone** ['sæksəfəun] *n* саксофо́н

**say** [seɪ] (*pt*, *pp* said) *vt* говори́ть (сказа́ть *pf*) ♦ *n*: **to have one's ~** вы́разить (вы́разить *pf*) своё мне́ние; **to ~ yes** соглаша́ться (согласи́ться *pf*); **to ~ no** отка́зываться (отказа́ться *pf*); **could you ~ that again?** повтори́те, пожа́луйста; **that is to ~** то есть; **that goes without ~ing** э́то само́ собо́й разуме́ется; **~ing** *n* погово́рка

**scab** [skæb] *n* (*on wound*) струп

**scaffolding** ['skæfəldɪŋ] *n* леса́ *mpl*

**scald** [skɔ:ld] *n* ожо́г ♦ *vt* ошпа́ривать (ошпа́рить *pf*)

**scale** [skeɪl] *n* шкала́; (*usu pl*: *of fish*) чешуя́ *f no pl*; (*MUS*) га́мма; (*of map, project etc*) масшта́б ♦ *vt* взбира́ться (взобра́ться *pf*) на +*acc*; **~s** *npl* (*for weighing*) весы́ *pl*; **on a large ~** в широ́ком масшта́бе

**scalp** [skælp] *n* скальп

**scalpel** ['skælpl] *n* ска́льпель *m*

**scampi** ['skæmpɪ] *npl* (*BRIT*) панированные креве́тки *fpl*

**scan** [skæn] *vt* (*examine*) обсле́довать (*pf*); (*read quickly*) просма́тривать (просмотре́ть *pf*); (*RADAR*) скани́ровать (*impf*) ♦ *n* (*MED*) скани́рование; **ultrasound ~** ультразву́к

**scandal** ['skændl] *n* сканда́л; (*gossip*) спле́тни *fpl*; (*disgrace*) позо́р; **~ous** *adj* (*behaviour, story*) сканда́льный

**Scandinavia** [skændɪ'neɪvɪə] *n* Скандина́вия

**scant** [skænt] *adj* (*attention*) пове́рхностный

**scapegoat** ['skeɪpgəut] *n* козёл отпуще́ния

**scar** [skɑ:] *n* шрам; (*fig*) тра́вма ♦ *vt* травми́ровать (*impf/pf*); **his face is ~red** у него́ на лице́ шрам

**scarce** [skɛəs] *adj* ре́дкий; **to make o.s. ~** (*inf*) исчеза́ть (исче́знуть *pf*); **~ly** *adv* (*hardly*) едва́ ли; (*with numbers*) то́лько

**scare** [skɛər] *n* (*fright*) испу́г; (*public fear*) трево́га, па́ника ♦ *vt* пуга́ть (испуга́ть *pf*); **there was a bomb ~ at the station** опаса́лись, что на ста́нции подло́жена бо́мба; **~crow** *n* (огоро́дное) чу́чело; **~d** *adj* испу́ганный, напу́ганный; **he was ~d** он испуга́лся *или* был испу́ган

**scarf** [skɑ:f] (*pl* **~s** or **scarves**) *n* шарф; (*also*: **head~**) плато́к

**scarves** [skɑ:vz] *npl of* scarf

**scary** ['skɛərɪ] *adj* стра́шный

**scathing** ['skeɪðɪŋ] *adj* уничтожа́ющий

**scatter** ['skætər] *vt* (*papers, seeds*) разбра́сывать (разброса́ть *pf*) ♦ *vi* рассыпа́ться (рассы́паться *pf*)

**scenario** [sɪ'nɑ:rɪəu] *n* сцена́рий

**scene** [si:n] *n* (*THEAT, fig*) сце́на; (*of crime, accident*) ме́сто; (*sight, view*) карти́на; **~ry** *n* (*THEAT*) декора́ции *fpl*; (*landscape*) пейза́ж

**scenic** ['si:nɪk] *adj* живопи́сный

**scent** [sɛnt] *n* (*smell*) за́пах; (*track, also fig*) след; (*perfume*) духи́ *pl*

**sceptical** ['skɛptɪkl] (*US* **skeptical**) *adj* (*person*) скепти́чный; (*remarks*) скепти́ческий

**scepticism** ['skɛptɪsɪzəm] (*US* **skepticism**) *n* скептици́зм

**schedule** ['ʃɛdju:l, (*US*) 'skɛdju:l] *n* (*timetable*) расписа́ние, гра́фик; (*list of prices, details etc*) пе́речень

**scheme** 638 **scrape**

*m* ♦ *vt* (*timetable*) распи́сывать (расписа́ть *pf*); (*visit*) назнача́ть (назна́чить *pf*); **on ~** по расписа́нию *or* гра́фику; **to be ahead of ~** опережа́ть (опереди́ть *pf*) гра́фик; **to be behind ~** отстава́ть (отста́ть *pf*) от гра́фика

**scheme** [skiːm] *n* (*plan, idea*) за́мысел; (*plot*) про́иски *pl*, ко́зни *pl*; (*pension plan etc*) план

**schizophrenic** [skɪtsə'frɛnɪk] *adj* шизофрени́ческий

**scholar** ['skɔlər] *n* (*learned person*) учёный *m adj*; **~ship** *n* (*grant*) стипе́ндия

**school** [skuːl] *n* шко́ла; (*US : inf*) университе́т; (*BRIT: college*) институ́т ♦ *cpd* шко́льный; **~boy** *n* шко́льник; **~children** *npl* шко́льники *mpl*; **~girl** *n* шко́льница; **~ing** *n* шко́льное образова́ние

**science** ['saɪəns] *n* нау́ка; (*in school*) естествозна́ние; **~ fiction** *n* нау́чная фанта́стика

**scientific** [saɪən'tɪfɪk] *adj* нау́чный

**scientist** ['saɪəntɪst] *n* учёный *m adj*

**scintillating** ['sɪntɪleɪtɪŋ] *adj* (*fig: conversation, wit*) блестя́щий

**scissors** ['sɪzəz] *npl*: **(a pair of) ~** но́жницы *pl*

**scoff** [skɔf] *vi*: **to ~ (at)** насмеха́ться (*impf*) (над +*instr*)

**scold** [skəuld] *vt* брани́ть (вы́бранить *pf*), руга́ть (отруга́ть *pf*)

**scone** [skɔn] *n* (*CULIN*) кекс

**scooter** ['skuːtər] *n* (*also:* **motor ~**) мопе́д; (*toy*) самока́т

**scope** [skəup] *n* (*opportunity*) просто́р; (*of plan, undertaking*) масшта́б

**scorch** [skɔːtʃ] *vt* (*clothes*) сжига́ть (сжечь *pf*); (*earth, grass*) выжига́ть (вы́жечь *pf*)

**score** [skɔːr] *n* (*in game, test*) счёт ♦ *vt* (*goal*) забива́ть (заби́ть *pf*); (*point*) набира́ть (набра́ть *pf*); (*in test*) получа́ть (получи́ть *pf*) ♦ *vi* (*in game*) набира́ть (набра́ть *pf*) очки́; (*FOOTBALL*) забива́ть (заби́ть *pf*) гол; **~s of** деся́тки +*gen*; **on that ~** на э́тот счёт; **to ~ six out of ten** набира́ть (набра́ть *pf*) шесть ба́ллов из десяти́; **~ out** *vt* вычёркивать (вы́черкнуть *pf*); **~board** *n* табло́ *nt ind*

**scorn** [skɔːn] *n* презре́ние ♦ *vt* презира́ть (*impf*); **~ful** *adj* презри́тельный

**Scorpio** ['skɔːpɪəu] *n* Скорпио́н

**scorpion** ['skɔːpɪən] *n* скорпио́н

**Scot** [skɔt] *n* шотла́ндец(дка)

**Scotch** [skɔtʃ] *n* (шотла́ндское) ви́ски *nt ind*

**Scotland** ['skɔtlənd] *n* Шотла́ндия

**Scots** [skɔts] *adj* шотла́ндский

**Scottish** ['skɔtɪʃ] *adj* шотла́ндский

**scout** [skaut] *n* (*MIL*) разве́дчик; (*also:* **boy ~**) (бой)ска́ут

**scramble** ['skræmbl] *vi*: **to ~ out of** выкара́бкиваться (вы́карабкаться *pf*) из +*gen*; **to ~ for** дра́ться (подра́ться *pf*) за +*acc*; **~d eggs** *npl* яи́чница-болту́нья

**scrap** [skræp] *n* (*of paper*) клочо́к; (*of information*) обры́вок; (*of material*) лоску́т; (*also:* **~ metal**) металлоло́м, металли́ческий лом ♦ *vt* (*machines etc*) отдава́ть (отда́ть *pf*) на слом; (*plans etc*) отка́зываться (отказа́ться *pf*) от +*gen*; **~s** *npl* (*of food*) объе́дки *mpl*

**scrape** [skreɪp] *vt* (*remove*) соска́бливать (соскобли́ть *pf*); (*rub against*) цара́пать (поцара́пать *pf*), обдира́ть (ободра́ть *pf*) ♦ *vi*: **to ~ through** (*exam etc*) пролеза́ть (проле́зть *pf*) на +*prp*

**scratch** [skrætʃ] n цара́пина ♦ vt
цара́пать (поцара́пать pf); (an
itch) чеса́ть (почеса́ть pf) ♦ vi
чеса́ться (почеса́ться pf); **from ~**
с нуля́; **to be up to ~** быть (impf)
на до́лжном у́ровне

**scrawl** [skrɔːl] n кара́кули fpl ♦ vt
цара́пать (нацара́пать pf)

**scream** [skriːm] n вопль m, крик
♦ vi вопи́ть (impf), крича́ть (impf)

**screech** [skriːtʃ] vi визжа́ть (impf)

**screen** [skriːn] n экра́н; (barrier,
also fig) ши́рма ♦ vt (protect,
conceal) заслоня́ть (заслони́ть
pf); (show: film etc) выпуска́ть
(вы́пустить pf) на экра́н; (check:
candidates etc) проверя́ть
(прове́рить pf); **~ing** n (MED)
профилакти́ческий осмо́тр;
**~play** n сцена́рий; **~ saver** n
скрисе́йвер

**screw** [skruː] n винт ♦ vt (fasten)
приви́нчивать (привинти́ть pf);
**to ~ sth in** зави́нчивать
(завинти́ть pf) что-н; **~driver** n
отвёртка

**scribble** ['skrɪbl] vt черкну́ть (pf)
♦ vi исчёркивать (исчёркать pf)

**script** [skrɪpt] n (CINEMA etc)
сцена́рий; (Arabic etc) шрифт

**Scripture(s)** ['skrɪptʃəʳ(-əz)] n(pl)
Свяще́нное Писа́ние ntsg

**scroll** [skrəul] n сви́ток ♦ vi: **to ~
up/down** перемеща́ть
(перемести́ть pf) наве́рх/вниз

**scrub** [skrʌb] vt скрести́ (impf)

**scruffy** ['skrʌfɪ] adj потрёпанный

**scrupulous** ['skruːpjuləs] adj
(painstaking) тща́тельный,
скрупулёзный; (fair-minded)
щепети́льный

**scrutiny** ['skruːtɪnɪ] n тща́тельное
изуче́ние or рассмотре́ние

**scuffle** ['skʌfl] n потасо́вка

**sculptor** ['skʌlptəʳ] n ску́льптор

**sculpture** ['skʌlptʃəʳ] n скульпту́ра

**scum** [skʌm] n пе́на; (inf : pej:
people) подо́нки mpl

**scythe** [saɪð] n серп

**sea** [siː] n мо́ре ♦ cpd морско́й; **by
~** (travel) мо́рем; **on the ~** (town)
на мо́ре; **out to~**, **out at ~** в
мо́ре; **~food** n ры́бные блю́да
ntpl; **~front** n на́бережная f adj;
**~gull** n ча́йка

**seal** [siːl] n (ZOOL) тюле́нь m;
(stamp) печа́ть f ♦ vt (envelope)
запеча́тывать (запеча́тать pf);
(opening) заде́лывать (заде́лать
pf)

**sea level** n у́ровень m мо́ря

**sea lion** n морско́й лев

**seam** [siːm] n (of garment) шов

**search** [səːtʃ] n по́иск; (for criminal)
ро́зыск; (of sb's home etc) о́быск
♦ vt обы́скивать (обыска́ть pf)
♦ vi: **to ~ for** иска́ть (impf); **in ~ of**
в по́исках +gen; **~ing** adj (look)
пытли́вый; (question) наводя́щий

**seasick** ['siːsɪk] adj: **to be ~**
страда́ть (impf) морско́й
боле́знью

**seaside** ['siːsaɪd] n взмо́рье

**season** ['siːzn] n вре́мя nt го́да;
(for football, of films etc) сезо́н ♦ vt
(food) заправля́ть (запра́вить pf);
**~al** adj сезо́нный; **~ed** adj
(traveller) закалённый; **~ing** n
припра́ва

**seat** [siːt] n (chair, place) сиде́нье;
(in theatre, parliament) ме́сто; (of
trousers) зад ♦ vt (subj: venue)
вмеща́ть (вмести́ть pf); **to be ~ed**
сиде́ть (impf); **~ belt** n привязно́й
реме́нь m

**seaweed** ['siːwiːd] n во́доросли fpl

**sec.** abbr = **second²**

**secluded** [sɪ'kluːdɪd] adj
уединённый

**second¹** [sɪ'kɔnd] vt (BRIT:
employee) командирова́ть (impf)

**second²** ['sɛkənd] adj второ́й

♦ *adv* (*come*) вторы́м; (*when listing*) во-вторы́х ♦ *n* (*unit of time*) секу́нда; (*AUT : also:* ~ **gear**) втора́я ско́рость *f*; (*COMM*) некондицио́нный това́р; (*BRIT : SCOL*) дипло́м второ́го кла́сса ♦ *vt* (*motion*) подде́рживать (поддержа́ть *pf*); **~ary** *adj* втори́чный; **~ary school** *n* сре́дняя шко́ла; **~-class** *adj* второразря́дный; **~-class stamp** ма́рка второ́го кла́сса

---

**second-class postage** - в Великобрита́нии мо́жно приобрести́ почто́вые ма́рки пе́рвого и второ́го кла́сса. Ма́рки второ́го кла́сса деше́вле. Пи́сьма с таки́ми ма́рками доставля́ются по ме́сту назначе́ния че́рез 2-3 дня.

---

**second**: ['sɛkənd] ~ **hand** *n* (*on clock*) секу́ндная стре́лка; **~-hand** *adj* поде́ржанный, сэ́конд-хэнд *ind*; **~ly** *adv* во-вторы́х; **~-rate** *adj* (*film*) посре́дственный; (*restaurant*) второразря́дный; ~ **thoughts** *npl*: **to have** ~ **thoughts (about doing)** сомнева́ться (*impf*) (сле́дует ли +*infin*); **on** ~ **thoughts** *or* (*US*) **thought** по зре́лом размышле́нии

**secrecy** ['si:krəsɪ] *n* секре́тность *f*

**secret** ['si:krɪt] *adj* секре́тный, та́йный; (*admirer*) та́йный ♦ *n* секре́т, та́йна; **in** ~ (*do, meet*) секре́тно, та́йно

**secretarial** [sɛkrɪ'tɛərɪəl] *adj* секрета́рский; ~ **course** ку́рсы *mpl* секретаре́й

**secretary** ['sɛkrətərɪ] *n* секрета́рь *m*; **Secretary of State (for)** (*BRIT*) ≈ мини́стр (+*gen*)

**secretive** ['si:krətɪv] *adj* (*pej: person*)

скры́тный; **he is** ~ **about his plans** он де́ржит свои́ пла́ны в секре́те

**secretly** ['si:krɪtlɪ] *adv* (*do, meet*) секре́тно

**secret service** *n* секре́тная слу́жба

**sect** [sɛkt] *n* се́кта

**sectarian** [sɛk'tɛərɪən] *adj* секта́нтский

**section** ['sɛkʃən] *n* (*part*) часть *f*; (*of population, company*) се́ктор; (*of document, book*) разде́л

**sector** ['sɛktər] *n* (*part*) се́ктор

**secular** ['sɛkjulər] *adj* све́тский

**secure** [sɪ'kjuər] *adj* (*safe: person, money, job*) надёжный; (*firmly fixed: rope, shelf*) про́чный ♦ *vt* (*fix: rope, shelf etc*) (про́чно) закрепля́ть (закрепи́ть *pf*); (*get: job, loan etc*) обеспе́чивать (обеспе́чить *pf*)

**security** [sɪ'kjuərɪtɪ] *n* (*protection*) безопа́сность *f*; (*for one's future*) обеспе́ченность *f*

**sedate** [sɪ'deɪt] *adj* (*person*) степе́нный; (*pace*) разме́ренный ♦ *vt* дава́ть (дать *pf*) седати́вное *or* успокои́тельное сре́дство

**sedative** ['sɛdɪtɪv] *n* седати́вное *or* успокои́тельное сре́дство

**sediment** ['sɛdɪmənt] *n* оса́док

**seduce** [sɪ'dju:s] *vt* соблазня́ть (соблазни́ть *pf*)

**seduction** [sɪ'dʌkʃən] *n* (*act*) обольще́ние

**seductive** [sɪ'dʌktɪv] *adj* (*look, voice*) обольсти́тельный; (*offer*) соблазни́тельный

**see** [si:] (*pt* **saw**, *pp* **~n**) *vt* ви́деть (уви́деть *pf*) ♦ *vi* ви́деть (*impf*); (*find out*) выясня́ть (вы́яснить *pf*); **to** ~ **that** (*ensure*) следи́ть (проследи́ть *pf*), что́бы; ~ **you soon!** пока́!, до ско́рого!; ~ **off** *vt* провожа́ть (проводи́ть *pf*); ~

**through** vt доводить (довести pf) до конца ♦ vt fus видеть (impf) насквозь +acc; ~ **to** vt fus позаботиться (pf) о +prp

**seed** [siːd] n семя nt; **to go to ~** (fig) сдать (pf); **~ling** n рассада no pl; **~y** adj (place) захудалый

**seeing** ['siːɪŋ] conj: ~ **(that)** поскольку, так как

**seek** [siːk] (pt, pp **sought**) vt искать (impf)

**seem** [siːm] vi казаться (показаться pf); **there ~s to be ...** кажется, что имеется ...; **he ~s to be tired** он кажется усталым; **~ingly** adv по-видимому; (important) как представляется

**seen** [siːn] pp of **see**

**see-through** ['siːθruː] adj прозрачный

**segment** ['sɛɡmənt] n (of population) сектор; (of orange) долька

**seize** [siːz] vt хватать (схватить pf); (power, hostage, territory) захватывать (захватить pf); (opportunity) пользоваться (воспользоваться pf) +instr

**seizure** ['siːʒər] n (MED) приступ; (of power) захват; (of goods) конфискация

**seldom** ['sɛldəm] adv редко

**select** [sɪ'lɛkt] adj (school, area) элитный ♦ vt (choose) выбирать (выбрать pf); **~ion** [sɪ'lɛkʃən] n (process) отбор; (range) выбор; (medley) подборка; **~ive** adj (person) разборчивый; (not general) избирательный

**self** [sɛlf] (pl **selves**) n: **he became his usual ~ again** он стал опять самим собой

**self-** [sɛlf] prefix само-; **~assured** adj самоуверенный; **~catering** adj (BRIT): **~catering holiday**

туристическая путёвка, в которую включается проезд и жильё; **~centred** (US **~centered**) adj эгоцентричный; **~confidence** n уверенность f в себе; **~conscious** adj (nervous) застенчивый; **~control** n самообладание; **~defence** (US **~defense**) n самозащита, самооборона; **in ~defence** защищая себя; **~discipline** n самодисциплина; **~employed** adj работающий на себя; **~evident** adj самоочевидный; **~interest** n корысть f; **~ish** adj эгоистический; **~ishness** n (of person) эгоизм; **~less** adj самоотверженный; **~pity** n жалость f к (самому) себе; **~portrait** n автопортрет; **~respect** n самоуважение; **~righteous** adj убеждённый в своей правоте; **~satisfied** adj самодовольный; **~service** adj: **~service restaurant** кафе nt ind с самообслуживанием; **~sufficient** adj самостоятельный

**sell** [sɛl] (pt, pp **sold**) vt продавать (продать pf) ♦ vi продаваться (impf); **to ~ at** or **for 10 pounds** продаваться (impf) по 10 фунтов; **~ off** vt распродавать (распродать pf); **~ out** vi (book etc) расходиться (разойтись pf); (shop): **to ~ out of sth** распродавать (распродать pf) что-н; **the tickets are sold out** все билеты проданы

**Sellotape** ® ['sɛləuteɪp] n (BRIT) клейкая лента

**selves** [sɛlvz] pl of **self**

**semblance** ['sɛmblns] n видимость f

**semester** [sɪ'mɛstər] n (esp US) семестр

**semi-** ['sɛmɪ] prefix полу-

**semi** - полуособня́к. В Великобрита́нии мно́гие се́мьи живу́т в полуособняка́х - два двухэта́жных до́ма име́ют одну́ о́бщую сте́ну, но отде́льный вход и сад.

**semi**: ~**circle** n полукру́г; ~**colon** n то́чка с запято́й; ~**final** n полуфина́л

**seminar** ['semɪnɑːr] n семина́р

**senate** ['senɪt] n сена́т

**senator** ['senɪtər] n (US etc) сена́тор

**send** [send] (pt, pp **sent**) vt посыла́ть (посла́ть pf); ~ **away** vt (letter, goods) отсыла́ть (отосла́ть pf); (visitor) прогоня́ть (прогна́ть pf); ~ **back** vt посыла́ть (посла́ть pf) обра́тно; ~ **for** vt fus (by post) зака́зывать (заказа́ть pf); (person) посыла́ть (посла́ть pf) за +instr; ~ **off** vt (letter) отправля́ть (отпра́вить pf); (BRIT : SPORT) удаля́ть (удали́ть pf); ~ **out** vt (invitation) рассыла́ть (разосла́ть pf); (signal) посыла́ть (посла́ть pf); ~**er** n отправи́тель m

**senile** ['siːnaɪl] adj маразмати́ческий

**senior** ['siːnɪər] adj (staff, officer) ста́рший; (manager, consultant) гла́вный; **to be ~ to sb** (in rank) быть (impf) вы́ше кого́-н по положе́нию; **she is 15 years his ~** она́ ста́рше его́ на 15 лет; ~ **citizen** n (esp BRIT) пожило́й челове́к, челове́к пенсио́нного во́зраста; ~**ity** [siːnɪ'ɔrɪtɪ] n старшинство́

**sensation** [sen'seɪʃən] n (feeling) ощуще́ние; (great success) сенса́ция; ~**al** adj (wonderful) потряса́ющий; (dramatic) сенсацио́нный

**sense** [sens] vt чу́вствовать (почу́вствовать pf), ощуща́ть (ощути́ть pf) ♦ n (feeling) чу́вство, ощуще́ние; **it makes ~** в э́том есть смысл; **the ~s** пять чувств; ~**less** adj бессмы́сленный; (unconscious) бесчу́вственный; ~ **of humour** (US ~ **of humor**) n чу́вство ю́мора

**sensible** ['sensɪbl] adj разу́мный

**sensitive** ['sensɪtɪv] adj чувстви́тельный; (understanding) чу́ткий; (issue) щекотли́вый

**sensitivity** [sensɪ'tɪvɪtɪ] n (see adj) чувстви́тельность f; чу́ткость f; щекотли́вость f

**sensual** ['sensjuəl] adj чу́вственный

**sensuous** ['sensjuəs] adj (lips) чу́вственный; (material) не́жный

**sent** [sent] pt, pp of **send**

**sentence** ['sentns] n (LING) предложе́ние; (LAW) пригово́р ♦ vt: **to ~ sb to** пригова́ривать (приговори́ть pf) кого́-н к +dat

**sentiment** ['sentɪmənt] n (tender feelings) чу́вство; (opinion) настрое́ние; ~**al** [sentɪ'mentl] adj сентимента́льный

**sentry** ['sentrɪ] n часово́й m adj, карау́льный m adj

**separate** adj ['seprɪt] vb ['sepəreɪt] adj отде́льный; (ways) ра́зный ♦ vt (split up: people) разлуча́ть (разлучи́ть pf); (: things) разделя́ть (раздели́ть pf); (distinguish) различа́ть (различи́ть pf) ♦ vi расходи́ться (разойти́сь pf); ~**ly** ['seprɪtlɪ] adv отде́льно, по отде́льности

**separation** [sepə'reɪʃən] n (being apart) разлу́ка; (LAW) разде́льное прожива́ние

**September** [sep'tembər] n сентя́брь m

**septic** ['septɪk] adj заражённый

**sequel** ['si:kwl] n продолже́ние

**sequence** ['si:kwəns] n
после́довательность f

**Serbia** ['sə:bɪə] n Се́рбия

**Serbo-Croat** ['sə:bəu'krəuæt] adj
се́рбо-хорва́тский

**serene** [sɪ'ri:n] adj безмяте́жный

**sergeant** ['sɑ:dʒənt] n сержа́нт

**serial** ['sɪərɪəl] n (TV, RADIO) сериа́л;
(PRESS) публика́ция в не́скольких
частя́х

**series** ['sɪərɪz] n inv се́рия

**serious** ['sɪərɪəs] adj серьёзный;
**are you ~ (about it)?** Вы (э́то)
серьёзно?; **~ly** adv серьёзно;
**~ness** n серьёзность f

**sermon** ['sə:mən] n про́поведь f

**servant** ['sə:vənt] n слуга́(ужа́нка)
m(f)

**serve** [sə:v] vt (company, country)
служи́ть (impf) +dat; (customer)
обслу́живать (обслужи́ть pf);
(subj: train etc) обслу́живать
(impf); (apprenticeship) проходи́ть
(пройти́ pf); (prison term)
отбыва́ть (отбы́ть pf) ♦ vi (TENNIS)
подава́ть (пода́ть pf) ♦ n (TENNIS)
пода́ча; **it ~s him right** поде́лом
ему́; **to ~ on** (jury, committee)
состоя́ть (impf) в +prp; **to ~ as/for**
служи́ть (послужи́ть pf) +instr/
вме́сто +gen

**service** ['sə:vɪs] n (help) услу́га; (in
hotel) обслу́живание, се́рвис;
(REL) слу́жба; (AUT)
техобслу́живание; (TENNIS)
пода́ча ♦ vt (car) проводи́ть
(провести́ pf) техобслу́живание
+gen; **the Services** npl (MIL)
Вооружённые си́лы fpl; **military**
or **national ~** вое́нная слу́жба;
**train ~** железнодоро́жное
сообще́ние; **postal ~** почто́вая
связь

**serviette** [sə:vɪ'ɛt] n (BRIT)
салфе́тка

**session** ['sɛʃən] n (of treatment)
сеа́нс; **recording ~** за́пись f; **to be
in ~** (court etc) заседа́ть (impf)

**set** [sɛt] (pt, pp ~) n (collection)
набо́р; (of pans, clothes) компле́кт;
(also: **television ~**) телеви́зор;
(TENNIS) сет; (MATH) мно́жество;
(CINEMA, THEAT, stage) сце́на ♦ adj
(fixed) устано́вленный; (ready)
гото́вый ♦ vt (place: vertically)
ста́вить (поста́вить pf);
(: horizontally) класть (положи́ть
pf); (table) накрыва́ть (накры́ть
pf); (time) назнача́ть (назна́чить
pf); (price, record) устана́вливать
(установи́ть pf); (alarm, task)
ста́вить (поста́вить pf); (exam)
составля́ть (соста́вить pf) ♦ vi
(sun) сади́ться (сесть pf),
заходи́ть (зайти́ pf); (jam)
густе́ть (загусте́ть pf); (jelly,
concrete) застыва́ть (засты́ть pf);
**to ~ to music** класть (положи́ть
pf) на му́зыку; **to ~ on fire**
поджига́ть (подже́чь pf); **to ~ free**
освобожда́ть (освободи́ть pf); **~
about** vt fus (task) приступа́ть
(приступи́ть pf) к +dat; **~ aside** vt
(money) откла́дывать (отложи́ть
pf); (time) выделя́ть (вы́делить
pf); **~ back** vt (progress)
заде́рживать (задержа́ть pf); **to ~
sb back £5** обходи́ться
(обойти́сь pf) кому́-н в £5; **~ off**
vi отправля́ться (отпра́виться pf)
♦ vt (bomb) взрыва́ть (взорва́ть
pf); (alarm) приводи́ть (привести́
pf) в де́йствие; (events) повлека́ть
(повле́чь pf) (за собо́й); **~ out** vt
выставля́ть (вы́ставить pf) ♦ vi
(depart): **to ~ out (from)**
отправля́ться (отпра́виться pf)
(из +gen); **to ~ out to do**
намерева́ться (impf) +infin; **~ up** vt
(organization) учрежда́ть
(учреди́ть pf); **~back** n неуда́ча

**settee** [sɛˈtiː] n диван

**setting** [ˈsɛtɪŋ] n (background)
обстановка; (position: of controls)
положение

**settle** [ˈsɛtl] vt (argument, problem)
разрешать (разрешить pf);
(matter) улаживать (уладить pf);
(bill) рассчитываться
(рассчитаться pf) с +instr ♦ vi
(dust, sediment) оседать (осесть
pf); (also: ~ **down**)
обосновываться (обосноваться
pf); (: live sensibly) остепеняться
(остепениться pf); (calm down)
успокаиваться (успокоиться pf);
**to ~ for sth** соглашаться
(согласиться pf) на что-н; **to ~ on
sth** останавливаться
(остановиться pf) на чём-н; **~ in**
vi осваиваться (освоиться pf);
**~ment** n (payment) уплата;
(agreement) соглашение; (village,
colony) поселение; (of conflict)
урегулирование

**seven** [ˈsɛvn] n семь; **~teen** n
семнадцать; **~teenth** adj
семнадцатый; **~th** adj седьмой;
**~tieth** adj семидесятый; **~ty** n
семьдесят

**sever** [ˈsɛvər] vt (artery, pipe)
перерезать (перерезать pf);
(relations) прерывать (прервать
pf)

**several** [ˈsɛvərl] adj несколько +gen
♦ pron некоторые pl adj; **~ of us**
некоторые из нас

**severe** [sɪˈvɪər] adj (shortage, pain,
winter) жестокий; (damage)
серьёзный; (stern) жёсткий

**severity** [sɪˈvɛrɪtɪ] n жестокость f;
(of damage) серьёзность f

**sew** [səu] (pt **~ed**, pp **~n**) vti шить
(impf)

**sewage** [ˈsuːɪdʒ] n сточные воды
fpl; **~ system** канализация

**sewer** [ˈsuːər] n канализационная

труба

**sewing** [ˈsəuɪŋ] n шитьё; **~
machine** n швейная машинка

**sewn** [səun] pp of sew

**sex** [sɛks] n (gender) пол;
(lovemaking) секс; **to have ~ with
sb** переспать (pf) с кем-н; **~ist** adj
сексистский; **he is ~ist** он -
сексист; **~ual** adj половой; **~ual
equality** равенство полов; **~ual
harassment** сексуальное
преследование; **~y** adj
сексуальный; (woman)
сексопильная

**shabby** [ˈʃæbɪ] adj потрёпанный;
(treatment) недостойный

**shack** [ʃæk] n лачуга

**shade** [ʃeɪd] n (shelter) тень f; (for
lamp) абажур; (of colour) оттенок
♦ vt (shelter) затенять (затенить
pf); (eyes) заслонять (заслонить
pf); **in the ~** в тени

**shadow** [ˈʃædəu] n тень f ♦ vt
(follow) следовать (impf) как тень
за +instr; **~ cabinet** n (BRIT)
теневой кабинет

**shady** [ˈʃeɪdɪ] adj (place, trees)
тенистый; (fig: dishonest) тёмный

**shaft** [ʃɑːft] n (of mine, lift) шахта;
(of light) сноп

**shake** [ʃeɪk] (pt **shook**, pp **~n**) vt
трясти (impf); (bottle)
взбалтывать (взболтать pf);
(building) сотрясать (сотрясти pf);
(weaken: beliefs, resolve)
пошатнуть (pf); (upset, surprise)
потрясать (потрясти pf) ♦ vi
(voice) дрожать (impf); **to ~ one's
head** качать (покачать pf)
головой; **to ~ hands with sb**
жать (пожать pf) кому-н руку; **to
~ with** трястись (impf) от +gen; **~
off** vt стряхивать (стряхнуть pf);
(fig: pursuer) избавляться
(избавиться pf) от +gen; **~ up** vt
(fig: organization) встряхивать

(встряхну́ть *pf*)

**shaky** ['ʃeɪkɪ] *adj* (*hand, voice*)
дрожа́щий

**shall** [ʃæl] *aux vb*: **I ~ go** я пойду́; **~
I open the door?** (мне) откры́ть
дверь?; **I'll get some water; ~ I?** я
принесу́ воды́, хорошо́?

**shallow** ['ʃæləu] *adj* (*water*)
ме́лкий; (*box*) неглубо́кий;
(*breathing, also fig*)
пове́рхностный

**sham** [ʃæm] *n* притво́рство

**shambles** ['ʃæmblz] *n*
неразбери́ха

**shame** [ʃeɪm] *n* (*embarrassment*)
стыд; (*disgrace*) позо́р ♦ *vt*
позо́рить (опозо́рить *pf*); **it is a ~
that/to do** жаль, что/+*infin*; **what
a ~!** кака́я жа́лость!, как жаль!;
**~ful** *adj* позо́рный; **~less** *adj*
бессты́дный

**shampoo** [ʃæm'puː] *n* шампу́нь *m*
♦ *vt* мыть (помы́ть *or* вы́мыть *pf*)
шампу́нем

**shan't** [ʃɑːnt] = **shall not**

**shape** [ʃeɪp] *n* фо́рма ♦ *vt* (*ideas,
events*) формирова́ть
(сформирова́ть *pf*); (*clay*) лепи́ть
(слепи́ть *pf*); **to take ~** обрета́ть
(обрести́ *pf*) фо́рму; **-~d** *suffix*:
**heart~~d** сердцеви́дный; **~less**
*adj* бесфо́рменный; **~ly** *adj*
стро́йный

**share** [ʃɛər] *n* до́ля; (*COMM*) а́кция
♦ *vt* (*books, cost*) дели́ть
(подели́ть *pf*); (*toys*) дели́ться
(подели́ться *pf*) +*instr*; (*features,
qualities*) разделя́ть (*impf*);
(*opinion, concern*) разделя́ть
(раздели́ть *pf*); **~ out** *vt* дели́ть
(раздели́ть *pf*); **~holder** *n*
акционе́р

**shark** [ʃɑːk] *n* аку́ла

**sharp** [ʃɑːp] *adj* о́стрый; (*sound*)
ре́зкий; (*MUS*) дие́з *ind* ♦ *adv*
(*precisely*): **at 2 o'clock ~** ро́вно в

два часа́; **he is very ~** у него́
о́чень о́стрый ум; **~en** *vt* (*pencil,
knife*) точи́ть (поточи́ть *pf*); **~ener**
*n* (*also*: **pencil ~ener**) точи́лка;
**~ly** *adv* ре́зко

**shatter** ['ʃætər] *vt* (*vase, hopes*)
разбива́ть (разби́ть *pf*); (*upset:
person*) потряса́ть (потрясти́ *pf*)
♦ *vi* би́ться (разби́ться *pf*)

**shave** [ʃeɪv] *vt* брить (побри́ть *pf*)
♦ *vi* бри́ться (побри́ться *pf*) ♦ *n*:
**to have a ~** бри́ться (побри́ться
*pf*)

**shaving** ['ʃeɪvɪŋ] *n* бритьё; **~s** *npl*
(*of wood etc*) стру́жки *fpl*

**shawl** [ʃɔːl] *n* шаль *f*

**she** [ʃiː] *pron* она́

**sheaf** [ʃiːf] (*pl* **sheaves**) *n* (*of
papers*) сто́пка

**shears** ['ʃɪəz] *npl* (*for hedge*)
садо́вые но́жницы *pl*

**sheaves** [ʃiːvz] *npl of* **sheaf**

**shed** [ʃed] (*pt, pp* **~**) *n* (*in garden*)
сара́й ♦ *vt* (*skin, load*) сбра́сывать
(сбро́сить *pf*); (*tears*) лить (*impf*)

**she'd** [ʃiːd] = **she had, she would**

**sheen** [ʃiːn] *n* лоск

**sheep** [ʃiːp] *n inv* овца́; **~dog** *n*
овча́рка

**sheer** [ʃɪər] *adj* (*utter*) су́щий;
(*steep*) отве́сный

**sheet** [ʃiːt] *n* (*on bed*) простыня́;
(*of paper, glass etc*) лист; (*of ice*)
полоса́

**sheik(h)** [ʃeɪk] *n* шейх

**shelf** [ʃelf] (*pl* **shelves**) *n* по́лка

**shell** [ʃel] *n* (*of mollusc*) ра́ковина;
(*of egg, nut*) скорлупа́; (*explosive*)
снаря́д; (*of building*) карка́с; (*of
ship*) ко́рпус ♦ *vt* (*peas*) лущи́ть
(облущи́ть *pf*); (*MIL*)
обстре́ливать (обстреля́ть *pf*)

**she'll** [ʃiːl] = **she will, she shall**

**shellfish** ['ʃelfɪʃ] *n inv* (*crab*) рачки́
*pl*; (*scallop*) моллю́ски *mpl*

**shelter** ['ʃeltər] *n* (*refuge*) прию́т;

(*protection*) укры́тие ♦ vt (*protect*)
укрыва́ть (укры́ть pf); (*hide*)
дава́ть (дать pf) прию́т +dat ♦ vi
укрыва́ться (укры́ться pf); **~ed**
adj (*life*) беззабо́тный; (*spot*)
защищённый

**shelves** [ʃelvz] npl of **shelf**

**shepherd** [ˈʃepəd] n пасту́х

**sheriff** [ˈʃerɪf] n (US) шери́ф

**sherry** [ˈʃerɪ] n хе́рес

**she's** [ʃiːz] = **she is**, **she has**

**shield** [ʃiːld] n щит; (*trophy*)
трофе́й ♦ vt: **to ~ (from)**
заслоня́ть (заслони́ть pf) (от
+gen)

**shift** [ʃɪft] n (in direction,
conversation) переме́на; (in policy,
emphasis) сдвиг; (at work) сме́на
♦ vt передвига́ть (передви́нуть
pf), перемеща́ть (перемести́ть pf)
♦ vi перемеща́ться
(перемести́ться pf)

**shimmer** [ˈʃɪməʳ] vi мерца́ть (impf)

**shin** [ʃɪn] n го́лень f

**shine** [ʃaɪn] (pt, pp **shone**) n блеск
♦ vi (sun, light) свети́ть (impf);
(eyes, hair) блесте́ть (impf) ♦ vt: **to**
**~ a torch on sth** направля́ть
(напра́вить pf) фона́рь на что-н

**shiny** [ˈʃaɪnɪ] adj блестя́щий

**ship** [ʃɪp] n кора́бль m ♦ vt (by ship)
перевози́ть (перевезти́ pf) по
мо́рю; (send) отправля́ть
(отпра́вить pf), экспеди́ровать
(impf/pf); **~building** n
кораблестрое́ние,
судострое́ние; **~ment** n (goods)
па́ртия; **~ping** n (of cargo)
перево́зка; **~wreck** n (ship)
су́дно, потерпе́вшее круше́ние
♦ vt: **to be ~wrecked** терпе́ть
(потерпе́ть pf)
кораблекруше́ние; **~yard** n
(судострои́тельная) верфь f

**shirt** [ʃəːt] n (man's) руба́шка;
(woman's) блу́зка; **in (one's) ~**

**sleeves** в одно́й руба́шке

**shit** [ʃɪt] excl (inf!) чёрт!, блин!

**shiver** [ˈʃɪvəʳ] n дрожь f ♦ vi
дрожа́ть (impf)

**shoal** [ʃəul] n (of fish) коса́к

**shock** [ʃɔk] n (start, impact) толчо́к;
(ELEC, MED) шок; (emotional)
потрясе́ние ♦ vt (upset)
потряса́ть (потрясти́ pf); (offend)
возмуща́ть (возмути́ть pf),
шоки́ровать (impf/pf); **~ absorber**
n амортиза́тор; **~ing** adj
(outrageous) возмути́тельный;
(dreadful) кошма́рный

**shoddy** [ˈʃɔdɪ] adj (goods)
дрянно́й; (workmanship)
куста́рный

**shoe** [ʃuː] n (for person) ту́фля; (for
horse) подко́ва; **~s** (footwear)
о́бувь fsg; **~lace** n шнуро́к

**shone** [ʃɔn] pt, pp of **shine**

**shook** [ʃuk] pt of **shake**

**shoot** [ʃuːt] (pt, pp **shot**) n (BOT)
росто́к, побе́г ♦ vt (gun) стреля́ть
(impf) из +gen; (bird, robber etc: kill)
застре́ливать (застрели́ть pf);
(: wound) вы́стрелить (pf) в +acc;
(film) снима́ть (снять pf) ♦ vi: **to ~**
**(at)** стреля́ть (вы́стрелить pf) (в
+acc); (FOOTBALL etc) бить (impf)
(по +dat); **~ down** vt (plane)
сбива́ть (сбить pf); **~ing** n (shots,
attack) стрельба́; (HUNTING) охо́та

**shop** [ʃɔp] n магази́н; (also:
**~work**) мастерска́я f adj ♦ vi (also:
**go ~ping**) ходи́ть (impf) по
магази́нам, де́лать (сде́лать pf)
поку́пки; **~keeper** n
владе́лец(лица) магази́на;
**~lifting** n кра́жа това́ров (из
магази́нов); **~ping** n (goods)
поку́пки fpl; **~ping centre** (US
**~ping center**) n торго́вый центр;
**~ping mall** n (esp US) торго́вый
центр

**shore** [ʃɔːʳ] n бе́рег

**short** [ʃɔːt] *adj* коро́ткий; (*in height*) невысо́кий; (*curt*) ре́зкий; (*insufficient*) ску́дный; **we are ~ of milk** у нас ма́ло молока́; **in ~** коро́че говоря́; **it is ~ for ...** э́то сокраще́ние от +*gen* ...; **to cut ~** (*speech, visit*) прерыва́ть (прерва́ть *pf*); **everything ~ of ...** всё, кро́ме +*gen* ...; **~ of doing** кро́ме как +*infin*; **to fall ~ of** не выполня́ть (вы́полнить *pf*); **we're running ~ of time** у нас зака́нчивается вре́мя; **to stop ~** застыва́ть (засты́ть *pf*) на ме́сте; **to stop ~ of doing** не осме́ливаться (осме́литься *pf*) +*infin*; **~age** *n*: **a ~age of** нехва́тка +*gen*, дефици́т +*gen*; **~ cut** *n* (*on journey*) коро́ткий путь *m*; **~fall** *n* недоста́ток; **~hand** *n* (*BRIT*) стеногра́фия; **~-lived** *adj* кратковре́менный, недо́лгий; **~ly** *adv* вско́ре; **~s** *npl*: **(a pair of) ~s** шо́рты *pl*; **~sighted** *adj* (*BRIT*) близору́кий; **~ story** *n* расска́з; **~-term** *adj* (*effect*) кратковре́менный

**shot** [ʃɔt] *pt, pp of* **shoot** ♦ *n* (*of gun*) вы́стрел; (*FOOTBALL*) уда́р; (*injection*) уко́л; (*PHOT*) сни́мок; **a good/poor ~** (*person*) ме́ткий/плохо́й стрело́к; **like a ~** ми́гом; **~gun** *n* дробови́к

**should** [ʃʊd] *aux vb*: **I ~ go now** я до́лжен идти́; **I ~ go if I were you** на Ва́шем ме́сте я бы пошёл; **I ~ like to** я бы хоте́л

**shoulder** [ˈʃəʊldər] *n* (*ANAT*) плечо́ ♦ *vt* (*fig*) принима́ть (приня́ть *pf*) на себя́; **~ blade** *n* лопа́тка

**shouldn't** [ˈʃʊdnt] = **should not**

**shout** [ʃaʊt] *n* крик ♦ *vt* выкри́кивать (вы́крикнуть *pf*) ♦ *vi* (*also*: **~ out**) крича́ть (*impf*)

**shove** [ʃʌv] *vt* толка́ть (толкну́ть *pf*); (*inf: put*): **to ~ sth in**

запи́хивать (запиха́ть *or* запихну́ть *pf*) что-н в +*acc*

**shovel** [ˈʃʌvl] *n* лопа́та ♦ *vt* (*snow, coal*) грести́ (*impf*) (*лопа́той*)

**show** [ʃəʊ] (*pt* ~**ed**, *pp* ~**n**) *n* (*of emotion*) проявле́ние; (*semblance*) подо́бие; (*exhibition*) вы́ставка; (*THEAT*) спекта́кль *m*; (*TV*) програ́мма, шо́у *nt ind* ♦ *vt* пока́зывать (показа́ть *pf*); (*courage etc*) проявля́ть (прояви́ть *pf*) ♦ *vi* (*be evident*) проявля́ться (прояви́ться *pf*); **for ~** для ви́ду; **to be on ~** (*exhibits etc*) выставля́ться (*impf*); **~ in** *vt* (*person*) проводи́ть (провести́ *pf*); **~ off** *vi* хва́статься (*impf*) ♦ *vt* (*display*) хва́статься (похва́статься *pf*) +*instr*; **~ out** *vt* (*person*) провожа́ть (проводи́ть *pf*) к вы́ходу; **~ up** *vi* (*against background*) видне́ться (*impf*); (*fig*) обнару́живаться (обнару́житься *pf*); (*inf: turn up*) явля́ться (яви́ться *pf*) ♦ *vt* (*uncover*) выявля́ть (вы́явить *pf*); **~ business** *n* шо́у-би́знес

**shower** [ˈʃaʊər] *n* (*also*: **~ bath**) душ; (*of rain*) кратковре́менный дождь *m* ♦ *vi* принима́ть (приня́ть *pf*) душ ♦ *vt*: **to ~ sb with** ( *gifts, abuse etc*) осыпа́ть (осы́пать *pf*) кого́-н +*instr*; **to have** *or* **take a ~** принима́ть (приня́ть *pf*) душ

**show**: **~ing** *n* (*of film*) пока́з, демонстра́ция; **~ jumping** *n* конку́р; **~n** *pp of* **show**; **~-off** (*inf*) хвасту́н(ья); **~room** *n* демонстрацио́нный зал

**shrank** [ʃræŋk] *pt of* **shrink**

**shrapnel** [ˈʃræpnl] *n* шрапне́ль *f*

**shred** [ʃred] *n* (*usu pl*) клочо́к ♦ *vt* кроши́ть (накроши́ть *pf*)

**shrewd** [ʃruːd] *adj* проница́тельный

**shriek** [ʃriːk] n визг ♦ vi визжа́ть (impf)

**shrill** [ʃrɪl] adj визгли́вый

**shrimp** [ʃrɪmp] n (ме́лкая) креве́тка

**shrine** [ʃraɪn] n святы́ня; (tomb) ра́ка

**shrink** [ʃrɪŋk] (pt **shrank**, pp **shrunk**) vi (cloth) сади́ться (сесть pf); (profits, audiences) сокраща́ться (сократи́ться pf); (also: ~ **away**) отпря́нуть (pf)

**shrivel** [ˈʃrɪvl] (also: ~ **up**) vt высу́шивать (вы́сушить pf) ♦ vi высыха́ть (вы́сохнуть pf)

**shroud** [ʃraud] vt: ~ed in mystery оку́танный та́йной

Shrove Tuesday - Ма́сленица. За Ма́сленицей сле́дует пе́рвый день Вели́кого Поста́. По тради́ции на Ма́сленицу пеку́т блины́.

**shrub** [ʃrʌb] n куст

**shrug** [ʃrʌg] vi: to ~ (one's shoulders) пожима́ть (пожа́ть pf) плеча́ми; ~ **off** vt отма́хиваться (отмахну́ться pf) от +gen

**shrunk** [ʃrʌŋk] pp of **shrink**

**shudder** [ˈʃʌdər] vi содрога́ться (содрогну́ться pf)

**shuffle** [ˈʃʌfl] vt тасова́ть (стасова́ть pf) ♦ vi: to ~ (one's feet) волочи́ть (impf) но́ги

**shun** [ʃʌn] vt избега́ть (impf) +gen

**shut** [ʃʌt] (pt, pp ~) vt закрыва́ть (закры́ть pf) ♦ vi (factory) закрыва́ться (закры́ться pf); ~ **down** vt (factory etc) закрыва́ть (закры́ть pf) ♦ vi (factory) закрыва́ться (закры́ться pf); ~ **off** vt (supply etc) перекрыва́ть (перекры́ть pf); ~ **up** vi (keep quiet) заткну́ться (pf) ♦ vt (keep quiet) затыка́ть (заткну́ть pf) рот

+dat; ~**ter** n (on window) ста́вень m; (PHOT) затво́р

**shuttle** [ˈʃʌtl] n (plane) самолёт-челно́к; (also: **space** ~) шатл; (also: ~ **service**) регуля́рное сообще́ние

**shy** [ʃaɪ] adj (timid) засте́нчивый, стесни́тельный; (reserved) осторо́жный; ~**ness** n (see adj) засте́нчивость f, стесни́тельность f; осторо́жность f

**Siberia** [saɪˈbɪərɪə] n Сиби́рь f

**sibling** [ˈsɪblɪŋ] n (brother) родно́й брат; (sister) родна́я сестра́

**sick** [sɪk] adj (ill) больно́й; (humour) скве́рный; **he is/was ~** (vomiting) его́ рвёт/вы́рвало; **I feel ~** меня́ тошни́т; **I'm ~ of arguing/school** меня́ тошни́т от спо́ров/шко́лы; ~**en** vt вызыва́ть (вы́звать pf) отвраще́ние у +gen; ~**ening** adj проти́вный, тошнотво́рный

**sickly** [ˈsɪklɪ] adj (child) хи́лый; (smell) тошнотво́рный

**sickness** [ˈsɪknɪs] n (illness) боле́знь f; (vomiting) рво́та

**side** [saɪd] n сторона́; (of body) бок; (team) кома́нда, сторона́; (of hill) склон ♦ adj (door etc) боково́й; ~**board** n буфе́т; ~**burns** npl бакенба́рды pl; ~ **effect** n побо́чное де́йствие; ~ **street** n переу́лок; ~**walk** n (US) тротуа́р; ~**ways** adv (go in, lean) бо́ком; (look) и́скоса

**siding** [ˈsaɪdɪŋ] n запасно́й путь m

**siege** [siːdʒ] n оса́да

**sieve** [sɪv] n (CULIN) си́то ♦ vt просе́ивать (просе́ять pf)

**sift** [sɪft] vt просе́ивать (просе́ять pf)

**sigh** [saɪ] n вздох ♦ vi вздыха́ть (вздохну́ть pf)

**sight** [saɪt] n (faculty) зре́ние;

(*spectacle*) зре́лище, вид; (*on gun*) прице́л; **in** ~ в по́ле зре́ния; **out of** ~ из ви́да; **~seeing** n: **to go ~seeing** осма́тривать (осмотре́ть pf) достопримеча́тельности

**sign** [saɪn] n (*notice*) вы́веска; (*with hand*) знак; (*indication, evidence*) при́знак ♦ vt (*document*) подпи́сывать (подписа́ть pf); **to ~ sth over to sb** передава́ть (переда́ть pf) что-н кому́-н; ~ **on** vi (*BRIT: as unemployed*) отмеча́ться (отме́титься pf) как безрабо́тный; (*for course*) регистри́роваться (зарегистри́роваться pf); ~ **up** vi (*MIL*) нанима́ться (наня́ться pf); (*for course*) регистри́роваться (зарегистри́роваться pf) ♦ vt нанима́ть (наня́ть pf)

**signal** ['sɪɡnl] n сигна́л ♦ vi сигнализи́ровать (*impf/pf*); **to ~ to** подава́ть (пода́ть pf) знак +dat

**signature** ['sɪɡnətʃəʳ] n по́дпись f

**significance** [sɪɡ'nɪfɪkəns] n значе́ние

**significant** [sɪɡ'nɪfɪkənt] adj (*amount, discovery*) значи́тельный

**signify** ['sɪɡnɪfaɪ] vt означа́ть (*impf*)

**silence** ['saɪləns] n тишина́ ♦ vt заставля́ть (заста́вить pf) замолча́ть

**silent** ['saɪlənt] adj безмо́лвный; (*taciturn*) молчали́вый; (*film*) немо́й; **to remain** ~ молча́ть (*impf*)

**silhouette** [sɪlu:'ɛt] n силуэ́т

**silk** [sɪlk] n шёлк ♦ adj шёлковый; **~y** adj шелкови́стый

**silly** ['sɪlɪ] adj глу́пый

**silt** [sɪlt] n ил

**silver** ['sɪlvəʳ] n серебро́ ♦ adj серебри́стый; **~y** adj серебри́стый

**similar** ['sɪmɪləʳ] adj: ~ (**to**) схо́дный (с +instr), подо́бный

(+dat); **~ity** [sɪmɪ'lærɪtɪ] n схо́дство; **~ly** adv (*in a similar way*) подо́бным о́бразом

**simmer** ['sɪməʳ] vi туши́ться (*impf*)

**simple** ['sɪmpl] adj просто́й; (*foolish*) недалёкий

**simplicity** [sɪm'plɪsɪtɪ] n (*see adj*) простота́; недалёкость f

**simplify** ['sɪmplɪfaɪ] vt упроща́ть (упрости́ть pf)

**simply** ['sɪmplɪ] adv про́сто

**simulate** ['sɪmjuleɪt] vt изобража́ть (изобрази́ть pf)

**simultaneous** [sɪməl'teɪnɪəs] adj одновреме́нный; **~ly** adv одновреме́нно

**sin** [sɪn] n грех ♦ vi греши́ть (согреши́ть pf)

**since** [sɪns] adv с тех пор ♦ conj (*time*) с тех пор как; (*because*) так как ♦ prep: ~ **July** с ию́ля; ~ **then, ever** ~ с тех пор; **it's two weeks ~ I wrote** уже́ две неде́ли с (тех пор) как я написа́л; ~ **our last meeting** со вре́мени на́шей после́дней встре́чи

**sincere** [sɪn'sɪəʳ] adj и́скренний

**sincerity** [sɪn'sɛrɪtɪ] n и́скренность f

**sing** [sɪŋ] (*pt* **sang**, *pp* **sung**) vti петь (спеть pf)

**singe** [sɪndʒ] vt пали́ть (опали́ть pf)

**singer** ['sɪŋəʳ] n певе́ц(ви́ца)

**singing** ['sɪŋɪŋ] n пе́ние

**single** ['sɪŋɡl] adj (*person*) одино́кий; (*individual*) одино́чный; (*not double*) одина́рный ♦ n (*BRIT : also*: ~ **ticket**) биле́т в оди́н коне́ц; **not a ~ person** ни оди́н челове́к; ~ **out** vt (*choose*) выделя́ть (вы́делить pf); **~-minded** adj целеустремлённый; ~ **room** n (*in hotel*) одноме́стный но́мер

**singly** ['sɪŋɡlɪ] adv врозь, по

отде́льности

**singular** ['sɪŋgjʊləʳ] *adj*
необыкнове́нный ♦ *n* (*LING*)
еди́нственное число́

**sinister** ['sɪnɪstəʳ] *adj* злове́щий

**sink** [sɪŋk] (*pt* **sank**, *pp* **sunk**) *n*
ра́ковина ♦ *vt* (*ship*) топи́ть
(потопи́ть *pf*); (*well*) рыть
(вы́рыть *pf*); (*foundations*)
врыва́ть (врыть *pf*) ♦ *vi* (*ship*)
тону́ть (потону́ть *pf or* затону́ть
*pf*); (*heart, spirits*) па́дать (упа́сть
*pf*); (*also*: ~ **back**, ~ **down**)
отки́дываться (отки́нуться *pf*); **to**
~ **sth into** (*teeth, claws etc*)
вонза́ть (вонзи́ть *pf*) что-н в +*acc*;
~ **in** *vi* (*fig*): **it took a long time
for her words to ~ in** её слова́
дошли́ до меня́ неско́ро

**sinus** ['saɪnəs] *n* (*ANAT*) па́зуха

**sip** [sɪp] *n* ма́ленький глото́к ♦ *vt*
потя́гивать *impf*

**sir** [səʳ] *n* сэр, господи́н; **Sir John
Smith** Сэр Джон Смит

**siren** ['saɪərn] *n* сире́на

**sister** ['sɪstəʳ] *n* сестра́; (*BRIT : MED*)
(медици́нская *or* мед-) сестра́;
**~-in-law** *n* (*brother's wife*)
неве́стка; (*husband's sister*)
золо́вка; (*wife's sister*)
своя́ченица

**sit** [sɪt] (*pt, pp* **sat**) *vi* (*sit down*)
сади́ться (сесть *pf*); (*be sitting*)
сиде́ть (*impf*); (*assembly*) заседа́ть
(*impf*) ♦ *vt* (*exam*) сдава́ть (сдать
*pf*); ~ **down** *vi* сади́ться (сесть
*pf*); ~ **up** *vi* (*after lying*) сади́ться
(сесть *pf*)

**sitcom** ['sɪtkɔm] *n abbr* (*TV*: =
*situation comedy*) коме́дия
положе́ний

**site** [saɪt] *n* (*place*) ме́сто; (*also*:
**building** ~) строи́тельная
площа́дка

**sit-in** ['sɪtɪn] *n* сидя́чая
демонстра́ция

**sitting** ['sɪtɪŋ] *n* (*of assembly etc*)
заседа́ние; (*in canteen*) сме́на; ~
**room** *n* гости́ная *f adj*

**situated** ['sɪtjueɪtɪd] *adj*: **to be ~**
находи́ться (*impf*), располага́ться
(*impf*)

**situation** [sɪtju'eɪʃən] *n* ситуа́ция,
положе́ние; (*job*) ме́сто; (*location*)
положе́ние; "**~s vacant**" (*BRIT*)
"вака́нтные места́"

**six** [sɪks] *n* шесть; **~teen** *n*
шестна́дцать; **~teenth** *adj*
шестна́дцатый; **~th** *adj* шесто́й;
**~tieth** *adj* шестидеся́тый; **~ty** *n*
шестьдеся́т

**sixth form** - квалификацио́нный
курс. Этот курс состои́т из
двух ступе́ней - ни́жней и
ве́рхней. Курс дли́тся два го́да
и предлага́ется на вы́бор
шко́льникам, кото́рые к 16
года́м заверши́ли
обяза́тельную шко́льную
програ́мму. В тече́ние двух лет
ученики́ гото́вятся к
выпускны́м экза́менам,
даю́щим пра́во на поступле́ние
в университе́т.

**size** [saɪz] *n* разме́р; (*extent*)
величина́, масшта́б; **~able** *adj*
поря́дочный

**skate** [skeɪt] *n* (*also*: **ice ~**) конёк;
(*also*: **roller ~**) ро́ликовый конёк,
ро́лик ♦ *vi* ката́ться (*impf*) на
конька́х

**skating** ['skeɪtɪŋ] *n* (*for pleasure*)
ката́ние на конька́х

**skeleton** ['skɛlɪtn] *n* (*ANAT*) скеле́т;
(*outline*) схе́ма

**skeptical** *etc* (*US*) = **sceptical** *etc*

**sketch** [skɛtʃ] *n* эски́з, набро́сок;
(*outline*) набро́сок; (*THEAT, TV*)
сце́нка, скетч ♦ *vt* (*draw*)
наброса́ть (*impf*); (*also*: ~ **out**)

обрисо́вывать (обрисова́ть *pf*) в о́бщих черта́х; **~y** *adj* обры́вочный

**ski** [skiː] *n* лы́жа ♦ *vi* ката́ться *(impf)* на лы́жах

**skid** [skɪd] *vi (AUT)* идти́ (пойти́ *pf*) ю́зом

**skier** ['skiːəʳ] *n* лы́жник(и́ца)

**skiing** ['skiːɪŋ] *n (for pleasure)* ката́ние на лы́жах

**skilful** ['skɪlful] *(US* **skillful)** *adj* иску́сный, уме́лый; *(player)* техни́чный

**skill** [skɪl] *n (ability, dexterity)* мастерство́; *(in computing etc)* на́вык; **~ed** *adj (able)* иску́сный; *(worker)* квалифици́рованный; **~ful** *adj (US)* = **skilful**

**skim** [skɪm] *vt (milk)* снима́ть (снять *pf*) сли́вки с +*gen*; *(glide over)* скользи́ть *(impf)* над +*instr* ♦ *vi*: **to ~ through** пробега́ть (пробежа́ть *pf*)

**skin** [skɪn] *n (of person)* ко́жа; *(of animal)* шку́ра; *(of fruit, vegetable)* кожура́; *(of grape, tomato)* ко́жица ♦ *vt (animal)* снима́ть (снять *pf*) шку́ру с +*gen*; **~ny** *adj (thin)* то́щий

**skip** [skɪp] *n (BRIT: container)* скип ♦ *vi* подпры́гивать (подпры́гнуть *pf*); *(with rope)* скака́ть *(impf)* ♦ *vt (miss out)* пропуска́ть (пропусти́ть *pf*)

**skipper** ['skɪpəʳ] *n (NAUT)* шки́пер, капита́н; *(SPORT)* капита́н

**skirt** [skəːt] *n* ю́бка ♦ *vt* обходи́ть (обойти́ *pf*)

**skull** [skʌl] *n* че́реп

**skunk** [skʌŋk] *n (animal)* скунс

**sky** [skaɪ] *n* не́бо; **~light** *n* слухово́е окно́; **~scraper** *n* небоскрёб

**slab** [slæb] *n* плита́

**slack** [slæk] *adj (rope)* прови́сший; *(discipline)* сла́бый; *(security)* плохо́й

**slag** [slæg] *vt (BRIT : inf )*: **to ~ sb (off)** поноси́ть *(impf)* кого́-н

**slam** [slæm] *vt (door)* хло́пать (хло́пнуть *pf)* +*instr* ♦ *vi (door)* захло́пываться (захло́пнуться *pf)*

**slang** [slæŋ] *n (informal language)* сленг; *(jargon)* жарго́н

**slant** [slɑːnt] *n* накло́н; *(fig: approach)* укло́н

**slap** [slæp] *n* шлепо́к ♦ *vt* шлёпать (шлёпнуть *pf)*; **to ~ sb across the face** дава́ть (дать *pf)* кому́-н пощёчину; **to ~ sth on sth** *(paint etc)* ля́пать (наля́пать *pf)* что-н на что-н

**slash** [slæʃ] *vt* ре́зать (поре́зать *pf)*; *(fig: prices)* уре́зывать (уре́зать *pf)*

**slate** [sleɪt] *n (material)* сла́нец; *(tile)* кро́вельная пли́тка *(из гли́нистого сла́нца)* ♦ *vt (fig)* разноси́ть (разнести́ *pf)* в пух и прах

**slaughter** ['slɔːtəʳ] *n (see vt)* убо́й; резня́, бо́йня ♦ *vt (animals)* забива́ть (заби́ть *pf)*; *(people)* истребля́ть (истреби́ть *pf)*

**slave** [sleɪv] *n* раб(ы́ня); **~ry** *n* ра́бство

**Slavonic** [slə'vɔnɪk] *adj* славя́нский

**sleazy** ['sliːzɪ] *adj (place)* запу́щенный

**sledge** [slɛdʒ] *n* са́ни *pl*; *(for children)* са́нки *pl*; **~hammer** *n* кува́лда

**sleek** [sliːk] *adj (fur)* лосня́щийся; *(hair)* блестя́щий

**sleep** [sliːp] *(pt, pp* **slept)** *n* сон ♦ *vi* спать *(impf)*; *(spend night)* ночева́ть (переночева́ть *pf)*; **to go to ~** засыпа́ть (засну́ть *pf)*; **~ in** *vi* просыпа́ть (проспа́ть *pf)*; **~er** *n (RAIL, train)* по́езд со спа́льными ваго́нами; *(: berth)* спа́льное ме́сто; ~**ing bag** n спа́льный мешо́к; ~**less** adj (night) бессо́нный; ~**walker** n луна́тик; ~**y** adj со́нный

**sleet** [sli:t] n мо́крый снег

**sleeve** [sli:v] n (of jacket etc) рука́в; (of record) конве́рт

**slender** ['slɛndər] adj (figure) стро́йный; (majority) небольшо́й

**slept** [slɛpt] pt, pp of **sleep**

**slice** [slaɪs] n (of meat) кусо́к; (of bread, lemon) ло́мтик ♦ vt (bread, meat etc) наре́зать (наре́зать pf)

**slick** [slɪk] adj (performance) гла́дкий; (salesman, answer) бо́йкий ♦ n (also: **oil** ~) плёнка не́фти

**slide** [slaɪd] (pt, pp **slid**) n (in playground) де́тская го́рка; (PHOT) слайд; (BRIT: also: **hair** ~) зако́лка ♦ vt задвига́ть (задви́нуть pf) ♦ vi скользи́ть (impf)

**slight** [slaɪt] adj хру́пкий; (small) незначи́тельный; (: error) ме́лкий; (accent, voice) сла́бый ♦ n униже́ние; **not in the ~est** ниско́лько; ~**ly** adv (rather) слегка́

**slim** [slɪm] adj (figure) стро́йный; (chance) сла́бый ♦ vi худе́ть (похуде́ть pf)

**slimy** ['slaɪmɪ] adj (pond) и́листый

**sling** [slɪŋ] (pt, pp **slung**) n (MED) пе́ревязь f ♦ vt (throw) швыря́ть (швырну́ть pf)

**slip** [slɪp] n (mistake) про́мах; (underskirt) ни́жняя ю́бка; (of paper) поло́ска ♦ vt сова́ть (су́нуть pf) ♦ vi (slide) скользи́ть (скользну́ть f); (lose balance) поскользну́ться (pf); (decline) снижа́ться (сни́зиться pf); **to give sb the** ~ ускольза́ть (ускользну́ть pf) от кого́-н; **a** ~ **of the tongue** огово́рка; **to** ~ **sth**

**on/off** надева́ть (наде́ть pf)/ сбра́сывать (сбро́сить pf) что-н; **to** ~ **into** (room etc) скользну́ть (pf) в +acc; **to** ~ **out of** (room etc) выска́льзывать (вы́скользнуть pf) из +gen; ~ **away** vi ускольза́ть (ускользну́ть pf); ~ **in** vt сова́ть (су́нуть pf) ♦ vi (errors) закра́дываться (закра́сться pf)

**slipper** ['slɪpər] n та́почка

**slippery** ['slɪpərɪ] adj ско́льзкий

**slit** [slɪt] (pt, pp ~) n (cut) разре́з; (in skirt) шли́ца; (opening) щель f ♦ vt разреза́ть (разре́зать pf)

**slither** ['slɪðər] vi (person) скользи́ть (impf); (snake) извива́ться (impf)

**sliver** ['slɪvər] n (of glass) оско́лок

**slog** [slɔg] n: **it was a hard** ~ э́то была́ тяжёлая рабо́та

**slogan** ['sləugən] n ло́зунг

**slope** [sləup] n скло́н; (gentle hill) укло́н; (slant) накло́н

**sloppy** ['slɔpɪ] adj (work) халту́рный

**slot** [slɔt] n (in machine) про́резь f, паз ♦ vt: **to** ~ **sth into** опуска́ть (опусти́ть pf) что-н в +acc

**Slovakia** [sləu'vækɪə] n Слова́кия

**Slovakian** adj слова́цкий

**slow** [sləu] adj ме́дленный; (stupid) тупо́й ♦ adv ме́дленно ♦ vt (also: ~ **down**, ~ **up**: vehicle) замедля́ть (заме́длить pf) ♦ vi (traffic) замедля́ться (заме́длиться pf); (car, train etc) сбавля́ть (сба́вить pf) ход; **my watch is (20 minutes)** ~ мои́ часы́ отстаю́т (на 20 мину́т); ~**ly** adv ме́дленно; ~ **motion** ♦ n: **in** ~ **motion** в заме́дленном де́йствии

**slug** [slʌg] n (ZOOL) сли́зень m

**sluggish** ['slʌgɪʃ] adj вя́лый

**slum** [slʌm] n трущо́ба

**slump** [slʌmp] n (economic) спад; (in profits, sales) паде́ние

**slung** [slʌŋ] *pt, pp of* **sling**

**slur** [sləːr] *vt* (*words*) мя́млить (промя́млить *pf*) ♦ *n* (*fig*): ~ **(on)** пятно́ (на +*prp*)

**sly** [slaɪ] *adj* лука́вый

**smack** [smæk] *n*(*slap*) шлепо́к ♦ *vt* хло́пать (хло́пнуть *pf*); (*child*) шлёпать (отшлёпать *pf*) ♦ *vi*: **to ~ of** отдава́ть (*impf*) +*instr*

**small** [smɔːl] *adj* ма́ленький; (*quantity, amount*) небольшо́й, ма́лый; ~**pox** *n* о́спа; ~ **talk** *n* све́тская бесе́да

**smart** [smɑːt] *adj* (*neat, tidy*) опря́тный; (*clever*) толко́вый ♦ *vi* (*also fig*) жечь (*impf*); **my eyes are** ~**ing** у меня́ щи́плет глаза́

**smash** [smæʃ] *n* (*collision : also*: ~**-up**) ава́рия ♦ *vt* разбива́ть (разби́ть *pf*); (*SPORT, record*) побива́ть (поби́ть *pf*) ♦ *vi* (*break*) разбива́ться (разби́ться *pf*); **to ~ against** *or* **into** (*collide*) врезаться (вре́заться *pf*) в +*acc*; ~**ing** *adj* (*inf*) потряса́ющий

**smear** [smɪər] *n* (*trace*) след; (*MED : also*: ~ **test**) мазо́к ♦ *vt* (*spread*) ма́зать (нама́зать *pf*)

**smell** [smɛl] (*pt, pp* **smelt** *or* ~**ed**) *n* за́пах; (*sense*) обоня́ние ♦ *vt* чу́вствовать (почу́вствовать *pf*) за́пах +*gen* ♦ *vi* (*food etc*) па́хнуть (*impf*); **to ~ (of)** (*unpleasant*) воня́ть (*impf*) (+*instr*); ~**y** *adj* воню́чий, злово́нный

**smelt** [smɛlt] *pt, pp of* **smell**

**smile** [smaɪl] *n* улы́бка ♦ *vi* улыба́ться (улыбну́ться *pf*)

**smirk** [sməːk] *n* (*pej*) ухмы́лка

**smog** [smɔg] *n* смог

**smoke** [sməuk] *n* дым ♦ *vi* (*person*) кури́ть (*impf*); (*chimney*) дыми́ться (*impf*) ♦ *vt* (*cigarettes*) кури́ть (вы́курить *pf*); ~**d** *adj* (*bacon, fish*) копчёный; (*glass*) ды́мчатый; ~**r** *n* (*person*) куря́щий(ая) *m(f) adj*,

кури́льщик(щица)

**smoking** ['sməukɪŋ] *n* (*act*) куре́ние; **"no ~"** "не кури́ть"

**smoky** ['sməukɪ] *adj* (*room*) ды́мный

**smolder** ['sməuldər] *vi* (*US*) = **smoulder**

**smooth** [smuːð] *adj* гла́дкий; (*sauce*) однор óдный; (*flavour*) мя́гкий; (*movement*) пла́вный

**smother** ['smʌðər] *vt* (*fire*) туши́ть (потуши́ть *pf*); (*person*) души́ть (задуши́ть *pf*); (*emotions*) подавля́ть (подави́ть *pf*)

**smoulder** ['sməuldər] (*US* **smolder**) *vi* (*fire*) тлеть (*impf*); (*fig: anger*) таи́ться (*impf*)

**smudge** [smʌdʒ] *n* пятно́ ♦ *vt* разма́зывать (разма́зать *pf*)

**smug** [smʌg] *adj* дово́льный

**smuggle** ['smʌgl] *vt* (*goods*) провози́ть (провезти́ *pf*) (*контраба́ндой*)

**smuggling** ['smʌglɪŋ] *n* контраба́нда

**snack** [snæk] *n* заку́ска

**snag** [snæg] *n* поме́ха

**snail** [sneɪl] *n* ули́тка

**snake** [sneɪk] *n* змея́

**snap** [snæp] *adj* (*decision etc*) момента́льный ♦ *vt* (*break*) разла́мывать (разломи́ть *pf*); (*fingers*) щёлкать (щёлкнуть *pf*) +*instr* ♦ *vi* (*break*) разла́мываться (разломи́ться *pf*); (*speak sharply*) крича́ть (*impf*); **to ~ shut** (*trap, jaws etc*) защёлкиваться (защёлкнуться *pf*); ~ **up** *vt* расхва́тывать (расхвата́ть *pf*); ~**shot** *n* сни́мок

**snare** [snɛər] *n* сило́к

**snarl** [snɑːl] *vi* рыча́ть (*impf*)

**snatch** [snætʃ] *vt* (*grab*) хвата́ть (схвати́ть *pf*); (*handbag*) вырыва́ть (вы́рвать *pf*); (*child*) похища́ть (похи́тить *pf*); (*opportunity*) урыва́ть (урва́ть *pf*)

**sneak** [sni:k] *vi*: **to ~ into** проска́льзывать (проскользну́ть *pf*) в +*acc*; **to ~ out of** выска́льзывать (вы́скользнуть *pf*) из +*gen*; **to ~ up on** я́бедничать (ная́бедничать *pf*) на +*acc*; **~ers** *npl* кроссо́вки *fpl*

**sneer** [snɪəʳ] *vi* (*mock*): **to ~ at** глуми́ться (*impf*) над +*instr*

**sneeze** [sni:z] *vi* чиха́ть (чихну́ть *pf*)

**sniff** [snɪf] *n* (*sound*) сопе́ние ♦ *vi* шмы́гать (шмыгну́ть *pf*) но́сом; (*when crying*) всхли́пывать (*impf*) ♦ *vt* ню́хать (*impf*)

**snip** [snɪp] *vt* ре́зать (поре́зать *pf*)

**sniper** ['snaɪpəʳ] *n* сна́йпер

**snob** [snɔb] *n* сноб; **~bish** *adj* сноби́стский

**snooker** ['snu:kəʳ] *n* сну́кер

**snore** [snɔ:ʳ] *vi* храпе́ть (*impf*)

**snorkel** ['snɔ:kl] *n* тру́бка (ныря́льщика)

**snow** [snəu] *n* снег ♦ *vi*: **it's ~ing** идёт снег; **~ball** *n* снежо́к; **~drift** *n* сугро́б; **~drop** *n* подсне́жник; **~fall** *n* снегопа́д; **~flake** *n* снежи́нка; **~man** (*irreg*) *n* снегови́к, сне́жная ба́ба

**SNP** *n abbr* = *Scottish National Party*

**snub** [snʌb] *vt* пренебрежи́тельно обходи́ться (обойти́сь *pf*) с +*instr*

**snug** [snʌg] *adj* (*place*) ую́тный; (*well-fitting*) облега́ющий

KEYWORD

**so** [səu] *adv* 1 (*thus, likewise*) так; **if this is so** е́сли э́то так; **if so** е́сли так; **while she was so doing, he ...** пока́ она́ э́то де́лала, он ...; **I didn't do it - you did so!** я не де́лал э́того - а вот и сде́лал!; **you weren't there - I was so!** тебя́ там не́ было - а вот и был!; **I like him - so do I** он мне

нра́вится - мне то́же; **I'm still at school - so is he** я ещё учу́сь в шко́ле - он то́же; **so it is!** и действи́тельно!, и пра́вда!; **I hope/think so** наде́юсь/ду́маю, что так; **so far** пока́; **how do you like the book so far?** ну, как Вам кни́га?

2 (*in comparisons: +adv*) насто́лько, так; (: +*adj*) насто́лько, тако́й; **so quickly (that)** насто́лько *or* так бы́стро(, что); **so big (that)** тако́й большо́й(, что); **she's not so clever as her brother** она́ не так умна́, как её брат

3 (*describing degree, extent*) так; **I've got so much work** у меня́ так мно́го рабо́ты; **I love you so much** я тебя́ так люблю́; **thank you so much** спаси́бо Вам большо́е; **I'm so glad to see you** я так рад Вас ви́деть; **there are so many books I would like to read** есть так мно́го книг, кото́рые я бы хоте́л проче́сть; **so ... that ...** так ..., что ...

4 (*about*) о́коло +*gen*; **ten or so** о́коло десяти́; **I only have an hour or so** у меня́ есть о́коло ча́са

5 (*phrases*): **so long!** (*inf: bye*) пока́! ♦ *conj* 1 (*expressing purpose*): **so as to do** что́бы +*infin*; **I brought this wine so you could try it** я принёс э́то вино́, что́бы Вы могли́ его́ попро́бовать

2 (*expressing result*) так что; **so I was right** так что, я был прав; **so you see, I could have stayed** так что, ви́дите, я мог бы оста́ться

**soak** [səuk] *vt* (*drench*) промочи́ть (*pf*); (*steep*) зама́чивать (замочи́ть *pf*) ♦ *vi* (*steep*) отмока́ть (*impf*); **~ up** *vt* впи́тывать (впита́ть *pf*) (в себя́)

**soap** [səup] n мы́ло; ~ **opera** n (TV) мы́льная о́пера

**soar** [sɔːʳ] vi (price, temperature) подска́кивать (подскочи́ть pf)

**sob** [sɔb] n рыда́ние ♦ vi рыда́ть (impf)

**sober** ['səubəʳ] adj тре́звый; (colour, style) сде́ржанный

**soccer** ['sɔkəʳ] n футбо́л

**sociable** ['səuʃəbl] adj общи́тельный

**social** ['səuʃl] adj (history, structure etc) обще́ственный, социа́льный; **he has a good ~ life** он мно́го обща́ется с людьми́; ~**ism** n социали́зм; ~**ist** n социали́ст ♦ adj социалисти́ческий; ~**ize** vi: **to ~ize (with)** обща́ться (impf) (с +instr); ~**ly** adv: **to visit sb ~ly** заходи́ть (зайти́ pf) к кому́-н по-дру́жески; ~**ly acceptable** социа́льно прие́млемый; ~ **security** (BRIT) n социа́льная защи́та; ~ **work** n социа́льная рабо́та

**society** [sə'saɪətɪ] n о́бщество

**sociology** [səusɪ'ɔlədʒɪ] n социоло́гия

**sock** [sɔk] n носо́к

**socket** ['sɔkɪt] n глазни́ца; (BRIT : ELEC, in wall) розе́тка

**soda** ['səudə] n (also: ~ **water**) со́довая f adj; (US : also: ~ **pop**) газиро́вка

**sodden** ['sɔdn] adj (very wet) вы́мокший

**sodium** ['səudɪəm] n на́трий

**sofa** ['səufə] n дива́н

**soft** [sɔft] adj мя́гкий; ~ **drink** n безалкого́льный напи́ток; ~**ly** adv (gently) мя́гко; (quietly) ти́хо; ~**ness** n мя́гкость f; ~**ware** n програ́мма, програ́ммное обеспе́чение

**soggy** ['sɔgɪ] adj (ground) сыро́й

**soil** [sɔɪl] n (earth) по́чва; (territory)

земля́ ♦ vt па́чкать (запа́чкать pf)

**solar** ['səuləʳ] adj со́лнечный

**sold** [səuld] pt, pp of **sell**

**solder** ['səuldəʳ] vt спа́ивать (спая́ть pf)

**soldier** ['səuldʒəʳ] n (MIL) солда́т

**sole** [səul] n (of foot) подо́шва; (of shoe) подо́шва, подмётка ♦ n inv (fish) па́лтус ♦ adj (unique) еди́нственный; ~**ly** adv то́лько

**solemn** ['sɔləm] adj торже́ственный

**solicitor** [sə'lɪsɪtəʳ] n (BRIT) адвока́т

**solid** ['sɔlɪd] adj (not hollow) це́льный; (not liquid) твёрдый; (reliable) про́чный; (entire) це́лый; (gold) чи́стый ♦ n твёрдое те́ло; ~**s** npl (food) твёрдая пи́ща fsg

**solidarity** [sɔlɪ'dærɪtɪ] n солида́рность f

**solitary** ['sɔlɪtərɪ] adj одино́кий; (empty) уединённый; (single) едини́чный; ~ **confinement** n одино́чное заключе́ние

**solitude** ['sɔlɪtjuːd] n уедине́ние, одино́чество

**solo** ['səuləu] n со́ло nt ind ♦ adv (fly) в одино́чку; (play) со́ло; ~**ist** n соли́ст(ка)

**soluble** ['sɔljubl] adj раствори́мый

**solution** [sə'luːʃən] n (answer) реше́ние; (liquid) раство́р

**solve** [sɔlv] vt (problem) разреша́ть (разреши́ть pf); (mystery) раскрыва́ть (раскры́ть pf)

**solvent** ['sɔlvənt] adj платёжеспосо́бный ♦ n раствори́тель m

**sombre** ['sɔmbəʳ] (US **somber**) adj мра́чный

---
KEYWORD
---

**some** [sʌm] adj 1 (a certain amount or number of): **would you like some tea/biscuits?** хоти́те ча́ю/

печéнья?; **there's some milk in the fridge** в холодúльнике есть молокó; **he asked me some questions** он зáдал мне нéсколько вопрóсов; **there are some people waiting to see you** Вас ждут какúе-то лю́ди 2 (*certain: in contrasts*) нéкоторый; **some people say that ...** нéкоторые говорят, что ... 3 (*unspecified*) какóй-то; **some woman phoned you** Вам звонúла какáя-то жéнщина; **we'll meet again some day** мы когдá-нибудь опять встрéтимся; **shall we meet some day next week?** давáйте встрéтимся кáк-нибудь на слéдующей недéле!

♦ *pron* (*a certain number: people*) нéкоторые *pl*, однú *pl*; **some took the bus, and some walked** нéкоторые поéхали на автóбусе, а нéкоторые пошлú пешкóм; **I've got some** (*books etc*) у меня есть нéсколько; **who would like a piece of cake? - I'd like some** кто хóчет кусóк тóрта? - я хочý; **I've read some of the book** я прочёл часть кнúги

♦ *adv* óколо; **some ten people** óколо десятú человéк

**somebody** ['sʌmbədɪ] *pron* = **someone**
**somehow** ['sʌmhaʊ] *adv* (*in some way: in future*) кáк-нибудь; (*: in past*) кáк-то; (*for some reason*) почемý-то, каким-то óбразом
**someone** ['sʌmwʌn] *pron* (*specific person*) ктó-то; (*unspecified person*) ктó-нибудь; **I saw ~ in the garden** я вúдел когó-то в садý; **~ will help you** Вам ктó-нибудь помóжет
**somersault** ['sʌməsɔːlt] *n* (*in air*) сáльто *nt ind*; (*on ground*)

кувырóк
**something** ['sʌmθɪŋ] *pron* (*something specific*) чтó-то; (*something unspecified*) чтó-нибудь; **there's ~ wrong with my car** чтó-то случúлось с моéй машúной; **would you like ~ to eat/drink?** хотúте чегó-нибудь поéсть/выпить?; **I have ~ for you** у меня кóе-что для Вас есть
**sometime** ['sʌmtaɪm] *adv* (*in future*) когдá-нибудь; (*in past*) когдá-то, кáк-то
**sometimes** ['sʌmtaɪmz] *adv* иногдá
**somewhat** ['sʌmwɔt] *adv* нéсколько
**somewhere** ['sʌmwɛəʳ] *adv* (*be: somewhere specific*) гдé-то; (*: anywhere*) гдé-нибудь; (*go: somewhere specific*) кудá-то; (*: anywhere*) кудá-нибудь; (*come from*) откýда-то; **it's ~ or other in Scotland** это гдé-то в Шотлáндии; **is there a post office ~ around here?** здесь гдé-нибудь есть пóчта?; **let's go ~ else** давáйте поéдем кудá-нибудь в другóе мéсто
**son** [sʌn] *n* сын
**song** [sɒŋ] *n* пéсня
**son-in-law** ['sʌnɪnlɔː] *n* зять *m*
**soon** [suːn] *adv* (*in a short time*) скóро; (*early*) рáно; **~ (afterwards)** вскóре; *see also* **as**; **~er** *adv* скорéе; **I would ~er do that** я бы скорéе сдéлал это; **~er or later** рáно или пóздно
**soot** [sʊt] *n* сáжа
**soothe** [suːð] *vt* успокáивать (успокóить *pf*)
**sophisticated** [sə'fɪstɪkeɪtɪd] *adj* изощрённый; (*refined*) изысканный
**soprano** [sə'prɑːnəʊ] *n* сопрáно *f ind*
**sordid** ['sɔːdɪd] *adj* (*place*) убóгий; (*story etc*) гнýсный

**sore** [sɔːʳ] n я́зва, боля́чка ♦ adj
(esp US: offended) оби́женный;
(painful): **my arm is~, I've got a ~
arm** у меня́ боли́т рука́; **it's a ~
point** (fig) э́то больно́е ме́сто;
**~ly** adv: **I am ~ly tempted (to)** я
испы́тываю большо́й собла́зн
(+infin)

**sorrow** ['sɔrəu] n печа́ль
f, грусть f

**sorry** ['sɔrɪ] adj плаче́вный; **I'm ~**
мне жаль; **~!** извини́те,
пожа́луйста!; **~?** (pardon)
прости́те?; **I feel ~ for him** мне
его́ жаль or жа́лко

**sort** [sɔːt] n (type) сорт ♦ vt (mail)
сортирова́ть (рассортирова́ть
pf); (also: **~ out**: papers, belongings
etc) разбира́ть (разобра́ть pf);
(: problems) разбира́ться
(разобра́ться pf) в +prp

**SOS** n abbr (= save our souls)
SOS

**so-so** ['səusəu] adv так себе́

**sought** [sɔːt] pt, pp of **seek**

**soul** [səul] n (spirit, person) душа́

**sound** [saund] adj (healthy)
здоро́вый; (safe, not damaged)
це́лый; (secure: investment)
надёжный; (reliable, thorough)
соли́дный; (sensible: advice)
разу́мный ♦ n звук ♦ vt (alarm)
поднима́ть (подня́ть pf) ♦ vi
звуча́ть (impf) ♦ adv: **he is ~ asleep**
он кре́пко спит; **I don't like the ~
of it** мне э́то не нра́вится; **~ly**
adv (sleep) кре́пко; (beat etc)
здо́рово; **~track** n му́зыка (из
кинофи́льма)

**soup** [suːp] n суп

**sour** ['sauəʳ] adj ки́слый; (fig: bad-
tempered) угрю́мый

**source** [sɔːs] n (also fig) исто́чник

**south** [sauθ] n юг ♦ adj ю́жный
♦ adv (go) на юг; (be) на ю́ге;
**South America** n Ю́жная

Аме́рика; **~east** n юго-восто́к;
**~erly** ['sʌðəlɪ] adj обращённый к
ю́гу; (wind) ю́жный; **~ern** ['sʌðən]
adj ю́жный; **South Pole** n: **the
South Pole** Ю́жный по́люс;
**~west** n юго-за́пад

**souvenir** [suːvə'nɪəʳ] n сувени́р

**sovereign** ['sɔvrɪn] n (ruler)
госуда́р(ыня) m(f); **~ty** n
суверените́т

**Soviet** ['səuviət] adj сове́тский; **the
~ Union** (formerly) Сове́тский
Сою́з

**sow¹** [sau] n (pig) свинья́

**sow²** [səu] (pt **~ed**, pp **~n**) vt (also
fig) се́ять (посе́ять pf)

**soya** ['sɔɪə] (US **soy**) adj со́евый

**spa** [spɑː] n (US: also: **health ~**)
во́ды fpl

**space** [speɪs] n простра́нство;
(small place, room) ме́сто; (beyond
Earth) ко́смос; (interval, period)
промежу́ток ♦ cpd косми́ческий
♦ vt (also: **~ out**: payments, visits)
распределя́ть (распредели́ть pf);
**~craft** n косми́ческий кора́бль
m; **~ship** n = **spacecraft**

**spacious** ['speɪʃəs] adj просто́рный

**spade** [speɪd] n (tool) лопа́та;
(child's) лопа́тка; **~s** npl (CARDS)
пи́ки fpl

**spaghetti** [spə'getɪ] n спаге́тти pl
ind

**Spain** [speɪn] n Испа́ния

**spam** [spæm] n (COMPUT) рекла́ма
на Интерне́те

**span** [spæn] pt of **spin** ♦ n (of hand,
wings) разма́х; (in time)
промежу́ток ♦ vt охва́тывать
(охвати́ть pf)

**Spanish** ['spænɪʃ] adj испа́нский;
**the ~** npl испа́нцы mpl

**spank** [spæŋk] vt шлёпать
(отшлёпать pf)

**spanner** ['spænəʳ] n (BRIT)
(га́ечный) ключ

**spare** [spɛəʳ] adj (free: time, seat) свобо́дный; (surplus) ли́шний; (reserve) запасно́й ♦ vt (trouble, expense) избавля́ть (изба́вить pf) от +gen; (make available) выделя́ть (вы́делить pf); (refrain from hurting) щади́ть (пощади́ть pf); **I have some time to** ~ у меня́ есть немно́го свобо́дного вре́мени; **to have money to** ~ име́ть (impf) ли́шние де́ньги; ~ **time** n свобо́дное вре́мя nt

**sparingly** ['spɛərɪŋlɪ] adv эконо́мно

**spark** [spɑːk] n (also fig) и́скра

**sparkle** ['spɑːkl] n блеск ♦ vi (diamonds, water, eyes) сверка́ть (impf)

**sparkling** ['spɑːklɪŋ] adj (wine) игри́стый

**sparrow** ['spærəu] n воробе́й

**sparse** [spɑːs] adj ре́дкий

**spartan** ['spɑːtən] adj спарта́нский

**spasm** ['spæzəm] n (MED) спазм

**spat** [spæt] pt, pp of **spit**

**spate** [speɪt] n (fig): **a** ~ **of** пото́к +gen

**speak** [spiːk] (pt **spoke**, pp **spoken**) vi говори́ть (impf); (make a speech) выступа́ть (вы́ступить pf) ♦ vt (truth) говори́ть (сказа́ть pf); **to** ~ **to sb** разгова́ривать (impf) or говори́ть (impf) с кем-н; **to** ~ **of** or **about** говори́ть (impf) о +prp; ~**er** n (in public) ора́тор; (also: **loudspeaker**) громкоговори́тель m

**spear** [spɪəʳ] n копьё

**special** ['spɛʃl] adj (important) осо́бый, осо́бенный; (edition, adviser, school) специа́льный; ~**ist** n специали́ст; ~**ity** [spɛʃɪ'ælɪtɪ] n (dish) фи́рменное блю́до; (subject) специализа́ция; ~**ize** vi: **to** ~**ize (in)** специализи́роваться (impf/pf) (в/на +prp); ~**ly** adv (especially) осо́бенно

**species** ['spiːʃiːz] n inv вид

**specific** [spə'sɪfɪk] adj специфи́ческий, определённый; ~**ally** adv (exactly) точне́е; (specially) специа́льно; ~**ation** [spɛsɪfɪ'keɪʃən] n (TECH) специфика́ция; (requirement) тре́бование

**specify** ['spɛsɪfaɪ] vt уточня́ть (уточни́ть pf)

**specimen** ['spɛsɪmən] n (example) экземпля́р; (sample) образе́ц; **a** ~ **of urine** моча́ для ана́лиза

**speck** [spɛk] n (of dirt) пя́тнышко; (of dust) крупи́ца, крупи́нка

**specs** [spɛks] npl (inf: glasses) очки́ pl

**spectacle** ['spɛktəkl] n (scene, event) зре́лище; ~**s** npl (glasses) очки́ pl

**spectacular** [spɛk'tækjuləʳ] adj впечатля́ющий, порази́тельный

**spectator** [spɛk'teɪtəʳ] n зри́тель(ница) m(f)

**spectrum** ['spɛktrəm] (pl **spectra**) n спектр

**speculate** ['spɛkjuleɪt] vi (COMM) спекули́ровать (impf); (guess): **to** ~ **about** стро́ить (impf) предположе́ния о +prp

**speculation** [spɛkju'leɪʃən] n (see vb) спекуля́ция; предположе́ние

**sped** [spɛd] pt, pp of **speed**

**speech** [spiːtʃ] n речь f; ~**less** adj: **I was** ~**less with anger** от гне́ва я лиши́лся да́ра ре́чи; **she looked at him** ~**less** она́ посмотре́ла на него́ в онеме́нии

**speed** [spiːd] (pt, pp **sped**) n (rate) ско́рость f; (promptness) быстрота́ ♦ vi (move): **to** ~ **along/by** мча́ться (промча́ться pf) по +dat/ми́мо +gen; **at full** or **top** ~ на по́лной or преде́льной ско́рости; ~ **up** (pt, pp ~**ed up**) vi ускоря́ться (уско́риться pf) ♦ vt ускоря́ть (уско́рить pf); ~**ily** adv бы́стро;

~**ing** n превыше́ние ско́рости; ~
**limit** n преде́л ско́рости;
~**ometer** [spɪˈdɔmɪtəʳ] n
спидо́метр; ~**y** adj (prompt)
ско́рый

**spell** [spɛl] (pt, pp **spelt** (BRIT) or
~**ed**) n (also: **magic** ~)
колдовство́; (period of time)
пери́од ♦ vt (also: ~ **out**)
произноси́ть (произнести́ pf) по
бу́квам; (fig: explain) разъясня́ть
(разъясни́ть pf) ♦ vi: **he can't** ~ у
него́ плоха́я орфогра́фия;
~**bound** adj зачаро́ванный; ~**ing**
n орфогра́фия, правописа́ние

**spend** [spɛnd] (pt, pp **spent**) vt
(money) тра́тить (потра́тить pf);
(time, life) проводи́ть (провести́
pf)

**sperm** [spəːm] n спе́рма

**sphere** [sfɪəʳ] n сфе́ра

**spice** [spaɪs] n (pepper, salt etc)
спе́ция

**spicy** [ˈspaɪsɪ] adj (food) о́стрый;
(: with a strong flavour) пря́ный

**spider** [ˈspaɪdəʳ] n пау́к

**spike** [spaɪk] n (point) острие́

**spill** [spɪl] (pt, pp **spilt** or ~**ed**) vt
(liquid) пролива́ть (проли́ть pf),
разлива́ть (разли́ть pf) ♦ vi
(liquid) пролива́ться (проли́ться
pf), разлива́ться (разли́ться pf);
~**age** n (of oil) вы́брос

**spin** [spɪn] (pt **spun** or **span**, pp
**spun**) n (trip in car) ката́ние;
(AVIAT) што́пор; (POL) укло́н,
тенде́нция ♦ vt (BRIT: clothes)
выжима́ть (вы́жать pf) (в
стира́льной маши́не) ♦ vi (make
thread) прясть (impf); (person,
head) кружи́ться (impf)

**spinach** [ˈspɪnɪtʃ] n шпина́т

**spinal** [ˈspaɪnl] adj (relating to the
spine) позвоно́чный; (relating to
the spinal cord) спинномозгово́й;
~ **injury** поврежде́ние

позвоно́чника; ~ **cord** n
спинно́й мозг

**spine** [spaɪn] n (ANAT)
позвоно́чник; (thorn) колю́чка,
игла́

**spinning** [ˈspɪnɪŋ] n (craft)
пряде́ние

**spinster** [ˈspɪnstəʳ] n ста́рая де́ва

**spiral** [ˈspaɪərl] n спира́ль f

**spire** [ˈspaɪəʳ] n шпиль m

**spirit** [ˈspɪrɪt] n дух; (soul) душа́;
~**s** npl (alcohol) спиртны́е
напи́тки mpl, спиртно́е ntsg adj; **in
good/low** ~**s** в хоро́шем/
пода́вленном настрое́нии; ~**ed**
adj энерги́чный; (performance)
воодушевлённый

**spiritual** [ˈspɪrɪtjuəl] adj духо́вный

**spit** [spɪt] (pt, pp **spat**) n ве́ртел;
(saliva) слюна́ ♦ vi (person)
плева́ть (плю́нуть pf); (fire, hot
oil) бры́згать (impf); (inf: rain)
мороси́ть (impf)

**spite** [spaɪt] n зло́ба, злость f ♦ vt
досажда́ть (досади́ть pf) +dat; **in**
~ **of** несмотря́ на +acc; ~**ful** adj
зло́бный

**splash** [splæʃ] n (sound) всплеск
♦ vt бры́згать (бры́знуть pf) ♦ vi
(also: ~ **about**) плеска́ться (impf)

**splendid** [ˈsplɛndɪd] adj
великоле́пный

**splint** [splɪnt] n (MED) ши́на

**splinter** [ˈsplɪntəʳ] n (of wood)
ще́пка; (of glass) оско́лок; (in
finger) зано́за

**split** [splɪt] (pt, pp ~) n (crack, tear)
тре́щина; (POL, fig) раско́л ♦ vt
(atom, piece of wood) расщепля́ть
(расщепи́ть pf); (POL, fig)
раска́лывать (расколо́ть pf);
(work, profits) дели́ть (раздели́ть
pf) ♦ vi (divide) расщепля́ться
(расщепи́ться pf), разделя́ться
(раздели́ться pf); ~ **up** vi (couple)
расходи́ться (разойти́сь pf);

( *group* ) разделя́ться
(раздели́ться *pf* )

**splutter** ['splʌtər] *vi* (*engine*) чиха́ть
(*impf*); (*person*) лепета́ть (*impf*)

**spoil** [spɔɪl] (*pt, pp* ~**t** or ~**ed**) *vt*
по́ртить (испо́ртить *pf* )

**spoke** [spəʊk] *pt of* **speak** ♦ *n* (*of
wheel*) спи́ца; ~**n** *pp of* **speak**

**spokesman** ['spəʊksmən] (*irreg*) *n*
представи́тель *m*

**spokeswoman** ['spəʊkswumən]
(*irreg*) *n* представи́тельница

**sponge** [spʌndʒ] *n* гу́бка; (*also:* ~
**cake**) бискви́т

**sponsor** ['spɒnsər] *n* спо́нсор ♦ *vt*
финанси́ровать (*impf/pf*),
спонси́ровать (*impf/pf*); (*applicant*)
поруча́ться (поручи́ться *pf*) за
+*acc*; ~**ship** *n* спо́нсорство

---

**sponsorship** - В
Великобрита́нии
спонси́рование явля́ется
распространённым спо́собом
сбо́ра де́нег на
благотвори́тельность. При́нято
выполня́ть ра́зного ро́да
зада́чи, наприме́р, пла́вание,
ходьба́ на дли́нную диста́нцию
или да́же похуде́ние.
Предположи́м, вы хоти́те
собра́ть де́нег для
благотвори́тельной
организа́ции, финанси́рующей
иссле́дования ра́ковых
заболева́ний. Вы заявля́ете,
что пройдёте пешко́м 10 миль
и про́сите знако́мых, друзе́й
и тд спонси́ровать ва́ше
реше́ние, же́ртвуя де́ньги в
по́льзу э́той
благотвори́тельной
организа́ции.

---

**spontaneous** [spɒn'teɪnɪəs] *adj*
(*gesture*) спонта́нный,

непосре́дственный;
(*demonstration*) стихи́йный

**spool** [spu:l] *n* ( *for thread*)
кату́шка; ( *for film, tape etc*)
боби́на

**spoon** [spu:n] *n* ло́жка; ~**ful** *n*
(по́лная) ло́жка

**sporadic** [spə'rædɪk] *adj*
споради́ческий

**sport** [spɔ:t] *n* ( *game*) спорт *m no
pl*; ~**ing** *adj* (*event etc*)
спорти́вный; ~**sman** (*irreg*) *n*
спортсме́н; ~**swoman** (*irreg*) *n*
спортсме́нка; ~**y** *adj* спорти́вный

**spot** [spɒt] *n* (*mark*) пятно́; (*dot: on
pattern*) кра́пинка; (*on skin*)
пры́щик; (*place*) ме́сто ♦ *vt*
замеча́ть (заме́тить *pf*); **a** ~ **of
bother** ме́лкая неприя́тность *f*;
~**s of rain** ка́пли дождя́; **on the** ~
(*in that place*) на ме́сте;
(*immediately*) в тот же моме́нт;
~**less** *adj* чисте́йший; ~**light** *n*
прожёктор; ~**ted** *adj* (*pattern*)
пятни́стый; ~**ty** *adj* ( *face, youth*)
прыща́вый

**spouse** [spaʊs] *n* супру́г(а)

**spout** [spaʊt] *n* (*of jug*) но́сик

**sprang** [spræŋ] *pt of* **spring**

**sprawl** [sprɔ:l] *vi* (*person*)
разва́ливаться (развали́ться *pf*);
(*place*) раски́дываться
(раски́нуться *pf*)

**spray** [spreɪ] *n* (*drops of water*)
бры́зги *pl*; (*hair spray*) аэрозо́ль *m*
♦ *vt* опры́скивать (опры́скать *pf*)

**spread** [spred] (*pt, pp* ~) *n* (*range*)
спектр; (*distribution*)
распростране́ние; (*CULIN, butter*)
бутербро́дный маргари́н; (*inf:
food*) пир ♦ *vt* (*lay out*)
расстила́ть (расстели́ть *pf*);
(*scatter*) разбра́сывать
(разбро́сать *pf*); (*butter*)
нама́зывать (нама́зать *pf*);
(*wings*) расправля́ть (распра́вить

pf); (arms) раскрыва́ть (раскры́ть pf); (workload, wealth) распределя́ть (распредели́ть pf) ♦ vi (disease, news etc) распространя́ться (распространи́ться pf); ~ **out** vi (move apart) рассыпа́ться (рассы́паться pf); ~**sheet** n (крупноформа́тная) электро́нная табли́ца

**spree** [spri:] n разгу́л

**sprightly** ['spraɪtlɪ] adj бо́дрый

**spring** [sprɪŋ] (pt **sprang**, pp **sprung**) n (coiled metal) пружи́на; (season) весна́; (of water) исто́чник, родни́к ♦ vi (leap) пры́гать (пры́гнуть pf); **in** ~ весно́й; **to** ~ **from** (stem from) происходи́ть (произойти́ pf) из +gen; ~**time** n весе́нняя пора́

**sprinkle** ['sprɪŋkl] vt (salt, sugar) посыпа́ть (посы́пать pf) +instr; **to** ~ **water on sth**, ~ **sth with water** опры́скивать (опры́скать pf) что-н водо́й

**sprint** [sprɪnt] n (race) спринт ♦ vi (run fast) стреми́тельно бе́гать/ бежа́ть (impf)

**sprout** [spraut] vi (BOT) пуска́ть (пусти́ть pf) ростки́; ~**s** npl (also: **Brussels** ~**s**) брюссе́льская капу́ста fsg

**spruce** [spru:s] n inv (BOT) ель f ♦ adj (neat) опря́тный

**sprung** [sprʌŋ] pp of **spring**

**spun** [spʌn] pt, pp of **spin**

**spur** [spə:r] n (fig) сти́мул ♦ vt (also: ~ **on**) пришпо́ривать (пришпо́рить pf); **to** ~ **sb on to** побужда́ть (побуди́ть pf) кого́-н к +dat; **on the** ~ **of the moment** вдруг, не разду́мывая

**spurn** [spə:n] vt отверга́ть (отве́ргнуть pf)

**spy** [spaɪ] n шпио́н ♦ vi: **to** ~ **on** шпио́нить (impf) за +instr; ~**ing** n шпиона́ж

**sq.** abbr = **square**

**squabble** ['skwɔbl] vi вздо́рить (повздо́рить pf)

**squad** [skwɔd] n (MIL, POLICE) отря́д; (SPORT) кома́нда

**squadron** ['skwɔdrn] n (AVIAT) эскадри́лья

**squalid** ['skwɔlɪd] adj (place) убо́гий

**squalor** ['skwɔlər] n убо́гость f

**square** [skwɛər] n (shape) квадра́т; (in town) пло́щадь f ♦ adj квадра́тный ♦ vt (reconcile, settle) ула́живать (ула́дить pf); **a** ~ **meal** соли́дный обе́д; **2 metres** ~ 2 ме́тра в ширину́, 2 ме́тра в длину́; **2** ~ **metres** 2 квадра́тных ме́тра; ~**ly** adv пря́мо

**squash** [skwɔʃ] n (BRIT: drink) напи́ток; (SPORT) сквош ♦ vt дави́ть (раздави́ть pf)

**squat** [skwɔt] adj призе́мистый ♦ vi (also: ~ **down**: position) сиде́ть (impf) на ко́рточках; (: motion) сади́ться (сесть pf) на ко́рточки

**squeak** [skwi:k] vi (door) скрипе́ть (скри́пнуть pf); (mouse) пища́ть (пи́скнуть pf)

**squeal** [skwi:l] vi визжа́ть (impf)

**squeamish** ['skwi:mɪʃ] adj брезгли́вый

**squeeze** [skwi:z] n (of hand) пожа́тие; (ECON) ограниче́ние ♦ vt сжима́ть (сжать pf); (juice) выжима́ть (вы́жать pf)

**squid** [skwɪd] n кальма́р

**squint** [skwɪnt] n (MED) косогла́зие

**squirrel** ['skwɪrəl] n бе́лка

**squirt** [skwə:t] vi бры́згать (бры́знуть pf) ♦ vt бры́згать (бры́знуть pf) +instr

**Sr** abbr (in names) = **senior**

**St** abbr = **saint** св.; = **street** ул.

**stab** [stæb] vt наноси́ть (нанести́ pf) уда́р +dat; (kill): **to** ~ **sb (to**

**death)** заре́зать (pf) кого́-н ♦ n (of pain) уко́л; (inf: try): **to have a ~ at doing** пыта́ться (попыта́ться pf) +infin

**stability** [stə'bɪlɪtɪ] n усто́йчивость f, стаби́льность f

**stabilize** ['steɪbəlaɪz] vt (prices) стабилизи́ровать (impf/pf) ♦ vi стабилизи́роваться (impf/pf)

**stable** ['steɪbl] adj стаби́льный, усто́йчивый ♦ n (for horse) коню́шня

**stack** [stæk] n (of wood, plates) шта́бель m; (of papers) ки́па ♦ vt (also: ~ **up**: chairs etc) скла́дывать (сложи́ть pf)

**stadium** ['steɪdɪəm] (pl **stadia** or ~**s**) n (SPORT) стадио́н

**staff** [stɑːf] n (workforce) штат, сотру́дники mpl; (BRIT : SCOL : also: **teaching ~**) преподава́тельский соста́в or коллекти́в ♦ vt: **the firm is ~ed by 5 people** на фи́рму рабо́тает 5 челове́к

**stag** [stæg] n (ZOOL) саме́ц оле́ня

**stage** [steɪdʒ] n (in theatre) сце́на; (platform) подмо́стки pl; (point, period) ста́дия ♦ vt (play) ста́вить (поста́вить pf); (demonstration) устра́ивать (устро́ить pf); **in ~s** поэта́пно, по эта́пам

**stagger** ['stægər] vt (amaze) потряса́ть (потрясти́ pf); (holidays etc) распи́сывать (расписа́ть pf) ♦ vi: **he ~ed along the road** он шёл по доро́ге шата́ясь; ~**ing** adj потряса́ющий, порази́тельный

**stagnant** ['stægnənt] adj (water) стоя́чий; (economy) засто́йный

**staid** [steɪd] adj чи́нный

**stain** [steɪn] n пятно́ ♦ vt (mark) ста́вить (поста́вить pf) пятно́ на +acc; ~**less steel** n нержаве́ющая сталь f

**stair** [steər] n (step) ступе́нь f,

ступе́нька; ~**s** npl (steps) ле́стница fsg; ~**case** n ле́стница; ~**way** = **staircase**

**stake** [steɪk] n (post) кол; (investment) до́ля ♦ vt (money, reputation) рискова́ть (рискну́ть pf) +instr; **his reputation was at ~** его́ репута́ция была́ поста́влена на ка́рту; **to ~ a claim (to)** притяза́ть (impf) (на +acc)

**stale** [steɪl] adj (bread) чёрствый; (food) несве́жий; (air) за́тхлый

**stalemate** ['steɪlmeɪt] n (fig) тупи́к

**stalk** [stɔːk] n (of flower) сте́бель m; (of fruit) чере́шок

**stall** [stɔːl] n (in market) прила́вок; (in stable) сто́йло ♦ vi: **I ~ed (the car)** у меня́ загло́хла маши́на; ~**s** npl (BRIT : THEAT) парте́р msg

**stamina** ['stæmɪnə] n сто́йкость f, вы́держка

**stammer** ['stæmər] n заика́ние

**stamp** [stæmp] n (POST) ма́рка; (rubber stamp) печа́ть f, штамп; (mark, also fig) печа́ть f ♦ vi (also: ~ **one's foot**) то́пать (то́пнуть pf) (ного́й) ♦ vt (mark) клейми́ть (заклейми́ть pf); (: with rubber stamp) штампова́ть (проштампова́ть pf)

**stampede** [stæm'piːd] n да́вка

**stance** [stæns] n (also fig) пози́ция

**stand** [stænd] (pt, pp **stood**) n (stall) ларёк, кио́ск; (at exhibition) стенд; (SPORT) трибу́на; (for umbrellas) сто́йка; (for coats, hats) ве́шалка ♦ vi (be upright) стоя́ть (impf); (rise) встава́ть (встать pf); (remain: decision, offer) остава́ться (оста́ться pf) в си́ле; (in election etc) баллоти́роваться (impf) ♦ vt (place: object) ста́вить (поста́вить pf); (tolerate, withstand) терпе́ть (стерпе́ть pf), выноси́ть (вы́нести pf); **to make a ~ against sth** выступа́ть (вы́ступить pf) про́тив чего́-н; **to ~ for parliament** (*BRIT*) баллоти́роваться (*impf*) в парла́мент; **to ~ at** (*value, score etc*) составля́ть (соста́вить *pf*); **~ by** *vi* (*be ready*) быть (*impf*) нагото́ве ♦ *vt fus* не отступа́ть (отступи́ть *pf*) от +*gen*; **~ for** *vt fus* (*signify*) обознача́ть (*impf*); (*represent*) представля́ть (*impf*); **I won't ~ for it** я э́того не потерплю́; **~ out** *vi* (*be obvious*) выделя́ться (вы́делиться *pf*); **~ up** *vi* (*rise*) встава́ть (встать *pf*); **~ up for** *vt fus* (*defend*) стоя́ть (постоя́ть *pf*) за +*acc*; **~ up to** *vt fus* ока́зывать (оказа́ть *pf*) сопротивле́ние +*dat*

**standard** ['stændəd] *n* (*level*) у́ровень *m*; (*norm, criterion*) станда́рт ♦ *adj* (*normal: size etc*) станда́ртный; **~s** *npl* (*morals*) нра́вы *mpl*; **~ of living** *n* у́ровень *m* жи́зни

**stand-by** ['stændbaɪ] *n*: **to be on ~** (*doctor etc*) быть (*impf*) нагото́ве

**stand-in** ['stændɪn] *n* замести́тель *m*

**standpoint** ['stændpɔɪnt] *n* пози́ция

**standstill** ['stændstɪl] *n*: **to be at a ~** (*negotiations*) быть (*impf*) в тупике́; **to come to a ~** (*negotiations*) заходи́ть (зайти́ *pf*) в тупи́к; (*traffic*) стать (*pf*)

**stank** [stæŋk] *pt of* **stink**

**staple** ['steɪpl] *n* (*for papers*) скоба́ ♦ *adj* (*food etc*) основно́й ♦ *vt* (*fasten*) сшива́ть (сшить *pf*)

**star** [stɑː*r*] *n* звезда́ ♦ *vi*: **to ~ in** игра́ть (сыгра́ть *pf*) гла́вную роль в +*prp* ♦ *vt*: **the film ~s my brother** гла́вную роль в фи́льме игра́ет мой брат; **the ~s** *npl* (*horoscope*) звёзды *fpl*

**starch** [stɑːtʃ] *n* (*also CULIN*) крахма́л

**stare** [stɛə*r*] *vi*: **to ~ at** (*deep in thought*) при́стально смотре́ть (*impf*) на +*acc*; (*amazed*) тара́щиться (*impf*) на +*acc*

**stark** [stɑːk] *adj* (*bleak*) го́лый ♦ *adv*: **~ naked** соверше́нно го́лый

**starling** ['stɑːlɪŋ] *n* скворе́ц

**starry** ['stɑːrɪ] *adj* звёздный

**start** [stɑːt] *n* нача́ло; (*SPORT*) старт; (*in fright*) вздра́гивание; (*advantage*) преиму́щество ♦ *vt* (*begin, found*) начина́ть (нача́ть *pf*); (*cause*) вызыва́ть (вы́звать *pf*); (*engine*) заводи́ть (завести́ *pf*) ♦ *vi* (*begin*) начина́ться (нача́ться *pf*); (*begin moving*) отправля́ться (отпра́виться *pf*); (*engine, car*) заводи́ться (завести́сь *pf*); (*jump: in fright*) вздра́гивать (вздро́гнуть *pf*); **to ~ doing** *or* **to do** начина́ть (нача́ть *pf*) +*impf infin*; **~ off** *vi* (*begin*) начина́ться (нача́ться *pf*); (*begin moving*) тро́гаться (тро́нуться *pf*); (*leave*) отправля́ться (отпра́виться *pf*); **~ out** *vi* (*leave*) отправля́ться (отпра́виться *pf*); **~ up** *vi* (*engine, car*) заводи́ться (завести́сь *pf*) ♦ *vt* (*business*) начина́ть (нача́ть *pf*); (*car, engine*) заводи́ть (завести́ *pf*); **~er** *n* (*BRIT : CULIN*) заку́ска; **~ing point** *n* (*for journey*) отправно́й пункт

**startle** ['stɑːtl] *vt* вспу́гивать (вспугну́ть *pf*)

**startling** ['stɑːtlɪŋ] *adj* порази́тельный

**starvation** [stɑːˈveɪʃən] *n* го́лод

**starve** [stɑːv] *vi* (*to death*) умира́ть (умере́ть *pf*) от го́лода; (*be very hungry*) голода́ть (*impf*) ♦ *vt* (*person, animal*) мори́ть (замори́ть *pf*) го́лодом

**state** [steɪt] *n* (*condition*) состоя́ние; (*government*) госуда́рство ♦ *vt* (*say, declare*)

констати́ровать *(impf/pf)*; **the
States** *npl (GEO)* Соединённые
Шта́ты *mpl*; **to be in a ~** *(impf)* в па́нике; **~ly** *adj*: **~ly home**
дом-уса́дьба

**statement** ['steɪtmənt] *n
(declaration)* заявле́ние

**statesman** ['steɪtsmən] *(irreg) n*
госуда́рственный де́ятель *m*

**static** ['stætɪk] *adj (not moving)*
стати́чный, неподви́жный

**station** ['steɪʃən] *n* ста́нция; *(larger
railway station)* вокза́л; *(also:*
**police ~)** полице́йский уча́сток
♦ *vt (position: guards etc)*
выставля́ть (вы́ставить *pf*)

**stationary** ['steɪʃnərɪ] *adj (vehicle)*
неподви́жный

**stationery** ['steɪʃnərɪ] *n*
канцеля́рские принадле́жности
*fpl*

**statistic** [stə'tɪstɪk] *n* стати́стик;
**~al** *adj* статисти́ческий; **~s** *n
(science)* стати́стика

**statue** ['stætjuː] *n* ста́туя

**stature** ['stætʃəʳ] *n (size)* рост

**status** ['steɪtəs] *n* ста́тус;
*(importance)* значе́ние; **the ~ quo**
ста́тус-кво *m ind*

**statutory** ['stætjutrɪ] *adj*
устано́вленный зако́ном

**staunch** [stɔːntʃ] *adj* пре́данный,
непоколеби́мый

**stay** [steɪ] *n* пребыва́ние ♦ *vi
(remain)* остава́ться (оста́ться *pf*);
*(with sb, as guest)* гости́ть *(impf)*;
*(in place)* остана́вливаться
(останови́ться *pf*); **to ~ at home**
остава́ться (оста́ться *pf*) до́ма; **to
~ put** не дви́гаться (дви́нуться
*pf*) с ме́ста; **to ~ the night**
ночева́ть (переночева́ть *pf*); **~ in**
*vi (at home)* остава́ться (оста́ться
*pf*) до́ма; **~ on** *vi* остава́ться
(оста́ться *pf*); **~ out** *vi (of house)*
отсу́тствовать *(impf)*; **~ up** *vi (at*

*night)* не ложи́ться *(impf)* (спать)

**steadfast** ['stɛdfɑːst] *adj* сто́йкий

**steadily** ['stɛdɪlɪ] *adv (firmly)*
про́чно; *(constantly, fixedly)*
постоя́нно

**steady** ['stɛdɪ] *adj (constant)*
стаби́льный; *(boyfriend, speed)*
постоя́нный; *(person)*
уравнове́шенный; *(firm: hand etc)*
твёрдый; *(look, voice)* ро́вный ♦ *vt
(object)* придава́ть (прида́ть *pf*)
усто́йчивость +*dat*; *(nerves, voice)*
совлада́ть *(pf)* с +*instr*

**steak** [steɪk] *n* филе́ *nt ind*; *(fried
beef)* бифште́кс

**steal** [stiːl] *(pt stole, pp stolen) vt*
ворова́ть (сворова́ть *pf*), красть
(укра́сть *pf*) ♦ *vi* ворова́ть *(impf)*,
красть *(impf)*; *(creep)* кра́сться
*(impf)*

**steam** [stiːm] *n* пар ♦ *vt (CULIN)*
па́рить *(impf)* ♦ *vi (give off steam)*
выделя́ть *(impf)* пар; **~er** *n (ship)*
парохо́д

**steel** [stiːl] *n* сталь *f* ♦ *adj* стально́й

**steep** [stiːp] *adj* круто́й; *(price)*
высо́кий ♦ *vt (food)* выма́чивать
(вы́мочить *pf*); *(clothes)*
зама́чивать (замочи́ть *pf*)

**steeple** ['stiːpl] *n* шпиль *m*

**steer** [stɪəʳ] *vt* направля́ть
(напра́вить *pf*) ♦ *vi*
маневри́ровать *(impf)*; **~ing
wheel** *n* руль *m*

**stem** [stɛm] *n (of plant)* сте́бель *m*;
*(of glass)* но́жка ♦ *vt (stop)*
остана́вливать (останови́ть *pf*); **~
from** *vt fus* произраста́ть
(произрасти́ *pf*) из +*gen*

**stench** [stɛntʃ] *n (pej)* смрад

**stencil** ['stɛnsl] *n* трафаре́т

**step** [stɛp] *n (also fig)* шаг; *(of
stairs)* ступе́нь *f*, ступе́нька ♦ *vi
(forward, back)* ступа́ть (ступи́ть
*pf*); **~s** *npl (BRIT)* = **stepladder; to
be in/out of ~ (with)** идти́ *(impf)* в

ногу/не в ногу (с +instr); ~ **down**
vi (fig: resign) уходить (уйти pf) в
отставку; ~ **on** vt fus (walk on)
наступать (наступить pf) на +acc;
~ **up** vt (increase) усиливать
(усилить pf); ~**brother** n
сводный брат; ~**daughter** n
падчерица; ~**father** n отчим;
~**ladder** n (BRIT) стремянка;
~**mother** n мачеха; ~**sister** n
сводная сестра; ~**son** n пасынок

**stereo** ['stɛrɪəʊ] n (system)
стереосистема

**stereotype** ['stɪərɪətaɪp] n
стереотип

**sterile** ['stɛraɪl] adj бесплодный;
(clean) стерильный

**sterilize** ['stɛrɪlaɪz] vt
стерилизовать (impf/pf)

**sterling** ['stə:lɪŋ] n (ECON) фунт
стерлингов; ~ **silver** серебро
925-ой пробы

**stern** [stə:n] adj суровый

**stew** [stju:] n (meat) тушёное мясо
♦ vt тушить (потушить pf)

**steward** ['stju:əd] n (on plane)
бортпроводник; ~**ess** n (on
plane) стюардесса,
бортпроводница

**stick** [stɪk] (pt, pp **stuck**) n (of
wood) палка; (walking stick)
трость f ♦ vt (with glue etc) клеить
(приклеить pf); (inf: put) совать
(сунуть pf); (thrust) втыкать
(воткнуть pf) ♦ vi (become
attached) приклеиваться
(приклеиться pf); (in mind)
засесть (pf); ~ **out** vi (ears)
торчать (impf); ~ **up for** vt fus
(person) заступаться
(заступиться pf) за +acc; (principle)
отстаивать (отстоять pf); ~**er** n
наклейка; ~**y** adj (hands etc)
липкий; (label) клейкий; (fig:
situation) щекотливый

**stiff** [stɪf] adj (brush) жёсткий;

(person) деревянный; (zip) тугой;
(manner, smile) натянутый;
(competition) жёсткий; (severe:
sentence) суровый; (strong: drink)
крепкий; (: breeze) сильный ♦ adv
до смерти

**stifle** ['staɪfl] vt (yawn) подавлять
(подавить pf)

**stifling** ['staɪflɪŋ] adj (heat)
удушливый

**stigma** ['stɪɡmə] n (fig) клеймо

**still** [stɪl] adj тихий ♦ adv (up to this
time) всё ещё; (even, yet) ещё;
(nonetheless) всё-таки, тем не
менее; ~ **life** n (ART) натюрморт

**stimulant** ['stɪmjulənt] n
стимулирующее or
возбуждающее средство

**stimulate** ['stɪmjuleɪt] vt
стимулировать (impf/pf)

**stimulating** ['stɪmjuleɪtɪŋ] adj
вдохновляющий

**stimulus** ['stɪmjuləs] (pl **stimuli**) n
(encouragement) стимул

**sting** [stɪŋ] (pt, pp **stung**) n (from
insect) укус; (from plant) ожог;
(organ: of wasp etc) жало ♦ vt (also
fig) уязвлять (уязвить pf) ♦ vi
(insect, animal) жалиться (impf);
(plant) жечься (impf); (eyes,
ointment etc) жечь (impf)

**stink** [stɪŋk] (pt **stank**, pp **stunk**) vi
смердеть (impf), вонять (impf)
(разг)

**stir** [stə:r] n (fig) шум, сенсация
♦ vt (tea etc) мешать (помешать
pf); (fig: emotions) волновать
(взволновать pf) ♦ vi (move)
шевелиться (пошевелиться pf); ~
**up** vt (trouble) вызывать (вызвать
pf); ~**-fry** vt быстро обжаривать
(обжарить pf)

**stitch** [stɪtʃ] n (SEWING) стежок;
(KNITTING) петля; (MED) шов ♦ vt
(sew) шить (сшить pf); (MED)
зашивать (зашить pf); **I have a ~**

**in my side** у меня́ ко́лет в боку́

**stoat** [stəut] n горноста́й

**stock** [stɔk] n (supply) запа́с; (AGR) поголо́вье; (CULIN) бульо́н; (FINANCE, usu pl) це́нные бума́ги fpl ♦ adj (reply, excuse etc) дежу́рный ♦ vt (have in stock) име́ть (impf) в нали́чии; ~s and shares а́кции и це́нные бума́ги; to be in/out of ~ име́ться (impf)/ не име́ться (impf) в нали́чии; to take ~ of (fig) оце́нивать (оцени́ть pf); ~**broker** n (COMM) фо́ндовый бро́кер; ~ **exchange** n фо́ндовая би́ржа

**stocking** ['stɔkɪŋ] n чуло́к

**stock market** n (BRIT) фо́ндовая би́ржа

**stocky** ['stɔkɪ] adj корена́стый

**stoke** [stəuk] vt (fire) подде́рживать (impf); (boiler, furnace) подде́рживать (impf) ого́нь в +prp

**stole** [stəul] pt of **steal**; ~**n** pp of **steal**

**stomach** ['stʌmək] n (ANAT) желу́док; (belly) живо́т ♦ vt (fig) переноси́ть (перенести́ pf)

**stone** [stəun] n (also MED) ка́мень m; (pebble) ка́мешек; (in fruit) ко́сточка; (BRIT: weight) сто́ун (14 фу́нтов) ♦ adj ка́менный

**stone** - сто́ун. Ме́ра ве́са ра́вная 6.35 кг.

**stony** ['stəunɪ] adj (ground) камени́стый; (silence) холо́дный; (glance) ка́менный

**stood** [stud] pt, pp of **stand**

**stool** [stu:l] n табуре́т(ка)

**stoop** [stu:p] vi (also: ~ **down**: bend) наклоня́ться (наклони́ться pf), нагиба́ться (нагну́ться pf)

**stop** [stɔp] n остано́вка; (LING: also: **full** ~) то́чка ♦ vt

остана́вливать (останови́ть pf); (prevent : also: **put a ~ to**) прекраща́ть (прекрати́ть pf) ♦ vi (person, clock) остана́вливаться (останови́ться pf); (rain, noise etc) прекраща́ться (прекрати́ться pf); **to ~ doing** перестава́ть (переста́ть pf) +infin; ~ **by** vi заходи́ть (зайти́ pf); ~**page** ['stɔpɪdʒ] n (strike) забасто́вка; ~**watch** n секундоме́р

**storage** ['stɔːrɪdʒ] n хране́ние

**store** [stɔːr] n (stock, reserve) запа́с; (depot) склад; (BRIT: large shop) универма́г; (esp US: shop) магази́н ♦ vt храни́ть (impf); **in ~** в бу́дущем; ~**room** n кладова́я f adj

**storey** ['stɔːrɪ] (US **story**) n эта́ж

**stork** [stɔːk] n а́ист

**storm** [stɔːm] n (also fig) бу́ря; (of criticism) шквал; (of laughter) взрыв ♦ vt (attack: place) штурмова́ть (impf); ~**y** adj (fig) бу́рный; ~**y weather** нена́стье

**story** ['stɔːrɪ] n исто́рия; (lie) вы́думка, ска́зка; (US) = **storey**

**stout** [staut] adj (strong: branch etc) кре́пкий; (fat) доро́дный; (resolute: friend, supporter) сто́йкий

**stove** [stəuv] n печь f, пе́чка

**St Petersburg** [sənt'pi:təzbə:g] n Санкт-Петербу́рг

**straight** [streɪt] adj прямо́й; (simple: choice) я́сный ♦ adv пря́мо; **to put** or **get sth** ~ (make clear) вноси́ть (внести́ pf) я́сность во что-н; ~ **away**, ~ **off** (at once) сра́зу (же); ~**en** vt (skirt, tie, bed) поправля́ть (попра́вить pf); ~**forward** adj (simple) просто́й; (honest) прямо́й

**strain** [streɪn] n (pressure) нагру́зка; (MED, physical) растяже́ние; (: mental) напряже́ние ♦ vt (back etc) растя́гивать (растяну́ть pf);

(*voice*) напряга́ть (напря́чь *pf*); (*stretch: resources*) перенапряга́ть (перенапря́чь *pf*); (*CULIN*) проце́живать (проце́дить *pf*); **~ed** *adj* (*muscle*) растя́нутый; (*laugh, relations*) натя́нутый

**strand** [strænd] *n* нить *f*; (*of hair*) прядь *f*; **~ed** *adj*: **to be ~ed** застрева́ть (застря́ть *pf*)

**strange** [streɪndʒ] *adj* стра́нный; (*not known*) незнако́мый; **~ly** *adv* (*act, laugh*) стра́нно; *see also* **enough**; **~r** *n* (*unknown person*) незнако́мец, посторо́нний(яя) *m(f) adj*

**strangle** ['stræŋgl] *vt* (*also fig*) души́ть (задуши́ть *pf*)

**strap** [stræp] *n* реме́нь *m*; (*of dress*) брете́лька; (*of watch*) ремешо́к

**strategic** [strə'tiːdʒɪk] *adj* стратеги́ческий

**strategy** ['strætɪdʒɪ] *n* страте́гия

**straw** [strɔː] *n* соло́ма; (*drinking straw*) соло́минка; **that's the last ~!** э́то после́дняя ка́пля!

**strawberry** ['strɔːbərɪ] *n* клубни́ка *f no pl*; (*wild*) земляни́ка *f no pl*

**stray** [streɪ] *adj* (*animal*) бродя́чий; (*bullet*) шально́й ♦ *vi* заблуди́ться (*pf*); (*thoughts*) блужда́ть (*impf*)

**streak** [striːk] *n* (*stripe*) полоса́

**stream** [striːm] *n* руче́й; (*of people, vehicles, questions*) пото́к ♦ *vi* (*liquid*) течь (*impf*), ли́ться (*impf*); **to ~ in/out** (*people*) вали́ть (повали́ть *pf*) толпо́й в +*acc*/из +*gen*

**street** [striːt] *n* у́лица

**strength** [strɛŋθ] *n* си́ла; (*of girder, knot etc*) про́чность *f*; **~en** *vt* (*building, machine*) укрепля́ть (укрепи́ть *pf*); (*fig: group*) пополня́ть (попо́лнить *pf*); (*: argument*) подкрепля́ть (подкрепи́ть *pf*)

**strenuous** ['strɛnjuəs] *adj* (*exercise*)

уси́ленный; (*efforts*) напряжённый

**stress** [strɛs] *n* (*pressure*) давле́ние, напряже́ние; (*mental strain*) стресс; (*emphasis*) ударе́ние ♦ *vt* (*point, need etc*) де́лать (сде́лать *pf*) ударе́ние на +*acc*; (*syllable*) ста́вить (поста́вить *pf*) ударе́ние на +*acc*

**stretch** [strɛtʃ] *n* (*area*) отре́зок, простра́нство ♦ *vt* (*pull*) натя́гивать (натяну́ть *pf*) ♦ *vi* (*person, animal*) потя́гиваться (потяну́ться *pf*); (*extend*): **to ~ to** *or* **as far as** простира́ться (*impf*) до +*gen*; **~ out** *vi* растя́гиваться (растяну́ться *pf*) ♦ *vt* (*arm etc*) протя́гивать (протяну́ть *pf*)

**stretcher** ['strɛtʃər] *n* носи́лки *pl*

**strewn** [struːn] *adj*: **~ with** усы́панный +*instr*

**stricken** ['strɪkən] *adj*: **~ with** (*arthritis, disease*) поражённый +*instr*

**strict** [strɪkt] *adj* стро́гий; (*precise: meaning*) то́чный; **~ly** *adv* (*severely*) стро́го; (*exactly*) то́чно

**stride** [straɪd] (*pt* **strode**, *pp* **stridden**) *n* (*step*) шаг ♦ *vi* шага́ть (*impf*)

**strike** [straɪk] (*pt, pp* **struck**) *n* (*of workers*) забасто́вка; (*MIL, attack*) уда́р ♦ *vt* (*hit: person, thing*) ударя́ть (уда́рить *pf*); (*subj: idea, thought*) осеня́ть (осени́ть *pf*); (*oil etc*) открыва́ть (откры́ть *pf*) месторожде́ние +*gen*; (*bargain, deal*) заключа́ть (заключи́ть *pf*) ♦ *vi* (*workers*) бастова́ть (*impf*); (*disaster, illness*) обру́шиваться (обру́шиться *pf*); (*clock*) бить (проби́ть *pf*); **to be on ~** (*workers*) бастова́ть (*impf*); **to ~ a match** зажига́ть (заже́чь *pf*) спи́чку; **~r** *n* забасто́вщик(ица); (*SPORT*) напада́ющий(ая) *m(f) adj*

**striking** ['straıkıŋ] adj
поразительный

**string** [strıŋ] (pt, pp **strung**) n
верёвка; (MUS, for guitar etc)
струна; (of beads) нитка ♦ vt: **to ~
together** связывать (связать pf);
**the ~s** npl (MUS) струнные
инструменты mpl; **to ~ out**
растягивать (растянуть pf)

**strip** [strıp] n полоса, полоска ♦ vt
(undress) раздевать (раздеть pf);
(paint) обдирать (ободрать pf),
сдирать (содрать pf); (also: ~
**down**: machine) разбирать
(разобрать pf) ♦ vi раздеваться
(раздеться pf)

**stripe** [straıp] n полоска; (POLICE,
MIL) петлица; **~d** adj полосатый

**stripper** ['strıpər] n стриптизёрка

**strive** [straıv] (pt **strove**, pp **~n**) vi:
**to ~ for sth/to do** стремиться
(impf) к чему-н/+infin

**strode** [strəud] pt of **stride**

**stroke** [strəuk] n (also MED) удар;
(SWIMMING) стиль m ♦ vt гладить
(погладить pf); **at a ~** одним
махом

**stroll** [strəul] n прогулка ♦ vi
прогуливаться (прогуляться pf),
прохаживаться (пройтись pf)

**strong** [strɒŋ] adj сильный; **they
are 50 ~** их 50; **~hold** n (fig)
оплот, твердыня

**strove** [strəuv] pt of **strive**

**struck** [strʌk] pt, pp of **strike**

**structural** ['strʌktʃrəl] adj
структурный

**structure** ['strʌktʃər] n структура

**struggle** ['strʌgl] n (fight) борьба
♦ vi (try hard) силиться (impf),
прилагать (приложить pf)
большие усилия; (fight)
бороться (impf); (: to free o.s.)
сопротивляться (impf)

**strung** [strʌŋ] pt, pp of **string**

**stub** [stʌb] n (of cheque, ticket etc)

корешок; (of cigarette) окурок
♦ vt: **to ~ one's toe** больно
спотыкаться (споткнуться pf)

**stubble** ['stʌbl] n (on chin) щетина

**stubborn** ['stʌbən] adj
(determination, child) упрямый,
упорный

**stuck** [stʌk] pt, pp of **stick** ♦ adj: **to
be ~** застрять (pf)

**stud** [stʌd] n (on clothing etc)
кнопка, заклёпка; (earring)
серьга со штифтом; (on sole of
boot) шип ♦ vt (fig): **~ded with**
усыпанный +instr

**student** ['stju:dənt] n (at university)
студент(ка); (at school)
учащийся(аяся) m(f) adj ♦ adj
студенческий; (at school)
ученический

**studio** ['stju:dıəu] n студия

**study** ['stʌdı] n (activity) учёба;
(room) кабинет ♦ vt изучать
(изучить pf) ♦ vi учиться (pf)

**stuff** [stʌf] n (things) вещи fpl;
(substance) вещество ♦ vt
набивать (набить pf); (CULIN)
начинять (начинить pf),
фаршировать (нафаршировать
pf); (inf: push) запихивать
(запихать pf); **~ing** n набивка;
(CULIN) начинка, фарш; **~y** adj
(room) душный; (person, ideas)
чопорный

**stumble** ['stʌmbl] vi спотыкаться
(споткнуться pf); **to ~ across** or **on**
(fig) натыкаться (наткнуться pf)
на +acc

**stump** [stʌmp] n (of tree) пень m;
(of limb) обрубок ♦ vt
озадачивать (озадачить pf)

**stun** [stʌn] vt (subj: news)
потрясать (потрясти pf),
ошеломлять (ошеломить pf);
(: blow on head) оглушать
(оглушить pf)

**stung** [stʌŋ] pt, pp of **sting**

**stunk** [stʌŋk] *pp of* **stink**

**stunning** ['stʌnɪŋ] *adj (fabulous)* потрясающий

**stunted** ['stʌntɪd] *adj (trees)* подрубленный; *(growth)* замедленный

**stupendous** [stju:'pɛndəs] *adj (large)* колоссальный; *(impressive)* изумительный

**stupid** ['stju:pɪd] *adj* глупый; **~ity** [stju:'pɪdɪtɪ] *n* глупость *f*

**sturdy** ['stə:dɪ] *adj* крепкий

**stutter** ['stʌtə'] *n* заикание ♦ *vi* заикаться *(impf)*

**style** [staɪl] *n* стиль *m*

**stylish** ['staɪlɪʃ] *adj* стильный, элегантный

**subconscious** [sʌb'kɔnʃəs] *adj* подсознательный

**subdue** [səb'dju:] *vt* подавлять (подавить *pf*); **~d** *adj (light)* приглушённый; *(person)* подавленный

**subject** [n 'sʌbdʒɪkt] *vb* [səb'dʒɛkt] *n (topic)* тема; *(SCOL)* предмет; *(LING)* подлежащее *nt adj* ♦ *vt*: **to ~ sb to sth** подвергать (подвергнуть *pf*) кого-н чему-н; **to be ~ to** *(tax)* подлежать *(impf)* +*dat*; *(law)* подчиняться *(impf)* +*dat*; **~ive** [səb'dʒɛktɪv] *adj* субъективный

**submarine** [sʌbmə'ri:n] *n* подводная лодка

**submerge** [səb'mə:dʒ] *vt* погружать (погрузить *pf*) (в воду) ♦ *vi* погружаться (погрузиться *pf*) (в воду)

**submission** [səb'mɪʃən] *n (state)* подчинение, повиновение; *(of plan etc)* подача

**submissive** [səb'mɪsɪv] *adj* покорный

**submit** [səb'mɪt] *vt (proposal, application etc)* представлять (представить *pf*) на рассмотрение ♦ *vi*: **to ~ to sth** подчиняться (подчиниться *pf*) чему-н

**subordinate** [sə'bɔ:dɪnət] *adj*: **to be ~ to** *(in rank)* подчиняться *(impf)* +*dat* ♦ *n* подчинённый(ая) *m(f) adj*

**subscribe** [səb'skraɪb] *vi*: **to ~ to** *(opinion, fund)* поддерживать (поддержать *pf*); *(magazine etc)* подписываться (подписаться *pf*) на +*acc*

**subscription** [səb'skrɪpʃən] *n (to magazine etc)* подписка

**subsequent** ['sʌbsɪkwənt] *adj* последующий; **~ to** вслед +*dat*; **~ly** *adv* впоследствии

**subside** [səb'saɪd] *vi (feeling, wind)* утихать (утихнуть *pf*); *(flood)* убывать (убыть *pf*); **~nce** [səb'saɪdns] *n* оседание

**subsidiary** [səb'sɪdɪərɪ] *n (also: ~ company)* дочерняя компания

**subsidy** ['sʌbsɪdɪ] *n* субсидия, дотация

**substance** ['sʌbstəns] *n (product, material)* вещество

**substantial** [səb'stænʃl] *adj (solid)* прочный, основательный; *(fig: reward, meal)* солидный; **~ly** *adv (by a lot)* значительно; *(in essence)* существенно, основательно

**substitute** ['sʌbstɪtju:t] *n (person)* замена; *(: FOOTBALL etc)* запасной *m adj (игрок)*; *(thing)* заменитель *m* ♦ *vt*: **to ~ A for B** заменять (заменить *pf*) А на Б

**substitution** [sʌbstɪ'tju:ʃən] *n (act)* замена

**subtitle** ['sʌbtaɪtl] *n (in film)* субтитр

**subtle** ['sʌtl] *adj (change)* тонкий, едва уловимый; *(person)* тонкий, искусный; **~ty** *n (detail)* тонкость *f*; *(of person)* искусность *f*

**subtract** [səb'trækt] *vt* вычитать (вычесть *pf*)

**suburb** ['sʌbə:b] n при́город; **the ~s** npl (area) при́город msg; **~an** [sə'bə:bən] adj при́городный

**subversive** [səb'və:sɪv] adj подрывно́й

**subway** ['sʌbweɪ] n (US) метро́ nt ind, подзе́мка (разг); (BRIT: underpass) подзе́мный перехо́д

**succeed** [sək'si:d] vi (plan etc) удава́ться (уда́ться pf), име́ть (impf) успе́х; (person: in career etc) преуспева́ть (преуспе́ть pf) ♦ vt (in job, order) сменя́ть (смени́ть pf); **he ~ed in finishing the article** ему́ удало́сь зако́нчить статью́

**success** [sək'sɛs] n успе́х, уда́ча; **the book was a ~** кни́га име́ла успе́х; **he was a ~** он доби́лся успе́ха; **~ful** adj (venture) успе́шный; **he was ~ful in convincing her** ему́ удало́сь убеди́ть её; **~fully** adv успе́шно

**succession** [sək'sɛʃən] n (series) череда́, ряд; (to throne etc) насле́дование; **in ~** подря́д

**successive** [sək'sɛsɪv] adj (governments) сле́дующий оди́н за други́м

**successor** [sək'sɛsər] n прее́мник(ица); (to throne) насле́дник(ица)

**succinct** [sək'sɪŋkt] adj сжа́тый

**succulent** ['sʌkjulənt] adj (fruit, meat) со́чный

**succumb** [sə'kʌm] vi (to temptation) поддава́ться (подда́ться pf)

**such** [sʌtʃ] adj тако́й ♦ adv: **~ a long trip** така́я дли́нная пое́здка; **~ a book** така́я кни́га; **~ books** таки́е кни́ги; **~ a lot of** тако́е мно́жество +gen; **~ as** (like) таки́е как; **as ~** как таково́й; **~-and-~** adj таки́е-то и таки́е-то

**suck** [sʌk] vt (bottle, sweet) соса́ть (impf)

**suction** ['sʌkʃən] n вса́сывание

**sudden** ['sʌdn] adj внеза́пный; **all of a ~** внеза́пно, вдруг; **~ly** adv внеза́пно, вдруг

**sue** [su:] vt предъявля́ть (предъяви́ть pf) иск +dat

**suede** [sweɪd] n за́мша

**suet** ['sʊɪt] n жир

**suffer** ['sʌfər] vt (hardship etc) переноси́ть (перенести́ pf); (pain) страда́ть (impf) от +gen ♦ vi (person, results etc) страда́ть (пострада́ть pf); **to ~ from** страда́ть (impf) +instr; **~er** n (MED) страда́ющий(ая) m(f) adj; **~ing** n (hardship) страда́ние

**suffice** [sə'faɪs] vi: **this ~s ...** э́того доста́точно, ...

**sufficient** [sə'fɪʃənt] adj доста́точный; **~ly** adv доста́точно

**suffocate** ['sʌfəkeɪt] vi задыха́ться (задохну́ться pf)

**sugar** ['ʃugər] n са́хар; **~ cane** n са́харный тростни́к

**suggest** [sə'dʒɛst] vt (propose) предлага́ть (предложи́ть pf); (indicate) предполага́ть (предположи́ть pf); **~ion** [sə'dʒɛstʃən] n (see vb) предложе́ние; предположе́ние; **~ive** adj (remarks, looks) неприли́чный

**suicide** ['suɪsaɪd] n (death) самоуби́йство; see also **commit**

**suit** [su:t] n костю́м; (LAW) иск; (CARDS) масть f ♦ vt (be convenient, appropriate) подходи́ть (подойти́ pf) +dat; (colour, clothes) идти́ (impf) +dat; **to ~ sth to** (adapt) приспоса́бливать (приспосо́бить pf) что-н к +dat; **they are well ~ed** (couple) они́ хорошо́ друг дру́гу подхо́дят; **~able** adj подходя́щий; **~ably** adv надлежа́щим о́бразом

**suitcase** ['su:tkeɪs] n чемода́н

**suite** [swi:t] n (of rooms)
апартаме́нты mpl; ( furniture):
**bedroom/dining room ~**
спа́льный/столо́вый гарниту́р

**sulfur** ['sʌlfər] n (US) = **sulphur**

**sulk** [sʌlk] vi зло́бствовать (impf),
ду́ться (impf) (разг)

**sullen** ['sʌlən] adj угрю́мый

**sulphur** ['sʌlfər] (US **sulfur**) n се́ра

**sultana** [sʌl'tɑ:nə] n кишми́ш

**sultry** ['sʌltrɪ] adj (weather)
ду́шный

**sum** [sʌm] n (calculation)
арифме́тика, вычисле́ние;
(amount) су́мма; ~ **up** vt (describe)
сумми́ровать (impf/pf) ♦ vi
подводи́ть (подвести́ pf) ито́г

**summarize** ['sʌməraɪz] vt
сумми́ровать (impf/pf)

**summary** ['sʌmərɪ] n (of essay etc)
кра́ткое изложе́ние

**summer** ['sʌmər] n ле́то ♦ adj
ле́тний; **in ~** ле́том; ~**time** n
(season) ле́то, ле́тняя пора́

**summit** ['sʌmɪt] n (of mountain)
верши́на, пик; (also: ~ **meeting**)
встре́ча на вы́сшем у́ровне,
са́ммит

**sumptuous** ['sʌmptjuəs] adj
роско́шный

**sun** [sʌn] n со́лнце; ~**bathe** vi
загора́ть (impf); ~**burn** n
со́лнечный ожо́г

**Sunday** ['sʌndɪ] n воскресе́нье

**sunflower** ['sʌnflauər] n (BOT)
подсо́лнечник

**sung** [sʌŋ] pp of **sing**

**sunglasses** ['sʌnglɑ:sɪz] npl
солнцезащи́тные очки́ pl

**sunk** [sʌŋk] pp of **sink**

**sun**: ~**light** n со́лнечный свет;
~**ny** adj (weather, place)
со́лнечный; ~**rise** n восхо́д
(со́лнца); ~**set** n зака́т, захо́д
(со́лнца); ~**shine** n со́лнечный
свет; **in the ~shine** на со́лнце;

~**stroke** n со́лнечный уда́р; ~**tan**
n зага́р

**super** ['su:pər] adj мирово́й,
потряса́ющий

**superb** [su:'pə:b] adj
превосхо́дный, великоле́пный

**superficial** [su:pə'fɪʃəl] adj
пове́рхностный; (wound) лёгкий

**superfluous** [su:'pə:fluəs] adj
изли́шний, ненужный

**superintendent** [su:pərɪn'tɛndənt]
n (POLICE) нача́льник

**superior** [su:'pɪərɪər] adj (better)
лу́чший; (more senior)
вышестоя́щий; (smug)
высокоме́рный ♦ n нача́льник;
~**ity** [supɪərɪ'ɔrɪtɪ] n
превосхо́дство

**supermarket** ['su:pəmɑ:kɪt] n
суперма́ркет, универса́м

**supernatural** [su:pə'nætʃərəl] adj
сверхъесте́ственный

**superpower** ['su:pəpauər] n (POL)
вели́кая держа́ва, сверхдержа́ва

**superstition** [su:pə'stɪʃən] n
суеве́рие

**superstitious** [su:pə'stɪʃəs] adj
суеве́рный

**supervise** ['su:pəvaɪz] vt (person,
activity) кури́ровать (impf);
(dissertation) руководи́ть (impf)

**supervision** [su:pə'vɪʒən] n
руково́дство, надзо́р

**supervisor** ['su:pəvaɪzər] n (of
workers) нача́льник; (SCOL)
нау́чный(ая)
руководи́тель(ница) m(f)

**supper** ['sʌpər] n у́жин

**supple** ['sʌpl] adj (person, body)
ги́бкий; (leather) упру́гий

**supplement** ['sʌplɪmənt] n (of
vitamins) доба́вка, дополне́ние;
(of book, newspaper etc)
приложе́ние ♦ vt добавля́ть
(доба́вить pf) к +dat; ~**ary**
[sʌplɪ'mɛntərɪ] adj (question)

дополни́тельный

**supplier** [sə'plaɪəʳ] n поставщи́к

**supply** [sə'plaɪ] n (see vt) поста́вка; снабже́ние; (stock) запа́с ♦ vt ( goods) поставля́ть (поста́вить pf); ( gas) снабжа́ть (снабди́ть pf); **to ~ sb/sth with sth** (see vt) поставля́ть (поста́вить pf) что-н кому́-н/чему́-н; снабжа́ть (снабди́ть pf) кого́-н/что-н чем-н; **supplies** npl ( food) запа́сы mpl продово́льствия

**support** [sə'pɔːt] n (moral, financial etc) подде́ржка; (TECH) опо́ра ♦ vt (morally) подде́рживать (поддержа́ть pf); (financially: family etc) содержа́ть (impf); ( football team etc) боле́ть (impf) за +acc; (hold up) подде́рживать (impf); (theory etc) подтвержда́ть (подтверди́ть pf); **~er** n (POL etc) сторо́нник(ица); (SPORT) боле́льщик(ица); **~ive** adj: **to be ~ive of sb** подде́рживать (поддержа́ть pf) кого́-н

**suppose** [sə'pəuz] vt полага́ть (impf), предполага́ть (предположи́ть pf); **he was ~d to do it** (duty) он до́лжен был э́то сде́лать; **~dly** [sə'pəuzɪdlɪ] adv я́кобы

**supposing** [sə'pəuzɪŋ] conj предположи́м, допу́стим

**suppress** [sə'prɛs] vt (revolt) подавля́ть (подави́ть pf); **~ion** [sə'prɛʃən] n подавле́ние

**supremacy** [su'prɛməsɪ] n госпо́дство, превосхо́дство

**supreme** [su'priːm] adj (in titles) Верхо́вный; (effort, achievement) велича́йший

**surcharge** ['səːtʃɑːdʒ] n дополни́тельный сбор

**sure** [ʃuəʳ] adj (certain) уве́ренный; (reliable) ве́рный; **to make ~ of sth/that** удостоверя́ться

(удостове́риться pf) в чём-н/, что; **~!** (okay) коне́чно!; **~ enough** и пра́вда or впра́вду; **~ly** adv (certainly) наверняка́

**surf** [səːf] vt (COMPUT) ла́зить (impf) по +dat

**surface** ['səːfɪs] n пове́рхность f ♦ vi всплыва́ть (всплы́ть pf)

**surfing** ['səːfɪŋ] n сёрфинг

**surge** [səːdʒ] n (increase) рост; (fig: of emotion) прили́в

**surgeon** ['səːdʒən] n (MED) хиру́рг

**surgery** ['səːdʒərɪ] n (treatment) хирурги́я, хирурги́ческое вмеша́тельство; (BRIT: room) кабине́т; (: time) приём; **to undergo ~** переноси́ть (перенести́ pf) опера́цию

**surgical** ['səːdʒɪkl] adj хирурги́ческий

**surly** ['səːlɪ] adj угрю́мый

**surname** ['səːneɪm] n фами́лия

**surpass** [səː'pɑːs] vt (person, thing) превосходи́ть (превзойти́ pf)

**surplus** ['səːpləs] n избы́ток, изли́шек; (of trade, payments) акти́вное са́льдо nt ind ♦ adj (stock, grain) избы́точный

**surprise** [sə'praɪz] n удивле́ние; (unexpected event) неожи́данность f ♦ vt (astonish) удивля́ть (удиви́ть pf); (catch unawares) застава́ть (заста́ть pf) враспло́х

**surprising** [sə'praɪzɪŋ] adj (situation, announcement) неожи́данный; **~ly** adv удиви́тельно

**surrender** [sə'rɛndəʳ] n сда́ча, капитуля́ция ♦ vi (army, hijackers etc) сдава́ться (сда́ться pf)

**surround** [sə'raund] vt (subj: walls, hedge etc) окружа́ть (impf); (MIL, POLICE etc) окружа́ть (окружи́ть pf); **~ing** adj (countryside) окружа́ющий, окре́стный; **~ings** npl (place) окре́стности fpl; (conditions) окруже́ние ntsg

**surveillance** [sə'veɪləns] n
наблюде́ние
**survey** vb [sə:'veɪ] n ['sə:veɪ] vt
(scene, work etc) осма́тривать
(осмотре́ть pf) ♦ n (of land)
геодези́ческая съёмка; (of house)
инспе́кция; (of habits etc) обзо́р;
**~or** [sə'veɪə<sup>r</sup>] n (of land)
геодези́ст; (of house) инспе́ктор
**survival** [sə'vaɪvl] n выжива́ние
**survive** [sə'vaɪv] vi выжива́ть
(вы́жить pf), уцеле́ть (pf); (custom
etc) сохраня́ться (сохрани́ться
pf) ♦ vt (person) пережива́ть
(пережи́ть pf); (illness)
переноси́ть (перенести́ pf)
**survivor** [sə'vaɪvə<sup>r</sup>] n (of illness,
accident) вы́живший(ая) m(f) adj
**susceptible** [sə'sɛptəbl] adj: ~ (to)
(injury) подве́рженный (+dat); **to
be ~ to flattery** легко́
поддава́ться (impf) на лесть
**suspect** vb [səs'pɛkt] n, adj ['sʌspɛkt]
vt подозрева́ть (impf) ♦ n
подозрева́емый(ая) m(f)adj ♦ adj
подозри́тельный
**suspend** [səs'pɛnd] vt (delay)
приостана́вливать
(приостанови́ть pf); (stop)
прерыва́ть (прерва́ть pf); (from
employment) отстраня́ть
(отстрани́ть pf); **~ers** npl (BRIT)
подвя́зки fpl; (US) подтя́жки fpl
**suspense** [səs'pɛns] n трево́га,
напряже́ние; **to keep sb in ~**
держа́ть (impf) кого́-н во
взве́шенном состоя́нии
**suspension** [səs'pɛnʃən] n (from
job, team) отстране́ние; (AUT)
амортиза́тор; (of payment)
приостановле́ние
**suspicion** [səs'pɪʃən] n подозре́ние
**suspicious** [səs'pɪʃəs] adj
подозри́тельный
**sustain** [səs'teɪn] vt подде́рживать
(поддержа́ть pf); (losses) нести́

(понести́ pf); (injury) получа́ть
(получи́ть pf); **~able** adj
(development, progress)
стаби́льный, усто́йчивый; **~ed**
adj неослабева́ющий; (interest)
неосла́бный
**swagger** ['swægə<sup>r</sup>] vi ше́ствовать
(impf)
**swallow** ['swɔləu] n (ZOOL)
ла́сточка ♦ vt (food, pills) глота́ть
(проглоти́ть pf); (fig) подавля́ть
(подави́ть pf)
**swam** [swæm] pt of **swim**
**swamp** [swɔmp] n топь f ♦ vt (with
water) залива́ть (зали́ть pf); (fig:
person) зава́ливать (завали́ть pf)
**swan** [swɔn] n ле́бедь m
**swap** [swɔp] n обме́н ♦ vt: **to ~
(for)** (exchange (for)) меня́ть
(обменя́ть pf) (на +acc) (replace
(with)) меня́ть (поменя́ть pf) (на
+acc)
**swarm** [swɔ:m] n (of bees) рой; (of
people) тьма
**sway** [sweɪ] vi кача́ться (качну́ться
pf) ♦ vt: **to be ~ed by** поддава́ться
(подда́ться pf) на +acc
**swear** [swɛə<sup>r</sup>] (pt **swore**, pp
**sworn**) vi (curse) скверносло́вить
(impf), руга́ться (вы́ругаться pf)
♦ vt кля́сться (покля́сться pf)
**sweat** [swɛt] n пот ♦ vi поте́ть
(вспоте́ть pf); **~er** n сви́тер;
**~shirt** n спорти́вный сви́тер; **~y**
adj (clothes) пропоте́вший; (hands)
по́тный
**swede** [swi:d] n (BRIT) брю́ква
**Sweden** ['swi:dn] n Шве́ция
**Swedish** ['swi:dɪʃ] adj шве́дский;
**the ~** npl шве́ды
**sweep** [swi:p] (pt, pp **swept**) vt
(with brush) мести́ or подмета́ть
(подмести́ pf); (with arm)
сма́хивать (смахну́ть pf); (subj:
current) сноси́ть (снести́ pf),
смыва́ть (смыть pf) ♦ vi (wind)

бушева́ть (impf); ~**ing** adj (gesture)
широ́кий; (statement) огу́льный
**sweet** [swi:t] n (candy) конфе́та;
(BRIT : CULIN) сла́дкое nt adj no pl,
сла́дости fpl ♦ adj сла́дкий; (kind,
attractive) ми́лый; ~ **corn** n
кукуру́за; ~**ness** n сла́дость f;
(kindness) любе́зность f
**swell** [swɛl] (pt ~**ed**, pp **swollen** or
~**ed**) n (of sea) волне́ние ♦ adj
(US : inf) мирово́й ♦ vi (numbers)
расти́ (вы́расти pf); (also: ~ **up**:
face, ankle etc) опуха́ть (опу́хнуть
pf), вздува́ться (вздуться pf);
~**ing** n (MED) о́пухоль f, вздутие
**sweltering** ['swɛltərɪŋ] adj ду́шный
**swept** [swɛpt] pt, pp of **sweep**
**swift** [swɪft] adj стреми́тельный;
~**ly** adv стреми́тельно
**swim** [swɪm] (pt **swam**, pp **swum**)
vi пла́вать/плыть (impf); (as sport)
пла́вать (impf); (head) идти́
(пойти́ pf) кру́гом; (room) плыть
(поплы́ть pf) ♦ vt переплыва́ть
(переплы́ть pf); (a length)
проплыва́ть (проплы́ть pf); ~**mer**
n пловец(вчи́ха); ~**ming** n
пла́вание; ~**ming costume** n
(BRIT) купа́льный костю́м; ~**ming**
**pool** n пла́вательный бассе́йн;
~**ming trunks** npl пла́вки pl;
~**suit** n купа́льник
**swing** [swɪŋ] (pt, pp **swung**) n (in
playground) каче́ли pl; (change: in
opinions etc) крен, поворо́т ♦ vt
(arms) разма́хивать (impf) +instr;
(legs) болта́ть (impf) +instr; (also: ~
**round**: vehicle etc) развора́чивать
(разверну́ть pf) ♦ vi кача́ться
(impf); (also: ~ **round**: vehicle etc)
развора́чиваться (разверну́ться
pf); **to be in full** ~ (party etc) быть
(impf) в по́лном разга́ре
**swirl** [swə:l] vi кружи́ться (impf)
**Swiss** [swɪs] adj швейца́рский
**switch** [swɪtʃ] n (for light, radio etc)

выключа́тель m; (change)
переключе́ние ♦ vt (change)
переключа́ть (переключи́ть pf); ~
**off** vt выключа́ть (вы́ключить pf);
~ **on** vt включа́ть (включи́ть pf);
~**board** n (TEL) коммута́тор
**Switzerland** ['swɪtsələnd] n
Швейца́рия
**swivel** ['swɪvl] vi (also: ~ **round**)
повора́чиваться (impf)
**swollen** ['swəulən] pp of **swell**
**sword** [sɔ:d] n меч
**swore** [swɔ:r] pt of **swear**
**sworn** [swɔ:n] pp of **swear** ♦ adj
(statement, evidence) да́нный под
прися́гой; (enemy) закля́тый
**swum** [swʌm] pp of **swim**
**swung** [swʌŋ] pt, pp of **swing**
**sycamore** ['sɪkəmɔ:r] n я́вор
**syllable** ['sɪləbl] n слог
**syllabus** ['sɪləbəs] n (уче́бная)
програ́мма
**symbol** ['sɪmbl] n (sign) знак;
(representation) си́мвол; ~**ic(al)**
[sɪm'bɔlɪk(l)] adj символи́ческий
**symmetrical** [sɪ'mɛtrɪkl] adj
симметри́чный
**symmetry** ['sɪmɪtrɪ] n симме́трия
**sympathetic** [sɪmpə'θɛtɪk] adj
(person) уча́стливый; (remark,
opinion) сочу́вственный; (likeable:
character) прия́тный,
симпати́чный; **to be ~ to(wards)**
(supportive of ) сочу́вствовать
(impf) +dat
**sympathize** ['sɪmpəθaɪz] vi: **to ~**
**with** сочу́вствовать (impf) +dat
**sympathy** ['sɪmpəθɪ] n (pity)
сочу́вствие, уча́стие; **with our**
**deepest ~** с глубоча́йшими
соболе́знованиями; **to come out**
**in** ~ (workers) бастова́ть (impf) в
знак солида́рности
**symphony** ['sɪmfənɪ] n симфо́ния
**symptom** ['sɪmptəm] n симпто́м
**synagogue** ['sɪnəgɔg] n синаго́га

**syndicate** ['sɪndɪkɪt] n (of people, businesses) синдика́т
**syndrome** ['sɪndrəum] n синдро́м
**synonym** ['sɪnənɪm] n сино́ним
**synthetic** [sɪn'θetɪk] adj (materials) синтети́ческий, иску́сственный
**syringe** ['sɪrɪndʒ] n шприц
**syrup** ['sɪrəp] n (juice) сиро́п; (also: **golden ~**) (све́тлая or жёлтая) па́тока
**system** ['sɪstəm] n систе́ма; **~atic** [sɪstə'mætɪk] adj системати́ческий

# T, t

**ta** [tɑː] excl (BRIT: inf) спаси́бо
**table** ['teɪbl] n (furniture) стол; (MATH, CHEM etc) табли́ца; **to lay** or **set the ~** накрыва́ть (накры́ть pf) на стол; **~ of contents** оглавле́ние; **~cloth** n ска́терть f; **~ lamp** n насто́льная ла́мпа; **~mat** n подста́вка (под столо́вые прибо́ры); **~spoon** n столо́вая ло́жка; **~ tennis** n насто́льный те́ннис
**tabloid** ['tæblɔɪd] n табло́ид, малоформа́тная газе́та

> **tabloid** - табло́ид. Так называ́ют популя́рные малоформа́тные газе́ты. Они́ содержа́т мно́го фотогра́фий, больши́е заголо́вки и коро́ткие статьи́. Табло́иды освеща́ют сканда́льные исто́рии, жизнь звёзд шо́у-би́знеса и спорти́вные но́вости.

**taboo** [tə'buː] n табу́ nt ind ♦ adj запрещённый
**tacit** ['tæsɪt] adj молчали́вый
**tack** [tæk] n (nail) гвоздь m с широ́кой шля́пкой ♦ vt (nail) прибива́ть (приби́ть pf); (stitch)

мета́ть (смета́ть pf)
**tackle** ['tækl] n (for fishing etc) снасть f; (for lifting) сло́жный блок; (SPORT) блокиро́вка ♦ vt (difficulty) справля́ться (спра́виться pf) с +instr; (fight, challenge) схвати́ться (pf) с +instr; (SPORT) блоки́ровать (impf/pf)
**tacky** ['tækɪ] adj (sticky) ли́пкий; (pej: cheap) дешёвый
**tact** [tækt] n такт, такти́чность f; **~ful** adj такти́чный
**tactical** ['tæktɪkl] adj такти́ческий
**tactics** ['tæktɪks] npl та́ктика fsg
**tactless** ['tæktlɪs] adj беста́ктный
**tag** [tæg] n (label) этике́тка, ярлы́к
**tail** [teɪl] n (of animal, plane) хвост; (of shirt) коне́ц; (of coat) пола́ ♦ vt сади́ться (сесть pf) на хвост +dat; **~s** npl (suit) фрак msg; **~back** n (BRIT: AUT) хвост
**tailor** ['teɪləʳ] n (мужско́й) портно́й m adj
**take** [teɪk] (pt **took**, pp **~n**) vt брать (взять pf); (photo, measures) снима́ть (снять pf); (shower, decision, drug) принима́ть (приня́ть pf); (notes) де́лать (сде́лать pf); (grab: sb's arm etc) хвата́ть (схвати́ть pf); (require: courage, time) тре́бовать (потре́бовать pf); (tolerate: pain etc) переноси́ть (перенести́ pf); (hold: passengers etc) вмеща́ть (вмести́ть pf); (on foot: person) отводи́ть (отвести́ pf); (: thing) относи́ть (отнести́ pf); (by transport: person, thing) отвози́ть (отвезти́ pf); (exam) сдава́ть (сдать pf); **to ~ sth from** (drawer etc) вынима́ть (вы́нуть pf) что-н из +gen; (steal from) брать (взять pf) что-н у +gen; **I ~ it that** ... как я понима́ю, ...; **~ apart** vt разбира́ть (разобра́ть pf); **~ away** vt (remove) убира́ть

(убра́ть pf); (carry off ) забира́ть (забра́ть pf); (MATH) отнима́ть (отня́ть pf); ~ **back** vt (return: thing) относи́ть (отнести́ pf) обра́тно; (: person) отводи́ть (отвести́ pf) обра́тно; (one's words) брать (взять pf) наза́д; ~ **down** vt (building) сноси́ть (снести́ pf); (note) запи́сывать (записа́ть pf); ~ **in** vt (deceive) обма́нывать (обману́ть pf); (understand) воспринима́ть (восприня́ть pf); (lodger, orphan) брать (взять pf); ~ **off** vi (AVIAT) взлета́ть (взлете́ть pf) ♦ vt (remove) снима́ть (снять pf); ~ **on** vt (work, employee) брать (взять pf); (opponent) сража́ться (срази́ться pf) с +instr; ~ **out** vt (invite) води́ть/вести́ (повести́ pf); (remove) вынима́ть (вы́нуть pf); **to** ~ **sth out of** (drawer, pocket etc) вынима́ть (вы́нуть pf) что-н из +gen; **don't** ~ **your anger out on me!** не вымеща́й свой гнев на мне!; ~ **over** vt (business) поглоща́ть (поглоти́ть pf); (country) захва́тывать (захвати́ть pf) власть в +prp ♦ vi: **to** ~ **over from sb** сменя́ть (смени́ть pf) кого́-н; ~ **to** vt fus: **she took to him at once** он ей сра́зу понра́вился; ~ **up** vt (hobby) заня́ться (pf) +instr; (job) бра́ться (взя́ться pf) за +acc; (idea, story) подхва́тывать (подхвати́ть pf); (time, space) занима́ть (заня́ть pf); **I'll** ~ **you up on that!** ловлю́ Вас на сло́ве!; ~**away** n (BRIT: food) еда́ на вы́нос; ~**off** n (AVIAT) взлёт; ~**over** n (COMM) поглоще́ние

**takings** ['teɪkɪŋz] npl (COMM) вы́ручка fsg

**tale** [teɪl] n расска́з; **to tell** ~**s** (fig) я́бедничать (ная́бедничать pf)

**talent** ['tælnt] n тала́нт; ~**ed** adj тала́нтливый

**talk** [tɔ:k] n (speech) докла́д; (conversation, interview) бесе́да, разгово́р; (gossip) разгово́ры mpl ♦ vi (speak) говори́ть (impf); (to sb) разгова́ривать (impf); ~**s** npl (POL etc) перегово́ры pl; **to** ~ **about** говори́ть (поговори́ть pf) or разгова́ривать (impf) о +prp; **to** ~ **sb into doing** угова́ривать (уговори́ть pf) кого́-н +infin; **to** ~ **sb out of sth** отгова́ривать (отговори́ть pf) кого́-н от чего́-н; **to** ~ **shop** говори́ть (impf) о дела́х; ~ **over** vt (problem) обгова́ривать (обговори́ть pf); ~**ative** adj разгово́рчивый, болтли́вый

**tall** [tɔ:l] adj высо́кий; **he is 6 feet** ~ его́ рост - 6 фу́тов

**tally** ['tælɪ] n счёт

**tambourine** [tæmbə'ri:n] n (MUS) тамбури́н, бу́бен

**tame** [teɪm] adj ручно́й; (fig) вя́лый

**tampon** ['tæmpɔn] n тампо́н

**tan** [tæn] n (also: **sun~**) зага́р

**tandem** ['tændəm] n (cycle) танде́м; **in** ~ (together) совме́стно, вме́сте

**tang** [tæŋ] n си́льный за́пах

**tangerine** [tændʒə'ri:n] n мандари́н

**tangible** ['tændʒɪbl] adj (benefits) ощути́мый, осяза́емый; (proof ) реа́льный

**tank** [tæŋk] n (water tank) бак; (: large) цисте́рна; (for fish) аква́риум; (MIL) танк

**tanker** ['tæŋkər] n (ship) та́нкер; (truck, RAIL) цисте́рна

**tanned** [tænd] adj загоре́лый

**tantrum** ['tæntrəm] n исте́рика

**tap** [tæp] n (водопрово́дный) кран; (gentle blow) стук ♦ vt (hit) стуча́ть (постуча́ть *pf*) по +*dat*; (*resources*) испо́льзовать (*impf/pf*); (*telephone, conversation*) прослу́шивать (*impf*)

**tape** [teɪp] *n* (*also:* **magnetic ~**) (магни́тная) плёнка; (*cassette*) кассе́та; (*sticky tape*) кле́йкая ле́нта ♦ *vt* (*record*) запи́сывать (записа́ть *pf*); (*stick*) закле́ивать (закле́ить *pf*) кле́йкой ле́нтой

**taper** [ˈteɪpər] *vi* (*narrow*) сужа́ться (су́зиться *pf*)

**tape recorder** *n* магнитофо́н

**tapestry** [ˈtæpɪstrɪ] *n* (*object*) гобеле́н

**tar** [tɑː] *n* дёготь *m*

**tarantula** [təˈræntjulə] *n* тара́нтул

**target** [ˈtɑːgɪt] *n* цель *f*

**tariff** [ˈtærɪf] *n* (*on goods*) тари́ф; (*BRIT: in hotels etc*) прейскура́нт

**tarmac** [ˈtɑːmæk] *n* (*BRIT: on road*) асфа́льт

**tarot** [ˈtærəu] *adj*: **~ cards** гада́льные ка́рты *fpl*

**tart** [tɑːt] *n* (*CULIN, large*) пиро́г ♦ *adj* (*flavour*) те́рпкий

**tartan** [ˈtɑːtn] *adj* (*rug, scarf etc*) кле́тчатый

**tartar** [ˈtɑːtər] *n* (*on teeth*) зубно́й ка́мень *m*

**task** [tɑːsk] *n* зада́ча; **to take sb to ~** отчи́тывать (отчита́ть *pf*) кого́-н

**taste** [teɪst] *n* вкус; (*sample*) про́ба; (*fig: glimpse, idea*) представле́ние ♦ *vt* про́бовать (попро́бовать *pf*) ♦ *vi*: **to ~ of** *or* **like** име́ть (*impf*) вкус +*gen*; **you can ~ the garlic (in the dish)** (в блю́де) чу́вствуется чесно́к; **in bad/good ~** в дурно́м/ хоро́шем вку́се; **~ful** *adj* элега́нтный; **~less** *adj* безвку́сный

**tasty** [ˈteɪstɪ] *adj* (*food*) вку́сный

**tatters** [ˈtætəz] *npl*: **in ~** (*clothes*) изо́рванный в кло́чья

**tattoo** [təˈtuː] *n* (*on skin*) татуиро́вка

**taught** [tɔːt] *pt, pp of* **teach**

**taunt** [tɔːnt] *n* издева́тельство ♦ *vt* (*person*) издева́ться (*impf*) над +*instr*

**Taurus** [ˈtɔːrəs] *n* Теле́ц

**taut** [tɔːt] *adj* (*thread etc*) туго́й; (*skin*) упру́гий

**tax** [tæks] *n* нало́г ♦ *vt* (*earnings, goods etc*) облага́ть (обложи́ть *pf*) нало́гом; (*fig: memory, patience*) напряга́ть (напря́чь *pf*); **~ation** [tækˈseɪʃən] *n* (*system*) налогообложе́ние; (*money paid*) разме́р нало́га; **~-free** *adj* (*goods, services*) не облага́емый нало́гом

**taxi** [ˈtæksɪ] *n* такси́ *nt ind*

**taxpayer** [ˈtækspeɪər] *n* налогоплате́льщик(щица)

**TB** *n abbr* = **tuberculosis**

**tea** [tiː] *n* чай; (*BRIT: meal*) у́жин; **high ~** (*BRIT*) (по́здний) обе́д

**teach** [tiːtʃ] (*pt, pp* **taught**) *vi* преподава́ть (*impf*) ♦ *vt*: **to ~ sb sth, ~ sth to sb** учи́ть (научи́ть *pf*) кого́-н чему́-н; (*in school*) преподава́ть (*impf*) что-н кому́-н; **~er** *n* учи́тель(ница) *m(f)*; **~ing** *n* (*work*) преподава́ние

**teak** [tiːk] *n* тик

**team** [tiːm] *n* (*of people*) кома́нда; **~work** *n* коллекти́вная рабо́та

**teapot** [ˈtiːpɔt] *n* (зава́рочный) ча́йник

**tear**[1] [tɛər] (*pt* **tore**, *pp* **torn**) *n* дыра́, ды́рка ♦ *vt* (*rip*) рвать (порва́ть *pf*) ♦ *vi* (*rip*) рва́ться (порва́ться *pf*)

**tear**[2] [tɪər] *n* слеза́; **in ~s** в слеза́х; **~ful** *adj* запла́канный

**tease** [tiːz] *vt* дразни́ть (*impf*)

**teaspoon** [ˈtiːspuːn] *n* ча́йная ло́жка

**teatime** [ˈtiːtaɪm] *n* у́жин

**tea towel** *n* (*BRIT*) посу́дное

полоте́нце

**technical** ['tɛknɪkl] adj (terms, advances) техни́ческий; **~ly** adv (strictly speaking) форма́льно; (regarding technique) с техни́ческой то́чки зре́ния

**technician** [tɛk'nɪʃən] n те́хник

**technique** [tɛk'niːk] n те́хника

**technological** [tɛknə'lɔdʒɪkl] adj техни́ческий

**technology** [tɛk'nɔlədʒɪ] n те́хника; (in particular field) техноло́гия

**teddy (bear)** ['tɛdɪ(-)] n (плю́шевый) ми́шка

**tedious** ['tiːdɪəs] adj ну́дный

**tee** [tiː] n подста́вка для мяча́ (в го́льфе)

**teenage** ['tiːneɪdʒ] adj (problems) подро́стковый; (fashion) тине́йджеровский; **~ children** подро́стки mpl; **~r** n подро́сток, тине́йджер

**teens** [tiːnz] npl: **to be in one's ~** быть (impf) в подростко́вом во́зрасте

**teeth** [tiːθ] npl of **tooth**

**teetotal** ['tiː'təutl] adj непью́щий, тре́звый

**telecommunications** ['tɛlɪ-kəmjuːnɪ'keɪʃənz] n телекоммуника́ции fpl

**teleconferencing** ['tɛlɪkɔnfərənsɪŋ] n телеконфере́нция

**telegram** ['tɛlɪɡræm] n телегра́мма

**telegraph** ['tɛlɪɡrɑːf] n телегра́ф

**telepathy** [tə'lɛpəθɪ] n телепа́тия

**telephone** ['tɛlɪfəun] n телефо́н ♦ vt (person) звони́ть (позвони́ть pf) +dat; **he is on the ~** (talking) он говори́т по телефо́ну; **are you on the ~?** (possessing phone) у Вас есть телефо́н?; **~ call** n телефо́нный звоно́к; **there is a ~ call for Peter** Пи́тера про́сят к телефо́ну; **~ directory** n

телефо́нный спра́вочник; **~ number** n но́мер телефо́на, телефо́н (разг)

**telesales** ['tɛlɪseɪlz] n телефо́нная рекла́ма

**telescope** ['tɛlɪskəup] n телеско́п

**television** ['tɛlɪvɪʒən] n телеви́дение; (set) телеви́зор; **on ~** по телеви́дению

**telex** ['tɛlɛks] n те́лекс

**tell** [tɛl] (pt, pp **told**) vt (say) говори́ть (сказа́ть pf); (relate) расска́зывать (рассказа́ть pf); (distinguish): **to ~ sth from** отлича́ть (отличи́ть pf) что-н от +gen ♦ vi (have an effect): **to ~ (on)** ска́зываться (сказа́ться pf) (на +prp); **to ~ sb to do** говори́ть (сказа́ть pf) кому́-н +infin; **~ off** vt: **to ~ sb off** отчи́тывать (отчита́ть pf) кого́-н; **~er** n (in bank) касси́р; **~ing** adj (remark, detail) показа́тельный

**telly** ['tɛlɪ] n abbr (BRIT : inf = **television**) те́лик

**temper** ['tɛmpəʳ] n (nature) нрав; (mood) настрое́ние; (fit of anger) гнев; **to be in a ~** быть (impf) в раздражённом состоя́нии; **to lose one's ~** выходи́ть (вы́йти pf) из себя́

**temperament** ['tɛmprəmənt] n темпера́мент; **~al** [tɛmprə'mɛntl] adj темпера́ментный; (fig) капри́зный

**temperate** ['tɛmprət] adj уме́ренный

**temperature** ['tɛmprətʃəʳ] n температу́ра; **he has** or **is running a ~** у него́ температу́ра, он температу́рит (разг)

**tempi** ['tɛmpiː] npl of **tempo**

**temple** ['tɛmpl] n (REL) храм; (ANAT) висо́к

**tempo** ['tɛmpəu] (pl **~s** or **tempi**) n темп

**temporarily** [ˈtɛmpərərɪlɪ] *adv*
временно

**temporary** [ˈtɛmpərərɪ] *adj*
временный

**tempt** [tɛmpt] *vt* соблазнять
(соблазнить *pf*), искушать *(impf)*;
**to ~ sb into doing** соблазнять
(соблазнить *pf*) кого-н *+infin*;
**~ation** [tɛmpˈteɪʃən] *n* соблазн,
искушение; **~ing** *adj (offer)*
соблазнительный

**ten** [tɛn] *n* десять

**tenacity** [təˈnæsɪtɪ] *n* упорство

**tenancy** [ˈtɛnənsɪ] *n (of room, land
etc)* владение на правах аренды;
*(period)* срок аренды *or* найма

**tenant** [ˈtɛnənt] *n*
съёмщик(мщица)

**tend** [tɛnd] *vt (crops, patient)*
ухаживать *(impf)* за *+instr* ♦ *vi*: **to ~
to do** иметь *(impf)* склонность
*+infin*

**tendency** [ˈtɛndənsɪ] *n (habit)*
склонность *f*; *(trend)* тенденция

**tender** [ˈtɛndər] *adj* нежный; *(sore)*
чувствительный ♦ *n (COMM, offer)*
предложение ♦ *vt (apology)*
приносить (принести *pf*); **legal ~**
*(money)* законное платёжное
средство; **to ~ one's resignation**
подавать (подать *pf*) в отставку;
**~ness** *n* нежность *f*

**tendon** [ˈtɛndən] *n* сухожилие

**tennis** [ˈtɛnɪs] *n* теннис

**tenor** [ˈtɛnər] *n (MUS)* тенор

**tense** [tɛns] *adj* напряжённый

**tension** [ˈtɛnʃən] *n* напряжение

**tent** [tɛnt] *n* палатка

**tentative** [ˈtɛntətɪv] *adj (person,
smile)* осторожный; *(conclusion,
plans)* сдержанный

**tenth** [tɛnθ] *adj* десятый ♦ *n
(fraction)* одна десятая *f adj*

**tenuous** [ˈtɛnjuəs] *adj* слабый

**tepid** [ˈtɛpɪd] *adj (liquid)*
тепловатый

**term** [təːm] *n (expression)* термин;
*(period in power etc)* срок; *(SCOL, in
school)* четверть *f*; *(: at university)*
триместр ♦ *vt (call)* называть
(назвать *pf*); **~s** *npl (conditions)*
условия *ntpl*; **in abstract ~s** в
абстрактных выражениях; **in the
short ~** в ближайшем будущем;
**in the long ~** в перспективе; **to
be on good ~s with sb** быть *(impf)*
в хороших отношениях с кем-н;
**to come to ~s with** примиряться
(примириться *pf*) с *+instr*

**terminal** [ˈtəːmɪnl] *adj*
неизлечимый ♦ *n (ELEC)* клемма,
зажим; *(COMPUT)* терминал; *(also:
air ~)* аэровокзал, терминал;
*(BRIT: also: coach ~)* автобусный
вокзал

**terminate** [ˈtəːmɪneɪt] *vt*
прекращать (прекратить *pf*)

**terminology** [təːmɪˈnɔlədʒɪ] *n*
терминология

**terrace** [ˈtɛrəs] *n* терраса; **the ~s**
*npl (BRIT: standing areas)* трибуны
*fpl*; **~d** *adj (garden)* террасный; **~d
house** дом в ряду примыкающих
друг к другу однотипных домов

**terrain** [tɛˈreɪn] *n* ландшафт

**terrible** [ˈtɛrɪbl] *adj* ужасный

**terribly** [ˈtɛrɪblɪ] *adv* ужасно

**terrific** [təˈrɪfɪk] *adj (thunderstorm,
speed etc)* колоссальный; *(time,
party etc)* потрясающий

**terrify** [ˈtɛrɪfaɪ] *vt* ужасать
(ужаснуть *pf*)

**territorial** [tɛrɪˈtɔːrɪəl] *adj*
территориальный

**territory** [ˈtɛrɪtərɪ] *n* территория;
*(fig)* область *f*

**terror** [ˈtɛrər] *n* ужас; **~ism** *n*
терроризм; **~ist** *n* террорист(ка);
**~ize** *vt* терроризировать *(impf/pf)*

**terse** [təːs] *adj* сжатый, краткий

**test** [tɛst] *n (trial, check)* проверка,
тест; *(of courage etc)* испытание;

(*MED*) ана́лиз; (*CHEM*) о́пыт;
(*SCOL*) контро́льная рабо́та, тест;
(*also*: **driving ~**) экза́мен на
води́тельские права́ ♦ *vt*
проверя́ть (прове́рить *pf*);
(*courage*) испы́тывать (испыта́ть
*pf*); (*MED*) анализи́ровать
(проанализи́ровать *pf*)

**testament** ['testəmənt] *n*: **the Old/
New Testament** Ве́тхий/Но́вый
Заве́т

**testicle** ['testɪkl] *n* яи́чко

**testify** ['testɪfaɪ] *vi* (*LAW*) дава́ть
(дать *pf*) показа́ния; **to ~ to sth**
свиде́тельствовать (*impf*) о чём-н

**testimony** ['testɪmənɪ] *n* (*LAW*)
показа́ние, свиде́тельство; (*clear
proof*): **to be (a) ~ to** явля́ться
(яви́ться *pf*) свиде́тельством
+*gen*

**test tube** *n* проби́рка

**text** [tekst] *n* текст; **~book** *n*
уче́бник

**textiles** ['tekstaɪlz] *npl* (*fabrics*)
тексти́льные изде́лия *ntpl*; (*textile
industry*) тексти́льная
промы́шленность *fsg*

**texture** ['tekstʃər] *n* (*structure*)
строе́ние, структу́ра; (*feel*)
факту́ра

**than** [ðæn] *conj* чем; (*with numerals*)
бо́льше +*gen*, бо́лее +*gen*; **I have
less work ~ you** у меня́ ме́ньше
рабо́ты, чем у Вас; **more ~ once**
не раз; **more ~ three times** бо́лее
*or*бо́льше трёх раз

**thank** [θæŋk] *vt* благодари́ть
(поблагодари́ть *pf*); **~ you (very
much)** (большо́е) спаси́бо; **~
God!** сла́ва Бо́гу!; **~ful** *adj*: **~ful
(for)** благода́рный (за +*acc*);
**~less** *adj* неблагода́рный; **~s** *npl*
благода́рность *fsg* ♦ *excl* спаси́бо;
**many ~s, ~s a lot** большо́е
спаси́бо; **~s to** благодаря́
+*dat*

**that** [ðæt] (*pl* **those**) *adj*
(*demonstrative*) тот (*f* та, *nt* то);
**that man** тот мужчи́на; **which
book would you like? - that one
over there** каку́ю кни́гу Вы
хоти́те? - вон ту; **I like this film
better than that one** мне э́тот
фильм нра́вится бо́льше, чем
тот
♦ *pron* 1 (*demonstrative*) э́то;
**who's/what's that?** кто/что э́то?;
**is that you?** э́то Вы?; **we talked
of this and that** мы говори́ли об
э́том и о том *or* сём; **that's what
he said** вот что он сказа́л; **what
happened after that?** а что
произошло́ по́сле э́того?; **that is
(to say)** то́ есть
2 (*direct object*) кото́рый (*f*
кото́рую, *nt* кото́рое, *pl*
кото́рые); (*indirect object*)
кото́рому (*f* кото́рой, *pl*
кото́рым); (*after prep*: +*acc*)
кото́рый (*f* кото́рую, *nt* кото́рое,
*pl* кото́рые); (: +*gen*) кото́рого (*f*
кото́рой, *pl* кото́рых); (: +*dat*)
кото́рому (*f* кото́рой, *pl*
кото́рым); (: +*instr*) кото́рым (*f*
кото́рой, *pl* кото́рыми); (: +*prp*)
кото́ром (*f* кото́рой, *pl* кото́рых);
**the theory that we discussed**
тео́рия, кото́рую мы обсужда́ли;
**all (that) I have** всё, что у меня́
есть
3 (*of time*) когда́; **the day (that) he
died** день, когда́ он у́мер
♦ *conj* что; (*introducing purpose*)
что́бы; **he thought that I was ill**
он ду́мал, что я был бо́лен; **she
suggested that I phone you** она́
предложи́ла, что́бы я Вам
позвони́л
♦ *adv* (*demonstrative*): **I can't work
that much** я не могу́ так мно́го

работать; **it can't be that bad** не
так уж всё плохо; **the wall's
about that high** стена́ приме́рно
вот тако́й высоты́

**thaw** [θɔ:] n о́ттепель f

KEYWORD

**the** [ði:, ðə] def art 1: **the books/
children are at home** кни́ги/де́ти
до́ма; **the rich and the poor**
бога́тые pl adj и бе́дные pl adj; **to
attempt the impossible** пыта́ться
(попыта́ться pf) сде́лать
невозмо́жное
2 (in titles): **Elizabeth the First**
Елизаве́та Пе́рвая
3 (in comparisons): **the more ... the
more ...** чем бо́льше ..., тем
бо́льше ...; (+adj) чем бо́лее ...,
тем бо́лее ...

**theatre** ['θɪətər] (US **theater**) n
теа́тр; (MED: also: **operating ~**)
операцио́нная f adj
**theatrical** [θɪ'ætrɪkl] adj
театра́льный
**theft** [θeft] n кра́жа
**their** [ðeər] adj их; (referring to
subject of sentence) свой; see also
**my**; **~s** pron их; (referring to subject
of sentence) свой; see also **mine**[1]
**them** [ðem] pron (direct) их;
(indirect) им; (after prep: +gen,
+prp) них; (: +dat) ним; (: +instr)
ни́ми; **a few of ~** не́которые из
них; **give me a few of ~** да́йте
мне не́сколько из них; see also
**me**
**theme** [θi:m] n те́ма
**themselves** [ðəm'selvz] pl pron
(reflexive) себя́; (emphatic) са́ми;
(after prep: +gen) себя́; (: +dat,
+prp) себе́; (: +instr) собо́й;
(alone): **(all) by ~** одни́; **they
shared the money between ~** они́

раздели́ли де́ньги ме́жду собо́й;
see also **myself**
**then** [ðen] adv пото́м; (at that time)
тогда́ ♦ conj (therefore) тогда́ ♦ adj
(at the time) тогда́шний; **from ~
on** с тех пор; **by ~** к тому́
вре́мени; **if ... ~ ...** е́сли ... то ...
**theology** [θɪ'ɔlədʒɪ] n теоло́гия,
богосло́вие
**theoretical** [θɪə'retɪkl] adj
теорети́ческий
**theory** ['θɪərɪ] n тео́рия; **in ~**
теорети́чески
**therapeutic(al)** [θerə'pju:tɪk(l)] adj
терапевти́ческий
**therapist** ['θerəpɪst] n врач
**therapy** ['θerəpɪ] n терапи́я

KEYWORD

**there** [ðeər] adv 1: **there is some
milk in the fridge** в
холоди́льнике есть молоко́;
**there is someone in the room** в
ко́мнате кто́-то есть; **there were
many problems** бы́ло мно́го
пробле́м; **there will be a lot of
people at the concert** на
конце́рте бу́дет мно́го наро́ду;
**there was a book/there were
flowers on the table** на столе́
лежа́ла кни́га/стоя́ли цветы́;
**there has been an accident**
произошла́ ава́рия
2 (referring to place: motion) туда́;
(: position) там; (: closer) тут; **I
agree with you there** тут or в
э́том я с тобо́й согла́сен; **there
you go!** (inf) вот!; **there he is!**
вот он!; **get out of there!** уходи́
отту́да!

**thereabouts** ['ðeərə'bauts] adv
(place) поблизости; (amount)
о́коло э́того
**thereafter** [ðeər'ɑ:ftər] adv с того́
вре́мени

**thereby** ['ðɛəbaɪ] *adv* такѝм о́бразом

**therefore** ['ðɛəfɔː*r*] *adv* поэ́тому

**there's** ['ðɛəz] = **there is, there has**

**thermal** ['θəːml] *adj* (*springs*) горя́чий; (*underwear*) утеплённый

**thermometer** [θə'mɒmɪtə*r*] *n* термо́метр, гра́дусник

**Thermos** ® ['θəːməs] *n* (*also:* ~ **flask**) те́рмос

**these** [ðiːz] *pl adj, pron* э́ти

**thesis** ['θiːsɪs] (*pl* **theses**) *n* (*SCOL*) диссерта́ция

**they** [ðeɪ] *pron* они́; ~ **say that ...** говоря́т, что ...; ~'**d** = **they had, they would**; ~'**ll** = **they shall, they will**; ~'**re** = **they are**; ~'**ve** = **they have**

**thick** [θɪk] *adj* (*in shape*) то́лстый; (*in consistency*) густо́й; (*inf: stupid*) тупо́й ♦ *n*: **in the ~ of the battle** в са́мой гу́ще би́твы; **the wall is 20 cm** ~ толщина́ стены́ - 20 см; ~**en** *vi* (*plot*) усложня́ться (усложни́ться *pf*) ♦ *vt* (*sauce etc*) де́лать (сде́лать *pf*) гу́ще; ~**ness** *n* (*size*) толщина́; ~**-skinned** *adj* (*fig*) толстоко́жий

**thief** [θiːf] (*pl* **thieves**) *n* вор(о́вка)

**thigh** [θaɪ] *n* бедро́

**thimble** ['θɪmbl] *n* напёрсток

**thin** [θɪn] *adj* то́нкий; (*person, animal*) худо́й; (*soup, sauce*) жи́дкий ♦ *vt*: **to ~ (down)** (*sauce, paint*) разбавля́ть (разба́вить *pf*)

**thing** [θɪŋ] *n* вещь *f*; ~**s** *npl* (*belongings*) ве́щи *fpl*; **poor ~** бедня́жка *m/f*; **the best ~ would be to ...** са́мое лу́чшее бы́ло бы +*infin* ...; **how are ~s?** как дела́?

**think** [θɪŋk] (*pt, pp* **thought**) *vt* (*reflect, believe*) ду́мать (*impf*); **to ~ of** (*come up with*) приводи́ть (привести́ *pf*); (*consider*) ду́мать (подумать *pf*) о +*prp*; **what did you ~ of them?** что Вы о них ду́маете?; **to ~ about** ду́мать (подумать *pf*) о +*prp*; **I'll ~ about it** я подумаю об э́том; **I am ~ing of starting a business** я ду́маю нача́ть би́знес; **I ~ so/not** я ду́маю, что да/нет; **to ~ well of sb** ду́мать (*impf*) о ком-н хорошо́; ~ **over** *vt* обду́мывать (обду́мать *pf*); ~ **up** *vt* приду́мывать (приду́мать *pf*)

**thinly** ['θɪnlɪ] *adv* то́нко

**third** [θəːd] *adj* тре́тий ♦ *n* (*fraction*) треть *f*, одна́ тре́тья *f adj*; (*AUT: also:* ~ **gear**) тре́тья ско́рость *f*; (*BRIT : SCOL*) дипло́м тре́тьей сте́пени; ~**ly** *adv* в-тре́тьих; **Third World** *n*: **the Third World** Тре́тий мир

**thirst** [θəːst] *n* жа́жда; ~**y** *adj*: **I am ~y** я хочу́ *or* мне хо́чется пить

**thirteen** [θəː'tiːn] *n* трина́дцать; ~**th** *adj* трина́дцатый

**thirtieth** ['θəːtɪɪθ] *adj* тридца́тый

**thirty** ['θəːtɪ] *n* три́дцать

---

KEYWORD

---

**this** [ðɪs] (*pl* **these**) *adj* (*demonstrative*) э́тот (*f* э́та, *nt* э́то); **this man** э́тот мужчи́на; **which book would you like? - this one please** каку́ю кни́гу Вы хоти́те? - вот э́ту, пожа́луйста

♦ *pron* (*demonstrative*) э́тот (*f* э́та, *nt* э́то); **who/what is this?** кто/что э́то?; **this is where I live** вот здесь я живу́; **this is what he said** вот, что он сказа́л; **this is Mr Brown** э́то ми́стер Бра́ун

♦ *adv* (*demonstrative*): **this high/ long** вот тако́й высоты́/длины́; **the dog was about this big** соба́ка была́ вот така́я больша́я; **we can't stop now we've gone this far** тепе́рь, когда́ мы так

далеко́ зашли́, мы не мо́жем
останови́ться

**thistle** ['θɪsl] n чертополо́х
**thorn** [θɔːn] n шип, колю́чка
**thorough** ['θʌrə] adj (search, wash)
тща́тельный; (knowledge, research)
основа́тельный; (person)
скрупулёзный; **~bred** n
чистокро́вная or чистопоро́дная
ло́шадь f; **~ly** adv по́лностью,
тща́тельно; (very: satisfied)
соверше́нно, вполне́; (: ashamed)
соверше́нно
**those** [ðəuz] pl adj, pron те
**though** [ðəu] conj хотя́ ♦ adv
впро́чем, одна́ко
**thought** [θɔːt] pt, pp of **think** ♦ n
мысль f; (reflection)
размышле́ние; (opinion)
соображе́ние; **~ful** adj (deep in
thought) заду́мчивый; (serious)
проду́манный, глубо́кий;
(considerate) внима́тельный;
**~less** adj безду́мный
**thousand** ['θauzənd] n ты́сяча;
**two ~** две ты́сячи; **five ~** пять
ты́сяч; **~s of** ты́сячи +gen; **~th** adj
ты́сячный
**thrash** [θræʃ] vt поро́ть (вы́пороть
pf); (inf: defeat) громи́ть
(разгроми́ть pf)
**thread** [θred] n (yarn) нить f,
ни́тка; (of screw) резьба́ ♦ vt
(needle) продева́ть (проде́ть pf)
ни́тку в +acc
**threat** [θret] n угро́за; **~en** vi
(storm, danger) грози́ть (impf) ♦ vt:
**to ~en sb with** угрожа́ть (impf) or
грози́ть (пригрози́ть pf) кому́-н
+instr; **to ~en to do** угрожа́ть (impf) or
грози́ть (пригрози́ть pf) +infin
**three** [θriː] n три; **~-dimensional**
adj (object) трёхме́рный; **~-piece
suite** n мя́гкая ме́бель f
**threshold** ['θreʃhəuld] n поро́г

**threw** [θruː] pt of **throw**
**thrifty** ['θrɪftɪ] adj бережли́вый
**thrill** [θrɪl] n (excitement) восто́рг;
(fear) тре́пет ♦ vt приводи́ть
(привести́ pf) в тре́пет,
восхища́ть (восхити́ть pf); **to be
~ed** быть (impf) в восто́рге; **~er** n
три́ллер; **~ing** adj
захва́тывающий
**thrive** [θraɪv] (pt **~d** or **throve**, pp
**~d**) vi процвета́ть (impf); (plant)
разраста́ться (разрасти́сь pf); **to
~ on** процвета́ть (impf) на +prp
**throat** [θrəut] n го́рло; **I have a
sore ~** у меня́ боли́т го́рло
**throes** [θrəuz] npl: **in the ~ of** в
лихора́дке +gen
**throne** [θrəun] n трон
**throng** ['θrɒŋ] n толпа́ ♦ vt
заполня́ть (запо́лнить pf)
**throttle** ['θrɒtl] n (AUT) дро́ссель m
♦ vt души́ть (задуши́ть pf)
**through** [θruː] prep (space) че́рез
+acc; (time) в тече́ние +gen; (by
means of) че́рез +acc,
посре́дством +gen; (because of)
из-за +gen ♦ adj (ticket, train)
прямо́й ♦ adv наскво́зь; **he is
absent ~ illness** он отсу́тствовал
по боле́зни; **to put sb ~ to sb**
(TEL) соединя́ть (соедини́ть pf)
кого́-н с кем-н; **to be ~ with**
поко́нчить (pf) с +instr; **"no ~
road"** (BRIT) "нет сквозно́го
прое́зда"; **~out** prep (place) по
+dat; (time) в тече́ние +gen ♦ adv
везде́, повсю́ду
**throve** [θrəuv] pt of **thrive**
**throw** [θrəu] (pt **threw**, pp **~n**) n
бросо́к ♦ vt (object) броса́ть
(бро́сить pf); (fig: person) сбива́ть
(сбить pf) с то́лку; **to ~ a party**
зака́тывать (закати́ть pf) ве́чер;
**~ away** vt (rubbish) выбра́сывать
(вы́бросить pf); (money) броса́ть
(impf) на ве́тер; **~ off** vt

сбра́сывать (сбро́сить pf); **~ out** vt (rubbish, person) выбра́сывать (вы́бросить pf); (idea) отверга́ть (отве́ргнуть pf); **~ up** vi (vomit): **he threw up** его́ вы́рвало; **~-in** n вбра́сывание

**thrush** [θrʌʃ] n (ZOOL) дрозд

**thrust** [θrʌst] (pt, pp ~) n (TECH) дви́жущая си́ла ♦ vt толка́ть (толкну́ть pf)

**thud** [θʌd] n глухо́й стук

**thug** [θʌɡ] n (criminal) хулига́н

**thumb** [θʌm] n (ANAT) большо́й па́лец (ки́сти) ♦ vt: **to ~ a lift** (inf) голосова́ть (impf) (на доро́ге)

**thump** [θʌmp] n (blow) уда́р; (sound) глухо́й стук ♦ vt (person) сту́кнуть (pf) ♦ vi (heart etc) стуча́ть (impf)

**thunder** ['θʌndər] n гром; **~storm** n гроза́

**Thursday** ['θəːzdɪ] n четве́рг

**thus** [ðʌs] adv ита́к, таки́м о́бразом

**thwart** [θwɔːt] vt (person) чини́ть (impf) препя́тствия +dat; (plans) расстра́ивать (расстро́ить pf)

**thyme** [taɪm] n тимья́н, чабре́ц

**thyroid** ['θaɪrɔɪd] n (also: **~ gland**) щитови́дная железа́

**tick** [tɪk] n (of clock) ти́канье; (mark) га́лочка, пти́чка; (ZOOL) клещ ♦ vi (clock) ти́кать (impf) ♦ vt отмеча́ть (отме́тить pf) га́лочкой; **in a ~** (BRIT: inf) ми́гом

**ticket** ['tɪkɪt] n биле́т; (price tag) этике́тка; (also: **parking ~**) штраф за наруше́ние пра́вил парко́вания

**tickle** ['tɪkl] vt щекота́ть (пощекота́ть pf) ♦ vi щекота́ть (impf)

**ticklish** ['tɪklɪʃ] adj (problem) щекотли́вый; (person): **to be ~** боя́ться (impf) щеко́тки

**tidal** ['taɪdl] adj (estuary) прили́во-

отли́вный; **~ wave** n прили́вная волна́

**tide** [taɪd] n прили́в и отли́в; (fig: of events) волна́; (of fashion, opinion) направле́ние; **high ~** по́лная вода́, вы́сшая то́чка прили́ва; **low ~** ма́лая вода́, ни́зшая то́чка отли́ва; **~ over** vt: **this money will ~ me over till Monday** на э́ти де́ньги я смогу́ продержа́ться до понеде́льника

**tidy** ['taɪdɪ] adj опря́тный; (mind) аккура́тный ♦ vt (also: **~ up**) прибира́ть (прибра́ть pf)

**tie** [taɪ] n (string etc) шнуро́к; (BRIT: also: **neck~**) га́лстук; (fig: link) связь f; (SPORT) ничья́ ♦ vt завя́зывать (завяза́ть pf) ♦ vi (SPORT) игра́ть (сыгра́ть pf) вничью́; **to ~ sth in a bow** завя́зывать (завяза́ть pf) что-н ба́нтом; **to ~ a knot in sth** завя́зывать (завяза́ть pf) что-н узло́м; **~ up** vt (dog, boat) привя́зывать (привяза́ть pf); (prisoner, parcel) свя́зывать (связа́ть pf); **I'm ~d up at the moment** (busy) сейча́с я за́нят

**tier** [tɪər] n (of stadium etc) я́рус; (of cake) слой

**tiger** ['taɪɡər] n тигр

**tight** [taɪt] adj (rope) туго́й; (shoes, bend, clothes) у́зкий; (security) уси́ленный; (schedule, budget) жёсткий ♦ adv (hold, squeeze) кре́пко; (shut) пло́тно; **money is ~** у меня́ ту́го с деньга́ми; **~en** vt (rope) натя́гивать (натяну́ть pf); (screw) затя́гивать (затяну́ть pf); (grip) сжима́ть (сжать pf); (security) уси́ливать (уси́лить pf) ♦ vi (grip) сжима́ться (сжа́ться pf); (rope) натя́гиваться (натяну́ться pf); **~-lipped** adj скры́тный; (fig: through anger) серди́тый; **~ly** adv (grasp) кре́пко; **~rope** n

натя́нутый кана́т; **~s** npl (BRIT)
колго́тки pl

**tile** [taɪl] n (on roof ) черепи́ца; (on
floor) пли́тка

**till** [tɪl] n ка́сса ♦ prep, conj = **until**

**tilt** [tɪlt] vt наклоня́ть (наклони́ть
pf); (head) склоня́ть (склони́ть pf)
♦ vi наклоня́ться (наклони́ться
pf)

**timber** ['tɪmbər] n (wood)
древеси́на

**time** [taɪm] n вре́мя nt; (occasion)
раз ♦ vt (measure time of )
засека́ть (засе́чь pf) вре́мя +gen;
( fix moment for) выбира́ть
(вы́брать pf) вре́мя для +gen; **a
long ~** до́лго; **a long ~ ago** давно́;
**for the ~ being** пока́; **four at a ~**
по четы́ре; **from ~ to ~** вре́мя от
вре́мени; **at ~s** времена́ми; **in ~**
( soon enough) вво́время; (after some
time) со вре́менем; (MUS, play) в
такт; **in a week's ~** че́рез
неде́лю; **in no ~** в два счёта; **any
~** (whenever) в любо́е вре́мя; (as
response) не́ за что; **on ~**
во́время; **five ~s five** пя́тью пять;
**what ~ is it?** кото́рый час?; **to
have a good ~** хорошо́
проводи́ть (провести́ pf) вре́мя;
**~ bomb** n (device) бо́мба с
часовы́м механи́змом; **~less** adj
ве́чный; **~ limit** n преде́льный
срок; **~ly** adj своевре́менный; **~
off** n свобо́дное вре́мя nt; (break)
выходно́й m adj; **~r** n (time switch)
та́ймер; **~scale** n (BRIT) вре́мя nt,
пери́од вре́мени; **~table** n
расписа́ние

**timid** ['tɪmɪd] adj ро́бкий

**timing** ['taɪmɪŋ] n: **the ~ of his
resignation was unfortunate**
вы́бор вре́мени для его́
отста́вки был неуда́чен

**tin** [tɪn] n (material) о́лово;
(container) (жестяна́я) ба́нка;

(: BRIT: can) консе́рвная ба́нка;
**~foil** n фольга́

**tinge** [tɪndʒ] n отте́нок ♦ vt: **~d
with** с отте́нком +gen

**tinker** ['tɪŋkər] n бродя́чий
луди́льщик

**tinned** [tɪnd] adj (BRIT)
консерви́рованный

**tin-opener** ['tɪnəupnər] n (BRIT)
консе́рвный нож

**tinted** ['tɪntɪd] adj (hair)
подкра́шеный; (spectacles, glass)
ды́мчатый

**tiny** ['taɪnɪ] adj кро́шечный

**tip** [tɪp] n (of pen etc) ко́нчик;
( gratuity) чаевы́е pl adj; (BRIT: for
rubbish) сва́лка; (advice) сове́т ♦ vt
(waiter) дава́ть (дать pf) на чай
+dat; (tilt) наклоня́ть (наклони́ть
pf); (also: **~ over**) опроки́дывать
(опроки́нуть pf); (also: **~ out**)
выва́ливать (вы́валить pf); **~-off**
n предупрежде́ние

**tiptoe** ['tɪptəu] n: **on ~** на
цы́почках

**tire** ['taɪər] n (US) = **tyre** ♦ vt
утомля́ть (утоми́ть pf) ♦ vi
устава́ть (уста́ть pf); **~d** adj
уста́лый; **to be ~d of sth**
устава́ть (уста́ть pf) от чего́-н;
**~less** adj (worker) неутоми́мый;
(efforts) неуста́нный; **~some** adj
надое́дливый, зану́дный

**tiring** ['taɪərɪŋ] adj утоми́тельный

**tissue** ['tɪʃuː] n бума́жная
салфе́тка; (ANAT, BIO) ткань f

**tit** [tɪt] n (ZOOL) сини́ца; **~ for tat**
зуб за зуб

**title** ['taɪtl] n (of book etc)
назва́ние; (rank, in sport) ти́тул

KEYWORD

**to** [tuː, tə] prep **1** (direction) в/на
+acc; **to drive to school/the
station** е́здить/е́хать (пое́хать pf)
в шко́лу/на ста́нцию; **to the left**

налéво; **to the right** напрáво
2 (*as far as*) до +*gen*; **from Paris to London** от Парѝжа до Лóндона; **to count to ten** считáть (посчитáть *pf*) до десятѝ
3 (*with expressions of time*): **a quarter to five** без чéтверти пять
4 (*for, of*) к +*dat*; **the key to the front door** ключ (к) входнóй двéри; **a letter to his wife** письмó женé; **she is secretary to the director** онá секретáрь дирéктора
5 (*expressing indirect object*): **to give sth to sb** давáть (дать *pf*) что-н комý-н; **to talk to sb** разговáривать (*impf*) or говорѝть (*impf*) с кем-н; **what have you done to your hair?** что Вы сдéлали со своѝми волосáми?
6 (*in relation to*) к +*dat*; **three goals to two** три: два; **X miles to the gallon** ≈ X лѝтров на киломéтр; **30 roubles to the dollar** 30 рублéй за дóллар
7 (*purpose, result*) к +*dat*; **to my surprise** к моемý удивлéнию; **to come to sb's aid** приходѝть (прийтѝ *pf*) комý-н на пóмощь
♦ *with vb* 1: **to want/try to do** хотéть (захотéть *pf*)/пытáться (попытáться *pf*) +*infin*; **he has nothing to lose** емý нéчего терять; **I am happy to ...** я счáстлив +*infin* ...; **ready to use** готóвый к употреблéнию; **too old/young to ...** слѝшком стар/мóлод, чтóбы +*infin* ...
2 (*with vb omitted*): **I don't want to** я не хочý; **I don't feel like going - you really ought to** мне не хóчется идтѝ - но, Вы должнѝ
3 (*purpose, result*) чтóбы +*infin*; **I did it to help you** я сдéлал э́то, чтóбы помóчь Вам
♦ *adv*: **to push the door to, pull**

**the door to** закрывáть (закрыть *pf*) дверь

**toad** [təud] *n* (*ZOOL*) жáба; **~stool** *n* (*BOT*) погáнка
**toast** [təust] *n* тост ♦ *vt* (*CULIN*) поджáривать (поджáрить *pf*); (*drink to*) пить (выпить *pf*) за +*acc*; **~er** *n* тóстер
**tobacco** [tə'bækəu] *n* табáк
**today** [tə'deɪ] *adv, n* сегóдня
**toddler** ['tɔdlər] *n* малы́ш
**toe** [təu] *n* (*of foot*) пáлец (*ногѝ*); (*of shoe, sock*) носóк; **to ~ the line** (*fig*) соотвéтствовать (*impf*)
**toffee** ['tɔfɪ] *n* ирѝска, тянýчка
**together** [tə'gɛðər] *adv* вмéсте; (*at same time*) одновремéнно; **~ with** вмéсте с +*instr*
**toilet** ['tɔɪlət] *n* унитáз; (*BRIT: room*) туалéт ♦ *cpd* туалéтный; **~ries** *npl* туалéтные принадлéжности *fpl*
**token** ['təukən] *n* (*sign, souvenir*) знак; (*substitute coin*) жетóн ♦ *adj* (*strike, payment etc*) символѝческий; **book/gift ~** (*BRIT*) кнѝжный/подáрочный талóн; **record ~** (*BRIT*) талóн на пластѝнку
**told** [təuld] *pt, pp of* **tell**
**tolerable** ['tɔlərəbl] *adj* (*bearable*) терпѝмый; (*fairly good*) снóсный
**tolerance** ['tɔlərns] *n* (*patience*) терпѝмость *f*
**tolerant** ['tɔlərnt] *adj*: **~ (of)** терпѝмый (к +*dat*)
**tolerate** ['tɔləreɪt] *vt* терпéть (*impf*)
**toll** [təul] *n* (*of casualties etc*) числó; (*tax, charge*) сбор, плáта
**tomato** [tə'mɑːtəu] (*pl* **~es**) *n* помидóр
**tomb** [tuːm] *n* могѝла; **~stone** *n* надгрóбная плитá, надгрóбие
**tomorrow** [tə'mɔrəu] *adv, n* зáвтра; **the day after ~** послезáвтра; **~ morning** зáвтра

у́тром

**ton** [tʌn] n (BRIT) дли́нная то́нна; (US: also: **short ~**) коро́ткая то́нна; (also: **metric ~**) метри́ческая то́нна; **~s of** (inf) у́йма +gen

**tone** [təun] n (of voice, colour) тон ♦ vi (colours: also: **~ in**) сочета́ться (impf); **~ up** vt (muscles) укрепля́ть (укрепи́ть pf)

**tongue** [tʌŋ] n язы́к

**tonic** ['tɔnɪk] n (MED) тонизи́рующее сре́дство; (also: **~ water**) то́ник

**tonight** [tə'naɪt] adv (this evening) сего́дня ве́чером; (this night) сего́дня но́чью ♦ n (see adv) сего́дняшний ве́чер; сего́дняшняя ночь f

**tonsil** ['tɔnsl] n (usu pl) минда́лина; **~litis** [tɔnsɪ'laɪtɪs] n тонзилли́т

**too** [tu:] adv (excessively) сли́шком; (also: referring to subject) та́кже, то́же; (: referring to object) та́кже; **~ much**, **~ many** сли́шком мно́го

**took** [tuk] pt of **take**

**tool** [tu:l] n (instrument) инструме́нт

**tooth** [tu:θ] n (pl **teeth**) n (ANAT) зуб; (TECH) зубе́ц; **~ache** n зубна́я боль f; **~brush** n зубна́я щётка; **~paste** n зубна́я па́ста

**top** [tɔp] n (of mountain) верши́на; (of tree) верху́шка; (of head) маку́шка; (of page, list etc) нача́ло; (of ladder, cupboard, table, box) верх; (lid: of box, jar) кры́шка; (: bottle) про́бка; (also: **spinning ~**) юла́, волчо́к ♦ adj (shelf, step) ве́рхний; (marks) вы́сший; (scientist) веду́щий ♦ vt (poll, vote) лиди́ровать (impf) в +prp; (list) возглавля́ть (возгла́вить pf); (exceed: estimate etc) превыша́ть (превы́сить pf); **on ~ of** (above: be)

на +prp; (: put) на +acc; (in addition to) сверх +gen; **from ~ to bottom** све́рху до́низу; **~ up**, (US) **top off** vt (bottle) долива́ть (доли́ть pf)

**topic** ['tɔpɪk] n те́ма; **~al** adj актуа́льный

**topless** ['tɔplɪs] adj обнажённый до по́яса

**topple** ['tɔpl] vt (overthrow) ски́дывать (ски́нуть pf) ♦ vi опроки́дываться (опроки́нуться pf)

**top-secret** ['tɔp'si:krɪt] adj сверхсекре́тный

**torch** [tɔ:tʃ] n (with flame) фа́кел; (BRIT: electric) фона́рь m

**tore** [tɔ:ʳ] pt of **tear**[1]

**torment** n ['tɔ:mɛnt] vb [tɔ:'mɛnt] n муче́ние ♦ vt му́чить (impf)

**torn** [tɔ:n] pp of **tear**[1]

**tornado** [tɔ:'neɪdəu] (pl **~es**) n смерч

**torpedo** [tɔ:'pi:dəu] (pl **~es**) n торпе́да

**torrent** ['tɔrnt] n пото́к; **~ial** [tə'rɛnʃl] adj проливно́й

**torso** ['tɔ:səu] n ту́ловище, торс

**tortoise** ['tɔ:təs] n черепа́ха

**torture** ['tɔ:tʃəʳ] n пы́тка ♦ vt пыта́ть (impf)

**Tory** ['tɔ:rɪ] (BRIT: POL) adj консервати́вный ♦ n то́ри m/f ind, консерва́тор

**toss** [tɔs] vt (throw) подки́дывать (подки́нуть pf), подбра́сывать (подбро́сить pf); (head) отки́дывать (отки́нуть pf) ♦ vi: to **~ and turn** воро́чаться (impf); to **~ a coin** подбра́сывать (подбро́сить pf) моне́ту; to **~ up** to do подбра́сывать (подбро́сить pf) моне́ту, что́бы +infin

**total** ['təutl] adj (number, workforce etc) о́бщий; (failure, wreck etc)

по́лный ♦ *n* о́бщая су́мма ♦ *vt*
(*add up*) скла́дывать (сложи́ть *pf*);
(*add up to*) составля́ть (соста́вить
*pf*)

**totalitarian** [təutælɪ'tɛərɪən] *adj*
(POL) тоталита́рный

**totally** ['təutəlɪ] *adv* по́лностью;
(*unprepared*) соверше́нно

**touch** [tʌtʃ] *n* (*sense*) осяза́ние;
(*approach*) мане́ра; (*detail*) штрих;
(*contact*) прикоснове́ние ♦ *vt* (*with
hand, foot*) каса́ться (косну́ться
*pf*) +*gen*, тро́гать (тро́нуть *pf*);
(*tamper with*) тро́гать (*impf*); (*make
contact with*) прикаса́ться
(прикосну́ться *pf*) к +*dat*,
дотра́гиваться (дотро́нуться *pf*)
до +*gen*; (*move: emotionally*)
тро́гать (тро́нуть *pf*); **there's been
a ~ of frost** подморо́зило; **to get
in ~ with sb** свя́зываться
(связа́ться *pf*) с кем-н; **to lose ~**
(*friends*) теря́ть (потеря́ть *pf*)
связь; **~ on** *vt fus* каса́ться
(косну́ться *pf*) +*gen*; **~ed** *adj*
(*moved*) тро́нутый; **~ing** *adj*
тро́гательный; **~line** *n* боковая́
ли́ния; **~y** *adj* (*person*) оби́дчивый

**tough** [tʌf] *adj* (*hard-wearing*)
кре́пкий, про́чный; (*person:
physically*) выно́сливый;
(: *mentally*) сто́йкий; (*difficult*)
тяжёлый

**tour** ['tuər] *n* (*journey*) пое́здка; (*of
town, factory etc*) экску́рсия; (*by
pop group etc*) гастро́ли *pl* ♦ *vt*
(*country, city*) объезжа́ть
(объе́хать *pf*); (*factory*) обходи́ть
(обойти́ *pf*)

**tourism** ['tuərɪzm] *n* тури́зм

**tourist** ['tuərɪst] *n* тури́ст(ка) ♦ *cpd*
(*attractions, season*) туристи́ческий

**tournament** ['tuənəmənt] *n*
турни́р

**tow** [təu] *vt* вози́ть/везти́ (*impf*) на
букси́ре; **"on** *or* (US) **in ~"** (AUT)

"на букси́ре"

**toward(s)** [tə'wɔːd(z)] *prep* к +*dat*;
**toward(s) doing** с тем чтобы
+*infin*

**towel** ['tauəl] *n* (*also*: **hand ~**)
полоте́нце для рук; (*also*: **bath
~**) ба́нное полоте́нце

**tower** ['tauər] *n* ба́шня; **~ block** *n*
(BRIT) ба́шня, высо́тный дом

**town** [taun] *n* го́род; **to go to ~**
(*fig*) разоря́ться (разори́ться *pf*);
**~ centre** *n* центр (го́рода); **~
council** *n* городско́й сове́т; **~
hall** *n* ра́туша

**towrope** ['təurəup] *n* букси́рный
трос

**toxic** ['tɔksɪk] *adj* токси́чный

**toy** [tɔɪ] *n* игру́шка

**trace** [treɪs] *n* след ♦ *vt* (*draw*)
переводи́ть (перевести́ *pf*);
(*follow*) просле́живать
(проследи́ть *pf*); (*find*)
разы́скивать (разыска́ть *pf*)

**track** [træk] *n* след; (*path*) тропа́;
(*of bullet etc*) траекто́рия; (RAIL)
(железнодоро́жный) путь *m*;
(*song, also* SPORT) доро́жка ♦ *vt*
(*follow*) идти́ (*impf*) по сле́ду +*gen*;
**to keep ~ of** следи́ть (*impf*) за
+*instr*; **~ down** *vt* (*prey*)
высле́живать (вы́следить *pf*);
(*person*) оты́скивать (отыска́ть
*pf*); **~suit** *n* трениро́вочный
костю́м

**tract** [trækt] *n* (GEO) простра́нство

**tractor** ['træktər] *n* тра́ктор

**trade** [treɪd] *n* (*activity*) торго́вля;
(*skill, job*) ремесло́ ♦ *vi* (*do
business*) торгова́ть (*impf*) ♦ *vt*: **to
~ sth (for sth)** обме́нивать
(обменя́ть *pf*) что-н (на что-н); **~
in** *vt* (*car etc*) предлага́ть
(предложи́ть *pf*) для встре́чной
прода́жи; **~mark** *n* торго́вый
знак; **~r** *n* торго́вец; **~sman**
(*irreg*) *n* (*shopkeeper*) торго́вец,

ла́вочник; ~ **union** n (BRIT) профсою́з

**tradition** [trə'dɪʃən] n тради́ция; **~al** adj (also fig) традицио́нный

**traffic** ['træfɪk] n движе́ние; (of drugs) нелега́льная торго́вля; ~ **jam** n про́бка, зато́р; ~ **lights** npl светофо́р msg; ~ **warden** n (BRIT) регулиро́вщик парко́вания маши́н на городски́х у́лицах

**tragedy** ['trædʒədɪ] n траге́дия

**tragic** ['trædʒɪk] adj траги́ческий

**trail** [treɪl] n (path) доро́жка, тропи́нка; (track) след; (of smoke, dust) шлейф ♦ vt (drag) волочи́ть (impf); (follow) сле́довать (impf) по пята́м за +instr ♦ vi (hang loosely) волочи́ться (impf); (in game, contest) волочи́ться (impf) в хвосте́, отстава́ть (impf); **~er** n (AUT) прице́п; (US: caravan) автоприце́п; (CINEMA) рекла́мный ро́лик, ано́нс

**train** [treɪn] n по́езд; (of dress) шлейф ♦ vt (apprentice, doctor etc) обуча́ть (обучи́ть pf), гото́вить (impf); (athlete, mind) тренирова́ть (impf); (dog) дрессирова́ть (выдрессировать pf) ♦ vi учи́ться (обучи́ться pf); (SPORT) тренирова́ться (impf); **one's ~ of thought** ход чьих-н мы́слей; **to ~ sb as** учи́ть (обучи́ть pf) кого́-н на +acc; **to ~ sth on** (camera etc) направля́ть (напра́вить pf) что-н на +acc; **~ed** adj (worker) квалифици́рованный; (animal) дрессиро́ванный; **~ee** n (hairdresser) учени́к; **~ee teacher** практика́нт(ка); **~er** n (coach) тре́нер; (of animals) дрессиро́вщик(щица); **~ers** npl (shoes) кроссо́вки fpl; **~ing** n (for occupation) обуче́ние, подгото́вка; (SPORT) трениро́вка; **to be in ~ing** (SPORT)

тренирова́ться (impf)

**trait** [treɪt] n черта́

**traitor** ['treɪtər] n преда́тель(ница) m(f)

**tram** [træm] n (BRIT) трамва́й

**tramp** [træmp] n (person) бродя́га m/f

**trample** ['træmpl] vt: **to ~ (underfoot)** раста́птывать (растопта́ть pf)

**trampoline** ['træmpəli:n] n батут

**trance** [trɑ:ns] n (also fig) транс

**tranquil** ['træŋkwɪl] adj безмяте́жный; **~lity** [træŋ'kwɪlɪtɪ] (US **~ity**) n безмяте́жность f

**transaction** [træn'zækʃən] n опера́ция

**transatlantic** ['trænzət'læntɪk] adj трансатланти́ческий

**transcend** [træn'sɛnd] vt переступа́ть (переступи́ть pf)

**transcript** ['trænskrɪpt] n (typed) распеча́тка; (hand-written) ру́копись f

**transfer** ['trænsfər] n перево́д; (POL, of power) переда́ча; (SPORT) перехо́д; (design) переводна́я карти́нка ♦ vt (employees, money) переводи́ть (перевести́ pf); (POL, power) передава́ть (переда́ть pf)

**transform** [træns'fɔ:m] vt (completely) преобразо́вывать (преобразова́ть pf); (alter) преобража́ть (преобрази́ть pf); **~ation** [trænsfə'meɪʃən] n (see vt) преобразова́ние; преображе́ние

**transfusion** [træns'fju:ʒən] n (also: **blood ~**) перелива́ние кро́ви

**transient** ['trænzɪənt] adj мимолётный

**transit** ['trænzɪt] n транзи́т; **in ~** (people, things) при перево́зке, в транзи́те

**transition** [træn'zɪʃən] n перехо́д; **~al** adj перехо́дный

**translate** [trænz'leɪt] vt: **to ~**

**(from/into)** переводить
(перевести *pf*) (с +*gen*/на +*acc*)
**translation** [trænz'leɪʃən] *n*
перевод
**translator** [trænz'leɪtə<sup>r</sup>] *n*
переводчик(ица)
**transmission** [trænz'mɪʃən] *n*
передача
**transmit** [trænz'mɪt] *vt* передавать
(передать *pf*); **~ter** *n* передатчик
**transparency** [træns'pɛərnsɪ] *n* (*of
glass etc*) прозрачность *f*
**transparent** [træns'pærnt] *adj*
прозрачный
**transplant** *n* ['trænsplɑːnt] *vb*
[træns'plɑːnt] *n* пересадка ♦ *vt*
(*MED, BOT*) пересаживать
(пересадить *pf*)
**transport** *n* ['trænspɔːt] *vb*
[træns'pɔːt] *n* транспорт; (*of people,
goods*) перевозка ♦ *vt* (*carry*)
перевозить (перевезти *pf*)
**transportation** ['trænspɔː'teɪʃən] *n*
транспортировка, перевозка;
(*means of transport*) транспорт
**transvestite** [trænz'vɛstaɪt] *n*
трансвестит
**trap** [træp] *n* ловушка, западня
♦ *vt* ловить (поймать *pf*) в
ловушку; (*confine*) запирать
(запереть *pf*)
**trash** [træʃ] *n* мусор; (*pej, fig*)
дрянь *f*
**trauma** ['trɔːmə] *n* травма; **~tic**
[trɔː'mætɪk] *adj* (*fig*) мучительный
**travel** ['trævl] *n* (*travelling*)
путешествия *ntpl* ♦ *vi* (*for pleasure*)
путешествовать (*impf*); (*commute*)
ездить (*impf*); (*news, sound*)
распространяться
(распространиться *pf*) ♦ *vt*
(*distance: by transport*) проезжать
(проехать *pf*); **~s** *npl* (*journeys*)
разъезды *mpl*; **~ agent** *n*
турагент; **~ler** (*US* **~er**) *n*
путешественник(ица); **~ler's**

**cheque** (*US* **~er's check**) *n*
дорожный чек
**travesty** ['trævəstɪ] *n* пародия
**trawler** ['trɔːlə<sup>r</sup>] *n* траулер
**tray** [treɪ] *n* (*for carrying*) поднос;
(*on desk*) корзинка
**treacherous** ['trɛtʃərəs] *adj* (*person*)
вероломный; (*look, action*)
предательский; (*ground, tide*)
коварный
**treachery** ['trɛtʃərɪ] *n*
предательство, вероломство
**treacle** ['triːkl] *n* патока
**tread** [trɛd] (*pt* **trod**, *pp* **trodden**) *n*
(*of stair*) ступень *f*; (*of tyre*)
протектор ♦ *vi* ступать (*impf*)
**treason** ['triːzn] *n* измена
**treasure** ['trɛʒə<sup>r</sup>] *n* сокровище ♦ *vt*
дорожить (*impf*) +*instr*; (*thought*)
лелеять (*impf*); **~s** *npl* (*art treasures
etc*) сокровища *ntpl*; **~r** *n*
казначей
**treasury** ['trɛʒərɪ] *n*: **the Treasury**,
(*US*) **the Treasury Department**
Государственное Казначейство
**treat** [triːt] *n* (*present*)
удовольствие ♦ *vt* (*person, object*)
обращаться (*impf*) с +*instr*;
(*patient, illness*) лечить (*impf*); **to ~
sb to sth** угощать (угостить *pf*)
кого-н чем-н; **~ment** *n* (*attention,
handling*) обращение; (*MED*)
лечение
**treaty** ['triːtɪ] *n* соглашение
**treble** ['trɛbl] *vt* утраивать
(утроить *pf*) ♦ *vi* утраиваться
(утроиться *pf*)
**tree** [triː] *n* дерево
**trek** [trɛk] *n* (*trip*) поход, переход
**tremble** ['trɛmbl] *vi* дрожать (*impf*)
**tremendous** [trɪ'mɛndəs] *adj*
(*enormous*) громадный; (*excellent*)
великолепный
**tremor** ['trɛmə<sup>r</sup>] *n* (*trembling*)
дрожь *f*, содрогание; (*also*: **earth
~**) толчок (*при землетрясении*)

**trench** [trɛntʃ] n канáва; (MIL) траншéя, окóп

**trend** [trɛnd] n (tendency) тендéнция; (of events, fashion) направлéние; ~**y** adj мóдный

**trespass** ['trɛspəs] vi: **to ~ on** (private property) вторгáться (втóргнуться pf) в +acc; **"no ~ing"** "прохóд воспрещён"

**trial** ['traɪəl] n (LAW) процéсс, суд; (of machine etc) испытáние; (bad experiences) перипети́и fpl; **on ~** (LAW) под судóм; **by ~ and error** мéтодом проб и ошибок

**triangle** ['traɪæŋgl] n (MATH, MUS) треугóльник

**triangular** [traɪ'æŋgjuləʳ] adj треугóльный

**tribal** ['traɪbl] adj племеннóй

**tribe** [traɪb] n плéмя nt

**tribunal** [traɪ'bju:nl] n трибунáл

**tributary** ['trɪbjutərɪ] n притóк

**tribute** ['trɪbju:t] n (compliment) дань f; **to pay ~** отдавáть (отдáть pf) дань +dat

**trick** [trɪk] n (magic trick) фóкус; (prank) подвóх; (skill, knack) приём ♦ vt проводи́ть (провести́ pf); **to play a ~ on sb** разы́грывать (разыгрáть pf) когó-н; **that should do the ~** э́то должнó срабóтать

**trickle** ['trɪkl] n (of water etc) стрýйка ♦ vi (water, rain etc) струи́ться (impf)

**tricky** ['trɪkɪ] adj (job) непростóй; (business) хи́трый; (problem) кáверзный

**trifle** ['traɪfl] n (small detail) пустя́к ♦ adv: **a ~ long** чуть длинновáт

**trigger** ['trɪgəʳ] n (of gun) курóк

**trim** [trɪm] adj (house, garden) ухóженный; (figure) подтя́нутый ♦ vt (cut) подрáвнивать (подровня́ть pf); (decorate): **to ~ (with)** отдéлывать (отдéлать pf)

(+instr) ♦ n: **to give sb a ~** подрáвнивать (подровня́ть pf) вóлосы комý-н

**trip** [trɪp] n (journey) поéздка; (outing) экскýрсия ♦ vi (stumble) спотыкáться (споткнýться pf); **on a ~** на экскýрсии; **~ up** vi (stumble) спотыкáться (споткнýться pf) ♦ vt (person) стáвить (подстáвить pf) поднóжку +dat

**tripe** [traɪp] n (CULIN) требухá

**triple** ['trɪpl] adj тройнóй; **~ jump** n тройнóй прыжóк

**tripod** ['traɪpɔd] n тренóга

**trite** [traɪt] adj (pej) избитый

**triumph** ['traɪʌmf] n (satisfaction) торжествó; (achievement) триýмф ♦ vi: **to ~ (over)** торжествовáть (восторжествовáть pf) (над +instr); **~ant** [traɪ'ʌmfənt] adj (team, wave) торжествýющий; (return) побéдный

**trivial** ['trɪvɪəl] adj тривиáльный

**trod** [trɔd] pt of **tread**; **~den** pp of **tread**

**trolley** ['trɔlɪ] n телéжка; (also: ~ **bus**) троллéйбус

**trombone** [trɔm'bəun] n тромбóн

**troop** [tru:p] n (of soldiers) отря́д; (of people) грýппа; **~s** npl (MIL) войскá ntpl

**trophy** ['trəufɪ] n трофéй

**tropical** ['trɔpɪkl] adj тропи́ческий

**trot** [trɔt] n рысь f (спóсоб бéга)

**trouble** ['trʌbl] n (difficulty) затруднéние; (worry, unrest) беспокóйство; (bother, effort) хлóпоты pl ♦ vt (worry) беспокóить (impf); (disturb) беспокóить (побеспокóить pf) ♦ vi: **to ~ to do** побеспокóиться (pf) +infin; **~s** npl (personal) неприя́тности fpl; **to be in ~** (ship, climber etc) быть (impf) в бедé; **I am in ~** у меня́ неприя́тности; **to**

**have ~ doing** с трудо́м +infin; **~d** adj (person) встрево́женный; (times) сму́тный; (country) многострада́льный; **~maker** n смутья́н; **~some** adj (child) озорно́й

**trough** [trɒf] n (also: **drinking ~**) коры́то; (also: **feeding ~**) кормушка; (low point) впа́дина

**trousers** ['trauzəz] npl брю́ки pl; **short ~** шо́рты

**trout** [traut] n inv (ZOOL) форе́ль f

**truant** ['truənt] n (BRIT): **to play ~** прогу́ливать (прогуля́ть pf) уро́ки

**truce** [tru:s] n переми́рие

**truck** [trʌk] n (lorry) грузови́к; (RAIL) платфо́рма

**true** [tru:] adj и́стинный; (accurate: likeness) то́чный; (loyal) ве́рный; **to come ~** сбыва́ться (сбы́ться pf); **it is ~** э́то пра́вда or ве́рно

**truly** ['tru:lɪ] adv по-настоя́щему; (truthfully) по пра́вде говоря́; **yours ~** (in letter) и́скренне Ваш

**trump** [trʌmp] n (also: **~ card**) ко́зырь m, козы́рная ка́рта

**trumpet** ['trʌmpɪt] n (MUS) труба́

**truncheon** ['trʌntʃən] n (BRIT) дуби́нка

**trunk** [trʌŋk] n (of tree) ствол; (of elephant) хо́бот; (case) доро́жный сунду́к; (US: AUT) бага́жник; **~s** npl (also: **swimming ~s**) пла́вки pl

**trust** [trʌst] n (faith) дове́рие; (responsibility) долг; (LAW) довери́тельная со́бственность f ♦ vt (rely on, have faith in) доверя́ть (impf) +dat; (hope): **to ~ (that)** полага́ть (impf), что; (entrust): **to ~ sth to sb** доверя́ть (дове́рить pf) что-н кому́-н; **to take sth on ~** принима́ть (приня́ть pf) что-н на ве́ру; **~ed** adj пре́данный; **~ee** [trʌs'ti:] n

попечи́тель m; **~ing** adj дове́рчивый; **~worthy** adj надёжный

**truth** [tru:θ] n (pl **~s**) пра́вда; (principle) и́стина; **~ful** adj правди́вый

**try** [traɪ] n (attempt) попы́тка; (RUGBY) прохо́д с мячо́м ♦ vt (test) про́бовать (попро́бовать pf); (LAW) суди́ть (impf); (patience) испы́тывать (impf); (key, door) про́бовать (попро́бовать pf); (attempt): **to ~ to do** стара́ться (постара́ться pf) or пыта́ться (попыта́ться pf) +infin ♦ vi (make effort) стара́ться (impf); **to have a ~** про́бовать (попро́бовать pf); **~ on** vt (dress etc) примеря́ть (приме́рить pf); **~ing** adj утоми́тельный

**tsar** [zɑ:r] n царь m

**T-shirt** ['ti:ʃə:t] n футбо́лка

**tub** [tʌb] n (container) бо́чка; (bath) ва́нна

**tube** [tju:b] n (pipe) тру́бка; (container) тю́бик; (BRIT: metro) метро́ nt ind; (for tyre) ка́мера

**tuberculosis** [tjubə:kju'ləusɪs] n туберкулёз

**TUC** n abbr (BRIT: = Trades Union Congress) Конгре́сс (брита́нских) профсою́зов

**tuck** [tʌk] vt (put) су́нуть (pf)

**Tuesday** ['tju:zdɪ] n вто́рник

**tug** [tʌg] n (ship) букси́р ♦ vt дёргать (дёрнуть pf)

**tuition** [tju:'ɪʃən] n (BRIT) обуче́ние; (US: fees) пла́та за обуче́ние; **private ~** ча́стные уро́ки

**tulip** ['tju:lɪp] n тюльпа́н

**tumble** ['tʌmbl] n паде́ние ♦ vi (fall: person) вали́ться (свали́ться pf)

**tumbler** ['tʌmblər] n бока́л

**tummy** ['tʌmɪ] n (inf) живо́т

**tumour** ['tjuːmər] (*US* **tumor**) *n* (*MED*) όπухоль *f*

**tuna** ['tjuːnə] *n inv* (*also*: ~ **fish**) тунец

**tune** [tjuːn] *n* (*melody*) мотив ♦ *vt* настраивать (настроить *pf*); (*AUT*) налаживать (наладить *pf*); **the guitar is in/out of** ~ гитара настроена/расстроена; **to sing in** ~ петь (*impf*) в лад; **to sing out of** ~ фальшивить (*impf*); **to be in/out of** ~ **with** (*fig*) быть (*impf*) в ладу/не в ладу с +*instr*; ~ **in** *vi* (*RADIO, TV*): **to** ~ **in (to)** настраиваться (настроиться *pf*) (на +*acc*); ~**ful** *adj* мелодичный; ~**r** *n*: **piano** ~**r** настройщик фортепьяно

**tunic** ['tjuːnɪk] *n* туника

**tunnel** ['tʌnl] *n* (*passage*) туннель *m*

**turbine** ['təːbaɪn] *n* (*TECH*) турбина

**turbulent** ['təːbjulənt] *adj* бурный

**turf** [təːf] *n* (*grass*) дёрн

**Turkey** ['təːkɪ] *n* Турция

**turkey** ['təːkɪ] *n* индейка

**Turkish** ['təːkɪʃ] *adj* турецкий

**turmoil** ['təːmɔɪl] *n* смятение; **in** ~ в смятении

**turn** [təːn] *n* поворот; (*chance*) очередь *f*; (*inf*: *MED*) вывих ♦ *vt* поворачивать (повернуть *pf*) ♦ *vi* (*object*) поворачиваться (повернуться *pf*); (*person*: *look back*) оборачиваться (обернуться *pf*); (*reverse direction*) разворачиваться (развернуться *pf*); (*become*): **he's** ~**ed forty** ему исполнилось сорок; **a good/bad** ~ добрая/плохая услуга; **"no left** ~**"** (*AUT*) "нет левого поворота"; **it's your** ~ твоя очередь; **in** ~ по очереди; **to take** ~**s at sth** делать (*impf*) что-н по очереди; **to** ~ **nasty** озлобляться (озлобиться *pf*); ~ **away** *vi* отворачиваться

(отвернуться *pf*) ♦ *vt* (*business, applicant*) отклонять (отклонить *pf*); ~ **back** *vi* поворачивать (повернуть *pf*) назад ♦ *vt* (*person*) вернуть (*pf*); (*vehicle*) разворачивать (развернуть *pf*); **to** ~ **back the clock** (*fig*) повернуть (*pf*) время вспять; ~ **down** *vt* (*request*) отклонять (отклонить *pf*); (*heating*) уменьшать (уменьшить *pf*) подачу +*gen*; ~ **in** *vi* (*inf*) идти (пойти *pf*) на боковую; ~ **off** *vi* сворачивать (свернуть *pf*) ♦ *vt* выключать (выключить *pf*); ~ **on** *vt* включать (включить *pf*); ~ **out** *vt* (*light, gas*) выключать (выключить *pf*); (*produce*) выпускать (выпустить *pf*) ♦ *vi* (*troops, voters*) прибывать (прибыть *pf*); **to** ~ **out to be** оказываться (оказаться *pf*) +*instr*; ~ **over** *vi* (*person*) переворачиваться (перевернуться *pf*) ♦ *vt* (*object, page*) переворачивать (перевернуть *pf*); ~ **round** *vi* (*person, vehicle*) разворачиваться (развернуться *pf*); ~ **up** *vi* (*person*) объявляться (объявиться *pf*); (*lost object*) находиться (найтись *pf*) ♦ *vt* (*collar*) поднимать (поднять *pf*); (*radio*) делать (сделать *pf*) громче; (*heater*) увеличивать (увеличить *pf*) подачу +*gen*; ~**ing** *n* поворот; ~**ing point** *n* (*fig*) поворотный пункт, переломный момент

**turnip** ['təːnɪp] *n* (*BOT, CULIN*) репа

**turnout** ['təːnaut] *n*: **there was a high** ~ **for the local elections** в местных выборах приняло участие много людей

**turnover** ['təːnəuvər] *n* (*COMM*) оборот; (: *of staff*) текучесть *f*

**turn-up** ['təːnʌp] *n* (*BRIT*) манжета

**turquoise** ['tə:kwɔɪz] adj (colour)
бирюзо́вый

**turtle** ['tə:tl] n черепа́ха

**tussle** ['tʌsl] n (fight, scuffle)
потасо́вка

**tutor** ['tju:tər] n (SCOL)
преподава́тель(ница) m(f);
(: private tutor) репети́тор; ~ial
[tju:'tɔ:rɪəl] n (SCOL) семина́р

**TV** n abbr (= television) ТВ

**tweed** [twi:d] n твид

**twelfth** [twelfθ] adj двена́дцатый

**twelve** [twelv] n двена́дцать; at ~
(o'clock) в двена́дцать (часо́в)

**twentieth** ['twentɪɪθ] adj
двадца́тый

**twenty** ['twentɪ] n два́дцать

**twice** [twaɪs] adv два́жды; ~ as
much вдво́е бо́льше

**twig** [twɪg] n сучо́к

**twilight** ['twaɪlaɪt] n (evening)
су́мерки mpl

**twin** [twɪn] adj (towers) па́рный ♦ n
близне́ц ♦ vt: to be ~ned with
(towns etc) быть (impf)
побрати́мами с +instr; ~ sister
сестра́-близне́ц; ~ brother брат-
близне́ц

**twinkle** ['twɪŋkl] vi мерца́ть (impf);
(eyes) сверка́ть (impf)

**twist** [twɪst] n (action)
закру́чивание; (in road, coil, flex)
вито́к; (in story) поворо́т ♦ vt
(turn) изгиба́ть (изогну́ть pf);
(injure: ankle etc) вывихивать
(вы́вихнуть pf); (fig: meaning,
words) искажа́ть (исказить pf),
кове́ркать (исковеркать pf) ♦ vi
(road, river) извива́ться (impf)

**twitch** [twɪtʃ] n (nervous)
подёргивание

**two** [tu:] n два m/nt f (две); to put
~ and ~ together (fig)
сообража́ть (сообрази́ть pf) что
к чему́; ~-faced adj (pej)
двули́чный

**tycoon** [taɪ'ku:n] n: (business) ~
магна́т

**type** [taɪp] n тип; (TYP) шрифт ♦ vt
(letter etc) печа́тать (напеча́тать
pf); ~writer n пи́шущая маши́нка

**typhoid** ['taɪfɔɪd] n брюшно́й тиф

**typhoon** [taɪ'fu:n] n тайфу́н

**typical** ['tɪpɪkl] adj: ~ (of)
типи́чный (для +gen)

**typing** ['taɪpɪŋ] n маши́нопись f

**typist** ['taɪpɪst] n машини́стка

**tyranny** ['tɪrənɪ] n тирани́я

**tyrant** ['taɪərnt] n тира́н

**tyre** ['taɪər] (US tire) n ши́на

**tzar** [zɑ:r] n = **tsar**

## U, u

**udder** ['ʌdər] n вы́мя nt

**UFO** n abbr (= unidentified flying
object) НЛО

**ugly** ['ʌglɪ] adj (person, dress etc)
уро́дливый, безобра́зный;
(dangerous: situation) скве́рный

**UK** n abbr = **United Kingdom**

**Ukraine** [ju:'kreɪn] n Украи́на

**Ukrainian** [ju:'kreɪnɪən] adj
украи́нский

**ulcer** ['ʌlsər] n я́зва

**ultimata** [ʌltɪ'meɪtə] npl of
**ultimatum**

**ultimate** ['ʌltɪmət] adj (final)
оконча́тельный, коне́чный;
(greatest) преде́льный; ~ly adv в
коне́чном ито́ге; (basically) в
преде́льном счёте

**ultimatum** [ʌltɪ'meɪtəm] (pl ~s or
**ultimata**) n ультима́тум

**ultraviolet** ['ʌltrə'vaɪəlɪt] adj (light
etc) ультрафиоле́товый

**umbrella** [ʌm'brelə] n (for rain, sun)
зонт, зо́нтик

**umpire** ['ʌmpaɪər] n судья́ m,
рефери́ m ind

**UN** n abbr = **United Nations**

**unable** [ʌnˈeɪbl] *adj* неспосо́бный;
**he is ~ to pay** он неспосо́бен
заплати́ть

**unaccompanied** [ʌnəˈkʌmpənɪd]
*adj* (*child, bag*) без
сопровожде́ния

**unaccustomed** [ʌnəˈkʌstəmd] *adj*:
**he is ~ to ...** он непривы́чен к
+*dat* ...

**unanimous** [juːˈnænɪməs] *adj*
единоду́шный

**unarmed** [ʌnˈɑːmd] *adj*
безору́жный

**unashamed** [ʌnəˈʃeɪmd] *adj*
бессты́дный

**unassuming** [ʌnəˈsjuːmɪŋ] *adj*
непритяза́тельный

**unattached** [ʌnəˈtætʃt] *adj* (*person*)
одино́кий

**unattractive** [ʌnəˈtræktɪv] *adj*
непривлека́тельный

**unauthorized** [ʌnˈɔːθəraɪzd] *adj*
неразрешённый; (*actions*)
несанкциони́рованный

**unavoidable** [ʌnəˈvɔɪdəbl] *adj*
(*delay*) неизбе́жный

**unaware** [ʌnəˈwɛəʳ] *adj*: **to be ~ of**
не подозрева́ть (*impf*) о +*prp*; (*fail
to notice*) не осознава́ть (*impf*)

**unbalanced** [ʌnˈbælənst] *adj*
(*report*) несбаланси́рованный;
(*person*) неуравнове́шенный

**unbearable** [ʌnˈbɛərəbl] *adj*
невыноси́мый

**unbeatable** [ʌnˈbiːtəbl] *adj* (*price,
quality*) непревзойдённый

**unbelievable** [ʌnbɪˈliːvəbl] *adj*
невероя́тный

**unbias(s)ed** [ʌnˈbaɪəst] *adj* (*report*)
непредвзя́тый; (*person*)
беспристра́стный

**unbroken** [ʌnˈbrəukən] *adj* (*silence*)
непре́рванный; (*series*)
непреры́вный; (*SPORT, record*)
непобиты́й

**uncanny** [ʌnˈkænɪ] *adj* (*resemblance,*

*knack*) необъясни́мый; (*silence*)
жу́ткий

**uncertain** [ʌnˈsəːtn] *adj* (*unsure*): **~
about** неуве́ренный
относи́тельно +*gen*; **in no ~ terms**
без обиняко́в, вполне́
определённо; **~ty** *n* (*not knowing*)
неопределённость *f*; (*often pl*:
*doubt*) сомне́ние

**unchanged** [ʌnˈtʃeɪndʒd] *adj*
(*orders, habits*) неизме́нный

**unchecked** [ʌnˈtʃɛkt] *adv*
беспрепя́тственно

**uncle** [ˈʌŋkl] *n* дя́дя *m*

**uncomfortable** [ʌnˈkʌmfətəbl] *adj*
неудо́бный; (*unpleasant*)
гнету́щий

**uncommon** [ʌnˈkɔmən] *adj* (*rare,
unusual*) необы́чный

**uncompromising** [ʌnˈkɔmprə-
maɪzɪŋ] *adj* бескомпроми́ссный

**unconditional** [ʌnkənˈdɪʃənl] *adj*
(*acceptance, obedience*)
безусло́вный; (*discharge,
surrender*) безоговоро́чный

**unconscious** [ʌnˈkɔnʃəs] *adj* без
созна́ния; (*unaware*): **~ of** не
созна́ющий +*gen*; **~ly** *adv*
(*unawares*) подсозна́тельно

**uncontrollable** [ʌnkənˈtrəuləbl] *adj*
(*child, animal*) неуправля́емый;
(*laughter*) неудержи́мый

**unconventional** [ʌnkənˈvɛnʃənl]
*adj* нетрадицио́нный

**uncover** [ʌnˈkʌvəʳ] *vt* открыва́ть
(откры́ть *pf*); (*plot, secret*)
раскрыва́ть (раскры́ть *pf*)

**undecided** [ʌndɪˈsaɪdɪd] *adj* (*person*)
коле́блющийся; **he is ~ as to
whether he will go** он не реши́л
пойдёт ли он

**undeniable** [ʌndɪˈnaɪəbl] *adj* (*fact,
evidence*) неоспори́мый

**under** [ˈʌndəʳ] *adv* (*go, fly etc*) вниз
♦ *prep* (*position*) под +*instr*; (*motion*)
под +*acc*; (*less than: cost, pay*)

ме́ньше +gen; (according to) по +dat; (during) при +prp; **children ~ 16** де́ти до 16-ти лет; **~ there** там внизу́; **~ repair** в ремо́нте

**undercover** [ʌndəˈkʌvəʳ] adj та́йный

**underestimate** [ˈʌndərˈɛstɪmeɪt] vt недооце́нивать (недооцени́ть pf)

**undergo** [ʌndəˈgəu] (irreg) vt (repair) проходи́ть (пройти́ pf); (operation) переноси́ть (перенести́ pf); (change) претерпева́ть (претерпе́ть pf)

**undergraduate** [ʌndəˈgrædjuɪt] n студе́нт(ка)

**underground** [ˈʌndəgraund] adv (work) под землёй ♦ adj (car park) подзе́мный; (activities) подпо́льный ♦ n: **the ~** (BRIT : RAIL) метро́ nt ind (POL) подпо́лье

**underline** [ʌndəˈlaɪn] vt подчёркивать (подчеркну́ть pf)

**undermine** [ʌndəˈmaɪn] vt (authority) подрыва́ть (подорва́ть pf)

**underneath** [ʌndəˈniːθ] adv внизу́ ♦ prep (position) под +instr; (motion) под +acc

**underpants** [ˈʌndəpænts] npl (men's) трусы́ pl

**underprivileged** [ʌndəˈprɪvɪlɪdʒd] adj (family) неиму́щий

**understand** [ʌndəˈstænd] (irreg: like **stand**) vt понима́ть (поня́ть pf); (believe): **to ~ that** полага́ть (impf), что; **~able** adj поня́тный; **~ing** adj понима́ющий ♦ n понима́ние; (agreement) договорённость f

**understatement** [ˈʌndəsteɪtmənt] n: **that's an ~!** э́то сли́шком мя́гко ска́зано!

**understood** [ʌndəˈstud] pt, pp of **understand** ♦ adj (agreed) согласо́ванный; (implied) подразумева́емый

**undertake** [ʌndəˈteɪk] (irreg: like **take**) vt (task, duty) брать (взять pf) на себя́; **to ~ to do** обя́зываться (обяза́ться pf) +infin

**undertaker** [ˈʌndəteɪkəʳ] n владе́лец похоро́нного бюро́

**underwater** [ʌndəˈwɔːtəʳ] adv под водо́й ♦ adj подво́дный

**underwear** [ˈʌndəwɛəʳ] n ни́жнее бельё

**underworld** [ˈʌndəwəːld] n (of crime) престу́пный мир

**undesirable** [ʌndɪˈzaɪərəbl] adj нежела́тельный

**undisputed** [ˈʌndɪsˈpjuːtɪd] adj неоспори́мый

**undo** [ʌnˈduː] (irreg: like **do**) vt (laces, strings) развя́зывать (развяза́ть pf); (buttons) расстёгивать (расстегну́ть pf); (spoil) губи́ть (погуби́ть pf)

**undoubted** [ʌnˈdautɪd] adj несомне́нный, бесспо́рный; **~ly** adv несомне́нно, бесспо́рно

**undress** [ʌnˈdrɛs] vt раздева́ть (разде́ть pf) ♦ vi раздева́ться (разде́ться pf)

**undue** [ʌnˈdjuː] adj изли́шний

**undulating** [ˈʌndjuleɪtɪŋ] adj волни́стый

**unduly** [ʌnˈdjuːlɪ] adv изли́шне

**uneasy** [ʌnˈiːzɪ] adj (feeling) трево́жный; (peace, truce) напряжённый; **he is** or **feels ~** он неспоко́ен

**uneducated** [ʌnˈɛdjukeɪtɪd] adj необразо́ванный

**unemployed** [ʌnɪmˈplɔɪd] adj безрабо́тный ♦ npl: **the ~** безрабо́тные pl adj

**unemployment** [ʌnɪmˈplɔɪmənt] n безрабо́тица

**unending** [ʌnˈendɪŋ] adj несконча́емый

**uneven** [ʌnˈiːvn] adj неро́вный

**unexpected** [ʌnɪksˈpɛktɪd] adj

неожи́данный; **~ly** *adv* неожи́данно

**unfair** [ʌnˈfɛər] *adj*: ~ **(to)** несправедли́вый (к +*dat*)

**unfaithful** [ʌnˈfeɪθful] *adj* неве́рный

**unfamiliar** [ʌnfəˈmɪlɪər] *adj* незнако́мый

**unfashionable** [ʌnˈfæʃnəbl] *adj* немо́дный

**unfavourable** [ʌnˈfeɪvrəbl] (*US* **unfavorable**) *adj* неблагоприя́тный

**unfinished** [ʌnˈfɪnɪʃt] *adj* незако́нченный

**unfit** [ʌnˈfɪt] *adj* (*physically*): **she is ~** она́ в плохо́й спорти́вной фо́рме; **he is ~ for the job** он непригоден для э́той рабо́ты

**unfold** [ʌnˈfəuld] *vt* (*sheets, map*) развора́чивать (разверну́ть *pf*) ♦ *vi* (*situation*) развора́чиваться (разверну́ться *pf*)

**unforeseen** [ˈʌnfɔːˈsiːn] *adj* непредви́денный

**unforgettable** [ʌnfəˈgɛtəbl] *adj* незабыва́емый

**unforgivable** [ʌnfəˈgɪvəbl] *adj* непрости́тельный

**unfortunate** [ʌnˈfɔːtʃənət] *adj* (*unlucky*) несча́стный; (*regrettable*) неуда́чный; **~ly** *adv* к сожале́нию

**unfounded** [ʌnˈfaundɪd] *adj* необосно́ванный

**unfriendly** [ʌnˈfrɛndlɪ] *adj* недружелю́бный

**ungrateful** [ʌnˈgreɪtful] *adj* неблагода́рный

**unhappy** [ʌnˈhæpɪ] *adj* несча́стный; **~ with** (*dissatisfied*) недово́льный +*instr*

**unharmed** [ʌnˈhɑːmd] *adj* (*person*) невреди́мый

**unhealthy** [ʌnˈhɛlθɪ] *adj* нездоро́вый

**unhurt** [ʌnˈhəːt] *adj* невреди́мый

**unidentified** [ʌnaɪˈdɛntɪfaɪd] *adj* (*unnamed*) анони́мный; *see also* **UFO**

**uniform** [ˈjuːnɪfɔːm] *n* фо́рма ♦ *adj* (*length, width*) единообра́зный; (*temperature*) постоя́нный

**unilateral** [juːnɪˈlætərəl] *adj* (*disarmament etc*) односторо́нний

**uninhabited** [ʌnɪnˈhæbɪtd] *adj* необита́емый

**unintentional** [ʌnɪnˈtɛnʃənəl] *adj* неумы́шленный

**union** [ˈjuːnjən] *n* (*unification*) объедине́ние; (*also*: **trade ~**) профсою́з ♦ *cpd* профсою́зный

**unique** [juːˈniːk] *adj* уника́льный

**unison** [ˈjuːnɪsn] *n*: **in ~** (*say*) в оди́н го́лос; (*sing*) в унисо́н

**unit** [ˈjuːnɪt] *n* (*single whole*) це́лое nt *adj*; (*measurement*) едини́ца; (*section*: *of furniture etc*) се́кция

**unite** [juːˈnaɪt] *vt* объединя́ть (объедини́ть *pf*) ♦ *vi* объединя́ться (объедини́ться *pf*); **~d** объединённый; (*effort*) совме́стный; **United Kingdom** *n* Соединённое Короле́вство; **United Nations (Organization)** *n* (Организа́ция) Объединённых На́ций; **United States (of America)** *n* Соединённые Шта́ты (Аме́рики)

**unity** [ˈjuːnɪtɪ] *n* еди́нство

**universal** [juːnɪˈvəːsl] *adj* универса́льный

**universe** [ˈjuːnɪvəːs] *n* вселе́нная *f adj*

**university** [juːnɪˈvəːsɪtɪ] *n* университе́т

**unjust** [ʌnˈdʒʌst] *adj* несправедли́вый

**unkind** [ʌnˈkaɪnd] *adj* недо́брый; (*behaviour*) зло́бный

**unknown** [ʌnˈnəun] *adj* неизве́стный

**unlawful** [ʌnˈlɔːful] *adj*

незако́нный

**unleash** [ʌnˈliːʃ] vt (fig: feeling)
дава́ть (дать pf) во́лю +dat;
(: force) развя́зывать (развяза́ть
pf)

**unless** [ʌnˈlɛs] conj е́сли не; **he
won't come, ~ we ask** он не
придёт, е́сли мы не попро́сим

**unlike** [ʌnˈlaɪk] adj (not alike)
непохо́жий ♦ prep (different from) в
отли́чие от +gen; **he is ~ his
brother** (not like) он не похо́ж на
бра́та

**unlikely** [ʌnˈlaɪklɪ] adj (not likely)
маловероя́тный

**unlimited** [ʌnˈlɪmɪtɪd] adj
неограни́ченный

**unload** [ʌnˈləud] vt (box, car)
разгружа́ть (разгрузи́ть pf)

**unlucky** [ʌnˈlʌkɪ] adj невезу́чий;
(object) несчастли́вый; **he is ~** он
невезу́чий, ему́ не везёт

**unmarried** [ʌnˈmærɪd] adj (man)
жена́тый, холосто́й; (woman)
незаму́жняя

**unmistak(e)able** [ʌnmɪsˈteɪkəbl]
adj (voice, sound) характе́рный

**unnatural** [ʌnˈnætʃrəl] adj
неесте́ственный

**unnecessary** [ʌnˈnɛsəsərɪ] adj
нену́жный

**unnoticed** [ʌnˈnəutɪst] adj
незаме́ченный

**UNO** n abbr (= United Nations
Organization) ООН

**unobtrusive** [ʌnəbˈtruːsɪv] adj
(person) ненавя́зчивый

**unofficial** [ʌnəˈfɪʃl] adj
неофициа́льный

**unorthodox** [ʌnˈɔːθədɔks] adj (also
REL) неортодокса́льный

**unpack** [ʌnˈpæk] vi
распако́вываться
(распакова́ться pf) ♦ vt
распако́вывать (распакова́ть pf)

**unparalleled** [ʌnˈpærəleld] adj

непревзойдённый; (crisis)
небыва́лый

**unpleasant** [ʌnˈplɛznt] adj
неприя́тный

**unpopular** [ʌnˈpɔpjulər] adj
непопуля́рный

**unprecedented** [ʌnˈprɛsɪdəntɪd] adj
беспрецеде́нтный

**unpredictable** [ʌnprɪˈdɪktəbl] adj
непредсказу́емый

**unprofessional** [ʌnprəˈfɛʃənl] adj
непрофессиона́льный

**unqualified** [ʌnˈkwɔlɪfaɪd] adj
неквалифици́рованный; (total)
соверше́нный

**unravel** [ʌnˈrævl] vt (fig: mystery)
разга́дывать (разгада́ть pf)

**unreal** [ʌnˈrɪəl] adj (not real)
нереа́льный

**unrealistic** [ˈʌnrɪəˈlɪstɪk] adj
нереалисти́чный

**unreasonable** [ʌnˈriːznəbl] adj
неразу́мный; (length of time)
нереа́льный

**unrelated** [ʌnrɪˈleɪtɪd] adj (incident)
изоли́рованный, отде́льный; **to
be ~** (people) не состоя́ть (impf) в
родстве́

**unreliable** [ʌnrɪˈlaɪəbl] adj
ненадёжный

**unrest** [ʌnˈrɛst] n волне́ния ntpl

**unruly** [ʌnˈruːlɪ] adj
неуправля́емый

**unsafe** [ʌnˈseɪf] adj опа́сный

**unsatisfactory** [ˈʌnsætɪsˈfæktərɪ] adj
неудовлетвори́тельный

**unscathed** [ʌnˈskeɪðd] adj
невреди́мый

**unscrupulous** [ʌnˈskruːpjuləs] adj
бессо́вестный, беспринци́пный

**unsettled** [ʌnˈsɛtld] adj (person)
беспоко́йный; **the weather is ~**
пого́да не установи́лась

**unshaven** [ʌnˈʃeɪvn] adj небри́тый

**unsightly** [ʌnˈsaɪtlɪ] adj
непригля́дный

**unskilled** [ʌn'skɪld] *adj*
неквалифици́рованный

**unstable** [ʌn'steɪbl] *adj* (*government*) нестаби́льный; (*person: mentally*) неуравнове́шенный

**unsteady** [ʌn'stɛdɪ] *adj* нетвёрдый

**unsuccessful** [ʌnsək'sɛsful] *adj* (*attempt*) безуспе́шный; (*writer*) неуда́вшийся; **to be ~ (in sth)** терпе́ть (потерпе́ть *pf*) неуда́чу (в чём-н); **your application was ~** Ва́ше заявле́ние не при́нято; **~ly** *adv* безуспе́шно

**unsuitable** [ʌn'su:təbl] *adj* неподходя́щий

**unsure** [ʌn'ʃuəʳ] *adj* неуве́ренный; **he is ~ of himself** он неуве́рен в себе́

**unsuspecting** [ʌnsəs'pɛktɪŋ] *adj* ничего́ не подозрева́ющий

**unsympathetic** ['ʌnsɪmpə'θɛtɪk] *adj* безуча́стный

**unthinkable** [ʌn'θɪŋkəbl] *adj* немы́слимый

**untidy** [ʌn'taɪdɪ] *adj* неопря́тный

**until** [ən'tɪl] *prep* до +*gen* ♦ *conj* пока́ не; **~ he comes** пока́ он не придёт; **~ now/then** до сих/тех пор

**untimely** [ʌn'taɪmlɪ] *adj* (*moment*) неподходя́щий; (*arrival*) неуме́стный; (*death*) безвре́менный

**untold** [ʌn'təuld] *adj* (*joy, suffering*) несказа́нный

**unused¹** [ʌn'ju:zd] *adj* (*not used*) неиспо́льзованный

**unused²** [ʌn'ju:st] *adj*: **he is ~ to it** он к э́тому не привы́к; **she is ~ to flying** она́ не привы́кла лета́ть

**unusual** [ʌn'ju:ʒuəl] *adj* необы́чный; (*exceptional*) необыкнове́нный

**unveil** [ʌn'veɪl] *vt* (*statue*) открыва́ть (откры́ть *pf*)

**unwanted** [ʌn'wɔntɪd] *adj* (*child,* *pregnancy*) нежела́нный

**unwavering** [ʌn'weɪvərɪŋ] *adj* (*faith*) непоколеби́мый; (*gaze*) твёрдый

**unwelcome** [ʌn'wɛlkəm] *adj* (*guest*) незва́ный, непро́шеный; (*news*) неприя́тный

**unwell** [ʌn'wɛl] *adj*: **to feel ~** чу́вствовать (*impf*) себя́ пло́хо; **he is ~** он пло́хо себя́ чу́вствует, он нездоро́в

**unwilling** [ʌn'wɪlɪŋ] *adj*: **to be ~ to do** не хоте́ть (*impf*) +*infin*

**unwind** [ʌn'waɪnd] (*irreg: like* **wind²**) *vi* (*relax*) расслабля́ться (расслабиться *pf*)

**unwise** [ʌn'waɪz] *adj* неблагоразу́мный

**unwitting** [ʌn'wɪtɪŋ] *adj* нево́льный

**unworthy** [ʌn'wə:ðɪ] *adj* недосто́йный

---
KEYWORD
---

**up** [ʌp] *prep* (*motion*) на +*acc*; (*position*) на +*prp*; **he went up the stairs/the hill** он подня́лся по ле́стнице/на́ гору; **the cat was up a tree** ко́шка была́ на де́реве; **they live further up this street** они́ живу́т да́льше на э́той у́лице; **he has gone up to Scotland** он пое́хал в Шотла́ндию

♦ *adv* **1** (*upwards, higher*): **up in the sky/the mountains** высоко́ в не́бе/в гора́х; **put the picture a bit higher up** пове́сьте карти́ну повы́ше; **up there** (*up above*) там наверху́

**2**: **to be up** (*out of bed*) встава́ть (встать *pf*); (*prices, level*) поднима́ться (подня́ться *pf*); **the tent is up** пала́тка устано́влена

**3**: **up to** (*as far as*) до +*gen*; **up to now** до сих пор

4: **to be up to** (*depending on*) зави́сеть (*impf*) от +*gen*; **it's not up to me to decide** не мне реша́ть; **it's up to you** э́то на Ва́ше усмотре́ние

5: **to be up to** (*inf: be doing*) затева́ть (*impf*); (*be satisfactory*) соотве́тствовать (*impf*) +*dat*, отвеча́ть (*impf*) +*dat*; **he's not up to the job** он не справля́ется с э́той рабо́той; **his work is not up to the required standard** его́ рабо́та не соотве́тствует тре́буемым станда́ртам; **what's she up to these days?** а что она́ тепе́рь поде́лывает?

♦ *n*: **ups and downs** (*in life, career*) взлёты *mpl* и паде́ния *ntpl*

**upbringing** ['ʌpbrɪŋɪŋ] *n* воспита́ние
**update** [ʌp'deɪt] *vt* (*records*) обновля́ть (обнови́ть *pf*)
**upgrade** [ʌp'greɪd] *vt* (*house, equipment*) модернизи́ровать (*impf/pf*); (*employee*) повыша́ть (повы́сить *pf*) (в до́лжности)
**upheaval** [ʌp'hiːvl] *n* переворо́т
**uphill** [ʌp'hɪl] *adj* (*fig*) тяжёлый, напряжённый ♦ *adv* вверх; **to go ~** поднима́ться (подня́ться *pf*) в го́ру
**uphold** [ʌp'həuld] (*irreg: like* hold) *vt* подде́рживать (поддержа́ть *pf*)
**upholstery** [ʌp'həulstərɪ] *n* оби́вка
**upkeep** ['ʌpkiːp] *n* содержа́ние
**upon** [ə'pɔn] *prep* (*position*) на +*prp*; (*motion*) на +*acc*
**upper** ['ʌpər] *adj* ве́рхний ♦ *n* верх; **~most** *adj* ве́рхний; **what was ~most in my mind** что бо́льше всего́ занима́ло мои́ мы́сли
**upright** ['ʌpraɪt] *adj* (*vertical*) вертика́льный; (*honest*) безупре́чный

**uprising** ['ʌpraɪzɪŋ] *n* восста́ние
**uproar** ['ʌprɔːr] *n* (*protest*) возмуще́ние; (*shouts*) го́мон, кри́ки *mpl*
**upset** *vb, adj* [ʌp'sɛt] *n* ['ʌpsɛt] (*irreg: like* set) *vt* (*glass etc*) опроки́дывать (опроки́нуть *pf*); (*routine*) наруша́ть (нару́шить *pf*); (*person, plan*) расстра́ивать (расстро́ить *pf*) ♦ *adj* расстро́енный ♦ *n*: **I have a stomach ~** (*BRIT*) у меня́ расстро́йство желу́дка
**upside down** ['ʌpsaɪd-] *adv* (*hang, hold*) вверх нога́ми; (*turn*) вверх дном
**upstairs** [ʌp'stɛəz] *adv* (*be*) наверху́; (*go*) наве́рх ♦ *adj* ве́рхний ♦ *n* ве́рхний эта́ж
**upstream** [ʌp'striːm] *adv* про́тив тече́ния
**uptight** [ʌp'taɪt] *adj* (*inf*) натя́нутый
**up-to-date** ['ʌptə'deɪt] *adj* (*information*) после́дний; (*equipment*) нове́йший
**upturn** ['ʌptəːn] *n* (*ECON*) подъём
**upward** ['ʌpwəd] *adj*: **~ movement/glance** движе́ние/ взгляд вверх ♦ *adv* = **upwards**; **~s** *adv* вверх; (*more than*): **~s of** свы́ше +*gen*
**uranium** [juə'reɪnɪəm] *n* ура́н
**urban** ['əːbən] *adj* городско́й
**urge** [əːdʒ] *n* потре́бность *f* ♦ *vt*: **to ~ sb to do** настоя́тельно проси́ть (попроси́ть *pf*) кого́-н +*infin*
**urgency** ['əːdʒənsɪ] *n* (*of task etc*) неотло́жность *f*; (*of tone*) насто́йчивость *f*
**urgent** ['əːdʒənt] *adj* (*message*) сро́чный; (*need*) насу́щный, неотло́жный; (*voice*) насто́йчивый
**urinate** ['juərɪneɪt] *vi* мочи́ться (помочи́ться *pf*)

**urine** ['juərɪn] n моча́

**urn** [ə:n] n (also: **tea ~**) тита́н

**Uruguay** ['juərəgwaɪ] n Уругва́й

**US** n abbr (= United States) США

**us** [ʌs] pron (direct) нас; (indirect) нам; (after prep: +gen, +prp) нас; (: +dat) нам; (: +instr) на́ми; **a few of ~** не́которые из нас; see also **me**

**USA** n abbr (= United States of America) США

**use** vb [ju:z] n [ju:s] vt (object, tool) по́льзоваться (impf) +instr, испо́льзовать (impf/pf); (phrase) употребля́ть (употреби́ть pf) ♦ n (using) испо́льзование, употребле́ние; (usefulness) по́льза; (purpose) примене́ние; **she ~d to do it** она́ когда́-то занима́лась э́тим; **what's this ~d for?** для чего́ э́то испо́льзуется?; **to be ~d to** привы́кнуть (pf) к +dat; **to be in ~** употребля́ться (impf), быть (impf) в употребле́нии; **to be out of ~** не употребля́ться (impf); **of ~** поле́зный; **it's no ~** (э́то) бесполе́зно; **~ up** vt (food) расхо́довать (израсхо́довать pf); **~d** [ju:zd] adj (car) поде́ржанный; **~ful** ['ju:sful] adj поле́зный; **~fulness** ['ju:sfəlnɪs] n по́льза; **~less** ['ju:slɪs] adj (unusable) неприго́дный; (pointless) бесполе́зный; **~r** ['ju:zər] n по́льзователь m; **~r-friendly** ['ju:zə'frɛndlɪ] adj просто́й в испо́льзовании

**USSR** n abbr (formerly: = Union of Soviet Socialist Republics) СССР

**usual** ['ju:ʒuəl] adj (time, place etc) обы́чный; **as ~** как обы́чно; **~ly** adv обы́чно

**utensil** [ju:'tensl] n инструме́нт; (for cooking) принадле́жность f

**utility** [ju:'tɪlɪtɪ] n: **public utilities** коммуна́льные услу́ги fpl

**utilize** ['ju:tɪlaɪz] vt утилизи́ровать (impf/pf)

**utmost** ['ʌtməust] adj велича́йший ♦ n: **to do one's ~** де́лать (сде́лать pf) всё возмо́жное

**utter** ['ʌtər] adj (amazement) по́лный; (conviction) глубо́кий; (rubbish) соверше́нный ♦ vt (words) произноси́ть (произнести́ pf); **~ly** adv соверше́нно

**U-turn** ['ju:'tə:n] n (AUT) разворо́т на 180 гра́дусов

# V, v

**vacancy** ['veɪkənsɪ] n (BRIT: job) вака́нсия; (room) свобо́дный но́мер

**vacant** ['veɪkənt] adj (room, seat) свобо́дный; (look) пусто́й

**vacation** [və'keɪʃən] n (esp US: holiday) о́тпуск; (BRIT : SCOL) кани́кулы pl

**vaccinate** ['væksɪneɪt] vt: **to ~ sb (against sth)** де́лать (сде́лать pf) приви́вку кому́-н (от чего́-н)

**vaccine** ['væksi:n] n вакци́на

**vacuum** ['vækjum] n (empty space) ва́куум ♦ vt пылесо́сить (пропылесо́сить pf); **~ cleaner** n пылесо́с

**vagina** [və'dʒaɪnə] n влага́лище

**vague** [veɪg] adj (blurred: memory, outline) сму́тный; (look) рассе́янный; (idea, instructions, answer) неопределённый; **he was ~ about it** он не сказа́л ничего́ определённого об э́том; **~ly** adv (say) неопределённо; (look) рассе́янно; (suspect) сму́тно; (slightly) слегка́

**vain** [veɪn] adj тщесла́вный; (useless) тще́тный; **in ~** тще́тно, напра́сно

**valid** ['vælɪd] adj (ticket, document) действи́тельный; (reason, argument) ве́ский; **~ity** [və'lɪdɪtɪ] n (see adj) действи́тельность f; ве́скость f

**valley** ['vælɪ] n доли́на

**valuable** ['væljuəbl] adj це́нный; (time) драгоце́нный; **~s** npl (jewellery etc) це́нности fpl

**valuation** [vælju'eɪʃən] n оце́нка

**value** ['vælju:] n це́нность f ♦ vt оце́нивать (оцени́ть pf); (appreciate) цени́ть (impf); **~s** npl (principles) це́нности fpl; **~d** adj (customer, advice) це́нный

**valve** [vælv] n (also MED) кла́пан

**vampire** ['væmpaɪə'] n вампи́р

**van** [væn] n (AUT) фурго́н

**vandalism** ['vændəlɪzəm] n вандали́зм

**vanilla** [və'nɪlə] n вани́ль f

**vanish** ['vænɪʃ] vi исчеза́ть (исче́знуть pf)

**vanity** ['vænɪtɪ] n тщесла́вие

**vapour** ['veɪpə'] (US vapor) n пар

**variable** ['vɛərɪəbl] adj (likely to change) изме́нчивый; (able to be changed: speed) переме́нный

**variation** [vɛərɪ'eɪʃən] n (change) измене́ние; (different form) вариа́ция

**varied** ['vɛərɪd] adj разнообра́зный

**variety** [və'raɪətɪ] n разнообра́зие; (type) разнови́дность f

**various** ['vɛərɪəs] adj (different, several) разли́чный

**varnish** ['vɑːnɪʃ] n (product) лак; (also: nail ~) лак для ногте́й ♦ vt (wood, table) лакирова́ть (отлакирова́ть pf); (nails) кра́сить (покра́сить pf)

**vary** ['vɛərɪ] vt разнообра́зить (impf) ♦ vi (sizes, colours) различа́ться (impf); (become different): **to ~ with** (weather etc) меня́ться (impf) в зави́симости от

+gen

**vase** [vɑːz] n ва́за

**vast** [vɑːst] adj (knowledge, area) обши́рный; (expense) грома́дный

**VAT** [væt] n abbr (BRIT: = value-added tax) НДС

**vat** [væt] n ка́дка

**Vatican** ['vætɪkən] n: **the ~** Ватика́н

**vault** [vɔːlt] n (tomb) склеп; (in bank) сейф, храни́лище ♦ vt (also: ~ over) перепры́гивать (перепры́гнуть pf) (че́рез +acc)

**VCR** n abbr = **video cassette recorder**

**veal** [viːl] n (CULIN) теля́тина

**veer** [vɪə'] vi (vehicle) свора́чивать (сверну́ть pf); (wind) меня́ть (поменя́ть pf) направле́ние

**vegetable** ['vɛdʒtəbl] n (BOT) о́вощ ♦ adj (oil etc) расти́тельный; (dish) овощно́й

**vegetarian** [vɛdʒɪ'tɛərɪən] n вегетариа́нец(а́нка) ♦ adj вегетариа́нский

**vegetation** [vɛdʒɪ'teɪʃən] n (plants) расти́тельность f

**vehement** ['viːɪmənt] adj (attack, denial) я́ростный, гне́вный

**vehicle** ['viːɪkl] n автотра́нспортное сре́дство; (fig) сре́дство, ору́дие

**veil** [veɪl] n вуа́ль f

**vein** [veɪn] n (of leaf) жи́лка; (ANAT) ве́на; (of ore) жи́ла

**velocity** [vɪ'lɔsɪtɪ] n ско́рость f

**velvet** ['vɛlvɪt] n ба́рхат ♦ adj ба́рхатный

**vendor** ['vɛndə'] n: **street ~** у́личный(ая) торго́вец(вка)

**veneer** [və'nɪə'] n (on furniture) фанеро́вка

**vengeance** ['vɛndʒəns] n мще́ние, возме́здие; **with a ~** (fig) отча́янно

**venison** ['vɛnɪsn] n оле́нина

**venom** ['vɛnəm] n (also fig) яд

**vent** [vɛnt] n (also: **air ~**)
вентиляцио́нное отве́рстие ♦ vt
( fig) дава́ть (дать pf) вы́ход +dat

**ventilate** ['vɛntɪleɪt] vt (room,
building) прове́тривать
(прове́трить pf)

**ventilation** [vɛntɪ'leɪʃən] n
вентиля́ция

**ventilator** ['vɛntɪleɪtə<sup>r</sup>] n
вентиля́тор

**venture** ['vɛntʃə<sup>r</sup>] n предприя́тие
♦ vt (opinion) осме́ливаться
(осме́литься pf) на +acc ♦ vi
осме́ливаться (осме́литься pf);
**business ~** предприя́тие

**venue** ['vɛnjuː] n ме́сто
проведе́ния

**veranda(h)** [və'rændə] n вера́нда

**verb** [vəːb] n глаго́л

**verbal** ['vəːbl] adj (spoken) у́стный

**verdict** ['vəːdɪkt] n (LAW) верди́кт;
(fig: opinion) заключе́ние

**verge** [vəːdʒ] n (BRIT: of road)
обо́чина; **to be on the ~ of sth**
быть (impf) на гра́ни чего́-н

**verify** ['vɛrɪfaɪ] vt (confirm)
подтвержда́ть (подтверди́ть pf);
(check) сверя́ть (све́рить pf)

**veritable** ['vɛrɪtəbl] adj и́стинный,
су́щий

**vermin** ['vəːmɪn] npl вреди́тели
mpl

**versatile** ['vəːsətaɪl] adj (person)
разносторо́нний; (substance,
machine etc) универса́льный

**verse** [vəːs] n (poetry, in Bible) стих;
(part of poem) строфа́

**version** ['vəːʃən] n (form) вариа́нт;
(account: of events) ве́рсия

**versus** ['vəːsəs] prep про́тив +gen

**vertical** ['vəːtɪkl] adj вертика́льный

**vertigo** ['vəːtɪgəu] n
головокруже́ние

**verve** [vəːv] n воодушевле́ние

**very** ['vɛrɪ] adv о́чень ♦ adj са́мый;

**the ~ book which ...** та са́мая
кни́га, кото́рая ...; **thank you ~
much** большо́е (Вам) спаси́бо; **~
much better** гора́здо лу́чше; **I ~
much hope so** я о́чень наде́юсь;
**the ~ last** са́мый после́дний; **at
the ~ least** как ми́нимум

**vessel** ['vɛsl] n су́дно; (bowl)
сосу́д; **blood ~** кровено́сный
сосу́д

**vest** [vɛst] n (BRIT: underwear)
ма́йка; (US: waistcoat) жиле́т

**vet** [vɛt] n abbr (BRIT: = veterinary
surgeon) ветерина́р ♦ vt (check)
проверя́ть (прове́рить pf);
(approve) одобря́ть (одо́брить pf)

**veteran** ['vɛtərn] n (of war)
ветера́н

**veterinary** ['vɛtrɪnərɪ] adj
ветерина́рный

**veto** ['viːtəu] (pl **~es**) n ве́то nt ind
♦ vt (POL, LAW) налага́ть
(наложи́ть pf) ве́то на +acc

**vetting** ['vɛtɪŋ] n прове́рка

**via** ['vaɪə] prep че́рез +acc

**viable** ['vaɪəbl] adj
жизнеспосо́бный

**viaduct** ['vaɪədʌkt] n виаду́к

**vibrant** ['vaɪbrnt] adj (lively)
жизнера́достный; (light) я́ркий;
(colour) со́чный; (voice)
стра́стный

**vibrate** [vaɪ'breɪt] vi вибри́ровать
(impf)

**vibration** [vaɪ'breɪʃən] n вибра́ция

**vicar** ['vɪkə<sup>r</sup>] n (REL) прихо́дский
свяще́нник

**vice** [vaɪs] n поро́к; (TECH) тиски́ pl

**vice-chairman** [vaɪs'tʃɛəmən] (irreg)
n замести́тель m председа́теля

**vice president** n ви́це-президе́нт

**vice versa** ['vaɪsɪ'vəːsə] adv
наоборо́т

**vicinity** [vɪ'sɪnɪtɪ] n: **in the ~ (of)**
вблизи́ (от +gen)

**vicious** ['vɪʃəs] adj (attack, blow)

жесто́кий; (*words, look, dog*) злой;
~ **circle** n поро́чный круг
**victim** ['vɪktɪm] n же́ртва
**victor** ['vɪktər] n победи́тель(ница)
m(f)
**victorious** [vɪk'tɔːrɪəs] adj (*team*)
победоно́сный; (*shout*)
побе́дный
**victory** ['vɪktərɪ] n побе́да
**video** ['vɪdɪəu] cpd ви́део ind ♦ n
(*also*: ~ **film**) видеофи́льм; (*also*:
~ **cassette**) видеокассе́та; (*also*:
~ **cassette recorder**)
видеомагнитофо́н; (*also*: ~
**camera**) видеока́мера; ~ **game**
n видеоигра́; ~ **recorder** n
видеомагнитофо́н; ~ **tape** n
видеоле́нта
**vie** [vaɪ] vi: **to** ~ **with sb/for sth**
состяза́ться (*impf*) с кем-н/в
чём-н
**Vienna** [vɪ'ɛnə] n Ве́на
**view** [vjuː] n (*sight, outlook*) вид;
(*opinion*) взгляд ♦ vt
рассма́тривать (рассмотре́ть pf);
**in full** ~ (**of**) на виду́ (у +gen); **in** ~
**of the bad weather/the fact that**
ввиду́ плохо́й пого́ды/того́, что;
**in my** ~ на мой взгляд; ~**er** n
(*person*) зри́тель(ница) m(f);
~**finder** n (PHOT) видоиска́тель
m; ~**point** n (*attitude*) то́чка
зре́ния; (*place*) ме́сто обозре́ния
**vigil** ['vɪdʒɪl] n бде́ние; ~**ant** adj
бди́тельный
**vigor** ['vɪgər] (US) n = **vigour**
**vigorous** ['vɪgərəs] adj (*action,
campaign*) энерги́чный
**vigour** ['vɪgər] (US **vigor**) n си́ла,
мощь f
**vile** [vaɪl] adj гну́сный,
омерзи́тельный
**villa** ['vɪlə] n ви́лла
**village** ['vɪlɪdʒ] n дере́вня
**villain** ['vɪlən] n (*in novel etc*)
злоде́й; (BRIT: *criminal*)

престу́пник
**vindicate** ['vɪndɪkeɪt] vt (*actions*)
опра́вдывать (оправда́ть pf);
(*person*) реабилити́ровать (*impf/
pf*)
**vine** [vaɪn] n (*with grapes*)
(виногра́дная) лоза́
**vinegar** ['vɪnɪgər] n у́ксус
**vineyard** ['vɪnjɑːd] n виногра́дник
**vintage** ['vɪntɪdʒ] cpd (*comedy,
performance etc*) класси́ческий;
(*wine*) ма́рочный
**vinyl** ['vaɪnl] n вини́л
**viola** [vɪ'əulə] n (MUS) альт
**violation** [vaɪə'leɪʃən] n (*of
agreement etc*) наруше́ние
**violence** ['vaɪələns] n (*brutality*)
наси́лие
**violent** ['vaɪələnt] adj (*behaviour*)
жесто́кий; (*death*)
наси́льственный; (*debate,
criticism*) ожесточённый
**violet** ['vaɪələt] adj фиоле́товый
♦ n (*plant*) фиа́лка
**violin** [vaɪə'lɪn] n (MUS) скри́пка;
~**ist** n скрипа́ч(ка)
**VIP** n abbr (= *very important person*)
осо́бо ва́жное лицо́
**virgin** ['vəːdʒɪn] n де́вственница
♦ adj (*snow, forest etc*)
де́вственный; ~**ity** [vəː'dʒɪnɪtɪ] n
де́вственность f
**Virgo** ['vəːgəu] n Де́ва
**virile** ['vɪraɪl] adj вери́льный
**virtually** ['vəːtjuəlɪ] adv
факти́чески, практи́чески
**virtual reality** ['vəːtjuəl-] n
(COMPUT) виртуа́льная
реа́льность f
**virtue** ['vəːtjuː] n (*moral correctness*)
доброде́тель f; (*advantage*)
преиму́щество; (*good quality*)
досто́инство; **by** ~ **of** благодаря́
+dat
**virtuous** ['vəːtjuəs] adj (*morally
correct*) доброде́тельный

**virus** ['vaɪərəs] n (MED) ви́рус

**visa** ['viːzə] n (for travel) ви́за

**visibility** [vɪzɪ'bɪlɪtɪ] n ви́димость f

**visible** ['vɪzəbl] adj ви́димый; (results, growth) очеви́дный

**vision** ['vɪʒən] n (sight) зре́ние; (foresight) прови́дение, ви́дение

**visit** ['vɪzɪt] n посеще́ние, визи́т ♦ vt (person, place) посеща́ть (посети́ть pf); (elderly, disabled) навеща́ть (навести́ть pf); ~**or** n (person visiting) гость(я) m(f); (in public place) посети́тель(ница) m(f); (in town etc) прие́зжий(ая) m(f) adj

**visual** ['vɪzjuəl] adj (image) зри́тельный; ~**ize** vt представля́ть (предста́вить pf)

**vital** ['vaɪtl] adj (question) жи́зненный; (problem) насу́щный; (full of life: person) де́ятельный, по́лный жи́зни; (organization) жизнеде́ятельный; it is ~ ... необходи́мо ...; ~**ity** n [vaɪ'tælɪtɪ] (liveliness) жи́вость f; ~**ly** adv: ~**ly important** жи́зненно ва́жный

**vitamin** ['vɪtəmɪn] n витами́н

**vivid** ['vɪvɪd] adj (description, colour) я́ркий; (memory) отчётливый; (imagination) живо́й; ~**ly** adv (describe) я́рко; (remember) отчётливо

**vocabulary** [vəu'kæbjulərɪ] n (words known) слова́рный запа́с

**vocal** ['vəukl] adj (articulate) речи́стый

**vocation** [vəu'keɪʃən] n призва́ние; ~**al** adj профессиона́льный

**vodka** ['vɔdkə] n во́дка

**vogue** [vəug] n мо́да; in ~ в мо́де

**voice** [vɔɪs] n го́лос ♦ vt (opinion) выска́зывать (вы́сказать pf); ~ **mail** n у́стное сообще́ние

**void** [vɔɪd] n (emptiness) пустота́; (hole) прова́л ♦ adj (invalid) недействи́тельный

**volatile** ['vɔlətaɪl] adj (situation) изме́нчивый; (person) неусто́йчивый; (liquid) лету́чий

**volcanic** [vɔl'kænɪk] adj вулкани́ческий

**volcano** [vɔl'keɪnəu] (pl ~**es**) n вулка́н

**volley** ['vɔlɪ] n (of gunfire) залп; (of questions) град; (TENNIS etc) уда́р с лёта; ~**ball** n (SPORT) волейбо́л

**voltage** ['vəultɪdʒ] n (ELEC) напряже́ние

**volume** ['vɔljuːm] n объём; (book) том; (sound level) гро́мкость f

**voluntarily** ['vɔləntrɪlɪ] adv доброво́льно

**voluntary** ['vɔləntərɪ] adj (willing) доброво́льный; (unpaid) обще́ственный

**volunteer** [vɔlən'tɪər] n (unpaid helper) доброво́льный(ая) помо́щник(ица), волонтёр; (to army etc) доброво́лец ♦ vt (information) предлага́ть (предложи́ть pf) ♦ vi (for army etc) идти́ (пойти́ pf) доброво́льцем; to ~ to do вызыва́ться (вы́зваться pf) +infin

**vomit** ['vɔmɪt] n рво́та ♦ vi: he ~**ed** его́ вы́рвало

**vote** [vəut] n (indication of opinion) голосова́ние; (votes cast) число́ по́данных голосо́в; (right to vote) пра́во го́лоса ♦ vi голосова́ть (проголосова́ть pf) ♦ vt (Labour etc) голосова́ть (проголосова́ть pf) за +acc; (elect): he was ~**d chairman** он был и́збран председа́телем; (propose): to ~ **that** предлага́ть (предложи́ть pf), что́бы; to put sth to the~, take a ~ on sth ста́вить (поста́вить pf) что-н на голосова́ние; ~ of **thanks** благода́рственная речь f; to pass a ~ of confidence/no confidence выража́ть (вы́разить *pf*) во́тум дове́рия/недове́рия; **to ~ for** *or* **in favour of/against** голосова́ть (проголосова́ть *pf*) за +*acc*/про́тив +*gen*; **~r** *n* избира́тель(ница) *m(f)*

**voting** ['vəutɪŋ] *n* голосова́ние

**voucher** ['vautʃər] *n* (*with petrol, cigarettes etc*) ва́учер

**vow** [vau] *n* кля́тва ♦ *vt*: **to ~ to do/that** кля́сться (покля́сться *pf*) +*infin*; **~s** *npl* (*REL*) обе́т *msg*

**vowel** ['vauəl] *n* гла́сный *m adj*

**voyage** ['vɔɪdʒ] *n* (*by ship*) пла́вание; (*by spacecraft*) полёт

**vulgar** ['vʌlgər] *adj* (*rude*) вульга́рный; (*tasteless*) по́шлый

**vulnerable** ['vʌlnərəbl] *adj* (*position*) уязви́мый; (*person*) рани́мый; **he is ~ to ...** он подве́ржен +*dat* ...

**vulture** ['vʌltʃər] *n* (*ZOOL*) гриф

# W, w

**wad** [wɔd] *n* (*of cotton wool*) тампо́н; (*of banknotes, paper*) па́чка

**wade** [weɪd] *vi*: **to ~ through** (*water*) пробира́ться (пробра́ться *pf*) че́рез +*acc*

**waft** [wɔft] *vi* доноси́ться (донести́сь *pf*)

**wage** [weɪdʒ] *n* (*also*: **~s**) зарпла́та ♦ *vt*: **to ~ war** вести́ (*impf*) войну́

**wail** [weɪl] *n* (*of person*) вопль *m* ♦ *vi* (*person*) вопи́ть (*impf*); (*siren*) выть (*impf*)

**waist** [weɪst] *n* та́лия; **~coat** *n* (*BRIT*) жиле́т

**wait** [weɪt] *vi* ждать (*impf*) ♦ *n* ожида́ние; **to keep sb ~ing** заставля́ть (заста́вить *pf*) кого́-н ждать; **I can't ~ to go home** мне не те́рпится пойти́ домо́й; **to ~ for sb/sth** ждать (*impf*) кого́-н/ чего́-н; **we had a long ~ for the**

**bus** мы до́лго жда́ли авто́буса; **~ on** *vt fus* (*serve*) обслу́живать (обслужи́ть *pf*); **~er** *n* официа́нт; **~ing list** *n* о́чередь *f*, спи́сок очередни́ков; **~ing room** *n* (*in surgery*) приёмная *f adj*; (*in station*) зал ожида́ния; **~ress** *n* официа́нтка

**wake** [weɪk] (*pt* **woke** *or* **~d**, *pp* **woken** *or* **~d**) *vt* (*also*: **~ up**) буди́ть (разбуди́ть *pf*) ♦ *vi* (*also*: **~ up**) просыпа́ться (просну́ться *pf*) ♦ *n* бде́ние (у гро́ба); (*NAUT*) кильва́тер; **in the ~ of** (*fig*) всле́дствие +*gen*; **~n** *vti* = **wake**

**Wales** [weɪlz] *n* Уэ́льс

**walk** [wɔːk] *n* (*hike*) похо́д; (*shorter*) прогу́лка; (*gait*) похо́дка; (*path*) тропа́ ♦ *vi* (*go on foot*) ходи́ть/идти́ (*impf*) (пешко́м); (*baby*) ходи́ть (*impf*); (*for pleasure, exercise*) гуля́ть (*impf*) ♦ *vt* (*distance*) проходи́ть (пройти́ *pf*); (*dog*) выгу́ливать (вы́гулять *pf*); **10 minutes' ~ from here** в 10-ти́ мину́тах ходьбы́ отсю́да; **~ out** *vi* (*audience*) демонстрати́вно покида́ть (поки́нуть *pf*) зал; (*workers*) забастова́ть (*pf*); **~er** *n* (*hiker*) тури́ст(ка); **~ing stick** *n* трость *f*

**wall** [wɔːl] *n* стена́; **~ed** *adj* обнесённый стено́й

**wallet** ['wɔlɪt] *n* бума́жник

**wallpaper** ['wɔːlpeɪpər] *n* обо́и *pl* ♦ *vt* окле́ивать (окле́ить *pf*) обо́ями

**walnut** ['wɔːlnʌt] *n* (*nut*) гре́цкий оре́х; (*wood*) оре́х

**walrus** ['wɔːlrəs] (*pl* **~** *or* **~es**) *n* морж

**waltz** [wɔːlts] *n* вальс

**wander** ['wɔndər] *vi* (*person*) броди́ть (*impf*); (*mind, thoughts*) блужда́ть (*impf*) ♦ *vt* броди́ть (*impf*) по +*dat*

**wane** [weɪn] vi (enthusiasm, influence) ослабева́ть (ослабе́ть pf)

**want** [wɔnt] vt (wish for) хоте́ть (impf) +acc or +gen; (need) нужда́ться (impf) в +prp ♦ n: **for ~ of** за недоста́тком +gen; **to ~ to do** хоте́ть (impf) +infin; **I ~ you to apologize** я хочу́, что́бы Вы извини́лись; **~ed** adj (criminal etc) разы́скиваемый; **~ing** adj: **he was found ~ing** он оказа́лся не на высоте́ положе́ния

**wanton** ['wɔntn] adj (gratuitous) беспричи́нный

**war** [wɔːr] n война́; **to declare ~ (on)** объявля́ть (объяви́ть pf) войну́ (+dat)

**ward** [wɔːd] n (MED) пала́та; (BRIT: POL) о́круг; (LAW) ребёнок, под опе́кой; **~ off** vt (attack, enemy) отража́ть (отрази́ть pf); (danger, illness) отвраща́ть (отврати́ть pf)

**warden** ['wɔːdn] n (of park, reserve) смотри́тель(ница) m(f); (of prison) нача́льник; (of youth hostel) коменда́нт

**wardrobe** ['wɔːdrəub] n шифонье́р, платяно́й шкаф; (clothes) гардеро́б; (THEAT) костюме́рная f adj

**warehouse** ['wɛəhaus] n склад

**wares** [wɛəz] npl това́ры mpl

**warfare** ['wɔːfɛər] n вое́нные or боевы́е де́йствия ntpl

**warily** ['wɛərɪlɪ] adv насторо́женно

**warm** [wɔːm] adj тёплый; (thanks, supporter) горя́чий; (heart) до́брый; **it's ~ today** сего́дня тепло́; **I'm ~** мне тепло́; **~ up** vi (person, room) согрева́ться (согре́ться pf); (water) нагрева́ться (нагре́ться pf); (athlete) размина́ться (размя́ться pf) ♦ vt разогрева́ть (разогре́ть pf); **the weather ~ed up** на у́лице

потепле́ло; **~-hearted** adj серде́чный; **~ly** adv (applaud) горячо́; (dress, welcome) тепло́; **~th** n тепло́

**warn** [wɔːn] vt: **to ~ sb (not) to do/of/that** предупрежда́ть (предупреди́ть pf) кого́-н (не) +infin/о +prp/, что; **~ing** n предупрежде́ние

**warp** [wɔːp] vi (wood) коро́биться (покоро́биться pf) ♦ vt (fig) извраща́ть (изврати́ть pf)

**warrant** ['wɔrənt] n (also: **search ~**) о́рдер на о́быск; **~y** n гара́нтия

**Warsaw** ['wɔːsɔː] n Варша́ва

**warship** ['wɔːʃɪp] n вое́нный кора́бль m

**wart** [wɔːt] n борода́вка

**wartime** ['wɔːtaɪm] n: **in ~** в вое́нное вре́мя

**wary** ['wɛərɪ] adj: **to be ~ of sb/sth** относи́ться (impf) к кому́-н/ чему́-н с опа́ской

**was** [wɔz] pt of **be**

**wash** [wɔʃ] n мытьё; (clothes) сти́рка; (washing programme) режи́м сти́рки (в стира́льной маши́не); (of ship) пе́нистый след ♦ vt (hands, body) помы́ть pf); (clothes) стира́ть (постира́ть pf); (face) умыва́ть (умы́ть pf) ♦ vi (person) мы́ться (помы́ться pf); (sea etc): **to ~ over sth** перека́тываться (перекати́ться pf) че́рез что-н; **to have a ~** помы́ться (pf); **to give sth a ~** помы́ть (pf) что-н; (clothes) постира́ть (pf) что-н; **~ off** vi отмыва́ться (отмы́ться pf); (stain) отсти́рываться (отстира́ться pf); **~ up** vi (BRIT) мыть (вы́мыть pf) посу́ду; (US) мы́ться (помы́ться pf); **~er** n ша́йба; **~ing** n сти́рка; **~ing-up** n (гря́зная) посу́да

**wasn't** ['wɔznt] = **was not**

**wasp** [wɔsp] n оса́

**wastage** ['weɪstɪdʒ] n (waste) трáта
**waste** [weɪst] n (act) трáта;
(rubbish) отхóды mpl; (also: ~
**land**: in city) пустырь m ♦ adj
(rejected, damaged) бракóванный;
(left over) отрабóтанный ♦ vt
растрáчивать (растрáтить pf);
(opportunity) упускáть (упустить
pf); ~**s** npl (area) пустыня fsg; ~
**paper** испóльзованная бумáга;
~**ful** adj неэконóмный; ~**paper
basket** n корзина для
(ненýжных) бумáг

**watch** [wɔtʃ] n (also: **wrist**~)
(нарýчные) часы́ pl; (act of
watching) наблюдéние ♦ vt (look
at) наблюдáть (impf) за +instr;
(match, programme) смотрéть
(посмотрéть pf); (events, weight,
language) следить (impf) за +instr;
(be careful of: person) остерегáться
(impf) +gen; (look after) смотрéть
(impf) за +instr ♦ vi (take care)
смотрéть (impf); (keep guard)
дежýрить (impf); ~ **out** vi
остерегáться (остерéчься pf);
~**ful** adj бдительный

**water** ['wɔːtə'] n водá ♦ vt
поливáть (полить pf); vi (eyes)
слезиться (impf); in British ~s в
британских вóдах; ~ **down** vt
разбавля́ть (разбáвить pf)
(водóй); (fig) смягчáть (смягчить
pf); ~**colour** (US ~**color**) n (picture)
акварéль f; ~**fall** n водопáд; ~**ing
can** n лéйка; ~**logged** adj
затóпленный; ~**melon** n арбýз;
~**proof** adj непромокáемый;
~**shed** n водораздéл; ~**tight** adj
(seal, door) водонепроницáемый;
~**way** n вóдный путь m; ~**y** adj
(soup etc) водянистый

**watt** [wɔt] n ватт

**wave** [weɪv] n волнá; (of hand)
взмах ♦ vi (signal) махáть (impf);
(branches) качáться (impf); (flag)

развевáться (impf) ♦ vt махáть
(impf) +instr; (stick, gun)
размáхивать (impf) +instr; ~**length**
n (RADIO) длинá волны́; **they are
on the** ~**length** (fig) они
смóтрят на вéщи одинáково

**wax** [wæks] n (polish) воск; (: for
floor) мастика; (: for skis) мазь f;
(in ear) сéра ♦ vt (floor) натирáть
(натерéть pf) мастикой; (car)
натирáть (натерéть pf) вóском;
(skis) мáзать (смáзать pf) мáзью

**way** [weɪ] n (route) путь m, дорóга;
(manner, method) спóсоб; (usu pl:
habit) привычка; **which** ~? - **this** ~
кудá? - сюдá; **is it a long** ~ **from
here?** это далекó отсю́да?; **which
~ do we go now?** кудá нам
тепéрь идти?; **on the** ~ (en route)
по пути or дорóге; **to be on one's
** ~ быть (impf) в пути; **to go out of
one's** ~ **to do** стáраться
(постарáться pf) изо всех сил
+infin; **to be in sb's** ~ стоя́ть (impf)
на чьём-н пути; **to lose one's** ~
заблудиться (pf); **the plan is
under** ~ план осуществля́ется; **in
a** ~ в извéстном смы́сле; **in some
**~s в нéкоторых отношéниях; **no
**~! (inf) ни за чтó!; **by the** ~ ...
кстáти ..., мéжду прóчим ...; "~
**in"** (BRIT) "вход"; "~ **out"** (BRIT)
"вы́ход"; "**give** ~" (BRIT : AUT)
"уступите дорóгу"

**WC** n abbr (= water closet) туалéт

**we** [wiː] pron мы

**weak** [wiːk] adj слáбый; **to grow** ~
слабéть (ослабéть pf); ~**en** vi
(person) смягчáться (смягчиться
pf) ♦ vt (government, person)
ослабля́ть (ослáбить pf); ~**ness** n
слáбость f; **to have a** ~**ness for**
имéть (impf) слáбость к +dat

**wealth** [welθ] n (money, resources)
богáтство; (of details, knowledge
etc) обилие; ~**y** adj богáтый

**wean** [wiːn] *vt* (*baby*) отнима́ть (отня́ть *pf*) от груди́

**weapon** ['wɛpən] *n* ору́жие

**wear** [wɛəʳ] (*pt* **wore**, *pp* **worn**) *n* (*use*) но́ска; (*damage*) изно́с ♦ *vi* (*last*) носи́ться (*impf*); (*rub through*) изна́шиваться (износи́ться *pf*) ♦ *vt* (*generally*) носи́ть (*impf*); (*put on*) надева́ть (наде́ть *pf*); (*damage*) изна́шивать (износи́ть *pf*); **he was ~ing his new shirt** на нём была́ его́ но́вая руба́шка; **~ down** *vt* (*resistance*) сломи́ть (*pf*); **~ out** *vt* (*shoes, clothing*) изна́шивать (износи́ть *pf*); **~ and tear** *n* изно́с

**weary** ['wɪərɪ] *adj* утомлённый ♦ *vi*: **to ~ of** утомля́ться (утоми́ться *pf*) от +*gen*

**weasel** ['wiːzl] *n* (*ZOOL*) ла́ска

**weather** ['wɛðəʳ] *n* пого́да ♦ *vt* (*crisis*) выде́рживать (вы́держать *pf*); **I am under the ~** мне нездоро́вится; **~ forecast** *n* прогно́з пого́ды

**weave** [wiːv] (*pt* **wove**, *pp* **woven**) *vt* (*cloth*) ткать (сотка́ть *pf*); **~r** *n* ткач(и́ха)

**weaving** ['wiːvɪŋ] *n* (*craft*) тка́чество

**web** [wɛb] *n* паути́на; (*fig*) сеть *f*; (*COMPUT*) = (**World Wide**) **Web**; **~ page** *n* электро́нная страни́ца, страни́ца на интерне́те; **~site** *n* сайт

**wed** [wɛd] (*pt*, *pp* **~ded**) *vi* венча́ться (обвенча́ться *pf*)

**we'd** [wiːd] = **we had**, **we would**

**wedding** [wɛdɪŋ] *n* сва́дьба; (*in church*) венча́ние; **silver/golden ~** сере́бряная/золота́я сва́дьба

**wedge** [wɛdʒ] *n* клин ♦ *vt* закрепля́ть (закрепи́ть *pf*) кли́ном; (*pack tightly*): **to ~ in** вти́скивать (вти́снуть *pf*) в +*acc*

**Wednesday** ['wɛdnzdɪ] *n* среда́

**wee** [wiː] *adj* (*SCOTTISH*) ма́ленький

**weed** [wiːd] *n* сорня́к ♦ *vt* поло́ть (вы́полоть *pf*)

**week** [wiːk] *n* неде́ля; **a ~ today** че́рез неде́лю; **a ~ on Friday** в сле́дующую пя́тницу; **~day** *n* бу́дний день *m*; **~end** *n* выходны́е *pl adj* (дни), суббо́та и воскресе́нье; **~ly** *adv* еженеде́льно ♦ *adj* еженеде́льный

**weep** [wiːp] (*pt*, *pp* **wept**) *vi* (*person*) пла́кать (*impf*)

**weigh** [weɪ] *vt* взве́шивать (взве́сить *pf*) ♦ *vi* ве́сить (*impf*); **~ down** *vt* отягоща́ть (отяготи́ть *pf*); (*fig*) тяготи́ть (*impf*)

**weight** [weɪt] *n* вес; (*for scales*) ги́ря; **to lose ~** худе́ть (похуде́ть *pf*); **to put on ~** поправля́ться (попра́виться *pf*); **~y** *adj* (*important*) весо́мый

**weir** [wɪəʳ] *n* (*in river*) запру́да

**weird** [wɪəd] *adj* (*strange*) стра́нный, дико́винный

**welcome** ['wɛlkəm] *adj* жела́нный ♦ *n* (*hospitality*) приём; (*greeting*) приве́тствие ♦ *vt* (*also*: **bid ~**) приве́тствовать (*impf*); **thank you - you're ~!** спаси́бо - пожа́луйста!

**weld** [wɛld] *vt* сва́ривать (свари́ть *pf*)

**welfare** ['wɛlfɛəʳ] *n* (*well-being*) благополу́чие; (*US: social aid*) социа́льное посо́бие; **~ state** *n* госуда́рство всео́бщего благосостоя́ния

**well** [wɛl] *n* (*for water*) коло́дец; (*also*: **oil ~**) (нефтяна́я) сква́жина ♦ *adv* хорошо́ ♦ *excl* (*anyway*) ну; (*so*) ну вот ♦ *adj*: **he is ~** он здоро́в; **as ~** та́кже; **I woke ~ before dawn** я просну́лся задо́лго до рассве́та; **I've brought my anorak as ~ as a**

**jumper** кро́ме сви́тера я взял ещё и ку́ртку; **get ~ soon!** поправля́йтесь скоре́е!; **he is doing ~ at school** в шко́ле он успева́ет; **the business is doing ~** би́знес процвета́ет; **~ up** vi (tears) наверну́ться (pf)

**we'll** [wi:l] = **we will, we shall**

**well-being** ['wɛl'bi:ɪŋ] n благополу́чие

**well-dressed** ['wɛl'drɛst] adj хорошо́ оде́тый

**wellies** ['wɛlɪz] npl (inf) = **wellingtons**

**wellingtons** ['wɛlɪŋtənz] npl (also: **wellington boots**) рези́новые сапоги́ mpl

**well-known** ['wɛl'nəun] adj изве́стный

**well-off** ['wɛl'ɔf] adj (wealthy) обеспе́ченный

**Welsh** [wɛlʃ] adj уэ́льский; **the ~** npl (people) уэ́льцы mpl, валли́йцы mpl; **~ Assembly** n Ассамбле́я Уэ́льса; **~man** (irreg) n уэ́лец, валли́ец; **~woman** (irreg) n валли́йка, жи́тельница Уэ́льса

**went** [wɛnt] pt of **go**

**wept** [wɛpt] pt, pp of **weep**

**were** [wə:ʳ] pt of **be**

**we're** [wɪəʳ] = **we are**

**weren't** [wə:nt] = **were not**

**west** [wɛst] n за́пад ♦ adj за́падный ♦ adv на за́пад; **the West** (POL) За́пад; **~erly** adj за́падный; **~ern** adj за́падный ♦ n (CINEMA) ве́стерн

**wet** [wɛt] adj (damp, rainy) вла́жный, сыро́й; (soaking) мо́крый; **to get ~** мо́кнуть (промо́кнуть pf)

**we've** [wi:v] = **we have**

**whale** [weɪl] n кит

**wharf** [wɔ:f] (pl **wharves**) n при́стань f

**what** [wɔt] adj 1 (interrogative: direct, indirect) како́й (f кака́я, nt како́е, pl каки́е); **what books do you need?** каки́е кни́ги Вам нужны́?; **what size is the dress?** како́го разме́ра э́то пла́тье? 2 (emphatic) како́й (f кака́я, nt како́е, pl каки́е); **what a lovely day!** како́й чуде́сный день!; **what a fool I am!** како́й же я дура́к!

♦ pron 1 (interrogative) что; **what are you doing?** что Вы де́лаете?; **what are you talking about?** о чём Вы говори́те?; **what is it called?** как э́то называ́ется?; **what about me?** а как же я?; **what about doing ...?** как насчёт того́, что́бы +infin ...? 2 (relative) что; **I saw what was on the table** я ви́дел, что бы́ло на столе́; **tell me what you're thinking about** скажи́те мне, о чём Вы ду́маете; **what you say is wrong** то, что Вы говори́те, неве́рно

♦ excl (disbelieving) что; **I've crashed the car - what!** я разби́л маши́ну - что!

**whatever** [wɔt'ɛvəʳ] adj (any) любо́й; **~ book** люба́я кни́га ♦ pron (any) всё; (regardless of) что бы ни; **~ you do ...** что бы ты не де́лал ...; **~ the reason ...** какова́ бы ни была́ причи́на ...; **do ~ is necessary/you want** де́лайте всё, что необходи́мо/хоти́те; **~ happens** что бы ни случи́лось; **there is no reason ~** нет никако́й причи́ны; **nothing ~** абсолю́тно ничего́

**whatsoever** [wɔtsəu'ɛvəʳ] adj: **there is no reason ~** нет никако́й причи́ны

**wheat** [wi:t] *n* пшени́ца

**wheel** [wi:l] *n* (of car etc) колесо́; (also: **steering ~**) руль *m*; **~barrow** *n* та́чка; **~chair** *n* инвали́дная коля́ска

**wheeze** [wi:z] *vi* хрипе́ть (*impf*)

**when** [wɛn] *adv, conj* когда́; ~ you've read the book ... когда́ Вы прочита́ете кни́гу ...

**whenever** [wɛn'ɛvəʳ] *adv* в любо́е вре́мя ♦ *conj* (any time) когда́ то́лько; (every time that) ка́ждый раз, когда́

**where** [wɛəʳ] *adv* (position) где; (motion) куда́ ♦ *conj* где; ~ ... **from?** отку́да ...?; **this is ~** ... э́то там, где ...

**whereabouts** *adv* [wɛərə'bauts] *n* ['wɛərəbauts] *adv* (position) где; (motion) куда́ ♦ *n* местонахожде́ние; **~as** *conj* тогда́ *or* в то вре́мя как; **~by** *adv* (formal) посре́дством чего́; **~ver** [wɛər'ɛvəʳ] *conj* (no matter where): **~ver he was** где бы он ни был; (not knowing where): **~ver that is** где бы то ни́ было ♦ *adv* (interrogative: position) где же; (: motion) куда́ же; **~ver he goes** куда́ бы он ни шёл

**wherewithal** ['wɛəwɪðɔ:l] *n*: **the ~ (to do)** сре́дства *ntpl* (+infin)

**whether** ['wɛðəʳ] *conj* ли; **I doubt ~ she loves me** я сомнева́юсь, лю́бит ли она́ меня́; **I don't know ~ to accept this proposal** я не зна́ю, приня́ть ли э́то предложе́ние; **~ you go or not** пойдёте Вы и́ли нет

---
KEYWORD
---

**which** [wɪtʃ] *adj* **1** (interrogative: direct, indirect) како́й (*f* кака́я, *nt* како́е, *pl* каки́е); **which picture would you like?** каку́ю карти́ну

Вы хоти́те?; **which books are yours?** каки́е кни́ги Ва́ши?; **which one?** како́й? (*f* кака́я, *nt* како́е); **I've got two pens, which one do you want?** у меня́ есть две ру́чки, каку́ю Вы хоти́те?; **which one of you did it?** кто из Вас э́то сде́лал?

**2: in which case** в тако́м слу́чае; **by which time** к тому́ вре́мени ♦ *pron* **1** (interrogative) како́й (*f* кака́я, *nt* како́е, *pl* каки́е); **there are several museums, which shall we visit first?** здесь есть не́сколько музе́ев. В како́й мы пойдём снача́ла?; **which do you want, the apple or the banana?** что Вы хоти́те - я́блоко и́ли бана́н?; **which of you is staying?** кто из Вас остаётся?

**2** (relative) кото́рый (*f* кото́рая, *nt* кото́рое, *pl* кото́рые); **the apple which is on the table** я́блоко, кото́рое лежи́т на столе́; **the news was bad, which is what I had feared** ве́сти бы́ли плохи́е, чего́ я и опаса́лся; **I had lunch, after which I decided to go home** я пообе́дал, по́сле чего́ я реши́л пойти́ домо́й; **I made a speech, after which nobody spoke** я вы́ступил с ре́чью, по́сле кото́рой никто́ ничего́ не сказа́л

---

**whichever** [wɪtʃ'ɛvəʳ] *adj* (any) любо́й; (regardless of) како́й бы ни; **take ~ book you prefer** возьми́те любу́ю кни́гу; **~ book you take** каку́ю бы кни́гу Вы ни взя́ли

**whiff** [wɪf] *n* (smell): **he caught a ~ of her perfume** на него́ пахну́ло её духа́ми

**while** [waɪl] *n* (period of time) вре́мя *nt* ♦ *conj* пока́, в то вре́мя как; (although) хотя́; **for a ~**

ненадо́лго; **~ away** vt: **to ~ away
the time** корота́ть (скорота́ть pf)
вре́мя

**whim** [wɪm] n при́хоть f

**whimper** ['wɪmpər] n хны́канье
♦ vi хны́кать (impf)

**whimsical** ['wɪmzɪkl] adj чудно́й

**whine** [waɪn] vi (person, animal)
скули́ть (impf); (engine, siren) выть
(impf)

**whip** [wɪp] n кнут, хлыст; (POL,
person) организа́тор
парла́ментской фра́кции ♦ vt
(person, animal) хлеста́ть (impf);
(cream, eggs) взбива́ть (взбить
pf); **to ~ sth out** выхва́тывать
(вы́хватить pf) что-н; **to ~ sth
away** вырыва́ть (вы́рвать pf) что-н

**whirl** [wəːl] vi кружи́ться (impf),
враща́ться (impf); **~wind** n ви́хрь m

**whirr** [wəːr] vi треща́ть (impf)

**whisk** [wɪsk] n (CULIN) ве́нчик ♦ vt
(CULIN) взбива́ть (взбить pf); **to ~
sb away** or **off** увози́ть (увезти́ pf)
кого́-н

**whiskers** ['wɪskəz] npl (of animal)
усы́ mpl; (of man) бакенба́рды
fpl

**whisky** ['wɪskɪ] (US, IRELAND
**whiskey**) n ви́ски nt ind

**whisper** ['wɪspər] n шёпот ♦ vi
шепта́ться (impf) ♦ vt шепта́ть
(impf)

**whistle** ['wɪsl] n (sound) свист;
(object) свисто́к ♦ vi свисте́ть
(сви́стнуть pf)

**white** [waɪt] adj бе́лый ♦ n (colour)
бе́лый цвет; (person) бе́лый(ая)
m(f) adj; (of egg, eye) бело́к; **~ lie** n
безоби́дная ложь f; **~wash** n
(paint) известко́вый раство́р (для
побе́лки) ♦ vt (building) бели́ть
(побели́ть pf); (fig: incident)
обеля́ть (обели́ть pf)

**whiting** ['waɪtɪŋ] n inv хек

**whizz** [wɪz] vi: **to ~ past** or **by**

проноси́ться (пронести́сь pf)
ми́мо

---

KEYWORD

---

**who** [huː] pron **1** (interrogative) кто;
**who is it?, who's there?** кто э́то
or там?; **who did you see there?**
кого́ Вы там ви́дели?
**2** (relative) кото́рый (f кото́рая, nt
кото́рое, pl кото́рые); **the woman
who spoke to me** же́нщина,
кото́рая говори́ла со мной

**whole** [həul] adj це́лый ♦ n (entire
unit) це́лое nt adj; (all): **the ~ of
Europe** вся Евро́па; **on the~, as a
~** в це́лом; **~meal** adj (BRIT):
**~meal flour** мука́ гру́бого
помо́ла; **~meal bread** хлеб из
муки́ гру́бого помо́ла; **~sale** adj
(price) опто́вый; (destruction)
ма́ссовый ♦ adv (buy, sell) о́птом;
**~some** adj здоро́вый

**wholly** ['həulɪ] adv по́лностью,
целико́м

---

KEYWORD

---

**whom** [huːm] pron **1** (interrogative:
+acc, +gen) кого́; (: +dat) кому́;
(: +instr) кем; (: +prp) ком; **whom
did you see there?** кого́ Вы там
ви́дели?; **to whom did you give
the book?** кому́ Вы отда́ли
кни́гу?
**2** (relative: +acc) кото́рого (f
кото́рую, pl кото́рых); (: +gen)
кото́рого (f кото́рой, pl кото́рых);
(: +dat) кото́рому (f кото́рой, pl
кото́рым); (: +instr) кото́рым (f
кото́рой, pl кото́рыми); (: +prp)
кото́ром (f кото́рой, pl кото́рых);
**the man whom I saw/to whom I
spoke** челове́к, кото́рого я
ви́дел/с кото́рым я говори́л

**whore** [hɔːr] n (inf: pej) шлю́ха

**whose** [hu:z] *adj* **1** (*possessive: interrogative*) чей (*f* чья, *nt* чьё, *pl* чьи); **whose book is this?, whose is this book?** чья это книга?
**2** (*possessive: relative*) кото́рый (*f* кото́рая, *nt* кото́рое, *pl* кото́рые); **the woman whose son you rescued** же́нщина, сы́на кото́рой Вы спасли́
♦ *pron* чей (*f* чья, *nt* чьё, *pl* чьи); **whose is this?** э́то чьё?; **I know whose it is** я зна́ю, чьё э́то

**why** [waɪ] *adv, conj* почему́ ♦ *excl*: **~, it's you!** как, э́то Вы?; **~ is he always late?** почему́ он всегда́ опа́здывает?; **I'm not going - ~ not?** я не пойду́ - почему́?; **~ not do it now?** почему́ бы не сде́лать э́то сейча́с?; **I wonder ~ he said that** интере́сно, почему́ он э́то сказа́л; **that's not ~ I'm here** я здесь не по э́той причи́не; **that's ~** вот почему́; **there is a reason ~ I want to see him** у меня́ есть причи́на для встре́чи с ним; **~, it's obvious/that's impossible!** но ведь э́то же очеви́дно/невозмо́жно!
**wicked** ['wɪkɪd] *adj* зло́бный, злой; (*mischievous: smile*) лука́вый
**wide** [waɪd] *adj* широ́кий ♦ *adv*: **to open ~** широ́ко открыва́ть (откры́ть *pf*); **to shoot ~** стреля́ть (*impf*) ми́мо це́ли; **the bridge is 3 metres ~** ширина́ моста́ - 3 ме́тра; **~ly** *adv* (*believed, known*) широ́ко; (*travelled*) мно́го; (*differing*) значи́тельно; **~n** *vt* расширя́ть (расши́рить *pf*) ♦ *vi* расширя́ться (расши́риться *pf*); **~ open** *adj* широко́ раскры́тый; **~spread** *adj* (*belief etc*) широко́ распространённый

**widow** ['wɪdəʊ] *n* вдова́; **~ed** *adj* вдо́вый; **to be ~ed** овдове́ть (*pf*); **~er** *n* вдове́ц
**width** [wɪdθ] *n* ширина́
**wield** [wi:ld] *vt* (*power*) облада́ть (*impf*) +*instr*
**wife** [waɪf] (*pl* **wives**) *n* жена́
**wig** [wɪɡ] *n* пари́к
**wiggle** ['wɪɡl] *vt* (*hips*) трясти́ (*impf*) +*instr*; (*ears*) шевели́ть (пошевели́ть *pf*)
**wild** [waɪld] *adj* (*animal, plant, guess*) ди́кий; (*weather, sea*) бу́рный; (*person, behaviour*) бу́йный; **the ~s** *npl* (*remote area*) ди́кие места́ *ntpl*; **in the ~s of** в де́брях +*gen*; **~erness** ['wɪldənɪs] *n* ди́кая ме́стность *f*; (*desert*) пусты́ня; **~life** *n* ди́кая приро́да; **~ly** *adv* (*behave*) бу́йно, ди́ко; (*applaud*) бу́рно; (*hit*) нейстово; (*guess*) наобу́м
**wilful** ['wɪlful] (*US* **willful**) *adj* (*obstinate*) своенра́вный; (*deliberate*) умы́шленный

**will** [wɪl] *aux vb* **1** (*forming future tense*): **I will finish it tomorrow** я зако́нчу э́то за́втра; **I will be working all morning** я бу́ду рабо́тать всё у́тро; **I will have finished it by tomorrow** я зако́нчу э́то к за́втрашнему дню; **I will always remember you** я бу́ду по́мнить тебя́ всегда́; **will you do it? - yes, I will/no, I won't** Вы сде́лаете э́то? - да, сде́лаю/нет, не сде́лаю; **the car won't start** маши́на ника́к не заво́дится
**2** (*in conjectures, predictions*): **he will** *or* **he'll be there by now** он, наве́рное, уже́ там; **mistakes will happen** оши́бки неизбе́жны
**3** (*in commands, requests, offers*):

**will you be quiet!** а ну-ка, потише!; **will you help me?** Вы мне не поможете?; **will you have a cup of tea?** не хотите ли чашку чая?

♦ vt (pt,pp **willed**): **to will o.s. to do** заставлять (заставить pf) себя +infin; **to will sb to do** заклинать (impf) кого-н +infin
♦ n (volition) воля; (testament) завещание

**willful** ['wɪlful] adj (US) = **wilful**
**willing** ['wɪlɪŋ] adj (agreed) согласный; (enthusiastic) усердный; **he's ~ to do it** он готов сделать это; **~ly** adv с готовностью, охотно; **~ness** n готовность f
**willow** ['wɪləu] n (tree) ива
**willpower** ['wɪl'pauər] n сила воли
**wilt** [wɪlt] vi никнуть (поникнуть pf)
**wily** ['waɪlɪ] adj лукавый
**win** [wɪn] (pt, pp **won**) n победа
♦ vt выигрывать (выиграть pf); (support, popularity) завоёвывать (завоевать pf) ♦ vi побеждать (победить pf), выигрывать (выиграть pf); **~ over** vt (person) покорять (покорить pf)
**winch** [wɪntʃ] n лебёдка
**wind¹** [wɪnd] n ветер; (MED) газы mpl ♦ vt: **the blow ~ed him** от удара у него захватило дух
**wind²** [waɪnd] (pt, pp **wound**) vt (rope, thread) мотать (смотать pf); (toy, clock) заводить (завести pf)
♦ vi (road, river) виться (impf)
**~ up** vt (toy, clock) заводить (завести pf); (debate) завершать (завершить pf)
**windfall** ['wɪndfɔːl] n (money) неожиданный доход
**windmill** ['wɪndmɪl] n ветряная мельница

**window** ['wɪndəu] n окно; (in shop) витрина; **~sill** n подоконник
**windscreen** ['wɪndskriːn] n ветровое стекло
**windswept** ['wɪndswɛpt] adj (place) продуваемый ветрами; (person, hair) растрёпанный
**windy** ['wɪndɪ] adj ветреный; **it's ~ today** сегодня ветрено
**wine** [waɪn] n вино
**wing** [wɪŋ] n (also AUT) крыло; **~s** npl (THEAT) кулисы fpl; **~er** n (SPORT) крайний нападающий m adj
**wink** [wɪŋk] n подмигивание ♦ vi подмигивать (подмигнуть pf), мигать (мигнуть pf); (light) мигать (мигнуть pf)
**winner** ['wɪnər] n победитель(ница) m(f)
**winnings** ['wɪnɪŋz] npl выигрыш msg
**winter** ['wɪntər] n (season) зима; **in ~** зимой
**wintry** ['wɪntrɪ] adj зимний
**wipe** [waɪp] n: **to give sth a ~** протирать (протереть pf) что-н
♦ vt (rub) вытирать (вытереть pf); (erase) стирать (стереть pf); **~ out** vt (city, population) стирать (стереть pf) с лица земли
**wire** ['waɪər] n проволока; (ELEC) провод; (telegram) телеграмма
♦ vt (person) телеграфировать (impf/pf) +dat; (ELEC : also : **~ up**) подключать (подключить pf); **to ~ a house** делать (сделать pf) (электро)проводку в доме
**wireless** ['waɪəlɪs] n (BRIT) радио nt ind
**wiring** ['waɪərɪŋ] n (электро)проводка
**wiry** ['waɪərɪ] adj (person) жилистый; (hair) жёсткий
**wisdom** ['wɪzdəm] n мудрость f
**wise** [waɪz] adj мудрый
**...wise** [waɪz] suffix: **timewise** в

смысле времени
**wish** [wɪʃ] n жела́ние ♦ vt жела́ть
(пожела́ть pf); **best ~es** ( for
birthday etc) всего́ наилу́чшего;
**with best ~es** (in letter) с
наилу́чшими пожела́ниями; **to ~
sb goodbye** проща́ться
(попроща́ться pf) с кем-н; **he ~ed
me well** он пожела́л мне всего́
хоро́шего; **to ~ to do** хоте́ть
(impf) +infin; **I ~ him to come** я
хочу́, что́бы он пришёл; **to ~ for**
жела́ть (пожела́ть pf) +acc or +gen;
**~ful** adj: **it's ~ful thinking** э́то -
приня́тие жела́емого за
действи́тельное
**wistful** ['wɪstful] adj тоскли́вый
**wit** [wɪt] n (wittiness) остроу́мие;
(intelligence : also : **~s**) ум, ра́зум
**witch** [wɪtʃ] n ве́дьма; **~craft** n
колдовство́

---

KEYWORD

---

**with** [wɪð, wɪθ] prep **1**
(accompanying, in the company of )
с +instr; **I spent the day with him**
я провёл с ним день; **we stayed
with friends** мы останови́лись у
друзе́й; **I'll be with you in a
minute** я освобожу́сь че́рез
мину́ту; **I'm with you** (I
understand) я Вас понима́ю; **she
is really with it** (inf: fashionable)
она́ о́чень сти́льная; (: aware)
она́ всё сообража́ет
**2** (descriptive) с +instr; **a girl with
blue eyes** де́вушка с голубы́ми
глаза́ми; **a skirt with a silk lining**
ю́бка на шёлковой подкла́дке
**3** (indicating manner) с +instr;
(indicating cause) от +gen;
(indicating means): **to write with a
pencil** писа́ть (impf) карандашо́м;
**with tears in her eyes** со слеза́ми
на глаза́х; **red with anger**
кра́сный от гне́ва; **you can open**

the door with this key Вы
мо́жете откры́ть дверь э́тим
ключём; **to fill sth with water**
наполня́ть (напо́лнить pf) что-н
водо́й

---

**withdraw** [wɪθ'drɔ:] (irreg: like
**draw**) vt (object) извлека́ть
(извле́чь pf); (remark) брать
(взять pf) наза́д; (offer) снима́ть
(снять pf) ♦ vi (troops, person)
уходи́ть (уйти́ pf); **to ~ money
from an account** снима́ть (снять
pf) де́ньги со счёта; **~al** n (of
offer, remark) отка́з; (of troops)
вы́вод; (of money) сня́тие; **~n** pp
of **withdraw** ♦ adj за́мкнутый
**wither** ['wɪðə*] vi (plant) вя́нуть
(завя́нуть pf)
**withhold** [wɪθ'həuld] (irreg: like
**hold**) vt (money) уде́рживать
(удержа́ть pf); (information)
ута́ивать (утаи́ть pf)
**within** [wɪð'ɪn] prep (place, distance,
time) внутри́ +gen, в преде́лах
+gen ♦ adv внутри́; **~ reach** в
преде́лах досяга́емости; **~ sight
(of)** в по́ле зре́ния (+gen); **the
finish is ~ sight** коне́ц не за
гора́ми
**without** [wɪð'aut] prep без +gen; **~
a hat** без ша́пки; **~ saying a word**
не говоря́ ни сло́ва; **~ looking** не
гля́дя; **to go ~ sth** обходи́ться
(обойти́сь pf) без чего́-н
**withstand** [wɪθ'stænd] (irreg: like
**stand**) vt выде́рживать
(вы́держать pf)
**witness** ['wɪtnɪs] n
свиде́тель(ница) m(f) ♦ vt (event)
быть (impf) свиде́телем(льницей)
+gen; (document) заверя́ть
(заве́рить pf); **~ box** n
свиде́тельское ме́сто
**witty** ['wɪtɪ] adj остроу́мный
**wives** [waɪvz] npl of **wife**

**wobble** ['wɔbl] vi (legs) трясти́сь (impf); (chair) шата́ться (impf)

**wobbly** ['wɔblɪ] adj (table etc) ша́ткий

**woe** [wəu] n го́ре

**woke** [wəuk] pt of **wake**; **~n** pp of **wake**

**wolf** [wulf] (pl **wolves**) n волк

**woman** ['wumən] (pl **women**) n же́нщина

**womb** [wu:m] n ма́тка

**women** ['wimin] npl of **woman**

**won** [wʌn] pt, pp of **win**

**wonder** ['wʌndər] n (feeling) изумле́ние ♦ vi: **I ~ whether you could tell me ...** не мо́жете ли Вы сказа́ть мне ...; **I ~ why he is late** интере́сно, почему́ он опозда́л; **to ~ at** удивля́ться (impf) +dat; **to ~ about** разду́мывать (impf) о +prp; **it's no ~ (that)** не удиви́тельно(, что); **~ful** adj (excellent) чуде́сный; **~fully** adv чуде́сно

**won't** [wəunt] = **will not**

**wood** [wud] n (timber) де́рево; (forest) лес; **~en** adj (object) деревя́нный; (fig) дубо́вый; **~pecker** n дя́тел; **~work** n (skill) столя́рное де́ло; **~worm** n (larvae) личи́нка древото́чца

**wool** [wul] n (material, yarn) шерсть f; **to pull the ~ over sb's eyes** (fig) пуска́ть (пусти́ть pf) пыль в глаза́ кому́-н; **~len** (US **~en**) adj шерстяно́й; **~ly** (US **~y**) adj шерстяно́й; (fig: ideas) расплы́вчатый; (: person) вя́лый

**word** [wə:d] n сло́во; (news) слух ♦ vt формули́ровать (сформули́ровать pf); **in other ~s** други́ми слова́ми; **to break/keep one's ~** наруша́ть (нару́шить pf)/ держа́ть (сдержа́ть pf) своё сло́во; **to have ~s with sb** име́ть (impf) кру́пный разгово́р с кем-н;

**~ing** n формулиро́вка; **~ processor** n те́кстовый проце́ссор

**wore** [wɔːr] pt of **wear**

**work** [wə:k] n рабо́та; (ART, LITERATURE) произведе́ние ♦ vi рабо́тать (impf); (medicine etc) де́йствовать (поде́йствовать pf) ♦ vt (clay) рабо́тать (impf) с +instr; (wood, metal) рабо́тать (impf) по +dat; (land) обраба́тывать (обрабо́тать pf); (mine) разраба́тывать (разрабо́тать pf); (machine) управля́ть (impf) +instr; (miracle) соверша́ть (соверши́ть pf); **he has been out of ~ for three months** он был без рабо́ты три ме́сяца; **to ~ loose** (part) расша́тываться (расшата́ться pf); (knot) сла́бнуть (осла́бнуть pf); **~ on** vt fus (task) рабо́тать (impf) над +instr; (person) рабо́тать (impf) с +instr; (principle) исходи́ть (impf) из +gen; **~ out** vi (plans etc) удава́ться (уда́ться pf) ♦ vt (problem) разреша́ть (разреши́ть pf); (plan) разраба́тывать (разрабо́тать pf); **it ~s out at £100** (cost) выхо́дит £100; **~er** n (in factory) рабо́чий(ая) m(f) adj; (in community etc) рабо́тник(ница); **~force** n рабо́чая си́ла; **~ing-class** adj рабо́чий; **~ing order** n: **in ~ing order** в испра́вности; **~man** (irreg) n (квалифици́рованный) рабо́чий m adj; **~s** n (BRIT: factory) фа́брика; (: steel, brick) заво́д; **~shop** n мастерска́я f adj, цех; (session) семина́р; (THEAT, MUS) сту́дия

**world** [wə:ld] n мир ♦ adj мирово́й; **to think the ~ of sb** быть (impf) о́чень высо́кого мне́ния о ком-н; **~ champion** чемпио́н ми́ра; **~ly** adj

(*knowledgeable*) искушённый;
**~wide** *adj* всемирный; **(World
Wide) Web** *n* (Всемирная)
Паутина
**worm** [wə:m] *n* (*ZOOL*) червь *m*
**worn** [wɔ:n] *pp of* **wear** ♦ *adj*
(*carpet*) потёртый; **~-out** *adj*
(*object*) изношенный; (*person*)
измотанный
**worried** ['wʌrɪd] *adj*
обеспокоенный, встревоженный
**worry** ['wʌrɪ] *n* (*anxiety*)
беспокойство, волнение ♦ *vi*
беспокоиться (*impf*),
волноваться (*impf*) ♦ *vt* (*person*)
беспокоить (обеспокоить *pf*),
волновать (взволновать *pf*);
**~ing** *adj* тревожный
**worse** [wə:s] *adj* худший ♦ *adv*
хуже ♦ *n* худшее *nt adj*; **a change
for the ~** ухудшение; **~n** *vi*
ухудшаться (ухудшиться *pf*); **~
off** *adj* (*financially*) более бедный
**worship** ['wə:ʃɪp] *n* поклонение,
преклонение ♦ *vt* поклоняться
(*impf*) +*dat*, преклоняться (*impf*)
перед +*instr*
**worst** [wə:st] *adj* наихудший ♦ *adv*
хуже всего ♦ *n* наихудшее *nt adj*;
**at ~** в худшем случае
**worth** [wə:θ] *adj*: **to be ~** стоить
(*impf*); **it's ~ it** это того стоит;
**~less** *adj* никчёмный; **~while** *adj*
стоящий
**worthy** [wə:ðɪ] *adj*: **~ (of)**
достойный (+*gen*)

─────────
KEYWORD
─────────

**would** [wud] *aux vb* **1** (*conditional
tense*): **I would tell you if I could** я
бы сказал Вам, если бы мог; **if
you asked him he would do it**
если Вы его попросите, (то) он
сделает это; **if you had asked
him he would have done it** если
бы Вы попросили его, (то) он

**2** (*in offers, invitations, requests*):
**would you like a cake?** не хотите
(ли) пирога?; **would you ask him
to come in?** пожалуйста,
пригласите его войти!; **would
you open the window please?**
откройте, пожалуйста, окно!
**3** (*in indirect speech*): **I said I would
do it** я сказал, что сделаю это;
**he asked me if I would stay with
him** он попросил меня остаться
с ним; **he asked me if I would
resit the exam if I failed** он
спросил меня, буду ли я
пересдавать экзамен, если я
провалюсь
**4** (*emphatic*): **it WOULD have to
snow today!** именно сегодня
должен пойти снег!; **you
WOULD say that, wouldn't you!**
Вы, конечно, это скажете!
**5** (*insistence*): **she wouldn't behave**
она никак не хотела хорошо
себя вести
**6** (*conjecture*): **it would have been
midnight** должно быть, была
полночь; **it would seem so**
должно быть, так; **it would seem
that ...** похоже, что ...
**7** (*indicating habit*): **he would come
here on Mondays** он (обычно)
приходил сюда по
понедельникам

─────────

**would-be** ['wudbi:] *adj* (*pej*)
начинающий
**wouldn't** ['wudnt] = **would not**
**wound¹** [waund] *pt, pp of* **wind²**
**wound²** [wu:nd] *n* рана ♦ *vt*
ранить (*impf/pf*)
**wove** [wəuv] *pt of* **weave**; **~n** *pp of*
**weave**
**wrangle** ['ræŋgl] *n*
препирательства *ntpl*
**wrap** [ræp] *vt* (*also*: **~ up**)

заворáчивать (заверну́ть pf);
(wind): to ~ sth round sth (tape
etc) обора́чивать (оберну́ть pf)
что-н вокру́г чего́-н; ~**per** n (on
chocolate) обёртка
**wrath** [rɔθ] n гнев
**wreath** [riːθ] n (pl ~**s**) n (for dead)
вено́к
**wreck** [rɛk] n (vehicle, ship)
обло́мки mpl ♦ vt (car) разбива́ть
(разби́ть pf); (stereo) лома́ть
(слома́ть pf); (weekend) по́ртить
(испо́ртить pf); (relationship)
разруша́ть (разру́шить pf); (life,
health) губи́ть (погуби́ть pf);
~**age** n обло́мки mpl; (of building)
разва́лины fpl
**wren** [rɛn] n крапи́вник
**wrench** [rɛntʃ] n (TECH) гáечный
ключ; (tug) рыво́к; (fig) тоска́
♦ vt (twist) вывёртывать
(вы́вернуть pf); to ~ sth from sb
вырыва́ть (вы́рвать pf) что-н у
кого́-н
**wrestle** ['rɛsl] vi (SPORT): to ~ (with
sb) боро́ться (impf) (с кем-н)
**wrestling** ['rɛslɪŋ] n борьба́
**wretched** ['rɛtʃɪd] adj несчáстный
**wriggle** ['rɪɡl] vi (also: ~ **about**:
worm) извива́ться (impf); (person)
ёрзать (impf)
**wring** [rɪŋ] (pt, pp **wrung**) vt
(hands) лома́ть (impf); (also: ~ **out**:
clothes) выжима́ть (вы́жать pf);
(fig): to ~ sth out of sb
выжима́ть (вы́жать pf) что-н из
кого́-н
**wrinkle** ['rɪŋkl] n (on face)
морщи́на ♦ vt (nose etc) мо́рщить
(смо́рщить pf) ♦ vi (skin etc)
мо́рщиться (смо́рщиться pf)
**wrist** [rɪst] n (ANAT) запя́стье
**writ** [rɪt] n (LAW) о́рдер
**write** [raɪt] (pt **wrote**, pp **written**)
vt (letter, novel etc) писа́ть
(написа́ть pf); (cheque, receipt)

выпи́сывать (вы́писать pf) ♦ vi
писа́ть (impf); to ~ to sb писа́ть
(написа́ть pf) кому́-н; ~ **down** vt
(note) писа́ть (написа́ть pf); ~ **off**
vt (debt) спи́сывать (списа́ть pf);
(plan) отменя́ть (отмени́ть pf); ~**r**
n писа́тель n
**writhe** [raɪð] vi извива́ться (impf)
**writing** ['raɪtɪŋ] n (words written)
нáдпись f; (of letter, article)
(на)писа́ние; (also: **hand~**)
по́черк; ~ **is his favourite
occupation** бо́льше всего́ он
лю́бит писа́ть; **in** ~ в
пи́сьменном ви́де
**written** ['rɪtn] pp of **write**
**wrong** [rɔŋ] adj непрáвильный;
(information) невéрный; (immoral)
дурно́й ♦ adv непрáвильно ♦ n
(injustice) несправедли́вость f ♦ vt
нехорошо́ поступáть (поступи́ть
pf) с +instr; **you are ~ to do it** э́то
нехорошо́ с Вáшей стороны́;
**you are ~ about that, you've got
it ~** Вы непрáвы; **who is in the ~?**
чья э́то винá?; **what's ~?** в чём
дéло?; **to go ~** (plan) не
удавáться (удáться pf); **right and
~** хоро́шее и дурно́е; ~**ful** adj
несправедли́вый
**wrote** [rəut] pt of **write**
**wrought** [rɔːt] adj: ~ **iron**
свáрочная or ко́вкая сталь f
**wrung** [rʌŋ] pt, pp of **wring**
**wry** [raɪ] adj (humour, expression,
smile) лукáвый
**WWW** n abbr = **World Wide Web**

# X, x

**Xmas** ['ɛksməs] n abbr = **Christmas**
**X-ray** ['ɛksreɪ] n (ray)
рентгéновские лучи́ mpl; (photo)
рентгéновский сни́мок ♦ vt
просвéчивать (просвети́ть pf)

(рентге́новскими луча́ми)
**xylophone** [ˈzaɪləfəʊn] *n* ксилофо́н

## Y, y

**yacht** [jɒt] *n* я́хта
**yard** [jɑːd] *n* (*of house etc*) двор;
(*measure*) ярд

> **yard** - ярд. Ме́ра длины́ ра́вная
> 90.14 см.

**yawn** [jɔːn] *n* зево́к ♦ *vi* зева́ть
(зевну́ть *pf*)
**year** [jɪər] *n* год; **he is eight ~s old**
ему́ во́семь лет; **an eight-~-old**
**child** восьмиле́тний ребёнок; **~ly**
*adj* ежего́дный ♦ *adv* ежего́дно
**yearn** [jəːn] *vi*: **to ~ for sth**
тоскова́ть (*impf*) по чему́-н; **to ~**
**to do** жа́ждать (*impf*) +*infin*
**yeast** [jiːst] *n* дро́жжи *pl*
**yell** [jɛl] *vi* вопи́ть (*impf*)
**yellow** [ˈjɛləʊ] *adj* жёлтый
**yes** [jɛs] *particle* да; (*in reply to*
*negative*) нет ♦ *n*
проголосова́вший(ая) *m(f) adj*
“за”; **to say ~** говори́ть (сказа́ть
*pf*) да
**yesterday** [ˈjɛstədɪ] *adv* вчера́ ♦ *n*
вчера́шний день *m*; **~ morning/**
**evening** вчера́ у́тром/ве́чером;
**all day ~** вчера́ весь день
**yet** [jɛt] *adv* ещё, до сих пор ♦ *conj*
одна́ко, всё же; **the work is not**
**finished ~** рабо́та ещё не
око́нчена; **the best ~** са́мый
лу́чший на сего́дняшний день;
**as ~** ещё, пока́
**yew** [juː] *n* (*tree*) тис
**yield** [jiːld] *n* (*AGR*) урожа́й *m* ♦ *vt*
(*surrender*) сдава́ть (сдать *pf*);
(*produce*) приноси́ть (принести́
*pf*) ♦ *vi* (*surrender*) отступа́ть
(отступи́ть *pf*); (*US : AUT*) уступа́ть

(уступи́ть *pf*) доро́гу
**yog(h)ourt** [ˈjəʊgət] *n* йо́гурт
**yog(h)urt** [ˈjəʊgət] *n* = **yog(h)ourt**
**yoke** [jəʊk] *n* (*also fig*) ярмо́
**yolk** [jəʊk] *n* желто́к

---
KEYWORD
---

**you** [juː] *pron* **1** (*subject: familiar*)
ты; (: *polite*) Вы; (: *2nd person pl*)
вы; **you English are very polite**
вы, англича́не, о́чень ве́жливы;
**you and I will stay here** мы
с тобо́й/Ва́ми оста́немся
здесь
**2** (*direct: familiar*) тебя́; (: *polite*)
Вас; (: *2nd person pl*) вас; **I love**
**you** я тебя́/Вас люблю́
**3** (*indirect: familiar*) тебе́; (: *polite*)
Вам; (: *2nd person pl*) вам; **I’ll give**
**you a present** я тебе́/Вам что́-
нибудь подарю́
**4** (*after prep: +gen: familiar*) тебя́;
(: *polite*) Вас; (: *2nd person pl*) вас;
(: *+dat: familiar*) тебе́; (: *polite*)
Вам; (: *2nd person pl*) вам;
(: *+instr: familiar*) тобо́й; (: *polite*)
Ва́ми; (: *2nd person pl*) ва́ми;
(: *+prp: familiar*) тебе́; (: *polite*)
Вас; (: *2nd person pl*) вас; **they’ve**
**been talking about you** они́
говори́ли о тебе́/Вас
**5** (*after prep: referring to subject of*
*sentence: +gen*) себя́; (: *+dat, +prp*)
себе́; (: *+instr*) собо́й; **will you**
**take the children with you?** Вы
возьмёте дете́й с собо́й?; **she’s**
**younger than you** она́ моло́же
тебя́/Вас
**6** (*impersonal: one*): **you never**
**know what can happen** никогда́
не зна́ешь, что мо́жет
случи́ться; **you can’t do that!** так
нельзя́!; **fresh air does you good**
све́жий во́здух поле́зен для
здоро́вья

**you'd** [juːd] = **you had, you would**

**you'll** [juːl] = **you shall, you will**

**young** [jʌŋ] adj молодо́й; (child) ма́ленький ♦ npl (of animal) молодня́к msg; **the ~** (people) молодёжь f; **~er** adj мла́дший; **~ster** n ребёнок

**your** [jɔːʳ] adj (familiar) твой; (polite) Ваш; (2nd person pl) ваш; see also **my**

**you're** [juəʳ] = **you are**

**yours** [jɔːz] pron (familiar) твой; (polite) Ваш; (2nd person pl) ваш; (referring to subject of sentence) свой; **is this ~?** э́то твоё/Ва́ше?; **~ sincerely, ~ faithfully** и́скренне Ваш; see also **mine**[1]

**yourself** [jɔːˈsɛlf] pron (reflexive) себя́; (after prep: +gen) себя́; (: +dat, +prp) себе́; (: +instr) собо́й; (emphatic) сам (f сама́, pl са́ми); (alone) сам, оди́н; **(all) by ~** ты сам or оди́н; **you ~ told me** Вы са́ми сказа́ли мне; see also **myself**

**yourselves** [jɔːˈsɛlvz] pl pron (reflexive) себя́; (after prep: +gen) себя́; (: +dat, +prp) себе́; (: +instr) собо́й; (emphatic) са́ми; (alone) са́ми, одни́; **(all) by ~** са́ми, одни́; **talk amongst ~ for a moment** поговори́те ме́жду собо́й пока́; see also **myself**

**youth** [juːθ] n (young days) ю́ность

f, мо́лодость f; (young people) молодёжь f; (pl **~s**; young man) ю́ноша m; **~ful** adj ю́ношеский; (person, looks) ю́ный

**you've** [juːv] = **you have**

# Z, z

**zany** [ˈzeɪnɪ] adj заба́вный

**zap** [zæp] vt (COMPUT) стира́ть (стере́ть pf)

**zeal** [ziːl] n рве́ние; **~ous** [ˈzɛləs] adj ре́вностный

**zebra** [ˈziːbrə] n зе́бра; **~ crossing** n (BRIT) зе́бра, пешехо́дный перехо́д

**zero** [ˈzɪərəu] n ноль m, нуль m

**zest** [zɛst] n (for life) жа́жда; (of orange) це́дра

**zigzag** [ˈzɪgzæg] n зигза́г

**zinc** [zɪŋk] n цинк

**zip** [zɪp] n (also: ~ **fastener**) мо́лния ♦ vt (also: ~ **up**) застёгивать (застегну́ть pf) на мо́лнию; **~per** n (US) = **zip**

**zodiac** [ˈzəudɪæk] n зодиа́к

**zombie** [ˈzɔmbɪ] n (fig) зо́мби ind

**zone** [zəun] n зо́на

**zoo** [zuː] n зоопа́рк

**zoology** [zuːˈɔlədʒɪ] n зооло́гия

**zoom** [zuːm] vi: **to ~ past** мелька́ть (промелькну́ть pf) ми́мо; **~ lens** n объекти́в с переме́нным фо́кусным расстоя́нием

# ENGLISH IRREGULAR VERBS

| present | pt | pp |
|---|---|---|
| arise | arose | arisen |
| awake | awoke | awoken |
| be (am, is, are; being) | was, were | been |
| bear | bore | born(e) |
| beat | beat | beaten |
| become | became | become |
| begin | began | begun |
| bend | bent | bent |
| bet | bet, betted | bet, betted |
| bid (at auction, cards) | bid | bid |
| bid (say) | bade | bidden |
| bind | bound | bound |
| bite | bit | bitten |
| bleed | bled | bled |
| blow | blew | blown |
| break | broke | broken |
| breed | bred | bred |
| bring | brought | brought |
| build | built | built |
| burn | burnt, burned | burnt, burned |
| burst | burst | burst |
| buy | bought | bought |
| can | could | (been able) |
| cast | cast | cast |
| catch | caught | caught |
| choose | chose | chosen |
| cling | clung | clung |
| come | came | come |
| cost | cost | cost |
| cost (work out price of) | costed | costed |
| creep | crept | crept |
| cut | cut | cut |
| deal | dealt | dealt |
| dig | dug | dug |
| do (does) | did | done |
| draw | drew | drawn |
| dream | dreamed, dreamt | dreamed, dreamt |
| drink | drank | drunk |
| drive | drove | driven |
| dwell | dwelt | dwelt |
| eat | ate | eaten |

| present | pt | pp |
|---|---|---|
| fall | fell | fallen |
| feed | fed | fed |
| feel | felt | felt |
| fight | fought | fought |
| find | found | found |
| flee | fled | fled |
| fling | flung | flung |
| fly | flew | flown |
| forbid | forbade | forbidden |
| forecast | forecast | forecast |
| forget | forgot | forgotten |
| forgive | forgave | forgiven |
| forsake | forsook | forsaken |
| freeze | froze | frozen |
| get | got | got, (US) gotten |
| give | gave | given |
| go (goes) | went | gone |
| grind | ground | ground |
| grow | grew | grown |
| hang | hung | hung |
| hang (execute) | hanged | hanged |
| have (has; having) | had | had |
| hear | heard | heard |
| hide | hid | hidden |
| hit | hit | hit |
| hold | held | held |
| hurt | hurt | hurt |
| keep | kept | kept |
| kneel | knelt, kneeled | knelt, kneeled |
| know | knew | known |
| lay | laid | laid |
| lead | led | led |
| lean | leant, leaned | leant, leaned |
| leap | leapt, leaped | leapt, leaped |
| learn | learnt, learned | learnt, learned |
| leave | left | left |
| lend | lent | lent |
| let | let | let |
| lie (lying) | lay | lain |
| light | lit, lighted | lit, lighted |

| present | pt | pp | present | pt | pp |
|---|---|---|---|---|---|
| **lose** | lost | lost | **speed** | sped, | sped, |
| **make** | made | made | | speeded | speeded |
| **may** | might | — | **spell** | spelt, | spelt, |
| **mean** | meant | meant | | spelled | spelled |
| **meet** | met | met | **spend** | spent | spent |
| **mistake** | mistook | mistaken | **spill** | spilt, | spilt, |
| **mow** | mowed | mown, | | spilled | spilled |
| | | mowed | **spin** | spun | spun |
| **must** | (had to) | (had to) | **spit** | spat | spat |
| **pay** | paid | paid | **split** | split | split |
| **put** | put | put | **spoil** | spoiled, | spoiled, |
| **quit** | quit, | quit, | | spoilt | spoilt |
| | quitted | quitted | **spread** | spread | spread |
| **read** | read | read | **spring** | sprang | sprung |
| **rid** | rid | rid | **stand** | stood | stood |
| **ride** | rode | ridden | **steal** | stole | stolen |
| **ring** | rang | rung | **stick** | stuck | stuck |
| **rise** | rose | risen | **sting** | stung | stung |
| **run** | ran | run | **stink** | stank | stunk |
| **saw** | sawed | sawed, | **stride** | strode | stridden |
| | | sawn | **strike** | struck | struck, |
| **say** | said | said | | | stricken |
| **see** | saw | seen | **strive** | strove | striven |
| **seek** | sought | sought | **swear** | swore | sworn |
| **sell** | sold | sold | **sweep** | swept | swept |
| **send** | sent | sent | **swell** | swelled | swollen, |
| **set** | set | set | | | swelled |
| **sew** | sewed | sewn | **swim** | swam | swum |
| **shake** | shook | shaken | **swing** | swung | swung |
| **shear** | sheared | shorn, | **take** | took | taken |
| | | sheared | **teach** | taught | taught |
| **shed** | shed | shed | **tear** | tore | torn |
| **shine** | shone | shone | **tell** | told | told |
| **shoot** | shot | shot | **think** | thought | thought |
| **show** | showed | shown | **throw** | threw | thrown |
| **shrink** | shrank | shrunk | **thrust** | thrust | thrust |
| **shut** | shut | shut | **tread** | trod | trodden |
| **sing** | sang | sung | **wake** | woke, | woken, |
| **sink** | sank | sunk | | waked | waked |
| **sit** | sat | sat | **wear** | wore | worn |
| **slay** | slew | slain | **weave** | wove, | woven, |
| **sleep** | slept | slept | | weaved | weaved |
| **slide** | slid | slid | **wed** | wedded, | wedded, |
| **sling** | slung | slung | | wed | wed |
| **slit** | slit | slit | **weep** | wept | wept |
| **smell** | smelt, | smelt, | **win** | won | won |
| | smelled | smelled | **wind** | wound | wound |
| **sow** | sowed | sown, | **wring** | wrung | wrung |
| | | sowed | **write** | wrote | written |
| **speak** | spoke | spoken | | | |

# GUIDE TO RUSSIAN GRAMMAR

It is not the purpose of this grammar section to attempt to give an exhaustive treatment of Russian grammar. Instead it is intended to outline the basic grammatical principles and to draw the user's attention to the most commonly encountered irregular forms.

## Spelling Rules

After **ж, ч, ш, щ, г, к** and **х**:

> **ы** becomes **и** e.g. ногá (*nom sg*) → ногú (*gen sg*)
> **я** becomes **а** e.g. молчáть (*infin*) → молчáт (*3rd pers pl*)
> **ю** becomes **у** e.g. молчáть (*infin*) → молчý (*1st pers sg*)

After **ж, ч, ш, щ** and **ц**:
**о** becomes **е** when unstressed e.g. хорóший (*m nom sg*) → хорóшего (*m gen sg*)

# NOUNS

## 1 Gender

All Russian nouns are masculine, feminine or neuter. In most cases the gender is determinable by the ending:

> дом *m*
> картú**на** *f*
> крéсло *nt*

Noun gender is significant since, for example, it determines the ending of a qualifying adjective:

> больш**óй** дом
> больш**áя** картúна
> больш**óе** крéсло

Masculine noun categories
i) All nouns ending in a hard consonant, e.g. кот, собóр, and all nouns ending in -й e.g. музéй.
ii) Some nouns ending in -а/-я including natural masculine nouns e.g. мужчúна, дáдя and masculine first names, including familiar forms e.g. Фóма, Мúтя.
iii) Numerous nouns ending in a soft sign, including:
    natural masculines e.g. парéнь, корóль.
    months of the year e.g. июль.

Feminine noun categories

i) The majority of nouns ending in -а/-я e.g. доро́га, ко́мната, тётя

ii) The majority of nouns ending in a soft sign including:
   natural feminines e.g. мать.
   all nouns ending in -жь, -чь, -шь, -щь, -знь, -мь, -пь, -фь.
   most nouns ending in -сть, -бь, -вь, -дь, -зь, -сь, -ть.

Neuter noun categories

i) Almost all nouns ending in -о e.g. ме́сто.

ii) Almost all nouns ending in -е e.g. со́лнце.

iii) All nouns ending in -ё e.g. копьё.

iv) All nouns ending in -мя e.g. вре́мя, и́мя.

v) Most indeclinable loan words e.g. ви́ски, ра́дио (a notable exception being ко́фе, which is masculine).

## 2 Cases

Russian nouns can decline into six cases:

**Nominative**: this case is used for the **subject** of a sentence.

**Accusative**: this case is used for the **direct object** of a sentence and after на and в to indicate **movement towards**.

**Genitive**: this case is used to indicate **possession** and with certain verbs and prepositions.

**Dative**: this case is used for the **indirect object** of a sentence and with certain verbs and prepositions.

**Instrumental**: this case is used to indicate the **means** by which an action is done, or the **passive agent** and with certain verbs and prepositions.

**Prepositional**: this case is used after на and в to indicate **location**, and with other prepositions, most notably о.

## 3 Declension

There are three declension patterns for nouns. The first declension contains most masculine and neuter nouns, the second contains most feminine nouns and the third is specific to feminine nouns ending in a soft sign. For the first declension, hard-ending masculine and neuter nouns (e.g. мост, о́зеро) have the genitive singular ending -а, whereas soft-ending masculine and neuter nouns (e.g. гость, го́ре) have the genitive ending -я. Similarly, the second declension pattern has a split between hard-ending feminine nouns (e.g. ла́мпа) with the genitive ending -ы and soft-ending feminine nouns (e.g. ба́шня) with the genitive ending -и. All nouns in the third declension pattern, as they are soft-ending, have the genitive ending -и. The genitive singular declension generally sets the pattern for the other oblique cases.

Plural animate nouns, that is to say nouns referring to living things such as people and animals, take genitive endings in the accusative case. In the singular, this rule applies to masculine animate nouns only.

The following tables sets out the most common declension patterns:

|  | masc hard завод | masc soft дви́гател\|ь | masc animate гост\|ь | neuter hard ме́ст\|о |
|---|---|---|---|---|
| Singular | | | | |
| Nom | заво́д | дви́гатель | гость | ме́сто |
| Acc | заво́д | дви́гатель | го́стя | ме́сто |
| Gen | заво́да | дви́гателя | го́стя | ме́ста |
| Dat | заво́ду | дви́гателю | го́стю | ме́сту |
| Instr | заво́дом | дви́гателем | го́стем | ме́стом |
| Prep | о заво́де | о дви́гателе | о го́сте | о ме́сте |
| Plural | | | | |
| Nom | заво́ды | дви́гатели | го́сти | места́ |
| Acc | заво́ды | дви́гатели | гостей | места́ |
| Gen | заво́дов | дви́гателей | гостей | мест |
| Dat | заво́дам | дви́гателям | гостя́м | места́м |
| Instr | заво́дами | дви́гателями | гостя́ми | места́ми |
| Prep | о заво́дах | о дви́гателях | о гостя́х | о места́х |

|  | *neuter soft* пол\|е | *fem hard* лáмп\|a | *fem soft* пол\|я́ | *fem soft sign* двер\|ь |
|---|---|---|---|---|
| | | **Singular** | | |
| *Nom* | пóле | лáмпа | поля́ | дверь |
| *Acc* | пóле | лáмпу | полю́ | дверь |
| *Gen* | пóля | лáмпы | поли́ | двери |
| *Dat* | пóлю | лáмпе | полé | двери |
| *Instr* | пóлем | лáмпой | полéй | дверью |
| *Prep* | о пóле | о лáмпе | о полé | о двери |
| | | **Plural** | | |
| *Nom* | поля́ | лáмпы | поли́ | двери́ |
| *Acc* | поля́ | лáмпы | поли | двери́ |
| *Gen* | полéй | лáмп | полéй | дверéй |
| *Dat* | поля́м | лáмпам | поля́м | дверя́м |
| *Instr* | поля́ми | лáмпами | поля́ми | дверя́ми |
| *Prep* | о поля́х | о лáмпах | о поля́х | о дверя́х |

Where nouns take a zero ending in the genitive plural, a buffer vowel (e, o or ё) may need to be inserted between the last two consonants. For example окнó has the genitive plural form óкон, сестрá → сестёр, бáшня → бáшен.

Feminine and neuter nouns ending in -ия/-ие take the ending -и in the singular prepositional case.

The table below shows the declensions of two of the most common irregular nouns, врéмя and мать:

|  | вре́мя | мать |
|---|---|---|
| | *Singular* | |
| Nom | вре́мя | мать |
| Acc | вре́мя | мать |
| Gen | вре́мени | ма́тери |
| Dat | вре́мени | ма́тери |
| Instr | вре́менем | ма́терью |
| Prep | о вре́мени | о ма́тери |
| | *Plural* | |
| Nom | времена́ | ма́тери |
| Acc | времена́ | ма́тере́й |
| Gen | времён | матере́й |
| Dat | времена́м | матеря́м |
| Instr | времена́ми | матеря́ми |
| Prep | о времена́х | о матеря́х |

И́мя, пле́мя and other nouns in -мя follow the same pattern as вре́мя. Дочь follows the same pattern as мать with the exception of the instrumental plural which is дочерьми́.

## ADJECTIVES

Russian adjectives generally have a long (attributive) form e.g. вежли́вый and a short (predicative) form e.g. вежли́в.

### 1 Long form adjectives

Russian long adjectives are used attributively and the majority have hard endings, the first vowel of the ending being -ы, -а, or -о. Note that the animate accusative/genitive rule which affects nouns also applies to long adjectives.

The following table shows the declension of hard-ending adjectives:

|      | m          | f        | nt       | pl         |
|------|------------|----------|----------|------------|
| Nom  | ста́рый     | ста́рая   | ста́рое   | ста́рые     |
| Acc  | ста́рый/ого | ста́рую   | ста́рое   | ста́рые/ых  |
| Gen  | ста́рого    | ста́рой   | ста́рого  | ста́рых     |
| Dat  | ста́рому    | ста́рой   | ста́рому  | ста́рым     |
| Instr| ста́рым     | ста́рой   | ста́рым   | ста́рыми    |
| Prep | о ста́ром   | о ста́рой | о ста́ром | о ста́рых   |

The alternative forms of the accusative are animate and identical with the genitive.
The feminine instrumental ending -ою also exists.

Adjectives ending in -ой, such as живо́й, decline similarly, with the only difference being the masculine nominative singular and inanimate accusative singular, where the ending -ой replaces -ый.

Note that Russian spelling rules may apply in some cases, so that adjectives such as гла́дкий, ти́хий and до́лгий decline as above with -и- in place of -ы-.

Adjectives ending in -ний are known as soft adjectives. They decline as follows:

|      | m           | f         | nt        | pl         |
|------|-------------|-----------|-----------|------------|
| Nom  | осе́нний     | осе́нняя   | осе́ннее   | осе́нние    |
| Acc  | осе́нний/его | осе́ннюю   | осе́ннее   | осе́нние/их |
| Gen  | осе́ннего    | осе́нней   | осе́ннего  | осе́нних    |
| Dat  | осе́ннему    | осе́нней   | осе́ннему  | осе́нним    |
| Instr| осе́нним     | осе́нней   | осе́нним   | осе́нними   |
| Prep | о осе́ннем   | о осе́нней | о осе́ннем | о осе́нних  |

The alternative forms of the accusative are animate and identical with the genitive.

The feminine instrumental ending -ею also exists.

Due to spelling rules, adjectives ending in -ший, -щий, -чий and -жий (e.g. хоро́ший, горя́чий) also decline like soft adjectives.

### 1.1 Possessive Adjectives

These follow one of two declension patterns. Possessive adjectives like соба́чий and де́вичий decline as follows:

|        | m              | f         | nt        | pl            |
|--------|----------------|-----------|-----------|---------------|
| Nom    | соба́чий        | соба́чья   | соба́чье   | соба́чьи       |
| Acc    | соба́чий/ьего   | соба́чью   | соба́чье   | соба́чьи/ьих   |
| Gen    | соба́чьего      | соба́чьей  | соба́чьего | соба́чьих      |
| Dat    | соба́чьему      | соба́чьей  | соба́чьему | соба́чьим      |
| Instr  | соба́чьим       | соба́чьей  | соба́чьим  | соба́чьими     |
| Prep   | о соба́чьем     | о соба́чьей| о соба́чьем| о соба́чьих    |

The alternative forms of the accusative are animate and identical with the genitive. The feminine instrumental ending -ьею also exists. The ordinal numeral тре́тий declines according to the above table.

In addition, there are possessive adjectives formed by adding the suffixes -ин, -нин or -ов to the stems of nouns. This form is mainly used with reference to particular family members such as ма́мин, му́жнин, and де́дов, but can also be derived from the familiar forms of first names e.g. Са́шин. These decline as follows:

|        | m           | f        | nt        | pl          |
|--------|-------------|----------|-----------|-------------|
| Nom    | Са́шин       | Са́шина   | Са́шино    | Са́шины      |
| Acc    | Са́шин/ого   | Са́шину   | Са́шино    | Са́шины/ых   |
| Gen    | Са́шиного    | Са́шиной  | Са́шиного  | Са́шиных     |

| | | | | |
|------|------------|------------|-----------|-------------|
| Dat | Сáшину | Сáшиной | Сáшину | Сáшиным |
| Instr | Сáшиным | Сáшиной | Сáшиным | Сáшиными |
| Prep | о Сáшином | о Сáшиной | о Сáшином | о Сáшиных |

The alternative forms of the accusative are animate and identical with the genitive. The feminine instrumental ending -ью also exists.

## 2 Short form adjectives

Short adjectives can be derived from most long adjectives. These are formed by replacing the long form endings with contracted ones. For example the adjective вéжливый declines as follows:

| | long form | short form |
|-----|-------------|-------------|
| m | вéжливый | вéжлив |
| f | вéжливая | вéжлива |
| nt | вéжливое | вéжливо |
| pl | вéжливые | вéжливы |

The masculine short form of many adjectives needs a buffer vowel (e, o or ё) to be inserted between the last two consonants or to replace a soft sign. For example вáжный has the masculine short form вáжен, лёгкий → лёгок, ýмный → умён. Masculine short forms of adjectives ending in -енный (i.e. unstressed) generally have -ен endings whereas those in -éнный (i.e. stressed) are replaced by the short form -éнен.

## 3 Usage

Long adjectives are typically used attributively, for example:

На ýлице стои́т **бéлая** маши́на.    A white car is parked in the street.
Он вóдит **бéлую** маши́ну.    He drives a white car.

Long adjectives may be used predicatively when they denote characteristics inherent to the nouns they refer to:

Эта ýлица – **дли́нная**.    This street is long.
Этот груз – **тяжёлый**.    This load is heavy.

In contrast, the short form is typically used predicatively, and when talking about a temporary state. For example он плох "he is unwell" contrasts with он плохо́й "he is bad."

## VERBS

### 1 Conjugation

Russian verbs can be divided into two groups according to their endings when conjugated. The two groups are referred to as 1st and 2nd conjugation. The following examples show the pattern encountered in the imperfective present tense and perfective future tense.

|  | 1st conjugation | 2nd conjugation |
|---|---|---|
| *infinitive* | рабо́тать | говори́ть |
| я | рабо́таю | говорю́ |
| ты | рабо́таешь | говори́шь |
| он/она́/оно́ | рабо́тает | говори́т |
| мы | рабо́таем | говори́м |
| вы | рабо́таете | говори́те |
| они́ | рабо́тают | говоря́т |

### 1.1 First-conjugation verbs

These include verbs with infinitive endings in -ать (e.g. рабо́тать), in -ять (e.g. стреля́ть), in -овать/-евать (e.g. интересова́ть, танцева́ть), in -уть (e.g. махну́ть), in -авать (e.g. узнава́ть), in -ыть (e.g. мыть) and in -зть, -оть, -сть and -ти, as well as monosyllabic verbs in -ить (e.g. шить).

Many first-conjugation verbs undergo a stem change in conjugation. Particularly common are consonant mutations in the final consonant before the ending. As general rules:

г becomes ж, д becomes ж, з becomes ж, к becomes ч, с becomes ш, ск becomes щ, ст becomes щ, т becomes ч. For example писа́ть declines пишу́, пи́шешь... пи́шут, and иска́ть declines ищу́, и́щешь... и́щут.

Another common stem change occurs in verbs ending in -овать/-евать. In the conjugation of these verbs, the -ева-/-ова- particle is replaced by

-y-. This category of verbs is important as it contains many borrowed and new verbs. For example, фотографи́ровать declines фотографи́рую, фотографи́руешь ... фотографи́руют.

## 1.2 Second-conjugation verbs

These include most verbs with infinitive endings in -ить (the main exception being monosyllabic ones), many verbs in -еть (e.g. смотре́ть), some in -ать (e.g. молча́ть) and two in -ять (боя́ться and стоя́ть).

Note that spelling rules may apply to the first person singular and third person plural of second-conjugation verbs. For example слы́шать conjugates слы́шу, слы́шишь... слы́шат.

As with first-conjugation verbs, many second-conjugation verbs have consonant mutations in the stem when conjugated. However, in the second conjugation, these mutations only affect the first person of the verb. For example, плати́ть declines плачу́, пла́тишь... пла́тят and суди́ть declines сужу́, су́дишь... су́дят.

Furthermore, a salient feature of the second conjugation is the addition of the letter л in the first person singular of verbs whose stem ends in б, в, м, п and ф, e.g. люби́ть: я люблю́ and корми́ть: я кормлю́.

## 1.3 Irregular Verbs

Some common Russian verbs have irregular conjugations. Below are the conjugations of three of the most useful irregular verbs:

| дать | |
|---|---|
| я дам | мы дади́м |
| ты дашь | вы дади́те |
| он/она́/оно́ даст | они́ даду́т |

| есть | |
|---|---|
| я ем | мы еди́м |
| ты ешь | вы еди́те |
| он/она́/оно́ ест | они́ едя́т |

Note that the invariable form есть is sometimes used as the present tense of быть.

| быть | |
|---|---|
| я бу́ду | мы бу́дем |
| ты бу́дешь | вы бу́дете |
| он/она́/оно́ бу́дет | они́ бу́дут |

Note that быть has no present tense form – the form given here is the future tense.

## 2 Past tense

The past tense for most Russian verbs is formed by replacing the infinitive ending by -л, -ла, -ло, -ли, giving the masculine, feminine, neuter, and plural forms respectively. For example:

|    | молча́ть       | упа́сть     | ко́нчить      |
|----|----------------|------------|---------------|
| m  | он молча́л      | он упа́л    | он ко́нчил     |
| f  | она́ молча́ла   | она́ упа́ла | она́ ко́нчила  |
| nt | оно́ молча́ло   | оно́ упа́ло | оно́ ко́нчило  |
| pl | они́ молча́ли   | они́ упа́ли | они́ ко́нчили  |

The singular past tense always agrees with the gender of the subject, so that even after the personal pronouns я and ты the gender is always marked, e.g. я сказа́л (masculine subject), я сказа́ла (feminine subject).

Verbs with infinitives ending in -ереть, -зть, -чь, and many in -ти have no -л in the masculine past tense, e.g. умере́ть (у́мер, умерла́), лезть (лез, ле́зла). This is also the case with some verbs in -нуть, e.g. привы́кнуть (привы́к, привы́кла).

The verb идти́ has an irregular stem in the past tense formed as follows: он шёл, она́ шла, оно́ шло, они́ шли. Compounds of идти́ such as прийти́ and уйти́ form the past tense similarly, e.g. прийти́ becomes он пришёл, она́ пришла́ etc.

## 3 Imperative Mood

The imperative mood has two forms – the familiar and the formal – which are used in accordance with the mode of address (i.e. the familiar ты or the formal Вы) appropriate in any given situation. The formal imperative is formed simply by adding -те to the end of the familiar form. The familiar imperative is formed by replacing the third person plural ending of a verb by -й where it is directly preceded by a vowel and и where it is preceded by a consonant and has mobile or end stress in conjugation.

For example:

де́лать (*infin*) → де́лают (*3rd pers pl*) → де́лай(те) (*imperative*)
подчеркну́ть → подчеркну́т → подчеркни́(те)
держа́ть → де́ржат → держи́(те)

The imperative ending -ь(те) is used where the third person plural ending is preceded by no more than one consonant and the verb has fixed stem stress in conjugation e.g.:

поста́вить → поста́вят → поста́вь(те)
оде́ть → оде́нут → оде́нь(те)

Some common exceptions:

– дава́ть and its compounds have дава́й(те)
– пить has imperative пе́й(те) (compare петь which has imperative по́й(те)). бить, вить, лить and шить also form the imperative like пить.
– The imperative of быть is бу́дь(те).

## 4 Aspect

The majority of Russian verbs have two verb aspects: the **imperfective** for conveying the **frequency** of an action, describing **repeated** or **habitual** actions or describing a **process**, and the **perfective** for emphasis on a **single** or a **completed action**. Each verb has two infinitives: an imperfective one and a perfective one. The conjugated form of an imperfective verb is the **present** tense, whereas the conjugated form of a perfective verb is a **future** tense. Perfective verbs have no present tense form.
Consider the following examples:

| | |
|---|---|
| Я не **чита́ю** кни́гу. | I am not reading the book. |
| Я не **прочита́ю** кни́гу. | I won't finish reading the book. |

There is no one simple way to differentiate aspectual pairs of infinitives. Some of the more common ways are by the presence of a prefix in the perfective aspect e.g. сде́лать (cf. imperfective де́лать), by the presence of a suffix in the imperfective aspect e.g. пока́зывать (cf. perfective показа́ть) or by a change in conjugation e.g. the perfective ко́нчить and its imperfective counterpart конча́ть. In addition, some aspectual pairs have infinitives deriving from two different roots, e.g. говори́ть (*impf*)/ сказа́ть (*perf*), брать (*impf*)/взять (*perf*).

A minority of verbs exist only in one aspect, e.g. стоя́ть (*impf*), while some verbs incorporate the two aspects in one form, e.g. иссле́довать (*impf/ perf*).

Aspect also has a bearing on the use of the imperative, where, generally speaking, the perfective aspect is used in positive commands (i.e. telling someone to do something), while the imperfective is used in negative commands (i.e. telling someone not to do something).

## 5 Future tense

There are two forms of the future tense in Russian: the perfective form and the imperfective form. The perfective future is formed by conjugating a perfective infinitive as shown under the conjugation section above. The imperfective future is formed by combining the future tense of быть with an imperfective infinitive as follows:

| я | бу́ду | чита́ть |
|---|---|---|
| ты | бу́дешь | чита́ть |
| он/она́/оно́ | бу́дет | чита́ть |
| мы | бу́дем | чита́ть |
| вы | бу́дете | чита́ть |
| они́ | бу́дут | чита́ть |

For example:

| Я не **прочита́ю** кни́гу. | I won't finish reading the book. |
|---|---|
| Я не **бу́ду чита́ть** кни́гу. | I won't read the book (= I won't start reading it). |
| Я **сде́лаю** поку́пки в суббо́ту. | I will do the shopping on Saturday. |
| Я **бу́ду де́лать** поку́пки ка́ждую суббо́ту. | I will do the shopping every Saturday. |

## TABLES OF RUSSIAN IRREGULAR FORMS

### PRONOUNS

#### Personal Pronouns

| Nom | я | ты | он | она́ | оно́ |
|---|---|---|---|---|---|
| Acc/Gen | меня́ | тебя́ | его́ | её | его́ |
| Dat | мне | тебе́ | ему́ | ей | ему́ |
| Instr | мной | тобо́й | им | ей | им |
| Prep | обо мне | о тебе́ | о нём | о ней | о нём |

The instrumental forms мной, тобо́й, and ей have alternatives мно́ю, тобо́ю, and е́ю respectively. The reflexive pronoun себя́ declines like тебя́.

| Nom | мы | вы | они́ |
|---|---|---|---|
| Acc/Gen | нас | вас | их |
| Dat | нам | вам | им |
| Instr | на́ми | ва́ми | и́ми |
| Prep | о нас | о вас | о них |

#### Interrogative Pronouns

The alternatives given at the accusative are animate forms which are identical with the genitive.

| Nom | кто | что |
|---|---|---|
| Acc | кого́ | что |
| Gen | кого́ | чего́ |
| Dat | кому́ | чему́ |
| Instr | кем | чем |
| Prep | о ком | о чём |

Similarly with никто́, ничто́ etc.

|       | m          | f     | nt    | pl         |
|-------|------------|-------|-------|------------|
| Nom   | чей        | чья   | чьё   | чьи        |
| Acc   | чей/чьего́  | чью   | чьё   | чьи/чьих   |
| Gen   | чьего́      | чьей  | чьего́ | чьих       |
| Dat   | чьему́      | чьей  | чьему́ | чьим       |
| Instr | чьим       | чьей  | чьим  | чьи́ми      |
| Prep  | о чьём     | о чьей | о чьём | о чьих    |

The instrumental form чьей has the alternative чьéю.

## Possessive Pronouns

|       | m          | f     | nt    | pl         |
|-------|------------|-------|-------|------------|
| Nom   | мой        | моя́   | моё   | мои́       |
| Acc   | мой/моего́ | мою́   | моё   | мои́/мои́х  |
| Gen   | моего́      | моéй  | моего́ | мои́х      |
| Dat   | моему́      | моéй  | моему́ | мои́м      |
| Instr | мои́м       | моéй  | мои́м  | мои́ми     |
| Prep  | о моём     | о моéй | о моём | о мои́х   |

твой and the reflexive possessive pronoun свой decline like мой. The instrumental form моéй has the alternative моéю.

|       | m            | f      | nt      | pl           |
|-------|--------------|--------|---------|--------------|
| Nom   | наш          | на́ша   | на́ше    | на́ши         |
| Acc   | наш/на́шего   | на́шу   | на́ше    | на́ши/на́ших  |
| Gen   | на́шего       | на́шей  | на́шего  | на́ших        |
| Dat   | на́шему       | на́шей  | на́шему  | на́шим        |
| Instr | на́шим        | на́шей  | на́шим   | на́шими       |
| Prep  | о на́шем      | о на́шей | о на́шем | о на́ших     |

ваш declines like наш. The instrumental form на́шей has the alternative
на́шею.

The possessive pronouns его́, её and их are invariable.

### Demonstrative Pronouns

|       | m           | f     | nt      | pl         |
|-------|-------------|-------|---------|------------|
| Nom   | э́тот        | э́та   | э́то     | э́ти        |
| Acc   | э́тот/э́того  | э́ту   | э́то     | э́ти/э́тих   |
| Gen   | э́того       | э́той  | э́того   | э́тих       |
| Dat   | э́тому       | э́той  | э́тому   | э́тим       |
| Instr | ээ́тим       | э́той  | э́тим    | э́тими      |
| Prep  | об э́том     | об э́той | об э́том | об э́тих   |

The instrumental form э́той has the alternative э́тою.

|       | m         | f    | nt    | pl        |
|-------|-----------|------|-------|-----------|
| Nom   | тот       | та   | то    | те        |
| Acc   | тот/того́  | ту   | то    | те/тех    |
| Gen   | того́      | той  | того́  | тех       |
| Dat   | тому́      | той  | тому́  | тем       |
| Instr | тем       | той  | тем   | те́ми      |
| Prep  | о то́м     | о той | о то́м | о те́х    |

The instrumental form той has the alternative то́ю.

|       | m         | f    | nt    | pl        |
|-------|-----------|------|-------|-----------|
| Nom   | сей       | сия́  | сиé   | сий       |
| Acc   | сей/сего́  | сию́  | сиé   | сий/сих   |
| Gen   | сего́      | сей  | сего́  | сих       |
| Dat   | сему́      | сей  | сему́  | сим       |
| Instr | сим       | сей  | сим   | си́ми      |
| Prep  | о сём     | о сей | о сём | о сих    |

The instrumental form сей has the alternative céю.

|       | m           | f        | nt      | pl        |
|-------|-------------|----------|---------|-----------|
| Nom   | весь        | вся      | всё     | все       |
| Acc   | весь/всего́ | всю      | всё     | все/всех  |
| Gen   | всего́      | всей     | всего́  | всех      |
| Dat   | всему́      | всей     | всему́  | всем      |
| Instr | всем        | всей     | всем    | все́ми    |
| Prep  | обо всём    | обо всей | обо всём | обо всех |

The instrumental form всей has the alternative всéю.

## NUMERALS

### Cardinal Numbers

The alternatives given at the accusative are animate forms which are identical with the genitive.

|       | m              | f        | nt       | pl          |
|-------|----------------|----------|----------|-------------|
| Nom   | оди́н          | одна́    | одно́    | одни́       |
| Acc   | оди́н/одного́  | одну́    | одно́    | одни́/одни́х |
| Gen   | одного́        | одно́й   | одного́  | одни́х      |
| Dat   | одному́        | одно́й   | одному́  | одни́м      |
| Instr | одни́м         | одно́й   | одни́м   | одни́ми     |
| Prep  | об одно́м      | об одно́й | об одно́м | об одни́х  |

The instrumental form одно́й has the alternative одно́ю.

|       | m        | f        | nt       |
|-------|----------|----------|----------|
| Nom   | два      | две      | два      |
| Acc   | два/двух | две/двух | два/двух |
| Gen   | двух     | двух     | двух     |
| Dat   | двум     | двум     | двум     |
| Instr | двумя́    | двумя́    | двумя́    |
| Prep  | о двух   | о двух   | о двух   |

| Nom   | три      |
|-------|----------|
| Acc   | три/трёх |
| Gen   | трёх     |
| Dat   | трём     |
| Instr | тремя́    |
| Prep  | о трёх   |

| Nom   | четы́ре          |
|-------|-----------------|
| Acc   | четы́ре/четырёх  |
| Gen   | четырёх         |
| Dat   | четырём         |
| Instr | четырьмя́        |
| Prep  | о четырёх       |

|       | m/nt       | f          |
|-------|------------|------------|
| Nom   | о́ба       | о́бе       |
| Acc   | о́ба/обо́их | о́бе/обе́их |
| Gen   | обо́их     | обе́их     |
| Dat   | обо́им     | обе́им     |
| Instr | обо́ими    | обе́ими    |
| Prep  | об обо́их  | об обе́их  |

| Nom   | пять    |
|-------|---------|
| Acc   | пять    |
| Gen   | пяти́   |
| Dat   | пяти́   |
| Instr | пятью́  |
| Prep  | о пяти́ |

The numerals шесть to два́дцать plus три́дцать decline like пять.

| Nom | со́рок |
|---|---|
| Acc | со́рок |
| Gen | сорока́ |
| Dat | сорока́ |
| Instr | сорока́ |
| Prep | о сорока́ |

| Nom | пятьдеся́т |
|---|---|
| Acc | пятьдеся́т |
| Gen | пяти́десяти |
| Dat | пяти́десяти |
| Instr | пятью́десятью |
| Prep | о пяти́десяти |

Similarly with шестьдеся́т and се́мьдесят.

| Nom | сто |
|---|---|
| Acc | сто |
| Gen | ста |
| Dat | ста |
| Instr | ста |
| Prep | о ста |

| Nom | две́сти |
|---|---|
| Acc | две́сти |
| Gen | двухсо́т |
| Dat | двумста́м |
| Instr | двумяста́ми |
| Prep | о двумста́х |

Similarly with девяно́сто.

| Nom | три́ста |
|---|---|
| Acc | три́ста |
| Gen | трёхсо́т |
| Dat | трёмста́м |
| Instr | тремяста́ми |
| Prep | о трёхста́х |

| Nom | четы́реста |
|---|---|
| Acc | четы́реста |
| Gen | четырёхсот |
| Dat | четырёмста́м |
| Instr | четырьмяста́ми |
| Prep | о четырёхста́х |

| Nom | пятьсо́т |
|---|---|
| Acc | пятьсо́т |
| Gen | пятисо́т |
| Dat | пятиста́м |
| Instr | пятьюста́ми |
| Prep | о пятиста́х |

Similarly with шестьсо́т, семьсо́т, восемьсо́т and девятьсо́т.

|  | singular | plural |
|---|---|---|
| Nom | ты́сяча | ты́сячи |
| Acc | ты́сячу | ты́сячи |
| Gen | ты́сячи | ты́сяч |
| Dat | ты́сяче | ты́сячам |
| Instr | ты́сячей | ты́сячами |
| Prep | о ты́сяче | о ты́сячах |

The instrumental singular form ты́сячью also exists.

## Collective Numerals

The following tables show how the collective numerals 2-7 decline.
The alternatives given at the accusative are animate forms which are
identical with the genitive.

| Nom | двóе | трóе | чéтверо |
|------|------|------|---------|
| Acc | двóе/двои́х | трóе/трои́х | чéтверо/ четверы́х |
| Gen | двои́х | трои́х | четверы́х |
| Dat | двои́м | трои́м | четверы́м |
| Instr | двои́ми | трои́ми | четверы́ми |
| Prep | о двои́х | о трои́х | о четверы́х |

| Nom | пя́теро | шéстеро | сéмеро |
|------|---------|---------|--------|
| Acc | пя́теро/пятеры́х | шéстеро/ шестеры́х | сéмеро/семеры́х |
| Gen | пятеры́х | шестеры́х | семеры́х |
| Dat | пятеры́м | шестеры́м | семеры́м |
| Instr | пятеры́ми | шестеры́ми | семеры́ми |
| Prep | о пятеры́х | о шестеры́х | о семеры́х |

## NUMBERS

| КОЛИЧЕСТВЕННЫЕ ЧИСЛИТЕЛЬНЫЕ | | Cardinal Numbers |
|---|---|---|
| оди́н (одна́, одно́, одни́) | 1 | one |
| два (две) | 2 | two |
| три | 3 | three |
| четы́ре | 4 | four |
| пять | 5 | five |
| шесть | 6 | six |
| семь | 7 | seven |
| во́семь | 8 | eight |
| де́вять | 9 | nine |
| де́сять | 10 | ten |
| оди́ннадцать | 11 | eleven |
| двена́дцать | 12 | twelve |
| трина́дцать | 13 | thirteen |
| четы́рнадцать | 14 | fourteen |
| пятна́дцать | 15 | fifteen |
| шестна́дцать | 16 | sixteen |
| семна́дцать | 17 | seventeen |
| восемна́дцать | 18 | eighteen |
| девятна́дцать | 19 | nineteen |
| два́дцать | 20 | twenty |
| два́дцать оди́н (одна́, одно́, одни́) | 21 | twenty-one |
| два́дцать два (две) | 22 | twenty-two |
| три́дцать | 30 | thirty |
| со́рок | 40 | forty |
| пятьдеся́т | 50 | fifty |
| шестьдеся́т | 60 | sixty |
| се́мьдесят | 70 | seventy |
| во́семьдесят | 80 | eighty |
| девяно́сто | 90 | ninety |
| сто | 100 | a hundred |
| сто оди́н (одна́, одно́, одни́) | 101 | a hundred and one |
| две́сти | 200 | two hundred |
| две́сти оди́н (одна́, одно́, одни́) | 201 | two hundred and one |
| три́ста | 300 | three hundred |

| четы́реста | 400 | four hundred |
| пятьсо́т | 500 | five hundred |
| ты́сяча | 1 000 | a thousand |
| миллио́н | 1 000 000 | a million |

## СОБИРАТЕЛЬНЫЕ ЧИСЛИТЕЛЬНЫЕ — Collective Numerals

дво́е
тро́е
че́тверо
пя́теро
ше́стеро
се́меро

## ПОРЯДКОВЫЕ ЧИСЛИТЕЛЬНЫЕ — Ordinal Numbers

| пе́рвый | 1-ый | first | 1st |
| второ́й | 2-ой | second | 2nd |
| тре́тий | 3-ий | third | 3rd |
| четвёртый | 4-ый | fourth | 4th |
| пя́тый | 5-ый | fifth | 5th |
| шесто́й | 6-ой | sixth | 6th |
| седмо́й | 7-ой | seventh | 7th |
| восьмо́й | 8-ой | eighth | 8th |
| девя́тый | 9-ый | ninth | 9th |
| деся́тый | 10-ый | tenth | 10th |
| оди́ннадцатый | | eleventh | |
| двена́дцатый | | twelfth | |
| трина́дцатый | | thirteenth | |
| четы́рнадцатый | | fourteenth | |
| пятна́дцатый | | fifteenth | |
| шестна́дцатый | | sixteenth | |
| семна́дцатый | | seventeenth | |
| восемна́дцатый | | eighteenth | |
| девятна́дцатый | | nineteenth | |
| двадца́тый | | twentieth | |

| | | |
|---|---|---|
| два́дцать пе́рвый | twenty-first | |
| два́дцать второ́й | twenty-second | |
| тридца́тый | thirtieth | |
| сороково́й | fortieth | |
| пятидеся́тый | fiftieth | |
| восьмидеся́тый | eightieth | |
| девяно́стый | ninetieth | |
| со́тый | hundredth | |
| сто пе́рвый | hundred-and-first | |
| ты́сячный | thousandth | |
| миллио́нный | millionth | |

## ДРОБИ     Fractions

| | | |
|---|---|---|
| полови́на | a half | ½ |
| треть (f) | a third | ⅓ |
| че́тверть (f) | a quarter | ¼ |
| одна́ пя́тая | a fifth | ⅕ |
| три че́тверти | three quarters | ¾ |
| две тре́ти | two thirds | ⅔ |
| полтора́ (полторы́) | one and a half | 1½ |
| ноль це́лых (и) пять деся́тых | (nought) point five | 0.5 |
| три це́лых (и) четы́ре деся́тых | three point four | 3.4 |
| шесть це́лых (и) во́семьдесят де́вять со́тых | six point eight nine | 6.89 |
| де́сять проце́нтов | ten per cent | 10% |
| сто проце́нтов | a hundred per cent | 100% |

# TIME AND DATE

| ВРЕМЯ | Time |
|---|---|
| который час? | what time is it? |
| сейча́с 5 часо́в | it is *or* it's 5 o'clock |
| в како́е вре́мя | at what time? |
| в +*acc* … | at… |
| в час дня | at one p.m. |
| | |
| по́лночь (*f*) | 00.00 midnight |
| де́сять мину́т пе́рвого | 00.10, ten past midnight, ten past twelve a.m. |
| де́сять мину́т второ́го, час де́сять | 01.10, ten past one, one ten |
| че́тверть второ́го, час пятна́дцать | 01.15, a quarter past one, one fifteen |
| полвторо́го, полови́на второ́го, час три́дцать | 01.30, half past one, one thirty |
| без че́тверти два, час со́рок пять | 01.45, a quarter to two, one forty-five |
| без десяти́ два, час пятьдеся́т | 01.50, ten to two, one fifty |
| по́лдень (*m*) | 12.00, midday |
| полпе́рвого, полови́на пе́рвого, двена́дцать три́дцать | 12.30, half past twelve, twelve thirty p.m. |
| час дня | 13.00, one (o'clock) (in the afternoon), one p.m. |
| семь часо́в ве́чера | 19.00, seven (o'clock) (in the evening), seven p.m. |
| де́вять три́дцать ве́чера | 21.30, nine thirty (p.m. *or* at night) |
| без че́тверти двена́дцать, оди́ннадцать со́рок пять | 23.25, a quarter to twelve, eleven forty-five p.m. |
| | |
| че́рез два́дцать мину́т | in twenty minutes |
| два́дцать мину́т наза́д | twenty minutes ago |
| в ближа́йшие два́дцать мину́т | in the next twenty minutes |
| за два́дцать мину́т | within twenty minutes |
| спустя́ два́дцать мину́т | after twenty minutes |

| | |
|---|---|
| сейча́с два́дцать мину́т четвёртого | it's twenty after three (US) |
| | |
| полчаса́ | half an hour |
| че́тверть часа́ | quarter of an hour |
| полтора́ часа́ | an hour and a half |
| час с че́твертью | an hour and a quarter |
| | |
| че́рез час | in an hour's time |
| че́рез час, ка́ждый час | every hour, on the hour |
| ка́ждый час | hourly |
| че́рез час | in an hour from now |
| | |
| разбуди́те меня́ в семь часо́в | wake me up at seven |
| уже́ нача́ло пя́того | it's just gone four |
| с девяти́ до пяти́ | from nine to five |
| с двух до трех (часо́в) | between two and three (o'clock) |
| сего́дня с девяти́ утра́ | since nine o'clock this morning |
| до десяти́ часо́в ве́чера | till ten o'clock tonight |
| о́коло трёх часо́в дня | at about three o'clock in the afternoon |
| три часа́ по Гри́нвичу | three o'clock GMT |

## ДАТЫ

## Date

| | |
|---|---|
| сего́дня | today |
| за́втра | tomorrow |
| вчера́ | yesterday |
| сего́дня у́тром | this morning |
| за́втра днём/ве́чером | tomorrow afternoon/night |
| позавчера́ ве́чером, позапро́шлой но́чью | the night before last |
| позавчера́ | the day before yesterday |
| вчера́ ве́чером, про́шлой но́чью | last night |
| послеза́втра | the day after tomorrow |
| два дня/шесть лет наза́д | two days/six years ago |
| ка́ждый день/вто́рник | every day/Tuesday |
| | |
| в сре́ду | on Wednesday |